s Latin America

Second Edition

Politics Latin America

Gavin O'Toole

Longman
is an imprint of

PEARSON

Harlow, England • London • New York • Boston • San Francisco • Toronto • Sydney • Singapore • Hong Kong
Tokyo • Seoul • Taipei • New Delhi • Cape Town • Madrid • Mexico City • Amsterdam • Munich • Paris • Milan

Pearson Education Limited
Edinburgh Gate
Harlow
Essex CM20 2JE
England

and Associated Companies throughout the world

Visit us on the World Wide Web at:
www.pearsoned.co.uk

First published 2007
Second edition published 2011

ISBN: 978-1-4082-3429-7

British Library Cataloguing-in-Publication Data
A catalogue record for this book is available from the British Library

Library of Congress Cataloging-in-Publication Data
A catalog record is available from the Library of Congress

10 9 8 7 6 5 4 3 2 1
13 12 11 10

Typeset in 10/12.5pt Sabon by 35
Printed and bound by Ashford Colour Press, Gosport.

To the memory of my parents, Bernard Joseph O'Toole and Patricia Ann O'Toole, née Edwards

Brief contents

Detailed contents

List of figures, tables and boxes

Chapter 4   Challenges facing democracy

Chapter 5   The presidency

Chapter 6   Legislatures, parties, the judiciary and public administration

Chapter 7   Established political actors

Chapter 13   Identities: Nationalism, Race and Feminism

Chapter 14   Structuralism and dependency

Chapter 15   Neoliberalism

Chapter 16   Redistributive models

Preface

This book introduces undergraduate students to the study of the domestic and international politics of Latin America and provides them with a roadmap to navigate this volcanic terrain. It proffers a self-contained introductory course in Latin American politics of 16 units that is intended to support the often unglamorous toil that goes on at the coalface of university life: teaching and learning. It makes no bold claims about being the definitive source of knowledge about this complex region of the world or a sophisticated research tool. Indeed, the work undertaken by the teacher is very different to that carried out by the researcher. It aspires only to be the equivalent of a blackboard and a piece of chalk – for the lecture hall and the seminar room are the lungs of academia: without them, there is no intellectual life.

Like all maps, this book's effectiveness depends upon how it is used. It aims to provide a sense of direction, but the map-reader must have a destination in mind and will have to stop along the way to take in supplies and gain further local knowledge at each landmark. Inevitably, there is a sense today in Latin America itself that the trajectory of political evolution since the early nineteenth century has been in the direction of democracy. This is the destination the book hopes its readers will, instinctively, have in mind. Latin Americans have travelled a long and often painful road towards an ideal of government based on the meaningful inclusion of the majority of people in the making of decisions that affect their lives, and in most cases they are still travelling along that route. Understanding why most Latin American countries failed to construct viable democratic systems of government until the recent era, and how to interpret the long overdue achievement of democracy and its strengths and flaws, must be the fundamental objective of the study of politics in the region. However, as we will see, democracy is a contested term over which no one can rightfully claim to have a monopoly, and one person's democracy can sometimes be another's tyranny.

This book also aims to provide the reader with some rudimentary tools for adopting a new *approach* to the study of Latin American politics. Until the 1990s, interest in history, geography, the humanities and broad sociological questions related to development, authoritarianism, urbanisation, peasant society, revolution, ethnicity and religion were prominent in the academic study of this region. There seemed to be little value dwelling on *institutional* forms in politics such as presidencies, legislatures and political parties because it appeared that, in Latin America, institutions were irremediably weak, instability was endemic and democratic norms were perpetually absent. Such an approach owed something to a tradition rooted in colonial scholarship that leaned towards descriptive analysis, and a perception that the study of politics within one region of the world – 'area studies' – was not a *scientific* activity. It also reflected Latin America's low position in the foreign policy pecking order, in part the result of an official posture during the Cold War dismissing the region as firmly within a US 'sphere of influence'. Reinforcing the sense that studying institutions was of limited value was the nature of politics in Latin America itself, where a problem traditionally faced in many countries has been *non-institutional* sources of power.

For scholars everywhere, the end of the Cold War in the late 1980s represented something of a crossroads in social science research. It contributed greatly to a climate in which grand, overarching theories of development influenced by Cold War categories gave way to a more empirical focus aiming to explain contemporary processes. Writing in 1995, the Latin Americanist Peter H. Smith said the momentous changes of the post-Cold War international arena demanded the application of two related methodologies in social science: comparative analysis, and in particular the comparison in a globalising world of processes in different *regions*; and quantitative research based on polls, electoral data etc. that can provide the means for *measuring* the extent of change. With the transition from authoritarian to democratic forms of government in Latin America in the 1980s and 1990s, interest has grown in political institutions, particularly the executive and legislative branches of government and parties. Electoral politics puts institutions at the heart of the competition for power and, accordingly, attention has turned to the structures and branches of government once considered marginal to understanding, and to how these shape political behaviour.

While there are some British and European academics who would bridle at the suggestion, the study of Latin American political institutions since the late 1980s has often departed from theoretical work developed in the US. This is not only because political studies within the US itself have had as their focus the institution of the presidency and its relations with congress, giving scholars well-honed theoretical tools to apply to the structures of Latin America, but for more obvious reasons also. By virtue of proximity and history, the US and Latin America have close relationships. US and Latin American scholars have long co-operated in research, and have led the way in intra-regional comparisons. The abundance of locally generated statistical analysis coming out of countries such as Mexico and Chile since the early 1990s attests to the development of an intellectual culture oriented to a pan-American audience. This book acknowledges these factors, and its underlying objective is to take a modest step towards ensuring the analysis of institutions is offered among other dishes on the menu of Latin American political studies everywhere. Some courses already do so, and this book aims to support these. At the same time, it does not seek to abandon an emphasis on broader historical and sociological phenomena, and introduces the student to more general developmental themes. Finally, it addresses the study of international relations and political ideas in Latin America – areas also sometimes neglected in courses.

The book is divided into five sections that introduce the student to the history, institutions and political actors, international relations, and political and economic ideas that have shaped Latin America. Each chapter summarises key points from the work of many dedicated academics who have explored different aspects of Latin American politics, and the book makes no attempt to claim that the ideas and approaches discussed within it are those of the author. It seeks to be an enabling work – a map identifying landmarks – and to find a middle way between disseminating, explaining and steering the student around these. It aims to strike a balance in the provision of sources for the points that are made, and references are provided in parentheses for: those statements or observations derived from research literature and works of theory that students may wish to explore further or even to challenge; that discuss a theme mentioned or expand on it; or that establish the source of specific information or data. The text steadfastly avoids exhaustive referencing of the type found in some academic monographs and journal articles, in the belief that there is nothing more off-putting to students at an introductory level than numerous in-text references. Page numbers are given in references only for quoted comments, and in most other cases, if students wish to locate the specific point in a work referred to, they will have to find that volume and read it themselves.

Each chapter incorporates many boxes to draw attention to important debates, case studies or phenomena related to the core theme. It is helpful when teaching to break up discussion in this way, and even at times to digress, in order to maintain a student's interest in the theme at hand. Boxes are classified in a self-evident way as: Landmarks, Theories and Debates, Institutions, Case Studies, Society and Trends.

In the text, parentheses are also used to spell out Spanish or Portuguese terms in translation, or to give either the dates in which an individual mentioned was in power or, alternatively, their lifespan. Unless otherwise stated, all translations from Spanish are the author's. Parentheses are also used to provide cross-references pointing the reader to other chapters and boxes elsewhere in the book that take a theme under discussion further. Each chapter incorporates discussion points, which aim to encourage students to think about the issues considered and explore these further. The questions provided should not be answered solely from information given in the text of this book: to provide fuller and better answers, students will have to look beyond it to other relevant literature in the field.

A list of websites is provided at the end of each chapter that it is hoped will be of practical value and interest to students. These are listed simply to complement a student's own reading, and no responsibility is taken for their content or the views expressed on them, which remain the responsibility of those who posted them. Students should also be aware of the many limitations and pitfalls of using material from the internet.

Finally, each chapter in the book incorporates a list of recommended reading. The titles, chapters or journal articles that it is proposed students follow up are classified as either essential, valuable or useful – but in all cases students should expand their reading beyond the lists given.

Lists of acronyms and abbreviations can be found at the start of the book. For each of the 21 countries included, short timelines for the recent period and political factboxes are included as a reference guide in Appendix A. A glossary of key terms to help students negotiate some of the language often used in political analysis and to provide a source of reference is provided as Appendix B. Students of Latin America are sometimes tripped up by Spanish or Portuguese names, especially if they do not speak or read these languages, and a dramatis personae with a brief note about the significance of key individuals is also incorporated as Appendix C and includes all the key figures in this book. Throughout the book, the use of the dollar symbol for monetary amounts or their equivalents refers to the US dollar.

I make no apology for coming to the study of Latin America from a background that has combined academic study with journalism. Journalists have made significant contributions to our knowledge of the region, and it was as a journalist working in Mexico that I became fascinated by the politics of this new world. I went on to undertake postgraduate studies and, eventually, to teach about Latin America at Queen Mary, University of London, where I discovered what a great privilege it is to sit down with students who share my fascination for the region and explore together its many dimensions. It is ironic that, in order to complete the first and second editions of this book, I have been exiled from the classroom – but perhaps there is a lesson for me there, too.

The first edition of this book was the result of a process of intellectual formation that began at what was then the Institute of Latin American Studies in London, where I studied while working at the *Guardian*. In my case, it is not stretching a point to say that it could never have been written, or even conceived, were it not for the instruction I received at ILAS from some towering figures in the field of Latin American studies, in particular Professor James Dunkerley, whose intellect and kindness are unbounded. I was fortunate to be able to combine doctoral studies with teaching at Queen Mary, where Pilar Domingo, a colleague and friend then heading off to Spain, bequeathed to me her course in Latin American politics. That lucky break was the genesis of this book, the ideas within which were fashioned thereafter from the many valuable observations by students at Queen Mary about how Latin America is, or should be, taught. If this book belongs to anyone, it is to them. The second edition strives to bring readers up to date with the many developments since 2007 that have confirmed the status of Latin America as one of the most fascinating and dynamic regions of the world.

Gavin O'Toole

Acknowledgements

Although compiled by one person, Politics Latin America reflects the expertise and labours of many people. I am grateful, first and foremost, to the team at Pearson Education: to Morten Fuglevand, for having had the vision to commission the first edition of this book, and to his colleagues Emma Travis, Janey Webb and Philip Langeskov for their support along the way; and more recently to Kate Ahl, Jessica Harrison, Jenny Oates, Joseph Howarth, Josie O'Donoghue, Joy Cash and Joe Vella for their helpful efforts to bring this second edition to fruition and their professional guidance. I am also grateful to all the perspicacious reviewers who assessed the proposals and drafts, and to the production staff more broadly, for the valuable contribution they have made.

I am also grateful to colleagues and friends who have encouraged me while I have laboured away, sometimes unwittingly through gestures of solidarity that have spoken much louder than words, in particular Margaret Broderick; Brendan O'Duffy of Queen Mary; Susan Wood and Ron Gillings of the *Times*; Tony Sablan of the *Times Higher Education Supplement*; Nick Smith, Lyndsey Jones and James Fitzgerald of the *Financial Times*; Richard Bartlett and the other creative minds behind the *Latin American Review of Books* and *Aflame Books*; Fiona Plowman, Paul Plant and Alfie; Jo Griffin; Martin Wilkins and Monica Houghton; Jay Kerr; Jonathan Cook; and Nik Lawrence. Last, but very definitely not least, I am grateful to my wife, Georgina, and our beautiful girls, Isabel, Nina and Caitlin, for tolerating my obsession with the geniality that can only come from their Mexican and Irish roots.

Publisher's Acknowledgements

We are grateful to the following for permission to reproduce copyright material:

Figures

Figure 4.2 adapted from *Economic Commission for Latin America and the Caribbean (ECLAC), Social Panorama of Latin America, 2009. Briefing paper, Santiago, Chile, November 2009, figure 5, p. 18*; Figure 11.1 from EuropeAid's Worldwide Operations: EuropeAid's commitments per programme and region 2008 (million euro's) in EuropeAid Corporation Office, 2009 Better Faster More – Implementing EC External Aid 2004–2009, Brussels: p. 30 Http://wwwec.europa.eu; Figure 14.1 from Percentage of total oil production exported to the US by the main Latin American producers, 2007, http://www.eia.doe.gov, Source: U.S. Energy Information Administration (2007).

Tables

Table 3.3 from *Governance Matters VIII Indicators: Aggregate and Individual Governance Indicators 1996–2008. Policy Research Working Paper 4978: World Bank Development Research Group pp. 80–82* (Kaufmann, D., Kraay, A., Mastruzzi, M.); Table 4.3 Reprinted from Transparency International. 2008a Corruptions Perceptions Index 2008. Copyright 2008. Transparency International: the global coalition against corruption. Used with permisison. For more information, visit http://www.transparency.org; Table 4.4 from *Economic Commission for Latin America and the Caribbean (ECLAC), Statistical Yearbook for Latin America and the Caribbean, 2008 (LC/G.2399-P), Santiago, Chile, February 2009, table 2.1.1.2, p. 86. United Nations publication, Sales No. E/S.09.II.G.1.*; Table 4.5 from *Economic Commission for Latin America and the Caribbean (ECLAC), Social Panorama of Latin America, 2009. Briefing paper, Santiago, Chile, November 2009, table 1, p. 11*; Table 4.6 from World Development Indicators, 2009a, Table 2.9a, p. 75; Table 5.2 adapted from Valenzuela, Arturo. Latin American Presidencies Interrupted. *Journal of Democracy* 15:4 (2004), table only, pp. 8–9. © 2004 The National Endowment for Democracy and The Johns Hopkins University Press. Reprinted with permission of The Johns Hopkins University Press; Table 6.1 from *Legislative Politics in Latin America*, Cambridge University Press (Cox, G. and Morgenstern, S. 2002); Table 6.3 adapted from Building Democratic Institutions, Party Systems in Latin America by Mainwaring, S. and Scully, T. Copyright © 1995 by the Board of Trustees of the Leland Stanford Jr. University. All rights reserved. Used with the permission of Stanford University Press, www.sup.org; Table 6.5 adapted from Exploring the Link between Decentralization and Democratic Governance, Tulchin, Joseph H. and Selee, Andrew (eds), http://www. wilsoncenter.org; Table 7.1 from *Business Politics and the State in Twentieth-Century Latin America*, Cambridge University Press (Scheider, Ben Ross. 2004); Table 7.2 from Princetown University Press (Stephen, A. 1988); Table 8.2 from *Building the Fourth Estate. Democratization and the Rise of a Free Press in Mexico*, University of California Press (Lawson, Chappell H. 2002); Table 9.1 from Network of world merchandise by region, 2007–2008 in WTO 2009 International Trade Statistics 2009. Geneva. p. 176, http://www.wto.org; Table 9.2 from Merchandise trade of selected regional trade agreements, 2000–2008 in WTO 2009 International Trade Statistics 2009. Geneva: p. 178, http://wto.org; Tables 10.1 and 10.2 from *Talons of the Eagle. Dynamics of US-Latin American Relations*, Oxford University Press (Smith, Peter H. 2000) p. 357; Tables 11.1 and 11.2 from Network of world merchandise trade by region, 2006–2008 in WTO 2009 International Trade Statistics 2009. Geneva. p. 176, http://wto.org; Table 12.1 adapted from *Reclaiming Latin America; Experiments in Radical Social Democracy*, Zed Books (Lievesley, Geraldine, Ludlam, Steve (eds) 2009) p. 4; Table 14.1 from *Economic Commission for Latin America and the Caribbean (ECLAC), Latin America and the Caribbean in the World Economy 2008–2009. Crisis and opportunities for regional cooperation (LC/G.2413-P), Santiago, Chile, December 2009, table, I.4, p. 31. United Nations publication, Sales No. E.09.II.G.62.*; Table 15.1 from *The Puzzle of Latin American Economic Development*, Rowman and Littlefield (1999); Table 15.2 adapted from Renato Baumann, "Integration in Latin America: trends and challenges" (LC/BRS/R.190), Brasilia, Economic Commission for Latin America and the Caribbean (ECLAC), January 2008 [online] http://www.eclac.org/publicaciones/xml/2/32312/LCBRSR190RenatoBaumannIntegration.pdf; Table 15.4 from Annual growth in Latin American countries, 1994–2004, Economic Survey of Latin America and the Caribbean 2002–2003, http://www.eclac.org; Table 15.5 from World Development Indicators 2009. p. 67 World Bank; Table 16.1 Excerpt from "Cuba's Trade Turnover by Trade Partner, 1965–1989" from *Cuba After the Cold War*, edited by Carmelo Mesa-Lago, © 1993. All rights are controlled by the University of Pittsburgh Press, Pittsburgh, PA 15260. Used by permission of the University of Pittsburgh Press; Table 16.2 from Consumption, Markets and Monetary Duality in Cuba. Togorcs, V. and Garcia, A. (eds), The David Rockerfeller Center for Latin American Studies, Harvard Univeristy, http://www.drclas.harvard.edu/.

Text

Box 3.4 from Democracy in Latin America. Towards a Citizens' Democracy, http://www.undp.org; Box 12.8 from the book **Conservative Thought in Twentieth Century Latin America** *by James D. Henderson. Reprinted with the permission of Ohio University Press, Athens, Ohio (www.ohioswallow.com)*; Box 13.4 from All Latin America, All the Time; New 24 hour TV Networks Aim to Unite Region with Tailored Coverage, *Washington Post*, 10/03/2005, A12 (Reel, M.); Box 13.6

from An Interview with Magdalena Cajia. White Racism and the Aymara in Bolivia, Counterpunch magazine online, 26 April 2007; Box 13.8 from Most Chileans reject Same-Sex Marriage, Angus Reid Global Monitor, Polls and Research. 24th April 2009, http://www.angus-reid.com; Box 13.9 from Peru's Red Sun of Terror Sets, *Observer*, 25/07/1993, p. 11 (O'Shaughnessy, S.), Copyright Guardian News & Media Ltd 1993; Box 14.3 from Economic Commission for Latin America and the Caribbean (ECLAC), "Background information – Evolution of ECLAC ideas" [online] http://www.eclac.org/cgi-bin/getprod.asp?xml=/noticias/paginas/4/14004/P14004.xml&xsl=/tpl-i/p18f-st.xsl&base=/tpl-i/top-bottom_acerca.xsl.

In some instances we have been unable to trace the owners of copyright material, and we would appreciate any information that would enable us to do so.

Acronyms and abbreviations (general)

ACIEL Acción Coordinadora de las Instituciones Empresariales Libres (Co-ordinating Action of Free Enterprise Institutions), Argentina

AEB Agência Espacial Brasileira (Brazilian Space Agency)

AECID Agencia Española de Cooperación al Desarrollo (Spanish Agency for Development Co-operation)

AFM Articulación Feminista Marcosur (Southern Framework for Feminist Articulation)

AICD Agencia Interamericana para la Cooperación y el Desarrollo (Inter-American Agency for Co-operation and Development, IACD)

ALADI Asociación Latinoamericana de Integración (Latin American Integration Association, LAIA)

ALALC Asociación Latinoamericana de Libre Comercio (Latin American Free Trade Association, LAFTA)

ALBA Alianza Bolivariana para los Pueblos de Nuestra América (Bolivarian Alliance for the Peoples of Our America, usually called the Bolivarian Alliance for the Americas)

ALN Ação Libertadora Nacional (National Liberation Action), Brazil

AMDH Academia Mexicana de Derechos Humanos (Mexican Academy of Human Rights)

AMNLAE Asociación de Mujeres Nicaragüenses Luisa Amanda Espinosa (Luisa Amanda Espinosa Association of Nicaraguan Women)

ANC Assembléia Nacional Constituinte (National Constituent Assembly), Brazil

ANDI Asociación Nacional de Industriales (National Association of Industrialists), Colombia

AP Andean Pact (see CAN)

APEC Asia-Pacific Economic Co-operation

APEGE Asamblea Permanente de Entidades Gremiales Empresarias (Permanent Assembly of Business Associations), Argentina

APPO Asamblea Popular de los Pueblos de Oaxaca (Popular Assembly of the Peoples of Oaxaca)

ASEAN Association of South-East Asian Nations

AUC Autodefensas Unidas de Colombia (United Self-defence Forces of Colombia)

AUP Uprooted People in Asia and Latin America Programme

Bancomext, Banco Mexicano de Comercio Exterior (Mexican Foreign Trade Bank) Mexico

BANINTER Banco Internacional, Dominican Republic

BFS Budgetary Finance System

CACM Central American Common Market (see MCCA)

CAEM Centro de Altos Estudios Militares (Centre for Advanced Military Studies), Peru

CAFTA (officially DR-CAFTA) Dominican Republic-Central American Free Trade Agreement, incorporating US

CAINCO Cámara de Industria y Comercio de Santa Cruz (Santa Cruz Chamber of Industry and Commerce), Bolivia

CAN Comunidad Andina de Naciones (Andean Community of Nations)

Canacintra, Cámara Nacional de la Industria de Transformación (National Chamber of Industry for Development), Mexico

CANF Cuban American National Foundation, United States

CAP Common Agricultural Policy

Caricom, Caribbean Community

CCE Consejo Coordinador Empresarial (Business Co-ordinating Council), Mexico

CDA Cuban Democracy Act (Torricelli Act), 1992

CDI Centrist Democrat International (see IDC)

CDR Comités de Defensa de la Revolución (Committees for the Defence of the Revolution), Cuba

CDS Consejo de Defensa Suramericano (South American Defence Council, SADC)

CEA Consejo Empresario Argentino (Argentine Business Council)

CEB Comunidades eclesiales de base / comunidades eclesiais de base (Catholic base communities)

CEDHA Fundación Centro de Derechos Humanos y Ambiente (Centre for Human Rights and Environment), Argentina

CELAM Consejo Episcopal Latinoamericano (Latin American Council of Bishops)

CEPAL Comisión Económica para América Latina (Economic Commission for Latin America, whose acronym in English was originally ECLA, later ECLAC to incorporate the Caribbean)

CEPRA Coordinadora Ejecutiva para la Reforma Agraria (Executive Co-ordinating Body for Agrarian Reform), Paraguay

CERIAJUS Comisión Especial para la Reforma Integral de la Administración de Justicia (Special Commission for the Integral Reform of Administration of Justice), Peru

CFR Council on Foreign Relations, independent US think-tank

CG Consejo Gremial (Business Association Council), Colombia

CGE Confederación General Económica (General Economic Confederation), Argentina

CGT RA Confederación General del Trabajo de la República Argentina (General Labour Confederation of the Argentine Republic)

CIA Central Intelligence Agency, United States

CICAD Comisión Interamericana para el Control del Abuso de Drogas (Inter-American Drug Abuse Control Commission, OAS)

CICIG Comisión Internacional Contra la Impunidad en Guatemala (International Commission Against Impunity in Guatemala)

CIDH Comisión Interamericana de Derechos Humanos (Inter-American Commission on Human Rights, IACHR)

CIDI Consejo Interamericano para el Desarollo Integral (Inter-American Council for Integral Development, OAS)

CLAD Centro Latinoamericano de Administración para el Desarollo (Latin American Centre of Administration for Development)

CMEA Council of Mutual Economic Assistance

CMHN Consejo Mexicano de Hombres de Negocios (Mexican Council of Businessmen)

CNC Confederación Nacional Campesina (CNC, National Peasant Confederation), Mexico

COECE Coordinadora Empresarial de Comercio Exterior (Co-ordinator for Foreign Trade Business Organisations), Mexico

CONAIE Confederación de Nacionalidades Indígenas del Ecuador (Confederation of Indigenous Nationalities of Ecuador)

Conatel Comisión Nacional de Telecomunicaciones (National Telecommunications Commission), Venezuela

Convergencia (Convergence of Civic Organisations for Democracy), Mexico

Coparmex, Confederación Patronal de la República Mexicana (Mexican Employers' Confederation)

CPC Confederación de la Producción y del Comercio (Confederation for Production and Commerce), Chile

CTH Confederación de Trabajadores de Honduras (Workers' Confederation of Honduras)

CTM Confederación de Trabajadores de México (Mexican Workers' Confederation)

CUT Central Única dos Trabalhadores (Central Workers' Confederation), Brazil

CVRD Companhia Vale do Rio Doce (Vale do Rio Doce Company, now Vale), Brazil

DAS Departamento Administrativo de Seguridad (Administrative Security Department), Colombia

DEA Drug Enforcement Administration, United States

DR-CAFTA Dominican Republic–Central American Free Trade Agreement, incorporating US

EALAF East Asia–Latin America Forum

ECLA/ECLAC see CEPAL

EDI Electoral Democracy Index

EEC European Economic Community

EGTK Ejército Guerrillero Túpac Katari (Tupac Katari Guerrilla Army), Bolivia

EIA Energy Information Administration, US

EIB European Investment Bank

ELN Ejército de Liberación Nacional (National Liberation Army), Bolivia, Colombia

Embraer, Empresa Brasileira de Aeronáutica (Brazilian Aviation Corporation)

Emfapa Tumbes, Empresa Prestadora del Servicio de Agua Potable y Alcantarillado de Tumbes (Drinking Water Provision and Drainage Company), Peru

Empreven, Empresarios por Venezuela (Business People for Venezuela)

ENAP Empresa Nacional del Petróleo (National Petroleum Company), Chile

Enarsa, Energía Argentina (Argentine Energy)

EOMs Election Observation Missions

EPB Ejército Popular Boricua (Boricua Popular Army), Puerto Rico

EPR Ejército Popular Revolucionario (Popular Revolutionary Army), Mexico

ERP Ejército Revolucionario del Pueblo (People's Revolutionary Army), Argentina

ESG Escola Superior de Guerra (Superior War School), Brazil

EuroLat, Euro-Latin American Parliamentary Assembly

EZLN Ejercito Zapatista de Liberación Nacional (Zapatista National Liberation Army), Mexico

FA Frente Amplio (Broad Front), Uruguay

FAES Fundacion para el Análisis y los Estudios Sociales (Foundation for Analysis and Social Studies)

FARC Fuerzas Armadas Revolucionarias de Colombia (Revolutionary Armed Forces of Colombia)

FAT Frente Auténtico del Trabajo (Authentic Labour Front), Mexico

FCO British Foreign and Commonwealth Office

FDI Foreign Direct Investment

FDN Fuerza Democrática Nicaraguense (Nicaraguan Democratic Force)

FDP Fuerzas de Defensa de Panamá (Panamanian Defence Forces)

FEALAC Forum for East Asia–Latin America Co-operation

Fedecámaras, Federación de Cámaras y Asociaciones de Comercio y Producción de Venezuela (Venezuelan Federation of Chambers and Associations of Commerce and Production)

Federacafé, Federación Nacional de Cafeteros de Colombia (National Coffee-growers Federation of Colombia)

Fejuve, Federación de Juntas Vecinales (Federation of Neighbourhood Councils), Bolivia

FEPALC, Federación de Periodistas de América Latina y del Caribe (Federation of Latin American and Caribbean Journalists)

FMRA, Foro Mundial sobre la Reforma Agraria (World Forum on Agrarian Reform)

FPMR Frente Patriótico Manuel Rodríguez (Manuel Rodríguez Patriotic Front), Chile

FPVA Federación de Partidos Verdes de las Américas (Federation of Green Parties of the Americas), Mexico City

FTA Free Trade Agreement

FTAA Free Trade Area of the Americas

FTAPP Free Trade Area of the Asia-Pacific

FUNAI Fundação Nacional do Índio (National Indian Foundation), Brazil

GATT General Agreement on Tariffs and Trade

GMB General Union (Britain)

GOU Grupo de Oficiales Unidos (United Officers Group), Argentina

GRIO Grupo de Río (Rio Group)

GSP Generalised System of Preferences, European Union

IACD Inter-American Agency for Co-Operation and Development (see AICD)

IACHR Inter-American Commission on Human Rights (see CIDH)

IADB Inter-American Development Bank (often IDB)

IAEA International Atomic Energy Agency

IAPA Inter-American Press Association
ICE Instituto Costarricense de Electricidad (Costa Rican Electricity Institute)
ICJ International Court of Justice in The Hague
IDB Inter-American Development Bank (sometimes IADB)
IDC Internacional Demócrata de Centro (Centrist Democrat International)
IDEA International Institute for Democracy and Electoral Assistance
IEDI Instituto de Estudos para o Desenvolvimento Industrial (Institute for the Study
 of Industrial Development), Brazil
IFE Instituto Federal Electoral (Federal Electoral Institute), Mexico
ILAS Institute of Latin American Studies, London
ILO International Labour Organisation
IMF International Monetary Fund
INTI Instituto Nacional de Tierra (National Land Institute), Venezuela
ISI Import-substitution industrialisation
ITUC International Trade Union Confederation
IV, Iniciativa Verde (Green Initiative), Argentina

LAC Latin American and the Caribbean
LAFTA Latin American Free Trade Association (Asociación Latinoamericana de
 Libre Comercio, ALALC)
LAIA Latin American Integration Association (Asociación Latinoamericana de
 Integración, ALADI)
LANIC Latin American Network Information Center, University of Texas, Austin
LGBT Lesbian, Gay, Bisexual and Transgender
Lidema Liga de Defensa del Medio Ambiente (Environmental Defence League), Bolivia
LNG Liquid Natural Gas

M-19 Movimiento 19 de Abril (19th of April Movement), Colombia
M&As Mergers and Acquisitions
MCCA Mercado Común Centroamericano (Central American Common Market,
 CACM)
Mercosur/Mercosul Mercado Común del Sur/Mercado Comum do Sul (Common
 Market of the South)
MINUGUA Misión de las Naciones Unidas para Guatemala (United Nations
 Mission to Guatemala)
MINVEC Ministerio para la Inversión Extranjera y la Collaboración Económica
 (Ministery for Foreign Investment and Economic Collaboration), Cuba
MIR Movimiento de Izquierda Revolucionaria (Revolutionary Left Movement),
 Chile
MLST Movimento de Libertação dos Sem Terra (Movement for the Liberation of
 the Landless), Brazil
MNCL Movimiento Nación Camba de Liberación (Movement for the Liberation
 of the Camba Nation), Bolivia
MRTA Movimiento Revolucionario Tupac Amaru (Tupac Amaru Revolutionary
 Movement), Peru
MST Movimento dos Trabalhadores Rurais Sem Terra (Landless Workers'
 Movement), Brazil

NAFTA North American Free Trade Agreement
NAM Non-Aligned Movement
NATO North Atlantic Treaty Organisation
NED National Endowment for Democracy
NPT Nuclear Non-Proliferation Treaty
NUS National Union of Students (Britain)

OAS Organization of American States
ODCA Organización Demócrata Cristiana de América (Christian Democrat Organisation of America)
OECD Organisation for Economic Co-operation and Development

Parlacen, Central American parliament
Parlandino, Andean parliament
Parlasur, Mercosur parliament
Parlatino, Latin American parliament
PBEC Pacific Basin Economic Council
PCS Public and Commercial Services Union (Britain)
PDVSA Petróleos de Venezuela (Petroleum of Venezuela)
PE, Partido Ecologista (Ecologist Party), Chile
PECC Pacific Economic Co-operation Council
Pemex, Petróleos Mexicanos (Mexican Petroleum), Mexico
Petrobras, Petróleo Brasileiro (Brazilian Petroleum), Brazil
PMPA Prefeitura Municipal de Porto Alegre (Porto Alegre Municipal Council), Brazil
PRODDAL Proyecto sobre el Desarrollo de la Democracia en América Latina (Latin American Democracy and Development Programme), UN
PRONASOL, Programa Nacional de Solidaridad (National Solidarity Programme), Mexico
PV, Partido Verde (Green Party), Brazil

RN Resistencia Nicaragüense (Nicaraguan Resistance i.e. *contras*)

SADC South American Defence Council (see CDS)
SECODAM Secretaría de Contraloría y Desarrollo Administrativo (Ministry of Auditing and Administrative Development), Mexico
SFP Secretaría de la Función Pública (Public Administration Ministry), Mexico
SHCP Secretaría de Hacienda y Crédito Público (Ministry of Finance and Public Credit), Mexico
SICLAC Socialist International Committee for Latin America and the Caribbean
SINAMOS Sistema Nacional en Apoyo de la Mobilización Social (National System for the Support of Social Mobilisation), Peru
Sofofa, Sociedad de Fomento Fabril (Society for Manufacturing Promotion), Chile
SUNTRACS Sindicato único nacional de trabajadores de la industria de la construcción y similares (National Union of Workers of Construction and Similar Industries), Panama

TeleSUR La Nueva Televisora del Sur (New Television Station of the South)
TPP Trans-Pacific Strategic Economic Partnership Agreement

UBE União Brasileira de Empresários (Brazilian Union of Businessmen)
UBPC Unidad Básica de Producción Cooperativa (Basic Unit of Co-operative Production), Cuba
UIA Unión Industrial Argentina (Argentine Industrial Union)
UN United Nations
Unasur, Unión de Naciones Suramericanas (Union of South American Nations)
UNCTAD United Nations Conference on Trade and Development
UNDP United Nations Development Programme
UNICEF United Nations Children's Fund
UNODC United Nations Office on Drugs and Crime
UNPAN United Nations Online Network in Public Administration and Finance
UNT Unión Nacional de Trabajadores (National Union of Workers), Mexico
UPLA Unión de Partidos Latinoamericanos (Union of Latin American Parties)
USAID, US Agency for International Development, United States
USAS United Students Against Sweatshops (United States)
USJFCOM United States Joint Forces Command

WFP World Food Programme
WTO World Trade Organisation
WWF World Wide Fund for Nature

YPF Yacimientos Petroliferos Fiscales (Fiscal Oilfields), Argentina

Acronyms and abbreviations (political parties and coalitions)

AD Acción Democrática (Democratic Action), Venezuela
AD-M19 Alianza Democrática Movimiento 19 de Abril (Democratic Alliance-19th of April Movement), Colombia
ADN Acción Democrática Nacionalista (Nationalist Democratic Action), Bolivia
ADOC Alianza Democrática de Oposición Civilista (Democratic Alliance of Civic Opposition), Panama
AL Alianza Liberal (Liberal Alliance), Nicaragua
Alianza PAIS, Patria Altiva y Soberana (Proud and Sovereign Fatherland Alliance), Ecuador
ANR-PC Asociación Nacional Republicana-Partido Colorado (Republican National Alliance-Colorado or Coloured Party), Paraguay
AP Acción Popular (Popular Action), Peru
APC Alianza Patriótica por el Cambio (Patriotic Alliance for Change), Paraguay
APRA Alianza Popular Revolucionaria Americana (American Revolutionary Popular Alliance, today referred to as the Partido Aprista Peruano, PAP), Peru
APU Alianza Pueblo Unido (United People's Alliance), Panama
ARENA Alianza Republicana Nacionalista (Nationalist Republican Alliance), El Salvador

CD Cambio Democrático (Democratic Change), Panama
CFP Concentración de Fuerzas Populares (Concentration of Popular Forces), Ecuador

COPEI Comité de Organización Política Electoral Independiente/Partido Demócrata Cristiano (Committee for Independent Electoral Political Organisation/ Christian Democrat Party), Venezuela

CPD Concertación de Partidos por la Democracia (Coalition of Parties for Democracy), Chile

CSD Convergencia Social Demócrata (Social Democrat Convergence), Guatemala

DCG Democracia Cristiana Guatemalteca (Guatemalan Christian Democracy party)

DPUDC Democracia Popular/Unión Demócrata Cristiana (Popular Democracy/ Christian Democrat Union), Ecuador

EP-FA Encuentro Progresista-Frente Amplio (Progressive Encounter-Broad Front), Uruguay

FL Fanmi Lavalas (Waterfall Family, or Lavalas Party), Haiti

FMLN Frente Farabundo Martí para la Liberación Nacional (Farabundo Marti National Liberation Front), El Salvador

FN Falange Nacional (National Falange), Chile

FNCD Front National pour le Changement et la Démocratie (National Front for Change and Democracy), Haiti

FNP Fuerza Nacional Progresista (National Progressive Force), Dominican Republic

Frepaso, Frente País Solidario (Federation for a Country in Solidarity), Argentina

FRG Frente Republicano Guatemalteco (Guatemalan Republican Front)

FSLN Frente Sandinista de Liberación Nacional (Sandinista National Liberation Front), Nicaragua

GANA Gran Alianza Nacional (Grand National Alliance), Guatemala

ID Izquierda Democrática (Democratic Left), Ecuador

IV Iniciativa Verde (Green Initiative), Argentina

MAS Movimiento al Socialismo (Movement Towards Socialism), Bolivia, Venezuela

MAS Movimiento de Acción Solidaria (Solidarity Action Movement), Guatemala

MCL Movimiento Cristiano Liberación (Christian Liberation Movement), Cuba

MFP Movimiento Femenino Popular (Women's Popular Movement), Peru

MIP Movimiento Indígena Pachakuti (Indigenous Pachakuti Movement), Bolivia

MIR-NM Movimiento de la Izquierda Revolucionaria-Nueva Mayoría (Revolutionary Left Movement-New Majority), Bolivia

MNP Movimiento Nacionalista Peruano (Peruvian Nationalist Movement, today known as Movimiento Etnocacerista)

MNR Movimiento Nacionalista Revolucionario (Revolutionary Nationalist Movement), Bolivia

MPD Movimiento Popular Democrático (Democratic Popular Movement), Ecuador

MPS Movimiento de Participación Solidaria (Movement of Co-operative Participation), Mexico

MSN Movimiento de Solidaridad Nacional (National Solidarity Movement), El Salvador

MVR Movimiento Quinta República (Fifth Republic Movement), Venezuela

NAM Non-Aligned Movement

NE Nuevo Espacio (New Space Party), Uruguay

NFD Nueva Fuerza Democrática (New Democratic Force), Colombia

NFR Nueva Fuerza Republicana (New Republican Force), Bolivia

NP Partido Nacional (National Party), Uruguay

OAS Organisation of American States

OFDI Outward Foreign Direct Investment

OPL Organisation du Peuple en Lutte (Organisation of People in Struggle, thereafter Organisation Politique Lavalas, Waterfall Political Organisation), Haiti

ORA Organización Renovadora Auténtica (Authentic Renewal Organisation), Venezuela

PAC Partido Acción Ciudadana (Citizen Action Party), Costa Rica

PAN Partido Acción Nacional (National Action Party), Mexico

PAN Partido de Avanzada Nacional (National Advancement Party), Guatemala

PAP Partido Aprista Peruano (Peruvian Aprista Party, official name today of APRA), Peru

PC Partido Colorado (Coloured Party, the Colorados), Uruguay

PC Partido Conservador (Conservative Party), Chile

PC Partido Convergencia (Convergence Party), Venezuela

PCC Partido Comunista de Cuba (Communist Party of Cuba), Cuba

PCC Partido Conservador Colombiano (Colombian Conservative Party), Colombia

PCCh Partido Comunista de Chile (Communist Party of Chile), Chile

PCN Partido Conservador de Nicaragua (Conservative Party of Nicaragua)

PCV Partido Comunista de Venezuela (Venezuelan Communist Party)

PDA Polo Democrático Alternativo (Alternative Democratic Force), Colombia

PDC Partido Demócrata Cristiano (Christian Democrat Party), Argentina, Bolivia, Chile, El Salvador, Honduras, Paraguay, Peru, Uruguay

PDC Proyecto Demócrata Cubano (Cuban Democrat Project)

PDI Polo Democrático Independiente (Independent Democratic Pole), Colombia

PDP Partido Democrático Progresista (Progressive Democratic Party), Paraguay

PDT Partido Democrático Trabalhista (Democratic Labour Party), Brazil

PE Partido Ecologista (Ecologist Party), Chile

PFL Partido da Frente Liberal (Liberal Front Party), Brazil

PFSDH Parti Fusion des Sociaux-Democrates Haitiens (Unified Party of Haitian Social Democrats), Haiti

PIC Partido Independiente de Color (Independent Party for Coloured People), Cuba

PID Partido Izquierda Democrática (Democratic Left Party), Ecuador

PIN Partido Integración Nacional (National Integration Party), Costa Rica

PIP Partido Independentista Puertorriqueño (Puerto Rican Independence Party)

PJ Partido Justicialista (Justicialist Party, i.e. Peronist), Argentina

PLC Partido Liberal Colombiano (Liberal Party of Colombia)

PLC Partido Liberal Constitucionalista (Liberal Constitutionalist Party), Nicaragua

PLD Partido de la Liberación Dominicana (Dominican Liberation Party), Dominican Republic

PLH Partido Liberal de Honduras (Liberal Party of Honduras)

PLN Partido Liberación Nacional (National Liberation Party), Costa Rica

PMDB Partido do Movimento Democrático Brasileiro (Brazilian Democratic Movement Party)

PN Partido Nacional (National Party, i.e. the Blancos), Uruguay

PNH Partido Nacional de Honduras (National Party of Honduras, often just PN)

PNOSP Partido Nuevo Orden Social Patriótico (New Order Social Patriotic Party), Argentina

PNP Partido Nacionalista Peruano (Peruvian Nationalist Party)

PNP Partido Nuevo Progresista (New Progressive Party), Puerto Rico

PNT Partido Nuevo Triunfo (New Triumph Party), Argentina

PODEMOS Poder Democrático y Social (Social and Democratic Power), Bolivia

PODEMOS Por la Democracia Social (For Social Democracy), Venezuela

PP Partido Panameñista (Panameñista Party), Panama

PP Partido Popular (Popular Party), Panama

PP Perú Posible (Possible Peru coalition)

PPC Partido Popular Cristiano (Christian Popular Party), Peru

PPD Partido Popular Democrático (Popular Democratic Party), Puerto Rico

PPD Partido por la Democracia (Party for Democracy), Chile

PPS Partido País Solidario (Country with Solidarity Party), Paraguay

PR Partido Reformista (Reformist Party), later to become PRSC, Dominican Republic

PRD Partido de la Revolución Democrática (Party of the Democratic Revolution), Mexico

PRD Partido Revolucionario Democrático (Democratic Revolutionary Party), Panama

PRD Partido Revolucionario Dominicano (Dominican Revolutionary Party), Dominican Republic

PRE Partido Roldosista Ecuatoriano (Ecuadorean Roldosist Party), Ecuador

PRF Partido Revolucionario Febrerista (Revolutionary Febrerista Party), Paraguay

PRI Partido Revolucionario Institucional (Institutional Revolutionary Party), Mexico

PRIAN Partido Renovador Institucional de Acción Nacional (Party of National Institutional Action and Renovation), Ecuador

PRSC Partido Reformista Social Cristiano (Social Christian Reformist Party), formerly PR, Dominican Republic

PRSD Partido Radical Social Demócrata (Radical Social Democrat Party), Chile

PS Partido Socialista (Socialist Party), Argentina

PSC Partido Social Cristiano (Social-Christian Party), Ecuador

PSCh Partido Socialista (Socialist Party), Chile

PSDB Partido da Social Democracia Brasileira (Party of Brazilian Social Democracy), Brazil

PS-FA Partido Socialista Ecuatoriano-Frente Amplio (Ecuadorean Socialist Party-Broad Front)

PSP Partido Sociedad Patriótica 21 de Enero (21st of January Patriotic Society Party), Ecuador

PSU Partido Socialista del Uruguay (Socialist Party of Uruguay)

PSUV Partido Socialista Unido de Venezuela (United Socialist Party of Venezuela)

PT Partido dos Trabalhadores (Workers' Party), Brazil

PU Partido Unionista (Unionist Party), Guatemala

PUC Partido Unión Cívica (Civic Union Party), Uruguay

PUR Partido de Unidad Republicana (Party of Republican Unity), Ecuador

PUSC Partido de Unidad Social Cristiana (Party of Social Christian Unity), Costa Rica

PV Partido Verde (Green Party), Brazil

PV Proyecto Venezuela (Project Venezuela)

PVEM Partido Verde Ecologista de México (Green Ecologist Party of Mexico)

RDNP Rassemblement des Democrates Nationaux Progressistes (Rally for Progressive National Democrats), Haiti

RECREAR Recrear para el Crecimiento (Recreate for Growth), Argentina

RN Partido Renovacion Nacional (National Renewal Party), Chile

UC Unión Cívica (Civic Union), Uruguay

UCEDE Union Del Centro Democratico (Union of the Democratic Centre), Argentina

UCR Unión Cívica Radical (Radical Civic Union), Argentina

UDI Unión Demócrata Independiente (Independent Democrat Union), Chile

UNE Unidad Nacional de la Esperanza (National Union of Hope), Guatemala

UNO Unión Nacional Opositora (National Opposition Union), Nicaragua

UNS Unión Nacional Sinarquista (National Synarchist Union), Mexico

UP Unidad Popular (Popular Unity), Chile

UPP Unión por el Perú (Union for Peru party)

URNG Unidad Revolucionaria Nacional Guatemalteca (Guatemalan National Revolutionary Unity)

Introduction

Latin America is an exciting region and, once under its exotic spell, a visitor rarely fails to return to it. From its breathtaking landscapes, bewitching music and pre-Columbian grandeur to its revolutionary traditions, the rebellious temperament of its people, and the unrivalled skill of its footballers, it never fails to capture the imagination. This vitality is often reflected in news reports, and in recent years the region has often been in the headlines. Journalists tend to concentrate on the negative, such as drug-trafficking violence in Mexico, the civil war in Colombia, riots and protests in Bolivia and Argentina, political intransigence in Honduras, or anti-US posturing in Venezuela and Cuba. However, behind the frequently bleak predictions and facile stereotypes there is much cause for hope and lessons for us all as Latin American people and their leaders push forward the bounds of political possibility and find innovative ways to tackle deep-seated problems. The election of José Mujica as the president of Uruguay in 2009 demonstrates how far some Latin American societies have progressed down the road of democracy: he is a former Tupamaros guerrilla who was imprisoned for 14 years in a military jail. Yet at the same time, the coup in Honduras that ousted President Manuel Zelaya in the same year shows how far some countries still have to travel.

Latin America is also of great importance to the study of politics, development, international relations and other disciplines, offering students, teachers and researchers many valuable opportunities to expand their knowledge. The study of Latin America today can:

■ provide us with theoretical tools for the analysis of key contemporary themes anywhere in the world – such as democratisation, institution-building or United States foreign policy. Those tools have often been fashioned from the study of Latin America's many and often startling contrasts, which are a characteristic feature of this region. Scholars of Latin America have made significant contributions to the most important debates in the social sciences and humanities, and have often been at the forefront of theoretical development in many areas. The study of Latin America has been distinctively *interdisciplinary*, and this has enabled it to attract experts from diverse fields and, in turn, to contribute to knowledge across many disciplines;

■ provide many rich examples to compare with our observations from other countries. As part of the 'developing world', Latin America has often been a laboratory for political and economic experiments, and so offers students of politics from across the world novel insights and experiences. It is also unique because, for the first time in history, almost an entire developing region suffering from significant levels of poverty and inequality is organised under democratic governments. At the same time, this vast region extends to the south of the most economically developed and powerful country, the US, offering us many opportunities to explore relations between neighbours from different cultural and political traditions enjoying different levels of development. As a region built through European colonialism upon the encounter between different races and cultures, Latin American countries offer valuable insights into how different groups co-exist and adapt to the juggernaut of change;

■ help us to understand phenomena closer to home, where so often we like to assume that we are immune to the ebb and flow of contemporary trends that find their most dramatic expression in the developing world. The Latin American republics are among the oldest independent states in the world, their borders largely fixed before the tumultuous wars that reshaped Europe until the late twentieth century. These republics have nearly two centuries of independent history to draw upon – Ireland, modern Italy and Germany, the Balkan states and much of central and eastern Europe do not have this depth of historical maturity. Yet the political evolution of the Latin American states has often proceeded in fits and starts, interrupted by military coups d'état, civil wars and economic collapse. Institutions have frequently failed, and political power has often been misused. Globalisation is having a profound impact on economies and international relations. We can learn from these experiences, and so we should.

But what is Latin America? When the World Trade Organisation published its annual international statistics in October 2005, it had made a subtle change to the way it compared the performance of countries in the Americas. Gone was the denomination 'Latin America' and, in its place, the hemisphere was divided into North America (Canada, the United States and Mexico) and South and Central America. A few months later, in January 2006, Evo Morales was inaugurated as president of Bolivia the day after celebrating his achievement in ceremonies at the archaeological remains of the Tiwanaku civilisation near La Paz. The 46-year-old former llama herder and coca leaf farmer made a private offering of sweets, wine and flowers to Pachamama – Mother Earth in Andean cosmology – before moving to the pre-Inca temple of Kalasasaya where, barefoot and dressed as a sun priest, he received a ceremonial baton and addressed thousands of supporters in the Aymara language. That same year, the Latin American and Caribbean Congress in Solidarity with the Independence of Puerto Rico brought together in Panama former presidents and 16 ruling parties from across the region. The summit called on the US to respect Puerto Rico's right to self-determination – yet Puerto Ricans themselves remain divided, or ambivalent, about choosing between being a member of the Latin American community of nations or a state of the US. Further north, Venezuela's radical president Hugo Chávez has revived notions of pan-Latin American unity under 'Bolivarian' ideals, bringing together economies and societies through regional institutions and initiatives that hark back to the nineteenth-century dreams of the great Liberator, Simón Bolívar.

All of these observations from positions rooted in the present and the past challenge the popular understanding of Latin America as a territorially defined region comprising nation-states that are linguistically Iberian – Spanish and Portuguese – and mainly Roman Catholic. They reveal that Latin America is, above all, an *idea* – and one that is constantly in motion and resistant to easy definitions. They illustrate that institutions and individuals can hold widely differing visions of Latin America and of its future. Such contrasting visions and the theories that have been built upon them have been at the very heart of political development in this complex region since the Spanish *conquistadores* first drew their swords to claim it as their own in the early sixteenth century. As a result, definitions of what comprises Latin America have always varied. The term itself has been attributed to different sources: from Latin American politicians and scholars themselves to the French under Napoleon III, who wanted to distinguish the Spanish-, Portuguese- and French-speaking areas of the American hemisphere to support his own imperial designs. This is a paradox, because many millions of people in the region do not speak languages derived from Latin as a mother tongue. When the Spaniards first arrived, about 2,000 indigenous languages were spoken in the region, and about 800 of these are still in use even now. The Andean language Quechua, for example, is spoken by as many as 14 million people, and has gained significantly greater status in recent years.

Today, Latin America has mainly sociological and geopolitical connotations: sociologically, it corresponds to those countries south of the US where Spanish and Portuguese (and some French or related creole languages) are spoken or which have Iberian cultural or ethnic antecedents or associations. The long era of Spanish and Portuguese colonial control prior to Independence in the early nineteenth century left an enduring legacy in these countries, and for visionary leaders bequeathed much material with which to dream of regional unity. Geopolitically, Latin America corresponds to 21 mostly independent countries south of the US, from Mexico in North America through Central America and the Caribbean and across the South American continent (see Figure I.1).

However, the status of Puerto Rico as a territory of the US has usually meant that it has been excluded from consideration when discussing Latin America, while at the same time it has been suggested that Latin America should incorporate dependent territories such as French Guiana and some people would like to include within it countries such as Belize, Guyana and Suriname because they are found in predominantly Latin American vicinities. Moreover, although the US itself is usually excluded from our understanding of Latin America because it is regarded as having primarily an Anglo-Saxon inheritance, large swathes of the southern US once formed part of Mexico and the Hispanic influence in these areas remains strong. Indeed, the settlement patterns of Hispanics or Latinos in the US are overwhelmingly concentrated in those states gained from Mexico in the mid-nineteenth century. US Census Bureau estimates show that Hispanics form the largest minority in the country, meaning that the US now has a Spanish-speaking population larger than that of most Latin American countries.

For the purposes of this book, Latin America comprises those 21 countries shown with their population figures and areas in Figure I.1, although reference will sometimes also be made to Hispanics in the US and other states. Puerto Rico, however,

Figure I.1 The countries of Latin America and their capitals, populations* and areas in sq. km. (sq. m.)

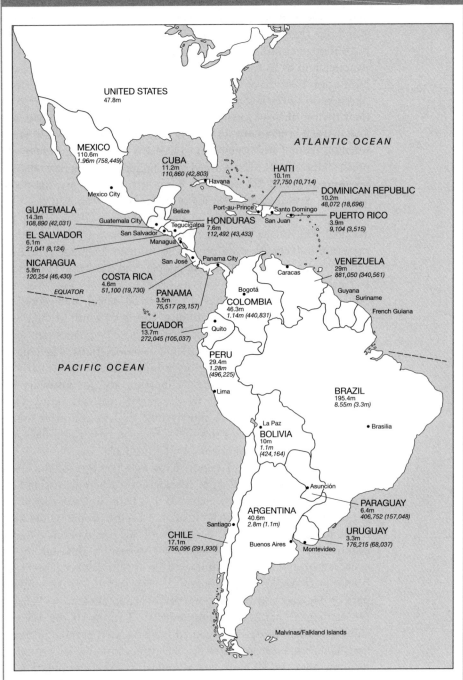

UNITED STATES
47.8m

ATLANTIC OCEAN

MEXICO
110.6m
1.96m (758,449)

CUBA
11.2m
110,860 (42,803)

Havana

HAITI
10.1m
27,750 (10,714)

Port-au-Prince

DOMINICAN REPUBLIC
10.2m
48,072 (18,696)

Santo Domingo

San Juan

PUERTO RICO
3.9m
9,104 (3,515)

Mexico City

GUATEMALA
14.3m
108,890 (42,031)

Belize

Guatemala City

Tegucigalpa

HONDURAS
7.6m
112,492 (43,433)

EL SALVADOR
6.1m
21,041 (8,124)

San Salvador

Managua

NICARAGUA
5.8m
120,254 (46,430)

San José

COSTA RICA
4.6m
51,100 (19,730)

Panama City

Caracas

VENEZUELA
29m
881,050 (340,561)

EQUATOR

Bogotá

PANAMA
3.5m
75,517 (29,157)

COLOMBIA
46.3m
1.14m (440,831)

Guyana

Suriname

French Guiana

ECUADOR
13.7m
272,045 (105,037)

Quito

PERU
29.4m
1.28m
(496,225)

PACIFIC OCEAN

Lima

BRAZIL
195.4m
8.55m (3.3m)

La Paz

Brasilia

BOLIVIA
10m
1.1m
(424,164)

Asunción

PARAGUAY
6.4m
406,752 (157,048)

ARGENTINA
40.6m
2.8m (1.1m)

Santiago

URUGUAY
3.3m
176,215 (68,037)

CHILE
17.1m
756,096 (291,930)

Buenos Aires

Montevideo

Malvinas/Falkland Islands

*2010 projections

Note: US figure refers to total Hispanic population only.

Source: UN Department of Economic and Social Affairs; US Census Bureau 2006.

continues to represent an anomaly in the compilation of statistics by multilateral bodies, and so its inclusion in comparative tables is contingent upon the availability of separate data for the country. The dominant language in the 21 countries dealt with here is Spanish, although it is the Portuguese-speaking Brazil that is the largest Latin American country, both in terms of area and population. It is from these Iberian roots that the study of politics in Latin America as a discernible region emerges, and it is impossible to separate the history and politics of this region from this inheritance. Moreover, these countries have at times shared so many traits such as presidentialism, ineffective institutions, central states that monopolise power at the expense of local governments, and the legacy of a strict hierarchy in society that it often seems natural and reasonable to group them together. Haiti also has something of an ambivalent status in the study of Latin America because, like many other Caribbean countries and Belize and the Guyanas, it does not share fully the Iberian heritage of the mainland states and is the only primarily francophone independent country whose roots, arguably, lie in French colonialism. One reflection of this is a political system that is semi-presidential in which parliament plays a greater role than in other Latin American states. Haiti is sometimes – but not always – incorporated in the study of Latin America because events in the country have at times influenced those elsewhere in the region, because of its proximity to Cuba and its role in US foreign policy, and because of its inescapable relationship with the larger Dominican Republic, with which it shares the island of Hispaniola and which has a closer historical relationship with Spain.

At the same time, Latin America is as much a product of its economic, political and cultural *diversity* as of the shared inheritance that gives its peoples a sense of separate identity. While Brazil's rapid development is turning it into a power in its own right complete with its own space programme under the auspices of the Agência Espacial Brasileira (Brazilian Space Agency), for example, in Honduras one in four children under five years old suffers chronic malnutrition, and in some rural communities this can reach 48.5 per cent. Diversity is both a challenge and an opportunity in the study of politics. It obliges us to identify common patterns of behaviour and to explain cases that digress from these. It forces us to dispense with the unnecessary and contradictory details that, at times, can overwhelm us in order to focus on what is really important. It demands that we make comparisons. It is the cornerstone of theory and comparative analysis.

The richness, complexity – and, at times, tragic consequences – of Latin American diversity is for students themselves to discover, ideally by throwing on a backpack and travelling through the region. However, any discussion of Latin American diversity will begin with the themes of race and ethnicity. In most cases the lands conquered and colonised by the Europeans in the sixteenth century had already been occupied for millennia by well-ordered indigenous communities, some of which, such as the Aztecs and Incas, had established by force their own sophisticated empires in the region. Indigenous history has not been as well documented as that of the European colonists who rapidly established their control over what would become Latin America. What is well known is that indigenous society collapsed during the period of Spanish Conquest as a result of mistreatment and the spread of diseases such as smallpox, measles and bubonic plague. Colonial policies and practices also sanctioned the seizure of indigenous lands. However, despite the domination of a white upper class, the countries of the region would develop during the colonial era as societies that combined European and indigenous cultural elements. The indigenous contribution to Latin American culture and society is still evident in many areas, from patterns of social organisation and land use to words such as chocolate, potato, tomato and tobacco that have been taken up or adapted by Spanish, Portuguese, English and other languages. This complex racial and cultural influence is best summarised by the Spanish term *mestizo* (mixed), used to refer to the biological but also the cultural fusion that distinguishes Latin America and its peoples to this day. To the European-indigenous encounter was added the impact of slavery, as Africans were shipped to Ibero-America to work the large estates and plantations established there and to serve their white owners. African culture has also had an important influence upon Latin America, particularly in the countries where most slaves were taken such as Brazil and Cuba.

In plural societies, diversity is the terra firma of democracy, and upon it sits the cornerstone of all democratic life: institutions. Although there is no single route through the constantly shifting terrain of politics, which is far too complex and contingent to allow us the luxury of a straightforward journey, one point of departure in our exploration of Latin America could be the degree to which the achievement of democracy has been delayed or obstructed by the nature of the governing institutions in which legitimate power is vested – the state. States in Latin America have so often been too weak or too strong, monopolised by interests that are too few or too many, or either too close or too far from the societies over which they preside. The nature of these governing institutions has been shaped by phenomena that will be discussed in the book – such as personalism, authoritarianism, revolution, lawlessness, populism, nationalism, corporatism and dependency – and, as a result, these have often been the main obstacles on the route towards democracy. This has meant that, although constitutions assign formal powers to executives, legislatures and judiciaries, real power has often resided with groups or individuals competing or co-operating outside the institutional structures of government such as leaders of powerful dynastic families, economic interest groups and trades unions, and with institutions such as the military that are not formally assigned a governing role. Governmental institutions such as national congresses have, until the recent era, often served as window-dressing for dictatorships or for the rule of a powerful clique. A survey in 2002 of Latin American leaders confirmed that many still believed *de facto* power often resides with groups acting outside of the formal institutions of politics (see Table I.1).

Yet institutions are of paramount importance for Latin America's future: weak institutions can make it more difficult to maintain political stability and can fuel uncertainty. They can foster scepticism about politics, resulting in immobilism, policy gridlock, a lack of government authority and, ultimately, political conflict. Most scholars agree that strong, stable, representative institutions are vital for the survival and well-being of democracy. This book aims to situate this consensus firmly at the heart of the study of Latin American politics.

Part I provides a brief introduction to the history of Latin America since Independence in the early nineteenth century. Chapter 1 examines developments from Independence until the Great Depression of the 1930s and Chapter 2 takes

Table I.1 Who exercises power in Latin America?*

Powers	Actors considered to exercise power	No. of mentions	% of interviewees who mentioned it
De facto powers	Economic groups/business executives/financial sector	150	(79.8)
	Communications media	122	(64.9)
Constitutional powers	Executive branch (i.e. president)	68	(36.2)
	Legislative branch (i.e. congress)	24	(12.8)
	Judicial branch (i.e. the courts)	16	(8.5)
Security forces	Armed forces	40	(21.3)
	Police	5	(2.7)
Political institutions and political leaders	Political parties	56	(29.8)
	Politicians/political operators/political leaders	13	(6.9)
Foreign factors	USA/Embassy of the USA	43	(22.9)
	Multilateral lending organisations	31	(16.5)
	International factors/external factors	13	(6.9)
	Transnational companies/multi-nationals	9	(4.8)

*According to the number of mentions by Latin American leaders consulted in 2002 by the Proyecto sobre el Desarrollo de la Democracia en América Latina (PRODDAL).

Source: UNDP, 2004b

the reader thereafter to the end of military rule on the eve of the democratic transitions of the 1980s.

Part II introduces the student to the study of democracy and the key political institutions and actors in Latin America. Chapters 3 and 4 explore what is meant by democracy, processes of democratic transition and consolidation, and the main challenges facing democracy today. Chapter 5 looks at the most important institution in Latin American politics, the presidency, and considers the impact of this office upon democratic governance. Chapter 6 looks at the legislative and judicial branches of government, political parties, developments in public administration, and decentralisation. Chapters 7 and 8 examine established and new political actors in Latin America, from business associations, trades unions, peasants, the Church and the military to social movements, non-governmental organisations, environmentalists and the media.

Part III introduces the student to international relations in Latin America. Chapter 9 examines the relationships between Latin American states themselves and the key foreign policy challenges facing countries in the region. Chapter 10 looks at the evolution and motives of US foreign policy towards Latin America, a key factor in the region's political development. Chapter 11 explores the evolving relationship between Latin America and two other regions of the world, Europe and Asia. European scholarship and the external policy of institutions such as the European Union are of great importance to Latin America's future development: Europeans have made significant contributions to peace processes, mechanisms to engender respect for human rights, social development and even regional integration in Latin America.

Part IV introduces the student to political ideas and the debates and behaviour they generate in Latin America. The study of political ideas in the region has not been consistent, and many courses have tended to neglect this area. Yet it is often political ideas that attract students to them in the first place. Chapter 12 explores formative themes in Latin American political thought and the clash of ideas on the left and right of the political spectrum. This has become the key tension shaping Latin American political development in recent years with the rise of a number of left-of-centre governments in the region. Chapter 13 looks at political ideas informed by a sense of identity, such as nationalism, racial and indigenous doctrines – which have become engines of mobilisation – feminism and gender politics.

Part V introduces the reader to the ideas that have influenced different models of political economy in Latin America. Chapter 14 explores the structuralist ideas that supported state-led industrialisation and the dependency approaches that emerged from these. Chapter 15 looks at neoliberalism – the most important influence upon economic development since the 1980s – and the relationship between the reforms this perspective inspired and the notion of globalisation. Finally, Chapter 16 considers strategies that have put redistribution and social justice at the heart of economic development, such as socialism, populism and social democracy. Inequality is a distinguishing characteristic of Latin American societies, which need to become fairer for all their citizens if democracy is to prosper.

Part I

AN INTRODUCTION TO LATIN AMERICAN HISTORY

Chapter 1

From Independence to the 1930s

This chapter examines the historical development of Latin America from the era in which new countries emerged out of the struggles for independence from Spain in the early nineteenth century until the birth of mass politics in the early twentieth century. The political history of modern Latin America begins with the quest for independence by countries that had been moulded for three centuries by Spanish and Portuguese imperial control. By the time of Independence, uniquely Latin American societies were developing from the fusion of Iberian, indigenous and African peoples and cultures. Landmarks in the development of indigenous society between Conquest and Independence are summarised in Table 1.1.

Indigenous society contributed to political development in many ways, creating complex and ethnically divided societies in which the desire for stability among post-colonial elites – members of powerful social groups ranging from landowners, soldiers and merchants of European origin in the early nineteenth century to career politicians, military officers, industrialists, financiers and professionals by the late twentieth century – has been at least as powerful as their desire for democracy and development. Institutional characteristics of some of the more powerful indigenous societies, such as that of the Aztecs, may also have been reflected in some ways in the development of politics since the early nineteenth century. The celebrated writer Octavio Paz, for example, likened the Mexican president to a *tlatoani* – an Aztec emperor who combined legal and sacred symbolic powers making him supreme in every respect (Paz, 1970). During the late colonial era prior to Independence, indigenous themes became prominent in the writing of non-indigenous priests and intellectuals developing early ideas of nationhood that rejected Spanish control (see Chapter 13). The fear among people of European descent of indigenous rebellion has also remained a feature of political culture into the twenty-first century, and was in evidence during the 1980s in Peru during the guerrilla war conducted by the Maoist organisation Sendero Luminoso (see Boxes 12.4, 13.9), during the 1990s, when a mainly indigenous guerrilla army rebelled in Chiapas, Mexico (see Boxes 12.6, 13.5), and more recently in Bolivia in the reaction among elites within resource-rich eastern provinces to political reforms that have greatly empowered the country's indigenous majority (see Chapter 6, Boxes 8.7, 12.11, 13.6).

The institution of slavery also influenced political and economic development, forming the mainstay of the colonial economy and the feudal social structures constructed around the large country estates of aristocratic Hispanic families. Debates

LANDMARKS
Table 1.1 Indigenous history prior to Independence

Year or period	Development
c.35,000–20,000BC	People from Asia settle in the North American region and spread south
c. 9000BC	Communities are now established as far south as Tierra del Fuego in modern Argentina
c.6000–2000BC	Intensive agriculture leads to the emergence of civilisations, particularly in Mexico, where hieroglyphic writing develops, and the Andes
ADc.990	Inca empire begins to expand in the Andes, eventually including modern Peru, Ecuador, Bolivia and parts of Argentina and Chile
1325	Aztecs found Tenochtitlán, the site of modern Mexico City, and this becomes the capital of an expansive military empire
1492	Christopher Columbus lands in what are now the Bahamas, convinced he has found the route to Asia. He makes four voyages between 1492 and 1504
1494	The Treaty of Tordesillas shares out the 'Indies' between Spain and Portugal
1495	The Spaniards begin a brutal enslavement of the indigenous people of Hispaniola, mainly in their search for gold. By 1502 so few survive that they start to import African slaves
1519–40	The main period of Spanish conquest of the Aztec, Maya and Inca civilisations and the escalation of the demographic collapse of indigenous society
1542	Spain tries to end the worst cruelty against indigenous people with the New Laws of the Indies
1560	The celebrated friar Bartolomé de las Casas estimates that by now up to 40 million indigenous people may have died
1600	At least 15 major epidemics have reduced the native population of the Americas to a fraction of its size prior to 1492
1697	The Spaniards finally conquer a Maya free-state, Tayasal, in the Petén jungle
1761	Mayas rebel against the Spaniards near Chichén Itza, Mexico
1780	Túpac Amaru II (José Gabriel Condorcanqui) leads a bloody revolt against the Spaniards in Tinta, Peru
1809–10	First revolts by creoles that would initiate lengthy struggles for Independence against Spanish rule

over slavery and race equality had a bearing on the political forms that were adopted in the post-Independence era and on subsequent immigration and development policies (see Chapter 13). The legacy of slavery informed the principle of racial and social equality enshrined in some of the early liberal constitutions of the independent republics of Latin America.

The Iberian imperial elite of aristocratic landowners, colonial officials, soldiers and members of the Roman Catholic Church's hierarchy maintained control over these divided and differentiated societies by force of arms, but also by the force of ideas. Populations wedded to tradition were inculcated with deeply-rooted notions of racial and social hierarchy. Although members of wealthy Hispanic families had the resources to travel and so were exposed to cosmopolitan influences, most of the population remained isolated until the late eighteenth century from some of the social and ideological influences that were reshaping Europe and parts of North America. The subsequent independence of the Latin American territories and their evolution from conditions of anarchy to orderly control under modern states overseeing mass political participation would be determined as much by events outside the region as within it.

Independence

Two centuries after the Conquest, the attitude of imperial Spain and Portugal towards their colonies had become one of neglect, and during the seventeenth century Spain also grew economically weaker while her colonies became more prosperous. A new dynasty of French Bourbons succeeded to the Spanish throne in 1713 holding 'absolutist' ideas – a belief that the monarchy had a divine right to rule without restrictions – that made them less willing to share power with the Roman Catholic Church. The Bourbons wanted to reverse Spain's decline and extract more from its colonies, and embarked on reforms that were felt most strongly in the Americas during the reigns of Carlos III (1759–88) and Carlos IV (1788–1808). Angry at British forays into its Caribbean colonies, the Spanish crown reorganised administration and commerce so as to stimulate the economy. Similar reforms were undertaken in Portugal by the Marquis of Pombal (1750–77), a powerful prime minister who saw Brazil as key to Portugal's revival.

Although Bourbon policies were successful because administration was more efficient, trade and government revenues grew, and military defences were strengthened, they generated discontent in the colonial population at a time when Enlightenment ideas also began to inform elite opinion (see Box 1.1), and so weakened the Spanish crown's legitimacy – its enjoyment of consent for its authority. Economic reforms damaged local traders and administrative reorganisation seeking to enhance the authority of Madrid meant people who had been born in Spain itself (*peninsulares*) replaced American-born whites, creoles (*criollos*), in official positions. Bourbon reforms also weakened the Church by tightening the control exercised by the crown, and in 1767 Carlos III expelled the Jesuit order from all of Spanish America. By the late eighteenth century, most creoles felt the Spaniards were taking their wealth and depriving them of power, and a number of revolts reflected the growing tension between Spain and its American colonies. Rebellions often involved indigenous people protesting against Spanish policies. Túpac Amaru II (b.*c.*1740–d.1781), a descendant of the Incas, led an indigenous army of 80,000 in revolt in what is now Peru; there were protests against taxes in New Granada (Colombia); and revolts by black slaves in Brazil.

Spain and Portugal were greatly affected by the aftermath of the French Revolution (1789). The decision of Carlos IV to join the French in 1796 exposed Spanish America to British attacks, and in 1805 the Spanish navy was destroyed in the Battle of Trafalgar. The British started raiding Spain's American colonies and in 1806 creole militias in Buenos Aires distinguished themselves by fighting off an attempted British invasion, demonstrating the Spanish crown's weakness. In 1807, Napoleon occupied Portugal and the throne was moved to Brazil. Carlos and his heir Ferdinand (1813–33) fell into the hands of Napoleon in 1808, and the French leader installed his brother Joseph as Spain's monarch. The French occupation of Spain led to a constitutional crisis in the American colonies, because the

THEORIES AND DEBATES	Box 1.1

The Enlightenment and ideology at Independence

Ideas generated by the Enlightenment, the period of European philosophical development in the eighteenth century in which the emphasis on reason displaced that on spirituality, contributed to the tensions in Iberian America that would lead to the Independence revolts. The Enlightenment informed thinking in three main areas – Church–state relations, popular sovereignty and national identity:

- *Church–state relations* Enlightenment thought emphasised secularism and rationality in the belief that religion was, in essence, superstition. Carlos III removed clerics from positions of authority and reduced ecclesiastical privileges. In the traditional societies of Spanish America, where rural inhabitants were profoundly religious, such ideas were considered heretical. Measures taken by the Church hierarchy in response to the Bourbon reforms hit both priests and parishioners. The expulsion of the Jesuits, for example, deprived many communities of teachers. The reforms forced disgruntled creole lower clergy into confrontation with the Spanish authorities, and priests in or from viceregal centres such as Peru and Mexico, for example, became prominent critics of Spain or conspired or took part in uprisings against it.

- *Popular sovereignty* The American War of Independence (1775–83) and the French Revolution (1789) gave great impetus to ideas of popular sovereignty in which the 'people' ended monarchic rule. US ships brought ideas about constitutional republicanism to Latin American ports and the French revolutionaries set out to establish republics across Europe. Notions of popular sovereignty and equality sparked slave revolts in the Caribbean, and the uprising in 1791 that led to Haiti's independence generated fears of social revolution among planters, increasing the stakes of colonial rule.

- *National identity* The American and French revolutions also generated early nationalist ideas, (sometimes called 'proto-nationalist'). Creole clerics, some of whom spent time in exile, such as the Mexican Fray Servando Teresa de Mier (b.1763–d.1827) and the Chilean Juan Ignacio Molina (b.1740–d.1829) challenged European notions that the New World was somehow inferior in works that extolled the spiritual, natural or social history of their motherlands. In New Spain (Mexico) and Peru, creole thought developed a patriotic strain and sometimes drew upon romantic notions of indigenous antiquity to give these ideas historical depth. Once the Independence insurgencies began, patriotism and early notions of national identity would be valuable to creole elites both in uniting their divided societies against the Spanish, but also in avoiding becoming the target of subordinated racial groups by having an identity to share with them.

disappearance of the sovereign begged the question about where legitimate authority now lay. Many creoles saw this as an opportunity to rebel, and between 1809 and 1810 they initiated uprisings that would last until 1825. Esteemed military figures such as the Venezuelan Simón Bolívar (b.1783–d.1830), who became known as the Liberator, emerged during the struggles of this period.

In Spain itself, there were uprisings in support of the deposed monarch, and in 1812 a rebel junta in Cadiz proclaimed a new constitution based on liberal ideas (see Chapter 12) that promised creoles a greater say in their affairs and convinced many people of the virtues of remaining tied to the mother country. This liberal constitution – and those that had preceded it in the revolutionary United States and France – had a significant influence on subsequent ideas about the importance of constitutions to politics in Latin America, constitutionalism. The importance placed upon the rules of political conduct codified in constitutions – even if in practice those rules were often ignored – can be seen as a precursor of the liberal political systems and democratic forms of government that some creoles in Latin America aspired to create (see Chapters 3, 12). Liberal ideas were considered to be revolutionary and justified the struggle to shake off control by a monarchy as well as providing principles upon which new systems of government could be based, such as individual freedom and equality. However, Ferdinand was restored to the Spanish throne with the defeat of Napoleon, annulled the 1812 constitution and decided to crush the American rebellions. This divided the creoles, and royalists regained the upper hand between 1815 and 1818. In 1820, a liberal revolt in Spain forced the king to restore the 1812 constitution, demonstrating once and for all that the monarchy could never regain its full authority. The Spanish liberals ordered the colonial authorities to seek a truce with the American rebels, undermining commanders in the field. Now, independence from a *liberal* Spain appeared attractive to *conservative* creoles in Latin America, who began to dream of having their own independent monarchy. Even the great Liberator, Bolívar, grew sceptical about the prospects for republicanism in Spanish America as he became convinced of the need for a strong central source of authority in these unruly societies.

Different countries followed different paths to independence. Much of Spanish America was rocked by rebellion and insurgencies that eventually resulted in independence (see Figure 1.1), while Brazil's path to self-rule was quite different (see Box 1.2).

Mexico's independence struggle was inaugurated in 1810 with the call to arms by a creole priest, Miguel Hidalgo y Costilla (b.1753–d.1811) in the name of

---

CASE STUDY   **Box 1.2**

Brazil's empire

Brazil followed a different path to independence than Spanish America and remained largely undisturbed by the turmoil after 1810. The country's economy was built on sugar, an industry dominated by wealthy white landowners. However, most people were black slaves, and the threat of a black revolt made allies of the white settler population and the Portuguese. As the Portuguese imperial administration had also devolved more power to local landowners, they saw no great benefit to independence. After fleeing Napoleon, the Portuguese court resided in Brazil from 1808, and the prince regent, who in 1816 would become King João VI (1816–26), enacted economic reforms that benefited Brazilian elites and ended the country's colonial status by declaring it a kingdom in its own right. In 1820, the French were driven from Portugal, leading to the establishment of a government committed to constitutional monarchy modelled on Spain's 1812 constitution. In Brazil, there was sympathy for the liberals and King João VI accepted the idea of a constitutional monarchy. He returned to Portugal in 1821, leaving as regent prince Dom Pedro who, in 1822, joined Brazilian planters, bureaucrats and businessmen to declare independence. Emperor Dom Pedro I of Brazil (1822–31) established Latin America's only independent monarchy, and it would survive until 1889. Brazil avoided the crisis of legitimacy that had occurred in Spanish America, and slave-owning elites were able to maintain a social system that allowed them to continue exercising control.

Figure 1.1 Rebellion and independence in Latin America 1791–1824

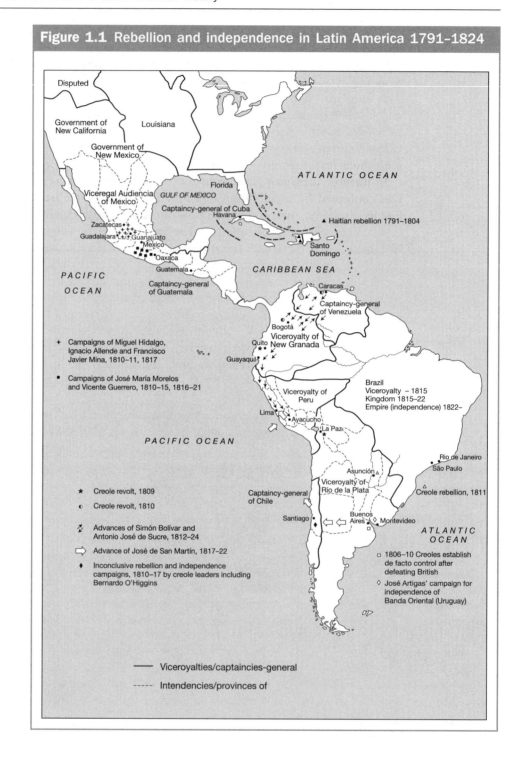

Disputed

Government of New California

Louisiana

Government of New Mexico

Viceregal Audiencia of Mexico

GULF OF MEXICO

Florida

Captaincy-general of Cuba

Havana

ATLANTIC OCEAN

Zacatecas
Guadalajara Guanajuato
Mexico
Oaxaca
Guatemala

PACIFIC OCEAN

Captaincy-general of Guatemala

Santo Domingo

▲ Haitian rebellion 1791–1804

CARIBBEAN SEA

Caracas

Captaincy-general of Venezuela

Bogotá

Viceroyalty of New Granada

Quito

Guayaquil

+ Campaigns of Miguel Hidalgo, Ignacio Allende and Francisco Javier Mina, 1810–11, 1817

■ Campaigns of José María Morelos and Vicente Guerrero, 1810–15, 1816–21

Viceroyalty of Peru

Lima

Ayacucho

La Paz

Brazil
Viceroyalty – 1815
Kingdom 1815–22
Empire (independence) 1822–

PACIFIC OCEAN

Rio de Janeiro
São Paulo

Asunción

Viceroyalty of Río de la Plata

Creole rebellion, 1811

★ Creole revolt, 1809

○ Creole revolt, 1810

Advances of Simón Bolívar and Antonio José de Sucre, 1812–24

⇨ Advance of José de San Martín, 1817–22

♦ Inconclusive rebellion and independence campaigns, 1810–17 by creole leaders including Bernardo O'Higgins

Captaincy-general of Chile

Santiago

Buenos Aires

Montevideo

ATLANTIC OCEAN

□ 1806–10 Creoles establish de facto control after defeating British

◇ José Artigas' campaign for independence of Banda Oriental (Uruguay)

—— Viceroyalties/captaincies-general

----- Intendencies/provinces of

Ferdinand and the Virgin of Guadalupe, Mexico's main religious icon. Yet it was the events in Spain that eventually led creole royalists to join forces with insurgents and declare independence, and Mexico began its independent existence as a monarchy under Emperor Agustín I (1822–23). The monarchical solution would soon break down as military leaders ejected Agustín and established a republic. In Central America, creole landowners felt threatened by the liberals in Spain and, in 1822, joined royalist Mexico. However, when Agustín fell, the provinces of Guatemala, El Salvador, Honduras, Nicaragua and Costa Rica joined together as the United Provinces of Central America.

In Buenos Aires, *de facto* creole control since the defeat of the British in 1806 was confirmed by a revolution in 1810. However, for the next 11 years creoles fought among themselves over economic policy and efforts by Buenos Aires to exert central control over the resistant provinces of Paraguay, Banda Oriental (modern Uruguay) and Upper Peru (now Bolivia). Between 1814 and 1817, the Argentine general José de San Martín (b.1778–d.1850) formed and trained a patriot army then crossed the Andes and seized Santiago. General Bernardo O'Higgins (b.1778–d.1842) became the first leader of independent Chile in 1817 and, aided by British mercenaries, San Martín's army headed north for Peru. Creoles rebelled in 1810 in Venezuela under Bolívar and Francisco de Miranda (b.1750–d.1816) and declared independence as a republic in 1811, sparking fighting that would last until 1823. However, non-whites supported the Spanish, Miranda was captured and Bolívar escaped to New Granada. By 1817, Bolívar had returned and he now included non-whites in his forces. From Venezuela, he moved against Bogotá in 1819, founding the Republic of Colombia. He moved back into Venezuela and defeated the Spanish in 1821, declaring the independence of Gran Colombia (incorporating Venezuela and Colombia), then moved on to conquer Ecuador. As a result, patriot armies would converge on Peru from south and north, and San Martín took Lima, cherishing a vision of an independent constitutional monarchy. However, San Martín came to a settlement with Bolívar that would have an important bearing on the fate of monarchy as an option in the region, and the newly independent countries of South America would be established with republican constitutions. Bolívar launched the final assault against royalist forces in Peru and, in 1824, won a decisive victory at Ayacucho, entering Bolivia in 1825.

From anarchy to neocolonialism

The wars of Independence devastated Latin America's economies, and the first 25 years of the new republics' independent existence were characterised by disunity, civil war, instability and foreign interventions. The main landmarks of the period of instability following Independence are summarised in Table 1.2. Trade came to a halt between 1810 and 1826, and the conflicts of the post-Independence period further suppressed economic activity. The new patriot armies cost a great deal to maintain, and the abolition of colonial-era taxes reduced the revenues of the new governments. The silver mines in Mexico and Peru were destroyed, and the civilian

LANDMARKS
Table 1.2 From Independence to instability

Year or period	Development
1804	Haiti wins independence from France
1805	French–Spanish naval defeat at Trafalgar by Britain
1806	Rebellion in Venezuela fails; creoles defeat British force in Buenos Aires
1807–08	Napoleon's forces invade Portugal then occupy Spain
1809	Revolts in Quito and La Paz
1810–25	Revolts leading to wars against the Spanish and between creoles across Latin America, eventually resulting in Independence
1812	Rebel junta in Cadiz proclaims liberal constitution
1822	Dom Pedro declares Independence in Brazil; Central American elites join Mexican empire
1823	Guatemala, El Salvador, Honduras, Nicaragua and Costa Rica abandon Mexico and join as the United Provinces of Central America; Monroe Doctrine claims Latin America within a US sphere of influence
1825–28	War between Argentina and Brazil, eventually concluding with Uruguay's independence
1827–29	Central America racked by civil wars; Spanish re-invasion of Mexico fails
1830	Gran Colombia breaks up as Ecuador and Venezuela secede
1833	Great Britain takes control of Las Malvinas (Falkland Islands)
1835–38	Texas breaks away from Mexico; secessionist revolts in several Brazilian states; Costa Rica and Nicaragua leave Central American confederation
1835–39	Short-lived Peru-Bolivia Confederation, ended by Chilean invasions after 1836 and eventual defeat in war
1844	Santo Domingo achieves independence from Haiti
1845–48	United States annexes Texas; US invades and defeats Mexico, which loses vast areas of territory; indigenous rebellion in Yucatán (Mexico); Central American confederation falls apart; Great Britain intervenes to consolidate protectorate on the Mosquito Coast in Central America, eventually yielding territory although retaining Belize

labour force was decimated. Communications were poor in the new republics and, because there were few banks in Latin America before 1850, new administrations lacked the capital required to improve transportation links and found themselves in debt to Great Britain. Elites mostly favoured free trade unencumbered by tariffs on imports, and from 1830–50, exports to Europe and the US increased but the control of trade often passed from the hands of Spanish merchants to British, French and US traders.

The Independence movements had come under the control of conservatives who wanted to maintain a social structure dominated by creoles and to avoid radical change. The new republics could export agricultural products and minerals, and their governments were controlled by creoles owning great estates or mines. Formally, laws establishing a social hierarchy based on caste (an individual's position in society based on their ethnic status, but usually determined by skin colour or other physical characteristics) disappeared with Independence, but the hierarchical structure of colonial society remained intact, with aristocratic whites ruling over indigenous or black labourers working the fields or mines. Conditions did not change for the indigenous masses, who survived through subsistence agriculture or as peons living on the land of a *hacienda* (estate) owner. Although colonial tithes on indigenous communities ('tribute') were abolished, in republics with large indigenous populations such as Bolivia, Peru and Colombia this measure was reversed because it depleted government revenues. Uprisings such as the caste war in Yucatán (1847), in which the native Maya tried to rid themselves of whites and *mestizos*, people of mixed white and indigenous backgrounds, continued to instill fear in the white elite. Slavery receded everywhere, except in republics with plantation economies such as Peru, Venezuela, Ecuador and Colombia, where proprietors feared economic ruin. But in some countries the practice actually grew, and from 1825–50, coffee and sugar planters in Brazil and Cuba imported record numbers of Africans.

The main problem faced by the newly independent countries of Latin America was the absence of a political consensus, with the creole ruling groups squabbling over values and national boundaries. Even though they had won self-rule, creoles disagreed over what system of government to adopt and numerous constitutions were implemented. The formula of monarchy in societies shaped by traditional, aristocratic norms had been considered, and in some cases was experimented with, but republicanism would prevail even though Latin America lacked a democratic tradition and institutions. These would have to be built from scratch by rulers who had no revenues and lacked public loyalty. In this atmosphere, patronage and clientelism prevailed by which politics – seen as a route to enrichment – was conducted through networks of alliances between dynasties and rival groups of elites in which individual powerbrokers rewarded their 'clients' with favours and resources (patronage) in return for support (see Boxes 1.3, 2.1, 7.1).

In particular, divisions emerged between conservatives and liberals that often, but by no means always, reflected an individual's position in society and the amount of land or wealth they possessed. Conservatives tended to hark back to an older order and regretted the monarchy's downfall. They feared democratic change and sought solace in the institutions of the former empire such as the Church and army (see Chapter 12). Powerful creole landowners and soldiers, for example, wanted to conserve the privileges they had long enjoyed; the Church had been closely identified with the monarchy, and sought to protect the great wealth it had amassed as a result. Liberals advocated models based on the political systems of the US, France and Britain and proclaimed sovereignty of the people, individual rights, equality before the law and accountable government founded on representative institutions. Many liberals were younger men influenced by radical ideas from Europe and the US who foresaw a new order in which countries achieved progress through the development of entrepreneurial activities in agriculture and industry. Often, they were not landowners, but it would not be correct to characterise liberals as urban progressives and conservatives as backward-looking country squires, because some wealthy landowners were liberal and some conservatives were pioneers of new entrepreneurial activities in Latin America such as banking. In general, individuals whose social position or family links put them closer to traditional structures of power, such as governing institutions and the Church, were more likely to end up being termed conservative than those further from such structures, who

The *caudillos*

The militarisation of society, the breakdown of law and order, and economic stagnation generated a power vacuum and anarchic conditions in which the *caudillo*, a regional chieftain, could dominate politics. From Independence until the 1850s, many Latin American countries were controlled by these strongmen, whose main role was to maintain order. *Caudillos* were often military leaders who had won a reputation in the Independence wars or ensuing revolts but nurtured an image as men of the people. The phenomenon of *caudillismo* reflected a pragmatic move to consolidate centralised power in a single source, presaging the emergence of stronger states – social institutions that together comprise the main source of power (see Box 2.1). Even Bolívar came to believe in the need for strong central authority and many elites began to believe that dictatorship was the only realistic way their troubled countries could be governed. However, *caudillismo* also reflected the enduring importance of clientelism and patronage – the relationship between a political 'patron' and a 'client' in which the latter gives the former support in exchange for favours – because *caudillos* existed in a mutually dependent relationship with aristocratic creoles by offering property holders protection in return for power. Moreover, *caudillismo* was not always inconsistent with the desire of elites for constitutional government and most *caudillos* did not ignore formal institutions such as congresses. Elections remained important symbols of popular sovereignty that allowed *caudillos* to demonstrate which regions they dominated and there was great interest in this period in constitutional ideals.

Perhaps the most notorious *caudillo* was Antonio López de Santa Anna (b.1794–d.1876) of Mexico, an opportunist whose many forays into politics worsened turmoil in his country and sparked conflict with the US, resulting in the loss of huge swathes of national territory. In Argentina, the conservative *caudillo* Juan Manuel de Rosas (b.1793–d.1877) dominated politics from 1829–52. Dr José Gaspar Rodríguez de Francia (b.1766–d.1840), a conservative dictator known as 'El Supremo', governed Paraguay from 1814–40 and isolated it from European cultural influences. Although *caudillismo* seemed to have a natural fit with traditional conservatism (see Chapter 12), there were also liberal *caudillos*. In Central America, the Honduran born *caudillo* Francisco Morazán (b.1799–d.1842) undertook liberal reforms that eroded the power of the Church. The creation of large armies following Independence had also created a new means for *mestizos* to rise in the social order based on their talents. *Caudillismo* offered an avenue to power for these ambitious men of mixed blood such as José Antonio Páez (b.1790–d.1873), the first president of Venezuela, and Andrés Santa Cruz (b.1792–d.1865) in Peru and Bolivia. In the late 1830s, the Guatemalan *mestizo* Rafael Carrera (b.1814–d.1865) took over from Morazán.

would in turn be more likely to become liberal (see Safford, 1987). The main differences between the positions taken by conservatives and liberals are summarised in Table 1.3 (see also Chapter 12).

Liberal ideas influenced by Spain's 1812 constitution shaped the new systems even in Brazil, which remained a monarchy (see Box 1.2). However, although liberals in government tried to put their ideas to work, their visions of change soon stalled in the face of the harsh realities of Latin America. In practice, many people did not accept the idea of racial equality; voting rights (suffrage) were restricted to property-owning elites; and the conservative defence of old-fashioned values often appealed to ordinary people. Where liberals and conservatives were most at odds

LANDMARKS

Table 1.3 The main differences between conservatives and liberals

Theme	Conservatives	Liberals
Change	Wanted to avoid radical change and criticised liberalism for being a spiritually impoverished materialist doctrine	Ideas considered revolutionary and in conflict with inherited colonial order
Vision of society	Attacked individualism for opening the door to anarchy. Wanted to maintain a hierarchical social structure dominated by creole landowners who preserved their privileges through legal and social restrictions on people of mixed race	Society based on principles of individual freedom, autonomy and equality before the law
Monarchy and government	Often saw themselves as descendants of the *conquistadores*, harked back to the colonial order and regretted the monarchy's downfall. Feared democracy and hostile to majority rule, preferring elite and authoritarian forms of representation	Wanted to shake off control by monarchy, proclaiming sovereignty of the people based upon universal suffrage. Liberalism and republicanism frequently came together
Institutions	Sought solace in the institutions of the former empire, such as the Church and army. Often sought to compensate for the loss of monarchy with heavily presidential and centralised systems	Advocated models based on the political systems of the US, France and Britain i.e. accountable government founded on representative institutions and constitutionalism. Often foresaw a society based on modern structures, such as federalism
Church-state relations	Wanted the Church to retain its dominant role as a source of cohesion in a hierarchical order that they dominated, and so sought to protect Church wealth and privileges. Saw attempts at Church–state separation as threatening anarchy	Wanted to reduce the power of the Church, expropriate its wealth and end its monopoly over education in order to nurture modern states overseeing secular, dynamic and enterprising societies
Economy	Mixed views about the benefits of foreign trade, investment and the role of the state. Instinctive preference for free market activities among elites, but not all opposed to state-directed industrialisation	Progress could be achieved through the development of entrepreneurial activities in agriculture and industry. Free market initially seen as the main source of progress in countries steeped in semi-feudal tradition

concerned the role of the Church, and battles over Church–state relations became an important influence on political perspectives in the nineteenth century (see Box 1.1). Liberals wanted to reduce the power of the Church in order to nurture modern states overseeing dynamic and enterprising societies, while conservatives wanted the Church to retain its dominant role as a source of cohesion in a hierarchical order of which they sat at the apex (see Chapters 7, 12). Popular resistance to liberal anticlerical reforms often provoked violence.

The result of economic devastation and disputes between liberals and conservatives was instability. Elite divisions were not contained within stable constitutional systems in most of the newly independent countries, and many liberal presidents and governments were thrown out after only a few years as conservatives called on the military to intervene. In these conditions, regional strongmen or *caudillos* often emerged to dominate politics (see Box 1.3).

The pressure among dominant groups in the provinces to maintain local power against central government by using the threat of secession also became a recurrent theme in the first 30 years of Independence. Such 'centrifugal' tendencies were aggravated by the inability of conservatives and liberals to agree about the ultimate source of legitimate authority in their countries. Tension was often a reflection of the desire among provincial or regional elites for more autonomy, and important sources of conflict in this period were the rival visions of federalists and centralists, both of whom often claimed to be following liberal precepts. Centralism, advocating the concentration of power in a single central authority, was often believed to be the only practical way of holding the weak new countries together at a time of instability and foreign threats. Federalists, by contrast, believed that only federal systems devolving power to states or provinces could work in such huge territories. Many *caudillos* adopted both federalist and centralist positions at different times during their careers.

Independent Mexico was ripped apart by such secessionist forces. The experiment with monarchy collapsed and a federal republic was declared in 1823 initiating a period of debilitating strife between liberals and conservatives and federalists and centralists. Pressure for independence grew in the 1830s in the states of Zacatecas, Texas and Yucatán. Texas seceded in 1836 and was subsequently annexed by the US, eventually sparking a crippling war (see below). In the late 1840s, large indigenous revolts shook Yucatán and Mexico's north-central mining states. In the United Provinces of Central America, disagreements among elites led to civil war and dismemberment as state governments resisted liberal control of the central government from 1829–40, and in 1838 Costa Rica and Nicaragua broke away from the confederation. Nine years of instability followed, and in 1847 Guatemala declared independence and the confederation fell apart. Bolívar's dream of pan-American unity collapsed and Gran Colombia fragmented. Brazil was also weakened by a series of regional revolts until the 1840s that helped to undermine the monarchy. Relations between Buenos Aires and outlying provinces of what was originally the viceroyalty of the River Plate collapsed and, following independence, the centralist 'unitarios' fought conservative 'federales' in the interior who resented the dominance of liberals in the former capital. Internal disputes also exacerbated tense relations between the new states of the region. Bloody wars were fought between Argentina and Brazil (1825–28), leading to the establishment of Uruguay as a buffer state, and between Chile and the combined forces of Peru and Bolivia (1836–39).

Foreign powers took advantage of instability in Latin America to extend their control and influence over territory, and the great imperial powers harassed the region's new states. Spain did not recognise the independence of its former colonies until the late 1830s and tried unsuccessfully to reconquer Mexico in 1829. In the 1830s and 1840s, Britain, France and the US attacked Latin American cities to protect their citizens or punish them for defaulting on debts. Britain, which had controlled Belize and coastal areas of Nicaragua and Honduras since the seventeenth century, increased its interventions in the region in the 1840s and took control of the Malvinas (Falkland) islands. Mexico's bitter divisions made the country weak and vulnerable to an expansionist US (see Box 1.4), and the war between the two countries and US occupation of 1846–48 – the largest intervention by a foreign power in Latin America following Independence – had an important symbolic effect on the region, inaugurating what has since often been described there as 'US

Box 1.4

The US displaces European powers

During the nineteenth century, Latin American countries brought an end to European military interventions but became the target of US attentions. President James Monroe (1817–25) believed his adversaries could use Latin America as a base to attack the US, and articulated the 'Monroe Doctrine' in 1823 which was aimed at dissuading European powers from engaging in a recolonisation effort of Latin America but also established an attitude of domination by the US over the Western hemisphere. The US began to advance its own claims over territory from ex-Spanish colonies in the 1840s. Its expansionist impulse was reinforced through the ideology of 'Manifest Destiny', which sought to justify taking land from Hispanic Europeans to extend 'civilisation', often a metaphor for an Anglo-Saxon and Protestant way of life. After its victory in Mexico in 1848, and the discovery of Gold in California, the US began challenging Britain in the region in earnest. In Mexico, in 1861 a debt default by Benito Juárez's government provoked France, Spain and Britain to occupy the country's main Atlantic ports, but Napoleon III used this as a pretext for extending French control over the country with the support of conservative monarchists. French forces occupied Mexico City in 1863 and Napoleon installed the Habsburg prince Maximilian (1864–67) as a puppet monarch. Juárez led a guerrilla war and, with the eventual French withdrawal, Maximilian was executed in 1867 – sending an unequivocal signal to the European powers that the era of their imperial ambitions in the region was over. Spain found it increasingly difficult to control Cuba and Puerto Rico, where nationalist sentiment aspiring to independence was growing. At the same time, by the mid-1880s the expansion of trade resulted in significant areas of the growing economies of Mexico and Central America coming under US control. The US began to intervene more directly in the region and, in the 1890s, its influence in Latin America began to overtake that of Britain. Its dominant role was confirmed in Cuba, where Spanish taxation on the sugar industry was pushing producers into the arms of the US. This, and strong expansionist sentiment within the US itself, provided Washington with a powerful incentive to intervene in the second Cuban War of Independence (1895–98), rapidly defeating the Spanish. Cuba became a US protectorate and Puerto Rico became a US possession after 1898 (see Boxes 10.6, 13.2). Alongside these interventions, however, there persisted a traditional hostility among US statesmen to the European concept of empire that had shaped notions of imperialism in the nineteenth century (see Box 10.1). This had an important bearing on the subsequent relationship between the US and Puerto Rico and helps, in part, to explain a failure to resolve the island's status to this day (see Box 10.6). In the recent era, Cuba's revolutionary government has pointed to the continuing US possession of Puerto Rico as evidence of an imperialist vocation in the Caribbean that goes back to the 1890s (see Schoultz, 2009). Interventions continued into the twentieth century, and in 1903, with US support, the republic of Panama broke away from Colombia. In 1905, President Theodore Roosevelt (1901–09) outlined a policy that claimed for the US the right to send forces to any country in the Western hemisphere whose political situation was deemed problematic for US interests. US forces occupied Nicaragua from 1912–33, and the Somoza family was established as a puppet dynasty after 1937. US forces intervened in Mexico in 1914 and 1916, and occupied the Dominican Republic from 1916–24 and Haiti from 1915–34. US investment in Latin America had risen significantly by the outbreak of the First World War, after which British trade and investment declined. US businesses invested more heavily than their British counterparts in processes of production. In Central America, for example, the United Fruit Company converted entire countries into so-called 'banana republics'. By 1929, the US was the main buyer of Latin America's minerals and agricultural products, and 40 per cent of all US international investments were in the region (Chasteen, 2001). This dependence and the presence of US businesses heightened nationalist sentiments and, during the 1920s, Latin American politicians began to describe large US corporations as symbols of imperialism and pledged to nationalise them (see Chapters 9, 13, 14).

imperialism' (see Boxes 9.3, 10.1). Imperialism refers to attempts by countries to form and maintain an empire by extending control over the territory and political and economic life of other countries. The ensuing 1848 Treaty of Guadalupe saw Mexico lose half its territory to its northern neighbour.

There were some exceptions to the instability of the Independence era and the decades that followed. In Brazil, the centralised monarchy largely maintained order, although the country did not escape the divisions caused by liberalism, particularly during the 1830s when liberal rebellions occurred in the provinces. In Chile, elites were relatively united and able to establish a tradition of stable constitutional government. The country's 1833 constitution would be one of the most enduring in Latin America and shaped political life into the twentieth century.

In much of Latin America, a semblance of order had been established by the mid-nineteenth century, although some countries such as Mexico would continue to be plagued by civil wars. From 1850 until the early twentieth century, the states of the region slowly began to establish control over their territories and elites began to consolidate their domination of political life and participate in the international economy. The main landmarks of this period are summarised in Table 1.4. By 1850, there were also signs of economic recovery as industrial growth in Europe stimulated foreign investment in Latin America and began to draw the region into the emerging global economy as an exporter of raw materials and agricultural products. Increasingly, landowners began to orient the production of their estates towards this international market. In turn, economic recovery spurred leaders to consolidate their political systems. A new generation of liberals, who had not lived under the Catholic monarchy and were inspired by the European revolutions of 1848, began to advocate more radical ideas. As the Church also began to recover from the turmoil of the Independence era, liberals renewed their efforts to end its privileges and expropriate its wealth. By the 1870s, liberals in some guise had triumphed throughout much of Latin America. In Mexico, the end of Santa Anna's domination in 1855 initiated *La Reforma* in which *mestizo* and indigenous liberal leaders such as Benito Juárez (1861–72) would inaugurate a 20-year process through which liberalism shaped the development of a secular state. None the less, it would take two civil wars (1854–55 and 1858–61) and the defeat of the Habsburg prince Maximilian (1864–67) installed by Napoleon III before the liberals triumphed (see Box 1.4). In Argentina, after 1862 Buenos Aires secured its position as the capital of a united republic under the liberal president Bartolomé Mitre (1862–68). Conservative rule began to end in Central America with the death of Carrera in Guatemala in 1865, and in Venezuela liberals came to power under Antonio Guzmán Blanco (1870–77, 1879–84, 1886–88). In Colombia, in 1861 the *caudillo* Tomás Cipriano de Mosquera imposed liberal rule, and in Chile liberals dominated power through elections from 1861–91. In Brazil, Pedro II (1841–89) avoided instability by pursuing liberal policies, but the War of the Triple Alliance (1864–70) between Paraguay and Brazil, Argentina and Uruguay gave radicals opportunities to call for reform of the monarchy and an end to slavery. Slavery was abolished in Brazil in 1888, and the monarchy collapsed the following year.

Both conservatives and liberals now accepted that a strong state was the only means of achieving progress and, in practice, when Latin American liberals gained power they often took steps to ensure strong central government, stability and order.

LANDMARKS
Table 1.4 From statebuilding to mass politics

Year or period	Development
1850–54	Slavery is abolished in a number of South American countries
1854–61	Mexican liberals advance radical reforms, provoking civil war
1859	Belize becomes British Honduras
1861–	Liberals begin to establish political control over many Latin American countries
1861–65	Annexation of Santo Domingo by Spain, leading thereafter to formation of the Dominican Republic
1862–67	French intervene in Mexico and install Habsburg prince Maximilian (1864–67), who is eventually defeated by liberals
1864–70	War of the Triple Alliance between Paraguay and Brazil, Argentina and Uruguay
1868–78	Patriot uprising in Cuba leads to the Ten Year War for independence from Spain
1879–84	War of the Pacific between Chile, Peru and Bolivia
1886–88	Slavery abolished in Cuba and Brazil
1889	Brazilian monarchy collapses and First Republic established
1895–98	Cuba's second major war of independence results in eventual defeat of Spain after US intervenes, establishing a protectorate
1899–1901	Devastating civil war in Colombia between liberals and conservatives
1903	Panama breaks away from Colombia with US support
1903–07	Radical José Batlle y Ordóñez becomes president of Uruguay
1910–17	Mexican Revolution
1912	Suffrage extended to large sectors of the population in Argentina
1912–33	US forces occupy Nicaragua
1915–16	US forces occupy Haiti then Dominican Republic
1916	Radicals under Hipólito Yrigoyen in Argentina take power from oligarchy, creating first truly mass party in Latin America
1925	Nationalist revolution in Chile allows Arturo Alessandri to push through reforms
1927–33	Augusto César Sandino leads rebellion against US forces in Nicaragua
1929	Wall Street Crash; Ecuador becomes the first Latin American country to extend the vote to women
1930	Brazilian armed forces hand presidency to Getúlio Vargas who establishes corporatist Estado Novo

From 1880, liberal governments were consolidated according to constitutional principles, but in fact often functioned as authoritarian regimes – governments that demanded obedience and paid little attention to liberal norms, often ruling through the use of force. Elections were often rigged so that elites remained in control and the mass of the population remained excluded from politics. In Brazil, for example, by the end of the nineteenth century only about 3 per cent of the population was eligible to vote. The emergence of a consensus about the need for greater stability to aid development of the export economy fostered a conservative-liberal synthesis in which liberals compromised on their democratic positions in favour of authoritarian solutions to underdevelopment. Social doctrines such as positivism stressing the rational exercise of state and bureaucratic power also grew in popularity in this period. Positivism encompassed a belief that it was possible, through 'scientific' policymaking by technically proficient administrators, to create the conditions in which modern liberal democracy could prosper, and was influential throughout Latin America, promoting strong government, social order, stability and economic growth (see Chapter 12). Liberals placed a premium on individual property ownership and believed it was necessary to use the state to break up communal lands and *haciendas* so that a new class of small landowners could emerge. The expansion of export economies based on free-market economics would be a characteristic feature of development until the 1930s.

Two main patterns of rule emerged in the second half of the nineteenth century: domination by a conservative oligarchy – a restricted group of wealthy elite creole landowners and merchants monopolising power; and domination by new form of *caudillo* stressing order and progress through development – centralised dictatorships with few limitations on their power (see Wiarda and Kline, eds, 1990). Both led to a form of authoritarian developmentalism – repressive rule whose main objective was rapid growth of the export sector – which reflected a consensus among elites of different political persuasions on the need to ensure order to facilitate the investment of foreign capital in the emergent economy. In Argentina and Chile, for example, landowners and other economic elites monopolised governments and excluded the masses, often with military support, while claiming to be legitimate because they obeyed constitutions. In Paraguay, a powerful oligarchy emerged in co-operation with liberal governments and foreign corporations between 1904 and 1923. Brazil's weak First Republic (1889–1930) survived because of an agreement between rival coffee and cattle oligarchs to alternate in power. In other countries, dictators established centralised control, often through repression, in support of development policies that mostly benefitted the landed elite. In Mexico, Porfirio Díaz (1876–1911) used violence to strengthen central power at the expense of regional forces yet maintained the appearance of constitutional rule. Díaz permitted a large increase in foreign control over sectors of Mexico's economy and, during the period of his rule (the *Porfiriato*), Mexico's import-export trade grew considerably. In Peru, General Andrés Cáceres (1886–90, 1894–95) put control over national revenues in the hands of a corporation of bondholders who took on the country's debt. In the Dominican Republic, the black general Ulíses Heureaux (1882–84, 1887–99) imposed conservative liberalism and fuelled the growth of the export economy.

Overseas demand began to pull a few Latin American economies out of stagnation and draw them into the global market. The *hacienda* economy began to expand and, by the 1880s, the larger Latin American countries were trading extensively with the outside world and modernising infrastructure and transportation links. Where conflicts between the young republics occurred in this period, the underlying cause was often control over territory or resources. The bloody War of the Triple Alliance (1864–70) between Paraguay and Brazil, Argentina and Uruguay was fought over control of the upper Paraná River, and the War of the Pacific (1879–84) between Chile, Peru and Bolivia originated in competition over nitrate deposits. Latin American countries became dependent for growth on overseas demand, often for single cash crops, and their development was only made possible by foreign investment. Britain and then the US displaced Spain and Portugal as dominant partners in emergent trading relationships, and were often able to secure a controlling interest in the export-oriented economies (see Box 1.4). In some cases, they were even able to control territory (such as the Panama Canal) or whole economic sectors. The Latin American economies of this period have often been described as 'neocolonial' – referring to a new form of foreign domination despite the achievement earlier in the century of formal political independence from Spain and Portugal – because of the way in which production processes were oriented to serving foreign markets and control was exerted by foreign powers. In Argentina, for example, Britain became the dominant source of capital and secured a commanding position through its control of railways and banks. This model of development had weaknesses. First, it generated little domestic industry, and the elites of most Latin American countries were not prepared to employ protectionism – the imposition of tariffs on imports in order to protect and encourage domestic production – because they benefitted so much from unrestricted free trade (see Chapters 14, 15). Second, growth in the period 1850–80 reinforced the highly stratified social structures inherited from the Independence era. By the late nineteenth century, elite sectors of the population were enjoying unprecedented prosperity, but the emphasis on agricultural products for export and mining meant labourers were very poorly paid. Finally, Latin America's reliance on exports made it acutely vulnerable to downturns in external markets and also dependent on imports of manufactured products.

The birth of mass politics

Rapid economic growth began to transform social structures in Latin America and generate new tensions. Sociological approaches to the history of this period have examined these tensions in terms of the formation of new social strata or classes, often as a result of different kinds of production, and the struggles between these (see, for example, Bauer, 1987; Knight, 1987; and Stolcke and Hall, 1987). A class is usually understood to be a social stratum defined by its relationship to the means of production or by its status.

The main beneficiaries of export growth were large landowners and a mercantile elite, the oligarchy, whose economic and political power grew in the late nineteenth century. Entrepreneurial landowners needed to ensure that they had access to a stable workforce and that they could extract from these workers the maximum productivity for the minimum in return. As a result, the main losers from Latin America's insertion in the world economy at this time were the *campesinos* or peasants. In order to maintain their supply of labour, for example, *haciendas* often kept peasants tied to them through 'debt peonage' by which they were obliged to continue working in order to pay off unmanageable debts. Indigenous people lost village lands as *haciendas* expanded, and many rural people either became impoverished working for low pay in the fields (a *rural proletariat* distinguished by the fact that they survived by earning wages as opposed to farming small plots of land for themselves) or migrated to the cities. The poor conditions endured by rural inhabitants provoked revolts, and peasants would play a key role in the great upheavals of the era, such as the Mexican Revolution (1910–17) (see Box 1.5).

CASE STUDY   Box 1.5

The Mexican Revolution

The Mexican Revolution (1910–17) was the product of rapid social change generated by economic modernisation and had an important influence upon the whole of Latin America by signalling the collapse of the oligarchic system and the birth of mass politics. The revolution began as an expression of middle-class discontent, but evolved into a mass rebellion fuelled by peasant disaffection. On the eve of the revolution in 1910, Mexico had been governed by Porfirio Díaz for more than 30 years, but his continuation in power became a problem when it became clear to elites that there were no clear rules for his succession. Other Latin American oligarchic systems had achieved transfers of power between rival elites who had alternated in the presidency. Elite discontent in Mexico was reflected in an anti re-election movement that emerged after 1904. In 1909, a northern landowner, Francisco Madero (1911–13), whose principal aim was to secure a share of power, started to campaign against Díaz. After failing to secure change by constitutional means, Madero fled to the US and called for an insurrection in 1910. Peasant and popular uprisings ensued, spawning the armies of Emiliano Zapata (b.1879–d.1919) and Pancho Villa (b.c.1878–1923). Díaz was ousted and Madero became president in 1911, but elite disagreements and Madero's resistance to peasant demands sparked a wider conflict. Conservative oligarchs and the middle classes abandoned Madero, provoking a military coup under General Victoriano Huerta (1913–14), who imposed an authoritarian dictatorship, sparking further rebellions in which rival armies competed for power across the country. A fragile consensus among the revolutionaries was achieved by Venustiano Carranza (1915–20), resulting in Huerta's downfall, but differences persisted. Carranza's Constitutionalist forces prevailed and he became president, drafting a new constitution in 1917 that reflected a nationalist inspiration by limiting the rights of foreign interests in economic development (see Chapters 13, 14). The landowning elites of the state of Sonora became predominant in the years following this period, laying the foundations for a system dominated by one party, the Partido Revolucionario Institucional (PRI, Institutional Revolutionary Party), until the late 1990s. The PRI remains today a formidable force in Mexican politics.

Export growth, urbanisation and immigration began to create new middle classes comprising professionals, bureaucrats, shopkeepers and small businessmen who were well educated, receptive to European ideas and increasingly desired some input in the policymaking process. In Mexico, the original goal of the revolution was for the middle classes to gain access to politics.

At the same time, a new working class moulded by the urban environment and immersion in a *market* or money economy as opposed to, say, production for subsistence in the countryside, began to emerge in countries such as Mexico (see Knight, 1987). The expansion of mining and some manufacturing reinforced this development. Urban workers were receptive to anarchist, Marxist and socialist ideas (see Chapter 12) and created new labour movements in Latin America, leading to a period of strikes and repression from 1914–27 and to the formation of socialist and communist parties. Strikes gave a platform to radical politicians such as Agustín Farabundo Martí (b.1893–d.1932) in El Salvador and Augusto César Sandino (b.1893–d.1934) in Nicaragua. The Church also began to address the development of the working classes and, in the 1890s, began to organise clubs and associations for Catholic workers. In need of labour to sustain the growth of the export economies, elites in some countries also turned to immigration from Europe (see Chapters 12,

13). Argentina pursued a policy of mass immigration, and migrants also headed to Brazil, Peru and Chile.

The migration of peasants to the cities, the emergence of light industry, and immigration contributed to rapid population growth and urbanisation in Latin America. Urban populations were vulnerable to changes in world trade because they could not survive like peasants on subsistence agriculture. Nor did the new urban classes fit into the traditional social hierarchy that had ensured the subordination of the peasantry. As a result, urban populations tended to be more politically volatile than rural populations. Growing social contrasts and the political pressures generated by economic growth did not go unnoticed by politicians. In Argentina, Chile and Uruguay, new parties representing urban middle and working classes began to demand political rights and social reform, challenging the creole oligarchies. In the first decades of the twentieth century, radical politicians such as José Batlle y Ordóñez (1903–07, 1911–15) in Uruguay, Hipólito Yrigoyen (1916–22, 1928–30) in Argentina, and Arturo Alessandri (1920–25) in Chile began to respond to middle- and working-class discontent.

As industry began to rebound in some countries after the First World War, workers found themselves in a stronger position and pressed for better conditions, inspired by the Russian Revolution (1917). Elements of the oligarchy began to see the need to co-opt – win over, and thereby neutralise – the organised working class, and in the 1920s laws to improve working conditions were passed. Oligarchical governments began to adapt by advocating more nationalist and protectionist policies (see Chapters 13, 14), yet continued to rig elections to exclude radicals, leading to agitation and political conflict.

Middle-class politicians represented a potent threat because they did not challenge the foundations of the liberal state but couched their demands for clean elections and an end to privileges in the language of liberalism (see Chapter 12). Urban classes were not strong enough by themselves to transform the political systems of Latin America and radical parties usually only secured gains in alliance with disaffected elites, such as Madero in Mexico. Oligarchical governments responded to social demands with both reform and repression – often extending limited political participation to the middle class but continuing to exclude lower classes. In Argentina, the Unión Cívica Radical (UCR, Radical Civic Union) mobilised the middle class and popular sectors seeking electoral reform, and in 1912 the suffrage was opened to large sectors of the population. The Radicals under Yrigoyen were able to overthrow the country's landowning oligarchy in 1916, creating the first truly mass party in Latin America. In Uruguay, Batlle y Ordóñez widened his constituency by extending the franchise, creating public employment and introducing social legislation – the first instance of social democracy in Latin America (see Chapters 12, 16).

Middle-class parties also often expressed resentment about the growing number of immigrants, and this xenophobia fuelled the nationalism that gained force as an ideology throughout Latin America in the early twentieth century, particularly after the shock of Spain's defeat in Cuba in 1898 (see Boxes 9.3, 10.1, 10.6, Chapter 13). Nationalist sentiments were an important factor in bringing to an end the neocolonial order by identifying local oligarchies with foreign interests, and nationalism would become a dominant doctrine by the late 1920s. Middle-class radicals often attacked foreign interests while advocating greater state intervention in the economy to ensure a fairer distribution of resources. In Uruguay, for example, Batlle y Ordóñez acted against what he called foreign economic imperialism by promoting protectionism to develop local industry and establishing Latin America's first welfare state.

However, the armed forces became the means by which nationalist movements would rise to power as the export economies began to falter from the mid-1920s, finally collapsing after the 1929 Wall Street crash. Chile was the first country to experience a nationalist revolution in 1925 when a coup finally allowed Alessandri to push through the radical reforms sought by his middle-class supporters. In 1930, the Brazilian armed forces dislodged the oligarchs and handed the presidency to Getúlio Vargas (1930–45, 1951–54), who created an Estado Novo (New State) modelled on fascism (see Box 12.9). In 1930, Argentina's military staged a coup but remained divided over policy and, in Cuba, junior officers staged an abortive nationalist revolution in 1933.

The global Great Depression after 1930 guaranteed the irreversible entry into politics of these new political forces, which began to replace oligarchic liberalism with a novel kind of state constructed to pursue economic development.

Summary

The Bourbon and Pombal reforms aimed to extract more from the Iberian colonies in the New World but generated discontent in the colonial population. Spain and Portugal were affected by the aftermath of French Revolution, and the decision of Carlos IV to join the French in 1796 exposed Spanish America to British attacks. These imperial struggles in Europe gave creole elites in Latin America the opportunity to rebel. In 1807, Napoleon occupied Portugal and the throne was moved to Brazil, and in 1808 the Spanish monarchs fell into Napoleon's hands, leading to a constitutional crisis in the American colonies. Between 1809 and 1810, the American creoles initiated uprisings that would last until 1825 and result in Independence across the region, although different countries followed different paths to self-determination. The first 25 years of the new republics' independent existence were characterised by civil war, instability and foreign interventions. There was little political consensus among the creole ruling classes, who were divided over what system of government to adopt. Few of the newly independent states were able to contain elite divisions within a stable constitutional system, resulting in the domination of regional strongmen or *caudillos*. The threat of secession became a recurrent theme in the first decades of Independence and gave foreign powers opportunities to intervene. However, in much of Latin America a semblance of order had been established by the mid-nineteenth century and there were signs of economic recovery as industrial growth in Europe began to draw Latin American exporters into the global economy. A new generation of liberals began to advocate radical ideas and, eventually, dominated politics. Both conservatives and liberals accepted that a strong state was the only means of achieving progress. Most Latin American states in the second half of the nineteenth century were either dominated by an oligarchy or under the control of centralised dictatorships, reflecting elite consensus about the need for stability. The *hacienda* economy began to expand and, by the 1880s, the larger Latin American countries were trading extensively with the outside world. Historians often characterise the Latin American economies of this period as neocolonial because of the way in which production processes were oriented to serving foreign markets. This model of development generated little domestic industry and reinforced highly stratified social structures. The main beneficiary of export growth was an oligarchy comprising large landowners and a mercantile elite.

However, rapid economic growth was transforming social structures in Latin America, creating a new middle class seeking access to political power and a small urban working class. At the same time, the poor conditions endured by rural inhabitants provoked revolts, and peasants would play a key role in upheavals such as the Mexican Revolution. Politicians were aware of the political pressures generated by economic growth, and elements of the oligarchy began to see the need to co-opt labour and to advocate more nationalist and protectionist policies, while radical politicians began to respond to middle- and working-class discontent. As the export economies began to falter from the mid-1920s, the armed forces became the means by which nationalist movements, often supporting middle-class aspirations, would rise to power. It was the Great Depression after 1930 that would lead to the irreversible entry into politics of these new forces and the establishment of a new kind of state dedicated to economic development.

Discussion points

- To what extent were the Bourbon reforms responsible for Independence?
- Would Latin America have risen up if Napoleon had not captured Carlos IV?
- Would the newly independent countries have been more stable as monarchies?
- In what senses did conservatives and liberals differ?
- Does the development of the export economy explain why stability was achieved?
- What made the new middle and working classes a potent threat to oligarchies?

Useful websites

www.h-net.org/~latam H-LatAm, international forum for the discussion of Latin American history

www.h-net.org/~clah/index.php Conference on Latin American History, an independent initiative affiliated with the American Historical Association

www.ibiblio.org/expo/1492.exhibit/Intro.html Library of Congress site on Columbus's encounter with the Americas

www.millersville.edu/~columbus Millersville University of Pennsylvania database of articles and essays on Columbus and the Age of Discovery

www.h-net.org/~latam/bibs/bibideas.html Useful bibliography on the history of ideas in Colonial Latin America maintained on H-LatAm site

www.cwis.org/fwdp Fourth World Documentation Project Archive of the Centre for World Indigenous Studies' Chief George Manuel Memorial Library containing some useful links about indigenous history

www.fordham.edu/halsall/mod/modsbook32.html Useful page on nineteenth-century Latin America with valuable links compiled by the Internet History Sourcebooks Project

lanic.utexas.edu/project/rla Religion in Latin America history page compiled by Father Edward Cleary of Providence College and now maintained by the Latin American Network Information Center (LANIC) at the University of Texas, Austin

www.unesco.org/culture/latinamerica/html_eng/index.html Ongoing but incomplete history of Latin America being compiled for UNESCO

www.hahr.pitt.edu/ Hispanic American Historical Review

www.yale.edu/glc/index.htm Gilder Lehrman Center for the Study of Slavery, Resistance, and Abolition, part of the Yale Center for International and Area Studies, dedicated to research on slavery

www.stanford.edu/group/LAEH/html/web.html Environmental History of Latin America, valuable bibliographical site compiled by academics at Stanford University

www.hartford-hwp.com/archives/ World History Archives by Hartford Web Publishing, offering essays from a working-class and non-Eurocentric perspective, including sections on Latin America

Recommended reading

Bethell, Leslie (ed.). 1985–86. *The Cambridge History of Latin America, Volumes 3 to 5.* Cambridge: Cambridge University Press

Essential introduction to the economic, social and political history of the region and key source of reference. Volume 3 covers the period from Independence to c.1870, and Volumes 4 and 5 from c.1870 to 1930

Williamson, Edwin. 1992. *The Penguin History of Latin America.* London: Penguin

Essential introduction to the history of Latin America with a valuable focus on themes such as nationalism and development

Halperín Donghi, Tulio. 1993. *The Contemporary History of Latin America.* Durham, NC: Macmillan

Valuable chronologically ordered overview of regional economic and political themes that also examines history by country, with a considerable focus on nineteenth-century developments

Chasteen, John Charles. 2001. *Born in Blood and Fire. A Concise History of Latin America.* New York: W.W.Norton

Useful and accessible history that often develops themes overlooked by other volumes such as the role of women in politics

Fowler, Will. 2002. *Latin America 1800–2000. Modern History for Modern Languages.* London: Arnold

Valuable and highly accessible introductory history of Latin America that is concise yet comprehensive, with useful features and definitions

Eakin, Marshall C. 2007. *The History of Latin America: Collision of Cultures.* Basingstoke: Palgrave Macmillan

Useful and accessible narrative survey of Latin American history from the pre-Columbian era to the twenty-first century stressing the collision of peoples and cultures in an explanation for the region's unity and diversity

Chapter 2

From the 1930s to the 1980s

This chapter explores the recent history of Latin America from the Great Depression of the early 1930s, through the development of modernising states overseeing rapid change in the postwar era and the military clampdown of the 1960s and 1970s, to the dawn of a new democratic era in the 1980s. The Great Depression that followed the Wall Street crash of 1929 had a significant impact on the form of economic development that would be pursued in much of Latin America and, as a result, upon the shape of the region's political systems. It initiated a process of industrialisation that gathered pace after the Second World War in which large state bureaucracies controlling public enterprises were created, and workers and middle-class professionals and bureaucrats were incorporated in new governing coalitions overseeing the region's own form of industrial revolution. However, the economic and political tensions generated by accelerated change, the constant threat of unrest among the main losers in this process such as the peasantry, and the waning fortunes of Latin America's first industries in the context of the tense Cold War struggle between the United States and the Soviet Union, contributed to the return of authoritarianism. Military regimes seized control in many Latin American countries from the 1960s until the 1980s, often employing repression to maintain power and purge the politics of their countries of leftwing elements. However, economic crisis, international change and internal tensions eventually made the pressure for a return to civilian rule irresistible. The military returned to the barracks and authoritarian rulers relinquished control throughout Latin America in the 1980s and 1990s.

The Great Depression

The Wall Street crash reduced demand for Latin American products and caused a recession that ended the neocolonial order by forcing countries to reconsider their dependence on the world economy. Some responded by seeking a special relationship with powerful countries that preserved access to their markets, as Argentina did by giving Britain preferential terms to purchase its beef. Most states in the region responded by taking the initial steps towards creating their own industries through import-substitution industrialisation (ISI) aiming to reduce their reliance on the import of manufactured goods (see Chapter 14). State-led ISI promised greater economic independence and to create jobs for an emerging working class. As a result, in the 1930s many Latin American governments began to restructure their economies by adopting protectionist policies that imposed tariffs on imports in order to nurture local industries. A nationalist climate made this easier by justifying hostility to foreign businesses (see Box 9.3, Chapter 13). The US administration of President Franklin D. Roosevelt responded to this climate by outlining a 'Good Neighbour Policy' towards Latin America in 1933 advocating that no American state should interfere in the affairs of others. FDR's foreign policy aimed to achieve more constructive economic relations with the region, laying the basis for subsequent US-Latin American co-operation during the Second World War. Protectionist policies in Latin America implied the need for greater government intervention in the economy than in the past, and by the end of the 1930s the state as a set of institutions had grown stronger across the region (see Box 2.1). Public ministries grew in size, new government agencies were created to promote manufacturing and in Mexico and Bolivia the state nationalised the oil industry.

THEORIES AND DEBATES   **Box 2.1**

The state

An important theme in the study of Latin America has been the strength of the state and its relationship with development. What comprises the state has been the subject of intense debate, but the most influential definition by Weber (1968) understood the state as a set of social institutions which exercised a monopoly over the legitimate use of force within a given territory. In Latin America, different types of state have emerged, but these have had common experiences and their capacities have almost always developed alongside the expansion of capitalism. The weakness of the state and the degree to which it has been the captive of powerful social groups, for example, have been factors that have repeatedly brought into question its legitimacy – authority based on consent – and held back economic modernisation. Whitehead (1994) argues that it is advantageous to trace the *effective* organisation of states in Latin America not from Independence but from later in the nineteenth century when stable administrations were established after many years in which dominant social groups had squabbled among themselves while excluding the mass of the population from politics. The stability of these administrations was related to the extent to which they were seen as legitimate by rival political and social forces. The first coherent efforts in Latin America from the 1850s at state-building – the active process of creating the formal institutions and procedures associated with the modern state, such as a government bureaucracy – reflected centralised attempts by oligarchic elites and authoritarian rulers to adapt property laws and develop infrastructure so that countries could integrate more effectively in the growing international economy. Prior to the 1930s, oligarchic states prevailed in which a limited bureaucracy served the interests of a small sector of the population which derived its power from land-ownership or international trade. The Depression after 1929, the rise of economic nationalism and industrialisation forced some states to assume new tasks and to find new sources of support in society to ensure stability. From the 1930s, modernising states developed by extending central public authority over greater areas of the national territory and taking on many more administrative responsibilities. During the Second World War these states were required to tighten centralised territorial control and the armed forces expanded. Public enterprises were also established in strategic sectors such as steel and power. These states often

▶

acted in the interests both of traditional oligarchs and newly emergent groups such as urban trades unions and professional bureaucrats. Their priorities and links with foreign markets limited development and often excluded the mass of the population from the benefits of economic growth. After the war, where ISI was underway it led to greater levels of state economic management and ownership, combined with public policies aiming to alleviate class conflict. In many cases, new, mainly urban classes were brought into the political process through populism – a form of political activity that championed the needs, concerns or preferences of ordinary people against powerful vested interests (see below, and Chapters 4, 12, 16). In the process, traditional political practices such as corporatism and clientelism gained a new lease of life (see Box 2.2, Chapter 7). Interest groups were maintained and controlled by the state while politicians distributed jobs and other payoffs to supporters. Corporatism both ensured state control over these groups but also limited the autonomy of the state, often preventing it from acting in the interests of the entire population. This lack of autonomy contributed significantly to underdevelopment because the big losers in this period were poorer people in the countryside (see Chapters 7, 14). As the Latin American states of the late 1950s began to respond to Cold War concerns about national security (see Box 10.2), they tightened their centralised control over territory, administration and economic resources. Revolutionary activity in the 1960s (see below) inspired states to assert further control over society while taking on more social welfare commitments. The state apparatus expanded and managers, bureaucrats, professionals and technocrats became more powerful and formed an important coalition underpinning the authoritarian regimes of the 1960s and 1970s. Technocrats are highly educated bureaucratic officials advocating technical solutions to economic and social problems. Their significance often lies in their non-political character and hence their apparent autonomy from special interests, and the greater emphasis they often place upon the efficient resolution of problems rather than on finding equitable solutions. However, the military juntas of the 1960s and 1970s (see below) were unable to create legitimate states based on popular consent, and these often were unable to act autonomously of foreign and domestic capital. In most of Latin America, state ownership in the economy expanded dramatically in the 1970s because of massive lending within international financial markets. States were able to enjoy legitimacy to the extent that economic intervention of this kind delivered benefits to society. However, the debt crisis after 1982 exposed a long-term crisis of these bloated states and, subsequently, radical economic reforms began to transform the relationship between states and societies in Latin America (see Vellinga, 1998; see also Chapter 15). Williamson (1992) argues that the restoration of democracy thereafter can be seen as an affirmation by the masses of the need for a legitimate state that could command the active consent of the people as a whole. However, even today in countries such as Mexico, Bolivia, Colombia and Brazil, the legitimacy of the state is sometimes challenged by guerrilla or indigenous organisations in remote regions where its ability to assert full control is, as a result, put into question. Guerrillas and drugs cartels operating from isolated areas sometimes act as quasi-states in regions under their control, enjoying some legitimacy among communities they protect or provide benefits to (see Box 4.3, Chapter 10, Figure 12.1). A state's legitimacy is also sometimes weakened by the activity of politicians and bureaucratic officials who act in the interests of powerful groups or sources of capital. Smaller states in Central America and some of the Andean countries such as Peru and Bolivia, for example, remained captive to landowning exporters well into the latter part of twentieth century. A corruption scandal in the Dominican Republic in 2003 exposed extensive links between one of the country's largest private banks, politicians and state officials. The state has returned to the forefront of debates about economic development and equality in Latin America since 1998, with a wave of left-of-centre governments in recent years enhancing its role and taking some private industries back into state control (see Chapters 12, 16).

Policy shifts and recession fostered political polarisation in the 1930s and new parties and movements – from communists to fascists – emerged to challenge elite conservative and liberal factions (see Chapter 12). However, economic recovery in the 1930s was achieved through the *traditional* export sector and policies adopted to survive the Depression required the state to balance the interests of the export sector, foreign capital and urban sectors. To do this, the state needed broad consent for its institutions and policies, and so power shifted to coalitions of landowners, middle classes, organised labour and the new state bureaucracy supported by the military. Most Latin American countries were ruled by authoritarian parties or military dictators stressing nationalism and some regimes had fascist trappings such as those led by Rafael Leonidas Trujillo (1930–61) in the Dominican Republic, Maximiliano Hernández Martínez (1931–44) in El Salvador, Jorge Ubico (1931–44) in Guatemala, Arturo Alessandri (1932–36) in Chile and José María Velasco Ibarra (1934–35) in Ecuador. The governments of Getúlio Vargas (1930–45) in Brazil, Lázaro Cárdenas (1934–40) in Mexico and David Toro (1936–37) in Bolivia had an authoritarian character while pursuing some progressive and socialistic reforms (see Chapter 16).

These political systems of the 1930s adapted by accommodating the new social forces generated by economic change yet did not end elite domination completely. Elements of the former hierarchy survived while new groups such as organised labour, peasant organisations and business groups were brought into the system under government control. In Brazil, for example, under Vargas trade unions were run by the ministry of labour. This development revived corporatism – a form of interest-group politics – that some scholars have argued has its roots in Iberian tradition (see Boxes 2.2, 7.1).

THEORIES AND DEBATES   **Box 2.2**

Corporatism

An important element of continuity in the evolution of Latin American political systems has been corporatism, which has often been a prominent feature of the relationship between state and society in the region.

The term corporatism has been employed in several ways in the study of Latin America (see Collier, 1995). First, it has been used to refer to a type of society distinguished by what are, in essence, cultural characteristics that some scholars have argued were inherited from the Iberian peninsula, such as social relations deriving from feudalism and a hierarchical Roman Catholic tradition, extended families governed by powerful patriarchs, essentially non-democratic links between the state and social groups, and hostility to the liberal capitalism of the modern era (see Wiarda, 1981, ed., 1974; Véliz, 1980). An ideological vision of society structured along these lines has at times been advanced by conservatives and Church thinkers in Latin America (see Chapters 7, 12). Second, corporatism has been used in a more functional sense to refer to ways in which hierarchically organised 'corporations' that represent distinct interest groups in society are incorporated into the state's policy-making process, allowing those groups both to represent their members' interests while at the same time ensuring their compliance with state policy – social and political control (see Schmitter, 1971, 1974; see also Box 7.1). Scholars employing the term in this way have not necessarily accepted the

▶

other sense in which it has been used. Under the functional definition, common examples of corporatist groups are the Church, trades unions, business organisations and the military. Often, the state gave these a monopoly of representation within the social sectors they catered for in exchange for control over the selection of their leaders and the articulation of their demands (see Schmitter, 1974).

Corporatism in both senses has been employed to characterise political relations from the colonial era to the present day. Wiarda (1998) has argued that colonial Latin America, like that of the Iberian peninsula, had corporatist features. Society was organised around largely autonomous groups such as the Church that enjoyed privileges in exchange for exercising responsibilities under royal authority. Independence ended the monarchy's role mediating between groups and, faced with anarchy, centralised control was imposed by *caudillos* (see Box 1.3) who tolerated corporatist structures like the Church and army, which in turn acted as *de facto* branches of government. As the liberal state itself developed in the late nineteenth century, it improved its ability to extend its control over more areas of national life and often sought to end the privileges of traditional corporations such as the Church and indigenous communities. At the same time, nineteenth-century Catholic thought developed influential notions of Christian corporatism that are still invoked in Latin America (see Chapter 12). Economic modernisation, however, generated new political and social forces and corporatism was revived as a means by which to accommodate and control these forces, especially following the Wall Street crash of 1929. The concept of corporatism has been applied, in particular, to political systems in which the state assumed a central role in regulating economic and political activity that emerged from the crisis of the 1930s. Latin American political systems that demonstrated corporatist influences included Brazil under Vargas, Argentina under Juan Domingo Perón (1946–55), Mexico under Cárdenas, and Chile under Carlos Ibáñez (1927–31, 1952–58). Populism was a reflection of what Williamson (1992) has called 'natural corporatism' by which a weak state bought stability by employing the traditional politics of clientelism in order to co-opt and reconcile rival interest-groups (see below, and Chapters 7, 16). In this way, many countries in Latin America continued to practise a disguised form of authoritarian corporatism while calling themselves democratic (see Malloy, 1977; Wiarda, 1981). In the 1960s, corporatist structures were revived by the military in bureaucratic-authoritarian regimes (see Box 2.5) that sought to regulate and control every aspect of life, and in this period corporatism became more identifiably associated with authoritarianism. Despite the return to democracy in the 1980s and 1990s, some scholars have pointed to the survival of corporatism in new forms – 'neocorporatism' – in some Latin American political systems (see Chapter 7).

However, corporatism in Latin America never gave the state complete control over society, was often combined with liberal elements, changed constantly and varied considerably from state to state (Wiarda, 1998; see also Mackinlay and Otero, 2004). Wiarda (1981) argued that various *different* forms of corporatism developed in Latin America ranging from leftwing (Cárdenas in Mexico) to rightwing (Augusto Pinochet, 1973–90, in Chile). Nor did corporate structures resolve social conflicts: the legacy of Vargas in Brazil and Perón in Argentina, for example, was social conflict, instability and military coups. In Argentina, the corporatist organisation of labour and business often resulted in stalemates that limited the country's ability to consolidate stable institutions.

In Chile and Venezuela, middle-class groups prevailed, while in Mexico control by a single party incorporating all social sectors was consolidated under an emergent bourgeoisie or capitalist class. Uruguay avoided the turmoil following the Wall Street crash but still experienced authoritarian regimes, and in Argentina, Brazil and Chile, ISI and nationalism exacerbated political conflict between urban powerbrokers and rural oligarchs. In Peru, disputes between industrialists and the small urban working class aggravated rivalry between conservative landowners and liberal export elites, provoking recurrent military coups. In Colombia, nationalism greatly exacerbated polarisation between rightwing figures such as Laureano Gómez (see Box 12.8) and leftwingers such as Jorge Eliécer Gaitán (b.1898–d.1948), whose assassination in 1948 unleashed a civil war known as La Violencia that established a persistent tradition of lawlessness.

Industrialisation accelerated during the Second World War as Latin America lost its access to the European market and there was rapid growth in US demand for strategic materials. The US also put Latin America under pressure to sever ties with the Axis powers, with countries supporting the Allies benefiting from preferential trade and investment relations. In Argentina, there was much sympathy for Italy and Germany, and the country remained neutral until towards the end of the war. In the larger countries of Latin America, the manufacturing encouraged by wartime economic policies began to have an impact on the class structure and political relations, strengthening industrialists and urban trades unions. By the end of the war, these supporters of industry had begun to challenge traditional export interests and gain the attention of government. With recovery in Europe after the war, however, demand for Latin American products began to fall and ISI faltered as imported goods flowed anew into the region. Government officials and economists began to argue that Latin America would need to invigorate its industrialisation process in order to compete. After 1949, the United Nations' Comisión Económica para América Latina (CEPAL, Economic Commission for Latin America, whose acronym in English was originally ECLA, later ECLAC to incorporate the Caribbean) supported efforts to develop ISI further (see Box 14.3). By the 1950s, most governments in the region had turned their backs on export-led growth policies, and this became the golden age of ISI. Table 2.1 summarises the main events in this period.

However, ISI policies were applied to a differing extent and according to different priorities in each Latin American country and, as a result, generated a wide range of experiences. In each case, the state had to meet or confront the vested interest of different social groups, particularly traditional landowning elites, and the resultant impact of ISI upon class structures varied considerably. ISI policies were most comprehensive and coherent in the larger economies of the region such as Mexico and the Southern Cone countries of Brazil, Argentina and Chile, where they fuelled the growth of discernible if small classes of domestic industrialists and urban workers and underpinned corporatism. The size of these countries, their existing infrastructure and their technological capacity meant that in many cases industrialisation occurred with little state intervention. In other parts of South America and in Central America, however, where traditional exporting elites retained considerable power, the state and other institutions such as CEPAL often played a more significant role in creating industry. In Peru, for example, traditional exporters held great economic and political power until the early 1960s, and ISI policies did not start until the administration of Fernando Belaúnde Terry (1963–68) and did not get seriously underway until the military had taken power under Juan Velasco Alvarado (1968–75). Thereafter, accelerated ISI in Peru based on comprehensive state intervention generated considerable economic and social problems for subsequent governments, serving to widen already significant inequalities. The Central American countries started to industrialise in the 1950s but were limited

LANDMARKS
Table 2.1 From the Depression until the 1950s

Year or period	Development
1928	Peruvian Marxist José Carlos Mariátegui publishes *Siete ensayos de interpretación de la realidad peruana* (Seven Interpretive Essays on Peruvian Reality)
1930–36	Nationalist or authoritarian regimes take power in the Dominican Republic, El Salvador, Guatemala, Chile, Cuba, Brazil, Honduras and Ecuador. Authoritarian leaders in Mexico, Brazil and Bolivia pursue socialistic reforms
1932–35	Chaco War between Bolivia and Paraguay over territorial claims
1933	US president Franklin D. Roosevelt outlines 'Good Neighbour Policy' towards Latin America advocating that no American state should interfere in the affairs of others
1937	Anastasio Somoza comes to power in Nicaragua; in Brazil the fascist Ação Integralista Brasileira (Integralists) comes close to pulling off a coup d'état but fails
1938	Lázaro Cárdenas nationalises the oil industry in Mexico
1939–45	Many Latin American countries remain neutral until late in the Second World War although supply the Allies with crucial raw materials. Some, such as Argentina, are sympathetic to the Axis powers, although several join the Allies as combatants in 1942 following attacks on their shipping and the raid on Pearl Harbor in December 1941. Brazil is the only Latin American country to send troops to Europe
1944–46	Democratic governments replace authoritarian regimes across the region and there is a general shift to the left as well as a period of labour militancy. In Guatemala, elections install nationalist presidents from 1944–54 who anger the US with their reformist policies
1946–48	Shift away from reformism as the Cold War begins to unfold and the US begins to place Latin American governments under pressure; states begin to bring organised labour under control and to repress Communist parties
1946	Juan Domingo Perón becomes president of Argentina, establishing a style of rule that has become synonymous with populism
1947	Organización Demócrata Cristiana de América (ODCA, Christian Democrat Organisation of America) founded
1948	Organisation of American States (OAS) formed; Comisión Económica para América Latina (CEPAL, Economic Commission for Latin America, ECLA) formed; assassination of populist Jorge Eliécer Gaitán in Colombia unleashes La Violencia; US backs dictatorship of Marcos Pérez Jiménez in Venezuela
1949	Costa Rica abolishes its armed forces
1952	Bolivian revolution installs populist Movimiento Nacionalista Revolucionario (MNR, Revolutionary Nationalist Movement); Puerto Ricans vote in support of US commonwealth status with autonomy in internal affairs
1953	Colombia's liberal-conservative coalition gives way to a repressive dictatorship under General Gustavo Rojas Pinilla; women get the vote in Mexico
1954	CIA supports overthrow of the constitutional government of Jacobo Arbenz in Guatemala; Vargas's populist government in Brazil collapses and he commits suicide after a military ultimatum; US supports Alfredo Stroessner's dictatorship in Paraguay
1955	Perón is toppled in a military coup in Argentina
1956	Somoza is assassinated in Nicaragua; Egypt's seizure of the Suez Canal generates nationalist tensions in Panama
1957	François 'Papa Doc' Duvalier becomes president in Haiti with US support
1959	Triumph of Cuban Revolution

by their small size. Under the aegis of CEPAL, ISI policies were the main impetus behind the first regional integration effort, and in 1960 the Mercado Común Centroamericano (MCCA, Central American Common Market, CACM) was formed by Guatemala, Honduras, El Salvador and Nicaragua as a mechanism to help nurture industry.

Populism

Democratic governments began to replace authoritarian regimes in several countries, including Brazil, Venezuela and Guatemala, for a brief period from 1945–47. In Chile, the changes generated by industrialisation had allowed for a form of democracy in which both industrialists and workers represented by their own parties competed for access to power. Several countries experienced the emergence of pro-industrial, multi-class and mainly urban 'populist' alliances behind a leader adopting nationalist rhetoric who used the power of the state to address issues of social justice. These alliances brought together classes that, under normal circumstances, were likely to come into conflict, such as workers and industrialists, and challenged the longstanding predominance of oligarchic and foreign economic interests by excluding them (see Chapter 14).

Populism is a term whose precise meaning has been hotly debated and that has been used in different ways in the Latin American context. Historians have tended to argue that populism was a reaction to the Depression of the early 1930s that reflected simultaneous processes of adaptation and modernisation in society and politics. Political scientists have used the term to refer variously to the characteristics of some of the movements like those above, to a style of political leadership, to a form of ideology (see Chapters 12, 13), or to a combination of all of these (see Conniff, ed., 1999). Di Tella (1965) applied the term populism to post-1945 mass movements in Latin America, understanding these not as a product of the autonomous organisational power of the working class and/or the peasantry but none the less enjoying the support of these social groups as well as the support of non-working class sectors upholding an anti-*status quo* ideology. Knight (1998) argued that populism in Latin America was best understood in terms of a political *style* adopted in order to obtain and maintain power involving a proclaimed rapport with 'the people', a 'them-and-us mentality', often during a period of crisis and mobilisation. Populist leaders and movements have usually championed the needs of ordinary people, regardless of the social group they belong to, against powerful vested interests and as an alternative to traditional institutions of political representation such as political parties (see Boxes 4.2, 6.2). They have often directed their message at the poor, using radical rhetoric to promise better living conditions, and at the lower middle classes, by attacking rural oligarchies, industrial elites and economic imperialism (see Kaufman and Stallings, 1991). Populist regimes were usually authoritarian and leaders sought legitimacy across classes through the unifying ideology of nationalism (see Chapter 13). Nationalists resisted any effort to encourage a return to export-led growth and insisted that industrialisation was the only way forward.

The most celebrated populist in Latin American history was Juan Domingo Perón, who ruled Argentina as president from 1946 until he was ousted in a coup in 1955. Perón's glamorous wife Evita became a global icon and has been celebrated in literature, music and cinema. Peronist economic policy tried to end foreign ownership in many sectors and raised workers' living standards, but an economic downturn and conflicts with the Vatican angered the middle class, and the military sent Perón into exile until 1973, when he returned to the presidency again briefly before his death. Other populist rulers with a nationalist message included Cárdenas in Mexico, José María Velasco Ibarra (1934–35, 1944–47, 1952–56, 1960–61, 1968–72) in Ecuador and Vargas in Brazil. Some populists such as Gaitán in Colombia and Victor Raúl Haya de la Torre (b.1895–d.1979) in Peru did not gain power but had an enduring impact on politics.

The Cold War

A climate of nationalism in Latin America developed before and during the Second World War while the US was strengthening its position as a global power (see Chapters 10, 13). After the war, the US focused on rebuilding Europe but, with the outbreak of the Cold War in the late 1940s, Washington again deepened its involvement in Latin American politics. FDR's cautious policy of the 1930s opposing foreign intervention in Latin American affairs was put aside. In 1948, the US was instrumental in setting up the Organisation of American States (OAS, see Box 9.5) which became a vehicle for its anti-communism, and by the 1950s the US had assumed the right to intervene against what it regarded as communist activity in the region. The Cold War altered the basis of inter-American relations by turning Latin America into a battleground in the conflict between US capitalism and Soviet communism. Washington pursued an anti-communist crusade until the late 1980s that had an important influence on the fate of democracy by helping to perpetuate authoritarian regimes. The democratic governments that had begun to replace authoritarian regimes in the immediate postwar period had often included reformists and members of communist or socialist parties. The US pressed friendly governments to outlaw these parties and their sources of support in labour movements. It also formalised the close working relationships it had established during the war with military forces, the main source of anti-communism. In this climate, and amid strains often generated by populism, most of Latin America's fragile postwar democratic experiments foundered. The logic of the Cold War also encouraged the US actively to undermine some reformist democracies. In Guatemala, between 1944 and 1954 democratic elections installed nationalist presidents who angered the US with their reformist policies. In 1954, a US-sponsored invasion from Honduras by a force recruited from enemies of the nationalist government of Jacobo Arbenz (1950–54), armed and trained by the Central Intelligence Agency (CIA), installed a repressive military junta in Guatemala. The US also backed dictatorships elsewhere, such as those of Marcos Pérez Jiménez (1948–58) in Venezuela and Alfredo Stroessner (1954–89) in Paraguay, although there were many inconsistencies in Washington's policy.

By the late 1950s, domestic demand for manufactured products remained weak and ISI had created only a limited number of jobs yet nurtured large, inefficient states with vast bureaucracies riddled with corruption. Latin America remained dependent on imports of capital goods – the equipment needed to set up factories for more sophisticated manufacturing processes – and so remained vulnerable to external economic factors. Proponents of ISI realised that the benefits of modernisation were not being distributed evenly or among most of the population, and peasants neglected by industrialisation policies had begun mobilising. Rising inflation and unemployment exacerbated social tensions and deep differences between protected industrialists, landowners and workers began to weaken governments.

In Colombia, the liberal–conservative coalition that overthrew Gómez gave way to a repressive dictatorship under General Gustavo Rojas Pinilla (1953–57). In Argentina, military hardliners began a purge against Peronists. In Brazil, Vargas's populist government was destroyed in 1954 by the irreconcilable demands of unions and industrialists and he committed suicide. Competition also developed between those advocating social reform and those who believed in more radical change. In Bolivia, the populist Movimiento Nacionalista Revolucionario (MNR, Revolutionary Nationalist Movement) took power in 1952 and pursued nationalist policies influenced by positions deriving from Marxism – a political philosophy advocating the achievement of workers' control of the means of production through revolution – to destroy the power of the traditional landed elites and mining interests. Although some countries such as Colombia, Venezuela, Costa Rica, Mexico, Chile and Uruguay were able to keep political differences under control, by the late 1950s much of Latin America had become mired in conflicts between rival social groups divided as to what direction their countries should take.

Until the 1960s, Marxism had played only a limited role in the evolution of Latin American politics, largely because the industrial working class was small and communist parties believed peasants would not be an important vector of revolution (see Chapter 12). However, the success of the Cuban Revolution in 1959 (see Box 2.3) challenged reformist perspectives and inspired armed revolts in Paraguay, Argentina and the Dominican Republic (1959), Venezuela and Colombia (1961), Guatemala and Ecuador (1962) and Peru (1963).

Cuba distorted US perceptions about the nature of the threat to its security and prompted the creation of the Alliance for Progress, a US programme of aid supporting reforms that was launched in Latin America in 1961. The objective of the

---

CASE STUDY   **Box 2.3**

The Cuban Revolution

The Cuban Revolution in 1959 was a turning point in the Cold War because it linked nationalist resistance to 'US imperialism' with insurgency and transformed the prospects of socialism in Latin America (see Chapters 9, 12, 13, 16, Box 10.8). The revolution which toppled the strongman Fulgencio Batista (1933–44, 1952–59) was the only successful armed insurgency in the region until the Sandinistas seized power in Nicaragua two decades later (see below). Cuba's revolution was led by middle-class

▶

professionals like Fidel Castro (1959–2008) and the Argentinean Ernesto 'Che' Guevara (b.1928–d.1967) who drew inspiration from a long nationalist tradition deriving from the anti-Americanism of the Cuban hero José Martí (b.1853–d.1895) (see Box 9.3, Chapter 13). Since 1898, Cuban development had been strongly dependent on the US, and Marxist theories of imperialism made sense to nationalists committed to ending the island's neocolonial relationship with its dominant neighbour (see Boxes 10.1, 10.6, Chapter 14). Castro became a dictator but oversaw a transformation of economic and social structures that tackled inequalities on the island (see Chapter 16). His regime nationalised foreign-owned estates and industries; turned sugar plantations into co-operatives and state owned farms; and placed a much greater emphasis on education and healthcare. As a result, the Cuban Revolution became a potent symbol for many people in the hemisphere of the ability of a small cadre of determined revolutionaries to bring about important social advances, and there was an upsurge of revolutionary socialism in Latin America during the 1960s outside established communist parties (see Figure 12.1). Once in power, however, Castro increasingly turned to Cuba's Communist Party for organisational support and in 1961 he formally proclaimed his allegiance to Marxism-Leninism after forging links with the Soviet Union. The revolution's survival – particularly after the tense confrontation between the US and the USSR during the 1962 Missile Crisis, in which President John. F. Kennedy (1961–63) threatened the Soviet leader Nikita Khrushchev (1953–64) with nuclear war if the Soviet Union did not withdraw missiles it had installed on the island – transformed the prospects of Marxism. A new generation now looked to Havana, not Moscow, for revolutionary inspiration, leading to the emergence of Marxist guerrilla movements throughout Latin America. Thereafter, the US saw revolutionary Cuba as a Soviet proxy, and this contributed greatly to Washington's support for repressive regimes and counter-insurgency strategies in the region during the 1960s and 1970s. Guevara's understanding of guerrilla warfare gave rise to the theory of the *foco*, a guerrilla focus based in the countryside spreading insurrection regardless of whether all the formal conditions for revolution were in place (see Box 12.2). He believed that even in the absence of conditions traditionally held to be necessary for a revolution – such as deep disenchantment with a regime considered to be illegitimate by several social classes – popular forces could still win a war against the army. The Argentinean revolutionary tried to export the revolution to Africa and Bolivia, where he was killed in 1967. However, Cuba's relationship with the Soviet Union developed into one of dependence not entirely dissimilar to that on the US prior to 1959 (see Chapters 11, 14, 16). As the first successful socialist revolution in the Americas, the Cuban Revolution had a profound impact upon politics in Latin America and globally, providing inspiration for a diverse range of followers from activists in other agrarian societies to the 'new Left' in the industrialised world and the Catholic Church (see Box 7.12, Chapter 12). US hostility to the Cuban revolutionary regime developed into and remains today a formative theme in Washington's relationship with Latin America as a whole (see Box 10.8). Latin American politicians critical of US foreign and economic policies have often nurtured ties with the Cuban government and provided support for Havana in its disputes with its powerful neighbour (see Box 16.1). Fidel Castro and Guevara have become potent icons of the Left's survival in Latin America and beyond. In 2006, an ailing Fidel Castro began to hand control over to his brother, Raúl, who took over as president in 2008. Although Raúl Castro has experimented with limited economic reforms, the direction of Cuban policy has not changed amid initial hopes for an improvement in relations with the US under President Barack Obama (2009–). Cuba was able to take advantage of economic growth in Latin America generated by vigorous commodities markets between 2003–08 and a more favourable diplomatic climate in the region among left-of-centre governments (see Chapters 12, 16) to strengthen its position vis-à-vis the US. It has also formed a strong bilateral relationship with the leftwing government of President Hugo Chávez (1998–) in Venezuela, institutionalised through the creation of a new trading bloc in the region, the Bolivarian Alliance for the Americas (ALBA).

Alliance was to nurture centrist, reformist alternatives to dictatorship premised on the notion that economic development and social reform could avert revolution. US capital was channelled to elected governments whose reforms – including some economic nationalism in the form of ISI combined with land reform and the reduction of income inequalities – met with Washington's approval. Reformers gaining US support in this period included Arturo Frondizi (1958–62) in Argentina, Rómulo Betancourt (1959–64) in Venezuela, Jânio Quadros (1961) in Brazil, Fernando Belaúnde Terry (1963–68) in Peru, Eduardo Frei (1964–70) in Chile, and Alberto Lleras Camargo (1958–62) and Carlos Lleras Restrepo (1966–70) in Colombia. However, the Alliance served, in fact, to demonstrate the *weakness* of democracy in Latin America by confirming that social tensions in countries such as Brazil, Chile and Argentina could not be contained by limited reformism. It suited political forces on both left and right to discredit the reformist option and, as the Alliance faltered and elites in Latin America began to turn to the military, Washington acquiesced in the establishment of repressive anti-communist regimes. Table 2.2 summarises the main events in this period.

Military regimes

Coups in Brazil and Bolivia in 1964 inaugurated a period of sweeping authoritarian rule across Latin America and signified a breakdown of the state under the stresses generated by industrial development. In Brazil, the growing radicalism of President João Goulart (1961–64), who had inherited the leadership of the populist constituency created by Vargas, alarmed the military. With the knowledge and collaboration of the US ambassador and military attaché, Brazil's armed forces seized control and would remain in power for 20 years. In Bolivia, a coup ended Víctor Paz Estenssoro's second term (1960–64), and the military remained in power for 18 years. In Peru, the reformist General Juan Velasco Alvarado (1968–75) took power in 1968, and the military remained until 1980. In Uruguay, the military began assuming more power during the 1960s as it tried to eradicate guerrilla activity and completed its formal takeover in 1973, remaining in power until 1984. Perhaps the most notorious coup of this era was in Chile in 1973, when the government of Salvador Allende (1970–73) was violently overthrown by General Augusto Pinochet, who remained in power for 17 years. It was the obsession with communism of the US president Richard Nixon (1969–74) that helps to explain why he instructed the CIA to undermine Allende after the Chilean Marxist had won the 1970 election (see Lowenthal, 1991). In Argentina, the military had staged recurrent interventions in politics since 1943, acting after 1955 against the Peronists, and in 1966 the armed forces again seized power. Perón was permitted to return to the country in 1973, but the military again intervened in 1976 and a series of hardline generals imposed a violent dictatorship until 1983. In Panama, a coup in 1968 brought the military to power until 1989, and in Honduras and El Salvador the armed forces stepped in from 1978–82 and 1979–83 respectively.

The military regimes of the 1960s–80s shared some characteristics. First, military interventions had hitherto often been in support of one civilian faction against another,

LANDMARKS
Table 2.2 From the Cuban Revolution to the 1980s

Year or period	Development
1959–63	Relations between the US and revolutionary Cuba collapse; Cuban-inspired armed revolts in Paraguay, Argentina, Dominican Republic, Venezuela, Colombia, Guatemala, Ecuador and Peru
1961	US-backed Bay of Pigs invasion of Cuba fails; US aid and reform programme, the Alliance for Progress, launched – reformers gain US support in Argentina, Venezuela, Brazil, Peru, Chile and Colombia; Paraguay becomes the last Latin American country to give women the vote
1962	Cuban Missile Crisis
1964	Coups in Brazil and Bolivia inaugurate a 20-year period of authoritarian military rule across Latin America; Eduardo Frei's Christian democrats come to power in Chile and benefit from US aid
1965	US forces invade Dominican Republic
1967	Che Guevara killed in Bolivia
1968	Reforming populist regime of General Juan Velasco Alvarado takes power in Peru; student demonstrators are massacred by the Mexican army at Tlatelolco on the eve of the Olympic games
1969	El Salvador attacks and fights the brief 'Soccer War' with Honduras
1970	Marxist Salvador Allende becomes president of Chile, provoking US campaign to undermine him
1973	Allende ousted amid great instability in a military coup that inaugurates the Pinochet dictatorship
1974	National Front pact between Colombia's Liberal and Conservative parties begins to unravel and guerrilla violence mounts
1976	Most repressive of Argentine military dictatorships comes to power and launches brutal 'Dirty War' against the Left
1977	Omar Torrijos signs a treaty with US that eventually gives back control of the Panama Canal to his country; FMLN guerrillas intensify attacks in El Salvador
1979	Nicaraguan Sandinistas overthrow the last Somoza in a successful revolution; confrontation with the US grows; in El Salvador army-backed rightwing death squads begin two-year eradication of tens of thousands of opponents; restoration of civilian government in Ecuador inaugurates slow process of democratisation across Latin America
1980	The Maoist guerrilla organisation Sendero Luminoso launches its war against the Peruvian state; Archbishop Oscar Romero is assassinated in El Salvador
1981	Ronald Reagan takes office in the US and initiates an aggressive anti-communist strategy in Latin America; *contra* war by US-backed Nicaraguan counter-revolutionaries begins against the Sandinista regime
1982	Mexico's inability to meet payments provokes the 'debt crisis'; Britain defeats Argentina in a war over the Malvinas/Falklands
1982–84	Colombian government under Belisario Betancur negotiates a ceasefire with the main guerrilla groups, which create political organisations to seek power through elections. These are subsequently targeted by rightwing paramilitaries and by 1986 the peace process is over, although the Movimiento 19 de Abril (M-19, 19th of April Movement) guerrilla organisation transforms into the AD-M19 political movement
1983	The Contadora negotiating process begins seeking a solution to the Central American civil wars through the mediation of (initially) Mexico, Venezuela, Colombia and Panama
1985	Radio Martí, affiliated to the US Information Agency, begins broadcasting to Cuba
1986–87	Further efforts unfold to find a negotiated solution to the civil wars in El Salvador and Guatemala, culminating in 1987 with the agreement by the Central American governments of the Esquipulas regional peace and democratisation plan
1989	US forces invade Panama

| THEORIES AND DEBATES | Box 2.4 |

Military antipolitics

During the 1960s and 70s, military officers in Latin America weighed up the problems facing their countries and many blamed corrupt and inept civilian politicians as well as dysfunctional institutions. They could only achieve modernisation, economic development and stability by curtailing 'politics' and ruling themselves for a long period. This attitude among military officers has been termed 'anti-politics' and Loveman and Davies (1997) traced the development of this phenomenon since the nineteenth century. An assumption that 'politics' was to blame for poverty, instability and economic backwardness was neither new nor confined solely to the military and, by advocating depoliticisation, military modernisers often found allies among civilian elites to whom democracy implied instability or unacceptable social reform. Loveman and Davies argued that antipolitics is committed neither to capitalism nor to socialism – it is antiliberal and anti-Marxist; it is repressive and coercive; it seeks order and places a high priority on orderly economic growth. In the 1960s and 1970s, antipolitics explicitly entailed hostility to labour protests, mobilisation by political parties and opposition to government authority, and placed an emphasis on more traditional Hispanic values of loyalty, authority and stability. To this it added the assumption widely held by Latin American military elites that economic development was an integral part of national security, and so was among the responsibilities of the armed forces (see Chapters 4, 7). The 'new professionalism' of the armed forces in the 1960s and 1970s now implied high levels of professional training in non-traditional areas that justified the establishment of military governments as instruments of development. This training took place at military colleges such as the Centro de Altos Estudios Militares (CAEM, Centre for Advanced Military Studies) in Peru and the Escola Superior de Guerra (ESG, Superior War School) in Brazil.

while the regimes of the 1960s and 70s often blamed the poor state of their countries on politicians and were distinctively *antipolitical* (see Box 2.4). As a result, the military often closed down democratic institutions such as congresses, parties, trades unions and the media, and took on administrative and managerial roles in the belief that they could act independently of squabbling civilians. Second, military leaderships in this period developed notions of national security (see Box 10.2), reflecting a concern with internal subversion. The US influenced this doctrine, and many Latin American officers were instructed in the US-run military School of the Americas in Panama and the CIA played a leading role in intelligence strategies. National security doctrine encouraged Latin American armed forces to take an increasingly active role in national life, and they often assumed responsibility for civic action programmes to help the poor in an effort to ease the conditions that were believed to foster insurgency. Third, most of the military regimes of the 1960s–1980s made systematic use of repression against thousands of civilians in this period and the use of torture, assassination and disappearances was common (see Table 7.2, Box 7.11). In Chile, thousands of supporters of Allende's Unidad Popular (UP, Popular Unity) coalition were rounded up and disappeared. In Argentina, the military conducted a brutal 'Dirty War' against the Left during the late 1970s in which at least 9,000 people, and perhaps up to 20,000, disappeared.

Many factors had contributed to the collapse of democracy in Latin America in the 1960s and 1970s. First, the military interventions occurred in the aftermath of the Cuban Revolution in the context of Cold War tension and, while the US cannot be blamed directly for most interventions, it often supported and even encouraged the military to act. The establishment of military governments both responded to and also fuelled guerrilla activity, and in societies where levels of economic and technological development were high, such as Uruguay, Argentina and Brazil, urban guerrillas appeared on the political landscape (see Figure 12.1). The guerrilla armies failed to overthrow the regimes they opposed and, in countries such as Uruguay, they contributed to the collapse of democratic government and the militarisation of politics. Second, even by the 1960s democratic institutions and values did not have deep roots in most Latin American societies. In conditions of social and political tension nurtured by severe inequality, rapid urbanisation, guerrilla activity and the aftermath of the Cuban Revolution, military intervention may have been inevitable. Third, military interventions coincided with the exhaustion of the first phase of ISI (see Chapter 14) or, in the case of Peru, with its initiation. An influential model of 'bureaucratic authoritarianism' was developed by O'Donnell (1973) to account for the relationship between the military regimes of the more industrialised economies of the Southern Cone and economic development (see Box 2.5). However, the economic policies adopted by military regimes in this period varied. The regime in Chile under Pinochet favoured economic liberalism and re-emphasised the role of the free market, and in Uruguay the military also tried to restructure the economy. Chile's regime developed policies in collaboration with the University of Chicago that would become influential in the late 1980s (see Chapter 15). It was easier to undertake reforms that might be unpopular with workers when repression could be used to silence opposition. Other regimes, such

---

THEORIES AND DEBATES   **Box 2.5**

Bureaucratic Authoritarianism

There were similarities among the military regimes of the Southern Cone in the 1960s–1980s. Coups tended to coincide with crises in civilian governments associated with the exhaustion of developmental models (see Chapter 14), and the ensuing regimes often placed an emphasis on restoring financial discipline through monetarism (see Chapter 15) and austerity packages. The notion of bureaucratic authoritarianism aimed to link economic modernisation and authoritarian rule by suggesting that the military stepped in to overcome the crisis associated with the exhaustion of ISI. Military elites believed that populism and communism were threatening economic progress and national security, and so took power in order to re-establish economic stability and political order. As a result, the notion of bureaucratic authoritarianism suggested that modernisation in the context of delayed development was more likely to lead to authoritarianism than to democracy.

Countries where bureaucratic authoritarianism was established had similar economic characteristics. To varying degrees, the economies of Argentina, Brazil, Chile, and Uruguay shared such factors as volatile growth, high and fluctuating inflation, recurrent balance-of-payments crises, capital shortages, capital flight and fiscal deficits. In short, they were deeply flawed capitalist economies and their poor performance made the very survival of capitalism debatable. These economic characteristics were combined with similar political issues: the emergence of an urban-based popular sector and, in particular, a rapidly growing working class concentrated in certain areas as a result of industrialisation. The growth of the urban popular sectors had generated conflicts over the allocation of resources and, as a result, growing politicisation that institutions struggled ever harder to control.

To the dominant classes inside these countries, but also those outside them linked to transnational capital, the absence of suitable conditions for normal economic functioning combined with perceptions of political instability raised the prospect that capitalism itself was at risk – a perception greatly heightened in the Cold War atmosphere. Moreover, as economic difficulties deepened, the demands of an increasingly politicised popular sector became more difficult to satisfy and pre-existing corporatist controls harder to maintain. At the same time, the state apparatus itself was becoming a battleground for competing social forces, and contributing to a general sense of uncertainty.

Rather than relying on the personal power of an individual military dictator, the form of rule established by bureaucratic–authoritarian regimes was based on the role of the military as an institution and premised on the idea that military personnel could govern better than civilians. As a result, these regimes employed military institutions to maintain social control. However, Mexico has also been described as having a modified version of bureaucratic authoritarianism in this period because the control its government had already been able to establish over popular forces without a military coup allowed it to exercise a similar sort of rule.

To O'Donnell (1988), bureaucratic-authoritarian states had several distinctive characteristics:

1) They maintained the domination in class-based societies of an 'upper bourgeoisie', that is, a powerful domestic and transnational capitalist class. None the less, at an institutional level, the 'specialists in coercion' – that is, the military – and those seeking to 'normalise' the economy, were the dominant actors. Bureaucratic–authoritarian states were, therefore, run by coalitions dominated by the military that often included domestic capitalists, transnational corporations, and economic technocrats, and which enjoyed the support of the US government. Together, these actors restored 'order' by deactivating the popular sectors and 'normalising' the economy. Government portfolios were allocated to military officers, civil servants or officials of large corporations, and economic decisionmaking was monopolised by generals and pro-business economists, sometimes trained at US institutions, such as Chile's so-called 'Chicago Boys' (see Chapter 15).

2) The working class and other popular forces were excluded from decisionmaking through repression, political activity was curbed, and stability enforced, allowing military regimes to dismantle social programmes that had been a source of patronage among politicians. There were exceptions to this, however, at least initially. In Argentina, for example, the 1966 coup enjoyed some support among popular sectors and was endorsed by many political and union leaders. It also had the support of Perón himself and the Peronists. The coup was widely seen as necessary because of an ineffectual government that was proving powerless in the face of widespread disorder, and not as an attack on the popular sector. None the less, the objectives of the Argentine bureaucratic–authoritarian regime ultimately proved to be the same as those elsewhere: to deactivate the popular sector in an effort to impose 'order' on society and so ensure its future viability. The implications of political exclusion in the bureaucratic–authoritarian regimes was the suppression of citizenship and of political rights, and the growth in influence of technocrats (see Box 2.1) who analysed and addressed social issues.

3) Bureaucratic–authoritarian governments often forged alliances with multi-national corporations and in Brazil and Chile key areas of the economy became effectively transnationalised. The military regimes relied on the availability at that time of cheap loans from international private banks to finance new large-scale infrastructure projects. These links with international economic forces reflected a new form of dependency. As a result, bureaucratic–authoritarian regimes promoted a model of growth biased in favour of large, oligopolistic units of private capital and that, in turn, implied the economic exclusion of the popular sector and the growth of inequality.

as that in Brazil, retained more statist approaches and did not radically restructure the economy, while forging close links with domestic and foreign capital. Most of the military regimes of this period instinctively preferred state ownership in strategic areas. A reformist approach taken by the Peruvian military government of 1968–75 distinguished this regime from the bureaucratic authoritarianism of the Southern Cone (see Chapter 16). The Peruvian military adopted policies of the revolutionary left, nationalised key economic sectors and pushed forward a strategy of ISI. This regime differed from those of Brazil, Argentina, Uruguay and Chile because it was largely autonomous of domestic capitalists and foreign investors; it attempted to build support through the inclusion of lower-class groups; and it did not indulge in the systematic terror characteristic of the Southern Cone regimes.

There were other important differences among the military regimes of the 1960s–1980s and, within each regime, rival currents. Military regimes were neither united nor autonomous of civilian politics and conflicts often emerged between moderates and hardliners over the use of repression. In most Latin American cases, after several years of authoritarian rule military–political leaderships sought some form of acceptance within society. In Chile, for example, control by Pinochet gradually evolved into personalist rule and a decisive stage was reached when a new constitution was approved by a plebiscite in 1980 giving the dictator a further eight years in office. In Brazil, the military regime claimed legitimacy after 1974 by laying out a framework for the transfer of power and balancing pro-regime forces. In Argentina, military regimes found it difficult to establish strong foundations within the institutions of government because of internal divisions, which weakened their efforts to seek support in society.

Some countries retained civilian-led governments in this period, although these often had an authoritarian character and ruled in conditions of instability. In Colombia, after 1974 the National Front pact between two traditionally dominant parties, the Partido Liberal (PL, Liberal Party) and the Partido Conservador (PC, Conservative Party), began to unravel and the stability that the pact had achieved was increasingly threatened by mounting guerrilla violence (see Chapter 12). In Venezuela, after 1968 the political system was monopolised by two main parties, Acción Democrática (AD, Democratic Action) and the Comité de Organización Política Electoral Independiente (COPEI, Committee for Independent Electoral Political Organisation), allowing it to maintain stability until the late 1980s, when economic crisis provoked a breakdown of the two-party system (see Box 4.2). In Mexico, the Partido Revolucionario Institucional (PRI, Institutional Revolutionary Party), maintained authoritarian control over government throughout the 1970s. Costa Rica maintained democratic rule during the 1970s despite deep economic problems both before and after the 1982 debt crisis in the region, largely because the main political forces agreed to alternate in power.

Guerrillas

The guerrilla option persisted in Central America, Colombia and Peru – where the Maoist organisation Sendero Luminoso launched a bloody war against the state (see Figure 12.1, Boxes 12.4, 13.9). The causes of revolutionary activity in Latin America have long been debated (see Box 2.6). Guerrilla insurgencies fared best in small agrarian countries ruled by corrupt and often dynastic elites who, by the 1970s, continued to prevail in much of Central America. Guerrilla movements, some of which had been established in the 1960s, grew in strength in Nicaragua, El Salvador and Guatemala and the proximity of these countries to the US meant that it intervened actively in the ensuing conflicts, often in support of dictatorships or military juntas. These revolutionaries and rightwing governments of Central America would fight the last major battles of the Cold War.

In Nicaragua, in 1979 the Sandinista revolutionaries overthrew Anastasio Somoza Debayle (1967–72, 1974–79), whose family had ruled the country tyrannically since

---

THEORIES AND DEBATES　　　　　　　　　　　　　　　　　　　　**Box 2.6**

What makes a revolution?

The causes of revolutions and the meaning of these sudden political, economic and social transitions have long been debated (see Selbin, 1993). An important cleavage in this debate has been between those whose arguments suggest that revolutionary movements 'make' revolutions, and those who have placed far more emphasis on the social and political structures in certain states and societies that make insurrections more likely. An orthodox position that chimed with classical Marxism suggested activities led by movements – such as strikes, peasant uprisings and guerrilla warfare – produced revolutions. Important contributions to this position have included those made by Wolf (1969), who stressed 'peasant wars' led to social revolutions in Mexico and Cuba among other countries; Paige (1975), who argued that certain types of peasantries were more likely to take part in revolutionary activities; and Tilly (1978), who examined patterns of social unrest among lower classes.

The idea that movements make revolutions was challenged by Skocpol (1979) who argued that, in certain cases, regimes collapsed because of their internal weaknesses as well as international factors. Skocpol argued that certain types of state or regime are more vulnerable to revolution than others. This approach directed attention away from opposition movements to the weaknesses within states and the characteristics of particular regimes. Wickham-Crowley (1992) examined this debate in the context of Latin America. He argued that the strength of a revolutionary movement itself cannot explain whether it is successful or not. The successful Cuban revolutionaries of 1956–59 were not stronger in military terms than revolutionaries in Colombia, Guatemala or Venezuela in the 1960s, and the victorious Sandinistas in Nicaragua were not as strong as the Salvadorean guerrilla fighters. It was the distinctive characteristics of the Cuban and Nicaraguan regimes that may have weakened them when confronted by revolutionary movements: both the Batista and Somoza regimes provoked the creation of a cross-class national opposition that brought together revolutionaries and moderates; both lacked support among *all* social classes and so could not mobilise a loyal defence; and both were personalist, which limited their nationalistic appeal (see also Selbin, 1993). Wickham-Crowley said three factors make for a likely revolution in Latin America: peasant support for a guerrilla movement is crucial; guerrilla movements must have enough military power to survive counterinsurgency measures; and a weak regime, when confronted by a guerrilla challenge, must engender a cross-class opposition. He identified Bolivia as a protoype for guerrilla *failure*. In 1966, the Argentinean revolutionary Che Guevara established a Cuban-led *foco* in the country, but the guerrillas lacked peasant support and they were destroyed by the army (see Box 12.2).

the 1930s. The dynasty's control had its origins in the US intervention against Augusto César Sandino (b.1895–d.1934) in the 1920s. The nationalist and anti-imperialist tradition exemplified by Sandino, and Guevara's notion of the *foco*, had been the inspiration for the formation in 1961 in Havana of the Frente Sandinista de Liberación Nacional (FSLN, Sandinista National Liberation Front). A devastating earthquake in 1972 and the theft by government officials of emergency aid transformed perceptions of the revolutionaries' cause and the Sandinistas were able to assume leadership after 1978 over a broad coalition that defeated Somoza's forces in a popular revolution. The revolution inaugurated the final phase of the Cold War in Latin America, which was characterised by the resurgence of aggressive anti-communism under President Ronald Reagan (1981–89) (see Chapter 10). Confrontation with the US grew as the Sandinistas accepted international support, including Cuban aid. Reagan imposed a trade embargo and sponsored the creation of a counter-revolutionary army in Honduras, the *contras*, who raided Nicaragua and destroyed its economy throughout the 1980s (see Box 16.2). In 1990, Violeta Chamorro (1990–97), a member of Nicaragua's conservative elite, became the first woman ever elected president in Latin America.

In El Salvador, by the late 1970s the suffering of the rural poor and the political monopoly of the country's landowning oligarchy had also generated an insurrectionary climate, unleashing a decade of civil war. The Salvadorean revolutionaries were also inspired by a nationalist figure from history, Agustín Farabundo Martí (b.1893–d.1932) who had served with Sandino. They gained moral and even material support from progressive and radical elements within the Church (see Boxes 7.12, 12.3). During the 1980s, Nicaragua's FSLN supported the Frente Farabundo Martí para la Liberación Nacional (FMLN, Farabundo Marti National Liberation Front) in its fight against the US-backed Salvadorean army, but the combatants fought to a stalemate and El Salvador's anti-communist elites sought a negotiated solution in 1992. In Guatemala, which had been under military control since 1954, there was also a resurgence of guerrilla activity in the late 1970s, eventually led by the Unidad Revolucionaria Nacional Guatemalteca (URNG, Guatemalan National Revolutionary Unity). The country's armed forces carried out a brutal campaign against the guerrillas, concentrated in the mainly indigenous western highlands and against the urban opposition, but after 1983 military leaders began to seek a negotiated transition to democracy and a civilian president was elected in 1985. Peace talks began in 1987 and agreements were finally concluded in 1996, ending a civil war that had begun in the 1960s and in which indigenous villagers had suffered greatly.

The triumph of democracy

By the end of the 1970s, many of Latin America's militaries were ready to return to the barracks and the region experienced a wave of democratisation, beginning with the restoration of civilian government in 1979 in Ecuador. By the mid-1990s, all of the countries in the region except Cuba were under some form of democratic rule, or were experiencing a transition to democracy.

In Ecuador, civilian rule was restored under Jaime Roldós (1979–81) after almost three decades of alternating military governments. The Nicaraguan guerrillas overthrew the Somoza dictatorship in 1979, but fully democratic elections did not occur until 1990. Peru's military handed over to civilian rule under Belaúnde Terry in 1980, but the following two decades were overshadowed by the brutal civil war against Sendero Luminoso in which the military took an increasingly prominent role (see Boxes 12.4, 13.9), followed by a decade of control under the autocratic populist Alberto Fujimori (1990–2000) whose administration became mired in corruption. Honduras formally began its democratic life in 1981 with the election of Roberto Suazo Córdova (1982–86) leading to the first civilian government in more than a century, but for another 10 years the country was affected by the Central American civil wars and the military retained disproportionate power. In Bolivia, in 1982 the military handed power to a civilian administration under Hernán Siles Zuazo (1952, 1956–60, 1982–85) and in Argentina, following the military's defeat in a war with Britain over the Malvinas/Falkland Islands (see Box 11.1), civilian rule returned in 1983 under Raúl Alfonsín (1983–89). In 1985, Uruguay's military handed back power to a civilian administration under Julio María Sanguinetti (1985–90, 1995–2000), and, in the same year, Brazil's military relinquished control to a civilian government under José Sarney (1985–90) and military rule formally ended in Guatemala with the election of Marco Vinicio Cerezo Arévalo (1986–91). However, Guatemala did not realistically resemble a democracy until after the peace deal in 1996. In Chile, Pinochet was defeated in 1988 in a plebiscite on the continuation of his rule and handed over power in 1990 to Patricio Aylwin (1990–94). In 1989, the US invasion of Panama ousted the military strongman Manuel Noriega (1981–89) and led to the re-establishment of civilian rule, and a coup in Paraguay deposed the ageing dictator General Alfredo Stroessner (1954–89) and led to a process of democratisation that culminated in 1993 with elections won by Juan Carlos Wasmosy (1993–98). In El Salvador, the recognition in 1991 of the FMLN as a political party and the signing of peace accords began a process of democratisation after a decade of civil war and the long domination of government by rightwing elites backed by the army. In Mexico, single-party control by the PRI ended when it finally lost congressional elections in 1997 and then presidential elections in 2000.

Military and authoritarian rule ended for several reasons (see Chapter 3). Rising international interest rates caused a severe debt crisis in 1982 (see Chapter 15) and eroded the belief among investors that military regimes could continue to manage economies by now heavily dependent on external borrowing. Nervousness among foreign investors put the fragile coalitions upon which bureaucratic–authoritarian regimes were founded under strain, and a new emphasis on free-market economics (neoliberalism) challenged the model of state-led economic development upon which corporatism had been based (see Chapters 7, 14, 15). Rivalries developed within the armed forces themselves as moderates began to argue that more could be gained from a negotiated transition to democracy than could be achieved with continued military rule. The international climate also became more hostile towards military regimes as Portugal, Greece and Spain underwent transitions to democracy. Lastly, a consensus began to emerge among key interest-groups in support of the idea of a revived liberal state founded on representative and accountable institutions. In particular, the late 1970s and 1980s witnessed the emergence of new social move-ments (see Chapter 8) and popular sentiment grew strongly in favour of a shift to democracy.

Forces on the political right were the initial political beneficiaries of democra-tisation, as Latin American countries undertook often painful 'neoliberal' eco-nomic restructuring processes that reduced the size of the state and promoted free markets during the 1980s and 1990s (see Chapter 15). However, in the late 1990s left-of-centre political forces began to make considerable gains across much of Latin America in what has sometimes been referred to as a 'pink tide' bringing socialist and social-democratic parties to power (see Chapters 12, 16). None the less, democratisation in much of the region remains flawed (see Chapter 4), and in some countries, reform has not eradicated the considerable influence enjoyed by the military, which has at times shown signs of unease following the election of presidents who are not on the right. In 2009, for example, in Honduras, President Manuel Zelaya (2006–09) was deposed in a coup, and in Paraguay, President Fernando Lugo (2008–) sacked the chiefs of the armed forces, warning that some officers were plotting a coup against him.

Summary

The 1929 Wall Street crash ended the neocolonial order as most countries took the first steps towards creating their own industries. Many Latin American countries were ruled by authoritarian parties or military dictators stressing nationalism as new groups such as organised labour were brought into politics under government control. Communist and fascist parties also emerged to challenge elite conserva-tive and liberal factions. The process of industrialisation gathered pace after the Second World War and large state bureaucracies controlling public enterprises were created. Workers and middle-class professionals and bureaucrats were incorpor-ated in new governing coalitions overseeing an industrial revolution. For a brief period from 1945–47, democratic governments began to replace authoritarian regimes, and in several countries pro-industrial, multi-class populist alliances were formed. After the late 1940s, the Cold War began to alter the basis of inter-American relations by turning Latin America into a battleground in the conflict between US capitalism and Soviet communism. Washington pursued an anti-communist crusade until the late 1980s that often helped to perpetuate authoritarian regimes. In the 1950s, industrialisation strategies also began to falter and inflation and un-employment exacerbated social tensions. The Cuban Revolution in 1959 transformed the prospects of Marxism in Latin America and inspired armed revolts through-out the region. It also distorted US perceptions about threats to its security and prompted the creation of the Alliance for Progress aid and reform programme. This had limited success and, as Latin American elites began to turn to the military, Washington acquiesced in the establishment of repressive anti-communist regimes. Military coups in Brazil and Bolivia in 1964 inaugurated a period of authoritarian rule across Latin America and signified a breakdown of the state under stresses generated by industrial development. The military regimes of the 1960s–1980s often blamed the poor state of their countries on politicians, justified their rule with ideas of national security, made systematic use of repression against thousands of civilians and favoured economic liberalism alongside state control of key strategic areas. Guerrilla activity persisted in Colombia, Peru and Central America, where revolutionaries and rightwing governments fought the last major battles of the Cold War. In Nicaragua, the Sandinistas led a successful revolution, leading to confrontation with the US, but in El Salvador the guerrillas and the army fought to a standstill. Guatemala's armed forces carried out a brutal campaign against guerrillas concentrated in mainly indigenous areas. From the late 1970s onwards, Latin American militaries began to return to the barracks and the region experienced a wave of democratisation. Authoritarian rule ended because of economic crisis, divisions within the armed forces, an international climate more hostile towards military regimes and a new consensus among key political actors in support of the idea of a revived liberal state. Since the late 1990s, left-of-centre political forces have been able to take advantage of democratisation to win power in many Latin American countries. None the less, democracy in the region faces many challenges and the military retains considerable influence in some countries.

Discussion points

- To what extent was the emergence of the modern state related to industrialisation?
- Was corporatism inevitable in Latin America, and was it a substitute for democracy?
- What was the relationship between populism and the organised working class?
- Did US anti-communism stifle democracy in Latin America during the Cold War?
- Why was the Cuban Revolution in 1959 so significant?
- Why were the military interventions of the 1960s and 1970s so distinctive?
- Assess the pros and cons of the model of bureaucratic authoritarianism.
- Do radical movements, or specific circumstances, make revolutions?
- What factors explain why military and authoritarian rule ended in Latin America?

Useful websites

oxlad.qeh.ox.ac.uk Oxford Latin American Economic History Database (OxLAD), compiled by the Latin American Centre of Oxford University

www.neha.nl/w3vl/latinamerica.html Latin American Economic and Business History section of the WWW Virtual Library, maintained in Amsterdam by the Netherlands Economic History Archive

www.evitaperon.org/Principal.htm Eva Perón Historical Research Foundation

http://historicaltextarchive.com Historical Text Archive run from Mississippi, containing useful articles and links about Latin American history

www.casahistoria.net/latam.html Useful site on Latin America within general history archive that has an independent left-of-centre perspective

www.wilsoncenter.org/index.cfm?topic_id=1409&fuseaction=topics.home Cold War International History Project (CWIHP) of the Woodrow Wilson International Center for Scholars

www.mtholyoke.edu/acad/intrel/cuba.htm Valuable site compiled at Mount Holyoke College containing documents surrounding the Cuban Missile Crisis

www.granma.cu/che/homeche.html Granma Internacional Digital website about Che Guevara

www.nottingham.ac.uk/SPLAS/Research/CRF/index.aspx Cuba Research Forum of the Department of Hispanic and Latin American Studies at the University of Nottingham, incorporating information on the Hennessy Collection of Cuban periodicals

www.ejercito.mil.ar Official site of the Argentine army

www.exercito.gov.br Official site of the Brazilian army

www.esg.br Brazil's Escola Superior de Guerra (ESG, Superior War School)

www.ejercito.cl Official site of the Chilean army

www.ejercito.mil.pe Official site of the Peruvian army

fmln.org.sv Frente Farabundo Martí para la Liberación Nacional (FMLN, Farabundo Martí National Liberation Front)

Recommended reading

Bethell, Leslie (ed.). 1990–95. *The Cambridge History of Latin America, Volumes 6 to 11.* Cambridge: Cambridge University Press

Essential introduction to the economic, social and political history of the region and a key source of reference. Volume 6 (Parts 1 and 2) covers key themes in the whole region from 1930 to 1990; Volume 7 provides separate histories of Mexico, Central America and the Caribbean; Volume 8 covers Spanish South America; Volumes 10 and 11 look at ideas, culture and society, and include bibliographical essays

Wiarda, Howard (ed.). 2004. *Authoritarianism and Corporatism in Latin America Revisited.* Gainesville, EL: University Press of Florida

Essential overview of corporatism in Latin America that explores this phenomenon at historical, theoretical and empirical levels and contains eight country studies as well as valuable introductory and concluding chapters pointing to new directions in research

Conniff, Michael L. (ed.). 1999. *Populism in Latin America.* Tuscaloosa, AL: University of Alabama Press

Essential collection of essays on Latin American populism past and present with a helpful introduction giving definitions and an overview of the study of this phenomenon and chapters that also explore its manifestations in the contemporary period

Loveman, Brian and Thomas M. Davies Jr (eds). 1997. *The Politics of Antipolitics. The Military in Latin America.* Wilmington, DE: Scholarly Resources

Valuable collection taking an historical approach to military interventions in Latin American politics with sections on the relationship between military establishments and the US, the policies and consequences of military rule and the persistence of anti-politics in the democratic era

O'Donnell, Guillermo. 1973. *Modernization and Bureaucratic Authoritarianism: Studies in South American Politics.* Berkeley, CA: Institute of International Studies, University of California

Influential work first published in 1973 developing a model of bureaucratic authoritarianism to account for the Latin American military regimes of that period, updated in the 1998 edition with a new preface

Wickham-Crowley, Timothy P. 1992. *Guerrillas and Revolution in Latin America. A Comparative Study of Insurgents and Regimes Since 1956.* Princeton, NJ: Princeton University Press

Essential survey of the origins and outcomes of rural insurgencies that represented the first systematic attempt to bring together case studies and sociological theories of revolution in Latin America

Part II

INSTITUTIONS, PROCESSES AND ACTORS

Chapter 3

Democratisation and the quality of democracy

This chapter considers how and why democracy became the norm across Latin America from the end of the 1970s following years of rule by authoritarian governments. However, in order to use the term 'democracy' it is necessary to begin by considering what it means. The democratic nature of politics in prosperous and developed regions such as Western Europe and most of North America is often taken for granted without realising that there is no single, self-contained definition of democracy that is universally accepted and the understanding of it has evolved over time: democracy is a *contested* concept. To what extent is democracy defined mainly by the presence of elections, for example, or is a minimum degree of economic equality necessary for all voters in a country to be incorporated fully in democratic life? How democracy is interpreted is of key importance for any theory that seeks to explain it and to provide a yardstick against which the process of democratisation in any given country can be assessed. The most difficult challenge in studying democratisation, therefore, has been reaching agreement on what 'democracy' actually is.

The study of politics in Latin America is valuable in such debates because the region poses key questions about how we understand democracy; about what conditions, if any, might be necessary for it to flourish; and about ways in which democratic systems can be measured and compared. Moreover, the largely uninterrupted trajectory towards the establishment of durable democratic practices in the developed industrial countries of Europe and most of North America has not been reproduced in Latin America, where democratic development has proceeded in fits and starts. The authoritarian military regimes that already held or took power in the 1960s and 1970s merely followed earlier democratic interludes.

In the 1980s and 1990s, the authoritarian and revolutionary regimes were replaced by elected civilian governments, and by 2000 most of Latin America could be described, on the basis of competitive elections, as democratic in some way. Only Cuba does not meet the most commonly used definitions of democracy because it does not have more than one political party and certain rights are suppressed, although the Cuban state argues that its political system *is* democratic.

That is not to say that the aspiration to establish democracy in Latin America has not always been present. It has been argued that the region's democratic tradition is robust and longstanding aspects of its political culture dating from Independence – such as constitutionalism and popular resistance to oppressive authority – complement modern democratic practices (Peeler, 1998; Forment,

2003; see also Chapter 1). None the less, the uneven and often interrupted nature of change in the region begs questions about what other factors may be involved in the broader move towards democratic political systems. It also allows academics to use examples from Latin America as a region and the individual countries within it to make comparisons with other parts of the world undergoing similar processes, such as the Middle East. Processes of democratisation in Latin America in the 1980s and 1990s, for example, formed part of what has been characterised more broadly as a global 'third wave' of democratisation since the early nineteenth century that began in the developing world in the early 1970s (Huntington, 1991). Data suggests that this 'third wave' has slowed considerably in recent years (EIU, 2008).

This chapter will survey these processes, investigate the key issues in theory that they draw attention to, and begin to explore the *quality* of the democratic systems that are evolving in Latin America and how this can be measured.

Democracy

In general, the term democracy is used loosely to refer to any country with a government chosen in an election, but there are many other interpretations of it. Rightwing conservatives subscribing to Catholic corporatism and even fascism (see Chapter 12) often spoke of creating hierarchical 'functional' democracies based upon the representation by elites of different social sectors. Cuba's regime says it has practised a 'revolutionary democracy' in which electoral competition takes place between candidates who can only belong to a single party. The Peruvian guerrilla organisation Sendero Luminoso subscribed to a Maoist vision of a peasant war spreading 'new democracy' that was neither capitalist nor socialist (see Boxes 12.4, 13.9).

A principal concern of the early literature about the shift from authoritarianism to democracy in Latin America was with seeing if minimal standards for the representation of citizens or their participation in politics could be achieved through the adoption of certain procedures such as elections. *Procedural* definitions of democracy emphasise the existence of formal political institutions and elections. They depict democracy, above all, as representative government and establish minimal conditions for this to be present such as contestation between political interests, constitutionalism and inclusiveness (see Hartlyn and Valenzuela, 1994). These conditions are usually met through: adherence to constitutional rules; secret ballots based on universal suffrage; free, regular and clean elections; competition between parties; and structures that ensure the executive (president) can be held to account for decisions he or she has made. They imply basic political *liberties* such as freedom of association and expression. Such minimalist procedural democracy is sometimes called 'polyarchy', a term associated with the ideas of Dahl (1971) that has been influential in the study of democracy and refers to a pluralist political system in which there is competition between many different interests. By procedural criteria, as long as basic conditions are met, a range of different institutional forms and procedures can be compatible with 'democracy'.

Elections are clearly very important: they confer *legitimacy* on the winner, establishing a president or party's right to govern in the public mind; they serve as safety valves, limiting frustrations by allowing for the expression of opposition views and preferences without overturning the political order; and they provide valuable information about the condition of a democracy and its institutions.

However, minimalist definitions of democracy that insist upon little more than an electoral process or certain procedural mechanisms are clearly unsatisfactory. Today, there is greater awareness that it is possible to have a poor quality of democracy and that elections in themselves are *not* a sign of democracy, as electoral systems may be unrepresentative or fraudulently manipulated.

For this reason, a distinction is often made between *electoral* democracy that meets the procedural requirements of a democratic process and *liberal* democracy where a democratic *spirit* based upon individual liberty prevails (Foweraker *et al.*, 2003). None the less, freedom and democracy are not the same thing, even though these terms are often used interchangeably. Even if some liberal conditions are met, a political system may still fall short of being truly democratic if it does not distribute power more evenly because of inequalities in society. The main alternative to procedural definitions of democracy, therefore, is a social conception of democracy – *social democracy* – that equates it with greater equality and justice (see Chapters 12, 16). Such a definition has clear relevance in Latin America, where inequalities are extreme (see Chapter 4). A discernible shift towards the political left in much of Latin America since democratic politics took hold has been marked by state policies aimed at fostering greater equality and justice that reflect social-democratic priorities.

Social democracy places a much greater emphasis than procedural democracy on the need for 'democratic governance'. The term governance refers to the ways in which any social unit organises the processes by which decisions are made and implemented and, in political terms, to the ways in which public institutions conduct their affairs and manage their resources. Governance can be understood broadly as the traditions and institutions by which authority is exercised in a country, and includes processes by which governments are selected, monitored and replaced; a government's capacity to effectively formulate and implement sound policies; and the respect of citizens and the state for those institutions that govern them. Good governance, therefore, describes how those institutions accomplish the task of guaranteeing basic *rights* for citizens without abuses of the system and within the law. The idea of *democratic governance* prescribes the criteria of good governance that are likely to be found within a democracy, including: the accountability of political leaders, freedom of association and participation, and an honest and accessible judicial system. Above all, democratic governance implies high levels of *participation* among political and social actors in all aspects of decisionmaking and the implementation of policy.

In recent years, initiatives at the level of local authorities (called municipalities) or below that promote an inclusive, *participatory* democracy, have been introduced in a number of Latin American countries, and the idea was enshrined in Venezuela's 1999 'Bolivarian Constitution' (Wilpert, 2006; see Chapter 12). What is distinctive about such initiatives is that they often respond to pressure from below, that is from among the population, as opposed to directives that come from above, that is, from the authorities themselves. Some investigators, therefore, identify potential tensions between participatory forms of democracy and *representative democracy* in which citizens do not take an active part in decisionmaking, which is undertaken by elected officials (see, for example, Selee and Peruzzotti eds, 2009).

The case of 'participatory budgeting' in Brazil (see Box 16.5), which involves citizens in decisions about local authority spending plans, is among the most well known examples of participatory democracy in Latin America, but innovative examples can also be found in Mexico, Bolivia, Chile, Brazil, and Argentina among other countries (see Avritzer, 2009; Selee and Peruzzotti eds, 2009). In Venezuela, for example, citizen participation in the allocation of resources under social programmes introduced by the Chávez government, such as local healthcare and education initiatives – sometimes called *misiones* – has been an important feature of contemporary political development (see Lievesley and Ludlam eds, 2009).

Democracy in Latin America

Anyone wishing to study democratisation in Latin America can do little better than to start with a comprehensive overview of the achievements and challenges of democracy in the region carried out on behalf of the United Nations Development Programme (UNDP, 2004b, 2004c). This was compiled by an independent team of academics and other experts with the help of political and social actors in Latin America, and has been the subject of much scrutiny (see, for example, Inter-American Dialogue/UNDP, 2005). It was followed up by a subsequent review, whose contributors made a case for stronger action by individual states to nurture and protect democracy in the region (UNDP, 2008).

The UNDP argued that since the late 1970s democratisation had made remarkable progress throughout Latin America. However, beneath this picture for the region as a whole, there had been considerable variation in the process and pace of democratisation between sub-regions such as Central America, the Andean region and the Southern Cone of Brazil, Argentina, Uruguay and Chile. By 1990, military regimes had disappeared in the Southern Cone but in Central America civil wars continued and democratisation occurred alongside peace processes. During the 1990s, the Andean countries – despite a continuing record of democracy or early progress in moving away from military regimes – had experienced serious political problems that at times threatened democracy. In Mexico, formal democracy was not achieved until the very end of the 1990s.

This variation derived from the different forms authoritarianism had taken across Latin America, which had a bearing on the timing and nature of democratisation in each country. Costa Rica is the only country to have escaped the complete breakdown of democracy. Some countries, such as Chile and Uruguay, experienced authoritarian rule under military regimes in the 1970s after having enjoyed stable democratic systems for many years. Others – often the poorest and least developed – were ruled by traditional dictators whose regimes were built upon their personal exercise of power. These included Nicaragua under various members of the Somoza dynasty between 1937 and 1979, and Paraguay under Alfredo

Stroessner (1954–89). From the 1960s until the 1980s, Brazil and Argentina came under the control of the armed forces. O'Donnell's (1973) model of 'bureaucratic authoritarianism' aimed to describe these and similar military regimes, which often articulated developmental goals, repressed labour to allow for economic restructuring, and stressed a national security doctrine aimed at resisting leftwing insurgency in the climate of the Cold War (see Boxes 2.5, 10.2, Figure 12.1, Chapters 4, 7). However, other military regimes in Peru (1968–78), Bolivia (1964–82) and Ecuador (1972–79) were more populist (see Chapters 2, 4) and stressed the need for economic redistribution (O'Donnell, 1986; see Chapter 16). In Guatemala, El Salvador and Honduras, entrenched conservative elites used repression and corruption to maintain power within what, on paper, were meant to be competitive political systems. In Mexico, power was monopolised by a single party, the Partido Revolucionario Institucional (PRI, Institutional Revolutionary Party), which retained control of congress (the legislature, or parliament) and the presidency until 1997–2000. In Cuba, the revolutionary leadership that has been in power since 1959 has combined personalism with the control of a single, mass authoritarian party.

Democratic transition

The 'third wave' of democratisation generated efforts to explain in a systematic way the shift from authoritarian, often military, regimes to competitive civilian political systems. Theoretical literature has adapted as political developments in Latin America have unfolded, and has asked several important questions: why do authoritarian regimes break down? What different forms does democratisation take? What factors determine the success of democracy?

The study of democracy in Latin America has never stopped evolving and has gone through a series of shifts in focus and priorities (for a useful summary of these, see O'Donnell *et al.*, 2008). However, two notional phases became prominent: the initial 'transition' to democracy and the subsequent 'consolidation' of democracy.

The analysis of democratic transition built upon a framework of ideas in the study of comparative politics that coalesced around the work of Rustow (1970), who rejected a commonly held assumption that certain 'preconditions' – such as relatively high levels of wealth and a commitment by the population to democratic values – were necessary for democracy to flourish (see Box 3.1). This position opened the way for democratic transition to be considered independently of factors that may keep a democracy *stable*, and so offered hope for countries hitherto seen as having little chance of meeting accepted preconditions. Rustow's approach assumed a dynamic process of change in which individual choices and bargaining played prominent roles in democratisation. Criticisms of this approach have mostly concerned what weight should be given within the equation to those factors on which the supposed preconditions that Rustow rejected had been based.

During the late 1970s and 1980s, scholars embraced Rustow's perspective or arrived at similar positions independently. Typically, they examined interactions between hardliners and moderates within an authoritarian regime and between

THEORIES AND DEBATES	Box 3.1

Are there 'preconditions' for democracy?

Why democracy emerged in some parts of the world and not others, and hence whether certain preconditions are necessary for democratic politics to flourish, has long been debated. Attempts to answer this question evolved out of the assumptions of 'modernisation' theory, a framework of understanding common in the 1950s, particularly in the US, that departed from the position that developed countries had also once been underdeveloped agrarian societies and so development could be understood as a series of successive stages through which all countries pass (see Box 14.2). Theoretical approaches often took the form of an effort to ascertain how different cultural, political or economic variables determined the presence of democracy. Modernisation theory implied that a democratic form of rule resulted from the process of economic and political evolution that had been experienced by the Western industrial nations.

Some studies explored the notion that the creation of a stable democratic regime might be linked to the type of culture found in a country, and stressed the presence of a *civic culture* of values based upon tolerance, rationalism or even Protestantism (see Almond and Verba, 1963; see also Box 7.13). Others searched for cultural obstacles to democracy in Latin America itself, such as the region's corporatist heritage (see Box 2.2, Chapter 7; see also Véliz, 1980; Wiarda, 1981). Diamond *et al.* eds (1989) argued that the development and maintenance of democracy is aided by citizens' values and attitudes of compromise, tolerance, conciliation, moderation and restraint. These values are important in any vigorous democratic system but academics still debate the extent to which they are *necessary* for democracy. Other studies investigated how social or political structures can help to explain the presence of democracy, such as the existence of certain institutions, forms of organisation or citizen associations (see Dahrendorf, 1959; Moore, 1966). A more contemporary variant of this structural approach has placed importance upon the existence and development of 'civil society' in which groups or associations autonomous of the state aggregate the activities of individuals and promote or defend their interests (Gill, 2000; see also Chapter 8).

Academics have also explored the relationship between socioeconomic factors and democracy, associating it with high per capita income, widespread literacy or urban residence. There is a positive correlation between levels of economic development and democracy at a global level, but not in Latin America. The assumptions of modernisation theory associate free-market economies with democracy in the belief that free markets produce growth and encourage liberal individualism, generating a conducive environment for this type of political system (see Chapters 4, 15). In Latin America, the argument that a link exists between free markets and democracy was given force by the re-emergence of democracy alongside the simultaneous adoption of market reforms during the 1980s and 1990s. However, critics of the association between free markets and democracy point out that capitalism can and often does prosper *without* competitive and participative political systems (China represents the best contemporary example of this).

The emphasis of modernisation perspectives on preconditions blended together the *causes* and the *conditions* of democracy, by assuming the conditions that prevailed in established democracies and that helped to maintain them may be the same as those required to *initiate* democratisation in other cases. Rustow, the pioneer of transition theory, rejected the idea that strict preconditions were necessary for democracy to take hold, an idea that is indeed difficult to sustain in the case of Latin America where democratisation has often taken place in adverse circumstances. It is safer to argue that cultural, political and economic factors are not so much preconditions as contributing factors helping to determine the *type* of democracy that may develop and its quality. Latin American leaders consulted for the UNDP's 2004 study asserted that two fundamental conditions for the survival of democracy in the region had to be broad political participation among citizens and the exercise of controls over how power is used (see UNDP, 2004b).

moderates and radicals in an opposition, and envisaged phases of regime break-down, transition and consolidation. A ground-breaking series of works published after 1986 edited by O'Donnell, Schmitter and Whitehead emphasised the *indeterminacy* of transitions from authoritarian rule. Other debates concerned the failure of authoritarian regimes to find mechanisms to make their rule appear legitimate in the eyes of the population; the roles played by elites within and outside regimes; the role of economic factors in regime change; the roles played by opposition groups and popular movements in transitions; the conditions necessary for transitions, and factors that may prevent or hinder them; and the role of international forces in the transition process.

Transition can best be understood as an uncertain process of regime change, where the rules of political competition are up for negotiation and it is not clear what the outcomes will be. Agüero (1998) argued that the varying analytical weight given to different *types* of transition had an important bearing on the different ways of evaluating democracy in the contemporary period. Therefore, it was valuable to distinguish between forms of transition because each establishes different rules and patterns that shape the prospects for future consolidation. Two broad forms of transition have been distinguished: those that occurred by the collapse or sudden rupture of authoritarian control, such as in Nicaragua in 1979 and Argentina in 1982; and those that occurred by transaction through talks between opposing groups leading to liberalisation by a regime, such as in Brazil, Peru and Chile.

In transitions by collapse, pressure on an authoritarian regime accumulates until active opposition – or, in the case of Argentina, defeat in the Malvinas/Falklands war – leads the military to retreat from politics. Revolutions clearly represent a transition by rupture, although they have rarely evolved into democratic patterns of competition. The Nicaraguan Revolution (1979) did not establish conditions for competitive multi-party democracy, which was only achieved by the defeat of the revolutionary regime in elections in 1990 that were, none the less, far from fair. Transitions by collapse are sudden, and authoritarian rulers have little control over the process. As a result, there are few constraints on the policies that can be undertaken by the democratic governments that succeed them, but at the same time these governments may be more threatened by disaffected actors.

Some transitions were preceded by efforts by military regimes to loosen constraints on activity – political liberalisation. Transitions by transaction, that is, through controlled political liberalisation, are typical of authoritarian regimes that believe they have successfully achieved economic development, as in the case of Brazil in 1985 and Chile in 1989. These often take the form of an elite 'pact' negotiated between the military rulers and the democratic opposition over a long period. The regime remains in control of the process and seeks to determine who is allowed to organise politically and compete in elections. Transitions by transaction can be more stable than those by collapse because disaffected actors such as the military will have had their interests accommodated. However, because the democratic opposition has negotiated with the armed forces, the resultant democracies are often born with guarantees that give the military a role in the new system – one that some high commands have since exercised. In 2009, for example, military chiefs in Honduras removed President Manuel Zelaya (2005–09) of the Partido Liberal de Honduras (PLH, Liberal Party) amid his power struggle with congress and the supreme court over plans for a vote on constitutional reform that they opposed (see Box 7.10). Zelaya went into exile and an interim government was formed under the speaker of congress, Roberto Micheletti, constitutionally second-in-line to the presidency. Micheletti and the armed forces argued that Zelaya had overstepped constitutional provisions and acted illegally by seeking to call a referendum on his own authority.

If the elite pact negotiated between military rulers and a democratic opposition is limited, a transition can be lengthy and unstable. Bolivia, for example, did not enjoy a durable elected government for four years after the regime of Hugo Banzer Suárez (1971–78) had ended because of squabbling between politicians and renewed military interventions, and the subsequent three-year presidency of Hernán Siles Zuazo (1982–85) was very unstable.

Factors that contribute to regime change

Transition theory was criticised for being premature in its assumption that substantive democratic change had, in fact, occurred (Carothers, 2002) and for downplaying the role of social mobilisation – the process by which a social group goes from being a passive collection of individuals to an active political force by organising, say, rallies and marches (Gill, 2000; Foweraker et al., 2003). Other theoretical emphases have also been advanced building on the idea of mobilisation and seeking to account for the role played in political change by social movements and organised labour, for example (see Foweraker et al., 2003; see also Chapters 7, 8). Transition theory has also been attacked as an ideological effort to promote the adoption of practices conducive to capitalism (Cammack, 1997).

However, despite disagreements about the best way of studying this stage of the democratisation process, the theoretical literature on transition was valuable for drawing attention to the many political, economic and international factors that can contribute to regime change and shape the type of democracy that emerges:

Political factors

Elites

Analyses of democratisation in Latin America have often focused upon elite choices, co-operation or conflict. Most of the transitions that occurred in the region took the form of agreements or pacts between political and economic elites both within and outside the authoritarian regime. O'Donnell (1986) argued that incumbents of an authoritarian regime often decided to open it up or 'depressurise' it, resulting in a series of deliberate agreements with the opposition. Przeworski (1991) suggested that transition processes often reached a critical moment in which political actors decided how best to extract themselves from military control and agree on the shape of the new democratic order by convening a constituent assembly to draft a new constitution, as in Peru (1979) and Brazil (1988) (see also Lijphart,

1993). Democracies established in this way are often born with guarantees that represent the armed forces in the new institutional system. Burton, Gunther and Higley (1992) employed the term 'elite settlement' to discuss ways in which rival factions suddenly and deliberately reorganised their relations. Such settlements create patterns of peaceful competition among elites, thereby providing the consensus necessary for stability, and characterised transitions in Brazil (1985), Uruguay (1984) and El Salvador (1989–92).

Legitimacy

Authoritarian regimes often had difficulties making their rule appear legitimate, that is, based on consent, which is crucial for ensuring political stability and so maintaining power. The PRI's loss of legitimacy in Mexico during the 1990s, for example, was an important factor in the eventual victory of the opposition Partido Acción Nacional (PAN, National Action Party). Violent challenges to authoritarian rulers were a feature of transitions in Central America, where powerful oligarchies or dynasties either lacked or lost legitimacy. Military regimes that continued in office ran the risk of splits, one key cause of which concerned the relationship between legitimacy and *repression* – the restraint of opposition through coercion. Repression allows a regime to dispense with the need for legitimacy in the short term, but in the longer term it is of limited effectiveness as a means of exercising control. However, if military leaders move away from repression they must seek broader support from within society in order to maintain their control over it. In most cases, military leaders sought some form of public acceptance after several years of authoritarian rule. In Brazil after 1974, the military regime used conservative politicians who supported it to forge limited links with society. Chile's dictator General Augusto Pinochet (1973–90) sought to establish his legitimacy through a new constitution approved by a plebiscite in 1980.

Parties

The process by which parties emerge or re-emerge in transitional politics is *important* because it will influence the type and durability of democracy that is established. Strong parties can channel and unite pressure for democratisation and negotiate a transition to a new regime, but weak parties can hamper the formation of coalitions and so impede democratisation (see Chapter 6). In Chile, the re-emergence of traditional parties during the 1980s channelled opposition to Pinochet's rule and spearheaded the 'No' campaign in the October 1988 referendum that would end his dictatorship. In Peru, the military chose the Alianza Popular Revolucionaria Americana (APRA, American Revolutionary Popular Alliance, today referred to as the Partido Aprista Peruano) with whom to negotiate the transition because this was the strongest political force and was more likely to ensure that agreements would be honoured.

Non-elite actors and civil society

The extent to which organised opposition and non-elite sectors of society contributed to the breakdown of authoritarian rule has also been debated (see Chapter 8).

The role played by groups representing middle-class professionals, businessmen, bureaucrats and movements of workers, peasants and the marginalised poor was often an important variable in transitions. At some point, all these groups may converge in a broad multi-class movement around the demand for democracy and an end to the abuse of power. In Brazil, middle-class organisations took the lead in pushing the military for increased representation, and unions and popular protests then added mass pressure by mobilising in demonstrations. In Mexico, protests against electoral fraud in the 1980s helped to erode the PRI's legitimacy. Non-elite actors can affect the transition process in several ways: as social movements, such as the Madres de Plaza de Mayo in Argentina, comprising the mothers of victims of military repression who were able to embarrass the regime; through political demonstrations, such as those that helped to push the Argentine military out of power following its defeat in the Malvinas/Falklands war; and through riots and rebellions, such as the Zapatista uprising in 1994 in southern Mexico that gave considerable impetus to the democratic opposition (see Boxes 11.1, 13.5). Such social mobilisation can influence how a transition occurs, but it can also raise the stakes for authoritarian regimes, increasing the fears of military hardliners and hence the risk that they will stage another coup.

Economic factors

Although there is no simple relationship between economic crisis and regime change, economic conditions clearly do affect the timing and terms of democratic transitions and shape the type of democracy that emerges. González (2008) has identified a degree of correlation since democratisation began between acute political instability in some Latin American countries and the failure or inability of their governments to meet the economic expectations of their populations (see Chapter 4).

Economic crises can isolate authoritarian rulers by undermining the alliances that keep them in power, causing business supporters to defect, and generating popular protests. Crisis conditions allow oppositions to link economic issues with political exclusion and increase the likelihood of splits within the military. In turn, where crises are avoided, authoritarian leaders enjoy greater leverage and are likely to maintain backing from elements in society when they leave office, allowing them to impose an institutional framework that maintains their privileges and favours their allies. In such cases, the economic policy of the new democratic government will be more constrained by parties and interests aligned with the outgoing authoritarian regime.

A distinction can be made between countries where democratisation occurred in a context of economic crisis, such as Argentina, and those where it occurred after more successful economic reform, such as Chile. In Argentina, economic difficulties and the dramatic loss of support following the Malvinas/Falklands war prevented the outgoing military rulers from preserving powers and political influence. Rightwing political parties that identified with the military's economic project fared badly in the 1980s, and the Unión Cívica Radical (UCR, Radical Party) government of President Raúl Alfonsín (1983–89) struggled with economic difficulties. In Chile, transition occurred on the terms of the outgoing military dictator, Pinochet, creating a limited framework within which democratic governments could operate. After 1989, rightwing candidates fared well in elections and the Left remained weak.

Economic conditions clearly have had a bearing on the outcomes of democratic politics in Latin America, and one indication of this was the electoral trend between 1998 and 2008 in which pro-market political forces were in retreat.

Since 2000, a number of presidents on the left and candidates critical of market policies or advocating some form of state control of the economy or expanded social provision have come to power or close to gaining it (see Chapters 12, 16). This was made possible by the new democratic politics, which empowers the sectors that benefitted least from economies shaped by non-democratic systems able to ignore their needs. Electoral competition and the freedom to organise politically opens the way to new social demands on governments while offering ambitious politicians the prospect of gaining the support of previously ignored constituents, and past policy choices do influence the preferences of these voters, parties and interest groups (see Haggard and Kaufman, 2008).

Democratic politics has often been associated with pressures for redistribution and democratic governments are, in general, considered to be more likely to expand welfare services or social insurance to new groups. In Latin America, countries with longer democratic traditions such as Costa Rica, Uruguay and Chile have established more generous welfare systems than in less democratic states. Given this, some scholars have asked whether authoritarian politics limited the scope of redistributive politics (see Haggard and Kaufman, 2008; and Chapter 16), although non-democratic regimes have at times expanded welfare provision to garner the support of key groups.

Although some governments on the left that have come to power following democratisation have made progress in reducing poverty (see Chapters 12, 16), interests linked to the old regime have sometimes limited the extent to which they have been able to address excluded social groups (see Box 16.4).

In Chile, for example, where centre-left Concertación coalitions were in power from the early 1990s until 2010, there has been a significant fall in poverty levels from 40 per cent in 1990 to 13 per cent today (Mideplan, 2008). However, the social policies introduced in Chile form part of a pragmatic effort to pursue reform alongside measures to ensure the capitalist economy remains competitive (see Chapter 16) and, explicitly, to avoid confrontation with powerful business and rightwing interests. Concertación governments, led after 2000 by socialist presidents, were constrained by constitutional rules and electoral laws ensuring the influence of the Right, by the coalition partners themselves, and by the influence of a 'política de acuerdo', or policy of consultation, with opposition parties and business organisations on economic policy.

In Bolivia, a broad range of policies and reforms pursued by the socialist president, Evo Morales (2006–) aimed at benefiting the poorest sectors of society have often met with stiff resistance among business groups and political interests in the more wealthy eastern parts of the country (see Boxes 4.1, 12.11). In 2009, for example, a government decision to commercialise its own foodstuffs in the battle against inflation was opposed vigorously by businessmen and some farmers.

International factors

External influences have also played an important role in regime change in Latin America and the subsequent evolution of democracy (see Whitehead, 2008, ed. 1996). International factors can influence a transition by making it more difficult for an authoritarian regime to stay in power and by strengthening moderates. In some cases, external actors have intervened directly in democratisation processes. From the late 1970s, the international climate became more hostile to authoritarian regimes and Latin America came under pressure from multilateral bodies and many countries to establish democracy and improve citizens' rights.

Whitehead (2008) has proposed an analytical framework for the study of the international dimensions of democratisation identifying four discernible processes that can be mutually reinforcing and, as a result, can generate regional momentum or 'convergence' in which democratic change occurs in several countries simultaneously:

Control, or the effort to engineer regime change and democratisation through invasion and occupation, as occurred in Haiti in 1994 ('Operation Uphold Democracy');

Conditionality, or the attaching of conditions about the standard of democratic practices in a country to membership in multilateral organisations or the ability to secure financial or other benefits from them;

Contagion, or the influence upon the politics of a country of media diffusion, and the example itself of democratisation elsewhere, particularly among its neighbours;

Consent, whereby democratic regimes can reinforce themselves and strengthen their international authority through mutual recognition, adjustment and support.

The United States

Some Latin American transitions took place under the pressure of the US (see Chapter 10). President Jimmy Carter (1976–81) began to challenge human rights violations by authoritarian regimes that had previously been allies of Washington and, since the 1980s, the US government has frequently expressed its support for democratisation in Latin America. Presidents Carter, George Bush Sr (1989–93), Bill Clinton (1993–2001) and George W. Bush (2001–09) all stated that the promotion of democracy was a central aim of US policy in the western hemisphere (van Klaveren, 2001).

Bush's successor, President Barack Obama (2009–), has distanced himself from the rhetoric of his predecessors, who strongly emphasised the need to achieve their vision of democracy in dealings with Latin American states. Obama has signalled his intention to change the tone of the relationship with Latin America to one based on dialogue and multilateralism (see Chapter 10). For example, the Obama administration was quick to send Latin America, and in particular those states with which Washington has had the most difficult relationship in recent years – Cuba and Venezuela – signals that it desired improved relations. When Obama has invoked democratic rhetoric, it has been a part of a more constructive and less intransigent approach to improving relations based on mutual respect and concrete deeds by both sides. The administration has taken concrete steps to improve ties with Cuba and Venezuela, and the president has refused to participate in the demonisation of Venezuelan President Hugo Chávez that has become common in the US press and among rightwing commentators.

At times, the US has acted directly in support of democratisation and has employed various tools to promote democracy in Latin America: from diplomacy to the scrutiny of human rights records to economic sanctions. In Mexico during the 1990s, Washington encouraged improvements in electoral procedures through constant, albeit largely unseen, pressure. Where democratic regimes have been at risk, as in Venezuela after 1990, Guatemala in 1993 and Paraguay in 1996, the US government has invested time and energy in defending them (Bulmer-Thomas and Dunkerley, 1999).

The US has even employed military intervention to achieve what its leaders have claimed are democratic outcomes, such as the invasion of Panama in 1989 to overthrow the dictatorship of General Manuel Antonio Noriega (1981–89), and the interventions in Haiti in 1994 and 2004 under UN auspices to establish or protect constitutional rule.

The US government has also spent large sums on nurturing inter-American civic life by providing funding for organisations that research democratic life such as Freedom House or through such initiatives as the National Endowment for Democracy (NED). The NED was created in 1983 under President Ronald Reagan (1981–89) to co-ordinate the efforts of parties, trade unions, and business organisations promoting democracy overseas (see Box 3.2), although the NED has many critics in the US and Latin America (see Box 10.7).

However, although the US has long expressed its support for democratisation in Latin America, at the same time it has also been criticised for inconsistency and for supporting non-democratic actors (see Chapters 9, 10). In 1982, for example, President Reagan called for an international effort to foster democracy; and in 1984 the Kissinger Commission proposed a long-term package of measures to promote democracy in Central America. The Reagan administration, however, simultaneously was intervening in conflicts in the region and taking sides against leftwing actors. Following the US invasion of Panama in 1989 to overthrow the dictatorship of General Manuel Antonio Noriega (1981–89), some Panamanians challenged US motives and there was armed resistance to its troops. Civilian casualties resulting from the invasion numbered at between 200 and 3,000, and Noriega's successor, Guillermo Endara (1989–94), was seen as a puppet of Washington and struggled to contain deep anti-American sentiment (see Box 9.3). In 2002, the US failed to condemn immediately an attempted coup against the Venezuelan president, Hugo Chávez (see Boxes 4.2, 7.2), subsequently prompting the chairman of a key US senate sub-committee, Christopher Dodd, to raise concerns that Washington had appeared to condone the removal of Chávez. The Venezuelan leader later claimed that he had evidence of US military involvement in the coup attempt, although this has not been proven. After its most recent intervention in Haiti in 2004, the US was forced to reject claims by the exiled president Jean-Bertrand Aristide (1991, 1993–94, 1994–96, 2001–04) that it had forced him out of the country against his will. In its response to the military's removal of President Zelaya in Honduras in June 2009 (see Box 7.10), Washington initially adopted a careful tone and acted

INSTITUTIONS   Box 3.2

The US National Endowment for Democracy

In 1983, during the Reagan presidency, the US congress created the NED as an independent, non-profit, non-governmental organisation receiving public funding to strengthen democratic pluralism through assistance to non-governmental organisations (NGOs) abroad (see Chapter 8). The NED builds upon the historical role assumed by the US as a model of democratic development and its creation evolved out of a growing emphasis upon human rights under President Carter in the 1970s. The establishment of the NED was influenced by foundations in Germany aligned to the main political parties and receiving government funding as part of the postwar effort to rebuild a democratic culture. The establishment of the NED as a grant-making foundation was followed by the creation of four organisations: the Center for International Private Enterprise (CIPE) and the Free Trade Union Institute (FTUI, later the American Center for International Labor Solidarity or Solidarity Center), and two institutes associated with the main US political parties, the National Democratic Institute for International Affairs (NDI) and the National Republican Institute for International Affairs (later the International Republican Institute, IRI). The NED serves as the umbrella organisation through which these institutions receive funding, and the US government allocates in the region of $30 million per year to it. Other countries have modelled democracy initiatives on the NED. In 1988, Canada's parliament established the International Centre for Human Rights and Democratic Development (now called Rights and Democracy). In 1992, the Westminster Foundation was created in Britain modelled on the NED. It receives government funding and each of the main parties is represented on its board.

behind the scenes as a broker, using its influence as an ally and trading partner to pressure both sides to reach a peaceful agreement. Later that year, Washington increased the pressure by halting non-humanitarian aid to the country worth $200 million, saying the replacement regime had failed to live up to commitments 'to restore democratic, constitutional rule'. However, eventually Washington came under criticism for accepting the outcome of elections for a new president in the country won by Porfirio Lobo (2010–), an opponent of Zelaya.

Critics have drawn attention to what they claim are double-standards in US foreign policy positions, not least in recent years because of the impact upon civil liberties within the country of assertive 'neoconservative' policies that gave rise to the global 'war on terror' (see Chapter 10; Livingstone, 2009). Whitehead (2008) argues that the dominant assumptions governing the form and content of what is understood to be a good democracy that the western media disseminates today has changed since a process launched in 1994 at the Summit of the Americas in Miami (see Chapter 9) that held out the prospect of a shared democratic project across the wider American hemisphere. Concerns about security, heightened by terrorism, have modified these assumptions to promote what has been called 'democradura', or limited democracy, which assembles democratic procedures and structures *constrained* by the fear of individuals or groups deemed sufficiently dangerous to warrant restrictions on their rights (see O'Donnell and Schmitter, 1986). This version of democracy may be considered among the peoples and governments of regions such as Latin America as unattractive and unnecessary, further limiting the influence of the US and its allies over the direction of political change elsewhere.

Other observers suggest that the potency of the democracy-promotion agenda of the US and other Western powers has been weakened by military interventions in the Middle East and also by the impact on emerging markets of the global financial crisis that unfolded in 2008 (see for example EIU, 2008). For example, poll data from an annual survey of attitudes towards democracy in 18 Latin American countries collected by the Chile-based Latinobarómetro organisation while President George W. Bush was still in office, revealed a considerable and consistent fall in his approval rating from 2005–08 in all but one Latin American country (Latinobarómetro, 2008; see Chapter 10). He was among the hemisphere's most unpopular leaders along with President Chávez of Venezuela.

Opponents of the foreign policy positions taken in Washington have also argued that its criticisms of democratic shortcomings in Latin American states have often been confined to countries with non-friendly leaders further to the left than counterparts allied to the US, such as Venezuela, Bolivia and Ecuador (see Boxes 9.8, 10.3, Chapter 12). US political leaders and editors have often demonised the elected presidents of these countries and attacked their policy positions. In 2006, for example, the then US defence secretary, Donald Rumsfeld, likened Venezuela's Chávez to the Nazi leader Adolf Hitler, reflecting continuing tension in relations between the two countries. In 2009, the film director Oliver Stone released a documentary called 'South of the Border' about the demonisation of Chávez in the US media. Rightwing critics of Obama's policy towards Latin America have also complained that, through his new approach to Venezuela, he has sent mixed messages to the region that do not leave Washington's positions clear (see Chapter 10).

US pressure for democratisation often accompanied calls for Latin American states to reform statist models of economic development – those in which the state played a leading role – and pursue policies identified with its Anglo-Saxon model of capitalist economy. Such reforms were identified with what eventually became loosely known as 'neoliberalism' and, in turn, with what was denominated the 'Washington Consensus' among the US Treasury and international financial institutions (IFIs) such as the World Bank and International Monetary Fund (see Chapters 15, 16). This was a set of prescriptions widely, if not universally, accepted by the US government and IFIs that advocated reforming the economies of developing countries by emulating the market-oriented policies of developed nations.

Such calls for reform could not be ignored when the high levels of debt held by countries in the region caused a serious economic crisis after 1982 (see Chapters 2, 15). However, a leftward shift in many Latin American governments as democratisation gathered pace has challenged this position – albeit in an uneven way – in what has been seen as a backlash against the economic model promoted by the US and other industrial countries (see Chapter 16; see also Corrales, 2008). Panizza (2009) has argued that the high point of the Washington Consensus in Latin America was the first presidential Summit of the Americas in Miami in December 1994, and that in the late 1990s the consensus began to unravel following economic crises in a number of countries and as the economic and social impact of the reforms became apparent. Many leftwing political leaders of Latin American countries have experience that predates the reforms of the late 1980s and early 1990s, and so remained opposed to ideas associated with neoliberalism and the

Washington Consensus. At the Summit of the Americas in 2009, for example, Nicaragua's president, Daniel Ortega, emerged as a vocal critic of US economic policy prescriptions and discussed these in talks with Obama.

Europe

In the 1970s and 1980s, the momentum of political change in southern European countries such as Spain helped to transform the European Community into an influential force promoting democratisation (see Chapter 11). For example, the European Union was a key source of funding for the ground-breaking UNDP report on democracy published in 2004 and the introduction of the Latinobarómetro surveys, which are now extensively employed to gauge attitudes in Latin America. The EU has also taken a close interest in the political development of Central and Eastern Europe (CEE) since the end of the Cold War, and studies of democratic transitions and other political and economic transformations frequently compare Latin America with the CEE region. It has at times used sanctions with which to press governments on their record. In 2008, for example, in an effort to encourage democratic reforms, the EU lifted sanctions on Cuba that had been imposed in 2003 in protest at Havana's imprisonment of more than 70 dissidents. However, in 2009, following inconclusive talks with Cuba on its human rights record, Brussels signalled that re-imposing sanctions remained up for review.

The EU has also used diplomatic pressure in its response to what it considers threats to democratic governance. Following the 2009 coup in Honduras, for example, EU countries withdrew their diplomats from Tegucigalpa.

However, there are also critics of procedures within the EU, who say that some of its practices, such as the selection of its Commission and the limited influence of its parliament, themselves fall short of being democratic. Such criticisms pose questions about the moral authority of multi-national bodies such as the EU when prescribing democratic reform in regions such as Latin America.

Consolidation and the quality of democracy

If democracy is understood primarily as an electoral phenomenon, there is no doubt that dramatic progress has been made towards the establishment and deepening of democratic rule in Latin America since the late 1970s. Electoral democracy has become firmly established across most of the region since the 1980s. Voting in clean elections in which citizens have gone to the polls in large numbers, a large selection of ideologically diverse parties and candidates have competed openly and fairly, electoral institutions have mostly functioned well, and the losing sides have not challenged the outcome in a violent way, has become the norm.

If we take participation in elections as just one indication of democratisation, this has extended significantly into large sectors of the population hitherto under-represented. A flourishing democracy presupposes that citizens are willing to take part in the political process, and participation, for example through the act of voting, is seen as a prerequisite of any stable democracy. Voter turnout in elections

Table 3.1 Voter turnout in legislative elections since 2000

Country					Year					
	2000	2001	2002	2003	2004	2005	2006	2007	2008	2009
Argentina		75.2				70.9		73.1		
Bolivia			72.1			84.5				
Brazil			68.7				83.3			
Chile		86.6				87.7				
Colombia			42.5				40.5			
Costa Rica			68.8				65.1			
Dominican Rep.			51.1				56.5			
Ecuador			63.5				63.5			75.7
El Salvador	38.1			28.4*			52.6			53.6
Guatemala				54.5				60.5		
Haiti	60.0						28.3			
Honduras		66.3				46.0				
Mexico	57.2			41.7			58.9			
Nicaragua		75.0					66.7			
Panama					76.3					71.8
Paraguay				64.0					65.5	
Peru	82.0	81.4					88.7			
Puerto Rico					81.7				79.0	
Uruguay					89.6					
Venezuela	56.6					25.3				

*Total vote includes valid vote only

Sources: International IDEA, 2009; elections in Puerto Rico: online database. Available at: http://electionspuertorico.org/ [accessed September 2009]

is one measure of political participation, although there is little consensus about what constitutes an acceptable or democratic level of turnout. Levels of turnout in legislative elections, for example, have increased in about half of Latin America since 2000 and in most cases have not varied wildly (see Table 3.1).

Some of the best examples of the democratic transformation in Latin America can be found in the Andean states, Bolivia, Ecuador, and Peru, where some of the more recent political crises since 2000 have occurred and hence democratic development has been turbulent. Yet in all three countries, there has been a dramatic expansion of democratic participation among previously excluded groups such as indigenous and illiterate peoples and qualitative improvements in citizenship (see Mainwaring, 2006; see also below).

Moreover, only in a few cases since the mid-1990s have democratically elected leaders been removed by force or through popular protests. Between 2000–09, there were at least 13 acute or other political crises, or lawful attempts to impeach presidents, in 10 countries in the region (see Table 4.1). None the less, most of the outcomes were a continuation of democratic governance and only three of the crises were standard coups with strong military participation (Paraguay, May 2000; Venezuela, April 2002; and Honduras, June 2009). The two former failed and the latter met with international condemnation, although there was a failure to reinstate the ousted president, Manuel Zelaya.

However, the history of democracy in Latin America has revealed recurrent problems of instability and authoritarian regimes have displaced civilian or democratic politics on many occasions. Given this, during the 1990s the attention of political scientists began to turn to the *consolidation* of the region's new democracies. Now the focus was on the conditions for the persistence of democratic governance and its stability in these countries.

The concept of consolidation has been more open to interpretation than transition and its emphasis is less on the role of elites and more on the relationship between the new system and society. Scholars have argued that democracy is consolidated when all political actors consider the democratic state to be the only legitimate means to settle competition for political office and formulate policy, by putting their faith in established institutions and adhering to democratic rules – that is, when democracy 'becomes the only game in town' (Przeworski, 1991). The new system gradually acquires legitimacy in the eyes of society and the threat from anti-system tendencies such as the military diminishes. In particular, consolidation can be understood in terms of respect for laws, rules and procedures. Linz and Stepan (1996) argued that democratic consolidation must be behavioural, attitudinal and constitutional, whereby rules are internalised by the population and valued: in such circumstances, overt rule-breaking alienates people. They summarised the conditions necessary for fully consolidated democracies as: a vibrant civil society; free and fair elections; the rule of law; a modern state apparatus that is politically impartial; and an economy in which the state regulates social and economic needs in ways that ensure the protection of property rights, the proper functioning of markets and economic growth. To these, Diamond (1999) added the need for effective regime *performance* to build the legitimacy necessary for democracy (see also Diamond *et al.* eds, 1999).

Researchers focused upon different aspects of the democratisation process, providing different standards against which to assess progress. Some highlighted the continuation of authoritarian legacies and efforts to limit the masses' access to power, generating a range of qualifying terms such as 'tutelary' or 'protected' democracy (Loveman, 1994; Collier and Levitsky, 1997). Others addressed institutional issues such as whether or not efficient electoral mechanisms and guarantees had been established. In Mexico, for example, reforms that loosened links between the PRI and electoral institutions came under scrutiny. A concern with the economic conditions in which the latest wave of democratisation has taken place, and in particular the complex relationship between globalised capitalism and democracy, also grew in importance (see Chapters 4, 15; also Przeworski, 1991; Rueschemeyer *et al.*, 1992; Cammack, 1997; Oxhorn and Ducatenzeiler eds, 1998).

However, some scholars drew attention to the limitations of the entire approach to democratic consolidation or even argued that the term is empty, clumsy or inadequate (see, for example, Agüero, 1998; Schneider, 1995; Przeworski *et al.*, 1996; Whitehead, 2001). The number of factors employed by which to gauge consolidation poses particular problems for this notion. Since the 1990s, the term 'unconsolidated' has been used sometimes to refer to those democracies still in the process of consolidation or that have not met the standard criteria established above. O'Donnell (1994) coined the term 'delegative democracy' to refer to a new 'species' of democracy that could be found in Latin America and that was not consolidated yet still able to endure (see Chapter 4). Philip (2003) argues that pre-democratic patterns of institutional, organisational and cultural behaviour have survived democratisation in Latin America, and their adaptive nature means that 'non-consolidated' democracies have endured.

The debate over consolidation, and the insertion of qualifying adjectives before the term 'democracy', inform the related and similarly inconclusive debate about how best to *measure* democracy (see Box 3.3).

Yet although it is likely that democratisation in Latin America cannot be fully understood within any single theoretical framework, the notion of consolidation remains valuable because it provides tools with which to compare processes of democratisation and to highlight its uneven development. Although Latin American countries have gained increasing experience of regular, competitive elections since

---

THEORIES AND DEBATES   Box 3.3

Measuring democracy

A nagging problem in the study of democracy is that there is no consensus about how best to *measure* it. Different approaches to measurement will, of necessity, reflect the different ways the term is understood in any given context (see above). Munck and Verkuilen (2002) assessed a number of influential indices of democracy and concluded that no single index satisfactorily meets the challenges of conceptualising and measuring it then aggregating the data. A helpful way of conceptualising different approaches to assessing democracy was provided by Coppedge (2005), who made a distinction between the use of 'thick' and 'thin' concepts in political analysis (see also Coppedge, 1999). Thick concepts refer to many aspects of what we observe, while thin concepts focus attention on only one or a few characteristics. By this approach, minimalist ways of assessing democracy, such as Dahl's polyarchy, can be considered 'thinner' than those measures that incorporate other variables such as political freedoms. One consequence of using a 'thin' concept of democracy is that many countries may qualify as being democratic, even though some are clearly more democratic than others. Freedom House, which is a well established source of data on democracy, produces a well known 'thin' measurement of democratic freedoms that designates countries that have met certain, minimal standards as 'electoral democracies'. The UNDP's overview of the achievements and challenges of democracy in Latin America refined a 'thicker' comparative measure that had long been under discussion, the Electoral Democracy Index (EDI) (UNDP, 2004b, 2004c). This generated a composite average value ranging from between 0 and 1.0 for countries or sub-regions based on four key variables considered to be crucial components of a democratic regime: the right to vote, how clean and free elections are, and the role elections actually play in securing access to public office. The UNDP's EDI showed that, by 2004, democratisation had made remarkable progress throughout Latin America since the late 1970s (see Figure 3.1).

A ranking developed by the Economist Intelligence Unit (2008) can be considered 'thicker' still because it is based on five criteria: electoral process and pluralism; civil liberties; the functioning of government; political participation; and political culture (see Table 3.2). Yet while the trend appears

▶

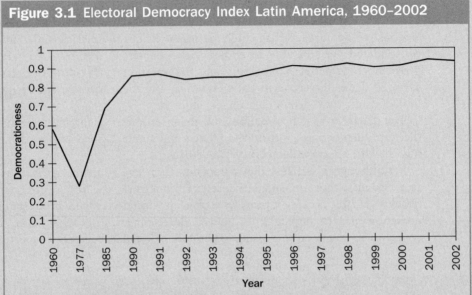

Figure 3.1 Electoral Democracy Index Latin America, 1960–2002

Note: The EDI is a 0–1 scale, with 0 indicating non-democracy and any number above 0 indicating a degree of democraticness, with higher scores referring to greater degrees of democraticness. The formula for calculating the EDI is: EDI = Right to Vote x Clean Elections x Free Elections x Elected Public Offices. Cuba and Haiti are not included.

Source: UNDP, 2004c

to have been towards collating ever more inclusive political measurements of democracy of this kind, a key theme of debate is the degree to which *social* and *economic well being* should form part of this democratic equation (see Chapter 16; and UNDP, 2004b, 2004c). This issue responds to questions about whether there are 'preconditions' for democracy (see Box 3.1). Although the EDI employed by the UNDP was based solely upon political criteria, its broader overview of the condition of democracy in Latin America incorporated a comprehensive picture of the levels of poverty and inequality in the region. In this way, the UNDP set out clear parameters by which to understand the state of electoral democracy in Latin America while advancing a comprehensive vision of democratic governance that combined electoral democracy with what it termed *citizenship* democracy (see Box 3.4). Another key theme has been the political sensitivity surrounding the issue of researchers based in one country measuring the democratic performance of others, which raises questions both about appropriate standards, ideological predispositions and even cultural issues. The UNDP, for example, has purposefully *not* developed a governance index, akin to the Human Development Index, that ranks countries, arguing that comparative indexes on democratic governance may act as catalysts in improving the domestic politics of countries by 'naming and shaming' those that perform poorly, but that this is not a role for the UNDP, whose focus is rather to help states identify problems that need to be addressed and ways to solve them (see UNDP, 2009a). In response to the proliferation of efforts to measure democracy on a global scale from outside the countries that are being examined, International IDEA has developed a methodology that endeavours to put the responsibility for evaluating the quality of democracy in the hands of the citizens and others who reside in the country being assessed, its 'State of Democracy (SoD)' assessment methodology (see Landman ed. with Beetham *et al.*, 2009; and Beetham *et al.*, 2008).

Table 3.2 EIU Index of Democracy 2008, Latin American countries

Country	Rank within overall index	Rank within Latin America	Overall score
Full democracies			
Uruguay	23	1	8.08
Costa Rica	27	2	8.04
Flawed democracies			
Chile	32	3	7.89
Brazil	41	4	7.38
Panama	43	5	7.35
Mexico	55	6	6.78
Argentina	56	7	6.63
Colombia	60	8	6.54
Paraguay	66	9	6.40
El Salvador	67	10	6.40
Peru	70	11	6.31
Dominican Republic	73	12	6.20
Honduras	74	13	6.18
Bolivia	75	14	6.15
Nicaragua	78	15	6.07
Guatemala	79	16	6.07
Hybrid regimes			
Ecuador	88	17	5.64
Venezuela	95	18	5.34
Haiti	110	19	4.19
Authoritarian regimes			
Cuba	125	20	3.52

Source: EIU, 2008

2000, leaving the impression that a level of democracy had been firmly established in the region, the idea that its new democracies had been or were being consolidated, and their condition, remains under scrutiny. The study of democracy in Latin America today tends to concentrate on three main areas of analysis: the study of institutions and questions about their efficiency and accountability; how democracy functions at sub-national levels, and hence questions of participation; and how issues of gender, race and ethnicity affect our understanding of democratic governance (see O'Donnell *et al.*, 2008).

In these areas and others, scholars draw attention to a number of problems that seriously call into question the *quality* of democratic governance established in Latin American countries, which many suggest has declined overall since the early years of the new millennium, and the many challenges faced by their political institutions. Some say that the prospects for a regionwide democratic convergence have, as a result, become discouraging (see Shifter, 2008; Whitehead, 2008). These problems include: deep levels of corruption; violence or recurrent political instability in countries such as Colombia, Guatemala and Bolivia; and persistent social and economic inequality and exclusion (see Chapter 4).

This explains why, although 19 of the 20 independent Latin American countries today have minimalist democracies, mostly established (or restored) during the 'third wave' of democratisation, only three of these are still generally regarded to have been consolidated: Costa Rica, Uruguay and Chile. The Economist Intelligence Unit (2008) ranking places only two of these, Uruguay and Costa Rica, in its category of 'Full democracies', with Chile towards the top of its category of 'Flawed democracies' (see Table 3.2). Inclusion in these categories is determined by the score countries achieve across the range of key variables.

Nicaragua was the only Latin American country that improved its category in the period 2006–08, moving from a hybrid regime to a flawed democracy, because of clean elections in 2006; a more constructive form of legislative politics; and constitutional reforms limiting executive power (see Chapters 5, 6).

In recent years there has been debate about the democratic status of Venezuela and Ecuador, classified according to the EIU as 'hybrid' systems that have both democratic and authoritarian characteristics. Some observers still regard both Venezuela and Ecuador as minimalist democracies (see González, 2008) although others believe they may represent examples of *deconsolidation* because forms of populist rule that sidestep institutional mechanisms have returned since the late 1990s (see Boxes 4.2, 6.2).

Citizenship

Given the complex, inconclusive picture of democratisation in Latin America, how can we best assess whether it is delivering concrete benefits for the citizens of the region?

The notion of rights is valuable as a way of judging the quality of democratic governance. Different definitions of democracy emphasise different categories of rights, with procedural definitions stressing political rights and social definitions stressing economic rights. In this way, definitions of democracy are also often debated according to the degree to which they ensure different forms of rights, making consensus about the term even more difficult to achieve.

Most Latin American countries subscribe to the international legal system of human rights, which include political and civil rights guaranteeing the individual's ability to participate in the political system and sanctity before the law; and social and economic rights, which promote development and individual self-esteem. Political rights are those that ensure participation in the political process and include the right to vote in clean, free and fair elections. Civil rights are those related to legal equality and protection, and include the right to life, equality under the law and protection against discrimination, personal security, information and freedom of expression. Social rights are those that allow individuals to develop their capacities and become fully integrated members of society, promoting self-development and individual self-esteem. They cover such rights as the right to subsistence, health, education and employment.

The UNDP vision of democracy for Latin America

'We maintain that democracy is more than a set of conditions for electing and being elected, which we call *electoral democracy*. It is also, as we have pointed out, a way of organising society with the object of assuring and expanding the rights of its people. This we define as a *citizenship democracy*. These two dimensions of democracy are closely connected, and the degree of development of both has a significant effect on the quality and sustainability of a democracy. The distinction between an electoral democracy and a citizenship democracy centres around four basic arguments, which guide this report:

1 The philosophical and normative foundation of democracy is to be found in the *concept of the human being as an individual with innate rights*. According to this idea the human being emerges clearly as an autonomous, rational and responsible person. This concept underlies all notions of citizenship, including political citizenship.

2 Democracy is a *means of organising society*, which guarantees that people can exercise their rights and work to expand their citizenship. It establishes rules for political relations, and for the organisation and exercise of power, which are consistent with the aforementioned concept of the human being.

3 Free, competitive and institutionalised elections, and the rules and procedures for forming and running a government – which together we will call *electoral democracy* – are essential components of democracy, and comprise its most basic sphere. But democracy is not limited to this realm either in terms of its reach or range of action.

4 The development of democracy in Latin America constitutes a *unique historical experience*, characterised by specifics that are closely linked to the processes involved in building Nations and societies, along with establishing all of their diverse cultural identities.'

Source: UNDP, 2004b, pp. 53–54 (italics in original); see also UNDP, 2004a

The UNDP report examined the degree to which, according to these categories of rights, Latin Americans enjoy full *citizenship* (2004b). It developed a vision for Latin America that goes beyond electoral democracy to advocate what it describes as *citizenship democracy* (see Box 3.4). This defines citizenship in this way: 'The notion of citizenship implies that each person is a member of the community with full rights. It embraces different spheres, each with its own rights and obligations. The broadening of citizenship is one condition for the success of a society and for strengthening its capacity to fulfil people's expectations' (UNDP, 2004b, p. 50).

Citizenship comprises the various rights of those who qualify as members of a society, and these can generally be measured:

Political rights

Foweraker *et al.* (2003) have shown that, in general, democratic transitions in Latin America have led to an improvement in political rights as measured by Freedom

House – an independent non-governmental organisation based in Washington that conducts research into democratic freedoms and supports democratic initiatives – illustrating the growth in electoral democracy in the region. Since the early 2000s, World Bank researchers have also aggregated a series of 'governance indicators' that gives an insight into the degree of political change in countries (see Kaufmann *et al.*, 2009). One of these indicators is that of 'Voice and Accountability', which captures perceptions of the extent to which a country's citizens are able to participate in selecting their government as well as enjoying other freedoms. These show a clear, if limited and at times erratic, improvement in many Latin American countries over time (see Table 3.3). None the less, the UNDP (2004b) argues that, while there have been clear gains in terms of electoral democracy, progress is uneven,

Table 3.3 'Voice and Accountability' governance indicator over time, Latin America, 1996–2008*

	Year		
Country	*1996*	*2002*	*2008*
Argentina	0.39	0.16	0.32
Bolivia	0.34	0.07	−0.01
Brazil	0.18	0.33	0.51
Chile	0.78	1.04	0.98
Colombia	−0.43	−0.50	−0.26
Costa Rica	1.13	1.10	0.98
Cuba	−1.78	−1.66	−1.85
Dominican Rep.	0.23	0.22	0.14
Ecuador	0.14	−0.09	−0.22
El Salvador	−0.01	0.10	0.06
Guatemala	−0.20	−0.41	−0.26
Haiti	−0.51	−1.31	−0.71
Honduras	−0.13	−0.23	−0.29
Mexico	−0.16	0.28	0.08
Nicaragua	0.17	−0.10	−0.14
Panama	0.24	0.57	0.59
Paraguay	0.06	−0.50	−0.33
Peru	−0.27	0.15	0.02
Puerto Rico	–	1.07	1.31
Uruguay	0.94	1.00	1.02
Venezuela	0.08	−0.56	−0.62

*Selected years only

Notes: Indicators based on individual variables measuring perceptions of governance, drawn from separate data sources constructed by different organisations from around the world. Individual measures are assigned to categories capturing six dimensions of governance. Estimates of governance for each country complemented with margins of error. The units in which governance is measured follow a normal distribution with a mean of zero and a standard deviation of one in each period. This implies that virtually all scores lie between −2.5 and 2.5, with higher scores corresponding to better outcomes.

Source: Kaufmann *et al.*, 2009

levels of participation are low, and deficiencies persist in the degree to which citizens can exercise control over the state's actions.

Civil rights

The UNDP also notes that important gains have been made with regard to the achievement and protection of rights that guarantee equality under the law for many social groups. Issues of gender, race and ethnicity and the degree to which social groups defined in these ways can participate in the political process particularly affect our assessment of democratic governance because they are especially important to our understanding of citizenship in Latin America (see O'Donnell *et al.*, 2008). There is clear evidence that rights have improved for many people in these groups. Women, for example, now participate in politics across Latin America at levels never before experienced (see Chapter 13). Freedom House assigns a numerical score to civil liberties in all countries compiled from a range of questions as part of its annual global assessment, and its data show that in no Latin American country did civil rights decline between 2002 and 2009 (see Table 3.4). However, the UNDP points out that the right to non-discrimination is not adequately guaranteed, inequalities persist in the treatment of people belonging to different social groups, and laws have often been ignored (see Tables 6.4, 8.1, 13.1). Progress in terms of the respect to the right to life, humane treatment, security and non-discrimination has been uneven and often inadequate, and Latin American citizens continue to experience violations of civil rights in ways traditionally associated with authoritarianism.

Social rights

Living conditions for millions of Latin Americans have improved in many areas, and key indicators suggest that much concrete progress has been made in enhancing social rights (see ECLAC, 2009c). One example of this can be found in improving infant mortality and life expectancy rates (see Table 3.5).

However, the UNDP says it is in this area, and in particular questions of poverty and inequality, that the least progress of all has been made, and that this poses the most serious challenge to Latin American democracies. Deep poverty in the countryside can also only come to light during a crisis. In Guatemala in 2009, for example, President Alvaro Colom declared a state of emergency to expedite the provision of food supplies to 54,000 families suffering severe food shortages in the east of the country. The UN's World Food Programme (WFP) operates a feeding programme in Guatemala for about 350,000 people, and the UN children's agency, Unicef, has estimated that almost half of the country's children suffer chronic malnutrition. Poverty, inequality and unemployment undermine social inclusion, and the UNDP warns that the deepening of democracy will require a significant expansion of the benefits associated with the notion of social citizenship (see Chapter 4).

Although the prominence of the notion of citizenship in the political vocabulary has grown alongside democratisation in Latin America, the meaning of this term has

Table 3.4 Civil liberties in Latin America, 2002 and 2009

Country	2002	2009
Argentina	3	2
Bolivia	3	3
Brazil	3	2
Chile	2	1
Colombia	4	4
Costa Rica	2	1
Dominican Rep.	2	2
Ecuador	3	3
El Salvador	3	3
Guatemala	4	4
Haiti	6	5
Honduras	3	3
Mexico	3	3
Nicaragua	3	3
Panama	2	2
Paraguay	3	3
Peru	3	3
Puerto Rico	2	1
Uruguay	1	1
Venezuela	5	4

Note: Each country and territory is assigned a numerical rating on a scale of 1 to 7 for civil liberties; a rating of 1 indicates the highest degree of liberties and 7 the lowest. A lower score is, therefore, normatively better. The ratings process is based on a checklist of 15 civil liberties questions. The civil liberties questions are grouped into four subcategories: Freedom of Expression and Belief (4 questions), Associational and Organisational Rights (3), Rule of Law (4), and Personal Autonomy and Individual Rights (4). Scores are awarded to each of these questions on a scale of 0 to 4, where a score of 0 represents the smallest degree and 4 the greatest degree of rights or liberties present. The highest score that can be awarded to the civil liberties checklist is 60 (or a total score of 4 for each of the 15 questions).

Source: Freedom House, 2002, 2009a

varied across the region and over time. Like democracy itself, political scientists have also debated its definition (see Dagnino, 2005; Tulchin and Ruthenburg eds, 2006).

None the less, citizenship has become an important point of reference for efforts to assess democratic governance in Latin America because the problems that continue to nag the region's democracies have limited the achievement of full rights for so many people. Rights cannot be properly enforced without an independent and effective judiciary (see Chapter 6) and, in many countries, the expansion of political rights has not been accompanied by the improvement or enforcement of civil and social rights.

Some scholars have suggested that citizens in the region only enjoy what they describe variously as low-intensity citizenship, a democracy of first- and second-class citizens or even democracy without citizenship (O'Donnell, 1993; Pinheiro, 1997; Vilas, 1997; see also Tulchin and Garland eds, 2000). Deficient citizenship

Table 3.5 Infant mortality and life expectancy in selected Latin American countries*

Country	Period					
	1970–75		*1990–95*		*2005–10*	
	IM	*LE*	*IM*	*LE*	*IM*	*LE*
Argentina	48.1	67.1	24.4	72.1	13.4	75.2
Bolivia	151.3	46.7	75.1	60.0	45.6	65.5
Brazil	90.5	59.5	42.5	67.5	23.6	72.4
Chile	68.6	63.4	14.1	74.3	7.2	78.5
Colombia	73.0	61.6	35.2	68.6	22.0	73.2
Costa Rica	52.5	67.9	14.5	76.2	9.9	78.8
Dominican Rep.	93.5	59.7	46.5	67.0	29.4	71.4
Ecuador	95.0	58.8	44.2	70.0	21.1	75.0
El Salvador	105.0	58.2	40.2	67.1	21.5	71.8
Guatemala	102.5	53.7	54.8	63.6	30.1	70.2
Honduras	103.7	53.8	43.0	67.7	27.8	72.1
Mexico	69.0	62.4	34.0	71.5	25.7	74.3
Nicaragua	97.9	55.1	48.0	66.1	26.1	71.0
Panama	43.4	66.2	27.0	72.9	18.2	75.6
Paraguay	53.1	65.9	43.3	68.5	34.0	71.9
Peru	110.3	55.4	55.5	66.7	28.7	71.2
Uruguay	46.3	68.7	20.1	73.0	12.0	76.1
Venezuela	48.7	65.7	23.1	71.5	15.8	73.8

*Selected periods only

Notes: Infant mortality is measured in terms of the probability of death between birth and exactly one year of age, expressed in deaths per each 1,000 births. Life expectancy figures measure the expected years of life from birth.

Sources: UNDP, 2008; UN Population Division, 2001; ECLAC, 2006a

adds to dangers facing the region. The failure of traditional forms of representation to channel social demands (see Chapter 4) and the inability of the state to address the basic problems of poverty and inequality may threaten stability by eroding popular support for democracy, encouraging alternatives to electoral politics and generating violent expressions of frustration about a lack of social progress.

The UNDP warns that, even though Latin America has largely moved away from authoritarian regimes, there remain threats to democracy deriving from incomplete citizenship rights and weak states that have been ineffective at expanding the rights implied by democracy (see, for example, Mariani, 2008; see also Box 2.1). It argues that in some countries democracy may be losing its vitality, not least because people are questioning its capacity to improve their living conditions and security. Most scholars accept that some authoritarian legacies have also survived the transitions (see Chapter 4).

Agüero (1998) used the metaphor of 'fault lines' to refer to the tensions that persist within democratic arrangements in Latin America.

Disenchantment

As a result, there is evidence of disillusionment with democracy and disenchantment with the working of democratic institutions in some countries. Latinobarómetro's annual surveys have demonstrated a fairly consistent average level of support for democracy as opposed to authoritarianism across Latin America since the mid-1990s (see Figure 3.2).

However, Latinobarómetro's figures conceal significant variation in levels of satisfaction with democracy across individual countries, and this system of government is often not compared favourably with the performance of individual administrations themselves (see Table 3.6). What this suggests is that individual governments enjoy greater levels of support than democracy as a system of government.

They show that support for democracy in Latin America as a whole has remained fairly steady between 1995 (58 per cent) and 2009 (59 per cent), while indifference among the public about *any* form of government has remained high (Latinobarómetro, 2009a). From 2005–08 public support for a democratic system of government over an authoritarian system declined in five Latin American countries, including more developed states such as Chile, Mexico, Costa Rica and Argentina (Latinobarómetro, 2005, 2008). Attitudes that show sympathy towards authoritarian rule in some circumstances are not disappearing: between 2002 and

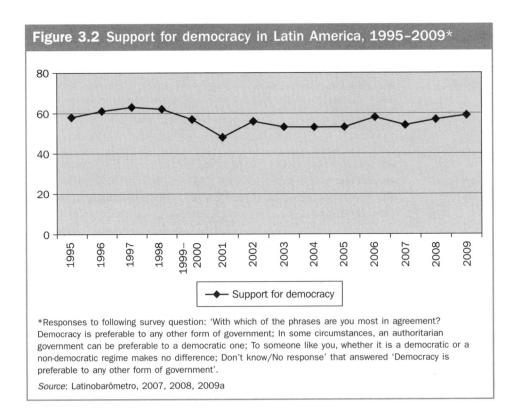

Figure 3.2 Support for democracy in Latin America, 1995–2009*

*Responses to following survey question: 'With which of the phrases are you most in agreement? Democracy is preferable to any other form of government; In some circumstances, an authoritarian government can be preferable to a democratic one; To someone like you, whether it is a democratic or a non-democratic regime makes no difference; Don't know/No response' that answered 'Democracy is preferable to any other form of government'.

Source: Latinobarómetro, 2007, 2008, 2009a

Table 3.6 Satisfaction with government performance and democracy in individual Latin American countries, 2009*

Country	Approval of government performance	Satisfaction with democracy
Argentina	25	36
Bolivia	57	50
Brazil	84	47
Chile	85	53
Colombia	72	42
Costa Rica	75	63
Dominican Republic	47	53
Ecuador	59	33
El Salvador	83	60
Guatemala	52	31
Honduras**	35	24
Mexico	52	28
Nicaragua	37	35
Panama	80	61
Paraguay	69	33
Peru	26	22
Uruguay	74	79
Venezuela	45	47

*Percentages

**2008

Note: Responses to the following questions: 'Do you approve or disapprove of the performance of the government headed by President (name)?' and 'In general, would you say that you are very satisfied, more or less satisfied, not very satisfied, or not at all satisfied with the functioning of democracy in (country)?'

Source: Latinobarómetro, 2008, 2009a

2008 the proportion of people who said that having a non-democratic government would not matter to them provided that it resolved their economic problems did not diminish. However, the 2008–09 economic crisis in Latin America appeared, if anything, to have strengthened support for democracy, and citizens are increasingly unwilling to put economic growth before democratic government (Latinobarómetro, 2009a).

Even if an individual expresses a preference for democracy, this may not imply *strong* support and may be accompanied by undemocratic attitudes towards some rules or issues. The UNDP (2004b) report on democracy offered a nuanced assessment of the degree of commitment to democracy in different sub-regions of Latin America based upon three categories of opinions and attitudes: democratic, ambivalent and non-democratic. This suggested that those with committed democratic attitudes, who prefer democracy over any other form of government, constituted the largest group of citizens in the region but, at 43 per cent of respondents, were not in the majority. Nor was support for democracy confined to any particular social group, but was evenly distributed across different sectors of society, although people with a higher education were more likely to be democratic.

Latinobarómetro data suggests, however, that although political institutions such as the presidency, congress, courts and police have not enjoyed a high level of public trust, confidence in some of them – particularly congresses and political parties – and hence their legitimacy in the eyes of the public, is growing slowly. The only institution that has enjoyed consistently high levels of confidence since 1996 is the Catholic Church.

Disenchantment is a problem for democracy because it can undermine the effectiveness of democratic institutions and result in indifference towards, or even support for, 'anti-system' elements such as extremist organisations, terrorist groups, guerrillas and paramilitaries. Those people categorised by the UNDP as non-democrats, for example, tend to trust institutions and public figures less than other groups (UNDP, 2004b). Attitudes towards extremist organisations vary widely across Latin America. When asked whether extremist parties should be permitted or prohibited, the citizens of different countries vary considerably in their responses: in Bolivia, for example, 57 per cent of respondents said extremist parties should be prohibited, whereas in Brazil only 23 per cent of people said these parties should be banned (Latinobarómetro, 2008).

Public support is essential to sustaining democracy, which becomes vulnerable when authoritarian forces can find support for their activities in the attitudes of citizens or when people turn a blind eye to those activities through indifference.

In Colombia, for example, Salvatore Mancuso, the military commander of the outlawed Autodefensas Unidas de Colombia (AUC, United Self-Defence Forces of Colombia) paramilitary organisation – which killed thousands of people in an illegal campaign against Marxist rebels and funded its activities by cocaine trafficking – actively tried to improve his public image after a process of disarmament had begun in 2003, and achieved significant levels of popularity among members of the public.

Disenchantment, limited progress on enhancing or enforcing citizenship rights and the failure of policymakers to meet expectations (see Chapter 4) have prompted some scholars to characterise the form of democracy that prevails in Latin America as a *restricted* political system which only serves the needs of a small elite, or to argue that the new democracies in the region are in fact hybrid regimes constructed with potent legacies from their authoritarian past in a context that accentuates social inequalities (see Weffort, 1998). The recurrence of authoritarianism in Latin America has prompted the question as to whether in recent years the region has merely been experiencing a wave of democratisation that may prove to be temporary.

Given the types of democracy that are emerging in Latin America, it is reasonable to ask whether the term democratic consolidation might be a misnomer. It has even been suggested that it is necessary to move beyond such categories as 'democratic' and 'authoritarian' and to concentrate on factors that transcend regime types or reconceptualise what we *mean* by democracy (see Remmer, 1990; Przeworski and Limongi, 1993; Oxhorn and Ducatenzeiler, 1998; Weffort, 1998).

Summary

There are different interpretations of the term democracy, the definition of which is important to the way processes of democratisation in Latin America are examined. The UNDP advances its own interpretation of democracy and, in a ground-breaking report in 2004, argued that democratisation has made significant progress in Latin America since the late 1970s. However, there has also been great variation in democratic experience across the region, and this derives from the different types of authoritarianism that had prevailed and the varied ways in which democratisation occurred. The analysis of democratic transition has built upon a framework of ideas established in the study of comparative politics by Rustow. He rejected the idea that strict cultural, economic or political preconditions were necessary for democracy to flourish in a country, and this position enabled scholars to consider democratic transition independently of the factors that are believed to maintain democracy in developed industrial countries. Transition is an uncertain process of regime change, several forms of which have been distinguished, from those that occurred because a military regime collapsed to those that were the outcome of negotiations between outgoing military rulers and their civilian opponents. Political, economic and international factors all contributed to regime change and shaped the type of democracy that emerged in each Latin American country differently. Following the transitions, scholars turned their attention to the degree to which the resulting democracies were being consolidated. A democracy is consolidated when all the political actors consider the democratic state to be the only legitimate means to settle competition for political office and formulate policy. The notion of consolidation implies that political actors have faith in democratic rules and are prepared to abide by them, and provides researchers with tools by which to compare processes of democratisation and the quality of democracy in Latin American countries. However, the idea of consolidation has been more open to interpretation than transition and it has been challenged by some scholars. Moreover, a number of different methodologies have been used to measure democracy, and these reflect the different ways the term is understood in any given context. Given the complex, inconclusive picture of democratisation in Latin America, the notion of citizenship based on a complex of political, civil and social rights has become valuable as a way of judging the quality of democratic governance. Despite progress towards democratisation, a particular problem faced by some Latin American democracies today is disenchantment, which can undermine the effectiveness of democratic institutions and result in support for 'anti-system' elements such as extremist organisations.

Discussion points

- How can democratic transition and consolidation be distinguished?
- What factors have contributed to democratisation in Latin America?
- How is a stable, consolidated democracy achieved?

■ Is capitalism necessary for democratisation?

■ Is liberal democracy unsuitable for Latin America because of the region's culture?

■ Can the quality of a country's democracy really be measured?

■ Should Cuba's political system be considered less democratic than Chile's?

Useful websites

www.undp.org/latinamerica/ UNDP regional site for Latin America and the Caribbean

www.undp.org/oslocentre/flagship/democratic_governance_assessments.html UNDP Oslo Governance Centre, Governance Assessments Portal which maintains a bibliography of publications on governance assessments and measurement

www.latinobarometro.org Latinobarómetro, Chile

www.ned.org The National Endowment for Democracy, US

www.dd-rd.ca/site/ Rights and Democracy (International Centre for Human Rights and Democratic Development), Canada

www.wfd.org The Westminster Foundation for Democracy, UK

www.idea.int International Institute for Democracy and Electoral Assistance (IDEA)

www.metagora.org Metagora project, a pilot international global statistics initiative supported by the World Bank, OECD, the United Nations and EU focusing on methods, tools and frameworks for measuring democracy, human rights and governance

http://info.worldbank.org/governance/wgi/index.asp World Bank's Worldwide Governance Indicators (WGI) project, which has produced aggregate and individual governance indicators for 212 countries and territories since 1996

www.worldpublicopinion.org Web resource on different public opinion surveys across the globe on the subjects of governance and human rights

http://graphics.eiu.com/PDF/Democracy%20Index%202008.pdf The Economist Intelligence Unit's Index of Democracy 2008

http://democraciaparticipativa.net/index.php Participatory Democracy net (English and Spanish)

www.freedomhouse.org Freedom House

www.wilsoncenter.org Woodrow Wilson International Center for Scholars

www.cartercenter.org The Carter Centre for human rights

Recommended reading

Linz, Juan and Alfred Stepan (eds). 1996. *Problems of Democratic Transition and Consolidation: southern Europe, South America, and post-communist Europe*. Baltimore: Johns Hopkins University Press

Valuable introduction to transition and consolidation containing a theoretical overview and conceptual definitions that can be used to compare processes of democratisation in Latin America with other regions

Domínguez, Jorge I. and Michael Shifter (eds). 2008. *Constructing Democratic Governance in Latin America*, 3rd Edition. Baltimore, MD: Johns Hopkins University Press

> *Valuable summary of progress in democratisation since transitions began in Latin America and new trends, with country studies*

United Nations Development Programme (UNDP). 2004. *Democracy in Latin America. Towards a Citizens' Democracy.* New York /Buenos Aires: UNDP/Alfaguara

> *Essential point of departure for a student seeking an overview of the condition of democracy in Latin America*

Tulchin, Joseph S. and Meg Ruthenburg (eds). 2006. *Citizenship in Latin America*. Boulder, CO: Lynne Rienner Publishers

> *Essential introduction to the concept of citizenship, its role in the assessment of democratic governance, and debates about it*

O'Donnell, Guillermo, Joseph S. Tulchin, and Augusto Varas (eds) with Adam Stubits. 2008. *New Voices in Studies in the Study of Democracy in Latin America.* Washington, DC: Woodrow Wilson International Center for Scholars; available at: http://www.wilsoncenter.org/topics/pubs/lap.newvoices.pdf [accessed September 2009]

> *Valuable introduction to the changing way in which democracy has been studied in Latin America with strong focus on key contemporary themes of analysis: the study of institutions; how democracy functions at sub-national levels; and issues of gender, race and ethnicity*

Selee, Andrew D. and Enrique Peruzzotti (eds). 2009. *Participatory Innovation and Representative Democracy in Latin America.* Baltimore, MD: Johns Hopkins University Press/ Woodrow Wilson Center Press

> *Useful examination of the growth of innovative participatory institutions in Latin American democracy and how these affect representative government, with case studies*

Chapter 4

The challenges facing democracy

Debates about the nature of democracy and the idea of consolidation outlined in Chapter 3 enable scholars to go far beyond a mere discussion of electoral procedures and who gets to vote when assessing democracy. It gives them useful tools to determine how democracy may be faring overall in a given country and which countries may, by certain measures, be more democratic than others. In short, it allows them to assess the quality of democracy in different countries and, where necessary, to recommend ways of improving it (see Diamond and Morlino eds, 2005). Has a country progressed beyond being merely an electoral democracy, which provides citizens with *access* to power, towards becoming a liberal democracy, which is distinguished by a distinctive mode of *exercising* power based upon limited government, the separation of powers, and the rule of law? Has it progressed even further towards dealing with pressing social issues that make it even more fully *inclusionary*, whereby the principle of equality before the law actively translates into equal opportunities (see Abente Brun, 2008)?

This chapter examines the political and economic factors that limit the quality of democracy found in Latin American countries today. Factors that inhibit full democratic consolidation include political instability deriving from presidentialism and difficult relations between the executive and legislature, and dissatisfaction with political parties that can strengthen populists (see Chapters 2, 5, 6) who are often tempted to break democratic rules or resort to authoritarian rule. Latin America is also plagued by factors that weaken the rule of law, fostering corruption and a sense among politicians, government officials and law enforcement officers that they can act illegally with impunity, and contributing to high crime and insecurity. Although the armed forces no longer threaten most democracies directly, civil-military relations remain a key issue for consolidation because military chiefs of staff may retain considerable influence in politics and may have the legal right to intervene in the political process in some circumstances. Another key issue for consolidation is the extent to which economic policy under democratic governments may be making a difference for populations that continue to suffer high levels of poverty and inequality, calling into question the *value* of democratic governance in the first place.

Political challenges to democratic consolidation

Instability

A key problem facing the new democracies of Latin America is political instability, especially in the Andean countries, which in many cases has cut short presidential terms (see Chapter 5). Political crises, some of them acute, occurred in a significant number of Latin American countries, particularly the Andean states, between 2000–09 (see Table 4.1).

González (2008) examined 17 continental Latin American states and found that more 'acute political crises' – those affecting the central political institutions – had occurred in the eight-year period of minimalist democracy between 2000–07 than during the preceding period 1992–99 when democratisation had just taken place or was still underway. Although the character of these recent crises had changed and they did not, in most cases, result in non-democratic regimes, the countries experiencing them could not be described as stable democracies, much less consolidated ones. Haiti and Honduras both experienced coups or military interventions in 2004 and 2009 respectively, although in neither case did the military as an institution remain in power.

Table 4.1 Acute and other political crises in Latin America, 2000–09

| Country | Crisis | Main characteristics of crisis | |
		Focused on*	Result**
Ecuador 1	January 2000	President	fell
Ecuador 2	April 2005	President	fell
Ecuador 3	March 2007	Legislature	57 lawmakers (out of 100) lost their seats
Ecuador 4	November 2004	President	lawful impeachment attempt failed
Paraguay 1	May 2000	President	did not fall
Paraguay 2	April 2002	President	lawful impeachment attempt failed
Peru	November 2000	President	fell
Argentina 1	December 2001	President	fell
Argentina 2	December 2001	President	fell
Venezuela	April 2002	President	did not fall
Bolivia 1	October 2003	President	fell
Bolivia 2	June 2005	President	fell
Haiti	February 2004	President	fell
Nicaragua	June 2005	President	did not fall
Honduras	June 2009	President	fell

*Initial focus of the crisis may be the president, the legislature, or both.

**Presidents may or may not fall, legislators (all or some) may retain or lose seats.

Sources: Adapted from González, 2008; news reports; Latinobarómetro, 2008

González looked for common factors that, if present, contribute to democratic consolidation but, when absent, promote instability. He argued that a central factor in most of the acute political crises in the period 2000–07, by comparison with the previous eight years, was *mass participation*. In his explanation for this instability, he examined the roles played by the effectiveness and independence of judicial systems in protecting rights (the political factor, see below) and the economic expectations of the population (the socioeconomic factor, see below). He found that the countries that score poorly in both categories (Ecuador, Bolivia and Venezuela) all experienced acute political crises during the period 2000–07, while among the countries that all scored well in both categories were the region's three consolidated democracies (see Table 4.2).

According to González, the data suggest a 'primacy of politics' in explaining instability: the link between crises and judicial-legal effectiveness is stronger than the link between crises and the growth of GDP per capita. However, the failure of economic growth to meet popular expectations does, none the less, play an important role in fostering instability (see below).

Political crises in Latin America often manifest themselves as challenges to sitting presidents, whose vulnerability may be exacerbated by constitutions or the composition of the judiciary that interprets these. The erosion of support for presidents may result from the perception of corruption, unpopular policies, the formation of hostile coalitions in congress, and even the role played by journalists

Table 4.2 Judicial-legal effectiveness, unsatisfied expectations and acute political crises, 2000–07*

Growth of GDP per capita at PPP, 1975–2003	Judicial–legal effectiveness circa 2002–2003		
	Least effective third	*Intermediate third*	*Most effective third*
Third with greatest GDP growth	‾‾‾	Panama Mexico	Chile Uruguay Costa Rica Colombia
	III	II	I
Intermediate third	Guatemala *Paraguay*** *Argentina***	‾‾‾	Brazil El Salvador
	IV	III	II
Third with least GDP growth	*Ecuador*** *Bolivia*** *Venezuela***	Honduras *Peru*** *Nicaragua***	‾‾‾
	V	IV	III

*Judicial–legal effectiveness circa 2002–2003; unsatisfied expectations according to average annual growth of GDP per capita at PPP, 1975–2003.

**Countries that experienced acute political crises during the period 2000–07. Within each cell countries are ordered (higher to lower) by diminishing levels of legal effectiveness.

Source: González, 2008

in exposing abuses of power. Guatemala's president, for example, came under heavy pressure in 2009 after allegations were made against him in connection with the killing of a prominent lawyer (see below). The allegations – which following an investigation turned out to have been baseless – prompted street demonstrations by thousands of citizens.

According to González, it has become more common in the recent period for presidents to be the target of political crises, and so it is necessary to look first, among the political factors contributing to instability, at presidentialism and difficult relations between the executive and legislature (see also Chapter 5).

Presidentialism

Among the institutional issues that still pose problems for Latin American democracies are those associated with presidentialism (see Mainwaring and Shugart eds, 1997). In Latin American countries, executive branches of government, which ensure that policies are carried out, are all presidential or semi-presidential, meaning that a president receives a popular mandate directly from the people through an election. Presidentialism became entrenched in the region because it offered a strong form of political leadership. However, it is often examined as a system in which the executive has undue powers compared to the legislative and judicial branches of government, which pass laws and interpret and apply them.

Presidentialism has often posed problems for democracy either because of a lack of clarity about the scope of formal presidential powers, resulting in a concentration of power by the executive, or because of problems with the legislature deriving from presidential *weakness*. Philip (2003) argues that a key explanatory factor behind non-consolidation is that Latin American presidentialism has become a contested, hybrid system of government prone to generating conflict and mistrust. One reason for this has been the separate election and functioning of the president and congress, meaning both can claim to have democratic authority through their mandates (Linz, 1994; see Chapter 5). It has resulted, among other things, in 'unbalanced presidentialism': cases where the president's powers are non-institutional but rather partisan or plebiscitary – exercised through party mechanisms or on the basis of direct appeals to the people over and above institutions – but also cases of executive weakness, where presidents cannot prevail against opposition-dominated legislatures (Philip, 2003). Corruption or the excessive use of patronage, by which presidents dispense benefits to political allies or supporters, also limit democratic consolidation by weakening the rule of law and respect for the presidency as an institution.

By the early 1990s, the new democracies of Argentina and Peru had become dominated by executives ruling in an autocratic way who saw the constitutional framework built upon the congress, judiciary and party system – the rules and regularities of party competition that give a political process continuity and stability (see Chapter 6) – as obstacles to policymaking, resulting sometimes in O'Donnell's 'delegative democracy' (see Chapter 3). This notion seeks to describe democracies that are not consolidated yet endure because they neither succumb to authoritarianism nor develop into the 'representative democracies' that can be found in most developed capitalist countries. Above all, O'Donnell's notion of delegative democracy aimed to describe the rule of a president who exercises power as if it were directly delegated to them by popular mandate and so ignores checks and balances built into the system, thereby eroding public faith in institutions and damaging party systems. He wrote: 'Delegative democracies tend to rest on the premise that whoever wins election to the presidency is thereby entitled to govern as he or she sees fit, constrained only by the hard facts of existing power relations and by a constitutionally limited term of office . . . other institutions – courts and legislatures, for instance – are nuisances that come attached to the domestic and international advantages of being a democratically elected president. Accountability to such institutions appears as a mere impediment to the full authority that the president has been delegated to exercise' (O'Donnell, 1994, pp. 59–60). The presidential styles adopted by Carlos Menem (1989–99) in Argentina and Alberto Fujimori (1990–2000) in Peru were characteristic of delegative democracy (see also 'Populism' below). The concentration of presidential power can manifest itself as *decretismo*, a president's ample use of legislative and emergency decree powers which Menem resorted to extensively. Unsuccessful legal challenges to the use of such powers can weaken the notion of judicial independence laid down by constitutions and, as a result, further strengthen presidentialism. Popular or ambitious presidents such as Menem and Fujimori have also often been tempted to extend their terms through constitutional reforms or challenges. In Colombia, for example, in October 2005 the constitutional court overturned a single-term presidential limit and ruled that Alvaro Uribe (2002–10) could stand for re-election in May 2006. His subsequent victory made him the first Colombian president to serve a consecutive term since 1886. Plans for what the Honduran congress and judiciary claimed were constitutional changes to extend the presidential term were at the heart of the dispute in 2009 that resulted in a coup that removed President Manuel Zelaya. The latest incumbent president to consider proposing extending his term was Daniel Ortega in Nicaragua, who announced plans in 2009 to change the constitution to allow him to stand again. In October 2009, Nicaragua's supreme court lifted a constitutional ban on re-election, clearing the way for Ortega to run in elections in 2011.

The separate executive and legislative branches of government need to be able to work together to avoid crisis, and so effective presidential government requires a working majority in congress (Mainwaring and Scully, 1995). Yet voting mechanisms in Latin America's multi-party systems – which usually combine the use of a plurality system for electing a president by majority with the use of proportional representation for electing legislatures, whereby congressional seats are distributed according to a party's share of the vote – can often mean that newly elected presidents take office without a working majority, weakening them and threatening impasse (see Chapter 5). Only a few Latin American political systems, such as Colombia, Costa Rica, Venezuela and Uruguay, have functioned to enable presidents to enjoy solid majorities or near majorities for long periods, and in many cases the executive has had difficulty pursuing a legislative agenda because of conflict with congress. In Mexico, for example, President Vicente Fox (2000–06) was embroiled in serious disputes with the legislature over the interpretation of his powers (see Box 5.3). Conflict with congresses due to lack of support among deputies has led to the forced resignation of presidents throughout Latin America since the 1990s.

It has also led recurrently to the removal of presidents or attempts to remove them through impeachment – the levelling of charges for misconduct – as a result of formal accusations of wrongdoing.

Representation through parties

The re-establishment of democracy returned parties to the centre of political activity in most of Latin America. It has been argued that a defining characteristic of democratic consolidation is the emergence of a party system that represents all the main political tendencies, because this restrains actors from pursuing other means of promoting their interests (see Chapter 6). However, a problem faced by Latin America's democracies is a decline in the ability of institutions such as parties to represent citizens effectively – that is, to act on their behalf and in their interests. Several scholars have argued that there are high levels of disenchantment with parties and they lack credibility, although the evidence suggests that confidence has been rising slowly in recent years even if it remains fragile. Disaffection with democracy originating in serious popular discontent with political parties is particularly high in the Andean countries – Venezuela, Colombia, Ecuador, Peru and Bolivia (see Mainwaring, 2008).

Writing in 1998, Hagopian argued that networks that link citizens to political institutions allowing them to be represented have decayed since the transition to democracy began at a faster rate than the emergence of new alternatives. The UNDP (2004b) suggested that there has been a significant increase in participation in politics through voting, and more broadly in terms of how the policies of elected governments are shaped, throughout most of Latin America. Latinobarómetro data in 2008–09 demonstrated greater interest in politics and overall participation in it compared with 2002 (Latinobarómetro, 2008, 2009a).

The implication of increased levels of participation through voting is that citizens enjoy a degree of representation that they may not have benefitted from previously. However, in countries with less well-established democracies, many people consulted by the UNDP believed that greater political participation results when citizens are involved in politics *outside established parties*, either by supporting independent candidates, joining civil society organisations that present themselves as alternatives to parties (see Chapter 8), or even demonstrating in street protests or other ways. Latinobarómetro data in 2009 suggested that many people consider that having the vote is not enough: 15 per cent of the population believe that, in order to change their circumstances, it is necessary to participate in protest movements (Latinobarómetro, 2009a). Parties themselves have sometimes been seen as *obstacles* to participation, and voter dissatisfaction with them remains high although confidence has grown consistently since 2001 (*ibid.*). Latin American political leaders consulted by the UNDP (2004b) also asserted that parties are not fulfilling their functions properly.

One example of how parties may not be functioning as well as they should in Latin America is the sheer number of them. In 2008, at least 11 Latin American countries had 10 or more parties in their lower houses and in Venezuela, for example, people could vote for at least 85 parties or movements (see Latinobarómetro, 2008).

Low or static levels of confidence in such traditional vehicles of political representation is often attributed to factors like corruption, public dissatisfaction with economic performance and even the increasingly important role of television, which disseminates political information in a way that parties once did (see below, and Box 8.11). Latin American political leaders consulted by the UNDP (2004b) often attributed declining party representativeness to such factors as personalistic leadership, the absence of internal party democracy, politicians' frequent use of clientelistic practices based on personal favours aimed at winning votes, and an absence of ideological differences between the parties.

Ways of illustrating dissatisfaction with the way parties represent demands include levels of voter turnout and abstention in elections and attitudes towards voting (see Table 3.1). In Mexico, Colombia, Brazil, Guatemala, El Salvador, Ecuador and Peru, for example, there were significant abstention rates during the 1990s (Hagopian, 1998). In other cases, voter turnout has oscillated in recent years: in the 1990s, turnout in Guatemala in presidential and parliamentary elections generally reached less than 50 per cent, but since then it has remained low for presidential elections (48.1 per cent in 2007) yet risen for parliamentary elections to 60.5 per cent in 2007 (IDEA, 2006, 2009). Even in some countries with a strong democratic tradition such as Costa Rica, voter turnout can decline: turnout as a proportion of registered voters fell in parliamentary elections from 81.8 per cent in 1990 to 65.1 per cent in 2006 and in presidential elections from 81.8 per cent in 1990 to 65.2 per cent in 2006 (*ibid.*). Hagopian (1998) examined declining representation by looking at continuity in parties' organisation and programmes. If parties do not have well-established organisations and if their representatives do not stay faithful to policies proposed during electoral campaigns, they will simply act as vehicles for their leaders' ambitions and will not be accountable to electors. Declining representation can also be measured by examining electoral 'dealignment' – the degree to which the loyalty of citizens to their preferred party erodes but is not replaced with loyalty to a competitor – and electoral 'volatility', the net change in the vote shares of all parties from one election to the next (*ibid.*). Non-identification on a left–right axis is a symptom of dealignment: Latinobarómetro data in 2008 demonstrated a decline to 19 per cent in the proportion of people across the region who, when asked about their political tendencies, did not place themselves on a left-right ideological spectrum, compared with 30 per cent in 2002. Hagopian argued that electoral dealignment was in a fairly advanced state in Latin America and that the evidence cast doubt on the idea that the decline in political representation is a temporary phenomenon. Mainwaring and Scully (1995) found striking levels of electoral volatility since the mid-1980s even in party systems with deep roots, such as Colombia, Venezuela and Argentina. Another indicator of how representative mainstream political parties are is the percentage of votes received by political parties that do not enjoy representation in the lower chamber of the legislature (UNDP, 2004b). In countries such as Brazil, Honduras, Paraguay and Uruguay this percentage has at times been very low, but in others such as Chile, Costa Rica and Guatemala, it has been as high as 12 per cent.

Although successes achieved by parties that have extended political participation to the left since the 1980s – such as the Partido dos Trabalhadores (PT, Workers' Party) in Brazil, the Frente Grande (Broad Front) in Argentina and the Alianza

Democrática Movimiento 19 de Abril (AD-M19, Democratic Alliance-19th of April Movement) in Colombia (see Chapter 12) – may suggest representation through traditional party systems is merely reorganising, new forms of representation have also emerged.

Mobilisation by social and popular movements – from human rights groups to religious organisations and self-help and civic associations, often articulating the demands of poor sectors of society – represents an important change in the conduct of Latin American politics (see Chapter 8; see also UNDP, 2004b). These movements have energised parts of the population never before mobilised, and have sometimes been more effective at securing concrete achievements than parties. At the same time, domestic and international non-governmental organisations (NGOs) have also expanded their reach in Latin America and forged new links with social movements.

Some scholars have argued that social movements and NGOs promise a novel form of representation through participation in which the force of social change is no longer from the top down but occurs in a decentralised way through local initiatives (see Baiocchi ed., 2003). There have also been many cases in which social actors have chosen to bypass the political process altogether and resort to direct action in pursuit of their demands. These actions often reflect the loss by political institutions of legitimacy and significant levels of frustration among the public. Street protests and popular uprisings have had a significant impact on politics in Latin America and have often forced out incumbent presidents (see above and Chapter 5). Another important phenomenon associated with the crisis of representation in Latin America has been the pressure for the decentralisation of power from central to provincial or municipal government, often from opponents of a new or incumbent administration, and a new emphasis upon constitutionalism to address what are perceived to be deficiencies in representation (see Box 4.1, Chapter 6).

None the less, careful analysis of the crisis of representation often attributed by both scholars and some populist leaders to the failure of political parties reveals that in some cases deficiencies in the performance and functioning of the *state itself* may be at the root of the problem (see Mainwaring, 2008). If states and their institutions were more effective, citizens would evaluate the situation in their country more favourably and this would strengthen their confidence in such institutions of democratic representation as political parties. This analysis would suggest that political reform should, first and foremost, concentrate on making states more effective before improving systems of representation.

The problem of populism

Autocratic presidentialism and the decline of parties as institutions of representation has sometimes left a void filled by leaders who promise to solve problems outside established political institutions. In particular, a lack of confidence in political parties can strengthen populists who offer a form of political representation outside parties and so do not rely on the latter as a source of support (see Boxes 4.2, 6.2, Chapter 2). Populism was a notable feature of Latin American

INSTITUTIONS   Box 4.1

Decentralisation and constitutionalism in Bolivia

In Bolivia, Evo Morales of the Movimiento al Socialismo (Movement Towards Socialism, MAS) was elected president in December 2005 following a campaign in which he railed against established political parties and promised a different, more participatory form of democracy (see Mainwaring, 2008; see also Chapter 3). Morales won on a ticket (the MAS) that had not even existed in the 1990s. Moreover, the polls were also the first in which local prefects (governors) were popularly elected in Bolivia's nine departments. This change was the result of a broad process of mobilisation by regional civic committees and other local groups demanding decentralisation, the most powerful of which were located in the eastern region of Santa Cruz – including the Comité Cívico Pro Santa Cruz (Pro Santa Cruz Civic Committee), the Cámara de Industria y Comercio (Chamber of Industry and Commerce), and the Cámara Agropecuaria del Oriente (Eastern Chamber of Agriculture) (see Boxes 8.7, 12.11). These groups – mostly opposed to the political programme of Morales – had been at the centre of demands for the convocation of a referendum on regional autonomy which was finally held in January 2006. Tensions and conflicts within the constituent assembly contributed to the huge December 2006 'million-person march' called by civic and business organisations in Santa Cruz with the aim of stopping the MAS from manipulating the outcome and hence 'defending democracy' (see Gamarra, 2008). According to Gamarra (2008), prefects citing regional autonomy have thus occupied the position historically held by political parties in Bolivia. Confrontational governors in Bolivia's four eastern departments, which tend to be wealthier and more ethnically mixed than the mainly indigenous departments of the western highlands but also contain most of the country's natural gas production and agribusiness, continued to press vigorously for more autonomy from the central state between 2006 and 2009, when the country's new constitution came into effect after it had been approved in a referendum.

The constitution gave significant levels of political and judicial autonomy to indigenous groups that are concentrated in the western highlands (see Chapter 8), asserted state control over natural resources such as oil, gas and minerals, and decentralised power, but many of its provisions were opposed by political and civic leaders in the eastern departments (see Box 13.6). Relations between the central and eastern provincial governments worsened following the discovery of what the Morales administration alleged was a plot to assassinate the president, and in May 2009 a state prosecutor accused the governor of Santa Cruz province of being implicated in this.

CASE STUDY   Box 4.2

Venezuela: party breakdown and populism

The rise of Hugo Chávez in Venezuela demonstrates one potential outcome of public disenchantment with political parties. From 1973 to the late 1980s, Venezuela enjoyed one of the most developed democratic party systems in Latin America dominated by two main parties, Acción Democrática (AD, Democratic Action) and Comité de Organización Política Electoral Independiente (COPEI, Committee for Independent Electoral Political Organisation) which alternated in office and together received between 85–90 per cent of the vote in presidential elections and about 75 per cent in congressional elections. These parties also dominated state and municipal offices and civil society organisations, maintaining control through patronage networks financed by the country's oil wealth and channelled through the state. The centre-left Movimiento al Socialismo (MAS, Movement Towards Socialism) led by former guerrillas became integrated into the party system, although it never rivalled the two main parties.

During the 1980s, Venezuela's political system came under increasing criticism, despite its achievements in comparison with other countries of the region. An important reason for this was its inability to provide better living standards for the country's growing population despite its substantial oil wealth, in large part because of corruption and the inability of the judicial system to deal with this. Opinion polls also suggested growing disenchantment with the excessive domination of the political process by AD and COPEI. As economic problems worsened, calls grew for reform of the two-party system to revitalise democracy by weakening their stranglehold on politics and decentralising the state. An important source of such calls was a host of social groups and movements – neighbourhood associations, co-operatives and human rights organisations – that had proliferated as civil society had grown *independently* of the party system. The habit of the main parties to centralise and seek control of social groups along party lines fuelled disenchantment among these organisations.

The decision in 1988 by the victorious AD presidential candidate, Carlos Andrés Pérez (1974–79, 1989–93), to implement a sweeping neoliberal adjustment plan shortly after his inauguration put the main parties under serious strain and caused massive riots. Pérez was widely condemned even from within AD, suggesting a breakdown in internal party discipline (see Chapter 6), and pursued his reforms independently through decrees. Two military rebellions in 1992 led by Chávez and his supporters shook the confidence of Venezuelans in their democracy and revealed growing splits in the military between younger officers committed to radical change and older, more senior officers who remained loyal to the system (Kornblith and Levine, 1995). In 1993, Pérez was impeached following accusations of corruption, and forced from office.

'Partisan dealignment' occurs when long-established parties see their support base migrating to new parties or political outsiders. In such an atmosphere, populists often emerge without party backing as outsider candidates who depict parties as corrupt and inefficient. In a clear early sign of partisan dealignment in Venezuela, Rafael Caldera (1969–74, 1994–99), the former president and founder of COPEI, won the presidency at the head of a loose coalition commanding just 30 per cent of the vote in opposition to both AD and COPEI and amid record abstention levels. This indicated a significant increase in electoral volatility since 1988 and the depth of disenchantment with politics. Caldera's failure to make inroads into solving Venezuela's problems heightened the sense of political crisis and, in 1998, Chávez, the popular former coup leader, won presidential elections. Chávez gained mass popular support at the expense of AD and COPEI at the head of the Movimiento Quinta República (MVR, Fifth Republic Movement), an electoral vehicle with no political pedigree. Since that time, he has employed a term that was frequently used by Fujimori in Peru to refer to a political system in thrall to a corrupt political class, the *partidocracia*, and promised to eliminate the corruption associated with those who had traditionally dominated politics. A key device for bypassing party politics has been the use of referendums outside the electoral calendar. However, the Venezuelan president has also attempted to unify fragmented forces on the left in a single party, creating the ruling Partido Socialista Unido de Venezuela (PSUV, United Socialist Party of Venezuela) after his victory in the 2006 presidential elections, now the largest leftwing party in Latin America by membership. Despite the proliferation of political parties in Venezuela (85 in 2008) which would tend to contribute to populism, data suggests that party politics in the country have grown in legitimacy, and citizens see parties as increasingly important to their democracy and, in general, doing a good job (see Latinobárometro, 2009a).

Populists often display an authoritarian streak implying the firm use of government and law and order. As a result, these leaders sometimes break democratic rules and leapfrog institutions that interfere with their exercise of power. Chávez used questionable means to force the closure of

▶

congress in 1999 and replace it with an assembly, and his opponents accused him of using fraud to win the referendum on his continued rule in 2004, although international observers and academics were split over the integrity of the result. In December 2004, a decision by legislators loyal to Chávez to appoint 17 new judges to an expanded supreme court was approved in the assembly by less than the constitutionally-stipulated two-thirds majority. Critics called the move an unconstitutional effort to control the court by stacking it with judges supportive of Chávez. Opposition parties boycotted assembly elections in November 2005 after accusing the country's electoral institute of favouring pro-government candidates, and this resulted in Chávez supporters gaining all 167 seats in the legislature. International observers were divided about whether the poll was free and fair, with European Union monitors believing it was but those from the Organisation of American States (OAS) expressing reservations. After his inauguration as president in 2007, Chávez proposed a law that was subsequently passed by the National Assembly that would send congress into recess for 18 months and allow the executive to legislate by decree in 13 critical policy areas (see Myers, 2008). There have also been signs that the Chávez administration's poor relations with certain media in Venezuela has fuelled his attempts to limit the freedom of the press (see Chapter 8).

However, scholars have disagreed about the nature of the Chávez regime, which has also been depicted as democratic for introducing reforms such as co-management and 'democratic planning' that includes workers in the decision-making processes of companies. Chávez won the 2006 presidential elections with a significant majority (63 per cent) and accepted defeat in 2007 in a referendum of proposals that would have extended his power. Opponents of Chávez claim, however, that although direct electoral fraud was not an issue in the 2006 election, the president had used state resources in ways that made it impossible for rivals to win (see Myers, 2008). The abolition of a three-term limit for elective offices was eventually passed in a referendum in 2009 in a vote described by most observers as free and fair.

None the less, there seems little doubt that Chávez has used a populist style to strengthen the state and pursue radical reforms that he has labeled the 'Bolivarian Revolution'. This has generated significant polarisation between marginalised and underprivileged groups mobilised in his support, and upper- and middle-class groups who have resisted his policies both through the institutional structure and demonstrations, marches and strikes, culminating in a failed coup attempt against him in April 2002 and a campaign thereafter that eventually forced him to hold the 2004 referendum in order to stay in power. Latinobarómetro data for 2004 showed Venezuela to be the most politically divided country in Latin America, with 49 per cent of respondents saying they would fight with their best friend about politics.

To some scholars, Chávez's political style and the opposition to this raises questions about the different visions of democracy that are competing in Venezuela and the broader region. Myers (2008) suggests that proponents and opponents of the Bolivarian Revolution each want a different type of democracy: in the case of the former, a direct democracy in which an elected leader embodying the general will acts without constraints; and in the case of the latter, a more traditional liberal democracy based upon checks and balances in government that guard against the tyranny of the majority.

politics before and after the Second World War and returned in a new form in the 1990s, when it was sometimes referred to as 'neo-populism' (see Knight, 1998).

The use of a party as a vehicle for the ambitions of one leading figure has been made easier by television, which allows an autocrat to woo a mass public. Television remains the dominant source of information about politics in Latin America, with 84 per cent of people in 2009 saying it is their main source compared with 55 per cent in the case of radio and 37 per cent for newspapers (see Latinobarómetro, 2009a). Menem in Argentina and Fernando Collor de Mello (1990–92) in Brazil, both of whom adopted populist styles of rule, used television skilfully to enhance their appeal over and above party politics. Contemporary leaders who have adopted a populistic style include Hugo Chávez (1999–) in Venezuela (see Box 4.2). Chávez has also been mindful of the power of television to support his objectives (see Boxes 8.11, 13.4).

Although populism has been understood in different ways (see Chapter 2), it remains valuable for characterising an important dimension and style of politics found in Latin America. The term is often used in the analysis of politics to describe a style of charismatic leadership that puts great store in the person of a leader, who derides politicians as corrupt and ineffective and displays an authoritarian streak intolerant of traditional political practices. As a result, populist leaders sometimes break democratic rules and leapfrog institutions that interfere with their exercise of power. This practice of bypassing parties and other institutions in a direct appeal to the people has been called *anti-politics* (see Box 2.4). The activity of populists reflects the weakness of a party system and they often emerge without the backing of an established party as outsider candidates who shun existing politicians. In Peru, for example, Fujimori won widespread popular support for his characterisation of established politicians as *obstacles* to reform.

Populists often enjoy success at times of crisis that allow them to present themselves as saviours of the nation embodying the popular will. Fujimori's populism reflected the failure of nominally democratic institutions to represent the interests of the majority and resolve Peru's serious problems, which were exacerbated by the violence of the guerrilla movements Sendero Luminoso (see Boxes 12.4, 13.9) and the Movimiento Revolucionario Tupac Amaru (MRTA, Tupac Amaru Revolutionary Movement) (see Figure 12.1). In Ecuador, President Rafael Correa (2007–) has been seen by many of his supporters as a saviour following a decade of political turmoil that involved three interrupted presidencies (see above, and Boxes 6.2, 8.4). Correa's populist presidency has been described as 'plebiscitary' for framing votes on political and constitutional reform as referenda on his rule, and for employing direct, unmediated appeals to public opinion in order to govern over the heads of existing institutions such as the legislature (see Conaghan, 2008). He has routinely attacked Ecuador's party system as a *partidocracia* – a term also routinely used by Chávez in Venezuela (see Boxes 4.2, 6.2) – dominated by an unrepresentative political elite. However, the price he has paid for this has, similarly, been to lack coherent organised backing in congress.

None the less, populist pressures do not surface only in times of crisis and can be found even in Latin America's consolidated democracies, where they also reflect disenchantment with established mechanisms of representation. In Chile in 2000, for example, despite the centre-left Concertación coalition's progress in improving socioeconomic conditions and democratic stability since the end of military rule, its candidate for the presidency, Ricardo Lagos (2000–06), faced a populist candidate on the right who capitalised on growing citizen alienation from the dominant parties and their leaders (see Valenzuela and Dammert, 2008).

In the 1990s, populistic appeals were couched in the language of neoliberalism – free-market liberalism – after years of economic stagnation (see Chapter 15; see also Demmers *et al.* eds, 2001). Leaders won support among the poor by appealing to them against established and often privileged organised interests such as trades unions and bureaucrats (see Chapters 6, 7). Where austerity programmes reduced inflation, attracted investment and generated growth, this allowed them to win re-election. More recently, the populism of Chávez in Venezuela has been based on a challenge to some central neoliberal economic tenets and efforts to re-establish state control over certain sectors of the economy (see Chapters 15, 16). Chávez has become a leading advocate in Latin America of economic policies associated with the socialist planning and forms of state control employed in Cuba and involving the nationalisation of key sectors and resources (see Boxes 9.1, 12.7, 16.1, Chapter 14). It is clear from these examples that populist leaders can adopt positions that have been associated traditionally either with the Left *or* the Right (see Chapters 12, 13).

The belief that political parties do not represent popular interests or are not fit to rule can encourage authoritarian behaviour seeking to bypass them and to centralise power. Once in power Fujimori, Menem, Collor and Chávez all began to concentrate power in the presidency (see Chapter 5). In 1992, Fujimori closed down the Peruvian congress which had opposed him and where he did not enjoy majority support. Critics of Chávez said he used unconstitutional means to close Venezuela's congress in 1999. Populist leaders are also prone to unexpected policy changes. Both Menem and Fujimori undertook radical neoliberal economic reforms (see Chapter 15) that went against their campaign promises. Fujimori, Menem, Collor de Mello and Pérez in Venezuela (see Box 4.2) all performed economic U-turns immediately after having been elected on anti-austerity programmes. In Ecuador, the populist president Lucio Gutiérrez (2003–05) lost the support of nearly all the groups that had brought him to power for contradicting promises that he would challenge neoliberal economic policies once in power, and was removed from office (see Box 6.2). To enact radical reforms, populists have often ignored democratic institutions, governing by decree to bypass congressional opposition and appealing directly to the masses to gain support for their actions. One sign of authoritarian tendencies has been the conflict between presidents and the media in several Latin American countries (see Chapters 5, 8).

The challenge to democratic consolidation of a weak rule of law

Democratic consolidation is more likely if lawfulness is the norm and laws are enforced effectively and impartially to ensure basic rights are protected and to protect political institutions from corruption and excessive partisanship – the tendency to favour one party's positions excessively. If the law-enforcement and judicial institutions of a democratic state are unable to guarantee citizens a basic level of security and a fair and effective rule of law, people may favour more authoritarian solutions to insecurity or take matters into their own hands.

However, evidence suggests that Latin American democracies are surviving *without* a fully effective rule of law and that crime, corruption and lawless behaviour by state agencies, and unequal access to lawyers and courts, have nurtured attitudes that corrode this and exacerbate a lack of respect among citizens for life and property. The Worldwide Governance Indicators for 2008 compiled for the World Bank, for example, suggest that four Latin American countries are among the 10 countries globally where there have been significant *declines* between 1998–2008 in the rule of law: Venezuela, Bolivia, Argentina and Ecuador (Kaufmann *et al.*, 2009).

Crime and insecurity

High crime rates and organised, often transnational crime pose a serious threat to democratic governance in Latin America and have at times threatened the functioning of the state itself. Everyday levels of crime are high in many Latin American countries, and in 2008 crime overtook unemployment for the first time since 1995 as the main problem facing citizens of the region (Latinobarómetro, 2008). According to Latinobarómetro's survey of 2009, 38 per cent of the Latin Americans asked said they had been a victim of crime in the previous 12 months (Latinobarómetro, 2009a).

However, the difference between the rate of recorded crime and the proportion of people who actually report having been victims of crime has varied considerably between 1995–2008, suggesting that perceptions of insecurity can change, particularly during times of economic downturn, despite crime rates that do not themselves change dramatically or rise only slowly. This means that the influence that the perception of crime can have on sentiments about democratic governance can be related to context. In Mexico, for example, in 2001, a year of economic downturn, 79 per cent of people said they had been victims of crime, yet only 18 per cent said that this was the principal problem facing the country (Latinobarómetro, 2008).

Concern about crime remains particularly high in Venezuela and Mexico, where 39 per cent and 38 per cent of people respectively said they were victims of crime in 2009 (Latinobarómetro, 2009a). Yet in absolute terms, Brazil and Colombia have the highest homicide levels within Latin America, and Colombia and El Salvador have the highest homicide levels in proportion to their populations (see UNDP, 2008).

Other than the impact on victims, high crime can contribute to attitudes about legality and the behaviour of public officials. Insecurity has meant that many Latin Americans see obeying the law as contingent upon one's circumstances, and this in turn has fuelled high levels of violence and crime. In Brazil, for example, in 2002 alone there were nearly 50,000 homicides (Amnesty International, 2005). Yet a proposal to ban the sale of guns in Brazil was defeated in a referendum in October 2005.

Examples of political violence or killing that may have had a political motive also persist throughout the region. Guatemala, for example, has experienced a number of political assassinations. In 2006, a congressman, Mario Pivaral of the opposition Unidad Nacional de la Esperanza (UNE, National Union of Hope) party, was assassinated by gunmen outside his party's headquarters in Guatemala City. Party officials linked the killing to the presidential and congressional elections due in 2007. Pivaral was the second legislator to be assassinated in the country since 2004. In 2007, three Salvadorean representatives to the Central American Parliament were murdered in Guatemala, and four policemen arrested in connection with the crime were themselves killed while in prison awaiting legal proceedings. Later that year, international election monitors expressed concern about the high murder rate among political candidates and activists in the run-up to Guatemala's polls in September.

In some instances, crime has even increased since democratisation and this is a significant problem for governments as it is likely to nurture growing disillusionment about the benefits of democratic governance. In Guatemala, for example, the annual number of homicides has almost doubled since the signing of the peace accords in 1996, and the rate of impunity for murders – those that remain unsolved – is 98 per cent. In 2008, there were an average of 17 murders per day in the country.

Drug-trafficking is the most high-profile source of violence in Latin America and in some countries, such as Mexico and Colombia, it has resulted in serious atrocities and human rights abuses (see Box 4.3, Chapter 10). Latin American leaders consulted by the UNDP (2004b) cite drug-trafficking as a serious threat to the democratic order. The activities of cartels and the violence associated with them – as well as the use of force in countering this – also have implications for international relations (see Chapters 9–11). Large crime syndicates in one part of the world can often fill the vacuum created by the retreat of syndicates in other regions. The Mexican cartels, for example, have grown more powerful since the retreat of the Cali and Medellín drug-trafficking organisations in Colombia; efforts to crack down against the Mexican cartels have, in turn, forced them to turn their attention to Guatemala.

High crime and weak law enforcement have resulted in the establishment of quasi-legal systems outside the reach of state judicial processes by drug barons, crime syndicates or guerrilla movements (see Boxes 9.8, 10.3, Figure 12.1). In 2008, for example, the human rights organisation, Amnesty International, reported that in Rio de Janeiro in the run-up to municipal elections, the control of large parts of the city by drug gangs and militias comprising off-duty or former police officers, firemen and soldiers had required deployment of the army in order to safeguard candidates' security (Amnesty International, 2009).

Drug-trafficking cartels in countries such as Mexico and Colombia control or are powerful in large parts of the territory and exercise considerable influence in politics. Ernesto Samper, the president of Colombia from 1994 to 1998, was at the centre of allegations that high-ranking officials in government had accepted political contributions from the Cali drug cartel. As a result of the allegations and the political turmoil that they led to, the US withdrew political assistance to Samper's government, criticized it recurrently for its supposed failure to fight the war against cocaine and the Cali cartel effectively, and eventually revoked Samper's visa, thereby effectively banning him from entering the country.

Funds generated by drug-trafficking have also often been implicated in the corrupt activities of judicial and law-enforcement officials (see below). In countries such as Honduras and Guatemala, corruption related to drug-trafficking is believed to have penetrated deep into the judicial system and public life. In November 2005,

Mexico's battle against drug-trafficking

Mexico is a major drug producing and transit country and the main foreign supplier of certain narcotics to the US, a key market because of the large number of drug consumers whose expenditure on drugs finances the activities of Mexican traffickers. The overall trade in illegal drug-smuggling into the US may be worth up to $48 billion annually, and about 70 per cent of that is thought to be controlled by the Mexican cartels. Recent levels of violence in Mexico reflect:

- growth in the activities of local cartels, which have filled the vacuum left by counter-narcotics activities in Colombia since the 1990s;
- increased competition, territorial disputes and changes in the balance of power between the cartels themselves since 2000, which fight over control of key smuggling corridors to the US;
- the breakdown of longstanding quasi-institutional links between the cartels and corrupt elements of the Partido Institucional Revolucionario (PRI), which ruled the country for much of the twentieth century;
- and the resistance by cartels to a major offensive against them launched by Mexico's president, Felipe Calderón, after coming to power in 2006.

Calderón's policy has been supported by the US since 2007 through the Mérida Initiative, a security co-operation arrangement (see Chapter 10). A key element of Mexico's strategy has been the deployment of the country's army against the cartels, and in 2009 about 45,000 Mexican troops in addition to state and federal police forces had been deployed across the country. There have also been efforts to root out corrupt officials from law enforcement and other agencies.

The conflict between the drug cartels and their confrontation with the state has escalated and, at times, has resulted in serious atrocities and human rights abuses. In 2005, warfare between rival drug gangs openly using rocket launchers, bazookas and machine guns on the streets of Nuevo Laredo forced the temporary closure of the US consulate there. In September 2009, amid the escalating conflict gunmen lined up patients in a drug treatment clinic in Ciudad Juárez against a wall and killed 17 people. Two months later, the severed heads of six policemen were dumped near a church in Durango state, northern Mexico, in a revenge attack by the Gulf cartel for the killing of 10 gang members. In January 2010, gunmen believed to have been linked to cartels opened fire on high-school students at a party in Ciudad Juárez, killing 16. When he visited the city in February 2010, Calderón was heckled and criticised by angry residents, who called for a de-escalation of the military presence.

Estimates of the number of people who have died in Mexico as a result of the conflict between drug-traffickers and the state between 2006 and 2010 have ranged from 5,000–30,000. In 2009, the murder rate in Ciudad Juárez reached an all-time high amid battles between rival cartels, with 1,986 killings for the year up to mid-October – an average of seven a day and 815 more than in 2008.

A recent dimension of the escalation in the conflict has been the use of terror tactics by Mexican traffickers to claim their territory and spread fear. Cartel members have broadcast executions on the internet and tossed severed heads into crowded nightclubs, for example. There have been suggestions that the cartels are engaging in copycat activity, mimicking through the use of beheadings and other such atrocities the style of violence used, for example, by terrorist organisations in the Middle East.

for example, Guatemala's top anti-drug investigator, Adán Castillo, was arrested and charged in the US with drug-trafficking following investigations by the US Drug Enforcement Administration. He denied wrongdoing.

The control of enclaves outside the formal reach of national institutions calls into question the nature of state power in Latin America, and the ability of the state to enforce the political, civil and social rights associated with democratic governance (see Box 2.1). A report by the US army's high command in 2009 into the security implications of the Mexican drug war, for example, discussed the potential for Mexico to become a 'failed state' as a result of the violence (USJFCOM, 2008).

Corruption

A weak rule of law begins with political corruption, which has serious implications for democracy (see Blake and Morris eds, 2009). To Philips (2003), democracy is non-consolidated if a person or group can expect to achieve or maintain public support in spite of or because of the open flouting of formal rules. Yet overtly lawless behaviour by powerful political and economic actors persists and is sometimes rewarded. In Venezuela, for example, President Carlos Andrés Pérez (1974–79, 1989–93) just avoided losing congressional immunity for alleged corruption as president from 1974–79, yet was elected again and assumed power in 1989, before being impeached for corruption and then removed in 1993.

Allegations of corruption and wrongdoing have been a normal part of Latin America's political landscape and have been levelled against many presidents (see Box 4.4).

Nor has the Left, which has come to power in a number of countries in Latin America since 2000 (see Chapter 12), been immune. In 2005, corruption allegations embroiled Brazil's leftwing government and damaged the popularity of President Luiz Inácio Lula da Silva (2003–10), much of whose public persona has been built upon an image of integrity. Members of the governing PT were accused of buying the support of coalition allies, a practice they subsequently claimed was common.

Allegations of corruption are often linked to the awarding of contracts by the government or to its procurement policies. In October 2008, for example, the entire Peruvian cabinet resigned after allegations that members of the governing Alianza Popular Revolucionaria Americana (APRA, American Revolutionary Popular Alliance, today referred to as the Partido Aprista Peruano) had taken bribes in the allocation of oil contracts. The case prompted Peru's congress to launch an investigation into all concessions hitherto granted in the country's gas and petroleum sectors, and sparked street protests by demonstrators angry at what many Peruvians see as endemic corruption and the failure of rapid economic growth to eradicate poverty.

Allegations of corruption are also often associated with the financing of political parties. An important challenge of democratic governance is ensuring that political parties and candidates have sufficient funds to compete fairly in elections and so present citizens with meaningful choices. At the same time, however, wealthy candidates and parties need to be prevented from deriving an unfair advantage

INSTITUTIONS   Box 4.4

Presidents in the dock

One of the most high-profile recent cases of a Latin American politician being accused of wrong-doing involved Peru's former president Alberto Fujimori (1990–2000) who, in September 2009, was sentenced by a court in Lima after a fourth and final trial to six years in jail for corruption. Fujimori was already serving prison sentences for abuse of power, ordering the security forces to carry out killings and kidnappings while in office, and embezzlement. In his fourth trial, Fujimori admitted to bugging and bribing opposition politicians, journalists and businessmen as part of a scandal that brought down his government in 2000.

In another high-profile case, the former president of Guatemala, Alfonso Portillo (2000–04) of the Frente Republicano Guatemalteco (Guatemalan Republican Front, FRG), was extradited from Mexico in 2008 to face charges linked to the disappearance of funds that had been earmarked for Guatemala's defence department, allegations that he has denied. The FRG has been accused of large-scale corruption in Guatemala in the period of Portillo's government, with accusations against government members of theft and money laundering, among other financial irregularities, amounting to more than $1 billion. Among other cases, the United Nations-sponsored International Commission against Impunity in Guatemala (CICIG) has investigated a $112 million fraud in which the former president and former members of the army were allegedly implicated.

Corruption allegations do not just affect newly democratising countries. In October 2004, Miguel Angel Rodríguez resigned as head of the Organisation of American States (OAS) to face allegations of accepting a bribe while president of Costa Rica between 1998 and 2002, which he denied. Rodríguez was accused of receiving a 'kickback' after a contract had been awarded to a French telecommunications company. He was arrested on his return to the capital San José and held in jail until being released to house arrest in March 2005 because of poor health while prosecutors continued investigations into the case. The case was one of a string of investigations into alleged corruption that have reached to the highest echelons of the Latin American political establishment. Another former Costa Rican president, Rafael Angel Calderón (1990–94), was also detained in 2004 while investigations were carried out into a separate bribery allegation, which he denied. In December 2003, Arnoldo Alemán, Nicaragua's president from 1997 to 2002, was convicted and sentenced to 20 years on corruption charges involving $100 million in public funds. Mireya Moscoso, who was Panama's president from 1999 until 2004, came under investigation after leaving office over government funds allegedly not accounted for during her administration. She denied any wrongdoing. In November 2005, Chile's former dictator Augusto Pinochet (1973–90) was also indicted on charges of fraud and corruption. In June 2006, Paraguay's former president Luis González Macchi (1993–2003) was sentenced to six years in prison after he was convicted of being involved in illegal bank transfers involving funds sent from Paraguay's central bank to the US in 2000. He had denied the charges.

High-level corruption is considered a major problem by multilateral institutions. In 1996, the Inter-American Convention Against Corruption was adopted by the OAS committing signatories to prevent, detect, punish and eradicate corruption in public administration, the first anti-corruption treaty of its kind in the world. This states that 'corruption undermines the legitimacy of public institutions and strikes at society, moral order and justice' (OAS, 2005). It laid out specific steps for states in the region to follow that included efforts to strengthen legal and accounting procedures. The UN has an Office on Drugs and Crime with specialist programmes against corruption, and the World Bank has also devoted considerable attention to researching the causes and impact of corruption.

However, even in cases where corruption is detected and perpetrators convicted, incarceration is rarely harsh for former presidents. Nicaragua's former president Alemán spent a few months in a special prison unit that included air conditioning, cable television and a massage service before returning to serve the rest of his 20-year term at his ranch.

from having greater resources, and donors must not be allowed to influence the decision-making processes of elected officials whose campaigns they financed. The regulation of campaign finance and ordinary party financing, therefore, is increasingly being seen as essential to a healthy democracy, and the key to such regulation is disclosure. The anti-corruption organisation Transparency International and the Carter Center developed methods for measuring the amount of disclosure in political finance and used these to measure this in eight Latin American countries (Crinis Project, 2007). They found deep flaws in the standards and practices governing transparency and accountability in party and campaign financing systems in the eight Latin American countries studied: Argentina, Colombia, Costa Rica, Guatemala, Nicaragua, Panama, Paraguay and Peru. Key problems identified included a lack of oversight for private donations, limited accountability by candidates, and unreliable data provided by parties, as well as the fact that information about political financing is not made public in most Latin American countries.

More broadly, Transparency International compiles an annual 'Corruption Perceptions Index' ranking countries according to a score derived from surveys conducted by 12 independent institutions reflecting the perceptions of business people and country analysts, both resident and non-resident, about levels of corruption in public contracting and government procurement. The higher the score, the lower the perceived corruption: a clean score is 10. It incorporates scores for the 20 Latin American republics among the countries ranked (see Table 4.3). A score of less than 3 out of 10 has traditionally been thought to indicate that corruption in a country is rampant: Transparency International's league table for 2008 suggested that this was the case in seven Latin American countries, with Venezuela and Haiti being the most corrupt, an improvement on 2005 when there were nine Latin American countries in this category.

Allegations of corruption are also routinely made against public officials as well as politicians in Latin America. Latinobarómetro data reveal that the perception of corruption is growing in Latin America, with respondents to its 2008 survey across the region believing that 68.6 out of every 100 public servants are corrupt, compared with 67.9 out of 100 in 2001 (Latinobarómetro, 2008). The public perception that it is possible to bribe a police officer, a civil servant or a judge was little changed between 2004–08, and remains very high in countries such as Paraguay, Venezuela and Argentina (see Figure 4.1). That said, the belief that progress is being made by states in reducing corruption has grown considerably, from 26 per cent in 2004 to 39 per cent in 2009 (Latinobarómetro, 2009a).

Inequality is a key component of corruption in Latin America, as well as determining access to fair and efficient legal processes. For example, Transparency International says that its research suggests poor families tend to pay bribes more frequently, depleting scarce household resources (Transparency International, 2008b). Inequality based on racial, gender and class prejudice within a legal process that favours the rich and powerful is common. Poor people and those from ethnic minorities or indigenous groups who find it hard to gain access to a lawyer often spend longer in prison awaiting trial, for example. The proportion of people detained in jail in Latin America who have neither been tried for or convicted of an offence is high in some countries.

Table 4.3 Transparency International Corruption Perceptions Index 2008 (for Latin American countries)

Country Rank	Country	CPI Score*
23	Chile	6.9
23	Uruguay	6.9
36	Puerto Rico	5.8
47	Costa Rica	5.1
65	Cuba	4.3
67	El Salvador	3.9
70	Colombia	3.8
72	Mexico	3.6
72	Peru	3.6
80	Brazil	3.5
85	Panama	3.4
96	Guatemala	3.1
102	Bolivia	3.0
102	Dominican Republic	3.0
109	Argentina	2.9
126	Honduras	2.6
134	Nicaragua	2.5
138	Paraguay	2.4
151	Ecuador	2.0
158	Venezuela	1.9
177	Haiti	1.4

*CPI Score relates to perceptions of the degree of corruption as seen by business people and country analysts and ranges between 10 (highly clean) and 0 (highly corrupt).

Source: Transparency International, 2008a

Poor law enforcement and impunity

Inequality in the legal process is also reinforced by inadequate or indifferent law enforcement throughout Latin America, and widespread impunity in some countries for powerful people with money or public officials. Authoritarian rule created a culture of impunity in Latin America and selective law enforcement has strengthened a culture of distrust (see Uildriks, 2009).

The murder of street children in countries such as Guatemala, Honduras and Brazil has frequently been met with indifference by judicial and law enforcement agencies, for example. Deaths in the countryside in conflicts over land and the murder of rural activists have been a persistent embarrassment for the government of Brazil where, in many cases, it has sometimes been discovered later that law enforcement officers have been involved in or connected to the killings (see below). Amnesty International said that in Brazil in 2008, for example, violence against landless workers continued to be carried out by unregulated or poorly regulated private security companies hired by landowners or by illegal militias, and forced evictions

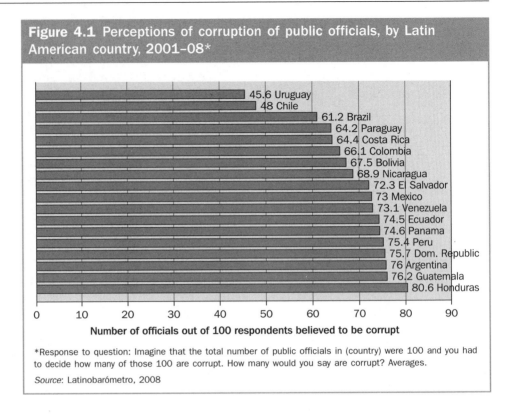

Figure 4.1 Perceptions of corruption of public officials, by Latin American country, 2001–08*

Number of officials out of 100 respondents believed to be corrupt

*Response to question: Imagine that the total number of public officials in (country) were 100 and you had to decide how many of those 100 are corrupt. How many would you say are corrupt? Averages.

Source: Latinobarómetro, 2008

took place in many instances with complete disregard for due process of law (see Amnesty International, 2009).

The weak enforcement of laws is an important aspect of democratic non-consolidation in much of Latin America: in some countries the level at which crimes are solved is pitifully low. In Guatemala, some estimates of the level of crimes that go unsolved are as high as 98 per cent (see CONGDP, 2009). Not only are law-enforcement agencies ineffective, they often see the law as an obstacle to their job and flout it themselves through corruption, torture and extra-judicial killing. In Guatemala in 2007, for example, four police officers were detained for the murder of three Salvadorean representatives to the Central American Parliament – then were themselves killed while in prison awaiting trial (see above). In 2006, mindful of how impunity in Guatemala contributed to the activities of illegal security groups and clandestine security organisations, the country's government allowed the UN to establish the International Commission Against Impunity in Guatemala (CICIG) to support the public prosecutor's office, the police and other state institutions in investigating sensitive and difficult cases (see also Box 4.4). In 2009, for example, CICIG played a key role in investigations into the death of the lawyer Rodrigo Rosenberg, and in exonerating the president of involvement.

The use of torture by police officers, who see this as a legitimate means of obtaining information, has at times been considered pervasive in countries like Mexico and Brazil. In its 2009 report, for example, Amnesty International says periodic military-style incursions by Brazil's police in largely unpoliced impoverished urban communities were often characterised by extra-judicial executions, torture and abusive behaviour towards residents (Amnesty International, 2009). In late 2009, Mexico's government said it would scale down its military presence in Ciudad Juárez and boost police numbers amid accusations of increased human rights abuses by soldiers in the war against drug-traffickers (see Box 4.3).

Inadequate law enforcement also encourages ordinary people to ignore rules or to take justice into their own hands (see Box 4.5). The state may turn a blind eye to violence by powerful private interests or may be too weak to prevent this. Powerful politicians and wealthy people sometimes maintain ties with the coercive state

---

SOCIETY   **Box 4.5**

What rule of law? Lynchings and vigilante justice

One sign of limited democratic consolidation is a culture of disregard for the rule of law and impunity. Lynching – the execution of suspected wrongdoers without due process – occurs frequently in some parts of Latin America, particularly rural areas. Lynchings carried out in a barbaric manner (victims are often burned alive) reflect inadequate law enforcement and a weak commitment to the rule of law, often because local aspirations for the dispensation of justice by official institutions are not met. The United Nations verification mission in Guatemala, Misión de las Naciones Unidas para Guatemala (MINUGUA), launched in 1997, recorded numerous cases of lynchings with a growing degree of cruelty and impunity for those responsible (see MINUGUA, 2000). The departments with the largest number of lynchings were Quiché and Alta Verapaz, both of which had been badly affected by the country's civil war. Lynchings continue to be a feature of Guatemalan life as the country struggles to cope with high crime and poor law enforcement: in the 12 months up to December 2009, mobs attacked more than 250 people in the country, killing at least 40 of them (*Mail*, 2009). Suspected criminals are the main target of mobs, but in one case a judge who had handed out a sentence for rape that was considered by some people to have been too lenient was attacked.

Most lynchings are carried out spontaneously in isolated rural areas with the participation of entire communities, and there have been many cases that are believed to have been planned or tolerated by local authorities. MINUGUA identified the participation in some cases of local officials belonging to structures that emerged during the counter-insurgency struggle such as volunteer 'civil defence' committees. In April 2006, Guatemala's president Oscar Berger deployed security forces in villages south of the capital after villagers threatened to lynch gang members they accused of robbing local buses and shops.

However, lynchings can also occur in urban contexts. In December 2009 in Guatemala City, a woman accused of being part of an armed gang that had tried to rob passengers on a bus was caught as she tried to flee. The passengers stripped and beat her in the street before dousing her with petrol and setting her alight. In November 2004, in the poor neighbourhood of San Juan Ixtayopan on the outskirts of Mexico City, two federal police agents purportedly sent to investigate drug dealing were beaten then burned to death in front of television cameras by a mob estimated at 2,000. The killings came amid rumours that children had been kidnapped from a local school and when residents saw three men taking photographs, they suspected them of wrongdoing. The incident underlined widespread mistrust in Mexican law-enforcement agencies, which are regarded by many citizens as corrupt, inept and in many cases the source of crime itself. It also underlined the failure of the government to tackle soaring levels of crime that included high rates of kidnapping.

agencies, such as the intelligence services, and take advantage of ineffective law enforcement to get their way. Middle classes and entrepreneurs may employ vigilantes to combat burglary or anti-social behaviour.

Where governments have made progress against impunity has been in cases involving former military officials that relate to previous periods of authoritarian rule (see Box 7.11). In some countries, progress has also been made in bringing to trial former presidents and their associates accused of more recent wrongdoing, seriously challenging the impunity from prosecution leaders may have enjoyed in the past. In 2009, for example, the former president of Bolivia, Gonzalo Sánchez de Lozada and 16 members of his former cabinet went on trial on charges of being responsible for the deaths in 2003 of 60 people during protests in the city of El Alto.

But even a firm rhetorical stand by a government on human rights can co-exist with the failure of courts to enforce rights in ways that benefit large sections of the population, and continuing corruption within the police force. Human rights groups continue to document rights violations in Latin America, including such practices as forced disappearances, execution, torture, political imprisonment, exile and restrictions on freedom of the press, expression, assembly and association. In March 2005, the Inter-American Commission on Human Rights of the OAS reported that, although there have been important advances in the protection of human rights in Latin America, it continues to face many challenges, including impunity in cases of serious violations, arbitrary detention, attacks on the independence and impartiality of the judiciary, and inhumane conditions in prisons (see Box 6.3). In its 2008 annual report, the IACHR pointed to situations that seriously or gravely affect the enjoyment and exercise of basic rights as enshrined in the American Convention on Human Rights within Colombia, Cuba and Venezuela, and voiced its concern about the persistent challenges facing human rights in Haiti deriving, in particular, from weaknesses in the administration of justice and impunity for violations (IACHR, 2009). Foweraker *et al.* (2003) used figures compiled by the research organisation Freedom House from 17 Latin American countries to demonstrate that the protection of civil liberties has lagged in the region. Some scholars have characterised the gap between constitutional principles and day-to-day legal practices as amounting to an 'unrule of law' in Latin America (Mendez *et al.* eds, 1999).

The military challenge to democratic consolidation

A central issue in the study of the military in Latin American politics has been its role both in the transition to democratic rule and its subsequent relationship with democracy (see Pion-Berlin ed., 2001; see also Chapter 7). Most transitions have involved some pact-making between civilians and the military or a military input into the transition process (see Chapter 3; see also Anderson, 1999). The pacted nature of transitions may have ensured their success by allowing the military to secure concessions in return for leaving power. As a result, transitions often did not involve a change in military attitudes but a shift in the balance of forces within military institutions. Military leaders and their civilian allies were often able to impose limitations on the transition process and on the constitutional framework within which the resulting democratic system would evolve. The challenge facing subsequent democratic governments was to exert civilian control over the military without provoking a backlash by balancing concerns about past abuses with present political needs. Most transitions between 1978 and 1993 included amnesties that enabled members of the police and military who had committed human rights crimes to enjoy impunity. They also involved accepting military-imposed limitations on political candidates, parties and procedures, and recognising some constraints on the authority of incoming governments.

A key factor shaping relations between the outgoing military and the incoming civilian administration was the extent to which they disputed the way the new government handled the legacy of human rights violations (see Box 7.11). In Brazil, conflict between the military and the civilian administration over what the armed forces had done while in power was minimal, but in Argentina there was considerable tension (Linz and Stepan eds, 1996; see also Pion-Berlin, 1997). In both countries, prisoners had been 'disappeared' – kidnapped and killed by the security forces – but in Argentina this problem had been much worse than in Brazil (see Table 7.2).

Latin America has a long tradition of the military serving as 'guarantors' of the institutional order, and they have often employed constitutional arguments to legitimise non-democratic forms of governance. In both Chile (1973–90) and Brazil (1964–85), the military claimed their interventions were to *protect* the constitution against incumbent presidents, attesting to the importance attributed to constitutional norms in Latin America (see Chapter 1). Most of the democratic transitions in Latin America did not eliminate the constitutional potential for such interventions. Loveman (1994) argued that the concept of democracy is, by definition, incompatible with the vesting of authority in political guardians in this way. He characterised this as 'protected democracy' which, he said, remained a feature of Latin America's transition process well into the 1990s. Hunter (1998) outlined a number of problems in the military's relationship with the democratic system that prevented civilian governments at times from exercising their full constitutional authority (see Chapter 7). These included:

i. the presence of institutional *prerogatives* that provide the military with a legal pretext to meddle in non-military affairs through 'regimes of exception', such as states of emergency at times of crisis in which the rights provided under normal laws are suspended;

ii. *de facto* military autonomy in a wide range of areas;

iii. and the persistence or emergence of military missions or roles that draw the armed forces into domestic functions.

Until recently, legal prerogatives that enhance military power and weaken the sovereignty of elected governments remained most substantial in Chile (Hunter, 1998), a country that reveals the continuing potential today for the legacies of military control to influence democratic politics. Although the socialist president Ricardo Lagos (2000–06) enjoyed a working majority in Chile's lower chamber, for example, his Concertación coalition was not dominant in the senate where pro-military rightwing parties maintained an equilibrium. The Lagos government did begin to remove some of the legal and constitutional vestiges of the period during which the country was controlled by the military dictator Augusto Pinochet (1973–90), but it was not until mid-2005 – a full 15 years after the return of democracy – that the senate restored a president's right to dismiss military commanders. The Lagos government made only limited progress in its efforts to try Pinochet for human rights crimes. In January 2006, Pinochet was granted bail after seven week's house arrest while facing charges related to the disappearance and presumed death of three leftwing activists during the 1970s (see Box 7.11). At the time of his death in December 2006, about 300 criminal charges were still pending against him in Chile for human rights violations, embezzlement and tax evasion, although he was never convicted of any crimes.

In some cases, the military continues to have missions that draw it into domestic functions. Since the early 1990s, for example, Brazil's army has been deployed regularly in the *favelas*, or slums, of Rio de Janeiro to tackle gang violence and drug-trafficking. In November 2005, El Salvador's government increased the deployment of army patrols on the streets to tackle escalating violence between rival gangs. The deployment of Mexico's military in the war against drug-traffickers has led to a number of allegations about human rights abuses in northern states such as Chihuahua (see New America Media, 2009; see also Box 4.3). In Honduras, military chiefs of staff insisted that when they ousted Manuel Zelaya in June 2009 they were acting in defence of a constitution threatened by a maverick president. However, Zelaya had made comments about sacking the head of the Honduran armed forces, Gen Romeo Vásquez Velásquez, just before the coup after the officer had refused to allow soldiers to provide logistical support in a vote on whether the constitution should be changed. In Honduras, it is a function of the military to assist with election logistics by, for example, distributing ballot boxes and other poll material. Gen Vásquez said he had refused because the supreme court had ruled the vote illegal. In Venezuela, President Hugo Chávez maintains a close relationship with his country's military, in which he served between 1975 and 1992 when he led an attempted coup that ended his military career but became important to his subsequent political ascent.

Renewed attention by Latin American governments to social problems have led to the military's expansion into civic roles. As a result, while democratic transition has removed militaries from direct control of government and their power has diminished, they retain considerable political influence, and politicians remain mindful of the risks that having the armed forces act in this way can pose.

None the less, the frequency of old-fashioned coups has clearly decreased in Latin America. In his study of political crises, González (2008) compared two periods in the post-Cold War years: 1992–99 and 2000–07. In the first period, of the eight acute political crises, five involved conventional military coups; and in the second, there were just two military interventions, Paraguay 2000 and Venezuela 2002, to which must be added the Honduran coup in 2009 – a decrease consistent with a pattern of long-term decline since the 1960s. González speculates that traditional coups may be becoming less frequent because, increasingly, they fail: most of the coups in the first period came to naught and in the second period, only the Honduran coup succeeded.

Critics of US foreign policy argue that its 'war on drugs' and more recently its 'War on Terror' following the 9/11 attacks in New York have had implications for Latin American democracies (see Box 10.4). This is because these have militarised foreign policy and put pressure on Latin American countries to increase military and counter-narcotics spending priorities – blurring the distinction between police and military functions in countries such as Mexico and Colombia; serving as a pretext for advancing other US interests in the region, and tighter border controls; and in some cases generating new violations of human rights (see for example Pilger, 2007; WOLA, 2009). Some indigenous groups demanding autonomy and protesting free-market policies in Latin America, for example, expressed concern that they had been identified as potential threats to domestic security in the climate generated by the 'War on Terror' (see González, 2005).

Economic challenges to democratic consolidation

An important debate in the study of democratisation concerns the role of economic factors in consolidation, attention to which grew with the downturn following the global financial crisis of 2008–09. The Economic Commission for Latin America and the Caribbean (ECLAC/CEPAL), for example, estimated that, after growing continuously for six years, the gross domestic product (GDP) of Latin America and the Caribbean would fall by 1.9 per cent in 2009, bringing about a reduction in per capita GDP of 3.1 per cent and pushing the unemployment rate up from the 7.5 per cent observed in 2008 to about 9 per cent in 2009 (ECLAC, 2009a). The World Bank says that growth in Latin America and the Caribbean in 2008 was 4.3 per cent, and the region was projected to contract around 2 per cent in 2009, before recovering to growth of approximately 3 per cent in 2010 (World Bank, 2009b).

The relationship between economic stability and political stability is important, but complex: there is evidence that the unfulfilled expectations of the population is among the factors that cause serious political crises (see González, 2008); however, data do not suggest a clear relationship between levels of satisfaction with democracy and GDP growth in Latin America (see Latinobarómetro, 2009a).

None the less, the apparent truth that prosperous countries tend to enjoy more stable democratic systems begs key questions: what are the implications of poverty and inequality for consolidation? And to what extent has the performance of democratic governments in Latin America met unfulfilled economic expectations? According to the UNDP (2004b), Latin America is unique because, for the first time in history, almost an entire developing region suffering from significant levels of poverty and with profoundly unequal societies is organised politically under democratic governments.

A common assumption among many policymakers and social scientists has been that capitalist development would inevitably result in some minimal level of social equality more amenable to sustaining democracy. The origins of this assumption lie in modernisation theory, the set of influential and optimistic assumptions about political development shaped by the stable democratic capitalist development of the US and Western Europe after the Second World War (see Boxes 3.1, 14.2). Such a perspective assumed that less developed countries would follow the same evolutionary path as the economically advanced countries. In particular, it associated free-market economies with political democracy: free markets would produce growth and encourage liberal individualism, generating socio-economic and cultural changes that engendered the attitudes and institutions associated with democracy. However, there are cases that undermine arguments which associate free-market economies with political democracy. In Chile, for example, Pinochet pursued radical free-market policies while ruling as a military dictator. Outside Latin America, China's communist regime has pursued a vigorous policy of market development. None the less, modernisation perspectives have persisted into the current era and some of the scholarly works about democratic transition and consolidation make similar evolutionary assumptions (for a useful critique of these, see Silva, 2004). In June 2005, for example, the US president, George W. Bush, reiterated in a speech to the OAS a longstanding belief among policymakers in his country that free trade would strengthen democracy in the American hemisphere. The assumed relationship between capitalist development and democracy was given force by the fact that democratisation in Latin America coincided with radical market reforms following the debt emergency in 1982. The stress of the debt crisis accelerated the end of authoritarianism, but also put Latin American governments under pressure to adopt a new model based on neoliberal economic ideas promoting private enterprise and free markets (see Chapters 2, 15). The neoliberal analysis argued that market reforms help all sectors of society to benefit from overall economic growth, including the poor, and so eventually reduce inequality.

Until about 2000, neoliberal policies constituted an orthodoxy in the region, and some countries such as Mexico and Chile institutionalised them by aligning with the US in free-trade treaties. The main objectives of Latin American trading associations such as Mercosur were premised upon neoliberal ideas about free trade, integration and globalisation (see Boxes 9.9, 15.5, 15.8, Table 15.2). Recently, however, more left-of-centre economic policies have been pursued in some Latin American countries (see Chapter 16). Democracy has meant that previously excluded groups are insisting on their share of national wealth, and although governments have responded to new demands in varied ways, a number of programmes have been launched in Latin American countries to transfer income to poorer groups (see below).

Contemporary assumptions about the relationship between the market economy and democracy, sometimes called the 'neo-modernisation' perspective, explain why neoliberal reforms were initially viewed favourably from the point of view of promoting democracy. This was reflected in the discourse of some policymakers in the US who used terms such as 'market democracy' to refer to the political systems that were emerging in the region. However, there is evidence that neoliberal reforms often worked *against* the needs of democratic consolidation (see Chapter 15). In many cases, the determination to reform the economy to the satisfaction of international investors but in the face of popular resistance strengthened the authoritarian tendencies of presidents. Reforms also weakened or changed the behaviour of social actors such as trades unions, and further excluded popular sectors such as the poor and marginalised from the formulation of policies. There has been considerable debate about the socioeconomic effects of neoliberal reform, with many scholars arguing that it has, on balance, been negative.

Growth

The rate of growth of GDP has been erratic in the Latin American and Caribbean region, ranging from 6.1 per cent in 2004 to a projection of –1.9 per cent in 2009, indicating how vulnerable the region is to global economic trends (ECLAC, 2009b). In overall terms, there has been an almost negligible increase in GDP per capita since 1980, at the beginning of the neoliberal economic reform process (see UNDP, 2004b). However, following a period of stagnation in the late 1990s, growth in per capita GDP in Latin America began to recover ground to reach impressive rates in some countries after 2004, although it has fallen back since then. Not only has the rate of growth of per capita GDP in Latin America been volatile, reflecting the vulnerability of people living in the region to international economic factors beyond their control, but it has varied considerably within the region. Countries such as Haiti and Honduras achieve consistently low growth rates when compared to countries such as Argentina and Uruguay (see Table 4.4).

Poverty and inequality

Latin American countries suffer from high levels of deprivation and, although in recent years the proportion of poor people has consistently declined in relation to the population, success in poverty reduction strategies has slowed (mainly because of rising food prices) and the downturn following the global financial crisis of 2008–09 is likely to push poverty levels back upwards. According to ECLAC, by 2008 33 per cent of the region's inhabitants were poor, including 12.9 per cent who were indigent, that is, when the per the per capita income of that person's household falls below a line based on the cost of satisfying their food needs only (see Table 4.5).

In November 2009, ECLAC estimated that, as a result of the downturn, a further 9 million people across the Latin American and Caribbean region would fall into poverty (ECLAC, 2009c; ECLAC IS, 2009a). It calculated that poverty in the region would increase by 1.1 per cent and indigence by 0.8 per cent with regard to 2008, pushing the total number of Latin Americans living in poverty to 189 million by the end of 2009 (34.1 per cent of the population), compared to 180 million in 2008, and indigence up from 71 million in 2008 to 76 million (13.7 per cent of the population) (see Figure 4.2).

None the less, the proportion of the overall population of Latin America that is poor has fallen dramatically: between 2002 and 2008, the percentage living in poverty fell by 11 points, and indigence fell by 7 points (ECLAC, 2009c). However, although these figures are encouraging, they conceal the scale of deprivation and the cyclical nature of poverty in the region: in absolute terms the number of people living below the poverty line has not fallen dramatically, and in some years has

Table 4.4 Growth rates of per capita gross domestic product, Latin America and the Caribbean*

Country	1995	2000	2004	2005	2006	2007	2008**
Argentina	−4.0	−1.8	8.0	8.1	7.4	7.6	5.8
Bolivia	2.3	0.1	1.9	2.2	2.6	2.4	3.7
Brazil	2.6	2.8	4.2	1.5	2.3	4.0	4.5
Chile	8.8	3.2	4.9	4.5	3.3	4.0	2.8
Colombia	3.3	1.3	3.1	4.2	5.5	6.8	1.7
Costa Rica	1.4	−0.5	2.4	4.0	6.9	5.5	1.6
Cuba	2.0	5.6	5.6	11.1	12.0	7.3	4.3
Dominican Republic	3.6	3.9	−0.3	7.6	9.0	6.9	3.0
Ecuador	−0.1	1.3	6.5	4.5	2.4	1.2	5.0
El Salvador	4.2	0.2	0.1	1.3	2.4	2.9	1.3
Guatemala	2.5	1.2	0.6	0.7	2.7	3.1	0.8
Haiti	7.8	−0.8	−5.0	0.2	0.7	1.5	−0.2
Honduras	1.6	3.6	4.1	3.9	4.2	4.2	1.7
Mexico	−7.8	5.1	3.2	2.3	3.7	2.0	0.6
Nicaragua	3.6	2.4	4.0	2.9	2.5	2.4	1.7
Panama	−0.3	0.8	5.6	5.4	6.8	9.4	7.5
Paraguay	3.0	−5.3	2.1	0.9	2.4	4.9	3.1
Peru	6.8	1.6	3.9	5.5	6.3	7.6	8.2
Uruguay	−2.1	−1.8	11.9	6.6	6.8	7.2	11.2
Venezuela	1.8	1.8	16.2	8.4	8.5	6.6	3.1
Latin America	−1.2	2.5	4.7	3.5	4.3	4.3	3.3

*Annual rate of variation

**Preliminary figures

Source: ECLAC, 2008a

increased (see Table 15.5); the 2008–09 crisis is likely to return to poverty about a quarter of the 41 million people who had made their way out of it in recent years (UNDP, 2004b; ECLAC, 2009c; World Bank, 2009a).

Despite poverty reduction, high levels of *inequality* have persisted, and today, Latin American societies remain among the most unequal in the world when compared with other regions (see Table 4.6; and World Bank, 2009a). Inequality is measured as the gap between those with highest incomes and those with the lowest. Surveys indicate that, in Latin America, the richest 10 per cent of individuals receive between 32 and 47 per cent of total income while the poorest 10 per cent receive only between 0.5 to 2.6 per cent (*ibid.*). These levels of inequality in the region – with the richest 10 per cent of individuals in countries such as Haiti and Colombia, for example, accounting for 47.8 and 45.9 per cent of total income respectively – can be compared to the share of wealth among the richest 10 per cent of people in countries such as the UK (28.5 per cent) and Canada (24.8 per cent).

Nor did the neoliberal model provide the number of jobs required to reduce unemployment to levels that will have a significant impact on inequality (see Chapter 15). Today, youth unemployment remains a particularly serious problem

Table 4.5 Persons living in poverty and indigence in Latin America around 2002 and 2007, and 2008*

Country	Around 2002		Around 2007		2008	
	Poverty	Indigence	Poverty	Indigence	Poverty	Indigence
Argentina[1]	45.4	20.9	21.0	7.2	–	–
Bolivia	62.4	37.1	54.0	31.2	–	–
Brazil	37.5	13.2	30.0	8.5	25.8	7.3
Chile	20.2	5.6	13.7	3.2	–	–
Colombia[2]	51.5	24.8	46.8	20.2	42.8	22.9
Costa Rica	20.3	8.2	18.6	5.3	16.4	5.5
Ecuador[1]	49.0	19.4	38.8	12.4	39.0	14.2
El Salvador	48.9	22.1	47.5	19.0	–	–
Dominican Republic	47.1	20.7	44.5	21.0	44.3	22.6
Guatemala	60.2	30.9	54.8	29.1	–	–
Honduras	77.3	54.4	68.9	45.6	–	–
Mexico	39.4	12.6	31.7	8.7	34.8	11.2
Nicaragua	69.4	42.5	61.9	31.9	–	–
Panama	36.9	18.6	29.0	12.0	27.7	13.5
Paraguay	61.0	33.2	60.5	31.6	58.2	30.8
Peru[3]	54.7	24.4	39.3	13.7	36.2	12.6
Uruguay[1]	15.4	2.5	18.1	3.1	14.0	3.5
Venezuela	48.6	22.2	28.5	8.5	27.6	9.9

*percentages
Notes:
According to the ECLAC, a person is classified as 'poor' when the per capita income of that person's household is below the poverty line, i.e., the minimum income needed to meet a person's basic needs. In the case of indigence, the line is based on the cost of satisfying a person's food needs only.

1 Urban areas.

2 The data for 2008 came from a new household survey, which was applied with the earlier series by the National Administrative Department of Statistics (DANE) and the National Planning Department (DNP) of Colombia. Since ECLAC had yet to complete internal processing of the new data, the figures for 2008 were estimated in a preliminary manner by applying to the 2005 values (calculated by ECLAC) the percentage variations implicit in the figures officially issued.

3 Figures from the National Institute of Statistics and Informatics (INEI) of Peru. These values are not comparable to those of previous years owing to changes in the sample framework used in the household survey. In addition, the figures given for 2001 correspond to the fourth quarter, whereas those shown for 2006 and 2007 refer to the entire year.

Source: Adapted from ECLAC, 2009c, which was compiled on the basis of special tabulations of data from household surveys conducted at years in the relevant countries approximating those in the table

confronting the societies of Latin America, with one in four young people aged between 18 and 29 neither working nor studying, such that the problems that young people face were the special focus of the eighteenth Ibero-American Summit of Heads of State and Governments held in San Salvador in 2008. The problems of youth help to explain high levels of tension between young people and the rest of society (see Latinobarómetro, 2008). The UNDP (2004b) points out that the *quality* of employment in general in Latin America has diminished since the 1990s, and today large numbers of people work in the unregulated or 'informal' sector – that part

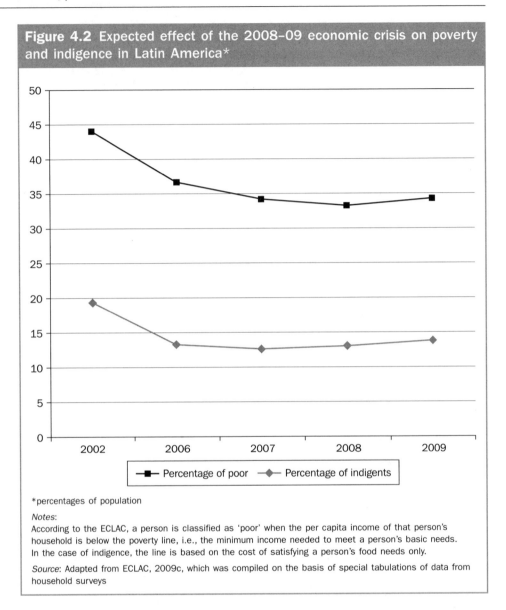

Figure 4.2 Expected effect of the 2008–09 economic crisis on poverty and indigence in Latin America*

*percentages of population

Notes:
According to the ECLAC, a person is classified as 'poor' when the per capita income of that person's household is below the poverty line, i.e., the minimum income needed to meet a person's basic needs. In the case of indigence, the line is based on the cost of satisfying a person's food needs only.

Source: Adapted from ECLAC, 2009c, which was compiled on the basis of special tabulations of data from household surveys

of the economy in which workers are not covered by insurance, welfare benefits or regulations (see Chapter 15).

Despite these bleak indicators, there is clear evidence that the sense of economic security among citizens in Latin America has been growing since the mid-2000s. Although there is volatility, Latinobarómetro data reveal a growing sense among people between 1996 and 2008 that economic prospects are improving at both a national and a personal level (see Figure 4.3).

Levels of economic insecurity may also be falling: after three years of growth, in 2008, more people than ever in the region reported feeling less fearful about becoming unemployed (Latinobarómetro, 2008). The impact of the 2008–09 financial crisis has once again pushed up the fear of unemployment.

Table 4.6 Distribution of income or consumption in Latin America c.2005–07*

Country	Survey year	Gini Index
Argentina	2005b	50.0
Bolivia	2005a	58.2
Brazil	2007b	55.0
Chile	2006b	52.0
Colombia	2006b	58.5
Costa Rica	2005b	47.2
Dominican Rep.	2006b	50.0
Ecuador	2007b	54.4
El Salvador	2005b	49.7
Guatemala	2006b	53.7
Haiti	2001b	59.5
Honduras	2006b	55.3
Mexico	2006a	48.1
Nicaragua	2005b	52.3
Panama	2006b	54.9
Paraguay	2007b	53.2
Peru	2006b	49.6
Uruguay	2006b	46.2
Venezuela	2006b	43.4
Canada	2000b	32.6
United Kingdom	1999b	36.0
United States	2000b	40.8

*And selected comparators.

Notes: Survey year is the year in which the underlying data were collected. 'a' refers to expenditure shares by percentiles of population, ranked by per capita expenditure; 'b' refers to income shares by percentiles of population, ranked by per capita income. Gini index measures the extent to which the distribution of income (or consumption expenditure) among individuals or households within an economy deviates from a perfectly equal distribution. A Lorenz curve plots the cumulative percentages of total income received against the cumulative number of recipients, starting with the poorest individual. The Gini index measures the area between the Lorenz curve and a hypothetical line of absolute equality, expressed as a percentage of the maximum area under the line. Thus a Gini index of 0 represents perfect equality, while an index of 100 implies perfect inequality.

Sources: World Bank, 2009a

However, these figures tell only part of the story. Across a range of indicators alongside high levels of poverty, inequality and unemployment – such as health and education provision – Latin American societies continue to suffer serious deficiencies. These worsen problems of poverty, making it more difficult to achieve the desired goals of progress and meaningful individual liberties.

The persistence of high levels of poverty and inequality in Latin America pose key questions about the relationship between economic development and democracy, and has prompted many scholars to reject the 'neo-modernisation' perspective. Critics argue that the minimum levels of economic development assumed to be necessary for sustaining democracy have generally not been present in the region, and so continuing poverty and inequality pose grave problems for democratic consolidation.

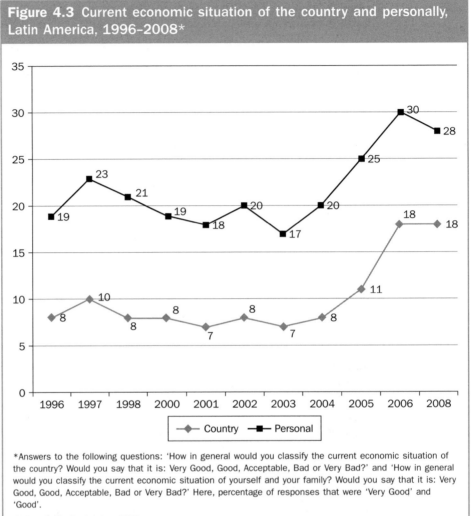

Figure 4.3 Current economic situation of the country and personally, Latin America, 1996–2008*

*Answers to the following questions: 'How in general would you classify the current economic situation of the country? Would you say that it is: Very Good, Good, Acceptable, Bad or Very Bad?' and 'How in general would you classify the current economic situation of yourself and your family? Would you say that it is: Very Good, Good, Acceptable, Bad or Very Bad?' Here, percentage of responses that were 'Very Good' and 'Good'.

Source: Latinobarómetro, 2008

This position derives from liberal theories of democracy, which suggest that there is a contradiction between a system based on the political equality of all citizens, and societies based on extremes of economic inequality. Oxhorn and Ducatenzeiler (1998), for example, challenge the notion that the liberalism underpinning economic reform – neoliberalism – is synonymous with democracy. Critics of the 'neo-modernisation' perspective argue that economic inequality *distorts* political equality and that a democratic system must include the majority of the country in the gains of growth if the system is to maintain public acceptance.

There is growing awareness that in Latin America the need to reduce inequality and consolidate a *meaningful* form of democracy are related. The UNDP (2004b) argues that thinking about democracy independent of economic questions is a mistake. It argues that the combination of political and economic freedom against a backdrop of poverty and inequality may not, in fact, lead to *either* stronger democracy or economic development. The UNDP maintains that only with more and *better* democracy can Latin American societies achieve greater equality and development. This is because only in a democracy can the poor and those who suffer most from inequality make claims and mobilise to improve their condition. In 2009, ECLAC argued in its *Social Panorama of Latin America* that perceptions of highly unfair income distribution are attributable primarily to the opinion among citizens that there is no basic social safety net and are related to distrust in political institutions and the belief that governments serve a privileged elite more than the majority (ECLAC, 2009c). It is these perceptions that continue to make inequality an important issue for democratic consolidation.

Summary

Significant political and economic challenges facing Latin America limit the quality of democracy in the region and pose problems for democratic consolidation (see Box 4.6). A lack of clarity about the scope of formal presidential powers, leading to excessively strong or weak presidents, generates conflict between executives and legislatures. High levels of dissatisfaction with political parties has limited their ability to represent the interests of citizens effectively, and parties are now often seen as obstacles to greater political participation. A lack of confidence in parties can, in turn, create the conditions for populism where a leader emerges outside the formal institutions of politics. Populists are tempted to break democratic rules and seek authoritarian solutions to problems.

Latin America is also plagued by weak judicial institutions, and this can foster corruption and a sense among politicians, government officials and law-enforcement officers that they can break laws with impunity. Weak judiciaries, ineffective law-enforcement and the impunity enjoyed by officials who break the law can exacerbate a lack of respect among citizens for life and property, fuelling crime, vigilantism and hence insecurity. Although the armed forces no longer threaten most democracies in Latin America directly, civil-military relations remain a key issue for consolidation, and the legal prerogatives enjoyed by the armed forces remain substantial in some countries and continue to influence democratic politics. An important debate in the study of democratisation concerns the role of economic factors in consolidation. The relationship between economic stability and political stability is important: there is evidence that the unfulfilled expectations of the population is among the factors that contribute to serious political crises. Democracy has had a limited impact on extreme poverty and severe inequality in Latin America, and this can make people question the value of democratic governance. Some scholars argue that the minimum levels of economic development necessary for sustaining democracy are not present in the region. However, there is also evidence that the sense of economic security among citizens has been growing. An important factor limiting the expansion of social and welfare policies as the region made its democratic transition were the economic constraints inherited from the previous era.

Challenges facing democracy

Political challenges

Presidentialism:

- Lack of clarity about presidential powers resulting in concentration of power or presidential weakness
- Corruption and excessive use of patronage
- Lack of a working majority in congress, fuelling conflict with legislators

Representation:

- Disenchantment with parties linked to corruption and economic dissatisfaction
- Growth of politics outside parties and partisan dealignment
- Lack of faith in the value of elections and abstention
- Populism, temptation of leaders to break rules and leapfrog institutions

Rule of law

- Endemic corruption
- Judicial systems that are neither independent nor effective
- Inequality within a legal process that favours the rich and powerful
- Lack of due process leading to miscarriages of justice
- Indifference by judicial and law enforcement agencies to human rights abuses
- Growth of vigilantism
- Corruption and lawless behaviour by state agents enjoying impunity
- Attitudes among citizens that exacerbate a lack of respect for life and property
- Establishment of quasi-legal systems outside the reach of the state

Civil–military relations

- Tensions over how democratic governments handle legacy of human rights abuses
- Continuation of military prerogatives that prevent civilian governments from exercising full constitutional authority
- *De facto* military autonomy in some areas
- Military missions that draw the armed forces into domestic functions

Economic challenges

- High levels of poverty and inequality
- Failure of neoliberal reforms to have an impact on poverty and inequality
- Unemployment, underemployment and financial insecurity
- Frustration about limited progress in improving living standards under democracy

Discussion points

■ Are strong presidencies in Latin America always bad for democracy?

■ To what extent do parties fulfil their role representing people in the region?

■ Why has populism been such a problem for democracy?

■ What factors best explain the weak rule of law in Latin America?

■ Do the armed forces pose a threat to democratic consolidation today?

■ Can Latin America be fully democratic with such high levels of inequality?

■ What has been the impact of neoliberal reform on democratic consolidation?

Useful websites

www.prd.org.mx Partido de la Revolución Democrática (PRD, Party of the Democratic Revolution), Mexico

www.pt.org.br Partido dos Trabalhadores (PT, Workers' Party), Brazil

http://acciondemocratica.org.ve Acción Democrática (AD, Democratic Action), Venezuela

www.psuv.org.ve Partido Socialista Unido de Venezuela (PSUV, United Socialist Party of Venezuela)

www.nadir.org/nadir/initiativ/mrta Movimiento Revolucionario Tupac Amaru (MRTA, Tupac Amaru Revolutionary Movement)

www.un.org/Depts/dpko/dpko/co_mission/minugua.htm United Nations verification mission in Guatamala, Misión de las Naciones Unidas para Guatemala (MINUGUA)

http://cicig.org United Nations-sponsored Comisión Internacional Contra la Impunidad en Guatemala (CICIG, International Commission against Impunity in Guatemala)

www.cidh.oas.org Organisation of American States' Inter-American Commission on Human Rights

www.idea.int International Institute for Democracy and Electoral Assistance (IDEA), Stockholm

www.alianzapais.com.ec Alianza PAIS (Patria Altiva I Soberana, PAIS Alliance), the party of Rafael Correa, the president of Ecuador

www.prian.org.ec Partido Renovador Institucional de Acción Nacional (PRIAN, Institutional Renewal Party of National Action), Ecuador

www.transparency.org Transparency International

www.freedomhouse.org Freedom House

www.oas.org/juridico/english OAS Department of Legal Affairs and Services, Office of Inter-American Law and Programmes

http://kellogg.nd.edu Kellogg Institute for International Studies at the University of Notre Dame, which promotes comparative international research with a core interest in Latin America

www.unodc.org/unodc/index.html United Nations Office on Drugs and Crime

www.wola.org Washington Office on Latin America human rights organisation

www.drogasedemocracia.org/English Latin American Initiative on Drugs and Democracy

www.justiceinitiative.org Open Society Justice Initiative

www.adc.org.ar La Asociación por los Derechos Civiles (Association for Civil Rights, ADC), Buenos Aires

Recommended reading

O'Donnell, Guillermo. 1992. *Delegative Democracy?* Working Paper 172, Helen Kellogg Institute. South Bend, IN: University of Notre Dame (see also: 1994. 'Delegative Democracy', *Journal of Democracy*, Vol. 5, No. 1 (January), pp. 55–70)

> *Essential work based on the Latin American experience setting out the case for a new species of democracy which can be contrasted with the representative democracy of developed capitalist countries*

Diamond, Larry, Marc F. Plattner and Diego Abente Brun. 2008. *Latin America's Struggle for Democracy.* Baltimore, MD: Johns Hopkins University Press and the National Endowment for Democracy

> *Essential overview of the key challenges facing the democracies in Latin America after a generation of reform*

Smith, William C. (ed.). 2009. *Latin American Democratic Transformations: Institutions, Actors, Processes.* Oxford: Wiley-Blackwell

> *Valuable and comprehensive introductory overview of the way in which Latin American societies seek to consolidate their democracies in adverse domestic and international circumstances that also examines the connections between democratic politics and neoliberal, market-oriented reforms*

Mendez, Juan, Guillermo O'Donnell and Paulo Sérgio Pinheiro (eds). 1999. *The (Un)Rule of Law and the Underprivileged in Latin America.* Notre Dame, IN: University of Notre Dame Press

> *Valuable collection examining the many different areas in which judicial processes in Latin America fail citizens, with a useful third section on issues of institutional reform*

Blake, Charles H. and Stephen D. Morris (eds). 2009. *Corruption and Democracy in Latin America.* Pittsburgh, PA: University of Pittsburgh Press

> *Valuable introduction to corruption in Latin America with a comparative focus that explores its negative impacts on democracy*

Haggard, Stephan and Robert R. Kaufman. 2008. *Development, Democracy, and Welfare States. Latin America, East Asia, and Eastern Europe.* Princeton, NJ: Princeton University Press

> *Useful exploration of the relationship between democracy and social policy in Latin America and other regions*

Chapter 5

The presidency

This chapter examines the presidency, the traditional source of formal power and of much of the imagery of strongmen, *caudillos* and charismatic populists that has come to characterise Latin America. The presidency stands at the apex of institutional politics in the region and builds upon centralist, authoritarian and even imperial traditions. Great symbolism is associated with the figure of the president, who is often seen as walking in the footsteps of patriotic legends such as Mexico's celebrated nineteenth-century president Benito Juárez (1861–63, 1867–72). The central position that presidents occupy in Latin American politics means that many of the institutional problems dogging the region derive from presidentialism, a type of system in which the president is always the chief executive. Most Latin American political systems conform to 'pure presidentialism', whereby the president is elected directly by the people so holding his or her own fixed electoral mandate separate to the fixed electoral mandate of the legislature (see Stepan and Skach, 1993); and whereby the president has the right to retain ministers of his or her choosing regardless of the composition of congress (see Mainwaring and Shugart, 1997). A mandate is the authority given by voters as the result of an election victory to a president or party to pursue certain policies or govern in a particular way, and so provides these with legitimacy.

One reason why political power has been concentrated in the presidency in Latin America is that presidentialism has long been interpreted by elites as a strong source of leadership over fractious societies that simultaneously embodies the idea of the 'state' (see Box 2.1), as opposed to being one component in a more complex *separation of powers* developed to avoid tyranny, as in the US. Some of the most successful presidents in Latin American history have been authoritarian centralists who resisted demands for checks and balances on their power. For this reason, Latin American executives comprising a president overseeing cabinet ministers have different relationships with legislatures and enjoy great influence over them. O'Donnell's notion of 'delegative democracy' (see Chapters 3, 4) characterised a type of exaggerated presidentialism, sometimes referred to as *hyper-presidentialism*, that is found in systems that are nominally democratic. However, there have been many clashes between different political actors in Latin America deriving from their different interpretations of the executive's role and powers. A key theme underlying literature on presidentialism since the 1990s has been how well it serves democratic stability (see Mainwaring, 1990). Philip (2003) argues that an important explanatory factor behind democratic non-consolidation is that Latin American

---

The voters decide – Brazil's 1993 referendum

In Brazil, a growing theme of debate after the transition of 1985 was about how to root democratic procedures in stable institutions. The Assembléia Nacional Constituinte (ANC, National Constituent Assembly), comprising both houses of congress, was convened in 1987–88 to rewrite the country's constitution. After first opting for a parliamentary system of government based on a mixed parliamentary-presidential model similar to that of Portugal, the ANC then backpedalled in favour of a presidential system, but one which was enhanced by giving the executive formidable temporary decree powers. Fierce disagreements between supporters of the presidential and parliamentary models were only resolved through a compromise by which it was agreed the issue and other momentous questions about the preferred form of government would be put to a referendum in 1993. Supporters and opponents of both options engaged the Brazilian public in this unique institutional debate through the press and on television in the run-up to the plebiscite, which the presidentialist forces won with 55 per cent of the vote against 25 per cent for those advocating a parliamentary system. The clear vote in favour of presidentialism came despite its poor record in Brazil in the years prior to the poll. Fernando Collor de Mello, Brazil's president from 1990 to 1992, was a political outsider who marginalised established parties, abused his decree powers to undertake draconian policies unilaterally without consulting congress, and was eventually impeached on corruption charges, although he was later declared not guilty of the allegations made against him. In 1991, Collor even intervened during senate deliberations to ratify the date of the referendum, thereby delaying the vote by a year, because he feared the 1992 date originally set would further damage his by then failing administration.

---

presidentialism has become a contested, hybrid system of government tending to generate conflict and mistrust (see Chapter 4). Nevertheless, when given the choice, Latin American voters prefer presidentialism over other systems (see Box 5.1).

Key characteristics of presidentialism

Presidentialism in Latin America has several distinguishing characteristics:

Winner takes all

Most presidential systems aim to ensure that the president gains a sufficient share of the vote to have a valid mandate, often through a second round of voting that gives the eventual winner clear democratic legitimacy. Whatever the share of the vote gained above a certain threshold, the victorious candidate takes over the *entire* executive branch and the losing candidate gains no stake in power whatsoever (Linz, 1994). This 'zero-sum' character of presidential elections can, in some cases, leave a majority of voters without representation, and in political systems in which there are many parties it can exacerbate polarisation (*ibid.*). In Chile, for example, the heterogeneous Unidad Popular (UP, Popular Unity) coalition led by Salvador

Allende (1970–73) gained a narrow plurality in presidential elections in 1970 with 36.2 per cent of the vote against 34.9 per cent for his main conservative rival. As a Marxist, Allende believed in the need to take radical steps to give workers much greater control over production and improve their conditions by nationalising private companies, redistributing land and expanding welfare provision. He embarked on an economic programme often described as revolutionary that generated bitter opposition from landowners, elements of the middle class, conservative politicians, the Church and the US, but also frustrated elements within UP who wanted to move further and faster against private property (see Sheahan, 1987; see also Chapter 12, Box 16.2). The result was political instability and economic crisis, and Allende's 'Chilean Road to Socialism' was cut short in the bloody military coup that brought Augusto Pinochet (1973–90) to power.

The winner-takes-all outcome can also give a president a sense of power and authority out of proportion to the size of his or her mandate. As we have seen, O'Donnell (1992) noted how presidentialism can favour delegative democracy emanating from the belief by whoever wins presidential elections that they can govern the country as they see fit. This plebiscitary character of presidential elections, the polarisation between the supporters of different candidates they can generate, and the appeals candidates often make outside of party politics frequently lead to high rates of approval for presidents at the start of a term but radical swings in support thereafter. In Peru, Alan García (1985–90, 2006–) enjoyed a 90 per cent approval rate when he began his first term of office, but this had fallen to 9 per cent by 1989. The personalised nature of presidential polls can also make the election of outsiders not identified with any party more possible, especially in the era of television (Linz, 1994; see also Box 8.11). The president's direct mandate can foster a propensity to identify closely with his or her voters and make constraints on exercising authority particularly frustrating (*ibid.*). As we have seen, autocratic presidentialism and a lack of confidence in parties can fuel populist forms of rule (see Chapters 2, 4). A president's power to appoint and dismiss a cabinet without congressional oversight can discourage independent-minded politicians from joining a cabinet, further limiting potential checks on presidential power (*ibid.*). The nature and timing of the presidential contest in relation to legislative elections can also influence the character of presidentialism; for example, Foweraker *et al.* (2003) argue that the rules governing the election of the executive influence the degree of presidential support in the assembly. The common combination in Latin America of a majoritarian election for president and election by proportional representation for congress can make it hard to build coalitions (Foweraker, 1998). This can be complicated by the detailed negotiations that sometimes take place over whether and how to hold elections in some Latin American countries, where legislators can often select from several electoral options (see Box 5.2).

Fixed terms

Linz (1994) argued that the fixed term presidents are elected for and the fact that this cannot normally be modified and is independent of the legislature can make presidential systems inflexible or 'rigid'. This means that the political process is

---

Argentina – the electoral menu

In Argentina during a political crisis in December 2001 that began with the resignation of President Fernando de la Rúa (1999–2001), the legislature faced a choice between three electoral options over how and whether to hold open elections the following March to pick a new executive. They could have chosen an election under the country's 'Lemas' law in which political parties are permitted to run several different candidates for president. Whoever wins the most votes is then credited with the votes of the rest of the bloc's candidates. The Peronists who controlled congress (i.e. the Partido Justicialista, PJ, Justicialist Party) favoured this method, which would have ensured them a greater share of the winning vote but would have needed the support in congress of other parties to get the two-thirds majority required to proceed with this type of election. Alternatively, legislators could have chosen to hold conventional open elections in March 2002 well before the end of De la Rúa's original term. The Peronists strongly resisted this option because it may have meant they would have suffered at the polls at a time of great disenchantment with politicians in general and because of their own internal divisions. Opposition parties, by contrast, lobbied for congress to call for open elections. Finally, legislators had the option of holding conventional elections at the end of De La Rúa's original term in December 2003, with the candidate winning the most votes becoming president. This was the option Argentina's legislature chose, allowing the Peronist Eduardo Duhalde (2002–03) to form a caretaker government and giving him time to take the first steps towards resolving the country's deep economic crisis prior to the polls.

---

governed solely by the duration of the presidential term, making adjustments to changing situations difficult. Fixed-term limits can also tempt an incumbent to seek extensions through constitutional change or provoke congresses to attempt to cut them short. Popular presidents have often sought extensions to their term. During the 1990s, for example, presidential terms were lengthened in Argentina, Peru, Venezuela, Ecuador and Brazil. At the same time, unpopular presidents have often faced premature removal from office. If there are no mechanisms to make extension or curtailment possible, frustrated actors might seek extra-constitutional or illegal means to lengthen or shorten presidential terms, putting democracy at risk.

No re-election

The principle of no re-election is common in Latin America and often has symbolic importance because of memories of past dictatorships. Some countries allow no immediate re-election, some allow immediate re-election but limit the presidency to two terms, and some allow candidates to stand again after a hiatus of one or two terms. It has become common since democratisation for presidents to seek constitutional changes that allow them to be re-elected. In 2004, for example, Colombia's conservative president Álvaro Uribe successfully sought a congressional amendment to the country's 1991 constitution that allowed him to run for a second term as president despite having disagreed with the idea of consecutive re-election during his campaign. He was re-elected as president in 2006. In Venezuela in 2009, President Hugo Chávez (1999–) won a referendum to eliminate presidential term limits that would prevent him from running for office in 2012. The suspicion that the Honduran president Manuel Zelaya (2006–09) wanted to end restrictions on re-election by rewriting the constitution was at the heart of a dispute with congress, the judiciary and the military that led to the coup that removed him in June 2009.

No re-election has the potential for generating certain patterns of behaviour. For an incumbent, it can encourage a sense of urgency leading to ill-designed policies, impatience with the opposition and political conflict or rapid spending (Linz, 1994). A president who cannot be re-elected cannot be held to account because voters will not get another chance to judge his or her performance at the polls. The desire for continuity may also encourage a president to seek a successor who will not challenge them while in office. If a president is prohibited from immediate re-election, but can run again after an interim period there can be tense relations between an incumbent and their predecessor. Conflicts between presidents and vice-presidents have also been frequent. In Paraguay in 1999, for example, President Raúl Cubas (1998–99) became involved in a bitter dispute with his vice-president, Luis María Argaña, whom he accused of trying to depose him amid efforts to launch impeachment proceedings against him. The political infighting split the ruling Colorado party which both men belonged to, with rival factions supporting Cubas and Argaña. In March 1999, Argaña was assassinated on his way to his office in Asunción. Paraguay's congress and most of civil society subsequently laid much of the blame for Argaña's death on Cubas and powerful allies of his, and the president resigned following street demonstrations.

Dual legitimacy

A key characteristic of presidentialism in Latin America is 'dual legitimacy' – the simultaneous democratic legitimacy of both president and congress and the source of many of the problems associated with presidentialism (Linz, 1994). Both the president and the legislature enjoy legitimacy because both are elected and it is always possible for both to point to their popular mandates, especially when they are at loggerheads. The potential for political conflict is latent in this system, particularly if the majority in the legislature represents voters that did not support the president. For example, Bolivia's president, Carlos Mesa (2003–05), was elected as an independent who was not a member of a political party and did not enjoy good relations with congress but at the time retained support among the public, with polls showing him enjoying the backing of 50 per cent of citizens.

Presidential powers

As chief executive, commander in chief of the armed forces and head of state, the Latin American president enjoys extensive power. Cox and Morgenstern (2002) examined two main categories of formal executive powers: *unilateral powers* and *integrative powers*.

Unilateral powers are those that can be used independently without the concurrence of the legislature or those that are used to change existing policy, and include decree powers, the ability to interpret and issue regulations in order to implement a general law, the authority to appoint ministers, judges and other officials, and the right to initiate bills and referendums. In Latin America, draft legislation is mostly introduced by the executive, who appoints and controls the cabinet. Latin American presidents routinely make policy decisions unilaterally and many have the ability to structure the budget, as legislatures are not, in most cases, constitutionally empowered to make significant changes (*ibid.*; see Box 5.3). In much of Latin America presidents have the right to make laws through decrees, a power largely distinct to this region which can include the ability to declare a 'state of emergency' giving them extensive emergency powers. Presidential powers to interpret and issue regulations that set out the applicability of legislation are not, in general, subject to judicial review (see Chapter 6). Where judges have ruled on presidential decisions, they have sometimes come under attack from the executive. In Argentina in 2002, for example, the supreme court declared aspects of the government's economic policy illegal, but President Eduardo Duhalde (2002–03) delayed implementing their decision while pressing congress to impeach the court.

INSTITUTIONS   **Box 5.3**

Outfoxed by congress

In December 2004, Mexico's supreme court froze spending on disputed infrastructure projects pending a final ruling on an intense dispute over the 2005 federal budget between congress and President Vicente Fox (2000–06), who had been embroiled in serious disagreements with legislators over the interpretation of his powers since taking office. Fox belonged to the conservative Partido Acción Nacional (PAN, National Action Party) and, since 2003, Mexico's congress had been dominated by the Partido Revolucionario Institucional (PRI, Institutional Revolutionary Party) the main opposition party, although no party had a majority.

Fox presented his budget in November 2004 and congressmen from the PRI and the left-of-centre Partido de la Revolución Democrática (PRD, Party of the Democratic Revolution) then decided to reallocate funds to projects they supported at the expense of funding for federal ministries. Fox criticised the decision, questioned their right to make it and then returned the budget to congress with 'observations'. Congress voted to reject the changes that Fox had proposed, which he said was the first time in history it had ever done so, triggering his constitutional challenge in the courts. It was the first time Mexico's supreme court had ever been called on to adjudicate in such a serious dispute between the executive and legislative branches. The separation of powers between executive and legislature had never been tested during the seven decades in which the PRI dominated all the branches of government in Mexico.

The main constitutional issues in dispute were whether the president had veto power over the budget; if so, whether this allowed rejection of specific parts of it; and whether congress had encroached on the executive's role. The supreme court was asked to intervene because it was not clear whether the president's veto power over legislation applied to the budget. Fox complained to the court that congress had encroached on the powers of the executive by introducing several new measures in the budget, and that he had the right to veto specific budget items. The court ruled by just six votes to five in May 2005 in favour of the president's power to veto the federal budget passed by congress, but a subsequent ruling confirmed that a two-thirds majority in congress could still overturn that veto.

The outcome of this constitutional confrontation was seen as important for the future of Mexico's democracy by establishing the basis for a clearer relationship between the three powers – executive, legislature and judiciary – and ultimately influencing whether Mexico would evolve as a presidential or as a parliamentary system. Fox himself said that, whatever the outcome, the constitutional dispute would strengthen democratic consolidation in Mexico. As it happened, the court's resolution singularly *failed* to clarify the separation of powers, and disputes over the 2005 budget dragged on until late in that year. None the less, the dispute underlined the declining power of the Mexican executive in the context of democratic reform. The presidency had contributed significantly to past authoritarianism by centralising power so much that the office was characterised as a form of dictatorship. A significant proportion of presidential power was informal (see above), that is, discretionary and non-institutional. Although the statutory constitutional powers of the executive were fairly restricted, the role of the president was greatly exaggerated by nationalism (see Chapter 13) and single-party rule, and under the PRI the executive gained an array of informal powers giving the individual in office great latitude to define both major policy initiatives and the extent of executive activities more broadly, and to subordinate the legislative and judicial branches. Informal presidential power rested in large part on the PRI's unassailable majority in congress, maintained mainly through electoral manipulation. However, Fox's tenure demonstrated the dramatic erosion of presidential authority that once derived from these informal powers. Fox ended the PRI's monopoly on power and gained a significant mandate to rule, but did not enjoy an absolute majority in either house and, therefore, did not enjoy the informal powers of previous presidents. One reflection of Fox's waning authority was the popularity of an unprecedented television satire in 2005, *El Privilegio de Mandar* (*The Privilege of Leading*), that portrayed the administration as paralysed by internecine strife over who would succeed him.

Integrative powers are those that allow the president to determine the policy agenda in the legislature by prioritising bills or empowering allies in congress. In particular, *urgency provisions* allow the executive to shape legislative agendas by forcing an assembly to deal with presidential requests quickly, and presidents also have extensive *veto powers*. In Chile or Uruguay, for example, if the executive declares a bill urgent, the legislature must make a decision about it within a specified period and in some cases inaction converts the bill into law. Shugart and Carey (1992) found significant variation in the use of these presidential powers across Latin America. When various measures of presidents' non-legislative and legislative prerogatives which allow an overall assessment of formal presidential powers are brought together, they reveal that presidents in Brazil, Chile and Ecuador enjoy high formal powers in regional terms, while those in Colombia, Guatemala and Venezuela have low formal powers (see Table 5.1). However, although a presidency may enjoy formidable powers on paper, officeholders are not always in a position to use these. In Chile, for example, although General Augusto Pinochet (1973–90) created a strong executive, the dictator's successors have held back from using the full powers available to them (Siavelis, 2002). Traditionally, Latin American presidents have also enjoyed significant *informal* powers that go beyond what is determined in

Table 5.1 Overall presidential powers*

Country	Index of formal presidential powers**	
Argentina	0.41	Medium high***
Bolivia	0.37	Medium low
Brazil	0.56	Very high
Chile	0.58	Very high
Colombia	0.29	Very low
Costa Rica	0.36	Medium low
Dominican Rep.	0.44	Medium high
Ecuador	0.55	Very high
El Salvador	0.42	Medium high
Guatemala	0.27	Very low
Honduras	0.38	Medium low
Mexico	0.37	Medium high
Nicaragua	0.38	Medium low
Panama	0.46	Medium high
Paraguay	0.34	Medium low
Peru	0.31	Medium low
Uruguay	0.38	Medium low
Venezuela	0.25	Very low

*2002

**General index of formal presidential powers is based on an average of non-legislative powers (given a score assigned according to the capacity of the legislature to cast a vote of censorship [censure] on the Cabinet and the capacity of the executive to dissolve the national legislature, standardised between zero and one) and legislative powers (weighted average).

***The level of any of these powers is assessed from a comparative regional perspective: 'Medium high' means that its score falls between the regional average and one positive standard deviation, etc.

Sources: UNDP, 2004b, based on: Shugart and Carey, 1992; Mainwaring and Shugart, eds, 1997; Carey and Shugart, eds, 1998; Samuels, 2000; Altman, 2001, 2002; Payne *et al.*, 2002; Georgetown University and the Organisation of American States, 2002

constitutions. They have an unparalleled ability to tap into party, military and business networks and can wield extensive influence by dispensing patronage. They often have unrivalled access to the media and hence the ability to generate public pressure in their favour.

Interrupted presidencies

In April 2005, Ecuador's president Lucio Gutiérrez (2003–05) was forced to seek refuge in the Brazilian embassy in Quito before fleeing his country and seeking asylum in Brazil four days after congress had dismissed him amid massive popular protests (see Box 6.2). Gutiérrez became the third Ecuadorean president since 1997 driven from office in this way. Within less than a year, violent nationwide demonstrations and strikes shook the presidency of his successor, Alfredo Palacio

(2005–07), prompting warnings in March 2006 that the country was at risk of a military coup. Rafael Correa became president in 2007 after winning elections. The turbulence that rocked Ecuador exemplifies the instability that can characterise the presidential regimes of Latin America, which have often been interrupted by crises, sometimes threatening democracy. The most recent example of an interrupted presidency was the removal of the Honduran president, Manuel Zelaya, in a coup that cut short his term in June 2009.

Valenzuela (2004) examined presidencies 'interrupted' before the expiry of their full term in the recent democratic era. Not only have many presidents left office with low approval ratings and few achievements, but on many occasions presidents have failed to complete their constitutionally prescribed terms and resigned or been removed early through impeachment based on formal accusations of wrongdoing or a coup, often in circumstances that threaten democratic stability (see Table 5.2, Box 7.10). Impeachment is a difficult last resort in Latin American politics and fraught with hazards for legislators who go down this route. It is often only where a president faces a backdrop of widespread popular opposition, as in the case of Gutiérrez in Ecuador, that legislators will be willing to impeach.

In most of the interrupted presidencies, presidents left office in response to a severe economic and political crisis either because they had performed badly or they were forced out after taking steps that threatened democratic rule, public unrest and disorder. In Ecuador, the removal of Gutiérrez in 2005 followed all the above elements: massive street protests fuelled by discontent over economic austerity policies approved by the IMF; anger at the president's interference in judicial independence; and the alienation of congress when he authorised the use of force to quell discontent. Military, congressional and judicial critics of Manuel Zelaya in Honduras claimed that he was taking steps that represented a threat to the democratic order, and that his removal was legal. When the military arrested Zelaya, they were acting on an arrest order issued by the supreme court, although his removal has been described as a coup because he was then taken to Costa Rica.

Two key factors can help to explain the breakdown of presidencies. First, presidents in Latin America can be placed under great pressure by protest movements because they are seen as the main source of power in the political system (*ibid.*). Protests against presidential policies raise the stakes in politics, because they can rapidly turn from unhappiness about a specific grievance into a protest against the perceived failure of the incumbent, thereby turning a government crisis into a constitutional crisis. Recurrent targets of protests against presidential policies have been measures taken to stabilise or reform the economy, and presidencies have frequently been interrupted amid serious protests against their economic policies. In 2003, for example, President Gonzalo Sánchez de Lozada (1993–97, 2002–03) fled Bolivia after 67 people died in the 'gas war', a month of protests led by the indigenous majority over plans to develop the country's gas reserves by exporting the fuel through Chile. In 2009, Sánchez de Lozada and members of his cabinet went on trial on charges of being responsible for the deaths in the city of El Alto. The presidency of Carlos Mesa (2003–05), who succeeded Sánchez de Lozada, was seriously weakened by recurrent protests demanding lower fuel prices, increases in taxes levied on foreign oil corporations, and a campaign for regional autonomy by the country's wealthiest region, and he also resigned amid crisis in 2005. According

Table 5.2 Interrupted presidencies in Latin America*

Country	President	Inaugurated	Resigned*	Explanation
Argentina	Raúl Alfonsín	1983	1989	President Alfonsín resigned five months before a scheduled transfer of power amid economic crisis and protests
	Fernando de la Rúa	1999	2001	President de la Rúa resigned amid economic crisis, civil disorder and corruption allegations
	Adolfo Rodríguez Saá	2001	2001	President Rodríguez Saá was in office for just one week during Argentina's political crisis and resigned in a dispute with members of his own Justicialist party
Bolivia	Hernán Siles Zuazo	1982	1985	President Siles Zuazo resigned by agreement amid economic crisis, widespread civil disorder, and corruption allegations
	Gonzalo Sánchez de Lozada	2002	2003	President Sánchez de Lozada resigned and fled to the US amid widespread violent civil disorder
	Carlos Mesa	2003	2005	President Mesa was unable to control escalating civil unrest over a range of issues that crystallised around energy taxes and resigned
Brazil	Fernando Collor de Mello	1990	1992	President Collor resigned amid impeachment proceedings, economic crisis, protests, and corruption allegations
Dominican Republic	Joaquín Balaguer	1994	1996	President Balaguer agreed to cut short his term after his election was marred by fraud allegations provoking mass protests
Ecuador	Abdalá Bucaram	1996	1997	President Bucaram resigned amid economic crisis, corruption allegations and conflicts with congress. Impeached
	Jamil Mahuad	1998	2000	President Mahuad resigned amid protests by indigenous groups and corruption allegations following a military ultimatum
	Lucio Gutiérrez	2002	2005	President Gutiérrez was dismissed by congress amid popular protests over economic policy and clashes, then sought refuge in the Brazilian embassy
Guatemala	Jorge Serrano	1991	1993	President Serrano resigned after a failed *auto-golpe* amid conflicts with congress over economic crisis
Haiti	Jean-Bertrand Aristide	i. 1990 ii. 2000	1991 2004	President Aristide was deposed in a coup in 1991. His 2000 election was marred by fraud allegations. He resigned in 2004 amid a rebellion and corruption allegations
Honduras	Manuel Zelaya	2006	2009	President Zelaya was deposed by the military in a coup following a dispute over plans for a referendum on calling a constituent assembly
Paraguay	Raúl Cubas	1998	1999	President Cubas resigned amid political divisions and protests following the assassination of his vice president
Peru	Alberto Fujimori	2000	2000	President Fujimori resigned amid conflicts with congress, allegations of electoral fraud and corruption, and protests
Venezuela	Carlos Andrés Pérez	1989	1993	President Pérez resigned amid economic crisis, military unrest and corruption allegations. Impeached

*Or deposed

Sources: Adapted from Valenzuela, 2004; updated from news reports

to Bolivia's constitution, the senate speaker, Hormando Vaca Diez, should have automatically taken over from Mesa, but he refused the job as protesters unhappy about the prospect of his leadership blockaded a session of congress to prevent his appointment. The next in line, the head of Bolivia's lower chamber, also indicated that he did not want the presidential job, meaning that it then passed to the head of Bolivia's supreme court, Eduardo Rodríguez (2005–06), who was subsequently sworn in as president. Presidential and congressional elections – originally scheduled for June 2007 – were brought forward to December 2005, and were won by Evo Morales (2006–), who had led many of the protests.

Second, Latin American presidencies are often bedevilled by the lack of a legislative majority. Kenney (2000) argued that between 1960 and 1997, for example, the president's lack of a supportive majority in the legislature came close to being a necessary condition for the breakdown of democracy (see Table 5.3).

A key factor determining the character of presidentialism in Latin America is the relationship between the executive and the legislature (see Jones, 2002). Conflicts between presidents and congresses have been common. In Mexico, for example, President Vicente Fox (2000–06) was embroiled in serious disputes with the legislature over the interpretation of his powers during his term of office (see Box 5.3).

In Ecuador, President Abdalá Bucaram (1996–97) was removed from office after congress charged him with 'mental incapacity', and Lucio Gutiérrez was dismissed by congress in 2005 after sanctioning heavy-handed tactics by security forces against protests over his economic policy. When Alfredo Palacio (2005–07) was sworn in as the new president, he immediately issued an arrest warrant for his predecessor who had fled the country. However, Palacio himself fell out with Ecuador's congress in his efforts to engineer political reform. In December 2005, he was forced

Table 5.3 Legislative majorities and economic failure in cases of democratic breakdowns,* 1960–93

Country	President	Years	Legislative majority	Loss of GDP/capita
Argentina	Arturo Illia	1963–66	✗	✔
	Isabel M. de Perón	1974–76	✗	✔
Brazil	João Goulart	1961–64	✗	✔
Chile	Salvador Allende	1970–73	✗	✔
Dominican Republic	Juan Bosch	1963	✔	✗
Ecuador	José María Velasco	1960–61	✗	✗
	José María Velasco	1968–70	✗	✗
Guatemala	Jorge Serrano	1991–93	✗	✗
Haiti	Jean-Bertrand Aristide	1991	✗	✔
Panama	Arnulfo Arias	1968	✔	✗
Peru	Fernando Belaúnde	1963–68	✗	✗
	Alberto Fujimori	1990–92	✗	✔
Uruguay	Juan María Bordaberry	1972–73	✗	✗

*Including both military and presidential coups ('*auto-golpes*')

Source: Adapted from Kenney, 2000

to abandon attempts to call a referendum on re-writing the constitution without going through the legislature. The move was denounced by congress and some legislators pledged to seek Palacio's impeachment.

The election of legislatures by proportional representation often means the executive does not have a working majority in congress, without which his or her initiatives can be blocked. Lack of congressional support and infighting were a key factor in the succession of five presidents over a two-week period during Argentina's political crisis in December 2001 (see Box 5.4). However, other factors can contribute to the poor performance of a minority president such as the policy position of the president's own party, the president's capacity to sustain a veto, and the legislative strength of the parties included in the cabinet (see Negretto, 2006).

Legislatures have been able to impose various limitations on presidential power and some, such as that of Mexico, have become much more assertive in recent years, directly challenging executive initiatives (see Box 5.3). In Argentina, the legislature has frustrated the executive's policy priorities, at times simply by failing to convene (Mustapic, 2002). In Brazil, weak presidents such as Collor de Mello often relied on decree powers to avoid legislative obstacles, but presidents have

---

| CASE STUDY | Box 5.4 |

Argentina – Five presidents in two weeks

During December 2001 two Argentine presidents, Fernando de la Rúa and Adolfo Rodríguez Saa, were forced to resign in close succession due to lack of political support from congress, provincial governors and the population. De la Rúa, the leader of the centre-left Unión Cívica Radical (UCR, Radical Civic Union), resigned on December 21 amid violent street demonstrations against his economic policies after serving two years of a four-year term. His government collapsed mainly because he had lacked support in congress – both houses of which were dominated after elections in October 2001 by the opposition Peronists – and among provincial governors. Peronist leaders in congress had refused to back his economic policies and Peronist governors had refused to accept central government requests to cut their spending. Moreover, De la Rúa could not generate consistent support within the coalition that had brought him to power in 1999 – leftwing groups in the coalition and even members of his own party had opposed his free-market policies. Powerbrokers within the Partido Justicialista (PJ, Justicialist Party i.e. the Peronists) settled upon Rodríguez Saa, the governor of the small state of San Luis, as a temporary leader to manage a caretaker government before new elections. However, Rodríguez Saa resigned on 30 December, saying lack of support from members of his own party had prevented him from leading the country out of its crisis. Following his resignation, the senate leader Ramón Puerta, who technically had been in line to take office and had already briefly served as acting president for 48 hours following De la Rúa's resignation, immediately resigned his leadership post to avoid being forced to reassume the executive position. That left the Peronist chamber of deputies leader, Eduardo Camaño, to take over on 31 December as a provisional president, again for 48 hours. On 2 January 2002, the Peronist senator Eduardo Duhalde was sworn in after being chosen during an emergency session of congress to complete De la Rúa's original term, lasting until 10 December 2003. Duhalde became the country's fifth president in two weeks.

not always been free to use decrees without restrictions and Brazil's legislature has the power to reject decrees and to prevent presidents reissuing them (Carey and Shugart eds, 1998; Amorim Neto, 2002a).

The strategies adopted by a president will depend on the type of legislature he or she has to deal with. Cox and Morgenstern (2002) argue that a 'central oscillation' in Latin American politics is the president's changing use of constitutional powers in response to changes in anticipated assembly support: when a president is weaker in congress, he or she typically resorts more frequently to unilateral powers, and when stronger, he or she tends to rely on integrative powers. In Argentina, for example, President Carlos Menem (1989–99) could not rely on the consistent support of his own Peronist deputies in congress and so pushed the limits of his constitutionally defined powers, seeking only enough support in the assembly to prevent his decrees being overridden. Presidents with a stronger political base in congress and with weaker institutional power to follow a unilateral strategy often aim to govern through, rather than around, the assembly.

Obstructions caused by legislatures have often tempted presidents to seek new powers through constitutional reforms, to resort to ruling by decree or to undertake 'self-coups' (*auto-golpes*) in which they suspend constitutions and assume direct rule, sometimes with the support of the armed forces. This was done by President Alberto Fujimori (1990–2000) in Peru in 1992 and attempted by President Jorge Serrano (1991–93) in Guatemala in 1993. Latin American presidents have also often reacted against legislatures they accused of being obstructive, corrupt or inefficient, by seeking to govern without involving them or to marginalise their role in the policymaking process. In Venezuela, for example, President Hugo Chávez sidestepped congress by organising a plebiscite to create a constituent assembly that eventually subsumed the existing legislature (see Boxes 4.2, 7.2). Some presidencies have even been accused of resorting to bribery to get their way. In Peru in September 2009, in a fourth trial of a range of charges against him, Fujimori was convicted of bugging and bribing opposition politicians, journalists and businessmen as part of a scandal that brought down his government in 2000.

Given the importance of conflicts and co-operation between the executive and the legislature in determining the character of presidentialism in Latin America, it is helpful to distinguish different types of relationship between these institutions. Based on their relationships with legislatures, Cox and Morgenstern (2002) proposed a typology of the presidencies that can be found in the region:

- Imperial presidency. The imperial president confronts an assembly that will reject their proposals and refuse to compromise, and so employs *unilateral* powers.
- Dominant presidency. The dominant president believes the assembly is subservient and will accept most of their proposals without bargaining. Congress may be subservient because the president has previously established their dominance through the control of nominations etc.
- Coalitional presidency. The coalitional president enjoys the co-operation of a workable assembly in which they head a coalition, and uses some payoffs to clinch deals but not as a main bargaining technique. The president seeks to implement policy through statutes using their *integrative* powers, and consults

legislative allies about the strategy for getting these passed, involving the assembly more closely in policymaking.

■ Nationally oriented presidency. A president faced with an assembly whose members seek payoffs and patronage may respond with 'pork-barreling' – buying the support of individual legislators through policymaking that supports benefits for that legislator's locale. In return, the legislature hands the president extensive authority over national policy by granting the executive decree powers to use as they see fit.

A key variable in the relationship between executives and legislatures is the extent of presidential support in the assembly. Effective presidential government requires either a working majority, or at least significant support, and the greater the backing a president has in the legislature, the less the likelihood of conflict. More enduring presidential democracies such as those of Colombia, Costa Rica and Uruguay have generally been those in which presidents have enjoyed majorities or near majorities. However, these are exceptions and few Latin American presidents have enjoyed majority support: of the interrupted presidencies mentioned above (Table 5.2), only three had come into office on the strength of absolute majorities won in a single round of voting (Aristide in Haiti, Pérez in Venezuela and Cubas in Paraguay). Kenney (2000) argues that between 1960 and 1997, 48 out of the 73 presidencies that began and ended in Latin America (65.8 per cent) lacked a legislative majority during part or all of their terms in office. A study by Payne *et al.* (2002) of 18 Latin American countries from 1978 to 2000 found that an incumbent enjoyed majority legislative support in only about one out of every four presidential terms covered. A key explanation for the breakdown of presidencies has been this absence of a legislative majority. In Bolivia, for example, the decision by the centre-right Nueva Fuerza Republicana (NFR, New Republican Force) to leave the fragile governing multi-party coalition supporting the centre-right president Sánchez de Lozada in October 2003, amid serious social unrest, deprived his administration of his working majority in congress and was the key factor leading to his resignation. Sánchez de Lozada had taken office in August 2002 with less than 25 per cent of the popular vote, and had lacked the congressional backing and popular support to govern by consensus. Similarly in Honduras, Zelaya had taken office in 2006 with only 25 per cent of the vote following an election in which turnout had been just 50 per cent (Latinobarómetro, 2009a). Zelaya's relations with congress were then greatly strained following his decision to issue a decree organising a poll on whether voters wanted to change the terms of general elections later that year to include a question about convening a constituent assembly.

Where presidents are weak, it is often because of the difficulties they face building coalitions in systems that lack strong political parties (see Chapter 6). Many presidents lacking an initial majority form coalitions in which different parties join together to support legislative initiatives as a bloc in congress or to be represented in the cabinet. Coalitions are common in Latin American government but many factors can work against successful coalition-building – from the motives of individual legislators to the reluctance of presidents to share authority with their coalition partners. Nor, as Valenzuela (2004) points out, is strong representation by the president's own party or allies in congress a guarantee of presidential success. A president may have a bad relationship with rival powerbrokers within his own party and problems dealing with them, such as Carlos Andrés Pérez during his second term as president of Venezuela from 1989–93, whose colleagues in the ruling Acción Democrática (AD, Democratic Action) grew resentful of his failure to consult them about policy and his autocratic style (see Box 4.2). Pérez's own party all but abandoned him following two coup attempts and, as unrest and corruption allegations against him mounted, he was impeached in 1993.

When coalition-building can create a presidential majority, the executive enjoys greater authority. In Brazil, the government of Fernando Henrique Cardoso (1995–2002) implemented radical reforms and a constitutional reform to allow re-election of the president. The failure to forge effective coalitions has often resulted in instability. In Ecuador, for example, it contributed to the downfall in 2000 of President Jamil Mahuad (1998–2000) who was forced to leave office by the army and indigenous protesters, becoming the first elected Latin American leader overthrown by the military since the Haitian president Jean-Bertrand Aristide was toppled in 1991. The lack of coherent party support in Ecuador's congress for Gutiérrez was also a key factor in his downfall in 2005 (see Box 6.2). Opposition to Zelaya's plans for a vote on whether a constituent assembly should be convened from within his own Partido Liberal de Honduras (Liberal Party, PLH) considerably weakened his position prior to the coup that removed him from power.

Presidentialism versus parliamentarianism, and semi-presidential systems

The pros and cons of presidentialism have long been debated in Latin America and scholars have been divided over the merits of presidential versus parliamentary systems (parliamentarianism). In a parliamentary system, the executive branch or head of government is not directly elected and is dependent on the support of the legislative branch, which can remove him or her through a vote of confidence. As a result, there is no clear separation of powers between the executive and legislature, and critics argue that this means fewer checks and balances on power than in a presidential system. However, parliamentary regimes have tended to be more stable than presidential regimes, a factor that can seem attractive in Latin America where presidencies have often been interrupted and democracy put at risk. It has even been argued that Latin America faces a choice between loyalty to the presidential tradition and hopes for full democratic consolidation (Valenzuela, 2004).

Linz and Valenzuela have been prominent in debates about presidentialism and potential alternatives to it (see Linz and Valenzuela eds, 1994; and Valenzuela, 2004). Linz (1994) has argued that presidentialism generates more political problems than parliamentarianism because it tends to encourage conflict not consensus, resulting in instability. Valenzuela believes arguments against moving away from presidentialism lie in the appeal of tradition and, given weak parties and legislatures, in the fear that parliamentarianism would lead to even greater instability. Comparisons between these systems have concentrated on several issues:

Dismissal

In presidential systems, the head of government is not chosen by the legislature and does not depend on the electoral success of supporters in the assembly to remain in office. The president not only holds executive power but is the symbolic head of state and cannot be removed by the legislature, except through impeachment proceedings initiated by a formal accusation of wrongdoing. Impeachment has become the main constitutional instrument employed by civilian elites in Latin America to depose rulers, but does not always succeed: lawful attempts at impeachment failed to remove presidents in both Paraguay in 2002 and Ecuador in 2004, for example (see Pérez-Liñán, 2010). Presidentialism tends to lessen the need for voting cohesion in the legislature and vests the power over its agenda with the leaders of parties in congress, especially the majority (Cox and Morgenstern, 2002). In parliamentary systems, the prime minister as the head of government is chosen by those controlling the legislature and can be dismissed through a vote of no confidence. This tends to result in the need for greater voting cohesion in the legislature and to give ministers greater control over the legislative agenda (*ibid.*).

Legitimacy, accountability and representativeness

In presidential systems, it is possible for the leaders of both executive and legislative branches of government to make claims about their own legitimacy based upon rival mandates. In parliamentary systems, the *only* institution with democratic legitimacy is the legislative assembly and the government is *responsible* to parliament, so there is no basis for a conflict of legitimation (Linz, 1994). It has been argued that presidentialism is, in fact, more accountable both because voters know exactly who they will get if the candidate they vote for wins the election and because the executive is personally responsible for policies, while in parliamentary systems it may not be known whom a winning party will choose to be prime minister. However, there is no mechanism for holding the executive to account in Latin America where, in general, presidents cannot be re-elected (*ibid.*). In parliamentary systems, it is easier for voters to hold a party to account at the next election. As a result, if a president suffers from weak legitimacy yet cannot be dismissed by a weak parliament, citizens may feel forced to take matters into their own hands. For example, questions about legitimacy dogged Haiti's president, Jean-Bertrand Aristide (1991, 1993–94, 1994–96, 2001–04), following controversial elections in 2000, contributing eventually to several coup attempts and violent anti-government protests that grew into a full-scale rebellion and forced him into exile in 2004.

Leadership, certainty and effective decisionmaking

It is often argued that presidentialism provides strong leadership and fixed terms reduce the *uncertainty* of parliamentary systems (which are disadvantaged by having many actors and potential realignments), and that the president's right to appoint and dismiss cabinet members without congressional input makes for decisive policymaking. However, presidential candidates are sometimes chosen through political *compromises*, and parliamentary systems are better at generating and preparing potential future leaders (*ibid.*). Once in power, an obstructive congress can make strong presidential leadership difficult. The rigidity of the presidential term can make it hard to adjust to changing situations, and a parliament's inherent flexibility may in fact be better suited to dealing with crises.

Given the problems associated with presidentialism, scholars have discussed the merits of *semi-presidential* systems that represent a halfway house between presidentialism and parliamentarianism (see Box 5.5). Parliamentary and semi-presidential systems were discussed in Latin America during the transition to democracy (see Box 5.1), but no existing presidential system has ever changed to a parliamentary system (Shugart and Carey, 1992).

Regardless of alternatives on offer, the difficulties generated by presidentialism have led to constitutional and *de facto* modifications of this system of government. Deviations from pure presidentialism have been identified at various times in Bolivia, Peru, Chile, Ecuador, Uruguay and Guatemala (Shugart and Carey, 1992). In some Latin American countries the legislative assembly has a say in the selection of the executive. This becomes especially valuable in cases where weak parties are unable to form durable coalitions during elections (Linz, 1994; Cox and Morgenstern, 2002; see Chapter 6). In Bolivia, for example, the legislature has played a uniquely assertive role among Latin American political systems, and if none of the candidates in a presidential election obtain an absolute majority of votes, congress has hitherto selected the executive (see Box 5.6).

THEORIES AND DEBATES   **Box 5.5**

Semi-presidentialism

Linz (1994) has argued that the negative experience many countries have had with presidentialism offer an opportunity for such constitutional innovations as semi-presidentialism. However, Valenzuela (2004) believes semi-presidentialism may not solve some of the inherent problems of presidentialism in Latin America and could, in fact, make them worse by exacerbating conflicts between the president and prime minister and making these personal. Semi-presidential systems (sometimes called 'dual-executive' systems) are those in which the president is elected by the people but there is also a prime minister who requires the confidence of a parliament. The president may appoint the prime minister, but needs the support of parliament to do so, and can also dissolve parliament, but needs the support of the prime minister to do so. The powers of the president and prime minister vary, and sometimes the president can bypass parliament by exercising emergency powers. Such systems can work well, especially when the party or parties supporting the president have a majority in the legislature, but they can also raise important constitutional issues, such as who controls the military or determines foreign policy. Valenzuela argues that practices which might promote greater stability in Latin America would include a presidential prerogative to dismiss congress and schedule the election of a new one, combined with a rule requiring the president to resign upon failure to command a majority in any new congress. The power to dissolve parliament has only been rarely incorporated into Latin American constitutions and was included, for example, in Chile's 1980 authoritarian constitution and in Paraguay and Uruguay (where it has never been invoked).

INSTITUTIONS	Box 5.6

Bolivia – empowered congress or vipers' den?

Bolivia's political process has often diverged from the norms of pure presidentialism and its congress has played a uniquely significant role in Latin America in determining the fate of executives, who have tended to wield less authority than those elsewhere. However, although the modifications that can be identified in Bolivia are more congruent with parliamentarianism, it remains a presidential system because, once elected, the executive should hold office for a full term without depending on the confidence of congress (Linz, 1994; Cox and Morgenstern, 2002). First, if none of the candidates in a presidential election obtains an absolute majority of votes, congress has selected the president from frontrunners in the popular vote (*ibid.*). This is likely in a situation where presidential votes tend to fragment between candidates because weak parties are unable to forge effective electoral coalitions (see Chapter 6). It occurred several times in the 1980s, with alliances in congress determining the winning candidate who, on several occasions, was not the candidate that had gained most votes in the popular election. In August 2002, Sánchez de Lozada was chosen president by Bolivia's congress, winning an 84–43 vote against Evo Morales. Where the executive is selected by congress in this way, the prospective president must build viable coalitions in the legislature from the outset. Second, although it is rare in Latin America for a president who has lost the confidence of his own parties or the legislature to be replaced during his term, this has occurred several times in Bolivia. Political crises caused by the strategy adopted for exploiting natural gas reserves rocked the country between 2003 and 2005 and brought down two presidents. Sánchez de Lozada resigned then fled the country in 2003 after just 14 months in office, and in June 2005 his successor, Mesa, resigned after just 19 months in office amid continuing unrest over the gas issue. Mesa was vice-president when Sánchez de Lozada was forced from office and his mandate had officially been due to end in 2007. In March 2005, congress had rejected an initial offer by Mesa to resign amid serious divisions among congressional leaders over a hydrocarbons bill. On that occasion, Mesa had blamed intransigence by congress in blocking the passage of the controversial hydrocarbons law, and in particular the stance of the leftwing Movimiento al Socialismo (MAS, Movement Towards Socialism), the second largest party in the assembly. As an independent, Mesa's support in congress was fragile. In June 2005, when Mesa again offered to resign, congress – by now forced to hold its session in Sucre because of chaos caused by protests in La Paz – accepted his offer. Mesa's successor, Eduardo Rodríguez, was able to bring a semblance of order to the country and an end to the protests mainly because, as a member of the judiciary, he was seen as untainted by politics. However, he also acceded to demands by the protesters for elections to a special constituent assembly to rewrite the country's constitution in 2006 and for a referendum on regional autonomy (see Boxes 4.1, 8.7, 12.11). Deep divisions within congress were at the heart of Bolivia's political crisis, with tense congressional debates about the new hydrocarbons law fuelling the unrest. Mesa had tried unsuccessfully to place responsibility for the hydrocarbons law with congress, and early into his term Rodríguez also insisted that congress had the last word on all matters to do with control of the country's gas reserves. Bolivia also demonstrates the importance of a strong mandate if presidentialism is to be effective and able to withstand challenges to the executive. Evo Morales (2006–) has faced significant opposition from within and outside the political process since coming to office, yet has been able to press ahead with unprecedented reforms on the basis of his strong mandate, one that was reaffirmed in his re-election in December 2009 with 63 per cent of the vote.

There have also been efforts in Latin America to limit or spread executive authority, although in general these have had little success. For example, Uruguay was governed by a 'plural executive' at various times in the early decades of the twentieth century and this was re-established after 1951 in an attempt to discourage a monopoly of power being achieved by one of the country's two main parties. Based on a Swiss multiple-executive model, the office of president was replaced by a nine-seat council allocated according to the parties' proportion of the vote, with a titular president chosen from the majority party to act as head of state. However, Uruguay's plural executive proved ineffectual and generated factionalism, preventing it from taking decisive action to solve the country's problems. In 1967, a new constitution abolished the council and re-established a strong presidency.

However, despite the academic debates about the merits or otherwise of reforming presidentialism and the frequency with which presidencies have been interrupted, this has remained the preferred form of government in Latin America. There are clear signs that, as an institution, the presidency is improving its performance relative to other institutions and that there is increasing approval of the performance of the governments that presidents lead (see Latinobarómetro, 2008, 2009a; Zovatto and Orozco Henríquez, 2008). Latinobarómetro data reveal that the approval rate of government performances in Latin America rose in 2009, at the height of the recent economic crisis, suggesting that strong executive power may be seen as preferable in times of uncertainty (Latinobarómetro, 2009a).

INSTITUTIONS **Box 5.7**

Strengths and weaknesses of presidential rule

Strengths

- strong source of leadership over fractious societies
- provides the certainty that legislative politics is unable to provide
- right to appoint and dismiss cabinet members without congressional input makes for decisive policymaking
- compensates for poorly disciplined parties because president does not depend on the electoral success of supporters in the assembly to remain in office
- legitimate and accountable, because voters know exactly who they are getting

Weaknesses

- contested interpretations of role and powers
- dual legitimacy of president and legislature can fuel conflict between them

Winner-takes-all election

- losing candidate gains no stake in power
- can leave voters without representation

▶

- can exacerbate polarisation
- can foster a disproportionate sense of power and authority, leading to delegative democracy
- can discourage independent-minded politicians from joining cabinet

Fixed terms and no re-election

- president cannot be held to account in an election
- rigidity of term can make adjustments to changing situations difficult
- can tempt incumbent to seek extra-constitutional or illegal means to extend term
- can encourage sense of urgency leading to ill-designed policies or rapid spending
- can exacerbate impatience with opposition and political conflict
- desire for continuity can encourage a president to seek an obedient successor

Difficult relationships with legislatures and parties

- voting systems can make it hard for a president to build coalitions and hence a working majority in congress
- can tempt presidents to seek new powers through constitutional reforms, to resort to ruling by decree, or to undertake 'self-coups'
- personalised nature of presidential polls makes election of outsiders not identified with any party more possible

Summary

The presidency is at the centre of institutional politics in Latin America and elites have interpreted presidencies as a strong source of leadership in fractious societies as opposed to being one component in a traditional separation of powers upon which European and US government is based. However, different interpretations among political actors of the executive's role and powers have been regarded as a factor behind democratic non-consolidation in Latin America. Distinguishing characteristics of Latin American presidencies include electoral systems that ensure the winner takes all power alongside multi-party legislative systems. This results in dual legitimacy, whereby both the executive and the legislature can claim to have a democratic mandate. The principle of no re-election is also common. Presidents enjoy a range of unilateral and integrative formal powers but they also have significant informal power deriving from their position at the heart of the political process. As an institution, the Latin American presidency has both strengths and weaknesses, and these are summarised in Box 5.7.

A president's relationship with the legislature – and the difficulties presidents often have building working coalitions – are key factors in determining the effectiveness of policymaking and political stability. The weaknesses of presidentialism, particularly those exacerbated by complex relations with congress, have often resulted in crises and the interruption of presidential terms. Scholars are divided over the merits of presidential versus parliamentary systems and have discussed whether semi-presidential systems that assign more power to the legislature would be more suitable for Latin America.

Discussion points

- What factors determine whether a Latin American president will be successful?
- Would parliamentary systems solve Latin America's political problems?
- Compare and contrast the different forms of presidential power.
- Are there ways of reducing conflict between the executive and legislature?
- Do electoral systems contribute to disproportionate presidential power?
- Why is the principle of no re-election so common in Latin America?
- To what extent does the legislature determine presidential strategies?

Useful websites

http://pdba.georgetown.edu/Executive/executive.html Valuable Georgetown University Political Database of the Americas Executive Branch site containing information about presidents, cabinets, ministries, reference materials and chronologies

www.cidob.org/en Valuable site with detailed biographies of Latin American presidents compiled by the Fundación CIDOB research centre at the University of Barcelona

www.worldstatesmen.org Useful independent encyclopaedia of presidents and *de facto* leaders

www.ps.org.uy Partido Socialista del Uruguay (PSU, Uruguayan Socialist Party), for Frente Amplio – Encuentro Progresista (FA-EP, Broad Front-Progressive Encounter)

www.observatorioelectoral.org Observatorio Electoral Latinoamericano (OEL, Latin American Electoral Observatory), valuable source of electoral data and analysis

www.presidencia.gob.pe Peruvian presidency

www.presidencia.gob.hn Honduran presidency

www.presidencia.gov.ar Argentine presidency

www.presidencia.gob.bo Bolivian presidency

www.masbolivia.com Movimiento al Socialismo (MAS, Movement towards Socialism), Bolivia

Recommended reading

Valenzuela, Arturo. 2004. 'Latin American Presidencies Interrupted'. *Journal of Democracy,* Vol. 15, No. 4 (October 2004), pp. 5–19

> *Essential and accessible starting point in the discussion of the problems associated with presidentialism in Latin America and hence the potential merits of other political systems*

Linz, Juan. J. and Arturo Valenzuela (eds). 1994. *The Failure of Presidential Democracy, The Case of Latin America. Volume 2.* Baltimore, MD: Johns Hopkins University Press

Essential introduction to the debate about the merits of presidential versus parliamentary systems, combined with case studies on individual countries

Pérez-Liñán, Aníbal. 2010. *Presidential Impeachment and the New Political Instability in Latin America.* Cambridge: Cambridge University Press

Essential introduction to the relationship between presidentialism and instability in democratic Latin America which explains why crises without breakdown have become the dominant form of instability in recent years

Mainwaring, S. 1993. 'Presidentialism, Multipartism, and Democracy: The Difficult Combination'. *Comparative Political Studies*, Vol. 26, No. 2 (July 1993), pp. 198–228

Useful examination of the relationship between presidentialism and multi-party systems that often lies at the heart of the tension between executive and legislature

Mainwaring, Scott, and Matthew Soberg Shugart (eds). 1997. *Presidentialism and Democracy in Latin America.* Cambridge: Cambridge University Press

Essential introduction to the consideration at a theoretical level of the degree to which presidentialism contributes to problems of democratic governance, with a valuable overview of variations among presidential systems in eight Latin American countries

Chapter 6

Legislatures, parties, the judiciary and public administration

This chapter examines the role played in Latin American politics by other branches of government that in established democracies such as those of Western Europe, the United States and Canada allow for a separation of powers. It looks at legislatures – often referred to as congresses – and the parties that inhabit them, the judiciary and the institutional structure of public administration whose role it is to deliver policy.

Latin American legislatures often appear subservient and weak, long overshadowed by a dominant presidency and populated by ineffectual and corrupt politicians. If it is doing its job properly, a legislature should act not just as a lawmaking assembly but as a check on the power of the executive. While in general that has not been the case in Latin America, legislatures are not as supine as the imagery we often have of them would give us to believe and they have grown in stature considerably since the return of democratic politics. The parties that populate legislatures should play an essential role in politics, representing citizens, bringing order and stability to the competition over resources, and acting to prevent the emergence of dictators and autocrats by guaranteeing institutional rules for political succession. One measure of whether a party system – the set of conventions and rules of competition between parties that generate continuity and stability – fulfils these roles is the degree to which patterns of party behaviour obey institutional norms. A number of problems are associated with parties that are weakly institutionalised – that is, parties that have failed to become established as institutions and whose survival is, as a result, in doubt (see below) – from populism to immobilism, policy gridlock, weak government authority and conflicts with the executive. All too often, the behaviour of parties has served to legitimise the excesses of presidential rulers. The judiciary should be an essential branch of government that exists to review and, if necessary, overturn executive actions. However, judges and the court system remain weak throughout Latin America, despite systematic efforts to reform them, and in many countries only a limited rule of law prevails (see Chapter 4). None the less, the spirit of reform characterising Latin American politics since the 1990s has had a discernible impact upon policy delivery by trimming down huge, centralised bureaucracies that were a product of corporatism and statism and were often plagued by severe inertia. Power is also increasingly being devolved to states, provinces and municipalities through strategies of decentralisation that can bring with them new hopes for democratic participation.

Legislatures

The traditional view of legislatures in Latin America is that they have been largely irrelevant to the policy process, often unable to remove presidents they dislike, yet ill-equipped to push forward their own proposals. However, at times, congresses have played an important role in politics and they are growing in importance across the region as the confidence of citizens in them rises. Recent studies have portrayed Latin American legislatures as important institutional players in the political process (see Alemán and Calvo, 2008). Latinobarómetro data, for example, reveal a slow but clear rise in the proportion of Latin American citizens who believe that there cannot be democracy without a congress, from 49 per cent in 2001 to 57 per cent in 2009; and an incremental rise in the favourable evaluation of the work done by congresses from 38 per cent in 2006 to 41 per cent in 2008 (Latinobarómetro, 2008, 2009a).

Half of Latin American countries have bicameral congresses that, unlike many of the bicameral legislatures in parliamentary regimes, have upper and lower houses that enjoy similar forms of power. This tends to make upper chambers, senates, highly relevant institutional players in the region, but can also mean that these can create another hurdle to efficient policymaking. If there is a significant difference in the way lower and upper chambers are elected or selected, what is known as incongruence, this can further complicate the relationship between them.

Other factors in the way the relationship between chambers may shape the passage of legislation are the rules used to reach a bicameral agreement on a law and the different decision-making procedures found in each chamber. Co-operation among members tends to be greater within senates – which often have more collegial working practices – than within the more uncertain and combative environment found in chambers of deputies. This difference can affect the enactment of presidential proposals, which are often more successful if a chamber is more cohesive and co-operative.

Morgenstern (2002a) has said legislatures in general can be characterised as either *originative*, making and breaking executives who shoulder the policy-making burden; *proactive*, initiating and passing their own policies; or *reactive*, amending or vetoing executive proposals. He has argued that Latin American legislatures are *reactive* because, while they rarely initiate legislation, they negotiate over policy issues and shape or halt executive initiatives (see also Morgenstern, 2002b).

The powers given to Latin American legislatures by constitutions vary considerably, with some enjoying real clout on paper – such as the ability to delay or amend presidential initiatives, revise the budget, overturn vetoes or even amend the constitution – yet others remaining weak (*ibid.*). Most legislatures have no say in the selection of the president and, as we have seen, executives have considerable power to shape the agenda of legislatures through such devices as urgency provisions. None the less, a president's powers – such as the ability to use decrees, for example – may be limited in practice according to the degree of support he or she enjoys in congress. Much legislative activity also takes place behind the scenes and can be difficult to factor into empirical studies, and this 'hidden influence' is a key methodological variable in the study of legislatures. Another important variable

THEORIES AND DEBATES

Box 6.1

Political ambition

Among the key variables influencing models that seek to explain legislative politics in countries such as the US are the aims and ambitions of members of the legislature and the strategies they adopt to achieve their goals (Morgenstern, 2002b). In the US, the most important goal of legislators is re-election, but in Latin America many legislators are less focused on re-election, more dependent on their party leaders for advancement, are often not members either of a single majority or opposition party, and work in systems in which constitutional powers vary considerably. Rates of re-election are comparatively low in Latin America and legislators are motivated by different ambitions, with some aiming for a career in national-level politics but others seeing their period in the legislature as a way of developing careers in state politics or in businesses. Where there are low re-election rates, legislators will devote more of their time towards shaping future careers, and this will influence the behaviour of any given legislature. Legislators who are not likely to return to their posts may, for example, be more responsive to presidents who control resources that they can use to improve their prospects once their term ends (*ibid.*). Chile has higher re-election rates than many other Latin American countries, and one result of this is that its legislators have professionalised many of their practices by employing press officers, for example. The Chilean deputies have shaped legislative structures such as the committee system to boost their electoral prospects and devoted more attention to the needs of their constituencies (Carey, 2002; Morgenstern, 2002a). By comparison, Mexico has low re-election rates, and its legislators have long complained about a lack of resources to do their jobs, have often depended on party leaders for careers once their terms ended, and have not taken great interest in the needs of their constituencies (Nacif, 2002).

influencing models of legislative behaviour are the aims and ambitions of members of congress (see Box 6.1).

Morgenstern (2002a) identified three key themes around which the study of legislative politics takes place – executive-legislative relations, legislative structure, and the policymaking process:

Executive-legislative relations

The degree of support a president enjoys in congress and the extent to which the executive is integrated into the legislative process influences the strategy they adopt. The main mechanism of that integration is often the cabinet: Latin American presidents use cabinet appointments to influence assembly support and it is common for individuals to hold cabinet and legislative office simultaneously. There is an inverse relationship between a president's support in the legislature and their recourse to unilateral powers: where a president has only weak support in congress and faces a hostile majority they will often have no chance of achieving policy goals through statutes and will be inclined to take unilateral action by using decree powers.

Statutes are more enduring than decrees and so are regarded as a preferable method of lawmaking. Where a president has a medium level of support in congress or a workable majority, they may be able to get statutes through using urgency provisions or by allocating cabinet posts and dispensing patronage. A president with strong support in congress can expect to have statutes passed by virtue of a large and pliant majority, and will not use decrees or vetoes (Cox and Morgenstern, 2002).

However, the relationship between a president's minority status and their recourse to the use of decrees when ordinary lawmaking is obstructed in congress is not straightforward, and a minority president who may be powerful in other ways may be able to foster workable compromises on legislation in congress and take advantage of a lack of incentives for coalition-formation among parties to build substantive congressional support for a law (see Alemán and Calvo, 2008). Some research has found that minority presidents tend to pass a majority of the bills they introduce and that their success rates are not strikingly different from those for majority presidents, with coalition-building one of their favoured strategies to avoid congressional stalemate (*ibid.*). Decrees may also be used less to force through policy and more as a bargaining tool or even to inform a congress about a president's broader objectives that still give legislators some influence.

Cox and Morgenstern (2002) identify four types of legislature and patterns of likely behaviour based upon their relationship with the president (see Table 6.1).

The *recalcitrant assembly* will provoke the president to use unilateral powers, and the *subservient* assembly will be dominated and dictated to. The other types of legislature are distinguished by what the president offers legislators in return for support. The *venal or parochial* assembly will support the president in return for patronage and payoffs. These legislatures prefer presidents to take broad authority over policy by granting the executive decree powers and sponsoring few of their own initiatives. *Workable assemblies* are brought into the policy process through concessions made by presidents in constructing viable coalitions.

Table 6.1 Presidential and assembly strategies

| | | Assembly strategies | | |
		Reject	Bargain	Demand payments	Acquiesce
Presidential strategies	**Undertake unilateral action**	Imperial president, recalcitrant assembly			
	Bargain		Coalitional president, workable assembly		
	Pay Off			Nationally-oriented president, venal or parochial assembly	
	Dictate				Dominant president, subservient assembly

Source: Cox and Morgenstern, 2002

Legislative structure and parties

The way a legislature is structured will influence how it operates and its power to shape the policy process. Morgenstern (2002a) identifies three prominent themes in the analytical literature on legislative behaviour: *procedural coalitions, committee systems* and *floor-voting patterns*. Procedural coalitions are those that form when legislators vote on the procedures the legislature will employ to elect house leaders, vote on bills, and allocate committee places. These coalitions will usually be different from those that form around policy issues. The number and size of the parties within the legislature have an important bearing on how it operates. In particular, the majority party monopolises procedural advantages and, as a result, has great influence over the content of legislation and the distribution of resources. The ways in which committee chairmanships are allocated and the control by party leaders of committee seats will have important implications for what policies will succeed and the legislature's ability to scrutinize presidential initiatives (*ibid.*). Floor-voting patterns, the ways legislators vote about policies on the floor of the house, are an important indicator of party behaviour, helping to identify the degree to which policy coalitions are coherent and united and the willingness of a party to work with the executive.

Policymaking role

Much of the literature on democratic transition and consolidation (see Chapter 3) characterised Latin American legislatures as marginal to the policy process. Legislatures in the region have limited policymaking powers, initiate less legislation than the US congress, for example, and have a less important role in amending legislation – but they are not completely irrelevant to the policy process. The main policy role they play has been in *blocking* legislation that assembly members consider unfavourable or *pressuring* a president to amend proposals or bills. By seeking to amend a presidential proposal or rejecting it, a legislature can force a president either to bargain, make concessions, buy votes with patronage, or resort to unilateral action through decrees.

Chile provides an example of a workable legislature that takes the initiative, sets the agenda, and whose leaders frequently consult with the president (Siavelis, 2002). Differences within the governing Concertación de Partidos por la Democracia (CPD, Coalition of Parties for Democracy) have often been suppressed by the strong desire of leaders of its constituent groups not to be seen as undermining unity, given the country's prior experience of dictatorship under Augusto Pinochet (1973–90) (Hershberg, 1997). Seniority has become important in Chile's lower house, with a hierarchical structure of committees operating to ensure all finance bills pass through committees overseen by party leaders (Carey, 2002). Chile's legislature also exercises significant 'hidden influence', with a large proportion of legislation requiring more than the legal minimum of steps to get through the legislature (Siavelis, 2002).

Argentina's legislature has not been as active as that of Chile, but nor has it been entirely subservient despite the executive's considerable powers and control over appointments and patronage. While the Argentine legislature's role is reactive,

Table 6.2 Legislative success and productivity in the Argentine Congress, December 1983–2001

Proponent	Chamber of Origin	Bills Introduced	Bills Passed	Success Rate (%)
Executive	Deputies	916	375	**40.9**
	Senate	919	566	**61.6**
Legislators	Deputies	20,632	780	**3.8**
	Senate	5,484	432	**7.9**

Note: Proponent refers to the actor that introduced the bill – president or legislators as party members or individuals; Chamber of Origin refers to the house in which the bill was introduced; Success Rate refers to the rate of approval of legislation introduced.

Source: Alemán and Calvo, 2008

it can disrupt the president's policy priorities and has been proactive enough to provoke presidential vetoes (Mustapic, 2002). The Peronist Partido Justicialista (PJ, Justicialist Party), which has frequently occupied a dominant position in both houses, has often relied on its party discipline (see below) and procedural advantages in areas such as the allocation of committee seats both to support and amend policies. We can gain an idea of the activity of the Argentine legislature by looking at the success rate of bills passed in the country (see Table 6.2). This reveals in the period studied that about 51 per cent of substantive bills introduced in congress by a president became law, but individual legislators were successful with only about 5 per cent of the legislation they introduced. Yet while presidents displayed higher rates of success, their productivity was lower than that of congressmen. The data also show that success rates are considerably higher for legislation initiated in the senate by both presidents and legislators.

Brazil's legislature sits somewhere between recalcitrant and workable, being both notoriously fractious yet also allowing some presidents to build working majorities. Weak presidents such as Fernando Collor de Mello (1989–92) have tended to rely on decrees, but others have been successful in the complex task of building support through the distribution of cabinet posts (Amorim Neto, 2002a). Although Brazil is known for the use by presidents of decrees, the legislature still shapes the policy process and important proposals rarely pass through congress unchanged (Ames, 2002). The most important legislation during the presidential term of Fernando Henrique Cardoso (1995–2003), including constitutional changes to allow for his re-election, had to undergo thorough legislative scrutiny. The interactions between President Luiz Inácio Lula da Silva (2003–10) and congress have been influenced by his relationship with his own Partido dos Trabalhadores (PT, Workers' Party) and the need to mediate between its factions. Resistance to some of his positions from within the PT has sometimes contributed to alliance building with conservative politicians. Relations between legislators and state governors – who control resources that are crucial to most political careers – also play a central role in Brazilian politics (Samuels, 2002). This has made the legislature's committee structure much more important, and has prompted legislators to structure this to support state, as opposed to partisan, interests. As a result, state delegations play an important part in procedural and agenda issues (*ibid.*). Prior to 1997, Mexico's legislature was fully subservient to the presidency, but it has undergone significant change since the PRI first lost control of the lower house and it has blocked or changed executive initiatives affecting social security legislation, fiscal measures and the relationship with Zapatista rebels in Chiapas (Casar, 2002). The PRI's loss of control brought about important changes in the composition and functioning of the committee system which previously served to further the goals of the dominant party (Casar, 2002; Nacif, 2002). Procedural reforms since the 1990s to allocate committee chairmanships proportionally have allowed other parties to negotiate for their share of leadership positions (Weldon, 2002). A subsequent revival in PRI fortunes in congress since 2003 has enabled the party to exercise an often decisive influence over policy, allowing it to extract concessions under President Felipe Calderón (2006–) in areas such as energy reform.

Parties and party systems

An influential definition of a party was provided by Sartori (1976), who described it as 'any political group that presents at elections, and is capable of placing through elections, candidates for public office' (p. 64). His definition was aimed, primarily, at *competitive* political systems and not those in which only one party predominated. A party is an organisation that exists, first and foremost, to compete for political power through elections, but parties fulfil many other roles in politics. They are the main agents of political representation for a range of social groups, and they also provide a key focus for ensuring that there is *accountability* in politics, by offering citizens the ability to hold governments to account at election time for what they have done. Parties provide access to government and opportunities for citizens to participate in politics, and are a means of recruiting and training new political leaders. They impose order on competing groups and demands while offering voters a choice between rival policy programmes. Parties also act as mechanisms of communication, providing links between a government and society and reducing the 'information cost' to the elector of voting – the time and effort required to find out about and assess rival policy platforms. Finally, political parties play a key role organising the business of the legislature by controlling the legislative agenda and affecting the behaviour of individual representatives in the legislature's broader mission to enact laws.

Political parties have taken many forms in Latin America, from those restricted to a small number of powerful politicians and their supporters in the nineteenth century to those with mass memberships in the twentieth century. The existence of parties that represent all the main political tendencies is held to be a defining characteristic of democratic consolidation because these restrain actors from pursuing extra-constitutional ways of promoting their interests.

Political parties have usually been examined as elements within a *system* in which at least two, and often many, parties compete for power (see Sartori, 1976; Carey, 1997; Foweraker, 1998). Parties and party systems are of particular importance to the *institutionalisation* of democracy, that is, the rooting of the democratic system in society through structured forms of participation, disagreement and competition.

A key theme in the analysis of both parties and party systems has, therefore, been the degree to which they are institutionalised.

There has been considerable debate about what factors constitute party institutionalisation – the process through which a party becomes established as an institution, increasing its prospects for survival – and this has often related to such factors as how parties are organised, the extent to which members and supporters value and obey them, and their links with society (see, for example, Duverger, 1964; Panebianco, 1988; McGuire, 1997; Gunther *et al.*, eds, 2002). Parties that can be considered strong, for example, include those that have established an organisational presence across a whole country or region; that have enjoyed stable levels of support or membership over time; that have built enduring relationships with social groups such as trades unions, peasant organisations or urban intellectuals; and that have maintained consistent policy programmes and platforms (see McGuire, 1997; Corrales, 2001). Learning and adaptation through policy innovations can also be an important mechanism by which politicians build programmatic parties, and this in turn can help to account for differences in the degree to which Latin American party systems have developed (see Kitschelt *et al.*, 2010).

Randall and Svåsand (2002) put forward a model by which to analyse the degree of institutionalisation of individual parties. They proposed that the process of party institutionalisation could be assessed in terms of four main elements: 'systemness', 'value infusion', 'decisional autonomy' and 'reification' (see also Huntington, 1968; Panebianco, 1988; Levitsky, 1998; Janda, 1980). Systemness refers to the increasing scope, density and regularity of the interactions that constitute the party as a structure. Value infusion refers to the extent to which party actors and supporters identify with the party above and beyond self-interested incentives for involvement in its activities. Decisional autonomy refers to a party's freedom from interference by groups it is closely linked to, such as trades unions, in determining its policies and strategies. Reification refers to the extent to which a party's existence is established in the public imagination.

Much of the analytical work on parties has concentrated on Western Europe and Randall and Svåsand (2002) argued that their model was of particular value when examining parties in developing regions, such as Latin America. In countries such as Brazil, for example, the evolution of parties has not always been gradual and has been interrupted regularly, the ability of parties to derive funding from membership dues has been limited, and clientelism persists (see Boxes 2.1, 2.2, 7.1).

The approach taken by Randall and Svåsand (2002) was also an effort to ensure that party institutionalisation is analysed as a separate phenomenon to party *system* institutionalisation, because aspects of each of these processes may sometimes be in conflict, particularly when there are uneven levels of institutionalisation among different parties within the same system. They believed that earlier work by Mainwaring and Scully (1995) advancing criteria for classifying party systems as either *institutionalised* or *inchoate*, that is, weakly-institutionalised (see Table 6.3), had not accounted for the possibility of such conflict. To Mainwaring and Scully, the institutionalisation of a party system implies stability in the rules of inter-party competition; the existence of parties that have stable roots in society and stable internal structures; the acceptance among all political actors that parties and elections are the most legitimate institutions for determining who governs; and a

Table 6.3 Criteria of party system institutionalisation

Institutionalised party system	Inchoate (non- or weakly-institutionalised) party system
Stability in the rules of inter-party competition	Relationships between parties are unstable and may change with each election
Parties have stable roots in society	The main parties do not inspire loyalty among citizens
Parties have stable internal structures	Parties are often small and poorly organised
All political actors accept that parties and elections are the most legitimate institutions for determining who governs	Citizens may not see parties and elections as the most legitimate institutions to determine who governs
Parties have a degree of ideological consistency over time	Parties are not ideologically consistent

Source: Adapted from Mainwaring and Scully, 1995

degree of ideological consistency over time. These factors are absent or qualified in inchoate systems.

Mainwaring and Scully developed an overall aggregate score of party system institutionalisation in Latin America. There have been marked differences across the region: in 1995, they identified strongly institutionalised party systems in Venezuela, Costa Rica, Chile, Uruguay, Colombia and Argentina; they classified Mexico and Paraguay as party systems in transition; and they described Peru, Brazil, Bolivia and Ecuador as inchoate systems. These categories are not fixed and even in countries where parties have been institutionalised, such as Venezuela, there can be a process of de-institutionalisation (see Box 4.2).

Stability in inter-party competition can be measured using the net change in seat or vote shares of parties from one election to the next. Mainwaring and Scully argued that low volatility in this measurement suggested patterns of party competition were stable in Uruguay, Colombia, Chile, Costa Rica, Argentina and Venezuela; but unstable in Mexico, Paraguay, Bolivia, Brazil, Ecuador and Peru. The degree to which parties have stable roots in society can also be analysed by examining different patterns of voting across consecutive legislative and presidential elections; the strength of connections between parties and organised interests; and the ability of parties to survive for a long time on the basis of long-term loyalties. The evidence compiled by Mainwaring and Scully suggested voters had weak attachments to parties, and that parties had weak links with social groups in Peru, Brazil, Bolivia and Ecuador.

The most well-established parties in Latin America have existed in Mexico, Costa Rica, Chile, Uruguay, Paraguay and, until recently, Venezuela. One measure of this has been the consistency with which political elites maintain or stay loyal to the party line in the legislature – party discipline. Chile has the oldest party system in the region and this helps to explain why, in spite of its presidentialist constitution and Pinochet's 17-year dictatorship, after 1990 parties reasserted their role as the backbone of democracy. Chile has been governed since democratisation by the centre-left Concertación coalition comprising the Partido Demócrata Cristiano (PDC, Christian Democrat Party), the Partido Socialista (PSCh, Socialist Party) and other socialists and centrists.

Mexico's party system remains in transition. Prior to the 1990s, legislative politics were dominated by the PRI which had a corporatist character in which sectoral groups such as peasants and workers were represented in large, vertically-organised confederations (see Chapter 7). Recurrent political reforms from the late 1970s and into the 1980s strengthened parties on both right and left. Growing co-operation between the PRI and the conservative Partido Acción Nacional (PAN, National Action Party) was reflected in PAN electoral gains. The PRI lost control of congress in 1997, and lost the presidency to the PAN in 2000, ending six decades of single-party rule. The democratic left rose rapidly then consolidated as a single party, the Partido de la Revolución Democrática (PRD, Democratic Revolution Party), elements of which had broken away from the PRI. Continuity since the 1990s and the predominance of these three main competing parties in an atmosphere of orderly inter-party relationships, combined with the ability of the PRI to stay intact despite deep internal divisions, reform itself and then restore its congressional fortunes, suggest that the party system has gradually become more institutionalised.

Parties have been less well organised in Colombia and Argentina. In Argentina, it was common for political leaders intentionally to weaken party organisations in order to enhance their personal position, yet there has also been stable inter-party competition between the main parties, the Radicals and the Peronists, and voting patterns have also been stable, even weathering the catastrophic loss of confidence in politicians that was generated by the crisis of 2001–02 in which the members of both main parties indulged in serious infighting (see Box 5.4). The main parties are well rooted in society, and voters have remained loyal to their preferences. However, the relationship between parties and the executive has been volatile and the Peronist party tends to remain dominated by a single personality.

In Bolivia, Ecuador, Peru and Guatemala, party organisation has traditionally been weak and personalism has prevailed. In Peru, during the 1980s and 1990s there was a discernible shift away from an institutionalised party system and significant volatility in electoral patterns. The collapse in fortunes of the Alianza Popular Revolucionaria Americana (APRA, American Popular Revolutionary Alliance, today referred to as the Partido Aprista Peruano) had by 1990 turned elections into highly personalised contests with party organisations playing a secondary role. Bolivia, Ecuador and Brazil have also suffered from weak party organisations and considerable electoral volatility. Parties in these countries have weak roots in society and suffer from low levels of allegiance. As a result, strong personalities often emerge and dominate electoral campaigns. Brazil's party system has been characterised by fluidity, resulting in almost constant coalition realignments through negotiations in congress, and also in the evolution of a personal dimension to political campaigns that echoes the emergence of past political outsiders such as Collor de Mello in 1989. Until recently, politicians would often switch parties, thereby changing the proportion of congressional seats held by each party, but a supreme court decision that elective terms belong to parties and not politicians will help to strengthen institutionalisation. Although the PT has evolved into a genuinely mass party and is driving the consolidation of a party system with a more institutionalised character, the country's PT president Lula da Silva (2003–10) has at times adopted a personalist style based on rhetoric that is characteristically populist (see Chapters 2, 4), and has alienated some PT factions through alliances with other parties.

Guatemala's party system is also weakly institutionalised. Since 1985 there have been at least 48 parties, most of which have disappeared after the first election that they contested (Puente and Linares, 2004). In 1999, for example, of 18 registered parties, 14 participated in national elections and eight of these were subsequently abolished under electoral rules for not obtaining 4 per cent of the valid votes or parliamentary representation; of the 10 parties that were in existence in 2004, only six had obtained parliamentary representation (*ibid.*). Puente and Linares (2004) highlighted estimates that, since the late 1980s, about 25 per cent of elected congressmen in Guatemala have abandoned the party that gained them election either to declare themselves as independents or to join other parties.

A number of political problems are associated with the lack of institutionalisation, including populism (see Box 4.2). The rise of Ecuador's president Lucio Gutiérrez (2003–05), for example, reflected weak party system institutionalisation (see Box 6.2). A lack of institutionalisation can also translate into scepticism about the legitimacy of the political system, and such systems are often characterised by immobilism, policy gridlock, weak government authority and conflicts within the executive's own party. By setting rules for political actors, institutions establish predictability and so weak institutionalisation can also engender uncertainty. In conditions of uncertainty political actors may put short-term gains before good policymaking. Incomplete institutionalisation can also exacerbate ideological polarisation, making it more difficult to maintain political stability. Inchoate party systems often have a large number of parties among which there is a significant degree of ideological polarisation.

The composition of the party system clearly has an effect on the behaviour of the legislature and executive, and the effectiveness of both is influenced by the *number* of parties or coalitions. Inevitably, if no party controls a majority this can immobilise the assembly, and even where parties share opposition to the executive they may be unable to unite in a coalition. It is generally felt that two-party systems are better suited to stable presidential democracy, but most Latin American democracies are multi-party systems which make it more difficult to achieve stability because this greatly complicates coalition-building. Mainwaring (1993) has argued that multi-party systems tend to exacerbate the problems of presidentialism (see Chapter 5), and Foweraker *et al.* (2003) suggest that the likelihood of a presidential majority or near majority diminishes as the number of political parties increases.

Stable competition between two or three parties or blocs in congress has been achieved in some Latin American political systems. In Uruguay, a two-party system dominated by the traditional parties, the Colorados and the Blancos, began to break down in the turbulent 1960s and the country moved towards a three-party system prior to the period of direct military control after 1973. Following the return to democracy in 1984, three main parties competed and provided significant stability. The Colorados and Blancos, and a leftwing alliance, the Frente Amplio (after 1994, the Encuentro Progresista-Frente Amplio, EP-FA, Progressive Encounter-Broad Front) were all represented in congress and in municipal authorities. However,

INSTITUTIONS	Box 6.2

Ecuador – A populist's contempt for politicians

The rise of the populist president Lucio Gutiérrez, who took office in January 2003 and was ousted in April 2005, reflected weak party system institutionalisation in Ecuador. The former colonel, dismissed from the army for leading the uprising that drove President Jamil Mahuad (1998–2000) from power, won an election runoff in November 2002 on promises to end corruption within the political system and judiciary by reducing the number of legislators, eliminating party influence over the court system and extraditing bankers implicated in a collapse of the banking system in 1999. The new president's populist style was based on hostility to Ecuador's traditional parties and court system, and he fashioned his image as a champion of judicial reform. Gutiérrez's formal party base was weak during his election campaign. He said he had no political ideology although his party, the Partido Sociedad Patriótica 21 de Enero (PSP, 21st of January Patriotic Society Party, named after the date Mahuad was driven out), was supported by Pachakutik, the country's leftwing indigenous movement, leftwing trades unions and a small Marxist party, the Movimiento Popular Democrático (MPD, Democratic Popular Movement), as well as some members of the Partido Socialista Ecuatoriano-Frente Amplio (PS-FA, Socialist Party-Broad Front). His hostile attitude towards the political establishment was much in evidence at the start of his administration. Gutiérrez declared he would not take the oath of office in congress but in front of 'the people' and threatened not to accept the presidential banner from the president of congress, whose election he said was unconstitutional. Initially, Gutiérrez's coalition had only 17 seats in the 100-member congress and his early months in office were marked by a failure to negotiate agreements with opposition parties that would allow him to gain control of the chamber, explaining why he announced that he would employ referendums to achieve his reforms. Yet despite Gutiérrez's stated disdain for political parties, he was only able to build a slim congressional majority by forging close links with the Partido Roldosista Ecuatoriana (PRE, Roldosista party) based on promises to its exiled leader and former president Abdalá Bucaram (1996–97), and with the Partido Renovador Institucional Acción Nacional (PRIAN, Party of National Institutional Action and Renovation). Congress had dismissed Bucaram as president in 1997 for 'mental incapacity' and alleged corruption, and he had gone into exile in Panama. Among the confrontational actions taken by Gutiérrez was the purging of the supreme court in late 2004. Under pressure from the president, congress voted narrowly to sack 27 of the 31 supreme court judges, most of whom were seen as having links with the opposition centre-right Partido Social Cristiano (PSC, Social-Christian Party). The move increased polarisation and led to protests by the Social Christians and counter-demonstrations by the Roldosista party in Guayaquil. In a highly politicised decision, the new court decided in early 2005 to drop criminal charges against Bucaram, initially paving the way for his return to Ecuador. Bucaram's Roldosista party helped to prevent efforts by congress to impeach Gutiérrez, and so was rewarded with this decision. The supreme court also enabled Gustavo Noboa (2000–03), the caretaker president prior to Gutiérrez, to return from exile in the Dominican Republic. However, Noboa was placed under house arrest later that year as an investigation into his handling of foreign debt talks began, and allegations against Bucaram were reinstated. In November 2005, a full complement of new supreme court judges was eventually installed after they had been appointed by an independent review panel. Another result of Gutiérrez's hostility to parties was to have polarised debates in Ecuador's legislature. In April 2005, a debate was delayed when MPs threw water bottles and coins during a fight in parliament, and some made gun signs and pretended to shoot at each other. Executive hostility to parties has continued under President Rafael Correa (2006–) who has routinely attacked Ecuador's party system as a *partidocracia* – a term also used elsewhere in the region referring to a political system dominated by an unrepresentative political party elite (see Box 4.2).

constitutional reforms adopted in 1996 that reflected efforts by the traditional parties to co-operate against the EP-FA, had an impact on this pattern of politics (see Cason, 2002). The EP-FA had been slowly eating into the dominant position of the two main parties since the early 1990s. The EP-FA victory in presidential elections in 2004 brought to an end this format and confirmed both the need for much closer co-operation among the traditional parties and a trend in Uruguayan politics towards competition between two blocs: the EP-FA and a centre-right alliance comprising the Colorados and Blancos. Even when there may be several or many parties in the legislature, one dominant traditional party such as the PRI in Mexico or the Peronists in Argentina is likely to structure competition.

The nature of parties and the degree to which the members of a party are united behind the same goals also influence the behaviour of legislatures. Party unity is important because it determines whether a party leader can enforce discipline on their legislators and this, in turn, will affect how parties behave within congress and their reliability as partners in a coalition. Even in cases where majorities have given parties control over procedural arrangements such as the legislative agenda and committee appointments, internal divisions can limit a dominant party's effectiveness and determine whether presidents will face a workable or a recalcitrant legislature (Morgenstern, 2002b). In Argentina, the Peronists have traditionally dominated legislative politics, yet have also suffered from persistent factionalism. The ability of a president to forge a coalition in order to win support for draft legislation may depend on the degree of party discipline in congress, that is, the extent to which the individual deputies of parties toe their party's line. Party discipline is stronger in some countries, such as Argentina and Chile, than in others such as Brazil, which traditionally was considered to have undisciplined parties unable to sustain strong coalitions, thereby frustrating the legislative agenda (see Amorim Neto, 2002b). In Chile, the multi-party centre-left Concertación coalition has been able to maintain discipline out of fear of the return of authoritarianism. Yet presidentialism may be able to function in Latin America as a *result* of weak, undisciplined parties, because a president without a clear majority confronted by disciplined parties would find it difficult to govern. Linz (1994) has argued that, since parties are not responsible or accountable for government stability and policy (because those are the tasks of the president), there are few incentives for parties to remain disciplined or to act responsibly.

Factors that determine party unity include ideology: central to the idea of a functioning democracy is a notion of well-organised parties that are ideologically coherent over time. Ideology and party programmes are considered to be an important factor in structuring party systems in Latin America and have a key role in the subsequent behaviour of legislatures (see Kitschelt *et al.*, 2010). The degree of ideological polarisation – the drift by parties away from the centre to increasingly extreme positions – will affect a president's ability to build coalitions in a legislature, with a lower degree of polarisation making coalitions more likely. The degree of ideological polarisation is also related to the number of parties, with two-party systems tending to experience patterns of competition that push political actors to the centre (see Sartori, 1976). Mainwaring and Scully (1995) argued that the combination of multi-partism and high polarisation can generate problems of governability.

In a measure employed by Morgenstern (2002b) some parties such as Brazil's PT and Chile's Socialists (PSCh) have demonstrated few internal differences and have been more ideologically cohesive over long periods. In Brazil, the PT has emerged as one of the most ideologically coherent parties, even though it is a heterogeneous coalition of positions often based on strong regional identities that have been hard, at times, to reconcile. The PRI in Mexico is among parties that should not be able to rely on ideology to generate party unity, for example, because of disagreements between its legislators. In 2003, serious divisions opened up within the PRI in congress over President Vicente Fox's (2000–06) proposed tax reforms between Elba Esther Gordillo, the leader of the PRI's congressional delegation, and another party leader Roberto Madrazo. Gordillo alleged that Madrazo had told lies, which he denied, prompting many PRI deputies to demand her replacement, and a new leader, Emilio Chauyffet, was then elected in a vote boycotted by more than 100 deputies. As a result, at one point both Gordillo and Chauyffet claimed to be leading the party in congress.

It is to be expected that bills introduced by members of the majority party have a higher probability of being passed than those introduced by members of other parties, but the success of legislators belonging to minor parties should vary based on their ideological positions. Centrists and independents tend to be at an advantage over more 'extremist' parties because of the former's value to a president when a specific threshold of support needs to be met and the fact that the latter are less likely to represent the preferences of the legislature.

The judiciary and judicial reform

The distinctive Iberian inheritance of Latin American legal systems helps to explain some of the characteristics of the judiciary in the region. Constitutions and legal principles derive from a code-law tradition that creates a self-contained framework within which judgements are made, unlike legal practices commonly found in countries with an Anglo-Saxon tradition based upon common law precedent, and hence upon interpretation. Such characteristics have implications for legal practice in Latin America, where codes are fixed and do not allow much room for interpretation. As a result, rulings can be resistant to compromise as courts and judges *apply* the law rather than *interpret* it. Larraín (2004) says that, at the same time, an important aspect of Latin American political culture that has survived since colonial times is a peculiar approach to legal norms, which tend to be formally upheld, but flouted in practice. He argues that this accounts both for excessive legalism – the formal and ritualistic adherence to rules – yet also to a readiness to ignore those rules in practice. This legal inheritance makes it more difficult to maintain the independence of the judiciary in Latin America – turning judges and lawyers into bureaucrats who do not enjoy the status of the legal profession elsewhere – and limits their power. It also helps to explain why, although Latin American constitutions provide for a division of powers between executive, legislature and judiciary, these branches of government are not equal in practice and it has been difficult for judges to challenge an executive by declaring a law unconstitutional. Historically, Latin

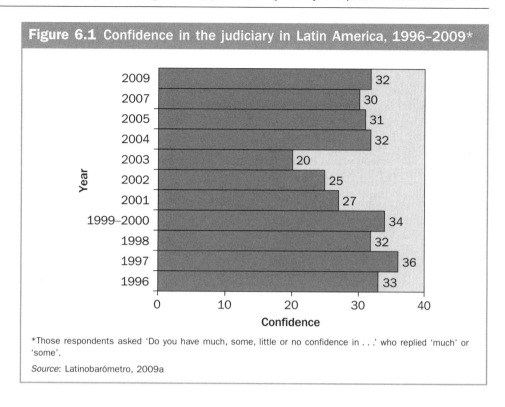

Figure 6.1 Confidence in the judiciary in Latin America, 1996–2009*

*Those respondents asked 'Do you have much, some, little or no confidence in . . .' who replied 'much' or 'some'.

Source: Latinobarómetro, 2009a

American judiciaries have lacked the power to assert themselves and have been vulnerable to political influence (see Wilson *et al.*, 2010). Public trust in the judicial system is also low and judiciaries offer the best examples of institutional failure in Latin America. Latinobarómetro surveys between 1996 and 2009, for example, suggested little change or only a slight increase in levels of confidence in the judiciary (see Figure 6.1).

The belief that many judges or court officials are corrupt also remains strong in Latin America. Data compiled by Latinobarómetro (2008) reveals little change among respondents in what they considered to be the probability of bribing a judge between 2004 (36 per cent) and 2008 (35 per cent). Alongside corruption are other persistent weaknesses in judicial systems. An independent and effective judicial system is an important pillar of democracy because judges play a key role in upholding constitutional rights and freedoms (Frühling, 1998). However, many of Latin America's judicial systems are neither independent nor effective, often fail to ensure citizens enjoy their constitutional rights and suffer from political interference. Inequality based on racial, gender and class prejudice within a legal process that favours the rich and powerful is also common. This inequality is reinforced by the lack of 'due process' – formal proceedings carried out fairly in accordance with established rules – which leads to many miscarriages of justice against vulnerable groups. Buscaglia (1998) argued that in Latin America there has been an absence of the basic elements of an effective judicial system: consistent and relatively predictable decisions; access to courts for the whole population irrespective of income; reasonable time for the resolution of cases; and adequate sentences.

Why is a strong judiciary so important? Prillaman (2000) argued that a strong judiciary is essential for checking executive and legislative breaches of the constitutional order, laying the foundations for economic development, and building popular support for democracy. An independent judiciary armed with judicial review – the power to rule on whether laws and decisions are constitutional that enables judges to ensure executive and legislative activities are legal – has been seen as the most important guarantee of constitutionality and a key obstacle to tyranny. An effective judiciary also helps to create the conditions for economic growth by safeguarding property rights, creating the predictability in the marketplace that is necessary for investors, and ensuring that all citizens can participate in the economy competitively and fairly (*ibid.*; see also Martínez, 1998). The recourse by citizens to the law in an effort to protect property rights was an important feature of the political mobilisation that characterised Argentine politics in late 2001 (see Smulovitz, 2006). Lastly, an effective judiciary is essential for enhancing public faith in the rule of law that underpins democratic governance (see Chapter 4).

According to Prillaman (2000), most Latin American judicial systems have fared badly according to three criteria: independence, efficiency and access.

Independence

Politicians have limited judicial independence in different ways. Some administrations use constitutional provisions allowing them to review appointments to limit the tenure of judges. This often occurs when a new president takes office with the assumption that he or she has full authority to replace personnel. Other executives have tried to pack courts with their appointees to make them serve their will. In 1990, President Carlos Menem (1989–99) packed Argentina's supreme court by increasing the number of judges from five to nine, ostensibly to improve its efficiency but most probably because he feared the court might block his government's economic reform programme. As a result of the decision, two of the original five sitting justices resigned, giving Menem's supporters an automatic majority in the court and resulting in supreme court judgements that were blatantly in his favour. Efforts by subsequent presidents to rid the court of Menem appointees were largely unsuccessful until the administration of Néstor Kirchner (2003–07), who was able to establish new criteria for allowing justices to be chosen through an independent process. Within a month of taking office as president in May 2003, for example, Kirchner persuaded congress to reopen impeachment proceedings against the supreme court that ultimately led to the resignation of key members.

In Venezuela, after taking power in 1999, President Hugo Chávez launched efforts to dissolve the supreme court *en masse*, suspended hundreds of judges in lower courts, and then appointed 101 new judges. Chávez and his supporters argued that this purge was necessary because of corruption and bias within the judiciary. As a result, the new supreme court regularly ruled in the president's favour. In late 2000, the former supreme court was again restructured and renamed the 'Supreme Tribunal of Justice', over which the president's Movimiento Quinta República (MVR, Fifth Republic Movement) had full control through appointment procedures.

Similarly, in Ecuador several purges have occurred and opposition generated by Gutiérrez's decision to tinker with the supreme court, and the subsequent decision by the judges he appointed to drop corruption charges against two former presidents, fuelled the public anger that contributed to his dismissal by congress in 2005 (see Box 6.2).

Another way of limiting the autonomy of courts has been to create special tribunals under the aegis of justice or interior ministries that bypass the court structure and can be controlled by the executive. The Sandinistas in Nicaragua created tribunals and popular courts dominated by party members and under the control of the interior ministry that ultimately answered to the president (Prillaman, 2000).

The independence of judges has also been compromised by judges higher up the court hierarchy sympathetic to a particular regime. In Chile, under Pinochet supreme court judges sympathetic to the military government removed or controlled lower-court judges who pursued human rights charges against military officers. Sometimes, judges have been threatened with violence by members of the state's security forces, drug traffickers or criminals. In Brazil, for example, Judge Antônio José Machado Dias was assassinated by gunmen in March 2003 as he drove home from a courthouse in President Prudente. Authorities investigated possible connections between the murder and a crime wave in Rio de Janeiro involving drug-trafficking cartels (ICJ, 2003). Lawyers investigating possible corruption are also at risk.

Causing judges to feel insecure makes them much more susceptible to partisan pressures and has implications for the integrity of court procedures, encouraging some of them to resort to corruption while sitting in the expectation that their tenure will be limited. Corruption usually takes the form of bribery and thrives in conditions where there is insecure tenure, low salaries, nepotism and unequal access to justice (Buscaglia, 1998). The huge wealth amassed by drug-traffickers has been a particular problem for the administration of justice in some Latin American countries. It is common in Latin American legal practice for judges to employ *ex parte* communication in which they meet lawyers and individual parties to cases separately, and this can create incentives for corruption and a lack of accountability in courts (*ibid.*). Making judges insecure can also encourage them to confine themselves to narrow administrative matters and avoid considering issues of legal principle or controversy.

Administrative inefficiency

Judiciaries in Latin America have tended to reflect the same problems of bureaucratic inefficiency as other sectors of the state, and this hampers the administration of justice (Prillaman, 2000). Latin American countries generally lack a professional managerial class to administer the court system and allow judges to run the show, limiting the time they spend on judicial matters. Measures of administrative inefficiency include pre-trial detention rates and the time it takes for a case to get to court, which tend to be lengthy in Latin America. In countries such as Argentina, the proportion of the prison population who have yet to be convicted often exceeds 60 per cent. The proportion of national budgets spent on justice in Latin America is also often low in comparison with more developed regions. A shortage of resources can mean low salaries, exacerbating corruption and restricting efforts by the judiciary to attract well trained personnel (Buscaglia, 1998). Suspects awaiting trial or offenders who have been convicted experience extremely poor conditions in prisons starved of resources (see Box 6.3). In Bolivia, an estimated 1,200 children live in prisons while their parents serve their sentences.

SOCIETY	Box 6.3

Penal systems in crisis

Bloody prison riots provide recurrent reminders of the serious problems faced by penal systems throughout Latin America and a measure of the task facing reformers. In January 2010, for example, violent clashes between rival gangs inside a prison in the Mexican state of Durango – housing 1,800 inmates, considerably more than its official capacity – left at least 23 inmates dead. Clashes at the same jail the previous August had left 20 prisoners dead. In October 2008, 21 inmates were killed in a riot at a prison in the state of Tamaulipas, and a month earlier, 21 were killed after two jail riots in Tijuana.

In the Dominican Republic in March 2005, at least 133 inmates were killed in a blaze at an over-crowded, vermin-infested prison in Higüey after rival gangs fighting over control of the drug trade set their bedding ablaze and blocked the entrance to a cell block known as 'Vietnam'. Only 26 prisoners were rescued from the jail. Prison officials said the violence began when members of three gangs began fighting for control of who would sell drugs and cigarettes and inmates blocked the cell block entrance in order to fight it out. The incident underlined the appalling conditions prisoners endure in the Dominican Republic, which the UN says has the most overcrowded jails in the Western Hemisphere. The country has 35 prisons with a built capacity for 9,000 prisoners but which at the end of 2004 held more than 13,500. Higüey is considered by Dominican human rights campaigners to have the worst conditions of any jail in the country and they have dubbed it 'hell on earth'. The Vietnam cell-block was designed for between 25 and 40 inmates but was in fact crammed with more than 150, and was so crowded that prisoners slept on top of toilets.

Gang fights and riots resulting from poor conditions, overcrowding and bad management are a frequent occurrence at prisons across Latin America. Gang culture fuelled by poverty is at the root of the problem of violence and helps to explain sophisticated levels of organisation that allow weapons to be smuggled into jails: at Higüey, rival groups set on each other with knives and machetes after a gang leader had been shot. Organised gangs in countries such as Honduras operate as criminal enterprises and fuel criminal and even political violence. In Guatemala, in August 2005 at least 30 prisoners died in battles in several prisons between rival gangs who co-ordinated the fighting using mobile phones. The gangs, the Mara Salvatrucha and the rival Mara 18, originally emerged in the US and, when their members returned or were deported, then spread to Central America. The Mara Salvatrucha was blamed for a massacre of bus passengers in the city of San Pedro Sula, Honduras, in late 2004 in which 28 people died. The gang's alleged leader was arrested in the US two months later. The deposed Honduran president, Manuel Zelaya (2006–09), had made efforts to tackle violence by the maras an important policy objective of his administration.

Sources: Various; news reports

Access to justice

A third area in which Latin American judicial systems are weak is access to justice, which tends to be more restricted the lower down the socioeconomic scale a citizen is situated. The perceptions of vulnerable social groups demonstrate, in some cases, what they regard as very limited access to justice (see Table 6.4). Access to the legal system is particularly poor in rural areas where the distances citizens need to travel to resolve conflicts are large. Buscaglia (1998) revealed that peasants in the remotest rural areas of Peru on average had to travel more than 50km to reach a court to solve a legal dispute. Remote and isolated court circuits can suffer problems of corruption and allow powerful local interests to influence proceedings. One result of this is that the formal channels of justice may not often be the main arenas for resolving disputes in large parts of the Latin American countryside. In urban areas too, poorer families also tend to have less access to courts. Buscaglia points to research showing a negative correlation between family income and the length of court procedures and costs of litigation.

Table 6.4 Perceptions of specific groups regarding equality before the law*

Country	Always or almost always have their rights respected**			
	Women	Indigenous people	Poor people	Immigrants
Argentina	69.7	9.1	7.9	21.4
Bolivia	54.8	21.2	13.9	38.51
Brazil	78.3	34.3	20.1	47.6
Chile	68.9	33.5	19.9	27.2
Colombia	70.3	22.1	18.1	24.1
Costa Rica	59.8	23.2	13.7	21.3
Dominican Rep.	76.4	11.5	22.2	40.2
Ecuador	60.4	40.2	25.2	30.6
El Salvador	72.0	32.3	32.4	30.9
Guatemala	65.3	38.7	24.8	18.7
Honduras	69.8	34.6	23.5	25.1
Mexico	54.8	7.5	5.6	9.9
Nicaragua	60.3	23.5	17.7	21.5
Panama	65.6	10.5	10.7	21.0
Paraguay	71.5	15.0	10.9	54.1
Peru	61.9	16.0	11.6	55.4
Uruguay	78.4	17.1	21.8	39.3
Venezuela	73.7	28.2	26.1	30.3
Latin America	67.0	23.1	17.8	30.8

*2002

**Includes the answers to both options 'always' and 'almost always'

Notes: The number of women, indigenous people, poor people and immigrants varies between 18,040 and 19,596.

Source: UNDP, 2004b; results of processing answers to questions p24u in the UNDP Proprietary Section of the Latinobarómetro report 2002

However, despite the commonly accepted negative characteristics of the judiciary, there have been occasions when courts have challenged legislation and executive power and resisted attempts by politicians to compromise their independence. Courts have greatly enhanced the human and civil rights agenda in Latin America, and at times have played a key role in impeaching incumbent presidents. Some have also turned against executives who appointed them in ways that challenge standard perceptions about constraints upon judicial independence (see Helmke, 2005). In Venezuela, judges appointed by Chávez came into direct conflict with the president following the short-lived coup of April 2002, in which he was politically weakened, by making a number of rulings that were unfavourable to him. During the abortive coup, the interim administration led by Pedro Carmona had identified the supreme court closely with Chávez and it was temporarily dissolved. Following the coup, the supreme court refused to support efforts by Chávez to punish military officers accused of taking part in the coup and struck down legislation he had previously passed. Venezuela's assembly, dominated by Chávez supporters, voted to impeach the supreme court's vice-president. One of the court's responses was to go on strike in protest at what it argued was political harassment.

In the 1990s public policies to ensure an independent, impartial and effective judicial system became an important theme of debate (Frühling, 1998). Since then, there has been a comprehensive agenda of judicial reform in Latin America, often backed by multilateral funding (see Biebesheimer and Mejía eds, 2000; Domingo and Sieder eds, 2001; Jarquín and Carrillo eds, 1998). Since the 1990s, an estimated $1 billion in financial support for judicial reform has been granted by the World Bank, the Inter-American Development Bank (IDB), the United Nations Development Program (UNDP), non-governmental institutions and countries to long-term projects to reform the administration of justice in the region (see DeShazo and Vargas, 2006). Accordingly, many countries in Latin America have undertaken projects to overhaul their judicial systems and institutions ranging from constitutional reform and the implementation of new civil and criminal codes, to changes in how justice is administered.

Although this reform process has had both successes and failures, the most recent regional evaluation of judicial reform efforts in Latin America, compiled in 2006, concluded that the overall record is disappointing, having failed to meet high expectations largely because of poorly functioning new systems that are slow, lack transparency, pay scant attention to users, and lack independence in decisionmaking (*ibid.*). The most successful examples of judicial reform have been in the area of criminal law, where there has been important progress in dismantling inquisitorial procedures that fostered authoritarian practices such as the widespread abuse of pre-trial detention. Reform of the criminal justice system in Chile, for example, is generally considered by observers to have been a success, given the ambitious scope of change, the resources allocated to reform, and the political commitment to undertake this process. An important element of reform was the adoption of a new code of criminal procedure, whose final implementation phase was in 2005. But progress in the area of criminal justice reform has not been matched in other areas, such as civil, family or labour law. Studies suggest that, despite efforts to reform Latin America's courts, they remain in crisis and bedevilled by underfunding, corruption, politicisation and cronyism (Helmke, 2005; see also UNDP, 2004b; Constance, 2003).

There are several reasons for limited progress in judicial reform in Latin America, some of which relate to the nature of the judiciary itself, which tends to be a conservative institution not given to short-term change and with a predilection to arcane practices. Judges are often reluctant to delegate or be open to the monitoring of their performance. Presidential pressure on the judiciary remains a challenge, with the judiciary in Argentina, Ecuador, Peru and Venezuela all coming under pressure from the executive in different ways. Judicial reform in Venezuela, for example, is often seen as a failure because reform efforts involving considerable investment were largely cancelled out by the Chávez presidency's interference in the judiciary, resulting in the loss of its independence. Peru provides an example of the degree to which economic and political crises can affect the progress of judicial reform and the constant challenge to judicial independence of executive pressure (see Box 6.4). Long-term political instability in countries such as Ecuador and Bolivia has prevented the judicial branch from establishing institutional authority, and judicial reform can face serious political obstacles and can become mired in partisanship. In Ecuador, for example, moves to reform the judiciary by President Gutiérrez provoked large protests, eventually prompting him to declare a state of emergency in April 2005 prior to his dismissal. After it had voted to remove 27 of the 31 supreme court judges, the fragile coalition supporting Gutiérrez was accused of sidestepping democratic institutions in order to concentrate his power. Gutiérrez argued the judges were supporters of the rightwing Partido Social Cristiano (PSC,

---

CASE STUDY   **Box 6.4**

Judicial reform in Peru

Peru's legal system and judges enjoy little public confidence and are seen by many citizens as neither impartial nor effective. The court system rarely extends to the municipal level of local government outside the main cities, and is considered by many to have long been subject to political influence and corruption. Yet a lack of sustained political support for the reform process has limited its progress. Following the end of Alberto Fujimori's administration in 2000, greater priority was placed on judicial reform, resulting in 2003 in the creation by congress of the Comisión Especial para la Reforma Integral de la Administración de Justicia (CERIAJUS, Special Commission for the Integral Reform of Administration of Justice). Government and civil society teams working under the auspices of CERIAJUS drew up a national plan of more than 170 projects, although few of these were eventually carried out. Improvements that did result included the creation of new anti-corruption courts to investigate crimes by public servants under the Fujimori regime and to monitor governmental ethics. Other concrete initiatives were the establishment of commercial courts in Lima to resolve disputes, better use of Peru's constitutional tribunal in interpreting the constitutionality of laws, and an extension in the use of justices of the peace to settle minor disputes. Yet only a small proportion of the CERIAJUS proposals were carried out, and some of the new tribunals produced limited results. The reform process in Peru failed to instil greater public confidence in the country's legal system and to overcome long backlogs in cases that remain pending, with a typical case brought to trial still taking two to three years to resolve. Nor did the reform efforts make inroads into the ineffective distribution of caseloads and widespread corruption among judicial branch employees (see Azabache, 2006; DeShazo and Vargas, 2006).

Social-Christian Party) headed by a rival, but congress replaced them with judges mostly affiliated with the populist Partido Roldosista Ecuatoriano (Ecuadorian Roldosist Party) and Partido Renovador Institucional de Acción Nacional (PRIAN, Institutional Renewal Party of National Action), which supported Gutiérrez.

Public administration

A distinguishing feature of the Latin American state has been the centralisation of decisionmaking and administration. Most of the countries in the region inherited centralised institutions from Spanish colonial rule (see Chapters 1, 12). During the twentieth century, the central state further concentrated power, authority and resources through policies of state-led economic development (see Box 2.1, Chapter 14) and, by the 1980s, most Latin American states retained a highly centralised institutional structure (Selee, 2004). However, at the same time strong regional identities, often reflecting the autonomy of provincial elites from central government, also emerged. Countries such as Brazil and Argentina have a long history of decentralised federal government by which authority has been devolved to states or provinces, although their political systems have alternated between periods of greater and lesser centralisation. Centralisation characterised state-led industrial development from the 1940s until the 1980s but also contributed to authoritarianism and limited pluralism. Centralisation also distorted policymaking priorities – fuelling inequality by concentrating public investment in urban areas – and it skewed public administration by generating ever larger bureaucracies that proliferated into a maze of ministries, secretariats and agencies with complex and redundant organisational structures often lacking a clear chain of accountability (Schmitter, 1971). Many Latin American bureaucracies were characterised by inefficiency, job insecurity, high staff turnover rates, an inadequate use of expertise, formalism, legalism, poor communication, a lack of co-ordination between departments and nepotism (Sloan, 1984). This was reinforced by the vested interest of politicians practising clientelism who sought access to the patronage offered by ministries and public agencies, and of bureaucrats and unions within those ministries themselves (see Boxes 2.1, 2.2, 7.1).

Reform of these administrative structures began with democratisation, and since the late 1980s, reform programmes have been launched seeking to depoliticise and professionalise these unwieldy centralised bureaucracies in an effort to foster good governance. In a democracy it is essential for a bureaucracy to be neutral and for public servants to put society's interests before partisan or personal agendas. It is also increasingly recognised that there is a link between the quality of public sector institutions and economic development. One result of these reform efforts is that Latin American state activity today is now relatively limited in comparison with more developed regions of the world. By the end of the 1990s, state spending as a proportion of GDP was lower in the region than in both the industrial Organisation for Economic Co-operation and Development (OECD) states and south-east Asia (Franko, 1999). The public sector in Latin America was about half the size of that of the average government of industrial countries, and the Latin American state spent less on social security, defence, health, and education (*ibid.*).

However, efforts to reform civil services have confronted significant political obstacles and, in a summary compiled on behalf of the UN and the Centro Latinoamericano de Administración para el Desarollo (CLAD, Latin American Centre of Administration for Development), Longo (2005) identified resistance by a number of political actors to civil service reform:

■ *Governing political classes:* Established politicians are likely to resist bureaucratic reform if the political cost to them of renouncing clientelism is greater than the benefits they will gain by introducing a more meritocratic system. For this reason, reformist governments can often encounter resistance to change from within a government's cabinet itself. In Brazil, for example, under President Fernando Henrique Cardoso (1995–2003) several cabinet ministers were among the most resistant individuals to civil service reform despite this being government policy.

■ *The political opposition:* Opponents of an incumbent government have a vested interest in rejecting their initiatives, and a minimum level of political consensus is therefore required for civil service reform to proceed. This may be difficult to forge in a divided congress.

■ *A government's own party:* According to Longo (2005), the functionaries of a governing party are likely to be intermediaries in clientelistic practices and so will tend to perceive control of public employment as a resource they cannot relinquish.

■ *Public employees:* Civil servants themselves are likely to resist reforms that may threaten their jobs and oppose the introduction of meritocratic practices, especially if they themselves have gained jobs as a result of nepotism or clientelism.

■ *Public service unions:* Unions representing civil servants are most likely to oppose reforms that threaten jobs, propose the privatisation of certain activities or imply any weakening of their collective bargaining by, say, the introduction of personalised contracts.

Given the potential scale of opposition and resistance to public service reform, some governments have kept the process strictly under the control of the executive and excluded other interested parties. In Uruguay, for example, President Julio María Sanguinetti (1985–90, 1995–2000) maintained the design and implementation of civil service reforms firmly within the executive and avoided consulting the legislature, political parties and social groups about it. Although there is considerable national variation, the civil services of Latin America continue to share similar problems. Longo (2005) identified these as:

- weak observance of codified rules on salaries and remuneration, promotion and dismissal;
- high levels of discretion in public-sector management that frequently give rise to arbitrary practices or political clientelism;
- a significant lack of professionalism;

- rigid procedural structures that obstruct the efficient implementation of public policies and the ability to adapt to change;
- significant shortfalls in internal structures, processes and capacities when it comes to personnel management.

Mexico provides a good example of restructuring efforts to engender professionalism and accountability in public administration. The absence of genuine party competition until the 1980s meant that the federal bureaucracy had developed intimate relationships with the bureaucracy of the governing PRI and was politically loyal to the executive. Over many decades, this relationship had engendered a huge, inefficient and corrupt federal administration comprising between 300,000 and 500,000 workers over which the president had absolute control. The president was free to appoint officials at almost every level and operate a system of rewards and sanctions that bolstered executive control. The change of administration every six years usually meant an accompanying change of thousands of federal officials, creating uncertainty throughout the public sector and ample opportunities for last-minute corruption. An absence of accountability meant that citizens were virtually powerless in the face of bureaucratic abuses.

A co-ordinated effort at reform began under the administration of President Ernesto Zedillo (1994–2000) with several programmes between 1995–2000 aimed at introducing accountability, evaluation, efficiency and a new professional service culture into public administration, and at tackling corruption and impunity. However, these reforms were complicated by differences in terms of overall vision and approach between the ministries charged with drawing them up, the Secretaría de Hacienda y Crédito Público (SHCP, Ministry of Finance and Public Credit) and the Secretaría de Contraloría y Desarrollo Administrativo (SECODAM, Ministry of Auditing and Administrative Development). They were also premised on internal self-regulation and, given the scale of the task and political resistance, had a limited impact.

Mexico turned to countries such as the United Kingdom and New Zealand for advice and, following the defeat of the PRI in presidential elections in 2000, more wholesale reforms became possible. In late 2002, Mexico's senate took the first steps in approving a combination of proposals put forward by the PRI and the PAN, and in early 2003 legislation was adopted to remove civil service appointments from political control. The administration of President Vicente Fox (2000–06) reorganised an auditing ministry into the Secretaría de la Función Pública (SFP, Public Administration Ministry) with the aim of targeting corruption in public services. The core principle of Mexico's reforms has been to introduce performance indicators so that appointments and progression within public administration are based on professional criteria such as merit as opposed to political loyalty, corruption or nepotism.

Decentralisation

In the 1980s and 1990s, decentralisation reforms driven by political and economic considerations and aiming to strengthen the role of local and regional (i.e. 'sub-national') governments also rose up the political agenda throughout Latin America. The crisis of the 1980s had cast doubt over the legitimacy of established political elites, who saw decentralisation as a way of redirecting discontent to local arenas. The devolution of powers and responsibilities in one sector of administration such as education and healthcare ('sectoral decentralisation') were also driven by concerns for efficiency or budgetary pressures (Selee, 2004). Supporters argued that, by allowing politically relevant action to take place 'beyond the state', decentralisation would strengthen democratic governance and improve policy delivery (see Montero and Samuels eds, 2004; Oxhorn *et al.* eds, 2004; Scott, 2009).

Decentralisation has changed the nature of the state in Latin America and reconfigured its relationship with society (see Box 2.1). In countries such as Mexico, Guatemala, Venezuela, Brazil and Argentina, reforms have transformed the role of local and regional governments.

In Mexico, economic crisis led to reforms in 1983 granting local authorities (*municipios* or municipalities) greater autonomy and resources. In response to its declining legitimacy and the increasing electoral success of opposition forces at a local level, the ruling PRI undertook further reforms in the 1990s that expanded state and municipal functions and increased their resources. Successive governments also pursued sectoral decentralisation to make health and education services more efficient. Since the mid-1990s, the desire of some indigenous groups for greater autonomy in local decisionmaking has been a key feature of disputes about decentralisation in Mexico. Although indigenous groups in the state of Oaxaca enjoy some meaningful autonomy at a municipal level, successive presidencies have largely resisted decentralisation of this kind. An indigenous law passed in 2001, that had its origin in negotiations following a rebellion in the state of Chiapas in 1994 (see Chapter 8, Boxes 12.6, 13.5), codified autonomous rights but was rejected by the country's main indigenous groups. This has resulted in the declaration by some indigenous groups of their own autonomy, not recognised by state authorities. The desire for greater recognition of indigenous rights and autonomy formed the backdrop to violent conflicts in Oaxaca in 2006.

In Venezuela, recommendations put forward by a commission on state reform in 1984 led to the creation of elected state and municipal governments for the first time in 1989. In Brazil and Argentina, the transition to democracy revived state and provincial government. Even in states such as Guatemala where most power resides in central structures – sometimes referred to as unitary states – decentralisation has had an important impact (see Box 6.5). A unitary state is one in which sub-national authorities either do not exist or have such little power that these are irrelevant to the political process.

In Bolivia, the debate about decentralisation and indigenous autonomy has fuelled serious secessionist tensions in the *media luna* region, the crescent or 'half-moon' shaped region comprising the country's northern, eastern and southern lowlands (see Boxes 4.1, 8.7, 12.11). The most public face of the autonomy movement in this region is the Movimiento Nación Camba de Liberación (Movement for the Liberation of the Camba Nation), a name referring to the heartland of Santa Cruz, which argues that federal institutions are beholden to *altiplano* (highland) indigenous groups and seeks to create a breakaway state in the resource-rich and more white and *mestizo* east. The response of President Evo Morales (2006–) has been

Decentralisation in Guatemala

Guatemala has a tradition of centralised government that was reinforced by military rule during the country's prolonged civil war. Centralisation meant that the rural areas in which most of Guatemala's large indigenous population live were greatly neglected. For example, by the end of the 1970s about 26 per cent of the population lived in the capital, Guatemala City, but this received 70 per cent of public investment (Puente and Molina, 2000). Constitutional changes in the 1980s, democratisation, and the peace process finally created a climate by the late 1990s in which progress on decentralisation could be made, and various political groups advanced proposals for devolving power from the capital. Guatemala's 1985 constitution increased the authority of municipal governments and amendments to the constitution in 1993, the municipal code of 1988, and a number of other laws about elections and political organisation together established the municipality – usually a town or district council – as the main decentralised authority enjoying considerable autonomy (Puente and Linares, 2004). Today there are 331 municipal governments in Guatemala. Peace accords signed in 1996 granted recognition to indigenous forms of association and dispute resolution within municipalities, and these became law in 2002 (Cardona, 2002). Municipal elections have become more transparent and fair as a result.

The administration and management of municipalities is carried out by a corporation (town council) comprising local elected representatives and presided over by the mayor. Guatemala's constitution and municipal code assign broad responsibilities to municipalities in several main areas: government and administration; budgeting; urban planning, land use and boundary maintenance; and the provision of public services such as transport, street lighting, refuse disposal and park maintenance (Puente and Linares, 2004). Because of uneven delivery, Guatemala has also experimented with 'associated municipalities' by which a group of small municipalities receive legal recognition as a collective entity allowing them to develop joint solutions to infrastructure and economic development problems by contracting loans (Cardona, 2002; Selee, 2004). Recent decentralisation initiatives in Latin America have addressed the administration of natural resources in an effort to increase forest production and promote the sustainable use of forests. The decentralisation of land and the management of natural resources was a key concession by Guatemala's government under the peace process that ended the civil war. Recent legislation in the country – which is still forested over 34.4 per cent of its territory – has transferred the regulation and administration of communal forests to the municipalities.

Among decentralised authorities, only municipalities have fiscal autonomy. They receive money from central government collected through federal taxation, can levy their own municipal taxes, and can generate income through fees for certain public services. Municipal revenues grew from 8 per cent of total state revenues mandated in the 1985 constitution to 10 per cent after 1993 and then to about 20 per cent by the late 1990s (Puente and Molina, 2000; Selee, 2004). Guatemala's constitution says municipal governments must spend 90 per cent of their revenues on investments in education, preventive health programmes, infrastructure and public services, which limits their ability to employ staff and their day-to-day operations. Congress keeps tight control over municipal taxation, which is collected once a year according to a formula based on income levels from all adults between 18 and 65 residing in the municipality. The central government also shares out other tax income with municipalities, such as VAT and taxes on the distribution of fuels. Special municipal taxes can also be levied on the owners of property who benefit from municipal improvements, such as drainage works, and municipalities can collect a levy on properties (Puente and Linares, 2004).

Polls suggest that citizens have a positive view of the role of municipalities and local elections often feature independent candidates put forward by 'civic committees' (Selee, 2004). Civic committees have been credited with allowing citizens to develop new forms of political action in a country where parties are known for indulging in patronage politics. Decentralisation has also enhanced the participation of indigenous people in the political process and recognised indigenous forms of governance (see Chapters 8, 13). Although few nationally elected officials are indigenous, local elections are increasingly being won by indigenous candidates. In 2002, while only 11 per cent of congressional deputies in Guatemala were indigenous, 52 of Guatemala's 330 municipalities had indigenous mayors (Cardona, 2002; Puente and Linares, 2004). The incorporation of traditional methods for selecting leaders and resolving disputes according to customary practices became law in 2002.

to seek a compromise in the development of decentralisation between groups of this kind in the east and *altiplano* indigenous groups that have also sought greater autonomy and a federal emphasis on the indigenous character of Bolivian nationality (see below, and Chapter 13).

There have been three main types of decentralisation: political, administrative and fiscal.

Political decentralisation

In the early 1980s, few Latin American countries had democratically elected local authorites. The most important element of decentralisation has been the establishment of elected governments at regional and local levels. Many countries have introduced or revived local government, and these have become important arenas of political debate (Selee, 2004).

Administrative decentralisation

Decentralisation reforms have laid down the functions of sub-national governments or authorities more clearly than before and given them more responsibility. Constitutional reforms in Brazil in 1986, the Mexican municipal reforms of 1983 and 1999, the Guatemalan constitution of 1985, and constitutional reforms in Venezuela in 1989 defined clear responsibilities for sub-national authorities. The creation of regions for specific public policy objectives, as opposed to self-government, is sometimes called 'regionalisation'. In Brazil, Argentina and Mexico, for example, central governments gave regional governments responsibilities for education and healthcare policies, but kept control over the curriculum and teachers' wages. Municipal governments have been given responsibility for functions such as local infrastructure, waste disposal, and planning and often enjoy wide autonomy. In Venezuela, 'asymmetric decentralisation' allows different local authorites to choose from a menu of functions they would like to assume based upon their needs and abilities (*ibid.*).

Fiscal decentralisation

A measure of the growing importance of decentralisation has been the increasing percentage of total government expenditures accounted for by sub-national governments since the mid-1980s. In Mexico, sub-national governments accounted for 28.66 per cent of total public expenditures in 1996 compared with 11.6 per cent in 1988 (Rowland and Ramírez, 2001; Mizrahi, 2004). Most sub-national governments remain dependent for resources on central government, and this limits their ability to shape policy, but some can generate their own revenue. In Argentina, for example, the city and province of Buenos Aires raise most of their own revenue (Falleti, 2004).

Different traditions, patterns of political development and rates at which decentralisation has been pursued have resulted in significant variation in the nature and responsibilities of sub-national government across Latin America today (see Table 6.5).

Selee (2004) has assessed the impact of decentralisation according to how much it has redistributed power by actually giving sub-national governments increased authority and resources, and how much it has redistributed power between the state and citizens in order to create a more responsive and accountable state. Many scholars and politicians reflexively believe decentralisation deepens democracy and reconnects citizens and the state. This belief is based on several assumptions: that

Table 6.5 Functions and finances of selected subnational authorities in Latin America

	Examples of functions decentralised			Subnational expenditure as a % of total public expenditure	Subnational government's dependence on fiscal transfers (%)	
	Significant	*Moderate*	*Limited*		*Regional*	*Local*
Mexico	Healthcare, urban planning	Education, social development		28.66	91.4	70.6
Venezuela		Education, healthcare		27.07	98	41
Brazil	Healthcare	Education, infrastructure		37	17	67
Argentina	Education	Healthcare	Housing	43.9	69.62	17
Guatemala	Water	Primary healthcare	Education, healthcare	20	N/A	30.18

Note: Data on subnational expenditures are somewhat unreliable and vary depending on sources used and, while useful for gauging approximate revenues and expenditures, should be viewed with caution.

Sources: Selee, 2004. Chapters in Tulchin and Selee eds, 2004. Subnational expenditure: for Mexico: Rowland and Ramírez, 2001; figures for 1996; for Venezuela, Mascareño, 2000; for Guatemala, Puente and Molina, 2000; for Argentina, Falleti, 2004; for Brazil, Burki, Perry, and Dillinger, 1999. Subnational governments' dependence: for Mexico, Mizrahi, 2004, for municipalities, 1991–98; for Venezuela, Mascareño, 2000; for Guatemala, Puente and Linares, 2004; for Argentine provinces, Falleti, 2004; for Brazil and for Argentine municipalities, Burki *et al.*, 1999

sub-national governments are more accountable to citizens because they are closer to them; that decentralisation allows for new forms of participation in policy-making in such areas as education, healthcare and welfare; and that decentralisation allows for the inclusion in policymaking of sectors previously excluded from the political process that have a stronger voice at a local level, such as women, the indigenous and the poor. The stated aim of ambitious decentralisation in Peru in 2002 was to give more power to people living in remote areas long neglected by Lima (see Box 6.6).

Selee (2004) has identified four important trends that shed light on the relationship between decentralisation and democracy. First, sub-national governments have become important arenas of electoral competition, and are often far more competitive than national governments. In Mexico, for example, much of the challenge to the PRI prior to the period in which it lost power, 1997–2000, came from within the regions, which provided a series of powerbases for opposition groups to contest its dominance. Second, sub-national governments across Latin America have sought to develop a more participatory relationship with citizens in policy-making and have used creative ways to engage citizens in planning and budget formulation. In Brazil, for example, municipalities have become influential democratic innovators, developing councils comprising representatives of government, civil society and business that oversee a broad range of sectoral responsibilities. Some Brazilian cities, such as Porto Alegre, have developed 'participatory budgeting' that engages citizens in municipal financial planning (see Box 16.5; and Baiocchi ed., 2003; Melo and Rezende, 2004). Third, municipal governments have pioneered important innovations in social policy. Since the 1990s, for example, there has been a large increase in the share of spending among municipalities in Brazil and Argentina on social policy (Selee, 2004). Fourth, in some countries decentralisation has contributed to greater recognition of pluralism by bringing indigenous people into the political process through increases in the number of indigenous elected officials (*ibid.*). In Mexican states with large indigenous populations such as Oaxaca, for example, customary law – indigenous tradition and custom – is recognised for the election of municipal authorities and the resolution of certain disputes (see Chapter 8).

However, despite these positive contributions to democratic governance decentralisation has sometimes had contradictory effects and an uneven impact. Established local and regional elites can sometimes be the main beneficiaries of decentralisation policies, which can reinforce local authoritarian power structures that centralisation had in fact weakened as well as clientelism (see García-Guadilla and Pérez, 2002; see also Box 7.1). Some critics of decentralisation argue that it can undermine democratic governance, fearing the resurgence of regional elites who use the resources available under decentralisation to restrict freedoms. In Colombia, for example, some local authorities are controlled either by guerrillas or drug cartels. Small municipalities can also become dominated by particular groups or families asserting local control. Critics of decentralisation also argue that it can undermine the coherence of national politics and co-ordinated social policies, and might threaten already fragile party systems (*ibid.*; see also Sabatini, 2003).

Decentralisation may also put at risk the capacity to promote fiscal balance by strengthening incentives for sub-national governments to generate revenues

CASE STUDY	Box 6.6

Decentralisation in Peru

In November 2002, elections in Peru ushered in a new devolved power structure by establishing new electoral regions with American-style state governments and regional presidencies. Voters elected 25 regional presidents and 229 members of regional councils, as well as 1,800 mayors. The regional governments were granted a range of powers formerly residing with central government, were allocated about a fifth of the national budget, and were given the right to raise their own taxes and auction state assets. Peru has long been a highly centralised country with power concentrated in the capital Lima, where a third of the country's population of 25 million people lives and controlling more than half of Peru's economic output, exacerbating problems of poverty and inequality elsewhere. There have been demands for decentralisation for decades and the law was promulgated by President Alejandro Toledo (2001–06) in fulfilment of campaign promises during the 2001 elections. Toledo's main argument for the reform was that the creation of regional governments would give more power to people in remote areas. An attempt at decentralisation by his predecessor, Alberto Fujimori (1990–2000), had failed when he had tightened his grip on power in the early 1990s in an atmosphere of repression and corruption. Critics of Toledo's move feared it may result in an another Argentine-style economic collapse related to the behaviour of free-spending provinces (see below, and Box 15.7), that corrupt local political powerbrokers would exploit decentralisation to enrich themselves, and that grassroots democracy may make it harder for a national president to govern. They suggested that a failure by the party in government to win the regional presidencies could affect its ability to govern and generate conflict. Critics also argued that because the law on how the regions would operate was hurried through congress just before the 2002 elections, it lacked clarity and was flawed. The new law defining the functions of the new regions was promulgated by Toledo just hours before voting began, with modifications designed to tighten budgetary oversight envisaged after the vote had taken place. Decentralisation also represented a considerable political risk for Toledo's own Perú Posible (Possible Peru) coalition, which won 10 per cent of the national vote as the regional elections were turned by Toledo's opponents into a referendum on his presidency. The opposition Alianza Popular Revolucionaria Americana (APRA, American Revolutionary Popular Alliance, today referred to as the Partido Aprista Peruano), the centre-left party of former president Alan García (1985–90, 2006–), who was planning another presidential bid in 2006 which he subsequently won, took 11 of the 25 regional presidencies. Four out of every 10 Peruvians voted for independent candidates. One of Perú Posible's founders later said the government had paid a high political price for putting the national interest ahead of those of the party. Toledo pursued further decentralisation measures after 2002, but was roundly defeated in an attempt to create five regional governments from 16 of the 24 departments in November 2005. He had argued that consolidation of this kind would allow local governments to pool their resources and help them to boost development. The defeat underlined the political risks of decentralisation, in no small measure reflecting Toledo's declining popularity among members of the public at that time.

autonomously and limiting the central state's control over overall borrowing (Franko, 1999). Argentina's provinces regained authority throughout the 1980s as a result of democratisation, and the arrival in 1989 of Carlos Menem, a Peronist president who had promised greater federalism, led central government to transfer responsibilities such as education and healthcare to the provinces. However, Menem's government did not give the provinces adequate resources with which to exercise their new responsibilities, and Peronist governors reached individual agreements with him on resources outside normal institutional rules (Falleti, 2004). Opposition governors refused to accept central government requests that they reduce state government expenditures, and borrowing by the provinces was a factor behind the country's economic crisis in 2001 (see Box 15.7). However, problems caused by excessive borrowing by sub-national governments in the expectation that they will be bailed out by the national government can also occur if they *lack* sufficient control over their economic affairs. In Colombia, for example, fiscal decentralisation during the 1990s resulted in significant departmental and municipal control over resources that were automatically allocated to areas of spending over which local authorities had little room for manoeuvre, such as education. This meant that local authorities were left with few 'discretionary' funds which could be diverted, if necessary, to service their debts (see Dillinger and Webb, 1999). The case of Colombia also draws attention to the importance of well-organised parties in the decentralisation equation (see above). Poorly organised national parties unable to assert their authority at a local level, combined with the threats to the autonomy of sub-national authorities posed by guerrilla and paramilitary organisations, tended to forestall efforts within Colombia's political process to tackle problems generated by these sub-national spending patterns (*ibid.*).

The decentralisation of fiscal arrangements can also exacerbate inequalities by enhancing disparities between regions, with sub-national governments least able to raise revenue often also being those that receive least from national governments. In Bolivia, decentralisation has become a divisive issue, fuelling existing tensions between regional and ethnic groups (see Boxes 4.1, 8.7, 12.11, 13.6). In January 2005, for example, protests demanding greater regional autonomy in Bolivia's wealthy eastern provinces forced President Carlos Mesa (2003–05) to allow direct elections for provincial governors (see Box 5.6). The protesters were led by local business leaders in Santa Cruz, who argued that the region's huge contribution to the national economy should allow them to have a greater say over managing taxes and local government. Santa Cruz accounts for about one-third of the country's production and its provincial capital is a commercial hub. Its demand for greater autonomy also reflects Bolivia's ethnic divisions, with many inhabitants of Santa Cruz descended from European immigrants adopting a market-oriented vision of economic management by contrast with the mainly indigenous, pro-state movement in the western Andean area dominated by poor indigenous communities. Past indigenous hostility to decentralisation in Bolivia has stemmed from a desire to ensure the national state retains control of natural resources so these can be put to greater use in social policies tackling the inequality that many indigenous groups suffer from (see Chapters 8, 13). However, a new constitution drawn up under President Morales and approved in 2009 gave Bolivia's 36 indigenous communities the opportunity to hold votes on autonomy – giving them new decisionmaking prerogatives in the areas of government, the judiciary and landholding – as part of a broader decentralisation of power that also granted greater autonomy to the country's nine departments. This gained significant levels of support among indigenous voters when it was passed. The country's wealthy eastern departments opposed the new charter on the basis that it did not go far enough in granting them control over how taxes on gas exports are spent.

Summary

Legislatures in Latin America have often been considered as marginal to the policy process but they are growing in stature. Three themes are of importance in the study of legislative politics: executive–legislative relations, legislative structure and the policymaking process. Relations between the executive and legislature are influenced by the type of assembly a president encounters. A *recalcitrant assembly* will provoke the president to use unilateral powers, a *subservient* assembly will be dominated and dictated to, a *venal or parochial* assembly will support the president in return for patronage and payoffs, and a *workable assembly* is brought into the policy process through concessions made by the president in constructing a viable coalition. The way a legislature is structured will also influence how it operates and its power to shape policy. The main policy role played by legislatures in Latin America has been in blocking legislation or pressuring a president to amend proposals or bills.

Parties and party systems are important to the institutionalisation of democracy by providing structured forms of participation, disagreement and competition. Randall and Svåsand (2002) put forward a model by which to analyse the degree of institutionalisation of individual parties based on four main elements: systemness, value infusion, decisional autonomy and reification. Mainwaring and Scully (1995) developed criteria for classifying party systems and noted marked differences in the degree of institutionalisation across Latin America. The political problems associated with the lack of party system institutionalisation include populism, immobilism, policy gridlock, weak government authority and conflict.

A strong judiciary is necessary to check executive and legislative breaches of the constitutional order, provide conditions for economic development and build popular support for democracy. However, Latin American judiciaries historically have been weak and vulnerable to political influence. Despite a comprehensive reform agenda in the 1990s, Latin American judicial systems fare badly in terms of their independence, efficiency and access.

By the 1980s, most Latin American states retained a highly centralised institutional structure which distorted public administration by generating large bureaucracies in the form of ministries, secretariats and agencies with complex hierarchies lacking accountability. Reforms since the 1980s have sought to depoliticise and professionalise these large centralised bureaucracies in an effort to foster good governance. Decentralisation aiming to strengthen the role of sub-national governments also rose up the political agenda in the 1980s and 1990s and has been driven by political and economic considerations. Supporters argue that decentralisation strengthens democratic governance and improves policy delivery. Decentralisation has changed the nature of the state in Latin America and reconfigured its relationship with society. Indigenous groups and regions that control significant natural resources have sought greater autonomy from the central state since democratisation began.

Discussion points

- How important are legislatures in Latin America, and should they have more power?

- What explains why some legislatures have a greater policymaking role than others?

- Why is it important for party systems to be institutionalised in Latin America?

- In what ways do Latin American political parties influence legislative behaviour?

- Does the weakness of judiciaries explain abuses of power?

- Under what circumstances have courts challenged executive power?

- Will decentralisation help or hinder democracy in Latin America?

Useful websites

www.e-fipa.org/news_en.htm Inter-Parliamentary Forum of the Americas (FIPA)

www.oas.org/sap/english/default.asp Secretariat for Political Affairs of the OAS, which supports democracy and governance initiatives in the region

http://pdba.georgetown.edu/Legislative/legislative.html Georgetown University Political Database of the Americas – Legislative Branch reference materials

http://pdba.georgetown.edu/Parties/parties.html Georgetown University Political Database of the Americas – Political parties by country. Contains party listings for each country

http://01.upla.net/modules/boletin09/ Unión de Partidos Latinamericanos (UPLA, Union of Latin American Parties), grouping of mainly conservative parties

www.cajpe.org.pe Comisión Andina de Juristas (Andean Commission of Jurists), human rights think-tank with a specialism in legal matters

www.cejamericas.org Centro de Estudios de Justicia de la Américas (CEJA, Justice Studies Centre of the Americas), Chile. Regional initiative to explore and research judicial systems and provision in the Americas

www.congreso.gob.pe/comisiones/2004/ceriajus/inicio.htm CERIAJUS judicial reform initiative in Peru

www.unpan.org/latin.asp Latin American and Caribbean site of United Nations Online Network in Public Administration and Finance (UNPAN), an initiative to promote best practice in public administration and efficient civil services

www.clad.org.ve Centro Latinoamericano de Administración para el Desarollo (CLAD, Latin American Centre of Administration for Development), an intergovernmental regional agency established at the UN's recommendation to promote the modernisation of public administration

Recommended reading

Morgenstern, Scott and Benito Nacif (eds). 2002. *Legislative Politics in Latin America.* Cambridge: Cambridge University Press

> *Essential introductory volume providing theoretical and empirical overview of legislative politics in Latin America*

Randall, Vicky and Lars Svåsand. 2002. 'Party Institutionalisation in New Democracies', *Party Politics*, Vol. 8, No. 1 (January 2002), pp. 5–29

> *Essential introduction to the discussion of institutionalisation that advances an important model of party institutionalisation*

Mainwaring, Scott and Timothy R. Scully (eds). 1995. *Building Democratic Institutions: Party Systems in Latin America.* Stanford, CA: Stanford University Press

> *Essential introduction to the theoretical and empirical questions concerning party system institutionalisation in Latin America*

Kitschelt, Herbert, Kirk A. Hawkins, Juan Pablo Luna, Guillermo Rosas, Elizabeth J. Zechmeister. 2010. *Latin American Party Systems.* Cambridge: Cambridge University Press

> *Valuable and up-to-date comparative focus on parties in Latin America that offers a theoretical explanation for how party systems become focused on ideologically informed policies*

Helmke, Gretchen. 2005. *Courts under Constraints. Judges, Generals, and Presidents in Argentina.* Cambridge: Cambridge University Press

> *Useful point of reference on judicial politics and reform containing theoretical framework for understanding how institutional instability affects judicial behaviour*

DeShazo, Peter and Juan Enrique Vargas. 2006. 'Judicial Reform in Latin America: An Assessment.' *Policy Papers on the Americas*, Vol. XVII, Study 2 (September 2006). Washington: Center for Strategic and International Studies (CSIS). Available at: http://csis.org/files/media/csis/pubs/0609_latin_judicial_reform.pdf

> *Valuable overview of progress in the effort to reform the judiciary across Latin America*

Tulchin, Joseph. S. and Andrew Selee (eds). 2004. *Decentralisation and Democratic Governance in Latin America.* Woodrow Wilson Center Report on the Americas #12. Washington: Woodrow Wilson International center for Scholars. Available at: www.wilsoncenter.org/topics/pubs/ACF18E5.pdf

> *Essential introductory text examining the relationship between decentralisation and democracy that contains valuable case studies*

Chapter 7

Established political actors

This chapter examines the state's relationship with society, in particular large, organised sectors of the population with the potential to assert themselves in pursuit of their demands. The nature of this relationship is an important theme in the study of politics in Latin America because it determines both the character of the state and the behaviour of key social groups (see Box 2.1).

The business lobby, large trades unions, confederations of peasants (*campesinos*), the military and the Church have often been able to challenge state power, and the state has either struggled against these groups or tried to control them. At times, this has meant that governability – the state's capacity to govern – has been much more of an issue in politics in Latin America than the *form* that government takes. The concept of corporatism has often been applied to the study of political systems in the region after the Second World War in which the state assumed a central role and maintained hierarchical links with organised sectors of society, 'corporations' (see Box 2.2). A distinction has sometimes been made between *state corporatism* and *societal corporatism*. State corporatism has been associated with authoritarian systems in which sectors such as labour are under centralised control, the political system is monopolised by one party, and there is an official ideology (Mackinlay and Otero, 2004). Corporations were often created directly by the state, which met their demands selectively through patron-client mechanisms or clientelism (see Box 7.1). In societal corporatism, corporations maintain a greater degree of independence from the state; they have negotiating power because they can eventually withdraw their support from it; their interests are represented effectively; and those in power must be less authoritarian (*ibid.*). Mexico under the Partido Revolucionario Institucional (PRI, Institutional Revolutionary Party) was often seen as the classic example of state corporatism. From 1940 until the late 1990s, social organisations affiliated to the PRI within its three sectors – worker, peasant and 'popular' or urban middle class – were practically the only channels for participating in political life and transmitting collective demands, and there were few independent groups. This resulted in enviable political stability, which in turn helps to explain the PRI's longevity and the country's delayed democratic transition.

THEORIES AND DEBATES   Box 7.1

Corporatism and clientelism

The functional definition of corporatism refers to a model of political participation in which powerful groups such as trades unions, peasant organisations and the military are linked to the state in a subordinate but mutually beneficial relationship. Corporatism has a long history in Latin America but has been used in particular in the analysis of political systems in which the state assumed a central role in regulating economic and political activity that emerged from the crisis of the 1930s (see Box 2.2, Chapter 14). Corporatist organisations in Latin America had two principal functions: representing their members' interests within the state, and controlling their members on behalf of the state, and they could be distinguished from organisations that were autonomous or 'independent' from the state (Mackinlay and Otero, 2004). In particular, the state assumed an active role in regulating the productive sectors – business groups, trades unions and peasant organisations – and corporatist influences were enshrined in labour codes, welfare systems and other public policies. Corporatist theory distinguished between countries in which organisations such as the labour movement or peasants had greater negotiating power with the state, and those in which the state had much greater authority (*ibid.*). Corporatism was also an institutional reflection of clientelism, a relationship between two notional political actors, patron and client, in which political support (usually votes) is exchanged for favours. The patron, usually a politician, rewards their clients – who are in a subordinate position in the relationship – for providing electoral support. Clientelism in Latin America has often taken a patrimonial form, by which an individual powerbroker controlling resources extends favours or patronage in a discretionary way. Historically, in Latin America such patterns of control were common and, by constraining popular participation in politics, limited the consolidation of democracy (Foweraker *et al.*, 2003). One reason there has been disillusionment with politicians, bureaucrats and parties in Latin America is that they are still often considered to indulge in clientelistic behaviour to further their own interests without regard for the rule of law, to the detriment of popular representation. Populism (see Chapters 2, 4) was a reflection of what Williamson (1992) has called 'natural corporatism' by which a weak state bought stability by using the traditional politics of clientelism to co-opt interest-groups.

Business

The state's relationship with sectors that have the potential to assert themselves in pursuit of their demands also calls to mind the concepts of 'civil society' or independent 'public' and 'private' spheres outside the state that have grown in importance in the study of democratisation (which are dealt with in more detail in Chapter 8). There has been debate about the degree to which some social sectors, such as organised business associations and private enterprise, for example, should be considered either as established actors in Latin American politics or studied as part of civil society. Schneider (2004) argues that the existence of business associations highlights the fact that the resources at the disposal of social groups vary greatly, and these present an important challenge to our understanding of civil society. First, the differences associated with business groups means it makes sense to distinguish between elite and non-elite organisations within society. Second, a key theme highlighted by business associations is the many links that exist between civil society organisations and the state. As a key variable in the evolution of business groups has been their relationship with the state, which in some cases has sought to embrace them through corporatism (see Box 7.1), they are dealt with here as established actors alongside trades unions and peasant organisations.

Entrepreneurs and private businesses have long shaped the evolution of Latin American economies alongside other sectors and the state, with their influence waxing and waning often in accordance with the prevailing ideological and economic climate. They have grown increasingly prominent and influential since neoliberal reforms were introduced in the region in the 1980s and democratisation took hold (see Chapters 3, 15), and until recently the power of the private sector was growing in relation to the public sector (Camp, 1989; Agüero, 2004). Latinobarómetro data also suggest that public confidence in the activities of private companies in Latin America has grown, and rose markedly between 2002 and 2009 (Latinobarómetro, 2009a). More recently, stable growth in the region since 2004 and a boom in the demand for commodities has favoured rapid growth and consolidation, creating growing multi-national corporations that compete on equal terms with those from developed regions of the world. A survey of the largest 500 companies in Latin America by the *Latin Trade* magazine, for example, suggested that the region's largest publicly traded companies, in aggregate, saw income rise 202 per cent in 2008 compared to the previous 12 months (*Latin Trade*, 2009). Utilities that are either state-owned or have a significant state holding dominate the corporate sector, but financial services companies are among the leading players in the region's private sector, with Brazil having some of the largest companies in the region. Private Brazilian companies recording impressive net sales gains in the year up to 2008 included the financial services companies Bradesco (27 per cent) and Itaú Unibanco (15 per cent) (*ibid.*).

In 2009, the online journal *Latin Business Chronicle* compiled its first annual ranking of the top 100 most powerful men and women in Latin American business, which included both those native to the region and foreign executives posted there who may have a significant impact on it (see *Latin Business Chronicle*, 2009). The journal listed figures well-known in the business affairs of their own countries and global markets, such as the Mexican tycoon Carlos Slim, who heads a conglomerate spanning telecommunications (América Móvil, Telmex), retail and energy interests; and the Peruvian businessman Dionisio Romero Paoletti, who heads several companies in his country and wields significant influence. It also identified the top 10 multi-national executives who wield influence on a regional basis across Latin America, including Vicente Trius, the president and chief executive officer of Wal-Mart Latin America, who supervises more than 325,000 employees in the region.

The private sector has played a significant role in some of the most high-profile achievements of engineering, resource extraction and manufacturing in Latin America, and has been a key player in the renegotiation and financing of debt. Business leaders have also played a prominent role in politics, with notable entrepreneurs or those who have been businessmen who have become presidents, or tried to, including Vicente Fox (2000–06) in Mexico, Ricardo Martinelli (2009–) in Panama, Sebastián Piñera in Chile (2010–), and Alvaro Fernando Noboa in Ecuador. Business-oriented newspapers that serve the specific needs of the private sector, such as *El Economista* in Mexico, also exist in most Latin American countries and are read by policymakers. The financial newspapers of the English-speaking world such as the *Wall Street Journal* also seek to penetrate this market with editions in Spanish and Portuguese.

Relations between the private sector and the state have varied considerably over time and are often determined by the regulatory environment for business established by a particular administration. Data compiled by the World Bank measuring perceptions of 'Regulatory Quality' – the ability of the government to formulate and implement sound policies and regulations that permit and promote private-sector development – show that of the 10 countries globally that have experienced a significant decline in estimates of governance between 1998–2008, five were in Latin America: Bolivia, Venezuela, Argentina, Ecuador and Uruguay (see Kaufmann *et al.*, 2009). This decline is related to the election of left-of-centre governments more ideologically ambivalent towards the activities of the private sector.

The public face of business is the plethora of associations that bring together sectoral and other interests in the private sector of each country. These business associations have evolved in different ways across Latin America. In some cases, such as Mexico, the government itself fostered the emergence of strong business groups with a broad, encompassing reach. In others, such as Argentina, polarised politics never allowed strong or stable business associations to emerge. Today there is striking variation between associations in different Latin American countries. The most important are those economy-wide groups that encompass broad segments or all of the private sector (see Table 7.1). Mexico, Chile and Colombia have strong encompassing associations; Argentina and Brazil have weak ones (Schneider, 2004).

A key variable in the evolution of business groups has been their relationship with the state, which in some cases has sought to incorporate businesses into economic governance through corporatism. Latin American states have often wanted to organise businesses in periods of crisis, and in the 1980s had strong incentives to nurture their associations. State actors also meddle in business organisations to generate support or reduce opposition; to gain information; to seek co-operation for policy implementation; and to force interests to compromise (*ibid.*).

The main role of business associations is economic, and they are influential actors in shaping market policies. Business associations and individual entrepreneurs routinely lobby governments, politicians and civil servants about policy and regulatory issues. Strong business groups collaborated closely with government negotiators in shaping the terms of free-trade agreements in Mexico, Chile and most recently Central America, for example, and associations can also help to co-ordinate areas of production to generate broader benefits for the economy as a whole. However, alongside their contribution to the economy, business associations play important political roles:

Democracy

A key question when studying associations that represent business elites is whether these act in favour of, or against, democratic governance. Schneider (2004) shows

Table 7.1 Voluntary encompassing business associations in five Latin American countries

	Association	*Scope*	*Staff*
Strong:			
Mexico	Coparmex (1929–)	Economy-wide	30
	CMHN (1962–)	Economy-wide	0
	CCE (1975–)	Economy-wide	80
Chile	CPC (1933–)	Economy-wide	8
	Sofofa (1883–)	Industry	50
Colombia	Federacafe (1927–)	Coffee	3,500
	ANDI (1944–)	Industry	150
	CG (1991–)	Economy-wide	3
Weak:			
Argentina	ACIEL (1958–73)	Economy-wide	0
	APEGE (1975–6)	Economy-wide	0
	CGE (1952–)	Economy-wide	10?
	UIA (1886–)	Industry	50
	CEA (1967–)	Economy-wide	2
Brazil	UBE (1987–8)	Economy-wide	Few to none
	IEDI (1989–)	Industry	8

Notes: See list of acronyms for full names. Figures for staff are rough estimates for average total employment in the last quarter of the twentieth century.

Sources: Schneider, 2004, from various

that both are possible. Some business associations supported the military interventions in Brazil in 1964, Argentina in 1966 and Chile in 1973. In Venezuela, the head of the economy-wide business association Fedecámaras served briefly as president during the short-lived coup against President Hugo Chávez (1999–) in April 2002 (see Box 7.2), yet business associations had opposed coup attempts in the country in 1992. However, associations have also helped to bring down dictatorships, as in Colombia in 1957, and when strong associations have lost access to authoritarian regimes they have sometimes shifted towards the opposition, as in Mexico both in the early 1970s and early 1980s.

Representation

The adequate representation of business is a core concern in most theories of democratic consolidation. Scholars of consolidation attribute an important role to associations that represent business because these provide information to citizens about state policy. Political leaders will also often call upon business associations in moments of crisis because they provide government with a means to consult elites about emergency measures. Business associations also have advantages over

---

Venezuela – The business of opposition

In Venezuela, relations between the business community and the populist president Hugo Chávez have been tense mainly because of legislation that the main business chamber, Fedecámaras, has argued is based on principles that violate the right to private property. In December 2001, Fedecámaras launched a series of nationwide work stoppages, backed by opposition labour unions, and in April 2002 its then president, Pedro Carmona, headed a 48-hour de facto government while Chávez was held prisoner following a coup attempt, which was ultimately unsuccessful. Attempts at reconciliation failed, and in December 2002 business leaders gave their implicit support to an all-out stoppage involving the oil industry, as a result of which the economy shrank by more than 7 per cent in 2003. Chávez has refused to talk to Fedecámaras, dealing instead with its member organisations in a bilateral way or with pro-government groups. This, in turn, has fostered the emergence of breakaway groups prepared to deal with the Chávez administration, such as Empresarios por Venezuela (Empreven, Business People for Venezuela) which was formed as a reaction to the alleged participation of Fedecámaras members in the failed 2002 coup. Such organisations provide examples of the benefits to business of maintaining supportive links with the state and identifying with its economic policies: by 2005, for example, Empreven members had received the equivalent of almost $12 million in government credits and its president had been appointed to the board of Bancoex, the government's export-promotion bank. In August 2009, Empreven Ecuador was launched in Quito with the support of Ecuadorean government. The group's stated mission now embraces the notion of economic integration in the region, but also the substitution of imports to Venezuela from Colombia with which Chávez has had tense relations (see Boxes 9.1, 9.8, 10.3, 16.1).

politicians by offering continuous representation in countries subject to frequent crises. Traditionally, there has been little contact between business associations and parties, not least because associations were either prohibited from engaging in party politics or remained neutral in order not to alienate potential winners (*ibid.*). As a result, business associations may strengthen civil society because citizens may in fact interact more with them than with the formal institutions of electoral democracy themselves.

Accountability

Business associations can contribute significantly to the broad role played by civil society in challenging and constraining potentially abusive states or protecting liberties from the encroachment of government (*ibid.*). For example, despite Colombia's many problems, the country's democratic stability is often explained by the influence of business associations: these have defended democracy in times of crisis and have used their influence on public opinion to pressure government to moderate its policies.

Governability

Business associations can help restrain divisive tendencies in fragmented societies. In Chile in the 1990s, for example, the Confederación de la Producción y del Comercio (CPC, Confederation for Production and Commerce) kept business in a unified dialogue with the government, and in Mexico the Coordinadora Empresarial de Comercio Exterior (COECE, Coordinator for Foreign Trade Business Organisations) brokered compromises among business sectors during the NAFTA negotiations (see Box 15.5). In Argentina and Brazil, by contrast, there have been no all-encompassing associations working against polarised debates and political conflict (*ibid.*).

However, even if they do not engage in direct partisanship, strong business associations can cause problems for democracy. First, business is often seen as an alternative source of power in societies with weakly institutionalised political structures. For example, a large proportion of Latin American political leaders consulted by the UNDP (2004b) highlighted the *de facto* power concentrated by business and financial sectors in their states. This power is very evident in countries such as Brazil, for example, whose president, Luiz Inácio Lula da Silva (2003–10) faced criticism for the so-called Mensalão vote-buying scandal that benefitted state and private companies and his own Partido dos Trabalhadores (Workers' Party, PT), and eventually led to the indictment in 2007 of 40 individuals, mostly former or current federal deputies. Brazil is home to Latin America's largest corporations, and some wield significant financial resources. The semi-public corporation Petrobras (Petróleo Brasileiro), for example, is one of the world's largest enterprises, with a market valuation of $200 billion, and is the second-largest oil company after ExxonMobil of the US, the world's largest publicly traded company. Large Brazilian groups dominate the organised business interests that are shaping policy in the Mercosur economic region (see, for example, Schelhase, 2008; see Box 9.9). Powerful conglomerates such as Organisações Globo, the group that owns the Globo Network and has interests in the food industry, real estate and financial markets, are not hesitant about political lobbying in defence of their interests. When Globo's media rival, Rede Record, launched Brazil's first free-to-view 24-hour news channel on terrestrial television, for example, Globo lobbied government officials including the communications minister to allege that the competitor was breaking the law. In Bolivia, business associations such as the Cámara de Industria y Comercio de Santa Cruz (CAINCO, Santa Cruz Chamber of Industry and Commerce) have been at the forefront of the campaign by the county's conservative *media luna* eastern provinces for greater autonomy and even secession (see Boxes 4.1, 12.11, 13.6; Eaton, 2007). The Brazilian and Bolivian cases suggest strongly that, when business groups behave in ways that may challenge democratic norms, it is primarily for economic reasons. In smaller countries, such as those of Central America, the private sector linked to an oligarchic power structure can have significant influence over governments.

Big business has options for exercising power that can *weaken* institutional politics, such as the use of corruption, personal networks and media leverage as well as capital flight (Schneider, 2004). Second, associations may over-represent business to the detriment of political equality, particularly where they are heavily dependent on states and the party system is weak (see Chapters 6, 15). Moreover, if a state creates or sustains associations, it is less likely that these will be effective counterweights if it abuses its power. A balanced position, therefore, suggests that business associations can both act against democracy and in favour of it (see Rueschemeyer *et al.*, 1992).

Trade unions

The relationship between organised labour and the state and parties has been of great importance in Latin American political development, although the strength of unions in the region has varied considerably among different countries (see Alexander, 2009). The criteria for determining the strength of organised labour include the proportion of the workforce that is unionised, the number of union confederations in a country, the extent of control these confederations have over member organisations, and the degree to which the main labour organisations in a country are united or divided on political and ideological matters. Argentina's economic and urban development was considered to have created conditions more conducive to the development of strong unions than in most other Latin American countries for much of the twentieth century (McGuire, 1997). Labour in Latin America was an important component of corporatist organisation because of the unions' close relationship with the state through policies of industrialisation (see Chapter 14; Collier and Collier, 2002). Corporatist relationships between the state and organised labour thrived under populist leaderships (see Chapters 2, 4) which delivered welfare benefits to workers through clientelistic mechanisms that, in return, secured for politicians electoral support. In countries like Mexico, politicians recognised labour as a political resource and took a direct role in stimulating and controlling labour organisations (see Box 7.3). Brazil's Estado Novo under Getúlio Vargas (1930–45, 1951–54) was another good example of corporatism. The Brazilian labour code of 1943 established rules of industrial relations that would survive into the 1990s through which the government kept the main unions under control and maintained mostly stable industrial relations. In several countries, the development of unions within a corporatist tradition fostered the emergence of labour-based parties (Levitsky, 2003). Labour-based parties have included the PRI in Mexico, the Peronists in Argentina (the Partido Justicialista, PJ, Justicialist Party), the Alianza Popular Revolucionaria Americana (APRA, American Revolutionary Popular Alliance, today referred to as the Partido Aprista Peruano) in Peru and Acción Democrática (AD, Democratic Action) in Venezuela.

In Argentina, efforts to consolidate fully corporatist relations between the state and labour were not completely successful, largely because strong unions developed (McGuire, 1997). The state made recurrent efforts from the 1940s to consolidate a corporatist relationship but the unions exercised considerable influence independently. However, organised labour became closely allied with the Peronist movement, although over time distance grew between Perón himself and Peronist unions. When Perón was in power, the unions mobilised supporters and delivered votes; when the government was not Peronist, the unions exerted

INSTITUTIONS   **Box 7.3**

Corporatist trades unions in Mexico

In Mexico, leaders of the 1910–17 revolution were quick to realise the potential of co-opting labour federations, and the PRI became skilled at courting corrupt union leaders, developing tighter control over workers than any other Latin American country. The PRI's labour sector was dominated by party loyalists such as Fidel Velázquez (b.1900–d.1997), the leader for more than half a century of Mexico's largest union organisation, the Confederación de Trabajadores de México (CTM, Mexican Workers' Confederation), who was openly hostile to independent union militants. The state used labour laws and other means of maintaining this system, and this implied state control over union registration, strikes and collective bargaining (de la Garza Toledo, 2004). This relationship discouraged autonomous union activity while providing benefits such as medical care to loyal unions. As a result, most unions identified with the regime and functioned as part of the political system (see Caulfield, 1998). Where union leaders demanded the right to take genuinely independent action, such as the railroad workers in 1959, they were often met with harsh repression. Labour relations in Mexico were subordinated to the economic and political needs of the industrialisation model (see Chapter 14) to ensure stable industrial relations, social peace and votes for the ruling party. Wage increases, benefits or social security were granted in exchange for support of public policies and votes (*ibid.*). Mexican trade unions and the political system overlapped, with trade union leaders often also being important PRI leaders in receipt of a quota of electoral positions within the administration. As a result, corporatism was characterised by a lack of democracy within trade union organisations themselves, because their political role came first and their function of representing workers' interests was subordinated. However, this did not always act against gains in wages or working conditions, both of which improved until the 1970s, although they declined thereafter.

pressure through extra-institutional channels, often in a destabilising way. Instability was one of the reasons Argentina's military deposed its civilian rulers, and unions were heavily repressed. Neoliberal reforms under President Carlos Menem (1989–99), a Peronist, caused divisions within organised labour, but there were indications of a revived corporatist relationship between the Peronist movement and the unions. Today, the PJ remains close to Argentina's powerful Confederación General del Trabajo de la República Argentina (CGTRA, General Labour Confederation of the Argentine Republic). Chile's relatively large labour movement was traditionally more independent of the state, in part because rival political parties competed for the support of individual unions and sought to maintain tight control over them once they had secured it. Although some Chilean unions mobilised in support of the state, others demonstrated their capacity to act as an oppositional force. Strikes and rallies by labour groups in support of and against Salvador Allende (1970–73), for example, were a key factor in the instability that led to the coup that toppled him (see Box 16.2).

The military regimes of the 1960s and 1970s suppressed the labour movement and strikes largely disappeared. One result of this was that in some countries, such as Brazil, what has been called 'new unionism' developed in the late 1970s, shifting workers' attention to matters that went beyond conditions on the shop floor towards broader issues of citizenship (see Rands Barros, 1999). Some unions mobilised workers against authoritarian regimes and provided the nucleus for democratic movements incorporating other social sectors.

Unions have played a role in shaping the character of democracy, not least because relationships between parties and unions are important to party, and party system, institutionalisation (see Chapter 6). Among the factors that determine the extent to which parties or party systems are institutionalised are the links between parties and key groups in society, such as trades unions, and the nature and stability of such relationships. The sequence by which democratic transition and neoliberal reform took place had a bearing on the degree to which unions were able to defend their interests, overall political stability and hence on the character of democratic consolidation. In transitions from dictatorships, subsequent reforms often extended labour rights denied under the previous regime (Cook, 2002). In some cases, where transitions began *before* neoliberal reform got underway, such as Argentina and Brazil, unions secured new rights and maintained their ability to bargain when the state proceeded to undertake market reforms. In Chile, neoliberal policies that had included reform of labour markets were enacted by the military dictatorship itself and, during the democratic transition, employers resisted reforms to expand labour rights, limiting the organisational capacity of unions (*ibid.*). In most cases, neoliberal reform changed the relationship between unions and parties (see Box 7.4, Chapter 15).

However, trades unions remain powerful actors in Latin America able to veto decisions, organise demonstrations and influence the public agenda (UNDP, 2004b; see also Wolfe, 2002). Although levels of public confidence in unions are not high in Latin America, they are greater than levels of confidence in political parties (Latinobarómetro, 2009a). Labour rights and the freedom of unions to organise remain key areas of conflict in the region, according to the International Labour Organisation (ILO) (see Box 7.5). Moreover, trade union corporatism has co-existed

---

CASE STUDY   Box 7.4

Argentine unions and neoliberal reform

McGuire (1997) argued that if a labour movement is weak, there will be less distributive conflict in society and the degree to which union leaders develop links with well-institutionalised parties will be less relevant for democratic consolidation. Levitsky (2003) examined the impact of neoliberalism on parties with a powerful labour base such as the Peronist PJ in Argentina. He argues that the huge changes of the 1990s weakened labour organisations and limited their ability to deliver the vote to parties they had traditionally had a corporatist relationship with. These factors encouraged labour-based parties to rethink their programmes, target new electoral constituencies and redefine their relations with unions. The PJ redefined its relationship with organised labour by dismantling traditional mechanisms of union participation and replacing its union-based mass linkages with patronage-based territorial organisation. By the early 1990s, it had transformed itself from a labour-based party in which unions were at times dominant into a clientelistic party in which they played a lesser role. As a result, organised labour's influence in the party declined, and this deunionisation contributed in an important way to the PJ's electoral success. By weakening an opponent of neoliberal reforms, de-unionisation also facilitated the PJ's shift to the right under Carlos Menem.

Box 7.5

Trade unionism – A dangerous occupation

Being a trade union activist or leader can be a dangerous occupation in Latin America, where anti-union violence is routine. According to its *Annual Survey of Violations of Trade Union Rights 2009*, the International Trade Union Confederation (ITUC) says many types of violations occurred in Latin America in 2008. Colombia continues to account for 60 per cent of the assassinations of trade unionists around the world, with 49 trade unionists assassinated in 2008 as part of a 25 per cent increase in cases of anti-union violence. According to the ITUC, Colombian labour law and policy still exclude more than two thirds of workers from social and worker protection measures, denying basic workers' rights to more than 12 million people. In Central America, the situation also worsened for trade unionists in 2008, according to the ITUC. Anti-union violence is a persistent problem in Guatemala, where more than 20 leaders of unions, indigenous groups and peasant farmers were murdered and the union movement was subjected to levels of persecution reminiscent of the practices used during the country's armed conflict. In Honduras, Rosa Altagracia Fuentes, the general secretary of the Confederación de Trabajadores de Honduras (CTH, Workers' Confederation of Honduras), was among trades unionists assassinated. In Panama, a leader of the national building workers' union, the Sindicato único nacional de trabajadores de la industria de la construcción y similares (SUNTRACS, National Union of Workers of Construction and Similar Industries) was murdered against a background of what ITUC describes as continuing violations of workers' rights.

Source: The ITUC, 2009

with neoliberal norms under certain conditions in states with a strong interventionist tradition, and new forms of corporatism, sometimes called 'neo-corporatism', have been identified (see, for example, Craske, 1994). There are indications that old patterns of behaviour persisted in countries like Mexico into the neoliberal era as unions continued to support state economic policies (de la Garza Toledo, 2004). This may help to explain why neoliberal reform under the PRI succeeded in suppressing wages under conditions of minimal industrial strife (*ibid.*). According to de la Garza Toledo (2004), the administration of President Vicente Fox (2000–06) of the Partido Acción Nacional (PAN, National Action Party) also sought to restore corporate relations based on the notion of a 'new labour culture' discussed in the 1990s between the CTM and the Confederación Patronal de la República Mexicana (Coparmex, Mexican Employers' Confederation). Fox also tried to develop his own style of corporatist labour relations based on Church social doctrine (*ibid.*). However, since the 1990s, independent unions rejecting the corporatism of the past have grown more powerful in Mexico in forums such as the Unión Nacional de Trabajadores (UNT, National Union of Workers). The Frente Auténtico del Trabajo (FAT, Authentic Labour Front), a union within the UNT, has succeeded in gaining rights to represent workers under Mexican law. In the state of Oaxaca in 2006, teachers' unions protesting poor conditions formed the core of a significant protest movement that brought together a diverse range of social and indigenous groups in a serious and violent confrontation with the state's PRI governor.

The representation of women and indigenous groups has become a key theme in labour organising in the democratic period, combining the notions of unionisation with other ideas such as empowerment in countries such as Honduras, Bolivia and Mexico (see Chapters 8, 13). In the banana-exporting countries of Central America, for example, women workers – *bananeras* – have gained increasing control over their unions and workplaces (see, for example, Frank, 2008).

Peasants

Rural society in Latin America is characterised by great poverty and inequalities in land ownership. Industrialisation failed to absorb flows of rural labour to the cities and the rural population continues to grow, increasing pressure on land. Two key themes have been prominent in the analysis of agricultural land use since colonial times: diversity, and concentration. There has been huge diversity in patterns of land tenure in Latin America and they have changed over time. Large landholdings, *latifundia,* usually in the form of modern corporate farms, often make up to 80–90 per cent of cultivable land; small-scale, traditional peasant agriculture makes up most of the rest. Although medium-sized producers exist, policy has been determined by this dualistic structure of production. The rapid expansion of capital-intensive forms of agriculture based around modern agro-technology has increased the pressure on land use and put rural smallholders at a disadvantage. Today, modernisation co-exists with traditional farming and rural social organisation, also making the defence of cultural integrity a key issue in rural development (see Chapters 8, 13). A recurrent response of governments to poor conditions in the countryside, the potential for peasant mobilisation, or low agricultural productivity, has been agrarian reform, especially through the redistribution of land.

An important dimension of the study of the countryside has been the degree to which land use has determined social relations. Communal land ownership was often associated with established ethnic identities producing for subsistence or local exchange. Large landholdings in Latin America were traditionally based on power relations which ensured the loyalty of peasants to landowners through paternalistic ties and a relationship of dependence that prevented the peasant from leaving. Middle-sized farms owned by their proprietors were often seen by liberals as the key to establishing a new, self-reliant bourgeois class of entrepreneurs who could drive forward national development (see Chapter 1). A key historical issue in agrarian development has been the extent to which the penetration of capitalism into rural society has transformed these social relations. The spread of commercial farming has progressively marginalised peasants from land, labour and credit markets and, as a result, land issues remain unresolved (see Box 7.6). Agribusiness tends to employ wage labour, often only seasonally, and there has been a large growth in the number of poor migrant labourers who oscillate between the rural sector and the outskirts of the urban sector as demands for labour change. Agribusiness has also shifted away from labour-intensive to more capital-intensive forms of production and large, transnational corporations now control a large proportion of agro-exports. Mechanisation and the impact of agrobusiness on traditional or small producers has forced them off the land.

SOCIETY

Box 7.6

Neoliberalism in agriculture

Since the 1990s, the main process shaping the rural economy and society has been neoliberal globalisation based on the export of primary commodities (Kay, 2004; see Chapter 15). Neoliberal policies have, first, displaced the distributive component of land reform by placing a new emphasis on agribusiness, individual farming and the breaking up of co-operative or collective forms of organisation. In countries such as Mexico and Bolivia, neoliberal reform led to changes in constitutional measures put in place to protect redistributed land, and in some instances led to the renewed concentration of land in fewer hands (*ibid.*). Second, neoliberal policies have deepened the *exclusionary* character of rural modernisation and further jeopardised the livelihoods of the peasantry (*ibid.*). Capitalist farmers are the main beneficiaries of market liberalisation and small landowners find it hard to compete, leading to indebtedness, the sale of lands and greater inequality. Third, neoliberal policies generally mean that agricultural produce cannot be subsidised or protected, and so the Latin American agrarian sector has found itself at a disadvantage in the face of protectionism by the US or EU. Lastly, neoliberal policies have led to far greater diversification of production in the countryside and, while Chile has successfully developed a diversified agricultural sector and the cultivation of new export crops such as soya beans or sunflower, other countries have not had so much success and rural production remains vulnerable to fluctuations in the world market and deteriorating international prices.

Kay (2004) identified five major changes in rural labour and employment as a result of modernisation: the replacement of tenant labour by wage labour; the growth of temporary and seasonal wage labour; the increasing feminisation of rural wage labour; the urbanisation of rural workers; and the growing importance of non-farm employment and income, such as rural industry and agro-industrial processing. These changes have led to differentiation and make it difficult today to talk of a single, homogeneous peasantry with shared interests. They have also transformed social relations, and today large landowners are, in effect, entrepreneurs running agribusinesses and no longer have traditional bonds of obligation to the rural poor. Neoliberal reforms have also had a political impact on the countryside, often restricting the peasant's room for manoeuvre. Kurtz (2004) examined the implications of neoliberal reforms for peasants in Chile and Mexico and argued that these undermined the communitarian bases of their social organisation by transforming a mostly settled peasant class into a seasonal rural proletariat – rural workers paid through wages as opposed to small landowners – and by introducing divisions among them based on self-interest that inhibited their ability to organise (see also Bruhn, 2005). As a result, rural associations and networks fell apart, leaving peasants with few forms of representation, while issues such as land reform disappeared from the political agenda amid a new commitment to private property. Kurtz argued that neoliberal economic reforms not only demobilised peasant organisations in Chile, but turned them into an electoral bastion for conservatives.

A key issue when examining the politics of the countryside are the conditions in which the poorest rural inhabitants live. Neither state-led industrialisation (see Chapter 14) nor neoliberal reforms have been able to resolve poverty, inequality

CASE STUDY   Box 7.7

Haiti and the Dominican Republic – Slaves in paradise?

Teenage labourers comprise a significant part of the estimated 20,000 Haitian farmhands who work in very poor conditions harvesting cane for the large sugar complexes of the neighbouring Dominican Republic. The children are often sent by their parents alone to work in the canefields and live in shacks in cane cutters' villages known as *bateyes* without electricity, water and sanitation during the harvesting season. Many face overwork, malnutrition and disease yet, given economic hardships in Haiti itself, do not wish to return to their country – a situation only made worse by natural disasters such as the catastrophic earthquake of 2010. Activists in the US have at times described the conditions of the workers as 'modern-day slavery'. Many cane cutters are recruited in Haiti and brought to the plantations by bus, but once there realise their wages will be low and try to head for the capital, Santo Domingo, to find better-paid jobs. Plantation foremen, occasionally armed, sometimes patrol the fields on horses to intercept escapees then lock them up for days. Workers often complain of mistreatment – from insults to beatings – for trying to leave. Three workers disappeared after they had been caught and beaten by plantation employees in November 2003, according to a complaint by the Dominican Centre for Advisory and Legal investigations. 'They are slaves in paradise,' said the Reverend Christopher Hartley, a priest at San José de los Llanos who has defended the farmworkers.

Source: Reyes, 2005

and exclusionary development, and in many countries such as Haiti conditions are bad (see Box 7.7). The issue of labour that has an element of compulsion in Paraguay, Bolivia and Brazil, sometimes described as slavery, has remained prominent (see Box 8.6). In 2007, for example, Brazilian labour ministry officials freed 1,000 workers on a sugar-cane plantation in the Amazon who they said were working in inhumane conditions akin to slavery. Brazil has one of the most unequal distributions of land in the world and about one-third of the rural population lives below the poverty line. Yet below Brazil's poorest farmers in the rural social order are the landless – former farmers, rural workers, and even urban workers unable to find work who often migrate in search of seasonal jobs and land. Brazil's Movimento dos Trabalhadores Rurais Sem Terra (MST, Landless Workers' Movement, see Chapter 8) now represents about 1.5 million landless workers.

Rural inhabitants often lack basic citizenship rights, such as economic and physical security, and have recurrently been caught between warring factions and displaced from their land in the civil wars that have ravaged countries such as Colombia and Guatemala. In April 2005, the United Nations' World Food Programme and the International Committee of the Red Cross said that Colombia had the world's third-largest population of internally displaced persons after Sudan and Angola (Green, 2005). The poor conditions in which rural inhabitants live is also a major source of conflict in the countryside. Labour disputes have led to violent confrontations between farm workers and landowners across Guatemala and Bolivia, for example.

Antiquated legal structures that have worked in favour of the rich and powerful have contributed to poverty and instability. Disputes over property rights, in

Property rights in Nicaragua

In Nicaragua, the Frente Sandinista de Liberación Nacional (FSLN, Sandinista National Liberation Front) forged a mixed economy following the revolution by redistributing agricultural assets expropriated and confiscated from an array of powerful landowning families and political enemies. However, a decade of civil war left the countryside in a desperate state of economic decline and social decay. Under these circumstances, the FSLN could not withstand the pressures of international isolation and national electoral competition, and Nicaragua underwent a transition from a revolutionary state to an electoral democracy with a neoliberal economy. The privatisation of millions of acres and hundreds of enterprises after 1990 reflected political preferences for the free market. Ultimately, squabbling between embattled Sandinista leaders, resurgent interests whose land had been confiscated, and rejuvenated conservative elements of the ruling Partido Liberal Constitucionalista (PLC, Constitutional Liberal Party), fostered an unstable institutional order and a great deal of legal ambiguity about the institution of property which has persisted into the contemporary period. Who owns what, and how much protection the law gives them, are key political issues in the country. Disputes between those who claim to be the former proprietors of estates who lost their land in the early years of the revolutionary government and landless people claiming title to the expropriated plots they farmed under the Sandinista regime have left many plantations in a legal limbo.

particular, can hamper the consolidation of democracy if they remain unresolved and exacerbate poverty (Lustig and Deutsch, 1998; ISPI, 2000). It has been argued that in Nicaragua, for example, protracted confrontation and violence over property rights have seriously threatened unconsolidated democratic institutions (Everingham, 2001; see also Box 7.8).

There has been a long debate about the political behaviour of rural inhabitants and this has boiled down to whether the peasantry is potentially a conservative force that will develop over time into a new agrarian petty bourgeoisie; or whether it is potentially a radical force whose revolutionary attitudes will be galvanised by changes in the countryside. One intellectual tradition suggests that peasants are frequently conservative, anti-revolutionary, and vulnerable to control by rural elites. A more recent contribution to this position was made by Kurtz (2004), who noted that Chilean peasants voted for conservatives throughout most of Chile's pre-coup history and that peasant quiescence, not radicalism, was the rule. Others have argued that agrarian reform can raise the revolutionary potential of the peasantry (see Wolf, 1969; Petras and Laporte, 1971). Peasants played a key role in the Mexican, Bolivian and Cuban Revolutions and were active in the Trotskyist guerrilla movement that provoked military intervention in Peru in 1968 and thereafter in the Maoist guerrilla movement Sendero Luminoso (see Boxes 12.4, 13.9, Figure 12.1). In Guatemala, peasants resisted military tactics against the guerrillas, and in Colombia they initially formed the basis of the insurgency by the Fuerzas Armadas Revolucionarias de Colombia (FARC, Revolutionary Armed Forces of Colombia). Some of the most well-known Latin American radical protest movements of the 1990s have been peasant organisations. Social movements continue to emerge across

Latin America among different sectors of the rural population. In Brazil – where only about 4 per cent of farmers control 79 per cent of the country's arable land – the MST was formed by Catholic and Marxist activists and has spearheaded land invasions of large estates demanding their expropriation. In Ecuador, indigenous Quichua peasants have led large mobilisations that have undermined governments (see Table 4.1, Box 6.2, Chapter 5). In Mexico, the Zapatista rebellion in Chiapas was undertaken by mainly Mayan peasants hit by agricultural modernisation (see Boxes 12.6, 13.5). Contemporary agrarian movements such as the Zapatistas have displayed great sophistication in their aims and activities, and have acquired an international profile. Leaders are more adept at promoting objectives through media such as the internet and at generating international pressure (Kay, 2004).

One reason that there have been opposing perspectives about the political character of peasants is that, like unions, their organisations often developed in a corporatist relationship with the state. In Mexico, the Confederación Nacional Campesina (CNC, National Peasant Confederation) was affiliated to the PRI and relied on the selective provision of benefits to peasants loyal to the party. In rural Mexico, the *ejido* – a form of social and territorial organisation – was the prime focus of corporatist activity. Ruling groups within *ejidos* became the channel used by the PRI to organise its activities in communities. Mackinlay and Otero (2004) have argued that corporatism persists in the Mexican countryside, albeit under new institutional arrangements.

Agrarian reform became a key political issue in Latin American politics in the wake of the Cuban Revolution (see Box 2.3), prior to which only Mexico and Bolivia had undertaken major land reforms as a result of revolutions. Reform has pursued two underlying objectives: to improve productivity and the efficient use of the land; and to respond to the demand for social justice through land redistribution. Land reform has been the result both of revolutionary change and political reformism. Extensive reforms have also been undertaken without a revolutionary process in countries such as Chile (1964–70) and Peru (1968–75). Yet the results of agrarian reform have been mixed and, in general, rural inhabitants remain worse off than their urban counterparts. The main legacy of land reform was to hasten the disappearance of the landed oligarchy and pave the way for the commercialisation of agriculture (Kay, 2004). Today, the need for agrarian reform persists and it remains an important political issue (see Box 7.9).

In 2006, Bolivia's leftwing president Evo Morales (2006–) launched a programme to distribute land to indigenous peasant communities, prompting dire warnings from landowners that they would take action to defend their estates. Bolivia's new constitution passed in 2009 made some concessions to these landowners, but also allowed land reform to take place by limiting the size of rural landholdings in future sales. The government of Paraguay became the latest in Latin America to propose land reform, with the creation of the Coordinadora Ejecutiva para la Reforma Agraria (Executive Co-ordinating Body for Agrarian Reform, CEPRA) being a central element of Fernando Lugo's campaign before he won the presidency in 2008, although subsequent progress has been limited. Paraguay has the most unequal land distribution in Latin America, with about 83 per cent of *campesinos* occupying just 6 per cent of the land, and 40 per cent of all property owned by just 351 hacienda owners

Box 7.9

Land reform in Venezuela

Venezuela's government began to undertake land reform after a law passed in 2001 empowered it to seize certain properties. Venezuela's president, Hugo Chávez (1999–), pledged to eliminate the *latifundio*, in a country where about three-quarters of arable land is owned by less than 5 per cent of the population, by breaking up estates of at least 12,350 acres that the government determined were idle. Chávez and his advisers saw land reform as a means of reviving agricultural production in a country that imports about 70 per cent of what it eats, and of ensuring greater social justice by providing farmland to peasants and attracting the poor out of overcrowded urban slums back to the countryside. Despite Venezuela's oil wealth, the majority of its population of 25 million people are poor and live in cities concentrated along the coastal strip. The development of a major oil export-ing industry led to the neglect of the country's agricultural sector, as foreign currency made it rela-tively cheap to import food. The rest of the country is sparsely inhabited, although much of the land is tropical wetland and savanna with poor soil used by cattle ranchers. In the initial period following the 2001 law, the government redistributed about 5 million acres of public land to peasants. It used oil money to set up co-operative ventures such as chicken farms and sugar mills and to train about 400,000 people in co-operative business practices. In 2005, Venezuela's Instituto Nacional de Tierra (INTI, National Land Institute) began to review the 6.6 million acres of land owned by private estates for redistribution. The government singled out a cattle ranch in central Venezuela owned by the British meat group Vestey's, much of which had already been occupied by peasants for several years, to ini-tiate redistribution. The land institute claimed that Vestey's and the owners of other ranches in Cojedes state had failed to demonstrate proof of ownership. Figures released in January 2009 suggested that nearly 2.7 million hectares (6.6 million acres) of *latifundio* land had been returned to productivity since the passage of the 2001 law, and about a third of the *latifundio* land existing in 1998 has been redistributed, benefiting 180,000 families (Schiavoni and Camacaro, 2009). Moreover, agricul-tural credit increased from approximately $164 million in 1999 to about $7.6 billion in 2008, boost-ing Venezuela's food production capacity by 24 per cent since 1998 (*ibid.*). By 2008, Venezuela had achieved self-sufficiency in corn, rice and pork, and had greatly increased the production of beef, chicken, eggs, milk, black beans, root vegetables and sunflowers. Critics said the land reform pro-gramme represented political posturing lacking in long-term strategic thinking and that Chávez's inflam-matory rhetoric was encouraging land invasions. At least 75 peasants were killed in land disputes from early 2002 to early 2004, for example. The critics argued that co-operative agro-industrial projects launched by the government are inefficient in the face of international competition and that expropriation will damage agribusinesses because the fear of confiscations turns away investors. However, there have been concrete gains for many small producers organised in co-operatives such as the cacao farmers in the coastal community of Chuao, who benefit from greatly increased government support in the form of new warehouses, offices, access to low-interest credit, technical assistance and loans to support new micro-enterprises.

(Howard, 2009). The country has a flourishing soyabean industrial agricultural export model that leaves little room for small *campesino* producers. It has become the world's fourth-largest exporter of soyabeans, a sector whose rapid growth over the last 15 years has generated significant tensions between industrial farmers and *campesinos* often encouraged to leave their land or compelled to relocate because of the problems caused through contamination of it by pesticides. Kay (2004) argues that agrarian reform can play a key role in successful economic development and that instability will continue as long as peasants continue to be marginalised.

The experience of Brazil under the administration of Fernando Henrique Cardoso (1995–2002), which distributed a considerable amount of land, reveals the constraints on governments pursuing agrarian reform today. From 1995 to 1998, roughly 287,000 landless families received land under the reform programme and about 20 million hectares, mostly in unused private holdings, were acquired for redistribution (see Pereira, 2003). However, critics of the Cardoso reforms such as Pereira (2003) argued that his policies in fact missed opportunities to help the rural poor and served to maintain an agricultural model that disproportionately benefits a small number of large producers.

The military

There have been scores of military interventions in Latin America and, until the 1980s, coups were as much a feature of politics as elections. The military has been both a corporate actor in politics and also an independent one prone to seeking control of the state. A central issue in the study of the military has been its role in the transition to civilian rule and within democratic politics (see Chapters 3, 4). Most democratising states underwent some form of demilitarisation – the reduction of the military's role, ranging from the simple exit of the military from the presidential palace to the complete abolition of the armed forces as an institution, as occurred in Costa Rica in 1948 (see Kincaid, 2000). One of the central questions of the newly established democracies of Latin America has been how to subordinate the military to civilian control.

Two key themes shaped the new relationship between the military and civilian government: the degree to which the military contested civilian policies, and the 'prerogatives' granted to the military by the new democratic leadership. Key to the new civil–military relationship was the extent of agreement over key issues such as how the new regime handled the legacy of human rights violations and the new mission established for the military in a democratic system. In several Latin American countries, prisoners were 'disappeared' or died while in the custody of the security forces while the military was in control (see Table 7.2).

Table 7.2 'Disappearances' in Brazil, Argentina and Uruguay during the bureaucratic–authoritarian regimes

Country	Disappeared	Population in 1975 (millions)	Disappeared per 100,000 people
Argentina	8,960*	28.0	32.0
Uruguay	26	2.6	1.0
Brazil	125	125.0	0.1

*Other estimates have put this much higher

Sources: Stepan, 1988; Argentine National Commission on the Disappeared. 1986; *Brasil: Nunca Mais* (see Arns, 1985); Gillespie, 1987

As a result, military officials wanted to protect themselves from legal reprisals for human rights abuses after the transition to democratic rule. The approach each country took to this issue depended on the relative strength of the military during the transition itself. In Brazil, congress voted in 1979 for an amnesty for crimes committed between 1964–79, this was accepted in the military and civil society as mutual, and attempts to challenge it later failed. In Argentina, by contrast, resentment of the military after 1983 allowed President Raúl Alfonsín (1983–89) to initiate proceedings that led to the conviction and imprisonment of eight senior junta officials. However, although Alfonsín assumed office with a strong democratic mandate strengthened by the disastrous performance of the military in the 1982 Malvinas/Falklands war (see Box 11.1), military–civil relations were characterised by tension: signs of resentment, lack of co-operation and periodic military revolts. In the face of resistance to prosecutions, Alfonsín also urged congress in 1986 to place a time limit on new proceedings to be filed. His administration also failed to nurture in the military a new respect for civilian control. Alfonsín's successor, Menem, used a general amnesty and careful negotiations to lower tensions and, ultimately, confirm the military's subordination to democratic governance.

Initiatives by democratic governments to redefine the role of the military and review its institutional prerogatives – areas of governance over which the military as an institution assumes it has a right to exercise control (see Chapter 4) – also varied. In Brazil, constitutional revisions formally established the military's mission as external, and put the civilian executive and legislature in control of any use of force internally. In Argentina, Alfonsín's reforms removed almost all the military's formal prerogatives, generating conflict that culminated in a barracks mutiny in 1987.

In some cases, demilitarisation was more comprehensive. In El Salvador, for example, the peace agreement signed in 1992 by representatives of the Salvadorean government and the Frente Farabundo Martí para la Liberación Nacional (FMLN, Farabundo Marti National Liberation Front) guerrilla organisation established the basis for changes in the Salvadorean security forces. The armed forces' mission and doctrine were redefined so that their primary responsibility would be national defence, and military doctrine was changed to reflect democratic values and respect for human rights (Kincaid, 2000).

The most important requirement of democratic civil–military relations is the political subordination of the armed forces to elected civilian authorities (Ruhl, 2005; see also Karl, 1996). Full democratic control means the subordination of the armed forces must be *institutionalised*, with the military accepting civilian policy controls over its internal activities through a defence ministry, congressional committees and civilian courts (Fitch, 1998, 2001). Progress has been slow in countries where military regimes exerted a strong hold over politics and society. It was not until August 2005 that Chile's congress approved constitutional reforms that allow the president to fire commanders, strip the military-dominated National Security Council of all but advisory powers, and do away with senatorial posts filled by individuals designated by the armed forces. Ruhl (2005) examined the limited progress that had been made in institutionalising civil–military relations in Guatemala by 2004. He argued that presidents after the 1996 peace accords were largely unable to reduce the role of the military and institutionalise democratic civil–military relations, and that the armed forces retained substantial institutional autonomy and *de facto* legal immunity. As we have seen, some scholars have highlighted the problems posed for democratic consolidation in Latin America by the inability to fully subordinate the military to civilian control (see Chapter 4; also Loveman, 1994; Hunter, 1998). Diamint (2004), for example, has argued that a prominent area in which civilian governments have failed to establish democratic decisionmaking is in security policy. He says there is still a considerable degree of military-to-military contact between the armed forces in Latin America and those in the US *outside* the scrutiny or control of democratic political institutions. Diamint suggests that such an absence of democratic civil control over the military could challenge, and potentially undermine, the consolidation of democracy in Latin America.

Today, most political leaders in Latin America believe that the armed forces still have significant influence, although there has been considerable progress in the institutionalisation of civilian control over them (UNDP, 2004b). In only three countries – Ecuador, Venezuela and Cuba – are the armed forces considered to be politicised and play a supervisory role with respect to the political process. In Honduras, where a coup cut short the presidency of Manuel Zelaya in 2009, the military has also retained considerable political influence. However, international scrutiny and a shared consensus on democratic values has made the cost of a coup much higher. A potential coup in Paraguay in 1996 was prevented by threats from its Mercosur partners to cut trade (see Box 9.9). A coup in Ecuador in 2000 lasted only a few hours before military leaders yielded, under pressure from the US and Latin American states. The coup in Honduras caused significant damage to the country's standing within Latin America and internationally (see Box 7.10).

In recent years, progress has also been made in pursuing military officials for past abuses (see Box 7.11). Yet in some countries the threat of military intervention remains and authoritarian legacies continue to have an important influence on the practice of politics (see Pion-Berlin, 2005). In Ecuador, in January 2000 the military and indigenous groups fomented a coup that led to the replacement of President Jamil Mahuad with Gustavo Noboa (2000–03). In March 2006, Ecuador's interior minister Alfredo Castillo resigned amid violent protests against free-trade talks with the US, again warning that the country faced the risk of a coup. In Venezuela, much of Hugo Chávez's public popularity derived from his role in leading a coup attempt in 1992 against President Carlos Andrés Pérez (1974–79, 1989–93). A coup attempt against Chávez himself failed in April 2002 (see Boxes 4.2, 7.2). During the political instability in Argentina in 2001, there were examples of excessive use of force by security personnel, prompting an angry backlash. In Paraguay, critics of the powerful former army chief, General Lino Oviedo, argue that he remains a destabilising force in politics. Oviedo was widely accused in Paraguay of involvement in the assassination of the vice-president, Luis María Argaña, in March 1999. He has denied being involved in the killing. He was arrested in June 2004 on his return from five years' exile in Brazil on charges related to a 1996 coup attempt but later freed. In Bolivia, in May 2005 instability caused by protests in La Paz by indigenous groups also provoked questions about the commitment of the military to civilian rule. Admiral Luis Aranda, the head of the country's armed forces, was forced to deny in the media that the military was planning a coup.

| CASE STUDY | Box 7.10 |

Honduran coup makes waves

Despite being a domestic political crisis, the coup in Honduras in 2009 had important international repercussions and damaged the country's standing within Latin America. At dawn on 28 June, up to 300 troops arrived at President Manuel Zelaya's home and, he has claimed, told him to surrender or they would shoot him. He was then taken to the airport and put on a flight to Costa Rica. Roberto Micheletti, the speaker of the Honduran congress who was constitutionally second-in-line to the presidency, was then sworn in as interim leader. The Organisation of American States (OAS) demanded the immediate reinstatement of Zelaya and suspended the membership of Honduras, the World Bank suspended the disbursement of loans to the country, and the United Nations General Assembly unanimously adopted a resolution calling for the ousted president's reinstatement. Zelaya's allies in Bolivia, Ecuador and Venezuela withdrew their ambassadors from Honduras, as did all European Union countries (see Chapter 11), and Brazil suspended visa-free travel for Hondurans. El Salvador, Guatemala and Nicaragua suspended overland trade with Honduras for two days, and Venezuela's president, Hugo Chávez, threatened to invade if the country's embassy or ambassador were attacked and said he would suspend oil shipments to Honduras. Other Latin American countries also reportedly began to take steps to suspend diplomatic relations with Honduras. Costa Rica's president, Oscar Arias, a Nobel peace laureate, was designated as a mediator by countries in the region, then hosted talks between Zelaya and the interim government and presented a detailed plan to try to end the crisis. The International Transport Workers' Union, which groups workers in 140 countries, began a boycott of Honduran-flagged ships. Brazil subsequently assumed a high profile in the affair after Zelaya had returned to his country covertly and sought refuge with his entourage in the Brazilian embassy. The Honduran military immediately imposed a cordon outside the diplomatic mission that prevented all but essential supplies to enter the compound for Brazilian diplomats and Zelaya's entourage. At one stage, they used tear gas against the compound and cut off electricity and water supplies to it. The Honduran regime also threatened to enter the diplomatic mission unless Brazil either granted Zelaya formal political asylum or handed him over to them, leading to a tense war of words about the legality of their acts under international law between the country's interim government and the Brazilian administration. The US was initially cautious in its response to the crisis, then refused to recognise Micheletti as president and pressed for Zelaya's return, suspending valuable development and military aid. Saying that Micheletti's interim government had failed to respect democratic processes, it later halted non-humanitarian aid to Honduras. However, the US ambassador to the OAS also criticised Zelaya's return to Honduras before a settlement had been reached as 'irresponsible and foolish'. In late September, Micheletti refused to admit an OAS delegation seeking talks with both sides and a negotiated settlement to the crisis into Honduras, and suspended civil liberties in the country that included the imposition of a curfew. Both sides entered negotiations in search of a solution, but talks stumbled repeatedly over Zelaya's demand to return to the presidency ahead of elections in November. The elections were held and won by the conservative candidate, Porfirio Lobo (2009–), dividing Latin American opinion. The US and several regional allies accepted the result but other countries did not. Charges brought by state prosecutors against the six commanders of the operation that alleged they had abused their power by originally removing Zelaya from the country were dismissed by the supreme court. President Lobo's first act after taking office was also to issue a decree that granted an amnesty to the soldiers, politicians and judges who had conducted the coup. The Honduran political crisis had a damaging effect on trade in Central America, with the country's neighbours, Guatemala, El Salvador and Costa Rica, losing millions of dollars of export business. In January 2010, Zelaya eventually went into formal exile in the Dominican Republic.

Amnesty no longer

Amnesty laws passed by outgoing military regimes are now proving to be no barrier to the prosecution of serving and former officers accused of human rights abuses during the period of authoritarian rule.

In Argentina, in June 2005 the supreme court ruled 7–1 that amnesty laws protecting former officers suspected of human rights abuses during military rule between 1976 and 1983 were unconstitutional, opening the way for the prosecution of hundreds of current and former military officials. In June 2006, in the first such case since the amnesty ruling, an Argentine court began the trial of a former police chief accused of murder during military rule. Argentina also requested the extradition of six men from Uruguay – five former military officers and a former policeman – in connection with the disappearance in 1976 of the daughter-in law of a famous Argentine poet. It has been estimated that between 9,000 and 20,000 people may have died at the hands of Argentina's military during the 'Dirty War' of the 1970s, often in brutal circumstances. For example, in Spain during the trial in 2005 of Adolfo Scilingo for genocide, terrorism and other crimes in this period, the former Argentine navy officer admitted participating in 'death flights' in which drugged, naked detainees were allegedly thrown from planes. He was sentenced to 640 years in prison for his crimes. The ruling by Argentina's supreme court upheld an earlier decision by a federal judge in 2001 that amnesty laws passed in 1986 and 1987 preventing charges against military officers involved in disappearances, torture and other crimes were unconstitutional and violated Argentina's obligations under international human rights treaties. The efforts of President Raúl Alfonsín (1983–89) to prosecute military leaders were hampered by army revolts and he sought to keep the peace by accepting amnesty provisions in 1986 and 1987, and his successor Carlos Menem pardoned former military commanders. Prosecutions against army, navy and air force officers have taken place, but mostly in Europe following the extradition of officers charged in the deaths of European nationals. After taking office in 2003, Argentina's president, Néstor Kirchner (2003–07), purged top military officials and in March 2004 announced that the Navy Mechanics School, which had been a death camp, would be turned into a museum honouring the military's victims. In June 2006, Kirchner brought into force a law originally passed by the Alfonsín government but not put into effect that clearly defined the mission of the military by saying they will only be deployed against external aggression. The country has maintained its efforts to bring to justice former military officers involved in past abuses. In October 2009, for example, Julio Alberto Poch, allegedly a former military pilot at the Navy Mechanics School and accused in Argentina of also flying the planes that were used to dump opponents of the military regime into the sea, was ordered to be kept in detention in Spain pending a decision on extradition. He denied the allegations.

In Chile, judicial moves against the former dictator Augusto Pinochet (1973–90) became emblematic, until his death in 2006, of efforts to confront past abuses. An independent commission for the civilian government that succeeded Pinochet calculated that 3,197 people died or disappeared during his regime. By December 2005, Pinochet had been stripped of his immunity in a number of lawsuits arising from human rights abuses and was facing charges in relation to several disappearances in the mid-1970s. Although he was never convicted of any crimes, at the time of his death, about 300 criminal charges were still pending against the former Chilean ruler for human rights violations, tax evasion and embezzlement. Other high-profile cases have also been reopened. In late 2009, six people, including four doctors, were charged over the death in 1982 of the country's former Christian democratic president, Eduardo Frei Montalva (1964–70). The judge said there was evidence that Frei, who had been a vocal critic of Pinochet, had been poisoned in hospital.

In Uruguay, in 2005 the leftwing government of Tabaré Vázquez (2005–09) brought charges of aggravated homicide against the former president Juan María Bordaberry (1972–76), who ruled as a puppet of the military, and his foreign minister, over the kidnapping and killing of two congressional leaders who had fled to Argentina after Uruguay's legislature was shut down in 1973. An amnesty law that applied to abuses committed inside Uruguay was passed in 1986 as the military prepared to hand power back to civilians, and was endorsed in a plebiscite in 1989. However, responding to a changed public opinion, the Vázquez administration found loopholes enabling it to reopen certain cases (see Rohter, 2005). In 2009, Uruguay's supreme court ruled that the amnesty law was illegal, setting a precedent for future trials of military officials, and General Gregorio Alvarez, who ruled from 1981–85, was jailed for 25 years for murder and human rights violations. In 2010, Bordaberry, now 81, was sentenced to 30 years in prison for murder and disappearances.

In late 2004, Paraguayan prosecutors requested the extradition from Brazil of the country's former military ruler, Alfredo Stroessner (1954–89), in relation to investigations into Operation Condor, a campaign involving military regimes across South America to eliminate opponents.

In Mexico, in June 2006 a court issued an arrest warrant against the former president Luis Echeverría (1970–76), whom special prosecutors accused of ordering a massacre of student protesters in Tlatelolco square, Mexico City, in 1968 when he was the country's interior minister, although several past attempts to prosecute him had failed. Critics of Echeverría argue that the Mexican state subsequently waged its own 'Dirty War' against leftwing activists during his presidency.

In Brazil, in 2009 the government of President Lula da Silva said it intended to create a truth commission to investigate crimes committed by the security forces between 1964 and 1985. Until then Brazil had been the only country in Latin America that had not investigated the deaths, disappearances and torture that took place during the dictatorship or tried alleged perpetrators. Attempts to bring them to justice had failed under the blanket provisions of a 1979 amnesty law.

There have also been moves in Central America to address the abuses of the past. Calls have also grown in El Salvador for the government to scrap amnesty laws protecting former military officials from being prosecuted for alleged abuses committed during the civil war. In November 2005, in a trial in a US federal court in Tennessee, El Salvador's former deputy defence minister Nicolas Carranza was found responsible for torture and murder during the 1980s. Carranza, who had become an American citizen, was being pursued for damages in the US because amnesty laws prevented such trials in El Salvador.

Spain has been at the forefront of efforts to pursue Latin American military officers. In October 2005 its highest court ruled that cases of genocide committed abroad could be judged in Spain even if no Spanish citizens have been involved, following a request by the Guatemalan indigenous activist Rigoberta Menchú for it to probe abuses in the 1970s and 1980s.

Although in some countries such as Argentina anti-democratic attitudes have been rooted out, with military leaders in 1995 publicly recognising the illegitimacy of state terror during the junta's control, scholars have argued that undemocratic attitudes persist elsewhere among officers (Hunter, 1998). In Guatemala, members of the country's truth commission seeking to ascertain the facts about past military abuses conducted much of their work without access to documentary evidence after having been told by security forces that no such evidence existed. In mid-2005, however, a huge archive about past cases stored by the former national police and containing 75 million pages of documents, as well as photographic and audio evidence, was discovered by investigators from the human rights ombudsman's office in a police compound in Guatemala City. In Honduras, a television appearance in August 2009 by the five generals in charge of the armed forces to explain their role in the coup against Zelaya and respond to international criticism of his removal from power (see Box 7.10), demonstrated that they continued to play a leading role in the country's politics (see Thompson, 2009). In Paraguay in late 2009, President Fernando Lugo replaced the heads of the army, navy and air force, after warning that coup-plotters were active in the military. In the absence of efforts to make militaries accountable through trials or truth commissions, officers will continue to believe they have immunity.

The Church

The role and power of the Church was a central factor shaping the political development of Latin American states following Independence. The Church has functioned, mainly in the countryside where there has been a large peasant sector, as an alternative or parallel source of corporatism – a concept that is also central to its teaching (see Chapter 12). It has been strong enough to resist becoming a subordinate political actor within state corporatism. In the twentieth century, the Church began to move away from an alliance with conservative elements to develop a reformist response to democracy. Christian democratic parties began to emerge and in 1955 bishops from across the region met in Rio de Janeiro for the first plenary meeting of the Consejo Episcopal Latinoamericano (CELAM, Latin American Council of Bishops). In Brazil, officials in the government of Juscelino Kubitschek (1956–61) often used Christian language to denounce social injustice and pursue accelerated development policies. At the same time, social questions gained a new prominence after the revolution in Cuba, which the Church hierarchy in Latin America believed required a religious response.

The most important influence in the modernisation of the Latin American Church was the Second Vatican Council held in the early 1960s in Rome. 'Vatican II' moved international Catholicism from a conservative position to one that supported democracy, human rights and social justice. It inaugurated a new openness in the Church allowing hitherto taboo themes such as the relationship between Christianity and Marxism to be discussed. CELAM took on board the implications of what was being discussed in Rome and, by 1968, the moral validity of the economic and political system in Latin America was firmly on its agenda. A CELAM conference in 1968 in Medellín, Colombia, has often been identified as the moment when 'liberation theology' emerged as an identifiable current of thought (see Box 12.3). However, in the longer term conservatism prevailed and was strengthened by Pope John Paul II (1978–2005), who believed that through liberation theology an alternative 'popular church' had emerged and had to be reined in. Cardinal Joseph Ratzinger served as John Paul II's main doctrinal policeman and, since becoming his successor as Pope Benedict XVI, has maintained the tough line against progressive priests (see Reel, 2005b).

A key factor shaping debates within the Church has been the specific national context in which these unfolded. Where there was a history of close association between the Church and state, as in Colombia and Venezuela, the Church hierarchy was often reluctant to attack the status quo; where there was past antagonism between Church and state, such as Mexico, Argentina and Cuba, Church influence has been limited. The structure of the Church itself has also led to diversity, disagreement and polarisation, and divisions can be identified between bishops, represented by CELAM; and between the priesthood, especially missionaries within more autonomous orders, such as the Jesuits, along with the laity (ordinary members of the congregation), in particular those churchgoers involved in *comunidades eclesiales de base* (CEBs, Catholic base communities). CEBs comprise small groups gathering regularly to study the bible and discuss local concerns. Bishops couched many of the pronouncements emphasising justice that came out of Medellín in terms that avoided a commitment to specific activities, often frustrating more radical, younger clergy. In Chile, for example, priests who supported Allende's socialist programme were repudiated by the Chilean hierarchy. A conservative reaction to Medellín was evident at CELAM's Puebla conference in 1979, although the bishops were divided. The Brazilian church is still known for its progressive bishops, for example, many of whom encouraged the growth of CEBs. There are also bishops elsewhere who have been characterised as supporters of liberation theology, such as Bishop Samuel Ruiz, who served as bishop of San Cristóbal de las Casas in Chiapas, Mexico, until 1999, although he rejected this label. Some bishops started out supporting radical forces, yet ended up in confrontation with them. In Nicaragua, bishops issued a pastoral letter in 1979 that legitimised the revolution, yet tensions later grew between them and the Sandinista government. There were also bishops formally described as conservatives but who confronted more regressive conservative forces, such as the Archbishop of San Salvador, Oscar Romero, who was assassinated in 1980 while saying Mass. Bishops who have challenged authoritarian actors remain targets of violence. In Guatemala in 1998, Bishop Juan Gerardi was murdered soon after publishing a report blaming the armed forces for most of the atrocities committed during the country's prolonged civil war (see Goldman, 2008). Lastly, there have also been reactionary bishops consistent in their opposition to liberation theology. In Argentina, the Church hierarchy was supportive of military authoritarianism and was criticised for staying silent about military repression.

The priesthood has been more progressive and radical than the hierarchy. Perhaps the most well-known radical priest in Latin America was the Colombian Camilo Torres (b.1929–d.1966), who joined a Marxist guerrilla movement (see Box 7.12).

The Nicaraguan Revolution of 1979 provided another example of the application of liberation theology and a number of priests joined the FSLN. The Church became polarised as some priests put Christian iconography at the service of the revolution and joined the Sandinista cabinet. In El Salvador, priests were killed by death squads in the late 1970s for helping to mobilise the poor. In 1989, rightwing paramilitaries executed a liberation theologian, Ignacio Ellacuria (b.1930–d.1989), along with five other Jesuit priests.

Vatican II and Medellín encouraged a new emphasis on participation by the laity and led to an upsurge in the creation of CEBs. These comprise a third organised tier of the Church and became associated with the socially-conscious dimensions

Box 7.12

Camilo Torres

Jorge Camilo Torres Restrepo studied law at the National University of Colombia before joining a seminary in Bogotá and being ordained as a priest in 1954. He travelled to Belgium where he studied sociology at the Catholic University of Louvain. In 1959, he returned to Bogotá and was appointed chaplain at the National University where he helped to found the faculty of sociology in 1960 and subsequently taught. He promoted community work among students in poor areas and enthusiastically implemented Vatican II reforms, but in 1961 fell out with Cardinal Concha Córdoba, who removed him from his post. Torres continued to collaborate in academic research projects and, under pressure from the Church hierarchy, resigned from the priesthood in 1965. He was the architect of the leftwing Frente Unido (United Front) political movement, which sought to unite opposition and revolutionary forces against the country's National Front governments. The United Front developed contacts with the nascent Marxist guerrilla organisation, the Ejército de Liberación Nacional (ELN, National Liberation Army) and was the target of government persecution. Frustrated with the inability to achieve change through peaceful means, Torres joined the ELN and died in his first armed engagement on 15 February 1966. His ideas reflected the norms of liberation theology in Latin America at that time, seeking to reconcile Christianity with Marxism (see Box 12.3). He became an icon for progressive Catholics and inspired the ideas of such figures as Father Ernesto Cardenal, who participated in Nicaragua's Sandinista revolution (see Cardenal, 2004). Other priests, such as the Spaniards Domingo Laín and Manuel Pérez, also died fighting with the ELN. A Spanish priest, Father Manuel Pérez, was a joint leader of the ELN from the late 1970s until his death in 1998 (see Boxes 12.3, 16.3, Figure 12.1).

of Church activity in the 1960s–1970s. Political channels such as parties and unions were being closed down by authoritarian regimes in much of Latin America, and so church-sponsored groups and activities inadvertently often became the only available political outlet. In this way, the Church helped to nurture the growth of civil society in the 1970s and 1980s (see Chapter 8). However, despite the fact that in countries such as Brazil Church progressives enjoyed a large network of CEBs and prestige for their defence of human rights, liberation theologians failed to establish an autonomous progressive Church in Latin America and the hierarchy prevailed. This failure has been explained, among other reasons, by the conditions generated by neoliberal reform (see Serbin, 2001; see also Chapter 15). Vasquez (1998) has argued that, because of the demands placed upon individuals in a neoliberal economy, activists lack time for engagement in CEBs and that unemployment, fragmentation of the working class, individualism and such factors as the need for women to work for basic survival also weakened popular church organisation.

Yet the idea of a popular church lives on in countries like Brazil and Nicaragua. Some radical priests in Brazil, for example, have adapted the rhetoric of liberation theology to contemporary circumstances, abandoning an emphasis on class in favour of the promotion of environmental conservation, women's rights and countering homelessness, Aids and landlessness. In Brazil, in September 2005 Bishop Luiz Flavio

Cappio staged a hunger strike to protest at controversial plans to divert water from the São Francisco river, and priests and nuns remain prominent in the activities of landless people to secure plots. In February 2005, Sister Dorothy Stang, a 73-year-old US nun who had been working with the landless and to protect the Amazon rain forests from loggers and ranchers for 37 years, was shot dead in Pará. By April 2006, three men had been jailed for her murder, one of whom testified that he had commissioned the two men who carried out the shooting on behalf of local ranchers. In late 2009, a witness in the Stang case was shot after being summoned to testify in a case against one of the ranchers accused of ordering the murder of the US nun. Reports following Stang's death suggested that Brother Henri Burin des Roziers, a French Catholic priest also working with the rural poor in Brazil, had been identified as a potential target of landowners.

The survival of radical positions explains continuing tensions within the Church in countries across the region. There were signs of divisions between the hierarchy and laity in Brazil with the election of the conservative Cardinal Ratzinger as Pope in 2005, and some members of the hierarchy have adopted positions that are openly critical of the Left. In Honduras, Cardinal Óscar Andrés Rodríguez Maradiaga, the Archbishop of Tegucigalpa, was a critic of Manuel Zelaya, who in turn accused him of conspiring and collaborating with the leaders of the coup that deposed him as president in June 2009. Archbishop Rodríguez was also a vociferous critic of comments by the Venezuelan leader, Hugo Chávez, that he had interpreted as interference in the sovereign affairs of Honduras following the coup. Church leaders in Venezuela itself have attacked some of Chávez's radical policies, such as the introduction of socialist ideas in aspects of teaching (see Box 12.7), and these have had a divisive effect on the main Christian denominations. In 2009, for example, a group of Venezuelan Anglican and Catholic priests who wanted to put more emphasis on helping the poor created what they called the 'Reformed Catholic Church'. The Venezuelan Episcopal Conference condemned the new religious group and its vice president, Archbishop Roberto Luckert, who has also been highly critical of Chávez, accused the group of taking government money and of mixing politics with religion.

Other priests or former priests have left the church – or been expelled by it – because of their decision to participate in politics. The former president of Haiti, Jean-Bertrand Aristide, was a Catholic priest from 1983–95 before being expelled from his order for his radical political activities. President Fernando Lugo (2008–) of Paraguay was the former Catholic bishop of San Pedro who, as a priest, was drawn to liberation theology (see above). Lugo resigned as a bishop in 2005, and the Pope granted him laicization after he had become president.

The limited fortunes of liberation theology and the efforts to establish a popular church that it gave rise to help, in part, to explain the growth of Protestant religious movements in Latin America. Evangelical Christianity began making inroads in the region during the 1970s–1980s in the context of civil war and at a time when the Catholic clergy was riven by political divisions. In Nicaragua, for example, conservative Christian relief agencies and evangelical missionaries preaching anti-communism were a regular presence at camps of the rightwing *contra* militias along the Nicaraguan-Honduran border (Chu, 2005). Evangelicals now constitute a significant religious minority and in Chile, Honduras and Brazil, for example, about

15 per cent of the population describes itself as Protestant. This figure rises to 22 per cent in El Salvador, 25 per cent in Guatemala and, in Mexico's southern Chiapas state, reports estimate it to be 36 per cent (*ibid.*). Analysts have long debated the political implications for Latin America of the growth in Protestantism (see Box 7.13).

Competition between religions has in some cases been the cause of violence or persecution. In Mexico, pastors and leaders of local evangelical congregations were among 34 men arrested for allegedly participating in a paramilitary attack on a Catholic prayer vigil in a chapel at Acteal in Chiapas in 1997 in which 45 people were killed. The Open Doors USA Christian organisation say the evangelicals were

---

THEORIES AND DEBATES **Box 7.13**

The politics of Protestantism

As the number of Protestants has grown, so have efforts by politicians to seek their support. Efraín Ríos Montt (1982–83) and Jorge Serrano Elías (1991–93) in Guatemala, Alberto Fujimori (1990–2000) in Peru, and Alvaro Uribe (2002–10) in Colombia are among the politicians to have courted Protestant groups. Protestants have also become more involved in politics themselves and some have created religious-based political parties or stood for office. In Paraguay in 2003, Oscar Nicanor Duarte (2003–08), a nominal Catholic who had attended a Mennonite church and had been critical of the Catholic hierarchy, was elected president. Protestant Evangelicals have also created their own political parties, such as Venezuela's Organización Renovadora Auténtica (ORA, Authentic Renewal Organisation) that gained several seats in congress and El Salvador's Movimiento de Solidaridad Nacional (MSN, National Solidarity Movement). The penetration of Protestantism in Latin America is an important phenomenon because many scholars believe religion shapes the way that individuals behave politically and economically. A key theme of debate has been the idea that Protestantism is more democratic than Catholicism, often because of its values. 'Neo-Weberian' views deriving from the work of the sociologist Max Weber (b.1864–d.1920) generally see Latin American evangelicals as favouring self-government, personal initiative, and gradual, peaceable change (see Martin, 1990; Smith, 1994). They suggest Protestantism changes individual attitudes about lifestyle, the work ethic and authority, which, over time, affect political culture (see Martin, 1990; Harrison, 1992; see also Weber, 1958). They argue that Protestantism will act as a catalyst for the development of the political attitudes necessary for democracy such as tolerance, social trust and support for democratic norms (see Martin, 1990; Swatos, 1994; Cleary and Stewart-Gambino, 1997; Sherman, 1997; Lynch, 1998). More recent research based on polling by the Gallup organisation has identified stronger entrepreneurial values among Protestants (Crabtree, 2008). The research conducted in 2007 suggested that members of Latin America's growing Protestant population were slightly more likely (57 per cent) than those in the majority Catholic population (49 per cent) to say they have a plan or idea to improve their standard of living. Other scholars reject the idea that the practice and structure of Protestantism has democratic potential and argue that evangelicals are contained within existing patron-client relationships or that Protestantism will have no long-term impact on the region (see Bastian, 1987; Martin, 1990; Chesnut, 1997; Corten, 1999). Research on Protestants in Brazil, Chile and Venezuela suggests that they are not significantly more politically active than Catholics and do not appear to behave politically in different ways to other groups (see Smilde, 2004; Patterson, 2005).

wrongly accused and used as scapegoats. However, the growth of Protestantism has also often been a fragile and reversible process, with evangelicals later drifting back toward Catholicism (Bowen, 1996). Catholics in Guatemala have employed tactics used by their rivals, such as operating radio stations and libraries, in an effort to arrest the growth of evangelicalism.

There have been various explanations for the growth of Protestantism. Some scholars suggest evangelical Protestant churches can offer a strong sense of community in a disorienting world, especially among internal migrants in countries such as Brazil (Chu, 2005). Many converts are also attracted to a style of worship more suited to contemporary tastes than what they regard as the staid Catholic Mass. The evangelical movement in Latin America has been particularly successful at using the media, with the Universal Church of the Kingdom of God in Brazil, for example, owning national TV networks. Brusco's (1995) study of Colombia showed that Pentecostalism appeals strongly to women and Brouwer *et al.* (1996) argued for a cultural explanation for the spread of Protestantism in Latin America, suggesting this religious approach offered US values in an era of consumerism. Latin American politicians have frequently claimed that an association exists between the work of evangelical Protestant churches and US interests. In November 2005, for example, Venezuela's president Hugo Chávez ordered the New Tribes US protestant missionary group to leave the country, alleging they were supplying information to the Central Intelligence Agency (CIA) and denouncing their work as 'imperialist' infiltrations.

Summary

The state's relationship with large, organised sectors of society is an important theme in the study of politics in Latin America because it helps to shape both the character of the state itself and the behaviour of key social groups. The concept of corporatism has often been applied to describe the hierarchical links maintained by the state with organised sectors of society, 'corporations', such as business groups, trades unions, peasant confederations, the military and the Church. Any discussion of the relationship between the state and business groups also draws attention to the concept of civil society (see Chapter 8). A key variable in the evolution of business groups has been their relationship with the state, which has often sought to organise business at times of crisis. Although the main role of business associations is economic, they play important political roles and have acted both to support democratic governance and to undermine it.

Organised labour was an important component of corporatist organisation because of many trades unions' close relationship with the state through its policies of industrialisation. The development of unions within a corporatist tradition sometimes fostered the emergence of powerful labour-based parties.

Organisations representing peasants also often developed in a corporatist relationship with the state. There has been a debate about whether the peasantry is potentially a conservative political actor that will develop over time into a new agrarian petty bourgeoisie, or whether it is potentially a radical force whose revolutionary attitudes will be galvanised by changes in the countryside. Some of the best known Latin American radical protest movements of the 1990s have been peasant organisations. Agrarian reform became a key political theme following the Cuban Revolution and remains an important issue today. Land reform hastened the disappearance of the landed oligarchy and created the conditions for the commercialisation of agriculture.

The military has been both a corporate actor and also an independent one seeking control of the state, and a central focus of study has been its role within democratic politics. A key question in the newly established democracies of Latin America has been how to subordinate the military to civilian control. Themes shaping the relationship between the military and civilian government include the degree to which the armed forces contest civilian policies and the 'prerogatives' granted to them by the new democratic leadership. Some scholars highlight the problems posed for democratic consolidation in Latin America by the inability to fully subordinate the military to civilian control. Latin American political leaders believe the armed forces still have significant influence, but also that there has been considerable progress in the institutionalisation of civilian control over them.

The Church has functioned as an alternative or parallel source of corporatism, particularly in the countryside. The most important influence in the modernisation of the Latin American Church was the Second Vatican Council in the 1960s in Rome, which moved Catholicism to a position that supported democracy, human rights and social justice. A conference in Colombia in 1968 is often considered to have been when 'liberation theology' emerged as an identifiable current of thought. The Vatican II and Medellín meetings encouraged a new emphasis on lay partici-pation and led to an upsurge in the creation of Catholic base communities. In some cases, these and progressive Church activities helped to nurture the growth of civil society in the 1970s and 1980s. However, liberation theologians did not establish an autonomous progressive Church in Latin America and the hierarchy prevailed. There have been various explanations for the growth of Protestantism in Latin America, and an important theme of debate has been the idea that it is more democratic than Catholicism.

Discussion points

- Why has state corporatism been associated with authoritarian systems?
- Are business associations a force for democracy or not?
- What determines whether corporatist relations develop between the state and labour?
- Are peasant movements generally conservative or progressive forces in politics?
- Has the military been subordinated to civilian control in Latin America?
- To what extent is the Church a unified political actor?

Useful websites

www.business-anti-corruption.com Business Anti-Corruption Portal

www.doingbusiness.org/exploreeconomies/?economyid=28 International Finance Corporation 'Doing Business' website offering valuable insights into the regulatory climate in different countries

www.empresariosporvenezuela.com.ve Empresarios por Venezuela (EMPREVEN)

www.americamovil.com/index_eng.htm América Móvil

www.telmex.com/mx/paises/pais.jsp Telmex

www.aico.org Asociación Iberoamericana de Cámaras de Comercio (AICC, IberoAmerican Association of Chambers of Commerce), brings together Spanish and Latin American chambers

www.coparmex.org.mx Confederación Patronal de la República Mexicana (COPARMEX, Mexican Employers' Confederation), one of Mexico's main business organisations

www.cce.org.mx Consejo Coordinador Empresarial (CCE, Business Co-ordinating Council), Mexico

www.sofofa.cl Federación Gremial de la Industria (Sofofa, Industrial Guilds Federation), Chile's main business organisation

www.cafedecolombia.com Federación Nacional de Cafeteros de Colombia (Federacafe, National Federation of Coffee Growers of Colombia), the heavyweight among business organisations in Latin America

www.ituc-csi.org International Trade Union Confederation (ITUC)

www.oit.org.pe/portal/index.php International Labour Organisation (ILO) regional office for Latin America and the Caribbean

http://portal.oit.or.cr/dmdocuments/empleo/pan_lab2009.pdf Labour Overview in Latin America and the Caribbean for 2009 (Panorama Laboral 2009 América Latina y el Caribe), ILO regional office for Latin America

www.cgtra.org.ar Confederación General del Trabajo de la República Argentina (CGT RA, General Labour Confederation of the Argentine Republic), Argentina's powerful main labour confederation

www.cta.org.ar Central de los Trabajadores Argentinos (CTA, Argentine Workers Union), union confederation founded to be independent of links with Peronism in 1992

http://congresodeltrabajo.org Congreso del Trabajo (CT, Mexican Union Congress), main trades union congress in Mexico

www.fatmexico.org Frente Auténtico del Trabajo (FAT, Authentic Labour Front), largest independent union within UNT in Mexico

http://movimientos.org/cloc Coordinadora Latinoamericana de Organizaciones del Campo (CLOC, Latin American Countryside Organisations Network), representing a number of independent peasant and rural organisations

http://movimientos.org/cloc/atc-ni Asociación del Trabajadores del Campo (ATC, Rural Workers' Assocation, Nicaragua), rural workers' union confederation

www.mst.org.br Movimento dos Trabalhadores Rurais Sem Terra (MST, Brazilian Landless Workers Movement)

www.iica.int Inter-American Institute for Co-operation on Agriculture, regional body supporting the efforts of member states to develop agriculture

www.ejercito.mil.uy/cea.htm Uruguayan military site listing national member sites of Conferencia de Ejércitos Americanos (CEA, Conference of American Armies), a co-operation forum for armed forces in the Americas

www.celam.org Consejo Episcopal Latinoamericano (CELAM, Council of Latin American Bishops)

www.iglesia.info Extensive list of links for the Catholic Church in Latin America

www.clar.org Confederación Latinoamericana de Religiosos y Religiosas (CLAR, Latin American Confederation of the Religious), Catholic site for those serving in religious orders

www.clailatino.org Consejo Latinoamericano de Iglesias (CLAI, Latin American Council of Churches), umbrella organisation for about 150 Protestant religious groups in the region

http://lanic.utexas.edu/project/rla/index.htm Valuable LANIC site linking to sources on religion in Latin America and downloadable books

Recommended reading

Collier, David. 1995. 'Trajectory of a Concept: "Corporatism" in the Study of Latin American Politics', in Peter H. Smith (ed.), *Latin America in Comparative Perspective. New Approaches to Methods and Analysis.* Boulder, CO: Westview Press

Valuable exploration and overview of how a key theme in the study of Latin American politics has been employed in theory

Schneider, Ben Ross. 2004. *Business Politics and the State in Twentieth-Century Latin America.* Cambridge: Cambridge University Press

Essential introduction to the history and structure of business associations in Latin America and the role they play in politics, providing a valuable theoretical overview

Schelhase, Marc. 2008. *Globalization, Regionalization and Business: Conflict, Convergence and Influence.* Basingstoke: Palgrave Macmillan

Valuable examination of how big business organises within Mercosur that gives insights into the interface between private enterprise and governments in the region

McGuire, James. 1997. *Peronism without Perón. Unions, Parties, and Democracy in Argentina.* Stanford, CA: Stanford University Press

Useful examination of the relationship between Argentine unions and Peronism and its impact upon party institutionalisation in Argentina, with a helpful first chapter on theory

Kay, Cristóbal. 2004. 'Rural livelihoods and peasant futures', in Robert N. Gwynne and Cristóbal Kay (eds), *Latin America Transformed: Globalization and Modernity*, 2nd Edition. London: Arnold

Valuable summary of the transformations resulting from economic modernisation in the Latin American countryside and the emergence of new peasant movements

Hite, Katherine and Paola Cesarini (eds). 2004. *Authoritarian Legacies and Democracy in Latin America and Southern Europe.* Notre Dame, IN: University of Notre Dame Press

Valuable comparative examination of the political structures and institutions bequeathed by authoritarian regimes whose contributors look at parties, executives, legislatures, constitutions and interest groups as well as cultural factors such as individual and collective memories

Smith, Christian and Joshua Prokopy (eds). 1999. *Latin American Religion in Motion.* London: Routledge

Valuable collection whose contributors examine the different faces of contemporary Catholicism and Protestantism in Latin America, containing useful case studies

Goldman, Francisco. 2008. *The Art of Political Murder: Who Killed the Bishop?* New York: Grove Press

Eloquent examination of the murder in Guatemala of Bishop Juan Gerardi that provides a valuable insight into the role of the Church in Latin America

Chapter 8

Civil society and emergent political actors

This chapter examines civil society in Latin America and the social movements and other interests that inhabit this independent 'public sphere' outside the state and use it to address societal problems. The concept of civil society has grown in importance in Latin American politics, providing the basis of new theoretical understandings of democratisation based on autonomous organisations (Alvarez *et al.*, 1998). The emphasis on civil society became an important characteristic of the study of democracy in the region in the 1990s when large multilateral financial institutions identified the potential in Latin America of organisations serving as intermediaries between the people and their governments for aiding the transition to democracy, and started to grant them generous funding (see O'Donnell *et al.*, eds, with Stubits, 2008). It was believed that civil society organisations could play an important role in changing conditions in some countries by opening and deepening democratic spaces. However, there has been considerable disagreement about what civil society is, not least because the large diversity of groups that are said to comprise it defy easy categorisation and some actors, such as business groups, the Church and trades unions, might at times be considered both 'established actors' yet also part of civil society (see Chapter 7). There has also been disagreement about civil society's contribution to democracy or otherwise (see Box 8.1; see also Encarnación, 2003).

The concept of civil society is important because in the last decades of the twentieth century many diverse social movements emerged in Latin America, from human rights organisations to Christian base communities (see Chapter 7), self-help groups giving voice to the poor, and charities. Non-governmental organisations developed alongside these social movements, and established interests such as business associations and the media began to assert their independence from the state. There is a consensus that Latin America experienced a sea change in terms of mobilisation outside the formal institutional arenas of politics as these 'new social movements' became a locus of political action among civilians and as businessmen and journalists began to challenge established norms. In some cases these forces played a key role in popular mobilisation against military dictatorships, and in Brazil, Uruguay and Chile increases in mobilisation coincided with democratic transitions. Today, the forms and degree to which citizens participate in addressing key issues of poverty, inequality, citizenship and environmentalism within their countries help to shape the quality of democracy (see Chapter 4). Citizens in societies with high levels of participation are generally better able to represent

Civil society

The term 'civil society' has been understood in a range of ways, from everything that is not the state or the market, to conceptions that restrict it to forms of *purposeful* associational life aimed at the expression of societal interests (Alvarez *et al.*, 1998; see also Cohen and Arato, 1992). In much democratic thought a distinction is made between the realm of the state – understood as a complex network of political institutions including the military, legal, administrative, productive and cultural organs – and civil society, understood as a public realm of associational social life such as privately owned, market-directed, voluntary run or friendship-based activities (Keane, 1988). MacDonald says: 'Civil society constitutes the arena of organised political activity between the private sphere (the household and the firm) and the formal political institutions of governance (the parliament, political parties, the army, the judiciary etc.)' (MacDonald, 1997, pp. 3–4). Diamond (1996) advanced an influential definition of civil society as *'the realm of organised social life that is voluntary, self-generating, (largely) self-supporting, autonomous from the state, and bound by a legal order or set of shared rules'* (Diamond, 1996, p. 228; italics in original; see also Diamond, 1994). He pointed out that civil society is distinct from 'society' in general in that it involves citizens acting collectively in a public sphere to express interests and make demands (*ibid.*). Civil society's autonomy from the state is seen both as a positive and as a negative quality, although this feature of civil society has increasingly come under scrutiny (see below). Classical liberals view civil society as the sphere of liberty and autonomy, while orthodox Marxists view it as an unequal terrain of oppression in capitalist societies built around class and state power (MacDonald, 1997). The essence of civil society is its *voluntary* nature and its role in maintaining society through the practices and values that persist in diverse groups such as families, households and religious and cultural organisations (Foweraker *et al.*, 2003). Some analysts stress the weakness of civil society in Latin America in the face of authoritarian legacies and neoliberal economic policies, and note how easily the leaders of popular groups can be co-opted into the state apparatus through agencies and funding programmes (*ibid.*). Others are more optimistic and stress civil society's strength, arguing that it embodies the formation of an increasingly activist citizenry that refuses to be subordinated to traditional political structures (*ibid.*; see also Cohen and Rogers, 1995).

their interests and policy preferences to those who govern than more quiescent citizenries. Their participation is sometimes gauged according to the extent to which it generates 'social capital', the networks, norms and trust within social life that enables people to act together more effectively to pursue shared objectives (see Putnam, 1995; Klesner, 2009). More recently, civil society has also been treated increasingly as an *international* concept because of alliances between social groups in Latin America and foreign NGOs. Some scholars now talk of the emergence of a 'global civil society' in which groups, such as indigenous movements, co-operate across borders and draw upon international law and transnational networks supported by new communications technologies to advance their causes (Radcliffe, 2004). The mainly indigenous guerrilla army in the southern Mexican state of Chiapas, the Ejercito Zapatista de Liberación Nacional (EZLN, Zapatista National Liberation Army) (see Box 8.2), and Amazonian indigenous groups in Brazil, for example, have used new communications media to help nurture transnational solidarities.

An important shared objective of many of these contemporary civil society groups has been to challenge the impact of neoliberal reform on Latin American society. In the 1990s, the changes brought about by neoliberalism interacted to transform the relationship between many citizens and the market and state because, as the state was rolled back, the market extended into spheres it had previously controlled (see Box 15.3). In particular, neoliberal reform has sometimes depoliticised sectors of society, such as organised labour, that have shown signs of resisting economic change. Citizens have responded to neoliberalism by forming social movements or coalitions of diverse groups whose interests have converged. One example of this was the El Barzón coalition of small and medium-sized farmers which came together in Mexico after 1993 because of high levels of indebtedness and the way production was organised in the countryside.

Social movements

Alvarez and Escobar (1992) characterised social movements as 'organized collective actors who engage in sustained political or cultural contestation through recourse to institutional and extra-institutional forms of action' (p. 321). Foweraker (1995) adopted a cautious approach to what can be described as a social movement, arguing that this must exhibit a sense of collective purpose and the kind of objectives that require interaction with other political actors – often state actors – and must also mobilise supporters in pursuit of its goals (see Box 8.2). Social movements today commonly include organisations of indigenous people, human rights groups, feminist organisations, environmental groups and independent trades unions. However, manifestations of popular protest taking a diverse range of forms – from organised demonstrations to guerrilla struggle – have long been a feature of Latin American politics. Eckstein (1989) argued that, after the 1960s, the fact that rapid urbanisation and marginalisation had not, in general, given rise to revolutionary movements shifted the focus of social scientists from society to the state and resulted in analyses of corporatist and bureaucratic–authoritarian views of state–society relations (see Boxes 2.2, 2.5, 7.1). Since the late 1970s, however, the weakening of traditional corporatism and of the strong central state has resulted in a new relationship between state and society, one that has been reflected in social mobilisation. The attention of scholars has, in turn, turned to the role of social movements in these processes and to explanations for mobilisation (see Slater, 1985). Under democracy, social movements in Latin America have played an important role in mobilising for change, and in many cases contributed significantly to a shift to the left in the region (see Silva, 2009; see also Chapter 12).

A collection of essays edited by Eckstein in 1989, for example, highlighted a range of theoretical explanations for social movement activity, from Marxist positions situating groups firmly within their historical–structural context, to 'resource mobilisation theory' explaining the activity of social movements in terms of their own organisational features and resources (see also McAdam *et al.*, 1988). Eckstein (1989) noted how, in fact, given the complexity and diversity of different movements, a wide range of economic, political, institutional and cultural factors

The character of social movements

New social movements generated a theoretical literature because they did not easily fit the traditional understanding of protest in terms of factors such as class or ideology (see Slater ed., 1985; Tarrow, 1994). They were often distinguished by their novelty, given the decline of older forms of representation such as unions. Slater (1985) developed an influential characterisation of new social movements as the reflection of new forms of struggle that emerge in relation to features of late capitalist society deriving from the increasing intervention of the state at all levels of social life. In general, social movements have not been concerned with capturing political power and their focus has often been on specific issues that respond to contemporary 'discourses' such as free trade, global warming and cultural imperialism rather than a comprehensive programme. New social movement theory argues that the meanings invested in struggles are not economic but social and cultural. As a result, social movements have often mobilised around identity and cultural differences as opposed to class identities (see Maheu ed., 1995; see Chapter 13). Womens' groups have often been seen as good examples of new social movements, affirming a gender identity that challenges patriarchal society. Another important source of new social movement mobilisation has been ethnicity (see below). A characteristic attributed to new social movements has been internal structures that stress participative decisionmaking and co-operative relationships making them less hierarchical and more decentralised than unions, peasant groups and parties. An example of this is the Zapatista movement in Chiapas formed out of the Ejercito Zapatista de Liberación Nacional (EZLN, Zapatista National Liberation Army), which has undertaken an exhaustive process of consultation and internal debate before taking strategic action (see Gilbreth and Otero, 2001). As a result, new social movements have tended to adopt a democratic discourse based on notions of citizenship (Radcliffe, 2004). It has been argued that they have played an important role in democratising social relations by changing popular perceptions, institutional cultures and political practices (Foweraker, 1995). It has been suggested that the popular politics practised by social movements challenges the explanatory models that have hitherto been used in political analysis, and in particular the categories used by social scientists based on their understanding of organisations, structures and forms of political activity (see Motta, 2009b). This has implications for how we understand such concepts as the state, domination and representation.

contributed to the activity of social movements. Consequently, the emergence of social movements has been explained in different ways: as an autonomous expression of interests; as a reflection of the growing use of the language of rights to express those interests; or as a 'structural' manifestation of the crisis of the strong central state (see Chalmers *et al.*, 1997; Foweraker *et al.*, 2003). Chalmers *et al.* (1997) argued that the dispersion of political decision-making activity in the post-war era away from the central state towards multiple decision-making centres had restructured popular representation into 'associative networks' suited to influencing public policy in a globalised and decentralised era. These networks of groups and institutions other than parties expanded access to representation. Given this representative role, underlying much of the literature since the 1990s has been the notion that the expansion of social movements, and hence of civil society, contributes to the functioning of a healthy democracy in several ways:

Representation

The contributions civil society can make to democratisation include providing representation outside ineffective institutions. Prior to democratisation, civil society demands were often channelled through corporatist parties or unions tied to the state. Social movements operate independently of the party system and offer new channels of representation. Chalmers *et al.* (1997) argued that in the contemporary era popular representation through 'associative networks' can be more well suited to influencing public policy. Moreover, a feature of social movements has often been a looser and more participatory form of organisation that suggests they are more internally democratic than traditional parties and unions.

Pluralism

Peeler (1998) argued that the term pluralism is appropriate for understanding civil society. Pluralism refers to the principle by which diverse groups co-exist and interact in society without conflict by tolerating each other. Whereas corporatism treats the state as recognising and even organising the corporations that represent society's interests, pluralism envisages the autonomous organisation of society. Political scientists often stress that a healthy democracy is built on the foundation of widespread political participation through organisations autonomous of the state that represent the diverse interests and demands of society (*ibid.*; see also Fox, 1997). Fox (1997) argued that the autonomy of civic associations is vital for the poorest members of society because they are the most vulnerable to incentives based on clientelism, that is, political subordination in exchange for material rewards (see Box 7.1). Associational autonomy enables the poor to move from being clients to *citizens* without losing access to the resources the state has to offer (*ibid.*; see Chapter 3).

Attitudes

Many observers argue that civil society can contribute to the development of a political culture supportive of democracy because social movements can help to foster democratic attitudes at both institutional and grassroots levels. Foweraker *et al.* (2003) suggested that civil society actors can raise levels of consciousness among their members by organising them and offering alternative models of political activity, and can shape public opinion by influencing legislative, judicial and party agendas.

However, although civil society was considered to be a significant force during and in the years following transitions from authoritarian rule, its political role has since become more complex and some scholars suggest that its potential is now limited (Peeler, 1998). First, some authors have argued that civil society is not homogeneous but also a terrain of struggle in which there can be undemocratic power relations and forms of exclusion (see Alvarez *et al.*, 1998; Foweraker *et al.*, 2003). Civil society comprises diverse organisations and movements with different goals that employ different means to achieve them: it can also host 'uncivil' anti-democratic elements such as paramilitary and guerrilla organisations seeking to destabilise society and challenge the state with violence (Foweraker *et al.*, 2003; see also Encarnación, 2002). Second, the boundary between civil society and the state has often become blurred and, increasingly, the state has itself tried to structure relationships within civil society, which has, in turn, become more institutionalised (Alvarez *et al.*, 1998; Radcliffe, 2004). Radcliffe (2004) argued that with the return of electoral democracy came the return of clientelism and corporatism linking civil society and the political system (see Box 7.1). States developed new forms of clientelistic relationship with organisations as they launched targeted assistance programmes such as the Programa Nacional de Solidaridad (PRONASOL, National Solidarity Programme) in Mexico from 1988–94, which aimed to cushion vulnerable sectors of the population from neoliberal reforms (see Craske, 1994). Social movements have often developed in a close relationship with the state because it is a source of resources. In some cases, the return to democracy was accompanied by the state reaching out to social movements and offering them funds. This enabled the state to create competition over resources and, by responding selectively, to divide these groups. In Bolivia, for example, the Federación de Juntas Vecinales (Fejuve, Federation of Neighbourhood Councils) of El Alto near La Paz was prominent in opposition to the privatisation of gas reserves in 2003, but was plagued by divisions which weakened it. One of its leaders, Abel Mamari, was appointed to head a new water ministry in 2006 then dismissed in 2007 (see Lievesley, 2009). In the 1990s, therefore, the *limitations* of social movements became apparent because they did not fit comfortably into the institutional structure that was evolving (see Dangl, 2010). Scholars began to reassess their capacity to provide alternative mechanisms of representation in Latin American society. A key theme of debate has been the relationship between social movements and parties, and the degree to which the former can grow independently and supplant party functions. Democratisation often placed parties back at the centre of political activity as a bridge between state and society by privileging a specific mode of participation: voting (see Chapters 3, 6). Some leftwing parties, such as the Partido dos Trabalhadores (PT, Workers' Party) in Brazil, have been effective in capturing the support of social movements, although even the PT has at times had tense relations with one of its key supporters, the Movimento dos Trabalhadores Rurais Sem Terra (MST, Landless Workers Movement). The MST accused the Brazilian president Luiz Inácio Lula da Silva (2003–10) of failing to live up to his election promises to find homes for 400,000 families. In November 2005, relations were strained further when a congressional inquiry in Brazil urged that land invasions be declared acts of terrorism and that leaders of the MST be prosecuted. A radical breakaway group within the MST, known as the Movimento de Libertação dos Sem Terra (MLST, Movement for the Liberation of the Landless), has been highly critical of the Da Silva government and demanded faster and more comprehensive land reform. After members of the organisation stormed a congressional building in Brasília in June 2006, it was revealed that one of the MLST leaders was Bruno Maranhão, a member of the PT's national executive, whose salary was promptly suspended by the party. By 2007 formal support within the MST for the PT had all but disappeared, with MST founder and national organiser João Pedro Stedile publicly acknowledging a fracture in relations because of his organisation's belief that the Da Silva administration had failed to implement the radical economic and social reforms that it had promised, especially agrarian reform.

Other parties, such as the Partido de la Revolución Democrática (PRD, Party of the Democratic Revolution) in Mexico, have had a more complex relationship with social movements, able to mobilise diverse sectors of civil society yet less able to forge stable, longer-term relationships with movements themselves. For example, in August 2005 Marcos, the leader of the Zapatistas, spoke publicly for the first time in four years to denounce the PRD's leftwing presidential candidate Andrés Manuel López Obrador as part of a broader attack on Mexican political parties (see Box 8.3).

With the return of democracy, political parties have often sought to control social movements because they are a source of competition for loyalties. Some scholars say that because of its very diversity, civil society cannot be a substitute for a viable, institutionalised party system (Peeler, 1998; see Chapter 6). Associations organised around specific demands do not enjoy permanent channels of access to the state, putting them at a disadvantage alongside institutionalised actors such as parties. In Peru, for example, weak political parties mean that community organisations have emerged *without* access to channels of political power, and such movements may be at a disadvantage alongside parties and in securing gains from the state. Recent literature on social movements has focused on the role they have played in the ascent of a new generation of leftwing leaders across Latin America (see

---

CASE STUDY **Box 8.3**

The power of civil society

Civil society demonstrated its power in Mexico in April 2005 when more than a million people marched through Mexico City in protest against a decision by congress that left the city's then mayor, Andrés Manuel López Obrador, facing prosecution in a land dispute. López Obrador was accused of breaching a court order after allowing work to build an access road to a hospital on a disputed plot of expropriated land to proceed. The decision to end his legal immunity – taken after Mexico's two biggest parties, the Partido Acción Nacional (PAN, National Action Party) and the Partido Revolucionario Institucional (PRI, Institutional Revolutionary Party), had joined forces in congress – was widely interpreted as a political tactic to block López Obrador's candidacy in the 2006 presidential election. Polls at that time suggested López Obrador, of the leftwing PRD, was the country's most popular politician and the favourite to win the election, which a prosecution would have prevented him from entering. Organisers said 1.2 million people marched into Mexico City's central square and surrounding streets in support of López Obrador, making it one of the biggest protests Mexico has ever seen, although officials put the number far lower. The size of the protest demonstrated the ability of the PRD to mobilise large segments of the population and progressive social movements. The party does not have a strong national following as much of its support is concentrated in certain regions. In an effort to defuse the crisis, President Vicente Fox (2000–06) sacked the attorney general, whose office subsequently abandoned efforts to prosecute López Obrador. Political observers say the reversal was a turning point for Mexico's democracy by demonstrating that popular pressure had successfully forced those in power to reverse efforts to play politics by older, undemocratic rules. In August, López Obrador stepped down as mayor of Mexico City to begin his campaign for the presidency officially (see Grayson, 2007).

Table 12.1) and the degree to which they have shaped the achievements of these administrations (see Petras and Veltmeyer, 2005). A question still being debated on the Latin American left today remains the extent to which social movements offer a greater chance of social change than formal institutional politics (see Chapter 12).

Indigenous movements

About 50 million people within 800 linguistic groups maintain indigenous lifestyles in Latin America which are often communitarian and rural, and in some countries they form the majority. In Bolivia and Guatemala, indigenous people comprise about 70 per cent of the population and in Peru and Ecuador, more than 40 per cent. Over the last 20 years, a significant new development in the rural politics of Latin America has been the rise of indigenous consciousness, which has thrust issues such as cultural diversity and autonomy to the top of the agenda of the region's young democracies and shaped the character of social movements in the countryside (Kay, 2004; see also Maybury-Lewis ed., 2003; Otero, 2003). The global prominence achieved by groups such as the Zapatistas in Mexico (see Box 13.5) and the election of an indigenous president in Bolivia, Evo Morales, has greatly increased attention to these issues and to the relationship more broadly between indigenous people in Latin America and development (see Forero, 2004b; Andolina *et al.*, 2009). However, some scholars argue that although the study of democratisation has begun to consider the effect of social hierarchies of class, race, and gender on citizenship in Latin America, relatively little attention has been paid to questions of multi-culturalism and so the question of how to integrate this into studies of democra-tisation remains unresolved (see Hooker, 2008). As a result, there has been little concrete guidance about which principles should guide the institutional design of multicultural policies in Latin America's diverse societies.

Indigenous groups have been mobilising to demand recognition of land rights since the nineteenth century, but since the 1970s a more politically self-conscious movement has emerged within Latin America and formed links with an international support network. The first wave of this recent phase of indigenous organisation was linked to mobilisation on local issues. In Bolivia, for example, the Katarista movement became prominent in 1974 after violent clashes between the army and Quechuas protesting about low agricultural prices. Military regimes often responded to indigenous mobilisation with repression. With the transition to democratic rule in the 1980s, some indigenous movements entered and remained in politics. The erosion of class-based socialist ideas following the end of the Cold War and the impact of neoliberalism have also acted as catalysts for the resurgence of indigenous protest movements (see Chapters 12, 15). This development within Latin America was reinforced by the emergence since the 1970s of an international indigenous movement originating in Church and United Nations initiatives to establish indigenous rights as a mainstream human rights issue across the world. In 1992–93, these trends came together in large, high-profile events such as the Earth Summit in Rio de Janeiro; commemorations to mark the 500th anniversary of the arrival of Columbus in the Americas; the award of the Nobel Peace Prize to the Guatemalan Mayan activist Rigoberta Menchú; and the naming by the UN of 1993 as the 'Year of Indigenous Peoples'. The 1994 EZLN rebellion in Chiapas put the conditions of indigenous people into the international spotlight and gave the idea of indigenous autonomy in Latin America a political profile and programme for the first time. Democratisation, which is empowering previously excluded social groups such as indigenous people, has combined with changing attitudes towards the Left in Latin America to open politics up to greater indigenous participation. In Bolivia, for example, this resulted in the election in 2005 of an indigenous president, Evo Morales. In Peru, President Alejandro Toledo (2001–06) made history when he became the country's first president of indigenous descent in 2001. Inspired by developments in Bolivia, indigenous organisations in Peru announced in 2008 that they would field their own presidential candidate in 2011.

Indigenous movements combine material and cultural demands in their opposition to economic and political exclusion (Foweraker *et al.*, 2003). They have often provided a unifying focus for a wide variety of organisations, particularly those on the left, around shared goals and have struck a chord among non-indigenous groups (Mattiace, 2005; Becker, 2008). The Confederación de Nacionalidades Indígenas del Ecuador (CONAIE, Confederation of Indigenous Nationalities of Ecuador), for example, has been at the heart of nationwide mobilisations since 1990 that have brought together opposition to privatisation, fuel price increases, neoliberal policies and free trade (see Chapter 15). In Mexico, the Zapatistas have been at the forefront of broader anti-globalisation protests and opposition to NAFTA, the proposed Free Trade Area of the Americas (FTAA), and large development projects such as the Plan Puebla-Panamá (see Boxes 13.5, 15.8; see also Mattiace, 2005). In Bolivia, President Morales has combined a strong commitment to improving indigenous rights with a mainstream leftwing policy platform. None the less, claims based on an indigenous heritage are often controversial and in countries such as Bolivia they have provoked significant debate as well as opposition within non-indigenous *mestizo* and ethnically European communities. The emphasis placed by Morales on his own ethnicity and the importance of Bolivia's indigenous heritage, for example, has been criticised by right-of-centre observers for allegedly fomenting racial divisions in an increasingly *mestizo* Latin America. Four main policy issues motivate indigenous movements today:

■ *Self-determination and autonomy:* Since the 1970s, indigenous organisations have often framed demands in terms of self-determination based upon legal recognition of their cultural distinctiveness. In practical terms, this has often been articulated through demands for regional autonomy to enhance their political participation and protect their cultural integrity (see Díaz Polanco, 1997).

■ *Territorial rights and control over natural resources:* The struggle for land and the protection of natural resources has been the main reason for indigenous mobilisation. In the 1970s and 1980s, land tensions increased as a result of population growth, sub-division and encroachment by commercial agriculture (see Box 7.6). Pressure on the land has grown with neoliberal reforms that encourage the privatisation and sale of communal or common lands, and greater exploitation of resources (see Chapter 15). Ethnic and environmental issues have also become increasingly intertwined. In Brazil, there have been recurrent and violent disputes in the Amazon Basin between indigenous groups such as the Yanomami and mining interests. In 2009, for example, Davi Kopenawa Yanomami, the leader of the Hutukara Yanomami Association and a spokesman for the Yanomami people, undertook a world tour to highlight the plight of his people if the Amazonian forest continues to be destroyed through mining and deforestation. In Peru in 2009, violent clashes between security forces and native Amazonians in the Bagua region – after months of rallies and blockades against decrees by the government of Alan García (1985–90, 2006–) to allow foreign corporations to begin oil and gas extraction, commercial forestry and large-scale agriculture in their ancestral lands – claimed at least 64 lives, with another 100–200 mainly indigenous people missing. In Bolivia, provisions in the 2009 constitution asserting state control over natural resources and limiting the size of landholdings are widely seen as an effort by the Morales administration to redistribute a greater share of the income generated by extractive industries to indigenous communities, for example.

■ *Political reform:* Indigenous organisations have often entered national politics in pursuit of constitutional and legislative reforms that address their demands for greater participation. Constitutional reforms in countries such as Paraguay, Colombia and Brazil have increased the participation of indigenous people in policy questions, although their movements have had a mixed record in electoral politics (see Barié, 2000). Electoral participation in Ecuador has been beset by tensions between traditional parties and a unified indigenous movement, whose own political success has strained its popularity (see Box 8.4). Some aspirant populists, such as Lucio Gutiérrez (2003–05) in Ecuador, made explicit appeals to indigenous people in an effort to sidestep traditional party politics. In Bolivia, Morales pledged to improve the political representation of indigenous people – who did not enjoy full voting rights until 1952 – and to increase the number of their representatives in his cabinet. The country's new constitution passed in 2009, for example, offers significantly more power to indigenous communities by allowing them to vote on local autonomy. A whole chapter of the new constitution was devoted to indigenous rights, and the document also grants indigenous systems of justice the same status as the national courts system. A new electoral law passed in 2009 reserves seven of the 130 seats in the country's lower house for indigenous groups.

■ *Military and police relations:* Indigenous people in countries such as Guatemala and Colombia have often been dragged into state counterinsurgency or counternarcotics strategies because they tend to live in the rural areas favoured by both guerrillas and drug-traffickers. As a result, indigenous-state relations have often become militarised and human rights abuses against indigenous people remain a persistent issue. In Guatemala, military regimes that suspected indigenous involvement in guerrilla movements often targeted Mayan communities, and in the early 1980s the military destroyed hundreds of villages and killed thousands of indigenous people (Foweraker *et al.*, 2003).

Today, prominent indigenous movements can be found in countries where indigenous people are most numerous, such as Ecuador, Bolivia and Guatemala,

---

CASE STUDY	Box 8.4

Ecuador's indigenous people and the problem with politics

Although Ecuador has one of Latin America's strongest indigenous movements, its participation in mainstream politics in recent years has damaged the popularity it once enjoyed. Indigenous social movements came to prominence in a nationwide uprising in 1990 aimed at gaining land rights and opposing economic policies backed by the International Monetary Fund (see Gerlach, 2003). These and subsequent civil society mobilisations by large organisations such as the Confederación de Nacionalidades Indígenas del Ecuador (CONAIE, Confederation of Indigenous Nationalities of Ecuador) led to the formation in 1996 of the Pachakutik alliance, a political party made up of indigenous and peasant groups and left-of-centre social movements that began winning local elections and, eventually, seats in congress. Pachakutik and CONAIE played an important role in pushing for a new constitution in 1998 that recognised Ecuador as a multicultural society, enabling the introduction of bilingual education and other reforms. Demonstrations by the indigenous movement were also pivotal in the removal of two presidents in 1997 and 2000 (see Table 5.2, Box 6.2) but Pachakutik began to lose support as a result of CONAIE's role in supporting the coup that removed President Jamil Mahuad in 2000. Among the army officers involved was Lucio Gutiérrez, who went on to become president in 2003. Many indigenous people have not supported Pachakutik, believing it has compromised in order to participate in party politics. Its support for Gutiérrez's election campaign also damaged its popularity after the president allocated it just four out of 17 cabinet posts. The indigenous movement broke ranks with the new president over his commitment to austere economic policies and free trade with the US, and it claimed he had failed to deliver on the promises he had made during his campaign, such as ending use of the US dollar as the country's currency. Gutiérrez sought closer links with Amazon and Christian indigenous organisations in what Pachakutik saw as a 'divide and conquer' strategy, and in mid-2004 Ecuador's main indigenous groups accused the government of trying to weaken their organisations. Some prominent indigenous leaders such as Luis Macas, who served as agriculture minister under Gutiérrez, went further and claimed the president was trying to eliminate the movement. Indigenous groups also asked the UN to step in to prevent bloodshed, claiming violent conflict was being stoked by the president. Steady economic growth and slowing inflation since the country adopted the US dollar in 2000 has also limited the ability of the indigenous movement to mobilise supporters (see Lucero, 2008). However, violent protests by indigenous groups against free trade talks with the US in March 2006 demonstrated anew their potential to dominate the political agenda (see also Clark and Becker eds, 2007).

---

and these have often mobilised. Ecuador's indigenous movement has played a key role both in removing and electing several presidents since 1997 (see Box 8.4). Bolivia is the latest country to experience mobilisations by indigenous groups demanding a greater say in decisionmaking, which have been instrumental in removing several presidents from office in the last few years (see Table 5.2, Box 5.6). Evo Morales, an Aymara, gained prominence leading coca farmers prior to the 2002 election and the street blockades of 2005 that led to the resignation of President Carlos Mesa (2003–05). Since Morales became president in 2006, mobilisation by indigenous groups in support of policies that have aimed to increase their representation and share of national resources has become a key feature of his presidency.

Latin American states have responded to indigenous demands with recognition of their identity and concessions in areas of rights (see also Chapter 13). Today,

Table 8.1 Collective rights for indigenous groups in Latin America

Country	Group Recognition	Customary Law	Land Rights	Autonomy or self-government	Bilingual Education	Anti-Racial Discrimination Rights
Argentina	Indirect	No	Yes	No	Yes	No
Brazil	Yes	No	Yes	No	Yes	No
Costa Rica	Yes	Yes	Yes	No	Yes	No
Colombia	Yes	Yes	Yes	Yes	Yes	No
Ecuador	Yes	Yes	Yes	No	Yes	No
Guatemala	Yes	No	Yes	No	Yes	Yes
Honduras	No	Yes	Yes	No	Yes	Yes
Mexico	Yes	Yes	Yes	No	No	No
Nicaragua	Yes	Yes	Yes	Yes	Yes	No
Panama	Yes	Yes	Yes	Yes	Yes	No
Peru	Yes	Yes	Yes	No	No	No
Venezuela	Yes	Yes	Yes	No	Yes	No

Source: Adapted from Hooker, 2008

most countries in the region recognise collective rights for indigenous peoples in the following terms: the multicultural nature of national societies and the existence of specific ethnic/racial sub-groups; indigenous customary law; collective property rights, especially in regard to land; official status for minority languages in predominantly minority regions; and guarantees of bilingual education (see Table 8.1; see also Hooker, 2008). Bolivia, for example, has changed its official name to the 'Plurinational State of Bolivia' to acknowledge the fact that it is a state that has several indigenous nations within it. Since 1990, 13 Latin American states have ratified the International Labour Organisation's Convention 169, considered to be the world's most progressive legislation on indigenous rights, that protects their land rights, obliges signatories to consult with indigenous peoples on development projects affecting their territories, and recognises them as equals. In 2007, the UN adopted the 'Declaration on the Rights of Indigenous Peoples', which endorses the right of native peoples to their own institutions and traditional lands. Although non-binding, it has been widely embraced by Latin American governments.

However, most states have resisted conceding regional autonomy and, in some cases, this has increased tensions between ethnic groups or provoked violence (see Box 8.5, Chapter 6). In Mexico, for example, the Zapatistas have been unable to secure meaningful regional autonomy in Chiapas after years of negotiations, souring relations with the government. In Nicaragua in the 1980s, constitutional reforms gave the Miskitu people some autonomous powers but subsequent governments reined these in. In Guatemala, rightwing non-indigenous organisations have blocked progress towards autonomous indigenous regions. The debate over regional or indigenous autonomy in Bolivia has fuelled separatist sentiments among conservative opponents of President Morales in the lowland eastern states and exacerbated ethnic tensions in the country (see Boxes 4.1, 12.11, 13.6).

Freedom for Araucania?

Members of the indigenous movement in Chile have raised their profile in pursuit of self-determination to control territories over which some of them have been in dispute with the state virtually since the Spanish Conquest. Although the Mapuche Indians of south-central Chile make up about 1 million of the country's 15 million people – accounting for more than 80 per cent of the country's indigenous population – and their communities still dot the forests of southern Chile, they have not gained the profile of other indigenous organisations in Latin America. However, since the late 1990s, some Mapuche communities have been waging an increasingly violent confrontation with corporate logging interests as they demand control over land they say is theirs. Forestry has become an important industry in Chile with exports to the US of wood, mostly from the country's southern region, worth about $600 million per year. Some Mapuche leaders complain that titles to disputed lands now held by loggers – who have planted hundreds of thousands of acres with non-native species that consume large amounts of water and fertilizer – are false and that they have been deprived of their territories illegally. They justify their position by reaching deep into the history of troubled relations between the Chilean state and the native peoples. The sixteenth-century *conquistadores* in what became Chile and Argentina met probably the fiercest resistance by indigenous people of the entire Americas in territory the Mapuches call Araucania. The Mapuches were able to fend off Spanish control until well after Independence from their enclaves south of the Bio-Bio River and had their independence formally recognised in treaties. Through a series of violent military expeditions they were incorporated into the Chilean state in the 1880s and relocated on reservations so that European colonists could settle and farm the region. By the 1920s, the Mapuches had lost title to their lands as a result of procedures they insist were illegal. Conflicts over the activities of corporate interests have grown since Chile's economy has become more comprehensively inserted in international markets. Much of the country's economic activity has become oriented to exportation, and export activities based upon the use of indigenous lands, water, forests and other natural resources which are important for their subsistence and culture have grown rapidly, encouraged by government policies. Ancestral Mapuche territory is among the richest in Chile in terms of natural resources and tourism potential. Indigenous activists and their supporters argue that past agreements from the early years of democratisation recognizing and offering some protection for indigenous peoples do not establish sufficient safeguards for the natural resources, such as forests, within indigenous lands. They also claim that export policies affecting their lands promoted by governments without their consultation are breaking the law. Since 1997, conflicts between indigenous and corporate interests have grown increasingly violent as indigenous activists have burned forests and farmhouses and destroyed forestry equipment. The Chilean government has invoked anti-terrorist legislation that had its origins in the period of Pinochet's dictatorship against some indigenous activists. Mapuche activists complain of judicial persecution and police brutality in response to their claims to ancestral lands. In January 2007, an international mission convened by the non-governmental Observatory for Indigenous Peoples' Rights documented many complaints of abuse. In an effort to lessen tensions, in 2001 the government of President Ricardo Lagos (2000–06) created the Commission for Historical Truth and New Treatment comprising politicians, academics and representatives of indigenous groups. The aim of the commission was to review and develop indigenous policy and examine the relationship between the state and indigenous groups. The commission's report in 2003 called for changes in the way Chile treats its indigenous people, recommending the formal recognition of political and territorial rights for them. Disagreements over the recommendations have delayed legislation, with socialists such as Lagos praising the document as an effort to correct errors of the past, but critics saying autonomy provisions will dismember the Chilean state. Lagos made efforts to develop a new dialogue with indigenous groups and frequently highlighted progress made in talks between the Mapuche and the government. In October 2009, President Michelle Bachelet put forward proposals to create a ministry for indigenous affairs, but the move was criticised by Mapuche activists who claimed it was an effort to create a smokescreen behind which government policy was unlikely to change.

Sources: Rohter, 2004; Aylwin, 1998; Hernández, 2003

The emergence of the indigenous movement has important implications for politics in Latin America:

The structure of the state

Indigenous movements have been reshaping the structure of the state and its relationship with society in their struggles to enhance rights and for greater decentralisation (Kay, 2004). Indigenous mobilisation often represents more than just a demand for greater inclusion and amounts to an effort to *redefine* statehood. Recognition of indigenous identity in law has implications for governance and democracy, implying the need for revised structures and policies that cater to excluded groups. Indigenous organisations have challenged states to move beyond formal democracy by linking it with economic and social policies that promote a more equal distribution of wealth (see Chapters 3, 4, 16). In Mexico, for example, the Chiapas rebellion in 1994 generated a debate about the institutional limitations of liberal democracy based upon party competition that is not accompanied by economic redistribution. In Bolivia, President Morales has linked his commitment to improving the standard of living and representation of indigenous communities to socialist policies that aim to redistribute income in the country more generally.

Indigenous organisations have also promoted decentralisation and challenged the unity of political authority based upon a tradition of centralism (see Chapters 6, 12). Latin America has had little experience of political structures that grant autonomy to culturally distinct communities, and states have tended to interpret demands for self-determination as a threat to sovereignty rather than a deepening of democratisation. Where there has been recognition of indigenous autonomy, it has been restricted to the local *municipio* level. For example, in talks with the Zapatistas between 1996 and 2001 Mexico's federal government manoeuvred to reduce the scope of indigenous autonomy originally agreed in peace accords, arguing that the original proposals were in conflict with the country's federal model. The state government of Chiapas also subsequently advanced initiatives aimed at limiting autonomy claims. An indigenous rights law was eventually approved by congress in 2001, but this was effectively a unilateral initiative from the centre restating municipalisation as the favoured approach to indigenous autonomy. Bolivia's 2009 constitution took a significant step towards granting indigenous communities autonomy, but was fiercely resisted by opponents in the eastern lowlands who none the less stood to gain significantly from the decentralisation proposals.

Laws to give indigenous people control over their communities can also discriminate against non-indigenous minorities. In Oaxaca, Mexico, the 16,000 residents of El Rosario, a new development of mostly state workers and professionals, far outnumber the indigenous Zapotecs who run the local government by custom, but cannot vote in local elections and have no say in how resources are spent.

Indigenous appeals for support to global actors such as the International Labour Organisation (ILO) also have important implications for national state sovereignty (see Box 8.6; see also Dunbar-Ortiz, 2001). Scholars have noted how indigenous and other marginalised citizens in Latin America have used the international arena to put pressure on national governments (see Keck and Sikkink, 1998; Brysk, 2000). The activities of indigenous movements raise important issues about the impact of international factors upon processes of democratisation in Latin America (see Chapters 3, 9).

INSTITUTIONS   **Box 8.6**

Indigenous people, forced labour and the ILO

The International Labour Organisation (ILO), an agency of the United Nations, is an example of a global organisation that has worked closely with indigenous people in ways that sometimes reveal the limits of national state sovereignty. It has taken an active role in scrutinizing the conditions in which indigenous people in Latin America live and work. In a report published in 2005, the ILO said that Andean countries had started taking steps to eradicate the problem facing indigenous people in some areas of forced labour, particularly through contemporary versions of debt bondage, in response to the findings of studies it had conducted in the sub-region. In the Ucayali and Madre de Dios departments of Peru's Amazon basin area, for example, investigations confirmed the use of forced labour within indigenous community lands in the context of illegal logging activities extracting mahogany and cedar. The ILO said intermediaries for loggers make advances to indigenous communities offering food or goods in exchange for a quantity of wood to be delivered later, giving rise to a debt which is then manipulated to extract unpaid labour. In the Chaco region of Bolivia and Paraguay, indigenous workers and sometimes whole communities have been held on large farms in conditions of 'serfdom', bound by debt obligations or even the threat of violence. In 2009, for example, members of the UN Permanent Forum on Indigenous Issues demanded an end to the semi-slavery of the Guaraní and other indigenous peoples in the Chaco region where they work on large estates, particularly those run by Mennonite religious communities (US Fed News, 2009). The ILO has highlighted other forms of forced labour used in Bolivian agriculture, such as the *enganche* or *habilitación* labour systems based on advances to workers before a harvest in exchange for a commitment to work. Although the bonded workers are usually male, their wives and children are often expected to provide free labour alongside them. The ILO says that, in response to its findings, in December 2004 the government of Bolivia created a National Commission for the Eradication of Forced Labour to work with the UN agency and other organisations in order to stamp out discrimination of this kind against indigenous people. Peru also responded with moves to develop policies that will eliminate forced labour. However, the UN Permanent Forum on Indigenous Issues reporting on the Chaco region in 2009 said much still needed to be done to end forced labour and the governments of both Bolivia and Paraguay needed to take further action.

Sources: ILO, 2002, 2005; US Fed News, 2009

Multiculturalism and national identity

Indigenous mobilisation in democratising societies can pose dilemmas for national identity and legal traditions. The indigenous question raises important questions about the past understanding of nationhood by representing a manifesto for multi-culturalism. In Bolivia, for example, the term 'nation' was until recently claimed both by the nation-state and by indigenous groups themselves (see Box 8.7). This has been addressed by appending the term 'plurinational' to the country's official name, which establishes its status as a state encompassing various groups that can each claim a culturally distinct status as separate 'nations'. In Peru, mobilisation has challenged the ethnic categories assigned to indigenous groups by non-indigenous policymakers: they have, for example, begun to insist that they are not just *campesinos* or '*nativos*', but Quechuas or Andeans, Amazonians or Shipibos (see Golash-Boza, 2008).

The existence of fully integrated 'nations' has been open to debate in Latin America because of its inheritance as a colonised region, and national identity has been a more explicitly constructed, modern notion (see Chapter 13). The policy of the nation-state in Latin America has been framed by this concern with the 'incomplete' nature of the nation and the subsequent need to 'integrate' diverse societies by constructing a national, homogeneous culture and ignoring or eradicating

---

CASE STUDY Box 8.7

Evo Morales and Bolivia

The Bolivian president, Evo Morales, has placed considerable emphasis on the indigenous heritage of his country and has spearheaded a number of initiatives to raise the status of indigenous culture while remaining faithful to his own origins. He makes a point of having lunch with indigenous guards at the national palace, for example. Bolivia's 2009 constitution recognised the country's 'plurinational' status and stresses the importance of ethnicity in Bolivia's make-up. Models of indigenous government, community justice and even healthcare are now on an equal legal footing with their non-indigenous counterparts. Self-rule restores elements of governing practices in the Bolivian highlands that precede the Inca empire by which local leaders called *mallkus* are democratically elected by their communities in public votes for terms of one year, then choose their senior officials. As many of the decisions involve communal resources, this form of local government has much in common with socialism (see Chapters 12, 16). Morales dissolved the ministry of indigenous affairs, arguing that in a country where indigenous people formed the majority its very existence amounted to a form of discrimination. He also founded three indigenous universities, established quotas for indigenous people in the military, and created a college for aspiring diplomats with native backgrounds. He has routinely employed indigenous symbolism such as the multi-coloured *wiphala* flag in official ceremonies, and has pioneered educational reforms that encourage the teaching of indigenous languages such as Aymara, Quechua, and Guaraní in schools and among government employees (see Gustafson, 2009). There are many signs that such efforts have established a much higher profile for indigenous culture in Bolivia. In La Paz, for example, Indian women in traditional bowler hats and embroidered shawls, sometimes called 'cholitas', became regular anchors on television newscasts, 'Miss Cholita' beauty pageants have become popular, and indigenous hip-hop stars now appear regularly at nightclubs.

diversity. However, indigenous organisations share a vision that reconceptualises Latin American society as multi-ethnic, or even as multi-national, and that rejects past strategies of integration, often pursued by non-indigenous elites through state agencies.

The multi-ethnic visions of indigenous organisations represent an effort to define a new quality of citizenship that often tests a dominant discourse based on universal, liberal norms of equality before the law (see Yashar, 1998; see also Chapter 3). In Latin America, inequality and *de facto* ethnic stratification have weakened citizens' shared identification with each other as members of the same civic community, and the sense of exclusion felt by indigenous people has generated tensions. Warren (1998) pointed out that in Guatemala, for example, critics of the Mayan movement and of ethnic nationalism routinely expressed fears that these would engender Balkanisation or separatism that could destroy the state. Separatist tensions are evident in Bolivia, but mainly within the non-indigenous community in the eastern provinces of the country (see Boxes 12.11, 13.6).

Organising on the basis of cultural difference has also posed dilemmas for indigenous movements themselves. As states and international organisations have recognised indigenous rights and provided resources to fund projects, the question of who speaks for indigenous people has become politicised (Mattiace, 2005). Cultural differences between indigenous organisations *themselves* can be a source of rivalry that weakens them as political actors (*ibid.*). A common source of division in countries such as Colombia and Ecuador has been between traditional local indigenous leaders and regional and national-level leaders (see Pallares, 2002; Warren and Jackson eds, 2002).

Individual versus collective rights

Indigenous mobilisation in Latin America has generated debates about the relationship between individual and collective or social rights. Latin American judicial systems emphasise the unitary nature of the law based upon universal individual rights deriving from the principles of liberalism (see Chapters 6, 12). Indigenous 'customary' law, however, is founded on a collective identity by which community norms take priority over the individual. Policies of multiculturalism can generate a conflict between the recognition of group rights and of universal individual human rights, and this in turn highlights tensions between different visions of democracy based on social or individual rights (see Eckstein and Wickham-Crowley eds, 2003; and Chapter 3). A common example of the dilemmas this has caused has occurred when the state has sought to interfere in customary practices that may compromise women's human rights (see Chapter 13).

Advocates for indigenous self-government in Mexico, for example, have proposed giving local communities control over local elections; the right to apply traditional methods of policing and justice for some crimes; and over land and natural resources. However, the women of tribes such as the Mixe have argued that they are routinely – and, in some cases, violently – discriminated against in the democratic process and that a male council of elders makes all the decisions. In Ecuador in 2006, a Pachakuthik congressman and the president of the national human rights commission, Estuardo Remache, was accused of domestic violence after allegedly severely beating his wife. Remache requested dismissal of the case in the national courts and that the matter be addressed through traditional indigenous justice within his own community in the province of Chimborazo (see Lavinas Picq, 2008). Lavinas Picq (2008) has argued that, if democratisation has coincided with the promotion of indigenous rights in recent decades, other rights – notably gender equality – seem to be lagging: the emergence of the indigenous movement in Ecuador, for example, has been accompanied by the atrophy of the women's movement in the country (see below, and Chapter 13), and patriarchal practices remain concealed in the name of ethnic cohesion. Devices such as ILO Convention 169 have attempted to reconcile individual and collective rights, but only in a few countries such as Colombia has there been progress in developing a new jurisprudence that attempts to balance indigenous autonomy against universally applied norms.

Non-governmental organisations (NGOs)

The growing predominance of NGOs in Latin America and their relationship both with small grassroots organisations, the state and international and private agencies has generated challenges for social movements. NGOs are private organisations funded either by voluntary contributions through membership, donations from larger organisations or through self-financing (Foweraker *et al.*, 2003). They began to flourish under military regimes in the 1970s, often implicitly as anti-government organisations, as a result of funding from the US and Europe. Their emergence coincided in the 1980s with neoliberal reform that encouraged the state to retreat from some of its traditional roles (see Chapter 15), and NGOs began to fill gaps in social provision. International bodies such as the World Bank saw the benefit of channelling development aid through NGOs, which began to connect local communities to international sources of funding and support for development projects (Foweraker *et al.*, 2003; Munck, 2003). However, a reduction in external funding following the transition to democracy subsequently forced many NGOs to turn towards the newly democratic states at a time when these were aiming to increase their legitimacy through social activities. The number of NGOs operating in Latin America has varied, but in 2004 Radcliffe suggested that about 25,000 were at work in the region.

Macdonald (1997) identified several approaches to understanding the role of NGOs in civil society: 'neo-conservative' positions see NGOs as private-sector actors capable of mobilising society without state intervention; 'liberal-pluralist positions' suggest that NGOs are organisations of civil society that provide a focus for individual political participation and counterbalance the power of authoritarian states; 'post-Marxist' perspectives build on Gramsci's argument that state power is maintained not just through the formal organisations of 'political society' (government, political parties and the military) but also through the institutions of civil society and so attribute to NGOs a role in promoting democracy (see Box 12.6; see also Gramsci, 1971). NGOs themselves often emphasise their democratic role in supporting civil society through popular participation and political empowerment.

| CASE STUDY | Box 8.8 |

No Sweat

The No Sweat organisation is an example of an NGO working alongside organisations in Latin America that draws upon international solidarities in order to campaign against the poor conditions that workers endure in 'sweatshops' in the region. The organisation based in Britain raises funds through individual membership and has been supported by large trades unions such as the Public and Commercial Services Union (PCS), General Union (GMB) and National Union of Students (NUS). It describes itself as a broad-based campaign looking to the anti-capitalist and international workers movement for support. It has campaigns and contacts throughout Latin America, and works to raise money for independent trades unions in countries such as Mexico, Colombia, El Salvador and Haiti and increase awareness about the conditions of workers by organising meetings and protests against global brands supplying high street chains that it accuses of exploiting them. No Sweat took as its inspiration similar campaigns in the US such as the United Students Against Sweatshops (USAS), Labour behind the Label and the Unite union which have organised large pickets of transnational clothing companies and blocked their deals with colleges. No Sweat argues that the rural poor, children and young women make up a large proportion of workers in sweatshop factories, and women often face sexual harassment, are obliged to take contraception and subjected to routine pregnancy tests, and are forbidden to have sexual relationships. Workers are often forced to do overtime, operate in unhealthy and unsafe conditions and are routinely abused, and violence is sometimes used against them if they try to unionise. A common target for No Sweat campaigns has been the clothing industry in which women work at sewing machines for up to 14 hours a day in dangerous conditions and for very low wages. No Sweat argues that its kind of activism can have direct benefits for workers. In 2001, for example, workers at KukDong International, a Korean-owned clothing transnational based in Atlixco de Puebla in Mexico that was producing clothes for some of the largest and most fashionable international brands, went on strike when five employees claimed to have been sacked for trying to organise an independent union because of poor conditions and low wages. Until then, the workers had been represented by a corporatist union linked to the PRI (see Chapter 7). The workers were backed by USAS and trades unions in the US, and forced the company, now called Mexmode, to rehire sacked workers including union leaders. They won the right to organise the only independent union with a signed collective agreement in Mexico's *maquiladora* or low-cost assembly industry.

Source: No Sweat, 2005a; 2005b

Many strive to improve the quality of citizenship and the conditions in which Latin American people live and work (see Box 8.8).

However, the main justification of most NGO projects, and in particular those with international funding, continues to be their contribution to economic development. They can be seen, above all, as brokers between civil society and sources of national and international funding for development (Radcliffe, 2004). Macdonald (1997) argues that the fact that many NGOs and their donors have recognised that NGOs have a role to play in strengthening civil society does not mean they have adopted a commitment to social justice.

Key themes emerge in efforts to determine the impact of NGOs in Latin America. First, they have often been portrayed as a reflection of an international consensus on neoliberal reform championed by the industrialised countries (see Box 15.1) because they provide services that the state has withdrawn from (Munck, 2003). This has generated a debate about whether NGOs can, in fact, be counted as part of civil society at all (Radcliffe, 2004). Today, NGOs get much of their funding from the state – which channels international grants to them. Some states, such as those in Nicaragua and Costa Rica, have intervened in civil society extensively, limiting the autonomy of NGOs and popular movements. In Mexico, NGOs emerged after the devastating 1985 earthquake and acquired a strong independent presence which the government then sought to co-opt through funding and the creation of a state council for NGOs (Munck, 2003). In Brazil, by contrast, the state has not tried to co-opt NGOs and they have preserved their grassroots orientation, called *basismo* (*ibid.*). Second, NGOs are often accountable to international donors, who can sometimes influence their activities. Serbin (2001) says there is a danger external funding might influence the agenda of NGOs to the detriment of local needs. In Central America, for example, the US government channelled aid to US-based NGOs as part of its broad counterinsurgency strategy in Honduras, El Salvador and Guatemala (see Chapter 10). Third, NGOs confront dilemmas similar to those faced by social movements about how far to work within existing structures while maintaining contact with the grassroots (Foweraker *et al.*, 2003). In some cases, the shift towards activity within the institutionalised structures of democracy has led to declining NGO activity and a diminishing emphasis on mobilisation (Munck, 2003).

Environmental movements

As a developing part of the world, Latin America has long faced the dilemma confronted by similar regions about the balance that must be reached between economic growth and its often harmful impact on the environment.

The natural environment in Latin America is as diverse as it is vast, and most scholars accept that the region as a whole contains the greatest biodiversity on the planet (see Miller, 2007). Most of the coral reefs of the American continent, for example, can be found in the waters off Latin American countries: Brazil, the Caribbean Sea and the eastern Pacific Ocean. Concerns about the environment often relate to the extraction of natural resources that result from models of economic development that have long been based on intensive exploitation and the export of natural resources (see Chapter 14). Environmental activists point to the resulting impact of ranching and farming on forests, of mining and industry on the air and water, and to unsustainable waste-management and water-use policies. They argue that these practices often destroy ecosystems, and even legally protected areas, while governments do nothing to halt them. Environmental issues in Latin America today include industrial waste hazards from the export assembly plants on the US–Mexico border down to a paper mill on the Uruguay River, deforestation in the Brazilian Amazon, the impact of mining upon water supplies in countries such as Ecuador and Peru, the struggle for accountability over the former US Navy bombing range at Isla de Vieques, Puerto Rico, and water policy in Chile, Bolivia and Mexico (see Figure 8.1). It is not only the activities of private manufacturers

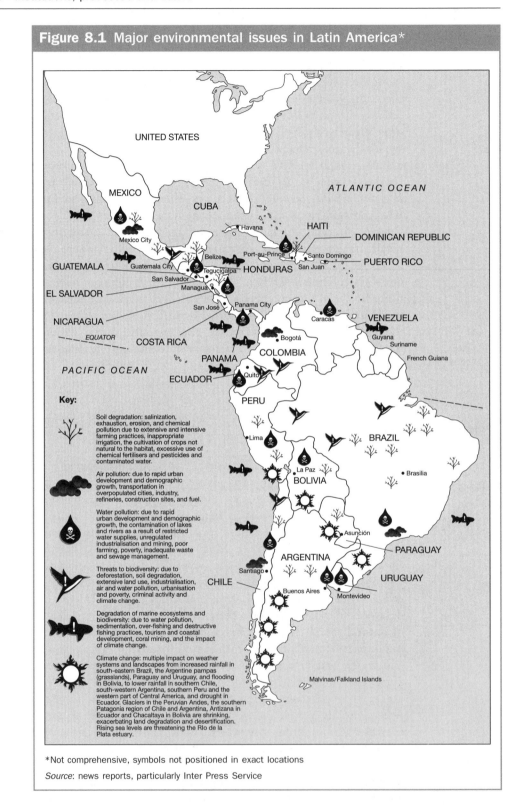

Figure 8.1 Major environmental issues in Latin America*

Key:

Soil degradation: salinization, exhaustion, erosion, and chemical pollution due to extensive and intensive farming practices, inappropriate irrigation, the cultivation of crops not natural to the habitat, excessive use of chemical fertilisers and pesticides and contaminated water.

Air pollution: due to rapid urban development and demographic growth, transportation in overpopulated cities, industry, refineries, construction sites, and fuel.

Water pollution: due to rapid urban development and demographic growth, the contamination of lakes and rivers as a result of restricted water supplies, unregulated industrialisation and mining, poor farming, poverty, inadequate waste and sewage management.

Threats to biodiversity: due to deforestation, soil degradation, extensive land use, industrialisation, air and water pollution, urbanisation and poverty, criminal activity and climate change.

Degradation of marine ecosystems and biodiversity: due to water pollution, sedimentation, over-fishing and destructive fishing practices, tourism and coastal development, coral mining, and the impact of climate change.

Climate change: multiple impact on weather systems and landscapes from increased rainfall in south-eastern Brazil, the Argentine pampas (grasslands), Paraguay and Uruguay, and flooding in Bolivia, to lower rainfall in southern Chile, south-western Argentina, southern Peru and the western part of Central America, and drought in Ecuador. Glaciers in the Peruvian Andes, the southern Patagonia region of Chile and Argentina, Antizana in Ecuador and Chacaltaya in Bolivia are shrinking, exacerbating land degradation and desertification. Rising sea levels are threatening the Río de la Plata estuary.

*Not comprehensive, symbols not positioned in exact locations

Source: news reports, particularly Inter Press Service

and the behaviour of mining corporations that threaten the environment. High poverty levels mean that Latin America can also be vulnerable to harmful activities that originate in the movements of global commodities markets. Record gold prices in 2009, for example, lured thousands of informal prospectors to the Madre de Dios region in Peru's southern Amazon rainforest where their alluvial mining practices threaten a key enclave of biological diversity. Deforestation in the region and high levels of mercury used in mining has fuelled concerns about serious ecological damage. More broadly, Latin American societies are also facing the consequences of global warming, such as melting glaciers in the Andes (see Carey, 2010).

An argument frequently voiced at the Second Latin American Congress on National Parks and other Protected Areas held in Argentina in 2007, the largest gathering of environmental organisations working in Latin America for a decade, was that environmentalists in the region have been advocating sustainable development for 30 years, but governments have still not taken this debate to heart. One of the main reasons for this is that the principal concerns of governments in the region over the last decade have been tackling poverty and ensuring political stability, not sustainable development, which has taken a back seat as they struggle to consolidate democracy and nurture growth.

Brazil represents a good example of the tensions that can exist within governments that are committed to improving the standards of living of large, poor populations, while coming under pressure from the international environmental movement. The division between a strong agricultural lobby alongside government interests keen to promote development, and environmental groups eager to protect natural resources and indigenous communities, have shaped debates over the Amazon, a region of international ecological importance because of the likely impact of deforestation there on the global climate (see Hemming, 2008). While Brazil has also pledged to end net deforestation by 2015, it has not been clear in its strategy for doing so, prompting some observers to suggest that ministries that have economic growth as their main objective are shaping Amazon policy. The tensions caused within Brazil's governing PT over the effort to maintain a balance in Amazon policy between growth and sustainability became evident in 2008, when Marina Silva resigned as environment minister in frustration at what she saw as misguided policies. Similarly, in Bolivia the social pressure to meet economic needs through extractive industries that destroy the natural environment – such as gas, mining and forestry – remains strong despite the election of an indigenous president, Evo Morales, whose own beliefs are supportive of a commitment to protecting the environment. About a quarter of Bolivia's national territory is thought to be environmentally degraded, according to the Liga de Defensa del Medio Ambiente (Lidema, Environmental Defence League), Bolivia's principal environmental coalition (see Farthing, 2009). Yet the environmental movement, which comprises indigenous groups and largely middle-class NGOs, remains small and the political demand for continued extraction of resources by government supporters within powerful social movements, who argue Bolivia's vast natural resources should benefit the country rather than foreigners, usually wins the day.

Environmental movements have developed in Latin America along the lines of those elsewhere in the world, lobbying against projects and practices that are deemed to be harmful to ecosystems that are often beautiful and fragile in equal measure and pressing for greater government protection of the environment and more sustainable use of resources. The profile of environmental movements has grown since democratisation, in some countries often in a relationship with indigenous movements, although the ideas about land use and sustainability of both groups do not always coincide (see Sawyer, 2004). Environmental movements were given significant momentum in the 1980s in the context of the growth of powerful international NGOs and campaign groups working for environmental change that became active throughout Latin America, such as Greenpeace. Conditionality, whereby international development assistance has required undertakings that aid and loans will not be used in ways that damage the environment, has also served to nurture the growth of the environmental lobby.

However, it is important to note that despite the limited growth of environmental organisations and parties (see below) in the region, Latin America has not merely imported the environmental concerns and politics of the developed world but has seen a significant number of endogenous, or locally generated, environmental initiatives, some of which have expanded beyond the region. In an examination of the evolution of the environmental movement in Brazil, for example, Hochstetler and Keck (2007) have contested what they call the 'transnational narrative' – by which environmentalism supposedly arrived in the country in the 1980s as a result of the international uproar over deforestation in the Amazon – and have argued that, as elsewhere, a 'new environmentalism' was already present in Brazil by the 1970s (see Box 8.9). Similarly, the Ecoclubs initiative for teenagers and young people who work with their communities through environmentally-related initiatives was created in Argentina 16 years ago and has since expanded to 30 countries in Latin America, Europe and Africa.

Key issues facing the environmental lobby are its heterogeneity, disagreements over values, expectations and demands among environmental social movements, and a lack of consensus about policy priorities and the best practical ways of securing change on ecological issues. Some groups, for example, argue that economic globalisation, free trade, privatisation, poverty and social inequality are the main causes of environmental degradation (see Chapters 4, 15), while others have a more nuanced focus on ecological issues and disregard sociopolitical factors (see García-Guadilla, 2005). Moreover, there remains considerable disagreement over the meaning of 'sustainable development' both among environmental social movements and the governments they seek to pressure. The term 'environmental justice' – which brings together broader issues of global injustice and local concerns about the environment – has grown in use as a way of addressing environmental issues, and especially the inequalities that may result in harmful environmental practices, in Latin America and elsewhere (see Carruthers ed., 2008). In 2005, García-Guadilla developed a useful typology that identified four types of environmental NGOs and social movements operating in Latin America:

- *Global ecologists:* Large, formal, institutionalised organisations that prioritise global ecological policies, such as the former Inter-Agency Committee on Sustainable Development.
- *Southern ecologists:* Latin American environmental social organisations and movements that prioritise the ecological dimension of sustainable development over

Greening Brazil

Hochstetler and Keck (2007) trace the development of the Brazilian green movement from 1972 to 1992 and identify three waves of environmentalism in the country according to periods of military dictatorship, democratisation and globalisation. The green movement's emergence during Brazil's democratic transition shaped an environmentalism that has generally been more politicised and further to the left than elsewhere, referred to by Brazilians as 'socio-environmentalism'. The creation of the Partido Verde (PV, Green Party) in 1987 was an important development in this process, as was the murder in 1988 of the rubber-tappers' leader Chico Mendes who had struggled against deforestation. This generated new awareness both nationally and internationally of Amazonian environmental politics, and what had hitherto been seen as a land reform issue gained an environmental hue. However, the concerns of environmentalists in Brazil were not solely focused on the Amazon and environmental awareness also grew in rapidly developing metropolitan areas such as São Paulo. In the 1970s, for example, the city of Cubatão in south-east Brazil became a focus for environmentalists because of debilitating air pollution caused by rapid industrial growth. Socio-environmentalism can be interpreted as the outcome of social pressures shaping policy and the development of domestic politics in Brazil. It helps to explain a resistance to environmentalism when it has been seen as a foreign idea pushed from outside the country, but acceptance of it as an integral part of national politics when it has come from within. Brazilians have, for example, been willing to tackle problems facing the Amazon region yet unwilling to internationalise these. The Brazilian government has, at times, reacted angrily to the interventions of external environmentalists in the debate about the future of the Amazon rainforest that have implied that its protection is too important to be left only to the Brazilian authorities. In 2008, for example, President Lula was forced to state in response to renewed international attention to the region that there could be no question about his country's sovereignty over it.

the economic and the social, and so focus on issues such as natural resource degradation, air, soil and water pollution, biodiversity conservation and climate change. Among this group are subsidiaries of large international organisations located in the south, and NGOs from southern countries, such as the Latin American branches of Friends of the Earth, Greenpeace and the World Wide Fund for Nature (WWF). They can have a high level of institutionalisation and are considered legitimate targets for international funding. They have some power to influence official agendas, but may face the problem of possible co-optation by governments and international multilateral institutions.

– *Political environmentalists:* This 'anti-system' group comprises anti-globalisation and pro-democratisation movements, such as environmental organisations and NGOs that lobby against economic globalisation, free trade and privatisation (see Chapter 15). They focus on the political and social dimensions of sustainable development more than on its ecological dimensions. These types of environmental organisations and social movements reject what is known as 'Agenda 21' – the official, mainstream agenda on the environment adopted at the UN Conference on Environment and Development, the so-called 'Earth Summit', in Rio de Janeiro in 1992 – and their power derives from 'informal' networking and mass mobilisation. They have a low level of institutionalisation and have difficulty obtaining funding.

- *Social environmentalists:* This group emphasises social equity and participatory democracy as prerequisites for sustainable development and their concerns are more oriented to the local and regional levels than the global. Their aims are social justice, greater equality, poverty elimination and democratic access to water, housing, food, land, health, sanitation, employment and education. This group includes many human rights, indigenous and women's organisations that incorporate such issues within their agendas. Other concerns include the social, cultural and health-related effects of pesticides and transgenic food, and the impacts of desertification and loss of biodiversity. They also act at a global level through informal networks that mobilise at summits. This group includes individual organisations such as En Defensa del Maíz in Mexico as well as networks of national, regional or international organisations. They have a medium-level of institutionalisation but are highly heterogeneous, with some being formal NGOs and others looser social movements. Their power derives from the inclusion in national constitutions of those whose rights they defend; alliances with other organisations; the use of electronic means to build alliances and form part of larger networks; and visibility from protest actions. Some receive government and international funding and so risk being co-opted. They also risk being displaced by large, international environmental NGOs and corporations.

By virtue of the international nature of environmental issues, campaign groups often have a focus that is non-national or transnational. The dispute over a Uruguayan paper mill, for example, brought together Uruguayan, Argentine and international green groups (see Box 8.10).

Environmental movements have at times thrown up political challenges within governing parties or the popular organisations they rely upon. Disagreements about the best ways to safeguard the environment can be a source of political tensions between former allies. In Brazil, for example, the former PT environment minister Marina Silva – a staunch defender of the Amazon rainforest – quit the party in 2009 following her resignation the previous year over environmental policy to pave the way for a possible presidential run in 2010 elections, probably on behalf of the country's Green Party. In Ecuador, the passing of a new constitution in 2008 that incorporated environmental measures considered to be among the most progressive in Latin America represented a moment of unity between the country's social movements and the Left, yet also engendered a national movement that has since challenged mining legislation over the question of environmental protection. After the constitution was ratified, Ecuador's president, Rafael Correa, promoted legislation that would greatly expand the operations of gold-, silver-, and copper-mining corporations as part of his vision of breaking the country's dependence on traditional extractive industries such as oil. The new mining law soon brought together social movements, led mainly by indigenous nationalities, mobilising against it and claiming that it violated the new constitution's environmental provisions, and weakened past support among popular organisations for the president.

In some countries of Latin America, green parties evolved out of environmental organisations and have existed for at least 20 years, although they remain small

Bitter pulp – the dispute over Uruguay's paper mill

A dispute between Argentina and Uruguay over the construction of a paper mill on the shared water-way between the two countries demonstrated the international implications of environmental disputes and the capacity of large projects to unite opposition across borders. Environmental groups from both countries have been involved in opposition to the mill on the Uruguay River, including REDES–Friends of the Earth Uruguay, Guayubira of Uruguay and Argentina's Fundación Centro de Derechos Humanos y Ambiente (CEDHA, Centre for Human Rights and Environment). The International Court of Justice (ICJ) in The Hague was expected to make a final ruling on a disagreement between the two countries over the mill in 2010. An initial ruling that the project could go ahead was followed by a World Bank announcement that the plant met its environmental standards and paved the way for the International Finance Corporation to approve loans for the project. The decision in 2007 by Uruguay's president, Tabaré Vázquez (2005–09), to allow the mill, constructed by a Finnish company, to begin its opera-tions provoked angry protests by tens of thousands of Argentine demonstrators and strained relations between the two countries. Every day it turns locally grown eucalyptus and other woods into about 2,600 tons of pulp, most of which heads for China and Europe. Company officials say the mill has created nearly 7,000 jobs and accounts for 1.7 per cent of Uruguay's gross domestic product. Under President Néstor Kirchner (2003–07), Argentina's government argued that Uruguay had violated the bilateral Uruguay River Treaty by failing to consult with Buenos Aires before authorising construction of the mill. Argentina has argued the mill will damage aquatic life and water quality, and referred the matter to the ICJ. Uruguay has insisted the $1.2 billion enterprise – the largest single capital invest-ment in the country – uses the latest technology and does not pollute the environment. At one stage, Uruguay closed its border crossing with Argentina closest to the mill, in Fray Bentos, after Argentine activists said they would protest there. Roadblocks by Argentine activists and confrontations with Uruguayan officials continued throughout 2008. However, Kirchner's successor, President Cristina Fernández (2007–), has shown impatience over the dispute, and told Argentine activists that she op-poses blockades of the bridge linking the two countries. Another potential environmental conflict between Argentina and a neighbouring country is also looming, with opposition growing to plans by Brazil to construct a hydroelectric dam 90 km north of the Iguazú falls, which are shared by both countries.

and have had a limited impact on politics in the region. The Partido Verde Ecologista de México (PVEM, Green Ecologist Party of Mexico), for example, was founded in 1986 and initially enjoyed fast growth. Brazil's Partido Verde (PV, Green Party) was formed in 1986 by environmentalists, artists, academics and anti-nuclear activists, many of whom had lived in exile and had been in contact with European environmental groups. The Green Party now has 14 members in Brazil's lower house of congress, 34 provincial legislators and 77 mayors. It was also represented in the cabinet of President Da Silva by the culture minister, Juca Ferreira. In Argentina and Chile, by contrast, green parties themselves are relatively new. In Argentina, the Iniciativa Verde (IV, Green Initiative) party was formed in 2006 and fielded its first political candidates in 2009. Its members include former directors of non-governmental organisations like Greenpeace, and social or environmental activists. In Chile, the Partido Ecologista (PE, Ecologist Party) was registered in early 2008 and is legally recognised in three northern regions, but its limited size precludes it from fielding candidates in presidential elections and hence limits its potential national influence. In 1997, the Federación de Partidos Verdes de las Américas (FPVA, Federation of Green Parties of the Americas) was created in Mexico City as a forum for like-minded parties. It now has Latin American member parties from Brazil, Chile, Colombia, Mexico, Nicaragua, Peru, Venezuela, Argentina and the Dominican Republic.

Although governments in Latin America have generally been limited in their ability to respond to calls for action on the environment, a new consciousness about ecological issues and pressure from social movements and green parties has made environmental awareness an important part of the language of governance. Politicians often seek to premise policymaking on the pledge that initiatives will not cause pollution and other problems. Governments have grown more sensitive to protests against what activists claim are environmentally damaging practices. At Isla de Vieques, an island municipality of Puerto Rico, for example, direct action protests by the local community over the environmental impact of the US Navy's use of the island as a bombing and weapons-testing range led to the navy's departure in 2003 and the designation of the area as a wildlife refuge. Governments are also more willing to enforce strict regulations to ensure that corporations extracting natural resources do not harm the environment. In 2009, for example, the Mexican government shut down a mine in the southern state of Chiapas operated by the Canadian company Blackfire, alleging that it had built roads without authorisation, caused pollution, generated toxic emissions, affected the direction and flow of water sources and changed land use without permission (Montgomery, 2009). Latin American governments have also begun to develop their own distinctive analysis of climate change and how to respond to international initiatives seeking low-carbon development (see De La Torre *et al.*, eds, 2009). Some countries, such as Costa Rica, have had significant success reversing past damage to the environment. In the 1970s and 1980s, Costa Rica had one of the highest rates of deforestation in the world, with forest cover dropping to about 21 per cent compared to about 75 per cent 50 years earlier, but policies to save the remaining forest and encourage new planting has increased forest cover to about 51 per cent today (see McMahon, 2009). In other countries, such as Brazil, environmental education now forms part of the primary and secondary school curriculum. Local governments have also played a key role in developing small-scale but none the less important initiatives to make such aspects of daily life as waste-management or water usage more sustainable (see, for example, Gutberlet, 2008).

Media

The media have always played an important role in politics and newspapers and broadcasting outlets have long served as mouthpieces for both rulers and their rivals regardless of the type of regime in power. All political initiatives involve a communication strategy to advocate social change and inform citizens. For example, media strategies formed an important component of rebellions and revolutions in Central America against authoritarian rule (see Darling, 2008).

However, the media gained new influence in Latin America in the context of democratisation for providing a voice to civil society and organised interests and, despite setbacks, there has been a trend in the region over the last decade towards gradual but sustainable progress in the area of free speech.

According to Latinobarómetro data, television and radio maintained their position between 1996–2009 as the main sources of information about politics, while the importance of the print media – newspapers and magazines – has declined considerably (Latinobarómetro, 2009a). In 2009, 12 per cent of respondents said that they now get their information about politics from the internet, whose use is growing considerably among young people aged between 18 and 25 in Latin America. In Venezuela, Peru, Argentina, Colombia and Brazil, more than three-quarters of young people in this category have used the internet at least once in their lives (Latinobarómetro, 2008).

On the one hand, the mass media are closely linked to economic interests and represent a means by which business groups shape opinion, set the agenda and manipulate the public image of officials, parties and institutions (UNDP, 2004b). On the other, the media provide a voice for non-elite sectors of civil society, and social movements have become skilled at manipulating their image through journalists.

In a study of the relationship between changes in the media and democratisation, Lawson (2002) argued that independent newspapers played an important role in the rebirth of Mexican civil society during the 1980s and 1990s. From the 1930s until the 1990s, Mexico's media establishment was governed by a sophisticated authoritarian system of state–media relations based on corruption and censorship, but between 1976 and 1996 this broke down. Independent publications emerged and devoted less coverage to officials of the ruling party and the state, shifting their attention instead to civil society. They conferred legitimacy on emerging social movements through a new 'civic discourse' and, as a result, reshaped the terms of political debate (*ibid.*). Civic discourse opened up spaces for non-partisan political action that were quickly filled by organisations such as the Convergencia (Convergence of Civic Organisations for Democracy), the Alianza Cívica (Civic Alliance), the Academia Mexicana de Derechos Humanos (AMDH, Mexican Academy of Human Rights) and other pro-democracy groups.

Social movements have recognised the importance of the media to their development and many actively seek coverage to spread their message. In Brazil, media interest in the MST has been intense since reporters filmed the 1996 massacre of 19 demonstrating landless farmworkers by military police in Eldorado do Carajás in the state of Para, and the landless movement has actively sought good relations with journalists (Berger, 1998; Hammond, 2004). In Mexico in late 2004, Mazahua indigenous women from Valle de Allende in the State of Mexico gained widespread publicity when they marched on Mexico City with rifles slung over traditional dresses demanding reparations for damage from a dam built in 1977. What had appeared as an authentic indigenous women's movement was in fact largely the creation of press advisers and, within eight weeks, they had won millions of pesos from the government (Bensinger, 2004).

The relationship between political change and media independence is unclear. Lawson (2002) argues that the Mexican case suggests a reciprocal relationship between political liberalisation and the emergence of independent media: the breakdown of Mexico's authoritarian regime made possible a media opening, but a media opening also contributed to democratisation. He says commercial competition was a crucial ingredient in breaking down the old system of press control and strengthening independent media outlets. However, reforms by the state also had a direct consequence on the media and President Carlos Salinas de Gortari (1988–94) took steps to modernise press–state relations. Between 1991 and 1993, Salinas restricted a time-honoured practice of paying for reporters' accommodations on presidential trips; stopped distributing bribes from the presidential palace; established a minimum wage for journalists; reduced official advertising and redirected it towards publications with larger circulations; cut longstanding subsidies to newspapers; extended VAT to newsprint; and forced newspapers to pay social security taxes in cash instead of in advertising space for the government (*ibid.*). These measures forced newspapers to rely more on commercial sources of revenue. Privatisation policies also gave banks, airlines, telephone companies and television stations control over their own advertising and the state, in effect, abdicated control over newspaper revenues (*ibid.*).

Media freedom is an ingredient both of theoretical conceptions of democracy and empirical measurements of it, and the term 'Fourth Estate' is sometimes used to characterise the role of the media as a guarantor of the separation of powers. As a result, liberalisation of the media can have important political consequences (see Table 8.2). In Nicaragua, for example, media freedom played an important role in the transition to democracy following the period of Sandinista revolutionary control. Nicaragua was the arena of fierce struggles over press freedom because of close links between the powerful family of Violeta Barrios de Chamorro, who became president in 1990, and the mass media.

A key theme on the agenda of scholars and organisations involved in efforts to strengthen democratic governance in Latin America today is 'media literacy' – the ability of citizens to access, analyse, evaluate and even create media content (see Martinsson, 2009). Proponents of greater media literacy argue that it allows citizens to acquire a well-founded position on societal issues and so be better equipped to express an opinion, and is an important contributing factor to participation in a healthy democracy. The media play several roles in a democracy:

■ *Legitimacy:* The media can strengthen or weaken the legitimacy of an administration by giving voice to competing perspectives and exposing the misdeeds of government officials. In Latin America, print and broadcast journalism has been

Table 8.2 Media opening in Mexico and its political consequences

Coverage under old system	Coverage by Mexico's emerging Fourth Estate	Political consequences of changes in coverage
1. Official agenda control 2. Selective silence 3. Electoral bias	1. Greater attention to non-official actors 2. Investigation of closed topics 3. More balanced campaign coverage	1. Promotion of civil society 2. Scandals and regime delegitimation 3. Increased support for opposition parties

Source: Lawson, 2002

increasingly critical of ruling elites. Waisbord (2000) pointed out how political conflicts and the increasing use of investigative reporting triggered the 'politics of scandal' in the region. Media scandals led to the impeachment of President Fernando Collor de Mello (1989–92) in Brazil, the removal of Carlos Andrés Pérez (1989–93) from the Venezuelan presidency, and the accusations of links with drug-traffickers against Ernesto Samper (1994–98) that debilitated his presidency in Colombia. Mainwaring (1999) argued that the media in Brazil contributed to anti-party attitudes and depoliticisation. Seligson (2002), by contrast, found no clear relationship between greater media exposure in Costa Rica and the declining levels of system support (see Box 8.11).

- *Voting:* The media play a crucial role in shaping public opinion and it is possible that impartiality and freedom of expression can have an impact on voting patterns. In Mexico, for example, some scholars have explored links between the result of the 1997 congressional elections – after which the PRI lost control of the chamber of deputies for the first time – and the decision by the Televisa broadcasting network to dramatically move away from blanket coverage of the party and to give opposition candidates substantial air time (see Lawson, 2002).

- *Accountability:* In theory, independent media guarantee the accountability of government officials, an important role in countries where parties and interest groups remain underdeveloped (*ibid.*). The press can oversee or constrain the actions of the political class, different branches of government and parties (UNDP, 2004b).

THEORIES AND DEBATES   Box 8.11

Media and parties

Research on the mass media has sought to explore its increasing power and the extent to which it is weakening or even replacing traditional institutions. In recent years, students of Latin American politics have shown a growing interest in the impact of television, which it has been argued represents a potential threat to political parties. Through television, candidates can appeal to citizens in direct ways without relying on party apparatuses, strengthening personalism (Grossman, 1995; Mainwaring and Scully, 1995; Weyland, 1998). Some authors have even claimed that the broadcast media are more powerful than political parties (Zuleta Puceiro, 1993). Pérez-Liñán (2002) examined whether increasing exposure to television news is related to the erosion of political partisanship among citizens of eight Latin American countries. The data suggested that television news encourages viewers to identify with particular parties in the short term, although the development of television may weaken Latin American parties in the long term. It has also been argued by some scholars that newspaper readership, by contrast, is an indicator of civicness, because newspapers disseminate a qualitatively different perspective from that offered by television, although not all scholars agree with this argument (see Sartori, 1989; Patterson, 1993). Television, however, is a valuable political resource when it comes to promoting political personalities and bringing them to public attention. A number of television journalists have entered politics in Latin America, the most recent being Mauricio Funes, who became president of El Salvador in 2009. Funes hosted a popular interview show on television, made appearances on large networks such as CNN en Español, and also hosted news programmes that were critical of previous governments.

Heads of government consulted by the UNDP describe constant interventions by the media as a counterbalance to the exercise of their power. The media can guarantee accountability because they provide the public with information, and without a relatively diverse and independent press, it is difficult to see how citizens can acquire sufficient information to make meaningful political choices or hold government representatives accountable for their decisions. If information on which citizens base political choices is distorted, it is difficult for them to evaluate official decisions.

However, it is important not to overstate the relationship between the mass media and democratisation, even where new media technologies rapidly become available. Boas (2000), for example, used the case of Cuba to argue that even highly accessible technologies such as the internet do not necessarily favour the emergence or consolidation of a democratic political system. The Cuban government has limited internet use and imposes a number of restrictions on websites that can be accessed. Other scholars have gone further and argued that repressive elements from the authoritarian period in Latin America have remained in place or been transformed into more subtle means of censorship and social control (see Lugo-Ocando ed., 2008). Despite the links that have been made between democratisation and press freedom, several barriers remain to a fully open media in Latin America:

The state

The persistence of state ownership in the economy continues to constrain advertising revenues in sectors that in a full market economy would be important sources of independent revenue for the media. An artificially restricted supply of advertising revenues accentuates the influence of existing large advertisers, such as the state. In some states, the executive has control over broadcast concessions, and this remains vulnerable to political manipulation. States can also punish and reward media owners through decisions on the enforcement of anti-monopoly regulations, for example. Powerful politicians can try to constrain the activity of the media through attacks on their integrity. In April 2006, for example, Colombia's president Alvaro Uribe accused sections of the media of undermining the country's democracy after two publications alleged there were ties between a state security agency and rightwing paramilitaries.

More recently, concern has been expressed by advocates of press freedom and rights groups about signs of state intolerance towards the media in countries with left-of-centre governments whose leaders feel that they have not been given fair coverage by outlets that represent or are identified with opposition or elite actors. In Venezuela, President Hugo Chávez increased his efforts to control the country's media with a series of new measures in 2009 that were criticised by rights groups. Venezuela's attorney general outlined new legislation on 'media crimes' by which anyone who provided information deemed harmful to state interests could be jailed. New rules were introduced requiring cable and satellite TV channels – including international broadcasters – to carry speeches by President Chávez, and the head of the Comisión Nacional de Telecomunicaciones (Conatel, National Telecommunications Commission) revoked the licences of 34 radio stations after they had failed to update documents with the agency. In its *Freedom of the Press 2009* report, Freedom House categorised Venezuela as 'not free' (Freedom House, 2009b; see also Chapter 4). In Argentina in 2009, tax inspectors raided the offices in Buenos Aires of the daily *Clarín* newspaper, which accused the government of President Cristina Fernández (2007–) of harassment. The move came during deliberations over a media reform bill that would force large media groups such as *Clarín* to sell some of their assets. In the past, President Fernández and her husband, the former president, Néstor Kirchner (2003–07), had accused *Clarín* of bias in its reporting. In Honduras, prior to his removal in a coup in June 2009, President Manuel Zelaya routinely complained that the main media outlets in the country were biased against him, and in 2007 ordered mandatory government broadcasts on all television and radio stations. While Zelaya was in office, the Inter-American Press Association (IAPA), the UN and the OAS (Organisation of American States) among others criticised threats to journalists and subtle forms of censorship in Honduras.

A report published by the Open Society Institute in 2008 criticized behind-the-scenes government interference with media freedom and editorial independence in Latin America, which it described as 'soft censorship' (see Open Society Institute, 2008). In particular, this documented what it claimed were government abuses of financial and regulatory powers over the media, such as those related to advertising and licensing processes.

Concentration

Private cartels and big businessmen often own large parts of an economy and can exert indirect control over the media through advertising (Lawson, 2002). Some big businessmen also own media outlets and, if these are not modern corporations but privately owned enterprises, editorial decisions can be vulnerable to their views (see Lugo-Ocando ed., 2008). For these reasons, market competition is seen as an important guarantor of a balanced and independent media in new democracies. If state ownership is merely replaced by private monopolies, economic reform is unlikely to promote fairer coverage (*ibid.*). The concentration of ownership raises questions about the degree to which the media themselves are accountable. Latin American heads of government consulted for the UNDP (2004b) believed the absence of controls on the press could threaten their ability to fulfil their duties. Political leaders voiced concerns that media organisations free of regulations can be used to express the interests of powerful economic groups.

Bias

Media outlets whose ownership is concentrated often display a rightwing bias and can be hostile to progressive positions. Brazilian media remains dominated by the Globo network, for example, and TV Globo's highly influential news coverage has in the past been accused of favouring conservative candidates and taking positions hostile to the PT. Mass media coverage can also reveal an establishment bias in how social movements are portrayed. Movement activists and critics of the media who have studied coverage of the MST in Brazil, for example, argue that this is mostly hostile and often distorted (see Berger, 1998; Hammond, 2004). Although media impartiality is seen as crucial to fair elections, this can also be reversed. In Mexico, during the 2000 presidential elections, for example, members of the directorate of the Instituto Federal Electoral (IFE, Federal Electoral Institute), the independent body organising and monitoring the elections, began to complain during the last week of campaigning about unbalanced coverage in favour of the PRI candidate, Francisco Labastida, after months of balance (Tuckman, 2000). The case of Notimex in Mexico, Latin America's largest state news agency, also illustrates how even a media gaining in autonomy in a new democratic environment can come under political pressure because of its critical coverage. For years Notimex was a propaganda vehicle of the PRI but the PAN president Vicente Fox promised to transform it into an independent source of news. The journalist Francisco Ortiz Pinchetti accepted this task on the condition that he would have full autonomy to restructure Notimex. By mid-2001, Mexico's interior ministry, which oversees Notimex and its budget, was reportedly growing unhappy with its unbiased coverage and state governors had complained that Notimex was quoting their critics (Quinones, 2002). Ortiz Pinchetti and 16 other top editors were dismissed in a move the interior ministry said was taken for administrative reasons and, in protest, 25 of their colleagues quit.

Summary

The concept of civil society has grown in importance in Latin American politics, providing the basis for new theoretical understandings of democratisation based on autonomous organisations. In the last decades of the twentieth century, many diverse social movements emerged in the region and became a locus of political action. Social mobilisation of this kind reflected a new relationship between state and society that resulted from the weakening of traditional corporatism and of the strong central state. Civil society was further strengthened by the development of non-governmental organisations, business associations and by an opening in the media. However, scholars remain divided about what civil society is, and the large diversity of groups that are said to comprise it complicate our understanding of it. Underlying much of the literature has been the idea that the expansion of civil society contributes to the functioning of a healthy democracy. The contributions that civil society can make to democratisation include providing representation outside ineffective institutions, nurturing pluralism and fostering democratic attitudes. However, the limitations of social movements operating outside the institutional structure have become apparent.

Indigenous organisations have grown increasingly prominent among social movements and combine material and cultural demands in their opposition to economic and political exclusion. The policy issues motivating indigenous movements today include self-determination and autonomy, the pursuit of territorial rights and control over natural resources, reforms enabling greater indigenous participation in politics, and the end of military and police abuses. The emergence of indigenous movements has important implications for politics in Latin America because their demands can amount to an effort to redefine statehood and can pose dilemmas for national identity and legal traditions.

The growth of non-governmental organisations (NGOs) in Latin America has challenged social movements. A reduction in external funding following the transition to democracy forced many NGOs to turn for funds towards newly democratic states, and this has fuelled a debate about whether NGOs can be counted as part of civil society. NGOs confront dilemmas similar to those faced by social movements about how far to work within existing structures while maintaining contact with the grassroots.

Environmental movements have developed across Latin America, often in response to slow progress by governments in addressing ecological degradation caused by economic models that have emphasised extraction for export over sustainability. In some countries, environmental organisations have spawned green political parties which have had some limited success in winning elections. A diverse range of movements has developed and these are often characterised by their heterogeneity and different priorities. Environmental movements have at times generated divisions within parties and governments. They have been able to apply some pressure on governments on individual environmental issues and the broader sustainability and carbon-reduction agendas. They also demonstrate the potential for non-national or transnational mobilisation.

The mass media act as an important mouthpiece for civil society, and social movements have recognised the importance of the media to their development. However, the relationship between political change and media independence is unclear. Media freedom is an ingredient of conceptions of democracy and the roles played by the media include strengthening or weakening the legitimacy of an administration, shaping public opinion prior to elections, and scrutinizing the activities of public officials and so holding them to account. However, barriers remain to a fully open media in Latin America such as the persistence of states' abilities to put the media under pressure, concentration of ownership and an establishment bias.

Discussion points

- What is civil society and what is its relationship with democracy?
- In what ways are 'new social movements' in Latin America new?
- Why do indigenous movements pose a challenge to the traditional state?
- Did NGOs occupy the roles abandoned by the retreating state in Latin America?
- To what extent does heterogeneity limit the impact of environmental movements?
- What roles have the mass media played in democratisation in Latin America?

Useful websites

www.devdir.org/la_caribbean.htm Extensive Directory of Development Organisations, Latin America and the Caribbean

www.movsoc.m2014.net/?lang=es Red Internacional de los Movimientos Sociales/Social Movements International Network, site linked to the World Social Forum in Porto Alegre with extensive lists of social groups

www.lacompa.org Convergencia de Movimientos de los Pueblos de las Américas (COMPA, Coalition of Popular Movements in the Americas), bringing together social movements in the region

www.cdi.gob.mx Comisión Nacional para el Desarrollo de los Pueblos Indígenas (CDI, National Commission for the Development of Indigenous Peoples), Mexico

www.ilo.org/public/english/indigenous International Labour Organisation (ILO) Indigenous and Tribal Peoples site

www.fmra.org/index_uk.html Foro Mundial sobre la Reforma Agraria (FMRA, World Forum on Agrarian Reform), an independent grouping of agrarian and social organisations

www.conaie.org Confederación de Nacionalidades Indígenas del Ecuador (CONAIE, Confederation of Indigenous Nationalities of Ecuador), most prominent indigenous organisation in Latin America

www.beingindigenous.org Chile's National Council of Culture and Arts website about indigenous culture

http://cscb.nativeweb.org/english.html Confederación Sindical de Colonizadores de Bolivia (CSCB, Bolivian Peasant Confederation), Bolivian indigenous peoples' (*colonizadores*) site

www.funai.gov.br Brazil's Fundação Nacional do Índio (FUNAI, National Indian Foundation)

www.mst.org.br/home.html Movimento dos Trabalhadores Rurais Sem Terra, Brazil's landless workers' movement

www.nosweat.org.uk No Sweat home page

www.wola.org Washington Office on Latin America (WOLA), independent human rights organisation promoting NGOs working mainly for human rights causes

www.lawg.org The Latin America Working Group, an independent civil society lobby and policy organisation in the US that is in frequent contact with social movements and NGOs in Latin America

http://lanic.utexas.edu/subject/society University of Texas at Austin's Latin American Network Information Center (LANIC) section on society and culture, with links to many social movements in Latin America

www.uia.org Union of International Associations (UIA), non-profitmaking organisation providing extensive listings of international NGOs and constituencies

www.infoamerica.org Portal Infoamérica, a comprehensive Spanish site with links to communications analysis and media

www.zonalatina.com Zona Latina, Latin American media and marketing site with links to media and articles about them

www.barnews.com/index.php BarNews portal containing extensive links to Latin American print and broadcast media

www.ifj.org/default.asp?Issue=LATAM&Language=EN Federación de Periodistas de América Latina y del Caribe (FEPALC, Federation of Latin American and Caribbean Journalists), the Latin American regional group of the International Federation of Journalists

www.ife.org.mx Mexico's Instituto Federal Electoral (IFE, Federal Electoral Institute)

www.endefensadelmaiz.org En Defensa del Maiz environmental organisation, Mexico

www.lidema.org.bo Liga de Defensa del Medio Ambiente (Lidema, Environmental Defence League), Bolivia

www.iniciativaverde.org.ar Iniciativa Verde (IV, Green Initiative) party, Argentina

www.guayubira.org.uy Guayubira environmental organisation, Uruguay

www.cedha.org.ar Fundación Centro de Derechos Humanos y Ambiente (CEDHA, Centre for Human Rights and Environment), Argentina

www.fpva.org.mx Federación de Partidos Verdes de las Américas (FPVA, Federation of Green Parties of the Americas)

Recommended reading

Foweraker, Joe, Todd Landman and Neil Harvey. 2003. *Governing Latin America*. Cambridge: Polity

> *Valuable survey of political processes in Latin America that places social movements firmly at the heart of the discipline*

Silva, Eduardo. 2009. *Challenging Neoliberalism in Latin America*. Cambridge: Cambridge University Press

> *Valuable comparative account of the role played by contemporary social movements in recent political change in key Latin American countries*

Sieder, Rachel (ed.). 2002. *Multiculturalism in Latin America: Indigenous Rights, Diversity and Democracy*. London: Institute of Latin American Studies/Palgrave

> *Essential introduction to the development of the indigenous movement and the implications for Latin American politics*

Lucero, Jose Antonio. 2008. *Struggles of Voice: The Politics of Indigenous Representation in the Andes*. Pittsburgh, PA: University of Pittsburgh Press

> *Valuable comparison of the indigenous movements in Ecuador and Bolivia that considers how conflicts within social movements, shifting identities and the politics of transnationalism contribute to political mobilisation*

Clark, Kim and Marc Becker (eds). 2007. *Highland Indians and the State in Modern Ecuador*. Pittsburgh, PA: University of Pittsburgh Press

> *Valuable introduction to the history of indigenous politics that shows the ways the Ecuadorean state has been shaped by its engagement with indigenous communities and how these are redefining ideas of citizenship and nationality*

Miller, Shawn W. 2007. *An Environmental History of Latin America*. Cambridge: Cambridge University Press

> *Essential introductory history of the impact of human society and development on the Latin American environment*

Carruthers, David V. (ed.). 2008. *Environmental Justice in Latin America: Problems, Promise, and Practice*. Cambridge, MA: MIT Press

Essential introduction to key environmental issues and movements that identifies the emergence of a distinctively Latin American environmental justice movement

Lawson, Chappell. 2002. *Building the Fourth Estate: Democratization and the Rise of a Free Press in Mexico*. Berkeley, CA: University of California Press

Essential introduction to theoretical dimensions of media politics in Latin America, although its focus is on Mexico

Lugo-Ocando, Jairo (ed.). 2008. *The Media in Latin America*. Maidenhead: Open University Press

Valuable and comprehensive overview of media systems in Latin America that provides a country-by-country analysis of media history, organization, relationships with the state, regulation and ownership

Part III

INTERNATIONAL RELATIONS

Chapter 9

Inter-state relations within Latin America

This chapter examines the relationships between the countries of Latin America and the main factors that influence the policies adopted by governments towards their neighbours. However, any discussion of foreign policies in Latin America cannot begin without acknowledging the overwhelming importance of the US in their evolution. Relations between states in the region have always been conducted under the umbrella of US predominance (see Chapter 10). A particularly important factor in the recent evolution of those relations was the Cold War, during which Washington aimed to ensure that its interests prevailed (see Chapter 2). The Cold War greatly restricted Latin America's room for manoeuvre in foreign policy-making by putting countries under pressure to align with the US in its struggle with the Soviet Union. Most foreign policy was considered in terms of how it would be viewed in Washington and this limited the ability of states to act autonomously in international arenas. Latin American countries had three options: they could co-operate with US security priorities; they could oppose the US, but risk sanctions; or they could seek isolation (Tulchin and Espach, 2001). As a result, many often pursued policies that reflected an introspective and defensive vision of national interests, were preoccupied with sovereignty, and also viewed each other as either communist or non-communist. Such perspectives suppressed mutual understanding within Latin America, fuelling distrust, and they help to explain both a lack of activity conducted at a regional level and competition between rival states. However, the end of the Cold War and democratisation has greatly expanded the opportunities open to countries to co-operate within the framework provided by economic integration and globalisation (see Cooper and Heine eds, 2009; Chapter 15). Scholars of international relations now seek to develop a theoretical framework in which to understand the ways in which Latin American states behave in the international arena and the tools they can use to further their interests.

Responses to US power

Latin American foreign policies have been shaped by the reality of US power and have adapted in response to changing US priorities (Smith, 2000). A central continuity in international relations has been this asymmetry between strong and weak neighbours, although there have been examples of interactions between small Latin

American states and their powerful northern neighbour in which the former have gained the advantage and, more recently, assertions of an independent foreign policy that challenge past US hegemony. Pastor (2001) cites the role played by General Omar Torrijos (1968–81) in negotiating back control of the Panama Canal through a treaty signed in September 1977, for example, as a watershed in US–Latin American relations. Pastor argues that Torrijos demonstrated that Latin Americans could achieve goals in the US by understanding the ways in which Washington works. Similarly, the administration in Mexico of Carlos Salinas de Gortari (1988–94) employed sophisticated lobbying to help persuade a sceptical US congress to accept the North American Free Trade Agreement (NAFTA), and secured gains as a result. Smith (2000) has argued that, over time, Latin America has developed distinct strategic alternatives to US power which became available in differing degrees and combinations at different periods. A number of Latin American policy alternatives can be identified:

- *The Bolivarian notion of unification:* Appeals to continental unity have recurred in Latin America and persist in the form of integration projects such as Mercosur (*ibid.*) (see Box 9.9, Table 15.2). Although the idea of continental unity has not taken a fixed institutional form, it demonstrated its potential by reinforcing Latin America's insistence on the principles of self-determination and non-intervention from the 1890s to the 1930s; in the formulation of a widely shared economic philosophy across the region after the 1940s; and in the settlement of the Central American conflicts by Latin American countries themselves in the 1980s. Globalisation and a shift towards the left in some countries of Latin America have given this idea a new lease of life (see Cooper and Heine eds, 2009). Venezuela's president, Hugo Chávez, has associated the Bolivarian idea with his vision of 'twenty-first-century socialism' (see Box 12.7), and has changed the official name of his country to the 'Bolivarian Republic of Venezuela'. Under Chávez, Venezuela has become a proponent of institutional initiatives that express the Bolivarian notion of unification, the most high-profile example of which is the Alianza Bolivariana para los Pueblos de Nuestra América (ALBA, the Bolivarian Alliance for the Peoples of Our America, usually called the Bolivarian Alliance for the Americas), an organisation promoting integration between Latin American states that has so far attracted the support of mainly left-of-centre leaders (see Box 9.1).

- *Support and protection from extrahemispheric powers:* A prominent feature of Latin America's strategic relations has been a balancing strategy to avoid excessive dependence on the US and increase the region's leverage vis-à-vis Washington within the global system through the consolidation of increased ties with other powers or regions (Tulchin and Espach, 2001). Some Latin American countries sought close ties with Great Britain in the nineteenth century (see Chapter 1), with the USSR during the Cold War (see Box 2.3), and to a more limited extent with Europe and the Asia-Pacific regions in the contemporary era (Smith, 2000; see also Chapter 11).

- *Sub-regional predominance:* Since Independence, some of the larger Latin American countries have entertained notions of being the dominant power in their vicinity, and Brazil and Mexico had emperors, albeit briefly (see Box 1.2).

INSTITUTIONS	Box 9.1

ALBA and oil diplomacy

Although initially created as an alternative to the Free Trade Area of the Americas (FTAA) proposed by the US (see Box 15.5), the Bolivarian Alliance for the Americas, ALBA, has extended beyond its original membership of Venezuela and Cuba and now has nine member states in Latin America and the Caribbean, most of which had left-of-centre presidents when they joined. In 2009, they agreed on the creation of a common currency for use mainly in trade, the sucre, which they later announced would be launched in 2010. Creation of the currency is aimed at helping the bloc's nine member states manage debts between their governments while reducing reliance on the US dollar. ALBA is now at the centre of a number of regional policy initiatives led by President Hugo Chávez, benefiting from the funds generated in Venezuela by high oil prices. These initiatives have attempted to counteract and lessen US influence in Latin America by appealing to a sense of continental solidarity, and are premised explicitly upon a rejection of neoliberal economic ideas promoting the role of the private sector in development and capitalist globalisation (see Chapter 15). They are based on bilateral trade and reciprocal aid agreements that have helped Chávez gain the support of countries in the region with like-minded leaders. The Venezuelan leader has advanced this policy through new multilateral institutions promoting a vision of Latin American integration based on concrete benefits, such as Petrocaribe, a Caribbean oil alliance with Venezuela allowing countries to buy its oil on preferential terms, and TeleSUR, a regional television network (see Box 13.4). Chávez has also extended the policy through a series of bilateral trade relationships with other Latin American countries. He has, for example, increased arms purchases from Brazil and exchanged Venezuelan oil, in innovative barter arrangements, for expertise and medical assistance with Cuba and Argentine meat and dairy products. This policy has been described as 'oil diplomacy' that represents a potent challenge to the former idea of US 'dollar diplomacy' in the Latin American region.

Argentina and Brazil competed to be the dominant power in the Southern Cone sub-region in the nineteenth century, and during the Cold War built up their military forces and engaged in a race to secure nuclear capabilities (see Box 9.2). In recent years, Brazil has sought a high-profile international role in trade negotiations, peacekeeping, arms control and within the United Nations, and is today emerging as a regional power. Venezuela has increasingly sought to assert itself in South America, pioneering its own integration initiatives such as ALBA (see above), and has often competed with Colombia for sub-regional pre-eminence.

■ *Use of international law:* Latin American states have at times tried to employ international law or sought the protection of international organisations as a strategic alternative to US domination, on the assumption that the principles of international law can protect weaker countries from arbitrary actions by stronger ones. In the early twentieth century, for example, many Latin American countries supported efforts to gain international recognition of the Drago Doctrine, named after an Argentine foreign minister, Luis María Drago (b.1859–d.1921), that challenged the legal right of the great powers, including the US, to use force to recover debts. Yet many of these legal principles were in abeyance during the Cold War, or are simply disregarded by powerful states.

CASE STUDY	Box 9.2

Nuclear weapons programmes in the Southern Cone

During the Cold War, Argentina and Brazil engaged in a race to develop nuclear capabilities despite a regional initiative to prohibit nuclear weaponry, the 1967 Treaty of Tlatelolco, and only scaled their programmes back with the inauguration of a new era of co-operation in the 1990s (see Sotomayor Velázquez, 2004). Argentina's nuclear programme was launched in 1949 under President Juan Domingo Perón (1946–55, 1973–74) and from an early stage envisaged a weapons capacity, with Argentina gaining the knowledge to produce the plutonium or highly enriched uranium necessary for bombs but not having sufficient raw material to do so. Argentina was dependent on the US for supplies of enriched uranium for its research programme and, in the 1970s, these were halted by Washington. It continued with plans to develop nuclear submarines, and experts on nuclear proliferation became convinced Argentina had the determination and capacity to become a nuclear power. With the end of military rule in the 1980s, the nuclear programme lost direction and the armed forces confirmed that the country had lost the technical capability to become a nuclear power. The Brazilian military government that took power in 1964 became worried about the progress Argentina had made in developing a nuclear capability and, in 1971, decided to acquire a nuclear reactor from the US. Like Argentina, Brazil needed to import supplies of enriched fuel and, as a result, had to accept the imposition of nuclear safeguards by the International Atomic Energy Agency (IAEA). Brazil's military junta then reached a deal with West Germany that it hoped would finally give the country an advanced nuclear capability, but US pressure imposed limitations on the project. However, another nuclear programme to build the equipment necessary to enrich uranium bought from China was run in secret and was not covered by nuclear safeguards. By 1979, the army had reportedly begun digging a huge shaft in the Amazon jungle to carry out atomic testing (Redick, 1972; Adler, 1987; Albright, 1989; Krasno, 1994; Sotomayor Velázquez, 2004). A congressional report published in 1990 revealed that the former military rulers had intended to build an atomic bomb through a programme not known to civilian authorities (see Sotomayor Velázquez, 2004). President Fernando Collor de Mello (1990–92) shut down the programme as soon as its existence was revealed. In November 1990, Presidents Collor de Mello and Carlos Menem (1989–99) of Argentina signed an international agreement renouncing the development of nuclear weapons and creating institutional verification mechanisms under the auspices of the IAEA. In 1991, under US pressure, Brazil and Argentina placed their nuclear facilities under the supervision of the IAEA and committed themselves to peaceful nuclear programmes, and in 1997 Brazil signed the Nuclear Non-Proliferation Treaty (NPT). These treaties ended the nuclear arms race in South America and heralded a new era of co-operation between Argentina and Brazil. In 2008, for example, Argentina and Brazil agreed to build a joint nuclear reactor to address potential energy shortages. However, in 2004 Brazil announced that it intended to build a uranium enrichment facility to produce fuel for its two nuclear power plants and for commercial export. The NPT allows signatory states under IAEA auspices to produce enriched uranium to power nuclear reactors, to store spent fuel, and to reprocess fuel. The announcement put further pressure on the NPT and generated renewed concern in Washington and among its allies, which fear states such as Iran, which has also been building uranium enrichment facilities, can use these to produce the plutonium needed for bombs. Brazil has the sixth largest uranium reserves in the world and has had the capacity to enrich uranium since 1980. The Brazilian constitution in fact bans the use and production of nuclear weapons, and international agreements signed by the country prohibit it as well. However, that has not stopped leading officials voicing the aspiration for Brazil to have a nuclear weapons capability. In 2003, Brazil's science and technology minister, Roberto Amaral, told the BBC's Brazilian service that his country should not rule out acquiring the scientific knowledge necessary to build an atomic bomb (bbc.co.uk, 2003). In 2009, Brazil's vice-president, José Alencar, made similar statements, arguing that Brazil should have the right to have nuclear weapons to give his country more 'respectability' in world affairs (Oppenheimer, 2009). In 2009, it was reported that Brazil is planning to co-operate with France on the construction of a hull for a nuclear-powered submarine that it wants in service by 2020 (Munks, 2009; see also Box 9.6).

■ *South–South solidarity:* Latin American states have at times tried to forge links with other developing countries in an effort to fashion an independent foreign policy, particularly during the Cold War, through affiliation with the Non-Aligned Movement (NAM) or the G77 movement that pressed for changes in international trading relations. Such initiatives have had little success, often because of differences within these movements themselves, although they have been important in shaping debates and perspectives on global affairs among their members. NAM has been influential in pushing forward the notion of 'South-South' solidarity that refers to co-operation between developing states and regions vis-à-vis the developed world. A number of Latin American countries belong to the NAM or, like Brazil, send observers to its meetings. Cuba has been at the forefront of efforts to forge links with other developing regions and has been influential within the NAM, hosting the organisation's summits in 1979 and 2006. Cuba has retained an internationalist perspective in a bid to mitigate the attempts of the US to isolate it. In September 2005, for example, Cuba announced the creation of an 'international brigade' of medics to assist countries hit by natural disasters. Cuba also provides specialist health services for thousands of poor Latin Americans who travel to the island for free medical treatment. Under an agreement with Panama, for example, Cuba promised to provide eye surgery for up to 12,000 Panamanian patients each year in a scheme that greatly helped the two countries improve diplomatic relations. In June 2006, Bolivian doctors staged protests against an influx of Cuban medics offering free care in rural and poor areas of the country. Cuba has also provided emergency medical aid for countries suffering natural disasters such as the devastating earthquake that hit Haiti in 2010.

■ *Social revolution:* The option of revolution represented a strategic alternative to US power during the Cold War, but this could only succeed with the protection of an extra-hemispheric power, and so the fate of revolutions became tied to relations between the superpowers (Smith, 2000). Revolutions in Cuba and Nicaragua provoked US hostility based on a fear of the relationship between the revolutionary regimes and the Soviet Union, although in both cases Washington's response was probably counterproductive (see Boxes 2.3, 16.2). The main questions that revolutions posed included whether the US pushed these countries closer to its adversaries, or whether they took such a step willingly for ideological reasons (Pastor, 2001).

To this list of the strategic alternatives to US dominance pursued in Latin America there can be added another option: cultural resistance (Smith, 2000). Latin American responses to US power have often taken the form of distinctive ideological outlooks and 'anti-Americanism' with an emphasis on national self-determination and identity (see Box 9.3).

At the same time, Latin American states always had the option of aligning themselves with the US in deference to its power or in pursuit of tactical advantage. The Cold War offered Latin American countries the prospect of a close association with the US, and gave the authoritarian right a strategic opportunity to invoke the cause of anti-communism to justify its claims on power (see Chapter 12). More recently, Mexico, Central American and Caribbean countries, and even those traditionally less close to Washington such as Argentina, have pursued this option by seeking an institutionalised relationship with the US through instruments such as the North American Free Trade Agreement (NAFTA) or even currency parity with the dollar. Parity with the dollar, or use of the dollar itself, has been adopted by several Latin American countries in the past. Smith (2000) has argued that such initiatives can suggest a tactical move that could unravel if it does not generate results.

The fall of the Berlin Wall in 1989 and the end of bipolar superpower tensions had important consequences for Latin America because, in the immediate term, it *further* limited the region's foreign policy options. Now there was little way of avoiding the reality of US power while the writ of international law and multilateral organisations remained limited. This has had several effects. First, without the geopolitical structure imposed by the Cold War, Latin America has received less attention from the big powers than before (Tulchin and Espach, 2001). The US and Europe both see Latin America as a promising market but not as a strategic priority (*ibid.*). The US has relegated regional issues in importance and its foreign policy priorities since 2001 have focused on the Middle East and the Islamic world. President George W. Bush (2001–09) and Secretary of State Condoleezza Rice left policymaking on Latin America to officials often portrayed as neoconservative ideologues, such as Roger Noriega, the Assistant Secretary of State for Western Hemisphere Affairs until September 2005, and the former White House aide Otto Reich. In February 2006, it was reported that Robert Zoellick, the US Deputy

SOCIETY	Box 9.3

Anti-Americanism

The danger inherent in any discussion of 'anti-Americanism' within Latin America, or any other region of the world for that matter, is that this can draw upon and reinforce generalisations and stereotypes that hinder more detailed explanations for hostile sentiments towards the US. It can also ignore the reality of 'anti-Latin American' sentiment within the US itself, which has been much in evidence from time to time among both politicians and the population, fuelled in particular by increases in Hispanic immigration (see Box 10.10). Finally, it can overlook *pro-American* sentiments that may exist in Latin America simultaneously with antipathy towards the US. In their examination of 'anti-Americanisms' across the world, Katzenstein and Keohane (2007) make a valuable distinction, for example, between 'anti-Americanism' and 'opposition to US policy', and also point out the many differences between opinion, distrust, and bias. In Venezuela, for example, Latinobarómetro data reveal that despite several years of rhetoric by political leaders hostile towards the US and a press that routinely criticises Washington, 41 per cent of Venezuelans in 2008 continued to have a favourable attitude towards the country and, in 2009, 62 per cent held favourable views of President Barack Obama (Latinobarómetro, 2008, 2009a).

McPherson (2003) has examined the phenomenon of anti-Americanism in inter-American diplomacy and points out that this co-existed with pro-Americanism in the region and was a diverse and variable sentiment, depending on the circumstances and country in which it could be found. McPherson argues that, in normal times, Latin American leaders and even fervent nationalists juggled a variety of positive and negative perceptions of the US *simultaneously*. He points out that it has been crises that have tended to intensify these perceptions, highlight their incompatibility and so test cultural and political loyalties to the US. In turn, US responses to anti-Americanism have tended to display a resilient belief that, under the right circumstances, such sentiments can be reversed. Expressions of anti-American sentiment within Latin America are, therefore, highly diverse, dynamic and very difficult to measure, and explanations for them in any given context may combine historical and cultural factors that draw upon a certain interpretation of past circumstances with more immediate political and economic factors based upon the relationship between a particular country and the US at a given moment. Latinobarómetro data also reveal, for example, that in 2001 – the year of the 9/11 attack on the World Trade Center – 73 per cent of Latin Americans had a favourable attitude towards the US, but that in 2008 this had declined to 58 per cent (Latinobarómetro, 2008). It is often implicit in media reports, for example, that the position towards the US adopted by a political leader is a reflection of the posture assumed by the population of his or her country as a whole, but this is highly misleading. The Colombian president Alvaro Uribe (2002–10) has maintained friendly relations with Washington and co-operated with its key foreign policy priorities, for example, making Colombia the key US ally and recipient of military aid in the region (see Box 10.3), while his neighbour in Venezuela, Hugo Chávez (1999–), has maintained hostile relations and used strident rhetoric denouncing US policies (see below). However, the Colombian left has long been an implacable critic of US 'imperialism' in Latin America and elements of the Venezuelan right have been in close, mutually supportive contact with Washington in their efforts to weaken the Chávez regime (see Box 7.2). Moreover, anti-Americanism is a very hard concept to define, and McPherson points out that scholars have used various terms to explain what they mean when they use this term, from an ideology, attitude, stance or tendency to a mindset, sense, predisposition, sentiment or type of bias.

Where expressions of hostility have been in evidence, these can often be explained as much by their historical and political context as by any deep-seated or residual hatred of North Americans. Expressions of hostility in Latin America to people from the North in the pre-Independence era often reflected mutual antipathy between the Anglo-Saxon and Hispanic crowns that was influenced by religious differences. Northern colonists inherited the attitudes of Great Britain and reviled the Spanish crown and its institutions as an enemy of their values, while Spanish colonists disliked and distrusted the northerners, whom they considered heretical (Smith, 2005). In the nineteenth century, expressions of mutual hostility grew more common as the young, expansionist US began to assert itself both in military terms and economically in the hemisphere and globally (see Box 1.4). Again, hostility to the cultural, political or economic influence of the US in Latin America existed alongside equally potent positive appraisals of the North as a model of republican virtue and liberal progress in all these areas. The emergence of nationalist ideology and the polarisation created by the Cold War gave anti-Americanism a more discernible political character during the twentieth century as a component of other ideologies, often subsuming it under the broader category of anti-imperialism (see Box 10.1). Anti-American sentiments that persist in the contemporary era are as contingent and variable as ever, often reflecting the political differences between an incumbent leader and

Washington in much the same way as the sentiments of antipathy that can be expressed between opposing political parties within the same legislature. Anti-American sentiments can also be associated with perceptions about an individual president. Only in Paraguay, for example, did evaluations of the US president George W. Bush during his second term (2005–09) improve. However, there are also frequent signs in Latin America of a more traditional resistance to US influence that tap into nationalistic sentiments. Violent anti-American protests were staged at the Summit of the Americas meeting of heads of state in Mar del Plata, Argentina, in November 2005, for example. Nationalism remains a potent force in Latin America and has been manifested in recent years by governments in the region questioning the neoliberal economic policies uncritically promoted by the US (see Chapters 13, 15). The Cuban government has maintained a strident anti-Americanism in the international arena and already poor relations between the Cuban regime and the US declined further during the presidency of George W. Bush (2001–09), with the Castro government putting up scores of posters in the capital Havana, for example, caricaturing Bush as both a fascist and a vampire. Venezuela's leader Chávez revived nationalist rhetoric that describes the US as a threat to regional interests and has pursued regional policies that directly challenge US influence (see Boxes 9.1, 16.1). In June 2005, at an Organisation of American States (OAS) summit in Florida, Chávez accused the US of seeking to impose a 'global dictatorship'. On other occasions, he characterised Latin American countries that supported US free-trade initiatives as 'lapdogs' and accused the US of planning to invade his country. Chávez has made high-profile purchases of Russian military hardware – including assault rifles with which to arm members of a million-strong reserve force he promised to create to resist invasion and, in 2009, also bought Sukhoi Su-30 fighter jets, T-72 battle tanks and air-defence systems (see Munks, 2009). The Venezuelan leader also proposed developing nuclear power capabilities with the help of Latin American neighbours like Brazil (see Box 9.2), and with Iran, whose own nuclear programme he vigorously defended. Angry at what he claimed were persistent destabilisation attempts by Washington, he threatened to stop oil supplies to the US and announced in June 2006 that the country would be substituting its fleet of US fighter jets with Russian aircraft. US responses to Chávez's posturing grew angrier over time, and in February 2006 the then defence secretary Donald Rumsfeld likened the Venezuelan leader's rise to power to that of Germany's Nazi leader Adolf Hitler. In April 2006, Washington accused Venezuelan officials of being complicit in an attack in Caracas on the car of the US ambassador to Venezuela. Bolivia's leftwing leader Evo Morales (2006–) has also adopted rhetoric that is highly critical of the US.

Yet at the same time, both the Cuban and Venezuelan governments have tried to reach out to poorer sectors of American society. In the aftermath of Hurricane Katrina in 2005, for example, Cuba offered to send 1,500 doctors to the US, although Washington did not respond to the offer. Alongside its strident criticisms, Venezuela has also courted US public opinion, offering help in the wake of Hurricane Katrina and concessionary fuel rates to poorer urban areas in the US.

Anti-American feelings when combined with nationalism are remarkably durable (see Katzenstein and Keohane, 2007). Cuban anti-Americanism is given force by continuing economic and political differences between the two countries that have their origins in the Cold War but also in a more complex and longer relationship that began during Cuba's nationalist struggle for independence in the late nineteenth century (see Boxes 2.3, 10.6). In Puerto Rico in mid-2005, the death of Filiberto Ojeda Rios, a fugitive nationalist, in a shootout with FBI agents provoked protests in San Juan, the capital. Puerto Rico was taken over by the US after its victory against Spain in Cuba in 1898 and is so thoroughly integrated into the political system that Puerto Ricans are US citizens. None the less, alongside currents of opinion that favour the status quo or enhancements to it, there continue to exist nationalist political sentiments and demands (see Box 13.2).

Secretary of State, had warned Rice about the danger of neglecting Latin America (Webb-Vidal, 2006). There have been signs that President Barack Obama (2009–) has been raising the importance of Latin America in US foreign policy.

One result of this disinterest has been the predominance of military-to-military ties between the US and Latin American armed forces, often outside the scrutiny of democratic institutions. Diamint (2004) argued that, as a result, the US Southern Command – responsible for all US military activities in Central America, the Caribbean and South America – has acquired a 'dangerous autonomy' resulting in proposals for forms of military co-operation that may in fact be unlawful (Diamint, 2004, p. 54). At the same time, Europe has become preoccupied with the tensions within its own integration project and security on its south-eastern borders (see Chapter 11). Latin America has not been a high priority partly because it does not pose a threat to the states that dominate world affairs. Nor have Latin American countries been assertive in projecting their power in the global system, and they are not among the most influential players in international affairs (*ibid.*). Tulchin and Espach (2001) argue that Latin American states were unsure how to take advantage of the new circumstances of the 1990s; have shown little confidence and a lack of strategic thinking in exploring options for enhanced global roles; and continue to fixate on the principle of sovereignty. While not being a US priority may have given Latin Americans more room for manoeuvre, Tulchin and Espach argue that the legacy of US power has continued to weigh heavily upon Latin American countries and these continue to define their strategic options in terms of how best to respond to the US. Smith (2000) agrees that Latin American leaders have little choice but to follow US policy prescriptions and seek accommodation with Washington and the advanced industrial countries.

However, by encouraging a shift away from anti-communist dictatorships and broadening the ideological spectrum of governments the US had to do business with, the new post-Cold War circumstances gradually renewed a need for Washington to employ *diplomacy*. The relaxation of Cold War security tensions offered the prospect of building a regional consensus on principles such as free trade and integration. Yet there have been contradictory tendencies in Latin American diplomatic relations. A round of hemispheric summits got underway in the 1990s, offering a new model of relations between Latin America and the US based on consensus (*ibid.*). These summits (usually excluding Cuba) were important because they treated all the region's democracies as equals and depended for their success on the co ordinated progress of all the participants. By contrast, proposals to establish NAFTA were perceived as an effort to create an exclusive bloc that threatened the access of other Latin American states to the US market. The deepening of US–Latin American relations was also slowed down by US domestic issues, with support for further integration waning in Washington and President Bill Clinton (1993–2001) unable to secure 'fast-track' negotiating power to press ahead with an extension of the free trade agenda (see Box 15.5). Observers in Latin America saw this as a sign that the US could be an unreliable partner in the project of hemispheric integration.

Since the fall of the socialist bloc, the watchwords of international relations in Latin America have been autonomy and globalisation, the increasingly transnational nature of capitalist development that reflects the emergence of a new international order since the end of the Cold War (see Box 15.6). In this new order, the US initially enjoyed military pre-eminence alongside a new economic 'multipolarity' based on centres of growth in different regions of the world. As a result, the post-Cold War world has become 'multi-layered' because of the uneven distribution of international economic and political power (*ibid.*). None the less, Western values have been spreading worldwide through democracy, the free market and communications technology, and these have been enshrined in emergent supra-national legal mechanisms such as the World Trade Organisation (WTO). The arrest in the UK in 1998 of Chile's former dictator Augusto Pinochet (1973–90) on murder charges at the request of Spain is evidence of an international discourse of universal human rights that challenges the principle of national sovereignty (see Farer ed., 1996). There is much evidence of the ability of the 'international community' to enforce its power upon national governments.

However, the damage to perceptions of the US generated by the war in Iraq and the rise of left-of-centre governments asserting an autonomous foreign policy have tested this new order. At the same time, there has been an inconsistency by global powers in the application of the values implied by the discourse of universal human rights. Washington has, at times, adopted apparently contradictory positions on human rights towards China and the Middle East, for example. The international debate about its incarceration of terrorist suspects at Guantánamo Bay in Cuba highlighted a contingent US approach to the universality of human rights. The rise of Brazil as a regional power and increased arms spending throughout Latin America by countries that have a difficult relationship with Washington, such as Venezuela, also suggest that US military pre-eminence can no longer be taken for granted in Latin America (see Munks, 2009).

Enhanced activity by multilateral institutions, non-state actors and transnational corporations, social movements and NGOs as well as organised crime (see Box 4.3, Chapter 8) have also complicated a picture of international relations traditionally based on sovereign-nation states, and thus challenge traditional ideas of sovereignty (Smith, 2001). International NGOs and social networks have demonstrated a capacity to influence domestic policies around the world on issues such as human rights and environmentalism. The internationalisation of investment has increased the power of multi-national corporations, and these increasingly influence the agendas of institutions such as the World Bank. When they fail, as during the financial crisis of 2008, their transnational visibility is reinforced as the impact of reduced investment bites hard in developing countries. Growing interest in the concept of economic globalisation is a product of this transformation (see Chapter 15; see also Cooper and Heine eds, 2009). But the establishment of alternative regional institutions that aim to temper globalisation – such as the Banco del Sur (see below) – are also a product of multipolarity.

Today, options available in the foreign relations of Latin American states are also shaped by widening differences between individual countries and between sub-regions such as the Andes and the Southern Cone. The effects of globalisation have been uneven and processes of regional integration are widening these differences, suggesting each country will pursue its own interests as it seeks greater insertion in the world economy. For example, Ecuador, Costa Rica and other Central American nations joined forces with the US banana industry in a lawsuit at the

WTO that had important implications for the industry in relatively close Caribbean countries (Tulchin and Espach, 2001). The creation of the Dominican Republic–Central American Free Trade Agreement (DR-CAFTA), a free trade agreement that also encompasses the US which came into force in 2009, is an example of sub-regional integration premised on a vision of globalisation, although past such efforts in Central America have not prospered (see below).

An international system characterised by increasing globalisation has important implications for domestic policies. First, economic integration means domestic policy decisions have *international* implications and so internal disputes can weaken foreign relations. In Brazil in 1999, for example, public disagreements between Itamar Franco, the governor of Minas Gerais state, and President Fernando Enrique Cardoso (1995–2003) over the repayment of federal loans precipitated a dramatic currency devaluation that contributed to economic recession across the Southern Cone. At the same time, the international community can modify domestic decisions. In Venezuela, scepticism among international investors forced Chávez to modify plans to close down congress and the supreme court as part of a commitment to rewriting the constitution. These links between domestic and foreign policy have prompted some scholars to develop the notion of 'intermestic' issues simultaneously involving both foreign and domestic actors and decisionmaking processes (van Klaveren, 2001).

Policy options

Tulchin and Espach (2001) argue that an 'institutionalist' account of international behaviour, by which a country's influence is partly determined by the nature and extent of its involvement in international institutions, is suitable for assessing Latin American policy options in the context of globalisation (see Box 9.4). Institutionalist theory suggests that international institutions benefit less powerful states in two ways: they offer them a more equal forum for the expression and pursuit of their interests; and the commitment of powerful countries to these institutions restrains these from acting unilaterally and gives them incentives to pursue their interests through multilateral initiatives (*ibid.*).

However, effective insertion into the international system is not a one-way process. On the one hand, it can imply the opening up of politics to foreign scrutiny in the quest for greater international legitimacy. The international monitoring of elections has grown considerably in Latin America, with countries such as Mexico overturning generations of tradition by opening up its polls to foreign observers in 1994, and the OAS and UN monitoring a string of elections in troubled countries such as El Salvador, Guatemala, Paraguay and Haiti. The OAS operates a Unit for the Promotion of Democracy which has observed elections in a majority of its member states and supports efforts to decentralise governments, modernise parties, strengthen legislatures and consolidate democratic values (see Box 9.5). On the other hand, effective insertion in the international system can imply even further political change. Chile, for example, embraced the rules of the emerging international system and enjoyed influence in the 1990s as a model of neoliberal reform and

---

THEORIES AND DEBATES **Box 9.4**

Institutionalism and realism

Institutionalist perspectives in international relations offer an alternative position to influential *realist* perspectives that assume the existence of an international arena without order characterised by inter-state conflict and the self-interested pursuit of power by sovereign nation-states (Tulchin and Espach, 2001; see also Goldstein and Pevehouse, 2009). Realists believe that, in the absence of a frame-work within which this pursuit of power can be managed – such as that provided by the Cold War rivalry between the US and Soviet Union – the world is dangerous and contentious. They argue that international institutions and alliances such as the United Nations or the North Atlantic Treaty Organisation (NATO) are valued by dominant parties pragmatically only to the extent that they are useful to them. Institutionalist perspectives, by contrast, point to growing interdependence and shared interests and values among states, which increasingly pursue their interests through international institutions based on rules and norms of conduct. Institutions are changing the relations between states and their behaviour and strategies, and raise the costs of conflict between states and provide incentives for their peaceful resolution. Power is defined not just by military might but by economic competitive-ness, skills and high-technology capacity, and the ability to assert influence abroad. Tulchin and Espach (2001) suggest that for countries in Latin America that have little power in the realist sense, partici-pation in international institutions offers ways of enhancing their influence. Critics of the institution-alist perspective argue that the patterns of behaviour it draws attention to will function so long as these benefit the powerful countries that dominate institutions, set the rules and pressure weaker countries to follow them in order to maintain their dominant position.

---

democratic transition, but this did not exempt it from further interventions by the international community regarding its human rights legacy and judicial processes following the arrest of Pinochet. International legitimacy requires more than rhetorical adherence to the values and objectives of the international community, and countries that do not measure up to its standards in punishing human rights violations are at particular risk of condemnation (Tulchin and Espach, 2001).

Five key themes emerge in the analysis of Latin American international relations today: sovereignty, multilateralism, regionalism, security and democracy.

Sovereignty

One product of the new international context has been the redefinition by Latin American governments of a traditional understanding of sovereignty that rejected any interference in the domestic affairs of a nation-state by an outside power. This traditional interpretation of sovereignty has long been a defining characteristic of international relations in Latin America and was embedded in Article 18 of the Charter of the OAS which prohibits member states from interference for any reason in the internal or external affairs of any state (Pastor, 2001; see Box 9.5). Acute Latin American sensitivities about sovereignty have often derived from memories of past interventions. Mexico and Nicaragua have been particularly vigorous in defending their sovereignty to prevent the US from interfering in their affairs (*ibid.*).

INSTITUTIONS	Box 9.5

The Organisation of American States

The idea of inter-American co-operation dates to the Independence era and first gained institutional form in 1890 when the Commercial Bureau of American Republics was formed by countries in the region. This evolved into the Pan-American Union and later into the OAS, which was created in 1948 when 21 countries in the hemisphere signed the OAS Charter outlining shared goals and mutual respect for sovereignty and adopted the American Declaration of the Rights and Duties of Man. The OAS expanded to include the nations of the English-speaking Caribbean and Canada after 1967, and all 35 independent countries of North, Central and South America and the Caribbean now belong to the organisation and have ratified its charter. It is based in Washington and has four official languages: English, Spanish, Portuguese and French. In 1962, the government of Cuba was excluded from participation in OAS affairs, although in 2009 the OAS voted to lift this long suspension. Although Cuba welcomed the decision, it said it had no immediate plans to participate in the OAS.

Once a year, OAS member states agree goals and policies through its general assembly comprising the foreign ministers of countries in the hemisphere. A permanent council made up of ambassadors appointed to the OAS by member states meets regularly. The OAS acts multilaterally to strengthen co-operation, and established from its inception a commitment to democracy, good governance, human rights, peace and security. Since the end of the Cold War, member states have intensified their co-operation and, at the landmark First Summit of the Americas in Miami in 1994, the region's democratically elected leaders agreed broad political, economic and development objectives. Key areas of activity in which the OAS has a prominent role include scrutinising human rights and strengthening democracy. In 1959, it created the Inter-American Commission on Human Rights (IACHR/CIDH), which is based in Washington, and in 1969 members agreed the American Convention on Human Rights which led to the establishment of the Inter-American Court of Human Rights based in Costa Rica. In June 1991, the OAS General Assembly approved the 'Santiago Commitment' containing resolutions on democracy, which mandated an immediate meeting of the OAS permanent council following the rupture of democratic rule in any country of the Americas and the adoption of procedures to promote and defend democracy regardless of the international repercussions (van Klaveren, 2001). In September 2001, member states of the OAS adopted the Inter-American Democratic Charter laying down the essential elements of democracy and establishing guidelines for responding when it is considered at risk in the region. In 2009, for example, the OAS suspended Honduras from participation in its affairs following the coup against President Manuel Zelaya (see Box 7.10). The OAS also works to enhance security co-operation and to counter drug-trafficking and corruption, issues which are often related (see for example Kaufmann, 2004). Its Inter-American Council for Integral Development (CIDI) promotes economic development, and the Inter-American Agency for Co-Operation and Development (IACD/AICD) was formed in 2000 to promote new and more effective forms of co-operation to fight poverty. Although the OAS has often been derided as a vehicle of US domination, Latin American countries have gained increasing influence over its affairs. In May 2005, the Chilean socialist interior minister José Miguel Insulza was elected secretary general of the OAS after gaining the support of a number of leftwing governments against a rival candidate from Mexico who was backed by the US. Insulza's election exposed divisions within the organisation, which had traditionally chosen a candidate that has US support. Most of South America and the Caribbean supported the Chilean, while North and Central America supported the Mexican. In February 2010 at a summit between members of the Rio Group (see Box 9.10) and the Caribbean Community (Caricom) in Cancún, Mexico, Latin American leaders reportedly discussed plans for a new pan-American alliance excluding the US and Canada that would serve as an alternative to the OAS.

In October 2005, for example, Nicaraguan politicians condemned comments by Robert Zoellick about a former president, Arnoldo Alemán (see Box 4.4), as an effort to interfere in the country's political process. In April 2006, the US State Department reportedly called on Nicaraguans not to vote for the former Sandinista leader, Daniel Ortega, in presidential elections scheduled for November and Washington's ambassador to Nicaragua held talks with rightwing politicians aimed at fostering an alliance to oppose Ortega.

Sensitivity towards sovereignty often takes the form of a reaction to territorial incursions. The bombing by the Colombian air force of a guerrilla camp within neighbouring Ecuador in 2008, for example, caused serious tensions in the region and resulted in the Ecuadorean president, Rafael Correa, severing diplomatic relations with his neighbour. Several other OAS member states also broke off relations with Colombia as a result of the cross-border raid.

However, the impact of globalisation has challenged the traditional understanding of sovereignty as a political phenomenon and has made it more *relative*. Economic interdependence, the extension of the discourse of human rights, the desire for legitimacy in international arenas, the emergence of transnational corporations, NGOs and social movements, and shared concerns about environmental degradation have all tested the sovereignty once enjoyed by nation-states. Universal human rights, for example, imply that individual human beings have rights that can be sustained *against* the sovereignty of the state in which they live, and violations of these rights are increasingly being met with co-ordinated political action by several states at once (van Klaveren, 2001). While still controversial, international intervention on behalf of democracy is also clearly no longer restrained by the principle of non-intervention (*ibid.*; see Chapter 3).

In 1990, the government of Mexico began to redefine its traditional position on sovereignty when President Salinas de Gortari abandoned the economic nationalism of the past and proposed free trade with the US (Pastor, 2001). The Mexican president argued that the best defence of a country's political and economic system is to open it up to free economic exchanges and commerce (*ibid.*). Mexico's relations with the US have since been strengthened in other areas, and disagreements surrounding policies concerning the US–Mexican border have increasingly been discussed in bilateral institutions of liaison and co-ordination (see Box 10.9). In Nicaragua in 1990, the nationalistic Sandinista government redefined the notion of political sovereignty by inviting the UN, OAS and Carter Centre to observe its elections – thereby linking sovereignty with democratic legitimacy (*ibid.*). In June 2005 at an OAS summit in Florida, Condoleezza Rice highlighted US concerns about political crises in Bolivia, Ecuador and Haiti and called for greater OAS intervention in promoting democracy in Latin America. This role of the OAS was invoked by Latin American states themselves following the coup in Honduras in 2009 against President Manuel Zelaya (see Box 7.10).

None the less, elements of the traditional state system endure and are resistant to these processes. Many countries are reluctant to accept compulsory jurisdiction of the International Court of Justice in The Hague, and the principle of sovereignty in interstate affairs remains strong in Latin America. Latin American politicians routinely complain that the US lacks respect for their sovereignty while demanding that its own sovereign rights be upheld, and there are many examples of continuing tensions deriving from a traditional defence of sovereignty. In 2004, for example, the US embassy complained to the Mexican government about actions 'inconsistent with diplomatic protocol' after Mexican troops had interrupted the funeral of a US marine who had died in Iraq and was being buried in the town of his birth, Guanajuato. At a meeting of the OAS in 2005, the US circulated a proposal calling for an institutionalised mechanism to monitor democratic trends in the Americas which was criticised by a number of countries as an invitation for political interference in their affairs. The OAS secretary general, José Miguel Insulza, said he thought such a mechanism would exceed the OAS charter.

Disputes over sovereignty also occur *between* Latin American states. In November 2005, the Bolivian government attacked what it considered to be interference in its internal affairs following critical comments by Venezuela's acting ambassador to the country about the rightwing candidate in the following month's presidential elections. Relations between Venezuela and Peru also suffered following derogatory exchanges between the Venezuelan leader Hugo Chávez and the candidate who went on to win Peru's April 2006 presidential elections, the former president Alan García (1985–90, 2006–). Chávez had made no secret of his preference for the nationalist candidate, Ollanta Humala, in the poll (see Box 13.3). Peru responded by recalling its ambassador from Venezuela, accusing Chávez of trying to interfere in its elections and prompting Venezuela to respond in the same way. García later declared that his election victory represented a blow to Chávez, but subsequently also sought to repair the strained relationship with Venezuela.

Multilateralism

In the 1990s there was a shift in favour of multilateralism, an approach to issues in which states act co-operatively and by consensus based on shared interests. Domínguez (2000) argues that the growth of multilateral approaches in Latin America resulted from four factors. First, the end of the Cold War freed the US from previous policy options in the region, allowing Latin Americans, in turn, to consider the US as an ally and seek its support for policy solutions. Second, the collapse of communism was accompanied by democratisation in Latin America, which seemed more effective when promoted multilaterally. Third, it was multilateral institutions that fostered the consensus in favour of free trade after the economic crises of the 1980s (see Chapter 15). Fourth, the US itself has come to rely on multilateral agencies as a substitute for its own economic aid to Latin American countries, which have turned to these institutions to cope with their own financial instability. Domínguez identifies several types of multilateral activity:

- *Commercial multilateralism* – Trade agreements are becoming important because of the growth in intra-regional exports (see Tables 9.1 and 9.2), and this commercial multilateralism has built upon inter-American institutions such as the Inter-American Development Bank (IADB or IDB) and the Economic Commission for Latin America and the Caribbean (ECLAC/CEPAL).

- *Political multilateralism* – Multilateralism has taken a political form in support of democratisation in Latin America, and democracy 'defence clauses' pledging to safeguard constitutional government have been written into a host of regional declarations by bodies such as the OAS (see Box 9.5). For example, concerns about the condition of democracy in Venezuela, and in particular the government's actions against media outlets in the country (see Chapter 8), held up progress of the ratification of Venezuela's application to join the South American trading bloc Mercosur in Brazil's senate until December 2009, and continues to hold this up in Paraguay (see Box 9.9).

■ *Security multilateralism* – Multilateralism has also spread to security areas. The UN and OAS played an important role in ending the Central American civil wars of the 1980s and 1990s, for example (see Chapters 2, 12), and were supported in this by such regional bodies as the European Community (see Chapter 11). Some countries have taken a more proactive position in security policy: Argentina became an active participant in UN peacekeeping efforts and sent forces to the Persian Gulf in 1991 and has been active in deployments in Croatia and Bosnia, the Central American Gulf of Fonseca, Cypus and Haiti. Troops from Bolivia, Brazil, Chile, Paraguay, Peru and Uruguay were also embedded in the Argentine mission in Cyprus, setting a precedent for the Latin American military. Troops from El Salvador, Honduras, the Dominican Republic and Nicaragua participated in the multi-national coalition based in Iraq following the US-led invasion of the country in 2003. Brazil, Argentina, Chile, Peru, Uruguay, Guatemala, Ecuador and Bolivia all contributed soldiers or police to the UN peacekeeping force in Haiti in 2004, the first time a UN force has been established with South American troops in a clear majority and with these leading the political and military sides of the operation. Latin American countries have also supported multilateral approaches to tackling international crime (see Domínguez, 2000). Brazil has assumed an increasingly prominent profile in regional security in recent years (see Box 9.6).

TRENDS   **Box 9.6**

Brazil – Latin America's first superpower?

Brazil's role in the Honduran crisis reflects a new assertiveness under President Luiz Inácio Lula da Silva (2003–10), who has systematically expanded his country's international influence with a foreign policy premised on the belief that it has become the logical South American 'pole' in a new multipolar order following the end of the Cold War. This assertiveness is borne of a confidence founded on impressive economic growth, which is turning Brazil, to all intents and purposes, into an agro-export superpower.

Da Silva's administration has sought allies across the world to support his country's vigorous bid for a permanent seat on the UN Security Council, which it is likely to gain. The administration has also, in the process, forged powerful alliances with China, India and South Africa, all of which have shared interests in reforming multilateral organisations. Brazil played a decisive influence in the displacement of the G8 grouping of major economies by the G20, for example.

Da Silva has also placed considerable emphasis on modernising Brazil's outdated armed forces while stressing that this is a non-offensive strategy, and the country's arms spending now vastly outpaces that of its neighbours, with $24.6 billion spent on defence in 2008 compared to $12.3

billion by its closest rival, Colombia. Recent arms deals by Brazil include plans to buy Scorpene attack submarines and Rafale fighter aircraft from France, and to build EC-725 transport helicopters under licence. As part of its effort to project its military power, in 2008 the Brazilian defence ministry formulated a strategy that placed considerable emphasis on the development of the country's defence industry and strategic partnerships with allied nations that include technology transfer. For example, in 2008 the Brazilian airline company Embraer showcased a transport aircraft, the KC-390, and the country also boasts a thriving helicopter industry (see Box 14.5). In 2009, ministers tasked the Brazilian navy with developing a 30-year security strategy based on expenditure in the region of $138 billion that will involve, among other things, buying or building two aircraft carriers and five nuclear submarines (see above). Leading Brazilian officials have also voiced an aspiration for the country to have a nuclear weapons capability (see Box 9.2), although this seems unlikely.

An impressive economic performance has provided a solid foundation for these developments. Brazil is fast becoming an agri-business superpower and a major exporter of energy and minerals (see Wheatley, 2009). It has become the world's biggest exporter of beef, chicken, orange juice, green coffee, sugar, ethanol, tobacco and soya beans, meal and oil, as well as the world's fourth largest exporter of maize and pork – and that is without having made use of a third of its available agricultural land (without even including environmentally off-limits regions such as the Amazon rainforest). Record prices for soya, iron ore and steel exports had helped Brazil to accrue international reserves of a record $224.2 billion by 2009 and bring infrastructure investment in new airports, highways, ports, and other facilities throughout the country by 2010 to a staggering $359 billion. The state-run oil company Petrobras has discovered huge reserves of oil in deep waters off the coast of Rio de Janeiro and São Paulo that could turn Brazil into one of the world's leading oil producers and exporters within a decade. Petrobras has begun a five-year, $174 billion investment programme to double Brazil's production to 3.5 million barrels a day by 2012. This performance has helped the country achieve investment-grade rating for its sovereign debt, putting it in the premier league of stable global economies, as well as almost unstoppable growth. Although the economy was expected to shrink in 2009, it was likely to recover to up to 5.3 per cent in 2010 by some estimates. Brazil has also been making its presence felt culturally. As if to underline its new status, it will host both the 2014 Fifa World Cup and the 2016 Summer Olympics. Brazil has also achieved growing importance as a centre of scientific innovation and, in 2007, its scientists produced over 12,000 papers – more than the combined output of Argentina, Chile and Mexico (Rocha, 2009). Although the Lula administration has tried to avoid creating the impression that Brazil is positioning itself to become a peacekeeping power in the style of the US, it is likely that Washington accepts Brazil's claim to regional leadership, largely because it cannot prevent this happening and sees it as the best way of counterbalancing the efforts by the Venezuelan president, Hugo Chávez, to create an anti-US bloc in the region based also on an increase in military capacity (see, for example, Munks, 2009). The military doctrine of Venezuela under the leadership of Chávez has been founded on a hypothetical US invasion launched from Colombia in an effort to engineer regime change or seize control of his country's oilfields, and Chávez has used this argument to justify a significant increase in spending on weapons from countries such as Russia (see Boxes 9.8, 10.3, 11.5). However, Brazil may also be nervous about Venezuela's support for Iran's nuclear programme and any suggestion that what has hitherto been only talk of nuclear co-operation between the countries may turn into reality (see Oppenheimer, 2009).

None the less, there have been signs that the relationship between Brazil and the US is one of rivalry as well as convenience. Da Silva has criticised the US for demonising Chávez and urged Washington to seek dialogue with the Venezuelan leader; Washington, meanwhile, criticised Brazil's role in 'facilitating' the return of Manuel Zelaya to Honduras following the coup that ousted him in 2009.

Table 9.1 Latin American intra-regional merchandise trade, 2006–08 (billions of dollars)

	Destination:	World	North America*		South and Central America**
Origin:			Total	United States	
World	**2006**	11812.00	2365.19	1816.55	362.78
	2007	13656.00	2517.69	1922.82	447.93
	2008	15717.00	2708.31	2058.99	582.70
North America*	**2006**	1664.08	902.39	528.41	106.22
	2007	1840.30	951.60	555.06	129.52
	2008	2035.68	1014.49	587.86	164.88
US	**2006**	1025.97	364.92	–	87.25
	2007	1148.20	385.42	–	105.35
	2008	1287.44	413.15	–	134.98
South and Central America*	**2006**	435.28	145.63	126.94	101.48
	2007	497.60	149.71	130.80	122.87
	2008	599.66	169.19	149.35	158.62

*Includes Mexico and Bermuda

**Includes the Caribbean

Source: WTO, 2009

Regionalism and integration

Regional integration has long been an aspiration of Latin American political elites, and has become an important theme in regional affairs (see Chapter 15; see also Mace *et al.*, 1999). A first wave of integration initiatives began in the 1960s as an effort to boost industrialisation under the aegis of CEPAL, and were inspired by the Treaty of Rome that had led to the creation of the European Economic Community in 1958 (see Chapter 2). CEPAL saw the abolition of barriers to exports and imports within Latin America itself as a way of promoting the development of a market for industrial goods and reducing the impact of external shocks on the region (see Box 14.3). The first integration effort was the creation of the Asociación Latinoamericana de Libre Comercio (ALALC, Latin American Free Trade Association, LAFTA) through the Treaty of Montevideo in 1960, which eventually incorporated 10 South American countries and Mexico. LAFTA had limited success and did not achieve its aim of abolishing intra-regional tariffs. The Treaty of Montevideo expired in 1980 and LAFTA was replaced by the Asociación Latinoamericana de Integración (ALADI, Latin American Integration Association, LAIA), but this was badly affected by the debt crisis that began in 1982, although it has since gained a new lease of life. In 1960, the Mercado Común Centroamericano (MCCA, Central American Common Market, CACM) was formed by Guatemala, Honduras, El Salvador and Nicaragua as a means of nurturing industry. It collapsed in 1969 because of tensions between member countries, but was revived in 1991 and is generally considered to have generated

Table 9.2 Latin American merchandise trade of selected regional trade agreements, 2000–08 (billions of dollars)

	2000	2001	2002	2003	2004	2005	2006	2007	2008
NAFTA									
Total exports	1225	1148	1106	1163	1320	1476	1664	1840	2036
Intra-exports	680	633	621	650	739	824	901	950	1013
Extra-exports	544	515	486	513	581	651	763	890	1022
Total imports	1687	1583	1604	1727	2012	2287	2545	2706	2911
Intra-imports	671	629	620	642	718	793	867	918	968
Extra-imports	1016	954	984	1085	1294	1494	1678	1788	1943
MERCOSUR									
Total exports	85	88	89	106	136	164	190	224	278
Intra-exports	18	15	10	13	17	21	26	32	42
Extra-exports	67	73	79	93	119	143	164	191	237
Total imports	90	84	62	69	95	114	141	184	259
Intra-imports	18	16	11	13	18	22	26	34	45
Extra-imports	72	68	52	56	77	91	114	150	214
Andean Community									
Total exports	26	25	26	30	39	51	65	77	94
Intra-exports	2	2	3	3	3	5	5	6	7
Extra-exports	24	23	23	27	36	47	60	71	87
Total imports	25	27	28	31	37	46	56	71	93
Intra-imports	2	3	3	3	4	5	6	7	9
Extra-imports	22	25	25	27	33	41	50	64	85

Source: WTO, 2009

net benefits to its members, although these have been uneven. In 1969, frustrated by limited progress under ALALC, Andean countries formed the Grupo Andino (Andean Pact, AP) whose original members were Bolivia, Chile, Colombia, Ecuador and Peru, with Venezuela joining in 1973. The AP also had limited success at establishing a common tariff and Chile withdrew in 1976 when its own economic policies proved incompatible with continued membership. AP has survived as the Comunidad Andina de Naciones (CAN, Andean Community of Nations), although Andean integration efforts faced a significant challenge in 2006 when Venezuela decided to leave CAN because some of its member states were negotiating and/or concluding free-trade agreements with the US. The four remaining countries renewed their commitment to the Andean Community and its regional integration process, however, and Chile later announced that it was interested in resuming its participation as an associate member.

These initial efforts at integration encountered considerable economic and political problems, and by the mid-1970s they had lost momentum even though intra-regional trade itself continued to increase. There had hitherto been little harmonisation of economic policies in the region, where there existed great economic disparities between different countries; only certain countries tended to dominate trade, which was also sensitive to international cycles; expectations for greater trade put much emphasis on the private sector, which in fact had a limited ability to expand; and states disagreed about removing protection for their individual industries. Latin American countries participating in these early integration experiments also lacked the political commitment to closer co-operation that their European counterparts had developed as a result of two world wars, and were weakened by their differences. Within the AP, for example, political differences between Chile's rightwing regime under General Augusto Pinochet (1973–90) and left-leaning governments in other states such as Peru exacerbated the pressure that led to Chile's withdrawal in 1976.

With the end of the Cold War a new spirit of continentalism based on regional integration was evident in the hemisphere (see Bulmer-Thomas ed., 2001). The largest regional integration initiative, ALADI, incorporates 12 member states from Mexico to Argentina and today serves as an institutional umbrella organisation promoting closer regional economic integration with the ambition of creating a common market. CAN and the South American trading bloc Mercosur (see Box 9.9) came together in 2008 to form the intergovernmental integration initiative, the Unión de Naciones Suramericanas (Unasur, Union of South American Nations) modelled on the European Union and backed by its own regional investment bank to fund economic and social projects, the Banco del Sur, which is likely to grow in importance following the 2008–09 global financial crisis. A key objective of Unasur is the creation of a single market by 2019 that eliminates cross-border tariffs by combining existing integration institutions. An important aim of integration established for Unasur in its founding treaty is the elimination of inequality, giving the initiative a social dimension. In this sense, it has been argued that its creation represents both the deepening of a social agenda alongside the Latin Americanisation of regional politics (see Lievesley and Ludlam, 2009). In 2009, the Dominican Republic–Central American Free Trade Agreement (DR-CAFTA), a free trade agreement that also encompasses the US came into force.

Such developments underline how trade has driven the integration process, and in the 1990s Latin America became the fastest growing market in the world for US goods. In 1994, NAFTA came into force and the Miami Summit launched the Free Trade Area of the Americas (FTAA) project (see Box 15.5), which has ultimately foundered but established the notion of hemispheric free trade as an important aspiration. Although it has fluctuated and has been hit by sub-regional downturns, intra-regional trade within Latin America, particularly trade between the Mercosur countries, has grown rapidly since the mid-1990s and today is vigorous (see Tables 9.1 and 9.2).

Large infrastructure and media projects that transcend national borders are also driving co-operation, such as the energy pipelines linking Argentina and Chile; a proposed $10 billion, 6,000-mile network of pipelines to pump Venezuela's natural gas across South America; and regional media initiatives such as TeleSUR (see Box 13.4). Ambitious engineers are even dreaming up projects on a previously unthinkable scale: in 2009, for example, Chilean architects proposed the construction of a 93-mile tunnel linking Bolivia to the Pacific Ocean to allow the landlocked country to regain access to the sea for the first time since it was defeated by Chile in the Pacific War in 1879. Chile's foreign minister, Mariano Fernández, called for further studies into the project, saying that Chile was open to suggestions of this kind that fostered Latin American integration (see Smink, 2009). The private sector is also playing an important role in forging economic ties (see Chapters 7, 15).

Regional integration initiatives have had important political implications in Latin America, contributing to the strengthening of stable, democratic governance. Political forums such as the Parlatino in Brazil have started to make a valuable contribution to regional affairs (see Box 9.7).

Security

The economic crisis of the 1980s, the end of the Cold War and growing multi-lateralism have eased military competition and bilateral tensions in some potential hotspots in Latin America, especially the Southern Cone and Central American countries, while exacerbating the potential for confrontation in others, particularly Venezuela and Colombia. Hotspots defined by disputes or tensions can be identified throughout Latin America (see Figure 9.1).

In Central America, since the peace processes of the 1990s there has been a trend towards demilitarisation and the redefinition of former 'national security' priorities

---

INSTITUTIONS	Box 9.7

Parlatino

The Parlamento Latinoamericano (Parlatino, Latin American Parliament) was created in Lima in 1964 as a forum representing different political tendencies whose initial aim was to promote and co-ordinate integration efforts within Latin America. It has developed into a permanent regional forum based in Brazil representing and bringing together Latin American legislatures, which send delegates to participate in it, and has received delegations from the European Parliament (see Chapter 11). Meetings have been held between representatives from the European Parliament and Parlatino since 1974, and mutual exchanges have taken place. Parlatino representatives also sit on EuroLat (the Euro-Latin American Parliamentary Assembly), a bi-regional assembly comprising members from the European Parliament and Latin American counterparts. Parlatino's objectives derived from the traditional foreign policy preoccupations of Latin American states, including non-intervention, self-determination and respect within international law for the juridical equality of states. It allows legislators to debate issues of common concern across borders and provides a regional platform for them to pronounce on international themes and raise controversial issues. In March 2003, for example, Parlatino rejected any attempt by the US to take unilateral action in Iraq and called for a multilateral solution through the UN in order to avoid war. It has also made vocal commitments to the defence of democracy and promotion of human rights. Parlatino deputies have on several occasions voiced support for the independence of Puerto Rico (see Boxes 10.6, 13.2). In 2009, for example, Carolus Wimmer, a member of Venezuela's Parlatino delegation, reiterated calls for the UN to reopen the debate on Puerto Rico's status in 2010 (see Milet, 2009).

Figure 9.1 Hotspots in Latin America*

Key:

Border/territorial disputes
1 Guatemala-Belize: Border demarcation
2 Honduras-El Salvador: Border demarcation; migration
3 Honduras-Nicaragua: Migration
4 Nicaragua-Costa Rica: Border demarcation; migration
5 Nicaragua-Colombia: Territorial dispute over San Andrés and Providencia Islands
6 Colombia-Venezuela: Thirty-four points on border in dispute; migration; guerrillas; contraband, including but not limited to drugs
7 Haiti-Dominican Republic: Migration; border demarcation
8 Bolivia-Chile: Territorial dispute; outlet to the Pacific
9 Peru-Ecuador: Border demarcation (largely resolved)

Maritime disputes
1 Honduras-El Salvador-Nicaragua: Demarcation of maritime borders in Gulf of Fonseca; depletion of fisheries
2 Honduras-Nicaragua: Demarcation of maritime border in Atlantic
3 Venezuela-Trinidad & Tobago: Maritime boundaries; resources
4 Peru-Chile: Maritime boundaries

Energy disputes
1 Bolivia-Brazil-Argentina: Tensions caused by Bolivian gas nationalisation
2 Argentina-Brazil: Disagreement over share of Bolivian gas
3 Paraguay-Brazil: Disagreement over benefits from Itaipú dam
4 Bolivia-Chile: Territorial issues likely to limit gas supplies
5 Peru-Chile: Maritime issues likely to limit gas supplies

*1995-present

Sources: Adapted from Mares, 2000; Rojas Aravena, 1997; news reports (see Chapter 7, Box 10.2). Democratisation proceeded alongside the reform of security institutions in El Salvador and Guatemala, where demilitarisation included the disarming of guerrilla forces, military demobilisation and the subordination of the armed forces to civilian control (Kincaid, 2000; see also Chapters 4, 7). Security co-operation in the region has improved, and in October 2005 Guatemala proposed the creation of a joint Central American peacekeeping force. In March 2009, members of Unasur (see above) held the first meeting in Chile of the newly formed Consejo de Defensa Suramericano (South American Defence Council, SADC), which was originally proposed by Venezuela and Brazil during deliberations on the creation of Unasur to serve as a security mechanism similar to the North Atlantic Treaty Organisation (NATO) that would promote military co-operation and regional defence. None the less, tensions preceded the SADC's formation, with Colombia reluctant to subscribe to it because of its own military ties with the US (see Box 10.3).

Tensions between Colombia and its neighbours have grown in recent years and have been exacerbated by political differences between the conservative Colombian president, Alvaro Uribe (2002–10), and his leftwing counterparts in Venezuela, Hugo Chávez (1998–), and Ecuador, Rafael Correa (2007–). A series of developments and incidents in 2008–09 gave rise to fears that tensions were escalating out of control and threatened armed conflict in the sub-region (see Box 9.8). At a meeting of regional leaders in Mexico in February 2010, Chávez and Uribe were embroiled in angry exchanges.

Outside these hotspots, Latin American governments continue to confront external and internal security challenges and a number of major interstate disputes have persisted.

Territorial and maritime border tensions have not disappeared and displays of force between Latin American countries continue (see Figure 9.1). A longstanding border dispute between Peru and Ecuador in 1995 led to military clashes that were only halted through US pressure and the intervention of the Rio Group – established in 1986 by eight Latin American countries as a mechanism for regional political co-operation (see Box 9.10). This dispute is regarded as significant in the study of international relations for demonstrating the possibility that *democracies can go to war*. Domínguez *et al.* (2003) noted that other militarised disputes took

---

CASE STUDY   Box 9.8

Colombia upsets the neighbours

Although a recent history of bad relations between Colombia and its neighbours distinguished by a string of accusations, counter-accusations and threats against each other has not resulted in armed conflict *per se*, the OAS has called on all the countries in the region to avoid escalating their disagreements. A particular source of friction has been Colombia's war against guerrillas, which has at times spilled over into neighbouring countries (see Figure 12.1; Tulchin and Espach, 2001). The Colombian government has long accused Ecuador of failing to tackle activity by Colombia's largest guerrilla group, the Fuerzas Armadas Revolucionarias de Colombia (FARC, Revolutionary Armed Forces of Colombia).

▶

The bombing in 2008 by the Colombian air force of a guerrilla camp within Ecuador generated serious tensions in the region (see above). Frictions between Ecuador and Colombia, which by the end of 2009 had still not restored formal diplomatic relations, were made worse by a series of Colombian accusations that President Rafael Correa's 2006 election campaign had benefited from FARC donations, an allegation that both Correa and FARC denied. Ecuador has accused Colombia of waging against it a 'media war' backed by the US (see EIU, 2009).

Colombia has also accused Venezuela's government of providing funds and weapons to FARC, charges it has also denied, while levelling the counter-accusations that Colombia is seeking a pretext to escalate conflict on behalf of its main backer, Washington. In 2008, Venezuela's response to Colombia's incursion into Ecuador was to mobilise troops at the border. Diplomatic ties between Colombia and Venezuela have been broken off several times, the latest occasion being in 2009 when Chávez recalled Venezuela's ambassador in response to charges by Uribe that Swedish-made weapons found in the possession of FARC had come via Venezuela. Tensions escalated later in 2009 after Venezuela accused Colombian military forces of entering its territory, an allegation that Colombia denied, and thereafter an announcement by Colombia that it is building a new military base on the Guajira peninsula on the border with Venezuela for up to 1,000 soldiers and had activated six new airborne battalions. In turn, Colombian officials justified the decision to create a new border base on the threat to the country from Venezuela.

The response of Chávez to growing tensions has been to steadily reinforce Venezuela's forces on the 2,200km border separating the countries. Colombia's guerrilla conflict was also made more complex in late 2009 by the announcement by FARC and the second main guerrilla group in Colombia, the Ejército de Liberación Nacional (ELN, National Liberation Army), that they are to join forces in their war against the state (see Chapter 12). Frictions have been exacerbated by US policy towards Colombia, its principal ally in the region, a source of oil and a key destination in Latin America for US foreign investment (see Chapter 15). Venezuela and other left-of-centre governments in South America were angered in 2009 by Colombia's agreement to allow the US to expand its military presence in the country as part of what both Colombia and Washington insist is a joint anti-drugs effort (see Box 4.3, Chapter 10). Chávez has alleged that the presence of US soldiers in Colombia is a threat to Venezuela and could enable a possible invasion.

The potential for a sub-regional conflict has focused attention on the military balance of power which, despite Chávez's high-profile purchases of Russian armaments, rests firmly in favour of Colombia. With 178,000 soldiers, Colombia's army is more than twice the size of the Venezuelan and Ecuadorean armies combined, and Colombian troops are experienced fighting rebels, paramilitaries and drug traffickers (Reuters, 2008). None the less, in August 2009 Chávez announced that he would be adding several battalions of Russian tanks to his armoury because of the perceived Colombian threat. According to the London-based International Institute for Strategic Studies, Venezuela already has nearly 200 tanks, while Colombia has no tank units (Sánchez, 2009). Another source of friction, generated by the Venezuelan leader's other responses to Colombian policy, is trade. Venezuela has pioneered its own trade and other integration initiatives such as ALBA (see Boxes 9.1, 16.1) and, in response to the tensions with Colombia, Chávez has promised to substitute imports from the neighbouring country, a direct threat to Colombian exporters. In August 2009, for example, Chávez said plans to import 10,000 automobiles from Colombia had been scrapped (*ibid.*). Imports from Colombia amounted to about $6 billion in 2008, making Venezuela Colombia's second-largest market after the US (EIU, 2009). Although it would be hard for Venezuela to substitute these imports with those produced locally or from within ALBA countries, efforts to do so could significantly disrupt Colombian exporters. It was the disruption to trade caused by Chávez's approach that was behind angry exchanges between him and Uribe at a meeting of regional leaders in Mexico in February 2010.

place in the 1990s and early 2000s between: Guatemala and Belize, Venezuela and Guyana, Venezuela and Trinidad-Tobago, Venezuela and Colombia, Nicaragua and Colombia, Nicaragua and Costa Rica, Nicaragua and El Salvador, Nicaragua and Honduras, Honduras and El Salvador, and Honduras and Guatemala. Since 2000, at least five boundary disputes between neighbouring Latin American states have resulted in the use of force, and two others in military deployments, and these incidents involved 10 Central and South American countries (*ibid.*). In October 2005, Costa Rica filed a lawsuit against Nicaragua at the International Court of Justice (ICJ) in a dispute over who should control the San Juan river following a decision by Nicaragua to recall its ambassador and to send troops to its southern border. Lesser disputes over borders and rights also persist. In November 2005, for example, Peru and Chile squabbled over fishing rights in the Pacific Ocean after the Peruvian president, Alejandro Toledo (2001–06), signed a law redrawing the country's maritime border in a way that granted it about 14,600sq miles of fishing waters that Chile was controlling. In October 2009, military exercises hosted by the Chilean air force in the Atacama Desert, close to the disputed border, angered Peruvian officials. The following month, another diplomatic row between Peru and Chile broke out after a Peruvian court ordered the arrest of two Chilean military officers for alleged spying. They were accused of paying a Peruvian air force officer to reveal secrets. The Peru–Chile maritime border dispute is being decided by the ICJ, but has also had implications for Bolivia, whose president, Evo Morales, has claimed that Peru's claim could put in jeopardy his country's chances of ever getting an outlet to the Pacific Ocean. Nicaragua also has a maritime border conflict with Colombia, and responded to the 2008 air raid on Ecuadorean territory by severing diplomatic ties with Bogotá. Even if they do not result in conflict, border disputes can have a damaging effect on relations and, because they may result in a lack of co-operation between national border agencies, may fuel transnational crime (see Chapter 4).

Another source of potential security tensions is energy, and in particular the need for countries to secure or protect stable supplies in an era of rising prices alongside growing competition for oil as emerging economies elsewhere identify new sources of long-term supply (see Korin and Luft eds, 2009). A key issue in Latin America is the distribution of energy resources: some countries have significant natural resources and at least six states in the region are oil exporters, while others such as Chile have meagre reserves and are net importers. Some like Brazil have significant oil reserves (see Box 9.6), yet meagre gas reserves, forcing the country to import gas from neighbouring Bolivia and Argentina. Others like Argentina have oil and gas reserves, but not in sufficient quantities to achieve a viable self-sufficiency. Argentina's desire to maximise its access to oil resources was at the heart of a dispute with the UK over drilling near the Malvinas/Falkland islands in 2010.

Latin America accounts for about 14 per cent of global oil production and possesses about 10 per cent of global oil reserves, with Venezuela and Mexico the two main producer nations. The region also has significant refining capacity, which has developed to serve the needs of the US in particular. Venezuela and Mexico consistently rank in the top four sources of US oil supply along with Canada and Saudi Arabia. Bolivia and Peru are important sources of natural gas, a resource that has had a significant influence on Bolivia's political development in recent years. Brazil has had some success diversifying its energy supplies and pioneered the development, for example, of biofuels such as ethanol (see Shattuck *et al.*, 2009). In February 2010, the Brazilian government granted an environmental licence for the construction of the Belo Monte hydro-electric dam in the Amazon rainforest in the northern state of Pará. But even diversification is no guarantee against blackouts: in 2009, for example, Ecuador introduced electricity rationing after a drought led to water shortages at the country's main hydro-electric power plant in Paute.

Resource nationalism, the desire to nationalise or ensure a significant state control over strategic energy sectors such as oil and gas, has grown in recent years in Venezuela, Argentina, Bolivia and Ecuador (see Chapters 14, 16). Even Brazil, which has generally welcomed foreign investment in the energy sector and required state-owned companies to compete with international companies, has tried to ensure that the state retains control of recently discovered offshore reserves. In some cases, recent nationalisations within and outside the energy sector have caused frictions between Latin American countries, such as Bolivia and its neighbours (see below). Venezuela's decision in 2008 to nationalise the local holdings of the Mexican cement corporation Cemex, for example, generated a long dispute with the company over compensation.

Energy policy has helped to shape inter-state relations in a number of countries, particularly within South America, in recent years. Blackouts are not uncommon in some countries, such as Venezuela and Ecuador, but major power shortages in several Latin American countries in 2009 increased concerns that the region is facing a more serious energy crisis. In February 2010, for example, the Venezuelan leader Hugo Chávez declared an 'electricity emergency' to help his government tackle shortages caused by the impact of drought on the hydro-electric power supplies that Venezuela is heavily reliant upon. Shortages can be explained by rising demand combined with a range of factors such as lower levels of water at hydroelectric dams because of climate change, poor planning, and a lack of infrastructure for the efficient distribution of energy in the region.

Other energy security issues concern access and control of resources, and changing markets for Latin America's chief energy exports (see Figure 14.1). Venezuela's security concerns are motivated in significant part by the desire to protect its oil industry: the country is the fifth largest oil producer in the world and the US is its main market. President Hugo Chávez has at times voiced fears that the country is vulnerable to a US invasion to secure oil supplies (see Boxes 9.1, 9.3, 9.8). In his effort to lessen dependence on the US as a market for Venezuelan oil, Chávez has moved closer to Russia in co-ordinating gas and oil policy on the international markets, and Russia has said it is possible that it could join with Venezuela and other gas-producing nations to form a cartel similar to OPEC (see Chapter 11). Chávez has also used energy to extend his foreign policy objectives within Latin America, pledging to guarantee the energy needs of his allies in the region through 'energy security treaties'. A key factor in the US relationship with Colombia has undoubtedly been the latter's oil reserves: although Colombia's oil industry has suffered from under-investment, there are thought to be significant areas still open for exploration. In Bolivia, the government of President Evo Morales (2006–) nationalised the oil and gas industry in 2006 and renegotiated the contracts of foreign energy corporations working in the country, causing tensions with neighbouring Brazil and

Argentina. Brazil's Petrobras – the biggest foreign investor in Bolivia which had invested more than $1 billion in Bolivian gas – was among companies required to reach a new agreement, angering the Brazilian government, who complained about the way Bolivia had conducted the negotiations. Bolivia has also signalled that it is unlikely to meet the energy needs of Chile, an energy importer, until the dispute over its access to the Pacific is resolved (see above). In 2010, Peru expected to begin operating Latin America's first liquefaction plant for the production of liquid natural gas (LNG), and could surpass Bolivia as the country with the second-highest proved gas reserves in the region after Venezuela. Peru's maritime dispute with Chile has reinforced nationalist calls in the country that it should not, however, sell piped LNG to its southern neighbour. Brazil and Argentina, meanwhile, have squabbled over the ratio of Bolivian gas supplied to them, with Bolivia prioritising exports to Brazil and Argentina seeking a bigger share to avoid energy shortages during winter months. In 2008, Argentina and Brazil agreed to build a joint nuclear reactor to address potential energy shortages. At the same time, relations between Chile and Argentina have been strained by the latter's approach to the delivery of natural gas to its neighbour (see Silva, 2009). Paraguay and Brazil have disagreed about the benefits they get from electricity generated at South America's largest hydroelectric dam, Itaipú, that they share: Brazil absorbs 95 per cent and Paraguay takes just 5 per cent. However, Paraguay is totally dependent on the dam's electricity: a power cut caused by a failure at the dam in late 2009 blacked out the entire country for 15 minutes.

Energy competition also has significant potential for influencing the relations of Latin American countries with other regions of the world. In February 2010, for example, Argentina formally objected to Britain about the start of oil and gas exploration in waters off the Falkland/Malvinas islands in the south Atlantic (see Box 11.1), and escalated the dispute by blocking a ship from leaving the port of Buenos Aires that it maintained was carrying drilling equipment to them. Concerns about energy security alongside recognition that energy policy is a potential source of inter-state tensions promoted the Inter-American Development Bank to establish a programme promoting integration and collaboration on energy policy in the Americas (see websites below). However, Latinobarómetro data suggest that a majority of Latin Americans believe energy problems in the region should be resolved through co-operation by countries, suggesting that energy policy is an area as ripe for potential collaboration as it is for conflict (see Latinobarómetro, 2009b). Within the infrastructure envisaged for Unasur (see above) is a protocol signed by members to develop the Anillo Energético Sudamericano (South American Energy Ring) that is intended to interconnect Argentina, Brazil, Chile, Paraguay and Uruguay with natural gas from several sources in the region, particularly Peru and Bolivia, although this initiative has suffered significant delays.

Transnational security issues also exist in Latin America, such as drug-trafficking, migration, international crime and arms trafficking.

The International Organisation for Migration (IOM) reports that international migration within Latin America is low in comparison with overall migration flows to the US and Canada (IOM, 2005a; see also IOM, 2005b). According to the IOM, the overall number of international migrants within Latin America and the Caribbean has changed little since 1980, oscillating between 5.8 million and

6 million, reaching a peak of 7 million in 1990. This declined considerably in the period 1990–2000, largely as a result of the repatriation of refugees from the Central American civil wars. The 1.2 million refugees reported by Latin American countries in 1990 had fallen to about 765,000 by 2002 (IOM, 2005a, 2005c). Officially, about 5 million Latin Americans are estimated to live outside their own countries within the region, although the real number is likely to be much higher because of the difficulties tracking migrants who, increasingly, are skilled workers. Some countries, such as Bolivia, are net exporters of people. Others, such as Argentina, Costa Rica, and Venezuela are popular destinations. Large numbers of Bolivians, Chileans, and Paraguayans live in Argentina; about 500,000 Nicaraguans live in Costa Rica; and several hundred thousand Colombians live in Venezuela.

Although migration within Latin America is considered to be low in international terms, migratory flows within some parts of the region, and in particular Central America and the Caribbean, have also been a source of tension between countries. Relations between the Dominican Republic and Haiti worsened considerably in 2005, for example, over a series of incidents in which Haitian migrants were either the targets of violence or themselves accused of violent acts. Officials in Mexico, which is itself an important source of undocumented or 'irregular' economic migrants into the US, often adopt a tough stance towards Central Americans entering the country in order to head north. Refugee flows can also generate domestic and international tensions. The IOM says a significant increase in the number of Colombian asylum seekers was noted in 2003–04 in Ecuador, which found it difficult to absorb and integrate the refugee population (IOM, 2005c). Militarisation of the battle against the drug trade by countries under pressure from the US has contributed to the high levels of violence in the region that fuel these refugee flows.

Latin American states have, at times, found their own solutions to regional security problems. In the late 1980s, for example, the Contadora Group – a regional peace initiative launched earlier in the decade by the foreign ministers of Colombia, Mexico, Panama and Venezuela – had significant success at helping armed guerrilla groups make the transition into political parties in Central America (Tulchin and Espach, 2001; see also Chapters 2, 12). Progress has also been achieved in specific areas, such as drug-trafficking, in which there is an established formula for co-operation through the Inter-American Drug Abuse Control Commission (CICAD) of the OAS (*ibid.*). Integration has also eased tensions and competition between historic rivals, and Mercosur has helped to foster stability and security in the Southern Cone (see Box 9.9). However, Tulchin and Espach (2001) argue that Latin America has been slow in developing institutional mechanisms that allow for a co-operative response to security crises, and the absence of these has strengthened the possibility of US unilateral action to resolve issues. None the less, definitive settlements to disputes remain more likely in circumstances where multilateral hemispheric solutions are sought (Domínguez, 2000). Joint military exercises in Latin America have often incorporated the US and there has been limited intra-regional military co-operation – Brazil and Argentina have developed the closest forms of defence collaboration in the region and formalised these through a number of pacts, although other countries periodically hold joint exercises. Moreover, the US is increasing its military presence in Latin America, particularly

Mercosur/Mercosul

The Mercado Común del Sur/Mercado Comum do Sul (Mercosur/Mercosul, Common Market of the South) was established in March 1991 through the Treaty of Asunción by which Argentina, Brazil, Paraguay and Uruguay agreed to a co-ordinated process of economic integration based on a common external tariff and trade policy. Between 1996 and 2004, Bolivia, Chile, Colombia, Ecuador, Peru and Venezuela became associate members. In December 2005, Mercosur leaders agreed to Venezuela's request to become a full member, although concerns in the Brazilian congress about its democratic credentials held up ratification of Venezuela's membership until December 2009, and by 2010 Paraguay had still not ratified this and an unclear timetable for congressional ratification could extend the process into 2013. While primarily an economic and commercial instrument, Mercosur is a good example of the extension of the economic integration process into other areas, and the treaty has become a strategic initiative that incorporates political, security and cultural dimensions. Today, Mercosur members stress as the basis of the integration project common values promoting democratic and plural societies, and commit themselves to democratic consolidation, sustainable development, environmental protection and social development. One reason for this is that Mercosur has eased tensions between historic rivals – by improving the security relations between countries that once saw each other as competitors – and now dominates the foreign policy priorities of its member states. In the 1990s, joint military exercises between its members became routine and in 1999, for example, Chile and Argentina resolved an outstanding territorial dispute and Brazil and Argentina agreed to joint production and repair of naval vessels. Mercosur declarations establish that peaceful relations between neighbouring states are an essential component of the integration process. Mercosur has also become institutionalised through the creation of mechanisms and channels for seeking political consensus between the members and associate member states on regional and other issues. In 2007, for example, the first session of the Mercosur Parliament was held after this institution was established to allow for greater scrutiny of shared issues. It is composed of 81 MPs, initially chosen from nominated members of the national parliaments of countries in the bloc but, since 2008, directly elected. Polls show a shift in Argentina towards closer ties with Brazil, and now both countries make relations with their neighbours a foreign policy priority (Muñoz, 2001). Mercosur has become a powerful tool for strengthening democracy. In 1996 the presidents of Argentina, Brazil, Paraguay and Uruguay signed a 'Presidential Declaration on Democratic Commitment', which was soon ratified by its associates, establishing democracy and respect for fundamental human rights as an 'indispensable condition' for the existence of Mercosur and its further development. Mercosur served as an instrument for defending constitutional government in Paraguay by helping to prevent a coup from succeeding in 1996, and a coup in Ecuador in 2000 lasted just a few hours because of external pressure on military leaders. Mercosur has also been prominent in attempts to find constitutional solutions to political crises that have plagued Bolivia and Ecuador since 2003. However, the integration agreement has not eliminated disputes between member countries entirely, and the way it functions has been criticised. In mid-2006, for example, Argentina appealed to the International Court of Justice to order Uruguay to halt the construction of a paper mill that it claimed would pollute the River Uruguay that separates the two neighbours, a dispute that continues to strain bilateral relations (see Box 8.10). Uruguay's president Tabaré Vázquez (2005–09) was at the forefront of calls for reform of Mercosur, arguing that in its current form the bloc benefited only Argentina and Brazil.

that of naval patrols (see Chapter 10). There have been a number of calls for a South American defence pact and, in 2008, Brazil's president, Lula da Silva, proposed the creation of a formal mechanism to deal with security and defence issues, an idea that met with the support of at least 10 countries in the region (see above). At the same time, however, Brazil is increasing its military co-operation with the US, which has offered it state-of-the-art F-18 Super Hornet fighter aircraft, for example, and there are signs that the US believes it may have a vested interest in permitting Brazilian military leadership in the South American theatre (see above). Some countries, however, continue to resist any move towards Latin American military co-operation and prefer to seek ties with traditional powers such as Russia (see Chapter 11). Venezuela has conducted joint naval exercises with Russia in the Caribbean, while limiting its defence collaboration with Latin American states to buying and selling arms. Other countries have also seen potential benefits in greater military co-operation with powers outside the region: even Colombia, Washington's closest ally in Latin America, reactivated a 1996 military co-operation agreement with Russia in 2008.

Democracy and human rights

Key themes to emerge in Latin American foreign relations have been the promotion of democracy and the protection of human rights, which have become major sources of consensus in international relations (van Klaveren, 2001). Governments in the US and European Union countries have also used political, economic, diplomatic or even military means to promote democratisation in Latin America (see Chapters 3, 10, 11). Many of these governmental actions have been supported or complemented by NGOs, political parties, foundations, religious institutions, trades unions, pressure groups and academics. International challenges to human rights abuses, support for NGOs and social movements, and solidarity between political parties have made an important contribution to democratisation in countries such as Chile, Paraguay and Uruguay (*ibid.*). External interventions of some kind have bolstered democratisation in the Dominican Republic (1978), El Salvador (1980), Honduras (1983), Bolivia (1984), Haiti (1991–94) and Guatemala (1993). Multilateral institutions such as the OAS have taken important steps to foster Latin American action on behalf of democracy (see Box 9.5), and to condemn developments considered harmful to it such as the 2009 coup in Honduras (see Box 7.10).

Democratisation itself has also become a factor of unity and co-operation between Latin American states. In the past, international action on human rights and democracy was limited by a strict interpretation of the principles of non-intervention and sovereignty. However, there is recognition today that international action in favour of democracy can be legitimate in some circumstances (*ibid.*). A salient tendency in Latin America since the 1980s has been regional political co-operation in processes of democratisation themselves, tapping into the 'snowball effect' of democratic transition whereby democratisation in one country can encourage similar changes in another (see Chapter 3). Argentina's democratisation process, for example, encouraged democratisation in Uruguay, and Central American democratisation can be seen as a *regional* process (*ibid.*). Latin American initiatives themselves have played an important part in this phenomenon. The Contadora Group's pioneering role in the Central American peace process led to the Esquipulas accords contributing decisively to the promotion of democracy; Mercosur has increasingly put democracy at the centre of its activities (see Box 9.9); and, when the Rio Group was established in 1986, it stated explicitly the defence of democracy as one of its main aims (see Box 9.10). Together, international scrutiny and the shared consensus on democracy has made the cost of a coup much higher than previously in Latin America. Brazil assumed a leading role among Latin American countries calling for the restoration of the Honduran president, Manuel Zelaya, following the coup in 2009, and Brazil has also asserted its democratic credentials well outside the South American continent. Honduran officials later took Brazil to the International Court of Justice for allowing the ousted president to remain in its embassy in Tegucigalpa, a move dismissed by Brazil as having no basis in law because of what it argued was the illegitimate status of the Honduran regime.

INSTITUTIONS   Box 9.10

The Rio Group

In 1986, eight Latin American countries established in Rio de Janeiro a permanent mechanism for regional political co-operation known as the Rio Group (GRIO), which now includes 23 participating members from Latin America and the Caribbean Community (Caricom). Cuba was permitted to join the organisation in 2008. The initiative resulted from the fusion of the Contadora Group (Mexico, Colombia, Venezuela and Panama) and the Support Group (Argentina, Brazil, Uruguay and Peru) which had met hitherto to analyse and develop solutions to the crises in Central America. Its formation was seen by some observers as an effort to create an alternative to the OAS (see Box 9.5) during the Cold War because of that organisation's domination by the US. The main objectives of GRIO were established in the 'Declaration of Rio de Janeiro' in 1986. These included: expanding political co-operation and improving inter-American relations; reaching common positions on international issues; fostering integration initiatives; and conflict resolution. In 1999, GRIO agreed on the principles that it stood for, that included: the defence of democracy; the protection of human rights; peace, security and disarmament; the establishment of viable institutions throughout the region; and the strengthening of multilateralism. The Rio Group played a decisive role in stopping military clashes in 1995 between Ecuador and Peru and provided the framework for a peace agreement between the two states in late 1998. It has promoted democracy as the main criterion for international legitimacy in Latin America. In 1997, the Summit of Heads of State and Government of the Rio Group issued a declaration on the defence of democracy that obliges signatories' foreign ministers to meet in cases in which there is an attempted upset of the democratic order (Muñoz, 2001). An emergency meeting of the Rio Group in Nicaragua in late June 2009, for example, condemned the coup in Honduras, refused to recognise the administration that had taken over from the ousted president Manuel Zelaya, and demanded his reinstatement (see Box 7.10).

Summary

A central factor in relations between the states of Latin America has been US predominance in the region. The Cold War restricted Latin America's room for manoeuvre and foreign policy was considered in terms of how it would be viewed in Washington. Latin America has developed alternatives to US power, including appeals to continental unity, balancing strategies to avoid dependence on the US, sub-regional dominance, the employment of international law, the development of links with other Third World nations and social revolution. Since the end of the Cold War, however, Latin America has received less attention from the US and Europe, which do not see relations with it as a strategic priority. Post-Cold War circumstances also renewed the US need to employ diplomacy and offered the prospect of a regional consensus on principles such as free trade and integration. The post-Cold War world is 'multi-layered' because of the uneven distribution of international economic and political power. The activity of multilateral institutions, non-state actors and transnational corporations, social movements and NGOs as well as organised crime have complicated international relations and challenged traditional ideas of sovereignty, with important implications for domestic policies. Economic integration means both that domestic decisions have international implications and that the international community can modify domestic decisions. In the context of globalisation, an institutionalist account of international behaviour is suitable for assessing Latin American policy options. Institutionalist theory suggests that international institutions benefit less powerful nations. At the same time, however, insertion into the international system can imply the opening up of politics to foreign scrutiny and political change. Today, the main themes shaping Latin American international relations are sovereignty, multilateralism, regionalism, security and democracy. Some Latin American governments have redefined a traditional understanding of sovereignty that rejected outside interference in domestic affairs. There has been a shift in favour of multilateralism, and trade as well as the politics of left-of-centre governments have driven new efforts at integration in Latin America. However, the end of the Cold War and multilateralism have not eradicated military tensions, which have been exacerbated by disputes over resources and by political differences between conservatives and those on the left.

Discussion points

- In what ways have Latin American states responded to the reality of US power?
- Is an institutionalist perspective suitable for assessing Latin American policy options?
- To what extent are efforts to redefine sovereignty related to globalisation?
- What factors have encouraged multilateral approaches by Latin American states?
- Has regional integration been confined to trade or is it a political process?
- What are the main security challenges faced by Latin American governments today?

■ Why has democratisation become a factor of unity between Latin American states?

Useful websites

www.oas.org Organisation of American States

www.parlatino.org Parlatino, the Latin American Parliament

www.mercosur.int Mercado Común del Sur/Mercado Comum do Sul (Mercosur/Mercosul, Common Market of the South)

www.oim.org.co International Organisation for Migration mission in Colombia

www.mre.gov.br Brazil's foreign ministry

www.haiti.mre.gov.br/pt-br Brazil's mission in Haiti

www.mrecic.gov.ar Argentina's foreign ministry

www.sre.gob.mx Mexico's foreign ministry

www.g77.org Group of 77, a caucus established at the United Nations by 77 developing countries representing the largest Third World coalition in the UN, which has many Latin American members

www.aladi.org Aladi (Asociación Latinoamericana de Integración, Latin American Integration Association), largest regional integration initiative aiming at eventual creation of a Latin American common market

www.alca-ftaa.org Area de Libre Comercio de las Américas (ALCA, Free Trade Area of the Americas, FTAA)

www.comunidadandina.org Andean Community, integration initiative of five Andean countries and the bodies and institutions comprising the Andean Integration System (AIS)

www.sica.int Sistema de Integración Centroamericana (SICA, Central American Integration System), organism created by Central American states in 1993 to foster integration

www.iadb.org/intal Instituto para la Integración de América Latina y el Caribe (BID-INTAL, Institute for the Integration of Latin America and the Caribbean) a think-tank created by the Inter-American Development Bank and the Argentine government

www.sela.org Sistema Económico Latinoamericano (SELA, Latin American Economic System), a regional intergovernmental organisation established in 1975 and seeking common positions on economic issues that brings together 26 Latin American and Caribbean countries

www.unasur.org Unión de Naciones Suramericanas (Unasur, Union of South American Nations)

www.opanal.org Organismo para la Proscripción de las Armas Nucleares en la América Latina y el Caribe (OPANAL, Agency for the Prohibition of Nuclear Weapons in Latin America and the Caribbean), an inter-governmental agency created to ensure compliance by signatories to the 1967 Treaty for the Prohibition of Nuclear Weapons in Latin America and the Caribbean, also known as the Treaty of Tlatelolco

www.jid.org/index.php?lang=en The Inter-American Defence Board, international committee of defence officials who develop collaborative approaches on security issues facing the Americas and advise the OAS

www.iadb.org/projects/project.cfm?id=RG-T1726&lang=en IDB technical co-operation pro-gramme promoting collaboration on energy policy in the Americas

www.cubanoal.cu/ingles/index.html Non-Aligned Movement

Recommended reading

Cooper, Andrew F. and Jorge Heine (eds). 2009. *Which Way Latin America?: Hemispheric Politics Meets Globalisation*. Tokyo: United Nations University Press

Essential introduction to international relations in Latin America which focuses on key themes determining the dynamic interaction between the region and the rapidly-changing global system

Tulchin, Joseph and Ralph Espach (eds). 2001. *Latin America in the New International System*. Boulder, CO: Lynne Rienner Publishers/Woodrow Wilson International Center for Scholars

Valuable introduction to international relations in Latin America combining theoretical overviews of the main issues with useful country case studies

McPherson, Alan. 2003. *Yankee No! Anti-Americanism in US-Latin American Relations*. London: Harvard University Press

Valuable insight into the nature of anti-Americanism in Latin America and how variable this can be

Domínguez, Jorge. 2000. *The Future of Inter-American Relations*. London: Routledge

Valuable overview of the key issues in Latin American international relations today

Prevost, Gary and Carlos Oliva Campos (eds). 2002. *NeoLiberalism and neoPanamericanism: The View from Latin America*. Basingstoke: Palgrave Macmillan

Interesting approach to regionalism based on an understanding of neoliberalism in Latin America as a new vector of pan-Americanism

Dabène, Olivier. 2009. *The Politics of Regional Integration in Latin America: Theoretical and Comparative Explorations*. Basingstoke: Palgrave Macmillan

Valuable overview of different experiences of regional integration in Latin America with case studies on Central America, Mercosur and the Andean region

Chapter 10

The US and Latin America

This chapter examines the policy of the United States towards Latin America and the inescapable relationship between them that has been of great importance to political and economic development in both. The US has been a key source of ideas, models, capital, expertise and political and military support for its allies in the region. It has been an implacable foe towards its enemies or those its leaders have disapproved of. Little that occurs at an international level in Latin America has escaped the attention of policymakers in Washington, and the US has been the main source of academic research on the region.

Since the late nineteenth century, the US has been in a different league to Latin America in terms of military and economic power, while enjoying enviable political stability. Interactions have been shaped by the reality of this asymmetry and a core problem in inter-American relations has been the propensity of the US to act unilaterally from its position of strength (Domínguez, 2000; see also Coerver and Hall, 1999; Dent, 1999; Hogan and Patterson eds, 2004). The essence of this relationship is often captured in the term 'hegemony', which in this case refers to the US ability to exert its influence beyond its formal borders and powers accounted for by international law. Latin America's responses to US predominance have often meant that relations have been characterised by confrontation and distrust, either because of a US tendency to intervene in Latin American affairs or US indifference towards developments in the region (see Rivarola Puntigliano, 2008). Bulmer-Thomas and Dunkerley (1999) suggested the weakness of diplomacy in Latin America itself has contributed towards US attitudes. However, although the western hemisphere has sometimes been regarded in international relations as a separate 'sub-system', many scholars have suggested that there is in fact nothing exceptional about the US–Latin American relationship. Smith (2000) has argued that the dynamics of US–Latin American relations have obeyed prevailing rules of conduct elsewhere in the global arena, and that changes in these rules have responded to several factors: the number of major powers; the nature of power resources; and the goals of international policy (see Table 10.1). Moreover, anti-American sentiment in Latin America is highly variable, and in many cases matched in equal measure by pro-American sentiment (see McPherson, 2003; Katzenstein and Keohane eds, 2007; see also Box 9.3).

Smith (2000) argues for three broad periods in inter-American relations: multilateral rivalry from the 1790s to the 1930s; the Cold War from the 1940s to the 1980s; and the contemporary post-Cold War 'Age of Uncertainty' since the late

Table 10.1 Global contexts for US–Latin American relations

Factor	Imperial Era 1790s–1930s	Cold War 1940s–1980s	Age of Uncertainty 1990s–
Distribution of power	Multipolar	Bipolar	Unipolar/multipolar
Policy goals	Territorial, commercial	Geopolitical, ideological	Economic, social
Rules of the game	Balance of power	Global containment	Undetermined

Source: *Talons of the Eagle: Dynamics of US–Latin American Relations*, Oxford University Press (Smith, Peter H. 2000) p. 357

1980s, in which there has been an absence of clear rules for international conduct. There is evidence that in this most recent period US influence in Latin America has been on the decline and Washington has increasingly had to compete for the support and attention of governments in the region. Following a period in which the presidency of George W. Bush (2001–09) damaged perceptions of the US in a Latin America increasingly turning to the left, the presidency of Barack Obama (2009–) is likely to be distinguished by efforts to project 'soft' power that aims to win hearts and minds and that is reflected in a commitment to multilateral solutions in the region.

The Cold War

As discussed in Chapter 9, the Cold War had a profound influence on the character of inter-American relations, placing the concept of 'national security' at the top of the US agenda (see Box 10.2, Chapter 2). Washington's preoccupation with the threat of communism both exaggerated the asymmetry of power between the US and Latin American countries, and encouraged the latter to focus their energies on security, often at the expense of democracy. It also reversed policies that had been adopted during the 1930s by US president Franklin D. Roosevelt (1933–45), who had sought to be a 'good neighbour' by advocating that no American state should interfere in the affairs of others. FDR's foreign policy had, in part, been an effort to achieve more constructive economic relations in a climate of growing nationalism in Latin America following the Great Depression, and it laid the basis for US–Latin American co-operation during the Second World War. As the Cold War unfolded, the US acted to ensure policies favourable to its interests, from covert involvement in domestic politics to military invasion. If democratic mechanisms allowed for advances by socialist forces, it allowed or aided the rise of anti-democratic authoritarian governments (Tulchin and Espach, 2001).

Several phases of the Cold War can be identified: an initial period shaped by US efforts to check the spread of communism, leading to the coup orchestrated by the CIA in 1954 in Guatemala; a second phase, characterised by broader concerns about revolution in the Third World sparked by the Cuban Revolution, leading to the Alliance for Progress policy of the 1960s; a third phase, in which policies of detente followed the trauma of the Vietnam War and the US under President Jimmy Carter (1977–81) demonstrated inconsistency in its backing for dictatorships;

and a final phase, characterised by the resurgence of aggressive anti-communism under President Ronald Reagan (1981–89).

Pastor (2001) identified as recurring issues in US–Latin American relations during this period problems caused by *succession* in friendly authoritarian regimes and by *revolutionary regimes*. Succession crises occurred when a dictator friendly to the US faced a challenge to unseat him. Pastor examined seven succession crises, five of them in Latin America – Cuba (1958–59), Dominican Republic (1960–61), Haiti (1961–63), Nicaragua (1978–79) and Chile (1988–89) – and argued that the US took a similar approach in all cases. Its preference for a democratic regime was often followed either by a continuation of an authoritarian but pro-US leadership or by a social revolution. If the US could not gain the first option, it would pursue the second in order to avoid the third. The worst outcomes for Washington occurred in Cuba and Nicaragua, where revolutions succeeded.

US policy towards revolutionary regimes in Latin America was shaped by its perception of the communist threat but was often out of proportion to the real risk of Soviet interference, and Washington did not seek to overthrow radical governments that it did not consider ideologically communist. For example, it did not view the revolution in Bolivia in 1952 as a communist threat, and so tolerated policies of nationalisation and gave the country aid and military training. However, in Guatemala in 1954 and in Chile in 1973 the US undertook covert interventions to confront what it perceived to be a communist threat. In 1976, Lowenthal assessed the findings of a report by the US senate on policy towards Chile showing that between 1963–73 Washington had engaged in a massive, systematic and sustained covert campaign against the Chilean left (Lowenthal, 1976). Similarly, Reagan's attitude to revolutionary Nicaragua was influenced by powerful rightwing interests in the US which interpreted retreat in Central America as an advance for the Soviet Union even though it could be argued that the Sandinista regime, although authoritarian, was ideologically diverse (see Whitehead, 1983; see also Chapter 12, Box 16.2).

In the post-Cold War era, the US emerged as the world's only military superpower while facing stiff economic competition, initially from Japan and the European Union, and in more recent years also from Russia and China. This was described as unipolar military supremacy and multipolar economic rivalry (Smith, 2000). It has resulted in uncertainty because the distribution of military power does not bear a clear relationship to the distribution of economic power. In the absence of recognised rules of international conduct, patterns of behaviour have become unpredictable. The end of the Cold War was the main contributing factor to the achievement of peace in Central America, and Cuba initially became more isolated, easing US security concerns. Washington welcomed the transition to democracy and an ideological preference for capitalism in Latin America, but in recent years it has still been accused of intervening in the affairs of countries such as Nicaragua, Bolivia and Venezuela to try to ensure political outcomes that are more to its liking (see Nieto, 2003). In the absence of extra-hemispheric rivals, the US acquired hegemony by *default* in the western hemisphere in the 1990s (Smith, 2000). Its military campaigns in the Middle East following the 9/11 attacks of 2001, and attention to the geopolitical dimensions of 'neoconservative' thought in the US associated with the administrations of George W. Bush renewed interest in debates about 'imperialism', a term that has been used frequently in Latin America with reference to US power in the region (see Boxes 1.4, 2.3, 10.1).

None the less, in the last few years the European Union, Russia and China have made it clear that they are prepared to test the limits of that hegemony by forging commercial, and in some cases, military ties in the region (see Chapter 11).

THEORIES AND DEBATES   **Box 10.1**

The US and the changing concept of imperialism

Although the administration of George W. Bush did not initially exhibit signs of digressing from the foreign policy of the Clinton era, this changed dramatically as a result of the 9/11 attacks which gave considerable impetus to foreign policy notions popular with 'neoconservatives' on the US right that combined a traditional belief in the duty of the US to promote liberal democracy around the world with a military doctrine that justified 'preemptive' actions to defuse perceived threats to the country before they were carried out. These ideas played a formative role in justifying US military action in Iraq and Afghanistan and its 'War on Terror' – with all the subsequent implications for diplomatic relations (see below, and Box 10.4) – as well as its policy in the Middle East more generally. Preemptive military action became a prominent tenet of the so-called 'Bush Doctrine' by which the administration's foreign policy became known after 2002. Although it can be associated mainly with neoconservative ideas about Islamic militancy, it caused alarm in Latin America where there has long been sensitivity to US interventionism. Ideas of preemptive war also revived interest in the theme of 'imperialism', a term that has been used frequently throughout Latin American political history with reference to US policy towards the region. A number of books and articles were published during the Bush years that explored the notion that the US was engaged in a new form of imperialism (see, for example, Foster, 2003, 2006; Tremblay, 2004; Harvey, 2005; Grandin, 2006; Kiely, 2006; McGowan, 2007; Hobsbawm, 2008). Imperialism is a complex term that has been extensively debated in political philosophy, particularly on the Left, given its association with Marxist ideas popular throughout the twentieth century about the development of monopoly capitalism (see Chapters 12, 15). The Latin American left has been prone to use the term, which complements their understanding of phenomena such as economic dependence (see Chapter 14) and the strong sense that the US has had an overbearing political and cultural influence in the region (see Box 1.4). Marxist theories of imperialism argue that it consists primarily in the economic exploitation of one region or group by another. Although these arguments have evolved considerably, they have long accorded a dominant or even a 'super-imperialist' role to the US as the world's most powerful capitalist economy. However, some important recent contributions to these debates, for example by William Robinson (2007) and Michael Hardt and Antonio Negri (2000), have taken the concept of globalisation (see Box 15.6) as the basis for a new, decentred supra-national capitalist order that may draw upon elements of US constitutionalism but in which the US is only one geopolitical player alongside, for example, transnational corporations. In support of this argument, for example, it has been suggested that US interventionism is *not* a departure from capitalist globalisation but merely a *response to its crisis* (see Robinson, 2007; Shor, 2010). By this interpretation, theories of a 'new imperialism' driven by the US effort to offset any potential decline in its hegemony against emergent rival powers ignore evidence about the transnationalisation of capital and the increasingly prominent role of supranational institutions in imposing capitalist domination upon a vulnerable inter-state system. In short, these interpretations argue that the recent manifestations of US 'imperialism' associated with the Bush era were merely symptoms of a larger, transnational phenomenon and the classical image of imperialism as a relationship of external domination involving a single, all-powerful state may be outdated.

In 2008, for example, Russia and Venezuela conducted joint naval exercises for three days, the first-ever presence of Russian naval forces in the Caribbean since the end of the Cold War (see Chapter 9). Moreover, the focus of US foreign policy towards the Middle East following the 9/11 attacks of 2001, the proliferation of left-of-centre governments in Latin America, and economic growth and democratisation have all combined to further dilute traditional US influence in the region. In an influential report published in May 2008, for example, a task force of the US Council on Foreign Relations declared the era of US hegemony in the Americas over (see Barshefsky *et al.* eds, 2008). New concerns now dominate US policymaking, and national security (see Box 10.2) has been redefined to place an emphasis on the drugs war, securing energy supplies, and on tackling illegal migration (see below).

Perspectives on US–Latin American relations

Because of the asymmetry in power and wealth between the US and Latin America, scholars have, inevitably, often portrayed the US as the subject in relationships and Latin America as a dependent object (see Schoultz, 1998; Smith, 2000). This position can convey a sense that Latin America will lose out in any dealings with the US. Pastor (2001) challenged this position by arguing that Latin Americans are also subjects with more room to pursue their interests than such a perspective would suggest. His approach pointed to caveats that must be acknowledged when studying US relations with Latin America: US attitudes towards Latin America are linked to its own development as a world power, but its interests have *changed* over time. During the Cold War, political and strategic considerations were of paramount importance in Washington, but in the post-Cold War period economic considerations have regained prominence.

Smith (2000) argued that four main factors have influenced US behaviour in Latin America over time: the relative importance of the region vis-à-vis other areas; perceptions of extra-hemispheric threats; US definitions of its own national interest; and the relationship between state actors and social groups in US policy formation. He summarised the determinants of US policy towards Latin America in different periods and how the combination of factors had a determining influence over resulting strategies (see Table 10.2).

It must also be recognised that, within the US foreign policy establishment overall, at times there has been a relative *lack of interest* in Latin America, and that today regions such as the Middle and Far East, and in particular China, are more of a priority. US policy priorities also vary according to the geographical position of countries and sub-regions within Latin America itself. Fear of upheaval in Mexico has been a key theme in relations and has resulted in exceptionalism in bilateral relations in comparison with other countries. A recent manifestation of this policy has been US support for the Mexican government's battle against drug-trafficking cartels (see below, and Box 4.3). The US has approached the rest of Latin America in terms of two distinct regions: the 'Caribbean Basin' comprising Central America, the Caribbean islands and to a lesser extent Venezuela and Colombia; and South America. Pastor (2001) suggests that 90 per cent of the time devoted by senior US

Table 10.2 Principal determinants of US policy

Determinant	Imperial Era 1790s–1930s	Cold War 1940s–1980s	Age of Uncertainty 1990s–
Importance of Latin America	Growing to very high	High	Ambiguous
Extrahemispheric rivals	European powers	Soviet Union	—
Primary goals	Spheres of influence	Anticommunism	Economic gain, social exclusion
Policy actors	Government + business	Government alone	Government + interest groups
General strategy	Territorial, commercial incorporation	Political penetration	Economic integration

Source: *Talons of the Eagle: Dynamics of US–Latin American Relations*, Oxford University Press (Smith, Peter H. 2000) p. 357

policymakers to Latin America has been to the Caribbean Basin, whose countries pose similar strategic issues for the US because of their proximity and instability. US relations with Cuba, for example, have also been characterised by exceptionalism (see Box 10.8). The countries of South America are larger and more stable, have enjoyed closer ties with Europe, and their political attention has often been more focused on each other than on Washington. None the less, there is significant variation in opinions about the relationship with the US in the sub-region, varying from 68 per cent of respondents in Colombia describing this in 2008 as very good or good to just 41 per cent in neighbouring Venezuela (Latinobarómetro, 2009b). Central Americans, by contrast, tend to have a more favourable perception of the US.

Policy objectives

Historically, US policies towards Latin America have had four main motives – territorial gain and strategic security, ideological predominance, and the advancement of economic interests – and US domestic politics has also often been at the heart of important issues affecting relations:

Territorial gain and security

The main period of US territorial expansion was in the nineteenth century, but where interventions in Latin America occurred these were often related to security considerations. Pastor (2001) argued that cycles of US behaviour towards Latin America – neglect followed by panic when events become adverse – are consistent with the view that US motives in its relations with the region are primarily *strategic*: it does not seek to impose political systems or to exploit economies, but seeks to avoid the possible emergence of hostile governments or policies. An important determinant of US–Latin American relations has been the fear of extra-hemispheric interference (Smith, 2000). Although no country in Latin America has had the ability to threaten the US, Washington has long feared that extra-hemispheric powers might secure a base in the region from which to attack it (Schoultz, 1998). The Monroe Doctrine of 1823 (see Box 1.4) established Latin America within the US sphere of influence in an effort to deter European reconquest in the Americas, and its late twentieth-century equivalent was national security doctrine (see Box 10.2; see also Sicker, 2001).

THEORIES AND DEBATES	Box 10.2

National security doctrine

The Cold War had a profound influence on the character of inter-American relations, placing the concept of 'national security' at the top of the US agenda. US policymaking was institutionalised with the creation of the National Security Council in 1947 as a forum for government advisers and cabinet members to consider security issues, and within two years this had been brought firmly under the control of the US presidency. The meaning of national security has changed over time, but during the Cold War it reflected a defensive posture aiming to protect an official vision of US national interests and values from both external and internal threats, principally communism. As a result, national security encompassed areas of both national defence and foreign relations, requiring the co-ordination of military, international and internal security affairs. The US has used many different mechanisms to guarantee its national security, including diplomacy, asserting its economic power, civil defence preparations and the expansion of intelligence operations. The concept of national security is relative and there is no simple formula for defining what is a threat or, in turn, what is the best response to a threat (Pastor, 2001). It is premised on a definition of national interests, and these include the need to preserve political integrity, stability and institutions, economic stability, and international order. Pastor (2001) examines in US history different positions taken by conservatives and liberals towards security and points out that, in his response to the Nicaraguan Revolution (1979), for example, Reagan stressed the national security threat to the US posed by the destabilisation of Central America and insisted upon a military response. Reagan was a conservative Republican, and his Democratic opponents agreed with his anti-Soviet and anti-Marxist goals but insisted that a military solution would be counterproductive. US experiences in Guatemala in 1954 had an important early influence on the application of national security doctrine to Latin America, leaving officials in Washington with the belief that, under certain circumstances, Latin Americans might welcome the presence of an adversary of the US. Officials came to the conclusion that, in order to confront such a challenge, the US had to ensure friendly governments held power – a major undertaking in a region where poverty, inequality and the behaviour of social elites inevitably favoured the development of ideologies such as communism. A broad definition of security, therefore, came to incorporate the need for support for greater development in the region, itself a potentially costly undertaking. The Alliance for Progress aid programme of the 1960s placed a priority upon initiatives to foster economic growth and social reform (see Chapter 2). However, US economic aid programmes were increasingly used to reinforce national security perspectives, and became associated with military assistance. Much of the economic aid provided to Latin America before the 1970s was given to special police forces that assisted the military in counterinsurgency operations. Through its extensive military assistance programmes, and at the US Army's School of the Americas in the Panama Canal Zone, the US passed its national security doctrine on to Latin American armed forces. At least 11 Latin American authoritarian rulers were among those trained at the School of the Americas (see Livingstone, 2009). Similar doctrines

▶

were adopted or developed by many of the military establishments in the region during the Cold War (see Chapter 2). Outspoken Latin American critics of the US such as Nieto (2003) have described the regimes that copied US national security doctrine as 'neo-fascist dictatorships' because of their militarism and authoritarian positions. In the 1990s, there was further evidence of how US national security doctrine has changed over time. Now, national security considerations led to militarisation of the drugs war: counter-narcotics replaced counterinsurgency as a US foreign policy priority (see below). National security remains a prominent feature of executive policymaking in the US and the National Security Adviser is one of the most influential figures in US government. It was given added force by the 'War on Terror' that followed the attacks against the World Trade Center on 11 September 2001 (see Box 10.4). An alternative vision of national security as well as of the appropriate foreign policy towards Latin America given the changes that have occurred since 2000 formed the backdrop to the declaration by the Council on Foreign Relations that US hegemony in the region was over (see Barshefsky et al. eds, 2008). The CFR task force that drew up the policy recommendations included R. Rand Beers, for example, who served in four positions on the National Security Council staff at the White House during four administrations and in 2009 was appointed by Obama to the Department of Homeland Security. The CFR document identified as critical issues in Latin America that merit special attention in US foreign policy today: poverty and inequality, public security, human mobility, and energy security. They argue that these issues represent fundamental challenges and opportunities for US–Latin American relations and will have a bearing on traditional US objectives of democracy promotion, economic expansion, and counter-narcotics. The failures of US immigration policy, in particular, affect the country's national security, economic growth, and foreign relations.

In Washington's view, the most tempting targets for adversaries of the US have been Latin America's smallest, poorest and least stable countries (Pastor, 2001). In principle, technological developments reduced any strategic value Latin America may have for an adversary by virtue of proximity many decades ago. However, US military predominance in the region has maintained a *symbolic* importance as an indicator of its credibility in international relations (Schoultz, 1998). During the Cold War, for example, Washington believed that any 'loss' of a country in Latin America to the Soviet Union would be interpreted around the world as a sign of US weakness. Since the dissolution of the Soviet Union, Latin America has no longer carried the same symbolic security significance. Smaller deployments of US forces have participated in anti-drug operations in several Latin American states, and US military advisers have at times been present in zones of conflict with guerrilla forces. The decision of the US to enhance its military presence in Colombia in 2009 generated significant debate within Latin America (see Box 10.3).

The US still considers Latin America to be within its sphere of influence and concerns about military credibility remain at the heart of its security policy (Schoultz, 1998). Key figures influential in devising Cold War-era policy towards Latin America under Reagan, for example, were given prominent foreign policy or national security roles by George W. Bush. The Bush administration placed a significant emphasis on security in its relations with Latin America as part of the 'War on Terror' that it pursued following the 9/11 attacks (see Box 10.4), to the apparent detriment of favourable attitudes in Latin America towards its powerful

| CASE STUDY | Box 10.3 |

US relations with Colombia

The militarisation of the campaign against drug-trafficking has revived some familiar strategic considerations, especially in Colombia, where US aid to the government in its battle against Marxist guerrillas has blurred the distinction between counter-narcotics, counterinsurgency (today designated 'counter-terrorism') and strategic security policies. Colombia is the world's third largest, and the largest Latin American, recipient of US military aid. Since 2000, the US has spent about $4 billion on programmes to fight drug-trafficking in Colombia, to train its army to fight insurgents, and to improve state institutions. As part of its commitment to the Colombian state, the US deployed hundreds of troops in the country to train and advise its military, and US involvement in its civil war became more or less direct. A decision in 2009 by Colombia's president, Alvaro Uribe, to permit US forces to increase its presence in the country for counter-narcotics and counter-terrorism operations by using Colombian military bases significantly increased tensions with neighbouring Venezuela and alarmed other Latin American states, deepening Colombia's diplomatic isolation in the region. The 10-year deal gave the US military access to seven Colombian army, navy and air force bases, permitted it also to use civilian airports, and granted US personnel and defence contractors diplomatic immunity.

In 1999, 'Plan Colombia' was devised as a Colombian initiative backed by US aid premised on an association between the main guerrilla organisations such as FARC (see Chapter 12, Box 16.3) and drug-trafficking. US officials have also tried to make connections between militant Islamic groups in the Middle East and Latin American drug-trafficking networks (see Diamint, 2004). More recently, the congressional Government Accountability Office released a report arguing that state corruption, covert aid to FARC, and a refusal to co-operate with US law enforcement agencies was turning Venezuela into a 'narcostate' at the centre of drug-trafficking in the region (Forero, 2009). Venezuela vigorously rejects the allegations, which President Hugo Chávez dismissed as a political device to weaken his government. Chávez has maintained political links with FARC, at one stage acting as an intermediary with the organisation on behalf of the Colombian government. He has also pushed for a solution to Colombia's civil war that has included the recognition of FARC as a political actor rather than a belligerent organisation, a move that would not be without precedent.

The centrepiece of Plan Colombia has been the aerial spraying of coca crops, which provide the raw material for cocaine and help to finance paramilitaries and rebels in the civil war. Initially, the US congress specified that aid under Plan Colombia should only be used in the fight against drug-trafficking, but the administration of George W. Bush admitted that some aid was being spent on counter-terrorism.

Critics of US policy such as Galen Carpenter (2003) say the war on drugs in Latin America has been disastrous for the region (see below), and that the US-funded battle against coca cultivation is not succeeding (see also Barshefsky *et al*. eds, 2008; Youngers and Rosin eds, 2004). Some evidence of that can be found in Mexico: drug flows north to the US continue and violence in Mexico has escalated (see Box 4.3) prompting new and costly US support for the Mexican government.

However, the UN Office on Drugs and Crime (2009) has indicated that there are signs that the counter-narcotics strategy in Colombia itself are working. In 2008, a significant decrease in cocaine production in Colombia, the world's largest cultivator of coca bush, brought the total area under cultivation down by about 8 per cent, and estimated global cocaine production was down as a result (UNODC, 2009). There was also a significant decline in trafficking in 2008 towards North America, the world's largest cocaine consumer market, reflected in rising prices and falling purity levels (*ibid*.). However, cultivation and production increased in Peru and Bolivia.

▶

None the less, critics say crop spraying from the air to eradicate coca kills all crops and destroys the livelihoods of poor peasant farmers, and they argue that US policy in Colombia has made a bad situation worse by fuelling violence. The human rights record of Colombia's military is one of the worst in Latin America, and critics accuse the armed forces of collaborating with rightwing paramilitaries accused of massacring civilians (Stokes, 2005). The links between FARC and drugs exports to the US have also been called into question, while evidence of links between rightwing paramilitary organisations countering the FARC and drug-trafficking has grown. FARC has imposed taxation on the production of drugs in the areas that it controls and, in some cases, it has co-operated with the UN in efforts to replace coca with alternative crops. Stokes (2005) argues that the record suggests the US has backed those actors who are in fact involved in drug trafficking by its support for a counterinsurgency strategy that has, at times, devolved military capability to paramilitaries.

The critics of US policy towards greater military engagement with Colombia also argue that there are other regional imperatives at work to explain it. Stokes (2005) argues that US intervention in Colombia has sought to stabilise social, economic and political arrangements in order to preserve the conditions for US investment, market access and the repatriation of profit by transnational corporations. The US is a key foreign investor in the country (see Chapter 15). The preservation of access to oil supplies is another important factor helping to explain US policy, particularly in the context of the effort to diversify sources of supply away from the Middle East and the enmity of the administration of Chávez in Venezuela, a major oil supplier to the US (see below, and Figure 14.1). The Venezuelan government itself argues that an expanded US military presence in Colombia represents a threat to its oil industry and is an effort to intimidate it because of its socialist policies and relations with Cuba. In response to the decision in 2009 to permit an increased US military presence in Colombia, Chávez urged his armed forces to be prepared for possible war, and Colombia said it would seek help from the UN Security Council and OAS to defuse tensions (see Box 9.8).

neighbour and its vision of democracy. Some scholars argue that it was prior US experience in Latin America itself that helped it shape the War on Terror associated with later engagements in the Middle East (see Grandin, 2006). According to the Pew Global Attitudes Project, for example, 82 per cent of Venezuelans, 34 per cent of Argentineans, and 51 per cent of Bolivians had a favourable view of the US in 2002, but by 2007 those proportions had fallen to 56, 16, and 43 per cent respectively (Pew Research Center, 2009). The percentage of Latin Americans who approved of US ideas on democracy decreased from 45 per cent in 2002 to 29 per cent in 2007 (*ibid.*). Those ideas place significant emphasis on the procedural aspect of democracy, namely elections, above all else (see Chapter 3). They were in evidence in the dispute that arose over policy throughout the Americas towards Honduras following efforts to broker a crisis to the coup of 2009. Although the US was eventually unable to negotiate the return of the ousted president, Manuel Zelaya, it accepted the decision to hold elections in the country in November 2009 as the only way to resolve the country's political crisis and restore democracy. The decision was condemned by Zelaya himself, and several Latin American countries, including Brazil and Argentina, said they would not recognise the election as legitimate. The conservative landowner Porfirio Lobo, Zelaya's main political rival who had supported his removal, was subsequently elected.

The 'War on Terror'

Security became a paramount consideration in US foreign policy after the 9/11 terrorist attacks in 2001. On the one hand, 9/11 shifted US priorities under President George W. Bush towards the Middle East, further demoting the importance of Latin America in US strategic policy, but, on the other, US tactics generated new tensions with Latin American governments as the Pentagon took a greater role that the State Department in shaping policy. Areas of tension generated in the relationship between Latin American governments and the US by the war on terror included:

– the US decision to allow its military aid to Colombia to be used against 'terrorists', that is, against FARC (see Boxes 9.8, 10.3);

– the legal limbo of US prisoners held at its military camp in Guantánamo Bay in Cuba, facilities that are retained under lease but that Cuba argues are held by force in violation of international law. The commitment of President Barack Obama (2009–) to close the camp's detention facility has eased these tensions;

– the secret US 'rendition' flights to ferry captives to countries where rules on torture may have differed;

– US demands for military personnel on Latin American soil to be granted immunity from the jurisdiction of the International Criminal Court;

– the pressure the US placed on Latin American countries to fall in line with its concern about the potential for activity by Islamic militants. Diamint (2004), for example, highlighted US concerns about the potential for activity by Islamic militants in South America, and in particular in the region where Argentina, Brazil and Paraguay meet known as the 'Triple Frontier'. These fears may not be entirely unfounded. US and Panamanian officials have acknowledged that a Saudi al-Qaeda operative was in Panama in April 2001, five months before the 9/11 attacks. In January 2006, Colombian authorities said they had broken up a ring that had provided false passports to members of al-Qaeda and Hamas who aimed to travel to Europe and the US (bbc.co.uk, 2006a). In 2009, Ronald Noble, the secretary general of Interpol, raised concerns about reports that the 'maras', Central American criminal gangs whose members also operate in the US, may have had contacts with al-Qaeda, and said that co-operation between these groups was not inconceivable (see Noble, 2009; *Chicago Tribune*, 2004; see also Box 6.3). However, the evidence for activity by Islamic militants in Latin America is thin on the ground, and a climate of nervousness not unlike that of the Cold War has led to false alarms. In May 2005, Nicaragua's national police declared an alert based on the 'possible presence' of two suspected members of the al-Qaeda network in Central America wanted by US authorities, although the US said later this had been a misunderstanding (AP, 2005a; Canadian Press, 2005).

A product of the climate generated by the War on Terror in the US has been to place much greater attention on immigration policy and human-trafficking across the US–Mexican border (see below). The decision by the Bush administration to reinforce and extend a physical barrier along the US–Mexican border in 2006 in response to security fears, without Mexican consultation, caused friction with Mexico at a time when it had been seeking concessions on migration because of the economic benefits to both countries and their partnership under NAFTA (see Boxes 10.9, 15.5).

Critics of the US war on terror in Latin America have also alleged that the US itself has, historically, been inconsistent with regard to terrorism in the region. For example, Washington has refused to extradite to Cuba or Venezuela Orlando Bosch and Luis Posada Carriles – Cuban exiles suspected of bombing a Cuban airliner in 1976, killing 73 civilians, and of other terrorist attacks.

The US still reserves the right for security reasons to intervene in Latin American states, even though these reject that it has any such right and often question its motives. Prior to 1999, the US military's Southern Command was based in Panama, and thereafter it began to operate from smaller bases leased for 10 years from Latin American countries, in particular those in Ecuador, Curaçao and Aruba in the Caribbean, and El Salvador. The decision by Ecuador not to renew the lease at its base in Manta when it expired in 2009 prompted the US to increase its military presence in Colombia and angered several neighbouring countries (see Boxes 9.8, 10.3). The US also maintains a large number of radar sites throughout Latin America, both fixed (particularly in Peru and Colombia) and mobile. It has also reserved the right to intervene in Latin American military policies. In 2005, Washington tried to block a $2 billion arms deal between Spain and Venezuela, for example, and Venezuela's president Hugo Chávez withdrew the diplomatic immunity of agents working for the US Drug Enforcement Administration, whom he said were spying on his country. In February 2006, Chávez expelled a naval attaché based at the US embassy in Caracas whom Venezuela accused of spying, and Washington responded by expelling a senior Venezuelan envoy. In 2008–09, the US revived its Fourth Fleet based in Florida as a naval command for the Latin America and Caribbean region. First created in 1943 to guard against enemy ships and submarines during the Second World War, the 4th Fleet was retired shortly after the end of the war. While officials said that its recent re-establishment did not change the US navy's mission in the area and that it would undertake work such as joint training, counter-narcotics operations and disaster relief, the move generated criticism in Latin America. Venezuela again described this as a potential threat to the country's oil resources, Cuba said it could be used to seize food and energy resources, Bolivia called its creation a form of intervention, and the governments of Argentina and Brazil made formal inquiries about its mission (see also Chapter 11).

Ideological hegemony

Ideological concerns have influenced US policy towards Latin America since the nineteenth century, shaped by a vision of tutelary duty towards a region whose people are generally regarded as inferior which Schoultz (1998) argues remains at the core of any explanation of US policy (see Box 10.5).

The Monroe Doctrine, for example, sought to deter not just European imperial power but also European absolutism. The ideological dimension of US foreign policy became apparent when the US first started to project its military power internationally with the war against Spain in Cuba in which Puerto Rico was also ceded to the US in 1898 (see Box 10.6), but was most apparent during the Cold War. Anti-communism pervaded every aspect of US policy towards Latin America from the late 1940s, when the US pressed countries to sever relations with the USSR and to ban communist parties, until the 1980s, when it promoted counter-revolutionary guerrilla movements (Smith, 2000). Anti-communist positions persisted into the post-Cold War era and were evident in legislation shaping policy on Cuba such as the 1992 Cuban Democracy Act, known as the Torricelli Act, and the

SOCIETY	Box 10.5

The US mindset

Schoultz (1998) has argued that a powerful mindset governs the thinking of US officials with regard to Latin America, prominent within which is 'a pervasive belief that Latin Americans constitute an inferior branch of the human species' (p. xv). He suggested that opinion poll data indicate that the rough outlines of this mindset are shared by a broad spectrum of the US public. He wrote: 'This is the mindset that led President Monroe to announce his Doctrine, that pushed President Polk to declare war against Mexico, that inspired President Roosevelt to wield a Big Stick, that induced President Taft to implement Dollar Diplomacy, that encouraged President Wilson to teach the Latin Americans to elect good leaders, that prompted President Kennedy to establish the Agency for International Development, that influenced President Reagan to create the National Endowment for Democracy, and that led President George Bush Sr (1989–93) to call Nicaragua's President an unwelcome dog at a garden party.' (p. xvii). Schoultz (2009) has also argued that this mindset has fuelled an 'uplifting mentality' among US government officials over many generations based on a belief that the country has a mission to teach neighbouring countries such as Cuba a better and higher form of civilisation. Livingstone (2009) has argued that such attitudes have been expressed by senior US officials as recently as the administration of George W. Bush. She writes: 'In a more subtle way, today's constant chiding of Latin American leaders by US secretaries of state, urging them to act "responsibly" and implement "responsible policies", has echoes of the parent–child relationship assumed in previous centuries' (Livingstone, 2009, p. 218). There is considerable support for this perspective among Latin American scholars. The Colombian Clara Nieto, for example, has criticised the neglect of teaching about Latin America within the US and argues that this derives from a fear of embarrassment about its role as an 'aggressive, expansionist imperial power' in the region (Nieto, 2003, p. 11). Latin American politicians have often spoken about a lack of respect in the dealings of the US towards them. Barack Obama (2009–) responded to this notion at the Summit of the Americas in Trinidad and Tobago in April 2009 by promising that, in future, relations will be characterised by mutual respect, although the continuities and discontinuities in foreign policy under his administration have been the subject of considerable debate (see below). The demand for respect still forms an important part of the rhetoric of countries that continue to have a difficult relationship with the US. Talks aimed at improving strained ties in late 2009 between Bolivia's president, Evo Morales, and the US Assistant Secretary of State for Western Hemisphere Affairs, Thomas Shannon, for example, were followed by comments by the Bolivian leader in which he urged 'mutual respect' between the two countries and said Washington should not interfere in Bolivia's affairs (see below).

1996 Cuban Liberty and Democratic Solidarity (Libertad) Act, also known as the Helms-Burton Act (see Box 10.8). A key recommendation by the Council on Foreign Relations task force on US foreign policy in 2008 was the repeal of the Helms-Burton law, which removed most of the executive branch's authority to eliminate economic sanctions against Cuba (see Barshefsky *et al.* eds, 2008).

Informing US anti-communism was a discourse on democracy that has been present since the nineteenth century and has been restated recurrently (see Lowenthal, 1991). Democracy promotion abroad has become the ideological cornerstone of US foreign policy in a context in which it is no longer able to appeal to anti-communism (Smith, 2000). Criticisms of this ideological discourse have concentrated less on the message – the underlying principle that democracy is a good thing has near universal support – but on *how* the US has promoted democracy abroad, in particular what is often seen as an over-emphasis on elections, as well as examples of double standards in its policies. Democracy promotion was an important part of the rhetoric of President George W. Bush, for example, who in June 2005 put democracy at the heart of his speech to the general assembly of the Organisation of American States (see Box 9.5). However, scholars such as Carothers (2009) have argued that the Bush administration bequeathed a highly problematic legacy on US democracy promotion by elevating its profile then tarnishing it. Carothers states: 'By relentlessly associating it with the Iraq war and regime change, he caused many in the world to see it as a hypocritical cover for aggressive interventionism serving US security needs' (2009, p. 1). This placed pressure on his successor, Barack Obama, to distance his administration from Bush's approach and pull back substantially from supporting democracy abroad; to dissociate the subject of democratisation from regime change and counter-terrorism; and to change the past emphasis in US policy on electoral democracy to one that concentrates instead on key elements of consolidation such as building the rule of law and an effective state (see Chapters 3, 4). Accordingly, in the first year of his administration, there was less emphasis in the rhetoric of Obama on democracy promotion in other countries than under his predecessor.

The US has used various policy tools to support its vision of democracy in Latin America (see Chapter 3), although Washington's record in promoting democracy has been inconsistent and often counterproductive, exposing it to charges of hypocrisy (see Hari, 2005). First, there are many examples in which the US has supported authoritarian regimes in Latin America or has turned a blind eye to electoral fraud in support of its strategic interests. While during the Cold War members of the Washington elite sought to combat authoritarian regimes, this was almost always overshadowed by the greater perceived need to combat communism. Second, in some cases, such as Guatemala in 1954 and Chile in 1973, the US has actively *undermined* democracy when Republican administrations believed communists had either captured government or would do so. Even Carter's support for improved human rights in Latin America was reined in out of fear of revolution in Nicaragua. Third, US actions have often weakened democratic mechanisms. Washington accepted the results of the 1988 presidential elections in Mexico which were widely considered to have been fraudulent, for example, and during the early 1990s tolerated the authoritarian behaviour of presidents who pursued economic reforms the US was promoting, such as Alberto Fujimori (1990–2000) in Peru. In September 2009, Fujimori was jailed in his country for corruption while he was already serving prison sentences for abuse of power, ordering the security forces to carry out killings and kidnappings while in office, and embezzlement. Fourth, there has been a longstanding US failure to respond to demands for a democratic resolution of the anomalous status of Puerto Rico that is only now being addressed more than a century after the island was ceded by Spain (see Box 10.6). During deliberations on the Puerto Rico Democracy Act of 2009 in the US House of Representatives, for example, the chairman of the committee on natural resources, Nick J. Rahall, said: 'When our union of states was comprised of renegade English colonies, we then stepped into a role that we previously had fought against. Given

Puerto Rico – a question of status

The unresolved nature of Puerto Rico's relationship with the US has long been the subject of debate on the Caribbean island itself and in the US congress and UN. It reflects both the complexities of US history – and in particular its ambivalent relationship with the concept of empire that, in principle, it has always opposed (see Box 10.1) – but also the ease with which a process of decolonisation can be delayed or postponed by virtue of the divisions that exist within a colonial society.

The island of nearly 4 million people is considered to be an unincorporated territory of the US, that is, belonging to it but not part of it. It is not a state of the union and has no voting representative in the US congress. US federal law applies, although most federal taxes do not because taxation is delegated to local authorities. People born on the island are US citizens and entitled to vote in federal elections, but not on the island itself because it is not incorporated, and as such are not fully enfranchised in the US political process. However, in 2006, the supreme court of Puerto Rico and the Puerto Rican secretary of justice determined that Puerto Rican citizenship itself exists and is recognised in the island's constitution.

In 1950, the US congress granted Puerto Ricans the right to establish a constitution for Puerto Rico – denoting it as a 'commonwealth' that supposed continued US sovereignty over the island but gave it a degree of autonomy that can be likened to that of a state – a measure that was accepted and came into force in 1952. The UN General Assembly then removed Puerto Rico's classification as a non-self governing territory, but did not determine if it had achieved full self-governing status. Nor did these congressional measures revoke provisions concerning the legal relationship of Puerto Rico to the US based on the territorial clause of the US constitution. In 1967, Puerto Rico's legislative assembly sought to determine the preference of the electorate according to three status options: commonwealth, pro-US statehood, and independence. The plebiscite was boycotted by the main pro-statehood and pro-independence parties, and the commonwealth option was approved. From 1952 to 2007, Puerto Rico's main parties have represented these different status scenarios: the Partido Popular Democrático (PPD, Popular Democratic Party) supports Puerto Rico's right to self-determination through 'association' status as a commonwealth of some kind, albeit one that does not have colonial status; the Partido Nuevo Progresista (PNP, New Progressive Party) advocates full US statehood through annexation; and the Partido Independentista Puertorriqueño (PIP, Puerto Rican Independence Party) seeks the island's independence. Status quo and pro-statehood forces have been evenly balanced as the two main political forces in this debate. A number of other organisations and nationalist groupings advocating independence or autonomy also exist. Plebiscites held in Puerto Rico in 1993 and 1998 have been inconclusive other than indicating dissatisfaction with the island's current status. Attempts in US congressional committees between the 1970s and 2000s to address the status issue have all foundered. In all, since the establishment of commonwealth status in 1952, four popular votes have been held on the status of Puerto Rico in three plebiscites and one referendum on the island, none of which has been sanctioned by the US congress itself. Since the 1970s, at least 40 measures have been introduced in the US congress to resolve or clarify the island's status, and it has held at least 12 hearings on the issue. In 2005 and 2007, reports issued by the US president's Task Force on Puerto Rico's Status concluded that it continues to be a territory of the US under the plenary powers of congress.

Meanwhile, pressure in Latin America for a resolution of the status issue has grown. In 2006, the Latin American and Caribbean Congress in Solidarity with the Independence of Puerto Rico was organised in Panama by the ruling Partido Revolucionario Democrático (PRD, Revolutionary Democratic Party)

▶

of President Martín Torrijos (2004–09). Former presidents and 15 other ruling parties from across Latin America were among those represented at the summit, which approved the so-called 'Panama Proclamation' calling on the US to respect Puerto Rico's right to self-determination. That year, the Latin American Parliament (Parlatino, see Box 9.7) added its weight to support for Puerto Rican self-determination, and in 2007 a number of prominent Latin American intellectuals including Gabriel García Márquez, Ernesto Sábato, Pablo Milanés, Eduardo Galeano, Mario Benedetti and Jorge Enrique Adoum also backed the Panama Proclamation. In March 2009, a meeting in Guatemala of the Socialist International's Committee for Latin America and the Caribbean adopted a 'Resolution on Puerto Rico' calling on member parties to intensify their efforts to encourage their governments to support a request by the UN Special Committee on Decolonisation to examine the case of Puerto Rico, and also calling for the release of Puerto Rican political prisoners. In June 2009, the UN Special Committee on Decolonisation, which several times has supported the case for Puerto Ricans to exercise their right to self-determination if they choose, approved a draft resolution calling on the US to expedite the process.

There have been two recent attempts to provide for referendums in Puerto Rico to determine the island's status through a Puerto Rico Democracy Act, introduced in the US congress in 2007 and then again in 2009. The 2007 bill gained bipartisan support in both the House of Representatives and Senate, but was not voted on before the 110th congress ended. The latest bill has been seen as offering the best chance to date of a resolution of Puerto Rico's status. It was introduced to the House of Representatives in May 2009 by Pedro Pierluisi, the Resident Commissioner of Puerto Rico, a non-voting member of the US house elected by the Puerto Rican voters, who is affiliated to the PNP. The Puerto Rico Democracy Act of 2009 would order a referendum giving Puerto Ricans the choice to retain their present status or choose a new one. If the latter were to prevail, a separate referendum would be held in which Puerto Ricans would vote on either being admitted as a US state or becoming a 'sovereign nation, either fully independent from or in free association with the United States'.

our own experience, would anyone have imagined that our new colony would be disenfranchised and kept unequal in our political framework?' (Rahall, 2009).

US actions have often taken little account of their impact on the democratic process, and have fuelled accusations against it, particularly on the left in Latin America, of 'imperialism' (see Box 10.1). Colombia's democracy was badly strained by the US attempt from 1995–98 to remove President Ernesto Samper (1994–98) from office. Bolivia's democracy has also been put under strain at various times by the priority placed by the US on policies to counter the production of coca, which has long played a traditional role in Andean culture but is also of commercial use in the cosmetics and food industries. The hostility of the Bush regime towards Evo Morales, the popular leader of Bolivia's leftwing Movimiento al Socialismo (MAS, Movement towards Socialism) and a spokesman for indigenous coca growers who became president in 2006, did not help efforts to find a solution to the country's political difficulties or to advance the US anti-drug agenda in the region. US officials, including the ambassador to Bolivia, suggested publicly that Washington might reconsider future aid to the country if Morales pursued policies that it did not approve of, including a commitment to strengthen ties with Venezuela and Cuba (Rieff, 2005; see also Box 16.1). In late 2008, Bolivia expelled the US ambassador, accusing him of fomenting civil unrest during anti-government protests, and Washington reciprocated by expelling the Bolivian ambassador. Two months later, Morales suspended the operations of the Drug Enforcement Administration in Bolivia. It was only a year later, in late 2009, that Morales and the US Assistant Secretary of State for Western Hemisphere Affairs, Thomas Shannon, held high-profile talks aimed at improving their strained ties. None the less, the cultivation of coca and its symbolic associations have become key political issues in Bolivia. In the run-up to elections in December 2009, for example, coca growers united to help finance Morales' re-election campaign.

Critics say the policy of the Bush administration towards Venezuela, which was characterised by a consistent deterioration in relations, also contradicted US rhetoric on democracy (see Box 9.3; Golinger, 2006). Washington gave *de facto* recognition of the government formed after a short-lived coup in 2002 that ousted President Chávez by industrialists who had, hitherto, reportedly been in contact with senior officials in the US State Department such as Reich (Nieto, 2003; see Box 7.2). Livingstone (2009) has examined these and other contacts between US officials and anti-Chávez forces that she argues amount to active intervention in attempts to remove the Venezuelan leader. Chávez himself has accused the US of a long list of covert interventions in the politics of his country and neighbours such as Bolivia, and accused Washington during the Bush administration of plotting to assassinate him. In September 2008, Chávez expelled the US ambassador to his country in solidarity with Bolivia, and diplomatic ties were only restored in mid-2009 after Obama had come to the presidency.

This inconsistency highlights the changing role democracy has played in the ideological justifications used by the US in foreign policy. Pastor (2001) argues that there has long been a debate in US policymaking circles about the promotion of democracy, with realists suggesting Latin America cannot sustain democracy and idealists asserting that the US should try to make democracy succeed. A persistent issue faced by the US has been the *model* of democracy it has promoted in Latin America. US statements promote a procedural model of democracy alongside liberal guarantees underpinning capitalism (see Chapters 3, 15). As a result, US policymakers have tended to view the Left with distrust, adopting a restrictive conception of democracy weighted in favour of dominant classes that precludes any form of social democracy (see Chapters 12, 16). This tension has become more evident as left-of-centre governments have come to power in Latin America by democratic means. The Council on Foreign Relations task force that examined US policy towards Latin America (see above) suggested that the longstanding focus on democracy, trade and drugs, while still relevant, is now an inadequate basis for conducting US relations in the region and that poverty and inequality should be among the key themes around which policy is reframed (see Barshefsky *et al.* eds, 2008). This suggests that the policy debate in the US has begun to incorporate a greater emphasis upon social democracy, probably in response to changes within Latin America itself. One of the initiatives undertaken by the US navy in the region since 2007, for example, has been visits by a navy hospital ship to 12 Latin American and Caribbean nations to provide free medical care, a clear response to similar initiatives by Cuba (see Chapter 9).

None the less, US discourse about democracy in Latin America has often found a receptive audience, and by the 1990s the development of a *shared* inter-American interest in the defence and promotion of democracy was evident (see Chapters 3, 9), enshrined in documents such as the OAS 'Santiago Commitment' (see Box 9.5). This convergence of values may reflect the emergence of an expanding 'inter-American civil society' fostered by governments and based upon links between interest groups, NGOs, businesses and ethnic communities across the hemisphere. It also reflects changes in US society itself as a result of significant growth in the US Latino population (see below). Growing family ties between Latinos in the US and their homelands amounts to a form of *de facto* US–Latin America integration. The US government has spent large sums on nurturing inter-American civic life through such initiatives as the National Endowment for Democracy, although at times these have been criticised both from within the US and Latin America (see Boxes 3.2, 10.7). Private organisations in the US such as the Ford, MacArthur and Carter foundations have also actively nurtured Latin American civil society.

Economic interests

Since the 1930s, the US has exerted its predominance in the Americas mostly in economic terms, and this has sometimes been seen as an underlying 'structural' explanation for its foreign policy. US politicians have always believed that their country must have access to Latin America to sustain a strong economy (Schoultz, 1998). The US has been both Latin America's most important economic partner but also its most important model. Economic relations between Latin America and the US during the Cold War were shaped by Washington's negative attitudes towards state intervention in the economy and its belief in export promotion. The US reacted with hostility to nationalist policies that proposed the expropriation of its interests, and actively tried to influence Latin American economic policies in the 1960s through John F. Kennedy's Alliance for Progress (see Chapter 2). Multi-national corporations became a prominent reflection of US economic activity in Latin America in the 1960s and 1970s, and relations also grew closer because oil revenues transformed US banks into an abundant source of investment. Development was curtailed by the debt crisis of 1982, and the US used its influence within financial institutions such as the IMF to shape the new neoliberal orthodoxy in Latin America (see Chapter 15). Neoliberalism moved the economic relationship between Latin America and the US further in the direction of interdependence, and in the early 1990s the Bush administration advocated a hemispheric Free Trade Area of the Americas (FTAA, see Box 15.5) modelled on the North American Free Trade Agreement (NAFTA) between the US, Canada and Mexico that came into force in 1994 (see below).

The desire for economic interdependence across the American hemisphere is not new. For more than a century, powerful interests in the US have sought to tie Latin American economies to its development, encouraging since the 1880s the emergence of an inter-American bureaucracy. Economic integration has also had a strategic objective and, at times, the US has used trade policy to strengthen its security. Generous concessions offered through the 1980s Caribbean Basin Initiative, for example, were shaped by Reagan's security agenda. Integration became more of a priority as the US became exposed to competition by powerful regional trading blocs such as Europe and lost influence in relative terms within multilateral

---

INSTITUTIONS	Box 10.7

NED – friend or foe?

Critics of the National Endowment for Democracy (see also Box 3.2) come from within and outside the US. At times, it has come under fire from within congress about its independence, organisation and accountability. The NED has been accused from the right of promoting a 'social-democratic' agenda through its labour institute, yet it has also been supported by rightwing organisations such as the Heritage Foundation and many of its external critics in fact see it as a rightwing initiative historically associated with Ronald Reagan's personal Cold War agenda. Latin American critics say the NED is a manifestation of US paternalistic attitudes towards the region and even an embodiment of imperialism (see Box 10.1). Nieto (2003) claims that in Venezuela the group of industrialists under Pedro Carmona who took power briefly following the 2002 coup against President Chávez had the support of the NED (see Box 7.2). Chávez himself publicised documents in 2004 purportedly demonstrating NED funding for NGOs and civil associations that had been actively opposing him, such as the election-monitoring group Súmate that organised the campaign to hold a recall referendum on his term in office that year. The Venezuelan leader denounced members of the group as conspirators and brought treason charges against some of them for receiving NED support, a move denounced by human rights organisations and the US government. The NED is also thought to have supported the work of several journalists in Venezuela who work for opposition media outlets that have come under pressure from the Venezuelan regime (see Box 4.2, Chapter 8). The NED and partner organisations such as the Center for International Private Enterprise (CIPE) have also granted funds to organisations in Bolivia that have been critical of policies pursued by its leftwing president, Evo Morales – including CAINCO, which has been active in the autonomy movement in the eastern part of the country (Bigwood, 2008; Dangl, 2008; see also Boxes 4.1, 12.11). The journalist Jeremy Bigwood (2008) says documents obtained under Freedom of Information rules clearly show the historic relationship between US funding institutions and the Santa Cruz opposition in Bolivia. Although at times the US congress has tasked the NED to carry out specific initiatives in countries of special interest, including Chile and Nicaragua, the NED itself insists its strengths derive from its status as a non-governmental and independent body. In its public statements, it says that democracy need not be based upon the US model but evolves according to the needs and traditions of diverse political cultures (see Lowe, 2005). Supporters of the NED say that it helps many groups with a social-democratic and liberal orientation across the world and has also supported, provided training for and consulted with groups that approve of democracy and criticise the US itself.

---

initiatives such as the General Agreement on Tariffs and Trade (GATT). The FTAA has been likened, in one respect, to the Monroe Doctrine, by seeking to restrict European and Asian influence in Latin America (see Box 1.4, Chapter 11).

Trade between the US and Latin America has increased significantly since the 1990s, and the rate of growth of trade between the regions has generally been higher than that in other parts of the world. By 2008, South and Central America exported goods worth $149 billion to the US, and was the destination for $135 billion of US exports (see Table 9.1). Much of the increase in intra-hemispheric trade has come as a result of NAFTA, although this agreement has not been without its critics (see Table 9.2). Intra-regional trade within NAFTA itself amounted to about $1,000 billion in 2008, of which Mexican exports to the US amounted to about \$215 billion and US exports to Mexico \$151 billion. In 2005, the World Trade Organisation changed its use of the category Latin America in its annual trade statistics to distinguish between North America (referring to the NAFTA economies, including Mexico) and South and Central America.

The desire to establish an FTAA can be seen as an effort to institutionalise existing trading links and to ensure US economic pre-eminence in the hemisphere against competition from Asia and Europe. Opposition to the FTAA grew in the period of economic growth in Latin America after 2002–08 and as a result of regional integration initiatives such as ALBA (see Boxes 9.1, 16.1). Large trading nations such as Brazil have been worried that key industries will find it difficult to compete with their US rivals, and suffer damage as a result. Hemispheric agreement on the FTAA missed its targeted deadline of 2005 and was not even on the agenda of the Trinidad & Tobago Summit of the Americas in 2009, suggesting that the appetite for a US-led pan-regional trade initiative and model for hemispheric integration has disappeared for the time being, a situation exacerbated by the impact of the 2008–09 financial crisis on trade in Latin America. The US has, instead, pursued free-trade integration through bilateral or bloc agreements extending the provisions of NAFTA, such as DR-CAFTA (see Chapter 9). The US trade relationship with Latin America has also changed under President Obama, who has been cooler towards commercial agreements than his predecessors. Moreover, the benefits and disadvantages of NAFTA itself – the first trade agreement between the US and a developing country – have come under scrutiny in recent years (see Gallagher and Wise, 2009; see also Chapter 15). There have been calls in both the US – including those of Obama during his election campaign – and in Mexico to renegotiate NAFTA, and in recent years Canada has also started to extend its own free trade agenda across the Americas independent of the US.

Targeted economic aid programmes reveal much about the traditional US objectives of achieving *stability* and *security* in Latin America. Financial instability in the region has created many challenges to policymaking and has had a direct impact on US interests. The 1982 debt crisis posed a serious threat to the solvency of major US banks; in late 1994, Mexico's financial crisis led the US government to arrange a complex \$50 billion rescue that protected international investors; Brazil's devaluation in 1999 provoked a region-wide recession; and the US played a pivotal role in efforts to deal with the aftermath of Argentina's crisis in 2001 (see Domínguez, 2000). Financial crises will recur in Latin America because of the behaviour of international capital markets and the region's dependence on the export of primary commodities such as oil. The impact of the most recent financial crisis in 2008–09 is again revealing the limited degree of autonomy Latin America has gained vis-à-vis US and international capital markets, despite recent growth that might suggest otherwise. The financial crisis did not have an immediate effect on Latin America because past instability in countries such as Argentina and Mexico had prompted their governments to take steps that limited financial speculation. Since 2000, for example, Latin American economies have been helped by huge windfall profits from high commodity prices and expanding markets in Asia, giving them greater financial autonomy with regard to the US. US financial and investment institutions were also at the centre of the global economic crisis of 2008–09 and, as these turned insolvent, their finance in Latin America began to flee or was repatriated, further weakening US economic leverage in the region. However, at the same time, the decline of export markets and the drying up of credit markets and foreign capital inflows engendered by the financial crisis had by mid-2009 again begun to expose weaknesses in Latin American economies and their relative dependence on export strategies (see Chapter 14). In order to underwrite the bailout to US financial institutions, the Obama administration absorbed credit in the region (see below), making it difficult for Latin American countries to finance their exports. This is because the US financial sector has been encouraged to expand capital reserves and direct lending to the domestic market at the expense of Latin American borrowers. In consequence, recession began to bite in Latin American countries during 2009, and will be watched carefully by the US, which will continue to perceive that its security remains affected by the stability of Latin America's economies.

Threats to US security have often prompted its policymakers to devise responses that include economic components. Variations in the level of US aid to Latin America reflect Washington's assessment of the security threat in the region (Pastor, 2001). For example, of all the foreign aid the US dispensed between 1945–90, more than 70 per cent was allocated between 1960 and 1980 (*ibid*.). With the end of the Cold War, however, the level of aid plummeted. US aid to assist in the fight against poverty in Latin America, administered by the US Agency for International Development (USAID), has remained fixed at an annual $600 million, roughly one-third of 1980 levels in real terms (see Barshefsky, Hill and O'Neil eds, 2008).

Domestic politics

Domestic US politics has played an important role in nearly every important issue affecting US–Latin American relations, from Independence to attitudes today towards Cuba. The politics of Florida, for example, has shaped policy on Cuba, not least because the US state has a large Cuban-American population of more than 800,000 (Schoultz, 1998). This helps to explain exceptionalism in US policy towards Cuba (see Box 10.8).

An important factor in shaping the role played by domestic issues in US policy towards Latin America has been the relative weight in the US of political actors vis-à-vis state elites. The Cold War gave US government elites – professional bureaucrats, career diplomats and politicians – unchallenged control over foreign policy doctrine, with business interests and organised labour playing a secondary role. With the end of the Cold War, foreign policy again became subject to an interplay of domestic interests – from ethnic groups in the US originating in Latin America, to business interests seeking free trade, to public opinion about drug-trafficking and migration. By the 1990s, pressure groups had been able to assert their influence over key foreign policy areas and Washington had assumed a position of responding to them (Smith, 2000). Latin America has also become a factor in the formulation of US domestic policy, with drug-trafficking and migration key themes that transcend borders.

Cuba and exceptionalism

Cuba's relationship with the US has differed greatly from that of most other Latin American countries. The Cuban Revolution (1959) occurred against the backdrop of an already exceptional relationship with the US that began when Cuba gained its independence from Spain in 1898 under US occupation. The US maintained its presence on the island and turned it into a political and economic protectorate (see also Box 10.6). As a result, the Cuban Revolution tapped into a deep seam of anti-Americanism (see Box 9.3), and subsequent relations between the US and Cuba have been shaped in part by a distinctive mindset among policymakers based on what US officialdom has traditionally seen as the country's civilising role in the region (see Box 10.5; Schoultz, 2009). The exceptionalism that distinguished US–Cuban relations has persisted since the collapse of the socialist bloc in the 1990s and US policy has become more inflexible with the passage of laws tightening the conditions on any future normalisation of relations. Cuba is required to repudiate communism if it wishes the US to lift its unilateral economic sanctions imposed in the aftermath of the 1959 revolution. The Cuban Democracy Act (CDA, or Torricelli Act) of 1992 and the Helms-Burton Act of 1996 tightened these sanctions and made the economic and political conditions that they demanded more explicit. The CDA marked a shift in policy by seeking for the first time to provide 'support for the Cuban people' by facilitating humanitarian donations from US NGOs (see Chapter 8), encouraging individual contacts, and increasing information flow between the two countries. One component of these provisions was the promotion of new telecommunications services, building on efforts that the US has undertaken through various media to wage a propaganda campaign against the Castro regime. Information and communication technologies have figured prominently in US–Cuban relations since the Cuban Revolution. As early as 1960, the CIA was transmitting clandestine radio broadcasts to Cuba, and since 1985 Radio Martí, affiliated to the US Information Agency, has broadcast politically oriented programming towards the island. In 1990, broadcasting from Florida of anti-Castro propaganda by a US government-funded television station, TV Martí, began. Plagued by technical hurdles and Cuban blocking, TV Martí had a limited impact, and in 2002 it came under congressional scrutiny after it was accused of having small or non-existent audiences, being grossly mismanaged and presenting an overtly biased viewpoint. The US has also tried to incorporate the internet into its propaganda policy, but the Castro regime has successfully resisted this (see Boas, 2000; see also Chapter 8). The limitations placed on public internet use in China, in some instances with the collaboration of large Western search corporations, has demonstrated the potential for non-democratic regimes to control this medium. The Helms-Burton Act authorised the US president to provide assistance to individuals and NGOs to support democracy-building efforts in Cuba. The powerful Cuban American National Foundation (CANF) formed by anti-Castro exiles was very influential in the drafting of this law, and grants have been directed towards anti-Castro groups. The laws of the 1990s set Cuba apart from the rest of Latin America with a detailed blueprint for the process, timetable and content of democratisation required on the island. These laws were 'codified', meaning that an act of congress and not just a presidential decision is required to vary their terms (Whitehead, 1999).

The impact of US attempts to stoke up internal dissent with the use of mass media has been limited, and US hardliners have shown increasing frustration with the failure of efforts to bring down the regime. At the same time, there has been a discernible change in the rhetoric both towards and from the island since the revolutionary leader Fidel Castro handed over control of the government to his brother, Raúl, who took over as president in 2008. Some of the economic and political changes undertaken by Raúl Castro, such as the relaxation of restrictions on the amount of land available to private farmers and moves to abandon strict salary equality, have been seen as signs of change (see Chapter 16). At the same time, the US president, Barack Obama, began his term in office by calling for a new beginning with Cuba and has made some symbolic gestures aimed at moving towards improved relations. In 2009, the US congress voted to lift Bush administration restrictions on Cuban-Americans visiting Havana and sending money from the US, for example.

There has also been an important rapprochement between Latin American countries and the Cuban regime, pioneered by Venezuela, which has forged a strong bilateral relationship with the island under President Hugo Chávez (see Boxes 9.1, 16.1), and made possible largely because of the ascent of a new generation of left-of-centre governments across Latin America (see Chapter 12). Left-of-centre governments in Latin American countries have openly been prepared to take a more supportive position towards Cuba, in defiance of the US. By 2009, nearly all the countries of Latin America had re-established formal diplomatic relations with Havana, the most recent being El Salvador in June 2009 under the country's new left-of-centre president Mauricio Funes (2009–) as soon as he took office. This has made it more difficult to isolate Cuba in multilateral forums. In 2009, the Organisation of American States (OAS) also voted to lift its ban on Cuban participation imposed in 1962 (see Box 9.5).

Today, the US continues its strategic effort to isolate the regime politically and economically with attempts to forge links with Cuban opposition movements and civil society. Cuba remains a potential flashpoint in US–Latin American relations, and Obama's policies towards the region are largely motivated by traditional US priorities (see below), suggesting that a dramatic change in attitude towards the island is unlikely. In September 2009, for example, Obama extended the 47-year-old trade embargo against Cuba for another year. Under the Helms-Burton Act, the embargo can only be lifted when the US deems Cuba to have begun a democratic transition. Such inflexibility in US policy has made it more difficult to respond to a Cuban crisis with non-military means. It has also been argued that the cost to the US of maintaining the status quo has so far been low, suggesting that, behind the rhetoric, the incentive to bring about a change of direction is in fact limited (Bulmer-Thomas and Dunkerley, 1999). None the less, the new willingness of Latin American countries to engage with Cuba diplomatically is likely to bring with it new opportunities for them to trade with the island, and in 2009 Russia signed agreements with Cuba to search for oil in its territorial waters in the Gulf of Mexico. Cuban authorities believe there may be up to 20 billion barrels of oil off its coast, offering a significant incentive to the US to improve ties.

The War on Drugs

The 'War on Drugs' in the US is the term given to a campaign against the illegal drugs trade that began in the 1960s and has extended abroad to participating countries such as Mexico (see Box 4.3) and Colombia (see Box 10.3; see also US Department of State, 2009a). Latin America is a key source of the supply of drugs to the US, although trafficking is fuelled as much by demand for drugs within the US itself, which is the largest global market for cocaine, as it is by organised cartels distributing them. Growing levels of drug-related violence in countries such as Mexico are also exacerbated by the trafficking of weapons across the US border. In 2008, the UN Office on Drugs and Crime noted a significant decline in trafficking towards North America, reflected in rapidly rising prices and falling purity

Figure 10.1 The War on Drugs in Latin America*

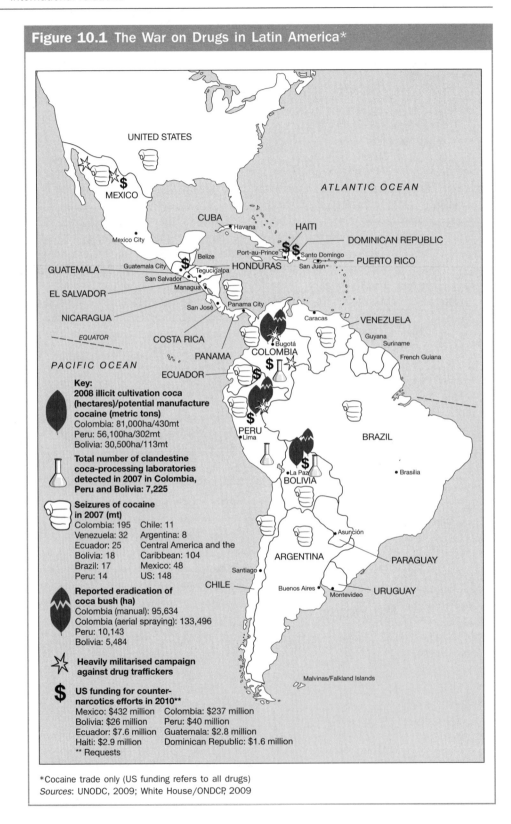

Key:

2008 illicit cultivation coca (hectares)/potential manufacture cocaine (metric tons)
Colombia: 81,000ha/430mt
Peru: 56,100ha/302mt
Bolivia: 30,500ha/113mt

Total number of clandestine coca-processing laboratories detected in 2007 in Colombia, Peru and Bolivia: 7,225

Seizures of cocaine in 2007 (mt)
Colombia: 195   Chile: 11
Venezuela: 32   Argentina: 8
Ecuador: 25   Central America and the
Bolivia: 18   Caribbean: 104
Brazil: 17   Mexico: 48
Peru: 14   US: 148

Reported eradication of coca bush (ha)
Colombia (manual): 95,634
Colombia (aerial spraying): 133,496
Peru: 10,143
Bolivia: 5,484

Heavily militarised campaign against drug traffickers

US funding for counter-narcotics efforts in 2010**
Mexico: $432 million   Colombia: $237 million
Bolivia: $26 million   Peru: $40 million
Ecuador: $7.6 million   Guatemala: $2.8 million
Haiti: $2.9 million   Dominican Republic: $1.6 million
** Requests

*Cocaine trade only (US funding refers to all drugs)
Sources: UNODC, 2009; White House/ONDCP, 2009

levels. One indication of the scale and public impact of drug-trafficking from Latin America to the US came in November 2009 when *Forbes* magazine included Mexico's most wanted man, Joaquín Guzmán, the head of the Sinaloa drug-trafficking cartel, in its list of the 'World's Most Powerful People' (Noer and Perlroth, 2009). Guzmán, who ranked 41st in the *Forbes* list, which includes President Barack Obama, is believed to have sent cocaine shipments to the US worth between $6 billion and $19 billion between 2001–09, and his struggle with Mexican security forces battling cartels has been responsible for thousands of deaths (see Box 4.3). There is also growing drug-consumption within Latin America itself, and increases in cocaine use in 2007 were reported by Venezuela, Ecuador, Brazil, Argentina, Uruguay, Guatemala, Honduras and Haiti.

The main centres of coca cultivation and cocaine production in clandestine laboratories are Colombia, Peru and Bolivia, and major transit routes for the smuggling of this as well as other drugs into the US are Central America, the Caribbean and Mexico (see Figure 10.1). Estimated global cocaine production, the vast majority of it in Latin America, decreased by 15 per cent from 994 metric tons in 2007 to 845 mt in 2008. The Caribbean and Mexico are also sources of cannabis production and, according to the World Drug Report 2009, methamphetamine precursors are increasingly being trafficked to Central and South America to manufacture amphetamine-type stimulants destined for the US (UNODC, 2009). Heroin is also trafficked from Mexico, and one of the country's most violent drug-traffickers, Arturo Beltrán Leyva, who was killed in a shootout with the security forces in December 2009, had been accused by the US of smuggling millions of dollars of heroin across the border as well as cocaine. Mexican and Colombian drug cartels distribute narcotics globally, and are believed to have established a foothold in West Africa, from where they can access the lucrative European market to the north.

As a result, US foreign policy in Latin America has increasingly been shaped with counter-narcotics strategy in mind, and the distinction between counter-insurgency ('counter-terrorism') and counter-narcotics policies has become blurred in Colombia. The US has pursued a range of policies to interrupt supply, beginning with traditional interdiction efforts that often involve international co-operation among security forces. Other countries have actively joined the US in international efforts to combat trafficking (see Chapter 11). The US has also pursued a policy of unilateral 'certification' of countries deemed to be co-operative in the 'War on Drugs', which allows it to use trade and aid incentives to apply direct pressure on governments, and fuel public pressure on them, to co-operate with its policies (see Hinojosa, 2007). Its most prominent regional initiatives have been Plan Colombia (see Box 10.3) and the Mérida Initiative, a security co-operation arrangement since 2007 between the US, Mexico and the countries of Central America established by George W. Bush and continued by Obama. Under this programme, the US provides financial and physical support for the efforts of these countries to tackle drug-trafficking. The Mérida Initiative is seen as crucial by US policymakers to the fate of President Felipe Calderón's increasingly militarised policy against traffickers in Mexico (see Box 4.3). In Peru, US support for anti-drug policies was tarnished by links between Vladimiro Montesinos, the intelligence chief of President Fujimori, and drug-trafficking cartels. The government of President Alan

García (1985–90, 2006–) launched Plan VRAE, a military offensive similar to Plan Colombia in the South Andean region of Ayacucho, which targets both drug-trafficking and surviving militias of the Shining Path guerrilla organisation that Peruvian officials say are involved in it (see Boxes 12.4, 13.9). Peru was one of the few countries in the region to support US plans to increase its military presence in Colombia (see Box 9.8), and the US Bureau of International Narcotics and Law Enforcement Affairs is actively supporting the Peruvian government's counter-narcotics strategy (see US Department of State, 2009b), which has grown increasingly militarised.

Washington has also gone to great lengths to change patterns of behaviour upon which drug-trafficking is based. Between 2000–04, for example, the US poured more than $500 million of development aid into Bolivia, much of it through the US Agency for International Development, and developed a micro-economic policy to reward farmers who shifted from coca to coffee production (see Dickerson, 2004). In 2004, as coffee prices fell, for example, the US shifted its efforts to helping Bolivian farmers develop premium beans that allow higher prices (*ibid.*).

However, US coca-eradication policies have encountered considerable opposition in countries such as Bolivia, with some political actors seeing them as interventionist and potentially damaging to rural development because of the collateral damage caused by the chemicals used. The use of aerial fumigation to destroy coca plants is at the core of the eradication strategy and local politicians, activists and environmentalists have all argued that this can have a significant impact on health and ecosystems (see Chapter 8). Coca eradication has also been criticised for threatening the livelihood of coca growers, for whom the leaf has traditionally been used in tea and chewed for religious, medicinal and nutritional purposes. The status of coca growers has become an important political issue in Bolivia, Colombia and Peru. In 2008, President Evo Morales, who was a coca-growers' leader earlier in his political career, suspended the activities of the DEA within Bolivia (see above), accusing its agents of conspiring against his leftwing government. As part of its response, the US announced in 2009 that it would cut trade benefits for Bolivia and reimpose import duties on some Bolivian goods. US officials argue that senior Bolivian officials encourage the production of coca.

Critics of US counter-narcotics strategy have argued that the 'War on Drugs' has damaged the progress of democratisation in Latin America by fuelling violence and rights abuses, and may be a pretext for military interventions in the region (see, for example, WOLA, 2009). Others have argued that the association of counter-narcotics strategy with counter-terrorism has been counterproductive, and has in fact helped strengthen the drug trade (Marcy, 2010). In 2008, for example, the Honduran president, Manuel Zelaya, called on the US to legalise drugs in order to prevent what he claimed was the main cause of murder in his country, which has been used as a transit point by Colombian cocaine traffickers. Violence in Mexico has clearly unnerved authorities in US border states, and the US Department of Homeland Security has considered using the national guard to prevent it spilling over into the US.

There is some evidence that Latin American countries themselves are beginning to influence the terms of the debate in the 'War on Drugs' within the US. They have consistently called for the US to make greater inroads in reducing domestic demand for drugs, which they argue is at the root of trafficking. The *World Drug*

Report 2009 noted a significant decline in cocaine use in the US, confirmed by the results of drug tests among the workforce that showed the proportion of people testing positive falling from 0.91 per cent in 1998 to 0.41 per cent in 2008, equivalent to a decline of more than 50 per cent over the last decade (UNODC, 2009). The Latin American Commission on Drugs and Democracy chaired by former presidents from the region made a major statement in 2009 on the use of force in the 'War on Drugs', which they said had failed to eradicate illegal drug consumption and the threats to democratic institutions this had generated (see Latin American Commission on Drugs and Democracy, 2009). They argued that more efficient counter-narcotics policies rooted in the respect for human rights are required that emphasise prevention and treatment.

President Obama has gone some way towards recognising factors for which the US is responsible that are fuelling drug violence in Latin America. In March 2009, for example, the Secretary of State, Hillary Clinton, conceded that the US must take part of the blame for drug-related violence in its southern neighbour and act to stem both demand for drugs at home and the trafficking of weapons over the border. Key debates in the US about the use of drugs have addressed such themes as legalisation and the use of treatment to reduce consumption, which critics of an increasingly militarised policy argue is more cost-effective than law-enforcement efforts alone. However, despite the willingness of Obama to acknowledge that the US must take some responsibility for drug violence, there are no signs of a change in the commitment to a militarised policy.

Migration

Another US domestic policy influenced by Latin America is migration, which is a complex and increasingly contentious issue. More than 18 million Latin American migrants, both legal and illegal are estimated to live in the US and the rate of immigration from the region has accelerated despite policies designed to halt it. The result is a large and growing Latino population of about 45 million people (27 million of whom were born in the US) who have both increasing spending power and political influence (see Box 10.10). Central Americans and Mexicans make up the largest proportion of the Latin American migrant community in the US (about 71 per cent) and, as a result, represent sizeable proportions of the global population of the countries from which they originate. For example, there are 11 million Mexicans in the US – about 10 per cent of Mexico's population.

While many Latin Americans once migrated to the US because of political turbulence or civil war, migration today is overwhelmingly caused by economic factors. The prospect of jobs pulls Latin Americans to the US, and poverty and lack of economic opportunity continue to push them there. On balance, most scholars believe the net economic impact of immigrants on the US economy has been positive. Given the economic causes, an important dimension of migration to the US is the way it provides stable income flows for the millions of family members who remain behind. Remittances, the money sent home by migrant workers, have become a crucial source of income for millions of families throughout Latin America – and now exceed total foreign direct investment and overseas aid to the region (see Boxes 11.2, 11.6; see also IDB, 2004). For example, about 2 million of El Salvador's 8 million citizens already live abroad, mostly in the US, and send home remittances equal to about 16 per cent of GDP. In 2008, Latin American and Caribbean expatriates transferred about $69.2 billion to their homelands, 0.9 per cent more than in 2007, according to the Inter-American Development Bank's Multilateral Investment Fund (IDB, 2009). Most of this money came from the US, with Spain also a key source of funds (see Box 11.2). However, after almost a decade of growth, the IDB projected a decline in remittances to Latin America and the Caribbean because of the 2008–09 financial crisis, rising unemployment in industrialised nations, a harsher climate against immigration and exchange rate fluctuations. One consequence of the scale of Latin American migration has been a US economy that is increasingly dependent on these workers, and Latinos now account for about 13 per cent of the US workforce. They are concentrated in lower-skilled sectors of the economy, and Latin American migrant workers are found in large numbers in sectors such as farming, fishing, forestry, construction and unskilled services such as cleaning and maintenance.

Immigration policy in the US was long characterised by weak enforcement of what were, on paper, tough laws. This has meant that for many years the law did not deter employers from hiring illegal immigrants and benefiting significantly from their low-cost labour. After the 9/11 attacks in 2001, the US government restructured the immigration system, bringing it under the control of the newly formed Department of Homeland Security and, in effect, combining a responsibility to control immigration with an emphasis on anti-terrorism. Resources for border patrols and surveillance equipment were increased, creating new obstacles to legal migration and encouraging migrants, including Latin Americans, to enter the US illegally. Illegal migrants are more likely to stay, because they have incurred expense and taken risks while entering the country and do not wish to repeat this experience.

Immigration became a key political issue in the US in 2006 as Republicans sought to retain control of congress in mid-term polls in November. Hundreds of thousands of people, many of them Latino, demonstrated across the country against proposals to tighten border security and greatly extend barriers on the border combined with plans to allow some illegal immigrants to seek US citizenship and provisions for guest-worker programmes. President George W. Bush had intended a comprehensive immigration reform to be the centrepiece of the US–Mexican relationship, but his bipartisan bill that combined tougher border security measures with plans to legalise illegal immigrants failed in 2007. Illegal migration remains unpopular among large sections of the population in the US and, to reduce the flow of illegal migrants, the US has adopted increasingly radical measures (see Box 10.9). In late 2008, for example, the outgoing Bush administration denied a request by Haiti's government to grant an estimated 30,000 undocumented migrants in the US temporary protected status while it recovered from damaging storms (see Semple, 2009).

While in the US itself immigration policy is largely considered a domestic issue, its shortcomings make it a foreign policy problem and an important issue in US–Latin American relations. The failure to reform immigration policy damaged US standing in Mexico and elsewhere in the region, for example, because many Latin

The Tortilla Wall

Thousands of illegal immigrants, mainly Latin Americans but also many Asians in transit, head north across the 1,950-mile (3,140km) border between Mexico and the US every year and drastic measures have been taken by the US to strengthen immigration controls. Separation barriers between the US and Mexico have slowly been extended in length since the 1990s as part of several operations to control illegal immigration in California, Arizona and Texas with the intention of forcing illegal immigrants to try crossing in more difficult terrain that makes it easier for US border agents to catch them. In California, since 1997 the Border Patrol has been building a barrier wall extending inland from the coastline where the US and Mexico meet (Broder, 2005; Schodolski, 2005). The barrier started as a wall made of surplus steel landing mats used for aircraft during the Vietnam War and has been supplemented by steel mesh, with a roadway between the two fences constantly patrolled by US Border Patrol vehicles. In early 2005, the US congress authorised the completion of a second layer of barriers behind an existing and incomplete corrugated metal barrier at Tijuana known as the 'Tortilla Wall' as part of a military spending bill, effectively using the threat of terrorism to overcome opposition to the project and ignoring Mexican protests. In November 2005, President George W. Bush angered Mexico when he announced the construction of further fences along the border in urban areas where there were no physical obstacles to crossing between the two countries. Proposals to extend barriers along the border have found favour with US conservatives but angered Mexican and Central American leaders. During a visit to the US in May 2006, Mexico's then president Vicente Fox (2000–06) said the construction of a wall was not the answer to illegal immigration, which was now the most pressing challenge in his country's relationship with the US. Critics of US policies dismiss the argument that terrorists have used the border to enter the country. The California barrier has sometimes merely shifted the problem along the frontier: as illegal crossing in California decreased, there has been a rise in crossings in Arizona. Barriers and patrols add to the hazards of crossing illegally, and some reports put the number of migrant bodies recovered in the US–Mexico borderlands between 1995 and late 2007 at more than 4,000 (see Nevins, 2008). Many die from exposure to extreme heat once they have actually made it across the border: it can reach 120 degrees at midday in San Diego and Imperial counties in southern California (*ibid.*). The build-up of boundary enforcement structures initiated during the presidency of Bill Clinton (1993–2001) has gradually pushed up the number of crossing-related fatalities. The number of US Border Patrol agents has been steadily increased and nationally it had about 15,000 agents in 2007 – three times the number of 1994 (*ibid.*) Innovative new methods are being employed to increase the level of monitoring. In Texas in 2008, for example, the Texas Border Sheriff's Coalition introduced a scheme whereby tens of thousands of people around the world volunteer to patrol the border via the web using live feeds from hidden surveillance cameras. The move has been criticised by human rights campaigners for encouraging vigilantism.

However, despite these controls, the scale of illegal immigration is vast and most illegal immigrants succeed in entering the US *anyway*. Deaths on the border have caused friction between the US and Latin American countries. There have also been incidents in which migrants have been targeted by vigilantes. Department of Homeland Security statistics show that, on the south-western US border, 705,022 foreign nationals were caught by the Border Patrol for being in the US illegally in 2008, 97.4 per cent of the total apprehended in the entire country (Rytina and Simanski, 2009). This compares with 1,171, 391 in 2005, indicating a significant fall in the number of apprehensions and, probably, in the number of illegal crossings. Of those migrants apprehended in 2008, 661,773

▶

were from Mexico, but many other potential migrants are prepared to go to desperate lengths to reach the US. In 2005, for example, 88 migrants from Peru and Ecuador seeking to reach the US were rescued at sea on a leaking boat near Costa Rica, and in 2009 Costa Rican officials intercepted a boat with 54 African migrants on board who had paid traffickers to reach the US (see AP, 2005b; AFP, 2009).

Americans perceive current laws as discriminatory and unfair. At the same time, Latin American countries have exhibited considerable forethought in their own immigration policies, largely deriving from an understanding of the benefits of integration. As a result, Latin American integration initiatives have been accompanied by efforts to manage immigration, with such measures as the development of complementary social-security arrangements among the countries participating in, for example, the Andean Community and within Mercosur (see Box 9.9, Table 15.2).

The future of US policy towards Latin America

Smith (2000) characterised the contemporary era in international relations as an 'Age of Uncertainty' that bears a resemblance to the Imperial Era of the nineteenth century, but argued that a principal difference from that period was the reality that US predominance within the western hemisphere was now uncontested. Whitehead (1999) argued that the 1995 'decertification' of Colombia as a country co-operating in the drugs war associated with US efforts to remove President Samper (see above); the 1996 Helms-Burton Act; and the 1997 denial by congress of 'fast-track' negotiating authority to President Bill Clinton (1993–2001) that would have enabled him to make rapid progress in advancing the country's free-trade agenda in Latin America; all reminded the region of the constraints implied by its relationship with such a dominant neighbour. Although US interventions and the broader content of inter-American relations will be conditioned by global international relations and trends, Smith anticipated continuing – or even accentuated – US predominance. A key theme at the heart of any effort to delineate the trajectory of US–Latin American relations, therefore, is the *fate* of US hegemony and how the administration of President Obama will respond to this issue (see Lowenthal *et al.* eds, 2009). A phrase that became prominent in speculation about Obama's desire to distance himself from the more bellicose foreign-policy style of the Bush administration and its association with military action was the determination to project 'soft power' that aims to secure influence and change through co-operative and persuasive means as opposed to coercive methods. Obama's personal image and popularity was generally seen as an important element of this approach. Some scholars suggest that US hegemony in Latin America has grown consistently over time and will continue to do so. In 1950, for example, GDP per capita in the US was just over seven times as large as in Latin America, but by 1990 it was nearly 10 times as large (Smith, 2001). Schoultz (1998) argued that when the Soviet Union disappeared, the US moved to *increase* its control over Latin America. However, today the debate about whether US influence in Latin America may in fact be declining has grown more relevant. Some scholars believe that the US is no longer the dominant variable in the foreign relations of most Latin American countries. Muñoz (2001) has argued that Latin Americans are both looking inward, promoting integration through agreements while cultivating partnerships with extra-regional powers such as the EU and Asia-Pacific Economic Co-operation (APEC) (see Chapter 11), and that most Latin American countries no longer base their domestic or foreign policy decisions on a calculation of how the US will react. There is also evidence that the ability of the US to influence developments in Latin America has been weakening since the 1990s and that this trend may have deepened since 2000, not least because of the ascent of a new generation of left-of-centre leaders in the region (see Table 12.1).

The election of leftwingers such as Evo Morales in a number of Latin American countries has been accompanied by declining loyalty to the US and a rapprochment in relations with Cuba that has allowed some leaders, such as Hugo Chávez in Venezuela, to assert their independence from the US (see Boxes 9.3, 12.7). Critics of US foreign policy openly deride Washington's obsession with Cuba's communist regime and what they see as efforts by the US to bully leaders it does not like, such as Chávez. In April 2005, Latin American influence over the OAS – a body traditionally dominated by Washington – was greatly enhanced by the withdrawal from the race of Francisco Flores, a rightwing former president of El Salvador who had been backed by the US (see Box 9.5). Flores withdrew after Washington failed to persuade small Caribbean countries to support him, and many of them shifted their vote to the Chilean socialist José Miguel Insulza backed by Brazil, Argentina and Venezuela, who subsequently won. During the Iraq war, only a handful of Central American countries such as El Salvador, one of the most loyal allies of the US in the region, sent troops in support of Washington. More powerful countries such as Mexico and Chile – both of which have sought to maintain good relations with Washington – resisted pressure to support the allied invasion and abstained from voting in the UN Security Council, angering the US. The foreign policy of George W. Bush's administration and the 'War on Terror' strained ties in the region and increased the unpopularity of the US (see Box 10.4). Chávez in Venezuela, Luiz Inácio Lula da Silva (2003–10) in Brazil and Morales in Bolivia were among Latin American leaders who were highly critical of US policy in the Middle East, and all worked to improve their countries' ties with Middle Eastern regimes. In late 2009, Brazil, Venezuela and Bolivia hosted a visit by Iran's president, Mahmoud Ahmadinejad, and voiced support for Iran's right to develop a peaceful nuclear programme, prompting the US Secretary of State, Hillary Clinton, to warn them about the consequences of their ties with the Islamic Republic.

Criticisms of the neoliberal economic orthodoxy championed by the US in the 1990s have also grown following crises in Mexico, Brazil and Argentina that exposed the region's continuing vulnerability to external economic factors (see Chapters 14, 15). The financial crisis of 2008–09 only served to strengthen these criticisms and to strengthen the notion that all is not well with US capitalism and, therefore that it does not offer a model of propriety. Larger countries such as Argentina and Brazil have challenged the US (and European) commitment to open markets, and have demanded a level playing field in international trade (see Box 15.5). Regional trade and integration initiatives such as Mercosur and ALBA have gained considerable momentum without US participation (see Chapter 9).

These examples confirm the view that a tension can be identified between a continuing, yet weakened, US propensity to act unilaterally and a growing multi-lateralism (Domínguez, 2000). Washington has traditionally been reluctant to accept multilateral authority and on many occasions has resorted to unilateral action (Bulmer-Thomas and Dunkerley, 1999). However, most US administrations have in fact swayed between unilateralism and multilateralism. The administration of George W. Bush, for example, began with a radical unilateralism but was forced to pursue a more multilateral agenda. One example of this was Washington's relation-ship with Lula da Silva in Brazil: despite initial signs that Da Silva's radical antecedents had unnerved the US administration, by November 2005 Washington was praising the 'good example' set by the South American country. Da Silva had not proved to be the leftwing demagogue many people had predicted he would be, and con-crete US interests in the region – its desire to woo Brazil's support for its free-trade agenda (see Box 15.5), to avoid radicalisation of the Latin American left, and to isolate Chávez in Venezuela – were better served through co-operative relations. Like all presidents, Obama is likely to change the balance between unilateralism and multilateralism in US foreign policy towards the region, but not to abandon either. In his first year in office, Obama gave signals that he favours a multilateral approach to regional issues that lend themselves to co-operative diplomacy, while retaining where necessary a unilateral style with regard to traditional US priorities. None the less, critics of US policy towards Latin America have suggested that the Obama administration's limited interest in, and commitment of economic resources to, Latin America reflects its continuing low status among foreign policy priorities (see Petras, 2009).

US unilateralism is most likely to remain a feature of relations over issues Washington considers to be linked to its domestic policy agenda (Domínguez, 2000). Cuba, drug-trafficking, migration and trade, for example, have all traditionally been more likely to generate unilateral US action.

Cuba was a prominent theme at the 2009 Summit of the Americas at which Obama signalled that he believed Washington would consider ending its economic embargo of the island. Prior to the summit, the White House lifted a ban on Cuban-Americans travelling and sending money to Cuba, and Cuba's president, Raúl Castro, also signalled a willingness to discuss all issues with Washington. None the less, powerful domestic US interests such as the Cuban exile lobby and the Republican right limit the ability of the White House to move beyond small, symbolic gestures and positive rhetoric. Despite the renewed diplomatic ties between Latin American states and Cuba, the US embargo continues (see Box 10.8), although support for this among anti-Castro Cuban exiles within the US has declined. After initially wel-coming the election of Obama, by late 2009 Cuba's former leader, Fidel Castro, was accusing the US president of plotting to overthrow leftwing governments in Latin America.

Unilateral US measures against drug-trafficking increased in the 1990s, gener-ating tensions with Latin American states. More recently, Latin American leaders have been asking Washington to reconsider its 'War on Drugs' (see above), which many believe has had a damaging impact on society and has largely failed. None the less, while the Obama administration has signalled that it is prepared to listen to Latin American concerns, the military focus of policy has not changed. The US tried a bilateral approach in countries like Mexico, but its efforts were sometimes undermined by actions that the Mexicans considered to have violated their sovereignty (*ibid.*). Policy towards drug-trafficking in Mexico has more recently been modelled on that taken in Colombia, with an emphasis on military aid. The US continues to provide funds for security training and equipment that militarises this anti-drugs campaign through the Mérida Initiative, which authorises nearly $1.6 billion of spending to Mexico, Central America and the Caribbean. Direct total US aid to Mexico for drug-control policies in 2010 under various programmes was set to amount to $432 million (see White House/ONDCP, 2009). This would make the country the hemisphere's top recipient of US security aid. The US has also proceeded with plans to incease its military presence in Colombia, despite the reservations of the country's neighbours (see Boxes 9.8, 10.3), and there have been signs that its support for counter-narcotics strategy in Peru is heading in the same direction. Relations with Bolivia have grown increasingly tense over coca production in the country. In 2009, the Latin American Commission on Drugs and Democracy described Obama's inauguration as an opportunity to establish an inter-American dialogue with the US government, legislators and civil society aimed at jointly developing more efficient and humane alternatives to the 'War on Drugs' modelled, in part, on European policies (Latin American Commission on Drugs and Democracy, 2009; see Chapter 11). Relations between the US and Ecuador arguably worsened after Obama took office. In February 2009, for example, Ecuador's president, Rafael Correa, expelled a senior US customs official from the country in a dispute over the US State Department's apparent desire to choose the head of Ecuador's anti-narcotics police (bbc.co.uk, 2009a). During a television address, Correa angrily claimed that the US customs attaché had treated Ecuador like a colony.

US attitudes on migration hardened in the 1990s under Republican majorities in congress, prompting protests from Central American governments, whose economies benefit from remittances sent home by migrants in the US (*ibid.*). Congressional Democrats favour comprehensive immigration reform that would offer a path to legal status for illegal immigrants already in the country, and Obama has signalled his support for new legislation – a key recommendation of the Council on Foreign Relations task force overview of US foreign policy (see Barshefsky *et al.* eds, 2008). It had been expected that a draft immigration bill would be introduced to congress by late 2009 and debate on it would begin in 2010. Obama has stated that while he supports offering some form of legalisation, he also wants tougher enforcement of existing laws that could appeal to both Democrats and Republicans. None the less, the administration gave signs in 2009 that it might be prepared to relax its position on humanitarian grounds in some cases. The dispute over immigration policy pursued by individual states such as Arizona has made reform more urgent.

Policy on trade with Latin America, worth about $550 billion annually, is one area where the US has strong unilateral reflexes, but which it may have to modify to changing realities. The past imposition by the US of 'anti-dumping' penalties on countries that tried to sell their exports cheaply in its market was interpreted as a tough unilateral measure that generated anxiety about whether Washington would live up to its free-trade commitments. Dumping occurs when exports are priced at a level lower than the price normally charged in an exporter's domestic market, and is considered to be damaging to the importing country's industry. The refusal of congress to authorise fast-track legislation for President Clinton's efforts to promote free trade (see above) also raised concerns among Latin American governments about the US commitment to trade deals it had previously agreed with them.

Under George W. Bush, congress ratified trade agreements with Chile in 2004, Central America and the Dominican Republic in 2007 (DR-CAFTA), and Peru in 2007, but the FTAA has receded (see above) and Obama inherited agreements with Colombia and Panama that Bush had completed but congress had not approved and so had become snared in US domestic politics. However, Obama signalled more protectionist instincts by indicating that he would like to renegotiate NAFTA and to rein in plans for further free trade agreements, further strengthening the sense that the US is prepared to shift on past commitments and making it harder for Washington to adopt a leadership role in the region, as was implied by the FTAA (see Box 15.5). At the same time, Latin American countries such as Chile and Mexico have reached bilateral agreements with the EU and Asian powers such as China (see Chapter 11) and the alternative 'Bolivarian' vision implied by ALBA has not foundered. The Council on Foreign Relations' recommendations for US foreign policy argued strongly in favour of US concessions enabling more open trade with Latin America, particularly in the areas of textile and agricultural imports, as an important step to reducing poverty and inequality in the region, to restore its standing, and to broaden long-term opportunities for US exporters (see Barshefsky *et al.* eds, 2008). Obama's decision to end Bolivia's trade preferences is a sign that, in the short-term, his administration is unlikely to proceed in this way, and the absence of a discernible trade policy in his first year in the White House indicated that this was not a top priority.

Domínguez (2000) argued that the traditional US view towards Latin America derived from a realist perspective in international affairs based on the fact of its power and scepticism about the role of multilateral organisations such as the OAS (see Box 9.5); however, the changes of the 1990s permitted the US and Latin America to find common cause in some areas, such as the defence of democracy, free trade and the maintenance of peaceful relations. At one level, this could reflect a convergence of values across the hemisphere, including those within the US itself, where the Hispanic population is growing rapidly (see Box 10.10). Domínguez argued that the predominant trend of the first decade of the twenty-first century has been a drift towards regionalist multilateralism in the effort to address a wide range of policy issues through hemispheric and sub-regional institutions (see also Fishlow and Jones eds, 1999). One example of this was the new preference for summitry that began with the Miami Summit in December 1994 when the FTAA concept was formally launched (see Chapter 9, Box 15.5). Although progress on the FTAA had stalled by 2005, American states continue to meet regularly to discuss trade and non-trade issues. In some cases, the multilateral approach accepted by the US has, in effect, been forced on Washington as a result of its commitments to trade associations such as the WTO or NAFTA. In other cases, such as the invasion of Haiti in 2004, the US has actively sought the support of the international community through the UN (*ibid.*). Since the Cold War, Washington has accepted much

Latinos in the US

The Hispanic or Latino community has a long history in the US and, today, is growing faster than any other minority, making the US home to one of the largest Spanish-speaking communities in the world (see Gutiérrez ed., 2004). Hispanics have surpassed African Americans as the largest minority group, with the US Census Bureau (2006) projecting that in 2010 there will be 47.8 million Hispanics in the country – 15.5 per cent of its population. Between 2000 and 2006, Hispanics accounted for one-half of the country's population growth, and the Hispanic growth rate (24.3 per cent) was more than three times that of the total population (6.1 per cent). A demographic growth rate that is significantly higher than that of the rest of the US population means that by 2020 Hispanics are likely to make up 17.8 per cent of the population. The number of Hispanic voters in the US is growing accordingly, and an estimated 9 per cent of the electorate in the 2008 presidential elections was Latino, higher by one percentage point than the share in 2004 (Lopez, 2009). However, many Latinos still do not register to vote and this means the community has been significantly under-represented in comparison with other minorities. In 2000, for example, the Hispanic and African American populations in the US were roughly the same size, but there were about 23 million eligible African American voters compared to 13 million Latinos (Pew Hispanic Center, 2004). None the less, the capacity of Hispanics for influencing the politics and society of the US is growing. An increasing number of further-generation Hispanic migrants, and in particular Puerto Ricans, are attaining top offices, the most high-profile of whom has arguably been Sonia Sotomayor, who became the first Hispanic supreme court justice in 2009.

The Hispanic vote was important to the Democratic victory in the 2008 presidential election, with an analysis by the Pew Hispanic Center of exit polls revealing that they voted for Democrats Barack Obama and Joe Biden over Republicans John McCain and Sarah Palin by a margin of more than two-to-one, 67 per cent versus 31 per cent (Lopez, 2009). Nationally, the Latino vote was significantly more Democratic in 2008 than in 2004, when President Bush captured an estimated 40 per cent of the Hispanic vote. Obama carried the Latino vote by big margins in all states with large Latino populations and his most significant breakthrough came in Florida, where he won 57 per cent of the Latino vote in a state where they have historically supported Republican presidential candidates. This decline in Hispanic Republicanism is likely to be a significant development in US politics in years to come and a key dilemma posed by Hispanics for the Republican Party coming out of the 2008 election defeat was evident in the debates surrounding the nomination of Sotomayor to the supreme court: how to maintain the support of its traditional base among white non-Hispanics, on the one hand, yet extend its appeal to women, Latinos and young people, on the other. In the US congress in 2009, the Congressional Hispanic Caucus comprised 23 Democratic and one independent member of Hispanic descent, and its Republican-controlled counterpart, the Congressional Hispanic Conference, had at least 11 members.

Hispanics in the US are also growing richer, and making their presence felt through their spending power. A study for the Telemundo Communications Group (2005) by the consultancy Global Insight suggested total consumer spending by the Hispanic population in the US stood at $531 billion in 2002 and would grow at an average annual rate of 9.1 per cent until 2020, much higher than the national growth rate of 6 per cent. In April 2006, immigrants in the US – many of them Hispanic – demonstrated their political potential when they protested against the tightening of laws against illegal immigration in large marches and rallies across the US. It is not known to what degree growing levels of political organisation among Latino communities will influence US foreign policy

▶

in Latin America. However, political and economic developments in New York City, New Jersey and Miami are already influenced by the national politics of the Dominican Republic, Puerto Rico and Cuba. Latin American countries have also grown increasingly aware of the value of maintaining ties with their expatriate communities and encouraging expatriate interest in issues that affect their country of origin. Mindful of the value to their economies of remittances from the US (see above), they have been progressive in terms of granting absentee voting rights to their citizens who may reside in foreign countries such as the US.

Latin Americans are also having a significant cultural impact upon the US itself. Latin American products such as salsa and wine are displacing domestic products and European imports; translated Latin American authors often outsell their US counterparts; and Latin American media compete in the US with news and cultural programmes translated into Spanish by English-language networks in order to tap into the Hispanic market. Television and radio networks devoted mainly to Spanish-language broadcasting have grown rapidly to meet the needs of this community, with large television networks such as the Los Angeles-based Univision Communications Inc competing with Florida-based Telemundo and a host of smaller rivals. Nor are there signs that the Hispanic community is losing its sense of identity through assimilation in a formally English-speaking society. There is much anec-dotal evidence that large numbers of the Puerto Rican community within the US, for example, which is arguably the country's most well-integrated Hispanic community, retain strong links with their home-land, families and heritage, and there are many active groups and initiatives that provide a strong cultural focus for the Puerto Rican diaspora within the US.

Alongside the growth of the Hispanic community within the US, there has been considerable specu-lation about the degree to which economic integration reflects or will nurture a *convergence* in values in the hemisphere. In an important study of values in Mexico, the US and Canada against the back-ground of the North American integration process, Inglehart *et al.* (1996) argued that the populations of the three countries have been converging over time in important ways: politically, through a shared trend toward increasingly democratic and participative systems and a loss of confidence in institu-tions; economically, through declining support for state interventions; and in terms of basic values concerning the family, religion and sexuality, with a trend towards a broader acceptance of divorce, abortion, and homosexuality, an increasing emphasis on the importance of the individual, and a more cosmopolitan identity that was more ambivalent towards nationalism. Inglehart, Nevitte and Basañez suggested that the convergences did not mean that Mexicans or Canadians were becoming 'Americanised' but that all three societies were evolving towards more global cultural positions.

more autonomy in Latin America by multilateral agencies such as the OAS, IADB, the Economic Commission for Latin America (ECLAC/CEPAL), the International Monetary Fund (IMF) and the World Bank. It has also engaged in some security co-operation in the region, working with Argentina, Brazil and Chile to try to resolve border disputes between Peru and Ecuador, for example (see Figure 9.1).

The balance in US actions in the Americas shifted towards hemispheric multi-lateralism during the Bush Sr and Clinton administrations for several reasons. Multilateralism can be more cost effective in securing a positive outcome. It was cheaper for the US to let the IMF take a leading role in containing the Brazilian financial crisis in 1999, for example, than it had been when it had acted alone to resolve the costly Mexican crisis of 1994–95 (Domínguez, 2000). Co-operation has often also yielded better results than unilateral action. US efforts to promote economic liberalisation, for example, have been more effective when done in co-operation with countries, and efforts to achieve democratic change through consent have been more effective than through threats or pressure. Co-operation can foster solidarity, an example of which came in September 2005 in the aftermath of the destruction caused by Hurricane Katrina to New Orleans in Louisiana when a Mexican military convoy carrying water treatment plants and mobile kitchens crossed into the US to help distribute aid to victims. Mexico dispatched a naval vessel with emergency rescue equipment towards the Mississippi coast.

However, what continues to be absent is an overall institutional commitment by the US to multilateralism that would impose rules and predictability in relations (Bulmer-Thomas and Dunkerley, 1999). The Obama presidency's foreign policy has been examined by scholars from the outset from the normative perspectives of either a growing realism about the limits of US military power or hopes for a greater commitment to multilateralism in world affairs (see, for example, Bacevich, 2008; Talbott, 2008; Zakaria, 2008; Gelb, 2009). Obama has come under significant pressure within the US to adopt a more multilateral approach in foreign policy (see Barshefsky *et al.* eds, 2008). But these sentiments have also been particularly prominent in the European allies of the US, as was confirmed by the award of the Nobel Peace Prize to the president in 2009. In its citation, the Nobel prize-giving committee said that, with Obama in office, 'multilateral diplomacy has regained a central position' and dialogue and negotiation had become the preferred instruments for conflict resolution. None the less, at the same time, European observers have pointed to the fact that, despite an apparent commitment to multilateralism, Obama's administration remained cool at the G20 summits in 2009 about proposals for co-ordinated attempts to impose a framework of regulations to limit transnational financial speculation, and that allied military engagement in countries such as Afghanistan still obeyed US security priorities. Moreover, perceptions of US foreign policy abroad are often out of kilter with those within the country itself. Conservative critics of Obama's policy, for example, restate a belief in US exceptionalism by which the unilateral promotion of its values abroad is seen as a key aspect of its national security, and there remained considerable mainstream opinion within the US in 2009 that favoured positions on a range of international issues that could be described as isolationist. This complex and often contradictory tension between rhetoric and reality has been evident in policy towards Latin America. Obama's first appearance at the Summit of the Americas in Trinidad and Tobago in April 2009, which brought together the 34 heads of government of the OAS, was closely watched for signs of rapprochement and was used by the new US president to signal a change in tone. Most observers came away satisfied with the gestures of goodwill that came out of it and the effort by the new US administration to listen and not to participate in the demonisation of leftwing leaders in the region that had been a feature of the Bush approach. None the less, the summit was short on *practical* achievements and generated only symbolic benefits for those present – it did not associate the US with a greater institutional commitment to multilateralism. Moreover, US efforts to broker a deal in late 2009 during the political crisis in Honduras following the coup that ousted President Zelaya demonstrated Washington's limited ability to effect change, but also the limitations of Latin American multilateralism *itself* in resolving such crises (see Chapter 9). Although what appeared to have been a definitive deal in Honduras that would have allowed Zelaya to return to office was brokered during a visit to the country by senior US officials, including Thomas Shannon, the Assistant Secretary of State for Western Hemisphere affairs, the accord broke down. While the US had stated its preference for Latin American governments to take the lead in resolving such regional crises, it was the US itself that was the only external actor able to make concrete progress in doing so, even though at the end of the day the outcome was disputed. The subsequent decision of the Obama administration to recognise the outcome of those elections was condemned by leading Latin American governments.

US energy policy is one area that suggests the benefits of a more multilateral approach as well as integrated policies in the Americas (see Deutch *et al.*, 2006; Isbell, 2009; and the Energy Institute of the Americas website, below). The US itself is highly dependent on imported oil and gas – with less than 5 per cent of the world's population yet using about 25 per cent of the world's oil – and Latin American countries such as Venezuela and Mexico are among its key foreign suppliers. A challenge recognised by government since the administration of George W. Bush has been to reduce this dependence and, as a result, strengthen the country's energy security. However, while this issue clearly has a bearing on US foreign policy and the strength of its economy, it is generally accepted that most of the concrete tools for reducing dependence potentially available to Washington are in domestic policy, and in particular the reduction of demand.

The foreign policy tools available to the US for reducing or mitigating its dependence on oil almost invariably imply multilateral actions, such as: encouraging the exploration for and production of petroleum outside traditional sources; contributing to existing efforts to ensure the transparent and fair operation of world oil and gas markets; subscribing to co-operative agreements that require signatories to follow agreed procedures for coping with disruptions in supply; encouraging a diversity of transit routes and cross-border infrastructure for moving supplies; and engaging with competitors for supplies that may be forced into political realignments that test US influence because of their own energy dependence, one example of which has been the EU's reluctance to confront difficult issues with Russia. The large revenues from oil and gas exports can sometimes compromise good governance by encouraging corruption and populism, and the US, therefore, also has an interest in promoting through existing multilateral bodies both good governance and a better use of hydrocarbon revenues.

Venezuela, one of the main Latin American suppliers of oil to the US, has the seventh largest proved reserves in the world. President Hugo Chávez has used oil as a way of projecting his country's influence and as a political tool against the US, at times threatening to halt supply (see Box 9.1). Although Venezuela's threat is not completely empty, any effort to act on it would have serious consequences for the country's attempt to gain a regional leadership role and would damage the government's revenues. Moreover, the US would be able to rely in the short term on its Strategic Petroleum Reserve to make up for shortfalls.

US energy policy was complicated by the global financial crisis of 2008–09, as a result of which stimulus funding was directed by the Obama administration to the creation of such initiatives as a 'smart' electricity grid, but also by the debate about climate change, which has placed Washington under pressure to move towards more sustainable energy policies. However, during his electoral campaign

Obama explicitly recognised the need for the US to participate in multilateral action by proposing a regional 'Energy Partnership for the Americas' that would work with multilateral institutions, such as the IDB and others to encourage investment in renewable and alternative energy sources, encourage technology sharing, and deploy an 'Energy Corps' of scientists throughout the region.

Summary

Inter-American relations have been shaped by the reality of asymmetry in the levels of power exercised by the US and by Latin American countries. A core problem in relations has been the propensity of the US to act unilaterally from its position of strength, often characterised by use of the term hegemony. Different periods in inter-American relations can be discerned, from the multilateral rivalry of 1790–1930; to the Cold War from the 1940s to the 1980s, which exaggerated the asymmetry of power between the US and Latin American countries; and, most recently, to the contemporary post-Cold War era, in which there has been an absence of clear rules for international conduct. The US emerged from the Cold War as the world's only military superpower while facing economic competition from other countries and regions, resulting in uncertainty. Washington welcomed the transition to democracy and an ideological preference for capitalism in Latin America, but is still accused of intervening in the region's affairs.

US interests have changed over time and different factors have influenced its behaviour towards Latin America. US policies towards the region have had four main motives: territorial gain, strategic security, ideological predominance and the advancement of economic interests. Security motives have derived from a fear of extra-hemispheric interference in the region. Ideological concerns have been shaped by a vision of tutelary duty towards Latin America and today democracy is the ideological cornerstone of US foreign policy. The furthering of economic interests has sometimes been seen as the underlying explanation for US foreign policy. Domestic US politics have also played an important role in issues affecting US–Latin American relations.

A key theme at the heart of any effort to delineate the trajectory of US–Latin American relations is the fate of US hegemony. Some scholars suggest that US control in Latin America has grown consistently over time and will continue to do so. However, others say US influence in Latin America is in decline. A phrase that became prominent in speculation about Obama's desire to distance himself from the style of the Bush administration and its association with military action was the determination to project 'soft power' that aims to secure influence and change through co-operative and persuasive means. As a result, a tension can be identified between a continuing US propensity to act unilaterally and multilateralism. The adoption of unilateralist positions by the US is most likely to occur in policy areas that Washington considers to be linked to domestic issues, such as drug-trafficking, migration and trade. However, the changes of the 1990s permitted the development of some consensus between the US and Latin America in such areas as the defence of democracy and free trade. This could reflect a convergence of values among the populations of the US, where the Hispanic population is rising rapidly, and Latin America. The search for energy security is also one area in which the US could benefit from multilateralism.

Discussion points

- Is hegemony an appropriate term for describing US predominance in the region?
- How did the Cold War shape US policy towards Latin America?
- What have been the main motives of US foreign policy in the region?
- To what extent do drug-trafficking and migration influence US policymaking today?
- Is US influence in Latin America growing or declining?
- Will the future of inter-American relations be determined by multilateralism?

Useful websites

www.wto.org/english/res_e/statis_e/statis_e.htm World Trade Organisation, International trade statistics, Trade by region for inter-American data

www.state.gov US Department of State

www.state.gov/p/wha US Department of State Bureau of Western Hemisphere Affairs

www.whitehouse.gov/issues/ White House site with links to key policy areas

www.whitehouse.gov/administration/eop/nsc National Security Council

www.cfr.org Council on Foreign Relations, New York

www.southcom.mil US Southern Command (USSOUTHCOM), the unified command that has responsibility for all US military activities on the land mass of Latin America south of Mexico and in adjacent waters

www.benning.army.mil/WHINSEC Western Hemisphere Institute for Security Co-operation, formerly the School of the Americas, at Fort Benning, Georgia

www.soaw.org/new School of the Americas Watch, an independent organisation that seeks to close the US Army School of the Americas in Georgia

www.canf.org Cuban American National Foundation (CANF, Fundación Nacional Cubano Americana), the most influential anti-Castro Cuban exile group in the US

www.cubavsbloqueo.cu Cuba vs Bloqueo, Cuban foreign ministry site about US blockade and diplomatic strategy towards it

www.usaid.gov US Agency for International Development (USAID)

www.ciponline.org Center for International Policy, independent US think-tank promoting a foreign policy based on international co-operation, demilitarisation and respect for basic human rights

http://justf.org Just the Facts, site about US defence and security assistance programmes in Latin America compiled by the Latin America Working Group Education Fund, Center for International Policy, and Washington Office on Latin America

http://pewhispanic.org Pew Hispanic Center, Washington, a non-partisan research organisation aiming to improve understanding of the US Hispanic population and to chronicle Latinos' growing impact on the country

www.ase.tufts.edu/gdae/policy_research/MexicoUnderNafta.html NAFTA at the Global Development and Environment Institute, Tufts University

www.sec.ou.edu/eia/index.php Energy Institute of the Americas (EIA)

Recommended reading

Bulmer-Thomas, Victor and James Dunkerley (eds). 1999. *The United States and Latin America: The New Agenda*. London/Cambridge, MA: Institute of Latin American Studies/ David Rockefeller Center for Latin American Studies

Valuable introduction to the main themes in the relationship between the regions in the post-Cold War context of free trade and multilateralism

Smith, Peter. 2007. *Talons of the Eagle: Latin America, the United States, and the World*, 3rd Edition. New York: Oxford University Press

Essential introduction to the underlying historical themes and political dynamics that have shaped US–Latin American international relations

Pastor, Robert. 2001. *Exiting the Whirlpool. US Foreign Policy Toward Latin America and the Caribbean*, 2nd Edition. Boulder, CO: Westview Press

Essential introduction to key themes in the study of US–Latin American relations that adopts a valuable analytical approach seeking to identify recurrent patterns of behaviour

Rivarola Puntigliano, Andrés. 2008. 'Suspicious Minds: Recent Books on US–Latin American Relations', *Latin American Politics and Society*, Vol. 50, Issue 4 (December), pp. 155–72.

Valuable review article examining recent works on US–Latin American relations that provides a useful overview of theories, themes and issue

Schoultz, Lars. 2009. *That Infernal Little Cuban Republic. The United States and the Cuban Revolution.* Chapel Hill, NC: University of North Carolina Press

Valuable historical overview of the key foreign policy issue in US–Latin American relations

Livingstone, Grace. 2009. *America's Backyard: The United States and Latin America from the Monroe Doctrine to the War on Terror.* London: Zed Books

Valuable if at times one-sided examination of US interventions in Latin America that provides a good introductory overview of the main issues that have strained relations

Lowenthal, Abraham F., Ted Piccone and Laurence Whitehead (eds). 2009. *The Obama Administration and the Americas: Agenda for Change.* Washington, DC: Brookings Institution Press

Valuable introduction to the key issues that confront the Obama administration as it shapes policy towards Latin America

Chapter 11

Latin America, Europe and Asia

This chapter looks at Latin America's relations with two key regions outside the American hemisphere: Europe and Asia. Latin American countries have diversified their diplomatic and commercial relationships with countries and large corporations in both regions, which since democratisation have, in turn, gained importance in Latin American affairs. Since the 1990s, the European Union has not only become a key market for Latin American exports and vice versa, but it has also engaged in political negotiations in support of regional peace processes, democracy and social development. Russia has raised its profile as a power in the region, developing economic and defence ties with countries such as Venezuela. Some Latin American countries have also developed links with countries in the Asia Pacific region through organisations such as Asia-Pacific Economic Co-operation (APEC). Investment by Japan, Korea and, increasingly, China has grown rapidly in Latin American countries, some of which also have communities that retain cultural ties with their countries of origin in Asia. Chile, Brazil, Mexico, Argentina, Peru and Venezuela also belong to the G15 group of developing countries from Latin America, Asia and Africa that meet to discuss shared economic and political concerns.

Latin America's relationships with Europe and Asia are important because these regions offer the prospect of providing a counterweight to US hegemony in the western hemisphere. Since 1991, a number of Ibero-American summits of heads of state and government have been held, and these are notable for including Cuba but excluding the US. Europe and Asia also provide successful models of integration, democratisation and economic development for Latin America to follow, and Europe shares much history and strong cultural affinities with the region. Europe's rolling programme of talks with Latin America have also shaped the parameters of a new type of relationship between asymmetrical regions based upon institutionalised political dialogue as opposed to the assertion of economic, diplomatic or military prowess. A commitment to multilateralism and collaboration based on shared interests are at the heart of this relationship. What this has meant is that, although EU and European private-sector interest in Latin America focuses primarily upon its markets and natural resources, a number of factors have contributed to a positive perception of European policies in the region that arguably give the EU significant influence. First, EU policies are evaluated in comparison with more unilateral US policies and often associated with a stress on democratic values, respect for human rights and sustainable development. Second, EU development aid and co-operation programmes tend to conceal its economic interests in Latin America and, as a result, discourse in Latin America about its relationship with Europe emphasises co-operation and political dialogue in a multipolar world.

Relations with Europe

Europe has always exercised a strong political and cultural influence in Latin America, a term probably coined by Europeans in the nineteenth century in an effort to distinguish the region from the US (see Introduction). Members of Latin America's elite have been crossing the Atlantic and seeking refuge and support in Europe throughout its history. Until the First World War, European countries were Latin America's main source of trade and capital, investment, technology and immigrants. Waves of European immigration had an important impact upon political culture and ideas throughout Latin America in the 1920s and 1930s (see Chapters 12, 13). In the period following the Second World War, Europe concentrated on reconstruction and was divided by the Cold War, and thereafter its energies were turned towards democratisation in its own southern countries and the process of regional integration that has evolved into the EU. Attention by the European community to the developing world concentrated heavily on Africa, mainly because of former colonial ties, and it was not until the 1970s that Europe as a political entity began to forge stronger relations with Latin America. Even today, much of European Commission official development aid goes to African countries among the ACP (Africa, Caribbean and Pacific) states.

The EU and institutionalised political dialogue

The tone of EU–Latin American relations has been established through institutionalised political dialogue leading to official multilateral, bi-regional or bilateral accords. The EU has increasingly favoured bi-regional institutional relations with an ever more integrated Latin America and, while there are tensions and occasionally disputes, in general these relationships represent an example of successful inter-regional policy co-ordination (see Soderbaum ed., 2009).

In its ties with Latin America, the European Economic Community (EEC) initially concentrated on trade and technical co-operation. The 'Brussels Dialogue' was launched, consisting of meetings between the European community member states and Latin American ambassadors in Brussels (Hoste, 1999). Economic relations between the regions also developed and, in 1971, members of the Andean Pact were allowed to benefit from Europe's generalised system of preferences (GSP), which grants products imported from beneficiary countries either duty-free access or a tariff reduction, although the debt crisis and the Malvinas/Falklands war in 1982 strained relations because of European community support for Britain (see Box 11.1).

Since 1974, regular meetings have been held between representatives from the European Parliament and their counterparts from the Latin American parliament,

CASE STUDY	Box 11.1

The Falklands War and the European community

In April 1982, Argentine forces invaded the Malvinas/Falklands islands in the South Atlantic, asserting with military force a longstanding claim on the territory. It was not the first time that the military authorities in Buenos Aires had considered such a drastic step. In documents made public at the National Archives in Britain in May 2005, it was revealed that a mini-Royal Navy task force led by the nuclear-powered submarine HMS *Dreadnaught* had been secretly sent to the Falklands to deter an Argentine attack in 1977 after a party of 50 Argentineans had landed on the island of South Thule, prompting fears of an invasion. Argentina's invasion in April 1982 led to the similar despatch by Britain of a naval task force amid frantic diplomatic efforts to end the crisis. In late April, the task force reached the islands and the armed forces engaged, leading to a short but bloody war that ended in June when Argentine forces relinquished the besieged capital, Port Stanley. The Argentine invasion was seen by the European community as a challenge to state sovereignty and, through its then foreign policy mechanisms, it supported Britain in response to what was regarded as an act of aggression. Argentina was condemned by EC member states and European foreign ministers appealed to the Argentine government to withdraw its forces. European states imposed a ban on the export of military equipment to Argentina and on imports from the Latin American country. The British government received strong support from Belgium, which held the presidency of the Council of Ministers when the invasion had taken place. At that time, European interests in Argentina were limited, and so the threat to member states caused by the dispute was not significant. However, the European consensus soon broke down because of the specific national interests of member states, and in May 1982 Ireland and Italy withdrew sanctions against Argentina. Ireland's position related in part to an historical neutrality, which it had in effect transgressed by backing Britain, and to its own complex and, at that time, tense relationship with its neighbour. Italy has traditionally had strong links with Argentina, and a large number of Italians emigrated to the South American country in the early twentieth century. The Italian government came under domestic political pressure to adopt a more neutral stance towards the dispute so as not to endanger its special relationship with Argentina. The Malvinas/Falkland islands continue to have the potential to influence Argentina's relationship with Europe. In February 2010, for example, the country formally objected to the start of oil and gas exploration in waters off the islands, and escalated the dispute with Britain by blocking a ship from leaving the port of Buenos Aires that it alleged was carrying drilling equipment to them.

Main source: Pinakas, 2004; see also Freedman, 1982; Edwards, 1984; Bulmer-Thomas ed., 1989; Gibran, 1998

Parlatino, and mutual exchange visits have taken place (see Box 9.7). The Vienna EU-LAC summit in 2006 led to the creation of EuroLat (the Euro–Latin American Parliamentary Assembly), a joint multilateral assembly comprising 150 members from the European Parliament and several counterparts in Latin America including Parlatino (Latin American parliament), Parlandino (Andean parliament), Parlacen (Central American parliament) and Parlasur (Mercosur parliament) as well as the Mexican and Chilean congresses. EuroLat has made high-profile public declarations about issues of shared interest such as the Honduran political crisis of 2009. While these represent largely rhetorical acts, they can contribute to broader multilateral initiatives and international efforts to uphold the rule of law and democracy. In late 2009, for example, EuroLat issued a declaration reiterating its support for a condemnation by the Organisation of American States of the coup in Honduras (see Boxes 7.10, 9.5).

It has only been since the mid-1980s that the European community has developed a strategic policy towards the Latin American region. The European Parliament began to show more interest in Latin America in the 1980s and adopted an increasing number of resolutions about the region following the accession to the European community of Spain and Portugal in 1986, which greatly enhanced interest in Ibero-America. Since the mid-1980s, the European community has begun to establish more constructive relations with Latin America based on a coherent policy framework vis-à-vis the region (see Bretherton and Vogler, 1999; Europa, 2004, 2005). Important political links also developed as a result of the 'San José Process', through which Europe began to develop a new relationship with Central America by assuming a role of political mediation (Whitehead, 1999; see also Roy ed., 1992). The San José Process was launched at the height of the final phase of the Cold War and involved annual talks by foreign ministers of European states and the five Central American governments about political reconciliation, economic reconstruction and regional integration (*ibid.*). These talks committed the European community to the promotion of peace and reconstruction in Central America; unlike US policy towards the sub-region, the European community sought to incorporate Nicaragua; and it relied on co-operation within international law as opposed to compulsion (*ibid.*). The San José Process helped to stabilise Central America by supporting moderates and their allies who designed the Contadora initiative and Esquipulas formula for a regional peace settlement (see Chapter 9). After peace processes were agreed, the European community became the main provider of reconstruction aid in Central America. The community was also active in other sub-regions of Latin America. It has supported Andean integration efforts since the Cartagena Agreement established the Andean Community (originally named the Andean Pact) in 1969. A first 'Framework Agreement on Co-operation' between the European community and the Andean Pact was concluded in 1983, replaced by a second agreement in 1993. At the end of the Cold War, the European community began to inject new life into the Andean Pact by negotiating a regionally specific variant of the GSP intended to reward the sub-region for collaboration in the war against drug-trafficking (*ibid.*).

In the 1990s, the EU became a more important economic and political partner for Latin America. Trade doubled between 1999 and 2008 and, today, the EU is Latin America's second largest trading partner and the largest investor in the region (see Table 11.1). The EU is also now the leading donor of development aid in the region, and between 1999–2009, the European Commission financed more than 450 projects and programmes in the region accounting for more than €3 billion (European Commission, 2009).

In 1997, in a context of growing competition between Europe and the US over Latin American markets, France proposed a presidential summit between the EU and Mercosur (see Box 9.9), and this was held at the landmark Rio summit in 1999. The meeting of more than 40 heads of state and government from the EU, Latin America and the Caribbean, hosted by Brazil, was the first such summit between the regions. Its objective was to strengthen political, economic and cultural

Table 11.1 European and Russian merchandise trade with the Americas, 2006 and 2008*

Destination		North America			Europe			CIS	
Origin		Total	US	South and C. America	Total	EU (27)	Other Europe	Total	Russian Federation
North	2006	902.39	528.41	106.22	276.20	249.52	26.68	8.26	5.52
America	2008	1014.49	587.86	164.88	369.06	323.26	45.81	16.03	10.86
US	2006	364.92	.	87.25	235.84	212.72	23.11	7.06	4.70
	2008	413.15	.	134.98	311.08	271.81	39.27	13.82	9.33
Sth and	2006	145.63	126.94	101.48	89.25	81.99	7.25	6.17	5.55
Central America	2008	169.19	149.35	158.62	121.30	109.43	11.87	8.98	7.49
Europe	2006	430.25	363.75	66.03	3667.21	3394.48	272.74	143.18	96.35
	2008	475.35	394.64	96.44	4695.03	4331.41	363.62	239.96	164.58
EU (27)	2006	393.03	334.37	61.48	3394.36	3135.56	258.80	131.66	89.90
	2008	434.71	362.67	88.99	4313.51	3973.53	339.99	218.34	153.16
Other Europe	2006	37.22	29.38	4.55	272.85	258.91	13.94	11.51	6.45
	2008	40.64	31.97	7.45	381.52	357.89	23.63	21.62	11.43
CIS	2006	23.86	21.20	5.74	257.40	215.65	41.74	79.42	21.48
	2008	36.12	32.78	10.05	405.55	338.41	67.14	134.67	35.52
Russian	2006	20.54	18.66	4.28	193.73	164.53	29.20	43.38	.
Federation	2008	26.91	25.14	5.26	297.79	254.92	42.87	71.15	.

*Billions of dollars

Source: WTO, 2009

understanding in order to encourage the development of a 'strategic partnership' leading to joint political and economic actions. A subsequent EU–Latin America and Caribbean summit was held in 2002 in Madrid, and in 2004 the first summit attended by the 10 states that had then just joined an expanding EU was held in Guadalajara, Mexico. Bi-annual summits now take place at which the regions discuss issues high on the international agenda such as climate change and poverty, with the last being in 2008 in Lima, Peru, and one scheduled for 2010. On alternate years to the EU-LAC summits, meetings between ministers within the EU and the Rio Group (see Box 9.10) are held. Talks at the EU–Rio Group ministerial meeting in Prague in 2009, for example, focused on the global financial crisis, renewable energy and energy security (see Chapters 9, 10).

At these summits, key documents outlining the shared values underlying the EU–Latin American relationship have been agreed. These include the 'Common Values and Positions paper' adopted at Madrid and the 'Guadalajara Declaration', which commit both regions to the preservation of democracy and the protection of human rights. In 2005, the European Commission issued a key strategy document that laid out its main policy objectives towards Latin America: to promote regional integration and negotiations to establish 'association agreements' with sub-regions in Latin America; and to steer development co-operation towards reducing poverty and inequality and improving educational levels (European Commission, 2005). Association agreements are accords that generally aim to foster dialogue and co-operation between political institutions and to advance free trade. Although these policy aims remain priorities, in recent years environmental issues, drugs and migration have risen up the bi-regional agenda. The Lima summit in 2008 led to the launch of the EUrocLIMA Programme, a joint EU–Latin America initiative to promote co-operation on climate change (see Chapter 8). A more recent summary that takes stock of 10 years of the 'strategic partnership' was published in 2009 (see European Commission, 2009).

These evolving institutionalised links between the EU and Latin America have resulted in a large number of official multilateral, bi-regional or bilateral accords. Since 1999, the European Commission has successfully negotiated a range of agreements with different Latin American countries and sub-regions through 'specialised dialogues'. In Central America, the San José Dialogue has continued since 1984 and involves annual ministerial meetings to discuss areas of mutual interest in support of progress towards democratisation, sub-regional peace and the fight against drugs. In 2003, the EU signed a political dialogue and co-operation agreement with Central America to broaden links and, at the 2004 Guadalajara summit, it agreed to move towards the negotiation of a closer association agreement.

The EU also conducts regular talks with Andean countries about their own process of regional integration, democracy and human rights, and drug-trafficking. In 2003, the EU and the Andean Community signed a new political and co-operation accord. Relations between the EU and Mercosur (see Box 9.9) gained a prominent position in inter-regional contacts and have had an important influence over the EU approach to Latin America as a whole (Whitehead, 1999). The European community has supported the consolidation of Mercosur since the South American trade pact was founded in 1991 and, within a year of its creation, the European Commission agreed to provide it with technical and institutional support. Links between the regions are based upon recognition of the potential of Argentine and Brazilian markets for European business, but there is also a political affinity between the Mercosur integration process and that of the EU and strong cultural ties between the regions (*ibid.*).

The EU has also developed institutionalised relationships with individual Latin American countries on a bilateral basis and reached similar 'association agreements' with Mexico in 1997 and Chile in 2002 (see IRELA, 1997). The EU–Mexico 'Economic Partnership, Political Co-ordination and Co-operation Agreement' that came into force in 2000 established a new kind of trading relationship based on tariff-free trade for 90 per cent of products and institutionalised political relations through a ministerial 'joint council' that meets regularly. Closer bilateral ties with Argentina and Brazil are developing, and the EU also envisages extending the policy of strengthening dialogue and co-ordination with other regional processes, such as the Ibero-American Summits and the OAS.

In this expanding nexus of dialogues and links between Europe and Latin America, a number of EU policy concerns have become prominent:

Migration

Migration to the EU from Latin America has been growing (see Box 11.2). Until recently, the issue had avoided the tone of debate commonly found in the US, where millions of immigrants from Latin America provide some politicians with a theme that lends itself well to populistic rhetoric. However, immigration and asylum have risen steadily up the political agenda in Europe, and have become strategic priorities in the EU's external relations. EU leaders have grown increasingly aware of the need for policies that balance the requirement to fill skill and labour shortages amid rapidly changing demographics with public concerns about security and social cohesion. In 2008, European leaders signed up to an immigration pact that began a process of harmonising policy towards non-EU migrants across the bloc's 27 member states. Tough new measures were agreed obliging member states to choose between issuing residency permits to illegal immigrants or returning them to their country of origin which, in some cases could mean jailing them before they are deported. Latin American leaders reacted angrily to the plans, and in July 2008 a summit of Mercosur leaders in Argentina ended with a joint declaration angrily condemning the EU policy. Latin American leaders variously described the EU pact as a threat to human rights, racist and even, according to Venezuela's president, Hugo Chávez, 'barbarism'. Chávez threatened to cut oil exports to Europe unless the EU retracted the measure, and other leaders talked about possible restrictions on grain and other agricultural exports. The Latin Americans believed the EU policy represented a populistic reflex that they associated more commonly with the US. They argued that European policymakers, by placing responsibility for illegal immigration on the immigrants themselves, were avoiding the responsibility of dealing with the issue in a proper legal and equitable way. In response to anger generated by the new policy, the EU began detailed talks with Latin America in 2009 aimed at addressing challenges generated by it. Brussels has also allocated funding to address the root causes of migration and border management issues, and support continues for countries such as Colombia under initiatives such as the 'Uprooted People in Asia and Latin America (AUP)' programme. Between 2002 and 2006, for example, the EC earmarked €63.8 million to Colombia in this way.

Climate change and the environment

Climate change has also risen up the EU's political agenda and this has been reflected in an intensification of contacts and talks with Latin American countries to give greater weight to environmental issues within the EU–LAC partnership. In 2006, talks aimed at closer contacts between the two regions began and, in 2008, the first meeting of environment ministers was held in Brussels to discuss climate change, renewable energy, biodiversity loss and deforestation. Combating climate change was one of the key topics of the Lima EU-LAC summit in 2008 and led to the creation of EUrocLIMA (see above). Between 2002 and 2007, the EU granted financial aid to a number of environmental initiatives in Latin America and the Caribbean for promoting renewable energy. It allocated €100 million to Latin America and the Caribbean for the period 2007–10 for projects in forest management,

Latin American migration to Europe

Latin American migration to Europe, particularly to countries that it has strong historical and cultural ties with such as Spain, Portugal and Italy, has grown rapidly in recent years. Most of the immigrants from Latin America and the Caribbean (LAC) head for southern Europe, taking advantage of diplomatic efforts to foster an Ibero-American community of nations and, in some cases, favourable visa regulations. This phenomenon demonstrates how quickly countries and regions can change from being sources of immigration to sources of emigration, as during the early twentieth century Latin America was the destination for millions of Europeans. Recent migration from Latin America began during the period of military dictatorship in the 1970s, but its magnitude grew significantly in the 1990s. Spain has the largest population originating in the LAC countries, of more than 1 million people (representing 35.2 per cent of its foreign population), Italy has 205,000, the UK 113,000, Germany 94,000 and Portugal 56,000. Legally resident migrants from Ecuador, Colombia, Peru and Argentina comprise the largest Latin American populations in Spain, Portugal and Italy. Migrant flows from Ecuador to Spain demonstrate how rapidly a population can increase in size: in 1996, there were just 2,913 Ecuadorean citizens holding residence permits in Spain (Pellegrino/IOM, 2004). In Portugal, by contrast, Latin American migration is a relatively recent phenomenon and, until the 1970s, Portuguese migrants were still heading for a new life in countries such as Brazil and Venezuela. A significant proportion of the recent inflow into Portugal, therefore, represents 'return migration' by members of the Portuguese diaspora in the Americas who have maintained links with their country of origin actively aided by government programmes. Many Brazilians in Portugal are well educated and middle class, allowing them to compete in the labour market on equal terms with the native population.

The majority of Latin Americans heading for Europe are economic migrants, and these send about $2 billion home in remittances annually. Individuals seeking political asylum represent only 2–3 per cent of the overall stock of asylum seekers in Europe. Most Latin American asylum seekers head for the US or Canada, although Colombia's civil war and exile from Cuba are still fuelling refugee flows to Spain. As Latin America has democratised, some of those destinations have sought to minimise asylum claims. The Canadian government, for example, clamped down on Mexican claims in 2009 in an effort to reduce the number of asylum seekers from its NAFTA partner entering the country. Colombians and Cubans have traditionally accounted for most LAC asylum applications filed in Spain.

There are several explanations for a growth in migration from Latin America, from economic crisis in countries like Argentina and its impact on its neighbours to the tightening of immigration controls in the US since the 9/11 terrorist attacks. Analysts believe the existence of an established Latin American diaspora in Europe will, in itself, become a driving force for further migration. Most Latin American migrants to Spain today are young people without children motivated to migrate for economic reasons, and the majority are women. This tends to reflect the needs of the labour market, where women are in higher demand than men, particularly in low-skilled service roles. However, once a woman migrant is settled it is not uncommon for her to be followed by other members of her family including a male spouse. While unskilled jobs in the service sector represent the main employment of migrants, a significant number of Latin Americans in Spain are professionals with university-level studies, prompting some analysts to warn about the negative consequences of a 'brain drain' for Latin America in the longer term.

Sources: Padilla and Peixoto, 2007; Pellegrino/IOM, 2004 (Ministry of the Interior, Spain, 2002, 2003; UNHCR, 2004)

deforestation, governance, and climate change adaptation. The European Investment Bank was also due to make available loans for environmental and renewable energy projects.

None the less, activists have at times pointed to a lack of transparency and hypocrisy in the EU's attitude to the responsibility of large European corporations for what they claim are environmentally damaging activities in Latin America. At the Vienna EU-LAC summit in 2006, for example, a parallel alternative 'Permanent People's Tribunal' involving NGOs and activist groups was held aiming to highlight the activities of the 30 largest European corporations in Latin America and the Caribbean. This included representatives from Brazil's Movimento dos Trabalhadores Rurais Sem Terra (MST, Landless Rural Workers Movement) and Vía Campesina, a global network of rural movements (see Chapter 8), whose targets included the Norwegian–Brazilian Aracruz Celulosa paper pulp company. Both the MST and Vía Campesina claimed Aracruz Celulosa has created the largest 'green desert' in Brazil, having planted more than 250,000 hectares with fast-growing pulp trees that deplete the soil and water sources (Godoy, 2006).

Drug-trafficking

Although Europe is the world's largest opiates market and the problem of cocaine is more prominent in the Americas, west and central Europe still represents a large cocaine market for drug-trafficking cartels, and it was only in 2008 following several years of significant increases in reported cocaine use that the European market stabilised. According to the UNODC (2009), between 4.3 and 4.6 million people in west and central Europe used cocaine between 2006–07, and the UK and Spain are the largest cocaine markets in the region. In some European countries the use of crack cocaine and other derivatives such as cocaine HDI has risen considerably (see UNODC, 2009). For the EU, key concerns are the crime-related activities caused by drug abuse and the cost of treatment. As a result, the co-ordination of counter-narcotics strategies has grown increasingly sophisticated. In 2007, 11 per cent of global cocaine seizures were in Europe, with Spain reporting the largest hauls (38 mt) as well as the highest number of clandestine coca processing laboratories detected outside the Americas (18).

Co-operation with Latin American countries has become a key element of the strategy against cocaine trafficking in EU states: according to the UNODC (2009), the most frequently mentioned country of origin for the cocaine trafficked to Europe is Colombia (which 48 per cent of countries reported as the source for their seizures), followed by Peru (30 per cent) and Bolivia (18 per cent). Key transit countries for the cocaine that finds its way to Europe are Venezuela (40 per cent in terms of volume), Ecuador, the Dominican Republic, Brazil, Argentina and Chile. The EU has developed formal mechanisms in its talks with LAC countries to co-ordinate and co-operate on counter-narcotics policies, and countries such as the UK have been actively involved in international drug-interdiction efforts in the region. In September 2009 off the coast of South America, for example, Britain's Royal Navy seized five tonnes of cocaine, with an estimated street value of $450 million, that was being transported from Colombia on a fishing boat.

Like the US, the EU has identified drug-trafficking from Latin America as a threat to its security. However, the EU counter-narcotics strategy towards the region has won praise there because it is based on an official recognition of Europe's 'shared responsibility' for the emergence of an illicit drugs market, and because co-operation with Latin America in the effort to combat the trade has focused heavily on alternative development projects (see Fukumi, 2008). Latin American leaders have also described the EU approach as more innovative, humane and efficient than that of the US for emphasising 'harm reduction' that focuses on confronting the damage caused by drugs in terms of public health, as opposed to 'prohibition' (Latin American Commission on Drugs and Democracy, 2009). None the less, Latin American countries have continued to stress the need for EU states to make greater efforts to reduce domestic drug consumption in order to curb the demand for illicit drugs that stimulates its production and exportation (*ibid.*).

While migration, climate change and drug-trafficking are the key themes that today shape the EU's efforts to interact with Latin America, as well as its broader agenda to enhance its influence in the region by promoting economic development and good governance, its influence can be examined in terms of three main themes: its role as a counterweight to US power; its economic interests in the region; and its support for integration and democratisation.

Europe as a counterweight

Latin American countries have long sought an external counterweight to the US (see Chapters 9, 10), a role fulfilled during the Cold War by the Soviet Union. Since the 1960s, some Latin American states have cultivated political and economic ties with other developed countries in a 'diversification of dependency' strategy that focused heavily on Western Europe (Muñoz, 2001). Since the end of the Cold War, both the EU and Latin America have shared the political perception that it is important to balance the tendency towards a unipolar world dominated by one superpower, and Europe began to play a greater role in Latin America as it was itself emerging from the Cold War tutelage of the US. In May 2006, for example, Venezuela – the world's fifth largest oil producer – hinted that it could begin to price its oil exports in euros rather than US dollars in a clear effort to weaken links with the US while strengthening ties with the EU.

The role of counterweight can be put to good use in diverse areas, particularly trade. Not only do Latin American countries already enjoy access to the US market, making the European market one in which there is significant growth potential for them, but they have at times expected better results from free trade with Europe than through hemispheric free-trade negotiations and have also seen the potential for using their relations with the EU as a bargaining chip in negotiations with Washington, such as on the FTAA (*ibid.*; see Box 15.5). Since the launch of the North American Free Trade Agreement (NAFTA) in 1994, Mexico's economy has become more closely integrated with that of the US and it has explicitly sought closer ties with Europe to offset its neighbour's dominant position (Bulmer-Thomas and Dunkerley, 1999). In 1997, the signing of an 'Economic Partnership, Political

Co-ordination and Co-operation Agreement' established ties between the EU and Mexico alone, as opposed to NAFTA.

The features of the EU that distinguish it from a conventional nation-state – especially its institutionalisation, negligible military capacity and limited strategic interests in Latin America – can make it an important mediator, as was the case in the San José Process. An EU insistence on democracy clauses and the process it must go through to ratify treaties promotes a higher standard of assessment for political and human rights than is written into such instruments as NAFTA, for example.

EU policy towards Cuba provides evidence of its independent approach: it has not followed the US line on economic sanctions; it has not taken the same view about the need to reverse revolutionary confiscations; and it has not endorsed the partisan version of democratisation advocated by the US (Whitehead, 1999). In the early 1990s, under the influence of Spain's socialist government, the EU experimented with an approach aiming to dismantle Cuba's closed system through a gradualist strategy, reintegration in the international market economy and constructive engagement (*ibid.*). Growing US–Cuban tensions in the 1990s turned EU attention to the extra-territorial pretensions of US laws. The Helms-Burton law (see Box 10.8) created instruments through which citizens and corporations outside US jurisdiction may be coerced into conforming with US policy, powers that the EU argued were at variance with Washington's obligations under international trading conventions. EU diplomacy and pressure secured *de facto* waivers of several of these measures against European firms.

The EU has at times also been seen in Latin America as a counterweight to the US in the negotiation of aspects of global trade policy (see below), although Europe has itself also looked to Latin America as a counterweight to the US in world trade talks, and EU resistance to addressing agricultural subsidies has been the main stumbling block to enhancing closer economic ties (see below). During the FTAA negotiations, for example, Brazil used the prospect of a deal with the EU as a bargaining chip to extract concessions from the US. EU and Latin American countries also shared concern about US unilateralism in the Middle East under President George W. Bush, and a common commitment to multilateralism and a reluctance to resort to military power is more amenable to the changed diplomatic climate that accompanied the inauguration of Barack Obama in 2009 (see Chapter 10). Internationally, the EU has a vested interest in multilateralism: it can only succeed in becoming a global actor by enhancing bi-regional relations through existing and new multilateral forms of partnership. Despite disagreements over migration and agricultural policy, there has been a greater convergence of interests between the EU and Mercosur on issues such as the environment, the International Criminal Court and development, for example, than between the US and Mercosur. The EU's development-oriented and consensus-seeking approach to problem solving, if bureaucratic, is also looked upon favourably in Latin America, a perspective enhanced by the ascent in a number of countries of governments espousing variants of social democracy that have much in common with European political tradition (see Chapter 12). The distance that has entered US–Latin American relations because of political changes in the region and perceptions of Washington's policy under Bush has created new spaces for the EU to project its influence, and the extent to which it does so will depend in large part both on the parameters of the relationship between the US and Europe and the degree to which the US accommodates Latin America's assertion of autonomy, particularly in areas of economic and security policy (see Chapters 9, 10). Despite Latin America's own regional initiatives, growing US trade with the region still offers the opportunity of leadership within a global trading system shaped by competing blocs such as the Americas, Europe and the Far East etc.

Economic interests

The EU has extensive economic interests in Latin America, which represents a large market for European consumer goods and is an important supplier of mineral resources and commodities. The European community's renewed interest in Latin America in the 1990s was, in part, fuelled by the large supply of cheap labour and investment opportunities that the region could offer. The EU has consistently strengthened its economic and trade links with the region and, by 2007, had become its second most important trading partner, and the main trading partner for Mercosur and Chile. Between 1999 and 2008, trade between the EU and Latin America and the Caribbean doubled, with EU imports from Latin America rising from €42.5 billion to €102.4 billion, and EU exports to the region increasing from €52.2 billion to €86.4 billion (Europa, 2009a). Trade is also likely to grow with the enlargement of the EU which, in January 2007, became an integrated market of 495.1 million people.

European investment in Latin America also grew considerably in the 1990s as a result of the privatisation programmes undertaken by most countries of the region (see Table 15.1). The EU is the most important source of foreign direct investment (FDI) for the region, although flows have varied. European FDI to Latin America peaked in 2000 at €46 billion, with the total stock of European investment in the region rising from €189.4 billion in 2000 to €227.8 in 2007 (*ibid.*). While most FDI is from private companies, the European Investment Bank (EIB), the EU's financing institution, began to target Latin America after 1992 and has made extensive loans there. In the period 2007–13, the EIB has allocated €2.8 billion in loans to finance operations that support the EU's co-operation strategy and complement its development programmes (EIB, 2009). It places special emphasis on projects that contribute to environmental sustainability and EU energy security. In 2009, for example, the EIB granted a $211 million loan to two subsidiaries of Gas de France-Suez Group to part-finance the construction and operation of the Guanaca, Lorena and Prudencia hydro-power plants on the Chiriqui river in western Panama. Panama hopes the project will help to meet rapidly growing demand for electricity in an environmentally sustainable way by using water resources.

The EU has signed economic agreements of one kind or another with most Latin American countries since the early 1990s, and its strategy has been to strengthen trade with the region both through free-trade agreements but also by supporting regional integration initiatives (see below). Chile and Mexico both reached free-trade agreements with the EU that came into effect between 2000 and 2002, for example, covering trade and investment and leading to a considerable increase in commerce. However, the extension of bilateral free-trade agreements between the US and Latin American countries, and the delineation of a hemispheric free-trade agenda modelled on NAFTA after 1994 (see Box 15.5), forced the EU to compete with the US on trade in the region. This has been made easier by Latin American efforts to diversify economies. Although the region's proximity to the US makes it a natural export market, many countries have sought to avoid dependence on the North American market. In recent years, for example, Central America, where the Dominican Republic–Central American Free Trade Agreement (DR-CAFTA) that also encompasses the US came into force in 2009, has actively sought to widen its export markets in Europe and elsewhere. Central American countries already benefit from the European GSP, but in 2007 talks began on an association agreement that will incorporate free trade. In recent years, the EU has moved away from the use of tariff preferences to encourage development such as the GSP towards compliance with multilateral rules under the General Agreement on Tariffs and Trade (GATT) and World Trade Organisation (WTO).

Reaching an agreement with Mercosur remains a priority for EU trade officials, who began negotiations with the bloc on a comprehensive free-trade deal as part of an inter-regional association agreement in 2000. Trade negotiations were suspended in 2004 pending the outcome of the Doha Round of WTO talks, although they continued in other areas and, by 2008, 16 negotiating rounds had been conducted. Trade with Mercosur is considerable and the EU is now the bloc's second largest trading partner after the US, representing 19.6 per cent of total Mercosur trade (Europa, 2009b). In 2007, the EU exported goods worth €32.12 billion to the regional bloc and imported goods worth €47.84 billion – as much as EU trade with the rest of Latin America taken together. EU investment stock in Mercosur countries amounted to €126.3 billion by 2006 (*ibid.*). Stumbling blocks in free-trade talks have been EU agricultural subsidies and the barriers this poses Mercosur: the EU is already its principal market for agricultural exports, which accounted for 21 per cent of total EU agricultural imports in 2007 (*ibid.*).

The European community has also targeted Latin America for development aid which, until the late 1980s, was devoted to agriculture. Since 1990, activities linked to human rights, democratisation and financial and technical assistance have been included in the aid agenda. The EU is now the leading donor of development aid to Latin America which, when combined with the contributions of individual member states, has totalled about €500 million per year since 1996 (Europa, 2009c). About €2.7 billion has been allocated by the EU for co-operative projects for the period 2007–13 and, alongside this, the European Investment Bank has earmarked €2.8 billion for loans in Latin America and the Caribbean (see Figure 11.1, and above).

The main objectives of development aid – administered by the EU's EuropeAid directorate and often allocated directly to government budgets so that the funds are spent wisely and there is 'local ownership' of the results – have been poverty reduction, sustainable development and improving social cohesion. In 2004, for example, the European Commission approved the EUROSociAL programme assisting Latin American countries to develop and implement social policies that help reduce the gap between the rich and poor (see Box 11.3). Other priorities of EU aid are good governance, sustainable development and higher education,

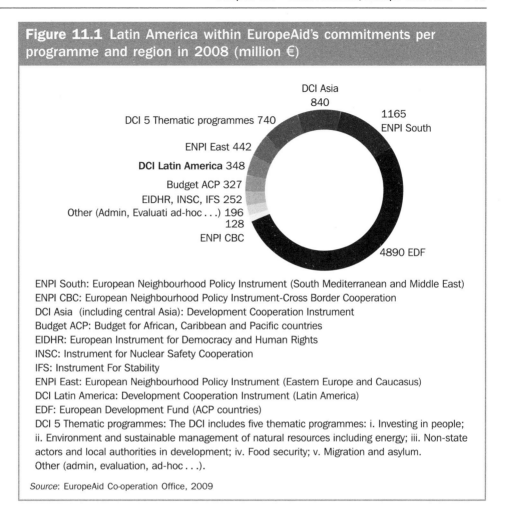

Figure 11.1 Latin America within EuropeAid's commitments per programme and region in 2008 (million €)

DCI Asia 840

1165 ENPI South

DCI 5 Thematic programmes 740

ENPI East 442

DCI Latin America 348

Budget ACP 327

EIDHR, INSC, IFS 252

Other (Admin, Evaluati ad-hoc . . .) 196

128 ENPI CBC

4890 EDF

ENPI South: European Neighbourhood Policy Instrument (South Mediterranean and Middle East)
ENPI CBC: European Neighbourhood Policy Instrument-Cross Border Cooperation
DCI Asia (including central Asia): Development Cooperation Instrument
Budget ACP: Budget for African, Caribbean and Pacific countries
EIDHR: European Instrument for Democracy and Human Rights
INSC: Instrument for Nuclear Safety Cooperation
IFS: Instrument For Stability
ENPI East: European Neighbourhood Policy Instrument (Eastern Europe and Caucasus)
DCI Latin America: Development Cooperation Instrument (Latin America)
EDF: European Development Fund (ACP countries)
DCI 5 Thematic programmes: The DCI includes five thematic programmes: i. Investing in people; ii. Environment and sustainable management of natural resources including energy; iii. Non-state actors and local authorities in development; iv. Food security; v. Migration and asylum. Other (admin, evaluation, ad-hoc . . .).

Source: EuropeAid Co-operation Office, 2009

although aid has also been allocated to areas of strategic interest to Europe such as the fight against drug-trafficking and migration projects. In Ecuador, for example, the EC has granted funding to projects aiming to improve the access to education of marginalised and disadvantaged communities. In the period 2005–08, more than €12 million was approved for migration projects in Latin America ranging from initiatives to optimise the benefits of remittances to action against human trafficking. In Colombia, the EU has funded 'Peace Laboratories' that contribute to the cultivation of alternative crops in coca-growing areas, which builds on the past use of trade preferences in the Central American and the wider Andean sub-regions to support development in the battle against drug-trafficking. Both sub-regions gained better terms of trade than other GSP recipients to help them shift production from coca to other crops. The EU also co-operates with countries in a large number of economic development schemes set up to increase the competitiveness of Latin American companies in international markets and to help small and medium-sized companies from both regions create joint ventures and projects involving technology transfer, telecommunications and transport.

| INSTITUTIONS | Box 11.3 |

EUROSociAL

One of the most recent EU projects in Latin America devised by the Commission's EuropeAid co-operation Office is called EUROSociAL, which began in 2005. Through the five-year, €30 million programme, the European Commission has aimed to help Latin American countries strengthen 'social cohesion' – a key theme at the Guadalajara summit – by developing and implementing social policies that contribute to reducing the gap between the rich and the poor in the region and promoting improved management of public policies. Social cohesion and the effort to combat poverty are key themes of the EU's development policy in general, and are based on its support for the UN 'Millennium Development Goals', a set of policy priorities to tackle these issues at a global level (see UN, 2005; European Commission, 2007). The EU's policy, 'The European Consensus on Development', was adopted by the European Parliament, the Council of Ministers, the Member States and the Commission in December 2005, and established as the overarching objective of EU development co-operation the eradication of poverty in the context of sustainable development. EUROSociAL aims to do this by helping policy-makers develop a capacity to take into account the social dimension of their work. This programme focuses on policies in health, education, the administration of justice, employment and taxation. It is based on the idea that inequality, poverty and social exclusion represent a barrier to economic development, create instability and dissatisfaction, and so ultimately threaten fragile democracies that have yet to deliver benefits for the poor (see Chapter 4). Social cohesion is a core value of the EU and has been a prominent theme in discussion about its own expansion. The EUROSociAL policy initiative is, therefore, a good example of one in which EU officials believe Europe's own experience can be successfully applied to Latin America. The programme seeks to transfer knowledge and experience between the public services of both regions in health, education, taxation and justice. It administers four significant grants of €6.4 million each to consortia of organisations carrying out programmes in these areas.

Integration

An important characteristic of the EU's policy towards Latin America since the mid-1980s has been support for regional integration, of which Europe has provided a powerful model. US interest in Latin American regional integration has varied in intensity and has been determined by trade and security interests (see Chapter 10). The EU, by contrast, has supported most Latin American integration initiatives *in principle* since it first began to exercise its influence internationally. It has often provided active support for integration efforts since the end of the Cold War. The European community has regarded Latin American integration as an important way of accelerating economic growth and strengthening the multi-lateral system. It has provided financial aid as well as technical assistance for regional integration processes and has shared the knowledge it has gained from its own experience of integration. Mercosur, the Andean Community and the Central American Common Market (CACM) are the three main regional focuses of integration within Latin America (see Box 9.9, Table 15.2). In 1992, the European Commission helped form a joint advisory committee with Mercosur through which it could share its experience of integration through training and technical assistance (*ibid.*). As early as 1985, the European Commission was granting funds to support and promote Andean Pact integration efforts (Hoste, 1999). The European community has supported the Andean integration process in three main ways:

- political support, which strengthens the ability of policymakers in the region pressing for closer relations with their neighbours and helps them in the resolution of disputes;
- technical assistance, through support and grants, for example, to projects harmonising statistical methodologies across the sub-region and market standards, and the sharing of expertise in such areas as disaster prevention;
- support for institution-building, with co-operation and the sharing of expertise to help strengthen and improve the capacity of Andean regional institutions such as the CAN general secretariat, the Andean Court of Justice, and the Andrés Bello Convention (a regional body that fosters educational, scientific, technological and cultural co-operation).

Democracy

Key themes in exchanges between Europe and Latin America have been democratisation and human rights (see Youngs, 2002). Since the 1970s, European governmental and non-governmental actors started to show increasing concern for democratic progress in the region, denouncing human rights violations, distancing themselves from authoritarian regimes, supporting political parties, aiding local NGOs and strengthening relations with newly democratic governments (van Klaveren, 2001). European-dominated political bodies such as the Socialist International also adopted active policies of support towards the region (see Chapter 12). The accession of Spain and Portugal to the European community in 1986 strengthened its role as a promoter of democratisation, and this became a characteristic of European policy after 1990 when concrete agreements were concluded with Latin American countries characterised by their commitment to democratic principles as a condition for co-operation and aid (Hoste, 1999). The co-operation and association agreements signed by the EU with its Latin American partners include clauses enshrining respect for democratic principles and human rights, which today remain under EU scrutiny and are frequently restated in mutual accords.

Europe's interest in the Latin American democratisation process is recent and has been pursued with pragmatism and consideration for more traditional interests, such as the promotion of trade, investment and arms sales (van Klaveren, 2001). However, Latin America has responded positively to EU pressure on democracy, in part because of shared preferences for democracy with a *social* character (Whitehead, 1999; see above and Chapter 3), but also because EU policies are often evaluated favourably for their intrinsically multilateral character in comparison with more unilateral US policies, and because the EU is able to assert an independent position vis-à-vis Washington. One example of this has been EU policy towards Cuba (see above), which has oscillated between supportive and punitive actions by seeking to engage in political dialogue with leaders on the island yet voicing its concern about political freedoms there. In recent years, the EU's relationship with Cuba has been shaped by the communist state's record on rights and the development of a common European response to this. In 2003, Brussels imposed sanctions on Cuba in protest at the imprisonment of dissidents, but these were formally lifted in 2008 to encourage democratic reforms, and the EU has re-established development aid to Cuba worth €40 million. EU policymakers argue that engaging with Cuba on areas of common interest such as trade and the environment will enable future discussions on political and human rights.

The EU has also supported electoral and constitutional processes in Latin America by deploying monitors in Election Observation Missions (EOMs). Between 2004–09, for example, EOMs were deployed in Bolivia, Ecuador, El Salvador Guatemala, Nicaragua, Peru and Venezuela, and their recommendations have made valuable contributions to the improvement of electoral systems (Europa, 2009c).

Problems and issues

The relationship between the European Union and Latin America has generally been positive and offers a potential model for peaceful, multilateral co-operation between large regions of the world. However, a number of caveats must be recognised in any examination of EU–Latin American relations and the co-operative themes outlined above:

The primacy of EU interests

Despite Latin American assumptions that Europe may offer a counterweight to the US, the EU's focus on the region has been determined largely by the pursuit of its own interests and has, at times, developed as a defensive response to US positions on trade. In this sense, EU attention to Latin America can be seen as an effort to diversify beyond the inward-looking bias of its own single market (Whitehead, 1999). For example, it can be argued that Europe had its own strategic objectives in addressing the crisis in Central America – a region in which it had few economic interests – at a time when it was believed in many European countries that President Ronald Reagan (1981–89) was using Nicaragua as the pretext for an escalation of the Cold War. The EU-Latin American summit in Vienna in May 2006, for example, was overshadowed by European concerns about its energy supplies following moves by Bolivia to nationalise its gas industry and the imposition of higher taxes on oil extraction by Venezuela. It is also no surprise that progress in establishing a free-trade agreement between the EU and Mercosur stalled alongside US efforts to consolidate a hemispheric Free Trade Area of the Americas (see below, and Boxes 9.9, 15.5, Table 15.2). An important incentive for the EU to make concessions to Mercosur had been to preempt the FTAA, which EU leaders believed would, in the absence of a trading agreement with them, damage European trade with the Southern Cone. Although EU pronouncements stress the importance of re-establishing trade talks with Mercosur, the fate of these remain closely tied to other developments, not least the emerging trade policy of the Obama administration in the US.

The EU's relationship with Latin America has also been constrained by recurrent tensions over trade. EU banana supplies have tended to come from former European colonies in the Caribbean which find it difficult to compete with lower-cost Latin American suppliers. A series of disputes in the 1990s over market access for Latin American countries became known as the 'banana wars'. After 1993, tension came to a head and the Latin Americans lined up alongside the US to appeal to the WTO, whose rulings demanded that the EU introduce new tariffs for the fruit. In 2005, the WTO again backed a claim brought by the Latin American countries that had argued the level of the proposed tariff would harm their economies. In 2009, the EU finally reached a deal, that will bring it in line with WTO rulings, to cut tariffs on Latin American banana imports gradually beginning in 2010.

The Mercosur countries have competitive agricultural export sectors and view Europe's Common Agricultural Policy (CAP) – a generous system of subsidies that, by 2013, will still represent about 32 per cent of the EU's budget – and the Lomé agreement, a trade and aid pact signed between the EU and selected African, Caribbean and Pacific nations conferring on them trade and investment benefits, as obstacles to free trade. Mercosur believes European expansion efforts mean that addressing agricultural subsidies will not be a priority in EU efforts to relax protectionism (Whitehead, 1999). Tensions over agricultural subsidies have meant that the search for mutual benefit has often focused on areas dominated by the private sector such as the auto trade, energy, privatised utilities, the financial sector and infrastructure projects (*ibid.*). Deadlock in trade negotiations between the EU and Mercosur over agricultural provisions suggests that any move to reform the EU budget to reduce the proportion of it accounted for by the CAP will have a positive impact on EU–Latin American relations.

As Latin American economies have grown and their integration initiatives have consolidated, the region has also demonstrated a greater assertiveness in its relationship with the EU. The EU and Mercosur, for example, failed to agree in talks on establishing a free-trade deal because of disagreements over access to their respective markets. In particular, Mercosur has been unwilling to make concessions in the area of most interest to EU countries – its manufacturing sector – until progress has been made on agriculture. Moreover, while a series of complex agreements have enhanced economic relationships between the EU and Latin America, these have often been criticised by aid organisations such as Oxfam for being based upon an excessive confidence in the contribution economic liberalisation will make to growth and poverty reduction, and for failing to make human development their central focus (see Oxfam, 1999).

The EU's institutional structure

The EU's relationship with Latin America has also been hampered by its own internal differences and policy diversity (see Box 11.4). There has been a tendency in Latin America to see Europe as a unitary actor, yet within the expanding EU there are many complex divisions and tensions, and these became particularly evident

INSTITUTIONS   Box 11.4

European policy diversity

Different regions of Europe articulate different interests in the overall conduct of EU relations with other regions. Spain and southern Europe have a greater interest in stronger relations with Latin America than the northern industrial countries, which tend to look eastwards (Whitehead, 1999). Different legal traditions and perspectives on human rights were also evident in the way in which European states approached the Pinochet affair, for example (see Box 7.11). Bulmer-Thomas and Dunkerley (1999) highlighted '. . . the erratic legal accords between Spain and the United Kingdom (in both bi- and multilateral forms), the division of powers and independence of the courts in both states, the military and political alliances and conflicts of the previous governments of both countries with Chile, the prospects for arms sales, the links between domestic political pacts in Chile and the claims to sovereignty sustained by Santiago abroad, the concern of Washington not to revisit its role in the coup of 1973, and, finally, the unfolding of a new agenda for the international prosecution of criminal cases concerned with genocide or the widespread violation of human rights on a consistent and enforceable basis' (p. 313). A more recent sign of the limits of unity in European affairs vis-à-vis Latin America, despite the EU integration process, came in policy towards climate change. In November 2009, France agreed with Brazil a common position on fighting global warming – to pursue the goal of reducing the emissions of industrialised nations to 50 per cent below 1990 levels by 2050 – before the scheduled UN climate change conference in Copenhagen aiming to establish a successor to the 1997 Kyoto treaty. The move came just days after the UK had said it was highly unlikely that a legally binding climate treaty could be agreed at Copenhagen and only a political deal was possible, angering developing countries which wanted a firmer commitment from the developed world to finance a climate deal.

during the progress towards ratification of the Lisbon Treaty, signed in 2007, that amended the European community's founding charters. The treaty was itself a replacement for the proposed European constitution, which was rejected by French and Dutch voters in 2005, and was intended to have been ratified by all member states by the end of 2008, a timetable that failed due to the initial rejection of the treaty in Ireland in 2008 (subsequently reversed in a second referendum in 2009).

The nature of the EU's relationship with Latin America is likely to remain limited, in comparison with that of the US, by its own institutional structure as a union of independent nations with executive and foreign policy representatives whose own authority is in flux. It was only in 2009, for example, that European Council leaders elected a president under the rules of the newly adopted Lisbon Treaty to represent the EU abroad. The new European president is a non-partisan consensus candidate, has no veto powers over legislation, serves a term of only two-and-a-half years and has no military prerogatives. The US president, by contrast, is a partisan candidate with a mandate to pursue his own policies gained through elections, has veto powers over legislation, serves for four years, and is the commander-in-chief of the world's most powerful armed forces and responsible for military strategy. Unlike the US, the EU's executive structure militates against prompt and authoritative decisionmaking, until recently one member state has been able to override all other EU members to block a policy, and many 'opt outs' remain.

As a result, the EU has shown nervousness when dealing with Latin America at times when its leaders appear to be divided among themselves. At the summit between EU and Latin American leaders in Vienna in May 2006, for example, some European officials voiced concern that their investments might not be secure in a Latin America plagued by political disputes. Expansion of the EU has also raised new issues and distractions. The expanding EU is increasingly focusing on its internal consolidation and the instability of its own external border, one sign of which has been its new immigration policy (see above).

The EU's relationship with the US

The EU's interest in Latin America also remains qualified by the reality of its relationship with the US as well as the future of the international system more generally. The banana disputes demonstrated that EU–Latin American relations are, in fact, often a 'triangular' affair in which the role of the US also figures prominently (*ibid.*; see also Kagan, 2004). Even by reaching an agreement with the US over Cuba, for example, the EU agreed to limit investment and sought common ground with Washington on democracy promotion (*ibid.*). Since 1998, EU foreign ministers have emphasised that the prospects for Cuba of future membership of the Lomé pact (today in the form of the Cotonou Agreement) depend upon progress on human rights, governance and political freedom. More recently, relations between the EU and Cuba have been turbulent, and Europe has struggled to maintain a common line and has at times appeared to be divided on the issue (see Box 10.8). Spain's socialist government resisted EU policy on limiting political ties with Cuba, and in July 2005 France signalled that it was normalising relations with Havana against an agreement by EU governments not to do so. Both Europe and Latin America continue to make their relations with the US a priority. Whitehead (1999) argued that Latin Americans would be unwise to place too much faith in the potential of closer ties with the EU because the US remains Europe's overriding strategic consideration. Bulmer-Thomas and Dunkerley (1999) cautioned that the issues and disputes raised by the EU's expansion and deepening mean that Latin America is not a priority and Europe will only be a source of token resistance to the hegemonic presence of the US in the region. Latin American republics should not assume that the EU will play a bigger role in hemispheric affairs. Some authors question the contemporary economic benefits of tighter relations with Europe or Asia anyway, arguing that in many ways the US domestic market is far more open to Latin America than the EU (see Smith, 2000). A strategic EU partnership with Mercosur could also have the effect of reducing the EU's commitment to other Latin American sub-regions, thereby strengthening the ability of other powers such as the US to further enhance their relationships with these.

It must be recognised also that ties between other European states and Latin America have developed *outside* the institutional and multilateral structures of the EU and Latin American regional bodies, further complicating EU–Latin American relations. Russia, for example, whose own relationship with the EU and its largest economies has deepened considerably in the last decade, has increased the effort to assert its influence and power in Latin America in recent years (see Box 11.5).

Box 11.5

Russia in Latin America

Since 2000, Russia has been strengthening its diplomatic and economic presence in Latin America but in 2008 it raised its profile in the region considerably with a series of presidential and ministerial visits, major arms, trade and energy deals, and military manoeuvres. A tour of the region by the Russian president, Dmitry Medvedev, took in Venezuela, the first by a Kremlin leader to the country, as well as Brazil, Cuba and Peru. Moscow has maintained political, economic and military links with Latin America since the era of the Soviet Union, engaging in limited competition with the US as a means of asserting its claim to great power status vis-à-vis Washington. Its recent activities in Latin America have had three main dimensions: economic, strategic and political.

Economic

Russia's key interest in Latin America is economic, with the region seen as a fertile market for arms, a potentially important customer of Russian energy infrastructure, and an ally in global energy markets. Russian trade with Latin America is very limited (see Table 11.1), and increasing this is considered important as the country attempts to compete in key markets such as defence, energy and aerospace with other emerging economies such as China (see below), India and Brazil.

Russia has been selling weapons in Latin America since 2004 and its principal customer has become Venezuela whose president, Hugo Chávez, signed contracts worth about $4.4 billion between 2005–09. In an effort to modernise its armed forces, but also to send a signal to Colombia with whom relations have deteriorated over its military relationship with the US (see Box 9.8), Venezuela has bought hardware including Mig-35 helicopters, Sukhoi fighter jets, and sniper and assault rifles, as well as arms-manufacturing facilities. Venezuela has also expressed interest in buying tankers, cargo and military transport planes, submarines and torpedoes. In September 2009, Chávez gave details of a deal with Russia that involved the purchase of 92 T-72S tanks, Smerch missiles and an advanced anti-aircraft defence system.

Russia has also aimed to raise its profile in the Latin American energy market and Venezuela has again been at the heart of its strategy, with an agreement between the state oil firm Petróleos de Venezuela (PDVSA) to form a $20 billion venture to develop the Junin 6 heavy-crude oil field in the Orinoco Belt with Russian energy companies, among them Rosneft Oil, Lukoil and Gazprom. Moscow has sought to take advantage of difficulties facing oil majors from other countries in operating in Venezuela, given a tougher contractual climate under the Chávez administration which, in 2007, forced multi-nationals to renegotiate contracts and seized the assets of those that did not comply. Venezuela also holds the second-largest reserves of gas in the western hemisphere and Gazprom and its European partners also hold licences for deposits in the Orinoco basin and are involved in projects to build new pipelines. Russia has also agreed to help Venezuela develop a nuclear energy programme and explore for raw materials such as uranium.

To support arms purchases and trade, Moscow has sometimes tied its development aid and loans in Latin America to the sale of Russian products. In 2008, for example, as the oil price sank limiting the revenues available to Chávez, Russia offered Venezuela a $1 billion credit line for further arms purchases, and the 2009 sales were supported by a credit line of $2.2 billion. Since 2008, Russia has also been repairing relations with Cuba, announcing plans to build a space centre on the island among other things, in an effort to restore trade damaged since the collapse of the Soviet Union. In early 2009, Russia also granted $20 million to Cuba and raised the possibility of future credits of $335 million to enable it to buy Russian products. The purchase by Bolivia of a new $20 million Russian-made Antonov-148 presidential aircraft accompanied a deal in which Russia will use a Bolivian air base to service its commercial aircraft flying in Latin America, regarded as symbolically important for the country as it seeks to revive its civil aerospace sector.

Strategic

Russia's military presence in Latin America has derived from its traditional rivalry with the US. In 2008, its military activities in the region included joint naval exercises with Venezuela led by a Russian nuclear-powered warship and visits to the country by long-range bombers, as well as fleet visits to Nicaragua and Cuba. This was seen, in part, as a rebuke to the US over its support for Georgia in the brief war in August 2008; its plans, now shelved, to install a missile shield in Poland, and encouragement for Ukraine and Georgia to join NATO; and the conviction that, if a US-led Western alliance can increase its presence in Russia's own sphere of interest, it can do so in the Americas.

Russia's collaboration on energy policy with Venezuela – both of which are heavily dependent on hydrocarbons for revenues – also has strategic objectives (see Chapter 9). Both countries want to influence developments in the global market and have a strong shared interest in a high oil price. Russia also wants a closer relationship with Venezuela and its regional allies on gas. Although much of South America's gas is traded locally and delivered through pipelines, the advent of liquid natural gas (LNG) is likely to transform the market by allowing countries such as Venezuela to transport this commodity all over the world. Russia subscribes to the idea of forming a gas-producing cartel that controls supply and wants to see South American gas exports head south and hence not to the US.

Political and diplomatic

Russian commercial activity and aid in Latin America has also had concrete political and diplomatic objectives. Venezuela and Nicaragua, for example, both recognised the independence of South Ossetia and Abkhazia, which broke away from Georgia with Russia's support in 2008. Bolivia turned to Russia to replace US funding in the fight against drug-trafficking through an agreement that would provide La Paz with helicopters, logistical support and military training (see Chapter 10). The move provided Moscow with valuable political capital in the effort to demonstrate its multilateral commitments in the fight against the drugs trade, and Russia has also collaborated in counter-narcotics activities with Venezuela and Nicaragua.

Russia shares anti-American sentiments with Latin America (see Box 9.3) but it has also developed its own foreign policy doctrine that, in formal terms, is based on the idea of a multipolar or polycentric world order in which multilateral and regional diplomacy are essential (see BBC Monitoring, 2009). Its support for Latin American integration derives from the commitment this makes to strengthening multipolarity, which in turn offers Moscow the opportunity to enhance its position as a global power. It has, for example, expressed its interest in becoming an observer at the South American Defence Council (see Chapter 9).

Russia's efforts to raise its profile in Latin America has not gone unnoticed in Washington, which has traditionally regarded the region as its sphere of influence (see Chapter 10). However, US concern has been limited, and Washington maintained the appearance of calm in response to Russia's 2008 military manoeuvres in the region, for example, while dispatching diplomats to ascertain its objectives. Russia's military might remains no match for that of the US; Russian companies are constrained from investing in Latin America by their lack of liquid assets; and the impact of the 2008–09 financial crisis on Russia is likely to further limit any ambition to assert its power outside its immediate vicinity. None the less, the US decision to revive its Fourth Fleet in Latin American waters can be seen, in part, as one response to the appearance of Russian ships off Venezuela (see Chapter 9). Of more immediate concern to Washington has been Russian arms sales to Venezuela, which the US argues is destabilising the region yet clearly tests its decision to increase its military presence in Colombia (see Blank, 2009). Chávez insists these arms purchases are for defensive purposes only and has voiced his fears about a US attack on his country. None the less, the missile systems being provided by Russia are capable of reaching into Colombia and US military installations in nearby Caribbean countries, and Venezuela's possession of air defences threaten US air power in the region. However, the 2008–09 financial crisis and falling oil prices are also likely to reduce Venezuela's appetite for further large arms purchases.

Lastly, while some Latin American countries such as Venezuela have seen in Russia, as in the EU, a potential counterweight to the US (see above), there is also resistance to any trend that would see them becoming pawns in struggles between external powers. During the Cold War, for example, it was this resistance among Latin American countries to alignment with *either* side that limited the ability of the Soviet Union to create a new front in its ideological struggle with the US (see Chapters 2, 10).

Relations with the Asia-Pacific region

Alongside the interest shown by Russia in Latin America, other countries have also explored economic opportunities in the region and closer political relationships with it, including Asian countries, India and Iran. These developments point to the changing nature of US hegemony in Latin America and, to some observers, suggest the end of the Monroe Doctrine that sought to resist outside interference in the Americas (see Box 1.4, Chapter 10), although the US and EU continue to have the largest foreign economic stakes in the region.

None the less, Asian countries such as Japan and China have long had links with Latin America both as trading partners and sources of immigration. The Japanese presence in Latin America, for example, dates back more than a century to an era when thousands of immigrants settled mainly in Brazil and Peru, and thereafter in Argentina, Bolivia, Mexico and Paraguay (see Box 11.6). From 1849–75, about 100,000 Chinese labourers were brought to Peru and integrated with its society so successfully that about 3 million Peruvians today claim Chinese descent and form the largest such community in Latin America.

Japan's powerful economic presence in Latin America is a more recent phenomenon that acquired significance after the 1960s when Japanese trade and investment in the region grew rapidly. Japanese automobiles, electronics and machinery began dominating the consumer market with new and improved technologies (Berríos, 2001). The country is now a key investor in Latin America and has reached free-trade agreements with Chile and Mexico. Japanese investments in Latin America and the Caribbean now account for about 10 per cent of the country's foreign direct investment worldwide (IDB, 2008), and it is the fourth largest source of foreign investment in Latin America's most dynamic economy, Brazil. Outside its Asian neighbourhood and the industrialised world, Latin America has become the main

Heading East and West

During the nineteenth and early twentieth centuries, Asian migrants began heading for the Americas in significant numbers. Migrants from China entered Mexico and migrants from Japan settled in Brazil and other parts of South America. In some cases, Asian migration was actively encouraged by governments. In Mexico, the government of Porfirio Díaz (1876–1911) encouraged Chinese immigration leading to the establishment of sizeable colonies, especially in the country's north-west (Knight, 1990). Even though the total Chinese population in Mexico in 1910 was less than 40,000, immigration generated resentment as the Chinese – originally brought in as cheap labour – became successful shopkeepers, traders and businessmen (*ibid*.) As a result, displays of xenophobic racism leading to the persecution of Chinese immigrants in the country influenced the policy of Mexico's revolutionary regime and resulted in mass expulsions in 1931 (*ibid*.). Japanese immigrants first went to Brazil in 1908 as farmers and labourers on coffee farms at a time when the country was short of farm workers. They have been highly successful and Brazil is now home to the largest ethnic Japanese community outside of Japan. Today, Latin America is home to about 1.5 million Japanese citizens, most of whom emigrated in the first half of the twentieth century (IADB/IDB, 2005). Japan itself is a favoured destination for the offspring of these original emigrants, particularly from Brazil and Peru.

A prominent example of the use to which Japanese Latin Americans can put these ties came with the self-exile of Peru's former president, Alberto Fujimori (1990–2000). A Peruvian of Japanese descent with dual Peruvian and Japanese citizenship, Fujimori fled to Japan in 2000 in the midst of a corruption scandal and remained there until 2005. While he was in Japan, Peru's congress removed him from office (see Box 4.4) and charges of corruption and human rights abuses were filed against him. He gained the support of several senior Japanese politicians, in part for what they saw as his decisive action in ending the 1997 Japanese embassy siege in Lima, and his continued presence generated a diplomatic dispute after Tokyo proved unwilling to accede to Peruvian extradition requests. Fujimori finally left Japan after announcing his intention to run in the Peruvian elections of 2006 and was detained in Chile then extradited to face criminal charges in Peru in September 2007.

As Japan's economic situation improved in the 1980s, many Japanese Brazilians went to Japan as contract workers to escape economic hardship at home. Japanese citizenship was offered to many of them in 1990, encouraging further immigration. A significant number of Latin Americans who are not ethnically Japanese have also headed east to find employment as migrant workers, mostly in labouring or manufacturing jobs. The IDB estimated in 2005 that there were more than 435,000 Latin American adults living in Japan, which has become a disproportionately important source of remittances to the region because wages are relatively high in comparison with other destinations. The IDB calculated that in 2005 more than $2.65 billion in remittances was likely to be sent back to Latin America by migrant workers living in Japan, mostly to Brazil ($2.2 billion) and to a lesser extent Peru ($356 million). Most Latin American migrant workers in Japan are aged under 35 and are well educated by comparison with migrants to the US. They send larger amounts of money home and more frequently than their counterparts in the US, aided greatly by lower transaction costs and easier access to banking. Significantly higher proportions of Latin Americans working in Japan both save money and develop plans to start their own businesses. According to the IDB, this combination of education, entrepreneurship and savings constitutes an important opportunity for Latin American migrants in Japan to contribute to the economic development of their own countries.

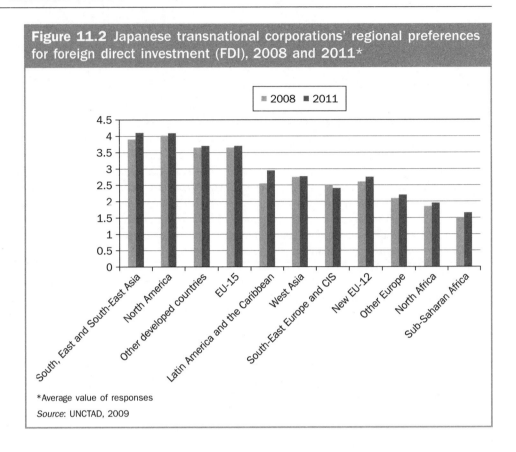

Figure 11.2 Japanese transnational corporations' regional preferences for foreign direct investment (FDI), 2008 and 2011*

*Average value of responses

Source: UNCTAD, 2009

focus of Japanese investors abroad (see Figure 11.2). Japanese investors are increasingly interested in the region's natural resources, and have signalled that they are likely to increase their stake in Latin America significantly over the next few years. Moreover, 48 per cent of large Latin American and Caribbean companies themselves now report having investments in Japan (UNCTAD, 2009).

In recent years, China has outpaced Japan in trade with Latin America, and in the first half of 2009, China became Brazil's biggest single export market for the first time (*Economist*, 2009). Other emerging Asian economies have also targeted the region for trade and investment, and the Inter-American Development Bank, the largest multilateral source of financing for Latin America and the Caribbean, maintains an office in Asia that actively encourages economic ties between Latin America and Japan as well as South Korea, a more recent investor in the region. China joined the IDB as a non-borrowing member in 2009, donating $350 million and thereby making it easier for Chinese companies to participate in infrastructure projects in Latin America, and Japan and South Korea are also members.

There are two main explanations for the deepening of ties between Latin American and Asian countries. First and foremost, relations have been driven by trade and economic opportunities. In terms of value, Latin American trade with Asia is rapidly catching up with that between the region and Europe (see Table 11.2).

Table 11.2 Asian merchandise trade with the Americas, 2006 and 2008*

| Destination | | North America | | South and C. America | Asia | | | | | |
Origin		Total	United States		Total	Japan	Australia/ New Zealand	Other Asia Total	China	Other
North	2006	902.39	528.41	106.22	308.34	68.36	22.78	217.20	62.22	154.98
America	2008	1014.49	587.86	164.88	375.51	77.66	27.93	269.92	81.55	188.37
United States	2006	364.92	.	87.25	274.21	58.46	20.35	195.40	53.65	141.75
	2008	413.15	.	134.98	329.41	65.14	24.75	239.51	69.71	169.80
South and	2006	145.63	126.94	101.48	60.60	12.84	1.00	46.76	23.50	23.26
Central America	2008	169.19	149.35	158.62	100.56	17.14	2.43	80.99	44.21	36.78
Asia	2006	705.15	629.13	69.46	1639.13	270.41	87.09	####	371.22	910.42
	2008	775.02	677.62	127.33	2181.40	341.87	123.47	####	474.71	####
Japan	2006	164.72	145.47	12.00	322.16	.	14.58	307.57	111.52	196.05
	2008	158.14	137.39	19.22	406.24	.	19.83	386.41	144.39	242.03
China	2006	284.20	254.97	26.64	329.45	112.03	18.78	198.64	.	198.64
	2008	349.93	308.18	56.62	476.15	138.50	29.88	307.77	.	307.77
Australia &	2006	13.08	10.54	1.76	99.32	26.72	11.33	61.27	16.61	44.66
New Zealand	2008	15.86	13.32	3.27	155.24	45.14	15.03	95.07	29.15	65.91
Other Asia	2006	243.15	218.14	29.07	888.20	131.67	42.39	714.15	243.09	471.06
	2008	251.10	218.74	48.23	1143.76	158.23	58.73	926.80	301.17	625.64

*Billions of dollars
Source: WTO, 2009

Strengthening ties with Asian countries can be seen as part of the broader effort by many Latin American countries to diversify or reduce economic dependence on the US (*ibid*.; see Chapter 14). Asian trading economies, and in particular the successful 'Tiger' economies, have also been influential models in Latin America since the 1990s, when neoliberal reforms were being introduced (see Chapter 15). Japan has sought secure access to Latin American markets to sell goods, obtain needed raw materials and establish a productive base with cheap labour to then export to other markets such as the US. As a result, for some Latin American countries, it has become the largest trading partner after the US and one of the largest investors. Japan's importance as a trade and investment partner has been most notable in Mexico, Brazil, Chile, Argentina, Peru and Panama. Mexico is of strategic importance because of its proximity to the US and membership of NAFTA, and Brazil because of Mercosur. China needs Latin American oil and raw materials to fuel its escalating growth, and its investments in the region have overwhelmingly been in oil and mining. Its demand for raw materials has pushed up world commodity prices and this, in turn, has fuelled growth in Latin America and, particularly South America, which is a major exporter of commodities. As a result, China has become a significant market for Brazil, Chile and Peru and trade with Latin America has grown at an annual average rate of about 40 per cent since 2003, much faster than its overall growth in trade (*ibid.*). Latin American exporters have also benefitted from the knock-on effect of Chinese trade with other countries, which has in turn increased their demand for commodities. Moreover, trade between Latin America and Asia has significant potential for growth, and this has been recognised in the negotiation of free trade deals and also by the Economic Commission for Latin American and the Caribbean (see ECLAC Press Centre, 2009). Japan has signed free-trade agreements (FTAs) with Mexico and Chile, China has signed an FTA with Chile and in 2008 concluded talks on a deal with Peru; and Taiwan, South Korea and Singapore all have FTAs with countries in the region. A large proportion of Chilean exports already head for Asia, and Chile has intensified its links with Australia, New Zealand and Malaysia. Chile is seen as a 'bridge' by Mercosur to the Asia Pacific region, and the terms of its association with the South American customs union make reference to this specific role. Mexico, by contrast and despite being a member of NAFTA, has to compete with China in the US market.

Second, Asian states also offer some limited potential to Latin America for diversifying diplomatic ties, and can contribute to efforts to seek a counterweight to the US (see above, and Chapters 9, 10) and, in the case of China, the desire led by Brazil to enhance alliances with other emerging economies such as India, Russia and South Africa that press for changes in what they consider to be an unfair distribution of global power.

US officials have been watching the economic and political relationships being developed by other countries in Latin America closely for a number of years. In April 2005, for example Roger Noriega, the then US Assistant Secretary of State for Western Hemisphere Affairs, told the House of Representatives' Western hemisphere sub-committee that China's growing role in Latin America did not threaten the US although it would be watching how this evolved closely (see Box 14.7). In May 2009, Hillary Clinton, the US Secretary of State, described the economic and political gains being made in Latin America by China and other countries such as Russia and Iran as 'disturbing' and said Washington could no longer afford to shun leaders who had been hostile to the US during the Bush administration (Pleming, 2009). One objective of China's involvement in Latin America has been to increase the isolation of Taiwan, over which it claims sovereignty. Of the 23 countries that recognise Taiwan (the Republic of China) as sovereign, for example, eight are Latin American, although these are mainly Central American and Paraguay is the only South American country that does so. In June 2007, for example, Costa Rica switched its diplomatic allegiance from Taiwan to China in a bid to attract Chinese investment.

However, China is also extending its influence as a natural consequence of rapid and sustained economic growth and liberalisation that has turned the country into a second superpower after the US. The US trade deficit with China grew from $6 billion in 1989 to $237 billion in 2009, for example, while in the same period China's foreign exchange reserves increased from $14 billion to a staggering $2,272 billion (Dyer and Luce, 2009). This dramatic shift in relative power was acknowledged in late 2009 by the visit of President Barack Obama to Beijing in which he formally recognised China's new profile and signalled that Washington foresaw the development of a unique partnership with Beijing in addressing international issues within a multipolar world order (*ibid.*). It was the first time in the post-Cold War world (see Chapters 2, 10) that Washington has acknowledged an equal global partner and ushered in a 'realist' diplomacy based on the development of a new multilateralism in which growing Chinese power will have important implications for Latin America as it seeks to chart a more independent foreign policy vis-à-vis the US (see Box 9.4, Chapter 10).

These implications have become apparent in the case of Chinese engagement with Venezuela and Cuba, which has strengthened the hand of leaders in both countries. China deepened its economic relationship with Cuba following the realignment at the end of the Cold War in the early 1990s, and has become the island's second largest trading partner after Venezuela with annual trade valued at about $2.3 billion. It has exported heavy goods and, in particular, modern transportation equipment to Cuba, while participating in Cuban efforts to revitalise nickel production and explore for oil. These growing economic ties have built on a longstanding ideological affinity characterised by a history of exchanges in the areas of science, technology, culture and defence and nurturing a strong bilateral relationship. There was much speculation when Raúl Castro took over from the ailing Fidel that the new Cuban leader favoured reforms that would lead to a liberalised, Chinese-style economy, although there have been few signs of this. China's more recent economic support for the island, in particular its investments, have provided significant relief to Cuba in a period of economic transition and uncertainty, and its diplomatic support for Cuba's communist government has also helped to lessen its international isolation (see Chapter 16). Economic agreements between China and Venezuela, such as a $16 billion investment deal for oil exploration in the Orinoco river agreed in 2009, form part of a strategy by President Chávez to increase his country's bilateral partnerships in the oil market and its economic independence vis-à-vis the US, which remains the main foreign market for Venezuelan oil. Chávez has indicated that he seeks to divert Venezuelan oil to China which, if exports rise as a result of Chinese economic support, can only be achieved by reducing supplies to the US.

None the less, there remain clear limits to the political influence of Asian countries in Latin America determined, in part, by their own relationships with the US. Japanese investment in Latin America is sensitive to the perception of instability and trouble spots such as Peru in the late 1980s and, more recently, Colombia, are considered high-risk targets for investment. Although a prime objective of many Latin American countries during the 1990s was to attract foreign direct investment, Japanese investors were often slow to respond, despite the opportunities offered by neoliberal reforms such as privatisation (see Table 15.1). Even though Japan has become more engaged internationally and its economic presence is very visible, it has also been reluctant to take a position of leadership in Latin America. Like Europe, Japanese policy towards the region has been shaped by its ties with the US. It has sought consensus and co-operation within a triangular relationship, rather than asserting itself in ways that might alienate Washington. An example of how Japan has been unable to chart a fully independent policy towards Latin America was its acceptance of the core tenets of the 'Washington Consensus' on economic reform in Latin American debtor nations (see Box 15.1). It also complied with a US request to deny credits to the Sandinista regime in Nicaragua, for example.

China's role in Latin America is also limited by a number of geopolitical and political factors. As the country has grown in stature, so has a debate among Chinese politicians and academics about its position in the world and to what extent Beijing should be taking a more active role in international affairs. While Obama may have signalled that the US sees China taking greater active responsibility, it remains unclear whether the country's political elite seeks to veer from a traditional low profile abroad, in large part because of fears that this may alarm China's neighbours and incur unwelcome costs. Suspicion of US policies in Asia also informs defensive reflexes aimed, in part, at limiting the ability of the US to take unilateral action. As a result, China's foreign policy has focused selectively on areas that will directly benefit its economic development, and Chinese leaders remain cautious about participating in broader international security issues. China also remains sensitive to discussion of its record on human rights, and although democratisation in Latin America has not precluded economic engagement with Beijing, the latter remains vulnerable to criticisms from the region about its own lack of progress on democracy.

A key feature of Latin American relations with Asia since the 1990s has been growing interdependence around the 'Pacific Rim' through trade and a consciousness of shared interests (see ECLAC/Peru, 2008). One example of this interdependence could be found in the impact of the Asian economic and financial crisis of 1997–98, which hit Latin America's trade because of a drop in demand for its exports. Economic ties were greatly strengthened by the formation in 1989 of Asia-Pacific Economic Co-operation (APEC), which now has 21 member economies including three Latin American states facing the Pacific – Mexico, Peru, and Chile (see Figure 11.3). Colombia and Ecuador have both sought to join the grouping and hope to become members in 2010. APEC's member economies now account for more than a third of the world's population, about 54 per cent of world GDP and 44 per cent of world trade. In the period 1989–2007, APEC's total exports increased from $1,200 billion to $6,200 billion, representing an annualised average growth rate of 9.5 per cent that outpaced the world average of 8.9 per cent, and total imports grew at the rate of 9.4 per cent a year, also outpacing world growth (Hyun-Hoon Lee and Jung Hur, 2009).

The organisation has worked to reduce trade barriers across the Asia-Pacific region in order to improve the efficiency of member economies and increase exports. APEC's Latin American members have all experienced an increase in trade within the region since APEC was established (see Table 11.3). Key to achieving APEC's vision are what are referred to as the 'Bogor Goals' of free and open trade and investment in the Asia-Pacific by 2010 for industrialised economies and 2020 for developing economies, culminating in the creation of a Free Trade Area of the Asia-Pacific (FTAAP). As a result, APEC can be seen as the embodiment of a commitment to commercial multilateralism (see Chapter 9). The 'Santiago Declaration' issued at the 12th APEC Economic Leaders' Meeting held in Chile in 2004, for example, 'reaffirmed the primacy of the rules-based multilateral trading system, which allows us to pursue trade liberalization on a global scale' through the WTO, and supported efforts to enhance regional integration and free trade agreements (APEC, 2005a, 2005b; see also APEC, 2005c; Nishijima and Smith eds, 1996). APEC has been criticised for not having clear objectives, but although its declarations have

Figure 11.3 Pacific Rim economies in APEC

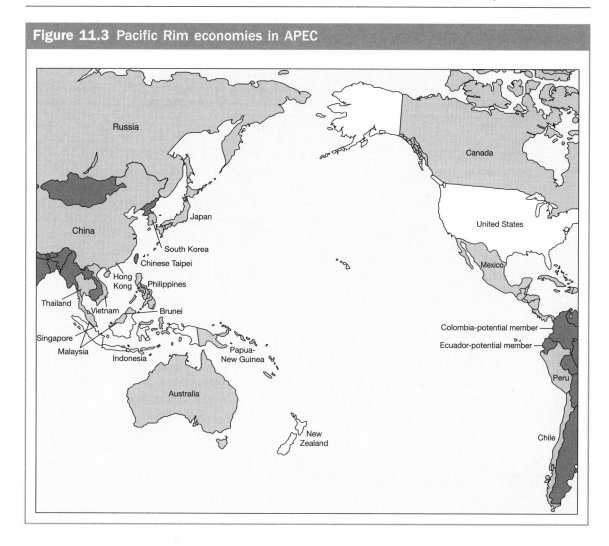

largely symbolic value, its commitment to promoting good governance – in particular by confronting corruption – could have a political impact. It has also debated the notion of collective security: the APEC ministerial meeting also held in Santiago in 2004 discussed security threats and terrorism in the Pacific region and examined the work of the organisation's Counter-Terrorism Task Force (APEC, 2005b).

Other initiatives also exist to promote trade and economic co-operation around the Pacific Rim, including the Pacific Economic Co-operation Council (PECC), whose members include Chile, Colombia, Ecuador, Mexico and Peru; the Pacific Basin Economic Council (PBEC), an independent business grouping whose members include corporations from Chile, Colombia, Ecuador, Mexico and Peru; and the East Asia–Latin America Forum (EALAF) which has 15 Latin American countries among its members and provides a platform for political, business and other leaders in the region to exchange views and to promote co-operation (Berríos, 2001). Chile has subscribed to a separate grouping known as the Trans-Pacific Strategic Economic Partnership Agreement (TPP) aimed at fostering free trade between

Table 11.3 Percentage shares of exports and imports in the APEC region (manufactured vs. non-manufactured products) for Latin American and selected countries, 1992 and 2007*

Country	Export of Manufactured		Export of Non-Manufactured		Import of Manufactured		Import of Non-Manufactured	
	1992	2007	1992	2007	1992	2007	1992	2007
Chile	0.2	0.5	1.4	2.8	0.4	0.4	0.2	0.9
Mexico	3.4	5.2	4.8	7.3	4.2	5.2	3.6	4.3
Peru	0.1	0.1	0.5	1.5	0.2	0.2	0.2	0.2
Canada	8.7	6.4	17.5	18.8	9.9	7.3	4.8	4.9
US	23.4	16.4	24.6	16.7	34.4	29.2	21.4	27.5
China	6.3	21.5	6.7	6.3	6.0	16.5	4.7	14.6
Japan	25.2	14.1	2.4	2.7	8.2	7.4	35.6	17.5
S Korea	5.6	6.6	2.3	4.0	4.6	5.0	7.6	7.4
Russia	–	0.4	–	3.7	–	1.6	–	0.7

*Will not add up to 100 because selected countries only

Source: Adapted from Hyun-Hoon Lee and Jung Hur, 2009 (with United Nations Comtrade Database)

it and Brunei, Singapore and New Zealand, and Peru has expressed an interest in joining this. The Inter-American Development Bank has also courted the Association of South-East Asian Nations (ASEAN) for new members who will be able to use it to enhance their commercial ties with Latin America.

Summary

Europe and Asia offer Latin America counterweights to US hegemony and also provide it with successful models of integration, democratisation and economic development. Europe has always exercised a strong political and cultural influence, but it was not until the 1970s that it began to forge stronger political relations with Latin America. Close economic relations have developed alongside an unfolding political dialogue whose milestones included the San José Process and the Rio summit of 1999. The tone of EU–Latin American relations has been set through institutionalised dialogue that has shaped the parameters of a new type of relationship between asymmetrical regions based upon negotiation as opposed to the assertion of economic, diplomatic or military prowess. As a result, the European Commission has reached a range of agreements with Latin American countries and sub-regions.

Prominent themes in the analysis of Europe's relationship with Latin America are its role as a counterweight to US power, its economic interests in the region, and its support for integration and democratisation. The EU's institutionalisation, negligible military capacity and limited strategic interests in Latin America can make it an important mediator, and EU policy towards Cuba provides evidence of its independent approach. The EU has considerable economic interests in Latin

America, and is deepening its economic, trade and development aid links with the region. An important characteristic of the EU's policy towards Latin America since the mid-1980s has been support for regional integration and democratisation. Latin America has responded positively to EU pressure, partly because of shared preferences for democracy with a social character. Positive perceptions of European policies derive from comparisons that are inevitably made between EU and more unilateral US approaches, and the way European economic interests are concealed by development aid and co-operation programmes. However, the EU's relationship with Latin America has been hampered by internal differences and tensions over trade. EU–Latin American relations are also often a 'triangular' affair in which the role of the US is prominent.

East Asian countries such as Japan and China have long had links with Latin America both as trading partners and sources of immigration. Japan's powerful economic presence acquired significance after the 1960s when Japanese trade and investment in Latin America grew rapidly. Strengthening ties with Asian countries can be seen as part of the broader effort by Latin American countries to diversify. None the less, clear limits to the political influence of Asian countries in Latin America are again determined by their own relationships with the US. A feature of relations with Asia since the 1990s has been growing interdependence around the 'Pacific Rim' through trade and a consciousness of shared interests. APEC's commitment to promoting good governance could have an important political impact in Latin America.

Discussion points

- How important have political links been in the EU–Latin American relationship?
- To what extent does Europe offer Latin America a counterweight to US power?
- Are there limits to the economic relationship between Europe and Latin America?
- What can Latin America learn from Europe's integration process?
- Is the positive perception of European policies in Latin America realistic?
- Will Latin American relations with Pacific Rim countries only ever be economic?

Useful websites

http://europa.eu/index_en.htm European Union 'Europa' information gateway

http://ec.europa.eu/europeaid/index_en.htm EC external co-operation programmes, with interactive map showing details of projects in individual Latin American countries

www.europarl.europa.eu/intcoop/eurolat/default_en.htm Euro-Latin American Parliamentary Assembly

www.eib.org European Investment Bank (EIB)

http://europa.eu/legislation_summaries/development/general_development_framework/r12544_en.htm Europa summary of 'The European Consensus on Development'

www.fco.gov.uk/resources/en/pdf/pdf16/fco_ukstrategypaperbooklet07 British Foreign and Commonwealth Office (FCO) strategy paper on relations with Latin America until 2020

www.cumbresiberoamericanas.com Cumbres Iberoamericanas de Jefes de Estado y de Gobierno, IberoAmerican Summit site

www.wto.org World Trade Organisation, WTO, Geneva

www.iadb.org Inter-American Development Bank, IDB, New York

www.iom.int International Organisation for Migration, Geneva

www.oas.org/atip/migration/iom%20report%20migration%20lac%20to%20eu.pdf Pellegrino, Adela. 2004. *Migration from Latin America to Europe, IOM Migration Research Series No 16*. Geneva: IOM

http://idbdocs.iadb.org/wsdocs/getdocument.aspx?docnum=546823 IADB. 2005. *Remittances to Latin American from Japan*. Okinawa: IADB, Multilateral Investment Fund

http://idbdocs.iadb.org/wsdocs/getdocument.aspx?docnum=547263 IADB. 2004. *Sending Money Home: Remittance to Latin America and the Caribbean*. New York: IADB Multilateral Investment Fund

www.apec.org Asia-Pacific Economic Co-operation (APEC)

www.apecsec.org.sg/apec/leaders__declarations/2004.html Santiago Declaration, Twelfth APEC Economic Leaders' Meeting, Santiago de Chile, 20–21 November 2004

www.pecc.org Pacific Economic Co-operation Council (PECC)

www.pbec.org Pacific Basin Economic Council (PBEC)

www.fealac.org Forum for East Asia–Latin America Co-operation (FEALAC)

www.g15.org Group of 15 nations

www.g20.org Group of 20 Korean host site

Recommended reading

Whitehead, Laurence. 1999. 'The European Union and the Americas', in Victor Bulmer-Thomas and James Dunkerley (eds), *The United States and Latin America: The New Agenda*. London/Cambridge, MA: Institute of Latin American Studies/David Rockefeller Center for Latin American Studies

Essential introduction to the main themes that have characterised the EU's unfolding relationship with Latin America that combines an historical overview with more analytical observations about the nature of contemporary linkages

Fukumi, Sayaka. 2008. *Cocaine Trafficking in Latin America: EU and US Policy Responses*. Aldershot: Ashgate

Valuable comparison of the US and EU counter-narcotics policies vis-à-vis Latin America, which offers insights into the differing multilateral relationships these have with the region

European Commission. 2009. 'The European Union and Latin America: Global Players in Partnership'. *Communication from the Commission to the European Parliament and the Council. COM(2009) 495/3, 30.09.2009*. Brussels: European Commission. Available online at: http://ec.europa.eu/external_relations/la/docs/com09_495_en.pdf [accessed November 2009]

Valuable summary and overview of the EU's developing relationship with Latin America and future priorities

Soderbaum, Fredrik (ed.). 2009. *The European Union and the Global South.* Boulder, CO: Lynne Rienner

Valuable overview of EU engagement with the developing world, focusing on economic co-operation, development co-operation, and conflict management, with case studies on regions that include Latin America

Smith, Peter. 2001. 'Strategic Options for Latin America' in Joseph Tulchin and Ralph Espach (eds), *Latin America in the New International System.* Boulder, CO: Lynne Rienner/ Woodrow Wilson International Center for Scholars

Useful chapter on Latin America's options in the international system that includes short but helpful sections on Europe and Asia

Berríos, Rubén. 2001. 'Japan's economic presence in Latin America'. Review article, *Latin American Politics and Society*, Vol. 43, No. 2 (Summer 2001), pp. 147–61

Valuable overview of the economic activity of what has until recently been the most important Asian actor in Latin America

Part IV

POLITICAL IDEAS

Chapter 12

Left and Right

Political ideas propose norms for the distribution and use of power, but how important are they? Ideas are only one factor influencing the behaviour of actors alongside other factors such as class, ethnicity or gender. Historians sometimes refer to a hegemonic *ideology* – a highly contested term often used to refer to a system of values, beliefs or ideas shared by a social group – through which, they argue, dominant elites shape values and culture. At the same time, individual ideas or norms themselves may be hegemonic in a society yet may not offer a comprehensive belief system that can be said to comprise an ideology *per se*. Ideas may also be expressed as much through the behaviour and approaches taken by political actors such as parties or social movements as by the conscious expression of a viewpoint or opinion by an intellectual or politician. Moreover, measuring the impact of ideas is difficult because they may be concealed deliberately by those who cherish them. At the same time, the context in which political ideas evolve is forever changing, and scholars interested in ideas and the broader concept of ideology have also understood and analysed them in many different ways. Given this, the study of political ideas is bedevilled by many variables, and one way of exploring them is to identify key strands and themes in political thought and to trace their evolution.

This chapter examines formative themes in Latin American political thought and explores a key division in debates since the nineteenth century – that between the Left and the Right. The Left is a broad term often used very loosely in politics traditionally referring to that part of the spectrum subscribing to ideas associated with socialism, social democracy and some forms of liberalism. In a continent distinguished by severe inequality and poverty, leftwing ideas advocating social or state ownership, or policies to redistribute wealth, in order to engineer greater equality have found many adherents among poorer social groups and their representatives in trades unions, labour parties, social movements and progressive elements of the Church etc. (see Chapters 7, 16). This has been reflected since democratisation – as a result of which social sectors previously marginalised in politics have become empowered – through electoral victories by a spectrum of left-of-centre parties and leaders across Latin America. Since 1998 in particular, a number of left-of-centre leaders have come to power, although because of the moderate and pragmatic stances most have adopted once in office, this drift leftwards has often been characterised as less of a red than a diverse 'pink' tide (see Table 12.1; see also Lievesley and Ludlam, 2009). By contrast, parties that have continued to denounce capitalism and advocate revolutionary change have enjoyed little popular support.

Table 12.1 The 'pink tide' of presidential election winners to the left of the political spectrum in Latin America between 1998 and 2009

Year	Country	Presidential election winner
1998	Venezuela	Hugo Chávez
2000	Chile	Ricardo Lagos
2001	Venezuela	Hugo Chávez
2002	Brazil	Luiz Inácio Lula da Silva
2003	Argentina	Néstor Kirchner
2004	Panama	Martín Torrijos
2004	Uruguay	Tabaré Vázquez
2005	Bolivia	Evo Morales
2005	Chile	Michelle Bachelet
2005	Honduras	Manuel Zelaya
2006	Brazil	Luiz Inácio Lula da Silva
2006	Costa Rica	Oscar Arias
2006	Ecuador	Rafael Correa
2006	Nicaragua	Daniel Ortega
2006	Venezuela	Hugo Chávez
2007	Argentina	Cristina Fernández
2007	Guatemala	Alvaro Colom
2008	Paraguay	Fernando Lugo
2009	Ecuador	Rafael Correa
2009	El Salvador	Mauricio Funes
2009	Uruguay	José Mujica
2009	Bolivia	Evo Morales
2010	Costa Rica	Laura Chinchilla

Source: Adapted from Lievesley and Ludlam (eds), 2009; news reports

By contrast, the Right is that part of the political spectrum associated with conservatism, fascism and, in some cases, nationalism (see Chapter 13). Rightwing and conservative ideas advocating the defence of a status quo based upon social hierarchy, and often embracing policies that favour or protect private ownership, have found adherents among wealthier and more privileged groups and their natural allies in the military and Church hierarchies.

The clash between leftwing and rightwing ideas has had an important influence upon Latin America's political evolution, often reflecting the deep class divisions found in the societies of the region. The struggle between left and right was best exemplified by the ideological competition between socialism and capitalism that was a distinguishing feature of the rivalry between the US and the Soviet Union in Latin America during the Cold War (see Chapters 2, 9, 10). However, the end of the Cold War transformed the prospects of the traditional left in the region and forced it to reassess cherished ideas, while also making it necessary for the Right to accommodate democratic politics for the first time. A shift in recent years on the left towards social-democratic positions and on the right towards greater acceptance of democratic pluralism – tolerance for other views – has sparked a debate about what is, indeed, now left and right. In overall terms, there has been a discernible convergence of ideas in the more moderate and mainstream 'centre' of Latin American politics, particularly in countries that have achieved stable growth such as Chile, although continuing inequality and instability suggest that the development of centrist politics could take much longer in other countries. In this respect, Latin America provides many examples of the changes in political ideas on the left and right that have occurred elsewhere in the world since the end of the Cold War.

Formative themes

Latin America's colonial inheritance, conflicts and inequalities have long enhanced its appeal to intellectuals analysing key contemporary problems and advocating solutions to them (see Hale, 1986). The Mexican scholar Jorge Castañeda (1994) has argued that intellectuals have played a disproportionately important role in Latin American politics because of the weakness of civil society (see Chapter 8), which they have sometimes acted as a substitute for. Since Independence, however, Latin America has been a net *importer* of ideas, ideology and social theory, and many of the political and social ideas advanced by intellectuals in the region have originated in Europe. Intellectuals in Latin America have often acted as conduits between a region in search of ideas and the outside world where these were produced, and this has given those intellectuals great influence. According to Castañeda, another characteristic of Latin American intellectuals has been their proximity to power – and their fascination with it. Throughout history, they have founded and led political movements and parties.

Imported ideas have been an important source of political debate in Latin America since the sixteenth century when the Catholic Church began to develop academic philosophy in schools, monasteries, convents and seminaries. In the eighteenth century Jesuit thinkers were influenced by the ideas of the Enlightenment, the European philosophical movement that stressed the superiority of reason as a guide to human concerns (see Box 1.1). This interest inaugurated a new era of political thought in Latin America, fuelling the turmoil of the Independence era. In the new republics, creoles embraced European notions of progress and often understood Latin American reality as barbarous and backward. The Western heritage of Latin America's elite and the ties that would develop subsequently between its independent republics and the international capitalist economy have shaped the ways in which political thought has developed ever since. Most of the main ideologies of the last 150 years were generated by the impact of the industrial revolution on northern European social structure and have no counterparts in the Iberian tradition. In Latin America, industrialisation occurred much later without similar changes in social structure (see Chapters 2, 14), and imported ideologies predominated, with modernity itself conceived of as a European or US phenomenon. The most potent ideologies to shape the twentieth century – communism, socialism, anarcho-syndicalism, fascism and national socialism – entered Latin America from Europe. US 'national security doctrine' and Soviet communist philosophy shaped the positions of Latin American elites and leftwing opposition movements during the Cold War (see Chapters 2, 9, Box 10.2). An international consensus on economic liberalism (neoliberalism) had a profound influence on Latin America in the 1980s and 1990s (see Chapter 15). Since 2000, this has been increasingly challenged by the ascent of left-of-centre governments in the region as a result of democratisation but also declining US influence (see Chapters 9, 10).

Yet at the same time, while tracing their origins to Europe and the US, many of the ideas permeating Latin American political thought have gained a distinctively local quality. Ideas have been shaped, in particular, by the turbulent interaction of Latin America's own historical legacies and resulting divisions around several formative themes whose origins are not specifically Latin American: centralism, the liberal heritage, the revolutionary tradition, scientific notions known as positivism, and corporatism. These themes have been prominent influences upon the development of political ideas in the region, although to varying degrees.

Centralism

Véliz (1980) argued that a dominant force in Latin American political culture since Independence has been a continuation of Iberian centralism, and that a centralist structure of government and bureaucratic tradition prevailed into the contemporary era. According to Véliz, the most concrete expression of centralism in the twentieth century could be found in the role played by strong central states during industrialisation from the 1930s onwards (see Box 2.1; see also Véliz ed., 1965). Centralism, often expressed through nationalism (see Chapter 13), was embraced by urban populist movements that dominated the political agenda in the postwar years. It found subsequent expression in the period of military authoritarianism that lasted from the early 1960s into the mid-1980s, since when it has been at the heart of the debate over neoliberal reform (see Chapters 2, 4, 7, 15). Centralism can be associated with another aspect of Latin American political tradition, authoritarianism, which attributes disproportionate importance to the role of and respect for authority.

Liberalism

Despite centralism, the most significant source of the programmes and theories that shaped politics in the newly independent Latin American states of the nineteenth century was liberalism (see Chapter 1). The origins of liberalism lie in the Enlightenment and the emergence of a small intellectual and social elite committed to the rights of the individual and popular sovereignty in opposition to the patriarchal order under a Catholic monarchy (see Box 1.1). The American War of Independence (1776–83) and the French Revolution (1789) inspired more radical individuals – often, but not always, liberals – who advocated republicanism to free their countries from Spanish control. Liberalism and republicanism frequently came together as white middle and upper classes agitated for more local power. As a result, for much of the early nineteenth century, liberalism was seen as an ideology in conflict with the inherited colonial order, although it was often out of step with the reality of highly stratified and economically backward societies characterised by deeply conservative elites, clerics and peasants. Many liberals foresaw a society based on modern structures, such as federalism, and often pointed to the US as a model of success. Liberalism gained ground after the 1848 revolutions in Europe, which inspired a new generation of younger, idealistic entrants to politics. Véliz (1980) argued that between 1850 and 1870, ideas that were derived from European commerical and political liberalism initiated a 'liberal pause' that would persist in an ever dwindling form until the 1960s.

Liberal principles placed a premium upon individual liberty, autonomy and enterprise based on equality before the law – a radical idea in Latin America's racially and ethnically stratified societies. The ideas of liberty, autonomy and enterprise sustained support for the free market, which many liberals initially believed would be the main source of progress in countries steeped in semi-feudal traditions. For this reason, liberals often advocated the disentailment – the removal of protective inheritance restrictions – of 'corporate' property held by the Church or indigenous communities as opposed to individuals. This economic liberalism helped to shape a model of capitalist development that has been a central focus of much ideology in Latin America since the nineteenth century. However, in time, some liberals began to circumscribe their belief in the free market and to advocate state intervention in the economy. In this context, free-market ideas were generally used most explicitly by liberals for their attacks on the Church, shaping their anti-clerical positions.

A renewed emphasis upon ideas derived from liberalism became evident in the period inaugurated by the Mexican Revolution (1910–17) as professionals and middle classes generated by rapid economic change became active in new parties demanding greater political inclusion (see Box 1.5). Conservative oligarchies found it increasingly difficult to resist demands based on liberal principles such as universal suffrage, and often resorted to electoral fraud and repression to stay in power (see Chapter 1). The 1920s and 1930s were, therefore, characterised by a growing liberal frustration at conservatism and the competition posed by new ideologies from Europe such as communism and fascism. Although the liberal pause would slowly come to an end between the end of the Second World War and the period of military authoritarianism in the 1960s and 1970s, economic liberalism whose central emphasis is the free market based upon individual liberty has developed into an orthodoxy in Latin America since the 1980s (see Chapter 15), and democratisation has restored the prominence of many liberal political ideas (see Chapter 3).

Revolution

Another key theme shaping social and political thought since the nineteenth century has been the idea of revolution. Even though they may advocate and employ constitutional methods, progressives in Latin America today continue to define themselves as 'revolutionaries' and often trace their political heritage to revolutionary figures such as the Liberator, Simón Bolívar (b.1783–d.1830); José Martí (b.1853–d.1895) and Ernesto 'Che' Guevara (b.1928–d.1967) in Cuba; Augusto César Sandino (b.1895–d.1934) in Nicaragua; and Emiliano Zapata (b.1879–d.1919) in Mexico. It has been argued that the idea of revolution lost force in Latin America after the collapse of the Socialist bloc in the late 1980s (see below) and the Nicaraguan election of 1990 in which the Sandinistas were ousted (see Castañeda, 1994). However, such revolutionary icons have remained a significant source of inspiration long after their deaths. In Cuba, for example, Martí's experience in the late nineteenth century influenced the revolutionary thought developed by Fidel Castro after 1959 (see Box 2.3). Che Guevara remains a global icon for radical progressives, and his ideas have had an important influence on contemporary political figures such as Hugo Chávez (1999–) in Venezuela, the latest in a long line of Latin American leaders to draw upon the region's revolutionary tradition (see Aleida Guevara, 2005; see also Box 12.2). Chávez's original Movimiento Quinta República (MVR, Fifth Republic Movement) espoused a 'revolutionary and Bolivarian' doctrine until its dissolution in 2007 when it merged into the Partido Socialista Unido de Venezuela (PSUV, United Socialist Party of Venezuela), now the largest leftwing party in Latin America. The PSUV was created from the forces in Venezuela that support the 'Bolivarian Revolution', a term that is used to refer to the political process pursued by Chávez in support of the 'socialism of the twenty-first century' that he advocates (see Box 12.7). Concrete manifestations of this idea include the economic and political integration effort led by Venezuela known as the Alianza Bolivariana para los Pueblos de Nuestra América (ALBA, see Boxes 9.1, 16.1). Other leaders on the left, such as Ecuador's Rafael Correa (2007–), claim to be leading a 'citizens' revolution'. Zapata's ideas continue to inspire peasant and guerrilla organisations across southern Mexico. Unrest in Oaxaca that began in 2006, for example, resulted in expressions of support for the Asamblea Popular de los Pueblos de Oaxaca (APPO, Popular Assembly of the Peoples of Oaxaca) and the restatement of Zapata's ideas by the older Ejército Zapatista de Liberación Nacional (EZLN, Zapatista Army of National Liberation) based in the state of Chiapas (see Box 13.5).

The definition of the term 'revolution' is hotly contested and the causes of revolutions have been complex and various (see Box 2.6). Revolution has been associated, in particular, both with the effort to modernise or reconstruct corrupted or traditional societies and with the notion of democracy. To the creole conservatives and liberals of the nineteenth century, for example, democracy itself was considered a *revolutionary* prospect threatening a race war. Successful revolutionary movements in Latin America have often produced similar forms of government based on mass legitimacy – often with a nationalistic flavour (see Chapter 13) – yet also on limited accountability and tightly controlled forms of participation. The Partido Revolucionario Institucional (PRI, Institutional Revolutionary Party) that controlled Mexico for much of the twentieth century derived its legitimacy from the Mexican Revolution (see Box 1.5). The Cuban Revolution in 1959 and the Nicaraguan Revolution in 1979 both sought to legitimise themselves by reference to the long nationalist struggle against oligarchic rule tied to US 'imperialism' (see Boxes 2.3, 10.1, 10.8, Chapter 16).

Positivism

A conflict that had been submerged by the economic growth of the late nineteenth century began to surface as the twentieth century dawned between the idealistic liberalism that had inspired political reforms after the 1850s and more authoritarian ideas associated with positivism that would eventually have a profound influence on Latin American thought. Positivism derived from the work of the French philosopher Auguste Comte (b.1798–d.1857) and encompassed a belief that human evolution had reached a 'positive' stage in which scientific method could be used to discover truth. Only propositions that could be demonstrated to be true scientifically were an acceptable basis for policymaking, and so it was possible through such 'scientific politics' to achieve the efficient management of society. Adherents of positivism believed strong government by technically proficient administrators was essential to rid society of backward elements and create the material conditions in which modern liberal democracy could prosper.

Positivism was influential throughout Latin America, promoting social order, stability and economic growth. The strength of positivist ideas reflected the commitment of dominant liberalism to pursue progress regardless of the cultural or religious obstacles that stood in the way. However, late nineteenth-century postivism also reflected the reassertion of authoritarian instincts and appealed to elites who sought to justify their privileged social position and their affinity for European culture. Positivists were often influenced by European ideas about race that reduced indigenous, *mestizo* and black populations to an inferior status (see Chapter 13). These ideas enabled them to justify rule by a small, creole elite and the postponement of democracy amid the accelerating demands for change that accompanied rapid economic growth. The eventual reaction against positivism in the early decades of the twentieth century weakened liberalism and had an important impact on the subsequent development of nationalism in Latin America. However, in contemporary Latin America the proliferation of technocrats – highly educated policymakers with a preference for technical solutions to social and economic problems – attests to the continuing tendency by elites to seek 'scientific' solutions to social problems in a positivist vein (see Box 2.1).

Corporatism

The term corporatism has been employed in different ways in the study of Latin America (see Boxes 2.2, 7.1). Corporatism as a formal ideology has not been common but a number of corporatist assumptions became popular in debate and policymaking in the early twentieth century and corporatist structures and practices have often prevailed (see Chapters 2, 7). Ideas advocating corporatism were developed within Roman Catholic social thought in the late nineteenth century in a bid to respond to a spirit of revolutionary change. These combined a cultural vision of society based on a hierarchical religious tradition with more functional dimensions of corporatism as a form of interest group politics by which organisations reflecting the concerns of social sectors are incorporated into the policymaking process through regulated links with the state, thereby reducing class conflict.

The emergence of more explicit conservative arguments in favour of corporatism in the 1920s revealed the persistence of an authoritarian tradition in Latin American politics, yet corporatist movements also developed in Mexico and Peru in the 1920s devoted to mass participation and social reform. Corporatist ideas have, therefore, influenced political themes on both the right and left in Latin American politics. By bringing peasants into politics, Mexico's revolutionary constitution of 1917 had a corporatist character, and the political party formed in 1929 that would become the PRI was explicitly corporatist in structure. In Peru, Raúl Haya de la Torre modelled the Alianza Popular Revolucionaria Americana (APRA, American Revolutionary Popular Alliance, today referred to as the Partido Aprista Peruano) on the Mexican revolutionary movement. He envisaged that the state created by a single party (APRA) would be organised not as a bourgeois (liberal) democracy but as a 'functional' democracy in which classes would be represented according to their role in production. The contemporary Bolivian left, in the form of the ruling Movimiento al Socialismo (MAS, Movement towards Socialism) under Evo Morales, builds upon a long corporatist tradition in the country's politics, sometimes called *movimientismo*, that is reflected in its approach to political representation and the role of the state in development and tackling inequality (see Gamarra, 2008). According to Gamarra (2008), a significant aspect of *movimientismo* is the push towards single-party rule, a reflex that is evident in the MAS. It has been argued that 'neo-corporatism' also exists in Latin American politics today. In Ecuador, for example, indigenous movements that have gained power in local government have created institutional frameworks that serve as channels for the expression of social movements' demands (see Ospina Peralta *et al.*, 2008).

The 1930s also witnessed the development of a more overtly ideological version of corporatism that encouraged a central focus on the state and was influenced by fascist and other European ideas found in Franco's Spain, Mussolini's Italy and Salazar's Portugal (see below). Fascism discredited corporatism as a formal ideology, although later authoritarian leaders such as General Augusto Pinochet (1973–90) in Chile were admirers of Franco's corporatist vision that endured in Spain long after the Second World War.

Ideas and themes on the Left

The origins of the Left in Latin America were diverse, ranging from an early social liberalism of the Independence era to the international anarcho-syndicalism of the late nineteenth century. As a result, leftwing thought in Latin America has taken many forms. Agrarian radicalism and anarcho-syndicalism – a radical and militant trade unionism that fought to improve working class conditions – were precursors of socialist and communist movements in the twentieth century. These ideas became appealing amid rapid social change as export economies expanded, an urban workforce evolved and immigration brought new workers to Latin America. Castañeda (1994) has traced the evolution of leftwing ideas in Latin America through socialist and communist movements and 'national populism' (see Chapter 16). After

1917, socialism and communism began to make headway among the organised working class, and communist parties were founded.

Marxist philosophy and its concern with redistribution has since been highly influential in Latin America, mainly because of the persistence of deep economic inequality (see Table 4.6, Chapter 15). An important feature of Marxism in Latin America, and its political application through Leninism, was their imported character. Communist parties in the region were often founded by immigrants, and this association would allow their critics to adopt nationalistic postures and portray these ideas as alien (see Chapter 13). At times, communists and socialists have participated in government and wielded considerable influence, but in general Marxist ideas have found it hard to adapt to Latin American conditions. Organised labour was generally weak in societies that were predominantly rural, and has often only gained influence only through a corporatist relationship with the state or dominant party (see Chapter 7). The close relationship between trades unions and labour-based parties such as the PRI in Mexico and the Peronists in Argentina are good examples of the influence of corporatism on the left in Latin America. None the less, a revival of interest in Marxist ideas in Latin America, among scholars in particular, has accompanied the rise of new left-of-centre administrations, and some key thinkers have used Marxist frameworks of analysis to interpret contemporary themes (see below, and Dussel, 2009).

Principal early themes of debate on the left in Latin America were the character of the forthcoming socialist revolution; the extent to which the proletariat – the industrial working class – should make alliances with other classes; and attitudes towards electoral politics. One of the Left's failures was its reluctance to come to terms with the issue that limited its relevance in the region: the peasant question. The Communist International, or Comintern, did not expect a revolution to take place in Latin America given its agrarian character and there was little incentive within communist movements to care about rural rebellion, explaining their commitment to a 'peaceful road' to power. Some thinkers recognised this failing and tried to address it, such as the writer José Carlos Mariátegui (b.1894–d.1930) who founded a socialist party in Peru in 1929 (see Box 12.1).

The cautionary strategy adopted by communist parties derives from another key issue of debate within Marxism in Latin America: whether local bourgeoisies were progressive or reactionary. Mariátegui argued that capitalism had reached Latin America too late for local bourgeoisies to follow in the footsteps of Europeans. Until the early 1960s most Latin American communist parties considered that local bourgeoisies were a *progressive* force and could struggle together with the proletariat in order to eliminate feudal legacies and end imperialism. This commitment to the progressive potential of the bourgeoise helps to explain why, in the 1930s, communists in Latin America pursued a 'popular front' strategy seeking alliances with nationalist, reformist and populist regimes. Popular-frontism in Latin America was underpinned by the idea that industrial development would result from a 'national democratic revolution' in which the progressive bourgeoisie would play a leading role. As a result, the Second World War was a period of communist support for the Allies, but this weakened the Left and after the end of the war communist activities were prohibited.

| THEORIES AND DEBATES | Box 12.1 |

Mariátegui

José Carlos Mariátegui was one of the leading South American social philosophers of the twentieth century. A journalist and social activist in Lima, Peru, he attempted to reconcile doctrinaire Marxism with a passionate concern for indigenous culture (see Chapter 13). In 1928, Mariátegui helped form the Socialist party of Peru that was led by declared Marxists but put forward a reformist programme and was open to the middle classes as well as the masses. Although he was criticised by contemporaries who went on to form the Peruvian Communist Party soon after his death, Mariátegui is extolled as the father of Peruvian and even South American communism.

In 1928, Mariátegui published *Siete ensayos de interpretación de la realidad peruana* (Seven Interpretive Essays on Peruvian Reality) which brought together articles he had written since 1925 published in journals (see Mariátegui, 1971). This analysed and set in an historical context key problems of Peru, such as land distribution and the status of indigenous people. One of the principal failures of emergent Latin American communism was its reluctance to come to terms with the peasant question. By 1928, communist parties were already well established in other countries in the region but these did not address the political and revolutionary importance of the rural sector. Mariátegui was one of the first to stress the revolutionary potential of peasants, arguing that the indigenous peasantry, not the industrial proletariat, were the true revolutionary class in Latin America. In this sense, he can be seen as a visionary and as an early exponent of an alternative to the orthodox communist line. Mariátegui saw socialism as a means of redeeming Peru's poor indigenous masses. He foresaw a united movement that incorporated peasants, workers, indigenous people, artisans and intellectuals. His Marxism was heavily influenced by concerns about indigenous cultural integrity and found inspiration in the communal aspects of Inca society.

Diverse elements on both left and right in Latin America have since drawn selectively upon Mariátegui's thought, which influenced among other things the anti-imperialism of the Left, the moral idealism of the Cuban Revolution (see Box 2.3, Chapter 16), liberation theology (see Box 12.3), and even the variant of Maoism advocated by the Peruvian guerrilla movement Sendero Luminoso (see Boxes 12.4, 13.9). His legacy was also evident in the populist programme carried out by the military government in Peru from 1968–75 that included radical land reform and the declaration of Quechua as an official language (see Chapter 16).

More recently, Mariátegui's ideas have come to the fore in countries such as Ecuador and Bolivia – where the relationship between indigenous movements and the political left has grown closer – providing a Marxist justification for the claims to self-determination of indigenous 'nations' (see Becker, 2008; see also Chapters 8, 13).

The Cuban Revolution (1959) was the first successful socialist revolution in the Americas and transformed the prospects of Marxism in Latin America at the height of the Cold War (see Box 2.3). The revolution split the Left by appearing to discredit the reformism of communist parties and firmly identifying socialism with Latin America's revolutionary tradition (see above). In particular, Cuba's revolution took place in an agrarian country without the aid of the Soviet Union, and so overturned accepted notions about the stages a society had to go through before revolution became possible. Castro's success gave new vigour to the revolutionary tradition, and a feature of Cuban ideology in the 1960s was revolutionary messianism, the promotion of revolution abroad by ideologues such as Che Guevara (see Box 12.2).

Cuba's revolution also tapped into continentalist sentiments (see Chapter 9, Box 13.1) and pro-Cuban thinkers argued in favour of a *hemispheric* revolution because all the countries in the region shared similar conditions. Guevara developed a theory of guerrilla warfare based upon a small revolutionary cadre of armed militants, the *foco*, which, like Mariátegui, assumed that the peasantry, not the small urban proletariat, offered the greatest revolutionary potential (see

---

THEORIES AND DEBATES   **Box 12.2**

Che Guevara

There has been a significant revival of interest in all aspects of the life of the Argentinean revolutionary Ernesto 'Che' Guevara since his remains were recovered from Bolivia in 1997 and reinterred in a mausoleum in Santa Clara, Cuba. Guevara is perhaps most recognisable through the iconic photograph of him taken in 1960 by Alberto Korda that has adorned millions of posters since the 1960s and has come to symbolise the charismatic radical across the world. Hundreds of books have been written about him and, more recently, filmmakers have interpreted the influences that helped shape the Argentinean revolutionary in hit movies. The Guevara phenomenon attests to the continuing potency of the romantic, self-sacrificing revolutionary martyr in popular imagination. One of its ironies, however, is that Guevara has become popularised through the consumer culture that he himself so vehemently opposed.

Guevara was born in 1928, the first child of middle-class parents in Rosario, Argentina, and went on to study medicine at the University of Buenos Aires. He became interested in Marxist ideas and travelled in South America, eventually heading for Guatemala, where he supported resistance to the CIA-sponsored coup in 1954 against the government of Jacobo Arbenz (see Chapter 2). Guevara fled to Mexico City, where he worked as a physician and met Fidel Castro, the exiled Cuban revolutionary. He joined Castro's 26th of July Revolutionary Movement as a medic, and was one of 12 members who escaped into the Sierra Maestra mountains after their group was decimated following the return to Cuba in 1956. Guevara distinguished himself subsequently as a military commander in the guerrilla struggle against the regime of Fulgencio Batista (1933–44, 1952–59), taking the strategic provincial capital of Santa Clara in a decisive battle that opened up the route to Havana. Following the guerrilla victory, Guevara served as president of Cuba's National Bank, head of the Department of Industrialisation and Minister of Industries from 1959–65 (see Yaffe, 2009). He also became the international face of the Cuban revolution, touring socialist and communist countries, including the Soviet Union and China, and in 1964 representing Cuba at a United Nations conference on development. Guevara was reviled by the US government, rightwingers and Cuban exiles as a key figure in the trials and execution of Batista loyalists and officials following the revolution, and his high profile also generated enmities within the Cuban revolutionary regime. His plans for rapid industrialisation, which had limited success, the differences he had regarding economic policies with other Cuban leaders, and his commitment to extend the revolution abroad, caused tensions within the government. Guevara was also ideologically influenced by Chinese communism and grew increasingly critical of the Soviet Union as the Sino-Soviet split grew more divisive, particularly between 1962–64. His pro-Chinese orientation means that he is often considered to have been an important advocate of Maoist strategy in Latin America and, like Mariátegui, Guevara attributed to the peasants the key role in revolutionary tactics (see Boxes 12.1, 12.4). In 1965, Guevara relinquished his official positions

▶

and Cuban nationality and disappeared from public life, leaving with a group of Cuban volunteers to lead guerrilla operations in the Congo and then later in Bolivia against that country's military regime. The Bolivian operation had little success, crucially failing to gain the support of local people, and Guevara's forces were outmanoeuvred. He was captured in October 1967 and most accounts indicate collaboration between Bolivian forces and the CIA in his subsequent execution at the age of 39.

Guevara's ideas and writing concentrated on the requirements for carrying out a successful revolution and for constructing a socialist society, and principal themes included:

- *Revolutionary warfare* Guevara placed much emphasis on the role played by military struggle in a revolution and his understanding of guerrilla warfare gave rise to the theory of the *foco*, a small cadre of armed militants based in the countryside spreading insurrection among the peasantry regardless of whether all the formal conditions for revolution were in place and, in particular, without the need for broad organisations (see Chapter 2). Many of his theories about guerrilla strategy were incorporated in his work *Guerrilla Warfare* (1961).

- *Consciousness and economic planning* Guevara played a prominent role in debates within Cuba between 1962–65 about how to build a non-capitalist order. He placed considerable emphasis on the role of consciousness in achieving true communism, articulating the notion of a 'new man' who responded to moral not material incentives, thereby allowing society to abandon market mechanisms (see 'Socialism and Man in Cuba', 1965, in Guevara, 2003). Until recently, Guevara's economic ideas have gained little attention but this has changed amid renewed debate about the form taken by global capitalism and the revival of state ownership across Latin America (see Chapter 16). Guevara had significant influence shaping Cuban economic policy and the transition from a free-enterprise economy dominated by US investment and trade to a socialist one in which the state controlled about 84 per cent of industry and trade. Key to his ideas was the formulation of the Budgetary Finance System (BFS) of economic management developed to deal with the problems created in Cuba by the extensive nationalisation of industry (see Yaffe, 2009). The BFS developed disciplined cost-centre financial accounting through which the surplus from profitable enterprises could be reallocated to struggling workshops and factories, applying the managerial precepts of the US monopolies that had been operating in Cuba before the revolution.

- *Anti-imperialism and international solidarity* The Guatemalan coup had confirmed Guevara in his belief that the US was an imperialist power (see Boxes 9.3, 10.1) that would oppose governments attempting to tackle inequality, and strengthened his conviction that the only way to achieve socialism was through armed struggle. The *foco* complemented Guevara's commitment to a *hemispheric* revolution, which in turn responded to continentalist sentiments (see Box 13.1). Guevara's notion of the *foco* was the inspiration for the formation of a number of guerrilla movements throughout Latin America following Cuba's revolution, including the Frente Sandinista de Liberación Nacional (FSLN, Sandinista National Liberation Front) which led a successful revolution in Nicaragua in 1979. Like Castro, Guevara drew some inspiration from the nationalist tradition (see Chapter 13), but anti-imperialism informed by Marxist ideas was much more central to the positions that he articulated. He viewed the entire world, and in particular the developing or Third World, as a theatre of revolution, steadfastly advocated international solidarity, and was a strong supporter of the Vietnamese Revolution – famously appealing to his South American comrades to create 'many Vietnams'. By 1965, Guevara had begun to situate the Soviet Union itself within his understanding of a broader, exploitative northern hemisphere oppressing an impoverished south, and he grew openly critical of Moscow (see 'Message to the Tricontinental', 1967, in Guevara, 2003). After his death, the Soviet Union put the Cuban regime under pressure to restrict its support for revolution in Latin America. (See also Guevara, 1961, 1968)

Chapter 7, Box 12.1). A host of armed *focos* inspired by Cuba emerged, but by the late 1960s it was clear that those following *foco* strategy had failed and *urban* guerrilla groups began to emerge in Argentina, Uruguay, Brazil and Colombia (see Figure 12.1). The ideological position of these groups was often unclear, although, in Brazil, Carlos Marighella (b.1911–d.1969) tried to develop a theory of urban guerrilla warfare.

These groups contributed significantly to the atmosphere of military repression of the late 1960s and 1970s and were swiftly destroyed. The military governments that took power in many countries in this period would be key influences on the subsequent evolution of the Left, which was repressed by the armed forces on the grounds that it was a source of instability and violence. In Argentina, where the 'Dirty War' unleashed by the military against elements of the population it considered subversive was most severe, military rule was seen by many on the right as a means of *ending* political violence (see Chapters 2, 7).

Cuba's revolution and the challenges it posed to accepted notions of revolution revived interest in Marxist theory and influenced the rise of an intellectual 'new Left' globally. It even influenced the emergence within the Church of an intellectual effort to reconcile Marxism with Catholic beliefs through liberation theology (see Box 12.3, Chapter 7).

In Chile, where a democratic tradition had survived into the 1970s, Salvador Allende (1970–73) pursued a 'peaceful road' to socialism. Although the Partido Comunista de Chile (PCCh, Communist Party of Chile) was only one member of Allende's broad multi-party Unidad Popular (UP, Popular Unity) coalition that came to power in 1970, it played an important role in his government (see Chapter 5, Box 16.2). The military intervention in 1973 demonstrated the dilemmas faced by a left confronted with a choice between the Cuban revolutionary option and the Chilean option of peaceful change in the face of stiff resistance. In both cases, centralism had rapidly become a characteristic feature of leftwing government (see above). The coup against Allende was a watershed for the Latin American left, and analyses of what had gone wrong under the Chilean leader became the basis of the different strategies that would evolve out of the military period: on the one hand, a renewed commitment to armed struggle or, on the other, a determination to press on with more moderate, democratic, reformist socialism (see Carr and Ellner, eds, 1993). In countries such as Peru, Colombia, El Salvador and Guatemala, existing guerrilla movements regrouped or new ones or new guerrilla alliances emerged (see Chapter 2). The successful 1979 revolution led by the Sandinistas in

---

THEORIES AND DEBATES   **Box 12.3**

A Church for the poor – liberation theology

Liberation theology is the name given to ideas developed by thinkers in the Catholic church who wanted a theologically grounded, radical response to the problems of Latin America, although outside the region some of its most ardent advocates have been Protestant thinkers. A theology is the systematic study of a religious belief in order to determine God's nature and purpose – a kind of religious mission statement. In the 1960s, social questions gained a new prominence within the

▶

teachings of the Roman Catholic Church and this was given momentum by the Cuban Revolution and the experience of Brazil. In Cuba, Christians played no significant role in the revolution and the Church became a refuge for those who opposed Castro. However, the Church hierarchy in Latin America viewed the Cuban Revolution as a challenge that required a response. The ideas that would become known in Latin America as liberation theology were given an important impetus by the deliberations of the Second Vatican Council (Vatican II) held in the early 1960s in Rome, which shifted the perspective of international Catholicism from a generally conservative position to one that supported democracy, human rights and social justice (see Chapter 7). The presence of Latin American bishops was greater than ever before, and this would have an impact on the Consejo Episcopal Latinoamericano (CELAM, Latin American Council of Bishops) that would take on board more explicitly the social and political implications of what was being discussed at Vatican II. Among the important decisions the Latin American bishops were to make was to schedule a conference at Medellín in Colombia. Liberation theology is closely identified with the writing of a Peruvian Catholic priest called Gustavo Gutiérrez, who coined the term and was an adviser at Medellín (see Gutiérrez, 1973). Gutiérrez had grown disillusioned with the development models adopted in Latin America, was sensitive to issues of dependency and underdevelopment, had a sophisticated knowledge of theories of capitalism and imperialism, and was directly immersed in poverty through his work. Between 1964 and 1967, he began to develop a conception of theology as a critical, religiously informed reflection on the material world. Liberation theology can be understood as an amalgamation of Marxist social analysis and a reinterpretation of a certain tradition within Christianity. On the one hand, it advanced a critique based on theories of dependency, underdevelopment and class analysis (see Chapter 14). On the other, it recalled a prophetic vision found within the Christian Bible and in Judaeo-Christian tradition constructed around such themes as slavery, exploitation and oppression. Liberation theology gained an international profile within Roman Catholicism between 1972–84 far beyond Latin America. However, it provoked a conservative reaction among members of the Church hierarchy alarmed by the open embrace by some priests of Marxism. There is much evidence that radical priests assisted revolutionary organisations, such as Camilo Torres in Colombia (see Box 7.12) and the Dominicans who may have helped urban guerrillas such as Carlos Marighella in Brazil in the late 1960s (see above; and Serbin, 2001). A Spanish priest, Father Manuel Pérez, became a joint leader of the Colombian Marxist guerrilla army, the Ejército de Liberación Nacional (ELN, National Liberation Army) from the late 1970s until his death in 1998. Pérez played a key role in shaping ELN ideology, which combined Cuban revolutionary theory with liberation theology and called for a Christian and communist solution to Colombia's problems through guerrilla warfare. Liberation theology was particularly influential in Central America during the civil wars of the 1980s, sometimes turning priests in countries such as El Salvador into targets of state violence. Father Ernesto Cardenal, who participated in Nicaragua's Sandinista revolution, became one of the most celebrated liberation theologians. The election of the Colombian bishop Alfonso López Trujillo as secretary general of CELAM in 1972 led to the removal of liberation theologians from its staff. Conservatives such as López Trujillo saw the liberationists as indulging in an effort to create a parallel 'church of the people'. The general meeting of CELAM in Puebla, Mexico, in 1979 was addressed by Pope John Paul II (1978–2005), who was hostile to liberation theology, and whose doctrinal guardian Cardinal Joseph Ratzinger went on to become his successor, Pope Benedict XVI (2005–). Pope Benedict XVI has also been hostile to certain elements of liberation theology and, as a cardinal while head of the Congregation for the Doctrine of the Faith, which oversees Catholic ideas, he issued condemnations of the acceptance of Marxist teaching and instances in which liberation theology may have been associated with violence, 'temporal messianism', and the fostering of class conflict within the Catholic communion. However, at the same time, he has also stressed the responsibility that Christians bear for the poor and oppressed.

Figure 12.1 Guerrilla movements in Latin America

UNITED STATES

MEXICO

Mexico City

ATLANTIC OCEAN

CUBA

Port-au-Prince

Santo Domingo

PUERTO RICO

GUATEMALA

EL SALVADOR

NICARAGUA

HONDURAS

San José

Panama City

PACIFIC OCEAN

Caracas

Bogotá

COLOMBIA

Quito

PERU

Lima

EQUATOR

BRAZIL

Brasilia

BOLIVIA

Asunción

ARGENTINA

Santiago

CHILE

Buenos Aires

Montevideo

URUGUAY

Key:

Guerrillas operating today:
Colombia: Fuerzas Armadas Revolucionarias de Colombia (FARC, Revolutionary Armed Forces of Colombia) 1964–, Ejército de Liberación Nacional (ELN, National Liberation Army), 1964–
Mexico: Ejército Zapatista de Liberación Nacional (EZLN, Zapatista Army of National Liberation), 1994– (limited combat); Ejército Popular Revolucionario (EPR, Popular Revolutionary Army), 1996–
Peru: Sendero Luminoso* (Shining Path ie Partido Comunista del Perú, Communist Party of Peru), 1980–

Organisations whose status is unclear:
Puerto Rico: Ejército Popular Boricua (EPB, Boricua Popular Army)

Significant indigenous dimension:

Guerrillas that played a leading role in successful revolutions:

Cuba, 1959: Movimiento 26, de Julio (26 July Movement)
Nicaragua, 1979: Frente Sandinista de Liberación Nacional (FSLN, Sandinista National Liberation Front)

Guerrillas engaged in lengthy civil wars that ended in peace accords:

Guatemala: Unidad Revolucionaria Nacional Guatemalteca (URNG, Guatemalan National Revolutionary Unity), umbrella group, 1982–96
El Salvador: Frente Farabundo Martí para la Liberación Nacional (FMLN, Farabundo Martí National Liberation Front), umbrella group, 1980–92
Nicaragua: Contras (Counter-revolutionaries, united in 1987 as Resistencia Nicaragüense, RN, Nicaraguan Resistance), US-backed counter-revolutionaries, 1979–90

Notable past guerrillas since 1959:

Rural
Bolivia: Ejército de Liberación Nacional (ELN, National Liberation Army i.e. Che Guevara), 1966–67
Chile: Destacamento Toqui Lautaro/Movimiento de Izquierda Revolucionaria (MIR, Revolutionary Left Movement, Toqui Lautaro Detachment,) 1980–81

Urban
Argentina: Ejército Revolucionario del Pueblo (ERP, People's Revolutionary Army), 1969–76 (some later activity by cadres)
Movimiento Peronista Montonero (Montonero Peronist Movement ie the Montoneros), 1970–77
Bolivia: Fuerzas Armadas de Liberación Zárate Willca (Zárate Willka Armed Forces of Liberation), 1985–91
Ejécito Guerrillero Túpac Katari (EGTK, Tupac Katari Guerrilla Army), 1991–92
Chile: Frente Patriótico Manuel Rodríguez (FPMR, Manuel Rodríguez Patriotic Front) 1983–97
Colombia: Movimiento 19 de Abril (M-19, 19th of April Movement), 1970–90
Peru: Movimiento Revolucionario Túpac Amaru (MRTA, Túpac Amaru Revolutionary Movement), 1980–97
Uruguay: Movimiento de Liberación Nacional (MNL, National Liberation Movement ie Tupamaros), main activity 1970–72
Brazil: Ação Libertadora Nacional (ALN, National Liberation Action)

Sources: Various; news reports

Nicaragua gave these movements encouragement and showed for a while that the armed option was not dead, and even today a number of guerrilla movements operate in Latin America (see Figure 12.1). However, Sandinista theory broke with the Cuban line because it stressed mass participation in an insurrection, challenging the idea of a revolutionary vanguard. The Nicaraguan Revolution was also pluralistic, comprising Marxists, social democrats, Christian democrats (see below) and even pro-business conservatives in a common popular front.

Elements of the strategy adopted by the Nicaraguans could also be identified in the activities of guerrilla organisations in other Latin American countries. In Peru, Sendero Luminoso (Shining Path), one of the most significant guerrilla organisations to emerge from rural society since the Cuban Revolution, reflected the potential for ideological innovation within traditional Marxism and, as in Cuba, challenged the position that the peasantry was a passive, conservative actor (see Boxes 12.4, 13.9, Chapter 7; see also Taylor, 2006).

The guerrilla movements that survived into the 1990s evolved differently to their predecessors inspired by the Cuban Revolution. In Peru, Colombia, El Salvador and Guatemala, their relative success derived from a decision not to pursue national strategies but to win over peasants in certain regions. They created fronts

---

THEORIES AND DEBATES   **Box 12.4**

Sendero Luminoso

The emergence of Sendero Luminoso in Peru stemmed from the divisions within a left that was both growing and radicalised as a result of the Sino-Soviet split in the 1960s, which divided communists into pro-Moscow and pro-Peking factions (see Taylor, 2006). Sendero's leader, Abimael Guzmán (b.1934–), subscribed loyally to Marxism-Leninism-Mao Zedong Thought (i.e. 'Maoism'). Guzmán (known to followers as 'Presidente Gonzalo') sought to apply directly Mao's theory of revolution beginning in the countryside and encircling the towns, with leadership passing from the peasants to the urban working class at a late stage. Sendero also tried to co-opt the legacy of Mariátegui, and another ideologue, Antonio Díaz Martínez, advanced a sophisticated vision of agrarian reform (see Chapters 7, 16). Like Mariátegui, Díaz Martínez paid great attention to indigenous questions, expressing a desire to prevent the 'deculturation' that had taken place in the northern Andes by rejecting Peru's *national* culture as an alien imposition (see Chapter 13). Díaz Martínez argued that national culture was destroying the emotional and ecological equilibrium that had enabled indigenous communities to withstand centuries of exploitation (Harding, 1988). Following his capture in 1992 and imprisonment, Guzmán began to espouse ideas that sought to distance the organisation from revolutionary warfare and diverged from those of the cadres that continued to fight. In turn, the guerrilla organisation's new leader in the field, Oscar Ramírez Durand ('Comrade Feliciano') tried to distance the organisation from any notion of an accommodation with the state and to reassert Guzmán's original ideas about revolution ('Gonzalo Thought'), while reorienting its work towards more political activities on the ground that reflected its weakened military capacity. Ramírez was himself captured in 1999 and, although sporadic activities by a few remaining militant factions of Sendero Luminoso continue today and occasionally claim casualties among government forces, their ideology is far less clear and they are alleged by the Peruvian government and the US to have become associated with drug-traffickers in the regions in which they operate (see Chapter 10).

with a political-military structure at the top and mass organisations at the base held together in ways that were not necessarily ideological. They abandoned the Cuban belief in a short guerrilla war leading to an insurrection and adopted the notion of 'prolonged popular war' associated with Maoism. However, armed actions were not aimed at defeating governments, but forcing them to negotiate, and this diluted the guerrillas' Marxist emphasis. By the early 1990s, they were no longer calling for a revolutionary transformation of society, but for the elimination of para-military groups, the purging of military officers responsible for human rights abuses, judicial reforms and democracy. Some guerrilla organisations, such as the Fuerzas Armadas Revolucionarias de Colombia (FARC, Revolutionary Armed Forces of Colombia) and the Ejército de Liberación Nacional (ELN, National Liberation Army) in Colombia, have either tried to form political organisations or have been engaged in stop-start peace negotiations. In recent years, the FARC has come under considerable pressure to lay down their arms from a range of prominent figures such as Hugo Chávez. The death from natural causes in 2008 of its veteran leader Manuel Marulanda represented a significant setback for the guerrilla organisation. In the case of the ELN, the urge to negotiate has reflected its declining capacity as a guerrilla organisation. It resumed peace talks with the Colombian government in December 2005 and has been involved in on-off negotiations since then. In 2008, for example, the Colombian president, Alvaro Uribe (2002–10), held talks in the presi-dential palace with an ELN spokesman, Francisco Galán, who later confirmed that the group would return to the negotiating table. However, internal differences have plagued ELN attempts to develop a political future: after Galán's talks in 2008, for example, ELN leaders dismissed him as their spokesman. None the less, the group has retained sufficient capacity to challenge the resources of the Colombian state, springing Carlos Marín Guarín, the highest-ranking ELN leader to have been captured, from jail in late 2009 in an audacious rescue. In December 2009, the FARC and ELN reportedly announced that, despite deep ideological differences, they intended to join forces and unite. Although such a move would pose a poten-tially greater threat to the country's security forces, it also reveals how the FARC is trying to recover ground lost by military setbacks.

By the 1980s, communist parties faced new ideological issues posed by the impact of *perestroika*, a further example of foreign influences in Latin American political thought. *Perestroika* refers to the restructuring by Mikhail Gorbachev of bureau-cratic management and of the communist party in the Soviet Union after 1985. It was associated also with the philosophy of *glasnost*, openness or transparency, which allowed for open debate about the problems that made such restructuring necessary. *Perestroika* threatened Castro's political model and Cuba's economy and, by ending the 'Brezhnev Doctrine' by which the Soviet Union claimed the right to intervene militarily to protect socialism from imperialism, it curtailed Soviet-Cuban military relations. *Glasnost* led to many criticisms of Cuba in the Soviet press after 1987, and further polarised the Left in Latin America between those who continued to advocate profound structural change and those who saw the merits of reformism. It reinforced a trend by which many communists embraced the ideas of Antonio Gramsci (b.1891–d.1937) advocating a 'war of position' in which the Left attempts to penetrate civil society and the government bureaucracy (see Gramsci, 1971; Box 12.6). As a result, some parties attempted to forge new

| THEORIES AND DEBATES | Box 12.5 |

Tendencies on the left at the end of the Cold War

Roberts (1997) identified four main tendencies on the Latin America left in the period following the end of the Cold War:

1 A **fundamentalist position** committed to Marxist-Leninist orthodoxy and the revolutionary conquest of state power in order to collectivise property and production. This stance rejected any drift towards the centre by the Left, and one example of it was the vestige of the Sendero Luminoso Maoist organisation in the 1990s (see Box 12.4).

2 **Class-based populism** that encouraged confrontational forms of mobilisation behind the bread-and-butter demands of popular groups as a tactic of political opposition. Parties such as the Partido Comunista de Chile (PCCh, Chilean Communist Party) assumed this orientation, emphasising class conflict yet unable to garner mass support.

3 A **radical democratic project** that identified capitalist relations and class exploitation as only several among many forms of social, economic, political or cultural domination. Radical democrats combine the struggle against capitalism with those against patriarchy, racial and ethnic discrimination and environmental destruction, and emphasise the role of grassroots organisations as important agents of change through whom political agency shifts from the state to civil society. The traditional idea of socialism as an alternative form of production is reconceptualised as the extension of democracy into the workplace and society (see Box 16.5). This position has been influential within the Partido dos Trabalhadores (PT, Workers' Party) in Brazil and the Mexican Zapatistas (see Box 13.5).

4 **Social democracy** that aspired within a democratic framework to transform the Left from an opposition force into a viable governing alternative using state power as an instrument for social and economic reform. The social-democratic position stresses an activist state that can govern market behaviour and redistribute income by modifying capitalist development to allow for more equitable patterns of growth, and seeks to ameliorate class conflict by incorporating organised labour into institutionalised decision-making processes (see Chapter 16). Venezuela's Acción Democrática (AD, Democratic Action) is a social-democratic party that shared in governing the country for many years prior to 1998 before the rise of Hugo Chávez (1999–).

Roberts said the third and fourth orientations were manifestations of the new emphasis on political democracy and that the social-democratic perspective may have practical advantages over its radical equivalent by adopting realistic postures that lessen opposition to it and enhance its appeal as a governing alternative.

broad-based tactical alliances redolent of popular frontism. The evolution of the Nicaraguan Revolution was said to be consistent with the Gramscian approach.

The events which *perestroika* gave rise to marked the definitive end of the Cold War. The socialist bloc in eastern Europe collapsed after 1989 and the Soviet Union dissolved in 1991. These events called into question the viability of socialism, and neoliberal reform also dented the notion of a 'traditional' organised working class and the orthodox left began to assign a less important role to workers in their debates as a result (see Chapter 15). Some leftwing parties supported a model of worker participation in companies and the leaders of some former radical movements, such as the Peronists in Argentina, became unlikely champions of neoliberalism while others promised not to reverse market reforms. By the mid-1990s, some leftwing parties were questioning not just the strategies socialists should follow, but socialism *per se*. In Nicaragua, the Sandinistas eschewed the term socialist, substituting for it vaguer developmentalist ideas. In Venezuela, the Movimiento al Socialismo (MAS, Movement Towards Socialism) all but discarded its leftwing label, implying that it was now obsolete. The collapse of the socialist bloc also discredited the notion of centrally planned economies and the role of the state in economic and social policy – cherished concepts on the Latin American left. Neoliberalism and the free trade agenda promulgated by the Western capitalist economies became a dominant orthodoxy, partly because the Left was devoid of alternatives other than a 'mixed economy' solution (see Chapters 15, 16).

By the mid-1990s, a range of different tendencies could be identified within the Latin American left (see Box 12.5).

The 'pink tide'

Until the 1980s, leftwing parties had rarely enjoyed widespread acceptance among voters but many began to participate fully within the institutional structures of democracy, and enjoyed rapid success: in Mexico, for example, an electoral coalition under Cuauhtémoc Cárdenas and backed by the Left nearly won the 1988 presidential elections within two years of its formation. In the 1990s, the prospects of the Latin American left began to change and democratic politics began to reward parties committed to the electoral path to power like never before, even in countries with powerful conservative elites (see Table 12.1). Since 1998, left-of-centre leaders and former radicals have come to power or remained in office in Venezuela, Chile, Brazil, Argentina, Panama, Uruguay, Bolivia, Honduras, Costa Rica, Ecuador, Nicaragua, Guatemala, Paraguay and El Salvador.

In Venezuela, in 1998 the radical populist Chávez won mass popular support in presidential elections at the head of the MVR. Chávez advocates a 'socialism of the twenty-first century' although his critics point to increasing authoritarianism. In Chile in 1999, the Partido Socialista (PSCh, Socialist Party) candidate Ricardo Lagos (2000–06) won presidential elections at the head of the Concertación coalition, becoming Chile's first socialist president since Allende, and he was succeeded in 2006 by another socialist, Michelle Bachelet (2006–10), the country's first woman president (see Chapter 13). In Brazil, in 2003 Lula da Silva of the Partido dos Trabalhadores (PT, Workers' Party) became president after many years of contesting elections. In Argentina, the centre-left Peronist Néstor Kirchner (2003–07) took office as president against a backdrop of severe economic weakness following the crisis that unfolded in 2001, and his wife, Cristina Fernández, succeeded him in 2007. In Panama in 2004, Martín Torrijos (2004–09) of the centre-left Partido Revolucionario Democrática (PRD, Democratic Revolutionary Party) won the first presidential elections since the US handed over control of the Panama Canal. In March 2005, Tabaré Vázquez of the Encuentro Progresista-Frente Amplio (EP-FA, Broad Front-Progressive Encounter) coalition that includes communists, former leftwing guerrillas and trades unionists, became Uruguay's first leftwing president, and in 2009 voters chose continuity by electing a leftwing successor, José Mujica, of the EP-FA, a former member of the Tupamaros guerrilla movement. In Bolivia, the Socialist leader Evo Morales (2006–) won elections at the head of the Movimiento al Socialismo (MAS, Movement towards Socialism), a heterogeneous political organisation that includes both Marxist militants and social movements such as coca growers' unions. In Honduras, Manuela Zelaya won elections in 2005 at the head of the Partido Liberal de Honduras (PLH, Honduran Liberal Party), whose mainstream position is centre-right, then proceeded to take positions arguably more to the left of his party before he was removed in a coup in 2009 (see Box 7.10). In Costa Rica, Oscar Arias of the social-democratic Partido Liberación Nacional (PLN, National Liberation Party) resumed power in 2006, and in 2010 the PLN's Laura Chinchilla was elected to succeed him. In Ecuador, the populist president Lucio Gutiérrez took office in 2003 with the support of a small Marxist party, some members of the Socialist Party, trades unions and Pachakutik, the country's leftwing indigenous movement, although Gutiérrez was ousted in April 2005 (see Box 6.2). In 2006, Rafael Correa won elections in Ecuador at the head of the Alianza PAIS (Patria Altiva y Soberana, Proud and Sovereign Fatherland Alliance) movement, that combines Christian socialism with ideas shared with Chávez of 'socialism of the twenty-first century'. Correa was re-elected for a second term in 2009, the first time in 30 years that the country had re-elected a president. In Nicaragua, the leftwing Sandinista leader Daniel Ortega made a comeback in elections in 2006. In Guatemala, in 2007 Alvaro Colom of the social-democratic and social-Christian Unidad Nacional de la Esperanza (UNE, National Union of Hope) won presidential elections, becoming the country's first left-of-centre president since Jacobo Arbenz was overthrown in a CIA-backed coup in 1954. In Paraguay, in 2008 Fernando Lugo, a former Roman Catholic bishop, won the presidency at the head of a centre-left coalition, the Alianza Patriótica por el Cambio (APC, Patriotic Alliance for Change). In El Salvador, in 2009 Mauricio Funes of the former guerrilla organisation, the Frente Farabundo Martí para la Liberación Nacional (FMLN, Farabundo Martí National Liberation Front), became the first leftwing leader to come to power in the country in 20 years.

None the less, this 'pink tide' remains fragile and there have been several reversals to it: the election in Panama of a conservative supermarket magnate, Ricardo Martinelli, as president in 2009; the election in Chile in 2010 of the conservative businessman Sebastián Piñera; and the removal in a coup of Zelaya in Honduras followed by the election of his main conservative rival, Porfirio Lobo (2010–).

There are a number of reasons why political support for the left has grown under electoral politics since the 1990s and it has had greater success in entering government:

Inequality and a 'backlash' against market reforms

High levels of disenchantment with neoliberal policies that have not had a discernible impact upon severe inequalities and are felt to have worsened problems of crime and insecurity have been an important factor in the ascent of most left-of-centre leaders (see Chapters 4, 15, 16). There has been a widespread perception in many Latin American countries that these policies have not been successful in empowering economies to address pressing social problems. As a result, in most of the countries that have elected left-of-centre presidents the successful candidates had campaigned on platforms that were less enthusiastic about market economics than their opponents, although they adopted a range of positions from open hostility to private property to a desire to strengthen regulation and limit foreign ownership (see below; see also Corrales, 2008). In turn, they mostly advocated a greater role for the state in the economy restricting market activities, from outright nationalisation and state control to greater regulation. Unsuccessful candidates who came close to winning elections – such as Andrés Manuel López Obrador of the Partido de la Revolución Democrática (PRD, Party of the Democratic Revolution) in Mexico in 2006, and Ollanta Humala of the Unión por el Perú/Partido Nacionalista Peruano (UPP/PNP, Union for Peru/Peruvian Nationalist Party) in Peru in 2006 – were also hostile to neoliberal economic policies.

However, a number of caveats must be made about the straightforward argument that the 'pink tide' in Latin America represents a backlash against market reforms. First, neoliberal policies that have sought to liberalise markets and limit the activities of the state in the economy were a relatively recent phenomenon in postwar Latin American politics (see Chapter 15). It was only in the 1970s that pro-market political forces began to gain momentum in the region, often under authoritarian regimes. Given that, the growth of support since the 1990s for left-of-centre politicians advocating a return to statist policies represents a return to the *status quo ante*. In some countries, the change from a pro-market position to a more statist one interpreted as a shift to the left has occurred among presidents belonging to the *same* political party. In Argentina, for example, presidents belonging to the Peronist Partido Justicialista (PJ, Justicialist Party) have both fallen into these camps: Carlos Menem (1989–99) campaigned on leftwing positions, then once in power adopted pro-market positions, whereas Néstor Kirchner (2003–07) responded to economic crisis by adopting much more statist policies. Second, electoral trends across Latin America have not been uniform, and in Chile, Colombia, Mexico and several Central American countries, pro-market political forces have maintained or regained power (see above). In Chile, moreover, centre-left coalition governments under leftwing leaders have maintained pro-market policies. Third, the record of neoliberal policies has been debatable and they have not conclusively failed to have achieved what was intended, especially the taming of inflation to create a long-term basis for stable, sustainable growth (*ibid.*). Furthermore, the governments of some countries (such as Argentina, Chile, Mexico and Peru) pursued neoliberal reforms much more aggressively than others (such as Ecuador, Paraguay and Venezuela), and even in countries that adopted similar reforms the outcomes have been highly uneven. Fourth, the public perception of market reforms has varied across and within countries, and over time. Corrales (2008), for example, points to general support for 'market reform' among the public as a concept alongside negative perceptions of privatisation and labour-market reforms.

Discontent and new political opportunities

Economic and political reforms generate winners and losers. A straightforward explanation for the arguable 'backlash' against neoliberal reform above would be that it generated a sufficiently powerful constituency of discontented losers to punish reforming incumbents and reorient politics leftwards. However, Corrales (2008) points out that the 1990s also produced new *economic* winners who turned anti-incumbent and *political* winners able to challenge the status quo due to new opportunities. He examines arguments that consider the possibility that the discontent with market reforms that has fuelled a leftward shift might *not* have originated with the 'losers' under neoliberal reform, but in part with the winners:

■ voters who gained from market reform might reward incumbents for delivering sustainable growth yet then turn their attention to new 'second-generation' issues. In Brazil, for example, after economic stabilisation the electorate began to prioritise issues such as inequality;

■ the rise of anti-incumbent leftwing movements might be associated with the beneficiaries of economic reform who remain dissatisfied with their gains in comparison with even bigger winners. In Argentina, Brazil and Peru, for example, the strongest support for the Left often occurred in comfortable middle-class neighbourhoods;

■ political changes associated with democratisation offered protest movements expanded opportunities for mobilising during the 1990s. A trend across the region was the growth of opportunities both for traditional leftwing parties but also new forces mobilising previously unorganised sectors, often as social movements, such as indigenous and ethnic communities (see Chapter 8). At the same time, the grip of traditional parties has weakened as corporatist and clientelistic mechanisms have withered and party systems have reconstituted (see Chapters 6, 7).

Organisational factors

While inequality in Latin America is widespread, some countries have not shifted leftwards: so other factors that explain the ability of the Left in some countries to take advantage of inequality as an issue in elections must be present, such as political mobilisation. Inequality has translated into electoral success mainly in countries that historically have had an organisational basis for mass mobilisation (see Cleary, 2008). In Brazil, for example, Lula da Silva has been able to benefit from the close relationship between his PT and organised labour and social movements. In Ecuador, support for the Left draws upon large, organised indigenous parties able to monilise their supporters to great effect for a range of political activities. A distinction has been made between 'elitist' and 'labour-mobilising' party systems in Latin America (see Roberts, 2002). In elitist party systems, parties tend to be organised vertically across class lines, which limits the ability of leftwing groups to mobilise voters on the grounds of socioeconomic divisions; labour-mobilising party systems, in which parties tend to be organised horizontally along class lines, arise in countries with larger trades unions and larger manufacturing sectors, and have often corresponded to the Left's electoral success.

International factors

Just as the changing international climate has been a factor contributing to democratisation in Latin America (see Chapter 3), it has also made coups overtly aiming to displace leftwing leaders much more difficult. The universal condemnation of the coup in Honduras against Manuel Zelaya in 2009, for example, and the efforts by the US among others to negotiate his return to power and to sanction the coup-plotters, are evidence of the difficulties faced by *golpistas* in Latin America today, even from traditional allies (see Box 7.10, Chapter 10). International democratic norms that require respect for the mandates of left-of-centre leaders have given the Left new security within the political process, and this in turn has made them more viable in the eyes of voters.

The embrace of democracy and programmatic change

Traditionally, much of the Latin American left had regarded democracy as a bourgeois device in the interests of capitalism, advocating in its place revolution leading to the dictatorship of the proletariat. In the 1960s and 1970s, most leftwing organisations in Latin America advocated Marxism, socialism, radical nationalism or other ideologies proposing revolutionary change. For some, military dictatorships appeared to vindicate the Marxist thesis advocating a non-democratic road to power through guerrilla activity. While these parties or movements were able to command significant mobilising capacity, the Cold War and authoritarian climate meant that, in large part, this was not deployed in electoral politics and, where it was, as in Allende's electoral success in Chile in 1970, it was subsequently reversed through coups. However, the Left became one of the champions of democracy and played a key role in the process of redemocratisation by joining in broad-based alliances. In the 1980s, parties on the left began to emphasise a commitment to representative democracy, respect for human rights and to democratise their own procedures. Most of the contemporary left no longer advocates revolution achieved through violent means, although Marxist ideas continue to inform debate (see below). The commitment to democracy, rights and inclusion owe much to the hegemony of what are, in essence, *liberal* political norms in contemporary capitalist societies. At least 29 Latin American parties on the left are now either members of the Socialist International – a worldwide organisation of parties that today has a strongly social-democratic orientation – or have some kind of relationship with it, and the organisation's secretary general in 2009 was a Chilean, Luis Ayala (see Table 12.2). The Latin American committee of the Socialist International has placed democracy and an empowered state at the top of its policy agenda (see SICLAC, 2004; Socialist International, 2009b).

Democratisation has had an important ideological impact on the left, filling some of the void left by the decline of socialist critiques. In Mexico, for example, the

Table 12.2 Socialist International member, consultative and observer parties from Latin America*

Country	Full member parties	Consultative parties	Observer parties
Argentina	Partido Socialista (PS, Socialist Party) Unión Cívica Radical (UCR, Radical Civic Union)		
Brazil	Partido Democrático Trabalhista (PDT, Democratic Labour Party)		
Chile	Partido por la Democracia (PPD, Party for Democracy) Partido Radical Social Demócrata (PRSD, Radical Social Democratic Party) Partido Socialista (PSCh, Socialist Party of Chile)		
Colombia	Partido Liberal Colombiano (PLC, Liberal Party of Colombia)		Polo Democrático Alternativo (PDA, Alternative Democratic Force)
Costa Rica	Partido Liberación Nacional (PLN, National Liberation Party)		
Dominican Republic	Partido Revolucionario Dominicano (PRD, Dominican Revolutionary Party)		
Ecuador	Partido Izquierda Democrática (PID, Democratic Left Party)		
Guatemala	Unidad Nacional de la Esperanza (UNE, National Unity for Hope)	Convergencia Social Demócrata (CSD, Social Democratic Convergence)	
Haiti	Parti Fusion des Sociaux-Democrates Haitiens (PFSDH, Unified Party of Haitian Social Democrats)		Organisation du Peuple en Lutte (OPL, Organisation of the People in Struggle)
Mexico	Partido de la Revolución Democrática (PRD, Party of the Democratic Revolution) Partido Revolucionario Institucional (PRI, Institutional Revolutionary Party)		
Nicaragua	Frente Sandinista de Liberación Nacional (FSLN, Sandinista National Liberation Front)		
Panama	Partido Revolucionario Democrático (PRD, Democratic Revolutionary Party)		
Paraguay	Partido Revolucionario Febrerista (PRF, Revolutionary Febrerista Party) Partido País Solidario (PPS, Party for a Country of Solidarity)	Partido Democrático Progresista (PDP, Progressive Democratic Party)	
Peru	Partido Aprista Peruano (PAP, Peruvian Aprista Party)		
Puerto Rico	Partido Independentista Puertorriqueño (PIP, Puerto Rican Independence Party)		
Uruguay	Nuevo Espacio (NE, New Space Party) Partido Socialista del Uruguay (PSU, Socialist Party of Uruguay)		
Venezuela	Acción Democrática (AD, Democratic Action) Movimiento al Socialismo (MAS, Movement Towards Socialism)	Por la Democracia Social (PODEMOS, For Social Democracy)	

*and the Latin American Caribbean; as of November 2009.
Note: Delegates from full member parties have the right to speak and vote at SI meetings, and the parties pay affiliation fees; delegates from consultative parties have the right to speak at SI meetings but do not have a vote, and the parties pay affiliation fees; representatives of observer parties have the right to attend SI meetings but do not have speaking or voting rights, and the parties pay an annual fee.
Source: Socialist International, 2009a

Partido de la Revolución Democrática (PRD, Party of the Democratic Revolution) defined itself by democratic, as opposed to leftwing, credentials. An important strain in leftwing thought in Latin America today is the idea of extending democracy beyond the notion of electoral inclusion through voting to a much more participative idea of democracy ('participatory democracy') often carried out at the level of local government and implicit in the idea of decentralisation (see Chapters 3, 6, Box 16.5). Participatory democracy derives from the radical democratic argument (see Box 12.5) in which the traditional idea of socialism as an alternative form of production is reconceptualised as the extension of democratic procedures deep into institutions. Since the 1980s, for example, Brazil's PT has been at the forefront of calls for decentralisation and mechanisms to foster popular participation in government, such as 'participatory budgeting' (see Baiocchi ed., 2003). In Venezuela, participatory democracy has been expanded significantly by President Chávez as part of the 'Bolivarian Revolution', with a large number of community organisations, councils and committees defined and created through legislation in 2005–06, and the expansion of worker self-management and co-operatives throughout the country. The Chávez government has tried to institutionalise participatory democracy through the creation of 'consejos comunales', neighbourhood councils that bypass traditional state structures (see Motta, 2009a).

At the same time, the end of the Cold War blurred the meaning of the term 'leftwing' and reduced the emphasis on themes such as public ownership. The strength of social-democratic arguments advocating a 'Third Way' between capitalism and socialism grew, and many socialist parties shifted to the centre on economic policy (see Chapter 16). In an influential set of prescriptions written at the end of the Cold War in 1993, Castañeda argued that the Left had to take advantage of alternative paradigms of capitalism, accepting the market if not the *spirit* of western capitalism (Castañeda, 1994). This 'new pragmatism' has been criticised from within the Left for idealising European social democracy and failing to acknowledge the many failures of reformist policies in Latin America (Petras with Vieux, 1999). None the less, alongside the reassertion of statism since 1998 through the nationalisation of strategic sectors of the economy in countries such as Bolivia, Venezuela and Argentina (see below; see also Chapter 16), a key characteristic of the 'pink tide' has been economic policy *continuity* that poses no radical threat to the workings of the free market. While leading figures on the left have been vociferous critics of neoliberal economic policies, they have been limited in their ability to make radical changes by the nature of their economies and globalisation (see Chapter 15). In Brazil, for example, Lula da Silva has come under attack from former supporters over his administration's economic policies, which critics argue put the needs of global capital before those of Brazilian workers (see Branford, 2009). In its first few years, for example, Da Silva's government followed the agenda of his predecessors by placing priority on macroeconomic stability and on meeting Brazil's commitments to multilateral lenders such as the IMF through tough monetary policies. Although a former critic of privatisation, Da Silva also created public-private partnerships for large infrastructure projects and oversaw significant growth in Brazil's financial sector (see Chapter 7).

Complementing a greater commitment to democracy has been the Left's embrace of pluralism, which found expression in new examples of intra-left alliances and coalitions. The end of the monolithic communist model offered the possibility for coalitions, but also the risk that ideology would be diluted. The willingness to accept diversity also led to tactical alliances between those on the left and those who might not agree with them ideologically, and the Church, in particular, is no longer seen as an opponent. The growth of social movements has also been an important focus of leftwing ideas (see Chapter 8), and the thesis that social movements are the precursors of a new type of participatory democracy has gained in importance. Some thinkers have sought an ideological mechanism to justify stronger links between the Left and social organisations, and in particular indigenous movements. Laclau and Mouffe (1985), for example, relegated worker–management conflict and pointed to the emergence of new forms of struggle generated by the penetration of capitalist relations into new spheres. Socialist scholars criticised this work for abandoning class analysis, although leftwing intellectuals in Latin America have played an important role in the emergence of civil society, and in the process also began to re-emphasise the ideas of Gramsci (see Box 12.6; Otero, 2004). Critics

---

THEORIES AND DEBATES   **Box 12.6**

Gramsci in the jungle

Contemporary Marxists have tried to situate international discussion about the importance of the Zapatista uprising in southern Mexico within Marxist debates in the post-Cold War era because the Ejército Zapatista de Liberación Nacional (EZLN, Zapatista National Liberation Army) was seen as the result of an encounter between urban Marxists and indigenous people in Chiapas (see Berger, 2001). Perhaps the most important strain of analysis that has emerged has tried to situate the rebellion within the framework provided by the ideas of Gramsci, who placed great emphasis on the relevance of civil society and culture in revolutionary strategy (see Gramsci, 1971). The Chiapas Marxists were compelled to find a new language that met the needs of their own analysis of history while addressing indigenous cultural concerns. Gramsci's work identified as one possibility the 'war of position' in which civil society alliances and struggles over cultural hegemony become resources in the fight for socialist transformation. Bruhn (1999) has argued that the EZLN demonstrates the spread of Gramscian tactics of 'cultural warfare' into armed leftwing movements. She argues that the Zapatistas' creative use of language is a key resource in the Gramscian war of position. Words are used to create an alternative truth in a form of ideological warfare and are also used to win allies in civil society. Indeed, so successful has the Zapatistas' use of ideological warfare been, that it has generated resentment among other guerrilla organisations in Latin America that have been fighting with guns for many years. Secondly, Bruhn argues that the EZLN has put civil society at the heart of its strategy, not only in its rhetoric but in its actions, attempting to build local coalitions reinforced by constant reiteration of the concept of 'dialogue'. Lastly, the EZLN leader Marcos is the epitome of the Gramscian intellectual – a person key to the transmission of ideas to civil society who is uniquely specialised in the elaboration of ideology and constantly challenging its accepted commonplaces. For this reason, EZLN imagery consciously seeks to blur cultural referents, mixing rural and urban ideas and icons and restating common political themes in new forms of language. Bruhn argues that the intellectual formation of Marcos (whom the Mexican government has claimed is Rafael Guillén, a former university communications lecturer) coincided in the late 1970s with the explosion of interest in Gramsci in Mexico, and that the discursive strategies Marcos has adopted in his voluminous communiques are, as a result, not incidental or arbitrary.

have argued that social movements are incompatible with traditional leftwing politics. More radical critiques denounce the ideology of many social movements as post-Marxist and compatible with neoliberalism (see Petras *et al.*, 1999). Moreover, the relationship between left-of-centre parties and social movements can be difficult if groups, such as the Zapatistas in Mexico, reject any participation in conventional politics, and if parties, once in power, do not meet expectations, as has happened in Brazil where the relationship between the PT and key social movements such as the MST has run into problems.

A prominent contemporary Latin American thinker whose work has been inspired by the new pluralism of the Left and social movements is Enrique Dussel, an Argentinean who now lives in Mexico. Dussel's philosophical reflections bring together some of the key influences on leftwing thought in Latin America – such as Marx, Gramsci, Emmanuel Levinas and liberation theology (see Dussel, 2009). Dussel has developed a philosophical interpretation of Marx – arguing that the nineteenth-century thinker was engaged in an *ethical* interpretation of the capitalist system – that attempts to revive his relevance for Latin America by providing the region with a meaningful critique of capitalism that can simultaneously avoid the dangers of totalitarianism. Dussel has also become identified with debates at the World Social Forum – an annual meeting in Brazil of a broad range of activists and social movements opposing neoliberalism (see Box 15.8) – by advocating an alternative to globalisation based on a plural, diverse, non-governmental and non-partisan politics that is simultaneously democratic and egalitarian.

Today, the Left in Latin America is even more heterogeneous and new attitudes towards socialism and global political developments have created a mosaic of positions and possibilities. These left-of-centre governments come from different traditions, have different aims, and are subject to different political and economic constraints (see Lievesley and Ludlam, 2009). Some, such as the Partido Socialista (PSCh, Socialist Party of Chile), have been elected at the head of coalitions within which the Left is weak or in a minority. Since 1998 the record of these parties and leaders in pursuing radical change once in office has been mixed, and a key distinguishing characteristic of the Left in Latin America today, therefore, is policy diversity, which challenges the very notion of a 'pink tide'. Moreover, although Chávez in Venezuela has used the most radical rhetoric among the recent crop of left-of-centre leaders, most of his colleagues no longer use the incendiary discourse full of Marxist references from the Cold War that sometimes provoked coups and political instability, and do not stress revolution as a means of alleviating inequality. That does not mean, however, that they are indistinguishable from their opponents. Kirchner's administration in Argentina, for example, adopted a confrontational stance towards the IMF, and Da Silva's administration in Brazil has led opposition to the hemispheric Free Trade Area of the Americas promoted by the US (see Box 15.5). The leftwing administrations also joined in denunciations of the US invasion of Iraq, and have been much more assertive about opposing the foreign policies of the Bush administration (see Chapters 9, 10). They have also acted as a bloc on bodies such as the Organisation of American States (see Box 9.5).

Policy diversity, the Left's record in power, and the limitations it faces, can be examined in several key areas:

Economic policy

Although critics of the drift towards the left in Latin America initially warned that these governments would renege on debt repayments and sideline private enterprise, these fears have not materialised. Radical policies of nationalisation and expropriation have only occurred in a few countries such as Venezuela, Bolivia (and, to a more limited extent, Argentina), although the role of the state in the economy has grown in much of Latin America. In many cases, even leaders with radical backgrounds have adopted pragmatic approaches obeying orthodox economic principles and international conventions. As a result, as early as 2005 some scholars were challenging the notion that power had shifted to the Left in Latin America and arguing that these administrations were not so different from their predecessors (see Petras and Veltmeyer, 2005, 2009). By accepting neoliberal reform, established social-democratic parties such as Acción Democrática in Venezuela may also have strengthened the appeal of alternatives advocating a rejection of it, such as Chávez (see Box 4.2). The shift towards social-democratic positions has, as a result challenged previous notions of what is left and right in Latin America. The 'pink tide' has incorporated a spectrum of policies from those that are radical and based on socialist principles to those that are moderate and accept much of the neoliberal agenda.

The most radical leftwing positions have been taken in Venezuela, where the Chávez government has been able to pursue an economic policy in keeping with his rhetoric because of record oil prices (see Chapter 16). These have given him considerable room for manoeuvre in policymaking and the ability to confront powerful business opposition, but have made his policies vulnerable to the impact of falling oil prices, which became evident in 2009. However, the Chávez government has not eradicated capitalism, Venezuela's economy remains mixed, and there has also been significant business opposition to Chávez's policies. Aided by record oil prices, Venezuela's economy returned to growth and the private sector changed its approach to Chávez and sought accommodation not confrontation. Radical measures have also been adopted in Bolivia, whose leader Evo Morales is a close ally of Chávez. However, Morales' room for manoeuvre has also been greatly limited by the depth of previous neoliberal policies in the country, its existing energy commitments to its neighbours, and its dependence on foreign investment and foreign assistance or loans to finance development projects. In Ecuador, Rafael Correa committed himself to socialism with economic promises that included higher social spending, increased state control over strategic sectors, and gaining a larger share of revenues from natural resources for the state through the renegotiation of contracts. However, Correa's administration has faced similar limitations to that of Morales and, after two years in office, Ecuador's economic policy was characterised above all else by uncertainty. In other countries that have formed part of the 'pink tide', less radical, social-democratic policies that do not aim to fundamentally challenge capitalism have been pursued (see Chapter 16).

Social policies

The social and welfare policies adopted by left-of-centre governments again vary in their extent and radicalism. Venezuela's 'misiones' – programmes that aim to provide social and economic rights to marginalised communities with a strong component of participatory democracy – represent the most radical policies in the region, although there have been large government programmes to tackle poverty and exclusion in much of Latin America in recent years (see Chapters 3, 4, 16). Across a range of indicators, the evidence suggests that these social policies have improved the quality of life for the most marginalised sectors of Venezuelan society. Latinobarómetro (2008) data reveal that a significantly larger proportion of Venezuelans perceive that inequalities have declined in recent years than in any other Latin American country. In Brazil, policy has been characterised by the broad continuity of economic policy with its predecessors and a continuing emphasis on macroeconomic stability, alongside targeted social programmes to reduce extreme poverty, such as the Bolsa Família initiative. There is also clear evidence that Brazil's poor have enjoyed improved living standards: whereas between 1995–2003 the proportion of Brazilians living below the absolute poverty level declined by only 2.2 per cent, between 2003–05 it declined by 19.2 per cent (see Samuels, 2008).

Despite the likely setbacks caused by the financial crisis of 2008–09, the Economic Commission for Latin America and the Caribbean has identified significant progress in the reduction of poverty and inequality in Latin America since 2002 (see ECLAC, 2009c). There was a discernible reduction in poverty and indigence rates between 2002–08 in countries with developed social policies such as Chile (from 25.8 per cent to 16.9 per cent), Brazil (from 50.7 per cent to 33.1 per cent) and Venezuela (from 70.8 per cent to 37.5 per cent), and inequality has also similarly declined since 2000 (*ibid.*). None the less, ECLAC argues that despite efforts to allocate more resources to meeting social needs, the amount of social spending in Latin America continues to be insufficient. Social policy is also an area in which the high expectations raised by the election of left-of-centre leaders have generated political hazards for them. In Brazil, for example, impatience grew over the slow speed of reform under Da Silva.

Democracy and pluralism

The deepening of democracy and the inclusion of new previously marginalised social groups has been a key commitment of the Left in recent years, and the notion of participatory democracy that gives ordinary people a measure of control over their affairs has been central to this (see Chapter 3, Box 16.5). Again, Venezuela offers the most radical examples of what participatory democracy can look like in practice. In his assessment of Chávez's programme, Wilpert (2006) has suggested that the democratic and participatory nature of the institutions created by the Chavéz's social policy is a distinguishing characteristic of 'twenty-first century socialism' (see Box 12.7; Wilpert, 2006). In Venezuela, the 1999 constitution expanded opportunities for democratic participation through, for example, referendums and the ability of citizens to participate in the nomination of judges and public officials. Citizens' assemblies have constitutional status and can force local public servants to be more accountable; local planning councils based on the model of participatory budgeting found in Porto Alegre, Brazil (see below, and Box 16.5) give ordinary people the opportunity to have a say in how municipal funds are spent; and co-operatives give workers a voice in how their enterprises are run. These

| THEORIES AND DEBATES | Box 12.7 |

Hugo Chávez and 'twenty-first-century socialism'

Venezuela's president, Hugo Chávez, has become a standard bearer for the Left in Latin America and beyond and, in turn, a hate figure for the Right internationally (see below). However, his political ideas have evolved since he came to power in 1998, and it was not until 2005 that he stated explicitly that his objective was socialism. Chávez came to power in 1999 as a political outsider amid considerable disenchantment in Venezuela with the country's then party system and political elite (see Box 4.2). In the first few years of his presidency, socialism did not figure prominently in his discourse, and his ideology was eclectic and loosely nationalist, looking backwards into Venezuelan history to draw heavily upon the figure of the Liberator, Simón Bolívar (see Buxton, 2009; see also Chapter 13). The programme of 'chavismo' initially concentrated on constitutional reform and was not based on an explicit critique of neoliberalism. Nor was nationalisation proposed, although Chávez expressed an interest in the so-called 'Third Way' steering a middle course between market policies and statist interventions that had been articulated by some European social democrats (see Chapter 16). However, after a new constitution was approved in 1999 and Chávez was re-elected in 2000, a commitment to tackling poverty, a critique of neoliberalism, and anti-Americanism (see Box 9.3) grew more prominent in the Venezuelan leader's discourse and began to take policy form. Statist policies and nationalisation informed an agenda distinguished by increasing references to socialism. Buxton (2009) highlights a process of radicalisation in this period in which Bolivarianism became explicitly identified with the Left. The defeat of attempts by opponents to remove Chávez from office (see Box 7.2) and the start of a new oil boom in 2004 strengthened his government's hand and gave him new leeway in policy-making. At the World Social Forum in Brazil in 2005 (see Box 15.8), the Venezuelan president declared that the goal of the 'Bolivarian Revolution' was to create a new socialist model that diverged from the failed twentieth-century socialist and communist experiments: 'twenty-first-century socialism'. Influences on Chávez's ideas are said to have ranged from Latin American Marxists and socialists such as Federico Brito Figueroa, Jorge Eliécer Gaitán, Salvador Allende (see Chapter 2), Che Guevara (see Box 12.2) and Fidel Castro (see Box 2.3), to liberal thinkers such as Noam Chomsky and religious figures such as Jesus. The term 'socialism of the twenty-first century' itself was coined in 1996 by Heinz Dieterich, a German sociologist who lives in Mexico, and grew in use on the left internationally after 2000. The ideas of Dieterich, who became a key adviser of the Chávez government, offer a socialist vision based on a critique of established notions of capitalism and socialism that he argues have hitherto both failed to solve the pressing problems that face mankind (Dieterich, 2005, 2006). Dieterich has argued for a non-violent socialist revolution achieved gradually through the construction of new institutions that prioritise participatory democracy, regional co-operation and workers' rights. Chávez himself has not articulated a distinctive definition of 'twenty-first-century socialism' although he has drawn distinctions with a centralising state socialism and his policies have reflected the main ideas of Dieterich above. None the less, Wilpert (2006) has argued that ideas expressed by Chávez about liberty, equality, social justice and solidarity make 'twenty-first-century socialism' largely indistinguishable from most other social projects of the era and twentieth century, and that it is only the institutions it aims to create, not the ideals that it is pursuing, that will make it distinctive. Moreover, Buxton (2009) has also argued that external factors – such as the rise in oil prices, the broader shift leftwards in Latin America, and the hostility of the US towards Chávez – shaped the initiatives that subsequently became central to the notion of 'twenty-first-century socialism', and that it is a specifically Venezuelan phenomenon that it may not be possible to replicate elsewhere. That is, the 'Bolivarian Revolution' has evolved a socialist identity rather than being a socialist project *per se*.

initiatives have had an impact on attitudes towards democracy. Latinobarómetro data reveal that a significantly larger proportion of Venezuelans perceive that they can change things through voting, as opposed to joining street protests, than in any other Latin American country (Latinobarómetro, 2008). The case of 'participatory budgeting' in Brazil is a well known example of participatory democracy, but innovative examples can be found throughout Latin America (see Avritzer, 2009; Selee and Peruzzotti eds, 2009). In Bolivia, the new constitution that came into effect in 2009 expanded democratic participation to indigenous people through a process of decentralisation that gives communities considerable autonomy over their affairs (see Chapter 6, Boxes 4.1, 8.7). However, according to Wilpert (2006) policies to expand participatory democracy have sometimes been contradicted or undermined by contravening tendencies: alongside efforts to increase citizen participation in state institutions, for example, the Chávez government has also greatly increased the strength of the presidency through constitutional reforms, and Chávez himself has employed an emotive style and has nurtured a personality cult, which can weaken democratic mechanisms and strengthen authoritarianism (see Chapters 4, 5). Chávez's commitment to participatory democracy has derived more from his critique of the country's party system and his hostility to established elites than from a pre-existing socialist analysis (see Box 12.7). Critics of participatory democracy have also claimed that, in practice, it can be long-winded and inconclusive, and that it does not necessarily exclude former elites from decisionmaking.

The Left's record when it comes to addressing the needs of marginalised and under-represented social groups has also been mixed across the region. Lievesley and Ludlam (2009) look at policies towards women as one way of examining this (see Chapter 13). They note progress in championing sexual and reproductive freedom by some women politicians on the left, such as Michelle Bachelet in Chile, while identifying examples in which male politicians such as Daniel Ortega in Nicaragua and Tabaré Vázquez in Uruguay have obstructed the same cause. The Right (see below) and the Church have often also resisted efforts to change the position of women in society. Lievesley and Ludlam suggest that, in general, the new governments have not challenged prevailing gender relations and that the 'pink tide' remains resolutely male.

The variety of positions on the Left in Latin America, within and outside government, have prompted efforts to classify contemporary left-of-centre forces in the region, although in their examination of the 'pink tide' Lievesley and Ludlam (2009) warn against the use of typologies because these beg a host of questions about methodologies and objectives. An alternative approach taken by Corrales (2008) has been to summarise the varieties of forms discontent about neoliberal economic policies has taken. He argues that, in order to gain power, the Left in Latin America has had to appeal to all these varieties of discontent and has not been able to rely exclusively on one issue or constituency:

Radicals – veteran revolutionaries who dislike markets, existing institutions and political parties, whose former commitment to violence has adapted into a commitment to contentious policies, often expressed through street protest. Radicals were in evidence, for example, in the 1999 constitutional assembly in

Venezuela, protests during the 2001 financial crisis in Argentina, and the 2003 street protests in Bolivia.

Protectionists – Opponents of efforts to open Latin American markets through free trade that include business owners and trade union leaders in a range of manufacturing, financial services and media sectors. Opponents of the Free Trade Area of the America initiative advocated by the US (see Box 15.5) would fall into this category, for example.

Hyper-nationalists – Fuelled by antipathy to the US and international financial institutions and their counter-narcotics and trade policies, this position is strong within universities, the media, military and middle class.

Commodity nationalists – Heirs of former economic nationalists who feel the state is not gaining sufficiently from the profits of key export sectors, such as mining, and seek higher taxation and state control in these sectors and less freedom for foreign interests.

Crusaders – Often found in citizen-based watchdog groups that are heirs of the human rights groups that emerged in the 1970s, they gravitated towards the Left in the 1990s but their connections with it have since weakened and their ideological positions are unclear. Many of the social groups that aligned to the PT in Brazil offer examples of this position.

Big-spenders – This group is not anti-market but tired of budget constraints and wants to invest in traditional progressive social policies such as health and education and statist infrastructure and energy projects, and includes both business groups and unions.

Egalitarians – These want the state to undertake redistributive policies to help the poor above all else, and represent a hybrid between the radicals and the big spenders. It is a position that can be identified, for example, with López Obrador of the PRD in Mexico.

Equalisers – This group also wants to help the poor, but by equalising their access to the market through targeted mechanisms while maintaining fiscal discipline. It is a position that can be identified with Chile's left-of-centre coalition governments.

Multiculturalists – This group wants to end what it regards as ethnic apartheid in parts of Latin America, especially the Andes, that led to the long-term political and economic neglect and exclusion of indigenous groups. It has been much in evidence in Ecuador, Peru and Bolivia.

Macho-bashers – This group represents a new trend on the Latin American left and challenges the patriarchal nature of societies, and the Left itself, in the region. It aims to strengthen womens' rights and increase their access to state office through 'gender parity' (see Chapter 13). The election of Bachelet in Chile in 2005 was an example of this position in action.

Despite the inherent diversity that characterises the 'pink tide', there has been a debate about whether the shift to the left represents a permanent realignment in Latin American politics deriving from significant changes in the nature of politics brought about by democratisation, new attitudes towards socialism following the end of the Cold War, and the deepening of social-democratic positions. The ripple effects of the financial crisis of 2008–09 are likely to provide the first major test of this notion. Economic and social policy in Latin America are heavily influenced by cyclical economic factors, making programmes vulnerable to changes in the international climate. By late 2009, there were signs that the global downturn would have a damaging impact on Latin American economies and on levels of poverty (see Chapter 4), and this will test support for the Left. Parties that are in power tend to be blamed for economic problems even if they may not be responsible for them. In Venezuela, for example, in 2009 there were growing signs of economic difficulties caused by falling oil prices to an economy now dominated by the public sector. Second, popular left-of-centre leaders such as Bachelet, Lula da Silva and Vázquez have had considerable difficulty finding young, charismatic successors (see Orihuela, 2009). In Uruguay, for example, the successful candidate fielded by the Frente Amplio (FA, Broad Front) leftwing coalition in the 2009 elections was José Mujica, who was 74. Third, in 2009 there were also signs of a resurgence on the right following several years in opposition (see above). The Right also lays claim to a strong recent tradition of economic management that recognises the reality of globalised production and finances that, its supporters argue, make it a better potential guarantor of Latin American development in the long term, and its ties with powerful business interests remain strong (see Chapter 7). They argue that those countries which undertook the most comprehensive neoliberal reforms championed by the Right (see Chapter 15), such as Chile, are precisely those best placed to ride out the storms caused by global financial turbulence.

Ideas and themes on the Right

The Left has made significant gains in Latin America in recent years, forcing the Right into opposition across the region. However, the Right remains a potent force in politics, has on several occasions disrupted the leftward trend (see above), and has regrouped in some countries to such an extent that at the end of 2009 some scholars were talking about a rightwing resurgence or even the emergence of a 'new right' in the region. Zibechi (2008) has argued the development of the Latin American right in recent years is characterised by three scenarios: countries where rightwing parties have gone into crisis, such as Venezuela, Bolivia and Ecuador; countries where the Right has shifted further to the right, creating an 'ultra-right' characterised by close ties with the US and a militarisation of security policy, such as Mexico and Colombia; and countries in which an electorally successful but moderate left has played a role once played by conservative parties, such as other Southern Cone and Central American 'pink tide' countries.

The Right has remained in government in Mexico, where a candidate of the Partido Acción Nacional (PAN, National Action Party) retained the presidency in 2006 in a close election result that was subsequently disputed by the left-of-centre challenger, the PRD; and in Colombia, where President Alvaro Uribe (2002–10) was re-elected by a comfortable margin in 2006 after spearheading constitutional changes that allowed him to stand for a second term. An independent, Uribe has remained popular in his country mainly as a result of his security successes against guerrilla organisations (see above). Despite conservative convictions, he has often adopted pragmatic positions in his relationships with other countries, maintaining diplomatic relations with Cuba, for example. In both Mexico and Colombia, the state is engaged in a conflict with drug-traffickers, and security has been a prominent theme of governance under conservative leaders. In some cases, the Right has regained power after a period in opposition. In Panama, the conservative businessman Ricardo Martinelli of the Cambio Democrático party (CD, Democratic Change) won presidential elections in 2009, displacing the centre-left Martín Torrijos; in Chile, Sebastián Piñera of the Coalición por el Cambio grouping won the presidency back from the centre-left in 2010, becoming the country's first right-of-centre leader since the departure of the dictator General Augusto Pinochet in 1990; and in Honduras, Porfirio Lobo of the centre-right Partido Nacional (PN, National Party), the main rival to Manuel Zelaya in the 2005 elections, won the presidency following a political crisis sparked by the coup that removed his predecessor.

The Right has also mounted stiff challenges to incumbent presidents in Venezuela and Bolivia, both through formal political mechanisms but also through popular mobilisation and street protests (see below; see also Chapter 7). In Uruguay, José Mujica, the candidate of the Frente Amplio (FA, Broad Front) leftwing coalition was unable to secure the required 50 per cent in the first round of presidential elections in late 2009 and struggled to fight off the candidate of the opposition rightwing Partido Nacional (National Party i.e. Blancos), Luis Alberto Lacalle, in a second round. In Brazil, the PT's presidential candidate for the October 2010 presidential elections, Dilma Rousseff, has lagged in polls behind potential opponents. In congressional elections in 2009 in both Mexico and Argentina, left-of-centre forces suffered significant losses at the hands of centrist and conservative parties. Rightwing political think-tanks such as the Fundacion para el Análisis y los Estudios Sociales (FAES, Foundation for Analysis and Social Studies), chaired by Spain's former leader José María Aznar, have also developed close links with conservatives in Latin America in recent years (see Zibechi, 2008).

Development

The Roman Catholic Church and Christian thought played a formative role in the evolution of political conservatism in Latin America following Independence (see Chapters 1, 7). Conservatives saw in the Church a source of social order and liberal attempts to effect Church–state separation as tantamount to abandoning moral law, threatening anarchy. The Mexican conservative Lucas Alamán (b.1792–d.1853), for example, saw Catholicism as the *only* common bond linking Mexicans divided by politics, caste and class. Therefore, a key factor in the formation of conservative parties in Latin America was conflict over the relationship between the Church and the emergent state. Middlebrook (2000) has examined the evolution of conservative parties according to these Church–state conflicts. In Chile and

Colombia, for example, religious cleavage contributed decisively to the formation of nationally organised centre-right and rightwing parties. In Argentina, Brazil, El Salvador and Peru, by contrast, it did not.

Early conservatives built upon an existing critique of liberalism deriving from disagreements about morality and the nature of mankind, and liberalism has remained an important target of conservative thought. Conservatives restated the virtues of Catholicism and criticised liberalism for following French theoretical works full of anti-Christian, spiritually impoverished materialist doctrines. The secular vision of liberals was based on the notion that man was an autonomous and rational being who must control his own destiny, and from these themes emerged ideas about individualism and the social contract. Conservatives saw men as imperfect beings who needed spiritual guidance to live good and productive lives, and attacked individualism for opening the door to dangerous egotism.

A problem faced by liberalism was that its roots remained shallow in societies whose political cultures were still steeped in traditional Iberian values of hierarchy and patronage. Traditionalism has been a core theme in conservative thought, and the conservatives of the nineteenth century saw themselves as descendants of the *conquistadores* and regretted the loss of the Catholic monarchy. They wanted to preserve a hierarchical society around the privileged positions of the Church and army, a separate 'republic' for indigenous people, and legal and social restrictions on those of mixed race, the *castas*. They identified with Spanish traditions and the values of the colonial era – Hispanism. Yet these beliefs posed dilemmas: the hierarchical values conservatives espoused required a monarch; if they embraced Hispanic traditions, how could they justify breaking with Spain; and how could they advocate a union between Church and state yet also republicanism? Some conservatives in Latin America were conspiring to bring monarchy back up until the 1860s, but others found a solution to these dilemmas in centralism. The Chilean conservative strongman Diego Portales (b.1793–d.1837), for example, drew up a constitution in 1833 compensating for the loss of monarchy with a heavily presidential and centralised system. Another conservative dilemma was the desire to preserve traditional society, while accepting that traditional values can stand in the way of economic progress. As a result, conservatives held mixed views about the benefits of foreign trade, investment and the role of the state. In Mexico, early advocates of state-directed industrialisation were conservatives such as Alamán and Esteban de Antuñano (b.1792–d.1847).

Later in the nineteenth century, divisions among conservatives developed between moderates less wedded to tradition who were more inclined to accept positivist ideas and those on the right who were more doctrinaire and saw conservative ideas as organic, divinely inspired and not something man could change (Henderson, 1988). Corporatist ideas also influenced the Right as it began to respond to arguments based on the theme of class conflict (see above; see also Boxes 2.2, 7.1). However, Church thought continued to be the most important source of ideas for many conservatives. In the late nineteenth century, the Church had accepted that it could no longer limit itself to the realm of the spiritual, and 'social Catholicism' represented its alternative to the main movements of the era, liberalism and socialism. A good example of the influence of Catholic social thought on Latin American conservatism can be found in the rightwing ideas of Laureano Gómez

THEORIES AND DEBATES   Box 12.8

The ideas of Laureano Gómez

Laureano Gómez (1950–53) of Colombia was one of Latin America's leading conservative thinkers of the twentieth century whose ideas embodied a strong reaction against nineteenth-century liberalism. He was elected president in 1949 during the country's bloody civil war known as the 'Violencia' and tried to restructure the constitution along corporatist lines, but was overthrown in a coup by General Gustavo Rojas Pinilla (1953–57) and exiled.

According to Henderson (1988), Gómez's vision began with the notion of a harmonious Christian community sustained by 'natural law', a kind of eternal law of divine origin to which all others must conform. While man enjoyed freedom, this was constrained by the standards of behaviour derived from natural law – God-given freedom did not imply licence. To Gómez, human salvation lay in the universal teachings of the Church, which provided the only way of achieving harmony within society. He insisted that because Colombia and her people were profoundly Roman Catholic, all efforts to deal with national problems had to be guided by that fact.

Man was a rational social being who formed, and was formed by, the various communities into which he was born or associated with, and through these 'corporate' communities men united to form a state (see above, and Boxes 2.1, 2.2, 7.1). Gómez's corporatism, and the popularity in this period of fascism (see Box 12.9), betrayed the influence of centralism on conservative thought, and the need for a strong central state was a key theme in both. God was the state's ultimate authority, but men could measure its effectiveness against natural laws. The state's position in the divine order meant that it did not derive its authority from free will or the transfer of individual rights based on the Rousseauian idea of a social contract.

This view of the state determined conservative attitudes to democracy, and conservatives such as Gómez were hostile to rule based on representation of the majority, preferring more limited, elite and authoritarian forms of representation. Rational men directing the state had to exercise leadership in the interest of all society – the 'common good'. The state also required homogeneity to remain strong and so leaders had to be sensitive to those who might corrupt the social organism – subversives. This notion could draw easily upon the racist ideas that had entered the mainstream through positivism (see above, and Chapter 13). Gómez, for example, believed Western societies were threatened by a liberal and Jewish-Communist-Masonic conspiracy against Christianity. He was convinced that Western liberalism had failed and had ill-served mankind by generating a crisis in society as a result of the damage to Christian unity of destructive individualism and materialism. His conservatism also included strong elements of nationalism (see Chapter 13) and romanticism.

Source: Henderson (1988)

(b.1889–d.1965), who dominated Colombian conservatism in the 1930s to the 1950s (see Box 12.8).

The growing popularity of fascism in Europe posed dilemmas for the Latin American right and fuelled divisions among conservative in countries such as Chile (see Box 12.9). On the one hand, many conservatives attacked fascism, arguing that fascist systems robbed man of individuality, dignity and humanity, and used fascism as a stick with which to beat liberalism by blaming liberal policies for opening the door to extremist ideologies. On the other, they reasserted the values of order and discipline in an effort to undercut the growth of fascist sympathies, and

Fascism in Latin America

In the 1930s, Latin American conservatives had to defend themselves against the competing ideology of fascism. Lower middle classes, rootless migrants to the city and immigrants were drawn to quasi-fascist movements that appeared between the 1920s and 1940s in every Latin American country and put forward authoritarian, corporatist, Catholic and racist ideas (see McGee Deutsch, 1999). Like other ideologies, fascism was imported into Latin America from Europe, and the fascist countries of Europe were also active in the region, giving ammunition to local anti-democratic and anti-liberal groups. Fascist attitudes towards hierarchy and race were heavily influenced by nineteenth-century positivist ideas (see above). In 1932, the Brazilian writer Plínio Salgado founded the fascist Ação Integralista Brasileira (the Integralists) preaching the need for order and corporatist rule. Integralist dogma was Christian, nationalist and traditionalist, and its style of political mobilisation was paramilitary. Prominent Integralists such as Gustavo Barroso took a strongly anti-Semitic line and the party's press reproduced Nazi propaganda against Jews. The Integralists came close to pulling off a coup d'état in 1937 but President Getúlio Vargas (1930–45, 1951–54) preempted Salgado's 'Greenshirts' by proclaiming the Estado Novo (New State), which also bore the corporatist trappings of fascism. Fascism was influential within the Argentine military and General José F. Uriburu (1930–32), who headed Argentina's first military government, admired fascist ideas. Uriburu envisioned a polity in which corporatist representation of functional groups (the army, Church, business, landowners and labour) would replace parties, elections and legislatures (see Boxes 2.2, 7.1). An important force behind a coup in Argentina in June 1943 was the Grupo de Oficiales Unidos (GOU, United Officers Group), officers united by anti-communism and advocating a pro-Axis neutrality in the Second World War. GOU blamed, among other things, Jewish businessmen for the country's problems. Its members included Juan Domingo Perón (1946–55, 1973–74) who, after becoming president, was sometimes denounced outside Argentina as a fascist.

in the 1930s conservatives accentuated hierarchical, organic, anti-majoritarian and corporatist aspects of their thought (Henderson, 1988). Other conservatives, by contrast, retreated into Catholic doctrines and placed a new emphasis on social activism in accordance with papal edicts, and the first signs of a conservative left wing began to emerge.

With the defeat of fascism and the onset of the Cold War, divisions grew as traditionalists continued to stress authority, order, centralism and hierarchy and progressives, often influenced by liberal ideas, stressed democracy, parliamentarianism and social justice. In Chile, splits between the traditional Partido Conservador (PC, Conservative Party) and the more progressive Falange Nacional (FN, National Falange) would lead to the emergence of the Partido Democrata Cristiano (PDC, Christian Democrat Party).

Christian democracy had its origins in the divisions of the 1930s, but grew rapidly in some countries in the Cold War atmosphere as a new political offering able to attract support from both left and right. The case of Venezuela demonstrates the continuing potential that religious issues had to generate party divisions well into the twentieth century, with religious conflict in the 1940s contributing to the development of the centre-right social-Christian political party, Comité de

Organización Política Electoral Independiente (COPEI, Committee for Independent Electoral Political Organisation) as the principal defender of Church interests in the country. In 1947, the Organización Demócrata Cristiana de América (ODCA, Christian Democrat Organisation of America), an international association of political parties and groups adhering to Christian humanist and Christian democratic ideology, was founded, and by the 1950s there were Christian democratic parties or movements in most Latin American countries (see Box 12.10).

Christian democracy also traces its roots to European ideas, such as those of the French intellectual Jacques Maritain (b.1882–d.1973). Parties do not break with Catholic humanistic values yet often have distanced themselves from the Church itself, mainly in order to broaden their political appeal. Although Christian democracy can be placed on the political spectrum as a centre-right philosophy, it has also at times been described as centre-left, and certainly moved leftwards as

---

INSTITUTIONS   Box 12.10

Christian democrats in Latin America

The ODCA was founded in 1947 in Montevideo by politicians from Argentina, Brazil, Chile and Uruguay with the support of others in Bolivia and Peru. Its first central committee comprised Manuel Ordoñez of Argentina, Alceu Amoroso Lima of Brazil, Eduardo Frei Montalva of Chile and Dardo Regules of Uruguay. The *Declaration of Montevideo* passed at its inaugural meeting committed the organisation to democratic Christian humanism aspiring to the achievement of social justice. The organisation also placed Latin American integration, human rights, modernisation and environmental protection as central to its agenda. In 2009, 27 parties in Latin America were affiliated as members or observers to the ODCA (see Table 12.3), which is based in Mexico City and claims a constituency representing 30 per cent of all registered voters in Latin America. It works closely with the Centrist Democrat International (CDI, in Spanish: Internacional Demócrata de Centro, IDC), its international equivalent, and with European, Asian and African regional Christian democratic groups. In 1998, the ODCA congress agreed to focus on six themes that were of priority according to the Christian humanist position:

- *Humanism* The need to 'humanise society' through efforts to confront a materialistic and individualistic way of life characterised by insecurity and mistrust.

- *Social Justice* The need to achieve greater social equity by modernising the notion of social justice in ways that integrate issues of poverty, income distribution, equality of opportunities and quality of life.

- *Family* Recognition of the importance of the family and the need to strengthen it for the consolidation of a more humane, solidarity-oriented, Christian society.

- *Education* The need to enhance education as a basic condition for overcoming inequity, through equality of opportunities, and as essential to growth and development.

- *Democracy* The need to deepen and improve democracy through enhanced participation.

- *Environment* Greater commitment to protecting the environment based on respect for the natural order of creation.

Source: ODCA, 2009

Table 12.3 Organización Demócrata Cristiana de América (ODCA) member parties in Latin America*

Country	Member parties
Argentina	Partido Demócrata Cristiano (PDC, Christian Democrat Party)
	Partido Justicialista (PJ, Justicialist Party)
Bolivia	Partido Demócrata Cristiano (PDC, Christian Democrat Party)
Brazil	Democratas (Democrats)
Chile	Partido Demócrata Cristiano (PDC, Christian Democrat Party)
Colombia	Partido Conservador Colombiano (PCC, Colombian Conservative Party)
Costa Rica	Partido Unidad Social Cristiana (PUSC, Social Christian Unity Party)
Cuba**	Movimiento Cristiano Liberación (MCL, Christian Liberation Movement)
	Proyecto Demócrata Cubano (PDC, Cuban Democrat Project)
Dominican Republic	Partido Reformista Social Cristiano (PRSC, Social Christian Reformist Party)
Ecuador	Unión Demócrata Cristiana (UDC, Christian Democrat Union)
El Salvador	Partido Demócrata Cristiano (PDC, Christian Democrat Party)
Guatemala	Democracia Cristiana Guatemalteca (DCG, Guatemalan Christian Democracy)
Haiti	Rassemblement des Democrates Nationaux Progressistes (RDNP, Rally for Progressive National Democrats)
Honduras	Partido Demócrata Cristiano (PDC, Christian Democrat Party)
Mexico	Partido Acción Nacional (PAN, National Action Party)
Panama	Partido Popular (PP, Popular Party)
Paraguay	Partido Demócrata Cristiano (PDC, Christian Democrat Party)
Peru	Partido Demócrata Cristiano (PDC, Christian Democrat Party)
	Partido Popular Cristiano (PPC, Christian Popular Party)
Uruguay	Partido Demócrata Cristiano (PDC, Christian Democrat Party)
Venezuela	Partido Demócrata Cristiano COPEI (COPEI, Christian Democrat-COPEI Party)
	Observer parties
Brazil	Partido da Social Democracia Brasileira (PSDB, Brazilian Social Democracy Party)
Paraguay	Patria Querida (Beloved Fatherland Party)
Uruguay	Partido Unión Cívica (PUC, Civic Union Party)
	Partido Nacional (NP, National Party)
Venezuela	Partido Convergencia (Convergence Party)

*As of November 2009

**Two further parties denominated as Cuban and affiliated to the ODCA that are, in fact, based in Florida have not been included

Source: ODCA, 2009

the Church did so in the 1960s. It has also been influenced by liberal ideas about human rights and the correct relationship between Church and state. The leftwards shift of the 1960s allowed politicians such as Eduardo Frei (1964–70) in Chile to identify the idea of a new Church that looked more favourably on social change, helping him to win power. Although the PDC in Chile offered a 'Revolution in Liberty', its programme proposed to reform Chilean capitalism to make it fairer and more efficient. PDC philosophy chimed well with US priorities in the region following the Cuban Revolution, and Frei's party benefitted from CIA funding. In power, the PDC pursued a centrist economic policy and eschewed the traditional conservative idea of a strong, corporate state for a more participatory democracy. The links it forged with social groups, in particular peasants, owed much to the broader corporatist tradition in politics (see above). While many PDC policies envisaged greater social harmony through reform, in practice they contributed to the political polarisation that would culminate in Chile's 1973 coup. Christian democracy has been more active in some countries than others. Christian democrats Luis Herrera Campíns (1979–84) of Venezuela, Belisario Betancur (1982–86) of Colombia and León Febres Cordero (1984–88) of Ecuador all won presidential elections. Eduardo Frei (1994–2000), the son of Chile's former president, became the head of the Concertación coalition government in 1993 promising 'growth with equity', and was the coalition's unsuccessful candidate in the 2009–10 presidential elections.

The period of military rule in much of Latin America in the 1960s and 1970s was important for understanding conservative ideas. Civilian conservative forces generally converged with military actors advancing political agendas of their own. Co-operation with military regimes revealed much about conservative attitudes towards democracy. Traditionally, conservatives saw in such radical ideas as democracy the danger of social revolution and supported authoritarianism to ensure leftwing governments did not come to power. However, it would not be correct to say that forces on the right have not themselves drawn upon Latin America's revolutionary traditions. In Nicaragua, for example, the *contra* counter-revolutionaries that fought during the 1980s against the Sandinista revolutionary regime and some of the conservatives who supported them *also* saw themselves as revolutionaries (see Figure 12.1).

The Right and democracy

Conservative and rightwing elites in Latin America have used different tactics to protect their interests in transitions to democracy and thereafter. Some rightwing military regimes, such as those of Chile and Brazil, tried to shape transitions to democracy so their interests were protected once they relinquished power, and subsequent political institutions and practices were similar to those of their authoritarian precursors (see Chapters 3, 4; see also Arceneaux, 2001). Following a transition to democracy, democratic regimes and conservative elites may act in concert to defend elite interests in order to ensure that those elites are not tempted to resort to the military option, and some conservative elites may even simultaneously use democratic institutions and violence to get their way (see Middlebrook, 2000; Payne, 2000).

Even today, the Right is often assessed from the position of fear of a re-emergence of coup coalitions between elites and the armed forces unnerved by popular mobilisation or unhappy with the policies of an incumbent president. In several countries there have been examples of the Right employing both democratic institutions but also extra-parliamentary resources to protect their interests, particularly in those countries that have experienced significant leftwing mobilisations (see below). Where the Right has not experienced an electoral resurgence, or has been on the defensive because of the progress of the Left, there have been instances in which its commitment to democratic institutions has been called into question and it has concentrated its efforts outside the electoral arena and instigated violent mass demonstrations and disinformation campaigns. In Venezuela, for example, there have been many examples of rightwing opposition outside the formal institutions of politics to Hugo Chávez since he came to power in 1999, and business groups were linked to the unsuccessful coup of 2002 (see Box 7.2). One arena of potential use to the Right has been the mass media, although its overt use can be as much a reflection of the Right's marginalisation as its extra-institutional capacities (see Chapter 8). In Venezuela, for example, significant media outlets supported the coup of 2002, when media employees reported being given directives to omit references in their reports by Chávez supporters and spokespeople (Zibechi, 2008). In Bolivia, rightwing forces have mounted vigorous opposition to the policies of Evo Morales (see above) and have, in particular, fuelled secessionist strains in eastern parts of the country in response to his agenda (see Box 12.11). In Honduras, a range of rightwing forces from within the country itself, the US and Venezuela were accused of being behind the coup that ousted President Zelaya in 2009 – including Venezuelans who may have been behind the unsuccessful coup against Chávez (see O'Shaughnessy, 2009).

In general, however, the restoration of democracy in the 1980s was accompanied by a new commitment to party pluralism and the creation of new conservative parties, not least because the armed forces were discredited as potential allies and business groups had grown disenchanted with bureaucratic states (see Chapter 7). Conservative parties were often prominent in the process of democratisation itself throughout Latin America. In Mexico, the PAN was a significant actor in the slow process of democratisation that unfolded after 1982. Its political activity was in contrast to a weak and fragmented left, and from 1983–88 the PAN gained prominence as a legitimate instrument for the expression of *mass* discontent. As a result, the role of the Right in shaping Latin America's democracies has generally become important to their future stability (see Chalmers, Campello de Souza and Borón eds, 1992). The Right's commitment to democratic practices has also changed the meaning of the term 'democracy' since the 1960s and 1970s, when it was commonly understood in Latin America as implying social objectives such as broadened participation and a more just distribution of wealth (see Chapter 3). In the 1980s, however, the Right's participation in democratisation contributed to an increasing emphasis on the *procedural* aspects of democracy, such as the construction of competitive institutions. Now, the Right tended to support the re-establishment of elections and parties as central to politics. In Chile, rightwing forces were able to draw upon earlier traditions of political organisation to establish strong, competitive parties. In El Salvador, social and economic elites successfully developed a new party, Alianza Republicana Nacionalista (ARENA, Nationalist Republican Alliance), capable of advancing their interests in a more competitive electoral environment, whose embrace of a neoliberal agenda boosted its appeal (see Box 12.12).

A hallmark of the Right in Latin America since the 1980s has been the neoliberal critique of the state's economic role (see Chapter 15). This gave conservatives

CASE STUDY · Box 12.11

The Right in Bolivia and secession

Rightwing forces concentrated in Bolivia's resource-rich eastern lowlands – the more conservative *media luna* provinces – have resisted the political initiatives of the leftwing president, Evo Morales, in a number of extra-parliamentary ways: a range of forces on the right were behind large demonstrations seeking regional autonomy and efforts to obstruct constitutional reforms that asserted national control over gas (see Boxes 4.1, 5.6). Alongside efforts to revive a conservative party nationally, the Right has also employed tactics more closely associated with the Left under authoritarian rule and indigenous mobilisation prior to the victory of Morales, such as marches and hunger strikes (see Gustafson, 2008). Some commentators have suggested that rightwing youth groups have employed street violence in civic strikes and to attack peasant and pro-MAS marches, and that landed elites have organised 'land defence councils' and 'self-defence committees' as potential precursors to paramilitary activity (see Gustafson, 2008). Similarly, newspapers and television channels owned mainly by representatives of the pro-autonomy business class concentrated in the east of the country have mounted vigorous campaigns against the MAS government (*ibid.*). More seriously, Bolivian officials have alleged that five Europeans captured or killed in La Paz in mid-2009 by security forces were involved in a plot to kill Morales and had links with rightwing businessmen in the country active in the anti-government opposition (see, for example, Fitsanakis, 2009).

Business groups with close links to the political right such as the Cámara de Industria y Comercio de Santa Cruz (CAINCO, Santa Cruz Chamber of Industry and Commerce), which represents about 1,500 companies, and the Cámara Agropecuaria del Oriente (Eastern Chamber of Agriculture), have been at the forefront of the campaign in the *media luna* for greater autonomy and even secession (see Eaton, 2007; see also Chapter 7). In 2005, for example, it was reported that the then CAINCO president had called for separation from the existing Bolivian state (Ballvé, 2005). These secessionist pressures can be understood as an attempt by conservative elites in the *media luna* – an area whose ethnic composition and economy differ significantly from the *altiplano* – to ensure the region's gas resources remain under their control. The *altiplano*, for example, is geared towards domestic markets, while the resource-rich *media luna* is export-oriented. More recently, the Bolivian state prosecutor investigating an alleged assassination plot against President Morales in 2009 reportedly accused Alejandro Melgar Pereyra, a figure linked by the Bolivian media to CAINCO, of being involved in financing the plot (see BBC Monitoring Americas, 2009). Tensions in Bolivia prompted the Union of South American Nations (Unasur) in late 2008 to pronounce the so-called 'Moneda Declaration' that gave unconditional support to the Morales government, warned the opposition against violence, and agreed to form a commission to investigate a massacre of anti-autonomy activist supporters of Morales in the northern Bolivian province of Pando.

a potent ideological tool in the new era and challenged the notion that their programmes did not advance agendas aimed at transforming society. In several countries conservative parties played a prominent role in promoting the market-oriented economic reforms that were widely adopted throughout Latin America. In Brazil, conservatives were able to shed their image as supporters of the 1964 authoritarian regime, adopting instead neoliberalism as a unifying idea. In Mexico, the PAN adopted an increasingly neoliberal discourse during the 1980s, generating splits between traditionalists and business-led *neopanismo*. One result of this was that, despite electoral failures, conservatives often enjoyed *programmatic* success

ARENA in El Salvador

The fortunes of ARENA in El Salvador demonstrate how conservatism has evolved in parts of Latin America. ARENA was formed in 1981 by rightwing military officers and landowners who combined fierce anti-communism with nationalism. The credibility of its first leader, Roberto D'Aubuisson (b.1943–d.1992), was weakened by links to death squads, although ARENA had gained sufficient support from the private sector and farmers to come close to winning elections by 1984. In this period, ARENA took a hardline approach to efforts to deal with an insurgency by leftwing guerrillas but in 1985, D'Aubuisson was replaced as party president by Alfredo Cristiani (1989–94), a coffee grower. By the late 1980s divisions were appearing within the party between the rightwing officers and oligarchs who had founded it and new members from within financial and industrial circles who believed the military were incapable of resolving the civil war. With the growing support of these business groups, ARENA achieved victories in the 1988 legislative and 1989 presidential elections. In 1990, business elements pressed Cristiani to suppress the right wing of the party and begin negotiations with the Frente Farabundo Martí para la Liberación Nacional (FMLN, Farabundo Marti Liberation Front). Cristiani's 1989–94 administration achieved a peace agreement to end the long civil war and improved the economy, but with the death of D'Aubuisson in 1992, further infighting broke out between rightwingers and moderates over control of the party. In elections in 1994, Armando Calderón Sol (1994–99), a rightwinger, won the presidency for ARENA and the party secured a working majority in the legislative assembly. FMLN electoral gains in 1997 prompted ARENA to portray a new image and it selected Francisco Guillermo Flores Pérez (1999–2004) – who was depicted as belonging to a new generation free from civil war associations – as its presidential candidate. His solid victory in 1999 consolidated ARENA's role as a governing party and he modernised the economy and strengthened relations with the US, sending troops to Iraq and playing a leading role in negotiations for the Central American Free Trade Agreement (DR-CAFTA, see Chapter 9). The FMLN won a significant victory against ARENA in elections in 2003, denying the conservative party a legislative majority. However, the ARENA candidate, Elias 'Tony' Saca (2004–09), was again victorious in presidential elections in 2004.

From its murky origins as an organisation linked to paramilitaries, ARENA has evolved into a modern political party with a sophisticated electoral machine and slick public relations. The party's principles place the individual at the heart of political action and recognise the family as the nucleus of society. ARENA characterises the state as an instrument for improving the individual's condition, and argues that achieving state power is not an end in itself. The role of the state is to guarantee work, the well-being of the fatherland and a productive, free-market economy. ARENA's principles state that three themes must determine the conduct of Salvadoreans, 'God, fatherland and liberty', and, in common with conservative parties that have religious antecedents, it develops a notion of human dignity as the basis of social development. The party says the right to own private property is indispensable to achieving and enriching that dignity and, in a reference to its anti-communist origins, rejects all doctrines based on 'class conflict'. However, while insisting that all are equal before God, it also takes a secular political position that insists religion must not be mixed with politics, distancing itself from the Church as an institution in a similar way to many Christian democratic parties.

whereby rivals such as Argentina's Peronist president Carlos Menem (1989–99) adopted elements of their neoliberal agenda. Recent left-of-centre administrations in Latin America have reacted against some elements of neoliberalism by enhancing the role of the state in the economy and introducing targeted social reforms (see above), while often accepting basic neoliberal premises, such as deregulation to encourage private enterprise, removing barriers to foreign investment, and free-trade agreements that support the effort to compete in a globalised economy. Only in a few cases have privatisations, for example, been reversed through nationalisation.

While there is little doubt that popular attitudes have changed towards the so-called 'Washington Consensus' – a loose set of policy prescriptions based on market liberalisation advocated by a range of international financial institutions, multilateral lenders and powerful countries such as the US – conservatives in Latin America continue to advocate these ideas (see Box 15.1). At the same time, economic stability and growth has created new corporate interests and in countries such as Brazil an increasingly powerful financial sector (see Chapter 7), groups that offer a natural constituency for the Right. Neoliberal ideas continue to provide politicians with the opportunity to present themselves as modernisers, particularly within their own parties, and to appeal to such new economic interests. In Paraguay, for example, the two main contenders for the Colorado Party's nomination prior to the 2008 presidential elections reflected the differences between a traditionalist 'old right' and a business-led 'new right' (see Dangl and Howard, 2008). Blanca Ovelar, a former minister of education, represented a more traditionalist strain within the party aiming to appeal paternalistically to the country's poor, while Luis Castiglioni, a former vice president, represented a new rightwing faction linked to interests whose power has grown since the end of the dictatorship of General Alfredo Stroessner (1954–89), such as soya growers, cattle ranchers and transnational agribusinesses. Castiglioni, who just failed to gain the nomination, is a promoter of neoliberal policies with whom Washington has cultivated close ties, especially on trade. A recurrent theme of neoliberals on the Latin American right today is tackling corruption, with contenders such as Castiglioni linking ideas such as the need to dismantle traditional corporatist structures (see above, and Box 7.1) with ideas of economic deregulation and private involvement in the provision of public services.

Alongside conservative ideas, there is considerable support for the free market in Latin America, although this has oscillated, and Latinobarómetro data in 2009 suggested that 47 per cent of Latin Americans believed the market economy was the only way a country could become developed (Latinobarómetro, 2009a). Satisfaction with privatised services has also grown steadily in the region, although support for the state and its role in the economy remains strong. Voters in countries that have experienced high rates of growth, such as Panama, have also responded to the message of rightwing candidates such as Ricardo Martinelli (2009–) that they are better placed to steer their countries through the global economic crisis.

Contemporary conservatism

Latin American parties on the Right today can be divided into those that are self-declared conservatives and those on the centre or centre-right that share a conservative perspective. At least 20 Latin American parties are affiliated in some way to the International Democrat Union – a grouping of conservative and, in

Table 12.4 Parties affiliated to the Unión de Partidos Latinoamericanos (UPLA), International Democrat Union (IDU) or Americas Democrat Union (ADU)*

Country	Member or associate member
Argentina	Union Del Centro Democratico (UCEDE, Union of the Democratic Centre) Recrear Para El Crecimiento (RECREAR, Recreate for Growth)
Bolivia	Acción Democrática Nacionalista (ADN, Nationalist Democratic Action) PODEMOS (Poder Democrático y Social, Social and Democratic Power)
Chile	Union Democrata Independiente (UDI, Independent Democrat Union) Partido Renovacion Nacional (RN, National Renewal Party)
Colombia	Partido Conservador Colombiano (PCC, Conservative Party of Colombia)
Costa Rica	Partido Integración Nacional (PIN, National Integration Party)
Dominican Republic	Partido Reformista Social Cristiano (PRSC, Social Christian Reformist Party) Fuerza Nacional Progresista (FNP, National Progressive Force)
Ecuador	Partido Social Cristiano (PSC, Social Christian Party)
El Salvador	Alianza Republicana Nacionalista (ARENA, Nationalist Republican Alliance)
Guatemala	Partido de Avanzada Nacional (PAN, National Advancement Party) Partido Unionista (PU, Unionist Party)
Honduras	Partido Nacional de Honduras (PNH, National Party of Honduras)
Nicaragua	Partido Conservador de Nicaragua (PCN, Conservative Party of Nicaragua)
Panama	Partido Panameñista (PP, Panameñista Party)
Paraguay	Asociación Nacional Republicana/Partido Colorado (ANR/PC, National Republican Association – Colorado Party)
Peru	Partido Popular Cristiano (PPC, Popular Christian Party)
Venezuela	Proyecto Venezuela (PV, Project Venezuela)

*As of November 2009

Source: UPLA, 2009; IDU, 2009

some cases, Christian democratic, parties based in Oslo – or to its regional grouping, the Unión de Partidos Latinoaméricanos (UPLA, Union of Latin American Parties, see Table 12.4).

The language of contemporary conservatism in Latin America blends traditional themes with new emphases, although fringe elements on the far-right that draw heavily on the racist themes which developed originally within positivism continue in existence (see Box 12.13, and above). Conservatives now speak more about economic development and social justice and less about order and discipline; continue to couch their programmes in terms of Catholic social philosophy and traditional principles; and continue to use concepts such as Christian morality, social harmony and the 'common good'. However, a key issue in the study of conservatives and the Right in Latin America today is their heterogeneity and, hence, the extent to which they can in fact be incorporated within one ideological category at all (see Seligson, 2003). Some observers argue that an 'ultra-right' has emerged in both Mexico and Colombia defined increasingly by the securitisation of policy against drug-trafficking and associated with paramilitary activity (Zibechi, 2008).

One result of conservative gains in politics has been a new relationship with the Church. In Mexico, Vicente Fox (2000–06) of the PAN became the country's first openly Catholic president since the 1920s. For the PAN and other conservative

Box 12.13

The far right

In the late 1990s, Argentina emerged as an important base for far-right and neo-Nazi groups in Latin America anxious to take advantage of what the Simon Wiesenthal Jewish human rights organisation argued were outdated anti-discrimination laws and ready access to the internet (Barraclough, 2002). Argentina also has the largest Jewish community in Latin America, with about 180,000 Jews out of a total population of over 40 million people, and this has been the target of terrorist attacks. In 1992, the Israeli embassy was bombed, killing 32 people, and in 1994, a Jewish community centre in Buenos Aires was bombed, killing 85 people. Argentine prosecutors have alleged Islamic militants carried out the community centre attack, although the militant group Hezbollah has denied this and independent investigators have expressed scepticism about the claim. The attack continues to have political ramifications: in October 2009, a judge indicted the former president Carlos Menem for allegedly trying to cover up evidence related to the case (bbc.co.uk, 2009c). He has denied wrongdoing.

The Stephen Roth Institute at Tel Aviv University has monitored neo-Nazi individuals and groups operating in Argentina. The main party on the far-right active in Argentina has been the Partido Nuevo Triunfo (PNT, New Triumph Party), led by Alejandro Biondini, who is alleged to have appeared at public meetings in SS-style uniforms giving the Nazi salute. The PNT became one of the first far-right groups in Latin America to start disseminating material on the internet. It was dissolved in March 2009 after Argentina's supreme court refused it recognition as a political party. A second and smaller organisation, the Partido Nuevo Orden Social Patriótico (PNOSP, New Order Social Patriotic Party) has also operated. Its members were alleged to have worn neo-Nazi uniforms and performed the fascist salute at gatherings. The PNT was at the centre of plans by neo-Nazi groups from Argentina, Brazil, Chile and Uruguay to hold a congress in 2000 in Chile on the anniversary of Adolf Hitler's birthday, but the event was banned by Chilean authorities.

Anti-fascism campaigners say a large number of extremist websites were launched in the late 1990s from within Argentina, where internet penetration was then one of the highest in Latin America. Outdated anti-discrimination rules that did not cover the internet and government promises not to interfere with internet activity were considered the main factors making the country attractive to extremists. Argentina's severe economic crisis after 2001 also made it a cheap place for foreign groups to set up hosting facilities. The Stephen Roth Institute says extreme rightwing groups continue to publish a number of anti-Semitic nationalistic journals and websites in Argentina. Far-right websites run from Argentina are also thought to have provided a point of contact for extremists in Chile, Uruguay, Brazil and Europe.

Paramilitary organisations operating in countries such as Colombia can also be classified as being on the far right (see Mazzei, 2009). In November 2005, the Autodefensas Unidas de Colombia (AUC, United Self-defence forces of Colombia) paramilitary organisation resumed disarmament after a long period of stop-start peace talks with the Colombian government. The organisation is an umbrella group of rightwing militias set up to protect the property of wealthy landowners and drug-traffickers from Marxist guerrillas, and it has been blamed for atrocities. Paramilitaries often have links with the political right and security forces. In October 2005, for example, Colombia's intelligence chief Jorge Noguera resigned amid allegations that his security agency, the Departamento Administrativo de Seguridad (DAS, Administrative Security Department) had been infiltrated by rightwing paramilitaries. In late 2009, a former Colombian general, Jaime Humberto Uscátegui, was sentenced to 40 years in jail after a court was told that he had knowingly let AUC death squads use his base (bbc.co.uk., 2009b). He pledged to appeal. Rightwing elements have also, at times, been influenced by religious ideas and radical Christianity (see Graziano, 1992).

Sources: Barraclough, 2002; The Stephen Roth Institute, 2000, 2007; bbc.co.uk, 2009b, 2009c

parties with religious roots, democracy is still put at the service of achieving the 'common good' and this principle lies at the heart of the PAN's party documents. Here, the common good stands for hostility to the liberal state, especially unrestrained liberal individualism. In Chile, the Unión Demócrata Independiente (UDI, Independent Democrat Union) begins its statement of principles with similarly traditional positions:

> There exists an objective moral order which is inscribed in human nature. The organization of society and all of its cultural, institutional and economic development must obey this moral order, which is the foundation of Western and Christian civilization. From the spiritual and transcendent dignity of the human being emanate rights inherent by their very nature that are anterior and superior to the State . . . The family, the basic nucleus of society, must be respected and strengthened. People have the right to form groups with the autonomy to pursue specific aims that are intermediate between the family and the State. The State exists to promote the common good, generally understood as a conjunction of social conditions that allow each member of the national community to realize their fullest material and spiritual possibilities.

Source: UDI, 2010

INSTITUTIONS   **Box 12.14**

El Yunque in Mexico

Ortiz (2008) has argued that a secretive socially conservative group within Mexico's ruling PAN called *El Yunque* (the Anvil) – which is heir to a tradition deriving from the country's 'cristero' movement that launched a rebellion in the 1920s against the secularisation of the Mexican state – has been engaged in an ideological confrontation with supporters of President Felipe Calderón (2006–). Ortiz claims that *Yunque* supporters occupied several key positions in the previous PAN administration of Vicente Fox (2000–06). In particular, Mexican journalists have identified Manuel Espino, president of the PAN from 2000–08, with the group (see Delgado, 2006). *El Yunque* has also been associated with the creation of a new Catholic party in Mexico that was officially registered in late 2007: the Movimiento de Participación Solidaria (MPS, Movement of Co-operative Participation) whose founders include former prominent *panistas* such as René Bolio, who resigned from Calderón's government to promote the party, and Enrique Pérez Luján, the leader of the Unión Nacional Sinarquista (UNS, National Synarchist Union), a rightwing Catholic movement whose positions have been likened to fascism (see Rodríguez, 2007). According to those who have studied *El Yunque*, its supporters want to replace what they see as a godless, secular state with a theocratic Catholic state, the 'City of God'. They are angry at what they see as a pragmatic, opportunistic drift by the 'humanist' centre of the Calderón administration away from the Catholic founding principles of the PAN and want stricter controls on the activities of women and sexual minorities, indigenous communities, trade unions, and the non-Catholic population in general. Lastly, they also regard as their historical mission opposing Judaism, and believe Zionism has become influential within the Calderón government. Ortiz (2008) argues that most new members of *El Yunque* are pious adolescents recruited from private Catholic schools, whose vow of secrecy makes it difficult to track the activities of the organisation. At the same time, more secular and humanist groups within the PAN have been closing ranks in support of Calderón, exacerbating divisions within the party, one reflection of which was the formation of the MPS.

Many contemporary Latin American conservative politicians, such as Ricardo Martinelli in Panama, are Catholics, even if they may not employ this openly to appeal to voters. However, the church and Catholic principles face considerable challenges in Latin America's rapidly changing societies. In 2007, for example, Pope Benedict XVI outlined these challenges in an address to the Pontifical Commission for Latin America (see Pope Benedict XVI, 2007). Among the key themes he identified were: cultural changes to morals and beliefs generated by the mass media; the repercussions on family life and religious practice of migration; questions generated by democratisation about the role of Catholicism in history; globalisation, secularism, violence and the drug trade. Cultural and social concerns have in some cases prompted Catholic activists to lobby for more conservative social policies, aiming to push their parties to the right. In Mexico, for example, attention has been given to the emergence of divisions within the PAN between supporters of the current president, Felipe Calderón, and religiously-inspired groups further to the right such as *El Yunque* (see Box 12.14) whose power-base in the party has apparently grown. In Nicaragua, Catholic and evangelical activists have often joined forces against feminism (see Chapter 13) and in 2006 influenced the debate on abortion, which was outlawed without exception (see Kampwirth, 2008).

Summary

Since Independence, Latin America has been a net importer of ideas, ideology and social theory. Ideas have been shaped by the interaction of Latin America's distinctive historical legacies and resulting divisions around centralism, the liberal heritage, the revolutionary tradition, scientific notions known as positivism, and corporatism.

The clash between leftwing and rightwing ideas has had a particularly important influence upon Latin America's political evolution, often reflecting deep class divisions. The origins of the Left in Latin America were diverse, but after 1917 socialism and communism began to make headway among the organised working class, although Marxist ideas have found it hard to adapt to Latin American conditions. Key themes of debate on the left in Latin America were the character of the forthcoming socialist revolution; the extent to which the proletariat should make alliances with other classes; and attitudes towards electoral politics. The Left failed to come to terms with the issue that limited its relevance in the region: the peasant question. The Cuban Revolution (1959) transformed the prospects of Marxism in Latin America at the height of the Cold War, but split the Left. It revived interest in Marxist theory and influenced the emergence within the Church of liberation theology. The military intervention in Chile against Allende (1970–73) demonstrated the dilemmas faced by a left confronted with a choice between the Cuban revolutionary option and the option of peaceful change. The different strategies that evolved out of the military period were either a renewed commitment to armed struggle or the acceptance of democratic, reformist socialism. However, the guerrilla movements that survived into the 1990s evolved differently to their predecessors inspired by the Cuban Revolution. Armed actions were not aimed at defeating governments, but forcing them to negotiate. The impact of *perestroika* and *glasnost* in the Soviet Union further polarised the Left in Latin America between those who continued to advocate profound structural change and reformists. Since the 1990s, positions on the left have been shaped by neoliberal reform, democratisation and the related emergence of social movements. The strength of social-democratic arguments advocating a third way between capitalism and socialism has grown. Until the 1980s, leftwing parties had rarely enjoyed widespread acceptance among voters, but many began to participate fully within the institutional structures of democracy. Since 1998, left-of-centre leaders and former radicals have come to power in many countries in Latin America, comprising what has been described as a 'pink tide' of mainly social-democratic positions. This has sparked a debate about what is now left and right. Democratisation filled the void left by the decline of socialist critiques and the growth of social movements has also been an important focus of leftwing ideas, which have gained new impetus through the notion of 'socialism for the twenty-first century' championed by some left-of-centre governments.

The Roman Catholic Church and Christian thought played a formative role in the evolution of political conservatism in Latin America. Traditionalism has been a core theme in conservative thought, but in the late nineteenth century divisions grew between moderates less wedded to tradition who were more inclined to accept positivist ideas and those who were more doctrinaire and saw conservative ideas as divinely inspired. The growing popularity of fascism in Europe posed dilemmas for the Latin American right and fuelled divisions among conservatives. Christian democracy grew rapidly in some countries in the Cold War atmosphere as a new political offering able to attract support from both left and right. During the period of military rule in much of Latin America in the 1960s and 1970s, civilian conservative forces generally converged with military actors. This co-operation revealed much about conservative attitudes towards democracy and, even today, the Right is often assessed from the position of a fear of coups and there are examples of it mounting opposition to a strengthened left outside the formal institutions of democratic politics. However, the restoration of democracy in the 1980s was in general accompanied by a new commitment to party pluralism and the creation of new conservative parties, which were often prominent in the process of democratisation itself. The role of the Right in shaping Latin America's democracies has become important to their future stability and has also changed the meaning of the term 'democracy' by contributing to an emphasis on its procedural aspects. The neoliberal critique of the state's economic role gave conservatives a potent ideological tool in the new era and challenged the notion that their programmes did not advance radical agendas. Today, Latin American parties on the right can be divided into those that are self-declared conservatives and those on the centre or centre-right that share a conservative perspective. The language of contemporary conservatism in Latin America blends traditional themes with new emphases, although fringe elements on the far right continue in existence. Despite leftwing gains throughout Latin America, the Right remains a potent force and some scholars suggest that it is enjoying a resurgence.

Discussion points

- Do the legacies of centralism and liberalism influence political ideas today?

- Why does Latin America have such a potent revolutionary tradition?

- Is the socialist model unrealistic following the collapse of the Soviet bloc?

- Does Gramsci offer a more appropriate basis for socialist debate in the twenty-first century?

- To what extent are Latin American conservatives committed to democracy?

- How do Christian democracy and traditional conservatism differ?

Useful websites

http://prdpanama.org/prdpa Partido Revolucionario Democrática of Panama

www.frenteamplio.org.uy Encuentro Progresista-Frente Amplio (EP-FA, Broad Front-Progressive Encounter), Uruguay

www.partidoliberaldehonduras.hn Partido Liberal de Honduras (PLH, Honduran Liberal Party)

www.psuv.org.ve Partido Socialista Unido de Venezuela (PSUV, United Socialist Party of Venezuela)

www.pcchile.cl Partido Comunista de Chile (PCCh, Chilean Communist Party)

www.partidoliberal.org.co/portal Partido Liberal Colombiano (PL, Colombian Liberal Party)

www.socialistinternational.org/viewArticle.cfm?ArticleID=1990 Socialist International Committee for Latin America and the Caribbean

www.pan.org.mx Partido Acción Nacional (PAN, National Action Party), main Mexican conservative party

www.partidoconservador.com Partido Conservador Colombiano (PCC, Colombian Conservative Party)

www.rn.cl Renovación Nacional (RN, National Renewal), Chilean conservative party

www.udi.cl Unión Demócrata Independiente (UDI, Independent Democratic Union), Chilean conservative party

www.idu.org International Democrat Union

www.odca.org.mx Organización Demócrata Cristiana de América

www.pdc.cl Partido Demócrata Cristiano de Chile (PDC, Chilean Christian Democractic Party)

www.ppc-peru.org Partido Popular Cristiano (PPC, Christian Popular Party), Peru

www.pfl.org.br Partido da Frente Liberal (PFL, 'Democratas', Liberal Front Party), Brazil

www.partidounidadsocialcristiana.com Partido Unidad Social Cristiana (PUSC, Social Christian Unity Party), Costa Rica

www.tau.ac.il/Anti-Semitism Stephen Roth Institute for the Study of Contemporary Antisemitism and Racism

Recommended reading

Bethell, Leslie (ed.). 1996. *Ideas and Ideologies in Twentieth Century Latin America.* Cambridge: Cambridge University Press

Essential introduction to the study of ideas in Latin American bringing together five essays that examine identity, political and economic ideas, liberation theology and scientific thought since the nineteenth century

Lievesley, Geraldine and Steve Ludlam (eds). 2009. *Reclaiming Latin America: Experiments in Radical Social Democracy.* London: Zed Books

Essential introduction to the contemporary left in Latin America that explores, above all, its diversity

Wilpert, Gregory. 2006. *Changing Venezuela by Taking Power.* London: Verso

Valuable critical examination of the social and economic record of the pioneer of 'twenty-first-century socialism', Hugo Chávez

Gutiérrez, Gustavo. 1973. *A Theology of Liberation.* New York: Orbis

Essential introduction to the core underlying arguments of liberation theology and the attempt to reconcile Catholic thought with Marxist ideas

Middlebrook, Kevin (ed.). 2000. *Conservative Parties, the Right, and Democracy in Latin America.* Baltimore, MD: Johns Hopkins University Press

Essential introduction to the evolution of the Right in Latin America that develops a valuable analytical approach for understanding the behaviour of conservative parties

Lynch, Edward. 1991. *Religion and Politics in Latin America. Liberation Theology and Christian Democracy.* New York: Praeger

Valuable theoretical exploration of the main underlying ideas of both Christian democracy and liberation theology that also looks more broadly at the relationship between religion and politics

Zibechi, Raúl. 2008. 'The New Latin American Right: Finding a Place in the World', *NACLA Report on the Americas*, Vol. 41, No. 1 (January), pp. 12–13

Valuable introduction to the contemporary Right in Latin America in a special edition of this journal devoted to this theme, with examples of how the Right has regrouped in the region

Chapter 13

Identities: Nationalism, Race and Feminism

This chapter examines ideas and themes concerning *identity* that have been important to Latin America's political evolution. Latin America's history as a conquered region colonised by European settlers who co-existed with large indigenous and imported slave populations has always made questions of personal and group identity prominent in political and social thought. Efforts by emergent states to forge unified national identities out of diverse and often fragmented societies have both been built upon, and come into conflict with, the reality of indigenous ethnicity. Slave populations, long ignored and discriminated against by dominant groups, have asserted their contribution to history and the cultural hybridity of modern Latin America.

Activity motivated by identification with a national idea, ethnicity and race, or gender have become an increasingly important theme in the study of politics since the end of the Cold War. That is partly the result of the challenges posed by the collapse of the socialist bloc to traditional class-based arguments (see Chapter 12), and of globalisation that tests loyalties to historical entities such as the nation-state (see Box 15.6). In Latin America, a growth in political activity motivated by such themes has also been the product of democratisation, which can bring with it new attitudes based on a new pluralism (see Chapter 3). Ethnicity and gender themes represent key examples of new directions in politics associated with the emergence of social movements (see Chapter 8).

Ideas deriving from a sense of identification with a nation, ethnicity, race or gender can be powerful forces in politics that both unite and divide societies. However, these ideas can at times compete for an individual's loyalties, and while political ideas deriving from identity often imply the pursuit of equality or fair treatment for certain social groups this can also, by implication, sometimes be at the expense of others. Moreover, while they may be potent mobilising forces, political ideas deriving from a sense of identification may not offer a coherent strategy and policy framework in a wide range of areas of modern governance.

Nationalism

Debates among scholars about the character and content of nationalism have been complex ever since they first started exploring what the 'nation' really means.

There is general agreement that nationalism as an ideology emerged from such Enlightenment and Romantic notions as popular sovereignty, self-determination and the idea of separate cultures with their own essences evolving organically as if they were living things (see Box 1.1). There is also agreement that nationalism appeared in Latin America in an early form at the time of Independence (see Chapter 1). The automatic framework for the region's post-Independence political systems was the nation-state, although continentalist ideas were popular (see Box 13.1).

THEORIES AND DEBATES   Box 13.1

Continentalism

A cousin of nationalism in Latin America has been continentalism, a form of pan-Latin American nationalism which emerged during the Independence struggles yet stills finds expression today and has been the natural bedfellow of anti-imperialism (see Chapter 9, Box 10.1). At the beginning of the nineteenth century, there were many proposals to model independent South America on the federal system of the US. The Liberator Simón Bolívar (b.1783–d.1830) hoped for a political association among the new Latin American republics and articulated a range of continentalist visions, ranging from a huge sub-continental federation to aspirations to unite sub-regions such as the Andes (Collier, 1983).

Continentalism has sometimes been understood as a synthesis of the individual nationalisms of Latin America, expressed in the notion of *la patria grande* – the greater fatherland. Although concrete ideas of continental unity have been based on political and economic criteria, they have often taken as their implicit point of reference the shared history and affinities of the peoples of this cultural region. Some nationalist writers, such as the Cuban Jorge Mañach (b.1898–d.1961) and the Mexican Leopoldo Zea (b.1912–d.2004), emphasised the existence of a discrete Latin American psychology. *Ariel*, a highly influential work written in 1900 by the Uruguayan essayist José Enrique Rodó (b.1872–d.1917), can be seen as an effort to give Latin American intellectuals a psychological basis for differentiating 'their' America and rejecting *nordomanía*, an uncritical obsession with the North (see below). The Peruvian philosopher Antenor Orrego (b.1892–d.1960) rejected all Latin American 'national cultures' as byproducts of colonialism.

Continentalist ideas reinforced the evolution of a politically oriented anti-imperialism, particularly on the left and among intellectuals developing ideas of 'Indo-Americanism' who identified more closely with Latin America's indigenous cultures (see below, and Box 12.1). They influenced the formation of the Alianza Popular Revolucionaria Americana (APRA, American Revolutionary Popular Alliance), which called for Latin American political unity in response to 'yankee imperialism'. The Left has often expressed Pan-Latin Americanist sentiments. In the 1930s and 1940s, communists made nationalism a prominent theme, largely because this helped to foster antagonism to the US. The anti-Americanism and anti-imperialism of Cuban revolutionaries such as Che Guevara (see Boxes 2.3, 9.3, 10.8, 12.2) were strongly infused with a continental nationalism, although it is also likely that Latin Americans disliked Castro's links with the Soviet bloc *because* of their continentalism. More recently, the foreign policy vision of prominent leftwing leaders such as Hugo Chávez in Venezuela has been founded on continentalist ideas and traditional notions of anti-imperialism. The Alianza Bolivariana para los Pueblos de Nuestra América (ALBA, the Bolivarian Alliance for the Peoples of Our America), an organisation created by Chávez to promote integration between Latin American states, is an institutional expression of this vision (see Boxes 9.1, 16.1).

From Independence to the late nineteenth century, Latin American leaders copied the liberal nationalism of Europe, where nationalist ideas had mainly political implications: popular sovereignty, individual rights and representative and constitutional government. Even to the great hero of Independence, Simón Bolívar (b.1783–d.1830), the main criterion of nationality was political and he did not develop ideas linking nationalism to cultural, linguistic or religious factors (Collier, 1983). However, Velíz (1980) has argued that the republican nationalism of nineteenth-century Latin America differed from the nationalism of Europe in one important respect: by being outward looking through a rejection of its own Hispanic past combined with attempts to imitate Britain and France. As a result, nationalist ideas were not a 'natural' development in Latin America in the same way they had been in Europe, and large sectors of the populations in the new republics were probably not aware of their potential nationality (Collier, 1983). One anomaly this bequeathed in Latin America was that the creation of the state *preceded* a generalised acceptance of the existence of the 'nation' in the ethnically diverse republics of the region. Independence created states without defined national identities whose borders were not based on pre-existing cultural divisions. This meant that awareness of a national consciousness or identity was usually an elite, intellectual affair long before it became a mass characteristic. As a result, one objective of the new states governed by elites became the *creation* of nations, and a key theme in nationalist thought in Latin America has been the notion of 'nation-building' – the forging of a unified nationality based on a discernible national identity. Although it varied significantly across Latin America, the process of nation-building could often be associated with the consolidation of a strong state in keeping with the centralist tradition (see Box 2.1, Chapter 12). In Mexico, national consciousness began to emerge from confrontation in the nineteenth century with outside powers such as the US. In Cuba and Nicaragua, the persistence of colonialism delayed the emergence of a strong sense of nationhood well into the twentieth century.

The underlying idea of a community of shared interests has retained its force in Latin America, although it has arguably been weakened by disparities in the levels of development achieved by individual countries. For example, several disputes between Brazil and Argentina within Mercosur (see Box 9.9) have been caused by such disparities. There have been many efforts at institutionalising regional economic or political co-operation, all revealing limited contintentalist aspirations of some kind. Yet nationalism has been stronger than continentalism as a mobilising force in Latin American politics, although the growth of such regional economic associations as Mercosur has fostered increasing levels of political co-operation between states. The decision by Venezuela to become a full member of Mercosur attests to the strong 'Bolivarian' commitment of its leader, Hugo Chávez (1999–). Ideas floated by Chávez with his Latin American counterparts have been behind the creation of a number of institutions to spearhead regional integration and eventually pave the way for a South American union, and Chávez has also developed plans for infrastructure to provide energy supplies at a continental level (see Chapter 9). He has also spearheaded cultural initiatives based on a contintentalist aspiration, such as the creation of the TeleSUR broadcasting network (see Box 13.4). Economic co-operation may help to offer an explanation for the limited impact of contintentalism in Latin America. The predominance of nation-states and the consequent evolution of nationalism may reflect the way in which it best suited elites to organise states in order to participate most beneficially in the world economy, just as growing levels of economic co-operation between states today is a response to an increasingly competitive globalised economy (see Chapter 15). The latest effort to unite the region took the form in 2008 of the intergovernmental integration initiative, the Union of South American Nations (Unasur) modelled on the European Union and backed by its own regional investment bank, the Banco del Sur. A key objective of Unasur is the creation of a single market by 2019 that eliminates cross-border tariffs (see Chapter 9).

As Latin America began to participate more fully in the export economy towards the end of the nineteenth century, hostility towards foreign capitalists grew, and in the 1890s an economic content was injected into nationalism. The desire of elites to win or assert national control over resources and economies has often found an expression as 'anti-imperialism' or taken the form of a xenophobic anti-Americanism (see Boxes 9.3, 10.1). In this way, expressions of nationalism in Latin America at the dawn of the twentieth century can, in part, be seen as a product of the developing world's *encounter* with the capitalism of the developed world. Latin American thinkers began to take more idealistic and romantic positions in the early decades of the twentieth century amid a backlash against positivist ideas (see Chapter 12), partly in response to the expansion in the region of capitalist development dominated by the US. The US had extended its borders at the expense of Mexico (see Box 1.4) and the existence of large US sugar interests in Cuba encouraged it to end Spanish rule on the island in 1898, turning Cuba into a protectorate (see Boxes 2.3, 10.8). The US also took control of Puerto Rico, the status of which is still being debated today, that provides an example of how durable nationalism can be in Latin America (see Box 13.2). Latin American republics began to feel that US doctrines threatened both territorial expansion at their expense and interference in their affairs. Cultural anxieties were articulated in 1900 by the Uruguayan writer José Enrique Rodó (see Box 13.1) in his essay, *Ariel*, an important statement of 'yankeephobia' that denounced US utilitarianism and materialism and fostered the stereotype of the avaricious North American who could become

---

CASE STUDY   **Box 13.2**

Puerto Rican nationalism

Puerto Rico provides an example of the enduring appeal of nationalism in Latin America, and organised political movements advocating independence first from Spain, and thereafter from the US, have existed on the island since the mid-nineteenth century. These have adopted both peaceful approaches to change as well as violent revolutionary tactics, and today a number of nationalist groups and parties exist. Ceded in 1898 following the Spanish-American War, Puerto Rico has been under US control for more than 111 years, and the status of this relationship has been debated and has risen up the political agenda in Latin America (see Box 10.6). Nationalism that has primarily had the political objective of independence has been an important current in Puerto Rican politics, and a history of nationalistic activism has punctuated its relationship with the US (see González-Cruz, 2006).

▶

Nationalists were involved in periodic clashes with security forces and assassination attempts in the run up to the Second World War and, in 1948, the US-appointed governor of Puerto Rico pushed through a law that made it illegal to display the Puerto Rican flag, sing patriotic songs and discuss independence. This set the scene for a nationalist uprising in 1950 that coincided with the start of a process that would result in 'commonwealth' status for the island. This supposed continued US sovereignty but gave Puerto Rico its own constitution and a degree of autonomy that can be likened to that of a state. The 1950 uprising was characterised by skirmishes in several towns on the island and, in Washington DC, by an unsuccessful attempt to assassinate the US president, Harry Truman. Nationalist tensions continued after commonwealth status had been established, and in 1954 a group of Puerto Rican nationalists opened fire with pistols at the US House of Representatives in Washington, wounding five legislators. In the 1960s, the main nationalist party split and several guerrilla organisations were formed aiming at independence, the most significant of which would become the Ejército Popular Boricua (EPB, Boricua Popular Army) whose leader, Filiberto Ojeda Ríos, was killed in 2005 by the FBI. The EPB also carried out activities within the continental US and remains extant, albeit inactive. US security agencies have long maintained surveillance of political activists seeking independence for the island, and have at times acted to disrupt their activities. Today, most nationalists in Puerto Rico belong to the main political organisation advocating independence, the Partido Independentista Puertorriqueño (PIP, Puerto Rican Independence Party), although this has struggled to gain sufficient voter support to maintain its official registration while enjoying considerable, high-profile international backing.

Puerto Rican nationalism has exhibited many of the characteristics common to most nationalisms, not least the notion of millennial origins. Puerto Ricans often identify themselves as Boricua, derived from a word of the country's original Taíno people, and allowing for an historical association with the island's pre-Columbian heritage. Patriotic sacrifice also forms part of nationalist mythology. In 1920, for example, nationalists successfully lobbied the island's assembly for the return from France of the remains of the patriot Ramón Emeterio Betances, thereby providing impetus for the unification of a fragmented independence movement. Puerto Rican nationalists have also been able to draw upon and share potent figures in the wider nationalist history of Latin America, and have enjoyed the vocal support of Cuba's revolutionary regime (see Schoultz, 2009). For example, José Martí, the Cuban national hero and a key figure in the delineation of Latin American identity, was the architect of the Cuban Revolutionary Party in 1892 whose founding statutes included among its aims aiding the achievement of Puerto Rican independence. In the more recent era, Cuba has recurrently raised at the UN the issue of Puerto Rican independence and linked it with Cuban history. Fidel Castro has answered the argument often made by US policymakers that only a tiny minority of Puerto Ricans favour independence with the idea that, prior to US independence, few North Americans wanted independence either (*ibid.*). Puerto Rico's economic dependence on the US – which accounts for 90 per cent of trade – has also been a key theme of nationalists (see Chapter 15). They argue that the foreign sector (i.e. the US) dominates both production and consumption and the dependent economy that has been created on the island is characterised by stagnation, over-exposure to crisis, and lower levels of development than in the US itself: personal income in Puerto Rico is significantly lower than in the US, for example, while unemployment is significantly higher (see US Fed News, 2008). The island's economy remains sensitive to developments in the US and, since 2005 has been contracting, with a deficit estimated in 2009 at $3.2 billion (see Cave, 2009). Confronted with a three-year recession, the island's governor, Luis Fortuño (2009–), unveiled an economic recovery plan that foresaw large spending cuts, prompting demonstrations in San Juan. In October 2009, his plan to lay off more than 20,000 workers provoked a general strike in the Puerto Rican capital.

a recognisable target for nationalists. Rodó called for a revival of idealism by invoking a common Latin American spirit.

An association between nationalism and economic and social themes also reflected the simultaneous development in politics in the early twentieth century of mass constituencies through the integration of new groups into the class structure (see Chapter 2). A nation could not be built without a popular constituency, so nationalists had to take up the demands of other sectors. Nationalism and anti-US feelings were often adopted by urban middle-class politicians ambitious to challenge the traditional oligarchies of landowners and merchants and seeking the support of workers. The potent attraction of nationalism in Latin America in this period can be linked to the development of mass politics, and alongside liberalism (and, many feminists would argue, patriarchy, see below) nationalism is the only ideology that can be said to have been hegemonic in many Latin American countries at a given phase in their evolution. Nationalist values, beliefs or ideas were often shared by social groups, and this could sometimes allow dominant elites to shape politics. The growth of nationalism as a political tool reinforced the search for an authentic national culture and fuelled the development of *cultural* nationalism, which began to find concrete expression in notions like 'Argentinidad' (the distinct quality of being Argentinean) developed by writers such as Ricardo Rojas (b.1882–d.1957). Argentine nationalism was expressed through nationalist education and xenophobia in terms of a positive image of the native Argentinean and a negative image of immigrants. Catholic writers were influential in the effort to delineate Argentine qualities and also fuelled anti-Semitism (see Chapter 12).

In Mexico, the fusion of economic and cultural ideas produced a revolutionary cocktail and the revolution of 1910–17 represented an important landmark in the evolution of Latin American nationalism, especially for republics with large indigenous populations. Mexico provided an example of the strong influence the revolutionary tradition has had upon nationalist ideas (see Box 1.5, Chapter 12). Most of the different revolutionary factions converged on the idea of nationalism or had a nationalistic objective at the heart of their agenda. In particular, the revolution gave impetus to the process of nation-building – *forjando patria* in the words of the writer Manuel Gamio (b.1883–d.1960). Intellectuals such as Gamio attributed the fundamental problems Mexico faced to its *failure* to construct a unified nationality, and the solution lay in a process of social integration that would bring different groups together under the aegis of a shared national culture. Masur (1966) used the term 'integral nationalism' to describe the framework of Mexico's revolution, with the state that it produced aiming, above all, to *integrate* society. The revolution gave expression to the first systematic effort by a Latin American state to inculcate in the population a coherent cultural nationalism. Mexico's history was rewritten, its pre-Columbian grandeur rediscovered and its art, folklore and dance revalued. A key strain of nationalist thought aimed to reconcile Mexico's indigenous and European races. Official recognition was given to the process of cultural mixing that led to the emergence of the Mexican people, and the cult of the *mestizo* blossomed. An influential figure in this effort was José Vasconcelos (b.1882–d.1959), revolutionary Mexico's education minister from 1921–24, who aspired to redeem indigenous people through education (see *indigenismo* below). Vasconcelos nurtured a new generation of artists and writers delineating the content of Mexican cultural nationalism. Mexican revolutionary ideology also gave force to the growing economic nationalism of the era, and new constitutional provisions placed natural resources in national hands.

By the mid-1920s, nationalist politicians generally remained too weak to win power through elections, which were often manipulated by conservative elites, and the armed forces became a vector of nationalism (see Chapter 1). In countries with large urban populations such as Brazil, Chile and Argentina, nationalism appealed to officers and, as the economic climate worsened, they began to intervene in politics. Chile was the first country to experience a nationalist revolution through a coup in 1925 that led to the dictatorship of General Carlos Ibáñez from 1927–31. Nationalism also formed the ideology of populist political movements that began to emerge in the 1920s and 1930s (see Chapter 2). Populism as a style of politics is often based upon charismatic leadership outside traditional parties and reflected in mass mobilisation. Notable populists included Juan Domingo Perón (1946–55, 1973–74) in Argentina, Getúlio Vargas (1930–45, 1951–54) in Brazil, and Victor Raúl Haya de la Torre (b.1895–d.1979) in Peru. Haya's Alianza Popular Revolucionaria Americana (APRA, American Revolutionary Popular Alliance) advocated Latin American unity, nationalisation in the economy, extensive social policies and anti-imperialism (see Chapters 9, 12). The impact of the Great Depression of the early 1930s generated nationalistic reactions, and in countries such as Brazil and Argentina nationalists proposed programmes of state-led industrialisation aiming to achieve sovereignty through self-sufficiency (see Chapter 14). The nationalistic mood and the persistence of external conditions favouring industrialisation would enhance the role of the state in promoting economic activity. By enhancing the role of the state, military and populist regimes with nationalist inclinations drew upon Latin America's traditions of centralism and authoritarianism. The Depression also increased political tensions, exacerbated by the growth of communism and the arrival of new radical ideas from Europe such as fascism (see Box 12.9), both of which saw nationalism as a valuable ideological tool.

Populism chimed well with the policymaking climate of the Depression era and had a natural affinity with nationalism by promoting a sense of inclusion for marginalised groups. However, populist coalitions were composed of rival interest groups and the nationalist message attracted different classes for different reasons at different times, ultimately preventing it from acting as a cohesive political ideology. While this national populism shared elements of the Left's programme, its nationalism, authoritarian streak and corporatist inclinations also suggested a rightwing inheritance (see Chapter 12). Such movements were often sympathetic to the Axis powers during the Second World War.

The war both discredited nationalism yet strengthened the conviction in Latin American countries that they would have to find their own way in a struggle for survival. As the victorious US began to advocate liberal-democracy abroad, nationalist governments began to seek an accommodation with liberalism. By the 1950s, populist movements were also being marginalised by more radical positions, such as those advanced by the Cuban Revolution (1959), and by the 1960s populism was becoming synonymous with the social-democratic aims of corporatist sectors of society that made claims on a strong central state (see Chapters 2, 7, 12). The military regimes of the 1970s advocated a form of autarkic (self-sufficient) nationalism, but also acted within a Cold War framework that highlighted Latin America's *dependent* status in a struggle between the superpowers (see Chapter 14). With democratisation in the 1980s, the armed forces were discredited and neoliberal ideas based on universal themes posed a stiff challenge to nationalist perspectives. In several Latin American countries in the 1990s, the leaders of parties with a strong national-populist tradition became champions of neoliberalism and overturned sacred revolutionary symbols (see Chapter 15). In Argentina, Carlos Menem (1989–99) turned traditional Peronist positions on their head and in Mexico, President Carlos Salinas de Gortari (1988–94) challenged the central tenets of the 'revolutionary nationalism' that had been developed as the official ideology of the ruling Partido Revolucionario Institucional (PRI, Institutional Revolutionary Party). However, nationalism may have been one reason these leaders were able to succeed with such radical policy shifts. Menem's assertive style and international prominence helped to nurture a new sense of national pride in an era of dizzying globalisation. Salinas was very aware of the ideological contradictions that existed between nationalism and the globalising neoliberal agenda. His response was to articulate through a slick presentation of policies a 'new nationalism' aiming to reconcile the competing claims of liberalism and nationalism (see O'Toole, 2003).

Strictly speaking, nationalism belongs to neither left nor right, although in Latin America there has been an affinity between nationalism and the Left because both have often shared the aspirations of nation-building, social integration and anti-imperialism. Nationalist positions have also often characterised social elites as being in an alliance with foreign capitalism and, in some countries, through references to the 'creole bourgeoisie', even as having a racial affinity with the stereotypical Anglo-Saxon or northern European. In Mexico and Peru, for example, nationalists have often made particular reference to the Hispanic or immigrant antecedents of ruling classes as opposed to the *mestizo* or indigenous origins of most ordinary people. In Peru in early 2005, militants advocating Inca nationalism were apprehended following a bloody siege in a town south-east of Lima (see Box 13.3). The group's programme made explicit reference to racial groups depicted as alien to the country. Positions based on racial arguments of this kind sometimes adopted by nationalists – especially when they express xenophobic sentiments – have much in common with arguments traditionally favoured by the Right and far right (see Chapter 12).

Given this language of anti-imperialism, anti-American sentiments have been an important component of nationalism on the left and have had a close relationship with revolutions (see Box 9.3). 'Revolutionary nationalism', which was refined into the official ideology of the PRI in Mexico, reflected the aspiration to protect economic sovereignty – principally against the US. The Cuban Revolution in 1959 also offered Latin Americans the hope of defeating 'imperialism', and nationalism was inserted into a Marxist framework that combined reformist notions of economic dependency with anti-Americanism. The revolutionary leader Fidel Castro was inspired by the romantic nationalism of José Martí (b.1853–d.1895), the poet-lawyer who had articulated a strong anti-Americanism. The idea that Latin Americans are vulnerable to powerful external forces and have to unite in order to protect their interests against foreigners is a potent undercurrent of both notions of

CASE STUDY	Box 13.3

The Inca nationalists

In January 2005, about 160 armed former soldiers led by retired army major Antauro Humala seized a police station in the southern Peruvian town of Andahuaylas to demand the resignation of President Alejandro Toledo (2001–06) whom they accused of 'selling out' the country to business interests in Chile. Humala's Movimiento Nacionalista Peruano (MNP, Peruvian Nationalist Movement) advocated a society based on indigenous culture and history modelled on the ancient Incan Empire, and espoused a message critical of Peru's European-descended elite. The retired officer first came to public attention in 2000 when he and his brother Ollanta Humala Tasso took part in a failed uprising against the then president Alberto Fujimori (1990–2000). In the 2005 incident, Toledo declared a state of emergency and the militants were apprehended after a four-day siege and Antauro Humala's surrender. The incident claimed six lives and led to the resignation of Peru's interior minister Javier Reategui. It added to the growing unpopularity of Toledo, who made history when he became Peru's first president of indigenous descent in 2001. Ollanta Humala, himself a former army officer, established the Partido Nacionalista Peruano (PNP, Peruvian Nationalist Party) and fought as a candidate in the country's 2006 presidential elections, winning 47 per cent of the vote against his victorious opponent's 52 per cent in a second round of voting. Some observers suggested the January 2005 uprising had been designed to boost his bid for the presidency. Today, the MNP is known as the Movimiento Etnocacerista, a name that evokes indigenous identity and the nineteenth-century guerrilla hero Andrés Avelino Cáceres (1833–1923). Central to its ideas remains a vision of a revived Incan society, and it advocates replacing an elite caste in Peru of Europeans, Asians and creoles or those descended from them with one composed of the country's indigenous people. Its supporters are mainly members of the military or veterans. The PNP, by contrast, characterises itself as a modern political party that respects democracy and is tolerant of its opponents. Its vision is not explicitly based on racial criteria and combines references to figures from Peru's Inca history such as Manco Cápac and Tupac Amaru II with influential leftwing thinkers such as José Carlos Mariátegui (see Box 12.1) and Víctor Raúl Haya de la Torre. The PNP platform is premised on the notion that, with the end of the Cold War, the ideological confrontation between socialism and capitalism ended, and has been displaced by a confrontation between nationalism and globalisation (see Box 15.6). At the same time, the party advocates anti-imperialism and Latin American continentalism in the spirit of Haya de la Torre (see Chapter 12).

imperialism and of continentalism, and continues to find many contemporary expressions in the region (see Box 13.1).

Leftwing leaders who have come to power in the region since 1998 have often combined the notion of anti-imperialism with the desire to assert greater control over the economy through policies such as the nationalisation of strategic sectors like oil and gas, sometimes called economic or resource nationalism, which are often formulated with US interests in mind but do not always end up targeting these (see Chapters 14, 16). For example, Venezuela's president, Hugo Chávez, extended his administration's policies of nationalisation to the country's banking sector during 2009, taking over Banco de Venezuela from its Spanish owner Santander and four other local banks. The political ideas of Chávez have evolved from a primarily nationalist position into one that is more explicitly socialist, much like the political ideas of Fidel Castro in Cuba (see Box 12.7). As a result, nationalistic posturing has remained a key feature of the Chávez administration's many disputes with neighbouring Colombia and asserts a traditional notion of sovereignty and territorial integrity (see Chapter 9). None the less, to these expressions of nationalism at a political and international level, the Chávez administration has appended a cultural policy based on a critique of past approaches considered elitist and centralising and, in response, stressing a philosophy of inclusion and unification (see Muñoz, 2008). As a result, the Venezuelan state has adopted a controlling role over many large cultural institutions, grouping all the museums together in a National Museums Foundation, for example. These institutions have been made more accessible to social groups beyond their traditional constituencies, and often politicised.

Other leaders such as Evo Morales in Bolivia have also combined nationalist and socialist positions that emphasise, above all, anti-imperialism and the assertion of economic and political independence. Morales has also sought to enhance the

---

TRENDS   **Box 13.4**

Towards Bolivarian TV?

There are many contemporary expressions of the continentalist aspiration in Latin America, reflecting both cultural affinities but also the degree to which a shared language can facilitate commercial expansion. The establishment in 2005 of the state-funded television networks La Nueva Televisora del Sur (TeleSUR) in Venezuela and TV Brasil in Brazil are potent examples of the ambition to forge a shared agenda among the countries of South America. TeleSUR began broadcasting in November 2005, and the Brazilian network's first test broadcast was transmitted via satellite in January 2005 from the World Social Forum in Porto Alegre to Argentina, Mexico and the US, with TV Brasil broadcasting regularly since 2007. Both networks have since established themselves as mainstream broadcasters, although TV Brasil reaches mainly a Brazilian audience. TeleSUR is available free to air via satellite in Latin America, the US, western Europe and northern Africa. The broadcasters have been compared to the al-Jazeera 24-hour Arabic-language news channel for their underlying ambition to assert local control over broadcast content. In early 2006, TeleSUR signed a co-operation agreement with the Arabic channel.

TeleSUR and TV Brasil executives share the aim of promoting a Latin American perspective on world and regional events through news bulletins, cultural programming and documentaries. Venezuela's populist president Hugo Chávez has long sought alternative sources of information to that broadcast by powerful non-Latin American networks such as CNN and the BBC, and has been a guiding force behind the development of TeleSUR. Argentina's president, Néstor Kirchner (2003–07) and Uruguay's president Tabaré Vázquez (2005–09) were early supporters of his initiative (see Reel, 2005a). Funding and support now comes from seven countries in the region.

The director of TeleSUR, Aram Aharonian, told the Washington Post: 'We need to see a point of view that comes from South America, not from Europe or the United States. Why can't we have our own point of view?'

In July 2005, the US House of Representatives voted to enable the administration of George W. Bush (2001–09) to begin its own television broadcasts to Venezuela in an effort to counter what Washington described as anti-US propaganda (see Chapters 9, 10).

Main source: Reel, 2005a

role of the country's indigenous heritage and pre-Columbian history in cultural discourses about the nation-state, employing indigenous rites in official functions and placing a newly positive emphasis on indigenous symbols and practices, such as the cultivation and use of coca. However, Bolivia reveals the extent to which nationalist positions can pose problems for the Left, and can be challenged with alternative visions. Nationalist discourses in Bolivia have been made more difficult for Morales by the argument that it is a 'plurinational' state – one that combines several nationalities – and are often rejected by his political opponents, who have themselves asserted a form of regional nationalism, based on a more European ethnic heritage, in their resistance to his initiatives (see below). Expressions of regional culture, linguistic diversity, street spectacles and symbolic manifestations have become an important part of the strategy of Bolivia's political right in the *media luna* provinces, and in particular Santa Cruz, to assert their autonomy from central government (Gustafson, 2008; see also Box 12.11). Such expressions of cultural nationalism can play a unifying role to bring together diverse social groups under one political banner.

It is also not uncommon to find conservatives expressing nationalist positions and a form of anti-imperialism, often deriving from an instinctive anti-Americanism, based upon a preference for Hispanic or national culture (see Box 9.3).

Racial and ethnic themes

Racial and ethnic themes have been prominent in Latin American thought since the Conquest, and many of the great debates of the twentieth century have related to agrarian issues and, by extension, to the indigenous question. Colonial rule maintained a degree of separation between communities with whites, *mestizos*, indigenous people and people of African heritage descended from slaves enjoying different levels of access to power and property. At Independence and during the nineteenth century, many creoles employed the emancipatory rhetoric of liberalism, proclaiming legal equality for all based on the idea of a shared national identity (see Chapters 1, 12). Yet in practice, liberal elites favouring a close connection with Europe excluded indigenous people from politics, and society remained characterised by discrimination.

Over time, miscegenation and liberal reforms increasingly replaced the caste-like social order of the colonial era with a class-based society in which racial divisions lost significance. However, during the nineteenth century new racial theories were developed, heavily influenced by positivist thought (see Chapter 12). In the period 1870–1940, the idea of race was given scientific respectability by European thinkers such as Herbert Spencer (b.1820–d.1903), who used the work of Charles Darwin (1809–82) to eschew hybridity in human reproduction by arguing that different races exhibited different capacities for survival. This 'social Darwinism' envisaged a classification of mankind into inferior and superior races and could be used to justify why some elites and nations maintained power. At that time, the spread of European colonialism and the rapid growth of the US appeared to provide support for those who claimed that white civilisation was superior. Such ideas influenced social policies regarding education, crime, health and immigration (see Skidmore, 1990; see also Leys Stepan, 1991). In some countries, ideological and economic factors nurtured a more virulent racism towards the end of the nineteenth century. In Mexico, under the dictator Porfirio Díaz (1876–1911) policymakers tried to attract white European immigrants while dispossessing indigenous and *mestizo* peasant communities of their land.

By placing a premium on whiteness, these ideas bolstered creole rule but also made it possible for mixed groups to justify their own socially higher position in relation to indigenous and black people. As a result, to become upwardly mobile one needed to be whitened. Brazil received more African slaves than any other country in the Americas, creating a multi-racial society with a large number of people occupying a mixed-race category. In Brazil, intellectuals tended to ignore the Spencerian bias against racial mixing and believed instead that the country would achieve progress through mixing that resulted in a gradual whitening of the population (see dos Santos, 2002). Even *opponents* of slavery believed that miscegenation would whiten – and so improve – the population, and racist stereotypes also had an important influence on progressive thinkers such as the anthropologist Gilberto Freyre (1900–87).

In countries with large indigenous and *mestizo* populations, a number of ideologies emerged as part of a broader reaction against positivism that urged the recovery of indigenous culture and rejected the view that indigenous people were anti-modern (Stavenhagen, 2002). The struggle of Emiliano Zapata (b.1879–d.1919) and his Zapotec peasants to win back ancestral lands during Mexico's revolution gave an impetus to the vindication of indigenous rights throughout Latin America (see Box 1.5, Chapter 8). From 1910 to 1940, writers, academics and politicians tried to come to terms with the place of indigenous people in revolutionary Mexico (Knight, 1990). The revolution had been fought with considerable indigenous participation, yet demands for agrarian reform were often couched in class terms. Mexico's revolutionary elite incorporated into their ideology *indigenismo*, which claimed to seek the emancipation of indigenous people through integration into the new revolutionary nation. Music, dance and rituals attributed to indigenous society were rehabilitated and woven into a new folkloric nationalism. Vasconcelos, the education minister, brought *indigenismo* to the forefront of cultural politics (see above).

Indigenismo flowered as an official ideology partly because Mexico's revolution created an interventionist state committed to nation-building (see above). However, *indigenismo* was a non-indigenous, elite formulation of the indigenous problem. It tended to repeat racist assumptions and reflected a new form of psychological determinism – the notion that a human's actions are always predetermined by their psychological inheritance. Efforts by *indigenistas* to recover a pristine indigenous culture would often take as their point of departure what was, in fact, a mixed, syncretic and, in essence, *mestizo* culture. *Indigenismo* complemented an emphasis on the *mestizo* because it aimed to integrate indigenous people into national society, in effect through a process of *mestizaje*. As a result, *indigenismo* and *mestizaje* both lent themselves readily to corporatist perspectives (see Chapters 2, 7, 12). Latin America's *mestizo* and mulatto (mixed African and European) population played an increasingly important role in the ideas of key thinkers throughout the region, from Andrés Molina Enríquez (b.1868–d.1970), who depicted the *mestizo* as the 'national race', to Vasconcelos, who argued that the *mestizo* was the apotheosis of human development, and Freyre in Brazil, who hailed *mestizaje* as a source of national pride. Influenced by Rodó, Vasconcelos formulated the idea of the 'cosmic race' based on a positive assessment of *mestizaje*.

The notion of *mestizaje* could be found throughout Latin America yet the idea of a *mestizo nation* remained revolutionary in the 1930s and 1940s when racist doctrines continued to influence political discourse. In Mexico, *indigenismo* and *mestizaje* found favour among the revolutionary elite because these ideas were nationalist (see above) and allowed elites to distinguish their revolutionary rhetoric from socialism or communism. Peruvian *indigenistas* argued that indigenous culture was the source of national values and sometimes based political platforms on these ideas. Haya de la Torre fused *indigenismo* and continentalism through the idea of 'Indo-America' (see Box 13.1). José Carlos Mariátegui (b.1894–d.1930) advanced a more extreme form of *indigenismo*, arguing that indigenous people formed the oppressed class (see Box 12.1). In Brazil, scholars such as Freyre and Arthur Ramos (b.1903–d.1949) began to show interest in the Afro-Brazilian heritage, although the whitening ideal remained entrenched among the political elite and a consensus that positively valued miscegenation encouraged the emergence of an official belief that Brazil did not have a race problem.

In Argentina, the number of European immigrants grew rapidly and by 1890 most of the country's indigenous people had either been killed or displaced. Intellectuals began to link Argentina's rapid development to racial ideas and to diffuse European racial notions. However, in the absence of indigenous people, racists turned their attention to European immigrants and anti-Semitic ideas flourished (Helg, 1990). Race was also a prominent theme in Cuba, where many intellectuals accepted European racist thought and hoped that blacks and mulattos would give way to whites or abandon African culture (*ibid.*). This radicalised some black thinkers into assuming segregationist positions. In 1908, a black political party, the Partido Independiente de Color (PIC, Independent Party for Coloured People), was created and was met with repression, leading to an army massacre of thousands of Afro-Cubans.

Official anti-racist positions slowly became the norm in Latin America and the integration of indigenous populations through *indigenismo* was given continental respectability in 1940 at the First Inter-American Indian Conference held in Mexico. For much of the Cold War era (see Chapters 2, 9, 10), political mobilisation adopted class categories. For Marxists, indigenous people were either part of the exploited peasantry, petit-bourgeois romantics or even counter-revolutionaries. Government anthropologists, by contrast, depicted the indigenous as deeply conservative and even anti-national. Yet although *indigenismo* contributed to new attitudes on race, it did not end racism. Revolution, modernisation and integration accelerated the breakdown of caste-like ethnic barriers and most Latin American countries developed an official line that racism was not a serious social problem. However, racist assumptions persisted and indigenous people continued to suffer informal discrimination, provoking backlashes. During the guerrilla struggles in Guatemala and Nicaragua, some indigenous intellectuals rejected Marxist ideology as a Western set of beliefs incapable of recognising indigenous cultural needs.

The attraction of indigenous people to Sendero Luminoso in Peru could also be seen as a partial rejection of orthodox Marxism (see Boxes 12.4, 13.9).

A resurgence of indigenous mobilisation since the 1970s gained force with democratisation in the 1980s and 1990s and has given indigenous issues a new prominence (see Chapter 8). Indigenous intellectuals such as Mario Juruna and David Yanomami in Brazil and Rigoberta Menchú in Guatemala have gained an international profile. One reflection of this phenomenon has been the development of new, indigenous perspectives on history and society by such groups as the Kaqchikel Maya in Guatemala (see Carey, 2001; see also Gustafson, 2009). Mayan nationalists and intellectuals such as Victor Montejo, Demetrio Cotjí and Enrique Sam Colop have played a key role in fostering a 'pan-Mayan' consciousness (see Warren, 1998; Nagel, 2002; del Valle Escalante, 2009). In Ecuador, indigenous activism since 1990 spawned a new generation of thinkers that became known as the 'Generation of 1990' (see Becker, 2008).

The rise of indigenous consciousness has thrust issues such as cultural diversity, autonomy and the impact of neoliberal reform on the countryside to the top of Latin America's political agenda (see Chapters 8, 15). The rebellion in 1994 by a mainly indigenous guerrilla force of Zapatistas in Chiapas, Mexico, put the poverty of indigenous people, discrimination, and the impact of neoliberal reform into the international spotlight, and may have created the basis for the first post-Communist ideology in Latin America (see Box 13.5). Indigenous people are disproportionately found surviving within the informal economy because of deprivation and a lack of skills (see Chapters 4, 15).

Indigenous organisations have forged an agenda with two main components. Some groups have demanded self-determination and autonomy based on their separate culture, posing serious questions about the past nature and the future of national identity in Latin America (see Chapters 6, 8). Through state- and nation-building policies, Latin American states have sought to construct a national, homogeneous culture based on a single administration by reducing diversity. But it has been argued that such has been the challenge in recent years by indigenous intellectuals from groups such as the Maya in Guatemala to established, hegemonic narratives of modernity, history, nation, and cultural identity written largely by non-indigenous scholars, that Latin American nation-states can no longer be conceived of in conventional terms as culturally and linguistically homogenous (del Valle Escalante, 2009). In some indigenous communities, local autonomy may respond to a long-standing tradition of participatory democracy: in Bolivia, for example, a pre-Inca form of political organisation based on extended family groups called the *ayllu* often involved high levels of participation in decisionmaking. Since the 1970s, many indigenous organisations have framed demands on the basis of their ethnic distinctiveness and have often argued that autonomy is essential if they are to overcome centuries of discrimination against their cultures by social groups with European or *mestizo* origins. They support this position by attributing discrimination against them to a longstanding racism. In April 2005, for example, five Guatemalan politicians were found guilty in the country's first trial for racial discrimination of shouting racist abuse at the indigenous activist and Nobel Prize winner Rigoberta Menchú. In March 2006, the UN Development Programme urged Guatemala to overcome what it called 'historically racist attitudes' towards

THEORIES AND DEBATES   Box 13.5

Zapatismo – an ideology of global significance?

In the early days of the brief uprising in January 1994 in Chiapas, southern Mexico, by the mainly indigenous Ejército Zapatista de Liberación Nacional (EZLN, Zapatista National Liberation Army), the Zapatistas consciously inserted their rebellion into the nationalist history of social struggle in Mexico, and used the figure of Emiliano Zapata to appropiate the progressive characteristics of the Mexican Revolution (see Box 1.5). In this respect, they provide a further example of the influence of the revolutionary tradition on the development of political ideas (see Chapter 12). *Zapatismo* today constitutes a rare example of a Latin American idea that has achieved international significance and may also have formed the basis for the first post-Marxist ideology of global reach (see, for example, Khasnabish, 2010). The EZLN's main spokesman and interlocutor has been an urban non-indigenous intellectual, Sub-comandante Marcos, whose eloquent articulation of Zapatista ideas has contributed to the growth of a global solidarity network, facilitated greatly by the use of contemporary communication technologies such as the internet.

Elements of contemporary *zapatismo* have their roots in the orthodox left, but have also been heavily influenced by a liberal and anarchist tradition in Mexico (see Chapter 12) and by contemporary liberal norms prevailing in the developed world. In an interview in 1997, Marcos explained how the EZLN was formed through an encounter between a small group of urban intellectuals with a revolutionary vision informed by Marxist-Leninist theory that in fact challenged the indigenous world view, and the indigenous communities of Chiapas themselves, who had a cultural belief system based on a long tradition of community struggle (Le Bot, 1997). As a result, the contemporary Zapatista ideology has both been hard to define using conventional categories, but also reflects the amorphous development of the original *zapatismo* that emerged from Mexico's revolution. The original *zapatismo* was first linked to the indigenous cause by planters warning about the danger of caste war, and thereafter taken up in retrospect by *indigenista* reformers like Manuel Gamio (see above) who depicted *zapatismo* as the awakening of the indigenous people of Morelos (Knight, 1990).

Contemporary *zapatismo* is first and foremost indigenist, putting the claims of ethnic groups for constitutional reform to enhance indigenous rights, for example, high on its agenda, but much like mainstream *indigenismo* this element of its discourse is incorporated within and balanced by more structural and political demands that interact with those found in non-indigenous society. The achievement of indigenous rights would not be seen as a culmination in itself, but as a point of departure for change in other arenas. Olesen (2004) has explored Zapatista ideology and pointed out that, had the EZLN limited itself to the quest for indigenous autonomy, it would have had less transnational resonance. The desire for some form of autonomy expresses a more substantive position seeking more meaningful citizenship for indigenous people (see Chapters 4, 8), and this has been stressed in another recurrent theme in Zapatista discourse, the demand for indigenous dignity, expressing the sense of exclusion that indigenous people in Latin America have felt for generations that they believe has turned them into second-class citizens.

The humanist aspiration underlying such themes as dignity helps to explain the global impact of the Zapatista cause. It has consciously sought to be universalist, and this is reflected in the popularity of expressions such as 'we are all Marcos' originally used by activist supporters. Olesen examined the way the EZLN invoked and formulated a global consciousness, generating a powerful sense of mutual solidarity. This universal aspiration may help to explain why Marcos has used anonymity, by wearing a ski mask, as a means of evincing consciousness, encouraging others to imagine themselves as him and reflect upon their own condition. This device has transformed him into a powerful symbol of the oppression of ordinary people.

Three other themes in *zapatismo* help to explain its ideological resonance outside Mexico. First, it is democratic, but advances a radical, social and participatory vision of democracy that challenges the institutionalised preference in Western capitalist society for liberal democracy at a time when this has become the dominant orthodoxy (see Chapter 3, Box 12.6). This may seem ironic, given the EZLN's initial prominence as an armed actor, but democracy has always been central to its rhetoric although it has grown in prominence in recent years. The vision of radical democracy advanced by the EZLN has been informed both by the practices and conventions of indigenous society, that balance strict individual obedience to the consensus derived from collective consultation with close accountability and scrutiny of those who govern, and by more theoretical positions informed by the sociological analysis of civil society and social movements (see Boxes 8.1, 8.2). It also forms part of the complex of ideas that make up the notion of a 'socialism for the twenty-first century' that has become popular on the left in countries such as Venezuela. In Zapatista communities, leadership is seen as a service to the community and not as a source of personal advantage. This has particular importance in Latin America if we consider such phenomena as populism, which often builds on a sense of deep alienation with the corrupt, self-serving practices of an established political class (see Chapter 4).

Second, *zapatismo* is pluralist, building relationships with social and political movements on the basis of respect for difference and tolerance, and respect sits at the heart of EZLN arguments in support of cultural and political autonomy for indigenous peoples. This pluralism differentiates the EZLN from previous armed movements from the left in Latin America and makes its guerrilla theory anti-vanguardist, with the organisation not only eschewing military activity where possible but also proposing to dismantle itself as a military force. It places a constant emphasis on civil society and sees its role less as a formal political actor and more as a means of creating a space for the empowerment of marginalised and popular sectors, what Marcos has described as '*zapatismo civil*' (see Chapter 8). One example of those to whom it would appeal is the informal sector of the economy, whose members exist outside a more traditional understanding of the class structure and have limited access to formal political representation (see Chapters 4, 8, 15). EZLN supporters have been critical of the traditional, bureaucratic organisations of the Left in Latin America, and *zapatismo* has been of particular appeal to anarchists and those working for social change outside formal political institutions. The EZLN would not back the candidate of Mexico's main left-of-centre party, the PRD, in the 2006 presidential election, for example. *Zapatismo* has also figured prominently in contemporary debates outside Mexico seeking to reconcile Marxism and anarchism (see, for example, Lynd and Grubacic, 2008; Khasnabish, 2010). At the same time, elements of the traditional left, such as militant Trotskyists, have criticised the Zapatistas and supporters for being 'liberal' and naive.

Finally, *zapatismo* has tapped into the existing critique of neoliberalism to advance a vision of political economy that has at its core a notion of injustice, to which it has added ideas about the alternative merits of traditional indigenous communalism and reciprocity. Its critique of neoliberal reform was initially national and specific to the impact of economic change on rural society (see Box 7.6), but Olesen argued that EZLN supporters conspicuously broadened the idea of injustice caused by neoliberal reform to a transnational arena after 1996 when they convened two conferences 'for humanity and against neoliberalism'. This broad notion of justice has also allowed Zapatistas to forge alliances with domestic and international groups of all political persuasions that share a hostility to economic liberalism. Taking the position of the traditional left, the EZLN has anchored its resistance to neoliberalism primarily on the grounds of the loss of sovereignty implied by such mechanisms as NAFTA (see Chapter 15), and this explains the guerrilla movement's self-depiction as an army of *national liberation*.

indigenous peoples, warning that if it did not the country could become ungovernable (bbc.co.uk, 2006b). In Bolivia, the longstanding marginalisation of indigenous people has been a recurrent theme of study and debate, and more recently scholars and other commentators have argued that rightwing opposition to the reforms of the indigenous, left-of-centre president, Evo Morales, is motivated in large part by racial antipathy among white elites driven by a rejection of people from the *altiplano* (see Boxes 12.11, 13.6; see also, for example, Gilly, 2008; Zibechi, 2008). Racial attributions that would not be regarded as acceptable in the politics of established democracies have until recently formed a normal part of the discourse of the Right in countries such as Guatemala and Bolivia.

However, behind arguments for indigenous autonomy on the basis that this may help to overcome longstanding ethnic discrimination are subtle variations and inconsistencies in how such language and ideas are used. Although coming from an identifiably indigenous background, politicians such as Morales in Bolivia, for example, may cultivate stronger ethnic discourse or employ indigenous symbols more overtly after coming to power as part of a broader strategy against their political opponents. Moreover, indigenous politicians themselves have at times also been accused of expressing racist ideas or using confrontational language that exaggerates the level of discrimination they face, what is sometimes called 'inverse racism' (Kozloff, 2007). There may also be divisions between and within communities that weaken the idea of a single, unified indigenous perspective. In Bolivia, for example, the two main indigenous communities, the Aymaras and the Quechuas, have sometimes competed for influence and adopted differing political strategies. During the 2005 presidential elections, Felipe Quispe – an Aymara representing the Movimiento Indígena Pachakuti (MIP, Indigenous Pachakuti Movement) – competed against Evo Morales of the Movimiento al Socialismo (MAS, Movement for Socialism), who is also of Aymara descent. Quispe advocates the establishment of an indigenous republic in the Aymara regions of Bolivia while Morales has adopted a more pragmatic discourse on decentralisation that recognises indigenous nationality but retains an emphasis on a unitary republic (see below, and Chapter 6).

Most Latin American governments reject claims to self-determination as a threat to national integrity and sovereignty, but a more assertive indigenous strain of thought has emerged that argues for autonomy by conceiving of indigenous populations as nations. By the 1990s, the traditional nationalist vision of an homogeneous mono-ethnic *mestizo* state premised on indigenous integration was under pressure. A common perspective to have emerged among indigenous groups has reconceptualised Latin American countries as multi-ethnic or even multi-national, and today many indigenous movements describe the nation-state by using such terms as pluriethnic, pluricultural or plurinational (see Chapter 8). In Bolivia, for example, the first article of the 2009 constitution changed references to the country in the previous 1967 charter as 'multi-ethnic and pluricultural' to a description of it as 'plurinational'. Indigenous self-determination has been a central theme of the Morales presidency, and Bolivia's 2009 constitution established a structure by which indigenous communities could gain a degree of autonomy (see Chapter 6, Boxes 4.1, 12.11). However, while large indigenous communities such as the Aymara in Bolivia may welcome gaining the status of a nationality, they may not be separatist or seek to create their own states (Kozloff, 2007). More extreme positions on self-determination may advocate a form of indigenous cultural or racial separatism as an 'authentic' alternative to Western civilisation (see above, and Box 13.3). Indigenous demands for self-determination can simultaneously confront both the tradition of centralism at the heart of Latin American politics and underlying assumptions inherited from positivist thought (see Chapter 12). The challenge this can pose to hegemonic ideas of national identity in some countries also makes it a potent threat in the eyes of dominant groups. In Bolivia, for example, ethnic tension has become a pressing issue (see Boxes 12.11, 13.6).

A second component of the indigenous agenda has been state policies that recognise or re-evaluate indigenous identity and culture. Multicultural rights or official recognition of indigenous cultures and languages have been enshrined in law throughout Latin America, in many cases since the 1980s (see Table 8.1). In Bolivia, for example, educational reforms under Morales have given a new status to Aymara, Quechua and Guaraní, and many civil servants are required to speak Aymara, which can also be found in some programming on national television and radio. Indigenous demands for bilingual education also challenge the idea cherished since Independence of a single national culture. Multiculturalism of this kind can challenge the mainstream *indigenista* position of integration and the tenets of liberalism. In particular, adjusting political and legal arrangements to multicultural criteria demands a reconceptualisation of the liberal inheritance of individual rights and the search for a new balance between communitarian and liberal conceptions of rights and obligations (Sieder, 2002).

Claims for self-determination also reinforce demands for greater pluralism in Latin American politics that have been supported by black organisations throughout the region. These demands have often been informed by prevailing liberal norms on human rights and democracy (see Chapters 3, 12) but also by the example of black people in the US. African-American groups in the US have provided an inspiration but also, in some cases, support for black organisations in Latin America. As a result, blacks throughout Latin America are increasingly expressing pride in

CASE STUDY   Box 13.6

Ethnic tension in Bolivia

The indigenous community's struggle for a greater say over economic policy to tackle deep inequalities has increased ethnic tensions in Bolivia. A small proportion of the population of 8 million people controls the country's resources while the majority are indigenous people, many of whom live on less than $2 a day. The election of the indigenous leader, Evo Morales, as president in 2006 has had an important influence on the development of ethnic relations. Bolivia is the most indigenous country in Latin America and its western Andean highland or *altiplano* regions are dominated by a poor Quechua and Aymara majority comprising rural communities, *collas*, that have repeatedly mobilised behind left-of-centre parties. The *media luna* eastern crescent, and in particular the city of Santa Cruz within Bolivia's wealthiest province, is home to many light-skinned or *mestizo* 'cambas' of mixed European and indigenous descent and, in this case, the largest indigenous group is the Guaraní. The area is wealthier, home to many ranchers and the middle classes working in a prosperous export economy, and the heartland of the Bolivian right. Santa Cruz has been at the centre of opposition to the left-of-centre programme of Morales and demands for regional autonomy that in some cases have amounted to calls for secession (see Chapters 6, 8, Box 4.1, 12.11). At one level, the confrontations between these forces have been a battle for control over the revenues generated by Bolivia's vast natural gas reserves as well as other natural resources such as agrarian and forestry lands and massive deposits of iron ore, all of which can be found in the eastern lowlands. Indigenous groups from the *altiplano* have long sought the nationalisation of resources such as gas so that the revenues generated by these can be deployed more equitably by the central state; while *media luna* groups have sought to retain control over the benefits generated by the extraction for export of the resources in their regions, often by multi-national corporations. Tensions have increased in line with growing expectations as the full scale of gas reserves in the country became apparent between 1996 and 2002.

Frustration in Santa Cruz came to a head after an indigenous revolt in the poor, mainly indigenous community of El Alto near La Paz in 2003 over the government's plans to exploit gas reserves, which would have involved the building of a pipeline to a Chilean port that offended nationalists (see Chapter 9) and which opponents claimed would not have benefitted Bolivia sufficiently. The El Alto revolt ignited what has since been called the 'Bolivian gas war' and led to the resignation of Gonzalo Sánchez de Lozada (1993–97, 2002–03), the US-educated president from Santa Cruz (see Box 5.6). The conflict over how hydrocarbons are exploited in the country shaped politics between 2003 and 2005, when it also claimed Sánchez de Lozada's successor, Carlos Mesa, and set the scene for the election of Morales, an Aymara whose Movimiento al Socialismo (MAS, Movement Towards Socialism) was among the political groups with a significant indigenous dimension that were at the centre of the gas protests. A hydrocarbons law passed by the Mesa government increased state control over natural resources and raised taxes on their exploitation, angering many people in Santa Cruz who argued that it had gone too far in meeting the demands of indigenous people. The response after 2005 of the Santa Cruz opposition, led by business leaders, was to seek autonomy that gives the region more control over how taxes are spent and provincial government is managed, while resisting the commitment of the Morales government to fully nationalise the gas sector.

However, it is too simple to characterise the dispute in Bolivia over natural resources as an ethnic conflict based on regional divisions, and politics and ideology remain important factors (see Gustafson, 2008). MAS support can be found in the east although it is strongest in western rural provinces, small towns and poor urban areas, while support for the Right can also be found in the *altiplano*, although it remains strongest in the country's big cities; the MAS advocates a strong central state that remains committed to nation-building and spearheading the process of development (see above); while the Right wants a weak state that favours regional poles of growth based on neoliberal export-led policies (see Chapters 15, 16); and the MAS in government inherits a tradition of corporatism in Bolivia that risks recreating authoritarian tendencies, while the Right's vision of electoral democracy is based on its natural majority in *media luna* provinces implied by decentralisation. At the same time, Bolivia's two main indigenous parties, MAS and the Movimiento Indígena Pachakuti (MIP, Indigenous Pachakuti Movement), have often been divided over policies towards key issues such as gas.

None the less, ethnic tensions have surfaced in other aspects of Bolivian life as the indigenous movement has grown stronger. In 2004, Gabriela Oviedo, the Bolivian candidate in the Miss Universe competition being held in Ecuador, angered indigenous groups when she told reporters that she was from Santa Cruz, where people were white, tall and spoke English, unlike the west of Bolivia, where she described the population as Indian, poor and short. Some outside observers have warned that, far from reflecting greater pluralism, indigenous mobilisation in Bolivia is polarising political positions, and it has been suggested that indigenous discourses about discrimination nurtured a backlash in parts of non-indigenous society that hardened racist positions (Kozloff, 2007).

Table 13.1 Collective Rights for Afro-descendant Groups in Latin America

Country	Group Recognition	Customary Law	Land Rights	Autonomy or self-government	Bilingual Education	Anti-Racial Discrimination Rights
Argentina	No	No	No	No	No	No
Brazil	Yes	No	Yes	No	No	Yes
Costa Rica	No	No	No	No	No	No
Colombia	Yes	No	Yes	Yes	Yes	Yes
Ecuador	Yes	No	Yes	Yes	No	Yes
Guatemala	Yes	No	Yes	No	Yes	No
Honduras	Yes	No	Yes	No	No	No
Mexico	No	No	No	No	No	No
Nicaragua	Yes	Yes	Yes	Yes	Yes	No
Panama	No	No	No	No	No	Yes
Peru	Yes	No	No	No	No	Yes
Venezuela	No	No	No	No	No	No

Source: Adapted from Hooker, 2008

their own history and culture and creating political movements to confront the inequality and discrimination many have suffered from. People of African descent have been present in Latin America since the Spanish Conquest (see Box 13.7) and an important reassessment of their role in the region's history is underway (see Reid Andrews, 2004). Progress in the recognition of collective rights for Afro-descendant groups – increasingly called Afro-Latin Americans – has been more limited than for indigenous groups, but is becoming a prominent theme of identity politics in some countries (see Table 13.1).

In Brazil, for example, 49 per cent of the population of 192 million people are descendants from black Africans, *pardo* (mixed race), or express some other self-identification as black. However, about 67 per cent of the black community is poor (Inter Press, 2009; see also Astor, 2004). In 2008, Brazilian blacks on average earned half as much as whites (and black women earned even less); at 500 large companies they accounted for just 3.5 per cent of the executives and 17 per cent of the managers; just over 5 per cent of blacks aged 30 had graduated from college against 18 per cent of whites; and of the 513 senators and deputies in congress, just 46 were Afro-Brazilians (Marotto, 2008). These legacies explain why over the past 15 years a black movement has emerged in Brazil to challenge the idea that there is no racism and to demand change. They also explain why the battle against racism has been a prominent policy of the ruling Partido dos Trabalhadores (PT, Workers' Party). Brazil's president, Luiz Inácio Lula da Silva (2003–10), included more black people in his cabinet than any former executive and created a cabinet-level secretariat to promote racial equality. In 2003, Da Silva appointed the country's first black supreme court justice, Joaquim Benedito Barbosa Gomes. Black members of the PT sought a racial equality statute to introduce quotas in areas such as public-sector recruitment. Black political mobilisation in Brazil has already had an effect and, in 2003, state universities began implementing racial entry quotas. By mid-2009, 20 out of 39 federal universities had already adopted quotas and plans to extend quotas to all public higher-education institutions were under discussion. There have also been more symbolic challenges to stereotypes: in 2009, for example, the São Paulo Fashion Week required at least 10 per cent of the models to be black or indigenous, after intense pressure from activists attacking a bias towards white models. However, the issue of race remains complicated by Brazil's long legacy of whitening policies, and quotas have also generated resentment among the white population, some of whom have responded with legal challenges. In 2008, 113 Brazilian intellectuals, academics and artists issued a protest denouncing the quotas on the grounds that they discriminated against poor students who are not black (Inter Press, 2009).

Black organisations have also been formed in Peru, Mexico (see Box 13.7) and Ecuador, and have often asked penetrating questions as to why the debate about multiculturalism in Latin America has sometimes brought concrete gains for indigenous peoples but has often overlooked blacks. Arguments put forward to explain this disparity have included the notion that Latin American elites have been unwilling to recognise blacks as possessors of a distinct cultural group identity like that of indigenous people, or the notion that blackness in the region often appears to be more related to social status than to culture (see Golash-Boza, 2008; Hooker, 2008). What is sometimes referred to as 'cultural citizenship' – a person's right to feel that they, and their community, belong to the nation – is important in a plural democracy (see Chapter 3). For this reason, policies of multiculturalism aiming to address inequalities in large sectors of the population have formed an important component of recent democratisation in Latin America. The lobbying of Afro-descendant groups alongside indigenous groups, therefore, has raised questions about how policies and institutions promoting multiculturalism are designed.

Some countries were pioneers in incorporating their black populations within the multicultural agenda. In 1997, Ecuador's congress recognised as an official commemoration the 'National Day of Black People' after intense lobbying by black organisations that have gained much of their inspiration from mobilisation by the country's indigenous people. In 2004, Afro-Colombian groups hosted a conference of black members of congress from throughout Latin America. The *Garifuna*, Afro-Latinos scattered along the coast of several Central American countries, have also begun to raise their profile.

Yet accusations of racial discrimination persist. In 2002, Erika Lizet Ramírez, the then Miss Honduras and the first Afro-Latina to win the national beauty title, spoke out about what she alleged was discrimination against her by organisers of the event because she is black. In October 2005, the Dominican Republic angrily rejected allegations of discrimination against Haitians born in its territory after the Inter-American Court of Human Rights had ordered it to give them birth certificates (see Box 7.7). Violent protests against the alleged abuse of Haitian migrants marred a visit to Haiti by the president of the Dominican Republic, Leonel Fernández Reyna (1996–2000, 2004–), in December 2005 (see Figure 9.1).

The historical links between Latin America and the Arab world are also being recognised. An estimated 17 million Latin Americans are of Arab descent, most of them Christians from Lebanon, Syria or Palestine, although about 6 million have

Africa in Mexico

Mexican social development is not often understood in terms of the contribution to the country's evolution by people descended from black slaves, but in recent years there has been a re-evaluation of the role played by those of African descent. The presence of Africans in Mexico extends back to the Spanish Conquest when Juan Garrido, a *conquistador*, was among several free Africans to accompany Hernán Cortés in subjugating the Aztecs. However, most Afro-Mexicans trace their heritage to slaves brought to the country by the Spanish. More than 200,000 African slaves were brought to Mexico and communities of slaves and free blacks from the US settled in certain areas of the country before and after Mexico abolished slavery in 1829. Most slaves were brought from Africa through Veracruz, the oldest port in Latin America, to work in the sugar cane fields and mines, and also as servants. As a result, many '*Afro-mestizos*' are concentrated in the state of Veracruz on the Gulf Coast and in Guerrero and Oaxaca states in the Costa Chica region on the Pacific Coast south of Acapulco (Pollard-Terry, 2005a). The African slave Gaspar Yanga, originally thought to have been from Gabon, led a slave revolt against the Spanish in Veracruz in about 1570, and established a maroon community (in Spanish, 'palenque') of freed slaves that survived for more than 30 years. In the nineteenth century, Yanga was incorporated into Mexico's nationalist history as an early hero, and a town called Yanga survives to this day in the region. One of Mexico's great Independence leaders, Vicente Guerrero (1782–1831), also had mixed African, indigenous and Spanish roots. However, in general Mexico's African ancestry was played down in nationalist historiography, particularly during the post-revolutionary era of state-building, by the emphasis that was placed upon the fusion of European and indigenous races and cultures in the creation of national identity. One example of indifference was the reaction to a book by Gonzalo Aguirre Beltrán, *La población negra de México* ('The Negro Population of Mexico') which was first published in 1946 but not reprinted until 1972 because of a lack of interest (see Aguirre Beltrán, 1981). In 1992, the Mexican government funded research to study and acknowledge the African contribution to the country's evolution. There has been considerable assimilation by people of African descent within the *mestizo* population and, other than a few enthusiasts and websites (see, for example, www.afromexico.com), this community has not been able to establish a significant profile. But elements of African heritage have endured and continue to influence the diet, music, dance and religious customs, and can be found in the names of cities and towns such as Mandinga. In Guerrero, women carry items on their heads without using their hands and on All Saints' Day perform a Dance of the Devil that is similar to dances performed in West Africa (Pollard-Terry, 2005b). In Coyolillo in Veracruz, a carnival with its roots in African culture is celebrated. However, public rhetoric has often betrayed the lack of recognition given to the contribution of black people to Mexico's diverse heritage. For example, comments made in 2005 by President Vicente Fox (2000–06) about how Mexicans take jobs 'not even' blacks want in the US were heavily criticised by black organisations, later prompting an expression of regret by the Mexican leader.

Muslim origins and Islam has grown as a religion among some indigenous communities in countries such as Mexico (see MacSwan, 2005). In Brazil, people of Syrian-Lebanese descent have achieved significant success in commerce as exporters, industrialists and powerbrokers (see Tofik Karam, 2007). Brazil's President Da Silva hosted the first South American–Arab Summit in Brasilia in 2005, and in 2009 a second Arab-Latin American summit was held in Doha, Qatar.

Feminism

The role of women in Latin American society is a key issue in contemporary social thought that has informed debates about citizenship, pluralism, participation and representation (see Chapters 3, 4). There has been concrete progress on many of the issues that have mobilised women in the past, such as equality in family law and male violence, through constitutional reforms and new laws across Latin America. There have also been signs that social norms confining women to subordinate or domestic roles have also been changing. Many women in the region now participate in political life and the job market as independent actors. Women's programmes have been institutionalised in government ministries, their political representation has increased, and in some cases has been promoted by quota rules – by 2008, at least 11 Latin American countries had adopted affirmative action measures to ensure a level of female participation in politics (see below). Together, these policy steps meant that, by 2007, women occupied 18.5 per cent of seats in Latin America's lower houses of congress or unicameral legislatures (see Figure 13.1), and women held 24.5 per cent of government ministries (see Llanos and Sample, 2008).

However, the progress of women in Latin America towards gaining full equality remains limited. Gains have been uneven and, while by 2008 in countries such as Costa Rica, Chile, Ecuador and Nicaragua women occupied at least a third of cabinet posts, they remained significantly under-represented in others such as Venezuela (18.5 per cent), Dominican Republic (17.6 per cent), El Salvador (15.4 per cent), Brazil (14.3 per cent) and Paraguay (10 per cent) (*ibid*.). Equality

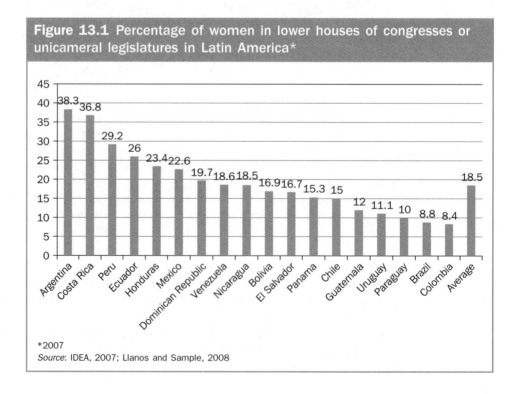

Figure 13.1 Percentage of women in lower houses of congresses or unicameral legislatures in Latin America*

*2007
Source: IDEA, 2007; Llanos and Sample, 2008

laws often are inadequately enforced; ministerial departments charged with improving women's lives often lack funds and do not have effective links with women's movements; quota laws are notoriously difficult to police; and there has been resistance to changes in reproductive rights and laws regarding sexual preference deriving from traditional *machismo* – a term referring to the exaggerated masculinity often attributed to or adopted by men in the region – as well as from social conservatives and powerful actors such as the Catholic Church (see Jaquette, 2009a; see also Chapters 7, 12). Moreover, women in Latin America have not developed a powerful feminist movement of the kind found in Europe and the US, and some scholars argue that the women's movement in Latin America has lost momentum in recent years (*ibid.*).

Feminist movements emerged in Latin America in the late nineteenth century, and were concerned with three main issues: the vote, protective labour laws, and education (Craske, 1999). Some radical movements emerged, often influenced by ideas brought by European immigrants, and in 1916 a conference in Mexico highlighted the close relationship between women and the Catholic Church in the region, explaining why many liberals and leftwingers were opposed to giving women the right to vote because they feared this would strengthen the Church's conservative influence. In the 1940s, several women's parties were formed, and in 1961 Paraguay became the last Latin American country to give women the vote.

During the 1960s and 1970s a 'second wave' of more class-conscious feminism was influenced by writing coming out of Europe and the US. The feminist struggle became intertwined with the struggle against military authoritarianism, and it would be a women's movement – the mothers of those 'disappeared' by the military regime in Argentina (see Chapters 2, 4, Table 7.2, Box 7.11) – that would mount the most effective challenge to authoritarian rule. While military regimes sometimes took socially conservative steps – measures deriving from conservative attitudes towards social issues like gender equality, such as ending public provision of contraceptives – in countries with leftwing regimes, women made concrete gains (see Chapter 12). In 1975, for example, the Cuban government passed legislation making childcare and housework the equal responsibility of men and women. The Nicaraguan Revolution (1979) offered hope to many feminists because the revolutionary party, the Frente Sandinista de Liberación Nacional (FSLN, Sandinista National Liberation Front), did not reject feminism as potentially counter-revolutionary. The Sandinista regime banned the use of women's bodies in advertising and promoted women to senior positions. Yet as the country entered deep crisis in the mid-1980s, these priorities were made secondary to that of defending the revolution, and women's emancipation faltered (Molyneux, 2001). Key Sandinista leaders have also grown more socially conservative as they have grown older.

In the 1980s, women's movements were prominent in the campaigns for democracy, which brought together individuals from diverse areas and sectors. A series of regional feminist meetings recognised the fractured internal politics of Latin American feminism and, by the late 1980s, growing acknowledgement of diversity, difference and plurality marked feminist thought (*ibid.*). Many feminists remained sceptical of the state's willingness to change the male bias of politics and saw more potential for advancing their cause in social movements, NGOs and development agencies (see Chapter 8). The idea of more active citizenship came to the fore and some feminists sought to provide a gender analysis of social movements that could allow women to develop a separate sphere of politics (see Jelin ed., 1990). By the 1990s, many feminist activists had begun to transcend some barriers to political activity, attitudes towards women had changed and feminists were able to influence legislation by employing the language of human rights and citizenship. These developments took advantage of and built upon new international norms that were emerging to promote gender equality by ending discrimination in such areas as education and employment. There were also signs that women were transcending the class divisions that had long weakened feminism. In Nicaragua, a 'National Coalition of Women' was created in 1996 bringing together women from both left and right (Blandón, 2001). None the less, women's groups and their objectives across Latin America remain heterogeneous and diverse (for reviews of literature, see Tiano, 2001; and Rakowski, 2003). Women have, for example, played prominent roles in the leadership and activism of indigenous movements, seeking greater inclusion and equal rights both as a gender and also as representatives of a culture (see above). In Ecuador, after 1986 women played a significant role in shaping the main movement behind indigenous mobilisation in the country, the Confederación de Nacionalidades Indígenas del Ecuador (CONAIE, Confederation of Indigenous Nationalities of Ecuador) (see Becker, 2008). Women have also been prominent in the leadership of the mainly indigenous Ejército Zapatista de Liberación Nacional (EZLN, Zapatista Army of National Liberation) in southern Mexico (see Boxes 12.6, 13.5).

Chile is an example of a country that has made significant progress in addressing the agenda of women's groups as part of a broader recognition of social pluralism and gender-related issues (see Box 13.8). Chile was once regarded as Latin America's most socially conservative country where old-fashioned attitudes towards gender equality prevailed even among sectors of the population that adopted progressive positions about equality in areas such as class. This meant that both men and women could be simultaneously progressive on political issues yet conservative on gender issues. Since democratisation, however, Chile has taken important strides in the struggle for women's rights. In 2005, for example, the two main contenders nominated for the presidential candidacy of the centre-left Concertación coalition were women former cabinet members: Michelle Bachelet of the Partido Socialista (PSCh, Socialist Party) and Soledad Alvear of the Partido Democrata Cristiano (PDC, Christian Democrat Party). A longstanding leftwing activist who was once tortured while under arrest during the Pinochet years, Bachelet trained as a surgeon and is a separated mother of three. She served as health minister in 2000–02 and defence minister in 2002–04. The more moderate Alvear – who withdrew to leave the way clear for Bachelet as Concertación candidate – served as justice minister in 1994–2000, and was credited with achieving free-trade agreements with the US and the EU as foreign minister from 2000–04. Bachelet's eventual victory in presidential elections in January 2006 was greeted with great enthusiasm by women across Latin America. She promptly unveiled a 20-strong cabinet comprising an equal number of women and men, with women being allocated such top ministerial positions as defence, economy and health. Bachelet extended this measure to positions beyond the cabinet, and brought an unprecedented

Chile's sexual revolution

At the time Richard's *Masculine/Feminine's* was first published in Chile, pioneering artists from the country were beginning to challenge gender-related themes that were formerly taboo. In 1994, a portrait of Simón Bolívar by the Chilean painter Juan Dávila caused diplomatic tensions by depicting the Independence hero wearing an open cassock exposing female breasts and hips (see Durán-Cogan, 2001). The publication and distribution of postcards incorporating Dávila's image, financed by the Chilean government, provoked formal diplomatic protests by the governments of Venezuela, Colombia, Ecuador and Bolivia. In March 2004, the *Financial Times* newspaper in London declared that a 'sexual revolution' was underway in Chile, where sex shops that would once have been the targets of harsh repression by the Pinochet regime now traded openly as the population questioned traditional values and mores (Mulligan, 2004). In 2002, about 5,000 people stripped off in public to pose in Santiago's Forestal Park for photographs by the performance photographer Spencer Tunick. Legislation to give homosexual couples the same conjugal rights as heterosexuals was put forward in 2003, divorce was finally legalised in March 2004, and television soap operas have started writing gay characters into their scripts. Mainstream politicians also now court these social groups. In 2003, transvestites in Santiago became celebrities during a campaign by Joaquín Lavin, the conservative mayor, to rid the streets of prostitutes. Lavin posed for the press with a group of transsexual prostitutes pledging to find them alternative work as hairdressers. However, resistance to giving same-sex couples the same rights as heterosexuals remains strong and demonstrates the persistence of social conservatism in Chile that was also in evidence in resistance to gender initiatives taken by President Michelle Bachelet (see above). By late 2009, Chilean legislators were still discussing the proposed civil union law and an Ipsos poll revealed that adults in the country were opposed to allowing gay and lesbian couples to wed, with 65.2 per cent of respondents not in favour of same-sex marriage (Angus Reid, 2009).

number of women into the state apparatus across a broad range of departments. In office, she championed sexual and reproductive freedom and gender equality played a prominent symbolic role in her political statements. Among other measures, Bachelet introduced a scheme to distribute free emergency contraception at public hospitals to teenage girls, introduced day-care initiatives for poor women, increased efforts to confront gender discrimination in the workplace, and promoted the idea of legal quotas in political parties for female candidates. However, Bachelet's tenure, which ended in 2010, has since been assessed as one in which she made limited gains on issues of gender equality (Lievesley, 2008; Llanos and Sample, 2008). There is also little consensus about the role played by feminism and the women's movement in her election (see Ríos Tobar, 2009). Bachelet struggled to find support within the Concertación coalition for women's policies, not least because her Christian democrat coalition partner, the PDC, holds conservative views on social issues such as reproductive rights and sexual freedom (Lievesley, 2009; see Chapter 12). Her proposals for quotas did not gain the consensus or support of congress. The country's feminist movement remains weak, and because of its limited role as a political force it was largely unable to support government policies or advocate changes (Ríos Tobar, 2009).

An influential contemporary Latin American feminist thinker, Nelly Richard, is also Chilean. Richard is a prominent cultural theorist and in her writing contemplates issues of Latin American identity, gender, postmodernism, neoliberalism and cultural resistance. Her most influential work, *Masculine/Feminine. Practices of difference(s)* (first published in English in 2004), came out in Chile in 1993 and was based on themes that emerged from the 1987 International Conference on Latin American Women's Literature in Santiago, one of the most important literary events to take place under the Pinochet dictatorship (1973–90). *Masculine/Feminine* is an influential work of Latin American feminist theory that seeks to explain why feminism has been important not only to the liberation of women but also to understanding how power was exercised under Chile's military regime. In it, Richard also explores broader gender construction, such as gay culture, and how feminists and gays work to break down the rigid structures of Chilean life. This work attests to the powerful challenge feminist ideas can pose to norms that have in the past been hegemonic in Latin America such as patriarchy, the male domination of power, based upon *machismo*. Gays and people with diverse sexual orientations continue to face considerable barriers to full equality in the region (see Corrales and Pecheny eds, 2010). Their treatment is regarded as an important barometer of tolerance in Latin American democracy and, despite the barriers to full equality, this has grown dramatically since 1998. Latinobarómetro data, for example, show that the proportion of people asked if they would not like to have a homosexual as a neighbour fell from 59 per cent in 1998 to 29 in 2009 (Latinobarómetro, 2009a). Buenos Aires became the first city in Latin America to approve civil unions for gay couples in 2002, but efforts by gays to test this law and marry since then have become mired in legal and religious wrangling. In late 2009, for example, plans by a couple in the Argentine city to take advantage of this rule – and thereby undertake what is thought to be the first gay marriage in Latin America – were suspended by a judge and referred to the supreme court. The couple then travelled to Tierra del Fuego province, where the provincial governor issued a special decree allowing them to wed. In 2009, Peru's interior ministry announced that it will ban homosexuals from the police force for damaging the image of the institution. The move was regarded as particularly controversial for having been put forward by a woman, the interior minister Mercedes Cabanillas of the centre-left Partido Aprista Peruano (the Alianza Popular Revolucionaria Americana, APRA, American Popular Revolutionary Alliance).

Various feminist analyses seeking to explain women's subordination and devise strategies for their emancipation, such as socialist feminism, have evolved in Latin America, alongside more moderate arguments emphasising female 'difference' deriving, for example, from motherhood.

Many early feminists combined their activities with membership of socialist and anarchist parties, obeying the maxim 'there's no feminism without socialism'. The social character of feminism in Latin America has often distinguished it from the rights-based individualism of US and European 'liberal' feminisms (Molyneux, 2001). Since the 1950s, ideas of community activism and participation originating on the left have been influencing many women's and feminist movements, which have often supported broader projects of social reform. Yet the relationship between socialism and feminism is complex, and in the 1960s and 1970s many on the left dismissed feminism as a bourgeois distraction and argued that women's subordination would automatically end with the development of socialism (Craske, 1999). The complexity of the relationship between feminism and socialism was revealed in Nicaragua where, despite progressive actions by the Sandinistas, feminist critiques of male power had little impact on official thinking and economic development policies took priority over the goal of female emancipation. The wave of left-of-centre movements and leaders that have taken power in Latin America since 1998 has also revealed the limits of the relationship between feminism and leftwing politics. The Left in Latin America has traditionally made women's rights a political priority, partly on the basis that efforts to fight poverty and tackle inequality must necessarily target women because they are still mainly responsible for family survival strategies. Yet Lievesley and Ludlam (2009) are among those who have argued that the left-of-centre governments in Latin America have not generally challenged prevailing gender relations, and have also struggled to overcome a conservative and Catholic backlash on policy proposals on issues such as abortion (see Chapters 7, 12).

In Latin America, the feminine was traditionally cherished and feminists often acted to protest against laws and conditions that prevented them from fulfilling such roles as the ability to nurture children and raise a family. In the nineteenth century, both supporters and opponents of female suffrage drew upon arguments that emphasised female 'difference' – deriving, above all, from motherhood – to support their positions (see Pieper Mooney, 2009). Motherhood was used by women to demonstrate their loyalty to the nation-state and hence their right to equal citizenship. Motherhood was idealised through *marianismo*, an equivalent idea to *machismo* exalting the virtues of womanhood derived from the role of the Virgin Mary in Catholic tradition. Motherhood also fitted neatly with nationalism – emphasising women's contribution to the forging of nationality through child bearing – and so political activity to defend it was acceptable to both men and women, right and left. In Argentina, the Peronist movement transformed motherhood into a political function imposed by the state (Craske, 1999). Eva Perón, (b.1919–d.1952), the popular wife of President Juan Domingo Perón (1946–55, 1973–74), became a powerful symbol of feminine virtues. In Nicaragua, both anti-Somocista women and many *contra* women used the rhetoric of motherhood (González, 2001; Kampwirth, 2001). The theme of motherhood also appeared within populism and the socialist iconography of revolutionary regimes. The emblem of the Sandinista women's organisation, the Asociación de Mujeres Nicaragüenses Luisa Amanda Espinosa (AMNLAE, the Luisa Amanda Espinosa Association of Nicaraguan Women) portrayed a woman bearing both gun and infant. Luisa Amanda was believed to be the first woman to die in combat against Somoza's National Guard. A newspaper cartoon about Mexico's Chiapas rebels depicted a pregnant indigenous woman with a grenade in her womb. Some Latin American feminists continue to use family arguments to secure rights and reject radical equality feminism. However, Jaquette (2009b) suggests that many women have concluded, in the Latin American context, that the approaches taken by 'difference' feminism and egalitarian feminism can be complementary, rather than opposed.

A number of key issues have been prominent in the evolution of feminism, such as class, organisational autonomy, citizenship and broad gender interests.

Feminism in Latin America was traditionally associated with the social elite, although women have played important political roles on both right and left. From 1900 to 1940 in Argentina, Brazil and Chile, upper- and middle-class women participated in rightwing organisations as an extension of their activities in the Church, spreading bourgeois notions of femininity and rejecting feminism as a set of ideas (McGee Deutsch, 1991; see also Chapter 12). In Chile, middle-class women mobilised against the Marxist president Salvador Allende (1970–73) and rejected feminist goals. In Bolivia, middle-class women have been active within the business-led rightwing opposition in eastern provinces to the reforms of the country's leftwing president, Evo Morales, through such organisations as the Comité Cívico Femenino (Feminine Civic Committees) (see Box 12.11). Rightwing parties and organisations have often emphasised the traditional Catholic view of women as mothers and housewives. Bolivia's feminine civic committees, for example, describe themselves as housewives and denounce what they argue is the impact of inflationary leftwing policies on household budgets. Yet women have also been prominent in radical upheavals – from the Mexican Revolution (1910–17) to the Chiapas rebellion (1994) – and have been just as influenced by the revolutionary tradition in Latin America as their male counterparts (see Boxes 1.5, 12.6, 13.5). They became armed combatants in the Sandinista revolutionary army and, at one stage, dominated the leadership of the Peruvian Maoist guerrilla organisation Sendero Luminoso (see Boxes 12.4, 13.9). Women have been prominent in the leadership of the Ejército Zapatista de Liberación Nacional (EZLN, Zapatista Army of National Liberation) in southern Mexico, and were behind the movement's proclamation of a 'Women's Revolutionary Law', a radical statement of equality. Women leaders of the Zapatistas have included Comandante Ramona, the *nom de guerre* of a Tzotzil Indian and a promoter of women's rights who died in 2006, and Subcomandante Elisa (María Gloria Benavides Guevara). The prominence of women in EZLN affairs has prompted some supporters to suggest that, while it is not a feminist movement, it is a *feminine* movement (see Blanc *et al.*, 2009). Other women have argued that a distinct form of 'indigenous feminism' exists in places like southern Mexico in which women struggle to draw on and navigate western ideologies while attempting to preserve and reclaim indigenous traditions (see Hymn, 2009).

CASE STUDY   Box 13.9

Sendero Luminoso – a woman's touch

According to Peruvian police, 56 per cent of the leadership of the Maoist guerrilla organisation Sendero Luminoso (Shining Path) was made up of women, making it a rebel army led by more women than men (BBC, 1993). Following the arrest of Sendero's leader Abimael Guzmán in September 1992 amid a comprehensive counter-insurgency campaign by the Peruvian military, the organisation's senior figures were able to meet to name a national co-ordinator whom police alleged was Teresa Durand Araujo, alias Comrade Doris. The Sendero leadership also formed a collegiate four-member presidency to replace Guzmán, two of whose members were thought to have been women: Comrade Doris and Margie Clavo Peralta, alias Comrade Nancy. The police claimed that the new Shining Path leader in

Lima, the organisation's fifth most senior official, was Jenny Rodríguez Mata. In July 1993, the Peruvian police disseminated a video that was broadcast by national television stations allegedly showing members of the organisation's central committee during a 1987 congress held secretly in Lima – 19 members (56 per cent) of whom were women. The police claimed to have arrested 15 top leaders from the 1987 congress, 10 of whom were women. Comrade Doris was Shining Path's military leader when Guzmán was arrested and had led the initial guerrilla insurgency in Ancash in northern Peru from 1980–82 before becoming Sendero's regional leader in Ayacucho in the south-east where the organisation had been created. Edith Lagos, a revered Sendero commander, led a raid on an Ayacucho prison, freeing more than 250 prisoners, and was killed in 1982 aged just 19.

Peruvian lawyers, psychologists and sociologists noted that Sendero's female members were often more well educated than their male counterparts and often appeared bolder in armed actions. The senderistas ordered to administer the *coup de grâce* to the victims of public assassinations were usually women. Their promotion to leadership positions also reflected Guzmán's rapport with women and his own commitment to women's issues. When he was 29, Guzmán married Augusta Latorre, the daughter of a communist leader in Ayacucho who became his closest political ally under the *nom de guerre* of Comrade Norah until her death in 1988. Norah's loyalty to Guzmán was among the reasons he promoted so many women in his organisation. Sendero also paid close ideological attention to the plight of Peruvian women based on ideas originating with Friedrich Engels about a woman's lack of control over material possessions. Catalina Adrianzen, one of the organisation's founders and most senior leaders until her capture in 1982, was Sendero's principal ideologue on the role of women. The wife of one of the guerrilla movement's most important ideologues, Antonio Díaz Martínez (see Box 12.4), Adrianzen was captured by Peruvian security forces and jailed for being a Sendero military commander in the Cuzco region. It is believed she died in captivity during the mid-1980s. In the 1970s, Adrianzen had founded and led the Movimiento Femenino Popular (MFP, Women's Popular Movement) in Ayacucho as a feminist adjunct to Sendero. Her only known work, *El marxismo, Mariátegui y el movimiento femenino* (1974) was an effort to analyse the condition of Peruvian women from a class perspective. She wrote:

> Marx, Engels, Lenin and Mao Zedong put forward the thesis of women's emancipation, not that of female liberation. The latter appears historically as a bourgeois thesis in whose depths is hidden the opposition of men and women through sex and which camouflages the root of the oppression of women.

Source: Peru's Red Sun of Terror Sets, *Observer*, 25/7/1993, p. 11 (O'Shaughnessy, S.) Copyright Guardian News & Media Ltd 1993

Given these diverse alignments, class divisions have tended to weaken feminism and efforts to forge a gender-based solidarity. A key issue has been whether women should put their gender or class interests first. Women's organisations in revolutionary Cuba and Nicaragua argued that the defence of the revolution was the prerequisite for feminine emancipation and so took precedence. Women have found it difficult to transcend the left–right political divide with successful coalition-building.

One of the things women on both right and left did have in common was a desire for autonomy from male-dominated political parties and guerrilla organisations. This desire was strengthened by the mobilisation of women against authoritarian governments, during which many leftwing organisations revealed themselves to be hostile to the idea of gender equality. A key issue in feminism, therefore, has been the appropriate extent of women's autonomy from male-dominated political organisations. Some feminists have sought to guard their autonomy from parties jealously while others who belong to political groups have promoted 'dual militancy' – advocating the struggle for women's liberation from male domination alongside a broad class struggle for distributive justice for all regardless of gender. Women on the right have often enjoyed greater autonomy in office than their left-wing counterparts. Other women have chosen to exert significant pressure from within a male-dominated political process. In Argentina, the left-of-centre Cristina Fernández of the Partido Justicialista (PJ, Justicialist Party i.e. the Peronists), a former senator and the wife of her presidential predecessor, Néstor Kirchner (2003–07), became the country's first elected female president in 2007. Fernández is a member of the Council of Women World Leaders, an international network of current and former women presidents and prime ministers. She is a lawyer by training and has carved out her own political career, but has adopted a subtle political strategy that combines an emphasis on her independent qualities while positioning herself as the heir to her husband's political legacy. None the less, this has not silenced a common refrain in commentary both within and outside Argentina that her husband and predecessor, Néstor Kirchner, remains the power behind the throne, indicating the persistence and strength of patriarchal ideas when confronted by women's political progress. Another common patriarchal position is the accusation made by men against presidents such as Michelle Bachelet in Chile, for example, of 'weak' leadership (see Lievesley and Ludlam, 2009).

Although women played a prominent role in the struggle for democracy in Latin America, few were subsequently elected to office once democratic institutions had become established. In response, gender quotas became a tool for increasing the representation of women, and are considered an important element of democracy. Argentina pioneered the use of quotas with a law in 1991 establishing that at least 30 per cent of candidates for elected office must be women. Other countries followed suit, although the proportion of seats allocated to women varies from 20 to 50 per cent. However, there remain differences among women themselves about the value and most appropriate form of quotas: having women in power does not guarantee that they will champion feminist concerns, and may absolve men of the sense that they share responsibility for women too. Quotas also work better in some countries than in others: in Argentina the proportion of women elected by 2008 stood at 38.3 per cent, while in Brazil it was only 8.8 per cent (Llanos and Sample, 2008). A study that compared the functioning of gender quotas in Argentina and Brazilian politics highlighted important differences in such factors as the wording of the quota laws and electoral systems (see Marx *et al.*, 2009).

Outside formal institutional politics, social movements have also proved alternative arenas allowing feminists to forge cross-class or cross-ethnic links more effectively. The proliferation of social movements and NGOs since the 1980s has given significant momentum to feminist organisations and provided new opportunities for women to engage in activist politics (see, for example, Rousseau, 2009). One important initiative in Latin America was the creation in 2000 of the Articulación Feminista Marcosur (AFM, Southern Framework for Feminist Articulation), which brings together groups in Uruguay, Brazil, Chile, Paraguay, Argentina, Bolivia and Peru. Feminists have been particularly active within the World Social Forum, the annual meeting in Brazil of activists and social movements, for example, and the AFM sits on this organisation's international committee (see Vargas,

2009; see also Box 15.8). At the same time, middle-class women have often participated in local schemes to alleviate poverty, such as the provision of street kitchens in Peru and Chile, and are often prominent in poverty-alleviation initiatives run by the Catholic Church (see Chapter 7).

Yet women remain victims of male discrimination – and often of male violence – in much of Latin America. The northern Mexican city of Ciudad Juárez, for example, became notorious after hundreds of women were murdered in a wave of killings between 1993 and 2003, often involving rape and mutilation but with no single apparent motive, in what activists and academics have sometimes described as 'femicide' (see Staudt and Montoya, 2009). Serious concerns about the threats to women in the city, and about the police disregard and corruption that had allowed the violence to persist, brought the issue to international attention, prompted the intervention of the federal government, and led to the creation of a number of women's initiatives and social movements aimed at confronting violence. In Brazil, a ruling in 2001 by the Comisión Interamericana de Derechos Humanos (CIDH, Inter-American Commission on Human Rights, IACHR) against the government in the case of María da Penha – who suffered two murder attempts and such serious attacks at the hands of her husband in the early 1980s that she was left paraplegic at the age of 38 – exposed the legal system's ineffectiveness in dealing with domestic violence. Her husband was able to take advantage of procedural appeals to remain free and the case was eventually taken to the IACHR, which found the Brazilian state guilty of negligence and a failure to act against domestic violence (see Piovesan, 2009). It was the first time a case of domestic violence resulted in a guilty verdict against a country within the inter-American system, and the ruling paved the way for an innovative new law in Brazil adopted in 2006 specifically addressing violence against women.

Such stark realities pose important questions about the quality of citizenship enjoyed by many women in Latin America (see Chapters 3, 4). Molyneux (2001) has discussed the issues of feminism with regard to the wider debate on citizenship, noting that feminist critiques have inspired a range of works on citizenship and challenged tenets of liberalism (see Jaquette, 2009b). In this sense, debates surrounding the formative themes of liberalism have been a key axis in the evolution of feminist ideas in Latin America (see Chapter 12). A feature of Latin American feminist politics has been the endorsement of active, participatory citizenship, and women have been identified as an important force in the reconstitution of civil society (see Box 8.1). As Craske has argued, women's participation in all aspects of any democratic society is crucial to the quality of democracy itself (see Chapter 4). Some Latin American feminists have joined criticisms of the liberal concept of citizenship based on individual rights, and have argued for a version of citizenship that is more participatory, socially responsible and responds to the practical issues of everyday life. This implies a definition of democracy that is less formal and procedural and more substantive and social (see Chapter 3). Jaquette (2009b) also points out that women's organisations form part of civil society in Latin America, and hence feminist deliberations are part of larger debates about civil society and the state, pluralism, and challenges to neoliberal globalisation (see Box 15.8). Feminist positions have also helped to revive questions of morality in debates on public policy and reinforced the idea of communitarianism, which enshrines a critique of liberal individualism and affirms collectivist moral positions. Some feminists have even argued that liberal individualism itself is premised on a *masculine* ideal of freedom. Others, however, challenge this notion and suggest that individual autonomy is a dimension of citizenship that is especially important for women who have lived under patriarchy and authoritarianism (see Valdés and Donoso, 2009).

Summary

Latin America's history as a region colonised by European settlers who co-existed with large indigenous and imported slave populations has always made questions of personal and group identity prominent in political and social thought. Nationalism as an ideology emerged in an early form at the time of Independence and, until the late nineteenth century, elites copied the liberal political nationalism of Europe. The creation of the state preceded a generalised acceptance of the existence of the 'nation', and so a key theme in nationalist thought in Latin America has been the notion of nation-building. As Latin America began to participate more fully in the export economy towards the end of the nineteenth century, an economic content was injected into nationalism and, in the face of US expansion, nationalist writers began to articulate cultural anxieties. An association between nationalism and economic and social themes also reflected the emergence of mass politics. Nationalism appealed to military officers and formed the ideology of populist movements advocating state-led industrialisation. The military regimes of the 1970s also advocated a form of autarkic nationalism, but democratisation and the rise of neoliberal ideas based on universal themes have challenged nationalist perspectives.

Racial and ethnic themes have been prominent in Latin American thought since the Conquest. Although nineteenth-century liberals employed emancipatory rhetoric proclaiming equality, in practice elites excluded indigenous people from politics. However, miscegenation and liberal reforms replaced the caste-like social order with a class-based society. New racial theories developed during the nineteenth century that helped to justify elite rule, although ideas that placed a premium on whiteness also made it possible for mixed groups to justify their own socially higher position in relation to indigenous and black people. In countries with large indigenous and *mestizo* populations, ideologies emerged urging the recovery of indigenous culture and claiming to seek the emancipation of indigenous people. These sometimes gained official recognition because they supported the creation of an interventionist state committed to nation-building. A racist orthodoxy gave way to official anti-racist positions in Latin America, and the integration of indigenous populations through *indigenismo* gained respectability. A resurgence of indigenous mobilisation since the 1970s gained force with democratisation. The rise of indigenous consciousness has pushed issues such as cultural diversity, autonomy and the impact of neoliberal reform up the political agenda. It has also given impetus to the claims of Afro-descendant groups. Indigenous demands for self-determination and autonomy pose questions about national identity in Latin America and reinforce demands for greater pluralism in politics that have been supported by black organisations.

The role of women in Latin American society is a key issue in contemporary social thought that has informed debates about citizenship. Feminist movements of the late nineteenth century were concerned with the vote, protective labour laws and education. During the 1960s and 1970s a 'second wave' of class-conscious feminism was influenced by writing coming out of Europe and the US. The feminist struggle became intertwined with opposition to authoritarianism and, in the 1980s, women's movements were prominent in campaigns for democracy. Various feminist analyses have evolved in Latin America, where the social character of feminism distinguishes these from the rights-based individualism of US and European 'liberal' feminisms. Issues prominent in the evolution of feminist ideas have included motherhood, class, organisational autonomy and citizenship. Although feminism in Latin America was traditionally associated with the social elite, women have also played a significant role in radical movements. However, class divisions have tended to weaken feminism and a key issue has been whether women should put their gender or class interests first. A feature of the feminist critique in Latin America has been the endorsement of active, participatory citizenship, and some feminists have criticised liberal concepts of citizenship based on individual rights. Women have made gains in terms of representation and achieving political office, but continue to face discrimination, and some scholars argue that the impact of the feminist movement has been limited.

Discussion points

- To what extent was nationalism a product of the encounter with capitalism?
- Is nationalism in a globalising world likely to survive as a political ideology?
- What roles have ideas about race and ethnicity played for elites in Latin America?
- Do notions of indigenous autonomy threaten the Latin American state?
- Is the emphasis on motherhood that influenced feminism a betrayal of its principles?
- Is the liberal feminism of the US and Europe unrealistic in *macho* Latin America?

Useful websites

http://mnp.tripod.com.pe Movimiento Nacionalista Peruano (MNP, Peruvian Nationalist Movement)

www.pndcuba.org Partido Nacionalista Democrático (PND, Democratic Nationalist Party), Cuban exile party based in Miami created by former opponents of Batista that uses theme of nationalism in its opposition to Castro

www.struggle.ws/mexico/ezlnco.html Translated communiques of the Ejército Zapatista de Liberación Nacional (EZLN, Zapatista National Liberation Army)

www.pachakutik.org.ec Movimiento Unidad Plurinacional Pachakutik – Nuevo País (Plurinational Pachakutik Unity-New Country Movement), Ecuador's pioneering indigenous party

www.masbolivia.com Movimiento al Socialismo (MAS, Movement Towards Socialism), ruling leftwing party in Bolivia that has become an important vehicle for indigenous people

www.cdi.gob.mx Comisión Nacional para el Desarollo de los Pueblos Indígenas (CDI, National Commission for the Development of Indigenous People), Mexico

www.laneta.apc.org/cni/mh.htm Congreso Nacional Indígena (CNI, National Indigenous Congress), umbrella organisation for indigenous groups in Mexico, contains links to other indigenous fora

www.TeleSURtv.net TeleSUR television station's website, Venezuela

www.gloobal.net/iepala/gloobal/fichas/ficha.php?entidad=Actividades&id=1062 Site for the 10th Latin American and Caribbean Feminist Encounter in São Paulo, 2005, containing a number of useful links to feminist groups

www.eclac.cl/mujer Comisión Económica para América Latina y el Caribe (CEPAL, Economic Commission for Latin America and the Caribbean, ECLAC) Gender Affairs Division

www.ciudadaniasexual.org Proyecto Sexualidades, Salud y Derechos Humanos en América Latina (Latin American Sexuality, Health and Human Rights Project)

www.cladem.org Comité de América Latina y el Caribe para la Defensa de los Derechos de la Mujer (CLADEM, The Latin American and Caribbean Committee for the Defence of Women's Rights), network and portal for women's groups supported by NGOs

www.oas.org/cim/defaults.htm La Comisión Interamericana de Mujeres (CIM, Interamerican Commission for Women), specialized OAS agency

www.cipacdh.org Centro de Investigación y Promoción para América Central de Derechos Humanos (CIPAC/DDHH, Central American Centre for Research and Promotion of Human Rights), Costa Rican gay and lesbian rights group

www.un.org/womenwatch/directory/latin_america_10474.htm United Nations Inter-Agency Network on Women and Gender Equality Latin America page, with useful links to official initiatives

www.cepal.org/oig ECLAC Gender Equality Observatory of Latin America and the Caribbean

www.unifem.org/worldwide/americas_caribbean UN Development Fund for Women Americas page, with useful links to Latin American initiatives

www.eurosur.org/FLACSO/mujeres Mujeres Latinoamericanas en Cifras (Latin American Women in Figures), site provided by the independent Facultad Latinoamericana de Ciencias Sociales (FLACSO, Latin American Social Sciences Faculty)

www.mujeresdelsur-afm.org.uy/index_e.htm Articulación Feminista Marcosur (AFM, Southern Framework for Feminist Articulation)

Recommended reading

Castro-Klarén, Sara and John Charles Chasteen (eds). 2003. *Beyond Imagined Communities: Reading and Writing the Nation in Nineteenth-Century Latin America.* Washington, DC: Woodrow Wilson Center Press/Baltimore, MD: Johns Hopkins University Press

Useful collection of essays on the development of national identities in nineteenth-century Latin America that is theoretically grounded in a reassessment of the work on nationalism in the region by Benedict Anderson (1991)

Williamson, Edwin. 1992. 'Nationalism and Development: An Overview', Chapter 9 in *The Penguin History of Latin America.* London: Penguin Books

> *Useful introduction to the relationship between nationalism and the development of the state and economy from the early twentieth century until the 1980s*

Appelbaum, Nancy, Anne MacPherson and Karin Alejandra Rosemblatt (eds). 2003. *Race and Nation in Modern Latin America.* Chapel Hill, NC: University of North Carolina Press

> *Essential introduction to the study of race and ethnicity that combines historical and anthropological analysis to explore race as a construct at the heart of Latin American political and social evolution*

Olesen, Thomas. 2004. *International Zapatismo. The Construction of Solidarity in the Age of Globalization.* London: Zed Books

> *Useful insight into how a localised social movement has formed the core of a global solidarity network that contains many lessons about the ideological role indigenous organisations can play*

Del Valle Escalante, Emilio. 2009. *Maya Nationalisms and Postcolonial Challenges in Guatemala: Coloniality, Modernity, and Identity Politics.* Santa Fe, NM: School for Advanced Research Press

> *Useful introduction to the impact of indigenous mobilisation in the realm of ideas, taking the Maya as its focus*

Reid Andrews, George. 2004. *Afro-Latin America, 1800–2000.* Oxford: Oxford University Press

> *Essential historical introduction to the history of people of African descent across Latin America that examines how they helped shape political, economic and cultural changes in these societies*

Jaquette, Jane S. (ed.). 2009. *Feminist Agendas and Democracy in Latin America.* Durham, NC: Duke University Press

> *Essential introduction to feminism in Latin America with chapters that explore a range of key issues in its study and case studies*

Corrales, Javier and Mario Pecheny (eds). 2010. *The Politics of Sexuality in Latin America: A Reader on Lesbian, Gay, Bisexual, and Transgender Rights.* Pittsburgh, PA: University of Pittsburgh Press

> *Essential reader on LGBT politics in Latin America bringing together scholarship around two core themes: inroads made in the struggle for rights, alongside limited progress in comparison with other social movements*

Part V

ECONOMIC IDEAS

Chapter 14

Structuralism and dependency

This chapter examines why many Latin American countries whose economic development until the Second World War had been shaped overwhelmingly by agriculture and mining embarked on strategies that, instead, made industrialisation a top priority. It looks at the main economic argument that justified this policy shift, called 'structuralism', and the profound implications this would have for the state and the character of politics in Latin America. The strategies proposed and adopted by economists to exploit a country's resources are of great importance to the ways in which social and political systems evolve. They determine who will be the main winners in a process of economic development – and who will be the losers. In turn, they shape the nature of the state and the behaviour of the political actors who seek to influence its policymaking role.

Until the 1930s, the model of development in Latin America had been dominated by a small, landowning oligarchy controlling agricultural production on vast estates. This model of development found its main political reflection in systems that excluded all but the elite from policymaking and in extreme levels of inequality. However, ideas that came out of the Great Depression eventually led to a transformation in the structure of the region's economies that placed a priority on industry. Industrialisation nurtured a form of development that benefitted urban social sectors and eroded the power of traditional landowners, but continued to exclude the peasants. It found new institutional expressions in the emergence of unwieldy, centralising states comprising large, bureaucratic ministries, and political expressions in the populism and corporatism that allowed elites dominating these states to maintain a core body of support to ensure stability (see Boxes 2.2, 7.1). However, like the models that had preceded it, rapid industrialisation generated social and political strains and began to run out of steam. The exclusion of large numbers of people from the benefits it promised and from the coalitions by which it was maintained fuelled unrest. Millions of peasants abandoned the countryside and headed for the city, swelling urbanisation. Radical economic perspectives based on the theme of 'dependence' gained force in the ideologically tense Cold War atmosphere. Political alternatives developed outside the formal institutions of politics and sought new sources of support in the countryside and among the urban poor. These stresses all contributed to authoritarian clampdowns by military regimes at a time when industrialisation had begun to falter. Once again, this set back the achievement of democracy (see Chapter 2).

From export-led growth to industrialisation

Before the Great Depression many policymakers and economists in Latin America had believed that the region's best prospects for growth could be found in exporting commodities that could be produced in abundance in their mainly agricultural and mining economies then sold to the growing industrial countries of Europe and to the US. This position was supported by the theory of comparative advantage in international trade, an influential doctrine that originated with the British economist David Ricardo (b.1772–d.1823). The notion of comparative advantage suggests that a country will gain the greatest economic benefit in a trading relationship with other countries by concentrating its production on commodities that it can provide at a lower overall cost, either because these are found in relative abundance or they can be produced relatively easily within its territory. In turn, other countries in a trading relationship are themselves better off if they accept the cost advantage the first country may have in producing that commodity, and themselves concentrate on producing other commodities in which they have advantages. Comparative advantage is the main basis for most economists' belief in free trade – international trade as free as possible from nationally imposed barriers such as tariffs and quotas on imports and exports. It is an important principle in economics because it implies an international *division of labour* in which some countries stick to producing agricultural or mineral commodities for sale to others that produce industrial goods. Comparative advantage and free trade are also important elements of the philosophy of economic liberalism, which places a premium on the benefits of free enterprise conducted within markets unimpeded by artificial barriers imposed by states.

In Argentina, Latin America's most prosperous economy by the early twentieth century, such ideas appeared to make sense and the country's role in the international economy as a supplier of agricultural commodities and raw materials from mining (together known as primary products) seemed natural. These ideas suggested that Argentina was best served by concentrating on the production and sale of beef, which could be produced intensively and cheaply from huge herds of cattle grazing on the vast pampas plains, and exchanged in a free international market with the highest or most reliable bidder in return for imported manufactured products. After all, until the Depression such a model had delivered unprecedented rates of growth and even small socialist organisations did not question the bias in favour of export-led agricultural production. This economic model had nurtured the development of distinctive political systems based on the exclusion of the vast majority of people (see Box 14.1).

The Great Depression that followed the Wall Street crash of 1929 hit Latin America hard as demand for its products withered and its ability to pay for imports declined, causing recessions and fuelling the growth of radical ideas and political unrest. The Depression forced Latin American countries to reconsider their relationship with the international economic system, with some thinkers arguing that the region had been forced into a disadvantaged position in the global division of labour. In particular, policymakers became aware of the need to reduce their reliance on the export of commodities and the import of manufactured goods, and in the 1930s

Export-led growth and the politics of exclusion

The most important political and social characteristics of societies with export-led economies, such as those of Latin America, were inequality and exclusion. This is because the main beneficiary of export growth was a powerful oligarchy comprising large landowners and merchants who tried to maintain their control over politics in their own interests well into the 1920s. In Argentina, for example, ranchers and export merchants worked hard to exclude others from politics, and political institutions were designed and administered by these powerful groups to support the main objectives of an economic model that benefited them. The main losers from Latin America's role in the international division of labour as a producer of agricultural goods and raw materials were poorly paid rural workers, many of whom began to head for the growing cities to find a better living, fuelling urbanisation. At the same time, economic growth created new, mainly urban middle-class professionals, bureaucrats, shopkeepers and small businessmen (see Chapter 1). The spontaneous development of small industries and mines, and increases in immigration, led to the emergence of a small working class. Growing urban populations did not fit easily into the social hierarchy that had supported the development of large estates and ranches for export-led growth, and tended to be more politically volatile than rural populations. As a result, the model of export-led growth adopted across Latin America generated new class tensions and in some countries such as Mexico, the continuing exclusion of the middle classes and rural poor led to agitation and political conflict (see Box 1.5).

The pressures generated by export-led growth helped to undermine the control of the oligarchs across much of Latin America, and political systems were in transition from the 1920s as elements of the oligarchy saw the need to incorporate the middle classes and workers into the policymaking process. Middle-class politicians often assumed nationalist positions that attacked foreign interests while advocating greater state intervention in the economy to ensure a fairer distribution of resources. Although oligarchical governments began to adapt by advocating more nationalist policies that proposed protectionism – the introduction of restrictions such as tariffs or quotas on some imports in order to favour local producers – it was the Great Depression that provided the stimulus for influential new ideas that would transform the economies and politics of Latin America (see Chapter 2).

most countries in the region took the first steps towards nurturing their own industries through import-substitution industrialisation (ISI, see Chapter 2). They began to restructure their economies by adopting protectionist policies in order to protect local industries from foreign competition, and this was made easier by the nationalist climate of the period that justified hostility to foreign economic activities (see Chapter 13). Some countries, such as Brazil, adopted policies that had, by the Second World War, allowed them to achieve substantial industrial growth. This early industrialisation coincided with a growing interest in Keynesianism – the body of thought developed by the British economist John Maynard Keynes (b.1883–d.1946) that advocated a greater role for the state in development – and with the apparent successes of central planning in the Soviet Union. These ideas all contributed in the 1940s to the emergence of the new 'structuralist' perspective in Latin America advocating the need for countries to create industry in order to rely less on the production of primary products. Structuralist ideas also represented a rejection of influential perspectives that were developing in the industrialised world about how agrarian societies developed into modern industrial economies (see Box 14.2).

Given Argentina's position in the vanguard of export-led growth, it is not surprising that the most influential Latin American structuralist to emerge from the period of reassessment following the Great Depression was an Argentinean, Raúl Prebisch (b.1901–d.1986). Prebisch was the first director of the United Nations' Comisión Económica para América Latina (CEPAL, Economic Commission for Latin America, whose acronym in English was originally ECLA, later ECLAC to incorporate the Caribbean) which, from 1948, became the source of many

---

THEORIES AND DEBATES   **Box 14.2**

Modernisation

The Marshall Plan pursued by the US following the Second World War pumped large amounts of aid into the devastated countries of Europe, enabling them to rebuild and modernise their economies in just a few years. This experience had an important influence on perspectives in the industrialised world about development in mainly agrarian societies. In this period, economists often began with an assumption that the industrialised countries had also once been underdeveloped agrarian societies, and so development could be understood as a series of successive stages through which all countries pass (Todaro, 1994). These evolutionary assumptions are the basis of modernisation theory, sometimes called linear-stage or stages-of-growth theory, and reflected the optimism and anti-communism of the postwar era. Modernisation perspectives became influential in US universities and are associated with the work of the sociologist Talcott Parsons (b.1902–d.1979) and the economic historian Walt W. Rostow (b.1916–d.2003) (see Box 3.1). They presented development as a move away from a traditional society shaped by communities to one based on individual values by imitating the developed world under the leadership of local entrepreneurial elites, passing through different stages en route to modernity (see Parsons, 1954; Rostow, 1962). All that was necessary to enable backward countries in regions such as Latin America to follow the same path as the developed world was the right mixture of investment, aid and savings. Perspectives originating in modernisation theory have been highly influential in shaping how development is understood in Latin America and the attitudes of the industrialised world towards the region. Such attitudes have a benign view of industrial capitalism and see the problems of developing countries as internal to them and not shaped by external factors. They emphasise the importance of culture and values, especially those of the middle class, by explaining development in terms of the characteristics of the US and Europe and how the absence of similar values is an obstacle for regions such as Latin America (*ibid.*). Lastly, modernisation perspectives assumed that the conditions (such as markets, transport facilities, educated workers and efficient administration) that had enabled rapid reconstruction of postwar Europe also existed in underdeveloped nations. There have been many criticisms of the modernisation perspective, and these criticisms formed the core of alternative models of political economy such as structuralism. Modernisation theory has been described as 'ethnocentric' because it understood development, and prescribed a formula for it, from the perspective of the industrialised West. It has been criticised for ignoring history and turning a blind eye both to the impact of colonialism in the developing world and the complex realities of Latin America, where power has often been concentrated in the hands of a small elite. Stages theories have also been criticised for failing to take into account the crucial role played by *international* factors in developing economies.

structuralist ideas (see Box 14.3). The ideas developed by Prebisch derived from his understanding of how the Depression had affected his native Argentina during the 1930s. They were refined in the years after the Second World War and were reinforced by the work of another UN economist, the German Hans Singer (b.1910–d.2006). The central argument that these economists developed is, as a result, sometimes referred to as the Prebisch-Singer thesis about unequal exchange in world trade. It had two underlying themes:

Centre-periphery

Prebisch believed the world comprised a 'centre' of developed industrialised countries and a 'periphery' of those that only produced agricultural goods and raw materials. He argued that the centre and periphery are closely interlinked through trade and that, because of the higher value of industrial products manufactured in the centre in relation to the raw materials and agricultural goods produced in the

---

INSTITUTIONS   **Box 14.3**

The Economic Commission for Latin America and the Caribbean

The Economic Commission for Latin America (ECLA) was established by the United Nations in 1948 to contribute to the economic development of the region, to co-ordinate actions towards that end, and to reinforce economic relationships between Latin American countries and other nations. Its scope was later broadened to include the countries of the Caribbean and it changed its name to ECLAC in 1984. ECLAC's theories and approaches have been recognised in many parts of the world. In its early years it developed its own method of analysis – 'historical structuralism' – which it has largely maintained to the present day. This approach focuses on the analysis of the ways in which Latin America's inherited institutional and production structure influence its economic dynamics. ECLAC does not recognise the existence of the uniform 'stages of development' foreseen by modernisation theory, arguing that circumstances are different for 'latecomers to development'. Five phases have been identified in ECLAC's theoretical work:

- 1950s: industrialisation through import substitution (ISI);
- 1960s: reforms to facilitate industrialisation;
- 1970s: reorientation of development 'styles' towards greater social homogeneity and diversification as a means of promoting exports;
- 1980s: overcoming the external debt crisis through 'adjustment with growth';
- 1990s: changing production patterns with social equity.

Since the end of the 1990s, ECLAC has sought to demonstrate how the conditions of Latin America and the Caribbean's integration in the global economy have a negative effect on the region and cause macroeconomic instability, low growth and adverse social effects. It has also warned about the impact of neoliberal reforms on the region's economies and has argued that there is a need to seek a more balanced form of globalisation, in order to 'reform the reforms' (see Chapters 15, 16).

Source: ECLAC, 2005a

periphery, peripheral countries were at a natural disadvantage in any trading relationship. Prebisch believed the prices of products made in the more technically advanced economies rose more quickly than those produced by backward economies, and pointed to Latin America's deteriorating terms of trade – the import prices of what countries in the region bought remained the same or rose, while the prices of what they sold on the world market declined. In the long term, this meant that Latin American economies would have to export more to buy the same quantity of manufactured imports. In this way, peripheral economies that persisted in exporting primary products would not benefit from free trade.

Surplus labour

Prebisch also argued that the pattern of economic development in peripheral countries under these arrangements was far more likely to generate a surplus of labour comprising workers squeezed out of primary products sectors such as agriculture by the constant need to control production costs because of the declining terms of trade. Unlike developed countries, however, it is more difficult in the periphery to redeploy these displaced workers to dynamic sectors such as manufacturing, because these sectors are so small and do not grow rapidly. If workers displaced from primary sectors are not absorbed, this pushes down the incomes of other workers. Low incomes are an important characteristic of underdevelopment and, in this way, it was believed that unequal exchange *caused* underdevelopment.

Prebisch concluded that the only way for Latin American countries to escape their disadvantaged position and hence underdevelopment was to reform the *structure* of their economies by creating industries and so relying less on the production of primary products. His ideas were influential in multilateral bodies and regional trade groupings, and shaped economic policies across Latin America. After 1949, ECLA advocated rapid industrialisation and was highly critical of the ways in which world trade operated, calling for international agreements to protect the prices of primary products in order to counter the impact of volatile terms of trade on developing economies. In Latin America, the 1950s was a period of unprecedented state intervention in the economy – statism – to direct the process of industrialisation. These ideas challenged the vision of development held by the industrialised countries (see Box 14.4).

ECLA ideas were criticised by many economists in the industrial countries, who rejected the centre-periphery division and argued that global trade would, in fact,

---

THEORIES AND DEBATES   Box 14.4

A challenge to economic liberalism

Structuralism posed a fundamental challenge to the orthodox positions adopted by economic liberals about the role of the state and market in the economy and about free trade. It was one of the first coherent expressions of what became known as 'development economics' that advocated state activism to tackle the problems faced by developing ('Third World') countries, and it adopted a pessimistic view about the ability of the free market to eradicate poverty. It coincided with nationalist perspectives in Latin America that proposed the achievement of greater economic independence and the sovereign control of resources. None the less, it was not fundamentally anti-capitalist and accepted that a form of national capitalism in which the state played a significant guiding role was the best hope for Latin American development.

State versus market

Economic liberalism suggests that rational, self-interested actors competing freely in the marketplace will produce the greatest good. The structuralists, by contrast, believed that the economy was shaped by power and politics and that Latin American markets were controlled by elites in ways that did little to generate growth. A dominant underlying theme of structuralism, therefore, was the notion that underdeveloped economies were characterised by *failures* of the free market, and this implied that state intervention to correct these failures was essential for development (see Box 15.3). The ECLA theorists believed the state should reform an economy's structure to create the right conditions for industrial development; that the domestic market should be enlarged through agrarian reform (see Chapter 7); and that income should be redistributed in order to raise the purchasing power of the majority. The state-versus-market debate continues to be reflected in longstanding disagreements between economists advocating planned industrialisation and those recommending that industrial growth in developing countries is best allowed to evolve spontaneously from the stimulus provided by free markets and trade. Advocates of planned industrialisation point to the example of rapidly growing Asian economies such as Korea to suggest that state direction within a capitalist economy may be essential for creating highly competitive, world-beating and technologically advanced industries. Each approach has different implications for the exercise of politics, as the former implies forms of corporatism and limitations upon the democratic pluralism frequently, if questionably, attributed to the latter (see Boxes 2.2, 7.1, Chapter 4).

Free trade

Classical economic liberalism argued that international trade free from impediments such as tariffs and quotas benefits all nations. Structuralists, by contrast, argued that trade relations between centre and periphery reinforced higher levels of development in the centre and so free trade could actually be *harmful* to less-developed nations. In this way, the structuralists highlighted for the first time the dangers of economic strategies that involved indiscriminate integration into the international market for countries that were in the early stages of development, and sought reform of the structure of the world economy through international agreements. Structuralists also argued that developing countries had to reduce their reliance on trade with the industrialised centre by increasing trade among themselves through regional integration initiatives. ECLA backed integration efforts during the 1950s and 1960s to allow ISI to be carried out at a broader level, such as the Latin American Free Trade Area (LAFTA), the Central American Common Market (CACM), the Andean Pact and the Caribbean Common Market (see Chapter 9, Table 15.2). A common market in Latin America might have provided the demand and competition that industrialisation required, but these early efforts at economic integration failed over disagreements between national states about removing protection for their individual industries or because of political instability.

equalise incomes among nations in the long term (Love, 1995). Many economists have since argued that the evidence supports the long-run deterioration of the real prices of raw materials since the last decades of the nineteenth century, tending to confirm Prebisch's broad hypothesis (see Ocampo, 1995). However, explanations for the decline in terms of trade may be far more complex than Prebisch suggested, because the prices of some primary products such as oil have performed much better than others; the deterioration in the terms of trade has not been the same for different Latin American countries; in most of the main Latin American economies, terms of trade have, in fact, improved in recent years; and it is unclear what effect changing technology has had on raw material prices. Until the 1980s, for example, it was not economically viable to extract oil from sandy, surface deposits found in large expanses in the northern hemisphere – today technological advances mean that it is, and this could eventually depress prices. Large 'oil sands' or 'tar sands' deposits can be found in Venezuela, for example (see Chapter 9).

ISI based on protectionist policies became a cornerstone of development strategies in Latin America until the 1980s, although each country had a different experience of it and in some, such as Peru, it began much later than in others (see Chapter 2). Strategies often began with the establishment of sectors seen as essential for industrialisation, such as iron and steel, engineering, transportation and communications. An important structuralist assumption was that the state was the only economic actor with the resources able to run heavy industrial sectors such as oil, petrochemicals and telecommunications, and so state-owned enterprises were formed throughout Latin America. Governments complemented these policies by taking measures in their overall administration of the national economy – that is, in their 'macroeconomic' policies – that were biased towards helping the new industries. In the first stages of ISI, for example, imports were usually allowed to rise so that emergent industries would have ready access to the inputs necessary for growth. To ease this development, states tended to maintain overvalued exchange rates in order to make some imports cheaper to purchase. The state also created national development banks to target investments in the economy; gave subsidies and tax credits to domestic companies; raised industrial wages to encourage internal demand and create a market for new products; and even encouraged foreign investment in areas where there was a shortage of local capital.

As a result of ISI, most countries in Latin America achieved the capacity to produce basic goods, and a few successfully created heavy industries. The larger economies, in particular, were able to diversify their exports beyond a single traditional primary product and provided an important source of employment (Alexander, 1995). Manufacturing sectors grew in importance as a proportion of GDP, and one measure of this was the declining share of the labour force employed in agriculture between 1930 and 1980. In Mexico, for example, the share of the labour force employed in agriculture fell from 63 per cent in 1940 to 37 per cent in 1980, and in Chile it declined from 41 per cent to 16 per cent (Cardoso and Helwege, 1992). Some countries were also able to establish the foundations of sophisticated and globally competitive modern industries. In Brazil, national production of all manufactured goods increased by 266 per cent from 1949 to 1964 (Alexander, 1995). Industrial products now make up a majority of Brazil's exports and the country has became a global force in sectors such as vehicle manufacturing, shipping and even aerospace (see Box 14.5). Protectionist policies also helped to stimulate growth. Throughout the 1950s, Latin American economies were growing faster than the industrialised economies – with annual growth rates thereafter averaging about 5.5 per cent between 1950–80 – and between 1950 and 1970 Latin American GDP trebled.

CASE STUDY **Box 14.5**

Embraer – a Brazilian success story

The remarkable growth of the Brazilian aeroplane manufacturer Empresa Brasileira de Aeronáutica (Embraer) is emblematic of the many successes within Latin America's industralisation strategy. Founded in 1969 by the Brazilian government under a military officer as its chairman, Embraer delivered its first plane to the Brazilian Air Force in 1973. Embraer was present for the first time at the Paris International Airshow in 1977 and opened an office in the US in 1980. By the early 1980s, it was producing several models, including the Tucano military training aircraft, AMX advanced pilot trainers, and small Brasília passenger jets, and by 1986 it was investing hundreds of millions of dollars in developing new planes. The company began developing the ERJ 145, its first regional jet, in 1989 and by the late 1980s it was producing a range of sophisticated military planes that included remote-sensing aircraft and maritime patrol and anti-submarine warfare aircraft. Amid a global downturn in the air-transport industry in 1990, and facing bankruptcy, the privatisation of Embraer began in 1991 and this was completed in 1994 with key shareholders including Brazilian investment and pension funds. Embraer began producing larger passenger aircraft and landed key contracts in the US, and in 1998 reported its first profit ($109 million) since becoming private. In 1999, Embraer signed a $4.9 billion contract for regional jetliners with the Swiss carrier Crossair, its largest to date. It began to develop a family of aircraft that included 98- and 108-passenger models through an Embraer-led, multi-national partnership among 16 aerospace companies. In 1999, a French aerospace consortium acquired 20 per cent of the Brazilian firm, and in 2000 Embraer was launched on the New York Stock Exchange. The company entered the market for business jets, targeted a rapidly growing China, and unveiled a new generation of larger planes for up to 110 passengers. Between 2001 and 2003, Embraer's sales to military and corporate customers more than doubled, although sales to commercial customers declined, in part because of the impact of the 9/11 terrorist attacks in the US on the air transport industry. In June 2003, Embraer won a $3 billion order from the US budget carrier JetBlue to produce 100 E190 jets, and JetBlue also took out an option to buy a further 100 E190s, which could increase the eventual value of the deal to $6 billion. Embraer is now the world's third-largest producer of commercial aircraft, with turnover in 2009 expected to be in the region of $5.5 billion. It makes passenger jets and turboprops, and its military aircraft are used by more than 20 air forces across the world. It is Brazil's second biggest exporter, with a total workforce of more than 17,000, and does about 90 per cent of its business outside Brazil, making it vulnerable to international crisis. None the less, the Asia Pacific market is seen as a key region of growth, particularly for executive and passenger jets, and the new phenomenon of air taxis (see Chapter 11). In 2009, Embraer started flying demo tours of its entry-level Phenom 100 in the Asia Pacific. It has signalled that it also aims to take advantage of Brazil's growing military budget, with increased domestic sales (see Box 9.6). Its KC-390 transport and cargo aircraft for the Brazilian military is expected to enter service in 2015, and Embraer has also sold Super Tucano fighters to other Latin American countries as well as to the Brazilian Air Force, and produces military reconnaissance aircraft for patrolling the Amazon.

Main sources: www.embraer.com; *Hoover's* (2003); *O Estado de São Paulo*, 2009; Downie, 2009; Sreenivasan, 2009

However, by the end of the 1950s the early phase of ISI was already becoming 'exhausted' as Brazil, Chile, Mexico, Argentina, Venezuela, Colombia and Peru began to run out of import-substitution possibilities (Cardoso and Helwege, 1992). ISI is exhausted when an economy has installed all those kinds of industries that can produce products formerly imported; if growth is to continue, the challenge then becomes one of amplifying existing markets (Alexander, 1995). A new 'post-import substitution strategy' becomes necessary involving more sophisticated forms of production to develop new products for local consumption and for export, and this requires greater efficiency, new skills and new consumption habits. By the 1960s, Prebisch himself was recommending a post-ISI strategy to remove protection from some industries and develop non-traditional exports. Other supporters of ISI, such as Brazil's president Juscelino Kubitschek (1956–61), proposed a post-ISI strategy of agricultural development and the stimulation of new industrial exports. In Chile, the Christian Democrat president Eduardo Frei (1964–70) also recognised the need to move on from ISI and promoted agrarian reform and the reorientation of industry towards exports. Frei's agrarian reforms were also recognition of the strains that had been generated by the exclusion of the peasantry from development at a time of heightened political mobilisation following the Cuban Revolution (see Box 2.3, Chapter 12).

Domestic industry was responsible for much of the industrial growth in Latin America until the 1950s, but as a shift towards more complex industrial products became necessary, its expansion was hampered by a lack of access to investment for large-scale projects and to the technology required for more sophisticated forms of manufacturing. ISI in Latin America had coincided in the postwar period with global expansion by many large US and later European corporations, and by the late 1950s many Latin American governments desperate for industrial investment began welcoming multi-national corporations into their countries. They increasingly saw them as allies in the later phase of ISI and wanted them to produce goods for higher-income urban consumers as well as for export. Multi-national companies brought capital, technology, skills and jobs, and helped to change consumption patterns, fitting the main objectives of the industrialisation strategies adopted in the region. Governments could attract them with tariff protection warding off imports that provided them with a captive market, subsidies on equipment, and overvalued exchange rates that made importing that equipment cheaper.

The coups of the 1960s and 1970s that inaugurated a period of military authoritarianism have been associated by some scholars with the exhaustion of the first phase of ISI (see Box 2.5). This position linked authoritarianism with the broad recognition among economic policymakers in some countries that it had become necessary to shift towards a more outward-looking economic policy combined with changes in the nature of local consumption patterns. Subsequently, the authoritarian regimes of Brazil, Chile, Uruguay and Argentina all made efforts to liberalise trade and promote non-traditional exports, although there was considerable variation in the policies they adopted and the extent to which they did, in fact, restructure their economies. By the late 1970s, ISI had come under sustained assault by neoliberals restating the ideas of economic liberalism who argued that it had wasted resources and created inefficient industries that had drained the economy (see Chapter 15). In the 1980s and 1990s, most Latin American leaders abandoned ISI and undertook radical trade reforms.

The industrialisation policies advocated by the structuralists had an important impact on the development of political systems in Latin America. By the 1970s, ISI had benefitted only limited sectors of the population, heightened inequalities, generated inflation, weakened the priority placed upon economic efficiency, and reinforced a tendency to adopt corporatist solutions to meeting political demands.

Growth of the state

Industrialisation policies implied the need for greater government intervention in the economy than in the past, and the state as a set of social institutions grew much larger in Latin America after the 1950s (see Box 2.1). Ministries grew in size and new government agencies were created to promote manufacturing as the public sector expanded (see Chapter 6). In many countries, the state nationalised key areas of production considered to be strategic, such as oil and minerals. Structuralists tended to hold to an idealised and benevolent notion of the state and a belief that its efforts to correct market failures would automatically result in better economic performance and welfare. One result of this was that structuralist strategies invariably failed to take into account the need for institutional and political ways of ensuring that state interventions were, in fact, effective and to the benefit of the majority of the population. Public services tended to be confined to urban industrial sectors, and the imposition of tariffs, the need to obtain import licences, and the imposition of quotas had all created new opportunities for corruption in government as bureaucrats and politicians began to profit from protectionism (see Chapter 4). The growth of the central state benefitted presidential rule at the expense of party systems, and legislative politics was often reduced to a struggle over the spoils offered by new opportunities for corruption created by growing state expenditure (see Chapters 5, 6). The state's role in setting up new industries, providing credit to private firms, subsidies and bureaucratic growth all fuelled public expenditure. This often led to inflation and deficit spending, by which governments spent money that they did not have in the expectation that they would be able to raise revenue in the future. Structuralists were more accepting of inflation than their critics, and it became embedded in Latin American economies (see Chapter 15).

Populism and corporatism

Meeting inflationary expectations became an important aspect of economic management and political negotiation. Some countries such as Mexico sought to control inflation by using corporatist and authoritarian mechanisms that ensured prices and wages were only increased by levels acceptable to the state (see Box 7.3). This was only possible if the government had effective control over the labour movement and industrialists and was able to forge or impose a consensus between them.

The industrialising state's compulsion to maintain control over organised labour helps to explain why early ISI in Latin America was sometimes accompanied by populist alliances that galvanised political support for statist economic policies (see Chapters 2, 4, 7). Populism is associated with such figures as Juan Domingo Perón (1946–55, 1973–74) in Argentina and Getúlio Vargas (1930–45, 1951–54) in Brazil, who opposed the status quo of primary product exports and favoured state ownership of key industries and intervention to protect workers. Populist movements helped to reduce class antagonisms by linking the working class and industrialists, often behind a shared nationalist ideology, and legitimised state corporatism (see Boxes 2.2, 7.1). The growth of public spending that accompanied the expansion of the state offered new opportunities for politicians to dispense patronage in return for support. Corporatism combined with protectionism, subsidised credit and price controls tended to nurture the emergence of privileged interest groups, such as unions and business circles, that directed their energies towards lobbying for state benefits by taking advantage of their favoured position in the industrialisation equation (see Chapter 7). Any mobilisation by these sectors increased the likelihood that the state would divert scarce funds to them and away from production and welfare in order to ensure their support. The close relationship the state maintained with some organised political interests could be counter-productive, substituting choices made on the basis of political calculations for those made on the basis of efficiency and national interest. Non-organised sectors of the population – in particular, the peasantry – were largely excluded from the benefits of industrial development, causing radicalisation and instability (see Boxes 12.1, 12.2). The Cuban Revolution (1959) and the strident rhetoric of its leaders inspired the development of political alternatives outside institutional structures, such as guerrilla movements (see Box 2.3, Figure 12.1).

Inequality

Using Brazil as an example, Evans (1979) argued that while industrialisation proceeded at a rapid pace, it delivered few benefits to the vast majority of the population. The political model he developed envisaged statist industrialisation based on a 'triple alliance' of the state, local capitalists and multi-national corporations, each element of which had few incentives to share the product of growth with the majority. In theory, ISI had promised initially to create jobs for a burgeoning working class, but, in fact, industrial growth under ISI was capital intensive and the amount of labour new plants absorbed was limited in relation to the growth in the labour force as workers moved from the countryside to the cities. This encouraged states to create jobs, further swelling the size of the state bureaucracy and agencies, and increasing the proportion of GDP committed to public expenditure. It also created a dual labour structure of relatively well paid workers alongside many unemployed or 'underemployed' workers in traditional sectors. An underemployed worker is one who works less than he or she would like to or needs to in order to survive. Although structuralists did not ignore the countryside, arguing that it was necessary to change patterns of land ownership through land reform, in practice ISI strengthened a tendency to disregard agricultural production as the state adopted measures that hurt traditional agricultural exporters in its effort to escape a reliance upon primary products. Credit was diverted to industry and public expenditures biased towards growing urban areas. Until the 1960s, there were only limited efforts to change the social structure of the countryside and landholding patterns (see Chapters 7, 15). Large landed estates remained in existence and low productivity persisted. Impoverished peasants abandoned the countryside to head for the city, fuelling urbanisation. The neglect of agriculture further reinforced a need to import foodstuffs, as the countryside was unable to supply urban areas with the food necessary to maintain the industrial workforce. The neglect of agriculture also worsened the unequal distribution of income between urban and rural populations. Latin America was the only region of the world where the share of income going to the poorest 20 per cent of the population consistently declined between 1950 and the late 1970s (Sheahan, 1987). At the same time, the growth in importance of urban political forces such as the labour movement also began to change the traditional balance of power in the countryside and weaken traditional landholders (Cardoso and Helwege, 1992).

Inefficiency

Industrialisation did not foster a new entrepreneurial class in Latin America, but generated a business class dependent on state protectionism for its existence. The behaviour of this group was sometimes referred to by economists as 'rent-seeking', meaning that they spent much time and energy seeking to capture the benefits that arose from the state's many interventions in economic life. The absence of foreign competition meant that there was little incentive to improve the efficiency of production processes, and the quality of locally manufactured products was often inferior. Leaders of domestic industries were also able to profit from artificially high prices and had no incentive to bring these down. Tax evasion by industrialists limited the revenues the state could use for public spending. Latin American economies relied excessively on tariffs and quotas beyond the early stages of industrialisation and, as a result, local industry failed to become competitive in world terms. Services such as electricity or telecommunications were frequently underpriced to stimulate growth, leading to heavy losses that were absorbed by the state and, in the longer term, resulting in underinvestment. By maintaining overvalued exchange rates to make some imports cheaper, the state hurt traditional exporters and so limited their ability to earn foreign exchange to pay for these imports, and so the cost of imports soon began to outstrip foreign exchange earnings from exports. As a result, Latin American imports and exports in the 1950s and 1960s grew below the world average (Cardoso and Helwege, 1992). Many governments began to respond to declining levels of foreign exchange – and rising levels of state expenditure – by borrowing large amounts of capital from international creditors and banks, particularly during the 1970s, and debts soared. ISI was also marked by overcapacity, with industrial plants being either more numerous or larger than was required to meet domestic demand and operating at high costs. In the late 1960s, for example, there were 90 automobile companies in Latin America producing 600,000 cars annually – an average output of just 6,700 each (Baer, 1972).

Authoritarianism

The notion of 'bureacratic authoritarianism' developed by O'Donnell (1973) was the most coherent effort to link the restructuring accompanying the exhaustion of the first phase of ISI with authoritarian rule (see Box 2.5). O'Donnell's model suggested that, while initially during ISI locally manufactured goods had been aimed at a broad spectrum of the population, in the bureaucratic-authoritarian phase from the mid-1960s onwards consumer durables such as cars and electrical appliances which only high-income sectors of the population could afford were seen as the main stimulus to growth. Therefore, continued growth required consumption to be concentrated in the high-income strata of the population, increasing inequality. Inevitably, governments would find it difficult to attract domestic support for such a policy shift among the popular sectors mobilised during the first phase of ISI that were now powerful and influential, particularly organised labour. Therefore, these sectors had to be brought under control to ensure that they did not obstruct economic change. Coalitions comprising the military, domestic and foreign capitalists, and technocrats took power in the most industrialised countries of the Southern Cone and exercised a characteristic form of rule that repressed labour and suppressed political opposition.

Dependency approaches

In the 1960s and 1970s, a more radical set of perspectives about development emerged from within the structuralist tradition, emphasising the severe limitations imposed by Latin America's *dependent* status within the international economy – the dependency or *dependencia* school. The notion of dependency had been formulated by Prebisch and debated by ECLA since its foundation, but it did not form a central focus until the 1960s. Prebisch believed that the crucial decisions affecting international trade were inevitably taken in the centre, meaning peripheral countries were dependent on it for growth and so incapable of achieving development on their own. The most substantial analysis of dependency by economists of the ECLA line was by the Chilean Oswaldo Sunkel (1969).

Dependency approaches grew in popularity in Latin America as criticisms that structuralist development policies had failed to tackle widespread poverty mounted and, as a result, these perspectives were more radical and political. Amid the broader ideological competition of the Cold War period, they coincided with ideas on the left about the objectives of development that were more hostile to capitalism, or advocated a form of capitalism in which social welfare was paramount (see Chapters 2, 12, 16). Dependency approaches began with the premise that the prospects of the developing world reproducing the type of capitalism found in the industrialised world were limited, and that the former could only escape its condition by restricting or even ending contact with the latter. They built upon the notion of a pre-established international capitalist economic system in which the possibilities open to peripheral countries had been rigidly determined by the expansion of the central economies. The policies adopted by the industrialised world perpetuated a condition of economic, political and cultural dependency in the Third World, whose role was to provide natural resources, cheap labour and markets that enabled industrialised countries to remain prosperous. These policies were enforced by the many ways in which industrialised countries set the rules of international trade, but also by the use of military force when necessary. This form of domination by the rich world ensured that the resources of poor countries were taken by industrialised countries, preventing reinvestment in developing nations and stunting their growth – and so the developed world was *responsible* for continuing underdevelopment in the Third World. Any attempt by dependent nations to resist this resulted in sanctions of some kind, and so economic development in the periphery was considered to be nearly impossible without drastic or, in some cases, revolutionary change.

Diverse dependency schools emerged and many economic thinkers adapted them to Marxist positions, giving them significant force following the Cuban Revolution. Several of these 'neo-Marxist' advocates of dependency theory were non-Latin Americans such as the Ukrainian-born American Paul A. Baran (b.1910–d.1964) and the German André Gunder Frank (b.1929–d.2005). However, dependency approaches also influenced many non-Marxists such as Pope John Paul II (1978–2005), and some dependency theorists took a reformist line that had more in common with structuralist positions. As a young economist, Fernando Henrique Cardoso (who went on to become Brazil's president from 1995–2003), together with a colleague, Enzo Faletto, argued that, despite dependency, there were opportunities to adopt strategies that allowed for national control of production and economic growth – 'associated dependent capitalism' – through, for example, limiting or taxing foreign capital, controlling capital flows and land reform (see Cardoso and Faletto, 1969). None the less, serious disagreements between social scientists and economists meant that there was no single unified 'dependency theory', and dependency approaches were roundly rejected by many economists in the industrial world (see Box 14.6).

Dependency approaches to international economics were also primarily theoretical and spawned few successful practical solutions to the problems of underdevelopment. The Cuban Revolution (1959) and the revolutionary regime's attempt to industrialise after it had severed ties of economic dependency with the US were of particular interest to theorists. However, in reality, Cuba substituted its economic dependence on the US for an equivalent dependence upon the Soviet Union (see Boxes 2.3, 10.8, and Chapter 16).

Dependency approaches built upon the core-periphery dichotomy in the international economic system envisaged by Prebisch, but diverged from structuralism in important respects:

Internal versus external causes of underdevelopment

Structuralism attributed underdevelopment mainly to internal constraints on economic development, and advocated changes in an economy's internal structure so that it was not as disadvantaged within the international economy. Dependency approaches, by contrast, argued that underdevelopment was *externally* induced

THEORIES AND DEBATES	Box 14.6

Criticisms of dependency approaches

Dependency perspectives were heavily criticised, particularly from within the countries they blamed for Latin America's economic ills, but remain influential today and often coincide with arguments deployed in opposition to free trade and economic globalisation (see Chapter 15). However, evidence does not always support the notion that the stronger the ties between rich and poor countries, the greater the latter's underdevelopment. Supporters of the idea of economic integration, for example, often argue that the *weaker* partner in an interdependent relationship gains more than the stronger, challenging the idea that centre develops at expense of periphery. None the less, there continue to be questions about the extent to which Mexico, for example, has gained long-term advantages from formal economic integration with the US and Canada within the North American Free Trade Agreement (NAFTA, see below). Liberal political economists insist that developing economies have reaped net benefits from their relationship with the industrialised world which, far from generating poverty, has been an agent of progress. They insist that without the access to markets and foreign capital that a close, co-operative relationship with the developed world can offer, developing countries will not be able to secure the investment and foreign exchange that are essential for growth (see Box 15.2). Critiques of dependency perspectives by economic liberals continue, attesting to their relevance today and the influence they still exert over the Left in Latin America (see below, Chapters 12, 16). However, intra-regional commercial integration within Latin America that obviates any potential for a traditional dependency – as opposed to agreements with developed countries outside the region – is becoming the norm, and preferential trade agreements have gained momentum in recent years (see Baumann, 2008). Until 1991, for example, preferential trade agreements accounted for about 8 per cent of total regional exports, but by 2005 there were 68 agreements, 51 of these intra-regional (*ibid.*). Moreover, the arguments for integration have evolved, and in some cases have become blurred, because of changes in the world economy, such as: the new mobility of international capital; the need to address shortcomings in energy, transportation and communication infrastructure in order to take advantage of markets; and the emergence of powerful new economic actors, such as China (see Box 14.7, Chapter 11). The complexity of the global market and the variation in economic circumstances throughout Latin America mean that integration is not necessarily the only way of diversifying or reducing dependence and should be pursued by regional leaders with a clear rationale. A collateral effect of the 2008–09 global financial crisis has also been that rapidly developing countries such as the 'BRICs' (Brazil, the Russian Federation, India and China) have assumed a greater role in international financial governance. The crisis also led to the displacement as the main international forum for economic decision-making of the traditional Group of Eight countries (G8) by the Group of Twenty (G20), which includes the main emerging economies. These developments have also challenged the notion of dependency.

by the existence and policies of the industrial capitalist countries constituting the centre. Some *dependencistas* reformulated theories of imperialism, arguing that the co-existence in the world economy of development and underdevelopment reflected a neo-colonial economic relationship (see Chapters 1, 9, Box 10.1). They believed that, by keeping the Third World underdeveloped, the bourgeoisie of the First World ensured a cheap supply of raw materials and a market for their manufactured goods, while stifling local capitalism by draining off the resources that could have been used for investment.

Capitalism and class

Dependency approaches were mostly hostile to capitalism and appealed, in particular, to Marxists because they drew naturally upon theories of class. Baran (1973) argued that the neo-colonial relationship between centre and periphery was sustained by a system of class relations in both. Certain groups within developing countries such as entrepreneurs, landlords and military rulers constituted an elite ruling class whose principal interest was in the perpetuation of the international capitalist system. Capitalists from the central countries dominated Latin America through these local elites. Industrialisation would, in fact, threaten this dependent bourgeoisie because it would challenge their privileged position. It was, therefore, against the interests of the advanced capitalist countries for underdeveloped regions to develop. Gunder Frank (1971) developed the notion of 'internal colonialism', which asserts that centre-periphery relations were reproduced *within* countries. Just as the developed centre grew at the expense of the periphery, thereby perpetuating underdevelopment, within countries urban areas absorbed resources from rural areas creating 'dual economies' and 'dual societies' that were simultaneously traditional and modern.

Pessimism

Dependency approaches were more pessimistic about the prospects of escaping underdevelopment than structuralist positions, which suggested that, with the correct mixture of industrialisation policies and state investment, a country could overcome its disadvantageous position in the international system. Dependency approaches suggested that the relations between dominant and dependent states were dynamic, and so dependency was an on-going and constantly changing process. These shifting interactions between centre and periphery tended to *intensify* unequal patterns of development. Later dependency analysis maintained that it would be hard for Third World countries to escape dependence through industrial development because ISI had, in practice, created *new* forms of dependency on foreign countries for machinery and capital, leading to indebtedness. First World countries had a vested interest in establishing capital-intensive forms of assembly in the Third World in order to take advantage of their cheap labour without losing technological advantages (see Sheahan, 1987).

National revolution

Advocates of dependency approaches placed great emphasis on international power imbalances and the need either for revolution or fundamental economic and political reforms, both within countries and the international system. As they were, in essence, pessimistic about the prospects of a developing country escaping dependence, and believed that the forms of domination by the centre were constantly changing, this left states with few options but to undergo revolutionary change. Marxists who employed dependency theory often advocated a socialist revolution as the only way to achieve the shift in power that was necessary for a country to escape its peripheral condition and achieve national economic autonomy. Gunder Frank, for example, argued that, given the complicity of the Latin American elites in imperialism, it was only by mobilising the working class and the peasants to seize power through revolution that the ties of dependency could be broken.

Foreign investment and sovereignty

Marxist *dependencistas* advocated egalitarian policies to reduce poverty and provide more diversified employment opportunities. Some called for the outright expropriation of privately owned companies in the belief that public ownership was essential to eradicating poverty and inequality. They argued that a much greater degree of national control over the economy and foreign investment was essential. Therefore, developing economies needed to limit their contacts with the industrialised countries, take control of national production, and become more self-sufficient. Dependency theorists were particularly critical of foreign investment and their positions appealed to nationalist sentiments that blamed foreign capital for underdevelopment at a time when multi-national corporations were investing heavily in Latin America. Latin Americans have long had a love–hate relationship with foreign companies, objecting to the extraction by foreign firms of profits yet also welcoming them as sources of technology and capital essential to achieving development (see Box 15.2). *Dependencistas* argued that the historical concentration of foreign investment in Latin America in agriculture and the production of raw materials had benefitted international capitalists and led to a net capital outflow from developing nations (see Cardoso and Helwege, 1992). They also argued that foreign investment affected political relations by creating a local bourgeoisie whose interests are tied to the success of foreign firms, which in turn gained disproportionate influence over economic policymaking. One of the ironies of the industrialisation process in Latin America was that it had been seen by many as a means of achieving greater national control over the economy by freeing a country from the constraints imposed by its reliance on agricultural commodities. However, in order to attract foreign investment, governments were often inclined to adopt policies that favoured foreign firms to the detriment of local producers or that kept organised labour or even the political opposition under control. By the 1960s, *dependencistas* were associating multi-national corporations with a lack of full national control over the economy because, in order to attract them, governments had been forced to adopt policies and permit conditions that they argued were not in the national interest and had limited the ability to take sovereign decisions.

The notion of dependency continues to influence perspectives in Latin America and is used to draw attention to the close economic relationship between more traditional centre-periphery relationships, such as that between Mexico and the US under NAFTA (see Chapters 10, 15), as well as the more recent appetite for Latin America's natural resources among rapidly developing countries such as China, which falls outside the traditional dependency school characterisations (see Box 14.7, Chapter 12).

NAFTA was the first trade agreement between the US and a developing country and has accounted for a large proportion of the increase in trade between the US and Latin America since the 1990s (see Table 9.2). Intra-regional trade within NAFTA itself amounted to about $1,000 billion in 2008, of which Mexican exports to the US amounted to about $215 billion and US exports to Mexico $151 billion. NAFTA has deepened Mexico's reliance on the US as an export market and a source of products significantly: about 82 per cent of Mexican exports by value head for the US, and about 50 per cent of its imports come from the US. However, the benefits and disadvantages of NAFTA have come under scrutiny in recent years and, in 2009, researchers at the Global Development and Environment Institute argued that, while Mexico benefitted from increased trade and investment, it did not gain the broad-based economic development that it had originally been assumed would result (see Gallagher and Wise, 2009). NAFTA has not created a European Union-style common market; Mexico has seen a net loss of jobs under the agreement; and delays for goods crossing the Mexican–US border have even lengthened because of security precautions to deal with terrorist threats to the US. Critics of NAFTA in Mexico and Latin America suggest it has strengthened the country's dependence on the US for limited gains.

Perspectives informed by dependency suggest that the neoliberal economic restructuring of Latin American economies from the mid-1970s into the 1990s may have increased the region's vulnerability to external factors, and hence did little to end its dependency (see Chapter 15). By these perspectives, a period of vigorous growth in Latin America between 2003 and 2008 demonstrates the region's *continuing* dependency on strategies based on the export of key natural resources, such as oil, gas and primary products. This is because the relative autonomy enjoyed by left-of-centre governments – particularly with regard to the pursuit of social policy – has in fact been tied closely to 'windfall profits' generated by unusually high commodity prices and demand in expanding Asian markets (see Petras, 2009; Chapter 11).

The end of this commodity boom and the impact of recession generated by the 2008–09 financial crisis will test these positions, particularly in more industrialised countries whose economies are more integrated into world markets and have followed an export-growth strategy, such as Brazil, Argentina, Colombia and Mexico. In late 2009, ECLAC suggested that, after growing continuously for six years, the GDP of Latin America and the Caribbean would fall by 1.9 per cent in 2009, reducing per capita GDP by about 3 per cent and pushing unemployment in the region to about 9 per cent (ECLAC, 2009b). Foreign trade was the chief victim of the global downturn, hit by a strong reduction of international demand and falling prices for raw materials: between the fourth quarter of 2008 and the first quarter of 2009, seven Latin American countries – Argentina, Venezuela, Brazil, Chile, Ecuador, Mexico and Peru – experienced a heavy drop in exports and capital flows were reversed in Brazil, Chile and Peru (*ibid.*). However, the extent to which the impact of 2008–09 financial crisis will expose Latin American 'dependency' is debatable. On the one hand, by mid-2009 there were growing signs of negative growth, rising unemployment, and rising levels of poverty in Latin America, alongside rising US protectionism and a shortage of capital in Latin America as a result of the US financial bailout (see, for example, ECLAC, 2009c). Phenomena of this kind have an important impact on the conduct of politics in the region: in Brazil in 2009, for example, unions that belong to the Central Única dos Trabalhadores (CUT, Central Workers' Confederation) usually allied to the ruling Partido dos Trabalhadores (PT, Workers' Party) joined social movements and landless workers in large demonstrations about unemployment, and in Argentina, Colombia, Peru and Ecuador there were also strikes and protests. Yet on the other hand, by late 2009 ECLAC was hinting at signs of an economic recovery in Latin America and the Caribbean beyond levels expected only a few months previously (see ECLAC, 2009b; ECLAC Press Centre, 2009). One reason for this is that, although the region has had to deal with a shock to its trade, it was better prepared to face the crisis than in the past because of greater fiscal discipline, lower public debt, healthy international reserves and current account surpluses. There was also evidence of a new Latin American response to external crisis that has enabled the region to attenuate some of the worst effects of the 2008–09 downturn and challenge the notion that the region lacks autonomy in economic management. In June 2009, for example, Latin American and Caribbean finance ministry officials met at ECLAC headquarters in Santiago to determine a regional position to the economic crisis and outline what they wanted in terms of international financial reforms.

There are also clear indications in the case of hydrocarbon exports that efforts to diversify combined, in some cases, with policy shifts related to the leftward turn in Latin America (see Chapter 12) may have a longer-term impact on the dependence on traditional markets for key exports such as oil and gas. Several Latin American countries remain heavily reliant on oil and gas revenues to finance public spending. A significant increase in the revenues available to governments in Latin America between 2002–08, for example, was closely related to the income they earned from natural-resource extraction: in Venezuela, Ecuador, Mexico and Bolivia more than 30 per cent of fiscal (i.e. tax) revenues in this period came from the natural-resource sectors (ECLAC, 2009a). Some of the main oil-exporting countries of Latin America have become heavily dependent on the US as their principal market (see Figure 14.1). Countries such as Venezuela have been forging closer links with emerging markets for oil such as China (see Table 14.1, Box 14.7, Chapter 12), while others, such as Argentina, have managed to achieve significant diversification in their markets.

None the less, the disruption to commodities resulting from the 2008–09 global downturn has drawn attention to the significant role China has played as a market for Latin American raw materials in recent years and new concern in the region about commodity dependency of this kind.

In August 2009, ECLAC reported that China had become the main destination for Brazilian and Chilean exports and the second market for products from Argentina, Costa Rica, Cuba and Peru (ECLAC Press Centre, 2009; see also ECLAC DITI, 2009a, 2009b). Vigorous demand for Latin American food, hydrocarbons, metals and minerals by a rapidly growing China – which accounts for about 11 per cent of world output – has benefitted the region's exporting countries, improving their terms of trade and stimulating growth. This is reflected in a dramatic change in the position of China as a trading partner for key Latin American economies (see Table 14.1, Box 14.7).

Figure 14.1 Percentage of total oil production exported to the US by the main Latin American producers, 2007

UNITED STATES

44%

MEXICO

Mexico City

CUBA

Havana

ATLANTIC OCEAN

Belize

Port-au-Prince

Santo Domingo

Guatemala City

Tegucigalpa

HONDURAS

San Juan

San Salvador

Managua

51%

San José

Panama City

Caracas

VENEZUELA

Guyana

29%

Suriname

Bogotá

COLOMBIA

French Guiana

EQUATOR

40%

PACIFIC OCEAN

Quito

ECUADOR

PERU

9%

30%

Lima

BRAZIL

La Paz

BOLIVIA

Brasília

Asunción

8%

ARGENTINA

Santiago

Buenos Aires

Montevideo

URUGUAY

Malvinas/Falkland Islands

Notes:
Totals (thousands of barrels per day)
Mexico
Total oil production: 3,500
Total oil exports to US: 1,532

Venezuela
Total oil production: 2,670
Total oil exports to US: 1,361

Brazil
Total oil production: 2,248
Total oil exports to US: 200

Ecuador
Total oil production: 511
Total oil exports to US: 203

Colombia
Total oil production: 543
Total oil exports to US: 155

Argentina
Total oil production: 799
Total oil exports to US: 64

Peru
Total oil production: 114
Total oil exports to US: 34

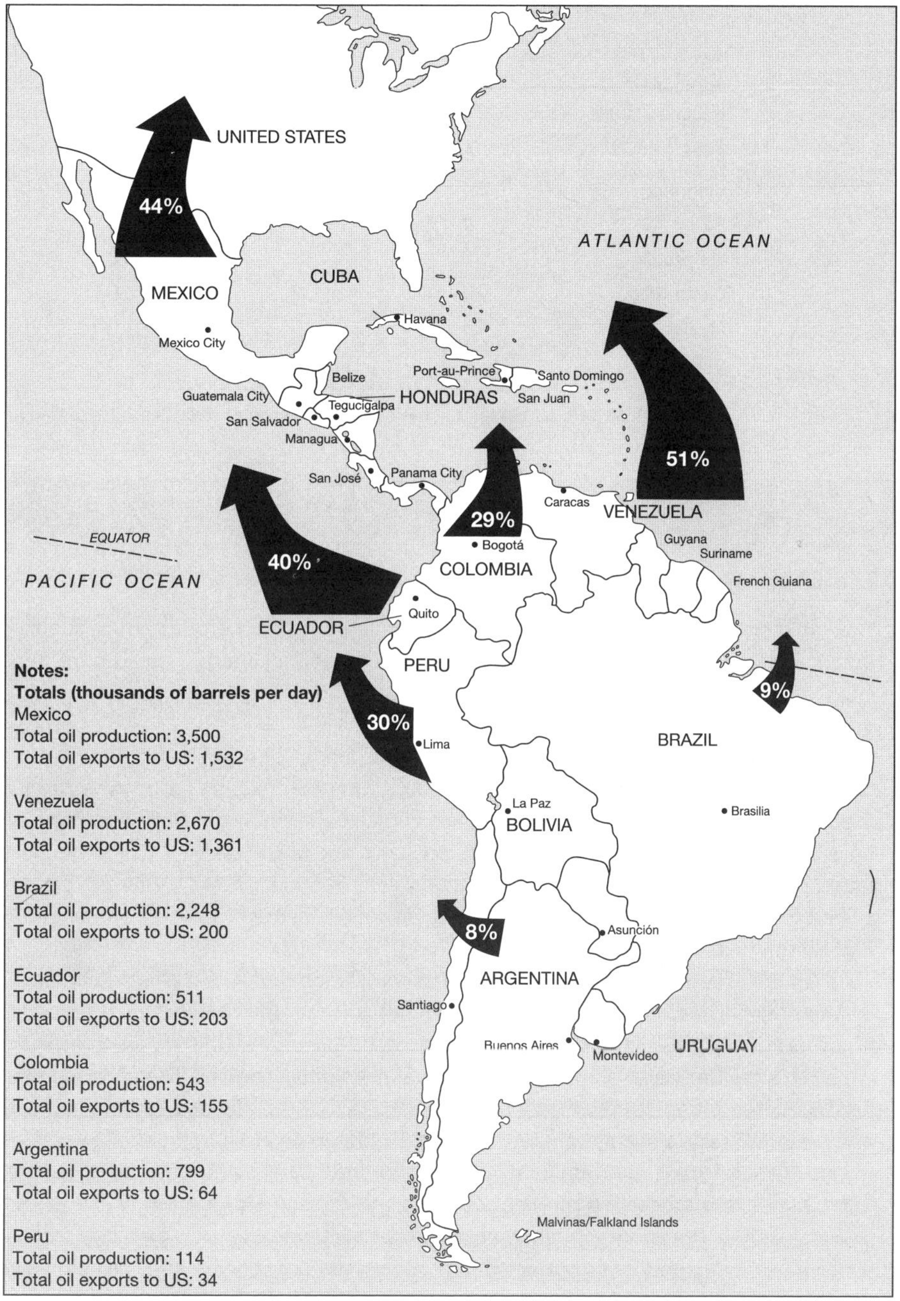

Source: Percentage of total oil production exported to the US by the main Latin American producers, 2007, http://www.eia.doe.gov, Source: US Energy Information Administration (2007)

Table 14.1 China's ranking as a trading partner for selected Latin American countries, 2000 and 2008

	Exports (destination)		Imports (origin)	
	2000	2008	2000	2008
Argentina	6	2	4	3
Brazil	12	1	11	2
Chile	5	1	4	2
Colombia	35	4	15	2
Peru	4	2	13	2
Venezuela	37	3	18	3
Costa Rica	26	2	16	3
Mexico	25	5	6	3
Cuba	5	2	5	2

Source: ECLAC DITI, 2009b (on the basis of IMF Direction of Trade Statistics [online])

TRENDS   Box 14.7

The China syndrome – good or bad?

The rapid growth of Chinese industry in recent years has generated an insatiable appetite for Latin American raw materials and is creating economic relationships that could have important geopolitical implications for the region. Growing links are being forged between the largest emerging markets of the western and eastern hemispheres.

Demand from China has helped push up the prices for many Latin American commodities since 1993 and the Chinese market helps to account for record sales among soya farmers from Argentina, Brazil, Paraguay and Bolivia and rapid growth in the copper mines of Chile and Peru. Brazil and Argentina have become important sources of the food and raw materials that China needs to feed a growing urban population and rapidly expanding industries. Optimists hope China can assume the role Europe played in the nineteenth century, providing insatiable demand for Latin American primary resources and solving persistent external deficits.

In its 2009 report on 'Latin America and the Caribbean in the World Economy', ECLAC's Division of International Trade and Integration recommended the development of a strategic relationship with China, which in 2007 in terms of global exports surpassed the US as the world's second-largest exporter after Germany, and hence offers Latin America and the Caribbean unprecedented production and export opportunities (see ECLAC DITI, 2009b). Despite a growing relationship with China and the APEC region in general (see Chapter 11), Latin America has so far been slow to exploit Asian-Pacific trade, giving countries such as China greater potential as a market in the short to medium term relative to established markets such as the US and EU.

Since 2004, there have been many signs across Latin America of new economic ties. China's trade with the region has grown at an annual average rate of about 40 per cent since 2003 – faster than overall trade – and in 2008 Chinese–Latin American trade amounted to about $140 billion. China has a trade deficit with Latin America and the Caribbean because it imports large quantities of commodities and natural resource-based manufactures. Latin American primary products – hydrocarbons, metals, minerals and some agricultural products such as soybean and oilseeds – are the exports to China that have grown most rapidly, from less than 40 per cent of the total exports to China from the region in 1995 to 62 per cent in 2006. Expanding Chinese demand for iron ore and copper has fuelled the profits of large Latin American corporations such as Brazil's CVRD (now Vale) and Codelco, Chile's state-owned copper company, which sends much of its total copper production to Asia, about half of which goes to China.

Chinese investment in Latin America has also risen considerably in recent years as it has grown into a key source of foreign direct investment, offering finance for oil pipelines and railway links that help to reduce the distribution costs for commodities it buys from Latin America. China has made no secret of its interest in gaining secure energy supplies from the region, with considerable implications for global energy markets (see Figure 14.1). It has begun to invest heavily in Latin American energy assets and resource extraction such as mining (see Box 15.2). Its companies have, for example, bought stakes in oilfields in Ecuador and Venezuela and have considered constructing a refinery in Costa Rica (see Chapter 11). In 2009, China agreed to lend Petrobras, Brazil's state-controlled oil company, $10 billion in return for up to 200,000 barrels a day (b/d) of crude oil, and reportedly bid at least $17 billion for an 84 per cent stake in YPF, Argentina's largest oil company. It is also investing in largely untapped energy markets like Peru and has explored projects in Bolivia and Colombia. China has also promised to build Bolivia's first satellite and a fast electric railway link for the country and is collaborating on energy and mining projects, taking particular interest in Bolivia's lithium deposits in the Uyuni desert.

Latin American companies are also taking advantage of China's growth to invest there, and exporters and investors from across the region have flocked to China to explore the market. Some larger Latin American companies such as the Brazilian aircraft manufacturer Embraer have made rapid inroads in the Chinese market (see Box 14.5). Alongside the trade in primary commodities, China has strengthened existing economic ties with Latin American countries and forged co-operation and free-trade agreements. In 2008, Cuba continued to step up co-operation with China, its second-largest trading partner, by signing several bilateral agreements and receiving a visit from the Chinese president, and in 2009 Peru signed a free trade agreement with China, Costa Rica began the first rounds of talks on a free-trade agreement (FTA), Panama signalled that it was likely to begin FTA talks, and a third Latin America–China Entrepreneurs Summit was held in Bogotá, Colombia, attended by hundreds of Chinese and Latin American business people. But it is not only large corporations that are exploring closer links with China: in La Paz, for example, Chinese language courses are growing rapidly among small traders and it is not uncommon even for market stallholders to travel to China in order to purchase products.

Alongside investment, China is entering Latin America's financial markets. In 2008, it joined the Inter-American Development Bank (IDB) and in 2009, the resources of a joint Chinese–Venezuelan fund reached $12 billion. A new financial infrastructure to facilitate co-operation is developing through banks such as SinoLatin Capital, the first merchant bank focused exclusively on cross-border transactions between China and Latin America. China's relations with Brazil are also being consolidated at a diplomatic level. The two countries have co-ordinated their approaches closely in the World Trade Organisation and Beijing has supported Brazil's efforts to become a permanent member of the UN Security Council (see Box 9.6).

China's growing presence in Latin America has at times been criticised for having an adverse impact on labour-intensive manufacturing. Soaring Chinese imports have alarmed some domestic producers and some Brazilian industrialists have warned of a threat to local industries, especially in vulnerable sectors, such as textiles. In 2004, for example, the Brazilian government revealed that it was investigating complaints about unfair competition practices involving the import of Chinese products that had caused losses to Brazilian companies. Brazil's shoe- and toy-making sectors have largely decamped to China itself and, for Mexico, China is a key competitor in the US market in sectors from textiles to electronics. China has also become a competitor for FDI, drawing capital away from Latin American countries because of its lower wages (see Box 15.2).

The velocity of China's expansion in Latin America and its demand for commodities – and, in particular, energy – has also provoked concerns about a new form of export dependency in Latin America. Sceptics have pointed to risks for Latin America of the Chinese boom and fear it could lock the region into a new cycle of dependence on producing raw materials, and that any Chinese downturn could hit the region badly (see above). The Chinese boom may even be threatening the environment: its consumer demand for popular aphrodisiacs such as sea cucumbers and shark fins, for example, has generated conflict in environmentally sensitive areas such as the Galapagos between local fishermen, commercial fishers and conservationists.

However, China's relationship with Latin America remains relatively under-developed, and does not appear to be recreating the potential for neo-colonial domination that forms a central theme of dependency theory. That is largely because, despite its insatiable appetite for Latin American commodities, China has so far provided the region with an opportunity to diversify its commerce in overall terms and not to concentrate it, and because trade with China represents South–South trade and not trade between the traditional centre and periphery. Moreover, recent evidence suggests that the economic relationship with China may have strengthened Latin America's relative autonomy by providing it with a means to avoid the worst impact of the 2008–09 crisis. In mid-2009, for example, ECLAC was reporting a rapid contraction in Latin American exports to China of 22 per cent year-on-year because of falling demand deriving from the global downturn, but by the end of 2009 it was suggesting that the fall in exports to China had been much milder compared to the region's other trading partners, the US and EU, and, to a certain extent, China's domestic market had even come to the rescue of Latin American exports. This was because only China has sustained the demand for basic products, allowing Latin American economies to counteract a more general reduction in foreign trade.

Sources: ECLAC/Peru, 2008; ECLAC Press Centre, 2009; ECLAC DITI, 2009a, 2009b; *China Daily*, 2009a, 2009b, 2009c, 2009d; *Economist*, 2009

Summary

The model of economic development adopted in a country has an important bearing on the character of the political system. Growth models based on the export of agricultural and mining products had, by the early twentieth century, nurtured political systems characterised by the domination of an oligarchic elite to the exclusion of almost everyone else. An established body of liberal theory justified the development of export-led growth as natural and inevitable, given Latin America's inheritance and position as a supplier of raw materials in the international economy. The Great Depression changed this, forcing Latin American countries to take the first steps towards creating industries that would lessen their reliance on the temperamental international commodities market and that promised the kind of prosperity enjoyed in the developed world. Countries in the region began to subscribe to the economic theory of structuralism, which argued that only if they transformed the structure of their economies by prioritising industry could they escape underdevelopment. Structuralism challenged some of the central ideas about trade and the role of the state held by economic liberalism. It also rejected the assumptions of the modernisation theory developing simultaneously in the industrialised world that assumed countries in regions like Latin America should develop along similar evolutionary lines to them. The creation of industries to manufacture products formerly imported was called import-substitution industrialisation (ISI), and this required the imposition of barriers to imports through protectionist measures such as tariffs. ISI led to substantial industrialisation in Latin America, and in some cases laid the basis for the creation of large, globally competitive industries. Industrialisation also had profound social and political implications, fuelling both urbanisation and poverty in the countryside, and leading to the creation of large central states that maintained stability through corporatism. The limitations of the rapid industrial growth of the 1950s had become apparent by the 1960s, when countries began to recognise the need to manufacture more sophisticated and valuable products that required greater levels of investment and technological know-how. Now policymakers began to stress the merits of industrial exports and the need for a change in the nature of local consumption patterns to allow more sophisticated forms of manufacturing to develop. One way of securing the high levels of investment and technical knowledge needed to produce more complex goods was by allowing multi-national corporations to set up. At the same time, the limited levels of political inclusion implied by industrialisation policies and the growth of inequality generated new social and political strains in Latin American countries. A radical theoretical response to the exhaustion of the first phase of ISI and to the social and political strains of the era developed in the form of dependency approaches, which often chimed with Marxist ideas. These advocated breaking Latin America's economic dependency on the industrialised economies completely. The change in the nature of industrialisation combined with growing social and political unrest in the 1960s has been associated by some scholars with the military clampdowns in this period, especially in the more industrially developed Southern Cone countries.

Discussion points

- By what criteria can the notions of 'centre' and 'periphery' be distinguished?
- What is protectionism and how can it be justified?
- Was state-led industrialisation in Latin America a success?
- How are dependency perspectives related to structuralism?
- Are internal or external economic factors more important for successful development?
- Is it possible to end dependence in Latin America?

Useful websites

www.eclac.cl Comisión Económica para América Latina (CEPAL, Economic Commission for Latin America and the Caribbean). See, in particular, 'About ECLAC – Evolution of ECLAC ideas'

www.oecd.org/home Organisation for Economic Co-operation and Development, a useful source of up-to-date information and assessment

www.oswego.edu/~economic/econweb.htm Useful site of internet resources for economists

www.embraer.com/english/content/home Empresa Brasileira de Aeronáutica (Embraer)

www.pdvsa.com Petróleos de Venezuela SA (PDVSA), Venezuela's state oil corporation

www.cut.org.br Central Única dos Trabalhadores (CUT, Central Workers' Confederation), Brazil

www2.petrobras.com.br/ingles/index.asp Petrobras, Brazil's state-controlled oil company

www.vale.com Vale, Brazilian mining giant, formerly Companhia Vale do Rio Doce (CVRD)

www.codelco.cl Codelco (Corporación Nacional del Cobre de Chile)

www.sinolatincapital.com SinoLatin Capital

Recommended reading

Bulmer-Thomas, Victor, John H. Coatsworth and Roberto Cortés Conde (eds). 2006. *The Cambridge Economic History of Latin America, Volume II. The Long Twentieth Century.* Cambridge: Cambridge University Press

   Essential, comprehensive yet accessible overview of Latin American economic development in the twentieth century and a valuable work of reference

Dietz, James (ed.). 1995. *Latin America's Economic Development. Confronting Crisis*, 2nd Edition. Boulder, CO: Lynne Rienner

   Useful collection containing essays by various authors that provides helpful theoretical discussions of some important schools of thought

Franko, Patrice. 2007. *The Puzzle of Latin American Economic Development*, 3rd Edition. Oxford: Rowman and Littlefield

   Essential introduction to the specific developmental problems faced by Latin America for students with varying levels of economic knowledge

Frieden, Jeffry A., Michael Tomz and Manuel Jr. Pastor. 2000. *Modern Political Economy and Latin America: Theory and Policy.* Boulder, CO: Westview Press

   Valuable introductory exploration of the relationship between economics and politics in Latin America with contributions that take theoretically informed thematic approaches to such issues as foreign trade, industrial policy and institutions

Esfahani, Hadi, Giovanni Facchini and Geoffrey J.D. Hewings (eds). 2010. *Economic Development in Latin America.* Basingstoke: Palgrave Macmillan

   Valuable introduction to the evolution of development strategies in Latin America focused mainly upon the Southern Cone that evaluates previous and current policies, with useful essays on ISI, institutions and the informal economy

Chapter 15

Neoliberalism

This chapter examines why most Latin American states abandoned strategies of inward-looking, state-led industrialisation during the 1980s and 1990s, and the social and political consequences of this dramatic policy shift. The catalyst for this change of heart was a debilitating crisis that began in 1982 during which Latin American countries struggled to meet payments on crippling foreign debts. Changes in policy were justified by a new 'neoliberal' consensus that formed around ideas restating the main themes of economic liberalism, the central emphasis of which is the free market. Neoliberalism transformed the character of the Latin American state that had evolved alongside industrialisation, and reconfigured the relative power of interest groups such as business organisations and trades unions. As neoliberal reforms also appeared to coincide with the end of military governments, they were often, albeit questionably, associated by policymakers in the developed world and financial institutions with democratisation (see Chapter 4). Initially, neoliberalism gave the political right a new and, at times, even popular banner to rally behind in the democratic era; more recently it has provided a strong focus of ideological opposition for Latin America's revived left (see Chapters 12, 16). It has thrown open Latin America's economies to flows of trade and investment from across the globe, deepening the region's incorporation into the momentous process of globalisation that has accelerated since the end of the Cold War. There is considerable interest in the social and political impact of globalisation upon Latin America because the region's fate has always been so closely tied to developments in the international economy. Globalisation has significant implications for the nature of the state, the character of political competition, inequality and culture. Regional integration, the growth of foreign investment and even the new opportunities offered by globalisation for Latin American companies to develop multi-national characteristics all have consequences for national sovereignty.

However, in the early years of the twenty-first century, neoliberalism has either been discredited or challenged, with policymakers from international financial institutions (IFIs) calling for 'second-generation' reforms that place greater emphasis on institution-building, governance and regulation and aim to open both local labour and capital markets and financial systems in an effort not to displace neoliberal reform, but to correct what are seen as its failures or weaknesses.

The nature of Latin American capitalism and the debt crisis

The character of capitalism in Latin America has been transformed recurrently since Independence (see Chapter 1). In the post-Independence period, Latin American economies developed on the basis of agro-exports controlled by a small number of oligarchic landowners. This model of development limited the emergence of industry and tied the fate of Latin American countries closely to the development of powerful external markets for their commodities and raw materials. In some societies, elements of the social structure that the agro-export economy created persisted well into the twentieth century, and their legacies are still evident. However, in the most dynamic Latin American economies, following a crisis in global capitalism exposed by the Great Depression, a model of national capitalist development emerged that tried to escape this reliance on agro-exports through import-substitution industrialisation (ISI, see Chapter 14). The structuralist ideas that advocated ISI were not anti-capitalist, and accepted that a form of national capitalism in which the state played a significant guiding role was the best hope for Latin American development. ISI laid the basis for inward-looking national development policies – sometimes assuming some of the characteristics of what has been called 'state capitalism' – while allowing Latin America to take advantage of capitalist expansion elsewhere in the world that provided markets for its products. As a result, Latin American capitalist development in the first half of the twentieth century tended to be distinguished from what was happening elsewhere by a much greater role for the state and public sectors; mass social mobilisation; and populist or corporatist political projects (see Chapters 2, 7, 14). In general, ISI based on protectionist policies became a cornerstone of development strategies in Latin America until the 1980s.

The oil crisis of the early 1970s, which hit Latin America hard, accelerated the exhaustion of ISI but also allowed governments in the region to borrow the 'petro-dollars' being earned by petroleum-exporting countries from higher oil prices and then banked in the global financial system. In this period, Latin American governments grew excessively over-exposed to foreign debt and, by late 1982, rising international interest rates and falling oil prices had begun to make it difficult for Mexico to keep up payments on its then $96 billion foreign debt. Investors lost confidence that their investments were safe and began to pull their money out of the country. However, as often happens in developing regions in which there are several countries sharing similar economic conditions, nervous investors also began to withdraw capital from the rest of Latin America, making it more difficult for all the countries in the region to pay their debts as well and stunting their growth. The debt crisis led to a 'lost decade' of stagnation and painful recovery during which large amounts of capital continued to be transferred out of Latin America in the form of debt payments while little came in. From 1983 until 1991, the net transfer of resources out of the region to countries in the developed world amounted to $218.6 billion (see Figure 15.1).

The debt crisis illustrated several important characteristics of the evolution of capitalism in Latin America that have shaped approaches to development such as dependency theory (see Chapter 14), in particular: the central role played by the

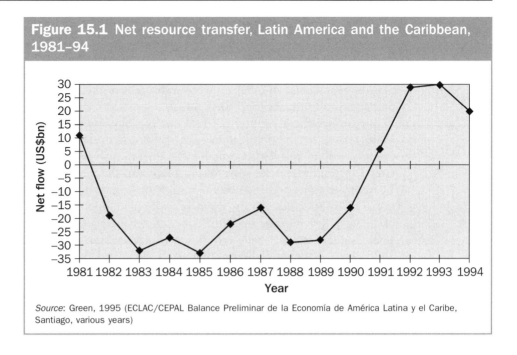

Figure 15.1 Net resource transfer, Latin America and the Caribbean, 1981–94

Source: Green, 1995 (ECLAC/CEPAL Balance Preliminar de la Economía de América Latina y el Caribe, Santiago, various years)

state in shaping internal markets; a reliance on exporting commodities to fluctuating world markets; and a reliance on external sources of capital for the investment needed to promote industrialisation.

The recent commodity boom between 2003–08 only served to illustrate both the difficulties governments in the region have always faced trying to wean themselves off a reliance on the export of primary goods, and the extent to which the fate of Latin America's economies has *always* been closely tied to global capital markets. A contemporary illustration of the continuing degree to which Latin America remains exposed to the behaviour of capital markets can be found in an indicator of corporate dynamism in the international economy: the number and value of mergers and acquisitions (M&As) involving Latin American corporations. M&As are one of the most common means that transnational corporations use to deploy their capital in foreign markets. Whereas the boom between 2003–07 saw record numbers of cross-border mergers and acquisitions, growing limitations on international finance in 2008–09 was expected to result in a dramatic fall in the number and value of M&As in Latin America.

None the less, the 1980s debt crisis was a turning point because it called into question the viability of ISI in Latin America, which had become dependent on a continuous infusion of capital, and so strengthened the hand of neoliberals. Neoliberal positions originated in critiques of structuralism that were voiced in the wake of the military coups of the 1960s and 1970s. In Chile, the military regime led by Augusto Pinochet (1973–90) relied on technocrats to develop its economic policies, and their ideas became influential throughout Latin America (see Boxes 2.1, 2.4, 2.5). Chile's most important technocratic policymakers had trained at the University of Chicago under the US champion of free markets Milton Friedman (1912–2006), and so were dubbed the 'Chicago Boys'. The Chicago school emphasised traditional comparative advantages in the export of primary products (see Chapter 14), the development of new industrial exports and the opening of Latin American economies to imports. Neoliberalism has also often been associated with the theory of monetarism refined by Friedman (see below). This argued that the main cause of inflation were states that printed money in order to finance public expenditures beyond their means.

A core neoliberal orthodoxy had emerged by the early 1980s, a period also characterised by the political ascendancy of conservative governments in the US, Canada, Britain and West Germany. Neoliberals also came to prominence in multilateral institutions such as the World Bank and the International Monetary Fund. These institutions and the administration of President Ronald Reagan (1981–89) in the US, among others, saw the debt crisis as an opportunity to promote market-oriented policy reforms in Latin America through aid with conditions attached. These policy reforms reflected the favoured agenda of international creditors and powerful economic actors that has been called the 'Washington Consensus', emphasising exchange rates that are not fixed by the state, trade liberalisation, foreign investment, public-spending cuts, privatisation, deregulation and property rights (Bulmer-Thomas, 1994; see Box 15.1). A new generation of leaders in countries such as Mexico wedded to economic liberalism now identified the *state* as the chief obstacle to development and embraced this policy agenda (see Vellinga, 1998).

Policies in the aftermath of the debt crisis initially sought short-term stabilisation to curb inflation. From 1982–83, Latin America endured a deep recession and most countries in the region implemented recovery programmes promoted by multilateral bodies such as the IMF based on austerity policies that involved curbing wage rises, ending subsidies and limiting welfare benefits. Neoliberals argued that the way to fight inflation was to reduce growth in the money supply (monetarism) by cutting public spending and raising interest rates. Different types of stabilisation plan were pursued, but by the late 1980s most Latin American governments were following neoliberal prescriptions in earnest.

International support for the efforts of Latin American countries to escape the economic difficulties caused by the debt crisis was co-ordinated after 1985 by the US Treasury. In 1989, the then US Treasury Secretary Nicholas Brady negotiated a range of measures that recognised, over and above the need to ease the burden of interest payments on Latin America's foreign debts, the need to *reduce* those debts. Although the Brady plan did not reduce debts by a great deal, it was a turning point because the confidence it inspired in Latin America's future opened the door anew to net inflows of foreign investment, which played a dominant role in recovery (see Box 15.2).

A second dimension of policies following the debt crisis aimed at long-term 'structural adjustment' which, like structuralism before it, sought to change the structure of economies in the region, but this time by reducing the role of the state. Many Latin American policymakers laid the blame for problems of debt, high inflation and slow growth on the interventionist state, which was portrayed outside the region as bloated and inefficient, allocating resources to favoured sectors such as public-sector workers or the owners of overprotected local industries (see Box 14.4). Neoliberals advocated radical changes to reduce the state's economic role through privatisation and deregulation, to nurture the private sector, and to reorient the

The Washington Consensus

The diverse set of policy reforms that reflected the agenda of international financial institutions, creditors and the treasuries of the industrialised world and came to be known as the 'Washington Consensus' has been the subject of extensive debate in Latin America and beyond. For Latin Americans, it is a symbolically loaded term, identifying the US rightly or wrongly as a central and, by implication, a potentially interventionist actor in a reform process based on classical economic ideas that began following the debt crisis and gained coherence through the term 'neoliberalism'. More recently, attacks on the Washington Consensus and neoliberalism have been key to the political appeal of left-of-centre candidates throughout Latin America and, with the rise of left-of-centre governments in the region since 1998, some scholars have identified something of a backlash amounting to a 'post-Washington Consensus' (see Panizza, 2009; see also Chapter 12). Panizza attributes the term 'Washington Consensus' to the economist John Williamson who, in 1990, listed a set of policy prescriptions that embodied a conventional wisdom at that time among economists based in Washington DC from the main IFIs, such as the IMF and World Bank, as well as the US Treasury, about the key issues facing Latin American economies following the debt crisis (see Williamson, 1990). These were:

- Fiscal discipline;
- Changes in public spending priorities (to areas that offered economic returns and the potential to improve income distribution, such as primary healthcare);
- Tax reform;
- Interest-rate liberalisation;
- Competitive exchange rates;
- Trade liberalisation;
- Liberalisation of foreign direct investment (FDI) inflows;
- Privatisation;
- Deregulation (to remove obstacles to market activity);
- and the need to secure property rights.

Importantly, this list encouraged other countries to adopt the relatively open policies that, it was assumed, developed nations already practised (see Boxes 14.2, 15.3). None the less, as Panizza points out, several of these prescriptions were flexible, and there was more consensus on some than on others, with disagreements over capital controls and industrial policy, for example. Moreover, the Washington Consensus did not address how to restart growth after the stabilisation policies following the debt crisis (see below), and its very identification with neoliberalism was in dispute. As Panizza points out, Williamson noted that there was no consensus among economists about what *model* of capitalist economy developing nations should follow – the Anglo-Saxon model, the European social market model, or the Japanese-style corporate capitalist model – and he even denounced the blind, ideological faith in markets of certain technocratic reformists. None the less, the Washington Consensus became established as the dominant economic discourse of the period following the end of the Cold War that ushered in a new phase in capitalist globalisation (see Box 15.6). Its resonance was heightened in Latin America because it coincided with the dramatic changes that had accompanied the end of ISI and with democratisation. Moreover, until that point a single narrative had not been developed to explain both the causes of the crisis facing the ISI models and to offer alternatives to it.

| TRENDS | Box 15.2 |

Foreign investment

The debt crisis had a dramatic impact upon levels of foreign investment in Latin America, which dried up as countries struggled to meet their debt obligations during the 1980s. However, debt relief schemes, the Brady Plan and neoliberal reforms created conditions in which foreign investors began to return to Latin America in droves. Since the early 1990s, attracting foreign investment has been a central plank of development strategy in Latin America. Despite variations in the average amount of capital that has flowed into the region every year, overall levels have grown considerably since the late 1990s. Today, foreign investment is seen by bodies such as ECLAC as essential to creating the conditions for sustained development. In 2008, for example, ECLAC reported that foreign direct investment (FDI) inflows in Latin America and the Caribbean rose to a new record high of $128 billion, even though FDI flows worldwide shrank by 15 per cent (ECLAC DPPM, 2009; see also ECLAC, 2008b). However, this vigorous flow of foreign finance to Latin America and the Caribbean disguises a profoundly uneven pattern of investment between countries and different economic sectors in the region. In 2008, there were marked sub-regional differences in FDI inflows within Latin America, with South America experiencing a rise of 24 per cent to $89.8 billion but Mexico, Central America and the Caribbean experiencing a 5 per cent fall to $38.4 billion. There were also significant differences within sub-regions themselves, with Brazil, Chile and Colombia accounting for 80 per cent of all the FDI heading for South America.

These different trends reflect the uneven effects that the international crisis has had on the region, and particularly on FDI destined for sectors that extract and export natural resources such as hydrocarbons and metal mining. The rise in FDI to South America was driven by high prices for key commodities such as hydrocarbons and metals, again highlighting Latin America's reliance on international markets, and large amounts of investment headed for the mining industry in Chile and Colombia. Mexico was worst hit in 2008, with FDI falling 20 per cent on the previous year, largely because of its close economic ties with the US economy, where recession limited the amount of outward investment heading for exporting sectors further south.

The US continues to be the largest single country source of FDI heading for Latin America, followed by Spain, Canada, the Netherlands and Japan. A large increase of FDI from Canada and Japan has been driven by the interest of investors in the natural resources of the region and its mining sector. Oil and gas exploration and production companies invested an estimated $96 billion in Latin America as a whole in 2008, 47 per cent more than in 2007.

Political conditions play a role in determining the levels of FDI that countries receive, with investors shying away from political instability. Argentina, for example, received investment totalling nearly $24 billion in 1999 but by 2002, following a serious economic and political crisis, this had fallen to $2 billion. Venezuela, where president Hugo Chávez (1999–) has nationalised key sectors of the economy and limited the role of foreign corporations, has seen a gradual but clear decline in levels of FDI from nearly $5 billion in 1998 to $1.7 billion in 2008. By contrast, its neighbour, Colombia, a staunch ally of the US, has experienced a rise of FDI from $2.8 billion in 1998 to $10.5 billion in 2008. Hostility to the presence of foreign corporations can also make investors nervous, although the impact of measures to increase taxes on their revenues or limit their stakes, for example, does not always result in the dire warnings they make about FDI abandoning countries with hostile policies coming true. In Bolivia, for example, violent protests led by the coca growers' leader Evo Morales and his Movimiento al Socialismo (MAS, Movement Toward Socialism) before he won the presidency in late 2005 were directed against the activities of multi-nationals that had invested over $3 billion to exploit the country's huge natural gas supply (see Boxes 5.6, 12.11). Bolivia has the second largest gas reserves in South America and multi-nationals such as BP, BG Group (British Gas) and Repsol have invested billions of dollars in the sector (see Chapters 9, 14). MAS was instrumental in violent protests over plans to export gas through Chile that led to the resignation of President Gonzalo Sánchez de Lozada in 2003, and encouraged the use of road blockades in an effort to press congress to increase royalties paid by foreign investors in the hydrocarbons sector significantly. MAS argued that plans to develop the country's resources allowed foreign companies to loot the country's natural wealth with no real benefit to its citizens. In response, Bolivia's then government insisted such demands would not be accepted by the international community, and foreign investors warned that such a move could make their continued presence in Bolivia unviable. In May 2006, the Morales government took control of the country's natural gas industry and told foreign firms to leave if they were not willing to renegotiate energy contracts (see Chapter 16). In 2004 and 2005, FDI flows fell dramatically then turned negative, just as the foreign investors had warned; but in 2006 FDI inflows picked up again, and by 2008 stood at $512 million, a level comparable to that of 2002. Much of this FDI was destined for Bolivia's natural resources sector, suggesting that foreign investors are both prepared to accommodate policies that may limit their activities provided the potential gains are high enough, and that new investors will move into areas vacated by others.

The international climate is also a key factor in determining levels of foreign investment: capital flows in Latin America in 2009 were expected to fall dramatically as a result of the global economic and financial crisis, with ECLAC projecting that FDI in the region in 2009 would fall by between 35 per cent and 45 per cent.

focus of economic growth back to exports. Policy reforms aimed to shift Latin America in a direction combining fast growth of exports with low rates of inflation. As a result, the region became more outward-looking, adopting policies of export-led growth. The ratio of exports to GDP rose rapidly in the 1990s and several Latin American countries such as Chile and Argentina made a significant effort to diversify away from traditional primary products. In such circumstances, it was clear that it would be necessary to dismantle trade barriers because companies that wanted to export needed access to inputs at prices similar to those paid by their competitors in other countries.

By the beginning of the 1990s two countries, Mexico and Chile, had laid the basis for sustainable long-term growth as a result of successful reforms (Bulmer-Thomas, 1994). Argentina, Bolivia, Colombia, Costa Rica, Ecuador, El Salvador, Uruguay and Venezuela had begun to make significant adjustments, although Ecuador and Venezuela remained heavily dependent on sales of oil (see Figure 14.1). Policy reforms in a last group of countries – Cuba, Dominican Republic, Guatemala, Haiti, Panama and Paraguay, Brazil, Honduras, Nicaragua and Peru – were slow or limited.

By the late 1990s, free-market economics had become dominant throughout most of Latin America, albeit in different forms and to varying extents, to the point where both supporters of the reform process itself and many of its critics on the left accepted that a new, market consensus had taken hold in the region. Part of the explanation for this change is that there was discernible popular support for many of the reforms, which despite belt-tightening often brought benefits to populations tired of economic instability and high inflation, and eager to make up for the 'lost decade' following the debt crisis. Between 1990 and 1997, Latin America experienced consistent economic growth, falling poverty and increased social spending (ECLAC, 1998). None the less, the record of neoliberal reform was mixed and, since 1998, this consensus has been challenged (see below).

Policy tools

The policy tools of neoliberal reform can be categorised under two main themes: policies that reduced the role of the state in the economy and aimed to remove constraints on market activity through privatisation and deregulation, thereby attracting foreign investment; and policies that liberalised trade to reorient the economy towards diversified export-led growth in a globalising economy.

Privatisation and deregulation

The term neoliberal refers to a range of policy positions adopted or pursued in a variety of ways in Latin America but their common denominator has been that they envisage economic development based upon free-market mechanisms and reject any distortion of market forces by the state (see Box 15.3). Neoliberals argue that growth in developing regions has been hampered not by lack of resources but by massive government interference with market mechanisms for political reasons and to propel industrialisation. Structural reform has, therefore, aimed to reduce the role of the state in the economy by cutting the size of the public sector and restricting social programmes and public services. An important reform tool has been privatisation, which became a visible symbol of a state's commitment to the new market model during the 1990s. Neoliberals believed that selling off state-owned enterprises – which accounted for about 12 per cent of GDP in the mid-1980s –

THEORIES AND DEBATES   **Box 15.3**

State versus market

At the heart of development debates in Latin America over the last 25 years has been the role of the state (see Box 2.1). Since the late nineteenth century, the state in Latin America has played a prominent and often proactive role in economic development. Structuralists assigned a key role to the state to spearhead industrialisation, encouraging it to create and protect local sources of production of a large range of goods formerly imported (see Chapter 14). As a result, state responsibilities and expenditures grew significantly. These interventionist models argued that government involvement was essential for overcoming barriers to growth.

However, by the late 1970s many policymakers outside Latin America and within multilateral institutions were arguing that states in the region were bloated and inefficient, acting mainly in favour of certain privileged groups (see Chapter 7). Governments had appeased politically powerful unions with legislation that raised costs above internationally competitive levels and protected local businessmen from foreign competition, reducing their incentive to produce cheaply and efficiently. By the 1980s, many Latin American policymakers themselves were beginning to blame the state for high inflation, indebtedness and slow growth, and the debt crisis finally convinced them that a new economic model was needed.

Neoliberal ideas demanded a radical restructuring of the state and opening of economies to market forces. Economists from the Chicago School argued that state-directed activity had a poor performance record and a free market was essential for development. They believed growth had been held back by extensive state interference with market mechanisms and this had disrupted efficiency and left economies worse off (Cardoso and Helwege, 1992). By responding to the 'invisible hand' of the market, private enterprise would ensure the most efficient allocation of resources and so generate the greatest good for all. Neoliberal positions were grounded in assumptions about the self-interest of economic actors and assigned the state a minimal role guaranteeing rules and property rights and providing limited public services (Franko, 1999). They advocated the privatisation of state enterprises, repealing minimum wage laws, eliminating tariffs, cutting welfare spending and giving businesses incentives to invest, such as lower taxes.

Many economists agree that much can be learned from neoliberalism when it comes to ensuring productive efficiency in technical terms. However, the economic structures of many developing countries are built upon ineffective institutions, inequality and political weaknesses that often make policymaking based purely on either market or state formulas difficult. 'Neostructuralist' critics of neoliberalism (see Chapter 16) say the history of Latin America provides ample evidence that economic development cannot occur *without* state intervention. They point out that social welfare programmes and minimum wage legislation provide the political stability that is essential to attracting investment.

Moreover, state activity in Latin America today still remains limited in comparison with that of other parts of the world after declining since the 1980s, and state spending is generally lower than in the developed industrial states and South-east Asia (Franko, 1999; see also Chapter 6). Central government expenditure as a proportion of national wealth also varies considerably throughout the region, from 15.3 per cent in El Salvador to 31.7 per cent in Bolivia in 2008 (ECLAC, 2009a).

Recent economic debates in Latin America have returned to the question of state regulation and, in some cases, state ownership through nationalisation, seeking more middle ground between structuralist and neoliberal positions (see Chapters 14, 16). Nationalisation is often politically popular but, since 2000, has largely been confined to Venezuela, Bolivia and Argentina, and in some cases is justified by governments not as the assertion of national control based on the revival of statism, but to correct a failing sector or address issues in the capital markets. In 2008, for example, the Argentine government took the country's flag-carrier airline, Aerolíneas Argentinas, which had originally been privatised in 1990, back into state control after several years in which it had teetered on the brink of bankruptcy and faced a series of industrial relations problems. Later in 2008, Argentina also nationalised the private pension system comprising about $30 billion in private pension funds. It justified this as an attempt to protect retirement investments from the international financial crisis, but was accused by critics of seizing retirement savings for cash to shore up public finances.

ECLAC (2009a) argues that a paradigm shift is taking place in Latin America and elsewhere that is repositioning the role of the state in the economy: in terms of regulating activity to ensure that the private sector's search for profitability does not compromise the well-being of the wider society; in developing a type of production atmosphere and infrastructure that rewards knowledge and environmental efficiency; and in protecting vulnerable sectors of society to ensure inclusive development. This revives questions about what kind of state is needed and what reforms are necessary to create it.

would enable the management of newly private firms to take decisions based on economic efficiency, rather than politics, and simultaneously would ease pressure on a state's budget.

A first wave of privatisation in Latin America in the 1980s generated resistance because state officials did not want to lose the political power that the control of these sectors conferred; managers and workers were threatened by job losses; nationalists argued that foreign capitalists would simply buy up key sectors; and the military grew nervous about who would control strategic industries. In some cases, measures were adopted to soften the blow of privatisation through delays in job reduction and generous severance packages. The scale of privatisation in Latin America gathered pace between 1990–94, when 56 per cent of all privatisations in the developing world took place there (Franko, 1999; see Table 15.1). Overall, ambitious privatisation programmes were undertaken in Chile, Argentina, Mexico and Brazil. In Chile, between 1974 and 1992 more than 500 firms were privatised, and state ownership in the economy accounted for 16 per cent of GDP by 1989 (*ibid.*). In Mexico and Argentina, privatisation was also extensive and one of the largest privatisations to take place in emerging markets was that of the huge Argentine state oil conglomerate Yacimientos Petroliferos Fiscales (Fiscal Oilfields, YPF) in 1993.

Table 15.1 Privatisation in Latin America 1990–95

Country	Privatisation revenues ($m)	Number of privatisation transactions	Privatisation revenue as % of GDP	Privatisation revenue from abroad as a % of total privatisation revenue
Mexico	24,271	174	2.0	28.7
Argentina	18,446	123	1.2	47.9
Brazil	9,136	45	0.3	14.5
Peru	4,358	72	1.6	82.4
Venezuela	2,510	29	0.6	66.6
Chile	1,259	14	0.5	51.9
Colombia	735	16	0.2	64.4
Bolivia	637	28	2.0	96.6
Nicaragua	126	75	1.5	3.7
Panama	100	9	0.3	62.9
Ecuador	96	9	0.1	55.9
Honduras	74	32	0.5	1.1
Costa Rica	46	4	0.1	0.0
Paraguay	22	1	0.1	50.0
Uruguay	17	7	0.0	94.1
Dominican R.	0	0	0	n/a
Guatemala	0	0	0	n/a
Haiti	0	0	0	n/a

Sources: Franko, 1999-IADB/IDB, 1996

Following legal changes, Brazil was a latecomer to privatisation in 1990, with the state continuing to hold 100 per cent stakes in public utilities, 67 per cent of steel, 67 per cent of chemicals and petrochemicals. Privatisation since then – initially in steel, petrochemicals and fertilisers, and thereafter in energy and transportation – was substantial, raising about $3 billion in 1996 and $5.5 billion in 1997 (*ibid*.). In 1997, Companhia Vale do Rio Doce (CVRD) – Latin America's biggest producer of gold, Brazil's largest exporter and the biggest foreign exchange earner in the country – was put up for sale with a price tag of $9.8 billion. Telebrás, the national telecommunications network was auctioned off in 12 restructured pieces for $19.1 billion, with Spain's Telefónica picking up the most valuable sector (*ibid*.).

The impact of privatisation has been the theme of significant debate, although most liberal economists believe it has, overall, been positive (see Smith, 2002; Chong and López de Silanes, eds, 2005). In general, it has led to improvements in the quality of services and has played an important role in bringing down inflation. By 1995, countries that had experienced hyperinflation such as Argentina, Nicaragua and Bolivia had brought inflation down to single figures. Privatisation has, in general, improved the competitiveness of some large Latin American companies. It has been particularly good news for local businessmen, who bought into privatising sectors: for example, Mexico's stock of billionaires rose from 2 to 24 during the presidency of Carlos Salinas (1988–94).

Latinobarómetro data also reveals growing levels of satisfaction with privatised public services, from 15 per cent in 2004 to 32 per cent in 2008 (Latinobarómetro, 2008). In some countries, such as Ecuador and Brazil, more than 50 per cent of people were satisfied with privatised services in 2008.

Deregulation involved a range of measures to remove constraints to market activity that included amending minimum wage laws, creating incentives for investment in the form of lower taxes and increasing the protection of private property. In particular, deregulation policies have sought to remove barriers to the movement of capital and the entry of foreign investment. Neoliberals argue that openness to foreign capital is beneficial because it increases investment that cannot be financed with local savings and so increases local production, with a potentially positive impact on welfare (Cardoso and Helwege, 1992). Foreign capital was a significant source of privatisation revenues, accounting for 39.7 per cent in Latin America between 1990–95 and jumping to 76.7 per cent in 1995 (Franko, 1999). In countries such as Bolivia, Peru and Uruguay, more than 80 per cent of privatisation revenues flowed from abroad (*ibid*.). Since 2008, the international climate has shifted strongly back in favour of regulation, especially of financial markets. As international financial systems come under much stricter regulation and oversight, suppressing the buoyancy of credit markets and pushing up interest rates, Latin American states may need to regulate further in order to ensure that domestic savings are maintained at adequate levels and can flow freely as investment to finance economic activity.

Foreign investment remains a significant plank of economic policymaking and is today seen as a crucial element of growth (see Box 15.2; see also Nelson, 2009). In Mexico, areas with the largest concentration of multi-nationals, such as the northern frontier region, are the most advanced sectors of the economy. An important recent trend in Latin America has been intra-regional investment (see Box 15.4).

The trans-Latins flex their muscles

A phenomenon of increasing interest to economists has been the growth of Latin American outward foreign direct investment (OFDI) – finance that is invested by Latin American corporations outside their countries, whether this is within the region itself or elsewhere in the world. OFDI is a measure of the region's ability to generate and deploy the capital that has long been something of a missing link in Latin American development (see above), and hence offers the potential to reduce its dependence on FDI (see Chapter 14).

Flows of OFDI from the countries of Latin America and the Caribbean have shown a consistent increase as economic growth has strengthened the fortunes of so-called 'trans-Latins', or Latin American transnationals. The development of this new generation of large Latin American corporations – mostly in Brazil, Chile, Argentina and Mexico, and representing an important new trend in the region – has been driven by economic reforms, saturated local markets, opportunities in neighbouring countries, the need to diversify risk, and recent growth. In 2008, Latin American and Caribbean OFDI rose to $34.5 billion, up 42 per cent from the previous year. Brazil has become a rich source of finance and is the region's leading foreign investor, accounting for $20.4 billion of OFDI (61 per cent) in 2008 – a staggering 190 per cent increase on the previous year and the second largest outflow of domestic capital in its history after 2006. Chile and Venezuela were the next main sources of Latin American OFDI in 2008 ($6.9 billion and $2.7 billion respectively).

The largest trans-Latins are involved in natural resource-based sectors such as oil and gas (Petrobras, PDVSA, ENAP), mining (CVRD/Vale), steel (Techint, Gerdau) and cement (Cemex). While many investments are in natural resources, iron and steel, and food, increasing amounts are being allocated by corporations to raising the productivity of their international operations. These corporations have generally enjoyed considerable state support to develop and some remain state-owned, but others have grown as a result of privatisation and competition. The US is the main destination for much of Brazil's and Colombia's outward investment (28 per cent and 57 per cent respectively in 2008), whereas South America was the target for 72 per cent of Chile's OFDI. Where the trans-Latins have been able to take advantage of local markets, in particular, has been in telecoms and services such as retailing. Chilean retailers such as Falabella, Ripley and FASA have focused their internationalisation strategies on Latin America. Some trans-nationals, such as Latin America's largest mining enterprise, Companhia Vale do Rio Doce (CVRD/Vale) of Brazil, have made ambitious investments throughout the world, with projects in 2009 extending to Oman, Indonesia, Australia and Mozambique.

The number and value of mergers and acquisitions (M&As) involving Latin American corporations – often considered by economic commentators to be a measure of their dynamism in the international economy – has grown considerably in recent years. In 2008, for example, large Brazilian corporations were involved in at least 12 foreign acquisitions, four of which were within the US and four within Latin America, including the $950 million purchase of LWB Refractories GmbH in Germany by Magnesita Refratarios. Among the acquisitions by Mexican corporations was the purchase by Grupo Bimbo of George Weston's Fresh Bread & Baked Goods Business in the US for $2.5 billion. Acquisitions are expected to decline as a result of the 2008–09 financial crisis.

However, intra-Latin American investment does not always guarantee advantages for the participants. Relations between Brazil and Bolivia were strained after President Evo Morales took control of Bolivia's gas industry, a large part of which was being developed by Petrobras. The move alarmed Brazil, which relies on Bolivia for half of its gas and called the action 'unfriendly'. The trans-Latins also face stiff global competition and the permanent threat of being absorbed by even larger foreign players, and in order to survive they must constantly renew and reinforce their competitive advantages. ECLAC says many of the flagship trans-Latins, such as Argentina's YPF and Pérez Companc, Chile's Enersis and Brazil's Ambev have become 'shooting stars', quickly snapped up by foreign transnationals seeking a quick way into Latin American markets.

Sources: ECLAC DPPM, 2009; ECLAC IS, 2009b

Trade reform

As part of their mission to reverse a bias under ISI against production for export, the neoliberals put trade reform at the top of their policy agenda in the belief that liberalising imports ultimately benefits everyone. Local factories can import the best available machinery and other inputs to improve their productivity, competition from abroad forces domestic producers to improve their products, and consumers can shop around for products at the best prices. From the late 1980s, trade reforms across Latin America dismantled protectionist measures despite the general lack of a reciprocal opening from the US or European governments. By the end of the 1980s, Latin American exports finally started to respond by growing in value, and diversification away from exporting a single commodity has been a key component of reform.

Neoliberal policymakers tried to institutionalise trade reforms through multilateral and regional free-trade agreements that co-ordinate the mutual reduction of tariff and other barriers to imports between countries. The General Agreement on Tariffs and Trade (GATT), an international body created in 1947 to promote the reduction of tariffs in goods and services, gained a new lease of life in the 1980s with the accession of Latin American states such as Mexico in 1986 and Bolivia, Costa Rica, El Salvador, Guatemala, Paraguay and Venezuela in the early 1990s. Free-trade agreements have become an important vehicle of regional integration in Latin America, although efforts to integrate markets are not new and many hark back to the ISI era (see Chapters 9, 14). A proliferation of sub-regional and bilateral free trade agreements within Latin America has created a complex 'variable geometry' of intra-regional trade preferences (see Table 15.2).

The latest round of integration began in 1991 with the formation of the Mercado Común del Sur/Mercado Comum do Sul (Mercosur/Mercosul, Common Market of the South) whose full members are Argentina, Brazil, Paraguay and Uruguay and whose associate members are Bolivia, Chile, Colombia, Ecuador and Peru (see Box 9.9). By 2010, the full membership of Venezuela was still pending ratification in Paraguay. In 1994, after several years of complex negotiations, Mexico joined with the US and Canada in the North American Free Trade Agreement (NAFTA). NAFTA was an important model at the heart of US aspirations to create a Free Trade Area of the Americas (FTAA) encompassing the entire western hemisphere (see Box 15.5). More recently, the establishment in 2008 of the Unión de Naciones Suramericanas (Unasur, Union of South American Nations) represents an effort to bring together Mercosur and the Comunidad Andina de Naciones (CAN, Andean Community of Nations), thereby extending the potential for a customs union encompassing almost the whole of South America.

Table 15.2 The 'Variable geometry' of free trade and economic integration initiatives in Latin America and the Caribbean

Sub-regional agreements	Year created	Current member economies
Mercado Común Centroamericano (MCCA, Central American Common Market, CACM)	1960	El Salvador, Guatemala, Honduras, Nicaragua, Costa Rica
Comunidad Andina de Naciones (CAN, Andean Community of Nations, ANCOM)	1969 (as Andean Pact)	Bolivia, Colombia, Ecuador, Peru
Caribbean Community (Caricom)	1973	Caribbean states, including Haiti
Asociación Latinoamericana de Integración (ALADI, Latin American Integration Association, LAIA)	1980 (to replace Latin American Free Trade Association, LAFTA, created in 1960)	Argentina, Bolivia, Brazil, Chile, Colombia, Cuba, Ecuador, Mexico, Paraguay, Peru, Uruguay and Venezuela
Mercado Común del Sur/Mercado Comum do Sul (Mercosur/Mercosul, Common Market of the South)	1991	Argentina, Brazil, Paraguay and Uruguay; Venezuelan membership pending ratification (associate members: Bolivia, Chile, Colombia, Ecuador and Peru)
North American Free Trade Agreement (NAFTA, Tratado de Libre Comercio de América del Norte, TLCAN)	1994	Mexico, US, Canada
Asociación de Estados del Caribe (AEC, Association of Caribbean States, ACS)	1994	Caribbean states, including Colombia, Costa Rica, Cuba, Dominican Republic, El Salvador, Guatemala, Haiti, Honduras, Mexico, Nicaragua, Panama and Venezuela
Alianza Bolivariana para los Pueblos de Nuestra América (ALBA, the Bolivarian Alliance for the Peoples of Our America, usually called the Bolivarian Alliance for the Americas) especially the Tratado de Comercio de los Pueblos (TCP i.e. Peoples' Trade Agreement)	2004	Venezuela, Cuba, Bolivia, Nicaragua, Ecuador, Honduras (suspended 2009) and Antigua & Barbuda, Dominica, St. Vincent and the Grenadines
Unión de Naciones Suramericanas (Unasur, Union of South American Nations i.e. Mercosur plus CAN)	2008	Argentina, Bolivia, Brazil, Chile, Colombia, Ecuador, Paraguay, Peru, Uruguay, Venezuela, Guyana, Suriname (observers: Mexico, Panama)
Tratado de Libre Comercio entre Estados Unidos, Centroamérica y República Dominicana (TLC, Dominican Republic–Central America Free Trade Agreement, DR-CAFTA)	2009	US, Costa Rica, El Salvador, Guatemala, Honduras, Nicaragua, Dominican Republic

Source: Adapted from ECLAC, 2006c; Baumann, 2008

INSTITUTIONS   **Box 15.5**

'NAFTA on steroids': free trade or forlorn hope?

Negotiations to create a Free Trade Area of the Americas (FTAA) that had been actively pursued by US policymakers since the early 1990s stalled in late 2003 and a deadline of January 2005 to finalise an agreement was missed. Negotiators did not give up hope of eventually striking a deal on what the FTAA's critics dubbed 'NAFTA on steroids'. In March 2005, US and Brazilian officials met to try to restart negotiations, but the window of opportunity for doing so grew progressively smaller with the approach of Latin America's 2006 electoral calendar. At the Summit of the Americas meeting of 34 heads of state in November 2005, 29 countries said they wanted to resume talks but five – Brazil, Argentina, Venezuela, Uruguay and Paraguay – decided to wait for results of a scheduled meeting of the World Trade Organisation (WTO). However, little progress was made thereafter, and hopes among supporters of the FTAA that the idea could be revived at the Fifth Summit of the Americas in Trinidad and Tobago in 2009 – the first to be attended by the President Barack Obama of the US – foundered, with trade low on the agenda. Critics of the FTAA, and in particular social movements in Latin America opposed to it as a key component of the neoliberal agenda, have now pronounced it dead. It is likely that the US will continue to seek bilateral trade deals throughout the Americas as an alternative.

Debate over the FTAA exacerbated divisions between some Latin American countries. In November 2005, Venezuela and Mexico withdrew their ambassadors from each other's capitals after disagreements following Mexico's support for the US effort to kickstart the FTAA talks degenerated into bitter exchanges. If an agreement were eventually reached, an FTAA accord would still need to be ratified by all member governments. Some observers concluded that the US should pronounce the FTAA dead and focus on completing global negotiations through the WTO.

The aim of the FTAA was to lower tariffs and open up borders between 34 western hemisphere countries – excluding Cuba – with a combined population of 800 million people and $13,000 billion in economic output, creating the world's largest free-trade zone based upon a common set of rules covering commerce and investment. Under such an arrangement, US manufacturers would benefit from lower tariffs and increased protection for intellectual property rights. Latin American companies would get easier access to US markets for industrial goods and farm products. Consumers across the region would gain from lower prices. Supporters of the FTAA said it should also be seen as more than just a way to boost trade and could be used to promote good governance, strengthen courts and other democratic institutions, and encourage greater regional co-operation.

The White House responded to the FTAA delays by pursuing smaller trade agreements in the region with sub-regions such as Central American and the Caribbean, and with individual countries such as Colombia, Peru and Ecuador. In 2004, the US reached an accord with six countries in the Dominican Republic-Central America Free Trade Agreement (DR-CAFTA), which came into force in 2009. Supporters of CAFTA believe this will be vital to helping Central American textile manufacturers to withstand increasing competition from China. Its opponents argue that any potential benefits will be outweighed by the effect of competition by US agribusinesses on Central America's small farmers, and in particular rice farmers. Passage of CAFTA was considered important to the eventual fate of the FTAA, with the White House believing it would send an important signal to Latin America about its willingness to make concessions. However, CAFTA met with stiff opposition in the US congress, where Democrats, labour leaders and religious groups argued that it lacked protections for workers and the environment. DR-CAFTA was approved in the House of Representatives by just two votes in the face of strong opposition, and became law in August 2005.

There was also considerable opposition to the FTAA in both the US and Latin America. US Democrats and labour officials argued it would endanger jobs and the environment in their country, and farmers suffering from increasing international competition said it would swamp the US market with cheap Latin commodities. The US trade surplus in agriculture has shrunk dramatically since the mid-1990s.

The election of left-of-centre governments in several Latin American countries (see Chapter 12) and resistance to the FTAA in the US by heavily protected farmers contributed to scepticism in Brazil and Argentina about Washington's willingness to reach a deal. Brazil, South America's largest exporter, was the source of many of the obstacles to concluding an FTAA agreement, mainly because of its opposition to US subsidies and demands for tariff reductions and greater protections for corporations overseas. Brazil initially refused to advance the FTAA talks unless the US agreed to put farm products on the negotiating table, and has sought much greater access to the US market for protected commodities such as sugar, ethanol, tobacco, orange juice and beef. The US has insisted that agricultural issues are negotiated in WTO-sanctioned global trade talks and that Latin American countries establish strong rules to protect intellectual property and investors in exchange for greater access to the US market, which Brazil has opposed. In an apparent concession to Brazil in November 2005, the US president, George W. Bush (2001–09) told his Brazilian counterpart, President Lula da Silva (2003–10), that the US would work towards eliminating agricultural subsidies but that this would depend on European willingness to do so also.

Delays to the FTAA encouraged South American countries to consolidate trading links with their neighbours through existing agreements such as Mercosur (see Box 9.9). Brazil has played a leading role in pushing for greater regional integration – including the creation of the Unión de Naciones Suramericanas (Unasur, Union of South American Nations) – to create a stronger negotiating front with the US (see Box 9.6, Chapter 10). Cuba's desire to join Mercosur also complicated discussions about the FTAA: Mercosur has made vigorous demands for the US to end its economic embargo of the island (see Box 10.8), and in 2006 Mercosur and Cuba signed agreements to eliminate tariffs and boost complementary trade. Venezuela has also created its own integration initiative, the Alianza Bolivariana para los Pueblos de Nuestra América (ALBA, Bolivarian Alliance for the Americas) as a socialist alternative to the FTAA (see Boxes 9.1, 16.1). As a result of the commodities boom between 2003–08, South America's big exporters also turned to growing markets such as China (see Chapter 11, Table 14.1, Box 14.7), prompting some observers to conclude that 'South-South' trade may offer a more promising return than the FTAA.

Globalisation

Policies removing barriers to foreign investment and liberalising trade favoured by neoliberals built on notions of global interdependence. Since the mid-1990s, the idea of 'globalisation' has been at the heart of debates about the impact of free trade upon Latin American development. Neoliberals embraced the concept of globalisation because it limits the ability of a national state to resist the dominant norms of the international economy by seeking to control trade and investment, and so represents an alternative to the statism epitomised by ISI.

A key aspect of globalisation is the predominance of liberal economic principles throughout the world, although it remains a contested idea that has been explained in different ways (see Box 15.6). Above all, globalisation can be characterised as the increasingly transnational nature of capitalist development that reflects the emergence of a new international order since the end of the Cold War. This blurs distinctions between economic activities within and outside countries and, by making national borders less significant, challenges a view of the world in terms of rich versus poor countries. By heightening competition, globalisation can engender economic success or failure for groups in *both* rich and poor nations (Payne and Nassar, 2003).

Perspectives on globalisation in Latin America

Latin America offers a valuable focus for the analysis of globalisation, a term that has been understood in different ways (see Held and McGrew, 2000; Harris, 2002; Ritzer, 2009; Whitman, 2009; Wunderlich, 2009). Scholars of politics in the region have often adopted the 'transformationalist' position arguing that globalisation is giving rise to complex transformations in economics, politics and culture that have an uneven and even contradictory impact on nations, regions and sectors.

In 2002, ECLAC developed its own perspective on globalisation and recommended ways Latin America could meet its challenges. The organisation argued that globalisation was a set of external economic, social and cultural processes that exerted progressively greater influences over regions and countries (ECLAC, 2002). As an economic phenomenon, globalisation brought opportunities for development, but also posed risks deriving from two key aspects of the globalisation process:

i) the current form of market globalisation, which is marked by the mobility of capital and of goods and services alongside severe restrictions on the mobility of labour. A good example of this is NAFTA (see above), which seeks to encourage the free movement of investment and goods across the US-Mexican border, while restricting the free movement of Mexican labour. To ECLAC, this aspect of globalisation reflects fundamental asymmetries in the global order, an analysis that coincides with those of structuralism and dependency theory by highlighting an unequal balance of power in the world economy;

ii) the absence of a suitable form of global governance both in economic terms but also other areas. ECLAC draws attention to one clear example of where effective global institutions are required: the financial markets, a position that has been greatly strengthened by the 2008–09 global financial crisis.

ECLAC put forward a positive agenda for Latin America and the Caribbean in the global era based on key principles: shared objectives; global institutions that respect diversity; the complementarity of global, regional and national institutions; and equitable participation in accordance with suitable rules of governance. Its agenda gives the new international order three main objectives: the provision of global public goods, the correction of international asymmetries, and the pursuit of a rights-based social agenda.

Robinson (2003, 2008) has developed an influential model of globalisation based upon his analysis of its impact on Central America, arguing that it is shaping a new 'transnational' economy and society that has disrupted past patterns of revolutionary upheaval and civil war in the region. He places significant emphasis on the rise in Latin American production of non-traditional agricultural exports, the proliferation of *maquiladora* assembly plants, international tourism, and the export of labour and consequent import of remittances. These developments help to explain how Latin America's political economy has changed as states integrate into the new global production and financial systems. His approach also bears some similarity to that of dependency theory by highlighting internal changes in the balance of power between different factions in society and the emergence of new transnational factions and new class groups as a result of economic restructuring. Just as local elements of a transnational working class or its equivalent are emerging in peripheral regions such as Latin America, so are those of a transnational bourgeoisie or capitalist class. Local capitalists act as 'national' contingents of the transnational capitalist class, shifting their wealth into and out of their own countries as needs be and adapting state structures to the new global environment. Robinson argues that development and underdevelopment should be reconceived in terms of global social groups, not nations, in which 'core-periphery' designates social position rather than geographic location.

▶

Gwynne and Kay (2004) also relate globalisation back to original ideas within structuralism and dependency theory, which they suggest remain relevant today. A central vision of structuralism was its conceptualisation of the international system as being constituted by asymmetric centre-periphery relations, and dependency theory also took as its point of departure a world system in which under-development was rooted within unequal economic relationships. Gwynne and Kay argue that there is evidence of increasing asymmetries as a result of globalisation between different regions in the world economy and between richer and poorer countries within regions. They distinguish between periphery and 'semi-periphery' in Latin America itself, arguing that the periphery comprises the poorest countries of the region and the semi-periphery comprises six countries with the highest per capita GNP – Argentina, Uruguay, Chile, Brazil, Mexico and Venezuela. Periphery and semi-periphery are becoming more differentiated, with those nation-states, regions or cities more inserted into the global economy better able to achieve sustained improvement in international competitiveness by their ability to attract capital, technology and labour. Gwynne and Kay say the new mobility of international capital since the 1970s has made Latin America's economies more dependent, increasing their vulnerability to changes in world capital markets and reducing their policy autonomy. They also point to studies confirming the deterioration of the periphery's terms of trade in relation to the core economies, a fact highlighted by structuralism and woven into the theory of unequal exchange.

Supporters of globalisation say it will intensify economic growth in ways that ultimately benefit everyone, and argue that global competition and free trade benefit most of the population by increasing job opportunities, weakening monopolies and reducing consumer prices as transnational capital flows into countries seeking lower costs and bringing with it jobs and technology. Others argue that the advancing global economy may have the power to improve and enrich lives through its capacity to distribute as well as create wealth, but may need mechanisms to ensure that this takes place according to human rights standards (see, for example, Kinley, 2009). In particular, globalisation has created poles of growth in the world economy based on regional integration, with multi-national corporations identifying regions in which to base their labour-intensive operations and develop markets for their products. Mexico and Brazil have been the two most important poles of attraction for foreign direct investment in Latin America. Annual 'globalisation indexes' based on trade and investment indicators are now produced that incorporate the economies of the region. In 2008, *Latin Business Chronicle*'s index suggested that Latin America was becoming far more globalised, and identified Panama and Costa Rica as the most globalised countries in the region (see *Latin Business Chronicle*, 2008).

Globalisation is having a significant impact upon Latin America's development. On the one hand, it may be deepening the region's traditional role as a source of raw materials and primary products by creating important new markets and export opportunities in countries such as China (see Table 14.1, Box 14.7, Chapter 11). The scale of the commodity boom and its impact on Latin American growth between 2003 and 2008 attest to this. On the other hand, technological development and the availability of global investment has made new types of economic activity that do not depend on traditional types of production possible in Latin America. In the late 1990s, for example, high-technology and information technology companies such as Intel, Acer and Microsoft began to locate in Costa

Rica or target it for investment, prompting the country's government to make the lofty claim that it was poised to become Latin America's 'high-tech capital' (Robinson, 2003). A potentially important area of growth in the most developed Latin American economies – and a good example of the economic activities that become possible through globalisation – is the offshore business services industry, which makes use of information technology to provide key components of a company's operations from abroad at a lower labour cost. Typical offshore business services include contact centres, business processes, information technology services, and knowledge-intensive, analytical services. This kind of offshoring is seen as important to the efforts of developing economies to attract 'high-quality FDI' – that which encourages local economic, technological and social development by allowing workers to develop new skills and paying them higher rates than they would find domestically – as opposed to just large quantities of FDI that may not necessarily help countries improve their skills base. Although Latin America's participation in the offshore services industry remains small, in recent years large corporations have shown an increasing interest in the region and ECLAC believes there is significant potential for growth. The A.T. Kearney Global Services Location Index, for example, reveals a rising profile of Latin American countries in the top 10 of those that are seen as most attractive globally for future offshore business services investments (see Table 15.3).

Globalisation has important implications for politics in Latin America. It has the potential for weakening the state's traditional role in economic management by shifting its focus towards meeting the requirements of international competitiveness and away from meeting the welfare needs of citizens or reducing inequality. To compete effectively, governments may be forced to adopt policies that could, in fact, promote greater inequality by reducing spending on healthcare, social services, subsidies for the poor and keeping wages low to attract investment (Payne and Nassar, 2003). Simultaneously, globalisation may diminish the ability of traditional political actors to represent and channel social interests while encouraging

Table 15.3 A. T. Kearney Global Services Location Index, 2004–07

	2004	*2005*	*2006/2007*
1	India	India	India
2	China	China	China
3	Malaysia	Malaysia	Malaysia
4	Czech Republic	Philippines	Thailand
5	Singapore	Singapore	Brazil
6	Philippines	Thailand	Indonesia
7	Brazil	Czech Republic	Chile
8	Canada	Chile	Philippines
9	Chile	Canada	Bulgaria
10	Poland	Brazil	Mexico
Others in the top 50	Mexico, Argentina, Costa Rica (in top 25)	Mexico, Costa Rica, Argentina	Uruguay, Argentina, Jamaica, Costa Rica, Panama

Source: ECLAC DPPM, 2009, on the basis of information from A.T. Kearney [online]

the emergence of new civil society actors such as the Zapatistas in Mexico (see Chapters 7, 8, Boxes 12.6, 13.5).

Globalisation also challenges the autonomy of states in the international arena in complex ways, increasing their room for manoeuvre in some respects while decreasing it in others. It may, for example, strengthen the opportunities for regional integration and multilateral approaches to decisionmaking, and weaken the influence of traditional actors such as the US (see Cooper and Heine eds, 2009; see also Chapters 9, 10). However, at the same time, important dimensions of globalisation that limit Latin American states' room for manoeuvre are the heightened risk of the withdrawal of capital and the detailed oversight of economic policy by international agencies and financial institutions such as the OECD and IMF. Modern states spend much time and energy trying to ensure a 'favourable investment climate' by developing economic policies that offer stability to large investors and do not conflict with the international norms. If they fail to do so, investment can dry up and international agencies can impose conditions on financial aid if they face a crisis. Argentina's crisis of 2001–03 (see Box 15.7) demonstrated how the

---

CASE STUDY   **Box 15.7**

Meltdown in Argentina

Argentina's crisis in 2001 demonstrates some of the paradoxes of neoliberal reform in Latin America. The country stopped servicing almost $100 billion of debt in the biggest sovereign default in history, exposing the fragility of the economy and generating a serious political, economic and social crisis. Hundreds of thousands of protesters took to Argentina's streets demanding a change in political leadership and five presidents came and went (see Box 5.4). The economic collapse was painful: GNP fell by about 20 per cent, unemployment rose to 20 per cent and about half of the population was thrust into poverty. Yet the IMF and multilateral institutions subscribing to the so-called Washington Consensus (see Box 15.1) had heralded Argentina as a *model* neoliberal economy and this praise was, in fact, a factor in the crisis. A report by the IMF's Independent Evaluation Office in July 2004 suggested that the IMF had been too indulgent towards Argentina in the years leading up to its financial crisis and that, instead of punishing the country for persistently missing its macroeconomic targets, it held it up as a model and even lavished praise on President Carlos Menem (1989–99) (Thomson, 2004a). For much of the 1990s, the IMF had shored up the Argentine economy with big loans that had, ultimately, compromised its structural reforms. Blustein (2005) has argued that the IMF was so impressed by the results of a decision to peg the country's peso to the dollar in 1991 that it suppressed its misgivings about Argentina's ability to balance its budget during the 1990s and ignored its own prescriptions for 'fiscal discipline' that lie at the heart of the Washington Consensus. The IMF, therefore, ignored Argentina's consequent need to borrow dollars on world capital markets at ever higher interest rates in order to maintain the currency's level. The report by the IMF's Independent Evaluation Office said the Fund was wrong, in particular, to have lent Argentina $8 billion in August 2001, just prior to its massive debt default (IMF, 2004). The response of the then Argentine economy minister, Roberto Lavagna, to the Independent Evaluation Office, argued that ideology, not evidence, had been behind the Fund's belief that all structural reforms would necessarily lead to increased growth, and that, while neither the IMF nor Argentina had benefited from the misguided policies that led to the 2001 crisis, it was Argentina that ended up having to pay both for its own errors but also for those of the IMF itself (see Panizza, 2009).

disapproval of international financial institutions and difficulties with international firms and investors can influence a government's response to crisis. Argentina stopped servicing almost $100 billion of commercial debt and interest in December 2001 in the biggest sovereign default in history. Several years of fraught negotiations ensued between Argentina and its creditors about how it could meet its obligations, during which Buenos Aires was accused by larger private investors of deliberately obstructing the renegotiation process. However, a hardening of attitudes by the IMF, the US government and the powerful Group of Seven (G7) industrialised countries in early 2004 forced Buenos Aires to begin accepting IMF demands. The US, which had acted as a mediator between Argentina and the IMF, began to lose patience with the lack of progress in resolving the crisis, and the G7 countries began to present a more united front. In early March 2005, the Argentine government announced that the majority of its private creditors had accepted the terms of a debt-reduction package – the largest ever achieved by a developing country.

Criticisms of neoliberalism

In recent years, the neoliberal orthodoxy and the export-led, market model have been the subjects of a broad reassessment (see, for example, Kingstone, 2010). In some countries, such as Brazil, left-of-centre governments have taken power with social agendas, and in others, such as Bolivia, a leftwing challenge to neoliberal policies has grown more militant and potent (see Chapters 12, 16). In Argentina, economic crisis prompted reflections about how the model is managed and the hype surrounding it, because the initial gains of neoliberal reform were lost in the disastrous collapse of 2001 (see Box 15.7). In Venezuela, Ecuador and Bolivia there has been a revival of populistic pressures subordinating economic decision-making to political criteria and re-establishing a strong role for the state in shaping social policies. Some scholars argue that the Washington Consensus has been replaced by a 'post-Washington Consensus' which combines adjustments that acknowledge the failures and weaknesses of neoliberal policy with elements of continuity (see Panizza, 2009, and below).

The take-up of neoliberal policies in Latin America occurred according to different phases in diverse countries, making an overall assessment of its impact on the region complex, but neoliberal reforms have been criticised on several fronts:

The politics of neoliberal reform

Neoliberalism often worked against the needs of democratic consolidation by strengthening authoritarian tendencies and limiting popular representation and participation through depoliticisation (see Chapter 4; see also Hellinger, 1999; Silva, Patricio, 2004). Economic adjustment sometimes reinforced a tendency towards the concentration of power in the executive and exacerbated tensions between the executive and other branches, weakening legislative and judicial institutions (see Chapters 5, 6). A number of autocratic presidents such as Alberto Fujimori (1990–2000) in

Peru pushed through painful reforms outside the parameters of traditional politics and concentrated their authority, especially in cases where very high inflation required complex stabilisation packages. Stabilisation and adjustment was easier when there was a strong, centralised presidency able to overrule congress and control the trade union movement and other sources of potential opposition.

Loans by international financial institutions such as the IMF that were conditional on reforms may also have had an impact on democracy. A government may act to reduce civil liberties, for example, in an effort to stifle unrest that results from structural adjustment policies pursued on the basis of a loan that demands as a condition the achievement of certain fiscal targets. In a study of loans to Latin American countries between 1998 to 2003, for example, Brown (2009) found that while the presence of an IMF loan in itself does not affect democracy, loans that require a high number of reforms can have a negative effect on democratic practices.

New civilian governments avoided actions that might cause division because of the need to stabilise their economies, to make the transition from authoritarian government, and to forge new civil–military relationships. In these circumstances, centrism, pragmatism and moderation replaced political debate and the concept of democracy was defined primarily in a procedural way and pared of any social implications (see Chapter 3). In Mexico, Bolivia, Argentina and Peru, highly educated technocrats were put in control of economic policy on the assumption that the public interest was better served by policymaking inoculated *against* an ill-informed public (see Box 2.1). One outcome of this was that, sometimes, prominent technocrats were able to pursue political careers on the back of their achievements, such as Fernando Henrique Cardoso in Brazil (1995–2002). Another outcome was a trend to technify problems and to target social policies, often diluting the political content of issues such as inequality (see Tulchin and Garland eds, 2000).

Neoliberal economic reforms also weakened or changed the behaviour of social actors such as trades unions and further excluded popular sectors such as the poor and marginalised from the formulation of policies. Reforms required the demobilisation of important sectors of society such as trade unions (see Chapter 7), whose resistance was at times met with repression, as in the Bolivian government's heavy-handed response to a miners' strike in 1985. Unions were also weakened by new laws aimed at enhancing labour market 'flexibility', making it easier for employers to hire and fire workers, and by the growth of the informal sector, often changing their strategies as a result (see above). In Argentina, for example, some unions began to participate in the process of privatising state enterprises and the pension and retirement systems. Organised labour throughout Latin America saw its bargaining power reduced, and in some countries rates of unionisation declined. The change in the role of the state transformed what parties on the left and centre-left could offer voters in terms of economic policy, and they responded by moving to the centre with issue-based promises (see Chapters 12, 16). The Left's shift to the centre has also served to deactivate politics itself, in some cases providing space for populists to fill. As parties such as MAS in Venezuela abandoned the aim of revolution and began to stress consensual change in the struggle against inequality, alternatives that appeared more radical, such as Chávez, were able to capture the popular mood. In the absence of potent alternative models, the most affected actors – workers, women and indigenous populations – have sought other ways to advance their demands, and much opposition to adjustment has taken place in civil society (see Chapters 8, 13). In some cases, neoliberal reforms provoked serious unrest, such as that which shook Bolivia in 2003 (see Box 5.6). New armed groups have also emerged, such as the Ejército Zapatista de Liberación Nacional (EZLN, Zapatista National Liberation Army) in Mexico that drew attention to the social exclusion of indigenous farmers unable to compete in newly liberalised markets (see Boxes 7.6, 12.6, 13.5). Policies inspired by neoliberal ideas continue to provoke conflicts between indigenous groups and states that wish to open their lands to greater economic use. In Peru in 2009, for example, bloody clashes between indigenous communities and security forces in Amazonian areas claimed many lives (see Chapter 8).

Privatisation

Assets owned by the state continue to be privatised in Latin America, albeit in a more limited way following the dramatic scale of privatisation in the 1990s (see below, Table 15.1). The way privatisation was carried out under neoliberal reforms in this period has often been criticised, particularly for a common failure to establish a strong regulatory structure to govern the activities of newly private utilities. Simply privatising corporations does not in itself resolve the inefficiencies associated with much state ownership: privatisation has to be accompanied by the establishment of regulations that prevent the emergence of monopolies and so protect consumers. Critics of privatisation say Latin American governments missed the chance to introduce strong regulatory frameworks and that this inhibited and delayed genuine competition. In some cases, governments desperate for funds merely transformed public monopolies into unregulated private monopolies. Following a serious economic crisis in Argentina in 2001 that put aspects of the neoliberal reform process in that country under the spotlight, for example, the Argentine economy minister, Roberto Lavagna (2002–05), criticised the privatisation process that his country had been encouraged to undertake by a range of international financial institutions for allowing monopolistic market structures to remain and for being conducted within an inadequate regulatory framework (see Box 15.7; and Panizza, 2009). Only where competition emerged did prices fall. In Chile, long-distance telephone rates fell 50 per cent as new competitors entered the market, while monopolised local rates rose by 35 per cent (Franko, 1999). In some cases, privatisation also led to the need to bail out incompetent businesses. A costly government bailout for Mexico's privatised banking system effectively sealed the fate of the ruling PRI in subsequent elections.

Privatisation has also had consequences for democratic consolidation in Latin America (see Chapters 3, 4). While privatisation was often hailed by supporters for its potential to create a healthy middle class that would play a significant role in reinforcing democratic stability, in countries such as Mexico most sales of industries were highly beneficial to the country's largest capitalists and helped them consolidate their position in markets they already operated in (see MacLeod, 2004). Privatisations in Argentina, Chile and Mexico allowed business groups to consolidate monopoly positions. Privatisation has reduced the contact citizens have with the state by handing functions once undertaken by corporations or agencies operated by the government to private providers. This can mean that citizens lose any input they may have once enjoyed in the process by which decisions are made about the provision of important services, and this may now put the logic of the market before the public interest. In this sense, privatisation can increase a fatalistic sense among citizens that important decisions are made by technocrats and the business community and are completely out of their hands. Privatisation processes were also often accompanied by a good deal of rhetoric about the state's inability to provide the service being privatised because of inherent inefficiencies and corruption. This did little to enhance public faith in state institutions and government more generally, and may have contributed to declining enthusiasm for politics. In some countries, such as Uruguay, there has been consistent resistance to sell-offs: in October 2004, for example, plans to privatise the country's water industry were rejected in a referendum when 64.5 per cent of voters said water should remain under state control. The vote gave the state exclusive control over water and sanitation and made access to them fundamental human rights.

Privatisation has also had implications for party systems in Latin America. In Mexico, privatisation helped to erode the centralised, single-party system under the PRI because it curtailed valuable sources of patronage in state corporations for the politicians who had controlled them (see Chapter 7). However, the awarding of public contracts to private providers creates new opportunities for corruption in government and sources of party finance as party membership withers, sometimes turning parties into vehicles that put their business sponsors first. As a result, privatisation has greatly empowered the private sector at the expense of groups formerly represented within the corporatist state, such as organised labour. MacLeod (2004) has suggested that, in the case of Mexico, the privatisation of state-led industries was not merely an act of state withdrawal but a process guided from the outset by private interests. This position is important because it suggests that privatisation in Latin America was shaped by collaboration between technocratic policymakers and private-sector groups. It challenges the notion promoted by advocates of neoliberal reform that technocrats were autonomous from special interests (see also Schamis, 2002). Finally, while neoliberals often argued that privatisation represented a healthy downsizing of the state in the interests of market reform, Schamis (2002) has suggested that privatisation can in fact lead to a strengthening, rather than a weakening, of state capacity. This is because in order to ensure that markets functioned correctly, states often sought to expand their institutional capacity in some areas by reorganising the civil service, creating a new infrastructure to support budgeting decisions, and developing new regulatory administrations.

Growth and investment

Neoliberal policies in Latin America have not produced the investment or growth rates required to have an impact on underdevelopment in the region, with consequences for democratic consolidation (see Chapters 3, 4). In most countries of Latin America, average annual growth rates during the period of neoliberal consensus after the early 1990s were below the 6 per cent ECLAC believes is necessary to tackle the problems of poverty and unemployment (see Table 15.4). Moreover, overall growth rates across the region were unpredictable, and varied considerably between 1994–2004, limiting the potential for attracting the large inflows of investment necessary to raise production.

In overall terms, there was an almost negligible increase in GDP per capita between 1980, at the very beginning of the neoliberal economic reform process, and 2003 (UNDP, 2004b). After a period of stagnation in the late 1990s, growth in per capita GDP in Latin America only began to recover ground when the effects of the commodity boom took hold after 2004–05 (see Table 4.4). According to Stallings and Peres (2000), of nine Latin American countries studied, only Bolivia, Chile and Costa Rica were successful in terms of raising the investment rates necessary to improve productivity. Changes in investment and productivity were insufficient to achieve the rapid rates of economic growth required for sustained development (Gwynne, 2004). Although Chile has tended to buck the general trend, with a strong record of investment and growth since 1985, it has still fallen behind comparable performance levels achieved in south-east Asian economies. An electoral resurgence

Table 15.4 Annual growth in Latin American countries, 1994–2004 (percentages)

Country	GDP annual growth rates (per cent)					
	1994	*1996*	*1998*	*2000*	*2002*	*2004*
Argentina	5.8	5.5	3.8	−0.8	−10.8	8.2
Bolivia	4.8	4.5	5.0	2.3	2.7	3.8
Brazil	6.2	2.5	0.1	4.0	1.5	5.2
Chile	5.0	6.9	3.3	4.2	2.0	5.8
Colombia	5.9	1.9	0.8	2.5	1.6	3.3
Costa Rica	4.6	0.8	8.3	1.8	2.8	4.1
Cuba	0.6	9.1	0.0	6.3	1.2	3.0
Dominican R.	4.7	7.2	7.4	7.3	4.3	1.8
Ecuador	3.7	3.0	2.2	0.9	3.8	6.3
El Salvador	6.0	1.8	3.8	2.1	2.1	1.8
Guatemala	4.1	3.0	5.1	3.4	2.2	2.6
Haiti	−17.6	5.6	2.9	2.0	−0.3	−3.0
Honduras	−1.9	3.7	3.3	5.6	2.6	4.3
Mexico	4.5	5.4	5.0	6.8	0.6	4.1
Nicaragua	4.0	5.1	4.1	6.5	0.7	4.0
Panama	3.1	2.7	4.6	2.6	2.2	6.0
Paraguay	3.0	1.1	−0.6	−0.6	−2.5	2.8
Peru	12.7	2.5	−0.5	2.5	5.4	4.6
Uruguay	7.0	5.0	4.4	−1.9	−12.0	12.0
Venezuela	−3.0	0.0	0.6	3.8	−9.0	18.0

Sources: ECLAC/CEPAL, 2003, 2004a, 2004b, 2005b, 2005c

by the Chilean right in the 2009–10 presidential elections reflected, in part, the desire of voters for policies that generate greater economic growth. A healthy economic performance throughout the global financial crisis of 2008–09 by countries such as Bolivia, whose leftwing president Evo Morales (2006–) has been a vociferous critic of neoliberal reforms, has also concentrated attention on the capacity for countries to grow through *alternatives* to neoliberalism (see Chapter 16).

Trade reform

Trade reform has brought greater benefits to the larger, industrialised, middle-income countries of Latin America such as Brazil, Mexico, Argentina and Chile, than to smaller, less industrialised and poorer countries such as Ecuador, Bolivia, Paraguay, Peru, El Salvador, Honduras and Guatemala. The record on rates of export growth in the neoliberal period is mixed. The direct impact of export-led growth was limited for much of the 1990s and the value of Latin America's exports did not keep pace with an expansion in world trade and failed to keep pace with an explosion in imports. However, neoliberal reform did leave Latin American and Caribbean countries much better placed as exporters to take advantage of a commodity boom that began in 2003, fuelled by Chinese demand for primary products (see Table 14.1, Box 14.7). This had a discernible impact on growth rates in the region: in 2004, Latin American and Caribbean economies grew overall by 6.1 per cent, in 2005 by 4.9 per cent, and in 2006 and 2007 by 5.7 and 5.8 per cent (ECLAC, 2004a, 2004b, 2006b, 2009b). This growth was closely tied to an expansion of world trade and demand in the US and China for oil, metals and minerals. None the less, rates of growth have been erratic in Latin America, ranging from 6.1 per cent in 2004 to a projected –1.9 per cent in 2009, indicating how exposed the region remains to trends in the demand for exports (ECLAC, 2009b). Growing demand helped Latin America's terms of trade, which improved significantly after 2004 in overall regional terms, although this began to fall back dramatically as a result of the 2008–09 downturn. There has also been considerable growth in the share of manufacturing exports as a proportion of GDP in Latin America, yet diversification and the rapid recent growth in demand has done little to change the continuing reliance on the export of commodities (see Chapter 14). None the less, export growth has strengthened the argument for the liberalisation of trade at a regional level in Latin America, and left-of-centre governments have played a formative role in recent initiatives on integration and preferential tariffs (see Table 15.2, Chapter 9).

Trade reform can bring problems as well as benefits to countries. In the short term, it can have a harmful impact on sectors that were previously protected, such as the manufacturers of consumer goods (see Box 14.7). Critics of trade liberalisation have at times pointed to a flood of imports into the region, bankrupting potentially competitive local producers and unleashing a consumer boom with harmful consequences for Latin America's trade balance. They also point to the high social cost of export diversification, exacerbating inequality and causing environmental problems. In smaller economies, trade reform can increase a reliance on the export of primary products. As commodity prices can be volatile, this can also derail macroeconomic planning. Small businesses complain about the ability of powerful foreign corporations to restrict competition in Latin America's open markets. In Mexico in November 2005, for example, a small shopkeeper won a landmark ruling against the Mexican subsidiary of Coca-Cola when competition authorities decided that the US drinks firm had tried to prevent her from selling the cheaper Peruvian rival Big Cola. Popular perceptions that free trade and capital mobility work to the disadvantage of local producers and can exacerbate existing inequalities have put Latin America at the forefront of opposition to globalisation (see Box 15.8).

SOCIETY   **Box 15.8**

Latin America and the anti-globalisation movement

Latin America has been at the forefront of the international 'anti-globalisation' movement that has emerged from social and popular organisations across the world opposing the impact of free-trade policies. One of the stated aims of the Zapatisa rebellion in the southern Mexican state of Chiapas in 1994, for example, was to oppose NAFTA on the grounds that this would harm indigenous communities (see Boxes 7.6, 12.6, 13.5, 15.5). During the 1990s, a global solidarity network, facilitated by the use of contemporary communication technologies such as the internet, developed in support of the Zapatista cause among civil society actors across the world (see Chapter 8). Two conferences, the 'encounters for humanity and against neoliberalism', attracted delegates to Chiapas in 1996 and began a process in which these Zapatista solidarity networks began overlapping with other groups. The networks that emerged were important precursors of the anti-globalisation movements, although rural social organisations had already emerged throughout Latin America in response to economic reforms (see Edelman, 1999; Welch, 2001; see also Box 7.6). Olesen (2004) has argued that, for many anti-globalisation activists, the Zapatistas were an important inspiration and some groups, like Peoples' Global Action formed in Geneva in 1998, were a direct outcome of the conferences in Chiapas to debate neoliberalism (see also Khasnabish, 2010). Italian delegates to the 1996 Chiapas meetings have been closely associated with the so-called 'White Overalls', a kind of protest movement vanguard that has become a potent symbol of the anti-capitalism movement. The anti-globalisation movement – often also loosely referred to as the global justice movement – came to prominence in 1999 in the Seattle anti-capitalism protests against the IMF, World Bank and the WTO.

In 2001, the World Social Forum was also established in Latin America, in the Brazilian city of Porto Alegre, to discuss ways of opposing the model of globalisation formulated in Davos, Switzerland, where large multi-national corporations, national governments, the IMF, the World Bank and the WTO meet at the annual World Economic Forum (see Correa Leite, 2005). The World Social Forum brings together thousands of representatives of NGOs, trade unions and other civil society organisations from across the world to discuss the impact of globalisation and neoliberalism on developing countries and to strengthen opposition alliances to this (see Box 15.6, Chapter 8). It has been held annually, mainly in Brazil, although its International Council meets at different venues across the world and, to mark its tenth anniversary in 2010, a single global centralised event was not planned and activities were scheduled throughout the world. Regional forums have also been created and the first Americas Social Forum took place in 2004 in Ecuador, which was chosen because of the strength of the country's indigenous social movements (see Box 8.4). National forums have also been set up in Argentina,

▶

Chile, Colombia and Puerto Rico. The first Puerto Rico Social Forum in Río Piedras in late 2006, for example, brought together 110 organisations in 200 workshops, panels, performances, exhibitions and conferences.

The World Social Forum is a concrete example of the degree to which some forms of political activity are becoming increasingly globalised, and is often portrayed as an example of grassroots participative democracy and pluralism (see Chapter 3, Box 16.5; see also Della Porta ed., 2009). However, it has also been criticised by some grassroots groups for becoming increasingly institutionalised by focusing its activities around organised and funded NGOs at the expense of popular social movements. Some leftwing political parties have attacked it for concentrating its fire on issues such as neoliberalism without developing a coherent economic or political agenda from which to advocate alternatives (see Hosseini, 2010). The World Social Forum has also been criticised for not developing a coherent set of procedures for decisionmaking and advocacy, while at the same time some anarchists have accused it of attempting to impose a form of centralised decisionmaking structure on otherwise democratic bodies.

Employment

Neoliberal policies did not create a sufficient number of jobs to bring down unemployment or have a considerable impact on reducing poverty and inequality. Between 1994 and 2004 unemployment rates increased in most of the countries of the Latin American and Caribbean region, and these only began falling to below 1998 levels between 2004–08 (ILO, 2009). In countries that experienced a rapid growth in exports in the 1990s, such as Chile, Mexico, Peru and Bolivia, employment levels grew. But others, including the larger economies of Brazil and Argentina, experienced slow or static rates of growth in employment. Official urban unemployment levels, related in part to labour market reforms that reduced the ability of trade unions to resist job losses, nearly doubled across Latin America between 1990 and 2002 (UNDP, 2004b). In Argentina they tripled, and in Paraguay and Uruguay they doubled or nearly doubled (*ibid*.).

The UNDP (2004b) has pointed out that the *quality* of employment in general in Latin America has diminished since the 1990s. According to the International Labour Organisation (ILO), nearly 60 per cent of new jobs created during the 1990s in Latin America were in the unregulated or 'informal' sector in which workers lack the most basic employment rights (Gwynne, 2004; see Chapter 4, Boxes 8.6, 8.8). The informal sector is that part of the economy in which workers are not covered by insurance, welfare benefits or regulations, and is a consequence of inadequate job growth. It can include a large range of different activities – from street vending on makeshift stalls to small restaurants and workshops, often referred to collectively as microenterprises. There is a relationship between urban poverty and informal employment, which tends to be associated with unskilled labour. In most countries of Latin America, the size of the informal sector grew in the 1990s, and in lower-income countries such as Bolivia, Paraguay, Peru and Ecuador the informal sector may now be larger than the formal sector.

Poverty and inequality

The nature of production under neoliberalism has not been sufficiently labour-intensive to have had a meaningful impact on levels of poverty and inequality in Latin America (Gwynne, 2004; see also World Bank, 2004, 2005). During the period of most intensive neoliberal reform, the 1990s until 2003, the absolute number of people in poverty and indigence according to international criteria grew in the region (see Table 15.5).

ECLAC (2004c) argued that Latin America and the Caribbean failed to gain much ground between 1997 and 2003 in its effort to combat poverty (see Table 4.5). Levels of poverty remain stubbornly high, although progress has been made in recent years – a period in which neoliberal orthodoxy has faced challenges – to bring these down. Between 2002 and 2008, the percentage living in poverty fell by 11 points, and indigence fell by 7 points (ECLAC, 2009c). Despite a recent downturn, stronger growth since 2003 suggests many countries may still succeed in halving extreme poverty by 2015.

Poverty reduction in recent years has failed to eradicate high levels of *inequality* in Latin America compared with other regions (see World Bank, 2009a). According to Stallings and Peres (2000), during the 1990s only in Chile was a sustained pattern of declining inequality achieved. In that period inequality continued to increase in Brazil, Mexico and Colombia, while in other countries such as Argentina, Bolivia and Peru it declined as inflation was brought under control but then rose again. Latin America and the Caribbean continue to experience among the worst levels of income inequality in the world (see Table 4.6).

Table 15.5 Poverty rate at international poverty lines, Latin America 1981–2005*

Region	People living on less than 2005 PPP $1.25 a day, millions (share %)								
	1981	1984	1987	1990	1993	1996	1999	2002	2005
Latin America and Caribbean	47 (12.9)	59 (15.3)	56 (13.7)	49 (11.3)	46 (10.1)	53 (10.9)	55 (10.9)	56 (10.7)	45 (8.2)
Europe and Central Asia	7 (1.8)	6 (1.4)	5 (1.1)	9 (2.1)	20 (4.4)	21 (4.8)	24 (5.3)	21 (4.8)	17 (3.8)

Region	People living on less than 2005 PPP $2.00 a day, millions (share %)								
Latin America and Caribbean	89 (24.6)	109 (28.1)	102 (24.9)	95 (21.9)	95 (20.7)	106 (22.0)	110 (21.8)	113 (21.5)	94 (17.1)
Europe and Central Asia	35 (8.7)	28 (6.8)	25 (5.9)	31 (7.1)	47 (10.8)	55 (12.4)	66 (14.9)	55 (12.5)	41 (9.2)

*And selected comparator

Note: International poverty line in local currency is the international poverty lines of $1.25 and $2 a day in 2005 prices, converted to local currency using the PPP conversion factors estimated by the International Comparison Programme.

Sources: World Bank, 2009a

Neoliberalism today

The ascendance of left-of-centre governments in Latin America since the late 1990s has challenged the dominance of neoliberal ideas and the Washington Consensus, although these challenges have often been rhetorical and neoliberal policy measures remain largely intact (see Chapter 12). Capitalism continues to provide the framework of ideas and behaviour within which economic development takes place in most of the region, despite the reversal of some elements of neoliberal reform and experiments with more radical redistributive models based on socialism (see Box 12.7, Chapter 16). However, the landscape of capitalism in Latin America is now varied and irregular, with some countries, such as Chile, building a sophisticated welfare infrastructure inspired by social-democratic ideas firmly upon strong neoliberal foundations, while others, such as Argentina, continuing to debate and test aspects of the neoliberal model in the search for a more heterodox policy-making formula that suits its domestic and regional politics.

Chile is often considered to be one of the most important strongholds of neoliberal ideas in Latin America, and these have penetrated so deeply that the existence of an open market and a privatised economy is not up for discussion. Silva (2009) argues that this is because: first, the neoliberal reforms undertaken from the 1970s onwards by a cohesive team of technocrats, with a high degree of co-operation by elites and the military regime, were seen as a potential solution to a broad range of economic, political and social problems; second, neoliberal policies were applied in all spheres of society; and, third, because the consolidation of the reforms has been facilitated by an awareness among Chileans that their country represents an exception of consistently stable growth within Latin America.

Argentina, by contrast, has had a more turbulent relationship with neoliberal ideas, largely because of its distinctive politics and the instability that came to be associated with neoliberalism following the crisis of 2001 (see Box 15.7). The crisis was the culmination of almost 20 years of conservative and neoliberal development strategies that some scholars have described as Argentine *transformismo* (transformation). Vivares *et al.* (2009) argue that *transformismo* was characterised by a capacity to *repackage* international neoliberal guidelines as domestic prescriptions by depoliticising them and presenting such policies as privatisation and free trade as universal technical solutions. Importantly, this was supported by the state's capacity to absorb and co-opt opposition political forces, and thereby defuse the social discontent that neoliberal policies generated. This discontent came to the fore as Argentina's financial problems developed into a political crisis after 2001 (see Box 5.4). The subsequent strategy to return the country to sustainable growth adopted by President Néstor Kirchner (2003–07) combined popular but 'unorthodox' measures to defy, for example, the recommendations of IFIs such as the IMF and enhance regionalism, with 'orthodox' policies inherited from the neoliberal period such as strict fiscal discipline and the accumulation of reserves (*ibid.*).

Panizza (2009) argues that a fundamental issue has been at the heart of a reassessment of neoliberalism by its erstwhile advocates since the late 1990s: whether the reforms were mistaken policy prescriptions or just insufficient and badly implemented. In partial answer to this question, a second generation of reforms has emerged among IFIs, particularly the World Bank, that implies some continuity with the original policy prescriptions together with changes to address their failures and shortcomings. These 'second-generation reforms' are aimed at strengthening the institutions that provide a foundation for market-oriented growth – in particular, enhancing the role of the state in development, better governance, and opening policymaking to wider political participation – while addressing the pressing need for adequate social policies in Latin America to tackle poverty. More importantly, greater importance is now placed upon the need to address some aspects of inequality, particularly with regard to opportunities for social mobility. One of the main political implications of 'second-generation' reforms is that they recognise the need for some state intervention and the strengthening of democratic governance. In practical terms, their institutional objectives – such as civil service reform and a strengthened rule of law – generally find support across the political spectrum (see Chapter 6).

However, some reforms, such as privatisation, remain firmly on the agenda of economic liberals, and the arguments for this could grow in economic sectors that require significant levels of investment, such as energy, especially in countries that have taken private assets into state control in recent years, such as Bolivia and Venezuela (see Chapters 9, 16). Ageing infrastructure, such as roads and railways, has become a new target for supporters of privatisation, and public–private partnerships also offer a new formula for private collaboration with the state. Privatisations can also be popularised by enhancing participation through public offerings of stock: in Colombia, the government privatised 20 per cent of the state-owned oil company Ecopetrol through a sale of its stock in 2007 in which more than 400,000 Colombians participated. Even left-of-centre governments have at times sold off large assets. In Bolivia, for example, the administration of Evo Morales sold development rights in the El Mutún state-owned iron ore deposit for $2.3 billion in 2006.

A narrow view of trade and financial liberalisation that aims for the complete removal of barriers to commerce and capital – as opposed to more cautious, regional integration initiatives that are premised on negotiated tariff preferences – also remains on the agenda of some neoliberals, although the notion of free trade has encountered considerable opposition in Latin America because of the strength of manufacturing exports relative to primary products. Arguments for financial liberalisation were also dealt a serious blow by the global crisis of 2008–09. The development of non-traditional exports are now seen on both left and right as an important way of ending a reliance on commodity exports. An example of the World Bank's effort to reconcile the notion of competitiveness within the global export market with that of inclusive growth can be found in its 2009 study of Bolivia, for example, which makes a range of recommendations for improving the government's ability to diversify exports (see Sakho and Calvo González eds, 2009).

Neoliberal ideas also continue to inspire right-of-centre candidates proposing visions of modernisation (see Chapter 12). For example, the Conservative billionaire, Sebastián Piñera, who won Chile's presidential elections in 2010, stood on a clear neoliberal platform by promising to be an 'entrepreneurial president' through policies that increase labour flexibility and cut regulation in an effort to increase competition and generally reduce the role of the state in the economy. In Uruguay, the conservative former president Luis Lacalle (1990–95), who was the unsuccessful candidate of the Partido Nacional (National Party, i.e. Blancos) in the country's 2009 presidential elections, promised more of the neoliberal policies that he had implemented as president in the first half of the 1990s. At that time, Lacalle was unable to push through one of the main aims of his administration – to privatise public utilities – with a 1992 referendum overthrowing privatisation legislation.

Summary

The 1982 debt crisis was a turning point in Latin America because it discredited the model of state-led industrialisation that had been justified by structuralist arguments. It gave significant impetus to neoliberal ideas already being pursued in countries such as Chile that restored an emphasis upon market economics and free trade. These neoliberal ideas proposed a return to export-led growth based on trade liberalisation and a radical restructuring of the bureaucratic state through privatisation and deregulation, and were supported by the Western industrial countries and multilateral institutions. These countries and institutions were often able to set conditions on the loans that Latin American states required to escape the stagnation caused by the debt crisis, thereby compelling them to undertake market reforms. Neoliberal structural reforms reduced the size of the Latin American state and cut the public sector. Privatisation policies often improved the efficiency of services for the public and brought down inflation. Support for free trade has been a key element of neoliberal policy and has led to multilateral and regional agreements that have tied Latin American countries into new integration initiatives such as NAFTA and Mercosur. Neoliberal reforms have thrust the idea of globalisation to the heart of debates about the impact of free trade upon Latin American development, and the region has been at the forefront of the international 'anti-globalisation' movement. Improved access to global markets has allowed powerful new players such as China to enter Latin America's development equation as a growing market hungry for the region's abundant raw materials. Globalisation has significant implications for Latin America's social and political development, by weakening the state's role in economic management in ways that could limit the ability to tackle inequality. Neoliberal reforms have often worked against the needs of democratic consolidation by strengthening authoritarian tendencies and depoliticising important sectors of the population or weakening groups such as organised labour while strengthening powerful business interests. Neoliberal policies have not produced the growth rates or increases in employment required to have a serious impact on poverty in Latin America. Continuing poverty and inequality can work against the long-term consolidation of democracy. A reassessment of neoliberal policies and globalisation gathered pace with the recent accession of left-of-centre governments in several Latin American countries. However, many aspects of the neoliberal reform agenda have not been reversed, and established neoliberal positions persist alongside proposals for 'second-generation' reforms that seek to correct past policy shortcomings. Neoliberal ideas continue to inspire candidates on the political right in Latin America.

Discussion points

- Can neoliberal reform be explained by the failure of structuralism?
- To what extent was the debt crisis a product of statism in Latin America?
- What role should the state play in countries characterised by deep inequality?
- What were the main policy tools employed by neoliberal reformers?
- In what ways are neoliberalism and economic globalisation related?
- Is free trade beneficial or harmful to Latin American economies and societies?
- What impact has the neoliberal economic model had in Latin America?
- How do 'second-generation' reforms differ from those of the 1990s?

Useful websites

http://economics.uchicago.edu University of Chicago Department of Economics

www.worldbank.org/lac World Bank, Latin America and the Caribbean site

www.imf.org International Monetary Fund (IMF), see Regional Reports

www.reaganlibrary.com Ronald Reagan Presidential Library

www.weforum.org World Economic Forum, an important global forum for neoliberal ideas

www.repsolypf.com Repsol YPF

www.csn.com.br Companhia Siderúrgica Nacional (CSN, National Steel Company), Brazil

www.telebras.com.br Telebrás, Brazil

www.telmex.com.mx Telmex, Mexico

www.cemex.com Cemex, Mexico

www.cencosud.cl Cencosud, South America

www.wto.org World Trade Organisation

www.wto.org/english/tratop_e/gatt_e/gatt_e.htm World Trade Organisation gateway to technical information on the Council for Trade in Goods (Goods Council), which is responsible for the working of the General Agreement on Tariffs and Trade (GATT)

www.nafta-sec-alena.org NAFTA Secretariat

www.mercosur.org.uy Mercosur/Mercosul

www.ftaa-alca.org Free Trade Area of the Americas

www.atkearney.com AT Kearney online

www.iadb.org Inter-American Development Bank IDB/IADB

www.ieo-imf.org Independent Evaluation Office (IEO) of the IMF www.nadir.org/nadir/initiativ/agp/en Peoples' Global Action

www.forumsocialmundial.org.br World Social Forum homepage

Recommended reading

Panizza, Francisco. 2009. *Contemporary Latin America: Development and Democracy beyond the Washington Consensus.* London: Zed Books

   Essential introduction to the neoliberal reform agenda and the subsequent evolution of a 'post-Washington Consensus'

Chong, Alberto and Florencio López de Silanes (eds). 2005. *Privatization in Latin America: Myths And Reality.* Palo Alto, CA: Stanford University Press/World Bank

   Valuable overview of privatisation in Latin America that evaluates the empirical evidence and assesses criticisms to identify where and why there have been shortcomings

Ritzer, George. 2009. *Globalisation: A Basic Text.* Oxford: Wiley-Blackwell

   Valuable textbook introduction to the major topics in globalisation studies

Stiglitz, Joseph. *Globalisation and its Discontents.* 2002. London: Penguin

   Useful polemic by former chief economist of the World Bank that highlights the negative impact globalisation can have on developing countries if it is not managed properly, with many references to Latin America

Gwynne, Robert M. and Cristóbal Kay (eds). 2004. *Latin America Transformed: Globalisation and Modernity.* London: Hodder

   Essential, comprehensive introduction to the economic, political, social and cultural consequences of globalisation in Latin America

Robinson, William I. 2008. *Latin America and Global Capitalism: A Critical Globalisation Perspective.* Baltimore, MD: Johns Hopkins University Press

   Valuable critical introduction to the impact of globalisation in Latin America that offers a theoretical model for understanding this complex process

Hosseini, S. A. Hamed. 2010. *Alternative Globalisations: An Integrative Approach to Studying Dissident Knowledge in the Global Justice Movement.* New York: Routledge

   Useful exploration of some of the ideas and ideologies that characterise the global justice movement that will help students identify common ground between highly diverse groups

Chapter 16

Redistributive models

This chapter examines development strategies pursued at various times in Latin America that have placed the need to tackle inequality through redistribution at the heart of the policy agenda. Severe inequality has long been a characteristic of development in the region, and today Latin American societies remain among the most unequal in the world. Inequality is a problem that politicians ignore at their peril, because it can fuel political unrest and instability and has serious implications for the character – and, indeed, the fate – of democracy (see Chapters 3, 4). Unfair societies are divided societies, and breeding grounds for the intolerance and violence that can work against democratic consolidation. The question of equality has long been at the heart of economic and political debate in Latin America. In the nineteenth century, the ideas held by oligarchs who dominated government were usually dismissive of inequality, regarding it as a natural phenomenon that reflected a social group's racial or ethnic inheritance (see Chapters 1, 13). Inequality was an inherent characteristic of export-led development prior to ISI, and informed the programmes of anarchist, socialist, communist and nationalist organisations dedicated to radical social change. Structuralists believed autonomous industrial development would inevitably lead to greater prosperity and a fairer distribution of resources, although industrialisation policies exacerbated the differences between social groups. Dependency perspectives advocated egalitarian societies, but were more theoretical than practical, often proposing revolutions that would level the social playing field by abolishing private property completely.

Only in Cuba since 1959 has a socialist model of development, in which private property rights are severely limited and the state plays a commanding role in economic management, been pursued coherently over a long period, with mixed results. Other models that had socialist components were also attempted in Chile under the Marxist president Salvador Allende (1970–73) and in revolutionary Nicaragua under the Sandinistas from 1979–90. Both governments challenged capitalist property relations, promoted redistribution and relied heavily on deficit spending, but both ended amid high inflation and economic instability, exacerbated by the hostility they provoked among powerful capitalist nations such as the US. Critics of the Chilean and Nicaraguan models argued that these governments failed because they paid little attention to the long-term consequences of spending beyond their means.

In other countries such as Peru, redistributive development models have also been adopted as part of a nationalist vision of development based upon multi-class populist alliances. While the policies pursued by the military regime in Peru from 1968–75, for example, had socialist components involving some expropriation of private property and the establishment of co-operative forms of production, they had more in common with populism because of their multi-class, corporatist and nationalist outlook (see Chapters 2, 4, 7).

More recently, the leftwing administrations of Venezuela and Bolivia have experimented with populist and socialist policies of some kind by constraining the room for manoeuvre of the free market. Throughout much of Latin America, left-of-centre governments have strengthened the role of the state in the economy in ways that hark back to the interventionist ideas of John Maynard Keynes (see below).

These policies can be placed along a contemporary spectrum of ideas justifying social-democratic approaches to economic policymaking that are associated with the rise of the Left in Latin America and the critique of neoliberalism (see Chapters 12, 15). This spectrum in opposition to neoliberalism is described variously as 'neostructuralist' or 'neodevelopmentalist', and revives some notions shared by structuralism and dependency theory while accepting elements of the neoliberal vision. Changes in the perspectives of powerful international financial institutions such as the World Bank, and the rise of developing economies, means that for the first time Latin America has the prospect of a model of development that, in broad terms, enjoys the consensus of both national governments and multilateral lenders. While there is considerable variation in policy positions, these ideas embrace the capitalist market while restoring the state's central role, to ensure a form of development that is as fair as possible to all social groups. The form of social democracy that has developed most comprehensively in countries such as Chile aims to mitigate harsher aspects of the neoliberal model within a framework of a dynamic market economy, while responding to popular pressures for fairer societies.

Socialism and the Cuban model

Cuba's socialist economic model has evolved under exceptional circumstances and is distinct from that of all the other Latin American states. Analysis of it reveals much about the difficulties of confronting dependency (see Chapter 14); the role of the state in economic policy (see Box 15.3); how effective non-material incentives are in fostering productivity and efficiency (see Box 12.2); and how political elites must reconcile their developmental aspirations with the objective conditions they inherit. The Cuban model represents a challenge to orthodox liberal economics that stress market freedom as the basis of sustainable development, not least because Cuba has survived adverse conditions exacerbated by the economic embargo of the US and external shocks such as the collapse of the socialist bloc in the late 1980s. Cuba's experience also poses questions within debates on the left about how to build socialism in countries with an economic legacy that is primarily agrarian.

Prior to the revolution of 1959, Cuba had a liberal economy in which the free play of market forces determined the allocation of resources. However, the country's independence from Spain was late and resulted in a heavy dependence upon US capital. Large sectors of Cuba's sugar agroindustry were owned by US corporations, economic policymaking became integrated into broader US decision-making priorities, and the island became heavily reliant on its neighbour for investment, technology, skills, tourism etc. As a result, land tenure developed in a way that did not support a traditional local landowning oligarchy, while the domination of US capital also stunted the emergence of a national capitalist industrial class.

At the time of the revolution, development indicators suggested that Cuba was not among the poorest Latin American countries and enjoyed relatively high levels of per capita income and life expectancy. However, Cuban society also suffered high levels of inequality, with the distribution of wealth heavily biased in favour of upper and professional classes. The land was concentrated in the hands of a few large landowners and US corporations, and impoverished landless peasants lived a harsh existence in the countryside, often with only seasonal employment. Few people had access to the fruits of capitalist development.

The Cuban Revolution transformed the economic model on the basis of a rejection of capitalist economic principles and the establishment of socialist policies oriented towards the achievement of greater equality. The period from 1959 until the 1970s was characterised by the extension of government control over production and distribution in which the revolutionary regime challenged the premises of dependent capitalist development. The new regime believed economic subordination to US economic interests was not compatible with their nationalistic or idealistic aspirations (see Boxes 9.3, 10.1). Short-term measures following the revolution included price freezes and wage rises for workers, the elimination of giant estates and prohibition of foreign ownership of land, and the nationalisation of large companies, banks and utilities. Washington reacted to the nationalisation of property owned by US citizens by cancelling Cuba's sugar quota and, eventually, by imposing an economic embargo on the island that has persisted to this day (see Box 10.8). These policies pushed the island towards closer ties with the Soviet Union (see Box 2.3, Chapters 10, 11).

Initially, there was a debate in revolutionary Cuba over economic strategy that would have a bearing on its relations with the Soviet Union, between those seeking to eliminate the market completely, such as the idealistic Che Guevara (see Box 12.2), and those who saw this as unrealistic (see Yaffe, 2009). An effort was made to free Cuba of its heavy reliance on the production of sugar through diversification and industrialisation, but this failed because the country lacked the capital, skills and raw materials necessary for such restructuring. None the less, by the late 1960s, revolutionary changes to class and property relations had eliminated dependent capitalism; the state had taken over production; agriculture had been reorganised into collective and state farms; and there had been significant improvements for citizens in health, education and social services (see WHOSIS, 2009). Between the revolution and 1980, per capita GDP in Cuba effectively doubled, and by 1978 levels of equality had been dramatically reduced: the 20 per cent of the population with the lowest incomes received 11 per cent of total income in comparison with 2.1 per cent in 1953 (Zimbalist and Brundenius, 1989; Centeno, 2004).

In the 1970s, more achievable development objectives were set, again with a focus on industry because agricultural production remained low. Some economic freedoms were permitted in agriculture that introduced limited market mechanisms and financial incentives within an overall model of central planning. The Cuban government introduced differential incomes for work effort, removed certain products from rationing lists, and increased access to some consumer durables at high prices. From 1971 to 1989, Cuba's economy grew at an annual average rate of 6 per cent, exceeding the growth of other Latin American states during the 1980s (Azicri, 2000). In the 1980s, the Cuban regime adopted a process of 'rectification' to rid the economic system of abuses and inequalities that had grown out of these reforms.

Key features of the Cuban model have been: the central role of the state and elimination of the free market; the reorientation of resources towards agriculture to achieve a more even process of development; until 1991, the substitution of dependence upon the US for that of the Soviet Union; and the response to external efforts to isolate the country internationally:

State not market

The Cuban economy has been inward looking and statist (see Box 15.3). The state has set priorities for the allocation of resources to sectors, eliminated private ownership and profit incomes in most productive activities, and redistributed wealth away from capital-owning classes to workers and the poor, initially through reductions in prices and rents and increases in wages. Rationing has been a recurrent feature of the economy and some supporters of this policy have argued that this is, in fact, a way of ensuring a fair distribution of food and social goods that avoids the emergence of inequalities. Cuba has pursued policies of full employment by encouraging state companies and farms to hire as many workers as possible, all but eliminating poverty due to unemployment yet greatly reducing efficiency. In the 1960s, the Cuban government also tried to inculcate in the population a new work ethic based on moral, as opposed to material, incentives, a theme often associated with the idealism of Guevara that challenged the idea of rational self-interest at the heart of economic liberalism (see Boxes 12.2, 14.4). Since taking over presidential duties in 2006, Raúl Castro has undertaken limited reforms to Cuba's socialist economy that introduce market mechanisms, such as lifting caps on bonus payments for productive workers and restrictions on the sale of consumer electronics goods. However, state ownership, regulation and centralised accounting have not been weakened, and arguably have been strengthened through his efforts to tackle bureaucratic inefficiencies. The state retains tight control over foreign trade and economic planning; it retains control of the growing resources generated by high-value activities, such as nickel production and, potentially, oil extraction; in recent years, it has increased its investments in key areas such as manufacturing and food processing, and has increased social expenditure in transport, communications and housing; the number of foreign and mixed enterprises has fluctuated according to its policy priorities and not because of market pressures; and the relationship between the state and workers mediated by the ruling party has not changed. Recent measures that have been portrayed outside Cuba as forms of economic liberalisation, such as the removal of caps on wage bonuses, in fact help the state to strengthen its control over salary policy and meet national plans. There has also been considerable speculation that, given its economic relationship and ideological affinities with China (see below and Chapters 11, 12), Cuba under Raúl Castro may adopt Chinese-style market reforms that have transformed the country's economy, yet there are few concrete signs of this occurring. Raúl Castro has been willing to experiment with markets and has responded to some popular pressures for change, but is not engineering a wholesale reorientation in economic policy.

Rural reorientation

The Cuban government initially reoriented productive investment towards rural areas in order to challenge what it called neocolonial conditions created by the US that had neglected the poorest sectors of the rural population. Agrarian reform laws limited the size of landholdings and redistributed large estates to *campesinos* (see Chapter 7). Co-operatives and state farms were formed and small private farms were encouraged to sell their land to the state. Although this collectivisation was based on the principle of large-scale agriculture, unlike the Soviet Union many private farmers working small plots were tolerated in Cuba. Efforts in the 1960s to diversify agriculture through a de-emphasis on sugar and industrialisation proved disappointing, and eventually the USSR insisted Cuba recognise the comparative advantage of sugar as a primary commodity with which to finance development. Fidel Castro made high sugar production targets in the 1970 harvest a political objective, but production fell short and the emphasis placed on them distorted priorities. The failure of the harvest exemplified the difficulties Cuba faced in trying to escape productive stagnation and to end its dependency on a single crop. The concentration of resources in agricultural production did not pay off and state farms were increasingly seen as wasteful and inefficient, resulting in the introduction of some economic freedoms to boost productivity. None the less, the reorientation of resources to the countryside limited the migration of landless *campesinos* to cities, as is common in other Latin American countries. During the special period, Cuban agriculture went into crisis – particularly by the country's inability to import crucial agricultural inputs such as pesticides and chemical fertilisers. The government responded by restructuring state farms as private co-operatives under close state regulation and by encouraging independent farmers' markets. One important dimension of these co-operatives is the ability to pay stakeholders according to their productivity, injecting incentives into production. These measures had a positive impact on food supplies, prices, and rural employment in the early 2000s but, in an effort to reduce Cuba's growing food import bill, the policy has been revisited in recent years by Raúl Castro, who has targeted sources of popular frustration, such as food prices, for change. Although Cuba has much cultivable land, it still imports about 70 per cent of its food at international prices – much of it from the US. Some private-sector farmers are now being encouraged to expand, and the land distribution programme has been decentralised to municipal authorities. The allocation of state land to self-employed farmers and co-operatives was speeded up following damaging hurricanes in 2008. Concessionary prices paid by the Soviet Union for sugar, one of Cuba's main exports, offset steadily falling prices, but production plummeted in the 1990s following the collapse of the Soviet bloc. Sugar production was reorganised as part of the broader shake-up of agriculture, but measures since 2002 to increase the efficiency of sugar production – particularly through downsizing, which halved the number of plantations and sugar mills – have had only limited success as the large-scale production of commercial competitors in countries such as Brazil continues to drive prices down.

Swing to the Soviet bloc and a new dependency

After 1970, Cuba's main trading partners became the Soviet Union and the communist bloc (see Table 16.1). Cuban trade with the USSR rose from an average 45 per cent in 1961–65 to about 70 per cent in 1985–88 and Havana grew reliant on other communist countries for aid and guaranteed exports in return for sugar. Cuba became closely tied to the Council of Mutual Economic Assistance (CMEA), an economic union based on barter trade comprising the Soviet Union, its Eastern European satellites and Mongolia. The CMEA gave Cuban products stable markets and access to key imports, and almost all of Cuba's oil was imported from the Soviet Union despite the proximity of Latin American producer countries with large reserves, such as Venezuela. Because of its political significance, Cuba benefitted from higher levels of Soviet support than other developing countries. In effect, Cuba became dependent on the Soviet Union and its satellites for its economic stability, although this was a more autonomous form of dependency than had existed prior to 1959 and one in which Cuba exercised greater flexibility in setting its own economic priorities (see Chapter 14).

The dissolution of the Soviet Union and the disappearance of the CMEA in the early 1990s confronted the Cuban economy with its most serious crisis since the imposition of the US embargo. Over the years, Cuba had made virtually no payments to the USSR on its debts, but in 1990 – when the overall Cuban debt to the Soviet Union at the official Soviet exchange rate amounted to about $27.6 billion – the USSR proposed that trade be conducted in freely convertible currency at world market prices. Unfavourable global economic conditions and a tightening of US economic pressure exacerbated Cuba's problems thereafter. In the period following the collapse of the Soviet bloc, it struggled to cope with the loss of about 80 per cent of trade and 40 per cent of national income (Ludlam, 2009). The loss of CMEA

Table 16.1 Cuba's trade turnover by trade partner, 1965–89 (per cent)

	1965	1975	1985	1989
CMEA (inc. USSR)	61.7	56.4	83.1	78.9
USSR	48.2	48.0	70.5	64.7
Market Economies	22.8	40.1	13.7	16.8

trading partners and sources of investment had a dramatic effect on conditions in Cuba, and in 1990 Castro declared that the country had entered a 'special period' of belt-tightening. Cubans experienced falling per capita income, blackouts, rationing, factory closures and shortages of essential goods (Saney, 2004). Whole sectors, from transport to construction, were forced to make cuts, rationing was tightened and malnutrition as a result of vitamin deficiencies became serious in 1992–93. The measures the Cuban government undertook to confront this crisis and reform the economy in the 1990s included the reintroduction of some market mechanisms. The government permitted self-employment and the establishment of small private enterprises, mostly in service sectors such as restaurants; it legalised the possession of US dollars, which allowed the state to tap into domestic sources of hard foreign currency; it introduced taxes on profits and investment income; it replaced state farms with co-operatives and opened private farmers' markets in order to stimulate food production (see above); and it gave state companies greater autonomy (see Table 16.2). Cuba's tourism industry was expanded and foreign investment was promoted. Tourism has since become a key driver of growth: international tourist arrivals on the island grew from less than 350,000 in 1990 to more than 2 million in 2007 (ECLAC DPPM, 2009). Today, tourism is a key source of foreign exchange for Cuba and large numbers of Europeans and Canadians visit the island. By 2002, more than 400 international companies were operating in Cuba in association with state enterprises, and joint ventures accounted for nearly half of the country's goods exports (Domínguez, 2005a). In July 2003, however, Cuba's government started reversing some of the market-oriented reforms of the 1990s by recentralising foreign exchange operations and forcing state-run companies to use the convertible peso that was pegged to the US dollar. Social spending initiatives and investments in infrastructure aimed to restore an emphasis on socialist ideals. The financial autonomy given to Cuban enterprises

Table 16.2 Economic and social transformations in Cuba in the 1990s

Decriminalisation of the holding of foreign currency

Opening to foreign investment

Geographical reorientation and decentralisation of foreign trade

Expansion of self-employment

Expansion of co-operatives in farming with the creation of UBPCs (Unidades Básicas de Producción Cooperativas, semi-private co-operatives) in agriculture

Re-sizing and re-structuring of state enterprises

Institutional and regulatory reorganisation of central state administrative agencies

Economic and financial reform

New salary scales for the labour force

Opening of farmer's markets

Opening of markets for small-scale industrial and craft goods

Decentralisation of decision-making and greater autonomy at the territorial level for policy implementation

New social programmes launched

Source: Togores and García, 2005

was rolled back and then removed in 2005 (see Yaffe, 2009). The number of mixed state and private or foreign enterprises operating in Cuba decreased by 41 per cent from 403 in 2002 to 236 in 2006 (*ibid.*).

The cumulative impact of these reforms meant that by 2005, Cuba's economy had recovered from the post-Soviet crisis. However, the country continues to be reliant on a limited number of key sectors and countries for its growth as it struggles to maintain a system of economic management that is radically different to the rest of Latin America. Centeno (2004) is among scholars who have suggested that a new form of dependence has returned to haunt Cuba in the form of a reliance on tourism and on remittances from abroad (see Chapter 14). More than a third of the over 300 firms operating with foreign capital in Cuba are involved in tourism-related activities, mainly in hotel management, for example. China and Venezuela have also become important guarantors of Cuban growth through concessionary prices and credits that bear some similarity to the economic mechanisms that defined Cuba's relationship with the Soviet Union (see below). It is arguable that Cuba's reliance on Venezuelan oil potentially forms the basis of a new form of dependent relationship (see Boxes 9.1, 16.1).

Response to external efforts to isolate the country

Cuba's close relations with the Soviet Union represented a political and economic response to efforts by governments hostile to the Castro regime to isolate the country in Latin America and on world markets. In the 1990s, intensifying US efforts to bring about regime change in Cuba following the end of the Cold War targeted its ability to overcome the economic blockade imposed on it by Washington since the 1960s (see Box 10.8). The focus of a new antagonism towards the Cuban regime in this period was largely economic and stemmed from an acknowledgement within the powerful Cuban American lobby and policymaking circles that the island no longer represented an overt security threat following the defeat of communism (see Gott, 2004). Considerable research, funded by the US government, was carried out into the country's socialist economy, and greater emphasis was placed by anti-Castro groups on the restoration of property confiscated from Cubans, many of them Batista supporters, who had fled to the US following the revolution. The Cuban Democracy Act (CDA, or Torricelli Act) of 1992 and the Helms-Burton Act of 1996 tightened the unilateral economic sanctions that had been imposed by the US in the aftermath of the 1959 revolution and made the economic and political conditions that they demanded for a return to normal relations more explicit. The CDA was aimed at frustrating Cuban trade, by prohibiting subsidiaries of US corporations from trading with Cuba and refusing permission to foreign ships that had entered Cuban ports to load or unload freight in the US. The Helms-Burton Act sought to prevent foreign investment in Cuba, although it originated in concern among US businesses that any political opening on the island may, in fact, work to the advantage of non-US corporations by favouring European, Canadian and Japanese investors (*ibid.*). One of its clauses established that any individual or corporation 'trafficking' in property belonging to an American that had been nationalised by Cuba could be sued in the US courts. This alarmed European corporations, and the EU opposed the measure vigorously as an obstacle to trade, securing an amendment that enabled the US president to waive the measure (see Chapter 11). In return, the EU began to take a stronger line towards Cuba on human rights. None the less, these measures remain on the US statute books and, while they have not been successful in toppling the communist regime, they continue to inhibit trade in all kinds of ways. In 2008, for example, at least two British banks closed Cuba-linked business accounts under the threat of US fines (Ludlam, 2009).

Cuba's response to isolation has been shaped by push and pull factors: it has continued to push for equal treatment in global forums and to diversify trade, while it has also been able to benefit from a changing international climate seeking better economic ties with the island, particularly within Latin America and global commodities markets. An important recent factor in Cuba's economic development has been the reversal of its diplomatic isolation within Latin America stemming from the Cold War (see Chapter 9). In recent years, most Latin American and Caribbean states have defied US pressure and normalised relations with the island, and this is having a significant impact on trade. In 2008, for example, Cuba became Brazil's second-largest trading partner within Latin America (Ludlam, 2009). Multilateral bodies such as the Organisation of American States (OAS) have also ended their isolation of the country, strengthening the ability of its diplomats to access world markets (see Box 9.5). Emerging economies such as China and Russia have also been pushing for closer economic ties with Cuba, and officials in Havana have even talked of forging a 'strategic partnership' with Beijing (see Chapter 11, Box 14.7; see also Frank, 2005). A series of agreements with China in recent years have led to a rapid increase in trade, and China has become the island's second largest trading partner after Venezuela, with annual trade valued at about $2.3 billion. China has sold transportation equipment to Cuba at concessionary prices, provided credits for it to buy machinery and supplies for communications and electronics, and has promoted tourism to the Caribbean island. In 2009, plans were unveiled for the construction of a new luxury 600-room hotel in Havana to be 49 per cent owned by China's Suntine International Economic Trading Company, and 51 per cent owned by Cuba's state tourism company, Cubanacán. Since 2005, China has been investing in Cuba's nickel industry. The international price for nickel, a key Cuban export, rose substantially during the recent commodity boom. Russia has also been repairing relations in an effort to restore trade damaged since the collapse of the Soviet Union, and in 2009 promised credits of $335 million to enable Cuba to buy Russian products.

A second important development has been the deepening of Cuba's bilateral economic relationship with Venezuela and its membership of the Alianza Bolivariana para los Pueblos de Nuestra América (ALBA, the Bolivarian Alliance for the Americas; see Box 16.1). Cuba has benefitted from concessionary oil prices through an agreement with Venezuela's president, Hugo Chávez (1999–), by which Venezuela supplies up to 100,000 barrels of crude oil a day at a steep discount in exchange for medical and other services in an arrangement estimated to be worth $750 million a year. ALBA has provided Cuba with a valuable opportunity to expand its trade both with member states in Latin America and the Caribbean but also in the wider world.

CASE STUDY	Box 16.1

Bolivarian bartering between Cuba and Venezuela

Since 2000, when Cuba's former president, Fidel Castro, and the Venezuelan leader, Hugo Chávez (1999–), reached an accord by which Venezuelan oil would, in effect, be bartered for Cuban goods and services, economic ties between the two countries have grown considerably. Under the agreement, Cuba gains petroleum at a concessionary rate, and in recent years has bought about 100,000 barrels a day, discounted by as much as 40 per cent, greatly easing its energy and transport problems. In 2001, Chávez amended the agreement in order to make separate payments to Cuba in hard currency for the provision of products and services originally intended as a payment for oil, leading to a rapid increase in Cuban exports to Venezuela. The value of trade between the two countries rose to about $7 billion in 2007, according to the Cuban government. Venezuelan government ministries have targeted Cuba as a major source of procurement for a range of goods and services – from minerals and transportation to health and education. In 2005, Castro and Chávez signed a series of agreements strengthening economic links even further, and tariffs on some products have been removed. Venezuela has also participated in the restoration of the dormant Cienfuegos oil refinery, south-east of Havana, further expansion of which was announced in 2009. Cuba and Venezuela have also co-operated on laying undersea fibre-optic cable between the countries which will help provide high-speed internet access to Cuban citizens by 2010, overcoming problems caused by Cuba's reliance on slow and expensive satellite links for internet connectivity.

Chávez has insisted the Cuban exchange agreements are not exceptional and come under the terms of existing accords by which Venezuela sells oil to neighbouring Latin American countries at a discount, and that Cuba pays at international rates and through the provision of services for everything it is provided with (see Guevara, 2005). He says that what makes these agreements appear exceptional is that, prior to them, the US had blocked the supply of Venezuelan oil to Cuba under the terms of its embargo and legislation (see Box 10.8, Chapter 9). This, he says, had prevented Venezuela doing business with a neighbouring country. The growing presence of Cuban medical personnel in poor areas of Venezuela is a visible sign of exchange relations and co-operation. Cuban medical assistance to Venezuela gathered pace in 2003 after a military coup and then a general strike had failed to topple Chávez (see Box 7.2). Cuba sent more than 14,000 doctors, 3,000 dentists, 1,500 eye specialists and 7,000 sports trainers to Venezuela between 2003–05 – as much as one-quarter of the island's entire medical establishment (Frank and Lapper, 2005). Those personnel either treat Venezuelans or train them as doctors or social workers. Thousands of Venezuelans have travelled to Cuba for medical treatment. Cuba also supported a Venezuelan programme to create 1,800 laboratories, rehabilitation centres and other clinics. Havana offered medical assistance under an existing Cuban aid programme in which poor host countries pay the Cuban doctors a small amount every month but make no further payment to the Cuban government.

The relationship between Cuba and Venezuela has been politically beneficial to both the Cuban government and Chávez. Medical aid has boosted the Venezuelan leader's popularity and helped him in a referendum on his continuation in power and in subsequent elections. The flow of Venezuelan oil gave Cuba's former leader, Fidel Castro, a chance to improve Cuban living standards for the first time since the collapse of the socialist bloc, and enabled the Cuban leadership to recentralise the economy.

In April 2006, Venezuela and Cuba extended elements of their growing co-operation to Bolivia when leaders of all three countries signed a three-way trade agreement under the Alternativa Bolivariana para América Latina y El Caribe (ALBA, Bolivarian Alternative for the Americas, see Box 9.1) which they promoted as a socialist integration plan that would be an alternative to proposals for a Washington-backed Free Trade Area of the Americas (see Box 15.5). The pact reduces or eliminates tariffs between countries participating in its trade regime as well as fostering co-operative medical and educational programmes and other economic projects. Cuba's continental eye-surgery programme, Misión Milagro (Miracle Mission), has been backed by ALBA finances and had restored sight to 1.2 million people by 2008 (Ludlam, 2009). The planned creation in 2010 of a trading currency for use by ALBA's nine member states, the sucre, would be of particular help to Cuba, which fell behind on its international debts amid the global downturn following the 2008–09 financial crisis. In December 2009, Cuba signed an agreement with Venezuela to pay for a shipment of rice in sucres.

Declining diplomatic and economic isolation has led to rapid growth in the value of Cuban merchandise exports, from $1.5 billion in 1998 to $3.5 billion in 2008, and in the value of its imports, from $4.1 billion in 1998 to $14.5 billion in 2008 (WTO, 2009). A well-educated and trained workforce has also allowed Cuba to become a growing provider of commercial services based on the knowledge economy.

Like most Latin American states, Cuba's development strategy has registered both successes and failures. Average standards of living have improved considerably since the revolution and Cuba's record in alleviating poverty has been superior to many states in the developing world. Cubans enjoy universal healthcare and education systems, and comprehensive social security. Infant mortality rates and life expectancy are comparable to those of developed countries. State funding in areas such as health and education has been maintained despite the economic crisis of the 1990s, and Cuba maintains relatively high indicators in these areas in comparison with other Latin American states. Cuban education levels are high, and the country continues to make progress in reducing class sizes, building schools and teacher-training centres, providing universal access to higher education and putting high technology in the classroom. The United Nations Development Programme's 2009 Human Development Index (HDI) ranked Cuba among societies with 'high human development' in 51st position of 182 countries examined, above regional neighbours such as Mexico and Costa Rica (UNDP, 2009b). The HDI reflects three measurable dimensions of human development: living a long and healthy life, being educated, and having a decent standard of living.

The reforms of the 1990s laid the basis for an eventual restoration of growth, and in 2004, the Cuban government reported a positive balance of payments for the first time since 1993. By 2005, Cuba's economy had recovered from the post-Soviet crisis, recording GDP growth of 11.2 per cent, followed by growth of 12.1 per cent in 2006 (ECLAC, 2009b). In March 2005, Fidel Castro's government revalued Cuba's peso by 7 per cent and its convertible peso by 8 per cent in a move reflecting their optimism in the country's economy. Cubans use the convertible peso to buy consumer goods that cannot be bought with the regular peso. The public consultation on economic problems held in 2007 by Raúl Castro reflected growing confidence among political leaders about the country's condition.

However, Cuban productivity remains stubbornly low, in part because of the US embargo and limited opportunities to use excess income for consumption, which have decreased the work incentive and made absenteeism and petty theft a persistent problem. Agricultural production for export remains inefficient, not least because of excessive state interference in production through regulation and price controls. Corruption has become a problem in the Cuban economy since 1990, fuelled in part by the growth of semi-private enterprises, the growth of dollar-generating sectors of the economy such as tourism, and low pay in state sectors. In 2005, for example, Castro vowed to tackle widespread theft from state enterprises and introduced measures to tackle the theft of motor fuel and corrupt relations between managers and foreign companies. Government salaries were raised significantly in an effort to reward workers with high productivity and postgraduate education, the first pay rises for some civil servants in 23 years. According to Domínguez (2005b), Cuba's approach to foreign investment, which is aimed at maintaining its control over the granting of concessions, has tended to limit the benefits to the island of international capital. Cuba also remains acutely vulnerable to external shocks, and was hit hard by the impact of the 9/11 terrorist attacks against the US on tourism globally and by rising oil costs.

The development of a unique economic strategy has accompanied the development of a distinctive political system. Cuba's regime insists its system represents a form of social democracy distinct from the competitive and plural democracy found in most capitalist countries (see Chapter 3). Cuba's unusual relationship with the international economy and the US has fostered the emergence of an authoritarian state that keeps tight control over social relations, its trade regime and economic management. The absence of political pluralism alongside signs of opposition to the regime, and the temptations generated by limited economic freedoms, has nurtured the development of repressive security structures to ensure stability. In February 2010, for example, a dissident, Orlando Zapata Tamayo, died in jail after a hunger strike of nearly three months. Zapata Tamayo had been arrested in 2003 in a crackdown on opposition activists, and it was the first time in 40 years that a Cuban dissident had starved to death in protest at the country's political system. However, the Cuban state is corporatist and workers' organisations are integrated into the policymaking process, ensuring they act as a mechanism of political control but also enabling them to influence government policy (see Chapter 7). Although Cuban trades unions are nominally independent of the Partido Comunista de Cuba (PCC, Cuban Communist Party) and entirely self-financing through union dues, they represent workers on the shop floor and exercise significant influence within the PCC and the legislature. At times, Cuban corporatism has been reflected in exhaustive consultation processes to test the mood about the direction of state policy. In 2007, at the start of Raúl Castro's leadership, a large public consultation about economic policy was held which produced more than 1.5 million proposals from 200,000 meetings (see Ludlam, 2009). Workers' rights and participation are important principles in the political culture of Cuba, institutionalised through progressive labour legislation, co-operative structures and consultation mechanisms.

Cuba reveals the difficulties states face in reconciling radical redistribution with the political pluralism implied by a procedural definition of democracy (see Chapter 3). To an extent, redistributive policies have been made easier by the exile of Cuba's small, formerly privileged class, who now form the core of the anti-Castro movement in Florida (see Box 10.8). This suppressed the development of rival political forces based on class and enabled the revolutionary regime to establish a system of representation based on state corporatism. The PCC is the only legal political party and there is no party competition, although it is not an electoral party and is prohibited from playing a role in the nomination of candidates. As a measure of the importance the PCC leadership places on economic conditions, the party's 6th congress planned for 2009 by the new leadership under Raúl Castro was postponed against the backdrop of uncertainty caused by the global economic downturn. Cuba's electoral process is tightly managed with the legislature, the Asamblea Nacional del Poder Popular (National Assembly of People's Power), comprising delegates elected directly by voters from lists selected by provincial and national candidacy commissions made up of representatives of mass organisations and unions. Therefore, electoral competition between candidates exists in principle, but formal campaigning is prohibited in an effort to avoid the emergence of a 'political class'. In practice, these arrangements ensure that the PCC dominates politics. However, despite its monolithic appearance, Cuba's political system is more decentralised than many others in Latin America (see Chapter 6), and constituents participate directly in the selection of local officials. This has allowed the Cuban system to devolve considerable power to community-level political structures. Since the 1990s, municipal governments working with neighbourhood councils (*consejos populares*) have become important providers of services. With about 7 million members, localised Comités de Defensa de la Revolución (CDRs, Committees for the Defence of the Revolution) comprising ordinary people have evolved into the system's largest mass organisation. Empowering citizens by giving them a say in their affairs at a local level helps to reduce tensions fostered by poor conditions.

The state aspires to redistribute all profit back into society and not to create stable conditions for the development of capitalism. However, the most negative impact of the special period on Cuban life in the 1990s was the re-emergence of inequalities, and Cuba is not entirely a 'classless' society. The economic crisis of the 1990s weakened Cuba's social safety net, and the policy response to it created new inequalities that have proven difficult for the government to address. Espina Prieto (2005) summarised a set of trends pointing to greater inequality by the end of the 1990s that included the impoverishment of large sectors of the labour force; the emergence of a worker elite; the exclusion of significant segments of the population from the consumption of certain products; and the state's relative loss of power both to set wages and redistribute income. Differential access to hard currency – the US dollar – has had an impact on equality. In 2006, one Cuban survey estimated that while 4 per cent of households had no hard currency income and relied on official salaries whose average value was about 20 convertible pesos per month, about 30 per cent of households had incomes above 200 convertible pesos and 8 per cent had incomes greater than 1,000 convertible pesos (Espina *et al.*, 2006; see Ludlam, 2009). Saney (2004) has discussed the re-emergence of racist attitudes towards Afro-Cubans (see Chapter 13) since the advent of economic crisis in the early 1990s and the introduction of some economic freedoms. The crisis also hit gender equality, as the burden of overcoming inadequate household budgets tends to fall disproportionately on women. Centeno (2004) has suggested that the informal economy comprising people who work in illegal sectors and often using dollars is now growing in importance in Cuba, bringing the country in line with the rest of Latin America (see Chapters 4, 15). In November 2005, for example, Castro blamed what he described as Cuba's 'new rich' – principally intermediaries and independent restaurant owners who had profited from the limited opening to private enterprise – for the country's problems. Although US policy towards Cubans sending remittances back to the island has been erratic, it has maintained an underlying tolerance of these important sources of foreign exchange (Domínguez, 2005b). The Cuban regime is aware of inequalities and has taken steps to tackle them, and some scholars argue that reforms portrayed outside Cuba as economic liberalisation do in fact strengthen the state's ability to tackle inequality through redistribution (see Ludlam, 2009). For example, indirect taxation has been introduced on remittances, tourist dollars, and through value-added tax on consumer electronics. Cubans themselves debated economic reform and the merits of greater private ownership in 2007 as part of the consultation exercise undertaken by the government. Economic 'liberalisers' on the island suggested it could be possible to increase private ownership and production – particularly in agriculture – without undermining socialism (see Yaffe, 2009).

Populist models

The term 'classical populism' is sometimes used to describe the urban political movements that developed in Latin America during the 1940s and 1950s opposing the primary product, export-oriented status quo and advocating accelerated industrialisation (see Chapters 2, 14). These movements often reflected cross-class demands for the state to pursue redistributive policies and, by constructing alliances linking the urban working class and the industrial bourgeoisie, reduced class antagonisms. The Argentine experience between 1945–52 under Juan Domingo Perón (1946–55, 1973–74), who forged an alliance between the urban working class and the local bourgeoisie to support industrialisation, is a good example of classical populism. Populism gave a central role in economic and social policy to the state, which tended to ignore the need to exercise restraints on spending.

Some scholars have used the term 'economic populism' to describe developmental strategies that emphasise growth and redistribution regardless of constraints, resulting in unsustainable levels of inflation, although others have rejected this term or what they suggest are attempts by critics of reform to use it pejoratively (see Dornbusch and Edwards eds, 1991; Cardoso and Helwege, 1992; Lievesley and Ludlam, 2009). Policies based on deficit spending that result in higher real wages for core political constituencies initially help to boost growth, but are achieved at the cost of foreign reserves and eventually fuel inflation. The policies pursued by Salvador Allende, the Marxist president of Chile from 1970–73, and by the Sandinista revolutionary regime in Nicaragua, have sometimes been characterised as economic populism because of the inflation and instability experienced under these regimes (see Box 16.2). However, the hostility of the US towards both the Chilean and Nicaraguan governments contributed significantly to economic crisis.

Peru has experienced a number of populist experiments. In the postwar era, Peru's economic model continued to be characterised by export-led growth, greatly

Economic populists? Allende in Chile and Nicaragua's Sandinistas

The policies pursued by the Marxist Salvador Allende, who was president of Chile from 1970 until the coup led by General Augusto Pinochet in 1973 (see Chapters 2, 12, Box 7.11), are sometimes described as an example of economic populism that resulted in instability and collapse. However, the objectives of the Unidad Popular (UP, Popular Unity) coalition led by Allende were socialist, challenging property rights and aiming at redistribution, and did not aim at satisfying both capitalists and workers or at making capitalism more benign. For this reason, they met strong resistance from capitalists and the US government, which withdrew aid, placed an embargo on exports to Chile, and funded Allende's opponents. Allende came to power in a country that already had a heavily protected industrial sector and welfare system in which agriculture had been neglected. He nationalised foreign firms, increased the minimum wage, expanded housing, food and educational assistance and undertook further agrarian reform through land takeovers. Initially, ample foreign reserves fuelled growth and rising industrial output, and unemployment fell. But a decline in prices for copper, the country's main source of export revenues, exacerbated a growing shortage of foreign exchange and the government deficit rose, exacerbating inflation and worsening the political polarisation generated by expropriation and takeovers.

In Nicaragua, the Sandinista revolutionary regime that came to power after 1979 also sought to pursue a redistributive programme but within a mixed economy. The regime initially concentrated on addressing high levels of poverty through agrarian, healthcare and educational reforms. The Sandinistas inherited a country with only basic industries and a large rural sector, and so did not envisage industrialisation, which was largely left to private capital although the government pumped expenditure into its own large agro-industrial projects (see Dijkstra, 1992). The Sandinistas benefited from significant amounts of foreign aid in the first years after the revolution. They also saw the need for a private sector and sought to balance distributive measures in the countryside with measures to retain the support of private producers that allocated disproportionate resources and credit to them. Mindful of the problems posed by inflation, the regime avoided large wage increases and the real wages of urban workers actually fell after 1981. Between 1980 and 1982, the Sandinistas were able to bring overall annual inflation down from 25 per cent to 22 per cent (Cardoso and Helwege, 1992). However, economic problems escalated. After 1980, world prices of the cotton and coffee accounting for about 60 per cent of Nicaragua's export earnings fell. As in Allende's Chile, Sandinista policies incurred the wrath of the US, which supported the *contra* counter-revolutionaries in a war that had devastating consequences for Nicaragua's economy and undermined the Sandinistas' development programme (see Chapters 9, 10, 12). By 1983, about half of government expenditure was devoted to the military, limiting social spending and fuelling the deficit. Military recruitment exacerbated labour shortages and rebel attacks destroyed infrastructure and prevented harvests. Socialist rhetoric and threats to expropriate property also created a climate of uncertainty for private producers (*ibid.*). By the late 1980s, consumption had fallen significantly and inflation was out of control, forcing the government to resort to deficit spending. Real wages and levels of individual consumption plummeted dramatically and, in 1988, Nicaragua suffered a record annual inflation rate of 33,600 per cent – one of the highest rates ever recorded in Latin America. By the late 1980s, the Sandinista government was pursuing increasingly orthodox adjustment programmes based on austerity policies that weakened support for the revolutionary regime. Despite Sandinista efforts in 1989 to implement IMF-approved stabilisation measures, the US sought to freeze Nicaraguan assets in Panama just before the 1990 election (see Stahler-Sholk, 1995).

inhibiting industrialisation and making the country vulnerable to external shocks. As a result, by the 1960s Peru was facing difficulties caused by fluctuations in world demand for its products. Export-led development meant Peru did not develop a strong national business sector, and industrialists were closely linked to foreign investment interests. A large urban working class did not develop and, in rural areas, semi-feudal structures based on large cotton and sugar plantations exacerbated problems of rural poverty which, in turn, led to rapid urbanisation and created a huge informal sector.

The military regime that came to power in 1968 under General Juan Velasco Alvarado (1968–75) challenged this development model and began a limited attempt at ISI, although his policies did not end dependency on imported industrial goods such as machinery. The nationalistic regime was less subservient to Peru's traditional creole oligarchy and adopted what has been called a 'Third Way' between capitalist and Marxist prescriptions (McClintock and Lowenthal eds, 1983). Once in power, the military called themselves revolutionary, but practised reform, and sought to bring about a radical change in the balance of forces within Peruvian society. The regime emphasised national autonomy, the elimination of the power of oligarchic landowners and greater participation by workers in industrial management and social policy (*ibid.*). The main planks of its policy were agrarian reform and redistribution, nationalisation and industrialisation, and statism and corporatism (see Boxes 2.2, 7.1, 14.4 and Chapter 14):

Land reform and redistribution

Velasco's administration undertook extensive land reform based on the expropriation of large landholdings and their redistribution to newly established co-operatives. Between 1969 and 1980, almost 360,000 families and members of farm co-operatives received land. This undermined the power of the traditional landowning oligarchy, forcing them to transfer their resources to more dynamic sectors of the economy in the cities. The middle classes were given new opportunities for development and social mobility (*ibid.*). The scale of Velasco's agrarian reform meant that it had a long-term impact on Peruvian society, popular memory and political developments into the 1990s (see Mayer, 2009). The Velasco government also adopted other redistributive measures. It required firms to distribute part of their profits to workers through shares, mainly in order to increase worker participation in running companies. Labour laws and regulations were changed to limit employers' rights and improve workers' conditions as part of an effort to restructure the balance of power within private companies and between classes. Programmes were launched to improve education and living standards for the poor, and newspapers were expropriated and reallocated to diverse social interests.

Nationalisation and industrialisation

The military also nationalised some key sectors of the economy, beginning with the International Petroleum Corporation, which had been at the centre of a dispute over oil between Peru and the US. Basic services as well as some foreign companies were expropriated and their owners were given compensation and incentives to reinvest in mining, fishing and agriculture. Velasco also pursued policies to protect industry and strengthen the private sector through tax incentives for private industrial investment and by improving opportunities for profit. Price controls on food and subsidised food imports were used to favour urban consumers. These policies represented an effort to improve on the experience of ISI elsewhere through the development, alongside state-led industrialisation, of primary and industrial exports (*ibid.*).

Statism and corporatism

Peru had never had a large state penetrating the entire country and the military regime expanded the state's influence and control by creating new ministries, agencies and banks (see Boxes 2.1, 15.3, Chapter 14). It tried to institutionalise these changes by creating corporatist institutions for the working class and peasant groups linking the regime with a mass support base (see Box 2.2, 7.1). There was extensive urban and rural unionisation, while established political parties and unions were marginalised. The military regime's most characteristic institution was the Sistema Nacional en Apoyo de la Mobilización Social (SINAMOS, National System for the Support of Social Mobilisation), created to co-ordinate the integration of newly mobilised peasant and worker groups.

Velasco's policies began to unravel after several years due to over-ambitious public investment projects and unrestrained expansion of the state. The regime's success had been premised on continued economic growth, but this ground to a halt after 1974. The regime also alienated supporters on the left who wanted more significant redistribution. Large landholdings were turned over to those who were already working them, and existing smallholders gained little. The distribution by owners to workers of equity rights – shares in an enterprise – was limited, and new labour regulations reduced productivity. The regime's industrialisation strategy lacked coherent policies to determine investment needs and employment priorities, and state firms were unable to break away from capital-intensive, import-dependent technology (*ibid.*). Despite its outspoken attitude towards foreign investment, the Velasco regime also borrowed to finance spending and investment as export earnings declined and inflation grew. As a result, Peru's external debt rose rapidly. In 1975, Peru's joint chiefs of staff replaced Velasco with General Francisco Morales Bermúdez (1975–80), whose efforts to get to grips with the country's economic crisis gradually reversed many of the reform initiatives and who adopted IMF-sponsored austerity measures. Bermúdez undermined the role of SINAMOS, transferred state assets back to private interests, and took the steps necessary for a transition back to civilian politics in 1980, when Fernando Belaúnde Terry (1963–68, 1980–85) of the centre-right Acción Popular (AP, Popular Action) party took power. The measures taken by Belaúnde Terry's government to control inflation by raising the prices of food and fuel and eliminating subsidies generated widespread discontent. In the early 1980s, Peru experienced serious labour unrest and growing guerrilla violence (see Box 12.4). By 1985, annual inflation was in the region of 230 per cent, Peru's $14 billion external debt had grown unmanageable, and nearly a third of the country's population of working age was unemployed.

In this climate, Peru experienced another experiment in populism under the young newcomer Alan García (1985–90, 2006–) of the Alianza Popular Revolucionaria Americana (APRA, American Popular Revolutionary Alliance), who came to power after winning elections with a sound mandate. García also pursued nationalistic, inward-looking expansionary policies, courting labour with higher wages and raising profits for local industrialists through protectionism and a range of policies that stimulated demand. He imposed restrictions on capital, announced that Peru would limit service payments on its foreign debt, and eventually nationalised the banking system. Initially, inflation fell and growth rose, but then prices began to rise rapidly, credit and investment dried up, the deficit swelled and reserves were exhausted. By 1990, inflation had topped 7,500 per cent, creating conditions of uncertainty and instability that the guerrilla organisation Sendero Luminoso used as a premise for escalating its offensive. García's disastrous presidency discredited APRA and allowed the then unknown Alberto Fujimori (1990–2000) to win elections at the head of a loose electoral coalition (see Chapter 4). The groups that had gained most under García were powerful urban, unionised workers as well as domestic capitalists, and his policies had little impact on poverty levels. García has made a political comeback – not surprisingly as a convert to free markets – and won Peru's presidential elections in 2006.

Since the 1990s, the term 'neo-populism' has sometimes been used to describe the autocratic style employed by presidents undertaking radical *neoliberal* reforms in Latin America (see Chapter 15). Argentina provides an example of neopopulism, with President Carlos Menem (1989–99) constructing a populist coalition in order to pass neoliberal reforms and using the links of his Peronist party to divide the labour movement in order to limit opposition.

The term 'populist' has been used both to support and to attack the programmes of radical leaders (see Box 16.2; and Edwards, 2010). In economic terms, left-of-centre populism can be seen as part of a continuum of social-democratic and socialist politics (see Lievesley and Ludlam eds, 2009). In Latin America, populist leaders and movements have usually championed the needs of ordinary people against powerful vested interests (see Chapter 2). Their message is often directed at the poor and promises better living conditions while attacking oligarchic or industrial elites and imperialism (see Kaufman and Stallings, 1991). Hostility to 'economic populism' is usually strong among multilateral lenders uneasy about inflation and in countries whose investors are nervous about the potential risk to their investments posed by instability and nationalisation.

The Venezuelan president, Hugo Chávez (1999–), occupies an important position on this continuum by pursuing policies similar to those of the national populism that prevailed in the period before neoliberal reform, yet by increasingly adopting a socialist critique and promising to create a 'socialism of the twenty-first Century' to justify and institutionalise these (see Boxes 4.2, 9.1, 12.7). The programme of 'chavismo' initially concentrated on constitutional reform and was not based on an explicit critique of neoliberalism, although Chávez expressed an interest in the so-called 'Third Way' between market policies and statist interventions. The most important characteristic of how this has subsequently evolved has been the effort by Chávez, whose political ascent derived from the populist alternative he provided to traditional institutions of political representation such as parties, to *institutionalise* radical policies through the consolidation of a broad socialist movement, the Partido Socialista Unido de Venezuela (PSUV, United Socialist Party of Venezuela). The PSUV unifies forces that support Chávez's 'Bolivarian Revolution', but there is a significant diversity of positions within it and it has been a product and not a source of change. The process of radicalisation through which the Bolivarianism of Chávez has become explicitly identified with socialism is better explained by a range of internal and external factors specific to Venezuela and the international climate (see Buxton, 2009). Record oil prices up to 2008, in particular, allowed Chávez to reintroduce statism in the economy without greatly fuelling the main problem of past populist policies: inflation. Chávez raised public spending to record levels on infrastructure projects such as highways and agrarian reform and, in January 2005, the government began taking control of large estates following a surge of land invasions by peasant groups. In 2007–08, a large programme of nationalisation resulted in the state taking over strategic sectors that it did not yet control such as telecoms. The state has seized assets it considers idle, such as silos belonging to Alimentos Polar, one of Venezuela's biggest food companies. Venezuela has also been leading new integration efforts in Latin America that challenge the economic position of the US in the region. The explicit purpose of ALBA, for example, was to challenge neoliberalism (see Box 9.1, Chapter 15). Where the private sector has remained a significant economic player, it has had to accept increasing state direction, tough regulation and, in areas such as food production, price controls. The Venezuelan state has insisted that private banks appoint state representatives to their boards, and businesses must ensure at least 20 per cent worker representation in boardrooms. In December 2009, Chávez told Toyota, Ford, General Motors and Fiat, multi-national car companies operating in the country, that they must share their technology with local businesses or leave. He said that Venezuela could easily replace them with Russian, Belorussian and Chinese plants if necessary (see Chapter 11, Box 14.7).

None the less, Chávez has not dismantled capitalism and Venezuela's economy remains mixed, with government spending as a proportion of GDP still lower than in other, more developed mixed economies such as France; foreign corporations still have large stakes in the oil sector as minority partners, and foreign participation remains crucial to the plans of the state oil monopoly PDVSA. Where Venezuela has nationalised assets such as banks, the government has agreed to pay compensation, often at market rates. In April 2009, for example, Venezuela took over its third largest lender, Banco de Venezuela, after agreeing to pay $1.05 billion to its Spanish owner, Banco Santander. In terms of social expenditure, Chávez has relied heavily on oil revenues to fund the 'misiones' – programmes to provide social and economic rights to marginalised communities (see Chapter 12). The Venezuelan *misiones* developed as part of a phase in the development of Chávéz's policy agenda that Buxton (2009) suggests began in about 2000 and ended in 2006 and was increasingly financed by PDVSA. By 2006, PDVSA was channelling about $6 billion to the 17 *misiones* that operated in different policy areas, from healthcare to subsidised food provision to education. The *misiones* are significant to the study of the Left in Latin America because they represent an institutional expression of the 'twenty-first-century socialism' advocated by the Venezuelan leader that has attracted interest on the left for offering a new sense of direction in the globalised post-Cold War world (see Boxes 12.7, 15.8).

Other leaders have also openly advocated socialist economic policies, while remaining constrained in the extent to which they can carry these out by the nature of their economies and politics. In Bolivia, the socialist president, Evo Morales (2006–), has been a vociferous critic of neoliberalism and what his finance minister Luis Arce (2006–) has described as a 'savage capitalism' that 'ransacks' a country's natural resources and fails to take account of a society's poorest (Mapstone and Schipani, 2009). None the less, Bolivian policymakers insist that legitimate businesses are not threatened, that their policies support private enterprise that invests in Bolivian social development, and that they are not opposed to foreign investment (*ibid.*). A key objective of Morales has been to assert greater state control over the economy through a policy of nationalisation, particularly of natural resource sectors. In 2006, Morales nationalised the country's gas sector and began a process of renegotiating contracts with hydrocarbons corporations to generate greater revenues for the government. His administration also took over some large international telecommunications and tin-smelting companies. However, the economic policies advocated by Morales and the Movimiento al Socialismo (MAS) resemble those of the other opposition parties in the country, and he has promised internationally to maintain macroeconomic stability and guarantees for foreign investments. Alongside the nationalisation of gas, for example, the Morales administration decided not to oppose the sale of development rights in Bolivia's El Mutún state-owned iron ore deposit – a form of privatisation – to Jindal of India in 2006. The scale of previous neoliberal reform and a dependence on foreign investment and foreign assistance or loans to finance development projects has limited Morales' room for manoeuvre. As a result of his nationalisation policies, foreign direct investment in Bolivia has declined considerably, and industrial sectors have struggled to secure long-term investment. In turn, production in key areas, such as gas, has fallen. Political resistance to Morales's programme has also grown, especially in the east of the country at the heart of its most productive sectors, where business associations are powerful actors in regional politics (see Boxes 4.1, 12.11, 13.6, Chapter 7). A dispute with the US over anti-narcotics policy led to Washington's withdrawal of trade preferences for Bolivia (see Chapters 9, 10). None the less, despite declining commodities markets, Bolivia was able to sustain strong growth in 2009, with GDP forecast to grow by 2.8 per cent to 4 per cent (*ibid.*). Like Venezuela, this achievement owed much to Bolivia's natural resources: its ability to avoid inflation was enhanced by a high level of foreign reserves and public savings, boosted by the revenues from taxes on foreign companies and the nationalisation of the hydrocarbons sector. Policymakers argued that an important factor in recent development, spurred by the state, has been the growth of the internal market.

In Ecuador, President Rafael Correa (2007–) adopted socialist rhetoric and promised higher social spending, increased state control over strategic sectors, and renegotiating contracts to gain for the state a larger share of revenues from natural resources. Correa promised to repudiate the foreign debt and has had difficult relations with the US, World bank and IMF. The first years of his administration were marked by attacks on foreign investment and growing uncertainty about the future of Ecuador's use of the US dollar as its currency. In 2008, the country defaulted on certain debt commitments and in 2009 began to restrict some imports, a move characterised by some observers as an effort to encourage local production (see Chapter 14). However, Ecuador's economic policy has been characterised more by uncertainty than by a clearly socialist sense of direction. One example of that was the decision to default on debts after honouring these for almost two years. Correa has been unable to reverse a decline in overall oil production; the government signalled in 2009 that it would need to limit public-sector spending; and, to meet its needs and cover its deficit, it negotiated international loans. Correa has also been criticised for not defining clear policies for foreign investment in the oil and mining sectors, and for generating a climate of contractual uncertainty that has resulted in a decline in private investment in the oil industry.

Neostructuralism

By the 1970s, a revised structuralist position (see Chapter 14) was being put forward that recommended the promotion of growth through more industrial exports. However, in this period foreign borrowing became easier and made it possible for many Latin American countries to postpone making changes, and only Brazil began serious restructuring by emphasising the export of manufactures and alternative sources of energy (Sunkel ed., 1993, 1995). Post-ISI policies of these kinds formed the core of a neostructuralist analysis, again associated with ECLAC economists (see Box 14.3), that did not wholly accept the neoliberal view that the market is the best source of development. Latin American neostructuralists such as Sunkel searched for a way of achieving sustainable and equitable growth that makes the best use of *both* the market and the public sector. This position expressed a desire for Latin America to develop from within in a way that could build upon the inheritance of structuralism while also taking sides with neoliberals about the importance of competitiveness within the world market.

In the 1990s, some multilateral institutions such as the World Bank began to identify social and economic shortcomings with neoliberal policies and the Washington Consensus (see Box 15.1), and to move closer to neostructuralist positions in an effort to reconcile adjustment policies with the need for more sustainable and equitable growth (Dietz ed., 1995). Panizza (2009) has identified a 'paradigm shift' based in redefinitions and reinterpretations of neoliberal reforms that amount to a 'post-Washington Consensus', the outcome of which has been a significant narrowing of the differences between the original advocates of reform and their mainstream critics among structuralist and developmentalist economists. The World Bank and the IMF have embraced some of these positions, which incorporate policies at the heart of the original neoliberal agenda – such as trade opening and flexible labour policies – with the new 'second-generation' reforms aimed at strengthening the institutions that are essential for creating conditions for market growth (see Chapter 15). Central to these ideas are an important economic role for the state and targeted social policies, which in some ways foresaw a resurgence of interest among policymakers in the developed world in Keynesian ideas as a result of the 2008–09 financial crisis (see Box 15.3). Keynes advocated a mixed economy that combined a predominant private sector with a large role for the state and public sector, which acted to maximise internal demand through fiscal stimulus and expansionary monetary policies.

Neostructuralist positions can be examined in terms of the market, the state and social justice:

The market

Neostructuralists accept the role of the market and export diversification in development, and insist on the need for macroeconomic stability. However, they have a more complex conception of the role of the free market in development that does not see it as the only solution to the problems of development and also takes into consideration social and political factors affecting how it functions in any given society. This is reflected in attitudes towards the competitiveness of companies, which neostructuralists argue may be influenced by social arrangements such as the conditions in which people work as well as by more traditional economic criteria such as the quality or price of a product. Neostructuralists also place a greater emphasis than their predecessors on developing exports – in particular industrial products – as opposed to the inward-looking policies that characterised ISI. They stress the importance of diversifying the exports that a country produces and making high-tech products. In order to achieve this, they advocate limited tariffs to protect certain infant industries against foreign competition. The main shift in perspective in this direction associated with the post-Washington Consensus is the recognition that the use of policy instruments that solely target growth through economic liberalisation is too narrow, and a broader approach to development taking in its social, institutional and political dimensions is needed. Markets continue to be key arenas for economic development, and macroeconomic stability remains of paramount importance, but IFIs such as the World Bank now recognise the role of broad political participation in achieving equitable development.

The state

Neoliberalism envisages an extremely limited role for the state whose only duty it considers to be ensuring the proper functioning of the market. Neostructuralism, by contrast, builds upon earlier structuralist foundations to argue that the market alone will not spur development and the state should step in where there has been a failure of the market to promote growth. Neostructuralists often argue that they seek to overcome the 'false dilemma' of state versus market by combining positive elements of both (see Box 15.3). They see development less as a spontaneous process and more as the result of planning by an activist state collaborating with civil society (see Chapter 8). They point to the highly competitive countries of south-east Asia as evidence of the positive role state intervention can play in development. The role neostructuralists attribute to the state has an implicitly political dimension because it includes co-ordinating the activities of different social actors, mediating between them when there are conflicts, and ensuring that the interests of weaker sectors are taken into consideration. An important shift in emphasis in this direction associated with the post-Washington Consensus is the recognition that the state should have a central role that, albeit still limited, goes beyond merely setting rules for markets to prosper and, through *effective* policies, acts as a catalyst for development within a wider political and social agenda. However, significant differences between neostructuralists and supporters of the post-Washington Consensus about the role of the state remain in such areas as the balance between state and market incentives, the role of state institutions and the relationship with foreign investors (Panizza, 2009). Some left-of-centre governments and 'neodevelopmentalists' also place significantly more emphasis on the proactive role of the state in development and on carving out space for independent, national action within the globalised economy, and reject the idea of a more liberal, hands-off 'night-watchman' state (see Kelly, 2008). The underlying principle of neodevelopmentalism, which is hostile to neither the market nor the state, is that economic policies and institutions should be formulated and implemented with *national interest* as their main criterion (see Bresser-Pereira, 2006).

The financial crisis of 2008–09 generated a favourable intellectual climate for a revival of Keynesian policies based on a more prominent role for the state based on public spending. Critics of neoliberal policies who have adopted Keynesian positions, such as Bolivia's president Evo Morales, can also point to vigorous growth amid the global financial crisis as an example of the potential for greater state intervention. None the less, while encompassing some nationalisation and more assertive social policies, Bolivian policies under Morales have maintained broad continuities with those of his neoliberal predecessors (see Chapter 15). Morales' appointment as finance minister of Luis Arce, for example, was heavily criticised by organised labour in the country for the latter's connections with IFIs (see Petras, 2006). Arce had been a supporter of the structural adjustment programmes identified with neoliberal reform, and has argued that the key to Bolivia's growth since 2006 has been the stimulus to internal consumption as opposed to external demand (*ibid.*).

Social justice and democracy

Neoliberals believe that allowing the state to transfer financial resources from one social group to another is unacceptable because it distorts the rules of the market, and the fight against poverty should largely be a question of human charity, not of distribution. Although structuralism and dependency theories placed an emphasis on questions of redistribution, neostructuralist positions have approximated those of the neoliberals. Neostructuralists do not advance egalitarianism, but argue that economic growth can be reconciled with social justice through state interventions to ensure equal *opportunities* for all social groups through targeted poverty reduction. At the same time, neostructuralists have a broader understanding of democracy than is found among neoliberals, and emphasise the importance of social democracy marked by high participation as an objective of development (see Chapter 3). These ideas reflect those that have emerged on the Latin American left since the end of the Cold War, when many leftwing parties began to embrace democratic politics and reassess their positions (see Chapter 12). The Left has undertaken a more systematic reassessment of economic strategies that have incorporated elements from the neoliberal policy menu. Some former Marxist guerrillas have even become successful capitalists, or try to combine their social philosophy with participation in the market by advocating a form of 'social capitalism' (see Box 16.3). The main shift in perspective in this direction among IFIs associated with the post-Washington Consensus is the recognition that effective public policies should be defined according to the degree to which they ensure that the benefits of market growth are shared, that growth helps to reduce poverty and inequality, and that people are protected against insecurity (see Panizza, 2009).

International financial institutions such as the Inter-American Development Bank, which was at the cutting edge of this reassessment, are today more willing than before to consider social-democratic solutions in the more economically advanced Latin American states. Roberts (1997) has argued that by the late 1990s a number of factors had converged to make social democracy attractive in Latin America (see Box 12.5). Social democracy as a political strategy aspires to use state power as an instrument for achieving reforms that modify capitalism to allow for fairer forms of development. Social democrats do not envisage reversing neoliberal policies and, in some cases, advocate continued privatisation, even though in other cases there has been talk of taking back into public ownership previously privatised sectors. Above all, social-democratic positions stress an activist state that can govern market behaviour through regulatory policies and redistribute income through taxation and social policy. They are wary of class confrontation and so opt for pragmatism over ideology, and multi-class electoral movements over class-based forms of political activity (Roberts, 1997). Social democrats seek to lessen class conflict by incorporating organised labour into institutionalised forms of political representation, and are instinctively corporatist (see Boxes 2.2, 7.1).

In recent years, most left-of-centre governments in Latin America have pursued social-democratic reformism that reconciles market competition with state regulation and redistribution (see Bresser Pereira *et al.*, 1993; Vellinga, 1993; and Castañeda, 1994). These policies have been influenced by neostructuralism and can be placed on a spectrum of social-democratic positions. Most of Latin America's incumbent left-of-centre leaders have been constrained by existing economic realities and have avoided radical policies when faced with the risk of a withdrawal of foreign capital and a collapse in investor confidence. Contemporary social democracy in Latin America has also evolved in a period of weak trades unions and its commitment to the market economy further limits union influence (see below).

In Brazil, the prospect of Lula da Silva's election caused alarm among conservatives in his own country and the US. However, Da Silva's domestic programme has been based on reform through market-led growth and was founded on an accord struck prior to the 2002 election with domestic investors and international financial institutions in which he committed a future Partido dos Trabalhadores (PT, Workers' Party) government to continuing the broad neoliberal outlines of existing economic policy (see Lievesley, 2009). In Argentina, prior to taking office, Néstor

From Marxist guerrillas to market guerrillas

The founding members of the Nuevo Arco Iris (New Rainbow) enterprise in Colombia were former Marxist guerrillas of the Cuban-inspired Ejército de Liberación Nacional (ELN, National Liberation Army) (see Chapters 2, 12) who embraced a social capitalism to distribute earnings from business ventures to aid programmes. Nuevo Arco Iris was created initially to co-ordinate the reintegration into society of about 800 former guerrillas who broke away from the ELN, and has since evolved into a sophisticated think tank and NGO promoting development and peace in 12 departments of the country. The group has ventured into running a hotel, a construction company and an agricultural brokerage, and explored the potential of internet cafes and manufacturing light fixtures for export. The programmes its earnings have financed have ranged from teaching children about conflict resolution to agricultural initiatives. In rural areas, it finances training programmes, supports the creation of small enterprises and co-operatives, and promotes sustainable development initiatives. In civil society, it supports the creation of peaceful and participatory mechanisms for conflict resolution, and has been involved in European Union human rights initiatives (see Chapter 11). It promotes the interests of the victims of violence and conducts research into a range of post-conflict issues. Many of the people employed by the organisation are former rebels. Nuevo Arco Iris has been funded by a range of Colombian central and local government agencies, through grants from the governments of other countries, the EU, aid agencies and international NGOs such as the Agencia Española de Cooperación al Desarrollo (AECID, Spanish Agency for Development Co-operation) and the Norwegian Refugee Council, and through contracts with the United Nations Development Programme (see Chapter 3). It has non-profit status and does not aim to make money, but operates like a company with a board and according to a business model. The organisation's survival is important in a country that has long struggled to end a civil war, because productive endeavours must be found for rebels from various guerrilla organisations who leave the field of combat, often as deserters, and because economic development can reduce social conflict. It is difficult for many former guerrillas to make the transition to an ordinary way of life: many are unemployed and homeless, and deserters are often seen as traitors by former comrades and killed. Rightwing paramilitary organisations have sometimes regarded programmes such as Nuevo Arco Iris as an effort by guerrilla organisations to pursue their former strategy by other means. A number of Nuevo Arco Iris employees have been killed, and it is believed that these murders were mostly committed by rightwing paramilitaries. The business environment can also work against former guerrillas who try to establish themselves in the market, as businesses often avoid dealing with them.

Source: Forero, 2004a

Kirchner (2003–07) criticised neoliberal reforms, promised a large public works programme to revive the economy, vowed to reduce dependence on foreign capital, and promised reforms to improve education and healthcare. Kirchner's record was more consistent in the adoption of traditional social-democratic positions on economic sovereignty and foreign investment, and he wrestled in complex financial negotiations with the World Bank, the International Monetary Fund and several European utility companies. After he called for a boycott of Shell oil, the corporation lowered the price of gasoline. He alarmed Argentine business leaders by re-nationalising some businesses privatised in the 1990s, among them postal services and a railway company (see Chapter 15). Kirchner's government also created a state-run oil company, Energía Argentina (Enarsa), and in March 2005, caused further alarm among managers of Argentina's privatised utilities in contractual disputes arising from the 2002 currency devaluation (see Box 15.7). Argentina's peso had been pegged to the US dollar since 1991 but, when the government allowed it to float, its value fell and this greatly reduced the utilities' revenues. Amid the renegotiation of contracts with the government by concessionaries providing public services, Kirchner effectively sought to rewrite the terms of the original privatisation. Cabinet ministers also hinted that they wanted to act against the Aguas Argentinas water company partly owned by French interests. In March 2006, the Argentine government terminated the Aguas Argentinas contract to supply drinking water to Buenos Aires and gave the concession to a new corporation owned by the state and workers. However, Kirchner's government was forced to accommodate international concerns generated by the debt default of 2001 in order to secure further lending, and began following orthodox prescriptions influenced by the IMF to further reform the country's economy. His successor, Cristina Fernández (2007–), has maintained a conciliatory line with international creditors and announced in 2008 that her government intended to pay its Paris Club debts with reserves. She faced considerable opposition in her efforts to redistribute through taxation policy from farmers angry at tax increases. In Panama, growth revived under Martín Torrijos (2004–09), unemployment declined, the country began pursuing free trade pacts with the US, Costa Rica and Nicaragua, and it won praise from the IMF for its targeted poverty-reduction programme. In the Dominican Republic, Leonel Fernández (2004–) took office promising to promote fiscal austerity and to fight corruption while supporting social concerns. The Fernández administration renegotiated its international debts, met fiscal and financial targets of the IMF and joined the Central American free trade agreement (DR-CAFTA) that includes the US, the Dominican Republic's most important trading partner. The Fernández administration encouraged considerable levels of foreign investment, although like most countries in the region began to suffer the impact of the financial crisis in 2009. In Uruguay, Tabaré Vázquez (2005–10) promised during his campaign to create a 'social emergency plan' to alleviate poverty, committed himself to Latin American integration, signalled that he would restore diplomatic relations with Cuba, and began his term with strong links to Chávez in Venezuela. However, Vázquez reiterated that he would respect Uruguay's international obligations in the form of a 2003 debt-restructuring arrangement and deal with the IMF, and won Wall Street's support for his choice of Danilo Astori as economy minister. In 2007, the country also signed a trade and investment agreement with the US that has been seen as a precursor to an eventual free trade agreement. Vázquez's policies were made easier by the realities of Uruguay's economic development, in which the state has long played a significant role, owning controlling or partial stakes in a large number of companies. In Paraguay, during Fernando Lugo's campaign for the presidency he described himself as a centrist and committed himself to addressing the need to tackle poverty and injustice but also promised to attract foreign investment and privatise public companies. In El Salvador, Mauricio Funes of the FMLN suggested that the party did not aspire to build socialism in the country, would not align with Venezuela against the US, and would not renegotiate its free trade relationships.

In terms of social policy, these left-of-centre governments have developed programmes that seek to address inequality in different ways (see Chapter 12). The transition to democratic rule had important implications for the course of social policy in Latin America, by empowering new interest groups and thereby placing new political pressures and constraints on governments. During the 1990s and early 2000s, the Latin American region was distinct when compared with similar regions such as Eastern Europe or East Asia for the extent of reform of core social insurance programmes, efforts to expand basic social services and the adoption of anti-poverty programmes (see Haggard and Kaufman, 2008). What that means is that, contrary to the belief that neoliberal reforms reduced the reach of the state, in some areas state activity increased. None the less, a key factor in the evolution of social and welfare policies in the region's democratising states until about 2004 were budget constraints inherited from the previous era, which limited the extent of policy reforms and determined their form. As a result, economic constraints and the shift towards the left in much of the region have not brought the discernible increase in social provision that might have been expected, and democracy in the region has not had a significant impact on social spending (*ibid.*). One example of this can be found in the share of government expenditure on health as a proportion of total health spending, which grew only slightly between 1996 and 2005 but remained low in comparison, for example, with East Asia. Until 2002, the ability of most Latin American countries to fund an expansion in welfare services was greatly limited by tight budgets or fears that government spending might fuel inflation. From 2002 until the international financial crisis that began in 2008, these spending constraints eased because of the resources generated through a boom in global commodities, but recession in the industrial world and a significant decline in Latin American exports in 2009 suggested strongly that they would return (see ILO, 2009). A key question that must be asked about social provision is whether it can be sustained through a severe downturn.

The political legacy of the costly and inefficient nature of welfare systems in Latin America and also their unequal coverage across different sectors of the population also helps to explain the limited expansion of social policies in the region under democracy. This is in part because democratic politics has also given opportunities to the existing beneficiaries of limited welfare services to defend their privileges against a potential dilution of their coverage as these services are extended to new groups.

Chile – a social democratic pioneer?

Although centre-left governments have made progress in reducing poverty, interests linked to the old regime have sometimes limited, or at least shaped, the extent to which they have been able to address excluded social groups. The social policies pursued by socialist presidents in Chile from 2000–09, for example, were distinguished by a pragmatic effort to pursue social reform alongside measures to ensure the capitalist economy remains competitive that are supported by the political right (see Chapters 12, 15). As a result, the ruling centre-left coalitions have not changed the neoliberal macroeconomic framework inherited from the Pinochet years.

Chile's military government under the Pinochet dictatorship (1973–90) was the first and most radical of the free market reformers. The regime took power through a coup in 1973 in the belief that the survival of capitalism was under threat. Its subsequent free-market policies were extensive and pervasive, aiming as much to impose an alternative social, political and economic order that would make it impossible for the Left to return as to reinvigorate economic growth.

The prospect of democratisation came at a time of economic growth in the late 1980s, which undermined both the case for continuing authoritarianism but also the revolutionary option for the Left, strengthening moderates who were arguing that it was necessary to modify, rather than abolish, capitalism. On the left, the balance of power shifted towards the Partido por la Democracia (PPD, Party for Democracy) and the Partido Socialista (PSCh, Socialist Party), which became important actors in the governing multi-party centre-left Concertación coalition (Roberts, 1997). The PPD was created by moderate socialists in 1987 to circumvent the legal proscriptions on traditional leftwing parties, portraying an image of modernity and non-ideological pragmatism and rapidly occupying the centre-left space. The PSCh abandoned past Marxist-Leninist revolutionary positions and embraced social democracy. These developments reflected the assumption of governmental responsibilities by the PSCh in the early 1990s within Concertación under the Christian Democrat president Patricio Aylwin (1990–94). The Left sought to demonstrate that it was capable of responsible economic management following the chaos under Allende (see Box 16.2, Chapter 12).

Aylwin inherited a strong economy in which radical neoliberal restructuring had already been carried out. He sought to reassure domestic and international capital of his commitment to preserve this model, and the cornerstones of his policy were liberalised trade and budgetary discipline. At the same time, the Concertación government also placed a greater emphasis on the need to reconcile growth with social justice. Aylwin's mild reformism resulted in a large majority in elections in 1993 for the Concertación's Christian Democrat presidential candidate Eduardo Frei (Hershberg, 1997). Frei's term from 1994–2000 was marked by the continuity of a mixed economic policy, and growth in Chile between 1990–98 was an impressive average 7 per cent a year, unemployment remained low, and GDP per capita doubled. In this context, the PSCh-PPD bloc was able to challenge the Christian Democrats for leadership of Concertación.

In 2000, the PSCh candidate Ricardo Lagos (2000–06) won presidential elections at the head of the Concertación coalition, becoming Chile's first socialist president since Allende. Although he inherited a recession, Lagos did not change the broad policy direction of his Concertación predecessors and established the basis for a strong economic recovery by 2005. He took power with a pledge that reflects the contemporary left's social-democratic priorities: to improve the free-market economy while helping the poor by correcting inequalities generated by the market. As a minister of public works from 1994–98, Lagos had refused to be bound by past socialist orthodoxy and was praised for his role presiding over the privatisation of Chile's motorways (see Table 15.1). He had favoured a deep involvement of the private sector in infrastructure investment and other key areas of the economy. As a keen advocate of the free market, Lagos signed a free-trade deal with the US (see Chapter 10). His successor, the socialist Michelle Bachelet (2006–10), identified closely with these policies and, as a result, during her administration had to contend with a series of strikes and protests by unions on the left. Also a former government minister, Bachelet adopted a pragmatic, non-ideological style that sought to reassure Chile's business community and win its backing against her conservative electoral rival. She spoke out against protectionism and in favour of further measures to keep the Chilean economy competitive by deepening its integration in the global economy, and signalled that she would maintain good relations with the US.

Chile's Concertación governments developed a brand of social democracy that aimed to sustain the country's economic dynamism while sharing out its benefits:

- The PSCh and PPD accepted the economic restructuring that took place under Pinochet as a fact, recognised private property as the engine of growth and did not try to reverse former policies such as privatisation. Now they promoted free trade, export-led growth, openness to foreign imports, investment, competition and regional integration. They resisted the temptation to undertake social spending at levels that exceeded rates of growth. For example, Bachelet's government revealed the extent to which the Concertación was prepared to risk criticism from core supporters for not allocating more of the profits of the copper producer Codelco to public spending, thereby exacerbating tensions with public-sector workers.

- The PSCh and PPD reconceptualised the role of the state to find a balance between the minimalism proposed by neoliberalism and the maximalist role of statism (see Box 15.3). They no longer viewed the state as the main producer or planner of economic activity and assigned these functions to the private sector operating in a competitive marketplace. The state was now seen as a strategic promoter of private economic activity that regulates the market in the public interest while seeking to integrate excluded sectors into the marketplace by promoting economic growth and social inclusion.

- The PSCh and PPD substituted a commitment to conscious redistribution for a position that advocated awarding state benefits selectively, but at the same time argued that the often contradictory objectives of growth and equity are compatible. As a result, the Left downplayed traditional welfare policies and emphasised targeted social programmes to give the poor greater access to the education and training that helps them participate in the market economy. Their poverty alleviation strategy rested upon generating employment rather than on a direct commitment to redistribution. Chile continues to suffer from one of the higher levels of inequality in Latin America (see Table 4.6) and the country still has more than 1 million unemployed or underemployed people. Concertación struggled to balance the gradual tightening of labour laws with the flexibility that enables small businesses to hire new workers. Changes to labour legislation are seen as a priority by the country's Right, which gained power in 2010. None the less, by most accounts, social-democratic stewardship of Chile's liberalised economy, and by implication the original neoliberal restructuring, has been successful: there has been a dramatic reduction in the level of poverty since 1990 (see Mideplan, 2008).

■ The PSCh and PPD abandoned the Left's past hostility to the US and integration in the global market. Lagos, for example, courted foreign investment and was a keen supporter of the free market, technological innovation and export diversification. He advocated free trade and the acceleration of Chile's integration in the global economy through bilateral agreements (see Box 15.5). Under Lagos, Chile signed agreements with the US, Europe and South Korea, and negotiated agreements with China and India. Lagos also won warm praise from Washington for his economic policies and for advocating closer ties between Latin America and the US. Chile has adopted a conscious, proactive policy to seeking free trade agreements with powerful economies and attracting foreign investment. Under Bachelet, policymakers began reaching out to establish or boost economic links with Indonesia, Malaysia, Pakistan, the Philippines, South Korea, Taiwan, Thailand and Vietnam, and Chile has also targeted the Middle East for trade.

However, the lessons that can be learned from Chile by other left-of-centre governments in Latin America may be limited. Silva (2009) has argued that the factors that shaped Chile's social-democratic model are almost exclusively connected to its own political development, and cannot be strongly linked to the recent 'pink tide' elsewhere in Latin America (see Chapter 12). These are:

– the profound impact of the experience of Allende's government from 1970–73 and the subsequent military regime on Chile's political culture in general, and on the Left in particular;

– the deep penetration of neoliberalism in all spheres of Chilean life and the support that market-oriented policies enjoy among the population;

– the strong political and institutional constraints on the moderate left as a result of a powerful rightwing opposition and the coalition nature of the Concertación. Tensions within the Concertación between the Left and Christian Democrats contributed to the decline of its electoral support in 2009 in favour of the rightwing Coalición por el Cambio (Coalition for Change), which is now more unified in comparison and whose candidate won the 2010 electoral run-off;

– the technocratic nature of economic policymaking, which has avoided populism and the politicisation of national debate.

Social-democratic reformism has confronted limitations, largely because of the compromises its advocates have to make in order to gain power and because of Latin America's relationship with the international economy (see Box 16.4). This has limited the gains achieved on behalf of needy sectors – the effect of economic policies pursued by the Concertación coalition in Chile, for example, has been falling

THEORIES AND DEBATES	Box 16.4

Social-democratic dilemmas

The limitations and dilemmas faced by social-democratic reformism in Chile and elsewhere include:

Institutional obstacles

In Chile a number of obstacles have stood in the way of even modest social reform since the centre-left parties of the Concertación have been in power. The constitution and political process were structured by the Pinochet regime to favour rightwing parties and interests, and the power of the state was constrained in ways that limited the potential for intervention to promote greater equality and expand participation. For example, Pinochet shifted responsibility for financing and implementing policy in several areas from central government to the regions, and insulated the central bank from democratic pressures (*ibid.*). Lagos repeatedly voiced his frustration at the limits imposed by the opposition of rightwing forces in congress upon his ability to undertake initiatives promoting greater equality in Chile.

Compromises

Roberts (1997) argued that the social-democratic perspective may have practical advantages over more redistributive policy alternatives such as socialism by sacrificing radical change in favour of realism and moderating its objectives in order to lessen opposition and so enhance its electoral appeal (see Box 12.5). Social democracy does not have the deep roots in Latin America that it possesses in Western Europe. Although positions on the left in Chile have similarities with those that have developed among social democrats in Europe, the Chilean socialists' sources of support are different due to the hetereogeneity of the country's workforce, low levels of unionisation and fragmented political loyalties on the left (*ibid.*). As a result, the Chilean social democrats have developed a catch-all electoralist orientation and a technocratic style. However, the desire to appeal to a broad cross-section of the population can often dilute the impulse to take more radical steps to solve pressing social problems that may challenge the interests of powerful political actors such as business groups.

Capital

Przeworski (1985) has argued that there is a contradiction between the processes by which capital operates at a global level and processes by which social-democratic forms of class compromise are constructed at a domestic level. In a globalised economy, capital markets have been liberalised in order to permit investment to flow effortlessly between countries. In Latin America, much existing private capital is already controlled by transnational corporations or domestic companies tied to foreign interests. Removing the constraints on capital means that those who control it can act against policies they find unfavourable in a given country by disinvesting. In this way, capitalists operating at a global level have great leverage to press national governments to adopt pro-business policies and to punish those that do not (see Box 15.6). This dependence on foreign capital can limit the autonomy of governments wishing to undertake social reforms, and governments whose policies diverge from international norms can be punished through capital flight. International capital flows can also weaken the power of organised labour and make it more difficult to reach a class compromise in domestic policy (Roberts, 1997). For this reason, social democracy relies on a *compromise* with capitalism which has often risked alienating its leftwing constituencies and has created political dilemmas for social-democratic politicians.

poverty, yet continuing inequality. However, there is also a corollary to broad agreement on the left over free-market reforms in Chile, and that is the acceptance of social policy by the Right. Sebastián Piñera, the victorious rightwing candidate in Chile's 2009–10 presidential elections, pledged to continue to deepen the social welfare provision currently granted by Concertación governments, confirming the consensus that exists on market-friendly policies within a social-democratic framework.

Chile also provides an example of the difficulties of reconciling the contradictory aims of growth and equity found within social democracy. In the primary campaign of Lagos, his advisers suggested that he would support a broad privatisation programme that would include selling Chile's giant state-run copper corporation Codelco (see Table 15.1). However, fearing that he would be labelled on the left as a neoliberal, Lagos subsequently shelved this idea. Yet at the same time, Lagos's programme did not meet expectations on the left. An important plank of his economic plans was to liberalise labour laws to make it easier for employers to hire and fire and to give them more flexibility in setting working hours. This angered organised labour and, in 2003, trade unionists seeking better pay and health and social security benefits staged Chile's first general strike since 1986. Observers suggested that, as a result of its economic policies, the Concertación found it increasingly hard to distinguish itself from the opposition rightwing coalition, the Alianza por Chile. At the same time, as a socialist, Lagos also had to contend with the suspicions of Chile's business community and the conservative opposition despite his record as a member of Concertación coalition governments that had nurtured the market-economy model. The constraints imposed by these groups and opposition by moderates within Concertación itself provided many examples of the limits of reformism within the social-democratic notion of growth with equity. Business vigorously resisted plans to allow for collective bargaining by trades unions on wages and conditions across industries; to prevent employers from hiring temporary workers during strikes; and to clamp down on tax evasion. Lagos argued that strong unions can act as a vehicle for ensuring greater labour flexibility, and therefore are in the best interests of employers. Conservatives, by contrast, have traditionally been hostile to trades unions, which they associate with the Left and with the economic instability under Allende that had preceded the Pinochet coup in 1973 (see Box 16.2, Chapters 7, 12).

Criticisms of neostructuralism

Neostructuralism has not gone unchallenged, and some scholars have argued that, because it is market-friendly, it may also have been tainted by association with the disappointing results of neoliberalism in Latin America and that traditional structuralist positions – 'post-neostructuralism' – are making a comeback in some economic circles (see Weyland, 2007). Growing support for neostructuralism on the left in Latin America, within policymaking circles, and among international bodies, derives in part from the search in the region for a broad counter 'discourse' to neoliberalism, and one of the most powerful recent critiques of neostructuralism has sought to emphasise this 'ideological' quality. In 2008, for example, Fernando Ignacio Leiva argued that the ability of neostructuralism to support the political discourse of left-of-centre coalitions intent on channelling rising popular discontent with dogmatic neoliberalism, and the absence of more radical alternatives, had shielded neostructrualism from critical evaluation (see Leiva, 2008a, 2008b). Leiva argues that Latin American neostructuralism is not an alternative to neoliberalism, but merely completes the historical task initiated by neoliberalism to consolide a new, export-led model of development. He says that the 'foundational myths' that distinguish neostructuralism from neoliberalism – and derive from the commitment to social consensus that originated in the trauma of authoritarianism in Latin America – conceal profound contradictions. These myths include the notion of relatively easy access to globalisation; the promotion of a regionalism compatible with the global rules of the World Trade Organisation; and the idea that a productive transformation with social equity can be achieved through export-led growth. Leiva suggests that neostructuralism fails to consider the nature of power relations that characterise the current dynamics of the international political economy, where transnational productive and finance capital exercise ever-increasing control over Latin American resources, economies, and societies; and that, by accepting the status quo of export-oriented development, neostructuralism compiles an analysis of Latin American economy and society that is sanitised of conflict and asymmetrical power relations. In effect, neostructuralism remains incapable of fully understanding the transformations in Latin American capitalism of the past decade and has, as a result, tended to emphasise short-term policies that make its promises of growth with social equity more ideological than evidence-based.

Because capital enjoys structural advantages in Latin America, many social democrats have argued for a powerful labour movement to press for redistribution. But another constraint faced by social democracy in the region is the relative *weakness* of organised labour and the fragmented character of popular organisations (see Chapters 7, 8). In Europe, social democracy emerged in conditions in which the working class in the form of an industrial proletariat comprised a far larger proportion of the population than in Latin America, where the working class remains a minority of the working population and workers in formal industries have little in common with those in informal sectors. These factors weaken the ability of workers to take collective action based on a shared class consciousness. Neoliberal policies have reinforced these obstacles to social democracy by deepening inequalities and so limiting the opportunity for consensus, and by generating differentiation within popular sectors, making it more difficult to form united organisations (see Chapter 15). One response by some local authorities in Latin America that places greater emphasis on the participatory and consensus-seeking components of social democracy has been democratic innovations in setting budgets. 'Participatory budgeting' was pioneered by the PT in more than 100 Brazilian municipalities, including cities such as Porto Alegre, São Paulo and Recife. This is a formula that allows local authorities to set spending priorities and so allocate resources based on direct and continuous consultation with local people at a ward level (see Box 16.5).

INSTITUTIONS	Box 16.5

Empowerment and democracy – participatory budgeting in Brazil

Participatory budgeting reflects a social interpretation of democracy that aims to empower ordinary citizens by giving them a say in how local authorities spend money in order to improve conditions and services (see Chapter 3). It has been pioneered in Brazil by the PT as an effort to *institutionalise* popular participation in local political processes that have traditionally been dominated by elites, thereby bridging the gap between state institutions and civil society (see Box 8.1). For this reason, participatory budgeting has often been used as an example of the promise offered by a more participatory democracy favouring ordinary people and civil society organisations that can be contrasted with a more elitist form of democracy dominated by career politicians and organised interests (see Nylen, 2003). In particular, participatory budgeting has been examined in terms of its potential for strengthening accountability and transparency in local politics (see Wampler, 2004). In Venezuela, participatory democracy under Hugo Chávez was meant to differentiate new forms of governance from what he argued was a former stranglehold maintained by political elites in a *partidocracía* (see Boxes 4.2, 6.2).

In Brazil, Porto Alegre has pioneered this form of local co-operation between city officials and civil society in the selection and implementation of policies and public works based on spending formulae developed from hundreds of public meetings involving up to 100,000 participants each year (see Goldfrank, 2003). Representatives from the 16 districts of the city vote on their priorities by investment sector, such as street lighting, refuse disposal etc. The city's budget and planning office then compiles the districts' scores and uses these to determine how to allocate investments by sector and then by district. The formula takes into account a district's need for a service in terms of existing or absent provision; its population; and the order in a list of priorities that people in each district place that particular investment sector.

In some cases, the impact of participatory budgeting on the conditions in which people live has been dramatic. Research by the World Bank (2003) examining the results of participatory budgeting in Porto Alegre found that between 1989 and 1996 the number of households with access to water services rose from 80 per cent to 98 per cent; the percentage of the population served by the municipal sewage system rose from 46 per cent to 85 per cent; the number of children enrolled in public schools doubled; and improved transparency and accountability increased the motivation of people to pay taxes and so taxation revenue rose by 50 per cent.

However, the success of participatory budgeting has varied and in some cases it can have unforeseen consequences. The role of municipal mayors has been of key importance to the fate of participatory budgeting and the most successful experiments have often been introduced by municipal mayors with links to social movements, progressive sectors of the Catholic Church, and trades unions (see Chapters 7, 8, Box 12.3). There are risks that a mayor with weak links and unable to generate sufficient participation to make participatory budgeting arrangements work well, or who is reluctant to devolve power to participatory forums in this way, could alienate key social groups and weaken local administration. If a municipal council is unwilling to support participatory budgeting, it is also difficult for a mayor to proceed.

Moreover the introduction of participatory budgeting is a time-consuming process that may not promise electoral benefits in the short term, and political opponents can also use the new participatory forums to try to damage a mayor. Wampler (2004) suggests that participatory budgeting may also have a mixed impact on accountability, strengthening it in some areas but weakening it in others. He argues that in Porto Alegre, while participatory budgeting has meant citizens have been incorporated into decisionmaking and the mayor's authority has increased, the municipal council's role in the budgetary process has been weakened. This suggests that, by only partially helping to improve accountability, participatory budgeting can be only one component of a strategy to deepen democratic practices. Participatory budgeting in Porto Alegre sometimes failed to sustain the image of clean government, brought tax increases and fiscal insecurity, and left expectations unfulfilled (see Goldfrank and Schneider, 2006; Panizza, 2009). In Brazil nationally, the federal administration did not adopt participatory forms of decisionmaking, limiting its impact. In Venezuela, local participatory democracy initiatives have been vulnerable to policy changes from above and grassroots organisations have sometimes been captured and controlled by political supporters of Chávez, who then operate a form of patronage politics (see Panizza, 2009). The personalisation of politics under Chávez further limits participation nationally.

Summary

Redistribution to tackle severe inequality has been a key theme in twentieth-century Latin American economic and political debate, although in only a few cases have governments placed this theme at the heart of their development programmes. Cuba's socialist economic model has been the most radical experiment in development in Latin America, eradicating most private property rights and relying solely on state planning to allocate resources through government control of almost all production and distribution. Cuba's revolutionary regime had, by the mid-1960s, ended the island's economic dependency on the US, but eventually substituted this for a dependent relationship with the Soviet Union, albeit one that was much more favourable to Cuba. Since then, the regime has made significant strides in reducing inequalities and creating a society in which most people have access to important public services such as education and healthcare, but at the cost of efficiency, competitiveness and political rights. During the 1990s, Cuba struggled to adapt to the new international order but has restored growth through reforms allowing some foreign investment and by seeking special relationships with countries such as Venezuela and China. Development strategies that emphasise growth and redistribution regardless of the potential inflationary consequences have sometimes been termed economic populism, and were pursued in Chile under the Marxist president Allende and in Nicaragua under the Sandinistas. Both regimes placed redistribution at the heart of their programmes but their economies nearly collapsed due to inflation, disinvestment, unrest, the resistance of domestic conservatives and the hostility of the US. A military regime in Peru fashioned a populist model of development with socialist and nationalist components that also placed a significant emphasis on redistribution. Key elements of this model were land reform and efforts to improve the conditions and rights of peasants and workers. However, an over-ambitious expansion of public investment and declining growth undermined the Peruvian experiment and it was abandoned by a subsequent regime. The expectations it had raised may have been a significant factor fuelling subsequent guerrilla violence in the 1980s. The limited impact of neoliberal policies upon poverty and inequality across Latin America, and ideological reorientation on the left following the end of the Cold War, have made neostructuralist ideas influential. These blend the neoliberal commitment to forging a dynamic economy within the global capitalist market with structuralist ideas about the positive role states can play in creating conditions for growth with equity. Neostructuralism supports the social-democratic policy framework that has been employed with some success in Chile since the 1990s, and the new role for the state promoted by left-of-centre governments that have come to power throughout Latin America. It has combined with a revival of attention to Keynesian ideas as a result of the global financial crisis of 2008–09, but is not without its critics.

Discussion points

- What does Cuba's economic development reveal about the notion of dependency?
- Is Cuba's growing relationship with Venezuela a new form of dependency?
- What characteristics are associated with populist development strategies?
- Are populist economic strategies destined to end in inflation and instability?
- To what extent do neostructuralists challenge the principles of capitalism?
- Why has the appeal of social democracy been so limited in Latin America?

Useful websites

www.cubagob.cu Cuban government homepage, with links to economic and social data from the Ministerio de Economía y Planificación (Ministry of the Economy and Planning)

www.cubaweb.cu CubaWeb pages with links on business and business associations

www.camaracuba.cu Cámara de Comercio de la República de Cuba, Cuba's state-run chamber of commerce

http://eurochambres.be/Content/Default.asp?PageID=98 AL-INVEST IV initiative through Eurochambres (the Association of European Chambers of Commerce and Industry) to help small and medium-sized enterprises in Latin America, including Cuba, internationalise

www.cubagov.cu/ingles/otras_info/cpi/index.htm Centro de Promoción de Inversiones (CPI, Investment Promotion Centre), an agency of Cuba's Ministerio para la Inversión Extranjera y la Colaboración Económica (MINVEC, Ministry for Foreign Investment and Economic Collaboration)

www.cubaindustria.cu Cuban industry portal

www.mincex.cu Ministerio del Comercio Exterior (Mincex, Trade Ministry), Cuba

www.cepec.cu Centro para Promoción de las Exportaciones de Cuba (CEPEC, Centre for the Promotion of Cuban Exports)

www.alternativabolivariana.org La Alternativa Bolivariana para América Latina y El Caribe (ALBA, Bolivarian Alliance for the Americas), TCP, Tratado de Comercio de los Pueblos www.alternativabolivariana.org/modules.php?name=Content&pa=showpage&pid=2059 ALBA documents in English

http://hdr.undp.org United Nations Development Programme's Human Development Reports

www.minci.gob.ve/actualidad/2/5573/convenio_cuba-venezuelarespuesta_inmediata.html Venezuelan government site containing information on the Convenio Cuba-Venezuela, a range of co-operation agreements between the countries

www.chinabuses.com/english/manufacturer/yutong.htm ChinaBuses.com website, for information on the Zhengzhou Yutong coach company

www.fundacionsalvadorallende.cl Fundación Salvador Allende (Salvador Allende Foundation)

www.salvador-allende.cl Useful archive of material about Salvador Allende

www.visionsandinista.com Visión Sandinista, web magazine produced by the Partido Frente Sandinista de Liberación Nacional (FSLN, Sandinista National Liberation Front party), Nicaragua

www.nuevoarcoiris.org.co Corporación Nuevo Arco Iris (New Rainbow Corporation), Colombia

www.santander.com Grupo Santander

www.economiayfinanzas.gob.bo Ministerio de Economía y Finanzas Públicas, Bolivia's finance ministry

www.aecid.es/web/es Agencia Española de Cooperación al Desarrollo (AECID, Spanish Agency for Development Co-operation)

www.nrc.no Norwegian Refugee Council

www.enarsa.com.ar/english/indexE.htm Energía Argentina SA, Enarsa

www.ppd.cl Partido por la Democracia (PPD, Party for Democracy), Chile

www.portoalegre.rs.gov.br Prefeitura Municipal de Porto Alegre (PMPA, Porto Alegre Municipal Council), Brazil

Recommended reading

Domínguez, Jorge, Omar Everleny Pérez Villanueva and Lorena Barberia (eds). 2005. *The Cuban Economy at the Start of the Twenty-First Century*. Cambridge, MA: Harvard University Press/The David Rockefeller Center for Latin American Studies

Essential overview of the macroeconomic issues, international dilemmas and welfare challenges facing the Cuban economy and the government's response to these, by scholars from both the US and Cuba

Yaffe, Helen. 2009. *Che Guevara: The Economics of Revolution*. Basingstoke: Palgrave Macmillan

Valuable economic history of revolutionary Cuba that explores the innovations of Che Guevara that still influence policymaking

Edwards, Sebastian. 2010. *Left Behind: Latin America and the False Promise of Populism*. Chicago, IL: University of Chicago Press

Valuable critique of left-of-centre economic policies in Latin America which argues that populist experiments have harmed growth and the lives of citizens

Mayer, Enrique. 2009. *Ugly Stories of the Peruvian Agrarian Reform*. Durham, NC: Duke University Press

> *Valuable insight into the human face of Peru's momentous agrarian reform under Velasco, demonstrating the social impact of large redistributive projects*

Sunkel, Osvaldo (ed.). 1993. *Development from Within: Toward a Neostructuralist Approach to Latin America*. Boulder, CO: Lynne Rienner

> *Useful and influential neostructuralist manifesto edited by the Chilean economist at the heart of the evolution of structuralist ideas*

Weyland, Kurt. 2007. 'The Political Economy of Market Reform and a Revival of Structuralism', *Latin American Research Review*, Vol. 42, No. 3 (January), pp. 235–50

> *Valuable introduction to the literature on the critique of neoliberalism that emerges from the revival of structuralist ideas*

Leiva, Fernando Ignacio. 2008. *Latin American Neostructuralism: The Contradictions of Post-Neoliberal Development*. Minneapolis, MN: University of Minnesota Press

> *Essential and timely critique of neostructuralism that aims to highlight what the author argues is its ideological nature*

Appendices

COUNTRY TIMELINES AND FACTBOXES, GLOSSARY AND DRAMATIS PERSONAE

Appendix A

Country timelines and factboxes

Mexico and North America

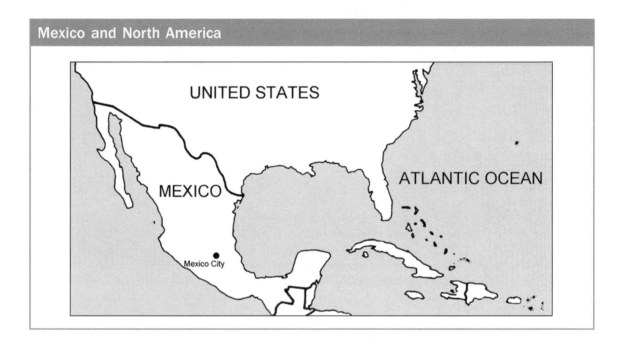

Mexico

1982	Debt crisis begins, with long-term implications for ruling PRI, dominant since the 1920s
1988	Technocrat Carlos Salinas de Gortari becomes president and begins neoliberal reforms
1989	Formation of the left-of-centre PRD
1992	Reforms culminate in signing of NAFTA with US and Canada
1994	Rebellion in southern state of Chiapas by mainly indigenous EZLN. PRI presidential candidate Luis Donaldo Colosio assassinated. PRI's Ernesto Zedillo Ponce de Leon elected president. Stock market plunges, peso collapses and deep recession begins
1995	Former president Salinas goes into exile after his brother is linked to the murder of a key PRI official, José Francisco Ruiz Massieu, although later exonerated
1996	EPR guerrilla organisation launches insurgency in south
1997	PRI suffers significant defeat in mid-term elections. Massacre of indigenous people by paramilitaries in Chiapas causes outcry and Zedillo launches investigation
1998	Governor of Chiapas resigns and peace talks with EZLN reactivated, then break down
2000	Vicente Fox Quesada of conservative PAN ends PRI rule in presidential elections
2001	Law increasing rights of indigenous people rejected by EZLN leaders. Fox appoints prosecutor to investigate disappearance of leftwing activists in 1970s and 1980s
2002	Former president Luis Echeverría questioned about massacres of students in 1968 and 1971. Three army officers charged with killing leftwing activists in 1970s
2003	Fox labour and energy reforms falter. PRI comeback in mid-term elections
2004	Investigator rules that shooting of students in 1971 was genocide, but judge refuses to order Echeverría's arrest
2005	Congress strips Mexico City mayor and PRD presidential hopeful Andrés Manuel López Obrador of immunity from prosecution in land dispute, but government abandons case
2006	Felipe Calderón of PAN narrowly defeats López Obrador in elections and he challenges result with large protests, but Federal Electoral Tribunal confirms Calderón's win. New president launches violent war on drug cartels. Echeverría placed under house arrest
2007	Genocide trial against Echeverría suspended over lack of evidence
2008	Deaths in war on drugs escalate. Hundreds of thousands of people protest against wave of killings and kidnappings. Faced with falling oil production, Calderón pushes through reforms that include plans to allow private investment in state oil monopoly Pemex
2009	Mexico's government takes emergency measures to protect economy from US downturn. Drug-related violence deepens. PRI makes significant gains in mid-term congressional elections, winning 48 per cent of seats in Chamber of Deputies
2010	Calderón heckled by residents of Ciudad Juárez angry at drug violence in the city

Factbox: Mexico

Federal presidential democratic republic of 31 states and one federal district.

Suffrage: Universal for those aged 18 or over, compulsory (in principle only).

Executive: President elected directly by the people for a six-year term.

Legislature: Bicameral Congreso de la Unión (Congress of the Union). The lower Cámara de Diputados (Chamber of Deputies) has 500 members – 300 elected by plurality and 200 by proportional representation – who serve three-year terms. The upper Cámara de Senadores (Chamber of Senators) has 128 members – 64 (two per state and the Federal District) elected by plurality; 32 (one per state and the Federal District) allocated to the first minority; and 32 elected by proportional representation from closed party lists, to serve six-year terms.

States: Governors and bicameral legislatures directly elected. States are subdivided into 2,438 municipalities (municipios) whose presidents and councils are directly elected.

Useful websites

www.presidencia.gob.mx **Presidency**
www.cddhcu.gob.mx **Chamber of Deputies**
www.senado.gob.mx **Senate**

Central America and the Caribbean

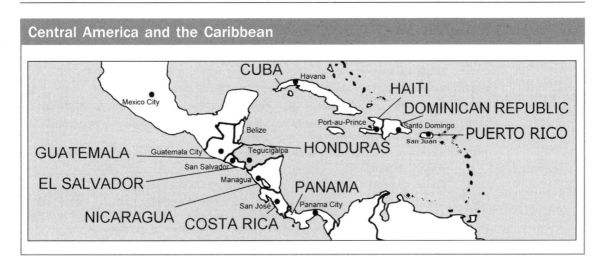

Guatemala

1970s	Military regimes attempt to eradicate left, resulting in tens of thousands of deaths
1981	Death squads and army kill at least 11,000 people in response to guerrilla activity
1982	General Efraín Ríos Montt takes power following military coup
1983	Ríos Montt ousted by General Mejia Victores, who declares an amnesty for guerrillas
1985	Military allows centrist civilian Marco Vinicio Cerezo Arévalo to assume power after DCG wins legislative elections under new constitution
1989	Attempt to overthrow Cerezo fails. Civil war toll since 1980 reaches 100,000 dead and 40,000 missing
1991	Cerezo succeeded by conservative Jorge Serrano Elías of MAS
1993	Serrano's inability to build congressional support sparks attempt to assume dictatorial powers through dissolution of congress. He is forced to resign, and former human rights commissioner Ramiró de León Carpio chosen by legislature to complete term
1994	De León Carpio makes progress in UN-brokered peace process between government forces and URNG guerrilla movement. Right wins legislative elections
1995	Rebels declare ceasefire. UN and US criticise Guatemala for widespread rights abuses
1996	Alvaro Arzú of centre-right PAN elected president and signs peace deal ending civil war
1998	Bishop Juan José Gerardi murdered just days after report highlighting military abuses
1999	UN-backed commission says security forces behind 93 per cent of all human rights atrocities during civil war, which claimed 200,000 lives. Alfonso Portillo of rightwing FRG wins presidential elections resulting in uneasy status quo in state's relations with military
2001	Portillo pays $1.8m in compensation to families of 226 men, women and children killed by soldiers and paramilitaries in northern village in 1982
2003	Conservative Oscar José Rafael Berger wins presidential elections for Gran Alianza Nacional. Guatemala and Central American states agree free-trade deal with US
2004	Ríos Montt placed under house arrest, major cuts to military, and damages paid to victims of civil war. UN mission set up to monitor post-civil war peace process winds up
2005	Ratification of the DR-CAFTA free-trade deal with US fuels street protests
2006	Spanish judge issues warrant for arrest of Ríos Montt over atrocities during civil war. Government and UN agree to create commission to tackle clandestine armed groups
2007	Three members of Central American Parliament murdered near Guatemala City
2007	Alvaro Colom of centre-left UNE wins presidential elections with 53 per cent of vote
2008	Former president Portillo extradited from Mexico to face corruption charges
2009	Colom hit by allegations of involvement in death of prominent lawyer, although subsequently exonerated. Former paramilitary becomes first person jailed for disappearance of civilians in civil war

Factbox: Guatemala

Presidential democratic republic with 22 departments.

Suffrage: Universal for those aged 18 or over (excluding members of the armed forces actively on duty).

Executive: President and vice-president elected directly by the people for a four-year term (majority runoff).

Legislature: Unicameral Congreso de la República (Congress of the Republic) has 158 members elected for a four-year term through a mixture of direct elections in constituencies and proportional representation.

Departments: Departmental governors are appointed by the president. The departments are subdivided into 333 municipalities plus Guatemala City, whose mayors or councils are directly elected.

Useful websites

www.guatemala.gob.gt **Presidency**
www.congreso.gob.gt **Congress**

El Salvador

1977	Guerrilla activities by leftwing FMLN intensify amid reports of increased human rights violations by army and death squads. General Carlos Romero elected president
1979	Success of revolution in Nicaragua ends El Salvador's military-oligarchic alliance. Romero ousted in coup by reformist officers, bringing hope that centrist alternative can be found to advance reform process, but this fails to curb army-backed political violence: between 1979–81, about 30,000 people are killed by army-backed rightwing death squads
1980	Archbishop of San Salvador, Oscar Romero, assassinated. Christian Democrat José Napoleón Duarte becomes first civilian president since 1931
1981	France and Mexico recognise FMLN as legitimate political force. US continues to assist Salvadorean government, whose forces continue to support death squads. Civil war gains international attention. US president Ronald Reagan presses for legislative elections
1982	Elections boycotted by Left and won by rightwing coalition dominated by ARENA
1984	Duarte wins elections and seeks negotiated deal with FMLN. While main political forces gain representation through party politics, military's conflict with FMLN intensifies
1989	Victory of ARENA candidate Alfredo Cristiani in elections, widely believed to have been fraudulent, threatens to undermine progress towards transition. FMLN attacks intensify
1991	FMLN recognised as political party
1992	Government and FMLN sign UN-sponsored peace accord
1993	Government declares amnesty for those implicated in human rights atrocities
1994	ARENA candidate Armando Calderón Sol elected president, but FMLN establishes itself as second-largest party
1997	FMLN makes gains in parliamentary polls. Leftwinger wins San Salvador mayoralty
1999	Francisco Flores of ARENA beats former guerrilla Facundo Guardado in presidential elections that divide FMLN
2001	El Salvador adopts US dollar as its currency
2002	US court holds two retired, US-based Salvadorean generals responsible for civil war atrocities and orders them to compensate victims
2003	Flores aligns foreign policy closely with that of the US, and Salvadorean troops sent to Iraq. El Salvador agrees on DR-CAFTA free-trade agreement with US
2004	Modernising liberal Elías Antonio Saca González wins ARENA's fourth presidential election in succession. Government ratifies DR-CAFTA
2005	OAS human rights court votes to re-open investigation into 1981 massacre of peasants
2006	El Salvador becomes first Central American country to implement DR-CAFTA
2008	More than 400 judges demonstrate over corruption allegations made against colleagues
2009	FMLN emerges as largest party in parliamentary elections. ARENA wins largest number of seats in local elections. Mauricio Funes of FMLN wins presidential elections

Factbox: El Salvador

Presidential democratic republic with 14 departments.

Suffrage: Universal for those aged 18 or over.

Executive: President and vice-president elected on the same ticket directly by the people for five-year terms (majority runoff).

Legislature: Unicameral Asamblea Legislativa (Legislative Assembly) of 84 seats whose members are elected for three-year terms through proportional representation: 20 deputies are elected nationally and 64 in 14 multi-member constituencies that correspond to the 14 departments.

Departments: Each department is administered by a governor appointed by the president. The departments are subdivided into 267 municipalities whose authorities are directly elected.

Useful websites

www.presidencia.gob.sv **Presidency**
www.asamblea.gob.sv **Legislative Assembly**

Honduras

1981	Military allows elections and accepts victory of centrist PLH candidate Roberto Suazo Córdova. Anti-communist general, Gustavo Alvarez Martínez, assumes leading role in government as US begins to use Honduras as base for attacks by *contra* counter-revolutionaries against Nicaragua's Sandinista regime
1982	Honduran military becomes embroiled in regional conflicts
1984	Alvarez deposed amid anti-US demonstrations. US-run training camps for Salvadorean counter-revolutionaries shut
1985	Another Liberal, José Azcona Hoyo, wins elections
1987	Both military and leftwing guerrillas gain amnesty for abuses of early 1980s
1988	Amnesty International alleges increase in human rights violations by armed forces
1989	Alvarez assassinated by leftwing guerrillas. Summit of Central American presidents reaches agreement on demobilisation of Nicaraguan *contras* based in Honduras
1990	Conservative Rafael Leonardo Callejas of PNH launches neoliberal economic reforms
1993	Government sets up commission to investigate alleged human rights violations by military. Liberal Carlos Roberto Reina wins elections and pledges to limit power of armed forces
1995	Compulsory military service abolished. Some officers charged with human rights abuses
1997	Conservative Liberal Carlos Roberto Flores Facussé wins elections and pledges to restructure armed forces
1998	Control of police transferred from military to civilian authorities
1999	Congress ratifies constitutional reforms that place armed forces under civilian control, but Flores has to dismiss leading officers amid reports of a coup plot
2000	Supreme Court rules that 1980s atrocities not covered by 1987 amnesty
2001	Honduran Committee for the Defence of Human Rights says more than 1,000 street children murdered in 2000 by police-backed death squads
2002	Conservative businessman Ricardo Maduro of PNH wins presidential elections
2003	Congress votes to send troops to Iraq. Honduras agrees on free-trade deal with the US
2004	Suspected gang members massacre 28 bus passengers in Chamalecon
2005	Honduran Congress approves DR-CAFTA
2006	Liberal Manuel Zelaya Rosales wins presidential elections
2008	Honduras joins leftwing Bolivarian Alternative for the Americas (ALBA)
2009	Zelaya removed in coup, ostensibly for initiating bid to change constitution allowing future term. Congress speaker Roberto Micheletti appointed acting president. US initially refuses to recognise Micheletti and suspends aid. OAS demands Zelaya's reinstatement and suspends Honduras. Latin American states protest coup. Zelaya returns to Honduras and takes refuge in Brazilian embassy. Talks fail to resolve crisis. Conservative Porfirio Lobo wins elections in November that are recognised by US and its allies, but rejected by other Latin American states. Honduran congress refuses to reinstate Zelaya to see out term
2010	Lobo assumes office and grants amnesty to soldiers, politicians and judges involved in removal of Zelaya, who goes into exile in Dominican Republic

Factbox: Honduras

Presidential democratic republic of 18 departments.

Suffrage: Universal for those aged 18 or over, and compulsory.

Executive: President is elected directly by the people for a four-year term.

Legislature: Unicameral Congreso Nacional (National Congress) has 128 members who are elected by proportional representation for four-year terms.

Departments: Departmental governors are appointed by the president for a four-year term. The departments are subdivided into 298 municipalities whose authorities are directly elected.

Useful websites

www.presidencia.gob.hn **Presidency**
www.congreso.gob.hn **Congress**

Nicaragua

1978	Assassination of leader of opposition Democratic Liberation Union brings together moderates and FSLN (Sandinistas) in united front against dictator Anastasio Somoza
1979	FSLN offensive ends with ouster of Somoza. Nicaragua's revolution begins the country's slow transition to democracy. Sandinistas lead broad anti-Somoza coalition but dominate and set out to institutionalise revolutionary project
1980	Somoza assassinated in Paraguay. Sandinista government led by Daniel Ortega nationalises lands held by Somoza family and turns these into co-operatives
1982	Attacks begin by CIA-organised National Guard soldiers who had fled to Honduras and formed the *contra* counter-revolutionaries
1984	Conservatives boycott elections for president, vice-president, and an interim national assembly to draw up new constitution. Ortega elected president. US mines Nicaraguan harbours and is condemned by the World Court
1988	Nicaraguan leadership signs peace agreement and holds talks with *contras*
1990	Violeta Barrios de Chamorro leading US-backed centre-right UNO coalition defeats Ortega in elections. Skirmishes between demobilised Sandinistas and former *contras*
1996	Arnoldo Alemán Lacayo of rightwing Alianza Liberal wins presidency and makes further reconciliation efforts
2000	FSLN wins Managua municipal elections
2001	Enrique Bolaños Geyer of conservative PLC wins landslide election victory. He pursues anti-corruption policy and prosecutes former president Arnoldo Alemán
2002	Opposition Sandinistas re-elect Ortega as party leader
2003	Former president Alemán jailed for 20 years for corruption
2004	World Bank writes off most of Nicaragua's debt, and Russia agrees to write-off multi-billion-dollar Soviet-era debt
2005	Disputes between Bolaños and Ortega over constitutional reforms to weaken power of presidency, and opposition allegations of campaign finance violations against Bolaños and PLC, develop into political crisis. OAS head José Miguel Insulza fails in mediation attempts. Crisis eases as congress agrees to delay constitutional reforms until 2007
2006	DR-CAFTA with the US takes effect. Bolaños unveils plans to build a canal linking Atlantic and Pacific Oceans. Ortega is returned to power in presidential elections
2007	Ortega takes Nicaragua into the leftwing Bolivarian Alternative for the Americas (ALBA)
2008	National and international criticism following irregularities in municipal elections. Nicaragua briefly cuts diplomatic ties with Colombia following the latter's military raid on Ecuadorean territory. Nicaragua becomes the first country after Russia to recognise the independence of Abkhazia and South Ossetia from Georgia
2009	Ortega declares that he would like to change Nicaragua's constitution to permit him to stand for another term in office

Factbox: Nicaragua

Presidential democratic republic of 15 departments and two autonomous regions.

Suffrage: Universal for those aged 16 or over.

Executive: President and vice-president directly elected on the same ticket (two rounds) for five-year terms.

Legislature: Unicameral Asamblea Nacional (National Assembly) of 92 members, 90 of whom elected by proportional representation and party lists to serve a five-year term. Seats reserved for previous president and runners-up in the previous presidential election.

Departments: Members of councils representing Atlantic Coast autonomous regions, and 153 municipal authorities, are directly elected.

Useful websites

www.presidencia.gob.ni **Presidency**
www.asamblea.gob.ni **National Assembly**

Costa Rica

1974	After years of conservative administrations, Daniel Oduber of the PLN is elected president and pursues socialist policies
1978	Conservative Rodrigo Carazo elected president amid deterioration in economy
1982	Luis Alberto Monge of PLN elected president and introduces austerity programme. Costa Rica comes under pressure from US to join fight against Sandinistas in Nicaragua. Some *contras* operate from Costa Rica
1985	US-trained anti-guerrilla force begins operating following clashes with Sandinista troops
1986	Oscar Arias Sánchez of PLN elected president on neutral platform. Initiates peace process in Central America
1987	Leaders of Nicaragua, El Salvador, Guatemala and Honduras sign Esquipulas accords of 1987, earning Arias the Nobel peace prize
1990	Rafael Angel Calderón of centrist PUSC elected president
1994	José María Figueres Olsen returns PLN to presidency and promises to cut public sector, sparking wave of strikes
1998	US-educated economist Miguel Angel Rodríguez of PUSC elected president and promotes economic reforms that provoke bitter struggle between supporters and opponents of neoliberalism. Rodríguez seeks to privatise state-controlled Instituto Costarricense de Electricidad (Costa Rican Electricity Institute) on recommendation of IMF, provoking unprecedented protests. Supreme court rules move unconstitutional, limiting further neoliberal reforms
2000	Rodríguez and his Nicaraguan counterpart resolve longstanding border dispute
2002	Abel Pacheco able to maintain PUSC hold on power by distancing himself from predecessor's neoliberal agenda. New third party, PAC, emerges
2003	Energy and telecommunications workers strike over Pacheco's privatisation plans and teachers strike over salary delays, prompting three ministers to resign
2004	Corruption allegations against former presidents that lead to arrest of Rodríguez – forcing him to resign as head of the OAS – and of Calderón
2006	After one of the closest results in Costa Rica's history, a recount, as well as legal challenges, Oscar Arias regains presidency for PLN when leftwing rival Ottón Solís of PAC concedes defeat
2006	Public workers strike in protest at proposed free-trade deal with the US
2007	Voters narrowly decide in referendum in favour of ratifying DR-CAFTA. Costa Rica becomes non-permanent member of UN Security Council
2009	Arias mediates in Honduran political crisis but is unable to broker agreement. He says Costa Rica will re-establish diplomatic relations with Cuba, 48 years after they were severed in 1961
2010	Laura Chinchilla of the PLN is elected Costa Rica's first woman president

Factbox: Costa Rica

Presidential democratic republic of seven provinces.

Suffrage: Universal for those aged 18 or over, and compulsory.

Executive: President and two vice-presidents elected on the same ticket directly by the people for four-year terms.

Legislature: Unicameral Asamblea Legislativa (Legislative Assembly) of 57 members who are elected by proportional representation for four-year terms.

Cantons: The seven provinces are subdivided into 81 cantons which have municipalities whose mayors and representatives are directly elected.

Useful websites

www.casapres.go.cr **Presidency**
www.asamblea.go.cr **Legislative Assembly**

Panama

1977	US agrees with Panamanian dictator General Omar Torrijos Herrera to transfer canal to Panama from 2000. US control of the 10-mile wide Panama Canal Zone has been the dominant theme in country's political development for most of the twentieth century
1981	Torrijos dies in a plane crash
1983	Former intelligence chief and CIA informant General Manuel Noriega becomes head of National Guard, which he renames Fuerzas de Defensa de Panamá. He greatly increases their power over political and economic life
1988	US charges Noriega with drug smuggling. He declares state of emergency in wake of failed coup
1989	Noriega annuls results of elections won by Guillermo Endara, a consensus candidate heading opposition alliance, ADOC. Noriega declares 'state of war' in face of US threats. US invades Panama, capturing Noriega, and taking him to Miami, where he is jailed. Noriega is replaced by Endara, ending 20 years of military control
1991	Parliament approves constitutional reforms. Privatisation begins
1994	Ernesto Pérez Balladares of the APU coalition dominated by PRD wins presidential elections and seeks rapprochement with the US, abolishing Panama's armed forces and pursuing neoliberal reforms
1999	Mireya Moscoso Rodríguez de Arias of rightwing Partido Arnulfista becomes Panama's first woman president. She oversees transfer of control of 50-mile canal to her country but her administration becomes mired in corruption allegations
2000	Moscoso announces creation of panel to investigate crimes committed while military governments in power from 1968–89
2002	Moscoso sets up commission to investigate corruption after protests against alleged graft
2003	Strike over management of social security fund paralyses public services and provokes violent clashes
2004	PRD's centre-left Martín Erasto Torrijos Espino, son of the former dictator, wins elections. Torrijos announces plans to widen canal in $5.3 billion expansion project, proposes laws to make government more transparent, and takes steps to confront corruption
2005	Plans to increase pension contributions and raise retirement age spark protests and strikes
2006	Voters in referendum back plan to upgrade Panama canal. Panama and US agree on a free-trade deal
2008	Russian warship sails through Panama canal for the first time since Second World War. Noriega released from prison after serving 17-year sentence
2009	US federal appeals court says Noriega can be extradited to France. Ricardo Martinelli of conservative Cambio Democrático coalition wins presidential elections

Factbox: Panama

Presidential democratic republic with nine provinces, three provincial-level indigenous regions, and two municipal-level indigenous areas.

Suffrage: Universal for those aged 18 or over, and compulsory.

Executive: President and vice-president elected on the same ticket directly by the people for five-year terms.

Legislature: Unicameral Asamblea Nacional (National Assembly) has 71 members who are elected for five-year terms in single- and multi-seat constituencies by plurality or proportional representation.

Provinces: Provincial governors are appointed by the president. There are 65 municipal authorities whose mayors and council members are directly elected.

Useful websites

www.presidencia.gob.pa **Presidency**
www.asamblea.gob.pa **National Assembly**

Cuba

1985–91	*Perestroika* and *glasnost* in Soviet Union deal blow to Cuban revolutionary model
1989–91	Downfall of communism in Eastern bloc and Soviet Union ends economic aid to Cuba
1993	US tightens embargo on Cuba, which introduces limited market reforms
1994	US agrees to admit 20,000 Cubans a year if Cuba halts exodus of refugees
1996	US trade embargo made permanent
1998	Pope John Paul II visits Cuba. US eases restrictions on money transfers to Cuba
2000	US House of Representatives approves sale of food and medicines to Cuba
2002	Captives from Afghanistan flown to US Guantánamo Bay base. UN Human Rights Commission criticizes Cuba's record. US Under Secretary of State John Bolton claims Cuba trying to develop biological weapons. Former US president, Jimmy Carter, makes goodwill visit in response. Cuban Asamblea Nacional amends constitution to make socialist system of government permanent
2003	Crackdown on dissidents provokes international criticism. EU halts high-level official visits to Cuba in protest
2004	US sanctions restrict US–Cuba family visits and remittances from expatriates. Cuba bans transactions in US dollars and taxes dollar-peso exchange conversions. Cuba and Venezuela initiate leftwing Bolivarian Alternative for the Americas (ALBA)
2005	Havana resumes diplomatic contacts with EU. Dissidents hold rare public meeting in Havana. Castro and Venezuela sign 49 economic agreements
2006	Castro undergoes surgery and temporarily hands control to brother Raúl
2008	Raúl Castro takes over as president. Ban on private ownership of mobile phones and computers lifted. Plans announced to abandon salary equality. Restrictions on land available to private farmers relaxed. State oil company says estimated 20bn barrels in offshore fields. Russia signs trade and economic accords and its warships visit Havana. Chinese president, Hu Jintao, visits to sign trade and investment accords
2009	First cabinet reshuffle since Raúl Castro took over. US congress votes to lift Bush administration restrictions on Cuban-Americans visiting Cuba and sending money to it. OAS votes to lift ban on Cuban membership imposed in 1962. Raúl Castro accuses Obama administration of trying to undermine his government

Factbox: Cuba

Presidential single-party republic with 14 provinces and one special municipality.

Suffrage: Universal for those aged 16 or over.

Executive: President of the Consejo de Estado and Consejo de Ministros (Council of State and Council of Ministers), which together comprise the executive, and several vice-presidents are elected by the Asamblea Nacional del Poder Popular (National Assembly of People's Power) every five years.

Legislature: Unicameral Asamblea Nacional del Poder Popular (National Assembly of People's Power) of 614 members elected for five-year terms in a popular vote from lists approved by special commissions. The Partido Comunista de Cuba (PCC, Cuban Communist Party) is the only legal political party and there is no formal campaigning during elections, but the party is proscribed from playing a role in nominating candidates.

Municipalities and Comités de Defensa de la Revolución (CDR): Delegates to provincial and municipal assemblies are elected in a similar way to those of the legislature. The CDRs (Committees for the Defence of the Revolution) were established in 1960 as a self-defence initiative but thereafter began carrying out social and community activities. With about 7 million members, these neighbourhood committees comprising ordinary people have evolved into the political system's largest mass organisation and a key element of governance.

Useful websites

www.cubagob.cu **Government portal**
www.parlamentocubano.cu **National Assembly**

Dominican Republic

1966	Conservative former acting president Joaquín Antonio Balaguer Ricardo, a veteran aide and protégé of the former dictator Rafael Leonidas Trujillo, who was assassinated in 1961, wins presidential elections and begins a period of 12 years in office
1978	In a reaction against Balaguer's decision to stand for a fourth term, voters elect Silvestre Antonio Guzmán Fernández, a moderate within the leftwing PRD. Guzmán proceeds to release about 200 political prisoners, ease media censorship and purge the armed forces of Balaguer supporters
1979	Hurricanes leave more than 200,000 people homeless
1982	Mired in corruption allegations, Guzmán commits suicide in 1982 and his successor, Salvador Jorge Blanco of the PRD, pursues economic austerity measures
1985	IMF-prescribed austerity measures provoke widespread riots
1986	Balaguer re-elected president and restores growth, but policies fuel inflation, causing strikes and protests
1988	Blanco tried in absentia and found guilty of corruption during presidential term
1990	Balaguer re-elected, and again able to restore growth
1994	Balaguer re-elected but, following allegations of massive electoral fraud, the veteran leader, by now 87, agrees to serve term of only two years. His PRSC agrees with PRD and centre-left PLD to a Pact for Democracy outlining political reforms and accepting new elections in late 1995 in which he will not stand
1996	Leonel Fernández Reyna of PLD elected president but pursues neoliberal reforms that provoke unrest
2000	Rafael Hipólito Mejía Domínguez of PRD wins presidential elections with promises of social reform
2001	Appeals court quashes conviction of former president Blanco for corruption
2003	Major scandal triggered by collapse of Banco Internacional (BANINTER). Investigators point to evidence of a massive fraud and allege that bank's most senior official had distributed millions of dollars to politicians, government officials and military officers. Economic crisis sparks violent protests
2004	Desire to reclaim stability under Fernández allows former president to win elections with promise to restore confidence
2005	Congress approves DR-CAFTA free-trade agreement with US and Central American states
2008	Fernández re-elected president

Factbox: Dominican Republic

Presidential democratic republic with 31 provinces and one district.

Suffrage: Universal for those aged 18 years or over and compulsory, although members of the armed forces and national police cannot vote.

Executive: President and vice-president elected on the same ticket directly by the people for four-year terms (majority runoff).

Legislature: Bicameral Congreso Nacional (National Congress). The lower Cámara de Diputados (Chamber of Deputies) has 178 members who are elected by proportional representation for a four-year term. The upper Senado (Senate) has 32 members who are elected by plurality for a four-year term.

Provinces: The governors of the provinces are appointed by the president. The provinces are sub-divided into 154 municipalities and 202 municipal districts whose mayors and councils are directly elected.

Useful websites

www.presidencia.gob.dov **Presidency**
www.senado.gov.do/PortalSILSenado **Senate**
www.camaradediputados.gov.do/portalsilcamara **Chamber of Deputies**

Puerto Rico

1946–48	US grants partial self-government enabling Puerto Ricans to elect governor. Luis Muñoz Marín of PPD becomes first democratically elected governor
1950–52	President Truman signs Commonwealth Bill paving way for Puerto Rican constitution. Nationalists oppose law and attempt to assassinate Truman, but Puerto Ricans vote in favour of commonwealth status in referendum. Constitution establishes commonwealth with internal autonomy
1954	Nationalists open fire in the US House of Representatives, injuring congressmen
1967	In a referendum on political status, 60 per cent of Puerto Rican voters back continued commonwealth status
1993	Nearly 49 per cent of voters back continued commonwealth status
1999	US practice fire kills security guard on Vieques island where there is a US navy bombing range, provoking large protests
2000	Sila Calderón of the PPD is elected to become Puerto Rico's first female governor
2001	President George W. Bush agrees to halt use of Vieques bombing range
2004	Aníbal Acevedo Vilá of PPD confirmed as governor after two months of legal disputes over a tiny margin of victory in elections
2005	Voters in a referendum support the idea of replacing Puerto Rico's senate and Cámara de Representantes with a unicameral legislature. Fugitive nationalist leader Filiberto Ojeda Rios killed by US agents in an incident that causes anger on the island
2006	US supreme court rejects move aimed at giving Puerto Ricans right to vote in presidential elections. Economic problems related to budget shortfall result in closure of schools and government offices, and provoke large protests. Sales tax adopted in an effort to address budget deficits. Latin American and Caribbean Congress in Solidarity with the Independence of Puerto Rico approves 'Panama Proclamation' calling on the US to respect Puerto Rico's right to self-determination
2008	Acevedo Vilá denies corruption charges linked to alleged election funding irregularities. He calls on UN to back Puerto Rico's right to self-determination. Luis Fortuño of pro-statehood PNP wins gubernatorial elections
2009	Fortuño announces major programme of public spending cuts. Thousands of workers protest in San Juan over planned layoffs. UN Special Committee on Decolonisation approves draft resolution calling on US to expedite process clarifying Puerto Rico's status

Factbox: Puerto Rico

Unincorporated territory of US with commonwealth status of 78 municipalities.

Suffrage: Universal for those aged 18 years or over, residents are US citizens but do not vote in US presidential elections.

Executive: Governor elected directly by the people for a four-year term; (head of state is the president of the US).

Legislature: Bicameral legislative assembly. The lower chamber, the Cámara de Representantes (House of Representatives) has 51 members who are elected directly (40 in constituencies and 11 by proportional representation) to serve four-year terms. The upper chamber, the Senado (Senate), has at least 27 members who are directly elected for four-year terms. Voters also elect a resident commissioner for a four-year term as a non-voting representative in the US House of Representatives.

Useful websites

www.fortaleza.gobierno.pr **Office of the Governor of Puerto Rico**
www.camaraderepresentantes.org **House of Representatives of Puerto Rico**
www.senadopr.us/Pages/default.aspx **Senate of Puerto Rico**
www.gobierno.pr/gprportal/inicio **Government portal**

Haiti

1971	Dictator François 'Papa Doc' Duvalier dies. Succeeded by son, Jean-Claude, 'Baby Doc'
1986	Baby Doc flees Haiti and Lieutenant-General Henri Namphy takes over
1988	Leslie Manigat elected president but ousted by Namphy, who is deposed by General Prosper Avril
1990	Protests force Avril into exile. Ertha Pascal-Trouillot leads country to elections won by Jean-Bertrand Aristide of Front National pour le Changement et la Démocratie coalition
1991	Aristide flees coup by Brigadier-General Raoul Cedras, triggering US and OAS sanctions
1993	UN imposes sanctions
1994	Facing US invasion, military regime relinquishes power. US forces oversee transition to civilian administration and Aristide returns
1995	UN peacekeepers start to replace US forces. Supporters of Aristide win parliamentary elections. René Préval of Organisation de Peuple en Lutte elected president
1996	Préval tries to introduce neoliberal reforms but is hampered by deadlock in parliament
1999	Préval dissolves parliament and begins ruling by decree
2000	Aristide returns to presidency at head of electoral vehicle called Fanmi Lavalas following elections boycotted by opposition groups and criticised by international observers
2001	Questions about Aristide's legitimacy contribute to coup attempts and protests
2004	Protests grow into full-scale rebellion against Aristide amid celebrations marking 200 years of independence as rebels seize towns and cities. Aristide loses support of US and France and leaves Haiti. Interim government under Boniface Alexandre takes over with support of UN stabilisation force led by Brazil. Growing political and gang violence, much of it by Aristide supporters. Polls scheduled for November 2005 postponed several times
2006	First elections since Aristide overthrown are inconclusive and marred by irregularities and violent clashes. Préval declared winner of presidential vote after deal over spoiled ballots. Government formed under Prime Minister Jacques-Edouard Alexis
2007	UN troops launch operations against gangs in lawless Cite Soleil shantytown
2008	Government introduces emergency cut in price of rice to halt food riots. Alexis dismissed by parliament. US and World Bank pledge extra food aid. Brazil strengthens peacekeeping force. Michèle Pierre-Louis appointed prime minister
2009	UN appoints the former US president, Bill Clinton, as special envoy to Haiti. World Bank and IMF cancel 80 per cent of Haiti's debt. Senate censures Pierre-Louis over economic stagnation and Jean-Max Bellerive is appointed prime minister
2010	Catastrophic earthquake leaving up to 300,000 dead compounds Haiti's many problems

Factbox: Haiti

Semi-presidential democratic republic of 10 departments.

Suffrage: Universal for those aged 18 or over.

Executive: President elected directly by the people for a five-year term. Prime minister is appointed by the president, ratified by the National Assembly, and selects cabinet in consultation with president.

Legislature: Bicameral Assemblée Nationale (National Assembly). The lower chamber, the Chambre des Députés (Chamber of Deputies), has 99 members elected directly for a four-year term. The upper chamber, the Sénat (Senate), has 30 members elected (one-third every two years) directly for six-year terms.

Departments: Departmental prefects are appointed by the central government. The departments are subdivided into 41 arrondissements and 133 communes (municipalities) whose mayors are directly elected.

Useful websites

www.haiti.org **Haiti's embassy in Washington**
www.lesenat.parlementhaitien.ht **Senate**
www.chambredesdeputes.parlementhaitien.ht **Chamber of Deputies**

South America

Venezuela

1989	Carlos Andrés Pérez of Acción Democrática elected president and launches austerity programme, generating violent unrest
1992	Colonel Hugo Chávez leads coup attempt
1993–95	Pérez impeached for corruption and Rafael Caldera of COPEI elected president
1996	Pérez jailed for corruption
1998	Election of Chávez as president reflects breakdown of party politics
2000	Chávez wins another term with mandate to pursue reform
2001	Chávez enacts land and oil reforms with powers that do not require congressional approval
2002	Chávez appoints new board to state oil monopoly PDVSA. Unions and Fedecámaras business chamber strike, and rallies lead to clashes. Military chiefs detain Chávez and name Pedro Carmona head of transitional government, but this collapses and Chávez returns to office. Strike led by opposition brings oil industry to standstill
2003	OAS brokers deal establishing framework for referendum on Chávez's rule. Opposition delivers large petitions demanding referendum
2004	Violent clashes between opponents and supporters of Chávez, who later wins recall referendum on serving out remaining two and a half years of term. Venezuela and Cuba initiate leftwing Bolivarian Alternative for the Americas (ALBA)
2005	Chávez signs land reform decree to eliminate large estates. Capture of FARC leader on Venezuelan soil sparks dispute with Colombia. Venezuela agrees to supply Caribbean states with cheap oil. Legislative elections see Chávez gains, but boycotted by opposition
2006	Chávez agrees $3 billion arms deal with Russia. He is elected to a third presidential term with 63 per cent of the vote
2007	Energy and telecommunications companies nationalised, large farms seized for redistribution and Orinoco oil projects taken over. Legislature allows Chávez to rule by decree for 18 months. Voters in referendum reject plans to extend Chávez's powers
2008	Colombian raid into Ecuador causes diplomatic crisis, and Chávez mobilises troops. Nationalisation of Spanish-owned Bank of Venezuela, household fuel distributors and petrol stations. Russian warplanes and warships visit Venezuela. US ambassador to Venezuela expelled in solidarity with similar decision by Bolivia. US reciprocates. Opposition makes gains in local elections and Caracas mayoralty
2009	Voters in a referendum back plans to abolish term limits for elected officials, a move that will allow Chávez to stand again in 2012. Relations with Colombia deteriorate over move to allow US troops to use its military bases. Tensions grow after Bogotá accuses Venezuela of supplying arms to FARC. Chávez orders 15,000 troops to border, citing violence by Colombian paramilitaries

Factbox: Venezuela

Federal democratic presidential republic of 23 states, one federal district (and one federal dependency comprising 72 islands).

Suffrage: Universal for those aged 18 or over.

Executive: President elected directly by the people for a six-year term.

Legislature: Unicameral Asamblea Nacional (National Assembly) of 167 members elected for five-year terms through a mixture of direct elections in constituencies and proportional representation. Several seats are reserved for indigenous groups.

States: State governors, legislators and the mayors and aldermen of 335 municipalities are directly elected.

Useful websites

www.presidencia.gob.ve **Presidency**
www.asambleanacional.gob.ve **National Assembly**

Colombia

1978	President Julio Turbay of Partido Liberal launches fight against drug-trafficking cartels
1982	President Belisario Betancur of Partido Conservador grants amnesty to guerrillas
1985	M-19 guerrillas attack Palace of Justice. Leftwing Patriotic Union party founded
1986	Liberal Virgilio Barco Vargas wins presidential elections. Rightwing paramilitaries begin murdering UP candidates
1989	M-19 reaches political agreement with government and becomes legal party
1993	Pablo Escobar, notorious leader of the Medellín drug cartel, killed
1995	Liberal Ernesto Samper elected president but accused of benefiting from drug money
1998	Conservative Andrés Pastrana Arango elected president and begins peace talks with guerrillas. Grants main guerrilla army, FARC, safe haven off-limits to national army
2000	Plan Colombia wins $1 billion in mainly military aid from US, nominally as part of counter-narcotics strategy. Peace talks with FARC break down
2001	Talks resume and FARC signs accord on negotiating ceasefire
2002	Pastrana breaks off talks with FARC, which steps up attacks. Independent Alvaro Uribe of Primero Colombia coalition wins presidential election promising crackdown on rebels. Before inauguration, FARC explosions hit Bogotá. Uribe declares state of emergency
2003	Voters reject Uribe's proposed austerity measures and political reforms in referendum. Paramilitaries of United Self-Defence Forces of Colombia (AUC) begin to disarm
2004	AUC and government begin peace talks
2005	Capture of FARC leader on Venezuelan soil provokes dispute with Venezuela. Exploratory talks with ELN begin in Cuba. Constitutional court rules Uribe can stand for re-election
2006	Colombia and US agree free-trade deal. Uribe supporters win legislative elections and he wins second term. Court investigates possible ties between politicians and paramilitaries
2007	Ecuador asks OAS for help over Colombia's coca crop-spraying programme. Large protests in Bogotá against conflict. Venezuela's president, Hugo Chávez, tries to broker FARC hostage release, then withdraws ambassador to Colombia in a dispute over role
2008	FARC releases hostages as a result of Chávez's mediation. Uribe rejects call by Chávez to stop treating rebels as terrorists. Colombian raid in Ecuador sparks diplomatic crisis. US hails move by Colombia to extradite paramilitary chiefs for drug trafficking. Colombia renews low-level diplomatic relations with Ecuador and Uribe visits Venezuela for talks
2009	FARC frees high-profile hostages. Uribe offers FARC talks. Relations with Venezuela deteriorate over plans allowing US to use Colombian bases. Uribe accuses Caracas of supplying arms to FARC, and Chávez accuses Colombia of military incursion

Factbox: Colombia

Presidential democratic republic of 32 departments and one capital district.

Suffrage: Universal for those aged 18 or over.

Executive: President and vice-president elected directly by the people for four-year terms (majority runoff).

Legislature: Bicameral Congreso (Congress). The lower chamber, the Cámara de Representantes (Chamber of Representatives), has 166 members elected by proportional representation for four-year terms. The upper chamber, the Senado (Senate), has 102 members elected by proportional representation for four-year terms. Indigenous peoples are allotted two Senate seats.

Departments: Departmental governors and legislative assemblies, and the mayors and councillors of 1,119 municipalities that the departments are subdivided into, are directly elected.

Useful websites

web.presidencia.gov.co **Presidency**
www.camara.gov.co **Chamber of Representatives**
www.senado.gov.co **Senate**

Ecuador

1979	Jaime Roldós Aguilera of Concentración de Fuerzas Populares becomes first civilian president following military rule
1981	Brief border war with Peru. Roldós dies in a plane crash and is replaced by vice-president, Osvaldo Hurtado
1984	Conservative León Febres Cordero of Partido Social Cristiano becomes president
1987	Febres Cordero kidnapped and beaten by army angry at privatisation and spending cuts
1988	Social democrat Rodrigo Borja Cevallos of Izquierda Democrática becomes president
1990	Indigenous organisations stage nationwide protests against austerity policies
1992	Sixto Alfonso Durán-Ballén of centre-right Partido de Unidad Republicana becomes president but neoliberal reforms alienate unions and indigenous groups
1996	Businessman Abdalá Jaime Bucaram Ortíz of populist Partido Roldosista Ecuatoriano elected president, but neoliberal reforms spark protests
1997	Bucaram deposed by congress for 'mental incapacity'
1998	Jamil Mahuad of centrist Democracia Popular-Unión Demócrata Cristiana elected president. Resistance to neoliberal policies persists
2000	Mahuad's decision to use US dollar as national currency provokes uprising under Colonel Lucio Edwin Gutiérrez, and he is forced from office by army and indigenous protesters. Vice-president, Gustavo Noboa, takes over
2002	Gutiérrez wins elections at head of newly created Partido Sociedad Patriótica 21 de Enero in alliance with indigenous and Marxist groups
2003	Noboa faces corruption charges and goes into exile
2004	Congress dismisses supreme court, which Gutiérrez accuses of supporting opposition
2005	Supreme court drops corruption charges against two former presidents, sparking protests. Congress replaces Gutiérrez with vice-president, Alfredo Palacio
2006	Protests over proposed free-trade deal with US. Ecuador cancels contract of US oil firm Occidental. Rafael Correa of left-of-centre Alianza PAIS wins presidential elections
2007	Ecuador seeks OAS help over Colombia's coca crop-spraying programme. Voters in a referendum support Correa's plan to rewrite constitution. Alianza PAIS wins majority on constituent assembly, which dissolves congress
2008	Colombian strike into Ecuador sparks diplomatic crisis. Correa wins 64 per cent of votes in referendum to increase powers. He pledges to default on foreign debts
2009	Ecuador expels two US diplomats, accusing them of interfering in police anti-narcotics appointments. Alianza PAIS dominates after legislative elections inaugurate new National Assembly. Correa wins second term. Government refuses to extend US military lease of Pacific air base. Ecuador joins leftwing Bolivarian Alternative for the Americas (ALBA)

Factbox: Ecuador

Presidential democratic republic of 24 provinces.

Suffrage: Universal for those aged 18 years or over, compulsory for the literate.

Executive: President and vice-president elected on the same ticket directly by the people for four-year terms.

Legislature: Unicameral Asamblea Nacional (National Assembly) has 124 members elected by proportional representation for four-year terms.

Provinces: Provincial governors are appointed by the president, provincial councillors are directly elected. The provinces are subdivided into 226 cantons (municipalities) whose mayors and councillors are directly elected.

Useful websites

www.presidencia.gov.ec **Presidency**
www.asambleanacional.gov.ec **National Assembly**

Peru

1980	After years of military control, civilian rule restored under Fernando Belaúnde Terry of centre-right Acción Popular. Sendero Luminoso launches guerrilla war
1981	Brief border war with Ecuador
1982	Deaths and disappearances escalate following army crackdown
1985	Alan García of APRA wins presidential elections and starts to reduce military influence
1987	Writer Mario Vargas Llosa leads movement against plans to nationalise banks
1988	Peru seeks IMF help over economy. Guerrilla campaign intensifies
1990	Political murders escalate. Centre-right outsider Alberto Fujimori elected president and launches austerity and privatisation programmes
1992	Fujimori assumes emergency powers. Shining Path leader captured
1993	New constitution passed allowing Fujimori to seek re-election
1994	About 6,000 Shining Path guerrillas surrender
1995	Fujimori re-elected
1996	Tupac Amaru guerrillas seize hostages at residence of Japanese ambassador
1997	Peruvian forces free hostages
2000	Vladimiro Montesinos, Fujimori's intelligence chief, causes scandal over bribery of opposition politicians. Human rights office estimates 4,000 'disappearances' since 1980 in civil war. Fujimori resigns while in Japan, but congress rejects this and impeaches him
2001	Judge orders Fujimori to face charges of dereliction of duty. Centre-left Alejandro Toledo of Perú Posible coalition wins presidential elections. Montesinos, now a fugitive, captured in Venezuela. International arrest warrant issued for Fujimori
2002	Truth and Reconciliation Commission begins hearings into civil war atrocities. Protests delay privatisation of power companies. Montesinos jailed for corruption
2003	Truth and Reconciliation Commission estimates 69,280 people died in civil war
2005	Uprising by nationalist army reservists in south. Congressional commission finds Toledo guilty of electoral fraud, but congress votes not to impeach him. Fujimori arrested in Chile. Peru and US agree free-trade deal. Shining Path guerrillas kill eight police officers
2006	García of APRA (now known as the Partido Aprista Peruano) wins presidential elections
2007	Congress grants García emergency powers to tackle drug-trafficking. Chile extradites Fujimori to face trial for murder
2008	Cabinet resigns after APRA embroiled in corruption scandal
2009	Fujimori sentenced to 25 years in jail for ordering killings and kidnappings. Scores die in Amazon in clashes between security forces and indigenous people over laws opening resources on their lands to foreign oil companies. Prime minister Yehude Simon quits after brokering talks that result in repeal of new land laws. Unions and opposition groups protest against free-trade policies. Chilean military exercise and spying scandal strain ties

Factbox: Peru

Presidential democratic republic of 25 regions.

Suffrage: Universal for those aged 18 or over, and compulsory until the age of 70.

Executive: President elected directly by the people for a five-year term (majority runoff).

Legislature: Unicameral Congreso de la República (Congress of the Republic) has 120 members elected by proportional representation for a five-year term.

Regions: Each of the 25 regions has a president, vice-president and a regional council, all of whom are directly elected. The regions are subdivided into 195 provinces and these are further sub-divided into 1,833 districts (municipalities), each with a directly-elected municipal mayor and council.

Useful websites

www.presidencia.gob.pe **Presidency**
www.congreso.gob.pe **Congress**

Bolivia

1982	Military leader General Celso Torrelio resigns amid economic crisis. Junta transfers power to civilian government led by left-of-centre MNR veteran Hernán Siles
1985	Siles resigns after general strike and coup attempt. Inconclusive elections result in congress choosing Víctor Paz Estenssoro of MNR as president. Paz Estenssoro begins radical neoliberal reforms with support of former dictator Hugo Banzer
1989	Social-democrat Jaime Paz Zamora of Movimiento de la Izquierda Revolucionaria-Nueva Mayoría becomes president with support of Banzer and continues reforms
1993	Banzer withdraws from presidential race; Gonzalo Sánchez de Lozada of MNR wins
1997	Banzer wins elections at the head of a fragile coalition to become first former Latin American dictator to return to presidency through ballot box
2000	Banzer hails comprehensive eradication of coca plant in Chapare region
2001	Vice-president, Jorge Quiroga, replaces Banzer, who is suffering from cancer
2002	Banzer dies. Sánchez de Lozada wins runoff in congress and becomes president
2003	Violent protests over tax plans and government proposals to export gas via Chile. Sánchez de Lozada resigns and is succeeded by independent Carlos Mesa
2004	Gas export deal with Argentina sparks more protests. Voters in referendum back greater state involvement in gas industry. Deal signed to allow Bolivia to export gas through a Peruvian port
2005	Rising fuel prices trigger anti-government protests in El Alto and Santa Cruz. Santa Cruz civic and business leaders demand autonomy. Congress rejects Mesa's resignation offer. Protests grow and Mesa promises new constitution and referendum on autonomy. Mesa resigns and indigenous Evo Morales of the Movimiento al Socialismo wins elections
2006	Morales takes energy industry into state control. He claims victory in elections for a constituent assembly to write new constitution. Reform bill to expropriate and redistribute land approved. Bolivia joins leftwing Bolivarian Alternative for the Americas (ALBA)
2008	Morales gains 67 per cent support in referendum on his leadership. Anti-government protests in east and north of Bolivia. Morales expels US ambassador, accusing him of encouraging unrest. US reciprocates. Congress approves new constitution. Morales suspends operations of US Drug Enforcement Administration in Bolivia
2009	New constitution approved giving indigenous majority greater rights and prospect of local autonomy. State prosecutor accuses Santa Cruz governor of involvement in alleged plot to assassinate Morales. Sánchez de Lozada and 16 members of his cabinet go on trial over deaths during 2003 El Alto protests. Morales re-elected president with 60 per cent of vote

Factbox: Bolivia

Presidential democratic republic with nine departments.

Suffrage: Universal and compulsory for those aged 18 or over if married or 21 if single.

Executive: President and vice-president elected on the same ticket directly by the people for five-year terms (indirect majority runoff).

Legislature: Bicameral Congreso Nacional (National Congress). The lower Camara de Diputados (Chamber of Deputies) has 130 members elected through a mixture of a vote in constituencies and proportional representation for five-year terms. The upper Camara de Senadores (Senate) has 27 members elected by plurality with minority representation for five-year terms.

Departments: Departmental governors (prefects) are directly elected. In 2008, four eastern departments – Santa Cruz, Beni, Pando and Tarija – declared autonomy from central government, although the move had no clear basis in law. The departments are further subdivided into provinces and 320 municipalities, whose mayors and councils are directly elected. Provisions providing for greater municipal autonomy under the 2009 constitution are being enacted.

Useful websites

www.presidencia.gov.bo **Presidency**
www.congreso.gov.bo **National Congress**

Brazil

1985	Tancredo Neves chosen by electoral college to be first civilian president for 21 years but falls ill and José Sarney of Partido do Movimento Democrático Brasileiro takes office
1988	A new constitution limits the powers of the presidency
1989	An outsider, Fernando Collor de Mello, becomes first directly-elected president since 1960 and introduces radical economic reforms, but these fail to curb inflation
1992	Collor resigns amid corruption allegations and replaced by vice-president, Itamar Franco
1994	Franco's finance minister, Fernando Henrique Cardoso, of Partido da Social Democracia Brasileira, elected president after success against inflation. Redistributes land
1997	Amended constitution allows president to run for re-election
1998	Cardoso is re-elected. Brazil receives IMF rescue package
2001	Government comes under pressure to amend ambitious development plans in Amazon basin
2002	Financial markets unsettled at prospect of electoral victory by leftwing Luiz Inácio Lula da Silva of Partido dos Trabalhadores (PT). Lula wins presidential elections to form first leftwing government for 40 years, and promises to end hunger
2004	Spate of land invasions. Brazil leads UN stabilisation force in Haiti, and applies for permanent seat on UN Security Council
2005	Murder of Amazon campaigner Dorothy Stang focuses international attention on Brazilian policy in region. Ruling PT shaken by corruption allegations and subsequent resignations. Death squad kills 30 people on outskirts of Rio de Janeiro. Voters in a referendum reject plans to ban sale of firearms
2006	Lula re-elected
2007	Government recognises human rights abuses carried out under military regime. Speaker of senate and a Lula ally quits amid corruption scandal
2008	Environment minister, Marina Silva, resigns in dispute with government colleagues over Amazon development. Brazil turns down invitation to join international oil cartel OPEC
2009	Brazil offers IMF $10 billion to help improve access to credit in developing countries. Government pledges to set up truth commission to investigate past military abuses. Rio de Janeiro and São Paulo hit by power blackouts. Brazil and France agree common position on global warming

Factbox: Brazil

Federal presidential democratic republic of 26 states and a federal district.

Suffrage: Universal (excluding military conscripts) for those over 18, and compulsory (voluntary for those between 16 and 18 and over 70).

Executive: President and vice-president elected on the same ticket directly by the people for four-year terms (majority runoff).

Legislature: Bicameral Congresso Nacional (National Congress). The lower Câmara dos Deputados (Chamber of Deputies) has 513 members elected by proportional representation for four-year terms. The Senado Federal (Federal Senate) has 81 members elected by plurality for an eight-year term (one-third and two-thirds elected alternately every four years).

States: State governors and legislators are directly elected. The states are subdivided into 5,564 municipalities, whose mayors and councils are directly elected.

Useful websites

www.presidencia.gov.br **Presidency**
www2.camara.gov.br **Chamber of Deputies**
www.senado.gov.br/sf **Federal Senate**

Paraguay

1989	General Andrés Rodríguez deposes Gen Alfredo Stroessner to become president and oversees elections for constituent assembly that redrafts constitution
1992	New democratic constitution
1993	Juan Carlos Wasmosy of centre-right Asociación Nacional Republicana-Partido Colorado wins first free presidential elections. Wasmosy becomes unpopular by appointing veteran Stroessner supporters to government posts
1996	Relations between Colorados and army chief General Lino Oviedo worsen, and Oviedo allegedly threatens coup
1998	Oviedo creates Colorado faction and leads in polls prior to presidential elections, but is sentenced to jail for 1996 threats. His running mate Raúl Cubas is elected president amid allegations of electoral fraud, and immediately frees Oviedo
1999	Congress begins process to remove Cubas, making vice-president, Luis María Argaña, likely leader. Argaña is assassinated, Cubas resigns and Oviedo goes into exile. Luis González Macchi appointed caretaker president, but relations with Oviedo supporters remain tense
2000	Government blames coup attempt on forces loyal to exiled Oviedo
2002	Violent protests seek González Macchi's resignation and changes to free-market policies. Congress supports impeachment proceedings against González Macchi, but he survives the bid to remove him
2003	Populistic Nicanor Duarte Frutos of a more statist Colorado faction wins presidential elections and pursues policies to the left of his predecessors. González Macchi goes on trial facing corruption charges
2004	Peasants stage land invasions. Oviedo returns from exile in Brazil and is arrested
2005	Rising crime. Lower chamber rejects plans to privatise utilities
2006	González Macchi jailed for embezzlement. Stroessner dies in exile
2008	A former bishop, Fernando Lugo of the centre-left Alianza Patriótica por el Cambio coalition, wins presidential elections. Lugo accuses Duarte and Oviedo of a conspiracy against his government
2009	Claims that Lugo fathered children while a bishop damage his image. Paraguay reaches a deal with Brazil to end an energy dispute. Lugo sacks armed forces chiefs after alleging that officers were plotting a coup

Factbox: Paraguay

Presidential democratic republic of 17 departments and the capital.

Suffrage: Universal for those aged 18 or over and compulsory until 75.

Executive: President and vice-president elected on the same ticket directly by the people for five-year terms.

Legislature: Bicameral Congreso Nacional (National Congress). The lower Cámara de Diputados (Chamber of Deputies) has 80 members elected by proportional representation for five-year terms. The upper Cámara de Senadores (Senate) has 45 members elected by proportional representation for five-year terms.

Departments: Departmental governors and councils are directly elected, but have limited powers. The departments are subdivided into 235 municipalities, whose mayors and councils are directly elected.

Useful websites

www.presidencia.gov.py **Presidency**
www.diputados.gov.py **Chamber of Deputies**
www.senado.gov.py **Senate**

Chile

1988	Opposition parties led by the Partido Demócrata Cristiano unite as the Concertación to defeat dictator Gen Augusto Pinochet in referendum on him remaining in power
1989	Patricio Aylwin of the PDC wins presidential elections for the Concertación. Although his achievements are limited, he establishes the basis for stability and reconciliation
1990	Pinochet steps down as head of state but remains army commander-in-chief
1993	Eduardo Frei, also of the PDC, wins elections, again for the Concertación coalition
1994	Frei succeeds Aylwin as president and begins moderate economic and social reforms that make concrete progress in reviving democratic institutions and improving conditions for the poor
1997	The strength demonstrated by rightwing parties loyal to Pinochet in legislative elections illustrate difficulties of efforts to reduce influence of military in politics
1998	Pinochet is made a senator for life, but is arrested in the UK on murder charges
2000	UK decides Pinochet not fit to be extradited and he returns to Chile. Decision to release him alleviates rightwing pressure on Frei administration, and strengthens conviction within Chile that judicial proceedings against the former dictator are inevitable. The socialist, Ricardo Lagos of the Concertación, is elected president and lays basis for recovery
2002	Pinochet resigns as a senator for life
2004	Law gives Chileans the right to divorce. Former head of secret police jailed over the death of a journalist in 1974. Supreme court strips Pinochet of legal immunity over murder allegations from the 1970s and he is placed under house arrest on human rights charges
2005	Senate approves changes to the constitution and restores president's right to dismiss military chiefs. Pinochet is temporarily freed from house arrest, then faces further charges for fraud and disappearances
2006	The socialist, Michelle Bachelet of the Concertación, wins presidential elections against the conservative Sebastián Piñera, becoming Chile's first woman president. Chile and China sign free-trade deal. Pinochet dies
2007	Government agrees to pay compensation to families of some Pinochet victims
2008	Peru files lawsuit at International Court of Justice in dispute with Chile over maritime borders. Political right gains ground in local elections
2009	Relations with Peru strained over Chilean military exercise close to disputed border. Tensions grow after Peruvian officer accused of spying for Chile. No outright winner in first round of presidential election
2010	Sebastián Piñera wins runoff to become first president on the right since re-establishment of democracy in 1990

Factbox: Chile

Presidential democratic republic of 15 regions and one overseas province.

Suffrage: Universal for those aged 18 or over, and compulsory.

Executive: President elected directly by the people for a four-year term (majority runoff).

Legislature: Bicameral Congreso Nacional (National Congress). The lower Cámara de Diputados (Chamber of Deputies) has 120 members elected by a distinctive binomial form of proportional representation for four-year terms. The upper Senado (Senate) has 38 members elected by a distinctive binomial form of proportional representation for an eight-year term.

Regions: Regional intendants and the governors of the 53 provinces that the regions are subdivided into are appointed by the president. The provinces are subdivided into 346 communes (municipalities) whose mayors and councillors are directly elected.

Useful websites

www.gobiernodechile.cl **Presidency**
www.camara.cl **Chamber of Deputies**
www.senado.cl **Senate**

Uruguay

1985	Army and political party leaders reach agreement in negotiations on return to democracy. Julio María Sanguinetti of centre-right Partido Colorado wins elections and becomes president
1986	National Accord between Colorados, Partido Nacional (i.e. Blancos), leftwing Frente Amplio and conservative Unión Cívica to ensure cross-party support for measures of general interest
1989	Referendum endorses amnesty for human rights abusers. Alberto Lacalle of Blancos elected president, and pursues neoliberal reforms
1992	Voters reject privatisation plans in referendums
1994	Sanguinetti returns to presidency, forms coalition government, pursues electoral and political reforms, and restores growth
1999	Growth allows Colorados to regain presidency under Jorge Batlle. Colorados and Blancos continue legislative coalition
2000	Batlle establishes commission to investigate fate of people who disappeared under dictatorship
2002	Uruguay in dispute with Cuba over UN resolution on human rights. Amid worsening economic conditions, Batlle announces emergency measures to limit impact of Argentina's financial crisis. General strike protests crisis
2003	Voters in referendum reject plans to allow foreign investment in state oil monopoly
2004	Voters in referendum reject plans to allow privatisation of state water utility. Economic problems help Tabaré Vázquez of leftwing Encuentro Progresista-Frente Amplio win presidential elections
2005	Within hours of inauguration, Vázquez restores ties with Cuba, signs energy deal with Venezuela and announces welfare package
2006	International Court of Justice rejects Argentina's attempt to halt construction of Uruguayan pulp mill. Former president Juan María Bordaberry and foreign minister arrested in connection with the killings in 1976 of opponents. Uruguay pays off large IMF debt
2007	Argentineans cross into Uruguay to protest outside pulp mill
2008	Vázquez reveals discovery of offshore gas field on Uruguay's coast
2009	Supreme court rules law protecting military officers from prosecution for past human-rights abuses is unconstitutional. General Gregorio Alvarez, who ruled from 1981–85, is jailed for 25 years for murder and human rights violations. Ruling Frente Amplio coalition and its presidential candidate José Mujica, a former Tupamaros guerrilla, win elections
2010	Bordaberry, 81, sentenced to 30 years in prison for the murder of two opposition supporters and the disappearance of nine others in the 1970s, becoming the second former ruler in months to be jailed for his role in past authoritarian regimes

Factbox: Uruguay

Presidential democratic republic with 19 departments.

Suffrage: Universal for those aged 18 or over, and compulsory.

Executive: President and vice-president elected on the same ticket directly by the people for five-year terms (majority runoff).

Legislature: Bicameral Asamblea General (General Assembly). The lower Cámara de Representantes (Chamber of Representatives) has 99 members elected by proportional representation for five-year terms. The upper Cámara de Senadores (Senate) has 30 members elected by proportional representation for five-year terms, plus the vice-president.

Departments: Departmental intendants and councils are directly elected.

Useful websites

www.presidencia.gub.uy **Presidency**
www.parlamento.gub.uy **General parliamentary portal**
www.diputados.gub.uy **Chamber of Representatives**

Argentina

1982	Defeat in Falklands/Malvinas war hastens end of military regime
1983	Raúl Alfonsín of centrist Unión Civica Radical becomes president. Economy plagued by hyperinflation. Alfonsín initiates prosecution of military officers for human rights abuses
1989	Carlos Menem of Partido Justicialista (i.e. Peronist) elected president, imposes austerity programme and pursues neoliberal reforms
1994	Bomb at Jewish community centre in Buenos Aires kills 86. Menem able to push through constitutional amendments that allow for re-election
1995	Menem re-elected
1996	Economic problems provoke general strike
1997	Spanish judge orders arrest of former Argentine officers. UCR and centre-left Frente País Solidario form anti-Peronist electoral coalition and make gains in congressional elections
1999	Fernando de la Rúa of Alianza coalition wins presidency and inherits economic problems
2000	Economic crisis grows. IMF grants Argentina $40 billion aid package
2001	De la Rua struggles to cope with cabinet resignations and protests over austerity policies. General strike against planned spending cuts. Opposition Peronists win control of congress. Share prices plummet. Restrictions imposed to halt capital flight. IMF suspends aid. General strike against curbs on bank withdrawals and delayed pensions. De la Rua resigns after protests. Adolfo Rodríguez Saa named president, but quits on 30 December
2002	Congress selects Peronist Eduardo Duhalde to complete De la Rúa's term. Devalues peso and country misses deadlines on debt repayments to IMF and World Bank. Suspension of banking and foreign exchange activities. Violent anti-government and IMF protests
2003	Peronist Néstor Kirchner wins presidential runoff. Congress scraps laws protecting former military officers from prosecution. Argentina and IMF agree on debt-refinancing deal
2004	International warrant for Menem issued over fraud allegations, but then cancelled
2005	Argentina puts together largest ever debt-reduction package by developing country. Supreme court scraps amnesty law protecting military officers
2006	Argentina repays IMF debt
2007	Police in Spain arrest former president Isabel Perón in connection with Argentine investigation into activities in 1970s of rightwing paramilitaries. Cristina Fernández de Kirchner succeeds husband as Argentine president
2008	Spanish court rejects request to extradite Isabel Perón. Fernández cancels tax increases on agro-exports. Two former generals jailed for Dirty War role. Pension funds nationalised
2009	Peronists lose majorities in both chambers in legislative elections
2010	Argentina protests to UK about offshore oil exploration near Falklands/Malvinas islands

Factbox: Argentina

Federal presidential democratic republic of 23 provinces and one federal district.

Suffrage: Universal for those aged 18 or over, and compulsory.

Executive: President and vice-president directly elected on the same ticket for four-year terms (runoff formula).

Legislature: Bicameral Congreso Nacional (National Congress). The lower Cámara de Diputados (Chamber of Deputies) has 257 members elected by proportional representation for four-year terms (one half every two years). The upper Senado (Senate) has 72 members elected by plurality with minority representation for six-year terms.

Provinces: Provincial governors, vice-governors and legislatures are directly elected. The provinces are subdivided into departments and further subdivided into 1,151 municipalities, whose intendants and councils are directly elected.

Useful websites

www.presidencia.gov.ar **Presidency**
www.diputados.gov.ar **Chamber of Deputies**
www.senado.gov.ar **Senate**

Glossary

This glossary is intended as a quick reference aide and, wherever possible, students should research the meaning of terms further and explore the disagreements that can usually be found about their precise definition.

A

absolutism – belief that the monarchy had a divine right to rule without restrictions

abstention – when people do not vote in elections

accountability – the principle that anyone exercising power or institutions given responsibility for public functions are answerable for their actions. There are many forms of accountability

administrative decentralisation – the devolution of mainly administrative functions to **sub-national authorities**. See **decentralisation, centralism, centralisation, political decentralisation, fiscal decentralisation, asymmetric decentralisation, sectoral decentralisation, sub-national authority,** *municipio*

Afro-Latino – term sometimes used to refer to Latin Americans of African descent. See *Garifuna*, **Afro-mestizo**

Afro-mestizo – term sometimes used to refer to *mestizos* who also have African antecedents. See **Afro-Latino**

agrarian reform – any of many type of reforms, principally in the countryside, to social relations, land ownership and agricultural production

agribusiness – an agricultural business, usually conducted on a large scale

altiplano – Andean plateau in Bolivia and Peru constituting notional highland 'regions' in both countries generally dominated by indigenous groups and distinct from lowland and more urban regions

anarchism – the belief that society can be organised without a state

anarcho-syndicalism – a type of **anarchism** that views organised labour as a revolutionary force that can transform society by replacing capitalism with worker self-management, often manifested in practice as a form of a radical and militant trade unionism

anti-Americanism – hostility to the US

anti-clericalism – opposition to the institutional influence of the Church in public and political life

anti-dumping – dumping occurs when exports are priced at a level lower than the price normally charged in the exporter's domestic market, often seen as damaging to industry in the importing country, and anti-dumping measures are those additional tariffs imposed by the importing country in these instances

anti-imperialism – opposition to **imperialism**

anti-politics – a style or form of politics that blames a country's poor condition on an established class of politicians, who are usually depicted as inept or corrupt, and the dysfunctional political institutions that they inhabit. Anti-political sentiments were commonly found within a military establishment that believed it could govern a country in a better way. See *partidocracia*

anti-system elements – actors whose behaviour threatens an existing political system, which in a democracy would include extremist organisations, terrorist groups, guerrillas and paramilitaries

association agreement – an agreement between the EU to foster dialogue and co-operation between political institutions in a country or region and those of Europe and to set out specific criteria for economic co-operation and free trade

associative networks – term used by Chalmers *et al.* (1997) to refer to networks of groups and institutions other than parties expanding popular access to representation and suited to influencing public policy in a globalised and decentralised era

asymmetric decentralisation – a form of **decentralisation** that allows **sub-national authorities** to choose from a menu of functions they would like to assume based upon their needs and abilities. See **decentralisation, centralism, centralisation, political decentralisation, administrative decentralisation, fiscal decentralisation, sectoral decentralisation, sub-national authority,** *municipio*

authoritarian developmentalism – term sometimes used to describe the priority placed on rapid economic development by an authoritarian state

authoritarianism – a form of government in which those who rule demand or enforce obedience from the population, usually without gaining its consent, and are not restricted by the formal requirements of constitutions, laws or elections

autocratic – the unrestricted exercise of power or authority. See **delegative democracy**

auto-golpe – see **self-coup**

autonomy – self-government, increasingly used with reference to **decentralisation**

ayllu – pre-Inca form of political organisation on the *altiplano* based on extended family groups, often involving high levels of participation in decisionmaking

B

Balkanisation – term derived from the history of the Balkans referring to the propensity of states in a region to break up into smaller territorial and political units that are often hostile towards each other

banana republic – originally a reference to Central American countries dominated by US banana plantations that enjoyed little ability to determine their own affairs as a result

bananeras – women workers in some banana-exporting countries of Central America

basismo – the grassroots orientation of **NGOs** in Brazil

bicameral – a legislature that has two chambers or houses

bilateral – involving two countries or parties. See **bi-regional**

biodiversity – the level of variation of species within a given ecosystem, often used as a measure of the condition or quality of a natural environment

bipolar – having two poles or protagonists

bi-regional – involving two regions. See **bilateral**

Bolivarianism – a broad notion of Latin American unification deriving from the ideas of Simón Bolívar, the nineteenth-century Independence hero

bourgeoisie – the dominant, capital-owning class in capitalist society which, according to Karl Marx, existed by exploiting the wage-labour of the **proletariat**

Brezhnev Doctrine – a foreign policy doctrine associated with Leonid Brezhnev that implicitly reserved for the Soviet Union the international right to intervene militarily on behalf of all socialist countries in order to protect socialism where it considered it to be under threat

BRICs – acronym used to refer collectively to the rapidly developing economies of Brazil, the Russian Federation, India and China

Budgetary Finance System (BFS) – Cuban accounting method pioneered by Che Guevara to enable centralised economic planning

bureaucracy – the apparatus of administration, usually referring to government based on a specialised set of offices, hierarchically organised

bureaucratic-authoritarianism – model developed by O'Donnell (1973) linking economic modernisation and authoritarian rule by suggesting that the military regimes that seized power in the Southern Cone from the 1960s–1980s did so to overcome the crisis associated with the exhaustion of **ISI**

Bush Doctrine – the assertive, unilateralist foreign policy pursued by President George W. Bush of the US and neoconservatives after 2002 in which preemptive military action became a prominent tenet. See, *democradura*, **neoconservative**

C

camba – Bolivian term for people from the country's lowlands, usually referring to a light-skinned person of European descent

campesinos (peasants) – Spanish term for peasant, a poor person with low social status working the land, often owning or controlling their own small plot. See **smallholder**

capital flight – large transfers abroad of money invested in a country usually as the result of fears about the future course of its economy, and in particular about the prospect of a debt default or currency devaluation

capital goods – the fixed assets used in producing goods such as machinery and equipment

capitalism – any of many variants of the system of social organisation based upon private ownership of the means of production. Capital is one of four factors of production (alongside land, labour and enterprise) and refers to any asset available for use in the production of further assets, from money itself to machinery or even tools

Caribbean Basin – region in US geopolitical strategy that comprises Central America, the Caribbean islands and to a lesser extent Venezuela and Colombia, as distinct from South America

caste system – a social hierarchy based upon an individual's position in society usually deriving from his or her ethnic or religious status or determined by physical characteristics

caudillo – a regional chieftain or military strongman often concentrating power and dominating politics. This phenomenon, common in the nineteenth century, was known as *caudillismo*

CEBs (Catholic base communities) – see *comunidades eclesiales de base/comunidades eclesiais de base*

centralism, centralisation – the concentration of power in a single central authority. A centralised state is one which monopolises power at the expense of regional or local authorities or agencies. See **decentralisation, political decentralisation, administrative decentralisation, asymmetric decentralisation, sectoral decentralisation, sub-national authority,** *municipio*

Christian democracy – a democratic political ideology inspired by Christian values and beliefs

citizenship – the rights, duties and privileges of anyone recognised as a legal member of a country. See **civil rights, political rights, social rights**

civil rights – those rights guaranteeing the sanctity of the individual before the law related to legal equality and protection such as the right to life, equality under the law, protection against discrimination and personal security. See **citizenship, political rights, social rights**

civil society – 'the realm of organised social life that is voluntary, self-generating, (largely) self-supporting, autonomous from the state, and bound by a legal order or set of shared rules' (Diamond, 1996, p. 228). See **private sphere, public sphere**

class – highly contested term often used loosely and usually employed to refer to a social stratum defined by its relationship to the means of production, by its status, or both

clientelism – the relationship between a political patron and a client in which the latter has little power but gives the former support in exchange for favours and resources, **patronage**

coalition – a combination of parties or social groups, usually formed to win or retain power. See **procedural coalition**

code law tradition – a tradition of laws within which judges work based upon written, hence codified laws, as opposed to a **common law tradition** based upon the precedent provided by past cases and custom, and hence on interpretation

Cold War – the era of hostility between the main superpowers (the US and Soviet Union) and their allies from the late 1940s until the late 1980s

collas – term originally referring to a pre-Inca people, now often used to refer to poor indigenous communities in Bolivia

common law tradition – a tradition of laws within which judges work based upon the precedent provided by past cases and custom, and hence on interpretation, as opposed to a **code law tradition** based on written, hence codified laws

commonwealth – term traditionally used to refer to the notionally consensual association of countries, such as Puerto Rico and the US, by which **sovereignty** may be shared or assigned in a mutually beneficial relationship

communism – any of several variants of the belief in a revolutionary struggle between classes leading to the victory of the **proletariat** and the establishment of a classless society based on **socialism**. See **Leninism, Maoism**

communitarian – a philosophical emphasis upon communities and societies, as opposed to the individual, that is not inconsistent with **liberalism**

comparative advantage – important principle in traditional theories of international trade associated in particular with the ideas of David Ricardo referring to one country's ability to produce a good at a lower cost (relative to other goods) compared to another country, based, for example, on its own natural endowments, implying that the former country has a natural advantage in exploiting such products in its trade

comunidades eclesiales de base/comunidades eclesiais de base (CEBs, Catholic base communities) – Spanish/Portuguese term for small Catholic grassroots groups that meet to study the Bible and discuss local concerns

conquistadores – Spanish term for the Spaniards who conquered what became Latin America

consolidation – democracy is consolidated when all political actors consider the democratic state to be the only legitimate means to settle competition for political office and formulate policy by putting their faith in established institutions and adhering to democratic rules. See **deconsolidation**

constituent assembly – an assembly convened to draft or adopt a new constitution

constitutionalism – government by an agreed set of rules over which the key sectors of society have some say, implying checks upon the exercise of power

contestation – competition between rival political forces

continentalism – a form of pan-Latin American (or pan-American) nationalism in which the main object of allegiance is the continent or region and so whose point of departure is a shared history or culture

contras – counter-revolutionaries who fought Nicaragua's Sandinista government during the 1980s

convergence – the regional momentum that can be generated by democratisation processes in which democratic change occurs in several countries simultaneously

co-opt – to win over by including, and thereby to neutralise

corporatism – any variant of the way in which hierarchically organised 'corporations' that represent distinct, functionally differentiated groups in society, such as the Church, trades unions, business organisations and the military, are incorporated into the state's policymaking process allowing those groups both to represent their members' interests while at the same time ensuring their compliance with state policy. Corporatism in Latin America has been commonly associated with the development of strong, centralised and **authoritarian states**. The term can also be used to refer to an **ideology** advocating the above or similar forms of social organisation

creole – see *criollo*

criollo (creole) – native born white (i.e. ethnically European) inhabitant of Latin America

cronyism – favouritism shown to friends or colleagues, especially by appointing them to public office regardless of their qualifications. See **nepotism**

D

debt peonage – the system by which **peons** were kept tied to *haciendas*, obliged to continue working in order to pay off unmanageable debts

decentralisation – when power is devolved from the central **state** to lower, regional and local authorities, known as **sub-national authorities**. See **autonomy, centralism, centralisation, political decentralisation, administrative decentralisation, sectoral decentralisation, fiscal decentralisation, asymmetric decentralisation,** *municipio*, **secession, separatism**

decertification – process employed by the US government by which it removes countries from a list of states it regards to be co-operating fully in certain policy areas, in particular the battle against drug-trafficking. See **narcostate, 'War on Drugs'**

decisional autonomy – term used in the analysis of party **institutionalisation** to refer to a party's freedom from interference by groups it is closely linked to, such as trades unions, in determining its policies and strategies. See **reification, systemness, value infusion, party system**

deconsolidation – the process by which a consolidated democracy unravels. See **consolidation**

decretismo – Spanish term referring to a president's ample use of legislative and emergency decree powers

deficit spending – a situation that arises when a government spends more than it receives in taxes, invariably financing the shortfall by borrowing. **Monetarists** argue this is the main cause of inflation. See **fiscal discipline, economic populism**

deforestation – the intentional clearance of natural forest through logging or slash-and-burn farming practices. See **sustainable development**

delegative democracy – term used by O'Donnell (1992) to describe the rule of a president who exercises power as if it were directly delegated to him or her by popular **mandate** and so ignoring checks and balances built into the system, eroding public trust in institutions and damaging **party systems**

demilitarisation – the reduction of the military's role, ranging from the simple exit of the military from politics to the complete abolition of the armed forces as an institution demobilisation – in political terms, the reversal of a process of social **mobilisation**; in military terms, the process of standing down armed forces from fighting status and integrating them into peaceful activities

democradura – a notion of limited democracy in which concerns about security, heightened by terrorism, have modified assumptions about a shared democratic project across the wider American hemisphere to promote democratic procedures and structures constrained by the fear of individuals or groups deemed sufficiently dangerous to warrant restrictions on their rights. See **neoconservative, 'War on Terror'**

democratic governance – the form of good **governance** likely to be found within a democracy that includes such characteristics as the accountability of political leaders, freedom of association and participation, and an honest and accessible judicial system

democratic pluralism – democracy characterised by **pluralism**

dependency – any of various perspectives in political economy that identify, usually as problematic, one country's financial, commercial or technological reliance upon another. In Latin America, these have often advanced the notion that local economic possibilities are a function of the expansion of the central, or developed industrial, economies which are, in consequence, responsible for underdevelopment. See **imperialism, structuralism**

depoliticisation – the reduction of political activity, participation or representation, often because of authoritarian or economic constraints on behaviour

deregulation – the removal of regulations governing the operation of a previously regulated economic sector or industry, usually with the intention of removing constraints to market activity, thereby improving efficiency and creating incentives for investment

deunionisation – the decline in membership or activity of trades unions

dictatorship – rule by a single individual with few limitations on the ruler's power

dirty war – the violent repression pursued by military regimes in several Latin American countries against individuals mainly associated with the Left during the late 1970s, involving systematic murder and **disappearances**, imprisonment, torture and human rights abuses

disappearance – this term usually refers to the kidnapping and, it is assumed but not always known, subsequent murder of an individual by political opponents, and has often been used with reference to the practices adopted by state security forces under **authoritarian** military regimes as part of a **dirty war** against the Left

disentailment – the removal of inheritance restrictions that ensured property remained in the hands of corporate estates such as the Church or indigenous communities. See **corporatism**

Drago Doctrine – doctrine named after an Argentine foreign minister, Luis María Drago, that challenged the legal right claimed by the great powers to justify the use of force to recover debts

dual legitimacy – the simultaneous democratic legitimacy of both president and congress gained through separate elections for each

dual militancy – feminist strategy advocating the struggle for women's liberation from male domination alongside a broad class struggle for distributive justice for all regardless of gender

due process – formal proceedings carried out fairly in accordance with established rules, usually employed with reference to legal proceedings

E

economic liberalism – an economic perspective informed by the main principles of **liberalism** implying that rational, self-interested actors competing freely in the market will produce the greatest good and that free international trade will benefit all nations. See **liberalism, neoliberalism, capitalism**

economic populism – a contested term used to describe developmental strategies that emphasise growth and redistribution regardless of budgetary constraints, often based on **deficit spending**, that result in unsustainable levels of inflation. See **populism, neo-populism**

ejido – a form of social and territorial organisation in the Mexican countryside

Election Observation Mission (EOM) – official scrutiny of an election by an outside agency such as the European Union

electoral dealignment – the degree to which the loyalty of citizens to their preferred party erodes but is not replaced with loyalty to a competitor

electoral fraud – any of many activities that consciously interfere with the process of an otherwise free and fair election in an effort to determine its outcome

electoral volatility – the net change in the vote shares of all parties from one election to the next, or the fragmentation of representation among a large number of small parties

elite – a small group of people enjoying a disproportionate amount of power, often by virtue of their wealth, social status, or control of force

elite settlement – an agreement among elites through which rival factions suddenly and deliberately reorganise relations

enclave economies – an economy is one in which 'enclaves' of production that are either capital intensive and so employ little local labour *or* geographically isolated in certain parts of the country can be found. These have often been based on energy production or mining and have developed within countries that produce primary products for export. In both cases growth in these enterprises – which are often controlled by foreign interests – may have little positive impact upon the local or national economy

energy security – a state's access to sufficient and stable energy resources. See **national security**

enganche – Spanish term that can mean 'enlistment' referring to a system of labour in which an advance is paid to a worker in exchange for a later commitment to work. See *habilitación*

Enlightenment – period of European philosophical development in the eighteenth century in which the emphasis on reason displaced that on spirituality

environmental justice – notion used to address environmental issues that combines broader themes of global injustice with local concerns about the environment, especially with reference to inequalities that may result in harmful environmental practices. See **deforestation, socio-environmentalism, sustainable development**

episcopal – relating to or governed by bishops

evangelical – relating to Protestant Christian sects, churches or movements

executive – the executive branch in politics is that concerned with carrying out policy, and usually refers to the presidency. See **legislative, judicial, plural executive**

extrahemispheric – originating from outside a hemisphere i.e. in the case of the Americas, non-American

F

failed state – term that has been used in the developed world with reference to states, usually in the developing world, where sufficient institutions have either broken down or do not function properly as to incapacitate the normal or desired functioning of the **state**. See **narcostate**

fascism – political philosophy that became predominant in Italy and Germany during the 1920s and 1930s arguing that the state or nation should be the guiding principle of politics and resulting in highly centralised dictatorial government based on repression

favelas – Brazilian term originating in Rio de Janeiro meaning shanty-towns or slums

FDI – see **foreign direct investment**

federalism – the devolution of central powers by the government of a **nation-state** to states or provinces. See **autonomy, decentralisation, centralism, centralisation, political decentralisation, administrative decentralisation, asymmetric decentralisation, sectoral decentralisation, sub-national authority,** *municipio*

femicide – term used, often in the context of discussions about **feminism,** to describe the murder of women specifically, in order to make a distinction with the literal meaning of the term 'homicide' i.e. the killing of men

feminism – any of various critiques, doctrines or beliefs based on the pursuit of equal social and political rights for women

feudalism – a social system predating capitalism in which aristocratic landowners stood at the apex of a hierarchical society, usually ruled over by a monarch, in which serfs (peasants) provided bonded labour in return for protection and security of tenure

fiscal decentralisation – the transfer of spending or revenue-raising powers from central government to **sub-national authorities**. See **decentralisation, centralism, centralisation, political decentralisation, administrative decentralisation, asymmetric decentralisation, sectoral decentralisation,** *municipio* fiscal discipline – any of various approaches to economic policymaking that do not result in **deficit spending** and the problems often associated with this, such as inflation

foco – Spanish term for focal point employed by the Argentine-born revolutionary Che Guevara to refer to a style of guerrilla warfare based upon a small revolutionary cadre of armed militants supported by local peasants

foreign direct investment (FDI) – investment in a real asset, such as a factory or building, in one country by a company based in another country. See **portfolio capital**

Fourth Estate – term sometimes used to characterise the role of the media as a guarantor of the **separation of powers**. See **media literacy**

free trade – trade between countries unencumbered by **protectionist** measures such as tariffs and quotas, ensuring the free flow of goods and services. See **comparative advantage, terms of trade, integration**

G

Garifuna – term mainly local to several Central American countries for citizens of mixed indigenous-African descent who live in communities along the coast. See **Afro-Latino**

GDP – see gross domestic product

glasnost – Russian term popularised by the Soviet leader Mikhail Gorbachev referring to the 'openness' that characterised a policy of self-criticism and transparency pursued in the late 1980s. See *perestroika*

globalisation – a contested idea often understood as the increasingly transnational nature of capitalist development that reflects the emergence of a new international order since the end of the Cold War. See **transformationalist position**

GNP – see gross national product

governability – the capacity of a government to govern

governance – the ways in which any social unit organises the processes by which decisions are made and implemented, that is, the ways in which public institutions conduct their affairs and manage their resources. See **democratic governance**

Great Depression – the economic slump in the US and other countries that followed the Wall Street crash of 1929

gross domestic product (GDP) – the total output of all goods and services produced within a country by both residents and non-residents. See **gross national product**

gross national product (GNP) – the total output of the residents of a country within its territory plus income earned abroad, but not including the income earned by foreigners working within that country. See **gross domestic product**

guerrilla – a member of an irregular armed force, usually fighting against state forces in the countryside as part of a revolutionary strategy. The term 'urban guerrilla' has been used to denote similar activity in cities

H

habilitación – Spanish term that can mean 'credit' referring to a system of labour in which an advance is paid to a worker before a harvest in exchange for a later commitment to work. See *enganche*

hacienda (country estate) – Spanish term for a large estate or ranch

hegemony – term originally refined by Antonio Gramsci referring to the preeminence of a dominant ideology but which has come to mean the dominance or leadership of one social group or country over others. See **imperialism**

Hispanics – people in the US with origins in the Hispanic countries of Latin America (or Spain). Often interchangeable with **Latinos**

Hispanism – an emphasis upon the traditions and values of Spain or the Spanish

humanism – a philosophy deriving from a belief in 'human nature' concerned principally with the capabilities, achievements and needs of human beings and often exalting such ideas as dignity

I

Iberian – pertaining to the Iberian Peninsula, i.e. Spain and Portugal

ideology – contested term often used to refer to a comprehensive and coherent system of political, economic and social values, beliefs or ideas shared or taken for granted by a social group that are usually concerned with the role of government and the policies it should adopt

impeachment – when a legislature levels charges of misconduct against a senior government official, usually a president, as the first step towards possible removal from office

imperialism – the efforts of some powerful countries to form and maintain an empire, that is to extend their control directly or indirectly over the territory and political and economic life of other countries. Opposition to this is called **anti-imperialism**. See **hegemony, sovereignty, super-imperialism**

import-substitution industrialisation (ISI) – a process of industrialisation based on efforts to substitute locally manufactured products for those formerly imported, usually relying on **protectionism**

impunity – when crimes or human rights abuses go unpunished

Indian – term commonly (but inaccurately) used to refer to an **indigenous** person in Latin America deriving from Christopher Columbus's belief that he had reached the Indies. See *indigenismo*

indigenismo – any of various forms of a political philosophy akin to nationalism and often related to it extolling the virtues of **indigenous** or **pre-Columbian** society, particularly associated with ideas developed in Mexico by such non-indigenous thinkers as José Vasconcelos, and often claiming to seek the emancipation of indigenous people. See **Indian**

indigenous – pertaining to the original, **pre-Columbian** inhabitants of what are now the Americas. See **Indian,** *indigenismo*

individualism – an approach to philosophy that emphasises the importance of individuals as opposed to social units

Indo-America – the focus of an alternative vision of what has hitherto been called Latin America that identifies with the region's **indigenous** culture and history. In the thought of the Peruvian thinker Victor Raúl Haya de la Torre, Indo-America represented an effort to fuse *indigenismo* and **continentalism**. See **Indian**

informal powers – the unwritten powers enjoyed by a president that are a function of his or her position and status and reinforce the incumbent's formal constitutional authority, such as the ability to tap into party, military and business networks, dispense **patronage** and secure access to the media in order to influence public opinion. See **integrative powers, unilateral powers, *decretismo***

informal sector – that sector of the economically active population whose activities lie outside any formal regulatory environment and so are rarely reflected in official statistics

institutionalisation – term that can have various meanings used both with reference to politics broadly, or more specifically, for example, to parties and **party systems,** characterising, according to Huntington (1968), the process by which organisations and procedures acquire value and stability. See **decisional autonomy, systemness, value infusion, reification, party discipline**

institutionalism – any of various approaches to the study of politics or history that stresses the analysis of institutions in the belief that these structure behaviour; also used in international relations to refer to an account of international behaviour by which a country's influence is partly determined by the nature and extent of its involvement in international institutions

integration – term that can have various meanings, usually employed to refer either to the process by which distinct groups in society (often classes or ethnic groups) lose their specificity and become less discernible components of the larger social whole, or to the process by which, through formal instruments such as economic treaties, countries create institutional mechanisms, procedures and rules by which to co-ordinate policymaking based on a common agenda

integrative powers – powers that allow a president to determine the policy agenda in the legislature by prioritising bills or empowering allies in congress, such as **urgency provisions** allowing the **executive** to force an assembly to deal with presidential requests quickly. See **legislative**

intermestic – involving both foreign and domestic actors or processes simultaneously

internal colonialism – idea sometimes used by Marxists and advocates of **dependency** perspectives asserting that the exploitative relationship between the industrial developed economies ('centre') and those of the Third World ('periphery') that perpetuate underdevelopment are reproduced within the latter as urban areas absorb resources from rural areas creating 'dual economies' and 'dual societies' which are simultaneously traditional and modern

international community – a notional community of like-minded states, existing above nation-states, that can exert supra-national power on individual countries through, for example, **international law**

international law – the laws that govern the conduct of independent countries in their relationships with each other. See **international community, sovereignty**

inverse racism – term sometimes used to refer to claims for preferential treatment based on allegations of **racism** that, by virtue of exaggeration for example, may in themselves resemble racism

J

judicial – the judicial branch in politics is that which interprets laws and thereby adjudicates legal disputes, and comprises judges, magistrates and the court system. See **judicial review, executive, legislative**

judicial review – the power to rule on whether laws and decisions are constitutional that enables judges or courts to ensure executive and legislative activities are legal, seen as an important obstacle to **tyranny**. See **judicial**

K

Keynesianism – the body of economic thought developed by the British economist John Maynard Keynes that advocated greater state intervention in the economy

L

laissez-faire – an economic philosophy advocating minimal government interference in or regulation of business or commerce based on the belief that private ownership and the free play of market forces at home and abroad will produce the greatest good. See **economic liberalism, liberalism, neoliberalism, capitalism**

landless – those without cultivable land who desire or require it for farming purposes, either because they are former *campesinos* displaced by the expansion of commercial agriculture, are awaiting plots or title under **land reform** or colonisation policies, or are simply destitute

land reform – government intervention to redistribute land, usually through expropriation and to *campesinos* or the landless, or to restructure the prevailing norms of tenure

latifundia – Spanish term for large landholdings, today usually modern corporate farms

Latinos – people in the US with origins in Latin America (or Spain and Portugal). Often interchangeable, but not strictly synonymous, with **Hispanics**

leftwing – broad term often used loosely to refer to that part of the political spectrum associated with **socialism, social democracy** and some forms of liberalism. See **rightwing**

legislative – the legislative branch in politics is that which makes laws and usually sets budgets, and refers to national assemblies, congresses and parliaments. See **executive, judicial**

legitimacy – authority based on consent that is considered crucial for ensuring political stability and so maintaining power. See **dual legitimacy**

Leninism – the interpretation of Marxist theory developed by the Bolshevik leader Vladimir Lenin that provided a political practice for Marxism and the guiding doctrine of the Soviet Union arguing, among other things, that **imperialism** is the highest form of capitalism. Often referred to as **Marxism-Leninism**. See **communism, socialism, social democracy**

liberal democracy – a democratic system characterised above all by rights, institutions and values based upon individual liberty. See **liberalism, social democracy**

liberalism – any of many variants of political and economic belief proclaiming that achieving or upholding the freedom of the individual is the purpose of government or economic activity. See **neoliberalism, social liberalism**

liberation theology – an amalgamation of Marxist social analysis and Christian theology that advanced a radical critique of development based on theories of **dependency**, underdevelopment and **class** analysis

lynching – the execution of suspected wrongdoers without **due process**

M

machismo – Spanish term also used in English referring to an exaggerated masculinity. See *marianismo*

macroeconomic – referring to the attributes or performance of an economy as a whole as opposed to individual sectors or industries

majoritarian – a majoritarian electoral system is one in which victory is achieved by gaining a majority or **plurality** of the vote as opposed to **proportional representation** in which representation is shared out according to participants' share of the vote. Presidential elections are majoritarian, although they may have a proportional element if they employ a double ballot system allowing people to vote first for their preferred candidate, and thereafter in a second round of voting for one of the final frontrunners

mallku – term in use in Bolivian highlands that harks back to governing practices that precede the Inca empire referring to an indigenous local leader democratically elected by a community in a public vote for a term of one year who then chooses his senior officials

mandate – the authority given by voters as the result of an election victory to a party or president to pursue certain policies or govern in a particular way with **legitimacy**

Manifest Destiny – ideology popular in the US in the 1840s that sought to justify taking land from Hispanic countries, namely Mexico, in order to extend 'civilisation'

Maoism – sometimes referred to as Marxism-Leninism-Mao Zedong Thought, Maoism constitutes the interpretation of Marxist ideas by the Chinese revolutionary Mao Zedong that placed the peasant at the heart of revolutionary struggle. See **Leninism, communism, socialism, social democracy**

maquiladora – Mexican term for the low-cost assembly sector of the economy

marianismo – Spanish term expressing a female equivalent of *machismo* that exalts the virtues of womanhood derived from the role of the Virgin Mary in Roman Catholic tradition

Marxism-Leninism – see **Leninism**

materialism – a branch of philosophy stressing the importance of material factors and well-being, as opposed to ideas or spiritual factors, that is often associated with Karl Marx's theories about history

media literacy – the ability of citizens to access, analyse and evaluate media content, and create it themselves. See **Fourth Estate**

mestizo, mestizaje (mixed, mixture) – Spanish terms used to refer to the biological and/or cultural fusion between the Spanish and the **indigenous** that distinguishes Latin America and many of its people. See **Afro-mestizo, mulatto**

military prerogatives – the areas of governance over which the military as an institution has a right, or assumes it has a right, to exercise control

miscegenation – the mixing of ethnic or racial groups. See *mestizo*, **mulatto**, *pardo*

mobilisation – the process by which a social group goes from being a passive collection of individuals to an active political force by organising and, say, staging rallies and marches, sometimes called social mobilisation. See **demobilisation**

monetarism – theory refined by the US economist Milton Friedman arguing that the main cause of inflation is spending by the **state** beyond its means through money creation, and so the way to bring down inflation is to curb the money supply, usually by restricting state spending. Monetarism and **neoliberalism** have sometimes been characterised as 'neoclassical' ideas for reviving classical **laissez-faire** economic principles. See **economic liberalism, capitalism, deficit spending, economic populism**

Monroe Doctrine – US foreign policy position advocated by President James Monroe in 1823 aimed at dissuading European powers from engaging in a recolonisation effort of Latin America, subsequently establishing an attitude of domination by the US over the western hemisphere. See **hegemony, imperialism, super-imperialism**

mulatto – term thought to have come from Spanish or Portuguese for a person of mixed African and European origin, considered in some English-speaking circles to be offensive and so avoided by them. See *mestizo*, **Afro-mestizo**, *pardo*

multiculturalism – a vision of society that conceptualises it as comprising distinct yet co-existing ethnicities. Terms such as **multi-ethnic** and **pluricultural** are also often used

multi-ethnic – See **multiculturalism**

multilateral – involving more than two countries, a term generally used in international relations, as opposed to **bilateral**. See **multilateralism, unilateralism**

multilateralism – an approach to issues in international relations by which states act co-operatively and by consensus based on shared interests. See **multilateral, unilateralism**

multi-national – a corporation that operates in more than one country, but usually many. See **globalisation**. This term has also been used, less commonly, to refer to the existence of more than one ethnic 'nation' within the territory of one state. See **multiculturalism, self-determination**

multi-party system – a political system in which there are more than two, but usually many, parties

multipolarity – the existence of multiples poles of development, growth, influence etc.

municipio (municipality) – usually the lowest tier of local government in Latin America. See **sub-national authority, decentralisation, centralism, centralisation, political decentralisation, administrative decentralisation, sectoral decentralisation, asymmetric decentralisation, federalism**

N

narcostate – term that has been used in the US with reference to Latin America to characterise a state that is dominated or heavily corrupted by drug-trafficking interests. See **failed state**

nation-building – a conscious effort to foster or create a unified nationality based on a discernible **national identity**

nation-state – a specific political entity comprising a **sovereign state** whose citizens are considered in cultural terms to comprise a nation because they share the attributes that make up a **national identity**. See **multi-national, multicultural-ism, sub-national authority, nationalism, globalisation**

national identity – the cultural and social attributes ascribed to a nation that are said to make it distinct. See **nation-state, nationalism**

nationalisation – when the state takes into public ownership an industry or economic sector formerly in private hands

nationalism – any of many variants of the belief in the existence of a distinct, given nation deserving of its own state and all that this implies, such as **sovereignty**, independence, social and cultural integrity etc. See **nation-state, globalisation**

national populism – see **populism**

national security – a condition aspired to by governments in which the nation-state is free from actual or potential external and internal threats, often generating policies that encompass military, economic, political, diplomatic and technological dimensions. See **energy security**

national socialism – a form of **socialism** based upon assumptions deriving from **nationalism**, such as racial or cultural distinctiveness, closely identified with Nazism in Germany under the Third Reich from 1933–45

neocolonial – term used by historians to characterise Latin American economies in the late nineteenth and early twentieth century referring to the way in which production processes were oriented to serving foreign markets and *de facto* control was exerted by foreign powers, and by Marxists and advocates of **dependency** perspectives to refer to a prevailing, exploitative relationship between Third World economies and the developed industrial countries that is sustained by a system of class relations in both

neoconservative – **rightwing** position associated in particular with the security policies of President George W. Bush in the US that gave rise to the '**War on Terror**' after 2001 which combined a traditional belief in the duty of the US to promote **liberal democracy** around the world with a military doctrine that justified preemptive actions to defuse perceived threats to the country before they were carried out. See **national security**

neocorporatism – term given by some scholars to the survival of **corporatism** in new forms in some Latin American political systems

neodevelopmentalism – economic position to the left of **neostructuralism** but sharing many of its themes that emphasises the proactive role of the state in development and in carving out space for independent, national action within the globalised economy. See **dependency**, **'post-Washington Consensus'**

neoliberalism – an economic doctrine that became dominant among policymakers in Latin America in the 1990s eschewing state intervention in the economy and promoting market-led growth, privatisation, deregulation and free trade. Neoliberalism and **monetarism** have sometimes been characterised as 'neoclassical' ideas for reviving classical **laissez-faire** principles. See **economic liberalism, capitalism, second-generation reforms**

neopanismo – Spanish term for a current that developed within the Mexican conservative Partido Acción Nacional (PAN, National Action Party) during the 1980s led by modernising businessmen that emphasised such ideas as **neoliberalism** as opposed to the party's traditional Catholic principles

neo-populism – term sometimes used to describe the **populist** political style employed by presidents since the 1990s, often associated with the autocratic behaviour adopted either by some executives to push through **neoliberal** reforms or, more recently, to challenge those reforms

neostructuralism – a contemporary economic strategy built upon earlier structuralist foundations arguing that the market alone will not spur development and that the state should step in where there has been a failure of the market to promote growth. See **post-neostructuralism, structuralism, 'post-Washington Consensus'**

nepotism – favouritism shown to one's relatives, especially in appointments or the bestowing of **patronage**. See **cronyism**

new social movement – organised social group exhibiting a sense of collective purpose that requires it to engage in political or cultural activity through institutional and extra-institutional forms of action that mobilise supporters in pursuit of its goals. See **resource mobilisation theory**

NGO – see **non-governmental organisation**

non-governmental organisation (NGO) – private organisations funded either by voluntary contributions through membership, donations from larger organisations or through self-financing with varied roles but often serving to channel international development aid

O

offshoring – the relocation of production or service provision to a lower-cost economy

oligarchy – government by a few people, the elite, which in the case of Latin America has usually referred to large landowners and merchants

oligopoly (oligopolistic) – a market in which control over the supply of commodities or capital is dominated by a small number of producers or interests

organised labour – the trades union movement

outward foreign direct investment (OFDI) – Latin American **foreign direct investment** (FDI) in a real asset, such as a factory or building, in another country. See **portfolio capital, trans-Latin**

overcapacity – having factories that are either more numerous or larger than required to meet demand and so operate at high cost relative to the returns on their production

P

paramilitary organisation – a group of civilians organised in a military fashion conducting armed activities that in Latin America often operates in place of or in support of state forces

pardo – Portuguese (and Spanish) term used in Brazil to refer to people of mixed race, i.e. mainly people of mixed black and white origin. See **mulatto,** *mestizo,* **Afro-mestizo,** *Garifuna*

parliamentarianism (parliamentarism) – a political system in which the executive branch of government is dependent on the confidence of the legislative branch which, typically, provides the former's personnel. See **presidentialism**

participatory budgeting – a system of local decisionmaking that allows local authorities to set spending priorities and so allocate resources based on direct and continuous consultation with local people at a ward level

participatory democracy – any of various forms of democratic practice that place a premium upon maximising the participation of ordinary people in decisionmaking

partidocracia – a term sometimes used by populistic leaders to attack a party system characterised as being dominated by an unrepresentative political elite. See **anti-politics**

party discipline – the extent to which the elected representatives of a political party obey its rules, programme, policy and ideas. See **decisional autonomy, institutionalisation, systemness, value infusion, reification, party system**

party system – the rules and regularities of party competition that give a political process continuity and stability. See **institutionalisation**

paternalism – power exercised over an individual or group, ostensibly in their best interest thus implying their lack of autonomy, that can be likened to that between a father and child

patriarchy – male domination of power

patronage – the resources, benefits, favours or ability to appoint that a power-broker can dispense by virtue of his or her political position in order to engender support

peasant/peasantry – see *campesino*

peninsulares – Spanish-born inhabitants of Latin America during the colonial and Independence eras

peon – an unskilled farm worker or peasant

perestroika – Russian term popularised by the Soviet leader Mikhail Gorbachev after 1985 referring to the restructuring of bureaucratic economic management and the communist party. See *glasnost*

personalism – the predominance of a single personality in politics such that loyalty is to a leader and not institutions or ideals

'pink tide' – collective term sometimes used to refer to the wave of governments led by left-of-centre parties or leaders that have come to power through electoral politics in Latin America since 1999

plebiscitary – pertaining to an expression of support by, or an appeal to, the population as a whole

plural executive – an executive comprising several members as opposed to a single president, tried in Uruguay as a nine-seat council. See **executive**

pluralism – the principle that diverse groups maintaining their distinctive characteristics fruitfully co-exist and interact in society without conflict by tolerating each other

plurality – a plurality is the largest single total of votes for any candidate, regardless of whether these amount to a majority of the votes cast

pluricultural – term that has often been used by **indigenous** movements to describe the multicultural composition of society. See **multiculturalism**

plurinational – term now incorporated in the official name of Bolivia that establishes its status as a state encompassing various nations in an effort to give international recognition to its **indigenous** identities, as opposed to a unitary **nation-state**. See **national identity**

polarisation – the drift from central to more extreme ideological positions

political culture – the unique combination of beliefs, attitudes and values held by individuals in any given society about how political and economic life should be conducted that together help to shape a political system's distinctive character

political decentralisation – the establishment of elected governments at sub-national levels. See **decentralisation, centralism, centralisation, administrative decentralisation, fiscal decentralisation, asymmetric decentralisation, sectoral decentralisation, sub-national authority,** *municipio*

political liberalisation – the loosening of constraints on political activity

political rights – those rights enjoyed by an individual that ensure participation in the political process such as the right to vote in clean, free and fair elections. See **civil rights, citizenship, social rights**

polyarchy – term coined by Robert Dahl (1971) to refer to **pluralist** forms of **liberal democracy** in which different interests compete

popular-frontism – political strategy adopted by communist parties before the Second World War with the principal aim of countering **fascism** based on alliances with nationalist, reformist and populist regimes. See **nationalism, populism**

popular sovereignty – the notion that legitimate authority derives from the consent of the 'people' as opposed to, say, a monarch. See **sovereignty, legitimacy, mandate**

populism – one of many variants of a form or style of politics deriving from a leader's identification with ordinary people as individuals and not as members of any particular social group and the challenge to powerful vested interests that this represents, usually implying the creation of alliances of classes outside formal party politics that, under normal circumstances, are likely to come into conflict, such as workers and industrialists. Populist regimes in Latin America have often been **authoritarian** and leaders have sought **legitimacy** across classes or in a **plebiscitary** way through the unifying **ideology** of **nationalism**, hence occasional use of the term **national populism**. The term 'classical populism' is sometimes used to describe urban populist movements that developed in Latin America during the 1940s and 1950s. See **neo-populism, economic populism**

portfolio capital – financial assets such as stocks, bonds and deposits, as opposed to real assets such as property, plant and equipment

positivism – a branch of philosophy emphasising the application of scientific method in reaching conclusions as opposed to theoretical or metaphysical abstraction. Positivist ideas in Latin America in the late nineteenth century were influential in policymaking and often justified **authoritarian** or racist positions. See **social Darwinism**

post-neostructuralism – the reassertion in economic thought of traditional **structuralist** positions that aims to avoid any association with the disappointing results of **neoliberalism**

'post-Washington Consensus' – term used by scholars such as Panizza (2009) to describe a new consensus, or a significant narrowing of the differences, between the original advocates of **neoliberalism** and their structuralist critics which incorporate policies at the heart of the original neoliberal agenda – such as trade opening and flexible labour policies – with **second-generation reforms** aimed at strengthening the institutions essential for market growth. Central to these ideas are an important economic role for the state and targeted social policies. See **neoliberalism, neostructuralism, post-neostructuralism, structuralism, Washington Consensus**

pre-Columbian – pertaining to the time before the arrival of Christopher Columbus in the Americas in 1492

presidentialism – a political system in which a president receives a popular **mandate** directly from the people through an election. See **parliamentarianism (parliamentarism)**

private sphere – an independent realm of activity, usually referred to in relation to freedoms and rights, where an individual notionally enjoys autonomy and authority free from state or institutional interventions, such as the home or a business. See **civil society, public sphere**

privatisation – the transfer of state-owned enterprises or a stake in them (often through shares), from the public to the private sector, usually through a sale. See **nationalisation**

procedural coalition – a **coalition** formed when legislators vote on the procedures the legislature will employ to conduct its affairs, as opposed to those coalitions that form around policy issues. See **legislative**

proletariat – the class under **capitalism** that works for wages, usually meaning industrial workers. See **rural proletariat**

prolonged popular war – guerrilla strategy associated with **Maoism** that foresaw the gradual encirclement by rural guerrillas of urban areas leading eventually to victory as opposed to a short guerrilla war leading to an insurrection

proportional representation – any of many variants of electoral formula by which parties win seats in a legislature in proportion to the share of the popular votes cast for them

protected democracy – term used by Loveman (1994) to refer to a political system that is nominally democratic but in which the military retains a significant supervisory role

protectionism – the imposition of tariffs, quotas or other barriers on imports in order to nurture domestic production. See **free trade, comparative advantage, trade liberalisation**

public sphere – an independent area of activity outside the state, usually referred to in relation to **social movements** or **civil society, where** people and groups can identify and debate social problems, thereby influencing political action. See **private sphere**

R

racism – complex term with many variants that refers, broadly, to the abuse of, mistreatment of, or discrimination against one group by another on the grounds of their 'racial' status. Such status is highly contested and controversial and often based on superficial physical traits, and racism is often used to refer to forms of discrimination that in fact have an ethnic or cultural basis. See **inverse racism**

realism – an account of inter-state behaviour assuming the existence of an international arena without order characterised by conflict and the self-interested pursuit of power by **sovereign nation-states**

real wage – wage adjusted for inflation, so as to take into account purchasing power

rectification – policies adopted by the Cuban regime in the 1980s to end what it saw as abuses and inequalities that had grown out of limited economic freedoms

regimes of exception – states of emergency or special provisions suspending normal constitutional norms and guarantees that provide the military with a legal basis for interfering in non-military affairs

regional autonomy – the powers enjoyed by a regional authority independent of central government. See **decentralisation, centralism, centralisation, political decentralisation, administrative decentralisation, sectoral decentralisation, fiscal decentralisation, asymmetric decentralisation, sub-national authority,** *municipio*

regionalism – an approach to international relations that defines the interests of a country in terms of a particular geographic region

regulatory quality – the ability of a government to formulate and implement sound policies and regulations that permit and promote private-sector development

reification – term used in the analysis of party **institutionalisation** to refer to the extent to which a party's existence is established in the public imagination. See **decisional autonomy, systemness, value infusion, party system**

remittances – the funds sent back to a country by migrants working in other countries, often making an important contribution to national wealth

representation – the process by which one political actor, usually meaning a party or politician, acts on behalf of others and so advances their interests. The term representative government usually refers to a government that has been freely elected

representative democracy – forms of democratic practice in which citizens do not take an active part in decisionmaking, which is undertaken by elected officials. See **participatory democracy**

repression – the use or threat of force to ensure control

republic – term used loosely to refer to any state without a monarchy. See **republicanism**

republicanism – the belief that a country should be a republic and not a monarchy, implying by some definitions the election of a head of state. Constitutional republicanism places an emphasis on the principles enshrined within a constitution upon which such a republic should be based

resource mobilisation theory – theoretical explanation for **social movement** activity that explains this in terms of their own organisational features and resources

resource nationalism – the desire to nationalise or ensure a significant level of state control over strategic resources, particularly energy sectors such as oil and gas

retail investors – ordinary individual savers owning shares in a company or bonds, as opposed to 'institutional' investors such as pension or private equity funds

revolutionary nationalism – any of many different forms of nationalism often reflecting the aspiration to protect economic sovereignty that have been associated with or the products of revolutions, in particular that of Mexico (1910–17), where revolutionary nationalism was subsequently developed by the PRI as an official ideology

rightwing – broad term often used loosely to refer to that part of the political spectrum associated with conservatism, fascism and in some cases nationalism. See **leftwing**

rural proletariat – a class of labourers in the countryside who work for wages as opposed to, say, farming small plots of land on their own account. See **proletariat, smallholder,** *campesino*

S

secession – the withdrawal of a state or region in order to exercise **autonomy** or **self-determination**

second-generation reforms – economic reforms that aim to correct what are seen as failures or weaknesses of **neoliberalism** by placing greater emphasis on institution-building, **governance** and regulation and opening local labour and capital markets and financial systems

sectoral decentralisation – the devolution of powers in distinct areas or sectors of responsibility, such as education or healthcare. See **decentralisation, centralism, centralisation, political decentralisation, administrative decentralisation, fiscal decentralisation, asymmetric decentralisation, sub-national authority,** *municipio*

secularism – the belief that reason should determine public affairs and that religious considerations should be excluded from them. See **Enlightenment, anti-clericalism** self-coup – (in Spanish *auto-golpe*) the suspension of constitutional norms and the assumption of direct rule by a civilian president, often with the support of the armed forces

self-determination – any of many different forms of political autonomy associated, in particular, with the pursuit of independence by 'national' groups within larger states. See **multi-national, nation-state, nationalism**

semi-presidentialism – political systems (sometimes called dual-executive systems) in which the president is elected by the people but there is also a prime minister who requires the confidence of a parliament. The president may appoint the prime minister, but needs the support of parliament to do so, and can also dissolve parliament, but needs the support of the prime minister to do so

separation of powers – the principle in politics that power should be divided between the **executive**, **legislative** and **judicial** branches of government in order to avoid **tyranny**

separatism – the ambition of some citizens within a state, often those sharing an ethnic identification, to separate and form their own state. See **autonomy, secession, self-determination**

smallholder – someone owning or controlling a small plot of land. See *campesino, latifundia*

social capital – the networks, norms and trust within social life that enables people to act together more effectively to pursue shared objectives

social Catholicism – a strain of Catholic thought and practice that placed a priority on meeting social needs and justice

social cohesion – the aim of social policies that contribute to reducing the gap between rich and poor in an effort to reduce crime and conflict in society and hence strengthen **governability, governance** and democracy

social conservatism – conservative attitudes towards such social issues as gender equality, that can exist alongside and irrespective of progressive attitudes advocating equality in areas such as class

social Darwinism – idea associated with the work of Herbert Spencer in the nineteenth century that envisaged a classification of mankind into inferior and superior races. See **positivism**

social democracy – political ideology arguing that the transition to **socialism** can be achieved gradually through democratic means rather than suddenly through revolution, implying as a result the need to reform the capitalist system in order to make it fairer and not to overthrow it. See **socialism, capitalism, structuralism, neostructuralism, post-neostructuralism**

socialism – any of many variants of the belief that society should be organised on the basis of collective, as opposed to individual, ownership of the means of production. See **communism, social democracy, social liberalism, capitalism, national socialism**

'socialism of the twenty-first century' – contemporary position popular in South America largely indistinct from traditional **socialism** although often placing significant emphasis on institutional reform, **participatory democracy** and **civil society**

social liberalism – liberalism in which there is greater emphasis upon social justice as opposed to individual or economic freedom. See **liberalism, neoliberalism**

social mobilisation – see **mobilisation**

social movement – see **new social movement**

social rights – those mainly economic rights enjoyed by an individual or group to develop their capacities and become fully integrated members of society such as the right to subsistence, health, education and employment. See **civil rights, citizenship, political rights**

socio-environmentalism – a strain of environmentalism, particularly associated with Brazil, considered to be more politicised and further to the left than counterparts elsewhere. See **environmental justice, sustainable development**

soft power – a foreign policy approach based on an effort to influence other states by winning hearts and minds that is reflected in a commitment to multilateral solutions as opposed to the unilateral assertion of military or other coercive power

South–South solidarity – co-operation between developing states and regions vis-à-vis the developed world

sovereignty – the unrestricted authority that a **state** enjoying **legitimacy** has over decisionmaking within its jurisdiction. See **international law, nation-state, nationalism**

state – the subject of much debate, but usually understood as a set of social institutions which exercises a monopoly over the legitimate use of force within a given territory. See **legitimacy, nation-state, statist**

state-building – the active process of creating the formal institutions and procedures associated with the modern state, such as a government bureaucracy. See **state, nation-state, statist**

statist (statism) – term characterising centralised state involvement in economic planning and activity, often implying extensive state ownership, thereby constraining if not eliminating free-market activities. See **state, nation-state, sovereignty**

statute – a formal, written and hence codified law enacted by a legislature and ratified by the **executive**. See **legislative**

structural adjustment – the strategic adjustment through policymaking of the whole structure of an economy, a term that has usually been used with reference to reforms associated with **neoliberalism** that entailed a reduction in the **state**'s role, nurturing of the private sector, and changing the focus of economic growth from **import-substitution** to exports. See **structuralism**

structuralism – the strategy adopted in Latin American political economy of reforming the structure of an economy, principally through state-led **import-substitution industrialisation (ISI)**, in order to escape the condition of underdevelopment that results from an over-reliance on the export of primary products. See **dependency, neodevelopmentalism, neoliberalism, neostructuralism, post-neostructuralism, 'post-Washington Consensus'** sub-national authority – a regional or local authority below that of the central state, such as a province, department or *municipio*. See **decentralisation, centralism, centralisation, political decentralisation, administrative decentralisation, federalism, fiscal decentralisation, asymmetric decentralisation, sectoral decentralisation**

sub-region – a discernible group of countries within a larger region, such as Central America, the Andes or the Southern Cone

super-imperialism – dominant global role accorded by Marxist theories of imperialism to the US as the world's most powerful capitalist economy

supra-national – term used to refer to structures or legal mechanisms that can be applied to individual countries by transnational forces or a notional **international community** existing above nation-states

sustainable development – the use of natural resources to generate economic growth that is not harmful to the environment, so that these can be further exploited by future generations. See **biodiversity, socio-environmentalism**

systemness – term used in the analysis of party **institutionalisation** to refer to the increasing scope, density and regularity of the interactions that constitute the party as a structure. See **decisional autonomy, reification, value infusion, party system**

T

technocrat – highly educated bureaucratic official advocating planned technical solutions to economic and social problems whose significance often lies in his or her non-political character and hence ostensible autonomy from special interests

terms of trade – a measure of a country's commercial well-being based upon the ratio of the average price of imports to the average price of exports

thick and thin – concepts in political analysis employed by Coppedge (1999, 2005) distinguishing between the observation of many characteristics of a phenomenon or process (thick) or only one or a few (thin). A consequence of using a 'thin' concept of democracy is that many countries may qualify as being democratic, even though some are clearly more democratic than others

trade liberalisation – the dismantling of barriers to **free trade** such as tariffs, quotas and regulations. See **protectionism**

transformationalist position – approach adopted in the study of **globalisation** arguing that this gives rise to complex transformations in economics, politics and culture that have an uneven and even contradictory impact on **nation-states,** regions and sectors

transformismo – term used with specific reference to Argentina to characterise the 20-year neoliberal reform process. See **neoliberalism**

transition – a process of regime change

trans-Latin – Latin American transnational corporation. See **outward foreign direct investment**

tribute – colonial tithes imposed on **indigenous** communities which persisted in some countries, in a modified form, into the twentieth century

Trotskyism – strain of **Marxism-Leninism** emphasising the ideas of Leon Trotsky, in particular internationalism, by contrast with the position adopted by Stalin of 'socialism in one country'. See **Leninism, Maoism**

tyranny – **dictatorship** that flouts the constitution or laws. See **authoritarian, repression**

U

underemployment – a situation in which workers work for fewer hours than they are able or want to, or have less desirable jobs than they would prefer or are qualified for, or are engaged in tasks that are not particularly productive, meaning in consequence that a portion of the labour force could be eliminated without reducing total output

unilateralism – an approach to international affairs by which a state acts only in its own interests without regard for the concerns of other states or **multilateral** organisations, hence the opposite of **multilateralism**

unilateral powers – **executive** powers that can be used independently without the concurrence of the legislature, such as decree powers. See *decretismo*, **informal powers, integrative powers**

unipolar – the existence of one dominant pole of growth, influence, power etc. See **multipolarity**

unitary state – a unitary state is one in which **sub-national authorities** either do not exist or have such little power that these are irrelevant to the political process

universal suffrage – the extension of the right to vote (suffrage) to all adults irrespective of social status, gender, ethnic distinctions etc.

urgency provision – a procedural device enabling an executive to ensure a legislature deals with a bill without delay. See **legislative**

V

value infusion – term used in the analysis of party **institutionalisation** to refer to the extent to which party actors and supporters identify with the party above and beyond self-interested incentives for involvement in its activities. See **decisional autonomy, reification, systemness, party system**

Vatican II – the Second Vatican Council, held in the early 1960s in Rome

veto – the power to prevent action or legislation by others

W

war of position – idea advocated by Antonio Gramsci by which the Left attempts to penetrate civil society and the government bureaucracy through reformist politics as opposed to adopting an armed or overtly revolutionary strategy

'War on Drugs' – term in the US given to a lengthy campaign against the illegal drugs trade that has extended abroad to participating countries such as Mexico, Colombia and Peru. See **decertification, narcostate**

'War on Terror' – the broad range of national security policies pursued by the administration of George W. Bush and favoured in particular by **neoconservatives** following the attacks against the World Trade Center on 11 September 2001 that involved punitive and 'preemptive' military interventions in the Middle East, a global covert conflict against mainly Islamic militants, significantly tightened domestic security and air transportation policies, greater attention to immigration policy, and the reassessment of traditionally held rights and liberties. See *democradura*, **Bush Doctrine**

Washington Consensus – the position shared by international creditors and economically powerful countries in the 1980s about what neoliberal policy reforms should be undertaken in Latin America, emphasising exchange rates that are not fixed by the state, **trade liberalisation, foreign direct investment**, public-spending cuts, **privatisation, deregulation** and property rights. See **neoliberalism, monetarism, second-generation reforms, 'post-Washington Consensus'**

X
xenophobia – hatred of foreigners

Z
Zapatista – a follower of the ideas or tactics of Emiliano Zapata

zapatismo – ideas associated with Emiliano Zapata and more recently the Ejercito Zapatista de Liberación Nacional (EZLN, Zapatista National Liberation Army) in Mexico advocating, initially, the restitution of indigenous lands and **land reform**, and more recently **participatory democracy, communitarianism**, the reversal of **neoliberal** economic reforms in agriculture and international solidarity between **civil society** groups, among other themes

Appendix C

Dramatis personae

This list contains a brief description of the individuals mentioned in this book to help students who may not be familiar with Hispanic names, in particular.

A

Adoum, Jorge Enrique – Latin American intellectual who backed the 'Panama Proclamation' on Puerto Rico

Adrianzen, Catalina – a founder of the Peruvian guerrilla movement Sendero Luminoso and ideologue

Agustín I – Mexican emperor, 1822–23 (born Agustín de Iturbide)

Aharonian, Aram – director of TeleSUR

Ahmadinejad, Mahmoud – President of Iran 2005–

Alamán, Lucas – b.1792–d.1853, Mexican politician

Alemán Lacayo, Arnoldo – President of Nicaragua 1997–2002

Alencar Gomes da Silva, José – Vice-President of Brazil 2003–

Alessandri, Arturo – President of Chile 1920–25, 1932–38

Alexandre, Boniface – Provisional President of Haiti 2004–06

Alfonsín, Raúl – President of Argentina 1983–89

Allende, Salvador – President of Chile 1970–73

Alvarez Martínez, Gustavo – Military strongman in Honduras 1982–84

Alvarez, Oscar – Honduran security minister in 2004

Alvear, Soledad – Chilean politician who withdrew from Concertación coalition's presidential primary race in 2005

Amaral, Roberto – Brazilian science and technology minister in 2003

Amoroso Lima, Alceu – Brazilian founding member of the ODCA in 1947

Aranda, Luis – Head of Bolivian armed forces in 2005

Arbenz, Jacobo – President of Guatemala 1951–54

Arce Catacora, Luis – Treasury then economy minister of Bolivia, 2006–

Argaña, Luis María – Paraguayan former foreign minister assassinated in 1999

Arias Sánchez, Oscar – President of Costa Rica 1986–90, 2006–10

Aristide, Jean-Bertrand – President of Haiti 1991, 1993–94, 1994–96, 2001–04

Arzú, Alvaro – President of Guatemala 1996–2000

Astori, Danilo – Uruguayan economy minister 2005–08

Atahualpa – b.1502–d.1533, last Inca emperor

Aylwin, Patricio – President of Chile 1990–94

Azcona del Hoyo, José – President of Honduras 1986–90

Aznar, José María – Prime Minister of Spain 1996–2004

B

Bachelet, Michelle – President of Chile 2006–10

Balaguer Ricardo, Joaquín Antonio – President of the Dominican Republic 1960–62, 1966–78, 1986–96

Banzer Suárez, Hugo – Bolivian dictator 1971–78 and president 1997–2001

Baran, Paul A. – b.1910–d.1964, Ukrainian-American economist who contributed to the development of dependency theory

Barbosa Gomes, Joaquim Benedito – Brazil's first black Supreme Court justice 2003–

Barrios de Chamorro, Violeta – President of Nicaragua 1990–97

Barroso, Gustavo – b.1888–d.1959, Brazilian writer and fascist

Batista, Fulgencio – Cuban military strongman and president 1933–44, dictator 1952–59

Batlle Ibañez, Jorge Luis – President of Uruguay 2000–05

Batlle y Ordóñez, José – President of Uruguay 1903–07, 1911–15

Beers, Rand – US Under Secretary for the National Protection and Programs Directorate (NPPD, Department of Homeland Security), 2009–

Belaúnde Terry, Fernando – President of Peru 1963–68, 1980–85

Benedetti, Mario – Latin American intellectual who backed the 'Panama Proclamation' on Puerto Rico

Benedict XVI (Joseph Ratzinger) – Roman Catholic Pope 2005–

Berger, Oscar José Rafael – President of Guatemala 2004–08

Betances y Alacán, Ramón Emeterio – b.1827–d.1898, celebrated Puerto Rican nationalist

Betancourt, Rómulo – President of Venezuela 1945–48, 1959–64

Betancur, Belisario – President of Colombia 1982–86

Biondini, Alejandro – leader of rightwing PNT in Argentina

Blanco, Salvador Jorge – President of the Dominican Republic 1982–86

Bolaños Geyer, Enrique – President of Nicaragua 2002–07

Bolio, René – One of the founders of the MPS, Mexico

Bolívar, Simón – b.1783–d.1830, Venezuelan independence leader known as the Liberator

Bonaparte, Joseph – b.1768–d.1844, brother of **Napoleon I** installed by him as King Joseph I of Spain (1808–13)

Bordaberry, Juan María – President of Uruguay 1972–76

Borja Cevallos, Rodrigo – President of Ecuador 1988–92

Bosch, Orlando – Anti-Castro exile accused by Cuba of terrorism

Brito Figueroa, Federico – b.1921–d.2000, Venezuelan Marxist historian

Bucaram Ortíz, Abdalá Jaime – President of Ecuador 1996–97

Burin des Roziers, Henri – French priest working with the rural poor in Brazil

Bush, George (Senior) – President of US 1989–93

Bush, George W. (Junior) – President of US 2001–09, son of **George Bush (Senior)**

C

Cabanillas, Mercedes – Interior minister of Peru 2009–

Cáceres, Andrés – President of Peru 1886–90, 1894–95

Caldera, Rafael – President of Venezuela 1969–74, 1994–99

Calderón Hinojosa, Felipe de Jesús – President of Mexico 2006–

Calderón, Rafael Angel – President of Costa Rica 1990–94

Calderón Sol, Armando – President of El Salvador 1994–99

Callejas, Rafael Leonardo – President of Honduras 1990–94

Camaño, Eduardo – Acting president of Argentina 2001–02

Cardenal, Ernesto – Nicaraguan priest, poet and minister in Sandinista revolutionary regime

Cárdenas, Cuauhtémoc – Mexican politician (PRD), presidential candidate 1988, 1994, 2000, son of **Lázaro Cárdenas**

Cárdenas, Lázaro – President of Mexico 1934–40

Cardoso, Fernando Henrique – President of Brazil 1995–2003

Carlos III – Spanish king 1759–88

Carlos IV – Spanish King 1788–1808

Carmona, Pedro – Transitional President of Venezuela during coup attempt 2002

Carpio, Ramiró de León – President of Guatemala 1993–96

Carranza, Nicolas – El Salvador's vice-minister of defence 1979–81

Carranza, Venustiano – Mexican revolutionary leader and president 1915–20

Carrera, Rafael – b.1814–d.1865, Guatemalan *caudillo*

Carter, Jimmy – President of US 1977–81

Castañeda, Jorge – Mexican academic

Castiglioni, Luis – Former Vice-President of Paraguay and contender for Colorado nomination in 2008

Castillo, Adán – Guatemala's top anti-drug investigator, arrested in the US for drug-trafficking in 2005

Castillo, Alfredo – Ecuador's interior minister who resigned in 2006

Castro, Fidel – Cuban revolutionary leader and head of state 1959–2008

Castro, Raúl – President of Cuba 2008–, brother of **Fidel Castro**

Cerezo Arévalo, Marco Vinicio – President of Guatemala 1986–91

Chauyffet, Emilio – Mexican politician (PRI)

Chávez Frías, Hugo Rafael – President of Venezuela 1999–

Chinchilla, Laura – President of Costa Rica 2010–

Chomsky, Noam – Influential US liberal intellectual

Cipriano de Mosquera, Tomás – b.1798–d.1878, Colombian *caudillo*

Clavo Peralta, Margie – Alleged to have been Comrade Nancy, a Sendero Luminoso leader

Clinton, Bill – President of US 1993–2001

Clinton, Hillary – US Secretary of State 2009–, wife of **Bill Clinton**

Collor de Mello, Fernando – President of Brazil 1990–92

Colom Caballeros, Alvaro – President of Guatemala 2008–

Colosio, Luis Donaldo – b.1950–d.1994, Mexican presidential candidate assassinated in 1994

Comte, Auguste – b.1798–d.1857, French philosopher

Córdoba, Concha – Colombian cardinal who removed **Camilo Torres** from his post in 1961

Correa Delgado, Rafael Vicente – President of Ecuador 2007–

Cortés, Hernán – b.1485–d.1547, Spanish conqueror of Mexico

Cotjí, Demetrio – Guatemalan Mayan writer, academic and former deputy education minister

Cristiani, Alfredo – President of El Salvador 1989–94

Cubas Grau, Raúl – President of Paraguay 1998–99

D

Darwin, Charles – b.1809–d.1882, English naturalist who developed the theory of evolution

da Penha, María – Brazilian victim of spousal abuse whose case became a *cause célèbre*

da Silva, Luiz Inácio (Lula) – President of Brazil 2003–10

D'Aubuisson, Roberto – b.1943–d.1992, first leader of ARENA in El Salvador

Dávila, Juan – Chilean painter

de Antuñano, Esteban – b.1792–d.1847, Mexican entrepreneur

de la Rúa, Fernando – President of Argentina 1999–2001

de la Vega, Garcilaso 'Inca' – b.1539–d.1616, Peruvian writer who recounted the origins and rise of the Inca empire

Díaz, Porfirio – Mexican dictator 1876–1911

Díaz Martínez, Antonio – Peruvian agronomist and Sendero Luminoso ideologue

Dieterich, Heinz – German sociologist who coined term 'socialism of the 21st century'

Drago, Luis María – b.1859–d.1921, Argentine foreign minister

Duarte, José Napoleón – President of El Salvador 1980–82, 1984–89

Duarte Frutos, Nicanor – President of Paraguay 2003–08

Duhalde, Eduardo – President of Argentina 2002–03

Durán-Ballén, Sixto Alfonso – President of Ecuador 1992–96

Durand Araujo, Teresa – Alleged to have been Comrade Doris, a Sendero Luminoso leader

Dussel, Enrique – Argentine political philosopher

Duvalier, François 'Papa Doc' – Dictator in Haiti, 1957–71

Duvalier, Jean-Claude 'Baby Doc' – Dictator in Haiti, 1971–86, son of **François 'Papa Doc' Duvalier**

E

Echeverría, Luis – President of Mexico 1970–76

Ellacuria, Ignacio – b.1930–d.1989, Spanish liberation theologian executed along with five other Jesuit priests by paramilitaries in El Salvador in 1989

Endara, Guillermo – President of Panama 1989–94

F

Farabundo Martí, Agustín – b.1893–d.1932, revolutionary in El Salvador

Febres Cordero, León – President of Ecuador 1984–88

Ferdinand VII – Spanish king 1813–33

Fernández Amunátegui, Mariano – Foreign minister of Chile 2009–

Fernández de Kirchner, Cristina – President of Argentina 2007–

Fernández Reyna, Leonel – President of the Dominican Republic 1996–2000, 2004–

Figueiredo, João – Brazilian military leader 1979–85

Figueres Olsen, José María – President of Costa Rica 1994–98

Flavio Cappio, Luiz – Brazilian bishop who staged a hunger strike in 2005 to protest against plans to divert water from the São Francisco river

Flores, Francisco – President of El Salvador 1999–2004

Flores Facussé, Carlos Roberto – President of Honduras 1998–2002

Fortuño, Luis – Governor of Puerto Rico 2009–

Fox Quesada, Vicente – President of Mexico 2000–06

Franco, Francisco – b.1892–d.1975, Spanish dictator

Franco, Itamar – President of Brazil 1992–95

Frei Montalva, Eduardo – President of Chile 1964–70

Frei Ruiz-Tagle, Eduardo – President of Chile 1994–2000, son of Eduardo **Frei Montalva**

Friedman, Milton – b.1912–d.2006, US economist

Freyre, Gilberto – b.1900–d.1987, Brazilian anthropologist

Frondizi, Arturo – President of Argentina 1958–62

Fuentes, Rosa Altagracia – Trade union leader assassinated in Honduras in 2008

Fujimori, Alberto – President of Peru 1990–2000

Funes, Mauricio – President of El Salvador 2009–

G

Gaitán, Jorge Eliécer – b.1898–d.1948, Colombian politician assassinated in 1948

Galeano, Eduardo – Latin American intellectual who backed the 'Panama Proclamation' on Puerto Rico

Gamio, Manuel – b.1883–d.1960, Mexican writer

García Márquez, Gabriel – Latin American intellectual who backed the 'Panama Proclamation' on Puerto Rico

García Pérez, Alan – President of Peru 1985–90, 2006–

Garrido, Juan – African *conquistador* who accompanied **Hernán Cortés** in subjugation of the Aztecs

Gaviria, César – President of Colombia 1990–94

Gerardi, Juan José – Catholic Bishop assassinated in Guatemala in 1998

Gómez, Laureano – President of Colombia 1950–53

González Macchi, Luis Angel – President of Paraguay 1999–2003

Gorbachev, Mikhail – Soviet leader 1985–91

Gordillo, Elba Esther – Mexican politician (PRI)

Goulart, João – President of Brazil 1961–64

Gramsci, Antonio – b.1891–d.1937, influential Italian Marxist political thinker

Guevara, 'Che' (Ernesto) – b.1928–d.1967, Argentine-born Cuban revolutionary leader

Gunder Frank, André – b.1929–d.2005, German economic historian who contributed to the development of dependency theory

Gutiérrez, Gustavo – Peruvian priest regarded as the founder of liberation theology

Gutiérrez Borbúa, Lucio Edwin – President of Ecuador 2003–05

Guzmán, Abimael ('Presidente Gonzalo') – Leader of Peruvian guerrilla organisation Sendero Luminoso

Guzmán Blanco, Antonio – President of Venezuela 1863, 1865, 1870–77, 1879–84, 1886–88

Guzmán Fernández, Silvestre Antonio – President of the Dominican Republic 1978–82

Guzmán, Joaquín – Leader of Mexico's Sinaloa drug-trafficking cartel

H

Haya de la Torre, Victor Raúl – b.1895–d.1979, Peruvian populist politician and ideologue who founded APRA

Hernández Martínez, Maximiliano – President of El Salvador 1931–44

Herrera Campíns, Luis – President of Venezuela 1979–84

Heureaux, Ulíses – President of the Dominican Republic 1882–84, 1887–99

Hidalgo, Miguel – b.1753–d.1811, creole priest who inaugurated Mexico's independence struggle

Huerta, Victoriano – Mexican general who imposed a dictatorship 1913–14

Hu Jintao – President of China 2003–

Humala, Antauro – retired Peruvian army major who led a brief rebellion in 2005

Humala Tasso, Ollanta – Peruvian former army officer and presidential candidate 2006, brother of **Antauro Humala**

Hurtado Larrea, Osvaldo – President of Ecuador 1981–84

I

Ibáñez, Carlos – President of Chile 1927–31, 1952–58

Insulza, José Miguel – Secretary-general of the OAS 2005–

J

João VI – Portuguese king 1816–26

John Paul II (Karol Józef Wojtyla) – Roman Catholic Pope 1978–2005

Juárez, Benito – President of Mexico 1861–63, 1867–72

Juruna, Mario – Brazilian indigenous politician

K

Kennedy, John. F. – President of US 1961–63

Keynes, John Maynard – b.1883–d.1946, British economist

Khrushchev, Nikita – Soviet leader 1953–64

Kirchner, Néstor – President of Argentina 2003–07

Kubitschek, Juscelino – President of Brazil 1956–61

L

Labastida Ochoa, Francisco – Mexican politician (PRI) and presidential candidate 2000

Lacalle, Luis Alberto – President of Uruguay 1990–95

Lagos, Edith – A revered Sendero Luminoso commander who led a raid on an Ayacucho prison

Lagos, Ricardo Froilán – President of Chile 2000–06

Laín, Domingo – Spanish priest who died fighting with Colombian guerrilla movement ELN

Latorre Carrasco, Augusta – Alias Comrade Norah, wife of the Sendero Luminoso leader **Abimael Guzmán**

Lavagna, Roberto – Argentina economy minister – 2002–05

Lavin, Joaquín – Chilean politician (UDI), presidential contender and former mayor of Santiago

Lleras Camargo, Alberto – President of Colombia 1945–46, 1958–62

Lleras Restrepo, Carlos – President of Colombia 1966–70

Lobo Sosa, Porfirio – President of Honduras 2010–

López Obrador, Andrés Manuel – Mexican politician (PRD) and former presidential candidate, mayor of Mexico City

López Trujillo, Alfonso – Colombian bishop, secretary general of CELAM 1972–84

Lückert León, Roberto – Archbishop of Coro 1998– and vice-president of the Venezuelan Episcopal Conference

Lugo, Fernando – President of Paraguay 2008–

M

Macas, Luis – An indigenous leader in Ecuador who served as agriculture minister under **Lucio Gutiérrez**

Machado Dias, Antônio José – Brazilian judge assassinated in 2003

Madero, Francisco – Mexican revolutionary leader and president 1911–13

Madrazo, Roberto – Mexican politician (PRI)

Maduro, Ricardo – President of Honduras 2002–06

Mahuad, Jamil – President of Ecuador 1998–2000

Mama Ocllo – Andean cosmological figure

Mañach, Jorge – b.1898–d.1961, Cuban writer

Manco Cápac – Andean cosmological figure

Maranhão, Bruno – Brazilian politician (PT) and a leader of the MLST

Marcos Subcomandante – Masked leader of the EZLN rebels in Chiapas, Mexico, whose name is not known, but whom the Mexican government claims is Rafael Guillén

Mariátegui, José Carlos – b.1894–d.1930, Peruvian Marxist thinker

Marighella, Carlos – b.1911–d.1969, Brazilian urban guerrilla and Marxist thinker

Maritain, Jacques – b.1882–d.1973, French Christian democratic thinker

Martí, José – b.1853–d.1895, Cuban independence leader

Martinelli Berrocal, Ricardo – President of Panama 2009–

Maximilian I – Habsburg prince installed as Mexican emperor (1864–67) by **Napoleon III**

Mayo Hernández, Mario Enrique – Cuban dissident

Medvedev, Dmitry – President of Russia 2008–

Mejía Domínguez, Rafael Hipólito – President of the Dominican Republic 2000–04

Menchú, Rigoberta – Guatemalan Mayan activist and 1992 Nobel Peace Prize winner

Mendes, Chico – Brazilian rubber-tappers' leader murdered in 1988

Menem, Carlos Saúl – President of Argentina 1989–99

Mesa, Carlos Diego – President of Bolivia 2003–05

Micheletti, Roberto – Acting President of Honduras 2009–10

Milanés, Pablo – Latin American intellectual who backed the 'Panama Proclamation' on Puerto Rico

Miranda, Francisco de – b.1750–d.1816, Venezuelan independence leader

Mitre, Bartolomé – President of Argentina 1862–68

Molina Enríquez, Andrés – b.1868–d.1970, Mexican writer whose work was an important precursor to the Revolution

Molina, Juan Ignacio – b.1740–d.1829 Chilean Jesuit priest forced into exile by the Spanish

Monroe, James – President of US 1817–25

Montejo, Victor – Guatemalan Mayan writer and academic

Montesinos, Vladimiro – Peruvian security chief under **Alberto Fujimori**

Morales Ayma, Evo – President of Bolivia 2006–

Morales Bermúdez, Francisco – Leader of Peruvian military regime 1975–80

Morazán, Francisco – b.1799–d.1842, Honduran-born Central American *caudillo*

Moscoso Rodríguez de Arias, Mireya – President of Panama 1999–2004

Mujica, José – President of Uruguay 2010–

Mussolini, Benito – b.1883–d.1945, Italian fascist dictator

N

Napoleon I – b.1769–d.1821, French general and emperor whose invasion of Spain and Portugal helped to precipitate Latin American Independence

Napoleon III – b.1808–d.1873, French emperor whose forces invaded Mexico (1861) and installed **Maximilian**

Nixon, Richard – President of US 1969–74

Noble, Ronald – Secretary-general of Interpol 2000–

Noboa, Alvaro Fernando – Ecuadorean businessman and politician (PRIAN)

Noboa, Gustavo – President of Ecuador 2000–03

Noguera, Jorge – Colombian intelligence chief who resigned in 2005

Noriega, Manuel Antonio – Panamanian dictator 1981–89

Noriega, Roger – US Assistant Secretary of State for Western Hemisphere affairs 2003–05

O

Obama, Barack – President of US 2009–

O'Higgins, Bernardo – b.1778–d.1842, Chilean independence leader

Ojeda Rios, Filiberto – Commander of the Puerto Rican clandestine nationalist organisation EPB killed by US security forces in 2005

Ordoñez, Manuel – Argentine founding member of the ODCA in 1947

Orrego, Antenor – b.1892–d.1960, Peruvian philosopher

Ortega, Daniel – President of Nicaragua 1985–90, 2007–

Ortiz Pinchetti, Francisco – Mexican journalist

Ovelar, Blanca – Paraguayan politician and contender for Colorado nomination in 2008

Oviedo, Lino César – Former Paraguayan army commander-in-chief 1993 and politician

P

Pacheco, Abel – President of Costa Rica 2002–06

Páez, José Antonio Páez – b.1790–d.1873, Venezuelan *caudillo*

Palacio, Alfredo – President of Ecuador 2005–07

Parsons, Talcott – b.1902–d.1979, influential US sociologist

Pascal-Trouillot, Ertha – Provisional President of Haiti, 1990–91

Pastrana Arango, Andrés – President of Colombia 1998–2002

Patterson, Anne – US State Department's Assistant Secretary for International Narcotics and Law Enforcement Affairs 2006

Paz Estenssoro, Víctor – President of Bolivia 1952–56, 1960–64, 1985–89

Paz Zamora, Jaime – President of Bolivia 1989–93

Pedro I – Brazilian emperor 1822–31, King of Portugal 1826

Pedro II – Brazilian emperor 1841–89

Pérez, Carlos Andrés – President of Venezuela 1974–79, 1989–93

Pérez, Manuel – Spanish priest who was a joint leader of the Colombian guerrilla movement ELN

Pérez Balladares, Ernesto – President of Panama 1994–99

Pérez Jiménez, Marcos – Venezuelan dictator 1948–58

Pérez Luján, Enrique – Leader of the UNS, Mexico

Perón, Evita (María Eva Duarte de Perón) – b.1919–d.1952, popular wife of **Juan Domingo Perón**

Perón, Juan Domingo – President of Argentina 1946–55, 1973–74

Pierluisi, Pedro – Resident Commissioner of Puerto Rico 2009–

Piñera, Sebastián – President of Chile 2010–

Pinochet, Augusto – Chilean military dictator 1973–90

Pivaral, Mario – Guatemalan congressman assassinated in 2006

Poch, Julio Alberto – Argentine held in Spain on 'Dirty War' charges

Pombal, Marquis of (Sebastião José de Carvalho e Melo) – Portuguese prime minister 1750–77

Portales, Diego – b.1793–d.1837, Chilean *caudillo*

Portillo, Alfonso – President of Guatemala 2000–04

Posada Carriles, Luis – Cuban-Venezuelan anti-Castro activist accused by Cuba of terrorism

Prebisch, Raúl – b.1901–d.1986, influential Argentine economist and the first director of CEPAL

Préval, René – President of Haiti, 1996–2001, 2006–

Puerta, Ramón – Acting president of Argentina 2001

Q

Quadros, Jânio – President of Brazil 1961

Quispe, Felipe – Bolivian Aymara indigenous leader

R

Rahall, Nick J. – Chairman of the committee on natural resources, US House of Representatives, 2007–

Ramos, Arthur – b.1903–d.1949, Brazilian scholar

Ratzinger, Joseph – Pope Benedict XVI (2005–)

Reagan, Ronald – President of US 1981–89

Reategui, Javier – Peruvian interior minister who resigned following the 2005 rebellion by Antauro Humala

Regules, Dardo – Uruguayan founding member of the ODCA in 1947

Reich, Otto – adviser, official or representative of US presidents, mainly under **Ronald Reagan** and **George W. Bush**. US special envoy to the western hemisphere 2003–04

Reina, Carlos Roberto – President of Honduras 1994–98

Remache, Estuardo – Pachakuthik congressman in Ecuador and president of the national human rights commission

Ricardo, David – b.1772–d.1823, British economist

Rice, Condoleezza – US secretary of state 2005–09

Richard, Nelly – Chilean cultural theorist

Ríos Montt, José Efraín – Military dictator in Guatemala 1982–83

Rodó, José Enrique – b.1872–d.1917, influential Uruguayan essayist

Rodríguez, Andrés – President of Paraguay 1989–93

Rodríguez, Eduardo – President of Bolivia 2005–06

Rodríguez, Miguel Angel – President of Costa Rica 1998–2002

Rodríguez de Francia, Dr José Gaspar – b.1766–d.1840, Paraguayan dictator

Rodríguez Maradiaga, Óscar Andrés – Archbishop of Tegucigalpa and a critic of the president, **Manuel Zelaya**

Rodríguez Mata, Jenny – Alleged to have been a Sendero Luminoso leader

Rojas, Ricardo – b.1882–d.1957, Argentine writer

Rojas Pinilla, Gustavo – President of Colombia 1953–57

Roldós Aguilera, Jaime – President of Ecuador 1979–81

Romero, Oscar – Archbishop of San Salvador assassinated in 1980

Romero Paoletti, Dionisio – Peruvian businessman

Roosevelt, Franklin D. ('FDR') – President of US 1933–45

Roosevelt, Theodore – President of US 1901–09

Rosas, Juan Manuel de – b.1793–d.1877, Argentine *caudillo*

Rostow, Walt W. – b.1916–d.2003, US economic historian

Rousseau, Jean-Jacques – b.1712–d.1778, Swiss political philosopher

Rousseff, Dilma – PT presidential candidate 2010, Brazil

Ruiz, Samuel – Bishop of San Cristóbal de las Casas, Chiapas, Mexico, 1959–99

Rumsfeld, Donald – US defence secretary 2001–06

S

Saa, Adolfo Rodríguez – Interim President of Argentina 2001

Sábato, Ernesto – Argentinean intellectual who backed the 'Panama Proclamation' on Puerto Rico and author of key probe into disappearances

Saca González, Elías Antonio – President of El Salvador 2004–09

Salazar, António de Oliveira – Prime minister and dictator of Portugal 1932–68

Salgado, Juan Ramón – b.1961–d.2006, deputy leader of the PLH in Honduras assassinated in 2006

Salgado, Plínio – b.1895–d.1975, Brazilian fascist leader

Salinas de Gortari, Carlos – President of Mexico 1988–94

Sam Colop, Enrique – Guatemalan Mayan writer

Samper, Ernesto – President of Colombia 1994–98

Sánchez de Lozada, Gonzalo – President of Bolivia 1993–97, 2002–03

Sandino, Augusto César – b.1895–d.1934, Nicaraguan revolutionary

Sanguinetti, Julio María – President of Uruguay 1985–90, 1995–2000

San Martín, José de – b.1778–d.1850, Argentine independence leader

Santa Anna, Antonio López de – b.1794–d.1876, Mexican *caudillo*

Santa Cruz, Andrés – b.1792–d.1865, *caudillo*, President of Peru (1827) and of Bolivia (1829–39)

Sarney, José – President of Brazil 1985–90

Scilingo, Adolfo – Former Argentine officer tried in Spain on 'Dirty War' charges

Serrano Elías, Jorge – President of Guatemala 1991–93

Servando Teresa de Mier, José – b.1763–d.1827, Mexican Dominican friar and early ideologue of independence

Shannon, Thomas – US Assistant Secretary of State for Western Hemisphere Affairs 2005–09, now ambassador to Brazil

Siles Zuazo, Hernán – President of Bolivia 1952, 1956–60, 1982–85

Silva, Marina – Brazilian environment minister (PT) who quit in 2008 over policy

Singer, Hans – b.1910–d.2006, German-born UN economist

Slim, Carlos – Mexican businessman

Solís, Ottón – Costa Rican politician (PAC) and presidential candidate 2006

Somoza Debayle, Anastasio – Nicaraguan dictator 1967–79

Soruco, Norah – Vice-president of Bolivian congress in 2005

Spencer, Herbert – b.1820–d.1903, English political theorist

Stang, Dorothy – US nun working with the landless in Brazil who was assassinated in 2005

Stone, Oliver – US film-maker

Stroessner, Alfredo – Paraguayan dictator 1954–89

Suazo Córdova, Roberto – President of Honduras 1982–86

Sunkel, Osvaldo – Chilean neostructuralist economist

T

Toledo Manrique, Alejandro – President of Peru 2001–06

Toro, José David – President of Bolivia 1936–37

Torres Restrepo, Camilo – b.1929–d.1966, Colombian liberation theologian and guerrilla

Torrijos Espino, Martín Erasto – President of Panama 2004–09, son of **Omar Torrijos Herrera**

Torrijos Herrera, Omar – Panamanian dictator 1968–81

Trius, Vicente – President and chief executive of Wal-Mart Latin America

Trujillo, Rafael Leonidas – Dictator in the Dominican Republic 1930–61

Túpac Amaru – last Inca emperor 1570–72

Túpac Amaru II (José Gabriel Condorcanqui) – b.c1740–d.1781, great-grandson of Túpac Amaru who led an indigenous uprising in colonial Peru

Túpac Katari (Julián Apasa) – bc.1750–d.1781, leader of an indigenous rebellion in Bolivia

U

Ubico, Jorge – President of Guatemala 1931–44

Uribe Velez, Alvaro – President of Colombia 2002–10

Uriburu, José Felix – Argentine military dictator 1930–32

Uscátegui, Jaime Humberto – Former Colombian general jailed in 2009 in connection with a massacre of civilians by paramilitaries at Mapiripán in 1997

V
Vaca Diez, Hormando – Bolivian Senate speaker in 2005
Vargas, Getúlio – President of Brazil 1930–45, 1951–54
Vargas Llosa, Mario – Peruvian author and politician
Vasconcelos, José – Mexican education minister 1921–24
Vásquez Velásquez, Romeo – Head of Honduran armed forces involved in the coup that removed **Manuel Zelaya**
Vázquez, Tabaré Ramón – President of Uruguay 2005–10
Velasco Alvarado, Juan – Military leader of Peru 1968–75
Velasco Ibarra, José María – President of Ecuador 1934–35, 1944–47, 1952–56, 1960–61, 1968–72
Velázquez, Fidel – b.1900–d.1997, Mexican trade union leader
Villa, Francisco 'Pancho' (José Doroteo Arango Arámbula) – b.c1878–1923, Mexican revolutionary leader

W
Wasmosy, Juan Carlos – President of Paraguay 1993–98
Weber, Max – b.1864–d.1920, German sociologist
Wimmer, Carolus – Foreign affairs spokesman of the PCV, Venezuela

Y
Yanga, Gaspar – African slave who led a revolt against the Spanish in Veracruz, Mexico, in about 1570
Yanomami, Davi Kopenawa – Leader of the Hutukara Yanomami Association and a spokesman for the Yanomami people, Brazilian Amazon
Yrigoyen, Hipólito – President of Argentina 1916–22, 1928–30

Z
Zapata, Emiliano – b.1879–d.1919, Mexican revolutionary leader
Zea, Leopoldo – b.1912–d.2004, Mexican philosopher
Zedillo Ponce de León, Ernesto – President of Mexico 1994–2000
Zelaya Rosales, Manuel – President of Honduras 2006–09
Zoellick, Robert – US Deputy Secretary of State 2005–06, now president of the World Bank

Bibliography

Abente Brun, Diego. 2008. 'Introduction', in Larry Diamond, Marc F. Plattner and Diego Abente Brun (eds), *Latin America's Struggle for Democracy*. Baltimore, MD: Johns Hopkins University Press/National Endowment for Democracy

Adler, Emmanuel. 1987. *The Power of Ideology: The Quest for Technical Autonomy in Argentina and Brazil*. Berkeley, CA: University of California Press

Adrianzen, Catalina. 1974. *El marxismo, Mariátegui y el movimiento femenino*. Lima: Ediciones Bandera Roja, No. 2 (April 1975); *Marxists Internet Archive*, October 2004. Available at: http://www.marxists.org/espanol/adrianzen [accessed February 2010]

AFP (Agence France-Presse). 2009. '54 African migrants arrest arrested off Costa Rica coast', AFP/Hindustan Times online, 13 September 2009. Available at: http://www. hindustantimes.com/News-Feed/africa/54-African-migrants-arrest-arrested-off-Costa-Rica-coast/Article1-453351.aspx [accessed February 2010]

Agüero, Felipe. 1998. 'Conflicting Assessments of Democratization: Exploring the Fault Lines', in Felipe Agüero and Jeffrey Stark (eds), *Fault Lines of Democracy in Post-Transition Latin America*. Coral Gables, FL: North-South Center Press

Agüero, Felipe. 2004. 'Globalization, Business, and Politics: Promoting Corporate Social Responsibility in Latin America', Paper presented at the annual meeting of the International Studies Association, Le Centre Sheraton Hotel, Montreal, Quebec, Canada, 17 March 2004. Tucson: ISA

Agüero, Felipe and Jeffrey Stark (eds). 1998. *Fault Lines of Democracy in Post-Transition Latin America*. Coral Gables, FL: North-South Center Press

Aguirre Beltrán, Gonzalo. 1981. *La población negra de México: Estudio etnohistórico*, Colección Fuentes para la historia del agrarismo en México. Mexico: SRA-CEHAM.

Albright, David. 1989. 'Bomb Potential for South America', *Bulletin of the Atomic Scientists*, Vol. 45, No. 4 (May), pp. 16–20

Alemán, Eduardo and Ernesto Calvo. 2008. 'Analyzing Legislative Success in Latin America: The Case of Democratic Argentina', in Guillermo O'Donnell, Joseph S. Tulchin, and Augusto Varas (eds), with Adam Stubits, *New Voices in the Study of Democracy in Latin America*. Washington, DC: Woodrow Wilson International Center for Scholars. Available at: http://www.wilsoncenter.org/index.cfm?topic_id=1425&fuseaction=topics.publications&group_id=7505 [accessed October 2009]

Alexander, Robert J. 1995. 'The Import Substitution Strategy of Economic Development', in James L. Dietz (ed.), *Latin America's Economic Development. Confronting Crisis*, 2nd Edition. Boulder, CO: Lynne Rienner

Alexander, Robert J. 2009. *International Labor Organizations and Organized Labor in Latin America and the Caribbean: A History*. Santa Barbara, CA: Praeger

Almond, Gabriel and Sidney Verba. 1963. *The Civic Culture. Political Attitudes and Democracy in Five Nations*. Princeton, NJ: Princeton University Press

Altman, David. 2001. *The Politics of Coalition Formation and Survival in Multiparty Presidential Regimes*. Doctoral thesis, Notre Dame, IN, Department of Government and International Studies, Notre Dame University

Altman, David. 2002. 'Prospects for E-Government in Latin America: Satisfaction with Democracy, Social Accountability and Direct Democracy', *International Review of Public Administration*, Vol. 7, No. 2, pp. 5–20

Alvarez, Sonia E. and Arturo Escobar. 1992. 'Conclusion: Theoretical and Political Horizons of Change in Contemporary Latin American Social Movements', in Arturo Escobar and Sonia Alvarez (eds), *The Making of Social Movements in Latin America· Identity, Strategy and Democracy*. Boulder, CO: Westview Press

Alvarez, Sonia E., Evelina Dagnino and Arturo Escobar. 1998. 'Introduction: The Cultural and the Political in Latin American Social Movements', in Sonia E. Alvarez *et al.* (eds), *Cultures of Politics. Politics of Cultures. Re-Visioning Latin American Social Movements*. Boulder, CO: Westview Press

Alvarez, Sonia E., Evelina Dagnino and Arturo Escobar (eds). 1998. *Cultures of Politics. Politics of Cultures. Re-Visioning Latin American Social Movements*. Boulder, CO: Westview Press

Ames, Barry. 2002. 'Party Discipline in the Chamber of Deputies,' in Scott Morgenstern and Benito Nacif (eds), *Legislative Politics in Latin America*. Cambridge: Cambridge University Press

Amnesty International. 2005. Brazil: *'They come in shooting'. Policing socially excluded communities*. London: AI, 2 December 2005, AI Index: AMR 19/025/2005. Available at: http://web.amnesty.org/library/Index/ENGAMR190252005 [accessed February 2010]

Amnesty International. 2009. *Amnesty International Report 2009. The State of the World's Human Rights*. London: Amnesty International. Available at: http://thereport.amnesty.org/sites/report2009.amnesty.org/files/documents/air09-en.pdf [accessed September 2009]

Amorim Neto, Octavio. 2002a. 'Presidential Cabinets, Electoral Cycles, and Coalition Discipline in Brazil', in Scott Morgenstern and Benito Nacif (eds), *Legislative Politics in Latin America*. Cambridge: Cambridge University Press

Amorim Neto, Octavio. 2002b. 'Critical Debates: The Puzzle of Party Discipline in Brazil', review article, *Latin American Politics and Society*, Vol. 44, No.1 (April), pp. 127–44

Anderson, Benedict. 1991. *Imagined Communities*, Revised Edition. London: Verso

Anderson, Lisa. 1999. *Transitions to Democracy*. New York: Columbia University Press

Andolina, Robert, Nina Laurie and Sarah A. Radcliffe. 2009. *Indigenous Development in the Andes: Culture, Power, and Transnationalism*. Durham, NC: Duke University Press

Angus Reid. 2009. 'Most Chileans Reject Same-Sex Marriage', Angus Reid Global Monitor (Angus Reid Strategies) online, Polls and Research, 24 April 2009. Available at: http://www.angus-reid.com/polls/view/most_chileans_reject_same_sex_marriage/ [accessed December 2009]

AP (Associated Press). 2005a. 'Nicaragua, El Salvador declare alert for al-Qaida suspects', Filadelfo Alemán, *Associated Press*, Managua, 24 May 2005. Factiva.com database [accessed March 2006]

AP (Associated Press). 2005b. 'Message in a bottle saves stranded refugees', Associated Press, Costa Rica, *Irish Examiner*, 31 May 2005. Factiva.com database [accessed March 2006]

APEC (Asia-Pacific Economic Co-operation). 2005a. 'About Apec'. Singapore: APEC. Available at: http://www.apecsec.org.sg/apec/about_apec.html [accessed February 2010]

APEC (Asia-Pacific Economic Co-operation). 2005b. 'One Community, Our Future: Santiago Declaration, Twelfth APEC Economic Leaders' Meeting, Santiago de Chile, 20–21 November 2004'. Singapore: APEC. Available at: http://www.apec.org/apec/leaders_declarations/2004.html [accessed February 2010]

APEC (Asia-Pacific Economic Co-operation). 2005c. 'Joint Statement, Sixteenth APEC Ministerial Meeting, Santiago, Chile, 17–18 November 2004'. Singapore: APEC. Available at: http://www.apec.org/apec/ministerial_statements/annual_ministerial/2004_16th_apec_ministerial.html [accessed February 2010]

Appelbaum, Nancy, Anne MacPherson and Karin Alejandra Rosemblatt (eds). 2003. *Race and Nation in Modern Latin America*. Chapel Hill, NC: University of North Carolina Press

Arceneaux, Craig L. 2001. *Bounded Missions: Military Regimes and Democratization in the Southern Cone and Brazil*. University Park, PA: Pennsylvania State University Press

Archetti, Eduardo, Paul Cammack and Bryan Roberts (eds). 1987. *Latin America. Sociology of Developing Societies*. Houndmills: Macmillan

Argentine National Commission on the Disappeared. 1986. *Nunca Más: The Report of the Argentine National Commission on the Disappeared*. New York: Farrar Straus Giroux

Arns, Dom Paulo Evaristo. 1985. *Brasil Nunca Mais*, 6th Edition. Petrópolis: Vozes

Astor, Michael. 2004. 'Flowers, race issues blooming in Brazil', Associated Press, *Houston Chronicle*, 29 February 2004, 2 Star, p. 31. Factiva.com database [accessed March 2006]

Avritzer, Leonardo. 2009. *Participatory Institutions in Democratic Brazil*. Baltimore, MD: Johns Hopkins University Press/Woodrow Wilson Center Press

Aylwin, José. 1998. 'Indigenous Peoples' Rights in Chile: Progresses and Contradictions in a Context of Economic Globalization', paper presented at the Canadian Association for Latin American and Caribbean Studies (CALACS) XXVIII Congress, Simon Fraser University, Vancouver, BC, 19–21 March 1998

Azabache, César. 2006. Submission to Peter DeShazo and Juan Enrique Vargas, 'Judicial Reform in Latin America: An Assessment', *Policy Papers on the Americas*, Vol. XVII, Study 2 (September). Washington: Center for Strategic and International Studies (CSIS). Available at: http://www.csis.org/media/csis/events/060607_judicial_azabache.pdf [accessed October 2009]

Azicri, Max. 2000. *Cuba Today and Tomorrow: Reinventing Socialism*. Miami, EL: University Press of Florida

Bacevich, Andrew J. 2008. *The Limits of Power: The End of American Exceptionalism*. New York: Metropolitan Books

Baer, W. 1972. 'Import Substitution and Industrialization in Latin America: Experiences and Interpretations', *Latin American Research Review*, Vol. 7, No.1 (Spring), pp. 95–122

Baiocchi, Gianpaolo (ed.). 2003. *Radicals in Power. The Workers' Party (PT) and Experiments in Urban Democracy in Brazil.* London: Zed Books

Ballvé, Teo. 2005. 'Bolivia's Separatist Movement', *NACLA Report on the Americas*, Vol. 38, No. 5 (March/April), p. 16

Baran, Paul. 1973. *The Political Economy of Growth.* Harmondsworth: Penguin

Barié, Cletus Gregor. 2000. *Pueblos indígenas y derechos constitucionales en América Latina: un panorama.* Mexico City: Instituto Indigenista Interamericano

Barraclough, Colin. 2002. 'Race-hate groups find virtual haven in Argentina; Lax laws and cheap Internet access have helped far-right groups thrive', *Christian Science Monitor*, 23 August 2002, p. 7. Factiva.com database [accessed March 2006]

Barshefsky, Charlene, James T. Hill and Shannon K. O'Neil (eds). 2008. *US-Latin America Relations A New Direction for a New Reality, Independent Task Force Report No. 60.* New York: Council on Foreign Relations. Available at: http://www.cfr.org/publication/16279/ [accessed November 2009]

Bastian, Jean-Pierre. 1987. *Protestantisme y modernidad latinoamericana: historia de unas minorias religiosas activas en América Latina.* Mexico City: Fondo de Cultura Economica

Bauer, Arnold J. 1987. 'Export-led Production. Rural Workers in Spanish America: Problems of Peonage and Oppression', in Eduardo Archetti, Paul Cammack anc Bryan Roberts (eds), *Latin America. Sociology of Developing Societies.* Houndmills: Macmillan

Baumann, Renato. 2008. 'Integration in Latin America – Trends and Challenges', Economic Commission for Latin America and the Caribbean Office in Brazil, LC/BRS/R.190, January 2008. Brazil: ECLAC/CEPAL. Available at: http://www.iadb.org/intal/intalcdi/PE/2008/01306.pdf [accessed December 2009]

BBC (British Broadcasting Corporation). 1993. 'Further report on alleged leadership of Shining Path', BBC Monitoring Service: Latin America, dispatch by Fernando Barrantes, Lima (ME/1728 D/2), 2 July 1993. Factiva.com database [accessed March 2006]

bbc.co.uk. 2003. 'Brazil to produce enriched uranium', BBC News website, UK, 7 October 2003. Available at: http://news.bbc.co.uk/1/hi/world/americas/3171276.stm [accessed February 2010]

bbc.co.uk. 2006a. '"Al-Qaeda link" to Colombia ring', BBC News website, UK, 27 January 2006. Available at: http://news.bbc.co.uk/1/hi/world/americas/4654162.stm [accessed February 2010]

bbc.co.uk. 2006b. 'UN in Guatemala "racism" warning'. BBC News website, UK, 15 March 2006. Available at: http://news.bbc.co.uk/2/hi/americas/4810566.stm [accessed February 2010]

bbc.co.uk. 2009a. 'US diplomat expelled from Ecuador', BBC News website, UK, 8 February 2009. Available at: http://news.bbc.co.uk/2/hi/americas/7877229.stm [accessed February 2010]

bbc.co.uk. 2009b. 'Colombia jails death squad general over massacre', BBC News website, UK, 26 November 2009. Available at: http://news.bbc.co.uk/2/hi/americas/8380025.stm [accessed February 2010]

bbc.co.uk. 2009c. 'Menem charged over bomb inquiry', BBC News website, UK, 1 October 2009. Available at: http://news.bbc.co.uk/2/hi/americas/8286134.stm [accessed February 2010]

BBC Monitoring. 2009. 'Russia's Lavrov writes article on international relations, global politics, Article of Minister of Foreign Affairs of Russia Sergey Lavrov, 'International Relations in the New Coordinate System', *Rossiiskaya Gazeta*, September 8, 2009', BBC Monitoring Former Soviet Union, 8 September 2009. Factiva.com database [accessed December 2009]

BBC Monitoring Americas. 2009. 'Bolivian prosecutor links Santa Cruz leaders to alleged terrorist cell', 10 May 2009, taken from *La Razón* website, La Paz, 5 May 2009. Factiva.com database [accessed December 2009]

Becker, Marc. 2008. *Indians and Leftists in the Making of Ecuador's Modern Indigenous Movements*. Durham, NC: Duke University Press

Beetham, David, Edzia Carvalho, Todd Landman and Stuart Weir. 2008. *Assessing the Quality of Democracy: A Practical Guide*. Stockholm: International Institute for Democracy and Electoral Assistance (IDEA). Available at: http://www.idea.int/publications/ [accessed September 2009]

Bensinger, Ken. 2004. 'Want a successful protest in Mexico? Arm your women', *Christian Science Monitor*, 18 November 2004, p. 4. Factiva.com database [accessed March 2006]

Berger, Christa. 1998. *Campos em confronta: a terra e o texto*. Porto Alegre: Editora da Universidade

Berger, Mark. 2001. 'Romancing the Zapatistas: International Intellectuals and the Chiapas Rebellion', *Latin American Perspectives*, Vol. 28, No. 2 (March), pp. 149–70

Berríos, Rubén. 2001. 'Japan's Economic Presence in Latin America', review article, *Latin American Politics and Society*, Vol. 43, No. 2 (July), pp. 147–61

Bethell, Leslie (ed.). 1985–95. *The Cambridge History of Latin America*, Volumes 3 to 11. Cambridge: Cambridge University Press

Bethell, Leslie (ed.). 1996. *Ideas and Ideologies in Twentieth Century Latin America*. Cambridge: Cambridge University Press

Biebesheimer, Christina and Francisco Mejía (eds). 2000. *Justice Beyond our Borders: Judicial Reforms for Latin America and the Caribbean*. Washington, DC: Inter-American Development Bank/The Johns Hopkins University Press

Bigwood, Jeremy. 2008. 'New discoveries reveal US intervention in Bolivia', Upside Down World: Covering Activisim and Politics in Latin America, online, 14 October 2008. Available at: http://upsidedownworld.org/main/content/view/1522/31/ [accessed November 2009]

Blake, Charles H. and Stephen D. Morris (eds). 2009. *Corruption and Democracy in Latin America*. Pittsburgh, PA: University of Pittsburgh Press

Blanc, Nicole, Gustavo Esteva and Beatriz Ramírez. 2009. '*Zapatismo*: a feminine movement', Mujeres Libres (Zapatista Women) online. Available at: http://www.mujereslibres.org/Articles/zapatismofeminine.htm [accessed December 2009]

Blandón, María Teresa. 2001. 'The Coalición Nacional de Mujeres: An Alliance of Left-Wing Women, Right-Wing Women, and Radical Feminists in Nicaragua', in Victoria González and Karen Kampwirth (eds), *Radical Women in Latin America. Left and Right*. University Park, PA: Pennsylvania State University Press

Blank, Stephen. 2009. *Russia in Latin America: Geopolitical Games in the US's Neighbourhood*. Paris: IFRI, Russia/NIS Center

Blustein, Paul. 2005. *And the Money Kept Rolling In (and Out). Wall Street, the IMF and the Bankrupting of Argentina*. New York: Public Affairs

Boas, Taylor C. 2000. 'The Dictator's Dilemma? The Internet and US Pol cy toward Cuba', *The Washington Quarterly*, Vol. 23, No. 3 (Summer 2000), pp. 57–67

Bowen, Kurt. 1996. *Evangelism and Apostasy: The Evolution and Impact of Evangelicals in Modern Mexico*. Montreal: McGill-Queen's University Press

Branford, Sue. 2009. 'Brazil: Has the Dream Ended?', Chapter 9 in Geraldine Lievesley and Steve Ludlam (eds), *Reclaiming Latin America: Experiments in Radical Social Democracy*. London: Zed Books

Bresser-Pereira, Luiz Carlos. 2006. 'The New Developmentalism and Conventional Orthodoxy', *Economie Appliquée*, Vol. 59, No. 3 (September), pp. 61–94. Available at: http://www.bresserpereira.org.br/papers/2006/06.3.NewDevelopmentalism-EconomieApplique.i.pdf [accessed December 2009]

Bresser Pereira, Luís Carlos, José María Maravall and Adam Przeworski. 1993. *Economic Reforms in New Democracies: A Social Democratic Approach*. Cambridge: Cambridge University Press

Bretherton Charlotte and John Vogler. 1999. *The European Union as a Global Actor*. London: Routledge

Broder, John M. 2005. 'With Congress's Blessing, a Border Fence May Finally Push Through to the Sea', *New York Times*, 4 July 2005, Late Edition – Final, p. 8. Factiva.com database [accessed March 2006]

Brouwer, Steve, Paul Gifford and Susan D. Rose. 1996. *Exporting the American Gospel: Global Christian Fundamentalism*. New York: Routledge

Brown, Chelsea. 2009. 'Democracy's Friend or Foe? The Effects of Recent IMF Conditional Lending in Latin America', *International Political Science Review*, Vol. 30, No. 4 (September), pp. 431–57

Bruhn, Kathleen. 1999. 'Antonio Gramsci and the *palabra verdadera*: The Political Discourse of Mexico's Guerrilla Forces', *Journal of Interamerican Studies and World Affairs* Vol. 41, No. 2 (Summer), pp. 29–55

Bruhn, Kathleen. 2005. 'Free Market Democracy and the Chilean and Mexican Countryside', review article, *Latin American Politics and Society*, Vol. 47, No. 1 (April), pp. 143–8

Brusco, Elizabeth. 1995. *The Reformation of Machismo: Evangelical Protestantism and Gender in Colombia*. Austin, TX: University of Texas Press

Brysk, Alison. 2000. *From Tribal Village to Global Village: Indian Rights and International Relations in Latin America*. Stanford, CA: Stanford University Press

Bulmer-Thomas, Victor. 1994. *The Economic History of Latin America Since Independence*. Cambridge: Cambridge University Press

Bulmer-Thomas, Victor (ed.). 1989. *Britain and Latin America: A Changing Relationship*. Cambridge: Cambridge University Press/Royal Institute of International Affairs

Bulmer-Thomas, Victor (ed.). 2001. *Regional Integration in Latin America and the Caribbean: The Political Economy of Open Regionalism*. London: Institute of Latin American Studies

Bulmer-Thomas, Victor and James Dunkerley. 1999. 'Conclusions', in Victor Bulmer-Thomas and James Dunkerley (eds), *The United States and Latin America: The New Agenda*. London: Institute of Latin American Studies, University of London/Harvard, MA: David Rockefeller Center for Latin American Studies

Bulmer-Thomas, Victor and James Dunkerley (eds). 1999. *The United States and Latin America: The New Agenda*. London: Institute of Latin American Studies, University of London/Harvard, MA: David Rockefeller Center for Latin American Studies

Bulmer-Thomas, Victor, John H. Coatsworth and Roberto Cortés Conde (eds). 2006. *The Cambridge Economic History of Latin America, Volume II. The Long Twentieth Century*. Cambridge: Cambridge University Press

Burki, Shahid Javed, Guillermo E. Perry and William R. Dillinger. 1999. *Beyond the Center: Decentralizing the State*. Washington, DC: World Bank

Burton, Michael, Richard Gunther and John Higley. 1992. 'Introduction: Elite Transformations and Democratic Regimes', in John Higley and Richard Gunther (eds), *Elites and Democratic Consolidation in Latin America and Southern Europe*. Cambridge: Cambridge University Press

Buscaglia, Edgardo. 1998. 'Obstacles to Judicial Reform in Latin America', in Edmundo Jarquín and Fernando Carrillo (eds), *Justice Delayed: Judicial Reform in Latin America*. Washington, DC: Inter-American Development Bank

Buxton, Julia. 2009. 'Venezuela: the political evolution of Bolivarianism', Chapter 3 in Geraldine Lievesley and Steve Ludlam (eds), *Reclaiming Latin America: Experiments in Radical Social Democracy*. London: Zed Books

Cammack, Paul. 1997. *Capitalism and Democracy in the Third World. The Doctrine for Political Development*. London: Leicester University Press/Cassell

Camp, Roderic A. 1989. *Entrepreneurs and Politics in Twentieth-Century Mexico*. New York: Oxford University Press

Canadian Press. 2005. 'US says Central American alert for al-Qaida suspects was a misunderstanding', Associated Press, Managua, *The Canadian Press*, 24 May 2005. Factiva.com database [accessed March 2006]

Cardenal, Ernesto. 2004. *La Revolución Perdida*. Madrid: Editorial Trotta

Cardona, Rokael. 2002. 'La situación de decentralización en Guatemala', presentation to the Preparatory Meeting of the Red Interamericana de Decentralización of the OAS, Cancún, Mexico, 11 September 2002

Cardoso, Eliana and Ann Helwege. 1992. *Latin America's Economy. Diversity, Trends, and Conflicts*. Cambridge, MA: MIT Press

Cardoso, Fernando Henrique and Enzo Faletto. 1969. *Dependencia y Desarollo en America Latina*. Mexico City: Siglo XXI. (1979. *Dependency and Development in Latin America*. London: University of California Press)

Carey, David, Jr. 2001. *Our Elders Teach Us: Maya-Kaqchikel Historical Perspectives*. Tuscaloosa, AC: University of Alabama Press

Carey, John M. 1997. 'Institutional Design and Party Systems', in Larry Diamond, Marc F. Plattner, Yun-han Chu and Hung-mao Tien (eds), *Consolidating the Third Wave Democracies. Themes and Perspectives*. Baltimore, MD: Johns Hopkins University Press

Carey, John M. 2002. 'Parties, Coalitions and the Chilean Congress in the 1990s', in Scott Morgenstern and Benito Nacif (eds), *Legislative Politics in Latin America*. Cambridge: Cambridge University Press

Carey, John M. and Matthew Soberg Shugart (eds). 1998. *Executive Decree Authority*. New York: Cambridge University Press

Carey, Mark. 2010. *In the Shadow of Melting Glaciers: Climate Change and Andean Society*. New York: Oxford University Press

Carothers, Thomas. 2002. 'The End of the Transition Paradigm', *Journal of Democracy*, Vol. 13, No. 1 (January), pp. 5–21

Carothers, Thomas. 2009. 'Democracy Promotion Under Obama: Finding a Way Forward', Carnegie Endowment for International Peace, Policy Brief 77, February 2009. Washington, DC: Carnegie Endowment for International Peace

Carr, Barry and Steve Ellner (eds). 1993. *The Latin American Left. From the Fall of Allende to Perestroika*. Boulder, CO: Westview Press/Latin America Bureau

Carruthers, David V. (ed.). 2008. *Environmental Justice in Latin America: Problems, Promise, and Practice*. Cambridge, MA: MIT Press

Casar, Ma. Amparo. 2002. 'Executive-Legislative Relations: The Case of Mexico (1946–1997)', in Scott Morgenstern and Benito Nacif (eds), *Legislative Politics in Latin America*. Cambridge: Cambridge University Press

Cason, Jeffrey. 2002. 'Electoral Reform, Institutional Change and Party Adaptation in Uruguay', *Latin American Politics and Society*, Vol. 44, No. 3 (September), pp. 89–109

Castañeda, Jorge. 1994. *Utopia Unarmed. The Latin American Left after the Cold War*. New York: Vintage Books

Castro-Klarén, Sara and John Charles Chasteen (eds). 2003. *Beyond Imagined Communities: Reading and Writing the Nation in Nineteenth-Century Latin America*. Washington: Woodrow Wilson Center Press/Baltimore, MD: Johns Hopkins University Press

Caulfield, Norman. 1998. *Mexican Workers and the State: From the Porfiriato to NAFTA*. Fort Worth, TX: Texas Christian University Press

Cave, Damien. 2009. 'Puerto Rico Unions Protest Job Cuts', *New York Times*, Late Edition – Final, 16 October 2009, p. 14. Factiva.com database [accessed December 2009]

Centeno, Miguel Angel. 2004. 'The Return of Cuba to Latin America: The End of Cuban Exceptionalism. Society for Latin American Studies 2004 Plenary Lecture', *Bulletin of Latin American Research*, Vol. 23, No. 4 (October), pp. 403–413

Chalmers, Douglas, Scott Martin and Kerianne Piester. 1997. 'Conclusion. Associative Networks: New Structures of Representation for the Popular Sectors?', in Douglas Chalmers *et al.* (eds), *The New Politics of Inequality in Latin America. Rethinking Participation and Representation*. Oxford: Oxford University Press

Chalmers, Douglas, Carlos Vilas, Katherine Hite, Scott Martin, Kerianne Piester and Monique Segarra (eds). 1997. *The New Politics of Inequality in Latin America. Rethinking Participation and Representation*. Oxford: Oxford University Press

Chalmers, Douglas, Maria do Carmo Campello de Souza and Atilio Borón (eds). 1992. *The Right and Democracy in Latin America*. New York: Praeger

Chasteen, John Charles. 2001. *Born in Blood and Fire. A Concise History of Latin America*. New York: W.W.Norton

Chesnut, Andrew R. 1997. *Born Again in Brazil: The Pentecostal Boom and the Pathogens of Poverty*. New Brunswick, NC: Rutgers University Press

Chicago Tribune. 2004. 'Official: Al Qaeda recruiting Latin gang members', *Chicago Tribune*, RedEye, 22 October 2004, p. 13. Factiva.com database [accessed March 2006]

China Daily. 2009a. 'ECLAC seeks deeper Latin America-China ties', China Daily online/ Xinhua news agency, 24 November 2009. Available at: http://www.chinadaily.com.cn/ bizchina/2009-11/24/content_9035932.htm [accessed December 2009]

China Daily. 2009b. 'Latin America must take advantage of trade with China: ECLAC', China Daily online/Xinhua news agency, 28 August 2009. Available at: http://www.chinadaily.com.cn/bizchina/2009-08/28/content_8629813.htm [accessed December 2009]

China Daily. 2009c. 'China's demand helps reduce commercial deficit in Latin America', China Daily online/Xinhua news agency, 26 August 2009. Available at: http://www.chinadaily.com.cn/bizchina/2009-08/26/content_8619048.htm [accessed December 2009]

China Daily. 2009d. 'Positive side of Beijing's imprint on Latin America', China Daily online/Xinhua news agency, 10 October 2009. Available at: http://www.chinadaily.com.cn/china/2009summerdavos/2009-09/10/content_8675228.htm [accessed December 2009]

Chong, Alberto and Florencio López de Silanes (eds). 2005. *Privatization in Latin America: Myths and Reality*. Palo Alto, CA: Stanford University Press/World Bank

Chu, Henry. 2005. 'In Latin America, a Religious Turf War', *Los Angeles Times*, Home Edition, 15 April 2005, p. A-1. Factiva.com database [accessed March 2006]

Clark, Kim and Marc Becker (eds). 2007. *Highland Indians and the State in Modern Ecuador*. Pittsburgh: University of Pittsburgh Press

Cleary, Matthew R. 2008. 'Explaining the Left's Resurgence', Chapter 5 in Larry Diamond, Marc F. Plattner and Diego Abente Brun (eds), *Latin America's Struggle for Democracy*. Baltimore: The Johns Hopkins University Press/National Endowment for Democracy

Cleary, Edward, and Hannah W. Stewart-Gambino. 1997. *Power, Politics, and Pentecostals in Latin America*. Boulder: Westview Press

Coerver, Don M. and Linda B. Hall. 1999. *Tangled Destinies: Latin America and the United States*. Albuquerque: University of New Mexico Press

Cohen, Jean and Andrew Arato. 1992. *Civil Society and Political Theory*. Cambridge, Mass.: MIT Press

Cohen, Joshua and Joel Rogers. 1995. *Associations and Democracy*. London: Verso

Collier, David. 1995. 'Trajectory of a Concept: "Corporatism" in the Study of Latin American Politics', in Peter H. Smith (ed.), *Latin America in Comparative Perspective. New Approaches to Methods and Analysis*. Boulder: Westview Press

Collier, David, and Steven Levitsky. 1997. 'Democracy with Adjectives: Conceptual Innovation in Comparative Research', *World Politics*, Vol. 49, No. 3 (April), pp. 430–51

Collier, Ruth. B. and David Collier. 2002. *Shaping the Political Arena. Critical Junctures, the Labor Movement, and Regime Dynamics in Latin America*. Notre Dame: University of Notre Dame Press

Collier, Simon. 1983. 'Nationality, Nationalism, and Supranationalism in the Writings of Simón Bolívar', *Hispanic American Historical Review*, Vol. 63, No. 1 (February), pp. 37–64

Comité Estatal de Estadísticas (CEE). 1989. *Anuario Estadístico de Cuba 1989*. Havana: CEE

Conaghan, Catherine M. 2008. 'Ecuador: Corea's Plebiscitary Presidency', Chapter 14 in Larry Diamond, Marc F. Plattner and Diego Abente Brun (eds), *Latin America's Struggle for Democracy*. Baltimore: The Johns Hopkins University Press/National Endowment for Democracy

CONGDP (Congressional Documents and Publications). 2009. 'House Foreign Affairs Subcommittee on Western Hemisphere Hearing – Guatemala at a Crossroads',

Testimony by Anita Isaacs, Benjamin R. Collins Professor of Social Science, Associate Professor of Political Science, Haverford College, 9 June 2009. Washington: Federal Document Clearing House

Conniff, Michael L. (ed.). 1999. *Populism in Latin America*. Tuscaloosa, AL: University of Alabama Press

Constance, Paul. 2003. 'Verdict Pending', *IDBAmérica*. Magazine of the Inter-American Development Bank, posted August 2003. Available at: http://www.iadb.org/ idbamerica/index.cfm?thisid=2361 [accessed February 2010]

Cook, Maria Lorena. 2002. 'Labor Reform and Dual Transitions in Brazil and the Southern Cone', *Latin American Politics and Society*, Vol. 44, No. 1 (April), pp. 1–34

Cooper, Andrew F. and Jorge Heine (eds). 2009. *Which Way Latin America? Hemispheric Politics Meets Globalization*. Tokyo: United Nations University Press

Coppedge, Michael. 1999. 'Thickening thin concepts and theories: combining large *N* and small in comparative politics', *Comparative Politics*, Vol. 31, No. 4 (July), pp. 465–76

Coppedge, Michael. 2005. 'Defining and Measuring Democracy', *IPSA/APSA Committee on Concepts and Methods Electronic Working Paper Series* (April). Available at: http://www.concepts-methods.org [accessed February 2010]

Corrales, Javier. 2001. 'Strong Societies, Weak Parties: Regime Change in Cuba and Venezuela in the 1950s and Today', *Latin American Politics and Society*, Vol. 43, No. 2 (July), pp. 81–113

Corrales, Javier. 2008. 'The Backlash against Market Reforms in Latin America in the 2000s', Chapter 3 in Jorge I. Domínguez and Michael Shifter (eds), *Constructing Democratic Governance in Latin America*, 3rd Edition. Baltimore, MD: Johns Hopkins University Press

Corrales, Javier and Mario Pecheny (eds). 2010. *The Politics of Sexuality in Latin America: A Reader on Lesbian, Gay, Bisexual, and Transgender Rights*. Pittsburgh, PA: University of Pittsburgh Press

Correa Leite, José. 2005. *The World Social Forum: Strategies of Resistance*. Chicago, IL: Haymarket Books

Corten, Andre. 1999. *Pentecostalism in Brazil: Emotion of the Poor and Theological Romanticism*. New York: St. Martin's Press

Cox, Gary W. and Scott Morgenstern. 2002. 'Epilogue: Latin America's Reactive Assemblies and Proactive Presidents', in Scott Morgenstern and Benito Nacif (eds), *Legislative Politics in Latin America*. Cambridge: Cambridge University Press

Crabtree, Steve. 2008. 'Latin America's Entrepreneurs: Catholics vs. Protestants: Protestants more likely to have plans to start businesses', 15 July 2008, *Gallup Daily News*, Gallup Inc. Available at: http://www.gallup.com/poll/108832/latin-americas-entrepreneurs-catholics-vs-protestants.aspx# [accessed October 2009]

Craske, Nikki. 1994. *Corporatism Revisited: Salinas and the Reform of the Popular Sector*. Research Paper 37, Institute of Latin American Studies, University of London. London: Institute of Latin American Studies

Craske, Nikki. 1999. *Women and Politics in Latin America*. Cambridge: Polity Press

Crinis Project. 2007. *The Crinis Project: Money in Politics – Everyone's Concern*. Berlin: Transparency International/The Carter Center. Available at: http://www.transparency.org/ regional_pages/americas/crinis [accessed October 2009]

Dabène, Olivier. 2009. *The Politics of Regional Integration in Latin America: Theoretical and Comparative Explorations*. Basingstoke: Palgrave Macmillan

Dagnino, Evelina. 2005. 'Meanings of Citizenship in Latin America', IDS Working Paper 258. Brighton: Institute of Development Studies, University of Sussex

Dahl, Robert. 1971. *Polyarchy: Participation and Opposition*. New Haven, CT: Yale University Press

Dahrendorf, Ralf. 1959. *Class and Class Conflict in Industrial Society*. Stanford, CA: Stanford University Press

Dangl, Benjamin. 2008. 'Undermining Bolivia', *The Progressive* online, February 2008. Available at: http://www.progressive.org/mag_dangl0208 [accessed November 2009]

Dangl, Benjamin. 2010. *Dancing with Dynamite: Social Movements and States in Latin America*. Oakland, CA: AK Press

Dangl, Benjamin and April Howard. 2008. 'New vs. Old Right in Paraguay's Election', *NACLA Report on the Americas*, Vol. 41, No. 1 (January/February), pp. 14–19

Darling, Juanita. 2008. *Latin America, Media, and Revolution: Communication in Modern Mesoamerica*. Basingstoke: Palgrave Macmillan

de la Garza Toledo, Enrique. 2004. 'Manufacturing Neoliberalism: Industrial Relations, Trade Union Corporatism and Politics', in Gerardo Otero (ed.), *Mexico in Transition: Neoliberal Globalism, the State and Civil Society*. London: Zed

de La Torre, Augusto, Pablo Fajnzylber and John Nash (eds). 2009. *Low-carbon Development: Latin American Responses to Climate Change*. Washington, DC: World Bank

Delgado, Alvaro. 2006. *El Yunque: La ultraderecha en el poder*. Barcelona: Plaza & Janes Editores

della Porta, Donatella (ed.). 2009. *Democracy in Social Movements*. Basingstoke: Palgrave Macmillan

del Valle Escalante, Emilio. 2009. *Maya Nationalisms and Postcolonial Challenges in Guatemala: Coloniality, Modernity, and Identity Politics*. Santa Fe, NM: School for Advanced Research Press

Demmers, Jolle, Alex E. Fernández Jilberto and Barbara Hogenboom (eds). 2001. *Miraculous Metamorphoses: The Neoliberalization of Latin American Populism*. London: Zed Books

Dent, David W. 1999. *The Legacy of the Monroe Doctrine: A Reference Guide to US Involvement in Latin America and the Caribbean*. London: Greenwood

DeShazo, Peter and Juan Enrique Vargas. 2006. 'Judicial Reform in Latin America: An Assessment.' *Policy Papers on the Americas*, Vol. XVII, Study 2 (September). Washington: Center for Strategic and International Studies (CSIS). Available at: http://csis.org/files/media/csis/pubs/0609_latin_judicial_reform.pdf [accessed October 2009]

Deutch, John, James R. Schlesinger and David G. Victor. 2006. 'National Security Consequences of US Oil Dependency', Independent Task Force Report No. 58. New York: Council on Foreign Relations. Available at: http://www.cfr.org/publication/11683/ [accessed November 2009]

Diamint, Rut. 2004. 'Security Challenges in Latin America', *Bulletin of Latin American Research*, Vol. 23, No. 1 (January), pp. 43–62

Diamond, Larry. 1994. 'Rethinking Civil Society: Toward Democratic Consolidation', *Journal of Democracy*, Vol. 5, No. 3 (July), pp. 4–17

Diamond, Larry. 1996. 'Toward Democratic Consolidation', in Larry Diamond and Marc F. Plattner (eds), *The Global Resurgence of Democracy*, 2nd Edition. Baltimore, MD: Johns Hopkins University Press/National Endowment for Democracy

Diamond, Larry. 1999. *Developing Democracy: Toward Consolidation*. Baltimore, MD: Johns Hopkins University Press

Diamond, Larry, Jonathan Hartlyn, Juan Linz and Seymour Martin Lipset (eds). 1999. *Democracy in Developing Countries: Latin America*, 2nd Edition. Boulder, CO: Lynne Rienner

Diamond, Larry, Juan Linz and Seymour Martin Lipset (eds) 1989. *Democracy in Developing Countries, Volume 4: Latin America*. Boulder, CO: Lynne Rienner

Diamond, Larry and Leonardo Morlino (eds). 2005. *Assessing the Quality of Democracy*. Baltimore, MD: Johns Hopkins University Press

Diamond, Larry and Marc F. Plattner (eds). 1996. *The Global Resurgence of Democracy*. Baltimore, MD: Johns Hopkins University Press

Diamond, Larry, Marc F. Plattner and Diego Abente Brun (eds). 2008. *Latin America's Struggle for Democracy*. Baltimore, MD: Johns Hopkins University Press/National Endowment for Democracy

Díaz Polanco, Héctor. 1997. *Indigenous Peoples in Latin America: The Quest for Self-determination*. Boulder, CO: Westview Press

Dickerson, Marla. 2004. 'Cultivating Change to Take Back the Land; The US is Helping Bolivian Farmers Improve the Quality of their Coffee in the Hope That They Don't Turn to Drug Crops', *Los Angeles Times*, 12 December 2004, Home Edition, p. C-1. Factiva. com database [accessed March 2006]

Dieterich, Heinz. 2005. *Hugo Chávez y el socialismo del siglo XXI*. Caracas: Instituto Municipal de Publicaciones de la Alcadía de Caracas

Dieterich, Heinz. 2006. *Der Sozialismus des 21 Jahrhunderts: Wirtschaft, Gesellschaft und Demokratie nach dem globalen Kapitalismus*. Berlin: Homilius

Dietz, James L. (ed.). 1995. *Latin America's Economic Development. Confronting Crisis*, 2nd Edition. Boulder, CO: Lynne Rienner

Dijkstra, Geske. 1992. *Industrialization in Sandinista Nicaragua: Policy and Practice in a Mixed Economy*. Boulder, CO: Westview Press

Dillinger, William and Steven B. Webb. 1999. *Decentralization and Fiscal Management in Colombia*. Draft Policy Research Working Paper 2122. Washington: World Bank Latin America and Caribbean Region, Poverty Reduction and Economic Management Sector Unit

Di Tella, Torcuato S. 1965. 'Populism and Reform in Latin America', in Claudio Véliz (ed.), *Obstacles to Change in Latin America*. London: Oxford University Press

Domingo, Pilar and Rachel Sieder (eds). 2001. *The Rule of Law in Latin America: The International Promotion of Judicial Reform*. London: University of London, Institute of Latin American Studies

Domínguez, Jorge. 2000. *The Future of Inter-American Relations*. New York: Routledge

Domínguez, Jorge. 2005a. 'The Cuban Economy at the Start of the Twenty-First Century: An Introductory Analysis', in Jorge Domínguez *et al.* (eds). *The Cuban Economy at the*

Start of the Twenty-First Century. Cambridge, MA: Harvard University Press/The David Rockefeller Center for Latin American Studies

Domínguez, Jorge. 2005b. 'Cuba's Economic Transition: Successes, Deficiencies and Challenges', in Jorge Domínguez *et al.* (eds), *The Cuban Economy at the Start of the Twenty-First Century*. Cambridge, MA: Harvard University Press/The David Rockefeller Center for Latin American Studies

Domínguez, Jorge, with David Mares, Manuel Orozco, David Scott Palmer, Francisco Rojas Aravena and Andrés Serbin. 2003. *Boundary Disputes in Latin America*. United States Institute of Peace, Peaceworks 50. Washington: USIP. Available at: http://www.usip.org/resources/boundary-disputes-latin-america [accessed February 2010]

Domínguez, Jorge and Michael Shifter (eds). 2003. *Constructing Democratic Governance*, 2nd Edition. Baltimore, MD: Johns Hopkins University Press

Domínguez, Jorge I. and Michael Shifter (eds). 2008. *Constructing Democratic Governance in Latin America*, 3rd Edition. Baltimore, MD: Johns Hopkins University Press

Domínguez, Jorge, Omar Everleny Pérez Villanueva and Lorena Barberia (eds). 2005. *The Cuban Economy at the Start of the Twenty-First Century*. Cambridge, MA: Harvard University Press/The David Rockefeller Center for Latin American Studies

Dornbusch, Rudiger and Sebastian Edwards (eds). 1991. *The Macroeconomics of Populism in Latin America*. Chicago, IL: University of Chicago Press/National Bureau of Economic Research Conference Reports

dos Santos, Sales Augusto. 2002. 'Historical Roots of the "Whitening" of Brazil', translated by Laurence Hallewell. *Latin American Perspectives*, Vol. 29, No. 1 (January), pp. 61–82

Downie, Andrew. 2009. 'Embraer: Brazilian group seeks military dividends', *Financial Times*, FT.com, 16 November 2009. Available at: http://www.ft.com/cms/s/0/523a0782-cfe9-11de-a36d-00144feabdc0.html [accessed February 2010]

Dunbar-Ortiz, Roxanne A. 2001. 'From Tribal Village to Global Village: Indian Rights and International Relations in Latin America', review article, *Latin American Politics and Society*, Vol. 43, No. 4 (December), pp. 146–50

Durán-Cogan, Mercedes. F. 2001. 'Words and Images. Figurating and Dis-Figurating Identity', in Mercedes. F. Durán-Cogan and Antonio Gómez-Moriana (eds), *National Identities and Sociopolitical Changes in Latin America*. London: Routledge

Durán-Cogan, Mercedes. F. and Antonio Gómez-Moriana (eds). 2001. *National Identities and Sociopolitical Changes in Latin America*. London: Routledge

Dussel, Enrique. 2009. *Twenty Theses on Politics*. Durham, NC: Duke University Press

Duverger, M. 1964. *Political Parties: Their Organization and Activity in the Modern State*. 3rd Edition. Translated by Barbara and Robert North. London: Methuen

Dyer, Geoff and Edward Luce. 2009. 'A wary willingness', *Financial Times*, FT.com, 19 November 2009. Available at: http://www.ft.com/cms/s/0/801443aa-d559-11de-81ee-00144feabdc0.html?nclick_check=1 [accessed February 2010]

Eakin, Marshall C. 2007. *The History of Latin America: Collision of Cultures*. Basingstoke: Palgrave Macmillan

Eaton, Kent 2007. 'Backlash in Bolivia: Regional Autonomy as a Reaction against Indigenous Mobilization', *Politics & Society*, Vol. 35, No. 1 (March), pp. 71–102

Eckstein, Susan. 1989. 'Power and Popular Protest in Latin America', in Susan Eckstein (ed.), *Power and Popular Protest: Latin American Social Movements*. Berkeley, CA: University of California Press

Eckstein, Susan (ed.). 1989. *Power and Popular Protest: Latin American Social Movements*. Berkeley: University of California Press

Eckstein, Susan E. and Timothy P. Wickham-Crowley (eds). 2003. *Struggles for Social Rights in Latin America*. New York: Routledge

ECLAC/CEPAL (Economic Commission for Latin America and the Caribbean/Comisión Económica para América Latina y el Caribe). 1998. *Social Panorama of Latin America*. Santiago: ECLAC. Available at: http://www.eclac.cl/publicaciones/default.asp?idioma=IN [accessed February 2010]

ECLAC/CEPAL (Economic Commission for Latin America and the Caribbean/Comisión Económica para América Latina y el Caribe). 2002. 'Globalization and Development, 29th Session, Brasilia, 6–10 May 2002.' Santiago: ECLAC. Available at: http://www.eclac.cl/cgi-bin/getProd.asp?xml=/publicaciones/xml/0/10030/P10030.xml&xsl=/tpl-i/p9f.xsl&base=/tpl/top-bottom.xsl [accessed December 2009]

ECLAC/CEPAL (Economic Commission for Latin America and the Caribbean/Comisión Económica para América Latina y el Caribe). 2003. *Economic Survey of Latin America and the Caribbean 2002–2003*. Santiago: ECLAC. Available at: http://www.eclac.cl/publicaciones/default.asp?idioma=IN [accessed February 2010]

ECLAC/CEPAL (Economic Commission for Latin America and the Caribbean/Comisión Económica para América Latina y el Caribe). 2004a. *Economic Survey of Latin America and the Caribbean, 2003–2004*. Santiago: ECLAC. Available at: http://www.eclac.cl/publicaciones/default.asp?idioma=IN [accessed February 2010]

ECLAC/CEPAL (Economic Commission for Latin America and the Caribbean/Comisión Económica para América Latina y el Caribe). 2004b. *Preliminary Overview of the Economies of Latin America and the Caribbean 2004*. Santiago: ECLAC. Available at: http://www.eclac.cl/publicaciones/default.asp?idioma=IN [accessed February 2010]

ECLAC/CEPAL (Economic Commission for Latin America and the Caribbean/Comisión Económica para América Latina y el Caribe). 2004c. *Social Panorama of Latin America 2004*. Santiago: ECLAC. Available at: http://www.eclac.cl/publicaciones/default.asp?idioma=IN [accessed February 2010]

ECLAC/CEPAL (Economic Commission for Latin America and the Caribbean/Comisión Económica para América Latina y el Caribe). 2005a. 'About ECLAC', 'History of ECLAC', 'Evolution of ECLAC ideas' and 'Background Information – Evolution of ECLAC Ideas'. Santiago: ECLAC. Available at: http://www.eclac.cl/cgi-bin/getprod.asp?xml=/noticias/paginas/0/21710/P21710.xml&xsl=/tpl-i/p18f-st.xsl&base=/tpl-i/top-bottom_acerca.xsl [accessed February 2010]

ECLAC/CEPAL (Economic Commission for Latin America and the Caribbean/Comisión Económica para América Latina y el Caribe). 2005b. *Economic Survey of Latin America and the Caribbean, 2004–2005*. Santiago: ECLAC. Available at: http://www.eclac.cl/publicaciones/default.asp?idioma=IN [accessed February 2010]

ECLAC/CEPAL (Economic Commission for Latin America and the Caribbean/Comisión Económica para América Latina y el Caribe). 2005c. *Preliminary Overview of the Economies of Latin America and the Caribbean 2005*. Santiago: ECLAC. Available at: http://www.eclac.cl/publicaciones/default.asp?idioma=IN [accessed February 2010]

ECLAC/CEPAL (Economic Commission for Latin America and the Caribbean/Comisión Económica para América Latina y el Caribe). 2006a. *Social Panorama of Latin America 2005, Preliminary Version.* Santiago: ECLAC. Available at: http://www.eclac.cl/cgi-bin/getProd.asp?xml=/publicaciones/xml/4/24054/P24054.xml&xsl=/dds/tpl-i/p9f.xsl&base=/tpl-i/top-bottom.xslt [accessed February 2010]

ECLAC/CEPAL (Economic Commission for Latin America and the Caribbean/Comisión Económica para América Latina y el Caribe). 2006b. *Anuario estadístico de América Latina y el Caribe 2005* (Statistical Yearbook). Santiago: ECLAC. Available at: http://www.eclac.cl/publicaciones/default.asp?idioma=IN [accessed February 2010]

ECLAC/CEPAL (Economic Commission for Latin America and the Caribbean/Comisión Económica para América Latina y el Caribe). 2006c. *Latin America and the Caribbean in the World Economy, 2005–2006.* Santiago: ECLAC. Available at: http://www.eclac.cl/publicaciones/default.asp?idioma=IN [accessed February 2010]

ECLAC/CEPAL (Economic Commission for Latin America and the Caribbean/Comisión Económica para América Latina y el Caribe). 2008a. *Statistical Yearbook for Latin America and the Caribbean, 2008.* Santiago: ECLAC. Available at: http://www.eclac.cl/publicaciones/default.asp?idioma=IN [accessed February 2010]

ECLAC/CEPAL (Economic Commission for Latin America and the Caribbean/Comisión Económica para América Latina y el Caribe). 2008b. *Foreign Direct Investment in Latin America and the Caribbean.* Santiago: ECLAC. Available at: http://www.eclac.org/cgi-bin/getProd.asp?xml=/publicaciones/xml/4/36094/P36094.xml&xsl=/ddpe/tpl/p9f.xsl&base=/tpl/top-bottom.xslt [accessed December 2009]

ECLAC/CEPAL (Economic Commission for Latin America and the Caribbean/Comisión Económica para América Latina y el Caribe). 2009a. *Economic Survey of Latin America and the Caribbean 2008–2009. Policies for creating quality jobs.* Briefing Paper. Santiago: ECLAC. Available at: http://www.eclac.cl/publicaciones/xml/5/36465/2009-254-EEI-2009-Lanzamiento-WEB.pdf [accessed February 2010]

ECLAC/CEPAL (Economic Commission for Latin America and the Caribbean/Comisión Económica para América Latina y el Caribe). 2009b. *Economic Survey of Latin America and the Caribbean: Policies for creating quality jobs.* Santiago: ECLAC. Available at: http://www.eclac.org/publicaciones/default.asp?idioma=IN [accessed December 2009]

ECLAC/CEPAL (Economic Commission for Latin America and the Caribbean/Comisión Económica para América Latina y el Caribe). 2009c. *Social Panorama of Latin America, 2009: Briefing Paper.* Santiago: ECLAC. Available at: http://www.eclac.org/publicaciones/xml/0/37840/PSI2009-Sintesis-Lanzamiento.pdf [accessed February 2010]

ECLAC Division of International Trade and Integration (DITI). 2009a. 'Latin America and the Caribbean in the World Economy 2008–2009: Crisis and opportunities for regional cooperation', Briefing Paper. Santiago: ECLAC Division of International Trade and Integration. Available at: http://www.eclac.org/publicaciones/default.asp?idioma=IN [accessed December 2009]

ECLAC Division of International Trade and Integration (DITI). 2009b. 'Latin America and the Caribbean in the World Economy 2008–2009: Crisis and opportunities for regional cooperation'. Santiago: ECLAC Division of International Trade and Integration. Available at: http://www.eclac.cl/publicaciones/xml/7/36907/Latin_America_and_the_Caribbean_in_the_World_Economy_2008_2009_vf.pdf

ECLAC Division of Production, Productivity and Management (DPPM). 2009. *Foreign Investment in Latin America and the Caribbean, 2008*. Santiago: ECLAC Division of Production, Productivity and Management. Available at: http://www.eclac.org/cgi-bin/getProd.asp?xml=/publicaciones/xml/4/36094/P36094.xml&xsl=/ddpe/tpl/p9f.xsl&base=/tpl-i/top-bottom.xslt [accessed December 2009]

ECLAC Information Services (IS). 2009a. 'Report Social Panorama of Latin America 2009: ECLAC Estimates that Nine Million People Will Fall in Poverty in 2009 Due to Crisis', Press release, ECLAC Information Services online, 19 November 2009. Santiago: ECLAC. Available at: http://www.eclac.org/cgi-bin/getProd.asp?xml=/prensa/noticias/comunicados/4/37834/P37834.xml&xsl=/prensa/tpl-i/p6f.xsl&base=/tpl-i/top-bottom.xsl [accessed November 2009]

ECLAC Information Services (IS). 2009b. '"Trans-Latins" the New Investment Trend in Latin America and the Caribbean', Press release, ECLAC Information Services online, 12 April 2006. Santiago: ECLAC. Available at: http://www.eclac.cl/cgi-bin/getprod.asp?xml=/prensa/noticias/comunicados/5/24305/P24305.xml&xsl=/prensa/tpl-i/p6f.xsl&base=/prensa/tpl-i/top-bottom.xsl [accessed December 2009]

ECLAC Press Centre. 2009. 'Latin America Should Take More Advantage of Trade Relations With China', press release, ECLAC, Press Centre, 26 August 2009. Santiago: ECLAC. Available at: http://www.eclac.org/cgi-bin/getProd.asp?xml=/prensa/noticias/comunicados/2/36932/P36932.xml&xsl=/prensa/tpl-i/p6f.xsl&base=/prensa/tpl-i/top-bottom.xsl [accessed December 2009]

ECLAC/Peru. 2008. *Opportunities for Trade and Investment between Latin America and Asia-Pacific: the link with APEC*. Santiago: ECLAC/Peru, Ministerio de Comercio Exterior. Available at: http://www.eclac.org/publicaciones/default.asp?idioma=IN [accessed December 2009]

Economist. 2009. 'The dragon in the backyard', *The Economist*, Economist.com, 15 August 2009. Factiva.com database [accessed December 2009]

Edelman, Marc. 1999. *Peasants Against Globalization: Rural Social Movements in Costa Rica*. Stanford, CA: Stanford University Press

Edwards, Geoffrey. 1984. 'Europe and the Falklands Islands Crisis 1982', *Journal of Common Market Studies*, Vol. 22, No. 4 (June), pp. 285–313

Edwards, Sebastian. 2010. *Left Behind: Latin America and the False Promise of Populism*. Chicago, IL: University of Chicago Press

EIA (Energy Information Administration). 2009a. 'U.S. Imports by Country of Origin, Total Crude Oil and Products, Annual-Thousand Barrels', US Energy Information Administration (EIA) statistics online. Washington: EIA. Available at: http://tonto.eia.doe.gov/dnav/pet/pet_move_impcus_a2_nus_ep00_im0_mbbl_a.htm [accessed December 2009]

EIA (Energy Information Administration). 2009b. 'Country Energy Profiles', US Energy Information Administration (EIA) online. Washington: EIA. Available at: http://tonto.eia.doe.gov/country/index.cfm?view=production [accessed December 2009]

EIB (European Investment Bank). 2009. 'Asia and Latin America (ALA)', European Investment Bank online. Luxembourg: EIB. Available at: http://www.eib.org/projects/regions/ala/index.htm [accessed November 2009]

EIU (Economist Intelligence Unit). 2008. *Index of Democracy 2008*. London: EIU. Available at: http://graphics.eiu.com/PDF/Democracy%20Index%202008.pdf

EIU (Economist Intelligence Unit). 2009. 'Colombia/Venezuela: Tensions spike', *Business Latin America*, London, 10 August 2009. London: EIU. Factiva.com database [accessed December 2009]

Encarnación, Omar. 2002. 'Venezuela's "Civil Society Coup"', *World Policy Journal*, Vol. 19, No. 2 (Summer), pp. 38–48

Encarnación, Omar. 2003. *The Myth of Civil Society: Social Capital and Democratic Consolidation in Spain and Brazil*. New York: Palgrave Macmillan

Escobar, Arturo and Sonia Alvarez (eds). 1992. *The Making of Social Movements in Latin America: Identity, Strategy and Democracy*. Boulder, CO: Westview Press

Esfahani, Hadi, Giovanni Facchini and Geoffrey J. D. Hewings (eds). 2010. *Economic Development in Latin America*. Basingstoke: Palgrave Macmillan

Espina Prieto, Mayra. 2005. 'Social Effects of Economic Adjustment: Equality, Inequality and Trends toward Greater Complexity in Cuban Society', in Jorge Domínguez *et al.* (eds), *The Cuban Economy at the Start of the Twenty-First Century*. Cambridge, MA: Harvard University Press/The David Rockefeller Center for Latin American Studies

Espina, Mayra, Ángel Hernández, Viviana Togores and Rafael Hernández. 2006. 'El consumo: economía, cultura y sociedad', *Revista Temas*, No. 47 (July–September). Available at: http://www.temas.cult.cu/sumario.php?numero=47 [accessed December 2009]

Europa (European Commission). 2004. 'EU's external assistance to Latin America, 2000–2004'; 'EU-Latin America co-operation at the biregional level'. Brussels: Europa. Available at http://www.europa-eu-un.org/articles/fr/article_4728_fr.htm [accessed February 2010]

Europa (European Commission). 2005. 'The EU's relations with Latin America'; 'EU-Latin America: growing relations MEMO/05/173 – Brussels, 25 May 2005'. Brussels: Europa. Available at: http://europa.eu/rapid/pressReleasesAction.do?reference= MEMO/05/173&format=HTML&aged=1&language=EN&guiLanguage=en [accessed February 2010]

Europa (European Commission). 2009a. 'Latin America and the Caribbean', European Commission, Trade, Europa online. Brussels: Europa. Available at: http://ec.europa.eu/trade/creating-opportunities/bilateral-relations/regions/latin-america-caribbean/ [accessed November 2009]

Europa (European Commission). 2009b. 'Mercosur', European Commission, Trade, Europa online. Brussels: Europa. Available at: http://ec.europa.eu/trade/creating-opportunities/bilateral-relations/regions/mercosur/ [accessed November 2009]

Europa (European Commission). 2009c. 'EU-Latin America: 10 years of Strategic Partnership', Europa, Press Release, MEMO/09/426, Brussels, 30 September 2009. Brussels: Europa. Available at: http://europa.eu/rapid/pressReleasesAction.do? reference=MEMO/09/426&format=HTML&aged=0&language=EN&guiLanguage=en [accessed November 2009]

EuropeAid Co-operation Office. 2009. *Better Faster More – Implementing EC External Aid 2004–2009*. Brussels: EuropeAid Cooperation Office. Available at: http://ec.europa.eu/europeaid/infopoint/publications/europeaid/better-faster-more_en.htm [accessed November 2009]

European Commission. 2005. 'A stronger partnership between the European Union and Latin America, European Commission', COM(2005) 636 of 08.12.2005. Brussels:

European Commission. Available at: http://ec.europa.eu/external_relations/la/docs/com05_636_en.pdf [accessed November 2009]

European Commission. 2007. *Latin America Regional Programming Document 2007–2013. 12.07.2007 (E/2007/1417)*. Brussels: European Commission. Available at: http://ec.europa.eu/external_relations/la/rsp/07_13_en.pdf [accessed November 2009]

European Commission. 2009. 'The European Union and Latin America: Global Players in Partnership', *Communication from the Commission to the European Parliament and the Council, COM(2009) 495/3, 30.09.2009*. Brussels: European Commission. Available at: http://ec.europa.eu/external_relations/la/docs/com09_495_en.pdf [accessed November 2009]

Evans, Peter. 1979. *Dependent Development: The Alliance of Multinational, State, and Local Capital in Brazil*. Princeton, NJ: Princeton University Press

Everingham, Mark. 2001. 'Agricultural Property Rights and Political Change in Nicaragua', *Latin American Politics and Society*, Vol. 43, No. 3 (October), pp. 61–93

Falleti, Tulia. 2004. 'Federalism and Decentralization in Argentina: Historical Background and New Intergovernmental Relations', in Joseph. S. Tulchin and Andrew Se ee (eds), *Decentralization and Democratic Governance in Latin America*. Woodrow Wilson Center Report on the Americas #12. Washington, DC: Woodrow Wilson International Center for Scholars

Farer, Tom (ed.). 1996. *Beyond Sovereignty: Collectively Defending Democracy in the Americas*. Baltimore, MD: Johns Hopkins University Press

Farthing, Linda. 2009. 'Bolivia's Dilemma: Development Confronts the Legacy of Extraction', *NACLA Report on the Americas*, Vol. 42, No. 5 (September/October). Available at: https://nacla.org/node/6096 [accessed February 2010]

Fishlow, Albert and James Jones (eds). 1999. *United States and the Americas: A Twenty-First Century View*. New York: W.W. Norton

Fitch, J. Samuel. 1998. *The Armed Forces and Democracy in Latin America*. Baltimore, MD: Johns Hopkins University Press

Fitch, J. Samuel. 2001. 'Military Attitudes Toward Democracy: How Do We Know If Anything Has Changed?', in David Pion-Berlin (ed.), *Civil-Military Relations in Latin America. New Analytical Perspectives*. Chapel Hill, NC: University of North Carolina Press

Fitsanakis, Joseph. 2009 'Mysterious International Mercenary Cell Uncovered in Bolivia', *Foreign Policy Journal* online, 21 April 2009. Available at: http://www.foreignpolicyjournal.com/2009/04/21/mysterious-international-mercenary-cell-uncovered-in-bolivia/ [accessed November 2009]

Forero, Juan. 2004a. 'Bogota's Social Capitalism, Led by a Marxist of Old', *New York Times*, 6 February 2004, Late Edition – Final, p. 1. Factiva.com database [accessed March 2006]

Forero, Juan. 2004b. 'Where the Incas Ruled, Indians Are Hoping for Power', *New York Times*, 17 July 2004, Late Edition – Final, p. 3. Factiva.com database [accessed March 2006]

Forero, Juan. 2009. 'Venezuela's Drug-Trafficking Role Is Growing Fast, U.S. Report Says', Washington Post Foreign Service, 19 July 2009, *Washington Post* online. Available at: http://www.washingtonpost.com/wp-dyn/content/article/2009/07/18/AR2009071801785.html [accessed November 2009]

Forment, Carlos A. 2003. *Democracy in Latin America 1760–1900. Volume I, Civic Selfhood and Public Life in Mexico and Peru*. Chicago, IL: University of Chicago Press

Foster, John Bellamy. 2003. 'The New Age of Imperialism', *Monthly Review*, Vol. 55, No. 3 (July–August), pp. 1–14

Foster, John Bellamy. 2006. *Naked Imperialism: The US Pursuit of Global Dominance*. New York: Monthly Review Press

Foweraker, Joe. 1995. *Theorizing Social Movements*. London: Pluto Press

Foweraker, Joe. 1998. 'Institutional Design, Party Systems and Governability – Differentiating the Presidential Regimes of Latin America', review article, *British Journal of Political Science*, Vol. 28, No. 4 (October), pp. 651–76

Foweraker, Joe, Todd Landman and Neil Harvey. 2003. *Governing Latin America*. Cambridge: Polity Press

Fowler, Will. 2002. *Latin America 1800–2000. Modern History for Modern Languages*. London: Arnold

Fox, Jonathan. 1997. 'The Difficult Transition from Clientelism to Citizenship: Lessons from Mexico', in Douglas A. Chalmers *et al.* (eds), *The New Politics of Inequality in Latin America. Rethinking Participation and Representation*. Oxford: Oxford University Press

Frank, Dana. 2008. *Bananeras: Women Transforming the Banana Unions of Latin America*. Brooklyn, NY: South End Press

Frank, Marc. 2005. 'Alliances with China and Venezuela bolster Cuba economic recovery', *Financial Times*, 7 April 2005, London Edition, p. 11.

Frank, Marc and Richard Lapper. 2005. 'Castro's doctors give Chavez shot in arm', *Financial Times*, 9 February 2005, London Edition, p. 8

Franko, Patrice. 1999. *The Puzzle of Latin American Economic Development*. Oxford: Rowman and Littlefield

Franko, Patrice. 2007. *The Puzzle of Latin American Economic Development*, 3rd Edition. Oxford: Rowman and Littlefield

Freedman, Lawrence D. 1982. 'Reconsiderations: The War of the Falkland Islands, 1982', *Foreign Affairs*, Vol. 61, No. 1 (Fall), pp. 196–210

Freedom House. 2002. *Country Reports*. Washington: Freedom House. Available at: http://www.freedomhouse.org [accessed September 2009]

Freedom House. 2009a. *Country Reports*. Washington: Freedom House. Available at: http://www.freedomhouse.org [accessed September 2009]

Freedom House. 2009b. *Freedom of the Press 2009. Further Declines in Global Media Independence*. Washington: Freedom House. Available at: http://www.freedomhouse.org/uploads/FreedomofthePress2009.pdf [accessed September 2009]

Frieden, Jeffry A., Michael Tomz and Manuel Jr. Pastor. 2000. *Modern Political Economy and Latin America: Theory and Policy*. Boulder, CO: Westview Press

Frühling, Hugo. 1998. 'Judicial Reform and Democratization in Latin America', in Felipe Agüero and Jeffrey Stark (eds), *Fault Lines of Democracy in Post-Transition Latin America*. Coral Gables, FL: North-South Center Press

Fukumi, Sayaka. 2008. *Cocaine Trafficking in Latin America: EU and US Policy Responses*. Aldershot: Ashgate

Galen Carpenter, Ted. 2003. *Bad Neighbor Policy: Washington's Futile War on Drugs in Latin America*. Houndmills: Palgrave Macmillan

Gallagher, Kevin and Timothy Wise. 2009. 'Nafta's unhappy anniversary', The Guardian online (guardian.co.uk), 1 January 2009. Available at: http://www.guardian.co.uk/commentisfree/cifamerica/2009/jan/01/nafta-anniversary-us-mexico-trade [accessed November 2009]

Gamarra, Eduardo A. 2008. 'Bolivia: Evo Morales and Democracy', Chapter 6, in Jorge I. Domínguez and Michael Shifter (eds), *Constructing Democratic Governance in Latin America*, 3rd Edition. Baltimore, MD: Johns Hopkins University Press

García-Guadilla, María Pilar. 2005. 'Environmental Movements, Politics and Agenda 21 in Latin America', Civil Society and Social Movements Programme Paper Number 16, October 2005, United Nations Research Institute for Social Development. Geneva: UNRISD

García-Guadilla, María Pilar and Carlos Pérez. 2002. 'Democracy, Decentralization, and Clientelism: New Relationships and Old Practices', *Latin American Perspectives*, Vol. 29, No. 5 (September), pp. 90–109

Gelb, Leslie H. 2009. *Power Rules: How Common Sense Can Rescue American Foreign Policy*. New York: Harper

Georgetown University and the Organisation of American States. 2002. *Political Database of the Americas*. Washington: Georgetown University/OAS. Available at: http://pdba.georgetown.edu [accessed February 2010]

Gerlach, Allen. 2003. *Indians, Oil and Politics: A Recent History of Ecuador*. Wilmington, DE: Scholarly Resources

Gibran, Daniel. 1998. *The Falklands War: Britain Versus the Past in the South Atlantic*. London: McFarland

Gilbreth, Chris and Gerardo Otero. 2001. 'Democratization in Mexico: The Zapatista Uprising and Civil Society', *Latin American Perspectives*, Vol. 28, No. 4 (July), pp. 7–29

Gill, Graeme. 2000. *The Dynamics of Democratization. Elites, Civil Society and the Transition Process*. Basingstoke: Macmillan

Gillespie, Charles. 1987. *Party Strategies and Redemocratization: Theoretical and Comparative Perspectives on the Uruguayan Case*. Doctoral thesis, Yale University, Department of Political Science

Gilly, Adolfo. 2008. 'Racism, Domination and Bolivia', *Counterpunch* magazine online, 1 October 2008. Available at: http://www.counterpunch.org/gilly10012008.html [accessed December 2009]

Godoy, Julio. 2006. 'Latin America-EU: Cooperation or Dependency?' Inter Press Service online, 11 May 2006, Vienna. Available at: http://ipsnews.net/news.asp?idnews=33205 [accessed November 2009]

Golash-Boza, Tanya. 2008. 'Afro-Peruvians in a Mestizo Nation: The Politics of Recognition, Cultural Citizenship, and Racial Democracy in Peru', in Guillermo O'Donnell, Joseph S. Tulchin, and Augusto Varas (eds) with Adam Stubits, *New Voices in Studies in the Study of Democracy in Latin America*. Washington, DC: Woodrow Wilson International Center for Scholars

Goldfrank, Benjamin. 2003. 'Making Participation Work in Porto Alegre', in Gianpaolo Baiocchi (ed.), *Radicals in Power. The Workers' Party (PT) and Experiments in Urban Democracy in Brazil*. London: Zed Books.

Goldfrank, Benjamin and Aaron Schneider. 2006. 'Competitive Institution Building: the PT and participatory budgeting in Rio Grande do Sul', *Latin American Politics and Society*, Vol. 48, No. 3 (September), pp. 1–31

Goldman, Francisco. 2008. *The Art of Political Murder: Who Killed the Bishop?* New York: Grove Press

Goldstein, Joshua and Jon C. Pevehouse. 2009. *International Relations*, 9th Edition. London: Longman.

Golinger, Eva. 2006. *The Chávez Code: Cracking US Intervention in Venezuela*. Northampton: Olive Branch Press

González, Gustavo. 2005. '"War on Terror" Has Latin American Indigenous People in Its Sights'. Inter Press Service online. Available at: http://ipsnews.net/news.asp?idnews= 28960 [accessed October 2009]

González, Luis E. 2008. 'Political Crises and Democracy in Latin America Since the End of the Cold War', Kellogg Institute for International Studies, Working Paper #353 (December 2008). Available at: http://kellogg.nd.edu/publications/workingpapers/ WPS/353.pdf

González, Victoria. 2001. 'Somocista Women, Right-Wing Politics, and Feminism in Nicaragua, 1936–1979', in Victoria González and Karen Kampwirth (eds), *Radical Women in Latin America. Left and Right*. University Park, PA: Pennsylvania State University Press

González, Victoria and Karen Kampwirth (eds). 2001. *Radical Women in Latin America. Left and Right*. University Park, PA: Pennsylvania State University Press

González-Cruz, Michael. 2006. *Nacionalismo Revolucionario Puertorriqueño, 1956–2005*. San Juan: Editorial Isla Negra

Gott, Richard. 2004. *Cuba: A New History*. New Haven, CT: Yale University Press

Graham, Richard (ed.). 1990. *The Idea of Race in Latin America, 1870–1940*. Austin, TX: University of Texas Press

Gramsci, Antonio. 1971. *Selections from Prison Notebooks*. London: Lawrence and Wishart

Grandin, Greg. 2006. *Empire's Workshop: Latin America, the United States, and the Rise of the New Imperialism*. New York: Henry Holt

Grayson, George W. 2007. *Mexican Messiah: Andrés Manuel López Obrador*. Pennsylvania: Pennsylvania State University Press

Graziano, Frank. 1992. *Divine Violence: Spectacle, Psychosexuality, and Radical Christianity in the Argentine 'Dirty War'*. Boulder, CO: Westview Press

Green, Duncan. 1995. *Silent Revolution. The Rise of Market Economics in Latin America*. London: Cassell

Green, Eric. 2005. 'Colombia's Displaced Populace Needs More Help, Report Says', Eric Green, *US Fed News*, Hindustan Times, Washington, 12 May 2005. Factiva.com database [accessed March 2006]

Grossman, Lawrence K. 1995. *The Electronic Republic. Reshaping Democracy in the Information Age*. New York: Viking

Guevara, Aleida. 2005. *Chávez, Venezuela and the New Latin America. An Interview with Hugo Chávez*. Melbourne: Ocean Press

Guevara, Ernesto. 1961. *Guerrilla Warfare*. New York: MR Press

Guevara, Ernesto. 1968. *Bolivian Diary*. London: Jonathan Cape

Guevara, Ernesto. 2003. *Che Guevara Reader. Writings on Politics and Revolution*. Melbourne: Ocean Press

Gunder Frank, André. 1971. *Capitalism and Underdevelopment in Latin America.* Harmondsworth: Penguin Books

Gunther, Richard, José Ramón Montero and Juan Linz (eds). 2002. *Political Parties: Old Concepts and New Challenges.* Oxford: Oxford University Press

Gustafson, Bret. 2008. 'By Means Legal and Otherwise: The Bolivian Right Regroups', *NACLA Report on the Americas*, Vol. 41, No. 1 (January/February), pp. 20–25

Gustafson, Bret. 2009. *New Languages of the State: Indigenous Resurgence and the Politics of Knowledge in Bolivia.* Durham: Duke University Press

Gutberlet, Jutta. 2008. *Recovering Resources – Recycling Citizenship: Urban Poverty Reduction in Latin America.* Farnham: Ashgate

Gutiérrez, David G. (ed.). 2004. T*he Columbia History of Latinos in the United States Since 1960.* New York: Columbia University Press

Gutiérrez, Gustavo. 1973. *A Theology of Liberation.* New York: Orbis

Gwynne, Robert N. 2004. 'Structural Reform in South America and Mexico: Economic and Regional Perspectives', in Robert N. Gwynne and Cristóbal Kay (eds), *Latin America Transformed: Globalization and Modernity*, 2nd Edition. London: Arnold

Gwynne, Robert N. and Cristóbal Kay. 2004. 'Latin America Transformed: Globalization and Neoliberalism', in Robert N. Gwynne and Cristóbal Kay (eds), *Latin America Transformed. Globalization and Modernity*, 2nd Edition. London: Arnold

Gwynne, Robert N. and Cristóbal Kay (eds). 2004. *Latin America Transformed. Globalization and Modernity*, 2nd Edition. London: Arnold

Haggard, Stephan and Robert R. Kaufman. 2008. *Development, Democracy, and Welfare States: Latin America, East Asia, and Eastern Europe.* Princeton, NJ: Princeton University Press

Hagopian, Frances. 1998. 'Democracy and Political Representation in Latin America in the 1990s: Pause, Reorganization, or Decline?', in Felipe Agüero and Jeffrey Stark (eds), *Fault Lines of Democracy in Post-Transition Latin America.* Coral Gables, FL: North-South Center Press

Hale, Charles A. 1986. 'Political and Social Ideas in Latin America, 1870–1930', in Leslie Bethell (ed.), *The Cambridge History of Latin America, Volume IV, c. 1870 to 1930.* Cambridge: Cambridge University Press.

Halperín Donghi, Tulio. 1993. *The Contemporary History of Latin America.* Durham, NC: Macmillan

Hammond, John L. 2004. 'The MST and the Media: Competing Images of the Brazilian Landless Farmworkers' Movement', *Latin American Politics and Society*, Vol. 46, No. 4 (December), pp. 61–90

Harding, Colin. 1988. 'Antonio Díaz Martínez and the Ideology of Sendero Luminoso', *Bulletin of Latin American Research*, Vol. 7, No. 1 (January), pp. 65–73

Hardt, Michael and Antonio Negri. 2000. *Empire.* London: Harvard University Press

Hari, Johann. 2005. 'US pushes style of democracy that suits its purposes', *Seattle Post-Intelligencer*, 13 March 2005, Final, p. D5. Factiva.com database [accessed March 2006]

Harris, Richard L. 2002. 'Globalisation and Globalism in Latin America: Contending Perspectives', *Latin American Perspectives*, Vol. 29, No. 6 (November), pp. 5–23

Harrison, Lawrence. 1992. *Who Prospers? How Cultural Values Shape Economic and Political Success.* New York: Basic Books.

Hartlyn, Jonathan and Arturo Valenzuela. 1994. 'Democracy in Latin America Since 1930', in Leslie Bethell (ed.), *The Cambridge History of Latin America, Vol. VI, part 2: Politics and Society*. Cambridge: Cambridge University Press.

Harvey, David. 2005. *The New Imperialism*, 2nd Edition. New York: Oxford University Press

Held, David and Anthony McGrew. 2000. 'The Great Globalization Debate: An Introduction', in David Held and Anthony McGrew (eds), *The Global Transformation Reader*. Oxford: Polity

Held, David and Anthony McGrew (eds). 2000. *The Global Transformation Reader*. Oxford: Polity

Helg, Aline. 1990. 'Race in Argentina and Cuba, 1880–1930: Theory, Policies, and Popular Reaction', in Richard Graham (ed.), *The Idea of Race in Latin America, 1870–1940*. Austin, TX: University of Texas Press

Hellinger, Daniel. 1999. 'Electoral and Party Politics', in Julia Buxton and Nicola Phillips (eds), *Developments in Latin American Political Economy: States, Markets and Actors*. Manchester: Manchester University Press

Helmke, Gretchen. 2005. *Courts under Constraints. Judges, Generals, and Presidents in Argentina*. Cambridge: Cambridge University Press

Hemming, John. 2008. *Tree of Rivers: The Story of the Amazon*. London: Thames and Hudson

Henderson, James D. 1988. *Conservative Thought in Twentieth-Century Latin America: The Ideas of Laureano Gómez*. Athens, Ohio: Ohio University Center for International Studies/Center for Latin American Studies

Hernández, Isabel. 2003. *Autonomía o Ciudadanía Incompleta: El Pueblo Mapuche en Chile y Argentina*. Santiago: CEPAL/Pehuén Editores

Hershberg, Eric. 1997. 'Market-Oriented Development Strategies and State-Society Relations in New Democracies: Lessons from Contemporary Chile and Spain', in Douglas A. Chalmers *et al.* (eds), *The New Politics of Inequality in Latin America. Rethinking Participation and Representation*. Oxford: Oxford University Press

Hinojosa, Victor J. 2007. *Domestic Politics and International Narcotics Control: US Relations with Mexico and Colombia, 1989–2000*. New York: Routledge

Hite, Katherine and Paola Cesarini (eds). 2004. *Authoritarian Legacies and Democracy in Latin America and Southern Europe*. Notre Dame, IN: University of Notre Dame Press

Hobsbawm, Eric J. 2008. *On Empire: America, War, and Global Supremacy*. New York: Pantheon Books

Hochstetler, Kathryn and Margaret E. Keck. 2007. *Greening Brazil: Environmental Activism in State and Society*. Durham, NC: Duke University Press

Hogan, Michael J. and Thomas G. Paterson. (eds). 2004. *Explaining the History of American Foreign Relations*. Cambridge: Cambridge University Press

Hooker, Juliet. 2008. 'The Institutional Design of Multiculturalism in Nicaragua: Effects on Indigenous and Afro-descendant Collective Identities and Political Attitudes', in Guillermo O'Donnell, Joseph S. Tulchin, and Augusto Varas (eds) with Adam Stubits, *New Voices in Studies in the Study of Democracy in Latin America*. Washington, DC: Woodrow Wilson International Center for Scholars

Hoover's. 2003. 'Embraer-Empresa Brasileira de Aeronautica S.A.', *Hoover's Company Profiles*, 10 December 2003. Austin, TX: Hoover's Inc. Factiva.com database [accessed March 2006]

Hosseini, S. A. Hamed. 2010. *Alternative Globalizations: An Integrative Approach to Studying Dissident Knowledge in the Global Justice Movement*. New York: Routledge

Hoste, Amaury. 1999. 'The New Latin American Policy of the EU', University of Bradford, Discussion Paper No. 11, European Development Policy Study Group, Development Studies Association, February 1999. Available at: http://www.edpsg.org/Documents/Dp11.doc [accessed February 2010]

Howard, April. 2009. 'Saying No to Soy: The Campesino Struggle for Sustainable Agriculture in Paraguay', *Monthly Review*, Vol. 61, No. 2 (June). Factiva.com database [accessed February 2010]

Hunter, Wendy. 1998. 'Civil-Military Relations in Argentina, Brazil, and Chile: Present Trends, Future Prospects', in Felipe Agüero and Jeffrey Stark (eds), *Fault Lines of Democracy in Post-Transition Latin America*. Coral Gables, FL: North-South Center Press

Huntington, Samuel. 1968. *Political Order in Changing Societies*. New Haven, CT: Yale University Press

Huntington, Samuel. 1991. *The Third Wave. Democratization in the Late Twentieth Century*. Norman, OK: University of Oklahoma Press

Hymn, Soneile. 2009. 'Indigenous Feminism in Southern Mexico', Mujeres Libres (Zapaista Women) online, July 2009. Available at: http://www.mujereslibres.org/Articles/indigenousfeminism.htm [accessed December 2009]

Hyun-Hoon Lee and Jung Hur, 2009. *Trade Creation in the APEC Region: Measurement of the Magnitude of and Changes in Intra-regional Trade since APEC's Inception*. Singapore: Asia-Pacific Economic Cooperation Policy Support Unit/Sogang University. Available at: http://www.apec.org/etc/medialib/apec_media_library/downloads/psu/2009/reports.Par.0001.File.tmp/MeasureIntraRegTrade.pdf [accessed November 2009]

IACHR (Inter-American Commission on Human Rights). 2009. *Annual Report 2008*. Washington: IACHR. Available at: http://www.cidh.oas.org/annualrep/2008eng/TOC.htm [accessed October 2009]

IADB/IDB (Inter-American Development Bank). 1996. *Economic and Social Progress in Latin America, 1996*. Washington, DC: Johns Hopkins University Press

IADB/IDB (Inter-American Development Bank). 2004. *Sending Money Home: Remittance to Latin America and the Caribbean*. New York: IADB Multilateral Investment Fund. Available at: http://www.iadb.org/news/docs/remittances_en.pdf [accessed February 2010]

IADB/IDB (Inter-American Development Bank). 2005. *Remittances to Latin America from Japan*. Okinawa: IADB/IDB, Multilateral Investment Fund

IADB/IDB (Inter-American Development Bank). 2008. 'IDB Promotes Japanese Investment in Latin America', Announcements, 22 February 2008. New York: IADB/IDB. Available at: http://www.iadb.org/news/detail.cfm?language=English&id=4431 [accessed November 2009]

IADB/IDB (Inter-American Development Bank). 2009. 'IDB sees remittances to Latin America and the Caribbean declining in 2009', News Release, 16 March 2009. New York: IADB/IDB. Available at: http://www.iadb.org/news/detail.cfm?id=5160 [accessed November 2009]

ICJ (International Commission of Jurists). 2003. 'Brazil – ICJ Deplores the Assassination of Judge Antônio José Machado Dias', ICJ Press Release, 17 March 2003. Geneva: ICJ. Available at: http://www.icj.org/IMG/pdf/doc-77.pdf [accessed February 2010]

IDEA (International Institute for Democracy and Electoral Assistance). 2006. *Voter Turnout. Presidential Elections* and *Parliamentary Elections*. Stockholm: IDEA. Available at: http://www.idea.int/vt/ [accessed February 2010]

IDEA (International Institute for Democracy and Electoral Assistance). 2007, 'Good Practices for Women's Participation in Latin America' Project (unpublished). Stockholm: IDEA

IDEA (International Institute for Democracy and Electoral Assistance). 2009. 'Voter Turnout', online database, based on data gathered from desk research by IDEA staff, surveys to Electoral Management Bodies and the IDEA publications. Stockholm: IDEA. Available at http://www.idea.int [accessed September 2009]

IDU (International Democrat Union). 2009. 'Member parties', International Democrat Union online. Oslo: IDU. Available at: http://www.idu.org/member.aspx [accessed November 2009]

ILO (International Labour Organisation). 2002. 'Indigenous Peoples'. San José: ILO/OIT MultiDisciplinary Team. Available at: http://www.ilo.org/public/english/region/ampro/mdtsanjose/indigenous [accessed February 2010]

ILO (International Labour Organisation). 2005. *Newsletter: The ILO and Indigenous and Tribal Peoples*, April 2005. Geneva: ILO. Available at: http://www.ilo.org/public/english/indigenous/newsletter/index.htm [accessed February 2010]

ILO (International Labour Organisation). 2009. *Global Employment Trends, January 2009*. Geneva: ILO

IMF (International Monetary Fund). 2004. *The IMF and Argentina, 1991–2001*. Washington: IMF. Available at: http://www.imf.org/External/NP/ieo/2004/arg/eng/pdf/report.pdf [accessed February 2010]

Inglehart, Ronald F., Neil Nevitte and Miguel Basañez. 1996. *The North American Trajectory: Cultural, Economic, and Political Ties Among the United States, Canada, and Mexico*. Hawthorne, NY: Aldine de Gruyter.

Inter-American Dialogue/United Nations Development Programme. 2005. *Scrutinizing Democracy in Latin America. A Discussion of the UNDP's Report on Democracy in Latin America, June 2005*. Washington/New York: Inter-American Dialogue/UNDP. Available at: http://www.thedialogue.org/PublicationFiles/Scrutinizing%20Democracy.pdf [accessed February 2010]

Inter Press. 2009. 'Brazil: University Racial Quotas Bogged Down in Congress', Inter Press Service online, ISI Emerging Markets Africawire, 29 April 2009. Factiva.com database [accessed February 2010]

IOM (International Organisation for Migration). 2005a. *World Migration Report 2005 – Press Kit*: 'International Migration in Latin America and the Caribbean'. Geneva: IOM.

IOM (International Organisation for Migration). 2005b. *Migration in the Americas*, No. 3 (September 2005). Geneva: IOM

IOM (International Organisation for Migration). 2005c. *World Migration 2005 – Costs and Benefits of International Migration. Section 1: Regional Overview, Selected Geographic Regions*. Geneva: IOM. Available at: http://www.iom.int/jahia/Jahia/cache/offonce/pid/1674;jsessionid=042962C4F823FE9ADE354E0CD8D81BAF.worker01?entryId=932 [accessed February 2010]

IRELA (Instituto de Relaciones Europeo-Latinoamericanas). 1997. *La Unión Europea y México: Una Nueva Relación Política y Económica*. Madrid: IRELA

Isbell, Paul. 2009. 'Energy for the Western Hemisphere: Revisiting Latin America's Energy Scene before the 5th Summit of the Americas', Real Instituto Elcano/Elcano Royal Institute ARI, ARI 10/2009, 14 January 2009. Madrid: Real Instituto Elcano. Available at: http://www.realinstitutoelcano.org/wps/portal/rielcano_eng/Content?WCM_GLOBAL_CONTEXT=/elcano/elcano_in/zonas_in/latin+america/ari10-2009 [accessed November 2009]

ISPI (Summit of the Americas. Inter-Summit Property Systems Initiative). 2000. *Property Registration*. Washington: Organisation of American States/USAID

ITUC (International Trade Union Confederation). 2009. Annual Survey of Violations of Trade Union Rights, 2009. Brussels: ITUC. Available at: http://survey09.ituc-csi.org/survey.php?IDContinent=2&Lang=EN [accessed October 2009]

Janda, Kenneth. 1980. *Political Parties: A Cross-National Survey*. London: Macmillan

Jaquette, Jane S. 2009a. 'Introduction', in Jane S. Jaquette (ed.), *Feminist Agendas and Democracy in Latin America*. Durham, NC: Duke University Press

Jaquette, Jane S. 2009b. 'Feminist Activism and the Challenges of Democracy', Chapter 10 in Jane S. Jaquette (ed.), *Feminist Agendas and Democracy in Latin America*. Durham, NC: Duke University Press

Jaquette, Jane S. (ed.). 2009. *Feminist Agendas and Democracy in Latin America*. Durham, NC: Duke University Press

Jarquín, Edmundo and Fernando Carrillo (eds). 1998. *Justice Delayed: Judicial Reform in Latin America*. Washington, DC: Inter-American Development Bank/Johns Hopkins University Press

Jelin, Elizabeth (ed.). 1990. *Women and Social Change in Latin America*. London: Zed Books

Jones, Mark P. 2002. 'Legislator Behaviour and Executive-Legislative Relations in Latin America', review article, *Latin American Research Review*, Vol. 37, No. 3 (Fall), pp. 176–88

Kagan, Robert. 2004. *Of Paradise and Power: America and Europe in the New World Order*. New York: Vintage Books

Kampwirth, Karen. 2001. 'Women in the Armed Struggles in Nicaragua: Sandinistas and Contras Compared', in Victoria González and Karen Kampwirth (eds), *Radical Women in Latin America. Left and Right*. University Park, PA: Pennsylvania State University Press

Kampwirth, Karen. 2008. 'Neither Left nor Right: Sandinismo in the Anti-Feminist Era', *NACLA Report on the Americas*, Vol. 41, No. 1 (January/February), pp. 30–34

Karl, Terry Lynn. 1996. 'Dilemmas of Democratization in Latin America', in Roderic Ai Camp (ed.), *Democracy in Latin America. Patterns and Cycles*. Wilmington, DE: Scholarly Resources

Katzenstein, Peter J. and Robert O. Keohane (eds). 2007. *Anti-Americanisms in World Politics*. Ithaca, NY: Cornell University Press

Kaufmann, Daniel. 2004. 'Corruption, Governance and Security: Challenges for the Rich Countries and the World', Chapter 2.1 in *Global Competitiveness Report 2004/2005*. Washington: World Bank. Available at: http://www.worldbank.org/wbi/governance/pdf/Kaufmann_GCR_101904_B.pdf [accessed April 2009]

Kaufmann, Daniel, Aart Kraay and Massimo Mastruzzi. 2009. *Governance Matters VIII: Aggregate and Individual Governance Indicators, 1996–2008. Policy Research Working Paper 4978*. Washington: World Bank Development Research Group. Available at: http://papers.ssrn.com/sol3/papers.cfm?abstract_id=1424591 [accessed September 2009]

Kaufman, Robert and Barbara Stallings. 1991. 'The Political Economy of Latin American Populism', in Rudiger Dornbusch and Sebastian Edwards (eds), *The Macroeconomics of Populism in Latin America*. Chicago: University of Chicago Press/National Bureau of Economic Research Conference Reports

Kay, Cristóbal. 2004. 'Rural Livelihoods and Peasant Futures', in Robert N. Gwynne and Cristóbal Kay (eds), *Latin America Transformed: Globalization and Modernity*, 2nd Edition. London: Arnold

Keane, John. 1988. *Democracy and Civil Society*. London: Verso

Keck, Margaret E. and Kathryn Sikkink. 1998. *Activists Beyond Borders. Advocacy Networks in International Politics*. Ithaca, NY: Cornell University Press

Kelly, Robert E. 2008. 'No "return to the state": dependency and developmentalism against neo-liberalism', *Development in Practice*, Vol. 18, No. 3 (June), pp. 319–32

Kenney, Charles D. 2000. 'Reflections on Horizontal Accountability: Democratic Legitimacy, Majority Parties and Democratic Stability in Latin America', draft paper prepared for the conference on Institutions, Accountability, and Democratic Governance in Latin America, Kellogg Institute for International Studies, University of Notre Dame, May 8–9, 2000

Khasnabish, Alex. 2010. *Zapatistas: Rebellion from the Grassroots to the Global*. London: Zed Books

Kiely, Ray. 2006. 'United States Hegemony and Globalisation: What Role for Theories of Imperialism?', *Cambridge Review of International Affairs*, Vol. 19, No. 2 (June), pp. 205–21

Kincaid, A. Douglas. 2000. 'Demilitarization and Security in El Salvador and Guatemala: Convergences of Success and Crisis', *Journal of Interamerican Studies and World Affairs*, Vol. 42, No. 4, Special Issue: Globalization and Democratization in Guatemala (Winter), pp. 39–58

Kingstone, Peter. 2010. *The Political Economy of Latin America: Reflections on Neoliberalism and Development*. New York: Routledge

Kinley, David. 2009. *Civilising Globalisation: Human Rights and the Global Economy*. Cambridge: Cambridge University Press

Kitschelt, Herbert *et al.* 2010. *Latin American Party Systems*. Cambridge: Cambridge University Press

Klesner, Joseph L. 2009. 'Who Participates? Determinants of Political Action in Mexico', *Latin American Politics and Society*, Vol. 51, No. 2 (Summer), pp. 59–90

Knight, Alan. 1987. 'The Working Class: The Working Class and the Mexican Revolution', in Eduardo Archetti, Paul Cammack and Bryan Roberts (eds), *Latin America. Sociology of Developing Societies*. Houndmills: Macmillan

Knight, Alan. 1998. 'Populism and Neo-populism in Latin America, Especially Mexico', *Journal of Latin American Studies*, Vol. 30, No. 2 (May), pp. 223–48

Knight, Alan. 1990. 'Racism, Revolution and Indigenismo: Mexico, 1910–1940', in Richard Graham (ed.), *The Idea of Race in Latin America, 1870–1940*. Austin, TX: University of Texas Press

Korin, Anne and Gal Luft (eds). 2009. *Energy Security Challenges for the 21st Century: A Reference Handbook*. Santa Barbara, CA: Praeger

Kornblith, Miriam and Daniel Levine. 1995. 'Venezuela: The Life and Times of the Party System', in Scott Mainwaring and Timothy Scully (eds), *Building Democratic Institutions. Party Systems in Latin America*. Stanford, CA: Stanford University Press

Kozloff, Nikolas. 2007. 'An Interview with Magdalena Cajias: White Racism and the Aymara in Bolivia', *Counterpunch* magazine online, 26 April 2007. Available at: http://www.counterpunch.org/kozloff04262007.html [accessed December 2009]

Krasno, Jean. 1994. 'Non-proliferation: Brazil's Secret Nuclear Program', *Orbis* Vol. 38, No. 3 (Summer), pp. 425–36

Kurtz, Marcus J. 2004. *Free Market Democracy and the Chilean and Mexican Countryside.* New York: Cambridge University Press

Laclau, Ernesto and Chantal Mouffe. 1985. *Hegemony and Socialist Strategy.* London: Verso

Landman, Todd (ed.) with David Beetham, Edzia Carvalho and Stuart Weir. 2009. *Evaluar la calidad de la democracia Una introducción al marco de trabajo de IDEA Internacional.* Stockholm: International Institute for Democracy and Electoral Assistance (IDEA). Available at: http://www.idea.int/publications/ [accessed September 2009]

Larraín, Jorge. 2004. 'Modernity and Identity: Cultural Change in Latin America', in Robert N. Gwynne and Cristóbal Kay (eds), *Latin America Transformed. Globalization and Modernity*, 2nd Edition. London: Arnold

Latin American Commission on Drugs and Democracy. 2009. *Drugs and Democracy: Toward a Paradigm Shift.* Latin American Commission on Drugs and Democracy, Open Society Institute, Instituto Fernando Henrique Cardoso, Viva Rio, Centro Edelsten de Pesquisas Sociais. Available at: http://www.ungassondrugs.org/images/stories/towards.pdf [accessed October 2009]

Latin Business Chronicle. 2008. 'Latin America More Globalized', fourth annual Latin Globalization Index, *Latin Business Chronicle* online, 10 December 2008. Available at: http://www.latinbusinesschronicle.com/app/article.aspx?id=2915 [accessed December 2009]

Latin Business Chronicle. 2009. 'Latin America: The 100 Most Powerful in Business', 9 September 2008. Florida: Latin Business Chronicle. Available online by subscription through: http://www.latinbusinesschronicle.com/app/article.aspx?id=3645

Latinobarómetro. 2005. *Informe. 1995–2005. Diez Años de Opinión Pública.* Santiago: Corporación Latinobarómetro

Latinobarómetro. 2007. *Informe 2007.* Santiago: Corporación Latinobarómetro

Latinobarómetro. 2008. *Informe 2008.* Santiago: Corporación Latinobarómetro. Available at: http://www.latinobarometro.org/docs/INFORME_LATINOBAROMETRO_2008.pdf [accessed April 2009]

Latinobarómetro. 2009a. *Informe 2009.* Santiago: Corporación Latinobarómetro. Available at: http://www.latinobarometro.org/ [accessed February 2010]

Latinobarómetro. 2009b. *América Latina Mira al Mundo: La economía y la política de las Relaciones Internacionales.* Santiago: Corporación Latinobarómetro. Available at: http://www.latinobarometro.org/ [accessed November 2009]

Latin Trade. 2009. 'LT 500: Latin America's Largest Companies'. Florida: Latin Trade. Available at: http://latintrade.com/rsrch/2009_LT_500.pdf [accessed October 2009]

Lavinas Picq, Manuela. 2008. 'Gender Within Ethnicity: Human Rights and Identity Politics in Ecuador', in Guillermo O'Donnell, Joseph S. Tulchin and Augusto Varas (eds) with Adam Stubits, *New Voices in Studies in the Study of Democracy in Latin America.* Washington, DC: Woodrow Wilson International Center for Scholars

Lawson, Chappell H. 2002. *Building the Fourth Estate. Democratization and the Rise of a Free Press in Mexico.* Berkeley, CA: University of California Press

Le Bot, Y. 1997. *El sueño zapatista*. Barcelona: Plaza y Janés

Leiva, Fernando Ignacio. 2008a. 'Toward a Critique of Latin American Neostructuralism', *Latin American Politics and Society*, Vol. 50, No. 4 (Winter), pp. 1–25

Leiva, Fernando Ignacio. 2008b. *Latin American Neostructuralism: The Contradictions of Post-Neoliberal Development*. Minneapolis, MN: University of Minnesota Press

Levitsky, Steven. 1998. 'Institutionalization and Peronism: The Concept, the Case and the Case for Unpacking the Concept', *Party Politics*, Vol. 4, No. 1 (January 1998), pp. 77–92

Levitsky, Steven. 2003. *Transforming Labour-Based Parties in Latin America*. Cambridge: Cambridge University Press

Leys Stepan, Nancy. 1991. *'The Hour of Eugenics': Race, Gender and Nation in Latin America*. Ithaca, NY: Cornell University Press

Lievesley, Geraldine. 2009. 'Is Latin America moving leftwards? Problems and Prospects', Chapter 1 in Geraldine Lievesley and Steve Ludlam (eds), *Reclaiming Latin America: Experiments in Radical Social Democracy*. London: Zed Books

Lievesley, Geraldine and Steve Ludlam. 2009. 'Introduction: a pink tide?', in Geraldine Lievesley and Steve Ludlam (eds), *Reclaiming Latin America: Experiments in Radical Social Democracy*. London: Zed Books

Lievesley, Geraldine and Steve Ludlam (eds). 2009. *Reclaiming Latin America: Experiments in Radical Social Democracy*. London: Zed Books

Lijphart, A. 1993. 'Constitutional Choices for New Democracies', in Larry Diamond and Marc F. Plattner (eds), *The Global Resurgence of Democracy*. Baltimore, MD: Johns Hopkins University Press

Linz, Juan J. 1994. 'Presidential or Parliamentary Democracy: Does it make a Difference?', in Juan. J. Linz and Arturo Valenzuela (eds), *The Failure of Presidential Democracy, The Case of Latin America. Volume 2*. Baltimore, MD: Johns Hopkins University Press

Linz, Juan and Alfred Stepan (eds). 1996. *Problems of Democratic Transition and Consolidation: southern Europe, South America, and post-communist Europe*. Baltimore, MD: Johns Hopkins University Press

Linz, Juan J. and Arturo Valenzuela (eds). 1994. *The Failure of Presidential Democracy, The Case of Latin America. Volume 2*. Baltimore, MD: Johns Hopkins University Press

Livingstone, Grace. 2009. *America's Backyard: The United States and Latin America from the Monroe Doctrine to the War on Terror*. London: Zed Books

Llanos, Beatriz and Kristen Sample. 2008. *30 Years of Democracy: Riding the Wave? Women's Political Participation in Latin America*. Stockholm: International Institute for Democracy and Electoral Assistance (IDEA). Available at: http://www.idea.int/publications/ [accessed September 2009]

Longo, Francisco. 2005. 'La implantación de la Carta Iberoamericana de la Función Pública: obstáculos y estrategias de reforma', presentation to the Foro Iberoamericano: Revitalización de la Administración Pública. Estrategias para la Implementación de la Carta Iberoamericana de la Función Pública, Mexico City, 5–6 May, 2005. Available at: unpan1.un.org/intradoc/groups/public/documents/CLAD/clad0051501.pdf [accessed February 2010]

Lopez, Mark Hugo. 2009. 'How Hispanics Voted in the 2008 Election', Pew Hispanic Center research, 5 November 2008. Washington: Pew Research Center. Available at: http:// pewresearch.org/pubs/1024/exit-poll-analysis-hispanics [accessed November 2009]

Love, Joseph. 1995. 'Raul Prebisch and the Origins of the Doctrine of Unequal Exchange', in James L. Dietz (ed.), *Latin America's Economic Development. Confronting Crisis*, 2nd Edition. Boulder, CO: Lynne Rienner

Loveman, Brian. 1994. '"Protected Democracies" and Military Guardianship: Political Transitions in Latin America 1978–1993', *Journal of Interamerican Studies and World Affairs*, Vol. 36, No. 2 (Summer), pp. 105–89

Loveman, Brian and Thomas M. Davies Jr. 1997. 'The Politics of Antipolitics', in Brian Loveman and Thomas M. Davies Jr (eds), *The Politics of Antipolitics. The Military in Latin America*. Wilmington, DE: Scholarly Resources

Loveman, Brian and Thomas M. Davies Jr. (eds). 1997. *The Politics of Antipolitics. The Military in Latin America*. Wilmington, DE: Scholarly Resources

Lowe, David. 2005. 'Idea to Reality: NED at 20'. Washington, DC: National Endowment for Democracy

Lowenthal, Abraham F. 1976. 'Two Hundred Years of American Foreign Policy: The United States and Latin America: Ending the Hegemonic Presumption', *Foreign Affairs*, Vol. 55, No. 1 (October), pp. 199–213

Lowenthal, Abraham F. 1991. *Exporting Democracy. The United States and Latin America. Case Studies*. Baltimore, MD: Johns Hopkins University Press

Lowenthal, Abraham F., Ted Piccone and Laurence Whitehead (eds). 2009. *The Obama Administration and the Americas: Agenda for Change*. Washington, DC: Brookings Institution Press

Lucero, José Antonio. 2008. *Struggles of Voice: The Politics of Indigenous Representation in the Andes*. Pittsburgh, PA: University of Pittsburgh Press

Ludlam, Steve. 2009. 'Cuban socialism: recovery and change', Chapter 7 in Geraldine Lievesley and Steve Ludlam (eds), *Reclaiming Latin America: Experiments in Radical Social Democracy*. London: Zed Books

Lugo-Ocando, Jairo (ed.). 2008. *The Media in Latin America*. Maidenhead: Open University Press

Lustig, Nora and Ruthanne Deutsch. 1998. 'The Inter-American Development Bank and Poverty Reduction: An Overview', POV-101-R. Washington, DC: Inter-American Development Bank

Lynch, Edward. 1991. *Religion and Politics in Latin America. Liberation Theology and Christian Democracy*. New York: Praeger

Lynch, Edward. 1998. 'Reform and Religion in Latin America', *Orbis*, Vol. 42, No. 2 (Spring), pp. 263–81

Lynd, Staughton and Andrej Grubacic. 2008. *Wobblies & Zapatistas: Conversations on Anarchism, Marxism and Radical History*. Oakland, CA: PM Press

McAdam, Doug, John McCarthy and Mayer Zald. 1988. 'Social Movements', in Neil J. Smelser (ed.), *Handbook of Sociology*. Beverley Hills, CA: Sage

McClintock, Cynthia and Abraham Lowenthal (eds). 1983. *The Peruvian Experiment Reconsidered*. Princeton, NS: Princeton University Press

MacDonald, Laura. 1997. *Supporting Civil Society: the Political Role of Non-governmental Organisations in Central America*. New York: St Martin's Press

McGee Deutsch, Sandra. 1991. 'Gender and Sociopolitical Change in Twentieth-Century Latin America', *Hispanic American Historical Review*, Vol. 71, No. 2 (May), pp. 259–306

McGee Deutsch, Sandra. 1999. *Las derechas: The Extreme Right in Argentina, Brazil and Chile, 1890–1939*. Stanford, CA: Stanford University Press

McGowan, John. 2007. *American Liberalism: An Interpretation for Our Time*. Chapel Hill, NC: University of North Carolina Press

McGuire, James W. 1997. *Peronism without Perón. Unions, Parties, and Democracy in Argentina*. Stanford, CA: Stanford University Press

Mackinlay, Horacio and Gerardo Otero. 2004. 'State Corporatism and Peasant Organizations: Towards New Institutional Arrangements', in Gerardo Otero (ed.), *Mexico in Transition: Neoliberal Globalism, the State and Civil Society*. London: Zed

MacLeod, Dag. 2004. *Downsizing the State: Privatization and the Limits of Neoliberal Reform in Mexico*. University Park, PA: Pennsylvania State University Press

McMahon, Paul. 2009. *Rainforests: The Burning Issue*. London: The Prince's Rainforests Project

McPherson, Alan. 2003. *Yankee No! Anti-Americanism in US-Latin American Relations*. London: Harvard University Press

MacSwan, Angus. 2005. 'Much Arab blood flows through Latin American veins', *Reuters* news agency, Brasilia, 10 May 2005. Factiva.com database [accessed March 2006]

Mace, Gordon, Louis Bélanger *et al.* 1999. *The Americas in Transition: The Contours of Regionalism*. Boulder, CO: Lynne Rienner

Maheu, Louis (ed.). 1995. *Social Movements and Social Classes: The Future of Collective Action*. London: Sage

Mail. 2009. 'Female armed robber stripped, beaten and set alight by angry lynch mob', Mail Foreign Service, *Daily Mail* online, 16 December 2009. Available at: http://www.dailymail.co.uk/news/worldnews/article-1236323/Female-armed-robber-stripped-beaten-set-alight-lynch-mob.html [accessed December 2009]

Mainwaring, Scott. 1990. 'Presidentialism in Latin America', *Latin American Research Review*, Vol. 25, No. 1 (Spring), pp. 157–79

Mainwaring, Scott. 1993. 'Presidentialism, Multipartism, and Democracy: The Difficult Combination', *Comparative Political Studies*, Vol. 26, No. 2 (July), pp. 198–228

Mainwaring, Scott. 1999. *Rethinking Party Systems in the Third Wave of Democratization. The Case of Brazil*. Stanford, CA: Stanford University Press

Mainwaring, Scott. 2006. 'State Deficiencies, Party Competition, and Confidence in Democratic Representation in the Andes', in Scott Mainwaring, Ana Maria Bejarano and Eduardo Pizarro Leongómez (eds), *The Crisis of Democratic Representation in the Andes*. Stanford, CA: Stanford University Press

Mainwaring, Scott. 2008. 'The Crisis of Representation in the Andes', Chapter 2 in Larry Diamond, Marc F. Plattner and Diego Abente Brun (eds), *Latin America's Struggle for Democracy*. Baltimore, MD: Johns Hopkins University Press

Mainwaring, Scott and Matthew Soberg Shugart. 1997. 'Juan Linz, Presidentialism and Democracy: A Critical Appraisal', *Comparative Politics*, Vol. 29, No. 4 (July), pp. 449–71

Mainwaring, Scott and Matthew Soberg Shugart (eds). 1997. *Presidentialism and Democracy in Latin America*. New York: Cambridge University Press

Mainwaring, Scott and Timothy Scully. 1995. 'Introduction: Party Systems in Latin America', in Scott Mainwaring and Timothy Scully (eds), *Building Democratic Institutions. Party Systems in Latin America*. Stanford, CA: Stanford University Press

Mainwaring, Scott and Timothy Scully (eds). 1995. *Building Democratic Institutions. Party Systems in Latin America*. Stanford, CA: Stanford University Press

Malloy, James (ed.). 1977. *Authoritarianism and Corporatism in Latin America*. Pittsburgh, PA: University of Pittsburgh Press

Mapstone, Naomi and Andres Schipani. 2009. 'Bolivia rejects "savage capitalism"', *Financial Times*, FT.com, 5 December 2009. Available at: http://www.ft.com/cms/s/0/4b3b2d70-e13d-11de-af7a-00144feab49a.html [accessed February 2010]

Marcy, William L. 2010. *The Politics of Cocaine: How US Foreign Policy has Created a Thriving Drug Industry in Central and South America*. Chicago, IL: Lawrence Hill Books

Mares, David. R. 2000. 'Securing Peace in the Americas in the Next Decade', in Jorge I. Domínguez (ed.), *The Future of Inter-American Relations*. London/New York: Routledge

Mariani, Rodolfo. 2008. 'Democracia, Estado y construcción del sujeto (ciudadanía)', in UNDP, *Democracia/Estado/Ciudanía: Hacia un Estado de y para la Democracia en América Latina*. Lima: Sede PNUD

Mariátegui, José Carlos. 1971. *Seven Interpretive Essays on Peruvian Reality*, translated by Marjory Urquidi. Austin, TX: University of Texas Press

Marotto, Telma. 2008. 'Brazilian Secret 93 Million Don't Want to Talk About Is Racism', Bloomberg news agency online, bloomberg.com, 27 June 2008. Available at: http://www.bloomberg.com/apps/news?sid=alezjRWRd5Tk&pid=20601109 [accessed February 2010]

Martin, David. 1990. *Tongues of Fire: The Explosion of Protestantism in Latin America*. Oxford: Blackwell

Martínez, Néstor Humberto. 1998. 'Rule of Law and Economic Efficiency', in Edmundo Jarquín and Fernando Carrillo (eds), *Justice Delayed: Judicial Reform in Latin America*. Washington, DC: Inter-American Development Bank

Martinsson, Johanna. 2009. 'The Role of Media Literacy in the Governance Reform Agenda'. CommGAP Discussion Paper. Washington: International Bank for Reconstruction and Development/World Bank, Communication for Governance & Accountability Programme (CommGAP)

Marx, Jutta, Jutta Borner and Mariana Caminotti. 2009. 'Gender Quotas, Candidate Selection, and Electoral Campaigns', Chapter 2 in Jane S. Jaquette (ed.), *Feminist Agendas and Democracy in Latin America*. Durham, NC: Duke University Press

Mascareño, Carlos. 2000. *Balance de la descentralización en Venezuela: logro, limitaciones y perspectivas*. Caracas: Nueva Sociedad

Masur, Gerhard. 1966. *Nationalism in Latin America*. New York: Macmillan

Mattiace, Shannan L. 2005. 'Representation and Rights: Recent Scholarship on Social Movements in Latin America', review article, *Latin American Research Review*, Vol. 40, No. 1 (Spring), pp. 237–50

Maybury-Lewis, David (ed.). 2003. *The Politics of Ethnicity: Indigenous Peoples in Latin American States*. Cambridge, MA: Harvard University/David Rockefeller Center for Latin American Studies

Mayer, Enrique. 2009. *Ugly Stories of the Peruvian Agrarian Reform*. Durham, NC: Duke University Press

Mazzei, Julie. 2009. *Death Squads or Self-Defense Forces? How Paramilitary Groups Emerge and Challenge Democracy in Latin America*. Chapel Hill, NC: University of North Carolina Press

Melo, Marcus and Flavio Rezende. 2004. 'Decentralization and Governance in Brazil', in Joseph. S. Tulchin and Andrew Selee (eds), *Decentralization and Democratic Governance in Latin America*. Woodrow Wilson Center Report on the Americas #12. Washington, DC: Woodrow Wilson International Center for Scholars

Mendez, Juan, Guillermo O'Donnell and Paulo Sérgio Pinheiro (eds). 1999. *The (Un)Rule of Law and the Underprivileged in Latin America*. Notre Dame, IN: University of Notre Dame Press

Mesa-Lago, Carmela (ed.). 1993. *Cuba after the Cold War*. Pittsburgh, PA: University of Pittsburgh Press

Middlebrook, Kevin J. 2000. 'Introduction: Conservative Parties, Elite Representation, and Democracy in Latin America', in Kevin J. Middlebrook (ed.), *Conservative Parties, the Right, and Democracy in Latin America*. Baltimore, MD: The Johns Hopkins University Press

Middlebrook, Kevin J. (ed.). 2000. *Conservative Parties, the Right, and Democracy in Latin America*. Baltimore, MD: Johns Hopkins University Press

Mideplan (Ministerio de Planficiación y Cooperación). 2008. 'Lucha contra la pobreza y reforma provisional destacan a Chile en foro internacional', Archivo de noticias, sala de prensa, www.mideplan.cl [accessed September 2009]

Milet, Claudia. 2009. 'Vicepresidente de Parlatino espera que Puerto Rico llegue a ser libre', YVKE Mundial/Prensa FDA, 26 March 2009. Available at: http://www.radiomundial.com.ve/yvke/noticia.php?22049 [accessed November 2009]

Miller, Shawn W. 2007. *An Environmental History of Latin America*. Cambridge: Cambridge University Press

Ministry of the Interior, Spain (Ministerio del Interior). 2002. *Anuario Estadístico de Extranjería*. Madrid: Ministerio del Interior, Delegación del Gobierno para la Extranjería y Migración

Ministry of the Interior, Spain (Ministerio del Interior). 2003. *Anuario Estadístico de Extranjería*. Madrid: Ministerio del Interior, Delegación del Gobierno para la Extranjería y Migración

MINUGUA (Misión de las Naciones Unidas para Guatemala). 2000. *Los linchamientos: un flagelo contra la dignidad humana*. Informe de verificación. December 2000. Guatemala: MINUGUA

Mizrahi, Yemile. 2004. 'Decentralization and Democratic Governance in Mexico', in Joseph. S. Tulchin and Andrew Selee (eds), *Decentralization and Democratic Governance in Latin America*. Woodrow Wilson Center Report on the Americas #12. Washington, DC: Woodrow Wilson International Center for Scholars. Available at: http://www.wilsoncenter.org/topics/pubs/ACF18E5.pdf [accessed February 2010]

Molyneux, Maxine. 2001. *Women's Movements in International Perspective. Latin America and Beyond*. Hampshire: Institute of Latin American Studies/Palgrave

Montero, Alfred P. and David J. Samuels (eds). 2004. *Decentralization and Democracy in Latin America*. Notre Dame, IN: University of Notre Dame Press

Montgomery, Shannon. 2009. 'Mexico shuts down Canadian mine', *Toronto Star*, 9 December 2009, p. A19

Moore, Barrington. 1966. *The Social Origins of Dictatorship and Democracy. Lord and Peasant in the Making of the Modern World*. Boston, MA: Beacon Press

Morgenstern, Scott. 2002a. 'Towards a Model of Latin American Legislatures', in Scott Morgenstern and Benito Nacif (eds), *Legislative Politics in Latin America*. Cambridge: Cambridge University Press

Morgenstern, Scott. 2002b. 'Explaining Legislative Politics in Latin America' in Scott Morgenstern and Benito Nacif (eds), *Legislative Politics in Latin America*. Cambridge: Cambridge University Press

Morgenstern, Scott and Benito Nacif (eds). 2002. *Legislative Politics in Latin America*. Cambridge: Cambridge University Press

Motta, Sara C. 2009a. 'Venezuela: reinventing social democracy', Chapter 4 in Geraldine Lievesley and Steve Ludlam (eds), *Reclaiming Latin America: Experiments in Radical Social Democracy*. London: Zed Books

Motta, Sara C. 2009b. 'Old Tools and New Movements in Latin America: Political Science as Gatekeeper or Intellectual Illuminator?', *Latin American Politics and Society*, Vol. 51, No. 1 (Spring), pp. 31–56

Mulligan, Mark. 2004. 'Sexual revolution catches up with Chile', *Financial Times*, 23 March 2004, London Edition, p. 11

Munck, Gerardo L. and Jay Verkuilen. 2002. 'Conceptualizing and Measuring Democracy. Evaluating Alternative Indices', *Comparative Political Studies*, Vol. 35 No. 1 (February), pp. 5–34

Munck, Ronaldo. 2003. *Contemporary Latin America*. Basingstoke: Palgrave

Munks, Robert. 2009. 'Could war erupt in arms-spree LatAm?' bbc.co.uk, 15 September 2009. Available at: http://news.bbc.co.uk/2/hi/americas/8256686 stm [accessed November 2009]

Muñoz, Boris. 2008. 'The Revolution of Conscience: Building a New Cultural Hegemony in Venezuela', Venezuela: The Chávez Effect, *ReVista: Harvard Review of Latin America* (Fall). Available at: http://www.drclas.harvard.edu/revista/articles/view/1127 [accessed November 2009]

Muñoz, Heraldo. 2001. 'Good-bye USA?' in Joseph Tulchin and Ralph Espach (eds), *Latin America in the New International System*. Boulder, CO: Lynne Rienner/Woodrow Wilson International Center for Scholars

Mustapic, Ana María. 2002. 'Oscillating Relations: President and Congress in Argentina', in Scott Morgenstern and Benito Nacif (eds), *Legislative Politics in Latin America*. Cambridge: Cambridge University Press

Myers, David J. 2008. 'Venezuela: Democracy or Autocracy', Chapter 12 in Jorge I. Domínguez and Michael Shifter (eds), *Constructing Democratic Governance in Latin America*, 3rd Edition. Baltimore, MD: Johns Hopkins University Press

Nacif, Benito. 2002. 'Understanding Party Discipline in the Mexican Chamber of Deputies: The Centralized Party Model', in Scott Morgenstern and Benito Nacif (eds), *Legislative Politics in Latin America*. Cambridge: Cambridge University Press

Nagel, Beverly. 2002. 'Indigenous Movements and Their Critics: Pan-Maya Activism in Guatemala', review article, *Latin American Politics and Society*, Vol. 44, No. 1 (April), pp. 189–92

Negretto, Gabriel L. 2006. 'Minority Presidents and Democratic Performance in Latin America, *Latin American Politics and Society*, Vol. 48, No. 3 (September), pp. 63–92

Nelson, Roy C. 2009. *Harnessing Globalization: The Promotion of Nontraditional Foreign Direct Investment in Latin America*. University Park, PA: Pennsylvania State University Press

Nevins, Joseph. 2008. *Dying to Live: A Story of US Immigration in an Age of Global Apartheid*. San Francisco, CA: City Lights Books

New America Media. 2009. 'New Report Reveals Accounts of Torture, Violence by Mexican Army', news report, 27 April 2009. Available at: http://news.newamericamedia.org/news/view_article.html?article_id=e2ab5bd64c610741e4d3e7ebc5556b53 [accessed October 2009]

Nieto, Clara. 2003. *Masters of War. Latin America and US Aggression from the Cuban Revolution Through the Clinton Years*. New York: Seven Stories Press

Nishijima, Shoji and Peter H. Smith. (eds). 1996. *Cooperation or Rivalry? Regional Integration in the Americas and the Pacific Rim*. Boulder, CO: Westview Press

Noble, Ronald K. 2009. 'Opening remarks to the Interpol 20th Americas Regional Conference, Viña del Mar, Chile 1 April 2009'. Speeches, Interpol online. Available at: http://www.interpol.int/Public/ICPO/speeches/2009/20090401SG_ARC20.asp [accessed November 2009]

Noer, Michael and Nicole Perlroth. 2009. 'The World's Most Powerful People: The 67 heads of state, criminals, financiers and philanthropists who really run the world', Special Report, Forbes.com. Available at: http://www.forbes.com/2009/11/09/world-most-powerful-leadership-power-09-intro.html [accessed November 2009]

No Sweat. 2005a. *Sweatshops and Globalisation: An Activist Response*. London: No Sweat

No Sweat. 2005b. *KukDong/Mexmode: Background to the Struggle for an Independent Union*, Document produced as Background to the KukDong Workers' Visit to Britain, November 2002. London: No Sweat

Nylen, William. 2003. *Participatory Democracy versus Elitist Democracy: Lessons from Brazil*. New York: Palgrave Macmillan

OAS (Organisation of American States). 2005. *Inter-American Convention on Corruption*, adopted at the third plenary session, held on 29 March 1996. Washington: OAS Department of Legal Affairs and Services, Office of Inter-American Law and Programmes

Ocampo, José Antonio. 1995. 'Terms of Trade and Center-Periphery Relations', in James L. Dietz (ed.). *Latin America's Economic Development. Confronting Crisis*, 2nd Edition. Boulder, CO: Lynne Rienner

ODCA (Organización Demócrata Cristiana de América). 2009. 'Partidos miembros', Organización Demócrata Cristiana de América online. Mexico City: ODCA. Available at: http://www.odca.org.mx/miembros.html [accessed November 2009]

O'Donnell, Guillermo. 1973. *Modernization and Bureaucratic Authoritarianism: Studies in South American Politics*. Berkeley, CA: Institute of International Studies, University of California

O'Donnell, Guillermo. 1986. 'Introduction to the Latin American Cases', in Guillermo O'Donnell, Philippe C. Schmitter and Laurence Whitehead (eds), *Transitions from Authoritarian Rule: Latin America*. Baltimore, MD: Woodrow Wilson International Center for Scholars/Johns Hopkins University Press

O'Donnell, Guillermo. 1988. *Bureaucratic Authoritarianism: Argentina 1966–1973 in Comparative Perspective*. Berkeley, CA: University of California Press. Available at: http://ark.cdlib.org/ark:/13030/ft4v19n9n2/ [accessed December 2009]

O'Donnell, Guillermo. 1992. 'Delegative Democracy?' Working Paper 172, Helen Kellogg Institute. South Bend, IN: University of Notre Dame

O'Donnell, Guillermo. 1993. 'On the State, Democratization and Some Conceptual Problems: A Latin American View with Glances at Some Post-Communist Countries', *World Development*, Vol. 21, No. 8 (August), pp. 1355–69. Also available at: http://kellogg.nd.edu/publications/workingpapers/WPS/192.pdf [accessed February 2010]

O'Donnell, Guillermo. 1994. 'Delegative Democracy', *Journal of Democracy*, Vol. 5, No. 1 (January), pp. 55–70

O'Donnell, Guillermo, Joseph S. Tulchin and Augusto Varas (eds) with Adam Stubits. 2008. *New Voices in the Study of Democracy in Latin America*. Washington, DC: Woodrow Wilson International Center for Scholars

O'Donnell, Guillermo and Philippe C. Schmitter. 1986. *Transitions From Authoritarian Rule: Tentative Conclusions About Uncertain Democracies*, Vol. 4. Baltimore, MD: Johns Hopkins University Press

O'Donnell, Guillermo, Philippe C. Schmitter and Laurence Whitehead (eds). 1986. *Transitions from Authoritarian Rule: Latin America*, Vol. 2. Baltimore, MD: Woodrow Wilson International Center for Scholars/Johns Hopkins University Press

O Estado de São Paulo. 2009. 'Brazil: Embraer increases national sales of aircraft', *O Estado de São Paulo* (English), 3 December 2009. Factiva.com database [accessed January 2010]

Olesen, Thomas. 2004. *International Zapatismo. The Construction of Solidarity in the Age of Globalization*. London: Zed Books

Open Society Institute. 2008. *The Price of Silence: The Growing Threat of Soft Censorship in Latin America*. Asociación por los Derechos Civiles/Open Society Justice Initiative New York: Open Society Institute. Available at: http://www.soros.org/initiatives/justice/focus/foi/articles_publications/publications/silence_20080811 [accessed October 2009]

Oppenheimer, Andres. 2009. 'Brazil a nuclear power? Probably not', *The Miami Herald*, 18 October 2009. Available at: http://www.miamiherald.com/news/columnists/andres-oppenheimer/story/1288046.html [accessed October 2009]

Orihuela, Rodrigo. 2009. 'Latin America's swing to the right', Guardian online, guardian.co.uk, London, 29 July 2009. Available at: http://www.guardian.co.uk/commentisfree/cifamerica/2009/jul/29/latin-america-right-elections [accessed November 2009]

Ortiz, Irene. 2008. 'Building the City of God: Mexico's Ultra-Right Yunque', *NACLA Report on the Americas*, Vol. 41, No. 1 (January/February), pp. 26–9

O'Shaughnessy, Hugh. 1993. 'Peru's Red Sun of Terror Sets', *Observer*, London, 25 July 1993, p. 11

O'Shaughnessy, Hugh. 2009. 'Democracy hangs by a thread in Honduras', *The Independent* online, 10 July 2009. Available at: http://www.independent.co.uk/news/world/americas/democracy-hangs-by-a-thread-in-honduras-1752315.html [accessed February 2010]

Ospina Peralta, Pablo, Alejandra Santillana Ortiz and María Arboleda. 2008. 'Neo-Corporatism and Territorial Economic Development: The Ecuadorian Indigenous Movement in Local Government', *World Development*, Vol. 36, No. 12 (December), pp. 2921–36

Otero, Gerardo. 2003. 'The "Indian Question" in Latin America: Class, State and Ethnic Identity Construction', review article, *Latin American Research Review*, Vol. 38, No. 1 (Spring), pp. 248–66

Otero, Gerardo. 2004. 'Mexico's Double Movement: Neoliberal Globalism, the State and Civil Society', in Gerardo Otero (ed.), *Mexico in Transition. Neoliberal Globalism, the State and Civil Society*. London: Zed Books

O'Toole, Gavin. 2003. 'A New Nationalism for a New Era: The Political Ideology of Mexican Neoliberalism', *Bulletin of Latin American Research*, Vol. 22, No. 3 (July), pp. 269–90

Oxfam. 1999. 'EU Association Agreements with Latin America: Good news for those in poverty?' Oxfam GB/Intermón/Novib briefing paper. Oxford: Oxfam. Available at: http://www.oxfam.org.uk/resources/policy/trade/downloads/trade_eu_latin.rtf [accessed February 2010]

Oxhorn, Philip and Graciela Ducatenzeiler. 1998. 'Economic Reform and Democratization in Latin America', in Philip Oxhorn and Graciela Ducatenzeiler (eds), *What Kind of Democracy? What Kind of Market?* University Park, PA: Pennsylvania State University Press

Oxhorn, Philip and Graciela Ducatenzeiler (eds). 1998. *What Kind of Democracy? What Kind of Market?* University Park, PA: Pennsylvania State University Press

Oxhorn, Philip, Joseph S. Tulchin and Andrew Selee (eds). 2004. *Decentralization, Democratic Governance, and Civil Society in Comparative Perspective: Africa, Asia, and Latin America*. Washington, DC: Woodrow Wilson Center Press/Johns Hopkins University Press

Padilla, Beatriz and João Peixoto. 2007. 'Latin American Immigration to Southern Europe', *Migration Information Source* (June). Washington: Migration Policy Institute. Available at: http://www.migrationinformation.org/Feature/display.cfm?id=609 [accessed November 2009]

Paige, Jeffery M. 1975. *Agrarian Revolution: Social Movements and Export Agriculture in the Underdeveloped World*. New York: The Free Press

Pallares, Amalia. 2002. *From Peasant Struggles to Indian Resistance: The Ecuadorian Andes in the Late Twentieth Century*. Norman, OK: University of Oklahoma Press

Panebianco, A. 1988. *Political Parties: Organization and Power*. Cambridge: Cambridge University Press

Panizza, Francisco. 2009. *Contemporary Latin America: Development and Democracy Beyond the Washington Consensus*. London: Zed Books

Parsons, Talcott. 1954. *Essays in Sociological Theory*. New York: The Free Press

Pastor, Robert A. 2001. *Exiting the Whirlpool. US Foreign Policy Toward Latin America and the Caribbean*, 2nd Edition. Boulder, CO: Westview Press

Patterson, Eric. 2005. 'Religious Activity and Political Participation: The Brazilian and Chilean Cases', *Latin American Politics and Society*, Vol. 47, No. 1 (April), pp. 1–29

Patterson, Thomas E. 1993. *Out of Order: An incisive and boldly original critique of the news media's domination of America's political process*. New York: Knopf

Payne, J., Daniel Zovatto, Fernando Carillo Floréz and Andrés Allamand Zavala. 2002. *Democracies in Development. Politics and Reform in Latin America*. Washington/Stockholm: IADB/IDB-IDEA

Payne, Leigh A. 2000. *Uncivil Movements: The Armed Right Wing and Democracy in Latin America*. Baltimore, MD: Johns Hopkins University Press

Payne, Richard J. and Jamal R. Nassar. 2003. *Politics and Culture in the Developing World. The Impact of Globalization*. New York: Pearson

Paz, Octavio. 1970. *Posdata*. Mexico City: Siglo XXI

Peeler, John. 1998. *Building Democracy in Latin America*. Boulder, CO: Lynne Renner.

Pellegrino, Adela/International Organization for Migration (IOM). 2004. *Migration from Latin America to Europe: Trends and Policy Challenges*. IOM Migration Research Series, No. 16. Geneva: IOM. Available at: http://www.oas.org/atip/migration/iom%20report%20migration%20lac%20to%20eu.pdf [accessed February 2010]

Pereira, Anthony. 2003. 'Brazil's agrarian reform: Democratic innovation or oligarchic exclusion redux?' *Latin American Politics and Society*, Vol. 45, No. 2 (July), pp. 41–61

Pérez-Liñán, Aníbal. 2002. 'Television News and Political Partisanship in Latin America', *Political Research Quarterly*, Vol. 55, No. 3 (September), pp. 571–88

Pérez-Liñán, Aníbal. 2010. *Presidential Impeachment and the New Political Instability in Latin America*. Cambridge: Cambridge University Press

Peruzzotti, Enrique and Catalina Smulovitz (eds). 2006. *Enforcing the Rule of Law: Social Accountability in the New Latin American Democracies*. Pittsburgh, PA: University of Pittsburgh Press

Petras, James. 2006. 'A Bizarre Beginning in Bolivia: Inside Evo Morales's Cabinet', *Counterpunch* online, 4/5 February 2006. Available at: http://www.counterpunch.org/petras02042006.html [accessed December 2009]

Petras, James. 2009. 'Rising Militarism: US-Latin American Relations', *The Palestine Chronicle*, 14 May 2009. Available at: http://www.palestinechronicle.com/view_article_details.php?id=15099 [accessed November 2009]

Petras, James and Henry Veltmeyer. 2005. *Social Movements and State Power. Argentina, Brazil, Bolivia, Ecuador*. London: Pluto Press

Petras, James and Henry Veltmeyer. 2009. *What's Left in Latin America? Regime Change in New Times*. Farnham: Ashgate

Petras, James and Robert Laporte. 1971. *Cultivating Revolution: The United States and Agrarian Reform in Latin America*. New York: Random House

Petras, James with Steve Vieux. 1999. 'Pragmatism Unarmed', in James Petras *et al.*, *The Left Srikes Back. Class Conflict in the Age of Neoliberalism*. Boulder, CO: Westview Press

Petras, James with Todd Cavaluzzi, Morris Morley and Steve Vieux. 1999. *The Left Srikes Back. Class Conflict in the Age of Neoliberalism*. Boulder, CO: Westview Press

Pew Hispanic Center. 2004. 'The Hispanic Electorate in 2004, Pew Hispanic Center, Fact Sheet'. Washington: Pew Hispanic Center. Available at: http://pewhispanic.org/files/factsheets/8.pdf [accessed February 2010]

Pew Research Center. 2009. 'Rising Environmental Concern in 47-Nation Survey: Global Unease with Major World Powers', The Pew Global Attitudes Project, 27 June 2007. Washington: Pew Research Center. Available at http://pewglobal.org/reports/pdf/256.pdf [accessed November 2009]

Philip, George. 2003. *Democracy in Latin America*. Cambridge: Polity

Pieper Mooney, Jadwiga E. 2009. *The Politics of Motherhood: Maternity and Women's Rights in Twentieth-Century Chile*. Pittsburgh, PA: University of Pittsburgh Press

Pilger, John and Christopher Martin. 2007. *The War on Democracy*. Documentary. Australia: Youngheart Entertainment

Pinakas, Thanasis. 2004. 'The Notion of Solidarity in European Foreign Policy: a Realist-Constructivist Approach', paper presented to European Foreign Policy Unit Research Student Conference on European Foreign Policy, London School of Economics, 2–3 July 2004

Pinheiro, Paulo Sérgio. 1997. 'Popular Responses to State-sponsored Violence in Brazil', in Douglas Chalmers *et al.* (eds), *The New Politics of Inequality in Latin America. Rethinking Participation and Representation*. Oxford: Oxford University Press

Pion-Berlin, David. 1997. *Through Corridors of Power: Institutions and Civil-Military Relations in Argentina*. University Park, PA: Pennsylvania State University Press

Pion-Berlin, David. 2005. 'Authoritarian Legacies and Their Impact on Latin America', *Latin American Politics and Society*, Vol. 47, No. 2 (July), pp. 159–70

Pion-Berlin, David (ed.). 2001. *Civil-Military Relations in Latin America: New Analytical Perspectives*. Chapel Hill, NC: University of North Carolina Press

Piovesan, Flávia. 2009. 'Violence against Women in Brazil', Chapter 5 in Jane S. Jaquette (ed.), *Feminist Agendas and Democracy in Latin America*. Durham, NC: Duke University Press

Pleming, Sue. 2009. 'China, Iran gains in Latam "disturbing": Clinton', *Reuters* news agency, Washington, 1 May 2009. Available at: http://www.reuters.com/article/politicsNews/idUSTRE54056120090501 [accessed November 2009]

Pollard-Terry, Gayle. 2005a. 'Documenting Mexico's Strong African legacy', *Los Angeles Times*, 21 February 2005, Home Edition, p. E-10. Factiva.com database [accessed March 2006]

Pollard-Terry, Gayle. 2005b. 'A long, intertwined history; "We are mixed, white and black," Soledad Camero says of her childhood community in Guerrero state, where African ways live on', *Los Angeles Times*, 21 February 2005, Home Edition, p. E-11. Factiva.com database [accessed March 2006]

Pope Benedict XVI. 2007. 'Great Challenges Facing the Church in Latin America', Address to Participants in the Plenary Assembly of the Pontifical Commission for Latin America, Vatican, 20 January 2007. Available at: http://www.catholicculture.org/culture/library/view.cfm?recnum=7409 [accessed November 2009]

Prevost, Gary and Carlos Oliva Campos (eds). 2002. *NeoLiberalism and neoPanamericanism: The View from Latin America*. Basingstoke: Palgrave Macmillan

Prillaman, William C. 2000. *The Judiciary and Democratic Decay in Latin America: Declining Confidence in the Rule of Law*. Westport, CT: Praeger.

Przeworski, Adam. 1985. *Capitalism and Social Democracy*. Cambridge: Cambridge University Press

Przeworski, Adam. 1991. *Democracy and the Market: Political and Economic Reforms in Eastern Europe and Latin America*. Cambridge: Cambridge University Press.

Przeworski, Adam and Fernando Limongi. 1993. 'Political Regimes and Economic Growth', *Journal of Economic Perspectives*, Vol. 7, No. 3 (Summer), pp. 51–69

Przeworski, Adam, Michael Alvarez, José Antonio Cheibub and Fernando Limongi. 1996. 'What Makes Democracies Endure?', *Journal of Democracy*, Vol. 7, No. 1 (January), pp. 39–55

Puente Alcaraz, Jesús and Juan Fernando Molina. 2000. 'Guatemala, Descentralización y Democracia: gobierno local y participación ciudadana, estudio de caso', in María

Antonieta Huerta Malbrán *et al.* (eds), *Descentralización, municipio y participación ciudadana: Chile, Colombia y Guatemala.* Bogotá: CEJA

Puente Alcaraz, Jesús and Luis Felipe Linares López. 2004. 'A General View of the Institutional State of Decentralization in Guatemala', in Joseph. S. Tulchin and Andrew Selee (eds), *Decentralization and Democratic Governance in Latin America.* Woodrow Wilson Center Report on the Americas #12. Washington, DC: Woodrow Wilson International Center for Scholars

Putnam, Robert D. 1995. 'Tuning In, Tuning Out: The Strange Disappearance of Social Capital in America', *PS: Political Science and Politics*, Vol. 28, No. 4 (December), pp. 664–83

Quinones, Sam. 2002. 'Old Politics Ends New Journalism. Notimex, the news agency funded by the government, was going to become a BBC-style organization', *Los Angeles Times*, 13 January 2002, Home Edition, p. M-3. Factiva.com database [accessed March 2006]

Radcliffe, Sarah A. 2004. 'Civil Society, Grassroots Politics and Livelihoods', in Robert N. Gwynne and Cristóbal Kay (eds), *Latin America Transformed: Globalization and Modernity.* London: Hodder

Rahall, Nick. 2009. 'Statement of the Hon. Nick J. Rahall, II, a representative in Congress from the State of West Virginia', Legislative Hearing on H.R. 2499, Puerto Rico Democracy Act of 2009, 24 June 2009, US House of Representatives Committee on Natural Resources, Washington. Available at: http://www.access.gpo.gov/congress/house/house12ch111.html [accessed November 2009]

Rakowski, Cathy A. 2003. 'Women as Political Actors: The Move from Maternalism to Citizenship Rights and Power', review article, *Latin American Research Review*, Vol. 38, No. 2 (Summer), pp. 180–94

Randall, Vicky and Lars Svåsand. 2002. 'Party Institutionalisation in New Democracies', *Party Politics*, Vol. 8, No. 1 (January), pp. 5–29

Rands Barros, Mauricio. 1999. *Labour Relations and the New Unionism in Contemporary Brazil.* New York: St Martin's

Redick, John R. 1972. *Military Potential of Latin American Nuclear Energy Programs.* Beverly Hills, CA: Sage

Reel, Monte. 2005a. 'All Latin America, All the Time; New 24-Hour TV Networks Aim to Unite Region With Tailored Coverage', *Washington Post*, 10 March 2005, Final, p. A12. Factiva.com database [accessed March 2006]

Reel, Monte. 2005b. 'Liberation theology lives on in Brazil', Washington Post, *Tulsa World*, 7 May 2005, Final Home Edition, p. A13. Factiva.com database [accessed March 2006]

Reid Andrews, George. 2004. *Afro-Latin America, 1800–2000.* Oxford: Oxford University Press

Remmer, Karen. 1990. 'Democracy and Economic Crisis: The Latin American Experience', *World Politics*, Vol. 42, No. 3 (April), pp. 315–35

Reuters. 2008. 'Factbox: Military power in Colombia, Venezuela and Ecuador', Reuters.com, *Reuters* news agency, 5 March 2008. Available at: http://www.reuters.com/article/idUSN0428234420080305 [accessed December 2009]

Reyes, Gerardo. 2005. 'Shuffling down one of . . .', *Miami Herald*, 6 March 2005, F1LA, p. 1. Factiva.com database [accessed March 2006]

Richard, Nelly. 2004. *Masculine/Feminine. Practices of difference(s).* Durham, NC: Duke University Press

Rieff, David. 2005. 'Che's Second Coming?', *New York Times*, 20 November 2005, Late Edition – Final, p. 72. Factiva.com database [accessed March 2006]

Ríos Tobar, Marcela. 2009. 'Feminist Politics in Contemporary Chile', Chapter 1 in Jane S. Jaquette (ed.), *Feminist Agendas and Democracy in Latin America*. Durham, NC: Duke University Press

Ritzer, George. 2009. *Globalization: A Basic Text*. Oxford: Wiley-Blackwell

Rivarola Puntigliano, Andrés. 2008. 'Suspicious Minds: Recent Books on US-Latin American Relations', *Latin American Politics and Society*, Vol. 50, No. 4 (Winter), pp. 155–72

Roberts, Kenneth M. 1997. 'Rethinking Economic Alternatives: Left Parties and the Articulation of Popular Demands in Chile and Peru', in Douglas Chalmers *et al.* (eds), *The New Politics of Inequality in Latin America. Rethinking Participation and Representation*. Oxford: Oxford University Press

Roberts, Kenneth. 2002. 'Social Inequalities without Class Cleavages in Latin America's Neoliberal Era', *Studies in Comparative International Development*, Vol. 36, No. 4 (December), pp. 3–33

Robinson, William. 2003. *Transnational Conflicts. Central America, Social Change, and Globalization*. London: Verso

Robinson, William I. 2007. 'Beyond the Theory of Imperialism: Global Capitalism and the Transnational State', *Societies Without Borders*, Vol. 2, pp. 5–26

Robinson, William I. 2008. *Latin America and Global Capitalism: A Critical Globalization Perspective*. Baltimore, MD: Johns Hopkins University Press

Rocha, Jan. 2009. 'Lula and Brazil: Abundant Energy', *World Today*, Vol. 65, No. 11 (November), p. 18

Rodríguez, Martín Diego. 2007. 'El Movimiento de Participación Solidaria supera *de panzazo* un requisito del IFE', *La Jornada* online, 3 September 2007. Available at: http://www.jornada.unam.mx/2007/09/03/index.php?section=politica&article=016n1pol [accessed November 2009]

Rohter, Larry. 2004. 'Mapuche Indians in Chile Struggle to Take Back Forests', *New York Times*, 11 August 2004, Late Edition – Final, p. 3. Factiva.com database [accessed March 2006]

Rohter, Larry. 2005. 'Uruguay Tackles Old Rights Cases, Charging Ex-President', *New York Times*, 31 July 2005, Late Edition – Final, p. 4. Factiva.com database [accessed March 2006]

Rojas Aravena, Francisco. 1997. 'Latin America: Alternatives and Mechanisms of Prevention in Situations Related to Territorial Sovereignty', *Peace and Security in the Americas*, FLACSO-Chile, No. 14 (October), pp. 2–7

Rostow, Walt W. 1962. *The Stages of Economic Growth: A Non-Communist Manifesto*. Cambridge: Cambridge University Press

Rousseau, Stephanie. 2009. *Women's Citizenship in Peru: The Paradoxes of Neopopulism in Latin America*. Basingstoke: Palgrave Macmillan

Rowland, Alison and Ramírez, Jesús. 2001. *La descentralización y los gobiernos sub-nacionales en México: una introducción*. Documento de Trabajo No. 93, División de Administración Pública. Mexico City: CIDE

Roy. J, (ed.). 1992. *The Reconstruction of Central America: The Role of the European Community*. Miami, FL: North-South Center Press, University of Miami

Rueschmeyer, Dietrich, Evelyne Huber-Stephens and John Stephens. 1992. *Capitalist Development and Democracy*. Chicago, IL: University of Chicago Press

Ruhl, Mark J. 2005. 'The Guatemalan Military Since the Peace Accords: The Fate of Reform Under Arzú and Portillo', *Latin American Politics and Society*. Vol. 47, No. 1 (April), pp. 55–85

Rustow, Dankwart A. 1970. 'Transitions to Democracy. Toward a Dynamic Model', *Comparative Politics*, Vol. 2, No. 3 (April), pp. 337–63

Rytina, Nancy and John Simanski. 2009. 'Apprehensions by the U.S. Border Patrol: 2005–2008', Department of Homeland Security, Office of Immigration Statistics Policy Directorate, Factsheet June 2009. Available at: http://www.dhs.gov/xlibrary/assets/statistics/publications/ois_apprehensions_fs_2005-2008.pdf [accessed November 2009]

Sabatini, Christopher. 2003. 'Decentralization and Political Parties in Latin America', *Journal of Democracy*, Vol. 14, No. 2 (April), pp. 138–50

Safford, Frank. 1987. 'Bases of Political Alignment in Early Republican Spanish America', in Eduardo Archetti, Paul Cammack and Bryan Roberts (eds), *Latin America. Sociology of Developing Societies*. Houndmills: Macmillan

Sakho, Yaye and Oscar Calvo González (eds). 2009. *Strengthening Bolivian Competitiveness: Export Diversification and Inclusive Growth*. World Bank Country Study. Washington, DC: World Bank Publications

Samuels, David. 2000. 'Fiscal Horizontal Accountability: Toward a Theory of Budgetary "Checks and Balances" in Presidential Systems', paper presented at the Conference on Horizontal Accountability in New Democracies, Kellogg Institute for International Studies, University of Notre Dame, Indiana, May 2000

Samuels, David. 2002. 'Progressive Ambition, Federalism, and Pork-Barreling in Brazil', in Scott Morgenstern and Benito Nacif (eds), *Legislative Politics in Latin America*. Cambridge: Cambridge University Press

Samuels, David. 2008. Brazil: 'Democracy under Lula and the PT', Chapter 7, in Jorge Domínguez and Michael Shifter (eds), *Constructing Democratic Governance in Latin America*, 3rd Edition. Baltimore, MD: Johns Hopkins University Press

Sánchez, Fabiola. 2009. 'Chavez: Venezuela to buy more tanks over US threat', Associated Press, Caracas, 6 August 2009

Saney, Isaac. 2004. *Cuba. A Revolution in Motion*. London: Zed Books

Sartori, Giovanni. 1976. *Parties and Party Systems: A Framework for Analysis*. New York: Cambridge University Press

Sartori, Giovanni. 1989. 'Video-Power', *Government and Opposition*, Vol. 24, No. 1 (Winter), pp. 39–53

Sawyer, Suzana. 2004. *Crude Chronicles: Indigenous Politics, Multinational Oil, and Neoliberalism in Ecuador*. Durham, NC: Duke University Press

Schamis, Hector E. 2002. *Re-Forming the State: The Politics of Privatization in Latin America and Europe*. Ann Arbor, MI: University of Michigan Press

Schelhase, Marc. 2008. *Globalization, Regionalization and Business: Conflict, Convergence and Influence*. Basingstoke: Palgrave Macmillan

Schiavoni, Christina and William Camacaro. 2009. 'The Venezuelan Effort to Build a New Food and Agriculture System', *Monthly Review*, Vol. 61, No. 3 (July). Factiva.com database [accessed February 2010]

Schmitter, Philippe. 1971. *Interest Conflict and Political Change in Brazil.* Stanford, California: Stanford University Press.

Schmitter, Philippe. 1974. 'Still the Century of Corporatism?', *The Review of Politics*, Vol. 36, No. 1 (January), pp. 85–131

Schneider, Ben Ross. 1995. 'Democratic Consolidations: Some Broad Comparisons and Sweeping Arguments', review article, *Latin American Research Review*, Vol. 30, No. 2 (Summer), pp. 215–34

Schneider, Ben Ross. 2004. *Business Politics and the State in Twentieth-Century Latin America.* Cambridge: Cambridge University Press

Schodolski, Vincent J. 2005. 'Border proposal a risk to marsh, ecologists say; GOP lawmakers seek to tighten crossing', *Chicago Tribune*, 6 March 2005, Chicago Final, p. 13. Factiva.com database [accessed March 2006]

Schoultz, Lars. 1998. *Beneath the United States. A History of US Policy Toward Latin America.* London: Harvard University Press

Schoultz, Lars. 2009. *That Infernal Little Cuban Republic. The United States and the Cuban Revolution.* Chapel Hill, NC: University of North Carolina Press

Scott, James W. 2009. *De-coding New Regionalism: Shifting Socio-political Contexts in Central Europe and Latin America.* Farnham: Ashgate

Selbin, Eric. 1993. *Modern Latin American Revolutions.* Boulder, CO: Westview Press

Selee, Andrew. 2004. 'Exploring the Link Between Decentralization and Democratic Governance', in Joseph. S. Tulchin and Andrew Selee (eds), *Decentralization and Democratic Governance in Latin America.* Woodrow Wilson Center Report on the Americas #12. Washington, DC: Woodrow Wilson International Center for Scholars.

Selee, Andrew D. and Enrique Peruzzotti (eds). 2009. *Participatory Innovation and Representative Democracy in Latin America.* Baltimore, MD: Johns Hopkins University Press/Woodrow Wilson Center Press

Seligson, Amber L. 2003. 'Critical Debates: The Right in Latin America: Strategies, Successes, and Failures', review article, *Latin American Politics and Society*, Vol. 45, No. 1 (April), pp. 135–45

Seligson, Mitchell A. 2002. 'Trouble in Paradise: The Impact of the Erosion of System Support in Costa Rica, 1978–1999', *Latin American Research Review*, Vol. 37, No. 1 (Spring), pp. 160–85

Semple, Kirk. 2009. 'Haitians in US Illegally Look for Signs of a Deporting Reprieve'. *New York Times* online, 27 May 2009. Available at: http://www.nytimes.com/2009/05/28/nyregion/28haitians.html [accessed November 2009]

Serbin, Kenneth P. 2001. '"Bowling Alone," Bishops' biographies, and Baptism by Blood: New Views of Progressive Catholicism in Brazil', review article, *Latin American Politics and Society*, Vol. 43, No. 4 (December), pp. 127–41

Shattuck, Annie *et al.* 2009. *Agrofuels in the Americas.* Oakland, CA: Food First Books

Sheahan, John. 1987. *Patterns of Development in Latin America. Poverty, Repression, and Economic Strategy.* Princeton, NJ: Princeton University Press

Sherman, Amy L. 1997. *The Soul of Development: Biblical Christianity and Economic Transformation in Guatemala*. New York: Oxford University Press

Shifter, Michael. 2008. 'Emerging trends and determining factors in democratic governance', Chapter 1 in Jorge I. Domínguez and Michael Shifter, *Constructing Democratic Governance in Latin America*, 3rd Edition. Baltimore, MD: Johns Hopkins University Press

Shor, Francis. 2010. *Dying Empire: US Imperialism and Global Resistance*. New York: Routledge

Shugart, Matthew Sobert and John Carey. 1992. *Presidents and Assemblies: Constitutional Design and Electoral Dynamics*. New York: Cambridge University Press

Siavelis, Peter M. 2002. 'Exaggerated Presidentialism and Moderate Presidents: Executive-Legislative Relations in Chile', in Scott Morgenstern and Benito Nacif (eds), *Legislative Politics in Latin America*. Cambridge: Cambridge University Press

Sicker, Martin. 2001. *The Geopolitics of Security in the Americas: Hemispheric Denial from Monroe to Clinton*. Westport, CT: Praeger

SICLAC (Socialist International Committee for Latin America and the Caribbean). 2004. 'Santa Marta Document. The Achievements and Deficiencies of Democracy'. Socialist International Committee for Latin America and the Caribbean, Colombia, 7–8 May 2004. Available at: http://www.socialistinternational.org/viewArticle.cfm?ArticleID=873 [accessed February 2010]

Sieder, Rachel. 2002. 'Introduction', in Rachel Sieder (ed.), *Multiculturalism in Latin America. Indigenous Rights, Diversity and Democracy*. Basingstoke: Palgrave/Institute of Latin American Studies

Sieder, Rachel (ed.). 2002. *Multiculturalism in Latin America. Indigenous Rights, Diversity and Democracy*. Basingstoke: Palgrave/Institute of Latin American Studies

Silva, Eduardo. 2004. 'Authoritarianism, Democracy and Development', in Robert Gwynne and Cristóbal Kay (eds), *Latin America Transformed. Globalization and Modernity*. London: Edward Arnold

Silva, Eduardo. 2009. *Challenging Neoliberalism in Latin America*. Cambridge: Cambridge University Press

Silva, Patricio. 2004. 'The New Political Order: Towards Technocratic Democracies', in Robert Gwynne and Cristóbal Kay (eds), *Latin America Transformed. Globalization and Modernity*. London: Arnold

Silva, Patricio. 2009. 'Chile: swimming against the tide?' Chapter 11 in Geraldine Lievesley and Steve Ludlam (eds), *Reclaiming Latin America: Experiments in Radical Social Democracy*. London: Zed Books

Skidmore, Thomas. 1990. 'Racial Ideas and Social Policy in Brazil, 1870–1940', in Richard Graham (ed.), *The Idea of Race in Latin America, 1870–1940*. Austin, TX: University of Texas Press

Skocpol, Theda. 1979. *States and Social Revolutions: A Comparative Analysis of France, Russia and China*. Cambridge: Cambridge University Press

Slater, David. 1985. 'Social Movements and a Recasting of the Political', in David Slater (ed.), *New Social Movements and the State in Latin America*. Amsterdam: CEDLA

Slater, David (ed.). 1985. *New Social Movements and the State in Latin America*. Amsterdam: CEDLA

Sloan, John. 1984. *Public Policy in Latin America*. Pittsburgh, PA: University of Pittsburgh Press

Smilde, David. 2004. 'Contradiction Without Paradox: Evangelical Political Culture in the 1998 Venezuelan Elections', *Latin American Politics and Society*, Vol. 46, No. 1 (April), pp. 75–102

Smink, Veronica. 2009. 'A tunnel to unite old rivals?', bbc.co.uk, 15 May 2009. Available at: http://news.bbc.co.uk/2/hi/americas/8049814.stm [accessed November 2009]

Smith, Christian. 1994. 'The Spirit and Democracy: Base Communities, Protestantism, and Democratization in Latin America', *Sociology of Religion*, Vol. 55, No. 2 (Summer), pp. 119–43

Smith, Christian and Joshua Prokopy (eds). 1999. *Latin American Religion in Motion*. London: Routledge

Smith, Joseph. 2005. *The United States and Latin America. A History of American Diplomacy, 1776–2000*. Abingdon: Routledge

Smith, Peter H. 1995. 'The Changing Agenda for Social Science Research in Latin America', in Peter H. Smith (ed.), *Latin America in Comparative Perspective: New Approaches to Methods and Analysis*. Boulder, CO: Westview Press

Smith, Peter H. 2000. *Talons of the Eagle: Dynamics of US-Latin American Relations*, 2nd Edition. Oxford: Oxford University Press

Smith, Peter H. 2007. *Talons of the Eagle: Latin America, the United States, and the World*, 3rd Edition. New York: Oxford University Press

Smith, Peter H. 2001. 'Strategic Options for Latin America' in Joseph Tulchin and Ralph Espach (eds), *Latin America in the New International System*. Boulder, CO: Lynne Rienner/Woodrow Wilson International Center for Scholars

Smith, Peter H. (ed.). 1995. *Latin America in Comparative Perspective: New Approaches to Methods and Analysis*. Boulder, CO: Westview Press

Smith, William C. (ed.). 2009. *Latin American Democratic Transformations: Institutions, Actors, Processes*. Oxford: Wiley-Blackwell

Smith, W. Rand. 2002. 'Privatization in Latin America: How Did it Work and What Difference Did it Make?', *Latin American Politics and Society*, Vol. 44, No. 4. (December), pp. 153–66

Smulovitz, Catalina. 2006. 'Judicialization of Protest in Argentina: The Case of Corralito', Chapter 3 in Enrique Peruzzotti and Catalina Smulovitz (eds), *Enforcing the Rule of Law: Social Accountability in the New Latin American Democracies*. Pittsburgh, PA: University of Pittsburgh Press

Socialist International. 2009a. 'Member Parties of the Socialist International, Latin America and the Caribbean', Socialist International online. Available at: http://www.socialistinternational.org/viewArticle.cfm?ArticlePageID=927 [accessed November 2009]

Socialist International. 2009b. 'Latin America and the Caribbean in the global financial crisis: Meeting of the SI Committee for Latin America and the Caribbean in Guatemala, 23–24 March 2009', Committees, Socialist International online. Available at: http://www.socialistinternational.org/viewarticle.cfm?articleid=1990 [accessed November 2009]

Soderbaum, Fredrik (ed.). 2009. *The European Union and the Global South*. Boulder, CO: Lynne Rienner

Sotomayor Velázquez, Arturo C. 2004. 'Civil-Military Affairs and Security Institutions in the Southern Cone: The Sources of Argentine–Brazilian Nuclear Cooperation', *Latin American Politics and Society*, Vol. 46, No. 4 (December), pp. 29–60

Sreenivasan, Ven. 2009. 'Embraer targets Asia Pacific for sales of business jet', *Shipping Times*, 7 December 2009. Factiva.com database [accessed January 2010]

Stahler-Sholk, Richard. 1995. 'Sandinista Economic and Social Policy: The Mixed Blessings of Hindsight', review article, *Latin American Research Review*, Vol. 30, No. 2 (Summer), pp. 235–50

Stallings, Barbara and Wilson Peres. 2000. *Growth, Employment, and Equity: The Impact of the Economic Reforms in Latin America and the Caribbean*. Washington, DC/Santiago: Brookings Institution/CEPAL

Staudt, Kathleen and Gabriela Montoya. 2009. 'Violence and Activism at the Mexico-United States Border', Chapter 9 in Jane S. Jaquette (ed.), *Feminist Agendas and Democracy in Latin America*. Durham, NC: Duke University Press

Stavenhagen, Rodolfo. 2002. 'Indigenous Peoples and the State in Latin America; An Ongoing Debate', in Rachel Sieder (ed.), *Multiculturalism in Latin America. Indigenous Rights, Diversity and Democracy*. Basingstoke: Palgrave/Institute of Latin American Studies

Stepan, Alfred. 1988. *Rethinking Military Politics. Brazil and the Southern Cone*. Princeton, NJ: Princeton University Press

Stepan, Alfred and Cindy Skach. 1993. 'Constitutional Frameworks and Democratic Consolidation: Parliamentarianism versus Presidentialism', in *World Politics* Vol. 46, No. 1 (October), pp. 1–22

Stephen Roth Institute. 2000. 'Anti-Semitism Worldwide 1999/2000. Annual reports, Country Reports, Argentina'. Tel Aviv: Tel Aviv University. Available at: http://www.tau.ac.il/Anti-Semitism/asw99-2000/argentina.htm [accessed February 2010]

Stephen Roth Institute. 2007. 'Argentina 2007', Country Reports, The Stephen Roth Institute for the Study of Antisemitism and Racism online. Available at: http://www.tau.ac.il/Anti-Semitism/asw2007/argentina.html [accessed November 2009]

Stiglitz, Joseph. *Globalization and its Discontents*. 2002. London: Penguin

Stokes, Doug. 2005. *America's Other War. Terrorizing Colombia*. London: Zed Books

Stolcke, Verena and Michael M. Hall. 1987. 'The Planter Class and Labour: The Introduction of Free Labour on São Paulo Coffee Plantations', in Eduardo Archetti, Paul Cammack and Bryan Roberts (eds), *Latin America. Sociology of Developing Societies*. Houndmills: Macmillan

Sunkel, Osvaldo. 1969. 'National Development Policy and External Dependence in Latin America', *Journal of Development Studies*, Vol. 6, No. 1 (October), pp. 23–48

Sunkel, Osvaldo. 1995. 'From Inward-Looking Development to Development from Within', in James L. Dietz (ed.), *Latin America's Economic Development. Confronting Crisis*, 2nd Edition. Boulder, CO: Lynne Rienner

Sunkel, Osvaldo (ed.) 1993. *Development from Within: Toward a Neostructualist Approach to Latin America*. Boulder, CO: Lynne Rienner

Swatos, William H. 1994. 'On Latin American Protestantism', *Sociology of Religion*, Vol. 55, No. 2 (Summer), pp. 84–97

Talbott, Strobe. 2008. *The Great Experiment: The Story of Ancient Empires, Modern States, and the Quest for a Global Nation*. New York: Simon & Schuster

Tarrow, Sidney. 1994. *Power in Movement: Social Movements, Collective Action, and Politics*. Cambridge: Cambridge University Press

Taylor, Lewis. 2006. *Shining Path: Guerilla War in Peru's Northern Highlands*. Liverpool: Liverpool University Press

Telemundo Communications Group/Global Insight. 2005. 'Snapshots of the US Hispanic Market'. Hialeah, Florida: Telemundo Communications Group/Global Insight, Business Economics and Custom Solutions Group

Thompson, Ginger. 2009. 'On TV, Honduran Generals Explain Their Role in Coup', *New York Times* online, 4 August 2009. Available at: http://www.nytimes.com/2009/08/05/world/americas/05honduras.html

Thomson, Adam. 2004a. 'IMF was "too lenient" over Argentina's deficits as economy headed for crisis', *Financial Times*, 28 July 2004, London Edition, p. 9

Thomson, Adam. 2004b. 'Chile: Increasingly drifting towards Asia', *Financial Times*, FT.com, 18 November 2004. Factiva.com database [accessed March 2006]

Tiano, Susan. 2001. 'From Victims to Agents: A New Generation of Literature on Women in Latin America', review article, *Latin American Research Review*, Vol. 36, No. 3 (Fall), pp. 183–203

Tilly, Charles. 1978. *Mobilization to Revolution*. Reading, MA: Addison-Wesley

Todaro, Michael P. 1994. *Economic Development*, 5th Edition. Essex: Longman

Tofik Karam, John. 2007. *Another Arabesque: Syrian-Lebanese Ethnicity in Neoliberal Brazil*. Philadelphia, PA: Temple University Press

Togores, Viviana and García, Anicia. 2005. 'Consumption, Markets and Monetary Duality in Cuba', in Jorge Domínguez *et al.* (eds), *The Cuban Economy at the Start of the Twenty-First Century*. Cambridge, MA: Harvard University Press/The David Rockefeller Center for Latin American Studies

Transparency International. 2008a. *Corruptions Perceptions Index 2008*. Available at: http://www.transparency.org/news_room/in_focus/2008/cpi2008/cpi_2008_table [accessed October 2009]

Transparency International. 2008b. *Corruption Perceptions Index. Regional Highlights: Americas*. Available at: http://www.transparency.org/policy_research/surveys_indices/cpi/2008/regional_highlights_factsheets [accessed October 2009]

Tremblay, Rodrigue. 2004. *The New American Empire: Causes and Consequences for the United States and for the World*. Haverford, PA: Infinity Publishers

Tuckman, Johanna. 2000. 'Flashy candidate used news media now opposed to him', *Washington Times*, 25 June 2000, 2, p. C10. Factiva.com database [accessed March 2006]

Tulchin, Joseph S. and Allison Garland (eds). 2000. *Social Development in Latin America. The Politics of Reform*. Boulder, CO: Lynne Rienner

Tulchin, Joseph S. and Andrew Selee (eds). 2004. *Decentralisation and Democratic Governance in Latin America*. Woodrow Wilson Center Report on the Americas #12. Washington: Woodrow Wilson International Center for Scholars. Available at: http://www.wilsoncenter.org/topics/pubs/ACF18E5.pdf [accessed February 2010]

Tulchin, Joseph S. and Meg Ruthenburg (eds). 2006. *Citizenship in Latin America*. Boulder, CO: Lynne Rienner

Tulchin, Joseph S. and Ralph H. Espach. 2001. 'Latin America in the New International System: A Call for Strategic Thinking', in Joseph S. Tulchin and Ralph H. Espach (eds), *Latin America in the New International System*. Boulder, CO: Lynne Rienner/Woodrow Wilson International Center for Scholars

Tulchin, Joseph S. and Ralph H. Espach (eds). 2001. *Latin America in the New International System*. Boulder, CO: Lynne Rienner/Woodrow Wilson International Center for Scholars

UDI (Unión Demócrata Independiente). 2010. 'Doctrina y Principios, Punta De Tralca 1991. 1.–Persona, Familia, Sociedad y Estado', UDI online. Santiago: UD . Available at: www.udi.cl/sitio/?page_id=389&preview=true [accessed February 2010]

Uildriks, Nils. 2009. *Policing Insecurity: Police Reform, Security, and Human Rights in Latin America*. Lanham, MD: Lexington Books

UN (United Nations). 2005. *The Millennium Development Goals: A Latin American and Caribbean Perspective*. New York: United Nations. Available at: http://www.cepal.org/publicaciones/xml/0/21540/lcg2331.pdf [accessed November 2009]

UNCTAD (United Nations Conference on Trade and Development). 2009. *World Investment Prospects Survey 2009–11. UNCTAD/DIAE/IA/2009/8*. Geneva: UNCTAD. Available at: http://www.unctad.org/en/docs/diaeia20098_en.pdf [accessed November 2009]

UN Department of Economic and Social Affairs. 2008. *World Population Prospects: The 2008 Revision*. New York: Population Division of the Department of Economic and Social Affairs of the United Nations Secretariat. Available at: http://esa.un.org/unpp [accessed December 2009]

UNDP (United Nations Development Programme). 2004a. *Human Development Report 2004. Cultural Liberty in Today's Diverse World*. New York: UNDP

UNDP (United Nations Development Programme). 2004b. *Democracy in Latin America. Towards a Citizens' Democracy*. New York /Buenos Aires: UNDP/Alfaguara. Available in Spanish at: http://www.gobernabilidaddemocratica-pnud.org/resultado.php [accessed February 2010]

UNDP (United Nations Development Programme). 2004c. *Democracy in Latin America. Towards a Citizens' Democracy. Statistical Compendium*. New York/Buenos Aires: UNDP/Alfaguara.

UNDP (United Nations Development Programme). 2008. *Democracia/Estado/Ciudanía: Hacia un Estado de y para la Democracia en América Latina*. Lima: Sede PNUD. Available at: http://www.undp.org/latinamerica/docs/Democracia_en_A%20_Latina.pdf [accessed September 2009]

UNDP (United Nations Development Programme). 2009a. *Supporting Country-led Democratic Governance Assessment: A UNDP Practice Note*. New York: UNDP. Available at: http://content.undp.org/go/cms-service/stream/asset/;jsessionid=auq0zh9xAXO8?asset_id=1793861 [accessed September 2009]

UNDP (United Nations Development Programme). 2009b. *Human Development Report 2009. Overcoming barriers: Human mobility and development*. New York: UNDP. Available at: http://hdr.undp.org/en/reports/global/hdr2009/ [accessed February 2010]

UNHCR (United Nations High Commissioner for Refugees). 2004. *Asylum Levels and Trends: Europe and non-European Industrialized Countries, 2003*. Geneva: UNHCR

UNODC (UN Office on Drugs and Crime). 2009. World Drug Report, 2009. Vienna: UNODC. Available at: http://www.unodc.org/documents/wdr/WDR_2009/WDR2009_eng_web.pdf [accessed February 2010]

UN Population Division. 2001. *World Population Prospects: The 2000 Revision*. New York: UN Population Division, Department of Economic and Social Affairs

UPLA (Unión de Partidos Latinoaméricanos). 2009. 'Miembros y asociados', Unión de Partidos Latinoaméricanos online. Available at: http://www.upla.net/index.php [accessed November 2009]

US Census Bureau. 2006. 'Hispanics in the United States', Presentation, Ethnicity and Ancestry Branch, Population Division, US Census Bureau. Available at: http://www.census.gov/population/www/socdemo/hispanic/files/Internet_Hispanic_in_US_2006.pdf [accessed December 2009]

US Department of State. 2009a. *International Narcotics Control Strategy Report 2009*. Washington: US Department of State, Bureau for International Narcotics and Law Enforcement Affairs. Available at: http://www.state.gov/p/inl/rls/nrcrpt/2009/ [accessed February 2010]

US Department of State. 2009b. 'Counternarcotics and Law Enforcement Country Program: Peru', Bureau of International Narcotics and Law Enforcement Affairs, Fact Sheet, 16 October 2009. Available at: http://www.state.gov/p/inl/rls/fs/130622.htm [accessed November 2009]

US Fed News. 2008. 'Trends, developments in economy of Puerto Rico', US Fed News/HT Media Limited, 28 March 2008. New Delhi: HTSyndication.com

US Fed News. 2009. 'Permanent Forum experts recount recent mission to Paraguay, Bolivia, urging end to "semi-slavery" of Guarani and other indigenous peoples of Chaco region.' US Fed News, 29 May 2009. New Delhi: HTSyndication.com

USJFCOM (United States Joint Forces Command). 2008. *The Joint Operating Environment: Challenges and Implications for the Future Joint Force*. Norfolk, VA: USJFCOM. Available at: http://www.jfcom.mil/newslink/storyarchive/2008/JOE2008.pdf [accessed September 2009]

Valdés, Teresa and Alina Donoso. 2009. 'Social Accountability and Citizen Participation: Are Latin American Governments Meeting their Commitments to Gender Equity?', Chapter 8 in Jane S. Jaquette (ed.), *Feminist Agendas and Democracy in Latin America*. Durham, NC: Duke University Press

Valenzuela, Arturo. 2004. 'Latin American Presidencies Interrupted', *Journal of Democracy*, Vol. 15, No. 4 (October), pp. 5–19.

Valenzuela, Arturo and Lucía Dammert. 2008. 'Problems of Success in Chile', Chapter 10 in Larry Diamond, Marc F. Plattner and Diego Abente Brun (eds), *Latin America's Struggle for Democracy*. Baltimore, MD: Johns Hopkins University Press

van Klaveren, Alberto. 2001. 'Political Globalisation and Latin America', in Joseph Tulchin and Ralph Espach (eds), *Latin America in the New International System*. Boulder, CO: Lynne Rienner/Woodrow Wilson International Center for Scholars

Vargas, Virginia. 2009. 'International Feminisms', Chapter 7 in Jane S. Jaquette (ed.), *Feminist Agendas and Democracy in Latin America*. Durham, NC: Duke University Press

Vasquez, Manuel A. 1998. *The Brazilian Popular Church and the Crisis of Modernity*. Cambridge: Cambridge University Press

Véliz, Claudio. 1980. *The Centralist Tradition of Latin America*. Princeton, NJ: Princeton University Press

Véliz, Claudio (ed.). 1965. *Obstacles to Change in Latin America*. London: Oxford University Press

Vellinga, Menno. 1993. *Social Democracy in Latin America. Prospects for Change*. Boulder, CO: Westview Press

Vellinga, Menno. 1998. 'The Changing Role of the State in Latin America', in Menno Vellinga (ed.), *The Changing Role of the State in Latin America*. Boulder, CO: Westview Press

Vellinga, Menno (ed.). 1998. *The Changing Role of the State in Latin America*. Boulder, CO: Westview Press

Vilas, Carlos M. 1997. 'Chapter 1, Introduction: Participation, Inequality, and the Whereabouts of Democracy', in Douglas Chalmers *et al.* (eds), *The New Politics of Inequality in Latin America. Rethinking Participation and Representation*. Oxford: Oxford University Press

Vivares, Ernesto, Leonardo Díaz Echenique and Javier Ozorio. 2009. 'Argentina: reforming neoliberal capitalism', Chapter 12 in Geraldine Lievesley and Steve Ludlam (eds), *Reclaiming Latin America: Experiments in Radical Social Democracy*. London: Zed Books

Waisbord, Silvio. 2000. *Watchdog Journalism in South America*. New York: Columbia University Press

Wampler, Brian. 2004. 'Expanding Accountability Through Participatory Institutions: Mayors, Citizens, and Budgeting in Three Brazilian Municipalities', *Latin American Politics and Society*, Vol. 46, No. 2 (July), pp. 73–99

Warren, Kay B. 1998. *Indigenous Movements and Their Critics. Pan-Maya Activism in Guatemala*. Princeton, NJ: Princeton University Press

Warren, Kay B. and Jean E. Jackson (eds). 2002. *Indigenous Movements, Self-Representation and the State in Latin America*. Austin, TX: University of Texas Press

Webb-Vidal, Andy. 2006. 'Chávez turns up heat in tit-for-tat political tussle with White House', *Financial Times*, 21 February 2006, London Edition, p. 8

Weber, Max. 1958. *The Protestant Ethic and the Spirit of Capitalism*. Translated by Talcott Parsons. New York: Charles Scribner's Sons

Weber, Max. 1968. *Politics as a Vocation*. Philadelphia, PA: Fortress Press

Weffort, Francisco. 1998. 'New Democracies and Economic Crisis in Latin America', in Philip Oxhorn and Graciela Ducatenzeiler (eds), *What Kind of Democracy? What Kind of Market?* University Park, PA: Pennsylvania State University Press

Welch, Cliff. 2001. 'Peasants Against Globalization: Rural Social Movements in Costa Rica', review article, *Latin American Politics and Society*, Vol. 43, No. 4 (December), pp. 166–8

Weldon, Jeffrey A. 2002. 'The Legal and Partisan Framework of the Legislative Delegation of the Budget in Mexico', in Scott Morgenstern and Benito Nacif (eds), *Legislative Politics in Latin America*. Cambridge: Cambridge University Press

Weyland, Kurt. 1998. 'The Politics of Corruption in Latin America', *Journal of Democracy*, Vol. 9, No. 2 (April), pp. 108–21

Weyland, Kurt. 2007. 'The Political Economy of Market Reform and a Revival of Structuralism', *Latin American Research Review*, Vol. 42, No. 3 (January), pp. 235–50

Wheatley, Jonathan. 2009. 'Agriculture: Superpower is ready to feed the world', *Financial Times*, 'Investing in Brazil Special Report', 4 November 2009. Available at: http://www. ft.com/cms/s/0/e079f622-c8d9-11de-8f9d-00144feabdc0,dwp_uuid=72323b5a-c8e0-11de-8f9d-00144feabdc0.html [accessed February 2010]

Whitehead, Laurence. 1983. 'Explaining Washington's Central American Policies', *Journal of Latin American Studies*, Vol. 15, No. 2 (November), pp. 321–63

Whitehead, Laurence. 1994. 'State Organization in Latin America Since 1930', in Leslie Bethell (ed.), *The Cambridge History of Latin America. Volume VI. Latin America since 1930: Economy, Society and Politics. Part 2. Politics and Society.* Cambridge: Cambridge University Press

Whitehead, Laurence. 1999. 'The European Union and the Americas', in Victor Bulmer-Thomas and James Dunkerley (eds), *The United States and Latin America: The New Agenda*. London: Institute of Latin American Studies, University of London/Harvard: David Rockefeller Center for Latin American Studies

Whitehead, Laurence. 2001. 'The Viability of Democracy', in John Crabtree and Laurence Whitehead (eds), *Towards Democratic Viability: the Bolivian Experience*. Basingstoke: Palgrave

Whitehead, Laurence. 2008. 'The Fading Regional Consensus on Democratic Convergence', Chapter 2 in Jorge I. Domínguez and Michael Shifter, *Constructing Democratic Governance in Latin America*, 3rd Edition. Baltimore, MD: Johns Hopkins University Press

Whitehead, Laurence (ed.) 1996. *The International Dimensions of Democratization: Europe and the Americas*. Oxford: Oxford University Press

White House/ONDCP. 2009. *National Drug Control Strategy, FY 2010 Budget Summary*. Washington: The White House/ONDCP. Available at: http://www.whitehousedrugpolicy.gov/ publications/policy/10budget/fy10budget.pdf [accessed November 2009]

Whitman, Jim. 2009. *Palgrave Advances in Global Governance*. Basingstoke: Palgrave Macmillan

WHOSIS (World Health Organization Statistical Information System). 2009. 'General government expenditure on health as percentage of total expenditure on health and private expenditure on health as percentage of total expenditure on health, 1996 and 2006'. Geneva: WHOSIS. Available at: http://www.who.int/whosis/en/ [accessed April 2009]

Wiarda, Howard J. 1981. *Corporatism and National Development in Latin America*. Boulder, CO: Westview Press

Wiarda, Howard J. 1998. 'Historical Determinants of the Latin American State', in Menno Vellinga (ed.), *The Changing Role of the State in Latin America*. Boulder, CO: Westview Press

Wiarda, Howard (ed.). 1974. *Politics and Social Change in Latin America: The Distinct Tradition*. Amherst, MA: University of Massachusetts Press

Wiarda, Howard (ed.). 2004. *Authoritarianism and Corporatism in Latin America Revisited*. Gainesville, FL: University Press of Florida

Wiarda, Howard J. and Harvey F. Kline (eds). 1990. *Latin American Politics and Development*, 3rd Edition. Boulder, CO: Westview Press

Wickham-Crowley, Timothy P. 1992. *Guerrillas and Revolution in Latin America. A Comparative Study of Insurgents and Regimes Since 1956*. Princetonn, NJ: Princeton University Press

Williamson, John (ed.). 1990. *Latin American Economic Adjustment: How Much has Happened?* Washington: Institute for International Economics

Williamson, Edwin. 1992. *The Penguin History of Latin America*. London: Penguin

Wilpert, Gregory. 2006. *Changing Venezuela by Taking Power*. London: Verso

Wilson, Bruce M. *et al.* 2010. *Courts and Power in Latin America and Africa*. Basingstoke: Palgrave Macmillan

WOLA (Washington Office on Latin America). 2009. 'WOLA Expresses Concerns on Palanquero Base', *Letter to US Secretary of State*, 7 August 2009. Washington, DC: WOLA

Wolf, Eric R. 1969. *Peasant Wars of the Twentieth Century*. New York: Harper and Row

Wolfe, Joel. 2002. 'The Social Subject Versus the Political: Latin American Labor Studies at a Crossroads', review article, *Latin American Research Review*, Vol. 37, No. 2 (Summer), pp. 244–62

World Bank. 2003. 'Case Study 2 – Porto Alegre, Brazil: Participatory Approaches in Budgeting and Public Expenditure Management', *Social Development Notes*, No. 71 (March 2003). Washington: World Bank Participation and Civic Engagement Group/Social Development Publications. Available at: http://www-wds.worldbank.org/servlet/WDS_IBank_Servlet?pcont=details&eid=000090341_20031216092121 [accessed February 2010]

World Bank. 2004. *Inequality in Latin America and the Caribbean: Breaking with History?* Washington: World Bank. Available at: http://siteresources.worldbank.org/BRAZILIN-POREXTN/Resources/3817166-1185895645304/4044168-1186325351029/10Full.pdf [accessed February 2010]

World Bank. 2005. *World Development Indicators*. Washington: World Bank. Available at: http://devdata.worldbank.org/wdi2005/Cover.htm [accessed February 2010]

World Bank. 2009a. *World Development Indicators 2009*. Washington: World Bank

World Bank. 2009b. 'Fast-track Recovery from Crisis Likely for Latin America'. Bulletin. Available at: http://go.worldbank.org/PP8LBGNLW0 [accessed October 2009]

WTO (World Trade Organisation). 2009. *International trade statistics 2009*. Geneva: WTO. Available at: http://www.wto.org/english/res_e/statis_e/its2009_e/its2009_e.pdf [accessed February 2010]

Wunderlich, Jens Uwe. 2009. *A Dictionary of Globalization*. New York: Routledge

Yaffe, Helen. 2009. *Che Guevara: The Economics of Revolution*. Basingstoke: Palgrave Macmillan

Yashar, Deborah. 1998. 'Contesting Citizenship: Indigenous Movements and Democracy in Latin America', *Comparative Politics*, Vol. 31, No. 1 (October), pp. 23–42

Youngers, Coletta A. and Eileen Rosin (eds). 2004. *Drugs And Democracy In Latin America: The Impact Of US Policy*. Boulder, CO: Lynne Rienner

Youngs, Richard. 2002. 'The European Union and Democracy in Latin America', *Latin American Politics and Society*, Vol. 44, No. 3 (September), pp. 111–39

Zakaria, Fareed. 2008. *The Post-American World*. New York: W.W. Norton & Co

Zibechi, Raúl. 2008. 'The New Latin American Right: Finding a Place in the World', *NACLA Report on the Americas*, Vol. 41, No. 1 (January/February), pp. 12–13

Zimbalist, Andrew and Claes Brundenius. 1989. 'Creciendo con equidad: El desarollo cubano en una perspectiva comparada', *Cuadernos de Nuestra América*, Havana: CEA, Vol. 6, No. 13 (July–December 1989)

Zovatto, Daniel and J. Jesús Orozco Henríquez (Co-ords.). 2008. *Reforma Política y Electoral en América Latina 1978–2007*. Mexico City: Universidad Nacional Autónoma de México/IDEA Internacional. Available at: http://www.idea.int/publications/perla/index.cfm [accessed October 2009]

Zuleta Puceiro, Enrique. 1993. 'The Argentine Case: Television in the 1989 Election', in Thomas Skidmore (ed.), *Television, Politics, and the Transition to Democracy in Latin America*. Washington, DC: Woodrow Wilson Center Press

Index

Page numbers in bold refer to entries in the Glossary

de Antuñano, Estevan 406, 635
De la Garza Toledo, Enrique 195, 197
De la Rúa, Fernando 134, 140, 142, 635
De La Torre, Augusto 246
de la Vega, Garcilaso -Inca- 635
death squads 46, 211, 413
'death' flights 208
debt crisis 36, 46, 50, 53, 75, 120, 276,
    310–12, 335, 487, 488–94, 518
debt default 541
debt peonage 27, **610**
decentralisation 153, 176–83, 184, 233, 440,
    610
   administrative 179, 605
   fiscal 180–3
   political 179, **623**
   sectoral 177, **626**
decertification 322, **610**
decision-making (presidential and
    parliamentary systems) 147–8
decisional autonomy 160, 184, **610**
Declaration of Montevideo 408
decolonisation 307–8
deconsolidation 82, **610**
decrees 156, 158
decretismo 98, **610**
deficit spending 471, 521, 534, **610**
deforestation 239, 241, 243, 246, **610**
del Valle Escalante, Emilio 435
delegative democracy 79, 97–8, 131, 133,
    610
Della Porte, Donatella 514
demilitarisation 204, 205, 279, 281, **610**
Demmers, Jolle 106
demobilisation 281, **611**
democracy 11, 36, 40, 41, 42, 45, 47–8,
    180, 181
   business associations (role) 190–1
   challenges facing 94–130
   Christian 407–10, 415–17, 419, **608**
   and civil society *see separate entry*
   consolidation *see* consolidation (of
     democracies)
   defence clauses 273–4
   definitions/uses 61–4
   delegative 79, 97–8, 131, 133, **610**
   empowerment and 554–5
   EU/Latin American relations 349–50
   human rights and 288–9, 349–50
   in Latin America 64–8
   liberal 63, 233, 376, 437
   limited 74
   meaning of term 61
   measuring 79–80
   participatory 63, 64, 237, 395, 396,
     399–401, 408, 410, 554–5

preconditions 65, 66, 80
   procedural 62, 63
   quality of 76–82
   representative 64
   and the Right 410–14
   social *see* social democracy
   social justice and 543–7
   support for 88–90, 91
   transition 7, 52–4, 65, 67–8, 116–17,
     118, 196, 203–4, 288–9, 410
   triumph of 52–4
   tutelary 78
democracy clauses 344
democradura **611**
Democratic Action (Venezuela) 50, 102, 103,
    145, 194, 388, 394
Democratic Alliance – 19th of April
    Movement (Colombia) 100
Democratic Change (Panama) 404
democratic consolidation 65, 67, 91, 196,
    609
   challenge from weak rule of law 106–16
   economic challenges 119–27
   military challenge to 116–18
   political challenges 94, 95–106
   quality of democracy and 76–82
democratic governance 63, 82, 168, 181,
    205, **611**
Democratic Labour Party (Brazil) 394
Democratic Left (Ecuador) 394
Democratic Party (Brazil) 409
democratic planning 104
democratic pluralism 373, 467, **611**
Democratic Popular Movement (Ecuador)
    164
Democratic Revolution Party (Mexico) 162
Democratic Revolutionary Party (Panama)
    389, 394
democratisation 72, 178, 318, 374, 388,
    393–7, 411, 418, 487
   consolidation 76–82
   contributory factors 68–76
   definitions 61–4
   explanation of 65–8
   in Latin America 64–8
demonstrations 411
Dent, David M. 293
dependencistas 478
dependency 343, 384, 488, 526–8, **611**
   criticisms of approach 476
   structuralism and 461, 474–84, 543
depoliticisation 507, **611**
deregulation 490, 493, 494–9, **611**
DeShazo, Peter 172, 173
deunionisation 196, **611**
Deutch, John 330